W9-BUR-866

Smiling Through the Apocalypse

Edited by Harold Hayes

Smiling
Through
the Apocalypse

Esquire's History of the Sixties

The McCall Publishing Co.
New York

Library of Congress Catalog Card Number: 70-96307

SBN-8415-0002-9

Printed in the United States of America

For Arnold

Contents

Part II

The Grass Roots of "Now"

Part III
Egos, Superegos and Ids

Part IV

The New Sentimentality

Part V

Some Failures in Communication

Section 1 / The Credibility Gap

Part VI

Living Up to Our Commitment in Vietnam

Part VII

Creative Agonies

"May you live in the most interesting of times"

—Traditional Chinese curse

Introduction

Decades seldom start on schedule. The Thirties began in '29 with the Depression; the Forties with World War II in '41; the Fifties with the election of Dwight Eisenhower in '52; and the Sixties ten months after the turn of the year when, in his television debate with Jack Kennedy, Richard Nixon's face signaled defeat. But for politicians and journalists, the first day of a decade opens a new epoch, ready or not, and Esquire reacted accordingly. In our January 1960 issue, the first paragraph of the lead article (by Arthur Schlesinger Jr.) read:

"At periodic moments in our history, our country has paused on the threshold of a new epoch in our national life, unable for a moment to open the door, but aware that it must advance if it is to preserve its natural vitality and identity. One feels that we are approaching such a moment now—that the mood which had dominated the nations for a decade is beginning to seem thin and irrelevant; that it no longer interprets our desires and needs as a people, that new forms, new energies, new values are straining for expression and release. The Eisenhower epoch—the present period of passivity and acquiescence in our national life—is drawing to a close."

Part prophecy, part wishful thinking. That January issue was published on December 14, having been assembled back in September of 1959. Actually, on Friday, January 1, 1960, no door opened. Khrushchev declared he would disarm Russia unilaterally, the French issued a one-franc coin worth twenty cents and N.A.S.A. announced plans to cut back space costs. If there were new energies and new values straining for release, most Americans were unaware of them. Rather, life seemed monotonously predictable. The average American was white, prosperous and torpid; a second car and a swimming pool were facts of his life, a new vacation home an immediate possibility. Though there was still plenty to fear from the Russians—perhaps a bomb shelter would prove a wiser investment than a beach house—the mood was benign. Of course the Negro was restless, and many people were distressed by news pictures of police dogs breaking up demonstrations in Alabama. But that was largely a regional problem; elsewhere, America was an ongoing enterprise. There was no war, the economy was sound (unemployment practically nonexistent) and our democratic institutions, God's church among them, were invulnerable. Arthur Schlesinger was right, however: The Fifties *were* drawing to a close. *Smiling Through the Apocalypse: Esquire's History of the Sixties*, is an account of what happened next.

A magazine is a promise, sometimes fulfilled, sometimes not. Responding to events of the day, it seeks to offer a bit more perspective than the shifting realities reported in the daily press, though the permanence of its views is only slightly less subject to change. Between the morning papers and the Cronkite show, there is often very little to add but—and this is the redeeming strength of all magazines today—attitude. The magazine engages its reader and holds him because it shares with him a certain point of view.

To land on the moon is to make news which transcends form: the faster the word gets out, the better. But once established, the fact moves from the simple to the complex, begging interpretation of a thousand varieties. A magazine's promise is the delivery, on a fixed schedule, of its own version of the world, its special attitude toward the reader.

The present-day attitude of Esquire was formed out of a reaction to the banality of the Fifties. From the raspberry to the hoax, in words and / or pictures (curiously the pictures always provoked the greatest outrage, especially George Lois's covers) and occasionally with some loss of dignity, the idea was to suggest alternate possibilities to a monolithic view. And how monolithic it was! The passivity of the Fifties was shared by garage mechanics and college presidents.

At Esquire our attitude took shape as we went along, stumbling past our traditional boundaries of fashion, leisure, entertainment and literature onto the more forbidding ground of politics, sociology, science and even, occasionally, religion. Any point of view was welcome as long as the writer was sufficiently skillful to carry it off, but we tended to avoid committing ourselves to doctrinaire programs even though advised on occasion that we might thereby serve better the interests of mankind. None of the programs available would permit us consistently to keep our lines open to the reader, so we stayed loose.

But despite this calloused lack of commitment—or perhaps because of it—we began to form the habit of searching for the right questions. If two superpowers have superbombs, how does one protect itself from the other? Should churches practice segregation? Should Arthur Miller be jailed for refusing to name those of his friends who were Communist? Was reverence due cherished institutions of American life, or irreverence? What evil lurked in the heart of Eisenhower, what virtue in the heart of Alger Hiss?

Raising such questions in the capacity of surrogate readers, we then moved as editors to find the appropriate writers, often the unexpected ones, to answer them. But the attitude, now roughly shaping, would become refined through more complicated means: the precise phrasing of titles—

> "JOE," SAID MARILYN MONROE,
> JUST BACK FROM KOREA,
> "YOU NEVER HEARD SUCH CHEERING."
> "YES I HAVE,"
> JOE DIMAGGIO ANSWERED

—the toning and sharpening "house copy," those introductory copy blocks and captions accompanying visual features; and sometimes—increasingly more often—planning features executed exclusively by the editors to remind readers that we were ever mindful of where their interests lay (the rococo phase of this cycle occurring well into the Sixties with a two-page list entitled "The 100 Best People in the World").

And always, always pounding away on the Idea, ten a week from each staff editor until he either mutinied, buckled or broke through to some dazzlingly fresh concept which gained for the magazine another inch of new ground.

Few magazines have successfully defined their own attitude, and Esquire is no exception. For a while we called ours an effort toward a rational view, then satire and then irony. But only humor—of a most complex, often unfunny sort—is sufficiently flexible to cover the larger part of our effort, from black wit to custard-pie burlesque. Against the aridity of the national landscape of the late Fifties we offered to our readers in our better moments the promise of outright laughter; by the end of the Sixties the best we could provide was a bleak grin.

Arriving slightly behind schedule, Jack Kennedy opened the door to an epoch releasing new energies indeed, though it is now clear that many of his constituents missed the point of his coming. What Kennedy wanted was the acceptance of conventional liberal measures to ensure minimum creature comforts, freedom and security; what the country wanted was to be like Jack—young, rich, powerful and attractive. Backing up, like electric currents in a cloudless sky, those new energies collected around him until the terrible spark of his assassination set them loose, traumatizing the country more than any event in recent memory.

"The Rise and Fall of Charisma," Part I of this book, traces through the Sixties the pathetic parabola of the Kennedy spirit, concluding with the Chicago Convention of 1968. But the Kennedy chronicle, like some medieval legend, seems endless. *The Last Kennedy,* a 1968 portrait of Edward by Burton Hersh, was turned in only days before the assassination of Robert and hastily revised to allow for this latest misfortune to strike the President's survivors. In the light of Edward Kennedy's disastrous experience in the Chappaquiddick affair of 1969, Hersh's appraisal appears now slightly out of chronology (and context). But here it stands. Although we are told the House of Kennedy at last has fallen, it will be seen that the theme of this section argues the decline of the Kennedy ideal began even before the President's death. The Hersh piece, like others throughout the book which may seem inconsistent in view of our later knowledge of events, is without further revision because it reflects our impressions of the moment. (At the end of each article is the date of its publication in Esquire, serving as a guide for the reader to his own memories of that moment.)

"The Grass Roots of 'Now,' " Part II, derives from the section preceding it. As Arthur Schlesinger had predicted, new forms and new values would come along with the new energies, and in Esquire's view the forms tended to define the values. Thus more than a casual interest was expressed by our editors and writers in the diversions of the period—from baton-twirling schools to Las Vegas casinos. No longer was there an archetypal American; standing in his place, self-absorbed and passionate to the point of militancy, was a cluster of groups, some of them harsh and disquieting.

So were some of their new values, six of which underline parts of this book:

Power is an absolute, like truth or justice. (Part I, "The Rise and Fall of Charisma")

Public image is more important than measurable achievement. (Part III, "Egos, Superegos and Ids")

The government lies. (Part V, Section 1, "The Credibility Gap")

Youth is incorruptible. (Part V, Section 2, "The Generation Gap")

Minority rights are secured more effectively by intimidation than by legislation or Christian example. (Part V, Section 3, "The Color Gap")

Patriotism is an irrelevant reason for going to war. (Part VI, "Living Up to Our Commitment in Vietnam")

But sentiments changed even more swiftly than values, and in 1964, midway through the period, two young editors named Robert Benton and David Newman stood back from the moment and cataloged with striking economy "The New Sentimentality," epiphenomenal moods of the day which rejected old illusions and appealed only to contemporary life "as it has to do with you, really just you, not what you were told or taught, but what goes on in your head, *really,* and in your heart, *really.*"* As a sort of way station along our seven-staged descent, "The New Sentimentality" stands alone as Part IV.

Only in Part IV, however, are value judgments themselves the subject of our attention. As this is a book about life in the Sixties, it is mostly concerned with the infinite variety of the odd and dissimilar: styles, conspiracies, education, sex, war, cars, establishments,** fads, drugs, Pepsi-Cola contests, murders, sports, riots and fashions. And with people of all kinds: winners, losers, clowns, revolutionaries, fools, mothers, actors, segregationists, topless waitresses, soldiers, villains, fighters, martyrs, hippies, yippies and L.B.J.

But the writer is the only hero.

"If any man have an ear," wrote St. John regarding a terminal point for readers of a wider audience than Esquire's, "let him hear." In the apocalyptic Sixties the message came through clearly, for writers were everywhere, sending back the word. "Creative Agonies," Part VII of this informal history, is concerned with the private lives of our writer kings.

It is doubtful whether even so egocentric an author as Ernest Hemingway saw himself as central to events as have some of the writers through these years, freedom-riding down South, slogging through the Mekong Delta, marching on the Pentagon, backtracking Kansas killers, running from cops in Chicago and so on—keeping witness in the truest sense, and all readers were the richer for it. So were writers, by the way,

---

* A fitting exegesis of the intentions of the same authors when they went on from Esquire to write the original screenplay of *Bonnie and Clyde*, a masterpiece of the Sixties.

** More than our share of them, perhaps: establishments on Wall Street, in the art world, the Washington press corps, the literary world, even a baseball establishment. In our pages, conspiracy lovers were fair game—until the Sixties turned around on us. See "The American Establishment" and "An Appreciation of the Nonmilitary Functions of War" in Part V. The former, published in 1962, spoofs the notion that there is an establishment; the latter, published in 1967, spoofs the notion that there is not.

some of them now millionaires whose celebrity had become international, but troublesome. Because instant communication allowed the possibility of instant success, writers and readers by mid-decade looked expectantly toward the coronation of the Writer of the Year. Saul Bellow, '65, *Herzog*; Truman Capote, '66, *In Cold Blood*; William Styron, '67 *The Confessions of Nat Turner*; Norman Mailer, '68, *The Armies of the Night*; Philip Roth, '69, *Portnoy's Complaint*. But sudden though it was, modern fame could pass quickly. Last year's writer found himself working under an excruciating pressure imposed by the mass reader's perfidy. Despite the unprecedented wealth and glory paid out by the Sixties for higher achievement, the time warp ultimately conspired against him. Talent got him there but publicity would have to keep him alive. Like everyone else, he too wanted to be young, rich, powerful and attractive. A prominent symptom of his unstrung condition was the emergence of his claims to new literary forms—the "nonfiction novel," "history as literature and literature as history," the "New Journalism." While identifying characteristics of at least two of these forms may be traced back to articles appearing first in this magazine, the claim was misleading. Demands of the language remain constant, and varieties in technique are relative matters, drawing from old sources. Separating the spurious from the authentic in most activities through this decade is a task continuing over into the future. But there can be no doubt that ours was a time uniquely blessed with an extraordinary abundance of writing talent, men of great originality and style exquisitely sensitive to the nature of change going on about them.

Most are present in this collection, a number of them having earlier established their reputations independently of Esquire. But a few of them first reached a national audience through this magazine and have continued throughout most of the period to identify their principal efforts with ours. These are Gay Talese, Tom Wolfe, Jack Richardson, Garry Wills,† and Martin Mayer; and, among our by-lined editors, Robert Benton, David Newman, Robert Brown, John Berendt and Alice Glaser.

Ironically, many of the better novelists weren't writing much fiction, perhaps because social disintegration forced the writer to view himself as his own protagonist; perhaps, as has been remarked elsewhere, because the times were too stimulating for the interior vision to contain. Although there is no fiction included in this selection, Esquire published throughout the Sixties a number of outstanding stories, even serializing through one hectic season the chapters of a Norman Mailer novel turned out to monthly deadline. Possibly the quality of the fiction was superior to that

† For the record, William F. Buckley Jr. sent over Garry Wills who had published, and continues to, in the *National Review*. But as Mr. Buckley would be the first to acknowledge, the editorial intentions of the two periodicals are so dissimilar as to allow the claim, on behalf of Esquire's readers at least, to stand.

of the nonfiction, the insights more lasting and—as our fiction department insists even to this day—more meaningful a way to view the period. Possibly. But in the Sixties, events seemed to move too swiftly to allow the osmotic process of art to keep abreast, and when we found a good novelist we immediately sought to seduce him with the sweet mysteries of current events.

Even so, for the very best of our writers, no single event yielded a key to the decade. There was too much going on—a fire in the street, a fight at the corner, a burglary in the house next door. The last two articles of our book—the *mano a mano* between William F. Buckley Jr. and Gore Vidal—are as appropriate a conclusion to the Sixties as any other, yielding as they do almost no direct information on the changing times other than by suggesting indirectly—through the bitterness, jealousy, ambition and despair of two of our most eloquent sensibilities—the character of America's collective confusion.

HAROLD HAYES

Part I

The Rise and Fall of Charisma

Superman Comes to the Supermarket

by Norman Mailer

For once let us try to think about a political convention without losing ourselves in housing projects of fact and issue. Politics has its virtues, all too many of them—it would not rank with baseball as a topic of conversation if it did not satisfy a great many things—but one can suspect that its secret appeal is close to nicotine. Smoking cigarettes insulates one from one's life, one does not feel as much, often happily so, and politics quarantines one from history; most of the people who nourish themselves in the political life are in the game not to make history but to be diverted from the history which is being made.

If that Democratic Convention which has now receded behind the brow of the Summer of 1960 is only half-remembered in the excitements of moving toward the election, it may be exactly the time to consider it again, because the mountain of facts which concealed its features last July has been blown away in the winds of High Television, and the man-in-the-street (that peculiar political term which refers to the quixotic voter who will pull the lever for some reason so salient as: "I had a brown-nose lieutenant once with Nixon's looks," or "that Kennedy must have false teeth"), the not so easily estimated man-in-the-street has forgotten most of what happened and could no more tell you who Kennedy was fighting against than you or I could place a bet on who was leading the American League in batting during the month of June.

So to try to talk about what happened is easier now than in the days of the convention, one does not have to put everything in—an act of writing which calls for a bulldozer rather than a pen—one can try to make one's little point and dress it with a ribbon or two of metaphor. All to the good. Because mysteries are irritated by facts, and the 1960 Democratic Convention began as one mystery and ended as another.

Since mystery is an emotion which is repugnant to a political animal (why else lead a life of bad banquet dinners, cigar smoke, camp chairs, foul breath, and excruciatingly dull jargon if not to avoid the echoes of what is not known), the psychic separation between what was happening on the floor, in the caucus rooms, in the headquarters, and what was happening in parallel to the history of the nation was mystery enough to drown the proceedings in gloom. It was on the one hand a dull convention, one of the less interesting by general agreement, relieved by local bits of color, given two half hours of excitement by two demonstrations for Stevenson, buoyed up by the class of the Kennedy machine, turned by the surprise of Johnson's nomination as vice-president, but, all the same, dull, depressed in its overall tone, the big fiestas subdued, the gossip flat, no real air of excitement, just moments—or as they say in bullfighting—details. Yet it was also, one could argue—and one may argue this yet—it was also one of the most important conventions in America's history, it could prove conceivably to be the most important. The man it nominated was unlike any politican who had ever run for President in the history of the land, and if elected he would come to power in a year when America was in danger of drifting into a profound decline.

A Descriptive of the Delegates: Sons and Daughters of the Republic in a Legitimate Panic; Small-time Practitioners of Small-town Political Judo in the Big Town and the Big Time

Depression obviously has its several roots: it is the doubtful protection which comes from not recognizing failure, it is the psychic burden of exhaustion, and it is also, and very often, that discipline of the will or the ego which enables one to continue working when one's unadmitted emotion is panic. And panic it was I think which sat as the largest single sentiment in the breast of the collective delegates as they came to convene in Los Angeles. Delegates are not the noblest sons and daughters of the Republic; a man of taste, arrived from Mars, would take one look at a convention floor and leave forever, convinced he had seen one of the drearier squats of Hell. If one still smells the faint living echo of a carnival wine, the pepper of a bullfight, the rag, drag, and panoply of a jousting tourney, it is all swallowed and regurgitated by the senses into the fouler cud of a death gas one must rid oneself of—a cigar-smoking, stale-aired, slack-jawed, butt-littered, foul, bleak, hard-working, bureaucratic death gas of language and faces ("Yes those *faces*," says the man from Mars: lawyers, judges, ward heelers, *mafiosos,* Southern goons and grandees, grand old ladies, trade unionists and finks), of pompous words and long pauses which lay like a leaden pain over fever, the fever that one is in, over, or is it that one is just behind history? A legitimate panic for a delegate. America is a nation of experts without roots; we are always creating tacticians who are blind to strategy and strategists who cannot take a step, and when the culture has finished its work the institutions handcuff the infirmity. A delegate is a man who picks a candidate for the largest office in the land, a President who must live with problems whose borders are in ethics, metaphysics, and now ontology; the delegate is prepared for this office of selection by emptying wastebaskets, toting garbage and saying yes at the right time for twenty years in the small political machine of some small or large town; his reward, one of them anyway, is that he arrives at an invitation to the convention. An expert on local catch-as-catch-can, a small-time, often mediocre practitioner of small-town political judo, he comes to the big city with nine-tenths of his mind made up, he will follow the orders of the boss who brought him. Yet of course it is not altogether so mean as that: his opinion is listened to—the boss will consider what he has to say as one interesting factor among five hundred, and what is most important to the delegate, he has the illusion of partial freedom. He can, unless he is severely honest with himself—and if he is, why sweat out the low levels of a political machine?—he can have the illusion that he has helped to choose the candidate, he can even worry most sincerely about his choice, flirt with defection from the boss, work out his own small political gains by the road of loyalty or the way of hard bargain. But even if he is there for no more than the ride, his vote a certainty in the mind of the political boss, able to be thrown here or switched there as the boss decides, still in some peculiar sense he is reality to the boss, the delegate is the great American public, the bar he owns or the law practice, the piece of the union he represents, or the real-estate office, is a part of the political landscape which the boss uses as his own image of how the votes will go, and if the people will like the candidate. And if the boss is depressed by what he sees, if the candidate does not feel right to him, if he has a dull intimation that the candidate is not his sort (as, let us say, Harry Truman was his sort, or Symington might be his sort, or Lyndon Johnson), then vote for him the boss will if he must; he cannot be caught on the wrong side, but he does not feel the pleasure of a personal choice. Which is the center of the panic.

Because if the boss is depressed, the delegate is doubly depressed, and the emotional fact is that Kennedy is not in focus, not in the old political focus, he is not comfortable; in fact it is a mystery to the boss how Kennedy got to where he is, not a mystery in its structures; Kennedy is rolling in money, Kennedy got the votes in primaries, and, most of all, Kennedy has a jewel of a political machine. It is as good as a crack Notre Dame team, all discipline and savvy and go-go-go, sound, drilled, never dull, quick as a knife, full of the salt of hipper-dipper, a beautiful machine; the boss could adore it if only a sensible candidate were driving it, a Truman, even a Stevenson, please God a Northern Lyndon Johnson, but it is run by a man who looks young enough to be coach of the Freshman team, and that is not comfortable at all. The boss knows political machines, he knows issues, farm parity, Forand health bill, Landrum-Griffin, but this is not all so adequate after all to revolutionaries in Cuba who look like beatniks, competitions in missiles, Negroes looting whites in the Congo, intricacies of nuclear fallout, and NAACP men one does well to call Sir. It is all out of hand, everything important is off the center, foreign affairs is now the lick of the heat, and senators are candidates instead of governors, a disaster to the old family style of political measure where a political boss knows his governor and knows who his governor knows. So the boss is depressed, profoundly depressed. He comes to this convention resigned to nominating a man he does not understand, or let us say that, so far as he understands the candidate who is to be nominated, he is not happy about the secrets of his appeal, not so far as he divines these secrets; they seem to have too little to do with politics and all too much to do with the private madnesses of the nation which had thousands—or was it hundreds of thousands—of people demonstrating in the long night before Chessman was killed, and a movie star, the greatest, Marlon the Brando out in the night with them. Yes, this candidate for all his record, his good, sound, conventional liberal record, has a patina of that other life, the second American life, the long electric night with the fires of neon leading down the highway to the murmur of jazz.

An Apparent Digression: A Vivid View of the "City of Lost Angels"; The Democrats Defined; A Pentagon of Traveling Salesmen; Some Pointed Portraits of the Politicians

"I was seeing Pershing Square, Los Angeles, now for the first time . . . the nervous fruithustlers darting in and out of the shadows, fugitives from Times Square, Market Street SF, the French Quarter—

masculine hustlers looking for lonely fruits to score from, anything from the legendary $20 to a pad at night and breakfast in the morning and whatever you can clinch or clip; and the heat in their holy cop uniforms, holy because of the Almighty Stick and the Almightier Vagrancy Law; the scattered junkies, the small-time pushers, the queens, the sad panhandlers, the lonely, exiled nymphs haunting the entrance to the men's head, the fruits with the hungry eyes and the jingling coins; the tough teen-age chicks—'dittybops'—making it with the lost hustlers . . . all amid the incongruous piped music and the flowers—twin fountains gushing rainbow colored: the world of Lonely America squeezed into Pershing Square, of the Cities of Terrible Night, downtown now trapped in the City of lost Angels . . . and the trees hang over it all like some type of apathetic fate." —John Rechy: *Big Table 3*

Seeing Los Angeles after ten years away, one realizes all over again that America is an unhappy contract between the East (that Faustian thrust of a most determined human will which reaches up and out above the eye into the skyscrapers of New York) and those flat lands of compromise and mediocre self-expression, those endless half-pretty repetitive small towns of the Middle and the West whose spirit is forever horizontal and whose marrow comes to rendezvous in the pastel monotonies of Los Angeles architecture.

So far as America has a history, one can see it in the severe heights of New York City, in the glare from the Pittsburgh mills, by the color in the brick of Louisburg Square, along the knotted greedy facades of the small mansions on Chicago's North Side, in Natchez's antebellum homes, the wrought-iron balconies off Bourbon Street, a captain's house in Nantucket, by the curve of Commercial Street in Provincetown. One can make a list; it is probably finite. What culture we have made and what history has collected to it can be found in those few hard examples of an architecture which came to its artistic term, was born, lived and so collected some history about it. Not all the roots of American life are uprooted, but almost all, and the spirit of the supermarket, that homogenous extension of stainless surfaces and psychoanalyzed people, packaged commodities and ranch homes, interchangeable, geographically unrecognizable, that essence of the new postwar SuperAmerica is found nowhere so perfectly as in Los Angeles' ubiquitous acres. One gets the impression that people come to Los Angeles in order to divorce themselves from the past, here to live or try to live in the rootless pleasure world of an adult child. One knows that if the cities of the world were destroyed by a new war, the architecture of the rebuilding would create a landscape which looked, subject to specifications of climate, exactly and entirely like the San Fernando Valley.

It is not that Los Angeles is altogether hideous, it is even by degrees pleasant, but for an Easterner there is never any salt in the wind; it is like

Mexican cooking without chile, or Chinese egg rolls missing their mustard; as one travels through the endless repetitions of that city which is the capital of suburbia with its milky pinks, its washed-out oranges, its tainted lime-yellows of pastel on one pretty little architectural monstrosity after another, the colors not intense enough, the styles never pure, and never sufficiently impure to collide on the eye, one conceives the people who live here—they have come out to express themselves, Los Angeles is the home of self-expression, but the artists are middle-class and middling-minded; no passions will calcify here for years in the gloom to be revealed a decade later as the tesselations of a hard and fertile work, no, it is all open, promiscuous, borrowed, half bought, a city without iron, eschewing wood, a kingdom of stucco, the playground for mass men—one has the feeling it was built by television sets giving orders to men. And in this land of the pretty-pretty, the virility is in the barbarisms, the vulgarities, it is in the huge billboards, the screamers of the neon lighting, the shouting farm-utensil colors of the gas stations and the monster drugstores, it is in the swing of the sports cars, hot rods, convertibles, Los Angeles is a city to drive in, the boulevards are wide, the traffic is nervous and fast, the radio stations play bouncing, blooping, rippling tunes, one digs the pop in a pop tune, no one of character would make love by it but the sound is good for swinging a car, electronic guitars and Hawaiian harps.

So this is the town the Democrats came to, and with their unerring instinct (after being with them a week, one thinks of this party as a crazy, half-rich family, loaded with poor cousins, traveling always in caravans with Cadillacs and Okie Fords, Lincolns and quarterhorse mules, putting up every night in tents to hear the chamber quartet of Great Cousin Eleanor invaded by the Texas-twanging steel-stringing geetarists of Bubber Lyndon, carrying its own mean high-school principal, Doc Symington, chided for its manners by good Uncle Adlai, told the route of march by Navigator Jack, cut off every six months from the rich will of Uncle Jim Farley, never listening to the mechanic of the caravan, Bald Sam Rayburn, who assures them they'll all break down unless Cousin Bubber gets the concession on the garage; it's the Snopes family married to Henry James, with the labor unions thrown in like a Yankee dollar, and yet it's true, in tranquility one recollects them with affection, their instinct is good, crazy family good) and this instinct now led the caravan to pick the Biltmore Hotel in downtown Los Angeles for their family get-together and reunion.

The Biltmore is one of the ugliest hotels in the world. Patterned after the flat roofs of an Italian Renaissance palace, it is eighty-eight times as large, and one-millionth as valuable to the continuation of man, and it would be intolerable if it were not for the presence of Pershing Square, that square block of park with cactus and palm trees, the three-hundred-and-sixty-five-day-a-year convention of every junkie, pot-head, pusher, queen (but you have read that good writing already). For years Pershing Square has been one of the three or four places in America famous to homosexuals, famous not for its posh, the chic is round-heeled here, but because it is one of the avatars of the good old masturbatory sex, dirty with the crusted sugars of smut, dirty rooming houses around the corner where the score is made, dirty book and photograph stores down the street, old-fashioned out-of-the-Thirties burlesque houses, cruising bars, jukeboxes, movie houses; Pershing Square is the town plaza for all those lonely, respectable, small-town homosexuals who lead a family life, make children, and have the Philbrick psychology (How I Joined the Communist Party and Led Three Lives). Yes, it is the open-air convention hall for the small-town inverts who live like spies, and it sits in the center of Los Angeles, facing the Biltmore, that hotel which is a mausoleum, that Pentagon of traveling salesmen the Party chose to house the headquarters of the Convention.

So here came that family, cursed before it began by the thundering absence of Great-Uncle Truman, the delegates dispersed over a run of thirty miles and twenty-seven hotels: the Olympian Motor Hotel, the Ambassador, the Beverly Wilshire, the Santa Ynez Inn (where rumor has it the delegates from Louisiana had some midnight swim), the Mayan, the Commodore, the Mayfair, the Sheraton-West, the Huntington-Sheraton, the Green, the Hayward, the Gates, the Figueroa, the Statler Hilton, the Hollywood Knickerbocker—does one have to be a collector to list such names?—beauties all, with that up-from-the-farm Los Angeles décor, plate-glass windows, patio and terrace, foam-rubber mattress, pastel paints, all of them pretty as an ad in full-page color, all but the Biltmore where everybody gathered every day—the newsmen, the TV, radio, magazine, and foreign newspapermen, the delegates, the politicos, the tourists, the campaign managers, the runners, the flunkies, the cousins and aunts, the wives, the grandfathers, the eight-year-old girls, and the twenty-eight-year-old girls in the Kennedy costumes, red and white and blue, the Symingteeners, the Johnson Ladies, the Stevenson Ladies, everybody —and for three days before the convention and four days into it, everybody collected at the Biltmore, in the lobby, in the grill, in the Biltmore Bowl, in the elevators, along the corridors, three hundred deep always outside the Kennedy suite, milling everywhere, every dark-carpeted grey-brown hall of the hotel, but it was in the Gallery of the Biltmore where one first felt the mood which pervaded all proceedings until the convention was almost over, that heavy, thick, witless depression which was to dominate every move as the delegates wandered and gawked and paraded and set for a spell, there in the Gallery of the Biltmore, that huge depressing alley with its inimitable hotel color, that faded depth of chiaroscuro which unhappily has no depth, that brown which is not a brown, that grey which has no pearl in it, that color which can be described only as hotel-color because the beiges, the tans, the walnuts, the mahoganies, the dull blood rugs, the moaning yellows, the sick greens, the greys and all those dumb browns merge into that lack of color which is an over-large hotel at convention time, with all the small-towners wearing their set, starched faces, that look they get at carnival, all fever and suspicion, and proud to be there, eddying slowly back and forth in that high block-long tunnel of a room with its arched ceiling and square recesses filling every rib of the arch with art work, escutcheons and blazons and other art, pictures I think, I cannot even remember, there was such a hill of cigar smoke the eye had to travel on its way to the ceiling, and at one end there was galvanized-pipe scaffolding and workmen repairing some part of the ceiling, one of them touching up one of the endless squares of painted plaster in the arch, and another worker, passing by, yelled up to the one who was working on the ceiling: "Hey, Michelangelo!"

Later, of course, it began to emerge and there were portraits one could keep, Symington, dogged at a press conference, declaring with no conviction that he knew he had a good chance to win, the disappointment eating at his good looks so that he came off hard-faced, mean, and yet slack—a desperate dullness came off the best of his intentions. There was Johnson who had compromised too many contradictions and now the contradictions were in his face: when he smiled the corners of his mouth squeezed gloom; when he was pious, his eyes twinkled irony; when he spoke in a righteous tone, he looked corrupt; when he jested, the ham in his jowls looked to quiver. He was not convincing. He was a Southern politician, a Texas Democrat, a liberal Eisenhower; he would do no harm, he would do no good, he would react to the machine, good fellow, nice friend—the Russians would understand him better than his own.

Stevenson had the patina. He came into the room and the room was different, not stronger perhaps (which is why ultimately he did not win), but warmer. One knew why some adored him; he did not look like other people, not with press lights on his flesh; he looked like a lover, the simple truth, he had the sweet happiness of an adolescent who has just been given his first major kiss. And so he glowed, and one was reminded of Chaplin, not because they were the least alike in features, but because Charlie Chaplin was luminous when one met him and Stevenson had something of that light.

There was Eleanor Roosevelt, fine, precise, hand-worked like ivory. Her voice was almost attractive as she explained in the firm, sad tones of the first lady in this small town why she could not admit Mr. Kennedy, who was no doubt a gentleman, into her political house. One had the impression of a lady who was finally becoming a woman, which is to say that she was just a little bitchy about it all; nice bitchy, charming, it had a touch of art to it, but it made one wonder if she were not now satisfying the last passion of them all, which was to become physically attractive, for she was better-looking than she had ever been as she spurned the possibilities of a young suitor.

Jim Farley. Huge. Cold as a bishop. The hell he would consign you to was cold as ice.

Bobby Kennedy, that archetype Bobby Kennedy, looked like a West Point cadet, or, better, one of those unreconstructed Irishmen from Kirkland House one always used to have to face in the line in Harvard house football games. "Hello," you would say to the ones who looked like him as you lined up for the scrimmage after the kickoff, and his type would nod and look away, one rock glint of recognition your due for living across the hall from one another all through Freshman year, and then bang, as the ball was passed back, you'd get a bony king-hell knee in the crotch. He was the kind of man never to put on the gloves with if you wanted to do some social boxing, because after two minutes it would be a war, and ego-bastards last long in a war.

Carmine DeSapio and Kenneth Galbraith on the same part of the convention floor. DeSapio is bigger than one expects, keen and florid, great big smoked glasses, a suntan like Man-tan—he is the kind of heavyweight Italian who could get by with a name like Romeo—and Galbraith is tall-tall, as actors say, six foot six it could be, terribly thin, enormously attentive, exquisitely polite, birdlike, he is sensitive to the stirring of reeds in a wind over the next hill. "Our grey eminence," whispered the intelligent observer next to me.

Bob Wagner, the mayor of New York, a little man, plump, groomed, blank. He had the blank, pomaded, slightly worried look of the first barber in a good barbershop, the kind who would go to the track on his day off and wear a green transparent stone in a gold ring,

Ar ' then there was Kennedy, the edge of the mystery. But a sketch will no longer suffice.

Perspective from the Biltmore Balcony: The Colorful Arrival of the Hero with the Orange-brown Suntan and Amazingly White Teeth; Revelation of the Two Rivers Political Theory

". . . it can be said with a fair amount of certainty that the essence of his political attractiveness is his extraordinary political intelligence. He has a mind quite unlike that of any other Democrat of this century. It is not literary, metaphysical and moral, as Adlai Stevenson's is. Kennedy is articulate and often witty, but he does not seek verbal polish. No one can doubt the seriousness of his concern with the most serious political matters, but one feels that whereas Mr. Stevenson's political views derive

from a view of life that holds politics to be a mere fraction of existence, Senator Kennedy's primary interest is in politics. The easy way in which he disposes of the question of Church and State—as if he felt that any reasonable man could quite easily resolve any possible conflict of loyalties—suggests that the organization of society is the one thing that really engages his interest."

—RICHARD ROVER *The New Yorker,* July 23, 1960

The afternoon he arrived at the convention from the airport, there was of course a large crowd on the street outside the Biltmore, and the best way to get a view was to get up on an outdoor balcony of the Biltmore, two flights above the street, and look down on the event. One waited thirty minutes, and then a honking of horns as wild as the getaway after an Italian wedding sounded around the corner, and the Kennedy cortege came into sight, circled Pershing Square, the men in the open and leading convertibles sitting backwards to look at their leader, and finally came to a halt in a space cleared for them by the police in the crowd. The television cameras were out, and a Kennedy band was playing some circus music. One saw him immediately. He had the deep orange-brown suntan of a ski instructor, and when he smiled at the crowd his teeth were amazingly white and clearly visible at a distance of fifty yards. For one moment he saluted Pershing Square, and Pershing Square saluted him back, the prince and the beggars of glamour staring at one another across a city street, one of those very special moments in the underground history of the world, and then with a quick move he was out of his car and by choice headed into the crowd instead of the lane cleared for him into the hotel by the police, so that he made his way inside surrounded by a mob, and one expected at any moment to see him lifted to its shoulders like a matador being carried back to the city after a triumph in the plaza. All the while the band kept playing the campaign tunes, sashaying circus music, and one had a moment of clarity, intense as a *déjà vu,* for the scene which had taken place had been glimpsed before in a dozen musical comedies; it was the scene where the hero, the matinee idol, the movie star comes to the palace to claim the princess, or what is the same, and more to our soil, the football hero, the campus king, arrives at the dean's home surrounded by a court of open-singing students to plead with the dean for his daughter's kiss and permission to put on the big musical that night. And suddenly I saw the convention, it came into focus for me, and I understood the mood of depression which had lain over the convention, because finally it was simple: the Democrats were going to nominate a man who, no matter how serious his political dedication might be, was indisputably and willy-nilly going to be seen as a great box-office actor, and the consequences of that were staggering and not at all easy to calculate.

Since the First World War Americans have been leading a double life, and our history has moved on two rivers, one visible, the other underground; there has been the history of politics which is concrete, factual, practical and unbelievably dull if not for the consequences of the actions of some of these men; and there is a subterranean river of untapped, ferocious, lonely and romantic desires, that concentration of ecstasy and violence which is the dream life of the nation.

The twentieth century may yet be seen as that era when civilized man and underprivileged man were melted together into mass man, the iron and steel of the nineteenth century giving way to electronic circuits which communicated their messages into men, the unmistakable tendency of the new century seeming to be the creation of men as interchangeable as commodities, their extremes of personality singed out of existence by the psychic fields of force the communicators would impose. This loss of personality was a catastrophe to the future of the imagination, but billions of people might first benefit from it by having enough to eat—one did not know—and there remained citadels of resistance in Europe where the culture was deep and roots were visible in the architecture of the past.

Nowhere, as in America, however, was this fall from individual man to mass man felt so acutely, for America was at once the first and most prolific creator of mass communications, and the most rootless of countries, since almost no American could lay claim to the line of a family which had not once at least severed its roots by migrating here. But, if rootless, it was then the most vulnerable of countries to its own homogenization. Yet America was also the country in which the dynamic myth of the Renaissance—that every man was potentially extraordinary—knew its most passionate persistence. Simply, America was the land where people still believed in heroes: George Washington; Billy the Kid; Lincoln, Jefferson; Mark Twain, Jack London, Hemingway; Joe Louis, Dempsey, Gentleman Jim; America believed in athletes, rum-runners, aviators; even lovers, by the time Valentino died. It was a country which had grown by the leap of one hero past another—is there a county in all of our ground which does not have its legendary figure? And when the West was filled, the expansion turned inward, became part of an agitated, overexcited, superheated dream life. The film studios threw up their searchlights as the frontier was finally sealed, and the romantic possibilities of the old conquest of land turned into a vertical myth, trapped within the skull, of a new kind of heroic life, each choosing his own archetype of a neo-renaissance man, be it Barrymore, Cagney, Flynn, Bogart, Brando or Sinatra, but it was almost as if there were no peace unless one could fight well, kill well (if always with honor), love well and love many, be cool, be daring, be dashing, be wild, be wily, be resourceful, be a brave gun. And this myth, that each of us was born to be free, to wander, to have adventure and to grow on the waves of the violent, the perfumed, and the unexpected, had a force which could not be tamed no matter how the nation's regulators—politicians, medicos, policemen, professors, priests, rabbis, ministers, ideologues, psychoanalysts, builders, executives and endless communicators—would brick-in the modern life with hygiene upon sanity, and middle-brow homily over platitude; the myth would not die. Indeed a quarter of the nation's business must have depended upon its existence. But it stayed alive for more than that—it was as if the message in the labyrinth of the genes would insist that violence was locked with creativity, and adventure was the secret of love.

Once, in the Second World War and in the year or two which followed, the underground river returned to earth, and the life of the nation was intense, of the present, electric; as a lady said, "That was the time when we gave parties which changed people's lives." The Forties was a decade when the speed with which one's own events occurred seemed as rapid as the history of the battlefields, and for the mass of people in America a forced march into a new jungle of emotion was the result. The surprises, the failures, and the dangers of that life must have terrified some nerve of awareness in the power and the mass, for, as if stricken by the orgiastic vistas the myth had carried up from underground, the retreat to a more conservative existence was disorderly, the fear of communism spread like an irrational hail of boils. To anyone who could see, the excessive hysteria of the Red wave was no preparation to face an enemy, but rather a terror of the national self: free-loving, lust-looting, atheistic, implacable—absurdity beyond absurdity to label communism so, for the moral products of Stalinism had been Victorian sex and a ponderous machine of material theology.

Forced underground again, deep beneath all *Reader's Digest* hospital dressings of Mental Health in Your Community, the myth continued to flow, fed by television and the film. The fissure in the national psyche widened to the danger point. The last large appearance of the myth was the vote which tricked the polls and gave Harry Truman his victory in '48. That was the last. Came the Korean War, the shadow of the H-bomb, and we were ready for the General. Uncle Harry gave way to Father, and security, regularity, order, and the life of no imagination were the command of the day. If one had any doubt of this, there was Joe McCarthy with his built-in treason detector, furnished by God, and the damage was done. In the totalitarian wind of those days, anyone who worked in Government formed the habit of being not too original, and many a mind atrophied from disuse and private shame. At the summit there was benevolence without leadership, regularity without vision, security without safety, rhetoric without life. The ship drifted on, that enormous warship of the United States, led by a Secretary of State whose cells were seceding to cancer, and as the world became more fantastic—Africa turning itself upside down, while some new kind of machine man was being made in China—two events occurred which stunned the confidence of America

into a new night: the Russians put up their Sputnik, and Civil Rights—
that reluctant gift to the American Negro, granted for its effect on foreign
affairs—spewed into real life at Little Rock. The national Ego was in
shock: the Russians were now in some ways our technological superiors,
and we had an internal problem of subject populations equal conceivably
in its difficulty to the Soviet and its satellites. The fatherly calm of the
General began to seem like the uxorious mellifluences of the undertaker.

Underneath it all was a larger problem. The life of politics and the life
of myth had diverged too far, and the energies of the people one knew
everywhere had slowed down. Twenty years ago a post-Depression generation had gone to war and formed a lively, grousing, by times inefficient,
carousing, pleasure-seeking, not altogether inadequate army. It did part of
what it was supposed to do, and many, out of combat, picked up a kind of
private life on the fly, and had their good time despite the yaws of the
military system. But today in America the generation which respected the
code of the myth was Beat, a horde of half-begotten Christs with scraggly
beards, heroes none, saints all, weak before the strong, empty conform-
isms of the authority. The sanction for finding one's growth was no longer
one's flag, one's career, one's sex, one's adventure, not even one's booze.
Among the best in this newest of the generations, the myth had found its
voice in marijuana, and the joke of the underground was that when the
Russians came over they could never dare to occupy us for long because
America was too Hip. Gallows humor. The poorer truth might be that
America was too Beat, the instinct of the nation so separated from its
public mind that apathy, schizophrenia, and private beatitudes might be
the pride of the welcoming committee any underground could offer.

Yes, the life of politics and the life of the myth had diverged too far.
There was nothing to return them to one another, no common danger, no
cause, no desire, and, most essentially, no hero. It was a hero America
needed, a hero central to his time, a man whose personality might suggest
contradictions and mysteries which could reach into the alienated circuits
of the underground, because only a hero can capture the secret imagination of a people, and so be good for the vitality of his nation; a hero
embodies the fantasy and so allows each private mind the liberty to
consider its fantasy and find a way to grow. Each mind can become more
conscious of its desire and waste less strength in hiding from itself.
Roosevelt was such a hero, and Churchill, Lenin and de Gaulle; even
Hitler, to take the most odious example of this thesis, was a hero, the
hero-as-monster, embodying what had become the monstrous fantasy of a
people, but the horror upon which the radical mind and liberal temperament foundered was that he gave outlet to the energies of the Germans and
so presented the twentieth century with an index of how horrible had
become the secret heart of its desire. Roosevelt is of course a happier
example of the hero; from his paralytic leg to the royal elegance of his

geniality he seemed to contain the country within himself; everyone from the meanest starving cripple to an ambitious young man could expand into the optimism of an improving future because the man offered an unspoken promise of a future which would be rich. The sexual and the sex-starved, the poor, the hard-working and the imaginative well-to-do could see themselves in the President, could believe him to be like themselves. So a large part of the country was able to discover its energies because not as much was wasted in feeling that the country was a poisonous nutrient which stifled the day.

Too simple? No doubt. One tries to construct a simple model. The thesis is after all not so mysterious; it would merely nudge the notion that a hero embodies his time and is not so very much better than his time, but he is larger than life and so is capable of giving direction to the time, able to encourage a nation to discover the deepest colors of its character. At bottom the concept of the hero is antagonistic to impersonal social progress, to the belief that social ills can be solved by social legislating, for it sees a country as all-but-trapped in its character until it has a hero who reveals the character of the country to itself. The implication is that without such a hero the nation turns sluggish. Truman for example was not such a hero, he was not sufficiently larger than life, he inspired familiarity without excitement, he was a character but his proportions came from soap opera: Uncle Harry, full of salty common-sense and small-minded certainty, a storekeeping uncle.

Whereas Eisenhower has been the anti-Hero, the regulator. Nations do not necessarily and inevitably seek for heroes. In periods of dull anxiety, one is more likely to look for security than a dramatic confrontation, and Eisenhower could stand as a hero only for that large number of Americans who were most proud of their lack of imagination. In American life, the unspoken war of the century has taken place between the city and the small town the city which is dynamic, orgiastic, unsettling, explosive and accelerating to the psyche; the small town which is rooted, narrow, cautious and planted in the life-logic of the family. The need of the city is to accelerate growth; the pride of the small town is to retard it. But since America has been passing through a period of enormous expansion since the war, the double-four years of Dwight Eisenhower could not retard the expansion, it could only denude it of color, character, and the development of novelty. The small-town mind is rooted—it is rooted in the small town—and when it attempts to direct history the results are disastrously colorless because the instrument of world power which is used by the small-town mind is the committee. Committees do not create, they merely proliferate, and the incredible dullness wreaked upon the American landscape in Eisenhower's eight years has been the triumph of the corporation. A tasteless, sexless, odorless sanctity in architecture, manners, modes, styles has been the result. Eisenhower embodied half the needs of the nation, the needs of the timid, the petrified, the sanctimonious, and the sluggish. What was even worse, he did not divide the nation as a hero might (with a dramatic dialogue as the result); he merely excluded one part of the nation from the other. The result was an alienation of the best minds and bravest impulses from the faltering history which was made. America's need in those years was to take an existential turn, to walk into the nightmare, to face into that terrible logic of history which demanded that the country and its people must become more extraordinary and more adventurous, or else perish, since the only alternative was to offer a false security in the power and the panacea of organized religion, family, and the F.B.I., a totalitarianization of the psyche by the stultifying techniques of the mass media which would seep into everyone's most private associations and so leave the country powerless against the Russians even if the denouement were to take fifty years, for in a competition between totalitarianisms the first maxim of the prizefight manager would doubtless apply: "Hungry fighters win fights."

The Hipster as Presidential Candidate: Thoughts on a Public Man's Eighteenth-Century Wife; Face-to-Face with the Hero; Significance of a Personal Note, or the Meaning of His Having Read an Author's Novel

Some part of these thoughts must have been in one's mind at the moment there was that first glimpse of Kennedy entering the Biltmore Hotel; and in the days which followed, the first mystery—the profound air of depression which hung over the convention—gave way to a second mystery which can be answered only by history. The depression of the delegates was understandable: no one had too much doubt that Kennedy would be nominated, but if elected he would be not only the youngest President ever to be chosen by voters, he would be the most conventionally attractive young man ever to sit in the White House, and his wife—some would claim it—might be the most beautiful first lady in our history. Of necessity the myth would emerge once more, because America's politics would now be also America's favorite movie, America's first soap opera, America's best-seller. One thinks of the talents of writers like Taylor Caldwell or Frank Yerby, or is it rather *The Fountainhead* which would contain such a fleshing of the romantic prescription? Or is it indeed one's own work which is called into question? "Well, there's your first hipster," says a writer one knows at the convention, "Sergius O'Shaugnessy born rich," and the temptation is to nod, for it could be true, a war hero, and the heroism is bona-fide, even exceptional, a man who has lived with death, who, crippled in the back, took on an operation which would kill him or restore him to power, who chose to marry a lady whose face might be too imaginative for the taste of a democracy which likes its first ladies to be executives of home-management, a man who courts political suicide by choosing to go all out for a nomination four, eight, or twelve years before his political elders think he is ready, a man who announces a week prior to the convention that the young are better fitted to direct history than the old. Yes, it captures the attention. This is no routine candidate calling every shot by safety's routine book ("Yes," Nixon said, naturally but terribly tired an hour after his nomination, the TV cameras and lights and microphones bringing out a sweat of fatigue on his face, the words coming very slowly from the tired brain, somber, modest, sober, slow, slow enough so that one could touch emphatically the cautions behind each word, "Yes, I want to say," said Nixon, "that whatever abilities I have, I got from my mother." A tired pause . . . dull moment of warning, ". . . and my father." The connection now made, the rest comes easy, ". . . and my school and my church." Such men are capable of anything.)

One had the opportunity to study Kennedy a bit in the days that followed. His style in the press conferences was interesting. Not terribly popular with the reporters (too much a contemporary, and yet too difficult to understand, he received nothing like the rounds of applause given to Eleanor Roosevelt, Stevenson, Humphrey, or even Johnson), he carried himself nonetheless with a cool grace which seemed indifferent to applause, his manner somehow similar to the poise of a fine boxer, quick with his hands, neat in his timing, and two feet away from his corner when the bell ended the round. There was a good lithe wit to his responses, a dry Harvard wit, a keen sense of proportion in disposing of difficult questions—invariably he gave enough of an answer to be formally satisfactory without ever opening himself to a new question which might go further than the first. Asked by a reporter, "Are you for Adlai as vice-president?" the grin came forth and the voice turned very dry, "No, I cannot say we have considered *Adlai* as a vice-president." Yet there was an elusive detachment to everything he did. One did not have the feeling of a man present in the room with all his weight and all his mind. Johnson gave you all of himself, he was a political animal, he breathed like an animal, sweated like one, you knew his mind was entirely absorbed with the compendium of political fact and maneuver; Kennedy seemed at times like a young professor whose manner was adequate for the classroom, but whose mind was off in some intricacy of the Ph. D. thesis he was writing. Perhaps one can give a sense of the discrepancy by saying that he was like an actor who had been cast as the candidate, a good actor, but not a great one—you were aware all the time that the role was one thing and the man another—they did not coincide, the actor seemed a touch too aloof (as, let us say, Gregory Peck is usually too aloof) to become the part. Yet one had little sense of whether to value this elusiveness, or to beware of it. One could be witnessing the fortitude of a superior sensitivity or the detachment of a man who was not quite real to himself. And his voice gave no clue. When Johnson spoke, one could separate what was fraudulent from what was felt, he would have been satisfying as an actor the way Broderick Crawford or Paul Douglas are satisfying; one saw into his emotions, or at least had the illusion that one did. Kennedy's voice, however, was only a fair voice, too reedy, near to strident, it had the metallic snap of a cricket in it somewhere, it was more impersonal than the man, and so became the least-impressive quality in a face, a body, a selection of language, and a style of movement which made up a better-than-decent presentation, better than one had expected.

With all of that, it would not do to pass over the quality in Kennedy which is most difficult to describe. And in fact some touches should be added to this hint of a portrait, for later (after the convention), one had a short session alone with him, and the next day, another. As one had suspected in advance, the interviews were not altogether satisfactory, they hardly could have been. A man running for President is altogether different from a man elected President: the hazards of the campaign make it impossible for a candidate to be as interesting as he might like to be (assuming he has such a desire). One kept advancing the argument that this campaign would be a contest of personalities, and Kennedy kept returning the discussion to politics. After a while one recognized this was an inevitable caution for him. So there would be not too much point to reconstructing the dialogue since Kennedy is hardly inarticulate about his political attitudes and there will be a library vault of text devoted to it in the newspapers. What struck me most about the interview was a passing remark whose importance was invisible on the scale of politics, but was altogether meaningful to my particular competence. As we sat down for the first time, Kennedy smiled nicely and said that he had read my books. One muttered one's pleasure. "Yes," he said, "I've read . . ." and then there was a short pause which did not last long enough to be embarrassing in which it was yet obvious no title came instantly to his mind, an omission one was not ready to mind altogether since a man in such a position must be obliged to carry a hundred thousand facts and names in his head, but the hesitation lasted no longer than three seconds or four, and then he said, "I've read *The Deer Park* and . . . the others," which startled me for it was the first time in a hundred similar situations, talking to someone whose knowledge of my work was casual, that the sentence did not come out, "I've read *The Naked and the Dead* . . . and the others." If one is to take the worst and assume that Kennedy was briefed for this interview (which is most doubtful), it still speaks well for the striking instincts of his advisers.

What was retained later is an impression of Kennedy's manners which were excellent, even artful, better than the formal good manners of Choate and Harvard, almost as if what was creative in the man had been given to the manners. In a room with one or two people, his voice improved, became low-pitched, even pleasant—it seemed obvious that in all these years he had never become a natural public speaker and so his voice was constricted in public, the symptom of all orators who are ambitious, throttled, and determined.

His personal quality had a subtle, not quite describable intensity, a suggestion of dry pent heat perhaps, his eyes large, the pupils grey, the whites prominent, almost shocking, his most forceful feature: he had the eyes of a mountaineer. His appearance changed with his mood, strikingly so, and this made him always more interesting than what he was saying. He would seem at one moment older than his age, forty-eight or fifty, a tall, slim, sunburned professor with a pleasant weathered face, not even particularly handsome; five minutes later, talking to a press conference on his lawn, three microphones before him, a television camera turning, his appearance would have gone through a metamorphosis, he would look again like a movie star, his coloring vivid, his manner rich, his gestures strong and quick, alive with that concentration of vitality a successful actor always seems to radiate. Kennedy had a dozen faces. Although they were not all similar as people, the quality was reminiscent of some one like Brando whose expression rarely changes, but whose appearance seems to shift from one person into another as the minutes go by, and one bothers with this comparison because, like Brando, Kennedy's most characteristic quality is the remote and private air of a man who has traversed some lonely terrain of experience, of loss and gain, of nearness to death, which leaves him isolated from the mass of others.

"The next day while they waited in vain for rescuers, the wrecked half of the boat turned over in the water and they saw that it would soon sink. The group decided to swim to a small island three miles away. There were other islands bigger and nearer, but the Navy officers knew that they were occupied by the Japanese. On one island, only one mile to the south, they could see a Japanese camp. McMahon, the engineer whose legs were disabled by burns, was unable to swim. Despite his own painfully crippled back, Kennedy swam the three miles with a breast stroke, towing behind him by a life-belt strap that he held between his teeth the helpless McMahon . . . it took Kennedy and the suffering engineer five hours to reach the island."

The quotation is from a book which has for its dedicated unilateral title, *The Remarkable Kennedys,* but the prose is by one of the best of the war reporters, the former *Yank* editor, Joe McCarthy, and so presumably may be trusted in such details as this. Physical bravery does not of course guarantee a man's abilities in the White House—all too often men with physical courage are disappointing in their moral imagination—but the heroism here is remarkable for its tenacity. The above is merely one episode in a continuing saga which went on for five days in and out of the water, and left Kennedy at one point "miraculously saved from drowning (in a storm) by a group of Solomon Island natives who suddenly came up beside him in a large dugout canoe." Afterward, his back still injured (that precise back injury which was to put him on crutches eleven years later, and have him search for "spinal-fusion surgery" despite a warning that his chances of living through the operation were "extremely limited") afterward, he asked to go back on duty and became so bold in the attacks he made with his PT boat "that the crew didn't like to go out with him because he took so many chances."

It is the wisdom of a man who senses death within him and gambles that he can cure it by risking his life. It is the therapy of the instinct, and who is so wise as to call it irrational? Before he went into the Navy, Kennedy had been ailing. Washed out of Freshman year at Princeton by a prolonged trough of yellow jaundice, sick for a year at Harvard, weak already in the back from an injury at football, his trials suggest the self-hatred of a man whose resentment and ambition are too large for his body. Not everyone can discharge their furies on an analyst's couch, for some angers can be relaxed only by winning power, some rages are sufficiently monumental to demand that one try to become a hero or else fall back into that death which is already within the cells. But if one succeeds, the energy aroused can be exceptional. Talking to a man who had been with Kennedy in Hyannis Port the week before the convention, I heard that he was in a state of deep fatigue.

"Well, he didn't look tired at the convention," one commented.

"Oh, he had three days of rest. Three days of rest for him is like six months for us."

One thinks of that three-mile swim with the belt in his mouth and McMahon holding it behind him. There are pestilences which sit in the mouth and rot the teeth—in those five hours how much of the psyche must have been remade, for to give vent to the bite in one's jaws and yet use that rage to save a life: it is not so very many men who have the apocalyptic sense that heroism is the First Doctor.

If one had a profound criticism of Kennedy it was that his public mind was too conventional, but that seemed to matter less than the fact of such a man in office because the law of political life had become so dreary that only a conventional mind could win an election. Indeed there could be no politics which gave warmth to one's body until the country had recovered its imagination, its pioneer lust for the unexpected and incalculable. It was the changes that might come afterward on which one could put one's hope. With such a man in office the myth of the nation would again be engaged, and the fact that he was Catholic would shiver a first existential vibration of consciousness into the mind of the White Protestant. For the first time in our history, the Protestant would have the pain and creative luxury of feeling himself in some tiny degree part of a minority, and that was an experience which might be incommensurable in its value to the best of them.

A Vignette of Adlai Stevenson; The Speeches: What Happened When the Teleprompter Jammed: How U.S. Senator Eugene McCarthy Played the Matador. An Observation on the Name Fitzgerald

As yet we have said hardly a word about Stevenson. And his actions must remain a puzzle unless one dares a speculation about his motive, or was it his need?

So far as the people at the convention had affection for anyone, it was Stevenson, so far as they were able to generate any spontaneous enthusiasm, their cheers were again for Stevenson. Yet it was obvious he never had much chance because so soon as a chance would present itself he seemed quick to dissipate the opportunity. The day before the nominations, he entered the Sports Arena to take his seat as a delegate—the demonstration was spontaneous, noisy and prolonged; it was quieted only by Governor Collins' invitation for Stevenson to speak to the delegates. In obedience perhaps to the scruple that a candidate must not appear before the convention until nominations are done, Stevenson said no more than: "I am grateful for this tumultuous and moving welcome. After getting in and out of the Biltmore Hotel and this hall, I have decided I know whom you are going to nominate. It will be the last survivor." This dry reminder of the ruthlessness of politics broke the roar of excitement for his presence. The applause as he left the platform was like the dying fall-and-moan of a baseball crowd when a home run curves foul. The next day, a New York columnist talking about it said bitterly, "If he'd only gone through the motions, if he had just said that now he wanted to run, that he would work hard, and he hoped the delegates would vote for him. Instead he made that lame joke." One wonders. It seems almost as if he did not wish to win unless victory came despite himself, and then was overwhelming. There are men who are not heroes because they are too good for their time, and it is natural that defeats leave them bitter, tired, and doubtful of their right to make new history. If Stevenson had campaigned for a year before the convention, it is possible that he could have stopped Kennedy. At the least, the convention would have been enormously more exciting, and the nominations might have gone through half-a-dozen ballots before a winner was hammered into shape. But then Stevenson might also have shortened his life. One had the impression of a tired man who (for a politician) was sickened unduly by compromise. A year of maneuvering, broken promises, and detestable partners might have gutted him for the election campaign. If elected, it might have ruined him as a President. There is the possibility that he sensed his situation exactly this way, and knew that if he were to run for President, win and make a good one, he would first have to be restored, as one can indeed be restored, by an exceptional demonstration of love—love, in this case, meaning that the Party had a profound desire to keep him as their leader. The emotional truth of a last-minute victory for Stevenson over the Kennedy machine might have given him new energy; it would certainly have given him new faith in a country and a party whose good motives he was possibly beginning to doubt. Perhaps the fault he saw with his candidacy was that he attracted only the nicest people to himself and there were not enough of them. (One of the private amusements of the convention was to divine some of the qualities of the candidates by the style of the young women who put on hats and clothing and politicked in the colors of one presidential gent or another. Of course, half of them must have been hired models, but someone did the hiring and so it was fair to look for a common denominator. The Johnson girls tended to be plump, pie-faced, dumb sexy Southern; the Symingteeners seemed a touch mulish, stubborn, good-looking pluggers; the Kennedy ladies were the handsomest; healthy, attractive, tough, a little spoiled—they looked like the kind of girls who had gotten all the dances in high school and/or worked for a year as an airline hostess before marrying well. But the Stevenson girls looked to be doing it for no money; they were good sorts, slightly horsy-faced, one had the impression they played field hockey in college.) It was indeed the pure, the saintly, the clean-living, the pacifistic, the vegetarian who seemed most for Stevenson, and the less humorous in the Kennedy camp were heard to remark bitterly that Stevenson had nothing going for him but a bunch of Goddamn Beatniks. This might even have had its sour truth. The demonstrations outside the Sports Arena for Stevenson seemed to have more than a fair proportion of tall, emaciated young men with thin, wry beards and three-string guitars accompanied (again in undue proportion) by a contingent of ascetic, face-washed young Beat ladies in sweaters and dungarees. Not to mention all the Holden Caulfields one could see from here to the horizon. But of course it is unfair to limit it so, for the Democratic gentry were also committed half en masse for Stevenson, as well as a considerable number of movie stars, Shelley Winters for one: after the convention she remarked sweetly, "Tell me something nice about Kennedy so I can get excited about him."

What was properly astonishing was the way this horde of political half-breeds and amateurs came within distance of turning the convention from its preconceived purpose, and managed at the least to bring the only hour of thoroughgoing excitement the convention could offer.

But then nominating day was the best day of the week and enough happened to suggest that a convention out of control would be a spectacle as extraordinary in the American scale of spectator values as a close seventh game in the World Series or a tied fourth quarter in a professional-football championship. A political convention is after all not a meeting of a corporation's board of directors; it is a fiesta, a carnival, a pig-rooting, horse-snorting, band-playing, voice-screaming medieval get-together of greed, practical lust, compromised idealism, career-advancement, meeting, feud, vendetta, conciliation, of rabble-rousers, fist fights (as it used to be), embraces, drunks (again as it used to be) and collective rivers of animal sweat. It is a reminder that no matter how the country might pretend it has grown up and become tidy in its manners, bodiless in its legislative language, hygienic in its separation of high politics from private life, that the roots still come grubby from the soil, and that politics in America is still different from politics anywhere else because the politics has arisen out of the immediate needs, ambitions, and cupidities of the people, that our politics still smell of the bedroom and the kitchen, rather than having descended to us from the chill punctilio of aristocratic negotiation.

So. The Sports Arena was new, too pretty of course, tasteless in its design—it was somehow pleasing that the acoustics were so bad for one did not wish the architects well; there had been so little imagination in their design, and this arena would have none of the harsh grandeur of Madison Square Garden when it was aged by spectators' phlegm and feet over the next twenty years. Still it had some atmosphere; seen from the streets, with the spectators moving to the ticket gates, the bands playing, the green hot-shot special editions of the Los Angeles newspapers being hawked by the newsboys, there was a touch of the air of promise that precedes a bullfight, not something so good as the approach to the Plaza Mexico, but good, let us say, like the entrance into El Toreo of Mexico City, another architectural monstrosity, also with seats painted, as I remember, in rose-pink, and dark, milky sky-blue.

Inside, it was also different this nominating day. On Monday and Tuesday the air had been desultory, no one listened to the speakers, and everybody milled from one easy chatting conversation to another—it had been like a tepid Kaffeeklatsch for fifteen thousand people. But today there was a whip of anticipation in the air, the seats on the floor were filled, the press section was working, and in the gallery people were sitting in the aisles.

Sam Rayburn had just finished nominating Johnson as one came in, and the rebel yells went up, delegates started filing out of their seats and climbing over seats, and a pullulating dance of bodies and bands began to snake through the aisles, the posters jogging and whirling in time to the music. The dun color of the floor (faces, suits, seats and floor boards), so monotonous the first two days, now lit up with life as if an iridescent caterpillar had emerged from a fold of wet leaves. It was more vivid than one had expected, it was right, it felt finally like a convention, and from up close when one got down to the floor (where your presence was illegal and so consummated by sneaking in one time as demonstrators were going out, and again by slipping a five-dollar bill to a guard) the nearness to the demonstrators took on high color, that electric vividness one feels on the side lines of a football game when it is necessary to duck back as the ballcarrier goes by, his face tortured in the concentration of the moment, the thwomp of his tackle as acute as if one had been hit oneself.

That was the way the demonstrators looked on the floor. Nearly all had the rapt, private look of a passion or a tension which would finally be worked off by one's limbs, three hundred football players, everything from seedy delegates with jowl-sweating shivers to livid models, paid for their work that day, but stomping out their beat on the floor with the hypnotic adulatory grimaces of ladies who had lived for Lyndon these last ten years.

Then from the funereal rostrum, whose color was not so rich as mahogany nor so dead as a cigar, came the last of the requests for the delegates to take their seats. The seconding speeches began, one minute each; they ran for three and four, the minor-league speakers running on the longest as if the electric antennae of television was the lure of the Sirens, leading them out. Bored cheers applauded their concluding Götterdämmerungen and the nominations were open again. A favorite son, a modest demonstration, five seconding speeches, tedium.

Next was Kennedy's occasion. Governor Freeman of Minnesota made the speech. On the second or third sentence his television prompter jammed, an accident. Few could be aware of it at the moment; the speech seemed merely flat and surprisingly void of bravura. He was obviously no giant of extempore. Then the demonstration. Well-run, bigger than Johnson's, jazzier, the caliber of the costumes and decorations better chosen: the placards were broad enough, "Let's Back Jack," the floats were garish, particularly a papier-mâché or plastic balloon of Kennedy's head, six feet in diameter, which had nonetheless the slightly shrunken, over-red, rubbery look of a toy for practical jokers in one of those sleazy off-Times Square magic-and-gimmick stores; the band was suitably corny; and yet one had the impression this demonstration had been designed by some hands-to-hip interior decorator who said, "Oh, joy, let's have fun, let's make this *true* beer hall."

Besides, the personnel had something of the Kennedy *élan*, those paper hats designed to look like straw boaters with Kennedy's face on the crown, and small photographs of him on the ribbon, those hats which had come to symbolize the crack speed of the Kennedy team, that Madison Avenue cachet which one finds in bars like P. J. Clarke's, the elegance always giving its subtle echo of the Twenties so that the raccoon coats seem more numerous than their real count, and the colored waistcoats are measured by the charm they would have drawn from Scott Fitzgerald's eye. But there, it occurred to one for the first time that Kennedy's middle name was just that, Fitzgerald, and the tone of his crack lieutenants, the unstated style, was true to Scott. The legend of Fitzgerald had an army at last, formed around the self-image in the mind of every superior Madison Avenue opportunist that he was hard, he was young, he was In, his conversation was lean as wit, and if the work was not always scrupulous, well the style could aspire. If there came a good day . . . he could meet the occasion.

The Kennedy snake dance ran its thirty lively minutes, cheered its seconding speeches, and sat back. They were so sure of winning, there had been so many victories before this one, and this one had been scouted and managed so well, that hysteria could hardly be the mood. Besides, everyone was waiting for the Stevenson barrage which should be at least diverting. But now came a long tedium. Favorite sons were nominated, fat mayors shook their hips, seconders told the word to constituents back in Ponderwaygot County, treacly demonstrations tried to hold the floor, and the afternoon went by; Symington's hour came and went, a good demonstration, good as Johnson's (for good cause—they had pooled their demonstrators). More favorite sons, Governor Docking of Kansas declared "a genius" by one of his lady speakers in a tense go-back-to-religion voice. The hours went by, two, three, four hours, it seemed forever before they would get to Stevenson. It was evening when Senator Eugene McCarthy of Minnesota got up to nominate him.

The gallery was ready, the floor was responsive, the demonstrators were milling like bulls in their pen waiting for the *toril* to fly open——it would have been hard not to wake the crowd up, not to make a good speech. McCarthy made a great one. Great it was by the measure of convention oratory, and he held the crowd like a matador, timing their *oles!*, building them up, easing them back, correcting any sag in attention, gathering their emotion, discharging it, creating new emotion on the wave of the last, driving his passes tighter and tighter as he readied for the kill. "Do not reject this man who made us all proud to be called Democrats, do not leave this prophet without honor in his own party." One had not heard a speech like this since 1948 when Vito Marcantonio's voice, his harsh, shrill, bitter, street urchin's voice screeched through the loud-speakers at Yankee Stadium and lashed seventy thousand people into an uproar.

"There was only one man who said let's talk sense to the American people," McCarthy went on, his muleta furled for the *naturales*. "There was only one man who said let's talk sense to the American people," he repeated. "He said the promise of America is the promise of greatness.

This was his call to greatness. . . . Do not forget this man. . . . Ladies and Gentlemen, I present to you not the favorite son of one state, but the favorite son of the fifty states, the favorite son of every country he has visited, the favorite son of every country which has not seen him but is secretly thrilled by his name." Bedlam. The kill. "Ladies and Gentlemen, I present to you Adlai Stevenson of Illinois." Ears and tail. Hooves and bull. A roar went up like the roar one heard the day Bobby Thomson hit his home run at the Polo Grounds and the Giants won the pennant from the Dodgers in the third playoff game of the 1951 season. The demonstration cascaded onto the floor, the gallery came to its feet, the Sports Arena sounded like the inside of a marching drum. A tidal pulse of hysteria, exaltation, defiance, exhilaration, anger and roaring desire flooded over the floor. The cry which had gone up on McCarthy's last sentence had not paused for breath in five minutes, and troop after troop of demonstrators jammed the floor (the Stevenson people to be scolded the next day for having collected floor passes and sent them out to bring in new demonstrators) and still the sound mounted. One felt the convention coming apart. There was a Kennedy girl in the seat in front of me, the Kennedy hat on her head, a dimpled healthy brunette; she had sat silently through McCarthy's speech, but now, like a woman paying her respects to the power of natural thrust, she took off her hat and began to clap herself. I saw a writer I knew in the next aisle; he had spent a year studying the Kennedy machine in order to write a book on how a nomination is won. If Stevenson stampeded the convention, his work was lost. Like a reporter at a mine cave-in I inquired the present view of the widow. "Who can think," was the answer, half frantic, half elated, "just watch it, that's all." I found a cool one, a New York reporter, who smiled in rueful respect. "It's the biggest demonstration I've seen since Wendell Willkie's in 1940," he said, and added, "God, if Stevenson takes it, I can wire my wife and move the family on to Hawaii."

"I don't get it."

"Well, every story I wrote said it was locked up for Kennedy."

Still it went on, twenty minutes, thirty minutes, the chairman could hardly be heard, the demonstrators refused to leave. The lights were turned out, giving a sudden theatrical shift to the sense of a crowded church at midnight, and a new roar went up, louder, more passionate than anything heard before. It was the voice, it was the passion, if one insisted to call it that, of everything in America which was defeated, idealistic, innocent, alienated, outside the Beat, it was the potential voice of a new third of the nation whose psyche was ill from cultural malnutrition, it was powerful, it was extraordinary, it was larger than the decent, humorous, finicky, half-noble man who had called it forth, it was a cry from the Thirties when Time was simple, it was a resentment of the slick technique, the oiled gears, and the superior generals of Fitzgerald's Army; but it was also—and for this reason one could not admire it altogether, except with one's excitement—it was also the plea of the bewildered who hunger for simplicity again, it was the adolescent counterpart of the boss's depression before the unpredictable dynamic of Kennedy as President, it was the return to the sentimental dream of Roosevelt rather than the approaching nightmare of history's oncoming night, and it was inspired by a terror of the future as much as a revulsion of the present.

Fitz's Army held; after the demonstration was finally down, the convention languished for ninety minutes while Meyner and others were nominated, a fatal lapse of time because Stevenson had perhaps a chance to stop Kennedy if the voting had begun on the echo of the last cry for him, but in an hour and a half depression crept in again and emotions spent, the delegates who had wavered were rounded into line. When the vote was taken, Stevenson had made no gains. The brunette who had taken off her hat was wearing it again, and she clapped and squealed when Wyoming delivered the duke and Kennedy was in. The air was sheepish, like the mood of a suburban couple who forgive each other for cutting in and out of somebody else's automobile while the country club dance is on. Again, tonight, no miracle would occur. In the morning the papers would be moderate in their description of Stevenson's last charge.

A Sketch of the Republicans Gathered in Convention: The Choice Between the Venturesome and the Safe; What May Happen at Three o'Clock in the Morning on a Long Dark Night

One did not go to the other convention. It was seen on television, and so too much cannot be said of that. It did however confirm one's earlier bias that the Republican Party was still a party of church ushers, undertakers, choirboys, prison wardens, bank presidents, small-town police chiefs, state troopers, psychiatrists, beauty-parlor operators, corporation executives, Boy-Scout leaders, fraternity presidents, tax-board assessors, community leaders, surgeons, Pullman porters, head nurses and the fat sons of rich fathers. Its candidate would be given the manufactured image of an ordinary man, and his campaign, so far as it was a psychological campaign (and this would be far indeed), would present him as a simple, honest, dependable, hard-working, ready-to-learn, modest, humble, decent, sober young man whose greatest qualification for President was his profound abasement before the glories of the Republic, the stability of the mediocre, and his own unworthiness. The apocalyptic hour of Uriah Heep.

It would then be a campaign unlike the ones which had preceded it. Counting by the full spectrum of complete Right to absolute Left, the political differences would be minor, but what would be not at all minor was the power of each man to radiate his appeal into some fundamental depths of the American character. One would have an inkling at last if the desire of America was for drama or stability, for adventure or monotony. And this, this appeal to the psychic direction America would now choose for itself was the element most promising about this election, for it gave the possibility that the country might be able finally to rise above the deadening verbiage of its issues, its politics, its jargon, and live again by an image of itself. For in some part of themselves the people might know (since these candidates were not old enough to be revered) that they had chosen one young man for his mystery, for his promise that the country would grow or disintegrate by the unwilling charge he gave to the intensity of the myth, or had chosen another young man for his unstated oath that he would do all in his power to keep the myth buried and so convert the remains of Renaissance man as rapidly as possible into mass man. One might expect them to choose the enigma in preference to the deadening certainty. Yet one must doubt America's bravery. This lurching, unhappy, pompous and most corrupt nation—could it have the courage finally to take on a new image for itself, was it brave enough to put into office not only one of its ablest men, its most efficient, its most conquistadorial (for Kennedy's capture of the Democratic Party deserves the word), but also one of its more mysterious men (the national psyche must shiver in its sleep at the image of Mickey Mantle-cum-Lindbergh in office, and a First Lady with an eighteenth-century face). Yes, America was at last engaging the fate of its myth, its consciousness about to be accelerated or cruelly depressed in its choice between two young men in their forties who, no matter how close, dull, or indifferent their stated politics might be, were radical poles apart, for one was sober, the apotheosis of opportunistic lead, all radium spent, the other handsome as a prince in the unstated aristocracy of the American dream. So, finally, would come a choice which history had never presented to a nation before—one could vote for glamour or for ugliness, a staggering and most stunning choice—would the nation be brave enough to enlist the romantic dream of itself, would it vote for the image in the mirror of its unconscious, were the people indeed brave enough to hope for an acceleration of Time, for that new life of drama which would come from choosing a son to lead them who was heir apparent to the psychic loins? One could pause: it might be more difficult to be a President than it ever had before. Nothing less than greatness would do.

Yet if the nation voted to improve its face, what an impetus might come to the arts, to the practices, to the lives and to the imagination of the American. If the nation so voted. But one knew the unadmitted specter in the minds of the Democratic delegates: that America would go to sleep on election eve with the polls promising Kennedy a victory on the day to come, yet in its sleep some millions of Democrats and Independents would suffer a nightmare before the mystery of uncharted possibilities their man would suggest, and in a terror of all the creativities (and some violences) that mass man might now have to dare again, the undetermined would go out in the morning to vote for the psychic security of Nixon the way a middle-aged man past adventure holds to the stale bread of his marriage. Yes, this election might be fearful enough to betray the polls and no one in America could plan the new direction until the last vote was counted by the last heeler in the last ambivalent ward, no one indeed could know until then what had happened the night before, what had happened at three o'clock in the morning on that long dark night of America's search for a security cheaper than her soul.

[November, 1960]

Kennedy Without Tears

by Tom Wicker

Shortly after President Kennedy was shot, the following inscription appeared on a plaque in one of the private bedrooms of the White House:

In this room Abraham Lincoln slept during his occupancy of the White House as President of the United States, March 4, 1861-April 13, 1865.

In this room lived John Fitzgerald Kennedy with his wife Jacqueline Kennedy during the two years, ten months and two days he was President of the United States, January 20, 1961-November 22, 1963.

Before many years pass, that deliberate linkage of two Presidents, that notice chiseled upon history by Jacqueline Kennedy, may seem as inevitable as the Washington Monument. Already, airports and spaceports and river bridges and a cultural center have been named for her husband. Books about him, even phonograph records, are at flood tide and *Profiles in Courage* has returned to the top of The New York *Times* best-seller list. It is almost as if he had never called businessmen sons of bitches, sent the troops to Ole Miss, the refugees to the Bay of Pigs, or kicked the budget sky-high.

Six months after his death, John F. Kennedy is certain to take his place in American lore as one of those sure-sell heroes out of whose face or words or monuments a souvenir dealer can turn a steady buck. There he soon will stand, perhaps in our lifetime—cold stone or heartless bronze, immortal as Jefferson, revered as Lincoln, bloodless as Washington. One can imagine the graven words on his pedestal:

"Ask not what your country can do for you. Ask what you can do for your country."

What his country inevitably will do for John Kennedy seems a curious fate for the vitality and intensity, the wry and derisive style of the man who was the Thirty-fifth President of the United States. His wit surely would have seared the notion of John F. Kennedy International Airport, much less Cape Kennedy—for this was the man who once told the great-great-grandson of John Adams, "It is a pleasure to live in your family's old house, and we hope that you will come by and see us."

One suspects the Eternal Flame might have embarrassed him as much as the Navy did that brilliant Pacific day last June when the strutting admirals put him literally on a flag-draped pedestal aboard an aircraft carrier while the band played *Hail to the Chief* and the jets screamed overhead on taxpayers' money; one of his favorite quips, after all, was that he had gone from Lieutenant J.G. to Commander-in-Chief without any qualifications at all.

I can almost hear that amused Boston voice inquiring, as he once did after reading a favorable Gallup Poll, where all those people who admired him so much were when Congress turned down his school bill in 1961. Staring from Valhalla at himself cast in stone in the middle of some downtown Washington traffic circle, he might well whisper to earthly passersby what he once told 12,000 Democrats in Harrisburg, Pennsylvania:

"I will introduce myself. I am Teddy Kennedy's brother."

And when children rise reverently in some future Fourth of July pageant to recite the chiastic prose of the Kennedy Inaugural Address—the stirring words that raced so many pulses among that "new generation of Americans" to which he appealed—some may recall instead the same rhythm, the same rhetoric, but different words and a more subtle imagination at work:

"We observe tonight not a celebration of freedom but a victory of party, for we have sworn to pay off the same party debt our forebears ran up nearly a year and three months ago. Our deficit will not be paid off in the next hundred days, nor will it be paid off in the first one thousand days, nor in the life of this Administration. Nor, perhaps, even in our lifetime on this planet. But let us begin—remembering that generosity is not a sign of weakness and that ambassadors are always subject to Senate confirmation. For if the Democratic party cannot be helped by the many who are poor, it cannot be saved by the few who are rich. So let us begin."

Now a politician who could laugh at a parody of his noblest speech—let alone make it himself, as Kennedy did the foregoing—obviously was something more intricate in life than the mere sum of the virtues symbolized by the Eternal Flame: purity, steadfastness, warmth, light. A President delighted by the political caricature of Everett McKinley Dirksen, but impatient with the solemn earnestness of Chester Bowles, obviously had a wide streak of Honey Fitz down his spine; yet that same President, confronted with an adulatory mob of hundreds of thousands of cheering Europeans, could not bring himself to respond with more than a halfhearted jab of the arm from the chest—something like a halfback straight-arming a tackler, apologetically. And lest it be imagined that he was merely unemotional, remember that it was the crowd's transmitted frenzy that led Kennedy to make the inspiring but not very wise cry: *Ich bin ein Berliner!*

In the early days of Kennedy's New Frontier (there was bound to be something roguish about a man who could bring the Ivy Leaguers—and himself—to Washington with a slogan that evoked echoes of the Wild West, which appalled most of them), I thought Richard Nixon was perhaps a more interesting *man* than Kennedy. I thought Nixon was, as Conrad wrote of Lord Jim, "one of us." But Kennedy, I thought then, for all his charm and fire and eloquence, was a straightforward political man, who listened to his own rhetoric, contrived his "image" in the comforting faith that a statesman had to get elected before he could do anyone any good, and believed sincerely that his causes were not only right but actually offered solutions to human problems. I thought Kennedy had what Senator Eugene McCarthy called the perfect political mentality— that of a football coach, combining the will to win with the belief that the game is important.

Now, I think that what Kennedy really had of that mentality was a rather peculiar form of the will to win. He wanted power, all right, but something more; "This ability," he once said, "to do things well, and to do them with precision and with modesty, attracts us all." It was a theme to which he often returned—the pursuit of excellence. And as the probability of his political canonization turns toward certainty, and the sad calcification of his humanity into stone and bronze continues, there is not much football coach in the man Kennedy who recalls himself to me most strongly.

If that human Kennedy still seems to me to have been altogether too detached and too controlled to have been, as were Nixon and Lord Jim, "one of us," with all those fascinating hesitancies and inadequacies and torments out of which literature is made, nevertheless he *was* a man "of few days and full of trouble," and for all I know he may even have played "such fantastic tricks before high heaven as to make the angels weep." But the statues will tell us nothing of that.

Not many of them, for instance, will bear inscriptions drawn from his wit—that derisive, barbed, spontaneous wit, just short of mordant, that played so steadily through his speeches and recurred in such stable patterns of wording and attitude that it strikes me in retrospect as the true expression of a point of view, of a way of thinking not subject to time or circumstance or conditions.

It is astonishing, in retrospect, how constantly and boldly this Irish Catholic President, this young man so publicly committed to things like patriotism and public affairs, lampooned politicians, politics, notions, men, systems, myths, himself, even his church. When *The Wall Street Journal* criticized Nixon, Kennedy said, it was like *"L'Osservatore Romano* criticizing the Pope." And Speaker John McCormack denies that Kennedy called him "Archbishop"; "He called me 'Cardinal,' " McCormack recalls.

When the Vatican implied some criticism of Kennedy's campaign efforts to prove himself free of papal influence, Kennedy said ruefully to a pair of reporters: "Now I understand why Henry the Eighth set up his own church."

He and McKinley were the only Presidents ever to address the National Association of Manufacturers, Kennedy told that august body, so "I suppose that President McKinley and I are the only two that are regarded as fiscally sound enough to be qualified." And to the $100-a-plate guests at a glittering political occasion, he confessed: "I could say I am deeply touched, but not as deeply touched as you have been in coming to this luncheon."

Not even the Kennedy family was spared its scion's irreverence. To a dinner of the Alfred E. Smith Foundation during the 1960 campaign, he remarked:

"I had announced earlier this year that if successful I would not consider campaign contributions as a substitute for experience in appointing ambassadors. Ever since I made that statement I have not received one single cent from my father."

Everyone remembers his remark, upon appointing Bob Kennedy Attorney General, that his brother might as well get a little experience before having to practice law; not so many heard him late one night at a Boston dinner last fall when he paid similar respects to the youthful Edward M. Kennedy:

"My last campaign may be coming up very shortly," he said, "but Teddy is around and, therefore, these dinners can go on indefinitely."

The Kennedy wit was so pronounced and so identifiable that it could be reproduced with near exactitude by Ted Sorensen, his speech writer. A deadly serious man, Sorensen's few recorded public jokes included one perfect specimen of Kennedy-style wit.

"There will be a meeting this afternoon of representatives from Baltimore, Atlantic City, San Francisco, Philadelphia, Chicago and other cities interested in holding the 1964 national convention," he said in a mock announcement to a Democratic party gathering. "The meeting will be held in Mayor Daley's room."

In order to laugh—as the Democrats did—one had to know of course that Richard Daley was mayor of Chicago and one of the most powerful figures in the Democratic party—and that the competition for the convention was cutthroat. But Sorensen, as Kennedy always did, had tuned his derision precisely to his audience and the circumstances. The target was the situation—Daley's power, the party's foibles, the audience's pretensions. But whatever the situation, the *point of view* remained constant in Kennedy-style wit; it was the point of view that marked the man.

That point of view, as these few examples show, was a blending of amiable irreverence into a faintly resigned tolerance. It was a point of view that did not expect too much of human beings, even of its possessor; even less did it count heavily upon the wisdom or majesty of politicians; and often enough the political process itself was seen with frank disrespect. Perhaps a British M.P., but no American politician in memory except John Kennedy, would have been capable of the devastating "endorsement" of Senator George Smathers that the President delivered at a fund-raising dinner in Miami Beach:

"I actually came down here tonight to pay a debt of obligation to an old friend and faithful adviser. He and I came to the Eightieth Congress together and have been associated for many years, and I regard him as one of my most valuable counselors in moments of great personal and public difficulty.

"In 1952, when I was thinking about running for the United States Senate, I went to the then Senator Smathers and said, 'George, what do you think?'

"He said, 'Don't do it. Can't win. Bad year.'

"In 1956, I was at the Democratic convention, and I said—I didn't know whether I would run for Vice President or not, so I said, 'George, what do you think?'

" 'This is it. They need a young man. It's your chance.' So I ran—and lost.

"And in 1960, I was wondering whether I ought to run in the West Virginia primary. 'Don't do it. That state you can't possibly carry.'

"And actually, the only time I really got nervous about the whole matter at the Democratic Convention of 1960 was just before the balloting and George came up and he said, 'I think it looks pretty good for you.' "

The audience was already in stitches, but Kennedy had saved the real barb of his wit to the last, for an astonishing punch line in which Smathers appears not only as a target but as part of an apparatus—the Presidency and its problems—that was in itself somewhat ridiculous in its pretensions:

"It will encourage you to know [Kennedy said] that every Tuesday morning . . . we have breakfast together and he advises with me—Cuba, anything else, Laos, Berlin, anything—George comes right out there and gives his views and I listen very carefully."

Nor did he stop with such small targets as Smathers. Composing a birthday telegram to his touchy Vice President, Lyndon Johnson, he once told a reporter, was like "drafting a state document."

When Prime Minister Lester B. Pearson of Canada arrived at Hyannis Port in the Spring of 1963, his reputation as a baseball expert had preceded him. The resident White House baseball nut was Dave Powers, an Irishman of jovial mien who could sing *Bill Bailey Won't You Please Come Home* with marvelous vigah at the drop of a Scotch and soda. After a chilly Cape Cod dinner, Pearson followed Kennedy into seclusion, only to find it shattered by a summons to Powers.

"Dave," the President said, "test him out."

Whereupon Powers put the Prime Minister through an exhaustive baseball catechism, while the President rocked silently in his rocking chair, puffing on a cigar inscrutably, either measuring his man or enjoying the incongruous match—or both. Back and forth flowed the batting averages, managers' names, World Series statistics, and other diamond esoterica, until finally it was Dave Powers, not Mike Pearson, who tripped on some southpaw's 1926 earned run average.

"He'll do," Kennedy said then, with some satisfaction. After which he and Pearson hit it off famously and jointly equipped Canada with nuclear warheads.

Probably the finest piece of work Kennedy did in his eight generally lackluster years in the Senate was his leadership of the fight against reform of the electoral college in 1956. He argued brilliantly for the system as it was and still is. His side prevailed for a number of sound reasons, but not least because Kennedy succeeded in convincing enough Senators that, as he put it, "Falkland's definition of conservatism is quite appropriate—'When it is not necessary to change, it is necessary not to change.' "

That might almost have been Lord Melbourne speaking: *If it was not absolutely necessary, it was the foolishest thing ever done,* Melbourne said of a Parliamentary act. Indeed, Melbourne may have been in Kennedy's mind; for in the course of that brutal exposure of all his habits and persuasions to which Americans subject their President, it was to become known that his favorite book was David Cecil's *Melbourne.*

Probably no monument of the future will record that fact; yet it ought to give biographers pause. If the Kennedy campaign of 1960 meant anything, in terms of the man who waged it, it ought to have meant that Kennedy was a man who aimed to set the country right, who saw no reason it couldn't be done, who intended to let nothing stand in the way of doing it. The President who took office that cold day in January, 1961, saying, "let us begin," seemed to promise that the nation's problems could be solved if only enough brains and vigor and determination and money were applied to them.

Why would such a man enjoy reading of Melbourne, who believed government, in fact most human effort, was futile; who counseled, *When in doubt do nothing*; who said of a proposal to reform the English municipal councils, *We have got on tolerably well with the councils for five hundred years; we may contrive to go on with them for another few years or so*; and who thought the most damaging part of reform was that it aroused extravagant hopes that government and society—even men— might actually be improved.

But perhaps Kennedy was never quite the man the 1960 campaign suggested—just as Melbourne was not quite the fogy a few random quotations might suggest. Melbourne, in fact, as his biographer pictures him, was a man of immense charm and wit, great learning, considerable understanding of human nature, and remarkable courage in going his way—attributes that might be aspired to by any man. Certainly Kennedy possessed some of them and there is evidence to suggest that he shared to some extent Melbourne's skepticism about political and other human efforts at improving the condition of man.

The Kennedy wit certainly implies that he did. So did his remarks on a famous television interview in December of 1962, when he reviewed his first two years in office.

"There is a limitation upon the ability of the United States to solve these problems," he said. " . . . there is a limitation, in other words, upon the power of the United States to bring about solutions. . . . The responsibilities placed on the United States are greater than I imagined them to be and there are greater limitations upon our ability to bring about a favorable result than I had imagined them to be. . . . It is much easier to make the speeches than it is finally to make the judgments. . . ."

And it might have been Melbourne speaking again when he said of his efforts to roll back steel prices: "There is no sense in raising hell and then not being successful. There is no sense in putting the office of the Presidency on the line on an issue and then being defeated."

A few months later, I asked Kennedy at a news conference if he would comment on what I said was a feeling in the country that his Administration seemed "to have lost its momentum and to be slowing down and to be moving on the defensive."

"There is a rhythm to a personal and national and international life and

it flows and ebbs," Kennedy replied. He even conceded—sounding not unlike Melbourne on the Reform Laws—that "Some of our difficulties in Europe have come because the military threat in Europe is less than it has been in the past. In other words, whatever successes we may have had in reducing that military threat to Europe brought with it in its wake other problems. . . ."

Later, Ted Sorensen was to publish a book that in its essence was a discussion of the limitations upon a President—the reasons why, as Kennedy wrote in a foreword, "Every President must endure a gap between *what he would like and what is possible"* (the italics are mine). Once again Sorensen had caught the spirit of his chief and reproduced it; politics was not after all simply a matter of brains and vigor and determination, or even money. Its events, life itself, flowed also from the contrary nature of men, the blind turns of chance, the inertia of custom. And in that same foreword Kennedy quoted Franklin Roosevelt as saying

"Lincoln was a sad man because he couldn't get it all at once. And nobody can."

On a more personal level, some who knew Kennedy well sensed something deeper than skepticism in him, though he was a private man who did not much reveal himself even to men who worked with him for years. He was absolutely fearless about airplanes, for instance, flying anywhere, at any time, in any weather in which he could get aloft, sleeping through anything, scarcely seeming aware that he was off the ground. Yet four persons in his family—his brother, his sister, Ethel Kennedy's parents—had died in aircraft accidents.

Kennedy sometimes discussed the possibility that he would be assassinated with members of his staff. They would be anxious to explain the details of security precautions to him, to show him that it was unlikely it could happen. "If someone is going to kill me," he would say, "they're going to kill me."

And one of those who was close to him believes that Kennedy bothered little about what he was going to do with all those years that presumably would be on his hands when he emerged from the White House at age fifty-one (assuming he won two terms).

"It didn't really concern him," the aide recalls. "He never thought he was going to live to be an old man anyway."

Yet he had his imperatives. A man owed something to the public service. He had to be a patriot. He ought to be physically fit and courageous. (Good war records received special consideration on the New Frontier, and Dave Powers remembers that Kennedy once learned by heart the citation for a medal that had been awarded to General Douglas MacArthur.) A man's job was to act, not talk—to begin, to take the first step in a journey of a thousand miles.

Kennedy has been compared to Franklin Roosevelt and he liked to pose in front of an F.D.R. portrait. In fact, some of his qualities more nearly recall Theodore Roosevelt, the apostle of the big stick, the strenuous life and the bully pulpit. Like T.R., for instance, Kennedy fancied himself in the role of national taste maker—Roosevelt picked up Edward Arlington Robinson and Kennedy adopted Robert Frost. Roosevelt let his rather rigid literary ideas get about and the Kennedys thought they ought to provide White House examples—Casals, Shakespeare and opera in the East Room—for the cultural uplift of the nation. Yet, after an American opera group had sung a scene from *The Magic Flute* in English, after a dinner for the President of India, Kennedy could confess to a group of guests: "I think they ought to sing it in the original language. It doesn't sound right any other way."

There is not much doubt that Kennedy's publicized delight in Ian Fleming's spoof-spy novels doubled Fleming's sales, although there has been no big run on Cecil's *Melbourne*. He kept green, graceful Lafayette Square in Washington from disappearing into the capital's Great Stone Face. One of his last interests was in a plan to redeem Pennsylvania Avenue from army-surplus stores, cheap steak houses and bumbling federal architects. But it was as if art and culture were in the National Interest, like the test-ban treaty and Project Mercury; and if Kennedy was an avid reader of history, he did not seem to suffer from a great personal involvement in drama, music, art. The movies shown in the White House screening room were often the commonplace of Hollywood, and, except in the East Room, Kennedy's favorite music was more nearly Sinatra than Schönberg. As President, his first venture to Broadway took him to the slick musical, *How to Succeed in Business Without Really Trying*. Once, when he had a group of newspapermen in his house at Palm Beach, I stole a look at a stack of recordings; the one on top was a Chubby Checker twist collection.

But the imperatives of taking part, of public service, seemed, like those that moved Teddy Roosevelt, to be genuine and even profound. To the Touchdown Club of New York, he quoted with obvious approval the rather fervent view of T.R. on the matter

"The credit belongs to the man who is actually in the arena—whose face is marred by dust and sweat and blood . . . a leader who knows the great enthusiasms, the great devotions—and spends himself in a worthy cause—who at best if he wins knows the thrills of high achievement—and if he fails at least fails while daring greatly—so that his place shall never be with those cold and timid souls who know neither victory nor defeat."

Many times, he voiced a similar sentiment in his own words. Oddly, the man of detachment, of cool wit and ironic view, preached the "long twilight struggle" in which the most certain thing was that there would be "neither victory nor defeat." Yet, the man of commitment, of action, rejected with robustious Teddy the "cold and timid souls" who had no blood and dust upon their faces. And another quotation he liked to throw at university audiences was the rhetorical question of George William Curtis of Massachusetts:

"Would you have counted him a friend of ancient Greece who quietly discussed the theory of patriotism on that hot summer day through whose hopeless and immortal hours Leonidas and the three hundred stood at Thermopylae for liberty? Was John Milton to conjugate Greek verbs in his library when the liberty of Englishmen was imperiled?"

To the students of George Washington University, Kennedy gave his own answer: "No, quite obviously, the duty of the educated man or woman, the duty of the scholar, is to give his objective sense, his sense of liberty to the maintenance of our society at the critical time."

But in the next breath he was telling the story of someone who went to Harvard years ago and "asked for President Lowell. They said, 'He's in Washington, seeing Mr. Taft.' I know that some other day, when they are asking for the President of your university, they will say that he is over at the White House seeing Mr. Kennedy. They understood at Harvard, and you understand here, the relative importance of a university president and a President of the United States."

If that was a joke, it did not come from one who often gave up "his objective sense, and his sense of liberty." Honey Fitz would sing *Sweet Adeline* until his tonsils gave out, but his grandson was never known to wear a funny hat in public. It may seem a small point, but John Kennedy maintained it literally to his dying day. On November 22, in Fort Worth, he went through the Texas ritual of being presented a cowboy hat—but steadfastly resisted the pleas of two thousand Texans that he put it on.

"Come to Washington Monday and I'll put it on for you in the White House," he joked. But even in that comparative privacy, had he reached it, he would not have worn that hat. The man of detachment had yielded himself enough; he would make his little pushing gesture at the crowds, but he would not wave his arms exuberantly above his head like Eisenhower, or thump his chest like Theodore Roosevelt.

So, despite their similarities, he was radically different from the ebullient T.R. Restraint was his style, not arm-waving. There was nothing detached, nothing ironic, about Roosevelt, who could say and believe it that in the White House "my teaching has been plain morality." Kennedy would never claim more than that he hoped he was a "responsible President"; he would not often speak on television because he believed people would tire of him and stop listening.

Sometimes, it seemed, he even thought of politics, the Presidency itself, as a sporting proposition. Kennedy never tired of exhorting college students to prepare themselves for the public service, but he was seldom stuffy about it. He did not propose, he told the University of North

Carolina student body, to adopt "from the Belgian constitution a provision giving three votes instead of one to college graduates—at least not until more Democrats go to college."

As the campaign of 1960 wore on, the atmosphere around the candidate sometimes seemed almost like one of those parlor games the Kennedys played so often. "Tell me a delegate and I'll tell you who he's for," Kennedy would say to members of his staff, in his best Twenty Questions manner. "Give me a state and I'll give you the delegate breakdown."

The election was so close it inhibited Kennedy; he would point out how closely divided was the country at every opportunity. Yet, he could compare his own disputed election to the plight of a Notre Dame football team that had won a game by means some thought illegal. "And we're not going to give it back," he told the National Football Foundation.

Kennedy disliked the solemn ideologues and myopic Babbitts who crowd American political life—Senator Karl Mundt of South Dakota, for instance—but he delighted in the skillful shenanigans of some who took the game of politics less seriously—even, in some cases, when the voters and taxpayers were taken too. With obvious relish, he once described the operations of the raffish but highly effective Senator Warren Magnuson of Washington as follows:

"He speaks in the Senate so quietly that few can hear him. He looks down at his desk—he comes into the Senate late in the afternoon—he is very hesitant about interrupting other members of the Senate—when he rises to speak, most members of the Senate have left—he sends his messages up to the Senate and everyone says, 'What is it?' And Senator Magnuson says, 'It's nothing important.' And Grand Coulee Dam is built."

The night before he died, Kennedy spoke in tribute to Representative Albert Thomas in Houston, Texas. Not the least of Thomas' achievements over the years had been the enrichment of Houston with federal investments; his most recent coup had been the somewhat controversial establishment there of the Manned Spacecraft Center. Kennedy recounted a bit floridly how Thomas had helped put the United States in a position to fire into space the largest booster rocket bearing the largest "payroll" in history. As the audience laughed, Kennedy hastily corrected the word to "payload."

That slip might have embarrassed most politicians, but it obviously struck Kennedy as funny. "It will be the largest payroll, too," he added, grinning, "and who should know that better than Houston. We put a little of it right in here." Wasn't that what made the wheels go round?

Kennedy laughed out loud when he heard that Everett Dirksen had said that one of his early economic measures would have "all the impact of a snowflake on the bosom of the Potomac." He once carried a letter from de Gaulle around the White House, pointing out its elegances to his staff. It mattered not who won or lost, but how they played the game.

Even the selection of winners of the Medal of Freedom, a sort of royal honors list Mrs. Kennedy and the President invented, was not free in Kennedy's mind from the sporting balance of politics—you scratch mine and I'll scratch yours. When the painter Andrew Wyeth was selected, Kennedy—who had put up an early argument for Ben Shahn—decreed: "Next year, we'll have to go abstract."

One night on his plane, returning to Washington from a speech in Trenton, he talked about his love of boating with a group of us, and confided: "I'd really like to have that yacht Eisenhower laid up in Phila-delphia [the old *Williamsburg*]. But he said he did it for economy reasons and if I took it out of mothballs now they'd never let me hear the end of it." That was how the game was played; all you could do was grin and bear it, and play the game yourself.

Thus, John Kennedy in his pursuit of excellence, his commitment to active service, spent a great deal of his short life playing and thinking politics—running and angling for office, first; pushing political solutions to social and economic problems, second. But that is not necessarily the same thing as being profoundly involved in politics; it is not the same thing as a belief in solutions or the efficacy of politics. Kennedy seemed sometimes to think of himself as taking the first steps he so often urged upon the country and the world; he would use politics, he would propose a program, not with much hope for either, but to raise a question, to start someone thinking, to bring a matter into whatever light there was.

One Saturday morning in 1963 in Los Angeles he appeared at the Hollywood Palladium to address a Democratic women's breakfast; it was the only time I ever heard *Hail to the Chief* played with a twist beat. He was supposed to make "brief remarks"; instead, he plunged in his familiar machine-gun delivery into a half hour of Democratic party evangelism so impassioned and so portentous of phrase that some of my colleagues wrote that he had "kicked off his 1964 campaign." I was so stirred by the speech that I phoned The New York *Times* to hold space for the full text of it. It was a "major address," I assured my editors.

When the transcript came spinning from the White House mimeograph an hour later, I thumbed through it in search of those memorable phrases, those ringing pledges, those grand calls to battle, that had rung through the Palladium. I have that transcript before me now and it confirms my disillusionment; there was nothing there, nothing but rhetoric and deliv-ery. We had seen a performance in which J.F.K. had been playing the game unusually well.

In 1962, Kennedy proposed a Cabinet-level Department of Urban Affairs. Robert C. Weaver, the Administration's housing chief, was to be its Secretary—the first Negro to sit in any President's Cabinet. The proposal was hailed as a political master-stroke. Who could vote, in effect, against Weaver except the Southerners? And who cared about them?

In any event, a great many members of Congress voted against the proposal and it became one of Kennedy's most embarrassing defeats. Not long afterward, I asked him how it had happened.

He took a cigar out of his mouth and answered bluntly: "I played it too cute. It was so obvious it made them mad." In short, he had played the game poorly. I think he often did.

He could go before a captive audience of Democratic old people in Madison Square Garden and shed crocodile tears in behalf of his medical-care plan—and look as political and as uncomfortable as he was. Before an audience in Miami Beach from which he had little further to gain, the A.F.L.-C.I.O., he was so palpably bored, his speech was so blatantly routine and uninspired, that men of more objective political judgment might have booed him from the platform. He went into General Eisenhower's home county during the 1962 campaign and delivered a speech so demagogic and so extravagant in its claims for Democratic virtue and Republican sloth that even the General was enraged and promptly proceeded to emerge from retirement to campaign against him—a development that might have been politically important had not the Cuban crisis changed the whole picture in October. On his Western trip in the Fall of 1963—his last extended tour in the country—Kennedy looked and felt so out of place talking about conservation and nature and wildlife that the reporters following him gave him the nickname "Smokey the Bear"; it was reported by Pierre Salinger at Jackson Lake Lodge that the President actually had seen a moose from the window of his room.

Shortly after Kennedy's death, Carroll Kilpatrick and I visited J. Frank Dobie at the University of Texas and asked him what was the difference between Kennedy and Lyndon Johnson. Mr. Dobie knew Johnson well; he knew Kennedy only as most Americans knew him—as a voice on the radio, a face on the screen, a presence in the land. "Johnson is concerned with means," Mr. Dobie said at once, as if the contrast was obvious. "Kennedy was interested in ends."

A generality, perhaps, but near enough to truth to *ring* true. Kennedy played the game as a political man had to, sometimes brilliantly, often with boredom and ineptitude. But it was not then that he stirred us. Even his memorable campaign of 1960, the finest exercise of his strictly political life, was not politics-as-usual; it was outside the ordinary rules, for Kennedy was a Roman Catholic, an inexperienced younger man, something of an intellectual, who put little trust in traditional politicians, and relied instead upon his own men, his own techniques, his own personality.

Perhaps he had to move beyond the rules, get out of the game, before he really involved himself—and therefore involved other men. His trip to

Europe in 1963 exhilarated him, for instance; he knew he had broken through the traditional wall of diplomatic niceties, spoken above the heads of politicians and governments, and he believed a new generation of Europeans had responded. At his death, his tax bill was mired in Congress, but its mere presentation may yet be the longest step toward lifting American economic policy out of twin ruts of ignorance and cliché. His civil-rights bill was fumbled and botched, but he was the first American President to recognize in the outpouring of events a "moral crisis" in race relations. The long shadow of de Gaulle darkened his European policy, but he had proclaimed on both sides of the Atlantic a commitment to the interdependence of two continents. Nobody could say there would be no nuclear war, but he had taken the "first step" of the test-ban treaty.

That is what haunts me about Kennedy—not just that he was a man of certain admirable visions, but that he had the kind of mind that could entertain vision, the kind of outlook that could put in perspective the gambits and maneuvers of the moment, see truly the futility of most means, the uncertain glory of most ends. Surely he was one of those men "educated in the liberal traditions, willing to take the long look, undisturbed by prejudices and slogans of the moment, who attempt to make an honest judgment on difficult events"; surely he tried to be one of those, to borrow his words again, who could "distinguish the real from the illusory, the long-range from the temporary, the significant from the petty. . . ."

And that is the real irony of John F. Kennedy's coming immortality. For when James Reston asked him in the Summer of 1961, during a long afternoon's talk at Hyannis Port, what kind of a world it was he had in mind, what vision he had of the future, John Kennedy—President of the United States for half a year, perpetrator of the Bay of Pigs, not long home from his "somber" meeting with Khrushchev in Vienna—could reply: "I haven't had time to think about that yet."

It is the classic story of the liberal man in politics. *I claim not to have controlled events,* Lincoln said, *but confess plainly that events have controlled me.* And perhaps it is symbolized in a compelling picture of Kennedy that comes to us from one of Washington's most imposing men.

It is a glimpse from the Cuban missile crisis of October, 1962, a period of great tension at the White House as throughout the world. The personage and the President were alone in Kennedy's oval office discussing what in New Frontier jargon were known as "the options"; that month, the options were pretty grim.

Kennedy rose from his rocking chair, leaving his visitor seated on a sofa. The President went across his office to the French doors that opened on the terrace of the West Executive Wing. Beyond the terrace lay the famous Rose Garden, redesigned like almost everything else about the White House by the elegant stylists who had come to live there. But at its end still towered the famous magnolia planted by Andrew Jackson.

Kennedy stood for a long time, silent, gazing at the garden and the magnolia, his hands behind his back, the burden of decision almost visible on his shoulders. "Well," he said at last, "I guess this is the week I earn my salary."

The detached thinker had been brought to bay by the necessities of the moment. That questing mind with its sensitivity to the complexity of things, to the illusory nature of answers and solutions, had come to the moment of black vs. white. That derisive and worldly wit was stilled in the sheer responsibility of choice. Action and events had overtaken contemplation and vision, and Kennedy shared the plight of Melbourne: *I am afraid the question of the Irish Church can neither be avoided or postponed. It must therefore be attempted to be solved.* And for Kennedy, that fall, humanity itself was the question.

So with his football coach's will to win, with his passion for "the ability to do things well," Kennedy had had his dreams and realized them. But I believe he stood on the sidelines, too, even while the game was going on, measuring his performance, wryly remarking upon it, not much impressed, not much deluded. Perhaps he knew all along that events would control, action overwhelm, means fail to reach ends. "There stands the decision," he wrote, "and there stands the President." Sooner or later, they would be as one.

The decisions he made, the slogans he spoke—let them be carved on the monuments. But for me his epitaph is inscribed on Dave Powers' silver beer mug, that John Kennedy gave him for his birthday last year. It reads:

> There are three things which
> are real:
> God, human folly and laughter.
> The first two are beyond our
> comprehension
> So we must do what we can
> with the third.

No one at the White House knew the source of those lines. I can find the words in no book of quotations. The Library of Congress has not been able to discover who wrote them. But I think I know.

[June, 1964]

Lee Oswald's Letters to his Mother (with footnotes by Mrs. Oswald)

Lee went to Russia in November of 1959. He was in Russia twenty months before I had the first letter from him.

I was in constant touch with the State Department with no result, so I made a personal trip to Washington, D.C., in January, 1961, and approximately in March I received an answer from the State Department informing me of my son's whereabouts. He was in Minsk, Russia, where he was working in a radio factory. When he first went to Russia it was in the paper that he was in the Metropole Hotel in Moscow, and then for twenty months I didn't know whether Lee was alive or dead.

Lee joined the Marines at age seventeen, on his birthday. Three years later he got out of the Marines and three days after that went to Russia. Lee wrote continuously while in the Marines, and then stayed with me for three days when coming out of the Marines, and there's much speculation about the three days because he did leave a mother who was partially ill. I had had an accident. But Lee and I discussed this immediately upon his return: I was destitute and matter of fact, Lee got a dire-need discharge because of this accident, but he was only out of the Marines three weeks before his time would have been up. I started through the Red Cross at

46

Lee's insistence, to see if he could help me in July. But it was September before he was released, and I have always said those three months of negotiations meant either that I could have been well and not needed my son, or that I could have been dead and not needed him, also. But someday I hope to do something about this, because I am sure there are very many other mothers who are ill and need their sons, and I would say that they need them immediately, and not go through the Government red tape for three months before they *are* sent home to help their mother out, however the case may be. So, after the three days—Lee said, "Mother, I have no background of work, and if I stay here the only salary I can demand would be $30 to $35 a week." Now we're talking about Texas, and not the Eastern states, because the salaries there are very, very low and actually that *is* the standard salary. And he said, "You're broke, so we would both be in the situation that you're in, so I've made up my mind that I'm going to work on a ship in the import and export business, where I can demand some money and I'll be able to help you."

I agreed with Lee because this is the way you help seventeen-, eighteen-, nineteen-year-olds, and I said, "It's a wonderful idea; but why don't you wait; Mother will settle her claim." It was not a suit, it was a compensation claim, I would be entitled to sixty percent of my salary, and the claim would have to be settled. In the meantime, probably I could baby-sit, and together we could manage. He said, "No, my mind's made up. We'll both be as bad off as you are now if I try to find work here, so I want to work on a ship." This was good thinking, and he was right, because a $35-to-$40-a-week job would not take care of a mother and a boy. So I accepted the fact that he has a right to his own mind. And so he left, and one week later I received a letter from Lee from New Orleans, stating that he had passage on a ship to Europe and he didn't expect me to understand, but to please try and understand—"This is something I must do," and so on, so then about a week later I picked up the paper and knew that he was in Russia.

Commission No. '80

Dear Mother

Received your letter today and was surprised that you are working on a ranch. Where is cromwell Texas, anyway? How is it you decided to go there?[1]

I am glad you think marina is beautiful[2] and I shall be good to her. She doesn't have a mother and father. They are dead. But she has a lot of aunts and uncles here in minsk and also in Leningrad where she was born. She was living at her aunts place when I met her they are real nice people her uncle is a major in the Soviet army. She work as a druggist. She finished the university two years ago for that occupation.

We are in good health and Im glad you are with good people also.

P.S. marina send her love, also.
Love
Lee

Commission No. 181   Aug. 3, 1968

Dear Mother

I received your packet today thanks alot for all the nice things. You really should not have bothered to send those little things its so expensive[3] I really now only need literature and every now and than some chewing gum like you sent me before. In the future please only send very light and necessary things.

I wrote Robert and he[4] was surprised that you are working at cromwell, Texas dont you write at all to each other?

We are getting ready to see you all, isn't it along[5] process especially for marina. Well, that's about all for now
Love
Lee

48 / The Rise and Fall of Charisma

1. LETTER RECEIVED JULY 18, 1961
   At this time, then I decided to devote my life to humanity, and I became a practical nurse, and I did "live-ins," which means living on the place twenty-four hours a day on duty. So I was in Crowell, Texas, on a case on my very first contact with Lee. This was an elderly woman who had a stroke. This was a ranch out of Crowell, Texas.

2. The first letter is lost. He mentions in it that he married a Russian girl, that Marina is beautiful, and he sent the wedding picture and also asks for some razor blades and a can of shaving cream, and some literature, "I very much miss literature." In my answer to the first letter I said Marina *is* beautiful.

3. LETTER RECEIVED AUGUST 10, 1961
   They had just married and I knew that she was a foreign girl—a Russian girl—so I thought probably she would like a little trinket, so I sent her a bracelet and a necklace—sort of a wedding gift—I mean it was something that was new, very unusual. Matter of fact, I'd had the bracelet for about twenty-five years; it was my own bracelet that I sent. And then I sent her the necklace, and a silk scarf.

4. Robert is Lee's brother. Lee has a half-brother that's older. Lee has two brothers, John and Robert, and Robert lived in Fort Worth, Texas.

5. I learned through a letter that he was coming home. I also learned through the very first letter from the State Department giving me Lee's address that Lee had contacted the Embassy in Moscow stating that he wished to return to the United States. This is my first contact with Lee, through the State Department, informing me of Lee's address and of his desire to return to the United States and then after my correspondence with Lee direct making provisions for coming home.

Commission No. ¹⁵²   *Oct. 2, 1961*

Dear Mother;

Recieved your package of books yesterday, thanks. alot for them I am very glad to have them.

I hope you are feeling well and are enjoying your stay in Vernon.

Here is the weather in Fort Worth and Vernon now. I suppose it must be still pretty low there although here it has already turned quiet cold.

Do you ever hear much from John? Where is he?

I am recieving a letter from Robert about once a month now.

In the future if you send me some books you can send me "time" magazine not

6. LETTER RECEIVED OCTOBER 10, 1961 Then I was on a case in Vernon, Texas. And this will explain why I have so many addresses, because I am a live-in nurse, and I go anyplace that I have a case. I'm on private duty, and I get my cases by word of mouth.

7. John, Lee's brother, is in the service of our country—he's in the Air Force, and has been since age seventeen. He's now been in fourteen years; this is his career. He moves around a lot.

"Ford times" and books like "close to the wind" I don't really want, they are too heavy and you could have sent me several smaller books instead, but its not important you made a very good choice in these books and I'm grateful.

Well thats about all for now Marina sends her love.

Love
Lee

8. I had had the books at the ranch and they had *Ford Times,* a magazine all about automobiles, and then I had a novel, *Close to the Wind,* and any other material that I could pick up I sent to Lee, because at this particular time I am working for $25 a week, and the postage alone for books and so on to Russia is very expensive, and I had no idea about the amount of books and postage—if I could afford it. And besides, since he asked for books, I wanted to immediately send him something, so whatever was around the house I gathered up and sent them the very first package.

Commission No. /. : — Oct. 22, 1959

9

Dear Mother,

Sorry to take so long to write but I thought something might have come up but we're still waiting.

I received your birthday card on the 14th thanks for the thought

I'll be glad to get any books you send in the future you might include some fashion magizines for marina also if you remember it.

Marines maiden name was Proosakava, her aunt and uncles address in Minsk is

MINSK
UL. KALININA 42,
APT 20
PROOCAKOBA

They don't speak any english, however, her uncle is a army Colonel, soon to retire.

You needn't worry about my losing american citizership I can

10

50 / The Rise and Fall of Charisma

9. LETTER RECEIVED OCTOBER 30, 1961 I just don't know what he could have been thinking of, dating this 1959.
10. Lee had married this Russian girl, and I thought possibly he would want to become a Soviet citizen, because he was working there, and had a wife who was a Russian girl, so I asked him if he had any idea of becoming a Soviet citizen.

only do that if I want too, and I don't want too.

"For my birthday marina sent me a gold and silver cup with the inscription "to my Dear Husband on his birthday 18/X/61" very nice don't you think, marina is on her vaction now, she is spending it with her aunt in the city of "KHARKOV" about 600 miles South-East of Kiev. She's just relaxing and taking it easy from work and the house work.

We both agreeled that she should go to a new enviroment on her vaction, but she comes back in a few more days on the 29th of October. Her aunt Palina's address is the city of— "KHARKOV"

VÉZO TREENKLERA
House 5, APT. 7
MIKHAILOVICH . P

Marina, unfortunatly, doesn't speak any English at all, I would like her to learn, and she bought some books for her on the subject**11** but for now she doesn't want to learn, she speaks a little French allready, (she learned in grammer school), and she doesn't want to study another lanuguage for now, she really does not have the time you know, what with her working from 10-5 and then the house-work but it doesn't matter for now. Well, that's about all for now.

I'll try to write more often.

Love
Lee

P.S.
Did you recieve my letter, with some pictures of minsk in it??

THE FIFTH LETTER

Commission No. _184_   — Nov. 1. 1961

Dear Mother,

I sent a letter a week ago, but I think I put the wrong address on it so am writing again, we recieved your post card it was very interesting for marina.

Well at the end of Febeary, begining of march we should have a baby. We want a boy.

There is very little information about the visas, we still have not recieved them and untill we do, we cannot leave the Soviet Union.

You can send me a few pennies if you like, alot of my friends are interested in collecting coins from america.

The weather here is cold and rather rainy now, although there still is no snow.

If you have any old photos

11. This to me is very important. This is the first time these letters are being released to the public, and I have stated over and over that I have actual documents in black and white to retract some of the awful statements that have been said against this boy. He's not perfect, but he has some very fine qualities. I think so, and the letters do show so. And so it states in the letter that Lee had brought literature and books for Marina for her to learn English, but she didn't want to, because of her housework and work, and he's gone along with that. However, I also know that Lee and Marina returned from Russia to Fort Worth, that Marina immediately started to take English lessons, also, through a university and Marina speaks broken English quite well. And so this will show you what the news media have done with my life and Lee's. This is actual proof. One particular story that they have exploited is that Lee treated her mean, and would not allow her to learn English, but we have it in black and white, and I state now that also in America that she was learning English. Lee wrote and spoke Russian very fluently. In fact Lee has the equivalent of one year of college education in Russian, and I have this in black and white, in the form of an application he made to the Albert Schweitzer School in Switzerland.

of myself and of you also, please send them. 12

Do you ever hear anything from aunt Lilian in New Orleans?

and how about John?

Marina sends her love and asks do you want to be a grandmother again??

are you still working for those people? You have changed address again haven't you?

Well that's about all for now. Write soon.

love Lee

Enclosed are some pictures of Leingrad where marina was bora (this is not minsk)

12. LETTER RECEIVED NOVEMBER 18, 1961
    I sent the one picture he had taken in New Orleans on Mother's Day, 1955. I sent a few baby pictures of Lee—just regular Kodak pictures.

Commission No. ⁎⁎ — Nov. 23

Dear Mother

Today we recived your grand gift. I am very surprised that you guesed my taste in color and fabric.

Here it is already very cold so your wool stole will be very useful.

It is very nice to feel that you are so attentive to me, more so, even, than to Lee.

I shall always remember your gift as a mark of our friendship.

I hope you won't be nervous for us, you shouden't worry about us too much.

I have never seen you(expept on a photograph) but I have alot of affection for you allready.

I hope you shall be well and thank you again for the fine present.

Marina

(I wrote it for her but the words are hers)

Commission No. 86

С новым годом!

Merry Christmas,
Dear mother, from
us both.
Lee, Марина

THE SEVENTH LETTER

Commission No. 87   Dec 13. 1961

Dear mother.
We received your post card today
and also the first package of books
which you sent us a month and a half
ago. I sure do appreciate your help.
I think we'll get together if
we finally get back to the states, and
maybe we'll be able to settle in Texas.
I hope everything is allright
with you, why so you change address
so often?
I sent you and Robert a
Christmas card, and even aunt Lilian
in New Orleans, do you write to them
at all? or to aunt Lilian.
Has Robert been writing to you
lately? 14
When you write you can
send us just post cards instead 15
of letters they are cheaper and
marina enjoys the pictures of

13. RECEIVED DECEMBER 12, 1961
The Christmas card says Merry Christmas, and what I find interesting, it has a pine cone and a clock with the numerals on, 12 o'clock. But the back of the Christmas card is blank, and this is what interests me most. This is a Russian Christmas card. There are no sentiments—you write your own words. All their Christmas cards are blank, which is wonderful—of course we do not have time to write our own words, particularly I would say people that have many, many acquaintances —in the hundreds—they don't even sign their name! But to me, this is ideal, because you have to sit down and write your own sentiments to your folks, and Lee did mention "Merry Christmas, Dear Mother—Lee," and Marina signed her name in Russian. So, see the Russian people are human beings after all, they do have many fine points to their way of life, just as we have to ours, but I believe that either today or tomorrow if we can recognize their fine points along with our fine points, along with their faults and our faults, and if we can nourish them then we will have peace.

14. LETTER RECEIVED DECEMBER 26, 1961
At this time I'm not having contact with any family at all. Matter of fact I've never been close to the family from the time they left home. We, as a family, were a close family, but when the boys married. . . . You have to understand that I'm a widow making my own living, and I am working twenty-four hours a day, and moving from place to place, and they have their own life, so we now have drifted to a certain extent, but I think most families do drift after the boys marry and leave home. And I have three boys, and boys are a little different than I believe a daughter would be. And I'm a very independent person, and I make my own living, and so it's a full-time job for a woman my age to be out in the busi-

[Handwritten letter, continued:]

Tepes and america.

Snow is on the ground deal and will be until april or may. Marina is feeling fine and everything is o.k. with that.

Marina laughed when she heard your question about babies born at home or in hospitals of course almost everyone here has their babys in the hospital

your choice of books is very good, thanks alot for them.

Marina sends her love and hopes you received her thank-you letter for the beautiful wrap you sent her

love Lee.

p.s. I wrote this letter on one day but didn't get to send it till today, when I received your second package of books, (cowboys & lines) so I shall thank you for them too. love Lee

THE EIGHTH LETTER

[Handwritten letter:]

Commission No. 196 — January 23.

Dear Mother

Please do me a big favor, go to the nearest office of the "Immigration and naturalization officer", and file an "affadavit of support" on behalf of my wife, this is a technical point in regards to permission to enter the U.S. for marina, and must be made in the U.S.. you simply fill out a blank (there may be a charge of a few dollars) and that's all.

Please do this now, as they are actually waiting for this document in moscow.

Personal information about marina which may be included in this blank are; Birth place and date city moloTSK, USSR July 17, 1941 name — marina nikolialava Oswald Place of residence, minsk KaluNINA st 4. APT 24 Thanks love Lee

[Right column text:]

ness world and take care of herself. So lately I don't have time for my family. I may be two hundred miles away.

15. I always did whatever the children asked me to do, because I knew it was very important. I also wrote letters. . . . Lee figured it was very expensive for me to mail letters, and I wrote quite frequently. And also, Marina enjoyed the pictures on the postcards. And he asked me to also write in the letters, and also send postcards, they're much cheaper, matter of fact, I believe he mentions this in a letter. And so he's always thinking: "Mother, don't spend everything you earn on us. We want to hear from you, but do it the easiest way." The same way with the packages; he keeps saying, "Don't send heavy packages." He's worried about the terrific postage that I pay . . . the expense, and he didn't want me to spend all of my money on things for them.

16. LETTER RECEIVED JANUARY 23, 1962; DATE ON THE LETTER IS THE SAME. UNDOUBTEDLY AN ERROR ON HIS PART. I got the affidavit for him, I wrote first to the naturalization and immigration office. I think now I'm in Vernon, Texas, on a case, or probably Crowell. These sections are all together—probably fifty or seventy-five miles away, bringing me back to Fort Worth all the time. The original place, Crowell, Texas, was two hundred miles away, and then I worked my way back to Fort Worth on cases. . . . So Wichita Falls was the closest place that I could get this information, because I'm in very small towns, Crowell, Vernon, and those towns are very small places, so Wichita Falls was the main place and I wrote and they sent me a form to fill out. Of course, then I would have to have a sponsor for the affidavit of support—an American sponsor, and I was working for a man at this particular time, taking care of his mother, who had had a stroke and he offered to be the sponsor.

THE NINTH LETTER

Commission No. 191 — January 20.

Dear Mother

I hope you recived my last letter of Dec 27. 17 As I then said we shall recive the exit visa's to leave the country in March or early april right now what we need is money for the tickets maybe you can try the Red Cross in Vernon about that they should notify the american Embassy, moscow, for information 18

We recived your package of magazines on about new years thanks alot for them, today I also recived a post card from you.

The weather is very cold and wet here, how is it in texas.

Mama is feeling fine and sends her love.

Did you recive the tea and candy from us? If so how did you like it

Thats about all for now, Write soon

Love xx
Lee

THE TENTH LETTER

Commission No. 192 — Feb. 1, 1962

Dear Mother

Today I recived 2 letters from you one from the 12th and the other from the 17th. as for the gifts we sent you, the can is of candy, eat it in good health.

As too your questions about the money problem I don't know if giving the story too the newspapers is too good, maybe you'd better hold off for awhile about that. I'll tell you when.

The Baby is due around march 1st.

we will probably fly into the U.S. on a airplane and I see no reason for you to come to New York to meet us. I want you to understand that although you can aid us in certain, small ways. This business about our coming to the U.S, is relatively simply don't make it more complicated than it is. 19

about all for now write soon
mama sends her love. Lee xxx

17. LETTER RECEIVED JANUARY 29, 1962
I don't believe there are any missing letters. What I think he's saying is that the letter following this would have been the one about the affidavit, and he wants to make sure that I receive the letter.

18. Lee needed help now. He's ready to come home. All documentations are secured for his wife and himself but he doesn't have the money to come home on so he asks me to contact the Red Cross and to contact several organizations who help people in these particular cases to come back.

19. LETTER RECEIVED EARLY IN FEBRUARY, 1962
I asked Lee if I should give his story to the newspaper because I am unable to get help. I had gone to several very prominent citizens and explained that this boy was in Russia and an American citizen who wanted to come home but for lack of money he was unable to. I also went to a very fine citizen who had a citizen award for helping people and I was turned down by him. The attitude was that if he went over to Russia to defect let him stay. Now this is a very fine, fine citizen with this attitude. And so I'm trying to get help for the boy and presenting my case that he is a young boy, he's an American citizen. He had been married and he has all documentation with him. The only thing lacking to bring him back to his native land would be money. And I am unable to get anyone to help in this endeavor. I thought if I would give the story to the newspaper that he wanted to come home, that his visas and everything were there, but it was the money lacking, then maybe some good American would finance his way home because I was not having any luck talking to the ones individually to help him to come home. He said he didn't want me to give the story to the newspaper. He'll tell me that. He didn't want to complicate his coming home any more than was

Feb 2, 762

Dear Marina,

Well it won't be long now until the baby is born and until we shall be seeing you, in the meantime you can do two things for me; file an affidavit of support on behalf of marina (this has to be done in the U.S.A.) it a technical point regarding U.S. permission to enter the United States and can be done at the offices of emigration and naturalization.

Also you can see about sending me some clippings or columns from the Ft. Worth papers for the month of Nov. 1959, I want to know just what was said about me in the Ft. World newspapers so I can be forwarded. If you don't have [21]

clipping yourself, you can always get back issues of newspapers by apply it their offices or the public library.

I received your package of newspapers and magazines, thanks!! [22] cutting those editorials was also good thinking on your part it gave me alot of news.

I suppose it is almost spring in Vernon by now, huh!

What is the latest news in Vernon?

Please write soon, we are getting your letters and so we always wait for more ha-ha

When you write please write Minsk 29. (zone) This helps me get your letters quicker

Love from us both

necessary. I think that then he wa negotiating with the Embassy abou money to come on a loan.

20. LETTER RECEIVED FEBRUARY 23, 196 I'm having trouble getting the affida vit of support out, though, but he wi have to have someone sponsor thi and I thought that the people I wa working for knew my problem an that they should offer and when the didn't I went to other people wh had turned me down and then when was talking about being turned dow then my employer offered to help.

21. I had written him and said now know you always know what you'r doing. You have a Russian wife, yo have a job. You have been in Russi for the last two years. You have ser me many, many fine gifts and yo write all the time and all of this take money and many, many photo graphs. Are you sure that this is wha you want to do because you are known defector and you may not b accepted and I have reason to sa this because I had already explaine how hard it was to get someone t help him to come home, how hard was to even get an affidavit of su port which was just a technicality and so I'm now realizing that th boy is going to have it very hard her in the United States and so I said t him are you sure that this is what yo want to do? And you exploited in th paper, very very much so, as a defe tor and that is why he is asking me t send the clippings of the papers so h would see what I am talking abou

22. The editorials were letters fro people in the newspapers. It ha nothing to do with the prior que tions he asked. I sent him som books and then I had wrapped th books up with newspaper editoria which are letters from people that had accumulated that I had thoug would be interesting reading. It ha nothing to do with the story of h defection. This is just extra readi and I wrapped the books up in man many of these papers, thinking th

Commission No. 74 — *Feb. 15, 1962*

Dear Mother,

Well, I have a little (6 lbs.) daughter, June Marina Oswald born at 10:00 A.M. February 15th. How about that?!!

Marina feels O.K. she only took an hour and a half to give birth at the hospital.

The possibility of our coming to the United States are very good although, of course, it'll be another couple of months.

Marina's exit visa to leave the U.S.S.R. is good until Dec. 1, 1962 so we have no worries about the visa's running out before everything is arranged.

The American Embassy in Moscow sent me an application for a loan (which I requested) so they will make the money available to us as soon as everything is arranged for Marina.[23]

The only thing holding us up now is the "affidavit of support" for Marina which I already told you about, once that is in, we can leave the U.S.S.R. any time we want.

How are things are yours end. If you don't have that letter from the marine corps. telling about the declary[24] below about getting a copy. I would like to have some material upon which to start, before going into the discharge matter further with the marines.

That's about all for now love from all three of us

Lee
Marina
June

P.S. Enclosed 3 pictures of Marina and I taken last summer on our balcony

he would enjoy the newspapers, and he wrote back and said it was quick thinking on my part. He enjoyed reading them. I sent him a book by Vincent Peale, *The Power of Positive Thinking,* and most of the other books that I sent were books that I had bought in a used-book place where I was—*Time, Life*—and just any, you know, everyday books, magazines, not books actually, just magazines. It kept running up into money. The postage was very expensive and I would get these books at half price because they were used magazines, *Reader's Digest,* anything. But they were in good condition and, you know, I would say up-to-date. So it would take two months to get the material. It would cost me anywhere from $2 to $5 to send a package. Oh, yes, he said he received them, thank you. But I knew he liked Vincent Peale's work, in fact on his application to Albert Schweitzer College the book that he said he most liked to read, Vincent Peale was one of the authors that he thinks of the most.

23. LETTER RECEIVED MARCH 1, 1962
The State Department loaned him the money to come home on. Lee had asked for $800 and the State Department loaned him, as has been publicized and made public by the State Department, $400 and some odd dollars, I think $463. They only brought home a few things, one radio, I might say, jewelry from Russia, clothing and some silverware and personal things.

24. I had written him and told him that I had a letter from the Marine Corps giving him an undesirable discharge. He had an honorable discharge from the Marines, serving three years, and a good-conduct medal, and the undesirable discharge was given because he had defected to Russia.

Commission No. *175*

Минск. Дом Правительства

Feb. 24.

Dear mother,

Well, I suppose you've already received our letter about the birth of little June Lee Oswald (not June marina) she weighted 9 lb at birth which was on Feb. 15th mother and child are doing well, she left the hospital on Feb. 24th

We will probably wait for a period of two or more months while little June gains weight for her trip to the U.S.

I don't think it is too advisable to leave earlier than may. our visas are good.

Was everything at your end OK?

The weather is rather cold here yet I guess in Texas it must be pretty hot by now.

Did you get those newspaper clipping I asked you for?

I hope you've already made out that afidivit of support for marina by now, like I asked you.

Thats about all for now.

Love Lee

Love from little June and marina

25. LETTER RECEIVED MARCH 7, 1962

Well, the envelope and the stationery . . . he's announcing the birth of his baby, and since this is the first fancy stationery I had, I'm to assume that possibly it's something special in Russia. I had another one of them—I think it was around Christmastime when another fancy one came. So I have to assume that this is probably the reason for it. But now he's telling me about the baby's right name and this might be interesting to the people. In Russia even if it's a female the middle name is always the name of the father. So her name is June Lee Oswald, and had it been a male and he wanted to name the boy Lee, he would have been named Lee Lee Oswald. They always take the middle name of the father. He then found out that it was June Lee Oswald.

Commission No. ___   March. 28.

Dear mother
        Today I received the official
from mr. Phillips.
        You asked weather I'll be
staying at your place or Robert in
Ft. Worth. I don't think I'll be
staying at either but I will be
writing both. In any event I'll
won't to live on my own and
probably will finally land in
Ft. Worth or New Orleans. we will
undoubtly come by ship to the
U.S. which will be a two
week Trip. I'll let you know
when we leave it first canceon.
I still don't know our exact
date of departure yet as there are
still a few things that be done before
we shove off.
        As I said in my last letter
we shall be coming probably in april

I allready told you I recieved
those clippings and so forth ok.
        The money situation is pretty
good although I'd like to have
enough to fly to the states,
but thats not too lightly at
this time, still its not very
important as regard the mode
of Transportation.
        Dear Lee, feels fine, she
allready weights 11 lbs. and is
it months old. marina feels
very well also.
        we are in constant touch
with the embassy so all is well.
        thats about all for now.
                        Lee

P. S.
marina sends. her love.
P.S. today we also recieved your
letter. Thanks.

26. LETTER RECEIVED APRIL 9, 1962
He had always lived with me and I was now working back in Crowell, Texas, and I asked him if he planned to come to Crowell and that's when he answered that he wanted to live on his own.

27. He was born in New Orleans, Louisiana, and lived there up until the age of five, when I remarried and left there and part of his life was spent in Fort Worth, Texas, so that was the two places he knew of.

28. Those were the clippings about his defection. I couldn't send him too many because I had to put them in letters, but I did give him the general idea.

29. I was getting a little concerned because it's been almost a year now that Lee is trying to come home. Documentations had been settled for quite a while and I said I was getting a little concerned and worried why they weren't coming home, since he had stated that money was going to be financed through the State Department and he said not to worry about it. I mentioned to him that I was getting a little concerned and upset and worried because I wanted the baby born here in America. It should have been born here in America, but for lack of money Lee didn't come home as fast as he should have. What I'm trying to say is, all of the visas and everything were settled, but the money problem is what kept him over there longer. Otherwise the baby would have been born here in the United States. And it's an awfully long trip, 10,000 miles, for a couple to come with a young baby. It's a very hard thing to do.

Commission No. *198* — *May 30. 1962*

Dear mother,

Well, here we all in Moscow getting ready to leave for the U.S.A., I'll be sending a telegram or otherwise informing you as to where we shall embark and so forth, everything is O.K. so don't worry about us. we shall be leaving from Holland by ship for the U.S. on June 4th however I expect to stay over in new york for a day or so and also Washington D.C. for sightseeing.

See you soon.

Yours Lee

30

30. LETTER RECEIVED JUNE 6, 1962
He arrived in New York. Now never did ask him about Washing and I have no way of knowing if went to Washington.

I received a postcard from Lee saying that they were leaving and th would be approximately about June 12 or 13 and later a speed letter fro the State Department informing me that my son and his wife had le Moscow and would arrive in New York on June 13.

Well, the case that I'm on now is a very elderly woman and it's just s and I in the house and so I'm unable to leave my patient in order to me my son. He's going to arrive in Dallas at the airport and Robert and h family are meeting him, but I'm unable to meet him and it's a week lat before I can find someone to take care of my patient temporarily so I cou go to Fort Worth, which I did for a weekend, to see Lee. Then I had to back on my case. It was awfully crowded in Robert's house. He has tw children and a wife and himself and with another couple and a child. I h then decided that I would terminate my services in Crowell, Texas, a come to Fort Worth where I could help the children as much as possib which I did. I had exactly $175 to my name. I had explained before that was working for $25 a week. Out of that I had to pay gasoline for my c to go to town because we're in little country towns way on the outskir which was approximately $6 a week, and then I sent all these packages Lee and postage and my insurance, so I didn't have anything left out of $ a week, and I did manage to save $175 in this year. So I rented a hou in Fort Worth, Texas, at the Rodeo Apartments, and Marina and L came to stay with me. I bought all the food and paid the first rent a then Lee got a job, I took him every day for a job, then he got a job and they went on their own. So here I am once again down to my last penny. I had been this way many, many a time and it's enough to say that I have a job and everything works out all right. What I'm trying to say is that the only money I had, I paid rent and bought food for these kids for one month and it took me three weeks to find a job. I took him every day job hunting and the first pay he kept and with his second pay had enough money to pay a month's rent and they went on their own.

I was never concerned about having a son in Russia. I made this perfectly plain in 1959 at the time of his so-called defection. They said that he had studied communism and that this is what he lived for—the time when he could go over there. Many, many statements. And I said then, and was criticized then very severely that if he had studied communism and if he had thought this out thoroughly and if this was what he wanted to do, I believed that as an individual that this was his right to do whichever he thought was the right thing to do, and that I would respect that right and I do—with everyone. And people in Russia are no different than the people here. I didn't know too much about Russia when he did defect, but I have now studied a little bit and feel that I can say, sincerely, that they live and breathe like we do and they think, and I see nothing different in Russia than we in America. I have a Russian daughter-in-law who I'm very proud of and would hope that the people would study other people's foreign ways a little so that we would have a deeper understanding. I will admit that I am very ignorant until Lee defected—I'm still ignorant, I don't mean to say otherwise, but I have no knowledge. I always said Russian people were peasant people and very poor and didn't have anything, and I subscribe to the *USSR*, which is a magazine put out by our government in Russia and we have an agreement with Russia—they put out *America* that goes to Russia, in Russian, and the *USSR* is written about Russia in English for us to read. It's a wonderful magazine and when I started to see the beautiful subways in Moscow then I realized how ignorant I was and that Russian people were normal people just like we. Their way of life is different. When we respect their way of life a little bit, as I said before, then I think we're on the road to peace.

I have never asked Lee why he went to Russia. As I said, I respected his view, I have my own ideas about why he went to Russia. Now it's evident that I'm trying to make it public. At the particular time I didn't question him about all this. This is what he wanted to do. If there was another reason why he went to Russia, I knew he wouldn't tell me. I just wouldn't ask. It wouldn't be the thing to do. Many people have asked since they knew I saw Lee in the jailhouse, if I asked him if he was guilty of killing President Kennedy, and I answered I wouldn't insult him and ask him that question. And the reason for that was I heard him with my own ears and saw him on television say "I didn't do it, I didn't do it," so why should I ask him if he did such a thing? I heard him say he didn't do it so that's enough for me whether it's my son or any other man.   [May, 1964]

"You All Know Me! I'm Jack Ruby!"

by Ovid Demaris and Garry Wills

At 1312½ Commerce Street in Dallas, across from the Adolphus Hotel and just down Commerce from the Baker and the Statler, there is a stairway up to a second-floor warren of rooms and corridors. The sign on the locked door reads:

DALLAS POLICE

GYM

FOR GOLDEN GLOVE BOXERS

SPONSORED BY

DALLAS POLICE ASSOCIATION

As before, the place is open only at night; but now its stairs temper the welcome rolled down them in thick red carpeting. Only two officers have a key to the gym, and a rubber treadway is clamped into the carpet with metal strips. The run of stairs, broken by a short landing, is capped with a dusty, unused box office. A door on the right takes one into a low room widened, on both flanks, beyond ceiling traces of thin walls removed. Back in the Thirties, Benny Binion ran his book out of these rooms, from a club called Pappy's 66, but for two decades number 1312½ gathered dust until, in 1960, S & R, Inc. (Slatin and Ruby) opened The Sovereign Club (private clubs apparently could evade the Dallas ban on public sale of mixed drinks). The club had its troubles, and Slatin's interest in S & R was soon taken over by Ruby's friend Ralph Paul, who insisted that the club be opened to the public and strippers be brought in. That is how The Sovereign Club became The Carousel, managed by Jack Ruby. Paul owned half of the club, and Ruby's brother Earl owned most of the other half; but for Jack it was the fulfillment of a dream.

Today, a boxing ring is built out from the stage where blue lights cooled the strippers' writhings. Only one of Ruby's short runways still projects beyond the ring's lip ("The Only Club in Dallas With Three Runways"). In the girls' dressing room, cops shower after their workout. Down the hall from dressing room to stage, one walks past scribbled-over walls: "Number four girl goes first." Eleven musicians' names are recorded in fading pencil: Tom Piesnor and Bill Willis top the list. Traces of the nightclub look dingy in the gymnasium's hard light. Tinny chandeliers are tied aslant. The pasteboard star on Jada's dressing room shrivels at its corners. A sequiny gold horse in bas-relief is punctured at two points and shows its papery insides. There is more (and more efficient) punching than in the club's old days, but less fighting. It is still, as in Ruby's lifetime, a policeman's world, but no longer a girl's world. Ruby's club was electric with the violence of exploited women.

Dingy as it seems, it marks the top of a ladder. The rungs, each laboriously reached, were: The Singapore Club, The Silver Spur, The Bob Wills Ranch House, The Vegas Club, Hernando's Hideaway, The Sovereign Club, The Carousel. In 1947 Ruby came to Dallas to help his sister Eva, who had taken over The Singapore Club. This was in South Dallas, a prowling ground of tough outcasts, of Texans with an oil millionaire's temperament and a janitor's pocketbook. It is a Dallas that was forgotten when the city's thin wedge of skyscrapers reared itself, after World War II, to yodel challenges across the continent at New York. But Jack and Eva were used to tough neighborhoods. They grew up in a Chicago ghetto; every step outside it was dangerous. "Jack was the girls' protector," Earl Ruby says; if anyone picked on the Ruby sisters (there were four of them), Jack would hunt him down. On Dallas' South Ervay Street, he was still protecting Eva—though the two squabbled like fishwives when they were together. (If Eva called Jack at his office, he would put the receiver on the desk and go about his business, checking every now and then to see if the indignant static had died away.)

The brother and sister changed their Singapore Club to The Silver Spur, specializing in hillbilly Western music. The club bruised along, and became known as Dallas' "bucket of blood." Ruby needed no bouncer; he had been a scrappy admirer and hanger-on of Barney Ross in Chicago, a haunter of fight circles, known for his own flare-ups and nicknamed

"Sparky." Bill Willis, Ruby's drummer in The Carousel, says: "Jack grew up in the same kind of neighborhood I did. If you have our background, you learn to be a jungle walker; you *sense* a fight coming on. Jack used to tell me, 'You have to take the play away. If *you* don't take the play, the other guy will.' Jack was a reactionary." A what? "A reactionary—he reacted fast." (A stripper who worked for him told us, "Jack was a spastic." He was? "Yes—he acted suddenly.")

At The Silver Spur, there were many plays Jack had to take away. He was not a big man—five-foot-nine, 175 pounds—but he was brawny in the arms and shoulders, and fast, and deft at his tactic of the seized initiative. We found no memory, in the jumbled fight stories from his "bucket-of-blood" days, of his ever losing the play. He struck fast. Once, though, having struck, he left his hand too long in an opponent's face: "Dub" Dickerson chomped down on his finger and would not let go. By the time Jack shook him off, the flesh was mangled and one joint of his left index finger had to be amputated. Typically, Jack and Dickerson were friends when they met after this.

Even on South Ervay, Jack maintained strict, if eccentric, standards of decorum. "He didn't let no 'characters' in," one character told us. ("Characters," in Ruby's world, is the truncated form of crime-story phrases, like "suspicious characters" and "questionable characters.") "He threw me out four or five thousand times." The speaker is a wry young man with a sullen pout, Gilbert "Corky" Crawford. "I have a record, you see" (a five-page record of arrests, to be precise, often on charges of pandering), "and police would come in and sometimes take me out and sometimes take me to jail. So Jack said he didn't need my business." Did he ever throw you out physically? "Oh no!" Buddy Walthers, one of Sheriff Bill Decker's most promising young understudies (one of those who wear Decker's Dick-Tracy-style hat, not a Stetson), snorted at this. "He beat the hell out of Corky." Ruby, who despised "punks" and "characters," rarely found other ways of expressing disapproval. He moralized with his fists.

Decorum meant a great deal to Jack Ruby. He did not smoke or drink (his father was a drunkard). He rarely talked Yiddish (the language of his childhood); he was intent on perfecting his Bottom-the-Weaver English (his mother could not write her own name). Alas, the only verbal mastery he achieved was in the realm of imaginative obscenity. ("He could cuss straight on, like saying his prayers," one of his friends said admiringly.) And his ardor for decorum manifested itself primarily in a readiness to flatten any patron who put his feet on the table. His determination to run a "clean club" made many strippers wonder how they could find protection from his protection. One girl told Jack she was given her black eye by her husband, and she was leaving him. The next time the poor fellow appeared at the club, Ruby pitched him down the stairs, though the couple had been reconciled and the girl was pleading, "Jack, I don't *want* you to hit him."

In 1952, Ruby tried to open a new place, and lost both it and The Silver Spur. It was the first, and the harshest, of his business failures in Dallas. Eventually he got The Silver Spur back, but by now he had his eye on the "respectable" downtown clubs. His first real advance toward that goal came when he went in with Joe Bonds at The Vegas Club—which meant a switch from hillbilly music to rock-and-roll. He ran dance contests to bring in the young crowd, and kept the place even cleaner of "characters." "Oh yeah," Corky says, "he threw me out of The Vegas, too." Jack lived for this club—as manager, bouncer, advertising agent, promotor, M.C.—until the day when he took his farthest step up and moved into the center of town, right next to Abe Weinstein's Colony Club, back at 1312½, where "Pappy" had started in the Thirties. In 1961 he opened The Carousel, which he thought of always as his "high-class place," his first club with strippers and a real "show." He left the old club for Eva to manage; Bob Larkin, a giant blarneyer, became the "houseman" (polite for bouncer) of The Vegas.

"He carried a lot of money," Larkin told us. "That's why he kept a gun in the bank bag. I often carried the gun. At the end of the night, Jack would take the money out of the cash register and put it in the deposit bag; that's when he took out his piece and put it in his pocket. Whenever he was carrying the money, he kept his piece handy. Sometimes he had me tote money from The Vegas to The Carousel, or to the bank, so I had the gun." Did you put it in your pocket? "No. I didn't want it. I just left it in the bag." But Jack put it in his pants pocket? "Yes." Ready, if anyone reached for the money bag or asked for his roll, to take the play away.

Was Jack a good fighter? "Sure. He never hesitated. Once he dropped by the club while I was at the door. I had to handle a troublemaker and, before I even got started, Jack stepped between us and nailed him. I asked him, 'Jack, why did you do that? That's what you pay me for.' 'Don't ever stop me,' he said; 'I might lose my nerve.'"

Did you get along well with him? "Sure. He was good to me. When I left him and went to work next door [at Abe's Colony Club], I got stabbed three times up in the Colony's telephone booth. By the time they got me down to the ambulance, Jack was there, leaning over and asking me how I felt. He followed the ambulance, and came into the emergency room. A priest was trying to give me the last sacraments, but Jack shouldered him aside and came straight at me: 'What the hell, Bob! Freddy Bass had to pick his guts up and carry them after he got stabbed. You're as good a man as he was.' I tell you, it was the best medicine I got in that hospital. When I went into the operating room, he came right with me. They told him he couldn't stand there. He said he could watch through the door, couldn't he, and they let him. He was with me all through, in the recovery room and everything. He even offered to give me blood. When my own boss came to see me, there was his next-door rival already there. In fact, Jack told me I should sue Abe for getting stabbed in his club. I said, 'Aw, Jack, what would I do with all that money?' 'Come in as a partner at The Carousel.' He was always figuring the angles.

"He was a stickler for the law. He thought of himself as a kind of cop. He liked to do their job for them. If people came in after hours, he would frisk them to make sure they weren't still carrying their bottle. He'd even frisk some of the girls. Other times, he'd have his girls take lie-detector tests if he thought they were hustling out of his club. We had one girl who liked to tell everybody her troubles; she kept Joe Johnson at the club till four one morning. When Jack and I came in from the restaurant, Jack hit the ceiling. 'This isn't a goddam bedroom.' The girl swore they had just been talking, but he took her over to Fort Worth to take the lie-detector test. He liked those tests and things the police use."

As Bill Willis, the drummer, puts it, "Most of my neighborhood friends became hoods or cops. When I started playing in clubs, old pals would drop by to say a raid was coming. I just got up and left my drums behind, while the old pals went after their paddy wagon. Jack was the same: he thought of cops as friends, as the ones who made good, who stayed out of the gangs." Jack made quite an impression on the police at the outset: on South Ervay, he came to the rescue of two policemen—Officers Blankenship and Carlson—who were being beaten by three toughs.

When Jack was at The Vegas, his bandleader was the shy, proud Negro musician, Joe Johnson. Joe now plays the piano at a supper club before lugging his saxophone over to The Pretty Kitty Kat Klub, out by Love Airport, where his band is playing. Thus is the kind of club Ruby moved up to from The Silver Spur. It is a small place throbbing with the amplified beat that keeps dancers at their puppet-jerks in the cramped area left them for maneuver. At intervals, a pomaded young man takes the microphone and grunts back at the drum—five feet of silk suit and half a foot of elevator heels, mouthing syllables as unshaped as the drum thuds. At unmercifully briefer intervals, two bovine girls make bare-limbed efforts at the spasm and lurch called "go-go dancing." It looks like a preternaturally violent form of hiccuping. Patrons shout ill-mannered "requests" at Johnson, who keeps his smile determinedly in place.

There is no talking to Johnson (or to anyone) in this club; but Denny's is just across the highway, and by one-thirty Joe can escape the inexplicable cries for more of the same ("same" being one of this exaggerating crowd's rare accuracies). Joe carries himself with a pained deference; Texas long ago "taught him his place"—or thinks it did. But he is accepted at Denny's, which, from one to five a.m., is taken over by "show-business folk." "They are night people," says Bill Willis (who does not join them but goes home to his wife, an interior decorator). "If success has to be bought by working from eight to five, they don't want it. It's a grimy world, but it has the promise of glamour, and they live on that. At

Denny's or Brinks—in Jack's day, at Lucas B and B Restaurant, right next to The Vegas—you meet the table-hoppers, coming to tell you that so-and-so is thinking of taking them into their act, or so-and-so is writing them a song."

The diner is crowded: aging charmers, male and female; sculpted coiffures, male and female; self-consciously "casual" outfits, girls with Tower-of-Pisa hairdos, raspberry-popsicle pants, dragonfly eyelashes. These fine-featured rough-skinned girls, their eyes framed in velvet, their figures not good enough for the tight pants that proclaim them, are treated to elaborately gallant leers. This is the world Ruby aspired to when he came to Dallas. He was on the outskirts of it for years, got one foot in it with The Vegas, moved into its center with Carousel.

Denny's is at its rush hour, and we cannot get a seat until Bob Larkin comes in and cons a booth from the diner's "mayder dee." Larkin is now a private investigator for a team of lawyers who have to know what is going on in this world. Bob knows. He moves from table to table histrionically hugging girls and ducking a short punch at each man's arm. Bill Howard, an old friend of Ruby's, arrives Thunderbird-wafted to talk about his renovated Stork Club ("I was the first to bring the go-go girl to Dallas"). Howard invests in oil, and once got Jack out of a disastrous venture in Oklahoma wells ("He plunged into things. Jack was always a first-puncher"). Howard ran a club in Miami for a while, where Jack stopped by to visit him while traveling on a free ticket to Havana. Sam and Joe Campisi, who run the Egyptian Lounge in Dallas but skip over to Las Vegas whenever they can, come into Denny's after their own restaurant closes. Joe Campisi liked to go to The Carousel to watch Ruby in action: "He was the best goddam show in town."

For this crowd, Dallas is partly a tryout town for Las Vegas, the new world's New Haven. Members of the Bottoms Up troupe, when they mince in, stir widening ripples: they have just played Vegas and are haloed with its neon. Anyone with a Vegas connection—especially if the connection carries a perfumy hint of the expensive underworld—is a celebrity. People who were children when Benny Binion and Herbert Noble ran the gambling in Dallas claim to have been their friends. Even now, when a man with a "reputation" (like R.D. Matthews) stops by Denny's the night people eat their scrambled eggs in awe. Just before the small-time Dallas gambler Lewis McWillie moved on to Vegas, he played the *padrone* to his old pal Jack Ruby, sending him that cut-rate ticket to visit Cuba. In an expansive mood, McWillie once thought he would acquire a gun like Jack's; but when Jack obligingly sent him one C.O.D. to Vegas, McWillie's wife would not let him pick it up; the package came back unpaid for. Disillusioning, no doubt; but the night people are still dazzled by the town Jack's "second club" was named for.

Joe Johnson does not talk except in short answers. Yes, he worked for

Jack a long time. Yes, Jack frisked customers. Yes, Jack took that girl to Fort Worth for a lie-detector test. Yes, Jack liked to show his club off to the cops. But what kind of man was he? "He made me part of his family. He never made me feel ill at ease because I'm a Negro. He always remembered to throw a party for me on my birthday." How would you compare the Kitty Kat to The Vegas? "Well, my band is more versatile now. We're getting so we will be able to play *all kinds* of engagements." Always the promise of glamour.

For Ruby the promise was fulfilled in The Carousel. "This is a f----- high-class place" he would assure doubters as he threw them down the stairs. To get some idea of that club, one must walk the block from Commerce Street to Jackson—from the dust of the Police Gym to the smoke that final-filters cellophane-dyed lights in Barney Weinstein's Theatre Lounge. It is a place still amused or made uneasy by memories of Jack. Every member of the band once worked for him—the drummer Bill Willis, "Mr. Texas" of 1952; trumpeter Johnny Anderson, once in Stan Kenton's band; pianist Billy Simmons, who wrote *M-i-s-s-i-s-s-i-p-p-i*. In this world men reach the top of their short ladder rapidly and take, without strong feelings of loss, the short fall down. It is a world of reputations won and lost, or never lost because not won; claimed anyway, and enjoyed as if bestowed by crowds enthusiastically.

Crammed backstage in a tiny dressing room, Bill Willis looks like an overgrown adolescent. A mild-mannered, non-smoking, non-drinking gymnast and devourer of books, he wears black suede boots and has long blond hair his hands mother and his eyes seek out in this wall or that of the mirrored room. "Hell, man, Dallas is still a shoot-out town. When I was wrestling as 'Mr. Texas,' I had people see me on television and pile in the car to come over and whip me. I knew the signs. 'Oh-oh,' I'd say, 'what can I do for *you*?' There are people who go out on the streets here looking for someone to 'draw' on them. They have the look. You stare it down; or, if that won't work, take them on. A smirk means they are confident you won't even draw. There's nothing to do with the smirk but mess it up, right now."

And Jack understood the shoot-out code? "He had to *live*, didn't he?" What about the view that he fought in sudden fits, not knowing what he did? "Well, the girl who said that is not very trustworthy. No, Jack knew. He didn't *want* to hesitate. He had to take the play. One time a rough boy started trouble and the M.C. hit him, then Jack hit him, but he kept getting up. I went over and put a pin on him, and we were at the top of the stairs, this boy kicking at Jack and Jack cussing him, when some well-dressed people started coming up the stairs. Jack instantly said, just as cool as you please, 'Come right up, folks! Step right over them! Just a couple of bums!'"

We told Bill a story given us by one of Jack's waitresses. She had just begun working for him, and was underage. When a drunk got boisterous, Jack took her back into the kitchen. "Stay here," he said, "there's going to be trouble; the police will come." He went out and pounded the fellow, then held him for the arrival of the officers. Does that sound like Jack? "Oh, yeah! One night he had two Vice Squad men at a table by the old hallway (he tore that wall out later, and moved the box office forward, but the hall used to lead to the stairs). There was a guy at the bar who wouldn't pay and wouldn't leave. Jack went over to him several times, but got nowhere. So Jack grabbed him, rushed him right into the hall past the Vice men, quietly beat the shit out of him, and threw him downstairs; then picked up the conversation with the Vice men, who never knew anything had happened."

What made him fight so much? "He used to say, 'This is my home. I don't want people spoiling it.' He wouldn't let anybody get away with anything." But his club became known as a rough place precisely because he fought so much! "Yeah, well, Jack tried to please, but he usually did the wrong thing for reaching his goal. It's like his big words to impress you. They always came out wrong. He'd say things like, 'It's been a lovely precarious evening.' Or he'd tell a girl, 'You make me feel very irascible.' " (Another of Jack's acquaintances told us he would say, "In lieu of the situation, let's do this.")

He was a Mr. Malaprop? "Yeah, he always did the very thing he was attacking. Like the time when Frank Fisher, our trumpeter, was lousing up his part, and shouting insults back at the audience. Jack called out to him across the club, 'Frank, you c--------, you got no *class*!' " (One of Ruby's employees told the F.B.I. that Jack beat him up because he had ordered the employees not to fight and this fellow got in a brawl anyway.)

Didn't Ruby's antics drive customers away? "No! They came to see *him*. The strippers would be working away up front and people would turn around to watch Jack. Man, we had a *club*. We had a *show*." Was it enjoyable for the employees then? "Sure, we all liked Jack. There was a circle of us, the steady ones. Tammi, and Andrew, and Alice the washroom attendant, and a couple of the waitresses: Diana the dingbat, and Alice, and Nisi, and Bonnie. Jack was hard on some, like Jada; but they asked for it. They were tough customers."

"Bill!" The M.C., a man named Benny, sticks his face in, a sad-eyed greenish face, wearing the greenish appendage that, out under lights, is only mildly unconvincing as a cigar—at any rate, more convincing than the slab of black moss he covers his baldness with. "Time to go." The intermission is over, and Bill must climb to his balcony seat out in front of the piano, behind his drums.

The Theatre Lounge is owned by Barney, one of the Weinstein brothers who monopolized the downtown strip business until Ruby came along.

The Weinsteins like to pretend that Ruby was not a competitor; but, looking around Barney's club (which is bigger than Abe's), one finds many veterans of The Carousel: all of the band; this week's star stripper; one of the best champagne girls; many of the "professionals" who drop in. The Theatre Lounge has a U-shaped balcony which is, technically, a "private club"—making Barney's the only strip joint that can serve mixed drinks. The lights are low; it makes the motions of the champagne girls less obvious. Up on the left there is an iridescent murk of bottles and a robin-breasted bartender. To the right, the glitter of metal on his drums marks the spot where Bill Willis is nested in darkness. On the stage, the first of the evening's four strippers is flouncing through her garmented overture ("Number four girl goes first"). There is a fringe of oglers around the runway, but most of the tables are empty. Back from the stage, below the overhang of balcony, things brighten near the cashier's lighted cranny (*her* motions are not to be obscure). An all-American college-boy type, the bouncer, takes us around through the kitchen into Barney's office.

Barney does not think much of Ruby's business practices. "He was unethical. He used to go and give out Carousel passes to people lined up in front of Abe's club. Besides, he raffled off turkeys, or dishes, or anything to bring in the customers." (This, in some way Barney takes to be obvious, sullied the purity of Strip.) "Jack had seven fights a week. I've had three fights in thirty years." Not that the business is without its risks. Abe Weinstein told us of the time when some hoodlum type was dating a young stripper, back in the Thirties. It was the girl's first job, her mother had asked Abe to look after her, and he told her to break it off. "So this character came in one afternoon while I was in the office alone. 'Abe,' he says, 'I'm going to kill you.' 'Well,' I said, 'I understand how you feel. But killing me won't do any good. I could see it a lot better if you just beat the shit out of me.' That got him, so he sat down and we talked a while. But that cured me. I never messed in the lives of my performers after that. They're not worth it. Do you know a moral, Christian, God-fearing girl who'll stand up there and take her clothes off?" Did Jack get involved in the girls' lives? "He was all mixed up with them. He had to be in on everything."

Barney agrees with his brother. "Jack had to *be* there, even when he wasn't wanted. I put on a benefit for one of our performers who died, and he came offering to sell ten tickets. But he never let well enough alone. He met people as they came in that night, and tried to get them to buy *more* tickets. I said, 'Jack, leave them alone. They already bought their tickets.' So then he wanted to sell *special* tickets for the best seats; he wanted to be my usher; he wanted to help, and he only got in the way. Once he dropped by when my houseman had not come in. He said, 'Don't worry, I'll stay and take care of any trouble.' I told him, 'I don't *want* you to, Jack.' You know, he doesn't stop trouble, he starts it. But he stayed anyway. He had a wonderful heart. When he hardly knew me, he read about my mother's funeral in the newspaper and came to it. He just had to get into everything, including the excitement of that weekend Kennedy died."

Do you think that was his attitude? "Sure, that's where the limelight was. He always wanted class. That's why he would hang around here. He said, 'Someday I'm going to buy a Cadillac and a Jaguar in the same week, like Barney.' That was his idea of class. But these are nothing to me. My idea of money is investing in the market; and my idea of a good time is going to Las Vegas. Jack never used to go there."

Barney is tolerant of Jack, considering his foibles as clumsy attempts to be Barney. It is a tolerance shared by others. Milton Joseph for instance, a jewelry store on the hoof, put it this way: "He wanted to be able to do this" (out comes a big roll, hundreds arranged around the outside as big strawberries are scattered on top in the supermarket). "He had one?" (Out with his gun.) "I have five." (We fear he will turn out pocket after lethal pocket to display this arsenal.) "He always wanted to be at the openings and closings of shows. But I was at more. He wanted to know the visiting movie stars. Face it, Jack was jealous of me. Now, you just met me, right?" Right. "If you were to see me again, would you remember me?" Undoubtedly. "Why?" It's hard to say. "The characteristics, perhaps?" (He shoots his cuffs with wide-flung hands as if stabbed from behind, then folds his arms with giant watch face flashing at us—a Victorian clock stand, china "Artful Dodger" from a line portraying Dickens' characters.) "The characteristics? The cigar? The star sapphire?" Yes, probably that. Did Jack shoot Oswald to be in the limelight? "Sure, I know. As soon as I heard Oswald was dead, I went down to help Tom Howard, Jack's lawyer. I became Tom's bailiff." His what? "I mean, if you came into his office, I would ask your name. 'Mr. X and Mr. Y? From Esquire? Fine, step in this room.' And then I would guard the door." Would what? "Guard the door. There was no telling what was going to happen. So when Jack's sister Eva came, with the newsmen Tony Zoppi and Hugh Aynesworth, I showed them straight into Tom's office, and stood guard. But Eva said I had to leave." You were guarding the door from the *inside?* "Yes." What did you do when she said you had to leave? "I guarded it from the outside." Would you say you and Jack were much like each other? "A little. So they tell me. But Jack had no class."

Barney takes us out of his office, which contains such exotica as a nude jigsaw puzzle, back into the kitchen. The atmosphere is homey; Barney's wife is giving out her cookies; no one drinks anything but coffee. Even the family pet is here, a forty-year-old parrot named Panama—one "exotic" whose wardrobe never dims. Pampered and taught bad words by the envious girls, he shifts his shot-silk eyes complacently and ruffles velvet feathers. He is the Weinstein bird. "It is time for Nikki." Barney takes us out to see his star, Nikki Joye, who is now working second billing. She cannot, for a while, turn fast on her athletic knees; a surgeon has just mined them for the cartilage ground loose when she works hard. She remains Barney's favorite, though she is disillusioningly thick below the waist. She has been with him twelve years, from the time she lied about her age at fifteen and bared the breasts that have been her visible means of support ever since. She twirls warily tonight, relying more on winks, pouts, serpenting tongue, mimed kisses than on drumbeat spasms. Makeup and shifting light do not blot out the incisions under each kneecap. Out at the end of the runway she whispers "Ouch" to her fond employer, who runs his thumb reflectively across a house matchbook (nudes on the cover, with little cardboard bosses for the breasts).

Above, in his aerie, Bill Willis concocts hysteria on his drums. "That's when I write my plays," he told us. What plays? "Oh, there is my *Bug in a Sycamore Tree.* A man is whittling on his porch one morning when something black splotches his hand. 'Son,' he says, 'what are we breeding in the bug way these days?' 'Wa-al,' says the boy, looking up, 'in that tree I see a ladybug, a cicada, and a Volkswagen.' The VW is driven by a candidate for office who wanted a divorce. He figured on holding out till after election, but his wife ran off the day before. He thought what the hell and took off with his girl. But a strong wind drove them off the road, off a cliff, and into the tree. The candidate, you see, is now parked illegally close to a voting booth. But they cannot take him away without chopping down the tree, and the tree is the last sycamore in Sycamore Junction." He winks at us, "How's that for a dramatic dilemma?" He was known for pulling Jack's leg, too. When Jack said he would match whatever his employees gave to charity at Christmastime, Bill (the one chosen to hold the money because he does not drink) came to him and said, "Here it is, Jack—four hundred dollars." Jack had his four hundred counted out before Bill told him they had only scraped up fifty.

Nikki has spun herself to a controlled climax, arching her upper torso out while, deftly, she veils her stomach bulge—a true pro can fake it. It is time for the penultimate thrill—the M.C.'s Al Jolson routine (it had to come, sooner or later; better sooner, so it comes later). Bill Willis leads the "spontaneous" applause when the lights go out and Benny moves around with tie, gloves and shoes lit up, a walking jukebox, Al Wurlitzer. Benny dampens the effect, of course, by his preliminary bustlings—turning on the amplifier, moving out the glow spot, starting the Jolson tape. It is like watching Houdini put the rabbit in his hat beforehand. Benny never gets beyond the obviousness of his wig.

Number one girl goes last: tonight, Tammi True, Barney's present star and Jack's alumna. She is short and energetic, throwing herself orgasmically back and back against the drive of Bill Willis' drum. Nikki's action was all above the waist, Tammi's is mainly below: she has what Jack called a "loose ass," which her act is designed to mix and stir with maximum agitation. One of Jack's waitresses, in a catty moment, accused her of having a *creased* ass. The next day Tammi came in with net stockings sewed to her G-string (which is waist-high in back). She pulls that G-string far out in front, and shrieks surrenderingly (a trick brought to Dallas by Jack's last star, the meteoric Jada).

Back into the dressing room with a perspiring Bill, followed in a moment by a blonde perspiring Tammi. She is smaller than she looked oscillating under lights. She blinks dark half-stars of eyelash down (chiming silently with the pasties that star her breasts), sets her tired doll's face (rosily mummified in makeup), and says: "I won't say anything against that man." Why not? "I understood him. I'm like him." How so? "I have a quick temper too. I don't normally do what Jack did; but when the time comes—did you hear what I did to Alice?" No. "Well, I caught her in the john and beat her into the trash barrel. I told her that was where she belonged." We hear Jack fired you that night. "Yes. I *told* you I understand him."

Bill levers his shoulders out of the room. Tammi, glancing after him, says in her gravelly warble, "A good boy, Bill. But he takes liberties." The Victorian locution sits oddly with this girl's truck-driverisms—until she makes it clear that Bill dreamily makes her throw, in mid-grind, an unprepared bump or two: "He's writing plays again." When we ask her about the story of Bill holding a man down at the top of the stairs while Jack welcomes customers and told them to ignore the bums, Tammi remembers it with great concern for the dancer left onstage when Bill abandoned the drums: the poor thing had to work her pelvis without acoustic punctuation.

What kind of man was Jack? "A good man." Why? "Well, he found out I was living with my children in an apartment house full of gay boys. It was $25 a week, all I could afford. He was shocked. He said, 'You shouldn't be living next to queers.' He paid the deposit on my apartment in the house where he lived." Did he have any designs on you? "No." Why not? Wasn't he interested in girls? "He laid some, and he liked the others." And he liked you? "Yes. Of course, we had our clashes." For instance. "Well, he never let an M.C. tell racial or religious jokes—not about any race. One time he thought I was off base. In December, I stitched 'Merry' across the net on one butt, and 'Xmas' on the other. He came backstage and said, 'I don't think it's good for you to have Christ's name on your ass.' I told him, 'For Christ's sake, Jack, it only says Xmas. Do you want me to put Yom on one butt and Kippur on the other?' That finished him. He just mumbled something about thinking it over."

Tammi had never been hit by Ruby, nor seen a woman hit by him. "Of course, he used to talk big. He was always going to beat our ass, but nothing ever came of it." She thinks him capable of hitting a woman. "*They* are ready to hit—*I* was—why shouldn't he be?" The girls Tammi works with are a tough crew; at the first hint of trouble, they have one shoe off, their weapon. After Tammi beat up her good friend Alice, they went on being good friends—like Jack and "Dub" Dickerson.

Did he ever talk to you about politics? "No. But he liked that picture of Caroline in high heels. And he always turned the TV on in the back of the club when the President spoke—an Inaugural Address or State of the Union Message. The press asked me whether Jack was a queer. I said no, and they took that as if I had been proving he wasn't in bed. It wasn't true, but I don't care what they say about me so long as they don't lie about Jack so much."

Time for the mummy-doll to dress again (so she can undress) and put on her stage pout. Shortly after she leaves, Bill returns. Tammi is loyal to Jack, isn't she? "She's a good girl. She's steady and hardworking, and keeps a good home for her grandmother and children. At least she's not a lesbian." Are most of the strippers? "Well, many. You should see them fight over the green girls who come in." Why is this? "Oh, it's narcissism, I guess. They're making love to *themselves* out there. The only bodies they're interested in are women's." (In the other Weinstein club, Buddy Raymon, an emaciated comedian turned bartender, gave us *his* interpretation: "When they have been pawed so many times by so many guys, they begin to think there *must* be something better." One of the strippers told us she amuses herself by dreaming up tortures; she is the one who supplements her income with labors to titillate an impotent old man.)

What did Jack think of these girls? "He worried about them. He said he wanted no prostitutes working for him. But he didn't know what went on. He was generous when they got in trouble, bailing them out, loaning them money to get home or come back to work. A girl named Bonnie called from New Orleans and asked for money to get out of a hot-check charge and back to Dallas. He said, 'Who the hell is Bonnie?' We told him, and he sent her the money; but he didn't remember who she was."

Did he ever talk about politics? "Nah, he wasn't really interested. He was patriotic and everything, but he would have been that way about any President. What impressed him about the Kennedys was that they were in authority *and* they had glamour. Just like movie stars, he'd say. One day he claimed he saw an actress out at Love Airport—I think it was Rhonda Fleming or Arlene Dahl—and went right over to join her for lunch. He came home happy as a lark. Another time, I had gone to see the American Ballet Theatre with my wife, and we showed him the program; in it Jackie Kennedy was posing with members of the troupe. He said, 'Isn't that wonderful? Her as famous as a star, and going to see something cultural like that!' He asked me later, 'Do you think she *really* cares about ballet?' 'Sure, Jack,' I said. He seemed relieved: 'Isn't that wonderful?' He would come up and ask me things like, 'Is Leonard Bernstein really that good a musician?' I told him he was, and he was happy. He didn't like phonies, and he didn't trust himself in sizing up the cultural ones. He knew I read a lot, and he used to ask me about them—or ask me what some big word meant.

"The night before Kennedy's assassination, he was up on the stage to demonstrate a twistboard he was promoting. 'Even President Kennedy tells us to get more exercise,' he said. A heckler shouted, 'That bum!' 'Don't ever talk that way about the President,' Jack shot back. The next day, when he called me all broken up by the assassination, he said, 'Remember that man making fun of President Kennedy in the club last night?' "

What else did he say? "Well, he was crying and carrying on: 'What do you think of a character like that killing the President?' I was trying to calm him down. I said, 'Jack, he's not normal; no normal man kills the President on his lunch hour and takes the bus home.' But he just kept saying, 'He killed our President.' "

"Pappy" Dolsen pokes his head into the little box where we are cramped perspiringly. He eases in, vested, suit-coated, overcoated, and stays for some time without visible discomfort. He is about seventy, a night animal, mothbally with age and wearied by a thousand petty violences; but under the liverish skin his bones still show the blueprint of a handsome man. In the Thirties he ran glamorous, dangerous places, he was like a club owner in some Bogart film—the gentleman tough, on equally good terms with the hoods and the cops and the leading citizens. But after giving up his partnership with Benny Binion (at Pappy's 66) and Abe Weinstein (at the Colony Club), Pappy lost his ambitious clubs out in the suburbs to the creeping local "dry" laws of Texas. Now he is a theatrical agent, booking girls in and out of the strip joints—not really needed around the two Weinstein clubs, but every night making the circuit of those cheap clubs that spread like brushfire along the edge of Dallas—places where the girls strip on the floor, not onstage; where the lights can work little of their magic; where they have little enough to work on in the first place. Pappy goes in, flirts with the studiously coy beginners, creakingly clarkgables them, takes the mike from young M.C.'s. Backstage now at the Theatre Lounge, he tells us how he keeps toughs off with his fists—or with *this* (with many fumblings and snags, he pulls out an ugly toy, a tear-gas gun). Could you beat Jack? "Hell, no. He hit you quick, and never backed up. Even if it wasn't his fight, he would step in, in a second. I remember once I was outside the Baker Hotel and there was some kind of demonstration over the Hungarian revolution. One guy was going to poke me for nothing, but Jack came along just then and in no time flattened this guy and someone else who came up to help him."

You were friends then? "Hell, no. He was always mad at me for not getting him bigger stars. He said I was favoring the Weinsteins, and he tried to get A.G.V.A. [the strippers' union] after me. But I got him his best star, Jada; and he cut me out of my commission on her."

Did that end your dealings with him? "Until the assassination [Jada left him a couple of days before it]. On the day before he killed Oswald, he called me and said, 'I did you wrong, Pappy; but I'll make it up to you. I'm going places in show business, and when I do, you're going with me. I'll call you back tonight.' " That was Saturday? "Yes." Did he call you back? "No." Have you told anyone about this? "Only Barney, on the day after Jack killed Oswald." (Barney confirmed this, but Pappy's memory, we were told, tends to get mixed with his imagination.)

Time for the third show out front. Bill suggests we talk to Diana. Diana Hunter is a champagne girl who worked for Jack five years. She is lustrous-eyed, teen-age-awkward, dishearteningly experienced, with a little-girl voice and fingernails cruelly gnawed; mother of four children, survivor of eight miscarriages, and just out of the hospital from a suicide attempt. "I did the pill bit—seventeen sleeping pills, a pint of whiskey, and twenty kidney pills. My husband left me. I was in Parkland Hospital when they brought Jack in with his cancer. Eva came to see me, crying and hysterical."

Diana is a good champagne girl. No one can help pitying her, doing things for her, helping her in immediate terms (thereby, over the long range, sinking her deeper in voracious spiritual acids). Jack used to say, "Alice, what can I do with Diana when she turns those spaniel eyes on me?" She knows her power, laughs at it and uses it even as she tells us of it. She has a kind of silly innocence that makes her always the seduced one, even for the thousandth time.

The economics of the champagne girl is vital to running a club in Dallas, where the law keeps strip joints like Jack's from serving liquor. The house can supply "setups"—expensive ice-and-mix accommodation for those who bring their own bottles in a bag. (If you arrive without the canonical paper bag, you are given one at the door.) But setups and beer will not give the clubs a working margin of profit; that must come from the second part of the "beer and wine" permit—from champagne. The clubs pay $1.98 a bottle for it, turban the label in the customary towel (never more welcome than here), and sell it for $18.50. The $1.50 change from a twenty usually goes to the waitress as her tip. The champagne girl gets $2.50 for every bottle she persuades "her fellow" to buy. It is her job to get rid of the bottles fast and move on to a second or third with this fellow, or to a second or third fellow. The indispensable instrument for this process is the "spit glass," a frosted glass of "ice water" (i.e. ice) frequently changed. The girl's mouth is simply a ladle for moving the cheap commodity from a thin-stemmed glass to a tall frosted one.

"I was so dumb," Diana tells us, "when I began. I was really *drinking* the stuff. I thought it dishonest not to. Jack had to take me aside and tell me: 'Diana, you're not going to make any money that way. All you'll do is ruin your kidneys. I like you, and I'd like for you to make me some money. So remember: selling champagne is a game, just like chess. The man wants to go to bed with you, and if he does, he wins. You want to get his money, and if you do, and don't give him anything in return, you win.' I've worked in a lot of places since, and that's the best advice I was ever given."

When did you go to work for Jack? "When I was eighteen. I had tried out in Barney's Amateur Night for strippers, but I couldn't dance, so I answered Jack's ad for a waitress. But I was so stupid, like a scared rabbit, I wasn't making any money. Then one day I had to bring my oldest girl into Dallas to the eye doctor." How many children did you have? "Three." You were eighteen? "Yes. I was married at fourteen. I told you I was stupid. Anyway, I knew Jack had Cokes and some food in the kitchen of the club, and I had no money to buy lunch for Lila, so I took her up there in the afternoon. Jack loved children. Children and dogs. He gave her grape soda and pie—Lila remembers that pie to this day. She wrote him a letter to thank him for it. Finally he said to her, 'Go to the kitchen, honey, and play with the dogs,' and he took me over to the bar. 'Diana, we've got to do something about that girl. Her eyes need to be fixed.' 'Why do you think I'm working here, Jack?' 'How much are you making a night?' 'Seven to ten dollars.' 'You'll never make it. Now, I saw you at Barney's, and you'll never be a dancer; and even if you could, I don't need a dancer. But if you go out on the strip circuit you can make $150 a week. I'll get you some lessons, and a wardrobe, and an agent. Then you'll be able to pay me back.' 'For what?' 'How much will your kid's operation cost?' 'Three thousand dollars.' 'I haven't got that; but here's fifteen hundred.' He wrote me a check, then acted as if he were angry: 'Now get the hell out of here and take care of that kid!' So I went out and made enough to pay Jack back." No interest? "No." No favors? "No."

"When I made enough to get the operation out of the way, I could quit dancing; so I came back to Jack as a waitress. I knew how to make them buy me champagne now. I learned a lot on that trip—what I'm trying to *un*learn now. I became a good champagne girl—along with Alice, the best—and I brought a lot of money in for Jack. But he never could have known that when he loaned me the money."

Did you get along with him? "Oh, we fought. He blew up at everyone. He fired me at least three hundred times—seven times in one night. But it didn't mean anything. Once a new girl named Bonnie, dumb as I had been, was following Jack's rules on who got what table. The rest of us ignored them, we had worked out our own system. But she tried to take a table away from me, a champagne party of twelve. So I slugged her. Jack stepped in and stopped us, and then fired me." Why you? "Because she was the new girl, the dumb girl. He always took the side of the underdog. Anyway, I was pregnant; Jack didn't know it, but Alice told the other girls, and they cut Bonnie out of everything. At last she asked them, 'What have I *done*?' and they told her about my three kids, and my going to college in the daytime, and not eating when tuition came around, and being pregnant and all. So she went to Jack and asked him to give me my job back. 'Welcome to the club,' Jack said; 'she got to you, too, eh?' Then he told Andrew to call me; he would never make up after a fight himself.

"When I got back, I was hemorrhaging. I've had eight miscarriages. I needed to go to the hospital, but I didn't have any money. Andrew heard about it and he took a collection for me at the bar. At the end of the night he gave me $150 for the hospital. But at home that night I lost the child—a boy, my first one; I had to cut the umbilical cord myself with a razor. Then I collapsed back into bed, but the afterbirth hadn't come out, and at five in the morning I woke up gushing blood all over the place. I lost four pints by the time they got me to the hospital. I'm Rh-negative, and they needed two more pints than they had; so they called the place where I worked and Jack came right over. It was such an emergency they took both pints from him. He gave blood to lots of people. He went out and never visited me. When I tried to thank him at the club, he just swore at me." How was that? "He wouldn't let us sit down unless we were drinking champagne, but my first night back I was still weak, so before the customers came in I was sitting there and I heard Jack coming up—you could always hear his dogs thumping up the stairs ahead of him. We would all jump up then and pretend to be busy, but this night I figured what the hell, and he stormed right over to me: 'Diana, if you're so tired you can't stand up, then get the hell out of here, you're fired.' " Did you go? "Sure, it was his way of saying I wasn't well enough to work yet. He had a soggy heart, but he covered it up with bluster."

Did he ever hit you? "No. I never saw him hit any girl." He hit Winnie, the girl who operated The Sovereign Club before he took it over from Joe Slatin. "Well, I have my doubts about that. Anyway, she was not one of his girls. He was proud of his girls. We fooled him. He liked the police to come up, to see what a clean club he ran. But I sure got him mad at times." For instance? "Once he was stuck on a Saturday night with only two dancers. He said, 'Diana, I know you're not much as a dancer. You're the only stripper I ever met who needs padded pasties. But I'm really stuck tonight. Can you go on?' I told him I only had my Diana the Huntress act—I did a Greek ballet, then a hunting scene, then a victory dance with one breast bare; I wrote the script myself, that's how I got my name. He said it would have to do, and I went home to get my bow and arrow. After I did the first show that night, Jack came back and said he loved it. He thought it was an act with class. Face it: falling on the floor and rolling around and sticking your tongue out is simply not class! It might be sex, but it's not class. Anyway, the bandleader came to me, very apologetic, and said, 'When you shoot your arrow down the entryway, you're scaring Bill Willis to death. He sits right by that door.' Funny, isn't it? The bigger they are, the more scared they are. But I said I would aim my bow somewhere else. In the second show, I shot it at the back of the stage, and it hit a big gold plaque with a horse on it. Remember, it was Saturday night, our big night, a full house, some standing at the bar; but when Jack saw that, he let out a scream and came shouting across the floor, onto the stage, up to the horse; he pulled out the arrow—I'm dancing all the time—and raged at me: 'Of all the goddam dancers in the *goddam* world I have to get a *goddam* huntress!'

" 'Alice' could tell you more stories, but I don't think she will talk to you. Her family didn't know where she worked, and she went away as soon as Jack killed Oswald so no one would talk to her. I don't think anybody ever did. Still, I'll try to get her for you." After much cloak-and-dagger negotiating—phone calls (for which others did the dialing), meetings on neutral ground, refusals, and a final knock on the door at two in the morning—Diana got her to talk to us: no name was to be used but "Alice."

Alice, it turned out, is a shrewd, cool woman who did the real managing of Jack's waitresses while he blustered. Just as there are romantic and realistic *managers* (Jack and the Weinsteins), so are there romantic and realistic *waitresses* (Diana and Alice). A conversation with both girls is tugged continually two ways.

Alice: "Jack was a frantic about 'my girls.' Now let me tell you: *we* had a *bunch*. We had some who did and some who didn't; we had some who went for girls and some who went for money; we had all kinds. We had some who went for Jack, and if they did they lasted no more than a week. He made us miserable for that week! But we managed to run them all off, because once he got it, that's all he wanted, and they went out the door. All you had to do was hold out against him to stay with him. If you put out with him, you didn't get anywhere. We'd just sit back and smile, and say, 'Well, three more days and two more pieces and we're rid of her.' "

Diana: "Jack expected us to be virgins."

Alice: "Well, not virgins; but not hustling out of his club, either. He thought if they would sleep with him, they weren't good enough to work in his place. The time that man took us all to the Ports O'Call for dinner, we got to work drunker 'n skunks, and all dressed up, but he couldn't get it out of us where we'd been."

Diana: "He only wanted us to go to church picnics."

Alice: "That was the night he fired Tammi for hitting me."

Did he ever set you up with men? Diana: "Never!" Alice: "Well, it was like his putting the make on you himself. He would introduce you to men as if daring you; but I said no, I would get my own men, and I think he was glad I did."

Diana: "He never set me up at all." Alice: "Well, he would introduce you if he wanted to impress people; but he wasn't promising one side or getting paid by the other, he was just getting people together." (Others told us that if a male patron in one party and a female in another were "odd men out," he would try to move them to the same table; he had to be arranging things, matchmaking, meddling.)

Did Jack, wanting class so badly, realize he could never have it as a strip-joint owner? Alice: "No. He thought he ran a very beautiful place." Diana: "He thought that *horse* was beautiful!" Alice: "He couldn't understand it when some people turned down ads for his place. He wanted it to be perfect. He even had his girls followed to make sure they weren't making arrangements to meet the patrons outside."

Was this because he was afraid of the Vice Squad? Diana: "No, it was the class bit." Alice: "He checked us beyond the point of protecting his license." Then why did he introduce girls to policemen who were interested in them? Diana: "He didn't." Alice: "He did too. But he never thought of that as hustling. Not if *he* did it. That was just getting 'my friends' together." Did he do many favors for the police? Alice: "Sure, he gave them free drinks, even after hours. He couldn't do enough for them—including some of the ones who belittled him after his arrest. He thought cops gave the club class!"

Was it a good club? Alice: "Everyone was going up there at the end, even those from other clubs when they got off. Jack was so determined to come up from the bottom and beat his competition." The Weinsteins? "Yes." Was he doing it? Alice: "He was on the verge, at the end." Diana: "Oh, we were beating hell out of the other clubs!" But they say Jack was in financial trouble. Alice: "I guess he was personally, but we were packing them in. We sold an awful lot of champagne. I used to make $500 some weeks. It was a bad night for us to make under $60." Diana: "Jack just liked to see that room fill up. And we had a team. Jack would fire one of us, and we'd all quit. We moved the bus-station girls right on back to the station." How would you do that? Alice: "Get them to sleep with him. If one refused, we'd kick in and *pay* her to. We paid them $50 or $100, and that finished them." Diana, did you donate to these funds? "Of course! That was the only way to keep things stable around the club. We all knew how to please Jack and get our way." Alice: "Sure, buy him a piece. Then, the first time she did something wrong in her work, he'd say, 'Get your ass out of here! We want high-class girls.' "

Weren't there any girls who refused to sleep with him and refused to go along with you? Alice: "One. But I fixed her. I asked a friend on the Vice Squad to tell Jack she was a prostitute. Jack had told me I would go before this girl did: she was a nice girl. But pretty soon he came up and said, 'Alice, did you know that girl was hooking?' 'No!' 'Yep, she was. I had to let her go.' "

What's this about his drifters? Diana: "Oh, he'd help anyone who came along and needed food or a place to stay. He'd put them up on the cot in the club." Alice: "He would cuss them out for not working, but he fed them all the same. And if he read about anyone in trouble, he used to send things to the victims."

We hear you could egg him on. Alice: "Oh, I was *good* at that. One man had been ugly to the girls, so I grabbed his money out of his hand. He said he was going to kill me, but I got to Jack first and said this fellow was being nasty. If they asked for trouble, we would make them buy us champagne or get Jack after them. He would stick up for his girls." Diana: "We called it planting the seed. Just suggest something to him, and he jumps to conclusions. He was so suspicious. He was always afraid someone in the next group was talking about him."

Alice: "One time he came in and those dogs had messed all over the club. It was near opening time, and I said, 'Jack, you better clean up after your dogs. I'm not going to.' 'Okay.' Then Buddy, the young M.C., said he'd help; 'But you take the soft ones, Jack. I'll help you with your dog shit, but only the hard ones.' Jack reared up and roared at him, 'Don't you ever talk like that around these ladies. Don't you *ever* say that!' 'My God, Jack, what did I do? I just said dog shit. What am I *supposed* to say?' 'Use a little finesse! Say. . . .' He snapped his fingers in the air, reaching for a word. 'Alice, tell him what that word is I'm thinking of . . . oh yes, I've got it. *Crap.* From now on you say dog *crap.*' "

Did you know Jada? Alice: "Sure. She tried to horn in on our fellows, and sell champagne, and take our men. One night she sat down where I had been and collected the tabs for my sales. I told Jack, but he only said, 'The waitress gave her the tabs? That's your fault.' So I was plotting against her, but Jack got rid of her before I had to." How much money was involved with these tabs? "Oh, not much." Two-fifty? "No, more than that. But not much." It was the principle of the thing? Both together: "That's right!"

What happened to Jada? "Well, she would get down on that tiger skin of hers and she'd . . . well, she'd lay it." That's right! What's that word Oh yes—say *lay*! "Yeah, wouldn't Jack love my finesse? Anyway, she would lay the rug, then climb up against her pole and lay it, and then 'flash'—pull her G-string way out; till Jack finally cut the lights out on her. She yelled *so much* at him that night!" Right from the stage? "Right there. And he yelled back. And pretty soon he'd cut the lights on again to see where she was." What were they yelling? "Oh, m--- f--- and what have you. He fired her, and she took him down to Judge Richburg on a peace bond."

Diana was fired three hundred times. Alice, how many times were you? "Not many. I could handle Jack. He could throw the rages; but I threw them just as good. Once he really blew up at me and told me to clear out forever. I went out and sat on those damn stairs, crying. After a while, he started down them. I expected him to throw me out, but he just went on by. In a little while, he came back up with a pizza and gave it to me. 'I thought you might be hungry.' It was his way of apologizing."

We understand he used to take coffee to the boys in the parking lot and sandwiches to the men at the dry cleaners where he got his shoes shined. Alice: "Yes, he always wanted to feed people. He would never let anyone else pick up the check when we went for coffee. Once, though, George Senator was cooking hamburgers in the back of the club and he put one on for me. Jack came into the kitchen, bitchin' as usual. I loved him dearly, but, face it, if he ever came into the club and he wasn't bitchin' we would have rushed him to the hospital. So he saw the hamburgers, and he said, 'What the hell, George, are we running a restaurant?' 'No, but I put one on for Alice.' 'Well, take it off.' Then he saw me standing there. He mumbled to George to go ahead and cook it, but I told him where he could put his hamburger and went out into the club. He followed me and said would I please eat that damn hamburger, and when I said no, he shouted toward the kitchen, "George, put on hamburgers for everyone in the house!' Poor George had to cook hamburgers all night.

"Once he threw a party for us after the show. George cooked up the big turkey we couldn't raffle off—no one who won it wanted to lug it away. Jack had rented a hotel suite for the night, and here comes George down the corridor with the hot turkey. But Jack stopped him, because Milt Joseph had crashed the party, as usual. 'I'll be damned if I'm going to feed that character,' he said. So we all had to wait till Milt left before we ate our cold turkey. He couldn't stand Joseph, who came from his old neighborhood in Chicago."

It is after one in the morning. Benny has become fluorescent for that last *Mammy* of the evening; now Tammi is doing her one-side twitch (the "Xmas" side, not the "Merry" one) to Bill's sustained drum roll. We get our coats from the all-American boy.

Out on the streets of Dallas, it is good to breathe air instead of champagne or smoke. Diana, back inside, is emptying her life into a spit glass; Benny is becoming the human equivalent of his own green cigar; Nikki and Tammi try to forget the day when a stomach becomes un-veil-able, a "loose ass" un-net-able; and Bill Willis "takes liberties" up in his drummer's perch—meditative bug in a dismal sycamore.

Out on the streets of Dallas, one encounters a city of promoters. The main industry is banking, and the main bank has a fourteen-story neon sign. It is a town full of imaginative middlemen scrambling for the big one. Jack Ruby was, to the bigtime promoters, a "foreigner." But he was not out of place on the Dallas streets. He always had a new scheme brewing—pizza ovens, British blades, twistboards, a new entertainer, a new club, a new advertising campaign. "He was always a-churnin' " we heard from many as their impression of Jack Ruby nodding and handshaking his way down the street.

"He never stuck with any of these projects," Barney told us. "The pizza oven he was pushing went over well. I've got one here. But he had moved on to something else by the time it became established." Ruby cruised the streets expectantly; if one angle does not work, and work fast, try another. Rebuffed here, go there, keep moving. The big deal is somewhere out there if one only gets in its way. Meanwhile, make contacts. "Whenever I drew up a contract for him," said Henry Klepak, the lawyer who managed his club purchases, "he wanted to know what my *connections* were. He thought law was a matter of who you knew. I tried to tell him I don't draw up contracts to please connections, but he thought I was just being modest."

Most of his bustling was done to promote his clubs, especially The Carousel. "You can't write about Jack's life outside the club," Andrew Armstrong said. "There *wasn't* any. Even when he was outside, he was at the newspapers or the radio stations trying to get more publicity; he was handing out passes to the club, or thinking of some new scheme to push it."

Andrew is a slim sober Negro, articulate, immaculate; Jack's bartender, second-in-command at The Carousel. "He wanted me to be the manager when it came to firing someone—not when it came to making decisions." Didn't he ask your advice? "Oh, yes, he would stand at the bar sketching ads for the next day's paper, and he asked my ideas then. He put a lot of time into those ads, he thought he was pretty good at them. Taking them in was a big thing for him." (Bill Willis says that when the show was finished Thursday night—actually Friday morning, toward the dawn of Kennedy's visit—he asked Jack if he planned to see the parade. The answer was: "Maybe. I don't know. I have to get some ads in.")

"He was proud," Andrew continued, "of his ad for Tammi. Barney had billed some girl as 'The Teacher Turned Stripper,' and Tammi was suing a man at the time, so Jack wrote an ad for her as 'The Stripper Turned Teacher'—teaching this guy not to break the law. When a new act was going on, he would get too nervous to watch it. He went off in the back and asked me, later, how it went. And, as I say, he tried to have me do the firing. 'What do you think of so-and-so?' he'd say. 'I think she's all right.' 'Well, I don't. Cut her loose.' '*You* cut her loose; you're the one that doesn't like her.' " Why did he want *you* to fire them? "He didn't have the heart to take a person's job away. Half these people, if I had fired them, he would have taken back." (There was a drunken pianist he could not get along with but could not fire; the band told Jack his toes had been frozen and amputated in a Korean prison camp. Jack shook his head and said, "Just like the Jews in the concentration camps." The tipsy musician was untouchable after that.) "Then, when Jack had fired someone, he would get to thinking about it and want them to come back, but he would never call them. He made me do it." We hear he used to make up arguments with food. "Well, he was always bringing food to people. He'd come up here every other day with sandwiches for me. I told him, 'Jack, I don't want these.' I never ate a one of them. But he kept on bringing them to me anyway."

Jack went out with the night people after his club closed around two in the morning. He often ended his day, near dawn, at the *Times Herald* office reworking his next day's ad. After such a night, Jack rose late; but he would get to the club around noon to meet Andrew and check the last night's receipts. "He was never satisfied. If we had a thousand-dollar night, he would still say, 'What can we do to bring more people in?' If he couldn't get to the club, he would give me a call to see how things were. I would say, 'Okay here; where are you?' Sometimes he'd be way out in some Negro district where there had been a flood or something. I'd say, 'What are you doing out there?' 'Oh, nothing, just driving around.' But I found out what he did those days from one of the bums who slept on the cot in back. He told me he had been picked up by Jack way out some-where. 'And what do you think he was doing?' the guy asked me. 'He was giving money to some kids that had been burnt out.' After that I began to notice that, after Jack read a newspaper, if you picked it up the way he left it, there would likely be news of some local disaster on that page."

Such excursions were not usual for Jack. After he came to The Carousel around noon, he normally spent his afternoon "a-churnin' " up and down Commerce Street. The nucleus of Dallas is very small. Once he had parked his car in the garage under the club and taken Sheba upstairs, he could go almost anywhere he wanted on foot. Down at one end of the street, he might drop in to see Max Rudberg, a bail bondsman Jack met ten years before the assassination when he was getting one of his girls out of jail. Since then, Max's wife and Eva have become good friends. "I used to see him at the Sheareth Israel Synagogue," Rudberg said. "He was a great admirer of Rabbi Silverman."

Rudberg, an imperturbable little elf, is wedged in a cubbyhole office which a plug-in heater makes an oven. A processor of little miseries, he floats on his sense of humor above the shabbiness around him. Dilapidated humans are lined up in the hall outside his hole, men who cannot make bond for their petty crimes, men glad to sit there in the darkness. Rudberg knows what it is all about, that it is a matter of the little blows, delivered one by one, unintermitted. "Jack had a good heart. If any of his girls ever called on him, he came. He put up money for the worst sort of risks. He was a soft touch.

"He used to stop in all the time. Whenever he came to the courthouse, just around the corner, he would 'make the rounds,' dropping in to see everyone he knew. Just a few days before the assassination, he was down here to fix some bad checks an employee had passed, and he came in here. He was all excited about Jada, his big-name stripper. She had hauled him in on a peace bond the night before, claiming she was afraid to go back to the club and get her clothes. There was a lawyer in here with me at the time, so Jack gave us a blow-by-blow description of his appearance before Judge Richburg. "Didn't I do right?' he would say. 'Could a lawyer have done better?' He wanted us to praise him. He had to be accepted. He was a *meshugana*."

Judge Richburg is a specialist on peace bonds—the story in Dallas is that he granted one woman a bond against her husband for breaking wind. He hastened to correct that story for us: "I gave it to her because her husband wouldn't bathe but three or four times a year." His most famous recent bond was Marina Oswald's against her second husband. Andrew told us about the night he and Jack had to appear before the judge: "Jada claimed Jack had hit her, but Alice, the washroom attendant, was right there, and she said no such thing happened. Judge Richburg was a circus, finding everybody in contempt every other sentence, talking on and on about his farm. We all came back to the club *howling* at him." Even Jada? "Sure. Jack fired her a little after that."

We asked Rudberg why he thought Jack killed Oswald. "Well, everyone was saying the sonvabitch needs killing, and Jack was anxious to please. He happened to be by the City Hall, sending money to that stripper, just like he always did, and he was bound to poke his head in and see what was happening. Wherever there was a crowd, he couldn't possibly pass it by. Then, as I say, he made the rounds wherever he was. After that, it was just a question of two nuts being in the right place at the right time." (Bill Willis said: "At the club, after the first shock, we all said, 'Well, it figures. Jack thought while he was downtown he might as well kill Oswald, too.' ")

Moving up Commerce Street from the courthouse, Jack would stop in at the Doubleday store; he liked to check the new diet books and visit with a man there who patronized his club. Today, the man says that he hardly ever went to The Carousel; that Jack came in because he admired his education; but that he himself did not like to associate with a person like Ruby.

Up near the club, Jack would put himself in the way of temptation against his diet at a nearby delicatessen; he usually left with sandwiches or rolls, which he carried to the Enquire Shine and Press Shop with him. He would glance at the papers lying there while he had a shine, and give out buns to his friends—if there was anything left, he ran it up to the club for Andrew. Still making his rounds, he stopped by the hotels; he knew all the doormen, and wanted them to direct visitors toward The Carousel.

He haunted the newspaper offices. A. C. Greene, of the *Times Herald,* told us that when Jack came in with his advertisements, he would visit the columnists and the entertainment editor, trying to pass off items from his ad as bits of news. "He even came to us in the editorial section and tried to persuade us that his stripper, Jada, deserved an editorial because she had a college degree. I don't think she did; but even if she did, what editorial point could be made of that? I guess he thought it would prove that education leads to success!"

Jack liked to visit the office of Gordon McLendon, who bills himself as "the old Scotchman" and plays teen-age atrocities on his "top forty" radio station KLIF. Jack thought McLendon one of Dallas' great intellectuals; he had been especially struck by a radio editorial McLendon put on the air after Stevenson was spit on in Dallas. This, said the editorial in effect, had put a blot of shame on the city. Jack, who had an unreciprocated passion for Dallas, used to quote that broadcast reverently. Asked, after his arrest, to name his best friends, Jack put McLendon among the six he mentioned—along with Andrew Armstrong and George Senator.

Mitch Lewis, McLendon's assistant, says he tried to protect Gordon from Jack's clogging attentions. "But he did get to Gordon, I forget how, with his damn twistboard. In fact, when I met Jack in the crowd of newsmen outside Captain Fritz's office, the day Kennedy died, he came up to me and wanted to know what Gordon was going to do about the twistboard idea. I remember thinking that was a hell of a thing to talk about at the time." Wasn't Jack interested in what was going on at City Hall? "Oh, he was excited by the cameras and lights. He liked to hang around newsmen. When Marina and Marguerite Oswald came by, I was jostled up close to them and so was Jack. I happened to see him when he first looked at them, and his eyes *glazed*. I think he was impressed that these frumps, one of them in a babushka, could suddenly be made the center of attention."

Did you know Jack well? "Yes, he was always pestering me, when I was with the Dallas *Morning News,* and even more when I came here. He wanted us to advertise his strippers on the air. I tried to tell him our station is all disc-jockey shows for the young folk. We can't plug burlesque shows to teen-agers. But he said his club was different. His star, Jada, was trained in ballet. He said she had studied psychology, and was a descendant of John Quincy Adams, and I don't know what all." (Bill Willis said he helped Jack frame an ad claiming Jada was a granddaughter of Pavlova.) " 'Mitch,' he would say, 'you're a writer, and she's a good subject for a book.' After she quit Jack, Jada came around to ask me if I would ghost a book about all the famous men she had gone around with. When she heard what Jack had done, she came running back to town to grab some of that publicity. She had quit a week or so too soon." (We asked Bill Willis if he thought Jada was an opportunist. "Man, she was no dope. She couldn't dance worth a damn, so she paid me ten dollars a week for the privilege of bawling me out in public whenever she missed a step—as if it had been my fault.")

Does Mitch Lewis like Jack? "No, he was always glancing over my shoulder to see if there was some bigger name he could talk to. He was a small-time whiner, whining because we didn't give him enough publicity. His suits were always ten years out of style."

McLendon's office is just a couple of blocks from the Statler, which was one of Ruby's favorite spots. He knew all the front personnel; he liked to drive up with friends—sometimes in Jada's gold Cadillac—and be greeted by the doorman. His old pal Leo Torti now runs the men's shop in the basement of the hotel, and his close friend Joe Cavagnaro is sales manager. Cavagnaro is brawny and well-dressed, soft-voiced but emphatic. "I met Jack in 1955. I had just come to Dallas, and I ate in the Lucas B and B Restaurant next to The Vegas. One day Jack walked in and said hello; we talked awhile, then Jack picked up my check. We became very close. I used to help him out at The Vegas, taking the cover charge at the door on Fridays and Saturdays. I even took the club's money over to the night-deposit slot, so I carried his gun, which was in the money bag. I never took it out, though." Where did he keep the money bag? "When it wasn't in the club, it was in his car trunk." Were you on his payroll? "Oh no, I did it as a favor to Jack. I just liked being with him. So did other young fellows who have become quite successful, like Heinz Simon and Leon Nowak. We were his friends; still are. We used to go around with him, servicing his pizza ovens, getting things for his clubs. He was fun to be with. He would take us to breakfast after the clubs closed, and treat us all. It was a good dance club, The Vegas, a bit tough but fun. Trini Lopez sang there when he was just getting started.

"Jack made his customers toe the line. I had a friend go to The Carousel with his wife. Jack had a gimmick—he would put a man up on the stage and have the stripper start undressing him. It didn't get very far; when the fellow's coat and tie were off, the M.C. would take a Polaroid picture and come on later threatening to blackmail him. Eventually, he would hand over the picture. Jack chose the men who were put up there carefully—they were ones he knew, or who were with their wives; not drunks. Even so, when Jack pushed my friend onstage he whispered to him, in a cold voice, 'Don't touch.'

"After I married, I didn't go to his clubs, except when my wife and I happened to be downtown at night; but he came out to visit us often. My wife would make him cheeseburgers—he loved them. And when my boys were born, he became very fond of them. He would bring his dogs out to play with them. He gave us one of Sheba's puppies; we called it Henry. The boys still think a lot of Jack." What did they think when they heard he had killed Oswald? Cavagnaro grins, a bit embarrassed: "They were proud of him. We tried to explain to them that what he did was wrong, but they were glad that Mr. Ruby got the man who killed the President. You know how kids are.

"When my mother and her sister came to visit us, Jack took them out to lunch. They were crazy about him. He was always very polite and gentle with them. And with his girl friend, Alice Nichols." Who was she? "A secretary at an insurance company; she's still there. Jack dated her, on and off for eleven years. She was a very nice, handsome woman, and he had an almost exaggerated respect for her." Did she love him? "I think so." Why were they never married? "He told me he promised one of his parents, I think his father on his deathbed, never to marry a gentile." (Mrs. Nichols, a shy widow, told the F.B.I. that Jack said he could not marry her because he was not worthy of her.)

Did you see many fights at The Vegas? "Sure, some people come to clubs like that itching to start trouble. If that's what they wanted, Jack took care of them. But he never looked for a fight. I only saw him hunt out a fight one time. The Hilltoppers were out at Memorial Auditorium, and I went to visit an old schoolmate of mine, Eddy Crowe, in the troupe. When I got to the dressing room, Jack was waiting outside the door, ready to jump Eddy. I asked him why; he had seen the show and he was going to beat up the guy who told the Jew joke. I told him there was no malice in the inoffensive Catholic and Jewish stories the Hilltoppers told, but he didn't like *any* racial or religious jokes. I finally got him cooled down.

"Though I didn't see him much at The Carousel, he dropped in here at least three times a week to have coffee with me. Once a week or so he would ask me to help him phrase a letter—he was writing a lot to the strippers' union claiming the Weinsteins violated union laws. When we finished working over the letter, he would dictate it to my secretary. He came in for coffee the day Kennedy was shot. He had been at City Hall, and he was writing an ad to say his club would be closed for three days. He asked me what *we* were going to do. I told him, 'Jack, you can't just close a hotel! People have to have a place to eat and sleep.' But he expected the whole city to close down. He was upset that Dallas would be shamed. I remember his telling me how much the Stevenson incident would hurt the convention business.

"When I was asked to testify at the change-of-venue hearing, there was some talk that the national corporation wouldn't be happy at my calling Jack a good friend there in the courtroom. My wife and I talked it over, and decided I had to give up my job if it would help Jack. He would have done the same for me." Do you think others in Dallas had this kind of pressure put on them? "Sure. I saw some important people in his clubs, people who would now deny they ever went there."

Was Jack's word good? "Like steel. Of course, you couldn't believe him when he said he was going to meet you at a certain time. He was always late. He would get caught talking to someone; and if he stopped talking to one person, he would start right up with someone else before he could get out the door. He seemed always to be on the run—glancing at a paper (he always had one with him), jumping up to leave, saying he was late for another appointment (he probably was)—but he hated to break off any conversation. He was a compulsive talker, even about the most personal things."

Would he boast of sexual conquests? "No. He was concerned it would get back to Alice. He never did anything that might hurt her." How did you hear about his murder of Oswald? "I had brought my two boys downtown to go to the Cathedral. We pulled up at the hotel—I was going to give them some milk and doughnuts before Mass—and we could see the crowd just up the way. The people were kept across the street, which was blocked off, and there was an armored car in the City Hall driveway. My boys—they were three and four then—wanted to go see what was happening (we had been listening to the car radio); so we started walking. Just as we came up, we heard the shot. It could have been a backfire, but someone came out shouting, 'He's been shot!' I grabbed up my boys to get them out of there. If only I had been on the other side of City Hall!"

As the day wore on, Ruby sometimes drove to The Vegas and "made the rounds" there—B and B Restaurant (though he had been feuding with Pete, the owner, just before the assassination and stayed out), Phil's delicatessen, Kaye's liquor store. The Kayes, old friends of Jack, said he would bring his dogs over and say hello; he was known in the neighborhood as a soft touch for bums and winos; he let people who didn't even have enough to pay the cover charge come into his club and hear the music, though they could buy nothing. The Kayes believe he shot Oswald to become a hero.

One afternoon a week Jack invariably made it to McLean Hair Experts for a treatment. "He was always late; and he stayed a long time, past closing, to get more attention from the girl who was working on him. He always wanted me to reassure him that he could keep what was left of his hair."

By six in the evening, Jack was at the Y.M.C.A. He belonged to the Health Club, which some men join to avoid being approached by homosexuals. Jack was not known at a neighboring fairy-rendezvous, and he did not linger at the Y. He worked out with the weights, showered, and was ready for a night at the club by seven.

He liked to attend local affairs. Perhaps his favorite entertainment was boxing. A policeman friend said he used to come down the aisle just as the lights went up between preliminaries and the main event, shaking hands, greeting people, handing out cards, telling jokes. He had a bantam-cock way of carrying himself; he tilted his head to one side, or perked it up, or nodded with almost a pecking motion, like some bright-eyed bird. "He always thought his next deal would be the one to make him a big man."

Sunday morning, November 24, 1963: 223 South Ewing Street—a concrete-block barn decorated at each end in the pastels that paint stores seem to unload on motel owners. Wings are built out at right angles from both barn ends, enclosing a swimming pool. The second-story rooms are reached by a gallery, so that every room opens on the court. The modern motel is much like a Shakespearean inn, with a swimming pool where the stage was.

This "apartment house" is a half-motel for slow-motion transients, mainly young working girls who share a two-bedroom apartment ($125) until they move on to marriage or a better job. The manager is a young girl too, Doris Warner, who lives in the ground-floor apartment nearest Ewing Street. Up the stairs, on the gallery, the first apartment one reaches is 207, where Mr. Ruby lives. He was drawn here by the swimming pool (where he splashes in a bathing cap, since Mr. McLean has warned him about chlorine in the hair); before this, he had to impose on a friend and swim in a hotel pool supposedly reserved for residents.

Ruby has brought other tenants in. Tammi True, one of his strippers, came for a while, with her children. George Senator, one of the hard-up people who lived on the cot in back of Ruby's club, moved here when his British blades began to catch on. At first he roomed with Stanley Corbat in 206. But Corbat got married, and Senator's chronic money troubles came round again, so on November 1 Ruby let him move in with him. He has let others use the extra bedroom in 207, including homeless strippers. Ruby is rarely "at home." His home is the club; and it was part of his bustling, oddly impersonal benevolence to find people places to live. If you needed anything, you mentioned it at your risk to Jack Ruby. He would press suggestions on you till you found your home, or car, or whatever—or until you feigned you had.

Sunday morning, at eight-thirty, the phone rings. George Senator is not in the apartment. Ruby paws his way out of sleep toward the phone and answers muzzily. Sheba stirs, too, and jumps off the bed. There is a picture of her dachshund sire, "big Clipper," over the bed. Ruby is having bad luck with his sleep these days. Yesterday, he got to bed at six a.m., only to have the current transient at The Carousel, Larry Crafard, wake him with an eight-thirty phone call. He answered that call so blisteringly that Crafard put what little he owned in his pockets and moved on—to Michigan, as F.B.I. men later discovered.

With this caller, Ruby is more patient; indeed, ineffectually so. His voice flares up, irritated, but gentles again when he remembers he is talking to a gentle, aging Negress.

"This is Elnora" (Elnora Pitts, who cleans his apartment on Sundays).

"Yes, well, what—you need some money?" Ruby has loaned money to "Eleanor," as he calls her, and she thinks he is referring to this. But he went to sleep with money on his mind. Sunday is payday for his employees, who get paid when they come to work. But the club has been closed since Friday—the only nights it has been closed in its history—and his staff will not come in at the regular time. These are people who cannot go an extra day without their thinly distributed money. Two of the girls have already been after him for money—last night, when he was too disturbed to come to grips with the problem.

"I was coming to clean today."

"Coming to clean?" What has that to do with payrolls?

Mrs. Pitts always calls ahead, so Ruby can clear the dogs out; she fears dogs. Today she tells him she cannot come in the morning. Should she come later?

"Well, yes; you can come, but you call me!"

"That's what I'm doing now, calling you so I won't have to call again."

"And you're coming to clean today?"

"Yes." (Long pause.) "Who am I talking to? Is this Mr. Jack Ruby?"

"Yes. Why?"

"Shall I come around two?"

"You call me before two, before you start."

"Well, what do I have to call you again for?"

"Well, so I can tell you where the key is and the money."

Ruby leaves change and bills scattered all over the tables and bureau tops, and Mrs. Pitts refuses even to touch those: "I don't dust them because I don't—by him being a Jewish man, I don't want him to say I taken the money." She is very sensitive on the point. Ruby has to tell her which money is set aside for her. (He owns antennae for sensing others' fear of racial rebuff.)

As usual, he cannot sleep after the call. Others, this morning, want to linger underwater in their sleep world, but Ruby is anxious to break the surface. He feels History all around him; he has been a demon of energy ever since that moment on Friday when the announcement momentarily stilled him (he sat in the *Morning News* building, numbed and staring fixedly).

First, to the paper; George brought it in before he left. Are the ads there? Yes. "Carousel closed, Vegas closed." How about the other clubs? You might know! They are reopening. There should be some way of forcing them to do the decent thing. They want to take advantage of the flow of people into Dallas—reporters, TV crews, investigators, the curious, the photographers—all those people he has been giving Carousel passes to since Friday. (When will they ever be used?) It is frustrating.

The assassination has made people unwilling to talk about the twistboard, too—though he did get the *Times Herald* staff interested in it yesterday. There should be some way of riding History's wave to success. But all it has done so far is make Ruby and his partner Ralph Paul lose their money. (Ralph was right about one thing—losing a weekend is serious for a club like ours. He wanted me to stay open, and it *is* his money I am losing. But I just couldn't—not after what happened.) What happened comes back to him like a blow. Of *course* he had to close the clubs; why didn't everybody else see that? Why were *they* open?

Coffee. Squeeze a grapefruit (his current health food). Turn on the TV. What is happening? He has not yet promoted any private schemes this weekend, but he put *himself* well forward. He got those scoops for KLIF. Gordon will *have* to notice that; he was credited with it on his own station. Already Ruby is getting known!

At what cost? The careful masks and thin controlled voices on the television screen remind him of the numbness that washes, periodically, across his buzz of opportunistic instincts and drowns their chatter. What else is in the paper? The funeral arrangements for Kennedy *("He read about my mother's funeral in the newspaper and came to it")*. A picture of the motorcade; the rifle; the rifle's wielder—he had stood not three feet from Ruby Friday night when he was shown to him and to the other reporters. (I would have thrown him out of my club, the smirking punk; yet here he is basking in attention, enjoying it, *enjoying* what he did to Jackie. And to Caroline.)

"My Dear Caroline" (the letter in the paper begins):

"Caroline, you must have a lot of courageous blood in your veins." [Like the Jews; Jews have guts.] ("You will cry. My children did. My wife did. And I did.) . . . Mentally sick and acutely evil men are very difficult to understand. . . ."

Yes, sick and evil, the kind Ruby roughs up and throws out; the kind he has grown up with, been forced to clear endlessly from his path, his besieged escape route from the ghetto. They would have smothered him, the sneerers, had he let them, coming at him from all sides. But he rose above them, took the play from them, hit out always at that sneer. He throws the newspaper down, too blur-eyed to read further. *("If you picked it up the way he left it, there would likely be news of some local disaster on that page.")*

Poor Caroline, poor Jackie. *("He was the girls' protector.")* Coming to Dallas for this. How can she ever face Dallas again; at the trial, for instance? How can Dallas face her? *("The Stevenson incident would hurt business.")* God, that sonvabitch needs killing! That's what they all say. Harry Olsen is right. He should be cut in little bits. *("We called it planting the seed. Just suggest something to him. . . .")*

It is after nine, and City Hall is swarming with newsmen. Chief Curry said last night they would not miss anything if they came by ten in the morning, but few believed him. They thought he was moving Oswald early, and meant to throw them off the track. Yet nothing has happened; maybe he *was* telling the truth. Inside Captain Fritz's office, question after question chips at that smug facade but cannot splinter it. The sneer acts as a bulwark here. In certain company, it could be a bull's eye.

George Senator returns—a puffy man of fifty, with a whipped-cream fluff of curls on top. Unlike Ruby, he was married, and has a son—the marriage, like everything else in his life, failed. Failure lends to his natural geniality the compliance people feel protective toward. No one dislikes George; nor respects him. They feel sorry for him. At the moment, he comes in carrying freshly tossed laundry; he has been working the washing machine downstairs.

Ruby shows him the letter to Caroline; says Jackie should be spared a return to Dallas; says that punk should be killed before he gets to trial. *("Of course, he always talked big. He was always going to beat our ass.")* George nods sympathetically. It is a comment he has heard many times in the last two days, from many lips. The TV drones mercilessly on, making the incredible inescapable. It *did* happen: look at the world telling itself, over and over, that it did. Ruby goes into the kitchen for more grapefruit and to scramble eggs. Senator cooks for people at The Carousel, and is considered an excellent chef. But Ruby is delicate about his food, accustomed to fixing minimal fare for himself on small stoves or hot plates. He has always lived in "a room" or rooms, not caring much which rooms. He has risen when others are at work, slept when they are getting up. South Ewing is simply a cot for him, or a dressing room attached to the swimming pool. His "home" was a place of raving foreigners, who could not even speak English—a crazy mother, a brutal, drunken father—a place to get out of. He has been getting out ever since. He wants no "home."

Ten-nineteen a.m. The phone in the apartment rings again. At this very moment Chief Curry is telling the newsmen that Oswald will be moved in an armored car (the urgent call went out to the Armored Motor Service half an hour ago, and the driver has been hauled from the Sunday School class he was teaching). Ruby answers, "Hello." "This is Lynn again." In Fort Worth. He gave her five dollars last night, when she came over to work and found the club still closed. She has no salary coming; it was all advanced to her long ago. But she and her husband must pay something on their rent and groceries or they cannot stay, cannot eat. They *have* to have twenty-five dollars.

Ruby remembers how angry he got, last night, at her phone call for money—how could she think of anything but the President's death! (He said this to her on the same day he demonstrated the twistboard to *Times Herald* employees. (He used to get angry at Eva for being so unpatriotic as not to pay her poll tax—which Ruby had not paid for four years.) He remembers, too, his storm of anger at poor Larry. He is angry at the world these days. (Larry! That's right! There's no one to feed the dogs. Sunday is Andrew's day off. I have to feed them. Poor Clipper.)

Lynn needs the money at once. They can't eat till they get it. All right. Can she get to the Western Union office in Fort Worth? Yes. "It will take me about twenty or thirty minutes to get dressed, and then I will go on down. I have to go near there anyway, to feed the dogs and let them out."

It is almost ten-thirty. The newsmen are getting restless; they had come to believe the ten-o'clock moving time. Ruby stretches his weight-lifter's arms, lifting the weight of full consciousness. Like many night people, he wakes up slowly, at no set time, against no regular deadline. He is used to dressing leisurely. This is the last morning he will be able to. Every morning after this, for the rest of his life, he will rise early, prodded against his protests to face increasingly empty days from their very outset. Today, though, not even Lynn's call can hurry him. Not even the thought of his hungry dogs.

First, a shower. Ban deodorant. McLean's hair lotion. (Eva will pick it up for him the next three years.) He studies and rubs, combs and studies. Disposing his remains of hair almost strand by strand, he achieves a slightly off-center part—a hairstyle very popular with the men of Dallas. The elaborate asymmetry of these few lines that cross his scalp rears thin barriers against the Enemy—Baldness, an enemy all the more dangerous because potentially comic. The one thing Ruby does not want to be is a clown. One of his recurrent key words is "dignified." Dignity is at issue as, after scrutiny, he moves two hairs across the divide, right to left, strong side to weak.

Must be at one's best when meeting History. He lathers up and shaves, once; British blade, the kind George was pushing; good product. He lathers again, and shaves slowly back and forth from every angle. Ruby has a heavy beard; any shadow of it would accentuate his jowliness. Even in jail, he will shave twice every day (still with a British blade, locked into the razor with a key the guard retains). His hands are hairy too, battle-scarred; chewed off at one point, that stump on his left hand. He has a ring on that hand, winking at him as he pulls his face back and forth to turn curves into planes for his blade's razing; not a big ring by Texas standards, though it has three diamonds in it. A recent acquisition. No one will remember a star sapphire among Ruby's "characteristics."

He studies himself in the mirror, challenging, hoping, asking approval from that face as he does from all other faces. He has brows that hood his eyes—Lloyd Nolan brows. Nose too big for Nolan, though; and too many chins, despite his sweating in the Y. (Chin up, eyes down, tie the Windsor knot, silk tie.) The eyes keep returning to his face. They do not rest easily on one thing, but slide on, always, wary of blows and wistful for "the big one." Eyes of someone forever being moved on *("He was always afraid someone in the next group was talking about him"*). Eyes of a promoter (*"He was always glancing over my shoulder to see if there was some bigger name to talk to"*). Eyes ready for challenge (*"You learn to be a jungle walker"*). Always in motion, they belong to a man always moving, looking for the next spot to jump, watching where the play is, ready to take the play away.

Flitting eyes, distrustful—fixing other eyes desperately in his conversation, loath to break off, lonely but afraid. Apprehensive about tenderness, which he shows provisionally, where it seems most safe, with a self-protective grouchiness (*"Get the hell out of here and take care of that kid"*). How much can he risk? Not much: surely benevolence toward bums; sex with the bus-station girls; love for brothers and sisters, as long as they are absent (too near, *they* too are dangerous, and must be abused); extravagant devotion to his parents—from the very moment that they died; vaguely warm companionship with a widow kept safely at a distance by "respect." Love slows the reflexes of jungle walkers. Even bums and bus-station girls can mock. Only the dogs stay loyal. It is safe to love them. Or is it? Leo Torti remembers the time when Ruby said, "Look at that dog. I actually love him, do everything I can for him. I wonder if the sonvabitch hates my guts."

Move your eyes, moving man, time to move. Suck in the gut. Dark suit jacket. Glasses in the pocket. Neat grey hat, name stamped in gold inside. Home is what the hat is, a moving marquee, its message not reaching the outside. No overcoat. Ducking in here and there and back out, he would have to shed and don and carry and check it. A coat is like affection, too unwieldy, slowing everything; impedes the swing of tightened shoulder (*"Jack was a first-puncher"*). Ruby owns no overcoat.

He'll be needing money. There is some locked in the closet ($131.41), more scattered around the apartment ($124.87). Not enough to meet the entire payroll. Besides, I have to treat the boys—and many of the boys are here now, newsmen from everywhere! Need my roll. I can do better than the sandwiches I bought them yesterday—that's what I do *every*day for my friends. Get the money and gun from the car. (*"Whenever he was carrying the money, he kept his piece handy."*)

He is pacing the rooms and mumbling to himself. Hard to remember all he has to do today. Hard to get the load of consciousness up in one weight-lifter's snatch. Why should he? In everything there is to be done, what can he *do*? There is no displacing that dead center of his numbness. No bringing a dead man back. No way to un-kill, erase the memory from Jackie's mind, spare Caroline. Senator watches him pace, hears him mutter, but makes out no words. Ruby's friends, asked what actor could play him in a movie, turn invariably to types like Marlon Brando, Telly Savalas, Ralph Meeker—men with fists for tongues, who mush out *s* to *sh*, blunt *th* to *t, t* to *d*. Ruby's lisp bothers him; he tries to talk slowly, to correct it ("as if he had had a few drinks and was being careful how he spoke," says Andrew). In prison he will practice over and over, pronouncing the names Shadrach, Meshach and Abednego. But when he is excited, the lisp and the ghetto accent fill his mouth with the thickening bitter porridge of his past; syntax disappears; he babbles. This morning he paces and babbles a full five minutes, all confused plans (what do I tell Eleanor, how to pay Andrew and the others?) the numb hurt (poor Caroline, my hungry dogs) and hate (Dallas, the rifle, the punk) and excitement (a real reporter, "The Only Three-Runway Club in Dallas With Jack Ruby").

"George, I'm taking the dog down to the club."

Ruby's car is his traveling office; the "office" in the club is home to a succession of bums. Even his files and "securities" are wheeled and on the move. There is nothing fixed or settled about Ruby. He houses transients because he is one. The car is white—a two-door Olds, a 1960 model; mustn't be flashy with the I.R.S. after him (as if jukeboxes were taxable "entertainment"). Sheba takes the back seat, which she keeps in a proprietary shabbiness. Ruby pulls his little transistor out of the glove compartment and flicks it on; turns it down a minute to talk with a neighbor, out at the end of the drive; then enters the Thornton Freeway (which runs right by his apartment). It is almost eleven. The armored car is on its way to City Hall. Andrew is arriving at the club, despite the fact that it is his day off—things are too unsettled; he has to find out what is going on; he is shocked to see the dogs have not been fed. Joe Cavagnaro is putting his boys in the car for Mass. Forrest Sorrels, of the Secret Service, is being allowed to question Oswald.

Ruby does not stay on the Thornton Freeway, veers, instead, left along Industrial Boulevard to the point where it meets Main, tugged insensibly toward Dealey Plaza, as thousands will be in future months and years Tomorrow, and for the next three years, Ruby himself will be one of the Plaza's attractions, when he lives above it in his prison corridor. He dips, now, under the Stemmons Freeway—where Kennedy, approaching from the other side, was hit. Rising out from the underpass, Ruby slows his car, snagged in the cobweb of trajectories already being spun by conjecture and hypothesis. It is scarred air he drives through. To the left, the wreaths. But up by Houston Street, a crowd turns from the wreaths and is facing the jail (Ruby's future home, the most settled dwelling he will ever have). Oswald must be in there, transferred by now from Chief Curry's City Hall to Sheriff Decker's Courthouse. The radio is vague about the time of transfer, but Ruby heard yesterday it would take place at ten.

On up Main, still reversing Kennedy's course, past Sanger's on the left, Neiman-Marcus on the right. Ten blocks, to Harwood, where City Hall is—in the same block as the only Western Union that is open on a Sunday. There are four or five people talking to a policeman as Ruby drives past the rabbit hole in City Hall that lets police cars underground to park. On the other side of the building, an armored car has just jockeyed with difficulty backward into the small mouth of the exit. Ruby hugs the curb to see what is going on *("He had to be in on everything")*. There is still something down there—TV crews, perhaps packing up their equipment *("He liked to hang around newsmen")*. Now he must get back to the left lane; he wants to pull into a parking lot across the street. But a moving bus blocks the other east-bound lane beside him; he cannot race ahead of the bus or ease in behind it in time to make the turn. He slows till he is even with the lot, waits for the taillight of the bus to clear, then swings hard left into the lot from the far-right lane *("He was a spastic—he acted suddenly")*. Ruby—who is almost superstitious about the law, reverencing it and tempted to break it and feeling remorse about it afterward—has just committed his penultimate infraction of the law.

The lot is on the corner of Main and Pearl, directly facing the Western Union office. Sheba jumps into the front seat and rustles in last week's newspapers *("He always had a paper with him")*. Stay here, girl. He puts the transistor in the glove compartment. No need to lock the doors. He opens the trunk, his file cabinet and bank and transient home's attic, throwing the keys down in the front part of this dreary treasure chest, and rummages through it. Receipts, junk, money; a moldering holster he never uses (it came with the gun); brass knuckles in the money bag, where he keeps his weapons. (Take the gun now. God! How I'd like to use it on that character!) The money is in two places. He takes the bigger amount ($2,015.33) and leaves the smaller ($837.50). He puts the gun in his right-hand pocket, the money in his left; it is one motion, the two go together. Slams trunk. (Damn! Forgot to pick the keys back up. My head is a hurricane these days.)

It's all right, though—extra trunk key in the glove compartment. He keeps it there always, with his wallet. George Senator has never seen a wallet on Ruby or in his room—it is good only for the license he needs when driving. Ruby saves his pockets for Carousel cards, and twistboard literature, and pictures of his girls. The glove-compartment key is there so Ruby can get to his second key ring—farther back in the trunk, in a box—if he mislays the first. Bill Willis remembers talking one night in the garage under The Carousel: "I told him I keep my extra keys under the hood, in case I lose my pocket set, and Jack said he kept a spare set in the trunk."

(I'll get out the keys when I come back. Over the street. Still those four or five people at the other end of the block. I wonder why?) Into Western Union. At the long counter one customer is ahead of him.

Oswald is pulling on a sweater in Captain Fritz's office. Ruby adjusts his glasses—bifocals, he wears them as little as possible—and prints Little Lynn's maiden name on the form: Karen Bennett. However, he neglects the bottom of the form; Doyle Lane, the clerk, must ask for his address, and writes it in: 1312½ Commerce. Not the apartment house. That is not home, there is no home; The Carousel comes closest. Lane copies the address, and other information, a second time; this is the receipt he will give to Ruby. The minutes click by now. Lane stamps the receipt: 1963 Nov 24 AM 11 16. Ruby puts his glasses away, hooking one of its dark wings on his breast pocket, while Lane writes a duplicate of the receipt, to keep in the office; writes it rapidly, with only a glance or two at the other slip of paper; copies the address the third time, wrong, 1313½; stamps the second receipt: 1963 Nov 24 AM 11 17. A new minute has cogged itself up in the machine, a controverted minute that men will haggle over and cling to and question. Ruby takes his copy and puts it in his pocket.

(Must get the keys out, drive Sheba to the club. The dogs need food and an airing; then leave Sheba with them; can't have her waiting for me in the car all day while I mix with the other reporters. But those people are still there, just down the street. Looks like the same ones, not just passersby. Well, it will only take a minute to find out what's happening.) *"He always made the rounds."* He turns left, west on Main.

Something strange *is* going on. A car is nosing out of the ramp, and this is an entrance door only! Ruby quickens his stride.

History has always broken her date with Jack Ruby before now, despite his careful efforts to arrange a meeting. In fifty-three seconds, she will keep it. A block over, on Commerce Street, Joe Cavagnaro has pulled up in front of the hotel, his boys in the car with him. "If I had been on Main Street, it would never have happened. The minute Jack saw my kids, he always picked them up. And he would never let them see violence." No, Jack saw too much of it when he was a kid. Cavagnaro kept him from hitting Eddy Crowe outside the dressing-room door. History will not be cheated, though; Joe is a block away when Ruby waits outside the door for Oswald.

The entrance to the ramp is narrow—twelve feet, six inches—just wide enough to let a car turn in (so narrow that the armored car eased clumsily into its counterpart on Commerce Street, and could not back down; low clearance blocked it). The policeman who had been in the middle of the Main Street ramp must move aside, and the knot of gazers with him. They back toward Harwood Street, to the driver's side of the car, away from the approaching Ruby. The car that is surfacing must turn left to circle the block and move up one-way Commerce Street. It is meant to lead the armored car in what, by a sudden change of plans, will be a decoy caravan. In Dallas, turning left on a two-way street is illegal for a car that comes out of a driveway or a parking lot. The policeman on guard here does not know what is happening. He leans down to the driver, just as the car's nose reaches the curb and points left, poised for the illegal turn. The driver tells the guard what he is going to do and, as they talk, Ruby arrives. The car's taillights have just cleared the entrance to the ramp. He will keep his date in less than fifty seconds *("He was never on time")*. Ruby glances down, sees lights, does not break his stride *("Jack was a reactionary—he reacted fast")*, but turns smoothly left, and down *("He plunged into things")*. As he is about to reach the line of men at the bottom, he hears a cry: "Here he comes!" The brightest TV lights blink on, turn the glow in City Hall's belly to a flare *("He used to come down the aisle just as the lights went up between preliminaries and the main event")*. "He's coming out!" He? The character? Ruby's shoulders tighten instinctively, a jungle walker's reaction when the natural enemy is near.

Just as he reaches the line of people, Captain Fritz's Stetson bobs into view, brilliant in the camera glare. At that moment, Ruby is looking straight ahead, on camera, though he does not know it. He stands in the penumbra of those lights *("He always wanted to be at the openings and closings of shows")*. At the edge. How short a step to the center. Like Marguerite and Marina *("His eyes glazed")*.

Detective Leavelle, a movie Texan, moves the human chain of handcuffed men toward the car. He wears a white Stetson and white suit—the good guy *("Hell, man, Dallas is still a shoot-out town")*. He dwarfs the young man beside him, tense in his dark sweater—the bad guy, face logy with fatigue and bruises, jaws faintly dusted with morning growth. Tomorrow Ruby will tell his old friend Buddy Walthers, "He looked just like Corky Crawford!"

The orange stab of light in this dark place turns Oswald's face to the side, for a moment—toward the dim figure just arrived. Some will later claim he looked at Ruby, looked *for* him—but he could not see in these first seconds of the dazzle. The glare makes him tighten his lips further, in a slight grimace *("There's nothing to do with the smirk but mess it up, right now.)* Ruby pushes through the line *("Jack shouldered the priest aside and came straight at me")*. No one has a chance of stopping him now *("Before I even got started, Jack stepped between us and nailed him")*, but one policeman raises his arm *("Don't ever stop me, I might lose my nerve")*. As usual, his first act is decisive—dead on target *("Jack was a first-puncher")*. He mates in one move *("You have to take the play away")*. The job is done.

Sergeant Pat Dean, who cleared the basement an hour ago, thinks, "My God, a cop has killed him" *("He liked to do the policemen's job for them")*. When police swarm toward him, Ruby the scuffler does not try to take *this* play. They are friends, they'll understand *("He usually did the wrong thing for reaching his goal")*. But why are they so rough? Don't they know he's on their side, just like on South Ervay, fighting at the side of Blankenship and Carlson? He came to their rescue. Why turn on him? *("He wanted to help, and he only got in the way")*. They must know I did it for Jackie *("Jack, I don't want you to hit him")*. For Dallas *("Even if it wasn't his fight, he would step in, in a second")*. For Caroline *("Diana, we've got to do something about that girl")*. They must see that: "YOU ALL KNOW ME!" *("Mr. Ruby got the man who killed the President")*. "I'M JACK RUBY!"

[May-June, 1967]

Robert's Character

by Patrick Anderson

From the moment I joined the Kennedy Administration I was determined to cling to my objectivity—to work long and hard, but deep within me to remain a neutral on the New Frontier.

The reasons for my reserve were perverse and personal. I grew up, a poor and rather puny lad, in a Texas city that applauded wealth and athletic ability in its young. As a result, although I have no religious or racial prejudice, I instinctively distrust the rich and athletic.

Add to this the usual suspicion of the Southwesterner for the Easterner and it is clear that although I was ready to work for Robert Kennedy, that most rich and athletic of Easterners, I was not likely to gaze upon him in unquestioning awe.

Kennedy, as Attorney General, was chairman of the President's Committee on Juvenile Delinquency, and one of his oldest and closest friends, David Hackett, was its executive director. On the recommendation of another Kennedy aide, Hackett hired me, in December of 1961, as information officer for this Committee. I was then a twenty-five-year-old newspaper reporter.

For the next three years my job kept me in and out of the Attorney

General's cavernous, fifth-floor office at the Justice Department, Hackett's office next door, and the press office across the hall. Yet despite this physical proximity, it must be clear that I am not attempting to picture myself as having been a close associate of Robert Kennedy. To the contrary, the point is that I was on the fringes, close enough to Kennedy to see his faults, but not close enough to see his virtues.

Kennedy was surrounded by a group of trusted aides—such as Hackett, Ed Guthman, his press officer, John Nolan, his administrative assistant, and Angie Novello, his personal secretary—and my business was carried on with them. My occasional conversations with Kennedy usually went something like:

"General, would you stand a little closer to the Governor for this next picture?"

"Okay."

In short, I was close enough to Kennedy to ghostwrite for him, but not close enough to rate more than a nod in the hall; close enough to issue invitations in his name, but not close enough to be sure he remembered my name; close enough to see the bickering in his office, but not close enough to see the grand designs in his mind.

It was from this vantage point—a frustrating one for a disciple, perhaps, but not a bad one for a determined neutral—that for two years I observed the second most powerful man in the United States. And in those days to know Robert Kennedy was to know the New Frontier.

Kennedy ran the Justice Department, and ran it well, but that was only the first of his many roles during his brother's Administration. The New Frontier operated on the assumption that there were many great jobs to be done and very few men who could do them correctly. One of the most important men in the Administration once said to me: "There aren't ten men in this country whose judgment I trust." Thus the trusted few worked to exhaustion (and loved it; the real sacrifices of the New Frontier were made by their wives and children), while hundreds of untrusted civil servants and political appointees sat idle.

To say that Kennedy performed many jobs is, of course, to say that he stepped on many toes. Although he was its youngest member, he in effect served as a straw boss over the Cabinet, and if a Cabinet member resented this, there was not a great deal he could do about it. It is true that Kennedy's authority stemmed in part from his own demonstrated abilities, as well as from the fact that he was the President's brother. (Teddy, after all, was not made Secretary of State.) But this factor should not be exaggerated, for Washington understands power much better than it understands talent. It was not Robert Kennedy's talent that caused J. Edgar Hoover to follow his orders after years of dealing directly with the White House, nor was it any loss of ability on Kennedy's part that led Hoover to revert to his old habits after the assassination.

Much of the Attorney General's moonlighting was political. The Kennedys believed that the Democratic National Committee, supposedly their party's political headquarters, could attract top men only during election years. Thus during 1961-63 Robert Kennedy was for all practical purposes the head of the Democratic political machine. While John Kennedy worried about Khrushchev and de Gaulle, Robert Kennedy handled the equally delicate negotiations with Chicago's Mayor Daley, Harlem's Congressman Adam Clayton Powell, Jr., and an endless stream of lesser politicos who had some claim to press the Kennedy flesh and bend the Kennedy ear. It is somewhere recorded that John Kennedy bathed and put on fresh clothing several times each day; one suspects that Robert Kennedy washed his hands many times each day.

It has been said that Kennedy successfully fused the two great traditions of American Attorneys General, the political and the legalistic. Nonetheless, he maintained clear lines between the two. Political matters were negotiable; matters of principle were not. Unsavory political deals were necessary from time to time. Harold Cox of Mississippi, the first Federal judge appointed by President Kennedy, who later referred from the bench to civil-rights workers as "a bunch of chimpanzees" and "a bunch of niggers," was the close friend of Senator James Eastland, chairman of the Senate Judiciary Committee; Judge Cox was the price the Administration had to pay for the confirmation of Judge Thurgood Marshall and other commendable appointments. But there were no negotiations when Democratic politicians were accused of breaking the law: during Kennedy's term, the Justice Department prosecuted two Democratic Congressmen, three State Supreme Court justices, five mayors, two chiefs of police, and three sheriffs.

Many high Administration officials had not had previous political experience and found the bread and butter of everyday politics mildly distasteful. A Democratic sheriff who was the protégé of an important Democratic Senator once sought a letter from Robert Kennedy praising the sheriff's "junior-deputies" program for teen-agers. I drafted a letter and took it for clearance to Byron ("Whizzer") White, the Deputy Attorney General, who later was elevated to the Supreme Court. White asked me if I thought we should endorse the program.

I recited the political background of the request, but White interrupted: "But is the man's program any good?" I was forced to admit that, although I was convinced the "junior-deputies" program was not subversive, I had not considered its merits a major factor. The letter was sent, but not until White had deleted several adjectives.

Another of Kennedy's part-time jobs was at the Defense Department. Although he admired the way Robert McNamara ran his shop, there were periodic crises when the military became involved in political matters and it was necessary for the Attorney General to take over as acting commander in chief. These emergencies included the occupation of Ole Miss, the "schoolhouse-door" confrontation with Governor Wallace at the University of Alabama, and the concealment at various military bases of that outspoken son of Cosa Nostra, Joe Valachi.

Because the underworld had reportedly offered $100,000 for Valachi's life, extreme measures were taken to keep his whereabouts secret prior to his Congressional testimony. But a reporter, acting on a tip, called the commanding general of the Army base where Valachi was concealed and asked the general if Valachi was there. "Sure, we've got him," the general reportedly replied, a bit of candor for which several high Administration officials urged that he be busted to private.

During these crises, I was assisting in the Attorney General's press office and my chief fringe benefit was having Pentagon colonels call me, an enlisted man in the National Guard, for clearance on various routine press announcements. I always suspected that Robert Kennedy, a deck-swabbing seaman during World War II, shared my pleasure in exercising civilian control over the military. Indeed, one of Seaman Kennedy's finest moments, I thought, came when he visited Korea early in 1964 and, according to wire-service reports, was told by a high-ranking general that it would be very difficult to grant his request for a trip to the front lines. "Why would it be difficult, General?" he asked, and got what he wanted. The general learned that there are few experiences in this world quite like having Robert Kennedy push his unsmiling face toward yours and ask, "Why?"

Kennedy also played a major role in Administration programs to help the young and the underprivileged, so much so that Anthony Celebrezze, a man who made the incredible blunder of resigning as Mayor of Cleveland to become Secretary of Health, Education and Welfare, once protested:

"If Bob Kennedy wants to run my Department, let him come take my job."

This was wishful thinking, of course, since Robert Kennedy, like any sensible man, would have jumped off the Capitol dome before he would have taken the H.E.W. job. It sufficed to have trusted Kennedy lieutenants placed in key positions throughout the government. All this was done, of course, in the name of "coordination." This is a popular word in government, but whenever it appears, it is wise to inquire: Who is coordinating whom? During his brother's Administration, Robert Kennedy was coordinating most of the government, either personally or through trusted aides.

One of Kennedy's most trusted aides was Dave Hackett, his close friend since they were schoolboys together at Milton Academy in the early war years. Justice Department legend has it that Hackett was once asked by a reporter if he had gone to school with the Attorney General and replied:

"In those days the Attorney General went to school with *me*."

The statement would have been true, for Hackett was a legendary athlete when Bob Kennedy was still scrambling to make the team. Another school friend, John Knowles, modeled the young athlete-hero of his prizewinning novel, *A Separate Peace,* on Hackett, who went on to be twice named to the U.S. Olympic hockey team.

When Kennedy moved into the Justice Department, Hackett moved into the office next to his. At a time when many young New Frontiersmen were sparing no effort to be popularly identified as such, Hackett was content to operate quietly out of an unmarked office, devoting himself entirely to Kennedy's interests. It was this tough, charming, handsome, calculating man who was given responsibility for the national juvenile-delinquency program, who was charged with launching the Kennedys' "domestic Peace Corps," and who represented Robert Kennedy's interests in the hard bargaining that led to the poverty legislation. It was because I worked for Hackett that I was able to see a great deal of the government, and more than a little of Robert Kennedy.

Kennedy was a strange, complex man, easier to respect than to like, easier to like than to understand; in all, a man to be taken seriously. His love for humanity, however real, seemed greater in the abstract than in individual cases. He was no intellectual, but he was more receptive to other men's ideas than most intellectuals. But even as you made excuses for his weaknesses, there was the fear that you were doing more than he would do for you.

He has been called a simple man; it would be more accurate to say he is many simple men.

There is the simple man who pursued Jimmy Hoffa with such relentlessness that he accomplished the truly stupendous feat of making many people feel sorry for Hoffa. There is the simple man who, introduced to a shy, embarrassed secretary, made an elaborate, boyish curtsy that both put the girl at ease and gave her something to remember for the rest of her life. There is the simple man who, after his brother's death, could tell a reporter in complete honesty that he was thinking about becoming a schoolteacher, while in another corner of his mind little engines were already pondering the complicated Johnson-Wagner-Powell-Buckley gambit that led to his Senate bid.

I once briefed a reporter on the many youth programs Kennedy took part in, and she asked why I thought he spent so much time with children. I suggested that they provided an antidote to the Hoffas and Governor Wallaces he was obliged to deal with so much of the time. During her interview the reporter asked Kennedy if this was true, and he replied with some annoyance: "I just like children; that's all."

Methinks he doth protest too much, that such determined simplicity springs necessarily from a basic complexity. Fitzgerald wrote of Dick and Nicole Diver: ". . . the simplicity of behavior also, the nursery-like peace and goodwill, the emphasis on the simpler virtues, was part of a desperate bargain with the gods and had been attained through struggles she could not have guessed at."

But I do not mean to romanticize Robert Kennedy. There is too much about him to dislike.

Kennedy's most obvious fault is rudeness. His face, when it lacks that boyish, photogenic grin, is not a pleasant sight. It has a certain bony harshness and those ice-blue eyes are not the smiling ones that Irishmen sing songs about. At best, he recalls Fitzgerald's description of Gatsby: "an elegant young roughneck."

It is with this stern visage that Kennedy confronts most of the world. The easy smile, the cheerful greeting—these are rare. He is too preoccupied with the salvation of humanity to be polite to individuals. His friends call this shyness, but the historians of the 1960 campaign do not record that he was ever shy in the pursuit of a stray delegate.

A more perceptive comment came from boxer Cassius Clay who told a writer during the 1964 campaign: "I see Robert Kennedy walking through the streets meeting everybody, shaking everybody's hands, and when he gets into office you gonna need a necktie to go and see him." Clay may have remembered the fate of another heavyweight champion, Floyd Patterson, whose autographed picture adorned Kennedy's office—until he lost the championship.

One summer afternoon in 1963 I saw him, within the space of ten minutes, at his very best and very worst. I went with him to a Washington school where, through his intervention, the swimming pool was being opened to neighborhood children for summer use for the first time. As he inspected the pool, a blustering bureaucrat from the recreation department approached him, hoping for commendation. Instead, he was met with a machine-gun burst of questions:

Q. How deep is the shallow end of the pool?

A. Three feet.

Q. What about children under three feet tall?

A. They can't use the pool.

Q. Why not use a wooden platform to raise the shallow end?

A. It would rot.

Q. Why wasn't the pool to be open on Sundays?

A. None of the pools was ever open on Sundays. . . .

By then the poor man, suddenly become an enemy of tiny tots and Sunday swimming, was almost incoherent. Kennedy turned and walked away without a word.

Grant that the man was a bumbler. A Southern politician would have thrown his arm around his shoulders, listened to his problems—and in five minutes had his promise to build the platform and open on Sundays. But Kennedy had no time for this.

Minutes later, as he left the pool, hundreds of Negro children ran after him, shouting his name and reaching out to touch him. Kennedy moved among them slowly, smiling, rubbing their heads, squeezing their hands, reaching out to the smaller ones who could not get near him. This was not done for show—there were no reporters or photographers along—but because he loved those slum children, loved them as much as he disdained the fool of a bureaucrat who could not give him the answers he wanted.

But I must cling to my viewpoint. It is well and good to love children. But it is a finer thing to be passably pleasant to all of the people all of the time than to play Santa Claus to the poor when the fancy strikes you.

Robert Kennedy's concern for Negro advancement, which won him such hate in the South, was less evident inside the Justice Department. There were plenty of Negroes to be seen—the waiters in his private dining room, the messengers who went out for coffee and sandwiches—but you'd have to look hard for one Negro lawyer in a job of importance.

One day a civil-rights group picketed the Justice Department in protest of its hiring practices and Kennedy went out to speak to them.

"We hire people for their ability, not their race," said Kennedy, who served in a Cabinet filled with men picked solely for their ability, such as Celebrezze and Gronouski.

But what I have called rudeness may more fairly be termed an unconscious assumption of superiority. The Kennedy crowd was above all else an ingroup. Jack was President. Bob made him President and could do sixty push-ups to boot. Jackie was Jackie. Ted was Senator. Sarge ran the Peace Corps like magic. Dave Hackett had been on the Olympic hockey team, twice. Art Schlesinger had a Pulitzer Prize. Pierre hadn't won a Pulitzer, but he had been a child prodigy on the piano. Dean Markham had been the meanest lineman in Harvard football history. Byron White had been a Rhodes Scholar *and* an all-American halfback.

And so it went. Our team can whip your team. (How fleeting, power; in 1961 I attended a party with Ken O'Donnell and Lyndon Johnson; people were debating which was more important.)

Although I never attended a party at Hickory Hill, Kennedy's home, I sometimes shared his guests' thrill vicariously as I helped Dave Hackett write the poems and paint the posters that played such a vital part in the Kennedy merrymaking. I remember one night helping Hackett rewrite a long poem which celebrated a yachting trip he had taken with Bob and Ted.

The gist of the poem was simply that Robert Kennedy was a hell of a fellow. All the other party props—the posters and the funny games—had the same moral. I could not understand a man who would let his closest friends pay homage to him, or friends who would do such a thing, or people who needed props and poems to have a party. Perhaps it is pertinent to remember that Fitzgerald is usually misquoted. He did not say the "rich" are different from you and me; he said the "very rich." I have friends who are rich, but the Kennedys are very rich and perhaps that is the difference. I know no better explanation.

An entire attitude toward life lies behind the simple act of pushing someone into a swimming pool. A man who sprang from modest beginnings, no matter how high he may have risen, will find his hand stayed by visions of the time when there was only one Sunday suit, bought at Easter time and handed down from brother to brother, patched, polished, pressed—preserved with desperate loving care and God forbid that it should ever be pushed into a swimming pool. I once knew a young Texas farmer who made a fortune in oil. In an effort to impress his dates he would rent the ballroom of a San Antonio hotel, hire a band, fly in exotic foods from around the world and after dinner have a cockfight staged on the ballroom floor. Yet I'm positive he could never have pushed anyone into a swimming pool; he knew the value of a good suit of clothing.

I was sometimes a ghost-writer for Robert Kennedy, a man whose intellectual level was forever fixed for me by a report that he listens to recordings of Shakespeare in the shower.

It was standard practice to end his speeches and articles with an erudite quotation. One Sunday, working at home on a piece for the *Saturday Review* on the proposed domestic Peace Corps, I found myself without Bartlett's *Familiar Quotations* and had to rely on memory. I used Donne's "no man is an island," only to be criticized by my wife for triteness. I argued that if Kennedy did in fact know any literary quotations (do you retain what you hear in the shower?) they probably would include "no man is an island." And I will further argue that if a man is going to know only a half-dozen quotations, they *should* include "no man is an island" and "give me liberty or give me death" and others equally trite. One of Kennedy's virtues, perhaps his greatest, is that he understands that truth is often quite simple.

For Kennedy is ruled by heart, not intellect. As one of his most perceptive admirers, Joseph Kraft, said of him: ". . . his view of the world is intensely personal. The Attorney General has almost no interest in abstract ideas." Like Barry Goldwater, he operates almost entirely by instinct. The difference is that Kennedy's instincts ("We must provide genuine opportunities for these people," "My brother cannot launch another Pearl Harbor") are good.

Kennedy's humor deserves more credit than it has received. It ranges from merciless joshing of his friends (as when they collapse halfway through a fifty-mile hike) to extremely caustic comment. One day not long after the Bay of Pigs a group of us watched a Presidential press conference on television in Ed Guthman's office. A reporter asked the President if he planned to unleash Chiang onto the Chinese mainland.

"That'll take their minds off Cuba," Robert Kennedy muttered.

To me, one of his most disturbing traits was his passion for statistics.

Statistics were always referred to as "facts," and his speeches, except for a six-month period in 1963 when novelist Richard Yates wrote them, were rarely more than collections of these statistical "facts," inspiring anecdotes, and erudite quotations. I was often called upon to supply these figures, a job made less tasteful by my utter disbelief in government statistics. But even leaving accuracy aside, I mistrust any man who thinks the best speech is the one with the most statistics.

As far as a speaker and his audience are concerned, it doesn't make the slightest difference whether 800,000 teen-agers are unemployed or a million. What does matter is whether he, or they, can understand what it is for just one child to live in a slum. And this understanding is not a fact that can be held in the fingertips, but a sorrow that must be carried in the heart.

My first doubts about John Kennedy came when I saw, firsthand, that he shared his brother's passion for facts. In October of 1963 I hurriedly wrote a statement on urban problems for the President to use in a Rose Garden ceremony announcing a grant to New Haven. My statement contained around a thousand words which aspired to Sorensenian eloquence, but prudently included several statistics on unemployment and population growth.

Minutes before the ceremony, the President skimmed my statement and then, using it as background, spoke off the cuff. This was standard procedure; both Kennedys could talk better than any of their writers could write.

But, I noted with a sinking heart, the President had used one item from my text verbatim—a statistic on the number of unemployed youth projected for 1970.

"So what?" it might be asked. But I cared about John Kennedy, this stranger to whom I was devoting several irredeemable years, and I found that the only firsthand knowledge I had of him was that he shared his younger brother's mania for "facts."

Skepticism is an occupational hazard of the image-making business. You know that the speeches are ghost-written, the spontaneous demonstrations are intricately planned, the press conferences are rigged so that a friendly reporter will ask the right question. You soon decide that you can learn more about a man from one unguarded handshake than from a dozen State of the Union Messages.

My doubts about Robert Kennedy were based on personal observation, and for all I knew Jack was just Bobby with an extra coat of polish or a better manager. I remembered that proud old Joe Kennedy once said, "Bobby is the one most like me," and I wondered if by Kennedy family standards Robert, not John, might be the ideal Kennedy. Perhaps Jack Kennedy, because of his childhood illnesses and because he was the second son, had merely been tolerated by his family as he read history books and grew soft on intellectuals. I was struck by the fear that perhaps Jack wanted to be like Bob more than Bob wanted to be like Jack.

Doubts such as these were in my mind one evening when, over my protests, one of the secretaries led me into the Attorney General's office to a party the staff was giving for his thirty-eighth birthday.

All office parties are bad, but this one was miserable. About forty employees, from Nick Katzenbach and Burke Marshall to the newest secretary, filed in and formed a circle about Kennedy, who stood alone beside his desk. No one came nearer than six feet to him, except when an aide handed him his "gifts." These included a plastic "hot-line" telephone to Paul Corbin, his political aide at the Democratic National Committee; a used putter (his own, brought from home, which he didn't recognize); and a laboriously designed "Anti-Monopoly" set. After slowly examining each gift he would say in his flat voice, "That's funny," and you suspected he meant funny like a crutch.

He stood in that circle for half an hour. Now and then Guthman or Jim McShane, the Chief U.S. Marshall and one of the funniest men alive, would toss a joke across the void and the girls would titter nervously. The only motion came when people in the circle jockeyed to get in line with the camera that was recording this awesome event.

After the gifts were opened, beer was served and perhaps the party livened up. I never knew because I left, embarrassed for all of us, the gawking guests and the lonely guest of honor.

That was the evening of November 20, 1963.

Two nights later, I read myself to sleep with a poem:

"What songs shall I sing for him that I love?"

I had learned that there is no neutrality. A man must choose and now, too late, I chose that sweet, star-crossed man who had passed beyond my love or sorrow to what we must believe to be a better world.

I did not see Kennedy again until four weeks later at his annual Christmas party for poor children. Several of his aides had been planning the party for months and his guests, seven hundred children from Washington's poorest families, were met with one treat after another from the moment they arrived at the Justice Department.

It was a clear, crisp December day. The children arrived at an inner courtyard where four burly Washington Redskins lifted them into horse-drawn sleighs for a fast ride around the courtyard over tons of artificial ice.

Next they went up the elevator to the Attorney General's office where a three-man clown band was playing and Santa stood beside a Christmas tree with a present for every child. Some of the presents had been sent from around the world to Caroline and John Kennedy, Jr. in the month preceding.

After receiving their presents, the children went down the elevator to the auditorium, where Carol Channing was to entertain after they had all assembled. I was among the staff people who were seeing that everyone got an ice-cream cone and found the bathroom. As the auditorium began to fill, someone suggested that I bring the clown band down to entertain the waiting children.

I went up the the Attorney General's office and was negotiating with the chief clown ("Hell, man, they just sent us up here!") when Robert Kennedy approached us. I explained that the auditorium was filling with children and we thought the clowns would do more good there. He nodded and walked away.

This was during the period when, according to the newspaper columnists, Kennedy was living in a trance. I don't know whether this was true, but I know I was living in a trance and so was everyone I knew who was worth a damn.

A moment later, as the chief clown protested to me that he and his boys weren't going anywhere until they'd had a smoke, Kennedy returned and spoke to me:

"The clowns should be where the children are."

Our eyes met for a long moment and it seemed, incredibly, as if he wanted my agreement.

"Yes, sir," I said, "they should be," and I herded the reluctant clowns downstairs.

[April, 1965]

The Holy Family

by Gore Vidal

From the beginning of the Republic, Americans have enjoyed accusing the first magistrate of kingly ambition. Sometimes seriously but more often derisively the President is denounced as a would-be king, subverting the Constitution for personal ends. From General Washington to the present incumbent, the wielder of power has usually been regarded with suspicion, a disagreeable but not unhealthy state of affairs for both governor and governed. Few Presidents, however, have been accused of wanting to establish family dynasties, if only because most Presidents have found it impossible to select a successor of any sort, much less promote a relative. Each of the Adamses and the Harrisons reigned at an interval of not less than a political generation from the other, while the two Roosevelts were close neither in blood nor in politics. But now something new is happening in the Republic, and, as the Chinese say, we are living "in interesting times."

In 1960, with the election of the thirty-fifth President, the famous ambition of Joseph P. Kennedy seemed at last fulfilled. He himself had come a long way from obscurity to great wealth and prominence; now his eldest surviving son, according to primogeniture, had gone the full distance and become President. It was a triumph for the patriarch. It was also a splendid moment for at least half the nation. What doubts one may have had about the Kennedys were obscured by the charm and intelligence of John F. Kennedy. He appeared to be beautifully onto himself; he was also onto us; there is even evidence that he was onto the family, too. As a result, there were few intellectuals in 1960 who were not beguiled by the spectacle of a President who seemed always to be standing at a certain remove from himself, watching with amusement his own performance. He was an ironist in a profession where the prize usually goes to the cornball. With such a man as chief of state, all things were possible. He would "get America moving again." But then mysteriously the thing went wrong. Despite fine rhetoric and wise commentary, despite the glamour of his presence, we did not move, and if historians are correct when they tell us that Presidents are "made" in their first eighteen months in office, then one can assume that the Kennedy administration would never have fulfilled our hopes, much less his own. Kennedy was of course ill-fated from the beginning. The Bay of Pigs used up much of his credit in the bank of public opinion, while his attempts at social legislation were resolutely blocked by a more than usually obstructive Congress. In foreign affairs he was overwhelmed by the masterful Khrushchev and not until the Cuban missile crisis did he achieve tactical parity with that sly gambler. His administration's one achievement was the test-ban treaty, an encouraging footnote to the Cold War.

Yet today Kennedy dead has infinitely more force than Kennedy living. Though his administration was not a success, he himself has become a world touchstone of political excellence. Part of this phenomenon is attributable to the race's need for heroes, even in deflationary times. But mostly the legend is the deliberate creation of the Kennedy family and its clients. Wanting to regain power, it is now necessary to show that once upon a time there was indeed a Camelot beside the Potomac, a golden age forever lost unless a second Kennedy should become the President. And so, to insure the restoration of that lovely time, the past must be transformed, dull facts transcended, and the dead hero extolled in films, through memorials, and in the pages of books.

Most notorious of the books has been William Manchester's *The Death of a President*. Hoping to stop Mr. Jim Bishop from writing one of his ghoulish *The Day They Shot* sagas, the Kennedys decided to "hire" Mr. Manchester to write their version of what happened at Dallas. Unfortunately, they have never understood that treason is the natural business of clerks. Mr. Manchester's use of Mrs. Kennedy's taped recollections did not please the family. The famous comedy of errors that ensued not only insured the book's success, but also made current certain intimate details which the family preferred for the electorate not to know, like the President's selection of Mrs. Kennedy's dress on that last day in order, as he put it, "to show up those cheap Texas broads," a remark not calculated to give pleasure to the clients of Neiman-Marcus. Also, the family's irrational dislike of President Johnson came through all too plainly, creating an unexpected amount of sympathy for that least sympathetic of magistrates. Aware of what was at stake, Mrs. Kennedy tried to alter a book which neither she nor her brothers-in-law had read. Not since Mary Todd Lincoln has a President's widow been so fiercely engaged with legend if not history. But then legend-making is necessary to the Kennedy future. As a result, most of the recent books about the late President are not so much political in approach as religious. There is the ritual beginning of the book which is the end: the death at Dallas. Then the witness goes back in time to the moment when he first met the Kennedys. He finds them strenuous but fun. Along with riotous good times, there is the constant question: How are we to elect Jack President? This sort of talk was in the open after 1956, but as long ago as 1943, Paul B. Fay, Jr.[1] made a bet that one day Jack would be J.F.K.

From the beginning the godhead shone for those who had the eyes to see. The witness then gives us his synoptic version of the making of the President. Once again we visit cold Wisconsin and dangerous West Virginia (can a young Catholic war hero defeat a Protestant accused of being a draft dodger in a poor mining state where primary votes are bought and sold?). From triumph to triumph the hero proceeds to the convention at Los Angeles where the god is recognized. The only shadow upon that perfect day is cast, significantly, by Lyndon B. Johnson. Like Lucifer he challenged the god at the convention; and was struck down only to be raised again as son of morning. The deal to make Johnson Vice-President still causes violent argument among the new theologians. Pierre Salinger[2] quotes J.F.K. as observing glumly, "The whole story will never be known, and it's just as well that it won't be." Then the campaign itself. The great television debates (Quemoy and Matsu) in which Nixon's obvious lack of class, as classy Jack duly noted, did him in—barely. The narrowness of the electoral victory was swiftly erased by the splendor of the inaugural ("It all began in the cold": Arthur Schlesinger, Jr.[3]). From this point on the thousand days unfold in familiar sequence and, though details differ from gospel to gospel, the story already possesses the quality of a passion play: disaster at Cuba One, triumph at Cuba Two; the eloquent speeches; the fine pageantry; and always the crowds and the glory, ending at Dallas.

With Lucifer now rampant upon the heights, the surviving Kennedys are again at work to regain the lost paradise, which means that books must be written not only about the new incarnation of the Kennedy godhead but

1. *The Pleasure of his Company,* by Paul B. Fay, Jr.
2. *With Kennedy,* by Pierre Salinger.
3. *A Thousand Days,* by Arthur Schlesinger, Jr.

the old. For it is the dead hero's magic that makes legitimate the family's pretensions. As an Osiris-Adonis-Christ figure, J.F.K. is already the subject of a cult that may persist, through the machinery of publicity, long after all memory of his administration has been absorbed by the golden myth now being created in a thousand books to the single end of maintaining in power our extraordinary holy family.

The most recent batch of books about J.F.K., though hagiographies, cannot help but at times illuminate the three themes which dominate any telling of the sacred story: money, image making, family. That is the trinity without which nothing. Mr. Salinger, the late President's press secretary, is necessarily concerned with the second theme, though he touches on the other two. Paul B. Fay, Jr. (a wartime buddy of J.F.K. and Under-Secretary of the Navy) is interesting on every count and since he seems not to know what he is saying, his book is the least calculated and the most lifelike of the ones so far published. Other books at hand are Richard J. Whalen's *The Founding Father* (particularly good on money and family) and Evelyn Lincoln's *My Twelve Years with John F. Kennedy* which, in its simple way, tells us a good deal about those who are drawn to the Kennedys.

While on the clerical staff of a Georgia congressman, Mrs. Lincoln decided in 1952 that she wanted to work for "someone in Congress who seemed to have what it takes to be President"; after a careful canvass, she picked the Representative from the Massachusetts 11th District. Like the other witnesses under review, she never says *why* she wants to work for a future President; it is taken for granted that anyone would, an interesting commentary on all the witnesses from Arthur Schlesinger (whose *A Thousand Days* is the best political novel since *Coningsby*) to Sorensen's more dour *Kennedy*. Needless to say, in all the books there is not only love and awe for the fallen hero who was, in most cases, the witness's only claim to public attention, but there are also a remarkable number of tributes to the holy family. From Jacqueline (Isis-Aphrodite-Madonna) to Bobby (Ares and perhaps Christ-to-be) the Kennedys appear at the very least as demigods, larger than life. Bobby's hardworking staff seldom complained, as Mr. Salinger put it, "because we all knew that Bob was working just a little harder than we were." For the same reason "we could accept without complaint [J.F.K.'s] bristling temper, his cold sarcasm, and his demands for always higher standards of excellence because we knew he was driving himself harder than he was driving us—despite great and persistent physical pain and personal tragedy." Mrs. Lincoln surprisingly finds the late President "humble"—doubtless since the popular wisdom requires all great men to be humble. She refers often to his "deep low voice" (sic), "his proud head held high, his eyes fixed firmly on the goals—sometimes seemingly impossible goals—he set for himself and all those around him." Mr. Schlesinger's lovely threnody at the close of *his* gospel makes it plain that we will not see J.F.K.'s like again, at least not until the administration of Kennedy II.

Of the lot so far, only Mr. Fay seems not to be writing a book with an eye to holding office in the next Kennedy administration. He is garrulous and indiscreet (the Kennedys are still displeased with his memoirs even though a few thousand words were cut from the manuscript on the narrow theological ground that, since certain things he witnessed do not enhance the image, they must be apocrypha). On the subject of the Kennedys and money, Mr. Fay tells a most revealing story. In December, 1959, at Palm Beach the family was assembled; someone mentioned money, "causing Mr. Kennedy to plunge in, fire blazing from his eyes. 'I don't know what is going to happen to this family when I die,' Mr. Kennedy said. 'There is no one in the entire family, except Joan and Teddy, who is living within their means. No one appears to have the slightest concern for how much they spend.' " The tirade ended with a Kennedy sister running from the room in tears, her extravagance condemned in open family session. Characteristically, Jack deflected the progenitor's wrath with the comment that the only "solution is to have Dad work harder." A story which contradicts, incidentally, Mr. Salinger's pious "despite his great wealth and his generosity in contributing all of his salaries as Congressman, Senator and President to charities, the President was not a man to waste pennies."

But for all the founding father's grumbling, the children's attitude toward money—like so much else—is pretty much what he wanted it to be. It is now a familiar part of the sacred story of how Zeus made each of the nine Olympians individually wealthy, creating trust funds which now total some ten million dollars per god or goddess. Also at the disposal of the celestials is the great fortune itself, estimated at one hundred two hundred three hundred or whatever hundred millions of dollars, administered from an office on Park Avenue, to which the Kennedys send their bills, for "the childhood habit of dependence persisted in adult life. As grown men and women the younger Kennedys still look to their father's staff of accountants to keep track of their expenditures and see to their personal finances."[4] There are, of course, obvious limitations to not understanding the role of money in the lives of the majority. The late President was aware of this limitation and he was forever asking his working friends how much money they made; on occasion, he was at a disadvantage because he did not understand the trader's mentality. He missed the point to Khrushchev at Vienna and took offense at what, after all, was simply the boorishness of the marketplace. His father, an old hand in Hollywood, would have understood better the mogul's bluffing.

It will probably never be known how much money Joe Kennedy has spent for the political promotion of his sons. At the moment, an estimated million dollars a year is being spent on Bobby's behalf, and this sum can

4. *The Founding Father,* by Richard J. Whalen.

be matched year after year until 1972, and longer. Needless to say, the sons are sensitive to the charge that their elections are bought. As J.F.K. said of his 1952 election to the Senate, "People say 'Kennedy bought the election. Kennedy could never have been elected if his father hadn't been a millionaire.'. Well, it wasn't the Kennedy name and the Kennedy money that won that election. I beat Lodge because I hustled for three years," etc.[4] But of course without the Kennedy name and the Kennedy money, he would not even have been a contender. Not only was a vast amount of money spent for his election in the usual ways, but a great deal was spent in not so usual ways. For instance, right after the pro-Lodge Boston *Post* unexpectedly endorsed Jack Kennedy for the Senate, Joe Kennedy loaned the paper's publisher $500,000.[4]

But the most expensive legitimate item in today's politics is the making of the image. Highly paid technicians are able to determine with alarming accuracy just what sort of characteristics the public desires at any given moment in a national figure and with adroit handling a personable candidate can be made to seem whatever the Zeitgeist demands. The Kennedys are not of course responsible for applying to politics the techniques of advertising (the two have always gone hand in hand), but of contemporary politicians (the Rockefellers excepted) the Kennedys alone possess the money to maintain one of the most remarkable self-publicizing machines in the history of advertising, a machine which for a time had the resources of the federal government at its disposal.

It is in describing the activities of a chief press officer at the White House that Mr. Salinger is most interesting. A talented image maker, he was responsible, among other things, for the televised press conferences in which the President was seen at his best responding to simple questions with careful and often charming answers. That these press conferences were not very informative was hardly the fault of Mr. Salinger or the President. If it is true that the medium is the message and television is the coolest of all media and to be cool is desirable, then the televised thirty-fifth President was positively glacial in his effectiveness. He was a natural for this time and place, largely because of his obsession with the appearance of things. In fact, much of his political timidity was the result of a quite uncanny ability to sense how others would respond to what he said or did, and if he foresaw a negative response, he was apt to avoid action altogether. There were times, however, when his superb sense of occasion led him astray. In the course of a speech to the Cuban refugees in Miami, he was so overwhelmed by the drama of the situation that he practically launched on the spot a second invasion of that beleaguered island. Yet generally he was cool. He enjoyed the game of pleasing others, which is the actor's art. He was also aware that vanity is perhaps the strongest of human emotions, particularly the closer one comes to the top of the slippery pole. Mrs. Kennedy once told a friend that the last thing Mrs.

Eisenhower had done before leaving the White House was to hang a portrait of herself in the entrance hall. The first thing Mrs. Kennedy had done on moving in was to put the portrait in the basement, on aesthetic, not political grounds. Overhearing this, the President told an usher to restore the painting to its original place. "The Eisenhowers are coming to lunch tomorrow," he explained patiently to his wife, "and that's the first thing she'll look for." Mrs. Lincoln records that before the new Cabinet met, the President and Bobby were about to enter the Cabinet room when the President "said to his brother, 'Why don't you go through the other door?' The President waited until the Attorney General entered the Cabinet room from the hall door, and then he walked into the room from my office."

In its relaxed way Mr. Fay's book illuminates the actual man much better than the other books if only because he was a friend to the President, and not just an employee. He is particularly interesting on the early days when Jack could discuss openly the uses to which he was being put by his father's ambition. Early in 1945 the future President told Mr. Fay how much he envied Fay his postwar life in sunny California while "I'll be back here with Dad trying to parlay a lost P.T. boat and a bad back into a political advantage. I tell you, Dad is ready right now and can't understand why Johnny boy isn't 'all engines full ahead.' " Yet the exploitation of son by father had begun long before the war. In 1940 a thesis written by Jack at Harvard was published under the title *Why England Slept,* with a foreword by longtime, balding, family friend Henry Luce. The book became a best seller and as Joe wrote at the time in a letter to his son,[4] "You would be surprised how a book that really makes the grade with high-class people stands you in good stead for years to come."

Joe was right of course and bookmaking is now an important part of the holy family's home industry. As Mrs. Lincoln observed when J.F.K.'s collection of political sketches "won the Pulitzer prize for biography in 1957, the Senator's prominence as a scholar and statesman grew. As his book continued to be a best seller, he climbed higher upon public-opinion polls and moved into a leading position among Presidential possibilities for 1960."[5] Later Bobby would "write" a book about how he almost nailed Jimmy Hoffa; and so great was the impact of this work that many people had the impression that Bobby had indeed put an end to the career of that turbulent figure.

Most interesting of all the mythmaking was the creation of Jack the war hero. John Hersey first described for *The New Yorker* how Jack's Navy boat was wrecked after colliding with a Japanese ship; in the course of a long swim, the young skipper saved the life of a crewman, an admirable thing to do. Later they were all rescued. Since the officer who survived was Ambassador Kennedy's son, the story was deliberately told and retold as

5. *My Twelve Years with John F. Kennedy,* by Evelyn Lincoln.

an example of heroism unequaled in war's history. Through constant repetition the simple facts of the story merged into a blurred impression that somehow at some point a unique act of heroism had been committed by Jack Kennedy. The last telling of the story was a film starring Cliff Robertson as J.F.K. (the President had wanted Warren Beatty for the part, but the producer thought Beatty's image was "too mixed up").

So the image was created early: the high-class book that made the grade; the much publicized heroism at war; the election to the House of Representatives in 1946. From that point on, the publicity was constant and though the Congressman's record of service was unimpressive, he himself was photogenic and appealing. Then came the Senate, the marriage, the illnesses, the second high-class book, and the rest is history. But though it was Joe Kennedy who paid the bills and to a certain extent managed the politics, the recipient of all this attention was meanwhile developing into a shrewd psychologist. Mr. Fay quotes a letter written him by the new Senator in 1953. The tone is jocular (part of the charm of Fay's book is that it captures as no one else has the preppish side to J.F.K.'s character; he was droll, particularly about himself, in a splendid sort of W. C. Fields way): "I gave everything a good deal of thought. I am getting married this fall. This means the end of a promising political career, as it has been based up to now almost completely on the old sex appeal." After a few more sentences in this vein the groom-to-be comes straight to the point. "Let me know the general reaction to this in the Bay area." He did indeed want to know, like a romantic film star, what effect marriage would have on his career. But then most of his life was governed, as Mrs. Lincoln wrote of the year 1959, "by the public-opinion polls. We were not unlike the people who check their horoscope each day before venturing out." And when they did venture out, it was always to create an illusion. As Mrs. Lincoln remarks in her guileless way: after Senator Kennedy returned to Washington from a four-week tour of Europe, "it was obvious that his stature as a Senator had grown, for he came back as an authority on the current situation in Poland."

It is not to denigrate the late President or the writers of his gospel that neither he nor they ever seemed at all concerned by the bland phoniness of so much of what he did and said, or of what they now say and do. After all, politicians have been pretty much the same since the beginning of history. Part of the game is creating illusion. In fact, the late President himself shortly after Cuba summed up what might very well have been not only his political philosophy but that of the age in which we live. When asked whether or not the Soviet's placement of missiles in Cuba would have actually shifted the balance of world power, he indicated that he thought not, "But it would have politically changed the balance of power. It would have appeared to, and appearances contribute to reality."

From the beginning the holy family has tried to make itself appear to be what it thinks people want rather than what the realities of any situation might require. Since Bobby is thought by some to be ruthless, he must therefore be photographed as often as possible with children, smiling and happy and athletic, in every way a boy's ideal man. Politically, he must *seem* to be at odds with the present administration without ever actually taking any important position that President Johnson does not already hold. Bobby's Vietnamese war dance was particulary illustrative of the technique. A step to the left (let's talk to the Vietcong), followed by two steps to the right, simultaneously giving "the beards"—as he calls them—the sense that he is for peace in Vietnam while maintaining his brother's war policy. Characteristically, the world at large believes that if J.F.K. were alive there would be no war in Vietnam. The mythmakers have obscured the fact that it was J.F.K. who began our active participation in the war when, in 1961, he added to the six hundred American observers the first of a gradual buildup of American troops, which reached twenty thousand at the time of his assassination. And there is no evidence that he would not have persisted in that war for, as he said to a friend shortly before he died, "I have to go all the way with this one." He could not suffer a second Cuba and hope to maintain the appearance of Defender of the Free World at the ballot box in 1964.

The authors of the latest Kennedy books are usually at their most interesting when they write about themselves. They are cautious, of course (except for the jaunty Mr. Fay), and most are thinking ahead to Kennedy II. Yet despite a hope of future preferment, Mr. Salinger's self-portrait is a most curious one. He veers between a coarse unawareness of what it was all about (he never, for instance, expresses an opinion of the war in Vietnam), and a solemn bogusness that is most putting off. Like an after-dinner speaker, he characterizes everyone ("Clark Clifford, the brilliant Washington lawyer"); he pays heavy tribute to his office staff; he praises Rusk and the State Department, remarking that "J.F.K. had more effective liaison with the State Department than any President in history." This would have come as news to the late President, not to mention quite a few of his thirty-four predecessors. Firmly Mr. Salinger puts Arthur Schlesinger in his place, saying that he himself never heard the President express a lack of confidence in Rusk. Mr. Salinger also remarks that though Schlesinger was "a strong friend" of the President (something Mr. Salinger, incidentally, was not), "J.F.K. occasionally was impatient with their [Schlesinger's memoranda] length and frequency." Mrs. Lincoln also weighs in on the subject of the historian-in-residence. Apparently J.F.K.'s "relationship with Schlesinger was never that close. He admired Schlesinger's brilliant mind, his enormous store of information . . . but Schlesinger was never more than an ally and assistant." It is a tribute to Kennedy's gift for compartmentalizing the people in his life that none knew to what extent he saw the others. Mr. Fay was an after-hours buddy.

Mrs. Lincoln was the girl in the office. Mr. Salinger was a technician and not a part of the President's social or private or even, as Mr. Salinger himself admits, political life. Contrasting his role with that of James Hagerty, he writes, "My only policy duties were in the information field. While Jim had a voice in deciding what the administration would do, I was responsible only for presenting that decision to the public in a way and at a time that would generate the best possible reception." His book is valuable only when he discusses the relations between press and government. And of course when he writes about himself. His 1964 campaign for the Senate is nicely told and it is good to know that he lost because he came out firmly for fair housing on the ground that "morally I had no choice—not after sweating out Birmingham and Oxford with John F. Kennedy." This is splendid but it might have made his present book more interesting had he told us something about that crucial period of sweating out. Although he devotes a chapter to telling how he did not take a fifty-mile hike, he never discusses Birmingham, Oxford or the Negro revolution. All in all, his book is pretty much what one might expect of a P.R. man. He papers over personalities with the reflexive and usually inaccurate phrase (Eisenhower and Kennedy "had deep respect for each other"; Mrs. Kennedy has "a keen understanding of the problems which beset mankind"). Yet for all his gift at creating images for others, Mr. Salinger seems not to have found his own. Uneasily he plays at being U.S. Senator, fat boy at court, thoughtful emissary to Khrushchev. Lately there has been a report in the press that he is contemplating writing a novel. If he does, Mr. Harold Robbins may be in the sort of danger that Mr. George Murphy never was. The evidence at hand shows that he has the gift. Describing his divorce from "Nancy, my wife of eight years," Mr. Salinger manages in a few lines to say everything. "An extremely artistic woman, she was determined to live a quieter life in which she could pursue her skills as a ceramicist. And we both knew that I could not be happy unless I was on the move. It was this difference in philosophies, not a lack of respect, that led to our decision to obtain a divorce. But a vacation in Palm Springs, as Frank Sinatra's guest, did much to revive my spirits."

Mr. Fay emerges as very much his own man and it is apparent that he amused the President at a level which was more that of a playmate escorting the actress Angie Dickinson to the Inaugural than as serious companion to the prince. Unlike the other witnesses, Mr. Fay has no pretensions about himself. He tells how "the President then began showing us the new paintings on the wall. 'Those two are Renoirs and that's a Cézanne,' he told us. Knowing next to nothing about painters or paintings, I asked, 'Who are they?' The President's response was predictable. 'My God, if you ask a question like that, do it in a whisper or wait till we get outside. We're trying to give this administration a semblance of class.' " The President saw the joke; he also saw the image which must at all times be projected. Parenthetically, a majority of the recorded anecdotes about Kennedy involve keeping up appearances; he was compulsively given to emphasizing, often with great charm, the division between how things must be made to seem, as opposed to the way they are. This division is noticeable, even in the censored version of Mr. Manchester's *The Death of a President*. The author records that when Kennedy spoke at Houston's coliseum, Jack Valenti, crouched below the lectern, was able to observe the extraordinary tremor of the President's hands, and the artful way in which he managed to conceal them from the audience. This tension between the serene appearance and that taut reality add to the poignancy of the true legend, so unlike the Parson Weems's version Mrs. Kennedy would like the world to accept.

Money, image, family: the three are extraordinarily intertwined. The origin of the Kennedy sense of family is the holy land of Ireland, priest-ridden, superstitious, clannish. While most of the West in the nineteenth century was industrialized and urbanized, Ireland remained a famine-ridden agrarian country, in thrall to politicians, homegrown and British, priest and lay. In 1848, the first Kennedy set up shop in Boston, where the Irish were exploited and patronized by the Wasps; not unnaturally, the Irish grew bitter and vengeful and finally asserted themselves at the ballot box. But the old resentment remained as late as Joe Kennedy's generation; with it flourished a powerful sense that the family is the only unit that could withstand the enemy, as long as each member remained loyal to the others, "regarding life as a joint venture between one generation and the next."[4] To Joe Kennedy, in Bobby's words, "the most important thing . . . was the advancement of his children . . . except for his influence and encouragement, my brother Jack might not have run for the Senate in 1952."[6] (So much for J.F.K.'s comment that it was his own "hustling" that got him Lodge's seat.)

The father is of course a far more interesting figure than any of his sons if only because his will to impose himself upon a society which he felt had snubbed him has been in the most extraordinary way fulfilled. He drove his sons to "win, win, win." But never at any point did he pause to ask himself or them just what it was they were supposed to win. He taught them to regard life as a game of Monopoly (a family favorite): you put up as many hotels as you can on Ventnor Avenue and win. Consequently, some of the failure of his son's administration can be ascribed to the family philosophy. All his life Jack Kennedy was driven by his father and then by himself to be first in politics, which meant to be the President. But once that goal had been achieved, he had no future, no place else to go. This absence of any sense of the whole emerged in the famous exchange between him and James Reston who naïvely (in the context) asked the newly elected President what his philosophy was, what vision did he have

6. *The Fruitful Bough,* privately printed.

of the good life. Mr. Reston got a blank stare for answer. Kennedy apologists are quick to use this exchange as proof of their man's essentially pragmatic nature (pragmatic was a favorite word of the era, even though its political meaning is opportunist). As they saw it: give the President a specific problem and he will solve it through intelligence and expertise. A "philosophy" was simply of no use to a man of action. For a time actual philosophers were charmed by the thought of an intelligent young empiricist fashioning a New Frontier.

Not until the second year of his administration did it become plain that Kennedy was not about to do much of anything. Since his concern was so much with the appearance of things, he was at his worst when confronted with those issues where a moral commitment might have informed not only with passion but with shrewdness his political response. On such bills as Medicare and Civil Rights, had he challenged the Congress in the Truman manner, he might at least have inspired the country, if not the Congress, to follow his lead. But he was reluctant to rock the boat and it is significant that he often quoted Hotspur on summoning spirits from the deep: any man can summon but will the spirits come? J.F.K. never found out; he would not take the chance. His excuse in private for his lack of force, particularly in dealing with the Congress, was the narrow electoral victory of 1960. The second term, he declared, would be the one in which all things might be accomplished. With a solid majority behind him, he could work wonders. But knowing his character, it is doubtful that the second term would have been much more useful than the first. After all, he would have been constitutionally a lame-duck President, perhaps interested in holding the franchise for his brother. The family, finally, was his only commitment and it colored all his deeds and judgment.

In 1960, after listening to him denounce Eleanor Roosevelt at some length, I asked him why he thought she was so much opposed to his candidacy. The answer was quick: "She hated my father and she can't stand it that his children turned out so much better than hers." I was startled at how little he understood Mrs. Roosevelt who, to be fair, did not at all understand him, though at the end she was won by his personal charm. Yet it was significant that he could not take seriously any of her political objections to him (e.g., his attitude to McCarthyism); he merely assumed that she, like himself, was essentially concerned with family, and, envying the father, would want to thwart the son. He was, finally, very much his father's son even though, as all the witnesses are at pains to remind us, he did not share that magnate's political philosophy—which goes without saying since anyone who did could not be elected to anything except possibly the Chamber of Commerce. But the father's confidence in his own wisdom ("I know more about Europe than anybody else in this country," he said in 1940, "because I've been closer to it longer"[4]) and the assumption that he alone knew the absolute inside story about everything is a trait inherited by the sons, particularly Bobby, whose principal objection to the "talking liberals" is that they never know what's really going on, as he in his privileged place does but will not tell. The Kennedy children have always observed our world from the heights.

The distinguished jurist Francis Morrissey tells a most revealing story of life upon Olympus. "During the Lodge campaign, the Ambassador told [Jack and me] clearly that the campaign . . . would be the toughest fight he could think of, but there was no question that Lodge would be beaten, and if that should come to pass Jack would be nominated and elected President. . . . In that clear and commanding voice of his he said to Jack, 'I will work out the plans to elect you President. It will not be any more difficult for you to be elected President than it will be to win the Lodge fight . . . you will need to get about twenty key men in the country to get the nomination for it is these men who will control the convention. . . .' "6

One of the most fascinating aspects of politician-watching is trying to determine to what extent any politician believes what he says. Most of course never do, regarding public statements as necessary noises to soothe the electorate or deflect the wrath of the passionate who are forever mucking things up for the man who wants decently and normally to rise. Yet there are cases of politicians who have swayed themselves by their own speeches. Take a man of conservative disposition and force him to give liberal speeches for a few years in order to be elected and he will, often as not, come to believe himself. There is evidence that J.F.K. often spellbound himself. Bobby is something else again. Andrew Kopkind in *The New Republic* once described Bobby's career as a series of "happenings." The McCarthy friend and fellow traveler of one year emerges as an intense New York liberal in another, and between these two happenings there is no thread at all to give a clue as to what the man actually thinks or who he really is. That consistency which liberals so furiously demanded of the hapless Nixon need not apply to any Kennedy. After all, as the recent gospels point out, J.F.K. himself was slow to become a liberal, to the extent he ever was (in our society no working politician can be radical). As J.F.K. said to James MacGregor Burns, "Some people have their liberalism 'made' by the time they reach their late twenties. I didn't. I was caught in crosscurrents and eddies. It was only later that I got into the stream of things." His comment made liberalism sound rather like something run up by a tailor, a necessary garment which he regrets that he never had time in his youth to be fitted for. Elsewhere he explains those "currents and eddies." Of his somewhat reactionary career in the House of Representatives he said, "I'd just come out of my father's house at the time, and these were the things I knew."7 It is of course a truism that character is formed in one's father's house. Ideas may change but the

7. *Portrait of a President,* by William Manchester.

attitude toward others does not. A father who teaches his sons that the only thing that matters is to be "first, not second, not third"[4] is obviously (should his example be followed) going to be rewarded with energetic sons. Yet it is hardly surprising that to date one cannot determine where the Junior Senator from New York stands on such a straightforward issue (morally if not politically) as the American adventure in Vietnam. Differing with the President as to which cities ought to be bombed in the North does not constitute an alternative policy. His sophisticated liberal admirers, however, do not seem in the least distressed by his lack of a position; instead they delight in the *uses* to which he has put the war in Vietnam in order to embarrass the usurper in the White House.

The cold-blooded jauntiness of the Kennedys in politics has a remarkable appeal for those who also want to rise and find annoying—to the extent they are aware of it at all—the moral sense. Also, the success of the three Kennedy brothers nicely makes hash of the old American belief that by working hard and being good one will deserve (and if fortunate, receive) promotion. A mediocre Representative, an absentee Senator, through wealth and family connections, becomes the President while his youngest brother inherits the Senate seat. Now Bobby is about to become R.F.K. because he is Bobby. It is as if the United States had suddenly reverted to the eighteenth century when the politics of many states were family affairs. In those days, if one wanted a political career in New York one had best be born a Livingston, a Clinton, or a Schuyler; failing that one must marry into the family like Alexander Hamilton, or go to work for them. In a way, the whole Kennedy episode is a fascinating throwback to an earlier phase of civilization. Because the Irish maintained the ancient village sense of the family longer than most places in the West and to the extent that the sons of Joe Kennedy reflect those values and prejudices, they are an anachronism in an urbanized non-family-minded society. Yet the fact that they are so plainly not of this time makes them fascinating; their family story is a glamorous continuing soap opera whose appeal few can resist, including the liberals who, though they may suspect that the Kennedys are not with them at heart, believe that the two boys are educable. At this very moment beside the Charles River a thousand Aristotles dream of their young Alexanders, and the coming heady conquest of the earth.

Meanwhile, the source of the holy family's power is the legend of the dead brother, who did not much resemble the hero of the books under review. Yet the myth that J.F.K. was a philosopher-king will continue as long as the Kennedys remain in politics. And much of the power they exert over the national imagination is a direct result of the ghastliness of what happened at Dallas. But though the world's grief and shock were genuine, it was not entirely for J.F.K. himself. The death of a young leader necessarily strikes an atavistic chord. For thousands of years the man-god was sacrificed to insure with blood the harvest, and there is always an element of ecstasy as well as awe in our collective grief. Also, Jack Kennedy was a television star, more seen by most people than their friends or relatives. His death in public was all the more stunning because he was not an abstraction called The President, but a man the people thought they knew. At the risk of *lèse-divinité,* however, the assassination of President Nixon at, let us say, Cambridge by what at first was thought to be a member of the A.D.A. but later turned out to be a dotty Bircher would have occasioned quite as much national horror, mourning and even hagiography. But in time the terrible deed would have been forgotten for there are no Nixon heirs.

Beyond what one thinks of the Kennedys themselves, there remains the large question: what sort of men ought we to be governed by in the coming years? With the high cost of politics and image making, it is plain that only the very wealthy or those allied with the very wealthy can afford the top prizes. And among the rich, only those who are able to please the people on television are Presidential. With the decline of the religions, the moral sense has become confused, to say the least, and intellectual or political commitments that go beyond the merely expedient are regarded with cheerful contempt not only by the great operators themselves, but also by their admirers and, perhaps, by the electorate itself. Also, to be fair, politicians working within a system like ours can never be much more than what the system will allow. Hypocrisy and self-deception are the traditional characteristics of the middle class in any place and time, and the United States today is the paradigmatic middle-class society. Therefore we can hardly blame our political gamesmen for being, literally, representative. Any public man has every right to try and trick us, not only for his own good but, if he is honorable, for ours as well. However, if he himself is not aware of what he is doing or to what end he is playing the game, then to entrust him with the first magistracy of what may be the last empire on earth is to endanger us all. One does not necessarily demand of our leaders passion (Hitler supplied the age with quite enough for this century) or reforming zeal (Mao Tse-tung is incomparable), but one does insist that they possess a sense of community larger than simply personal power for its own sake, being first because it's fun. Finally, in an age of super-communications, one must have a clear sense of the way things are, as opposed to the way they have been made to seem.

Since the politics of the Kennedys are so often the work of publicists, it is necessary to keep trying to find out just who they are and what they really mean. If only because should *they* be confused as to the realities of Cuba, say, or Vietnam, then the world's end is at hand.

At one time in the United States the popular wisdom maintained that there was no better work for a man to do than to set in motion some idea whose time had not yet arrived, even at the risk of becoming as unpopular as those politicians J.F.K. so much admired in his book and so little emulated in his career. It may well be that it is now impossible for such men to rise to the top in our present system. If so, this is a tragedy. Meanwhile, in their unimaginative fierce way, the Kennedys continue to play successfully the game as they found it. They create illusions and call them facts, and between what they are said to be and what they are falls the shadow of all the useful words not spoken, of all the actual deeds not done. But if it is true that in a rough way nations deserve the leadership they get, then a frivolous and apathetic electorate combined with a vain and greedy intellectual establishment will most certainly restore to power the illusion-making Kennedys. Holy family and bedazzled nation, in their faults at least, are well-matched. In any case, the age of the commune in which we have lived since the time of Jackson is drawing to a close and if historical analogies are of any use at all, the rise of the *signori* is about to begin, and we may soon find ourselves enjoying a strange new era in which all our lives and dreams are presided over by smiling, interchangeable, initial gods.

[April, 1967]

The Last Kennedy

by Burton Hersh

If the continuing story of the Family Kennedy ever finds literary format, it will probably be as a series of convulsive epilogues recounting all the foreshortened lifetimes, wiped away abruptly each in lunatic turn by yet another tide of fate. This the Kennedys were Irish enough to start out knowing. Edward Moore Kennedy, whose instincts are the most subtle among his generation of brothers, senses fate especially. Even after Eugene McCarthy's upset in New Hampshire forced on Robert Kennedy the expediency of running in the primaries, Ted was reportedly opposed. Once the decision was made, however, he slipped into the familiar harnesses and even worked up enough enthusiasm while in West Virginia to infer, with unaccustomed clumsiness, that he might be back in eight years to campaign for himself. "Bobby's therapy is going to cost the family $8,000,000," Victor Navasky reports Ted as having remarked gloomily once the primary battles started. His foreboding was more than financial.

When the worst was fulfilled, when he appeared at the center of the television screen, clearly in charge of the nation's latest trauma, always referred to as "Senator Edward," it was difficult to remember that only six years ago he had been lumbering, helpless Ted. Back then, well-informed opinion of every imaginable description—the right, the intellectual left, old college classmates, onlookers in general—decided in advance that Ted Kennedy was never going to be anything much more useful to society than a Winthrop House jock whose wind had gotten lousy.

One September evening in 1962, having just proposed to open his political career as the Junior Senator from Massachusetts, Kennedy glanced up from his prepared remarks to hear the issue of his candidacy itself being laid open savagely by his upset opponent. "What are your qualifications for the United States Senate?" Edward J. McCormack Jr. was intoning across a South Boston auditorium platform. "You graduated from law school three years ago. You never worked for a living. You have never run for or held elective office. You are running on a slogan—You can do more for Massachusetts. . . . This is the most insulting slogan I have seen in Massachusetts because it means vote for this man because he has influence, he has connections, he has relations. This is a slogan that insults the President of the United States. . . ."

McCormack's attack, despite the passion with which he was delivering it, had been meticulously calculated. Having already been elbowed out of this youngest Kennedy's way for the Democratic Party's formal endorsement, the ambitious thirty-eight-year-old Attorney General of Massachusetts was risking his chances in the primary on a personal assault uninhibited by even the canons of Boston-Irish character assassination.

"I listened to my opponent the other night," McCormack continued, "and he said, 'I want to serve because I care.' You didn't care very much, Ted, when you could have voted between 1953 and 1960 on sixteen occasions and you only voted three times. . . . Do you really care about civil rights? While I was fighting to eliminate the 'black belts' and the ghettos, you were attending a school that is almost totally segregated, the University of Virginia—"

There was a simple wooden rostrum in front of Kennedy; he seemed to hang onto it for balance, the knuckles of his heavy fingers whitening, the muscles of his ox pelvis of a jaw squirming each time he reset it. Kennedy's hewn, somewhat lipless and inexpressive face looked particularly drained for one so congenitally affable; sweat had begun its beading just below his widow's peak.

Late the previous spring, on the recommendation of tactical advisers who wanted to give the open secret of his misdemeanor a chance to ventilate itself, Kennedy had admitted to a Boston *Globe* reporter that he left Harvard after his freshman year because somebody else took a Spanish exam for him. Whatever the scandal-value of the incident, it had pretty much depleted itself over the months of the summer, but the impression lingered: weak. Weak.

By autumn the Massachusetts political air was overhung and threatening with rumors. One insisted that Joe, the Founding Father, and old Joe alone among the Kennedys had much of an appetite for Edward's candidacy. The seat in the Senate his brother the President had occupied—warmed reliably since 1960 by Benjamin Smith II, Jack's room-mate in college—Teddy wanted now. Political appointments out of Washington were reportedly delayed. There was recurrent talk that, win or lose, Ted Kennedy was going to oversee all patronage in Massachusetts after September of 1962.

The paranoia normal to workers for the good of the party grew and provided the Kennedy campaign a special leverage of its own. For McCormack, alliances of a political lifetime had now begun to dissolve. "I'm going after the anti-chutzpah vote," the angry young Attorney General had sworn to friends as he needled the inexperienced Kennedy into open confrontation.

"The thing that fascinates me is Teddy's constant reference to his trips," McCormack went on that embattled evening. "He made two European trips, visited eleven countries in twenty-four days. In South America he visited nine countries in twenty-seven days."

Much of the informed American community shared McCormack's indignation. "It was sporting of Teddy to wait until he was thirty instead of asking for an Act of Congress or a Constitutional Amendment to lower the qualifying age," Inez Robb had written. The Washington *Post,* praising this arriving Kennedy for his modesty, pointedly noted that he had "much to be modest about." The New York *Times* admitted that Kennedy was just old enough for the Senate, but had "few other qualifications," and suggested that "relatives of prominent officials" should "present some solid evidence of talent before they make the sacrifice of starting at the top." "Nepotism!" Scotty Reston exclaimed. Mark De Wolfe Howe of the Harvard Law School circulated a letter throughout the academic world calling Edward Kennedy's candidacy that of a "bumptious newcomer . . . both preposterous and insulting." McCormack himself let it be known that one of his cardinal motives in running was to ward off the most self-evident among Kennedy's domestic blunders: his brother's elevation to the Senate.

McCormack was leaving his audience no doubt at all that evening that he intended to spare his President chagrin. "I worked my way up the political ladder," McCormack, who is himself the nephew of the Speaker of the United States House of Representatives, reminded his audience. "I'm not starting at the top."

For what already seemed like hours Ted Kennedy had been reaching at, clutching at, anything that might somehow drive the exchange back to substantive political issues. Despite Kennedy's carefully rehearsed gestures, his dragged-out nasalized inflections, his decisive down-blading hand motions—in spite of everything, McCormack was somehow keeping real discussion pushed maddeningly away. McCormack lashed out; whatever Ted managed in return went awry, somehow. "We should not have any talk about personalities or families!" Kennedy attempted, finally.

McCormack cracked right down. "And so I ask, since the question of names and families has been injected, if his name was Edward Moore—with his qualifications, with your qualifications, Teddy—if it was Edward Moore your candidacy would be a joke. Nobody's laughing, because his name is not Edward Moore—it is Edward Moore Kennedy."

The debate was one of those exceptional public events helpful to everybody involved in it. Certainly Edward McCormack had gotten a beautiful opportunity to relieve his spleen in front of the television cameras. (Although, when he was later beaten in the primary, he went out of his way to berate the condition of Massachusetts politics generally, and sulked straight through until a chance at another important Democratic office came along a couple of years afterward.) Kennedy himself, as things worked out, profited immediately and measurably from an enormous sympathy backlash. He sensed the effect a couple of days afterward when, as he was campaigning at the door of a factory at quitting time, a seasoned old laborer asked suddenly: "Is it true, like I heard, that you never worked a day in your life, Kennedy?"

The candidate mumbled something to the effect that he hadn't worked much with his hands, really. . . .

"Well, let me tell ya somethin', kid," the seasoned old laborer said, "ya sure ain't missed a hell of a lot."

From that instant, Kennedy realized, he had his seat in the Senate.

This latest, last, most resented, least-seriously-taken of two generations of Kennedys to come to Washington now arrived to begin his career-at-the-top. Insiders around Washington, like academics around Boston, ignored any genuinely accurate picture of Edward Kennedy and devoted themselves to scrutinizing the negative: he was *not* a humorous, charming, detached, intellectualizing man, like Jack; he did not have the clarity, push, hard-edged aggressiveness that made Bobby so effective. The profile of whatever he had done that far in life looked utterly Kennedy-derivative: he went through prep school and, when they let him in again, Harvard; he played end on the football team; his grades were bad enough to keep him out of Harvard Law School but good enough for the University of Virginia, like Bobby's. He spent a season, like both his brothers, reporting for the International News Service. There had been two years as a private first class stationed near Paris in the U.S. Army. He managed Jack Kennedy's campaign for President in the Far West, and carpers at the time liked to blame him for losing California. What most people remembered best was his willingness to go off a major ski jump on somebody's challenge in Wisconsin: to casual knockers this meant he was crazy or irresponsible. After the 1960 election he worked for the office of the Attorney General of Massachusetts, rounded thirty, and ran for Senator.

For anybody interested in picking out more detail, certain other aspects of Kennedy's personality now began to recommend themselves. Once he was out of the Army, he had volunteered and worked in a settlement house in Boston's Negro South End. At Law School he was elected head of the Student Forum and, with John Tunney, now a California Congressman, won the Moot Case contest, a round-robin debate that, like the Ames at Harvard, suggests potential courtroom agility. People who knew him at all began to report that he was an excellent listener, that he remembered and combined ideas well, and that in the end his decisions were largely his own except—even then, except—when influenced directly and strenuously by Bobby. He worked very hard, it was said. He could demand a great deal of anybody who worked for him, but his ambiance, the state of tension he kept around himself, was livable with.

Ted's way with people was variously taken; some who ran into him found him empty, really: bland. "In my opinion he's just a pasteboard mask," somebody remarked to me.

"I don't know what makes Teddy tick, but I'm sure that the fact that he's the youngest son in a family of real abrasive people makes him want to make good. And he's making good," another more caustic and more knowledgeable Kennedy-watcher tipped me early.

Milton Gwirtzman, a young Washington lawyer who has worked one way or the other with most of the Kennedys, and who served as Kennedy's legislative assistant, had much the same viewpoint. Milton is a little oracular—the word in Kennedy circles was that you had to believe in Milton in order to be able to see him clearly—but I think his meaning is plain enough. "While he's growing up," Milton said, innocuous behind his dense Army-pink eyeglasses, "the youngest son doesn't have the physical or mental abilities of the others, so the way he gets along is to be good, nice, easy to get along with. When Ted got to Washington in 1963 he faced substantially the same situation in the Senate, where many envious Senators had *sons* older than he was then. . . . But he made a point of calling them all Senator, and he learned how to have a drink of bourbon with Jim Eastland and address him as Mister Chairman, and they saw that he did his homework, that he was ready to take on the dirty work, like presiding over the Senate, that nobody really likes, and after a while he was—people started to take to him here. His younger-brother characteristics stood him in good stead."

These younger-brother characteristics are well-documented in Kennedy family archives. In 1938, for example, when Joe was settling in as Ambassador to the Court of Saint James's, Edward brought an urgent request home. Might he be permitted to punch a classmate, who had been working him over daily? "You tell me I can't get into fights because Dad is the Ambassador," the six-year-old told Rose earnestly. Permission came; Kennedy already showed an unusual sense of the fitness of whatever he did.

Or even farther back: when Ted was born a full four years after Jean, and thus really the afterthought, the belated end of that generation's model run, Joe traded in the family sailboat *Tenovus* for something larger, *Onemore*. By the time Edward came along Joe's frenetic notorious years as the lone-wolf speculator of Wall Street were pretty much over; having found, at best, marginal acceptance among the Best People of either Boston or New York Society, the Kennedys had removed, spiritually at least, to their own privately mythologized duchy at Hyannis Port, from where they proceeded to establish diplomatic relations with the remainder of America. Joe, who backed Franklin D. Roosevelt early and reminded him of it often, received a series of appointments (Chairman of the Securities and Exchange Commission, head of the Maritime Commission, ultimately that choicest of Ambassadorships). Accordingly, during his impressionable earliest years, little Ted enjoyed very regular exposure to the men who (in a favorite phrase of his own, these days) "move affairs." Until Joe Kennedy's iron-willed America Firstism forced Roosevelt to allow him to resign, F.D.R. took a perverse delight in the machinations of this colicky redheaded Irish-American speculator he himself set loose among the university theorists and tea-table career people of the very early New Deal; the umbilical connection between The Family and the American Government, however slack it went just after World War II, was now unbrokenly established.

One of Joe's penchants had been for pedagogy. "Dad was always very very interested in what went on in school, in sports," Edward Kennedy said when I asked him about his earliest years. "He also took a very great interest in your conduct. For example, I remember he didn't feel I ought to have a bicycle unless others among my classmates did. He tended to keep this kind of discipline up until it became self-generating." Edward developed into the best sailor, tennis player, mountaineer, skier in the family. An exceptional listener always, he sensed beneath the unfettered dinner-table arguments about politics and international affairs the undertow of very large family second-generation governmental ambitions. Big, friendly, low-strung, and, in his father's phrase, affable as an Irish cop, Ted took on the anchor-man responsibilities for the family when his father started failing. He edited a private book, *The Fruitful Bough*, of vignettes about Joe, and put in a lot of weekend duty at Hyannis Port after his father's stroke. *Jack and Bob will run the show, while Ted's in charge of hiding Joe* went a pernicious little couplet just before the election in 1960; whoever wrote that had a maliciously delicate nose for character. "You can see the emotion in his eyes, the interest, but that's all," Ted Kennedy says currently of his father. "These days his concerns are pretty well limited to the activities of his grandchildren. . . ."

Instructions—requests, really—that I got some months ago from Edward Kennedy's very, very able and otherwise rather unbuttoned staff when I was first in Washington suggest the sensitivities that this has engendered. "Don't overplay the role of the staff," I was cautioned, "and don't refer to the Senator either to his face or—more particularly—in print as *Teddy*. This irks him and we hear him muttering about the Teddy treatment sometimes."

Early one otherwise unexceptional June evening in 1964 something happened to Edward Kennedy which may very well have amounted to the most important event in his life up to that time. The rented private aircraft in which he was doing some rather informal campaigning around back Massachusetts went into a spin somehow and crashed nose-first into an apple orchard not far outside Springfield. The pilot and Kennedy's administrative assistant, Edward Moss, were killed; Kennedy, who had been half-standing just behind them almost in the middle of the plane, was dragged out of the wreck in desperate condition. Surgeons at the nearest accessible hospital, after cleaning him up and putting him through a series of probes too sensitive to allow the use of pain-killers, found out little by little that three vertebrae in his lower back had been smashed together, two ribs were cracked, and internal hemorrhaging around his spleen and left kidney was so extensive that until some of it had dissipated there would be no way to discover how much, if any, permanent damage had been done his inner organs. The position of the third lumbar vertebra was especially precarious; it had been driven out sideways so far that one more inch would have snapped his spinal cord and left him a paralytic.

Radio and television reports went out immediately, of course; within hours a party of Kennedys had arrived. The student nurse on duty refused to leave her post or make clear to the group, which included Robert, Governor Peabody, and Ted's wife Joan, which room the Senator was in. The increasingly anxious visitors finally found the young Senator beneath an oxygen tent, "tubes up his nose, things dangling from both his arms," as his wife remembers.

"There are more of us than there is trouble," Bobby told an overtaking newsman shortly. "The Kennedys intend to stay in public life. Good luck is something you make, and bad luck is something you endure."

The near-corpse inside the translucent tent apron, recognizing, perhaps, his wife's characteristic pink dress, showed signs of saying something. "Hi, Joansie," he managed, with difficulty. Then, typically, "Don't worry!"

Kennedy spent the next six months in a series of hookups, most notably a rotating Stryker frame. His mind and his secretary Angelique Voutselas' stenographic pad were increasingly busy. One suspects that such a prolonged brush with death went deep into Edward Kennedy's thinking and feelings. There was a suggestive similarity between his own injury—which, he was told shortly, would leave him physically limited, half-crippled permanently, dependent on a back brace—and that of his assassinated brother Jack. This produced a strange result. People who had gone mountain climbing with Ted, for example, had always commented on his low-keyed calm and stamina and courage; now in times of danger or physical stress he began to show a peculiar detachment. "I could very well understand people's opposition to my original Senatorial candidacy," he told me once when he and I were discussing the subject. "The reservations of others. And I bore no ill feeling toward those people"—he talks like this, very often: those stilted political phrases, those long, cold, dragged-out vowels of Kennedyese—"Today, since then, a number of those people have been helpful. . . ." Then, thinking it over: "Perhaps, had I been somebody else, and had I been asked, I'd have opposed my nomination myself."

This detachment pervades. David Burke, Kennedy's serious, able executive assistant, admits to a palm-clamming tenseness the moment he climbs into any aircraft smaller than a DC-8; Kennedy, for his own macabre reasons, will fly almost anywhere in almost anything, and, since Burke accompanies him often, so must Dave. Kennedy has long since found this out about Burke and, having acquired a pilot's license early in his own life, Edward amuses himself quietly sometimes by unobtrusive little palms-up/palms-down gestures calculated to hint to Burke the way he himself would handle the stick. Circling into Topeka once in a privately owned jet, Kennedy speculated aloud about whether *he* could get the aircraft down, insisting that he could figure out the purpose of all the controls except one mysterious but presumably unimportant little red light. . . . Another time, during a very rugged passage indeed, Kennedy pulled together the deck of cards he was riffling idly and suggested that the ashen Burke pick one at random. Burke complied, fingers shaking. "Isn't it too bad nobody is going to know that is the last thing you ever did," his employer commented stonily.

"Liberalism," among the Kennedys originally, was the kind of term Old Joe liked to lay up in quotes whenever he needed to use it: the liberal in politics was somebody with a heart bleeding all over the carpet, and applesauce for brains. Edward, once his Senate seat was warmed properly, began to show symptoms of an instinctive gut liberalism of approach, a deeply effective, very detailed sense of whom the commonest of people were, and what they really needed. Recently turning over the pages of his photograph album he showed me a picture somebody had taken of him, early in that first campaign, shaking hands all around a machine shop. "If you look closely," he remarked, "you can see that half the people there are without at least *part* of one of their fingers." He turned the binder page over: the next picture showed him soliciting across some kind of conveyor belt tended by a gnomic flour-dusty old man. "That man was kneading the blueberries out as they came through that endless pie-making machine," Kennedy said. "He told me, 'If you want my vote, Kennedy, you'll have to shake my hand.' " The candidate was photographed dripping blueberries halfway to the elbow.

More and more, the legislation Kennedy began to be associated with concerned the plight of the scratch-dirt poor, people suffocating in the impacted slums, the dispossessed and homeless, the old, the immigrants, draftees. He began to spend a lot of his Massachusetts time talking with out-of-work fishermen, with workers in the cranberry bogs. Kennedy became the most knowledgeable man in the Senate about voting-rights problems, about refugee affairs. His concern was unmistakably deep. His sense of the corruptions and dislocations within postwar America became increasingly specific. He began working harder and harder. His day might last from an early tactical discussion in his McLean, Virginia, home at seven in the morning until a post-dinner-party stint with his willing but fading staff people that started at ten p.m. and went on into the morning following. An avid brain picker anyhow, the half-crippled young Senator, trying to formulate a piece of legislation, was likely to import an expert from Harvard or take a jet halfway around the world to find out for himself precisely the relevant facts; these facts had a way of coming back in debate on the floor of the Senate like machine-gun bullets. The legislation he proposed gained a name for being exceptionally well-backgrounded, clear in its intention, and limited in its intention. Typical was his recent amendment to the Administration's O.E.O. (Poverty) Act, which provided in complete detail for the establishment, staffing, and maintenance of forty "neighborhood health center" clinics throughout the worst American city slums. "His proposals are laid in with a rifle, accurately, not with a shotgun," a ranking Republican told me; this made them easier for his conservative opponents to vote for and justify at home. The Democratic leadership on The Hill began to prefer Kennedy's work to the often very abrupt, badly timed, frequently blanketing legislation being brought forward by the Junior Senator from New York.

While Kennedy's intensity at work now approached total preoccupation, his way with whichever people he cared about became more relaxed, simpler, more whimsical. His secretaries tried to stay out of giggling range when, as is most frequently true, he realized he wasn't going to make it home in time to put his three young kids to bed and so was forced to deliver, via telephone, the afternoon's installment of an ongoing animal saga in which he himself plays all the voices. Never ostentatious anyhow (he drives his own Chrysler around, frugally trading it every couple of years), he now made every effort to keep everything as unencumbered as possible for himself.

His reputation—his justification for being there at all—pretty much established in the Senate by 1964, he got himself reelected for a full term from his hospital bed and returned early in 1965 to receive his colleagues' heartfelt welcoming. Then, in September of 1965, came the Morrissey incident.

Francis Xavier Morrissey, Frank Morrissey, had been a municipal judge in the Boston city court system for a good many years before the trip he took to Washington, D.C. which was to make him momentarily famous. Morrissey, essentially an old-line Kennedy-family coat holder, aspired to the dignity of a place on the Federal Bench to cap his career. In fact, the Kennedys owed him. Frank Morrissey had done a great many services for Joe, and when first Jack, and finally Ted, decided to establish their political bases in Massachusetts, Morrissey guided both boys adeptly and with an unmistakable devotion. There had even been talk of a judgeship for Morrissey early in the Kennedy Administration; snooping at the time by the ever-vigilant Boston *Globe* seems to have scared the Administration off. When, much later on and largely as a personal courtesy, one suspects, Edward Kennedy sent along to Lyndon Johnson his recommendation of Morrissey for the judgeship, the political expectation overall was that the President would appoint one of his own among the Massachusetts devoted.

The expectation proved incorrect. In a special conference at the L.B.J. ranch, the President announced that he was going to forward to the Senate for its ratification the long-dormant Morrissey nomination. *Why* is disputed. Some claim that Johnson agreed to the Morrissey idea to hang a man of Morrissey's limited qualifications on the record of the Kennedys. Others regard it as a favor granted Edward in gratitude for the way he had floor-managed the Administration's regional development bill shortly before, and explained that the President had craftily waited until Autumn of 1965 to forward the nomination because The New York *Times* was struck; Johnson's intention here, supposedly, was to give the Kennedys at least a partial news blackout during which to drag hapless Frank Morrissey through.

Unfortunately for Morrissey The Boston *Globe* was not struck. The *Globe,* in an exhaustively researched series of exposés and editorials, exhumed Frank Morrissey's past, his graduation from a Georgia diploma mill, his struggle to pass the Massachusetts bar, his desultory achievements since. Local defenders of the honor of the Bench, like Judge Wyzanski and the Boston chapter of the American Bar Association, disapproved of Morrissey publicly and sternly.

The Washington *Post* picked the story up and attacked from the opposite flank. By the time Frank Morrissey got down to his Senate hearings, conservatives on the Judiciary Committee, scenting vulnerable game, were very nearly drooling. "Certain questions have arisen," Everett Dirksen began—too gently. Then—Morrissey showing up all loquaciousness, his inflections one moment affected and mincing, the next the low, whining South-Boston bleat, pure borderline Irish—Dirksen took him, a little more archly, further: "*Grave* questions have arisen." Finally, "Serious accusations have been leveled—" Morrissey talked some more; liberals all over the chamber were coming up hesitant. Edward Kennedy now spoke on Morrissey's behalf: under unmistakable personal pressure, the Cro-Magnon jaw trembling, very obviously near tears, Kennedy launched a diatribe, recalled the shoeless Irish boy Morrissey was in childhood, his battle for respectability, the regard he earned as a Justice within the Boston Courts. . . . Warming to his subject, Kennedy reprimanded the American Bar Association as an organization narrow-minded enough to have tried to stop the ratification of Louis Brandeis for the Supreme Court. . . .

Dirksen, in too deep to backpedal, called Washington's puzzled press corps together before the committee could vote: he had a "bombshell," which he intended to explode if Morrissey's nomination went further.

Everett Dirksen's "bombshell," when unearthed finally, was a particularly puny little operatic ladyfinger. In 1961 Frank Morrissey and Edward Kennedy, traveling together in Italy where Kennedy had received an award from the American Committee on Italian Migration, vacationed for a day or two on Capri. There they shared a meal with a fellow American who bragged around about it later. The fellow American turned out to be a deported Mafia gangster; apparently Dirksen, somehow digging up the item from an Italian newspaper four years afterward, had some intention of linking publicly the names of Edward Moore Kennedy, Frank Morrissey, and the American criminal underworld.

Appraised of what Dirksen's bombshell was, Kennedy painfully and reluctantly sent the nomination back to the Judiciary Committee to die: *I would want any nominee of mine to be confirmed on a record clear and complete enough. . . .*"I think Teddy learned then," Doyle of The Boston *Globe* told me years afterward, "that you can't buy the whole thing."

More vital than the Dirksen "bombshell" was the realization that no matter what happened, the Morrissey nomination was tarred with notoriety; any Senator who voted for Morrissey—and Kennedy could have compelled the vote, that is commonly agreed—would come away tarred to his constituents too. Every Senator around felt the strain of patronage obligations himself; all understood Kennedy's position; all appreciated the public humiliation—and the private judgment—that killing the nomination involved.

Conservative knives had probably been sharpening for Kennedy since his whirlwind unexpected decision, not months after he hobbled back into the Senate chambers on his silver-headed cane, to buck both the Conservative establishment and the Liberal leadership and try to stick an amendment outlawing local and state poll taxes onto the Administration's 1965 Voting Rights Bill. The oligarchs of Committee Power in the Senate hated the idea of another incursion by Northerners into the sanctified inequities of their vespertine political world; the Liberal wing feared that the Kennedy amendment would cost them votes enough to endanger the bill.

From the vantage point of his Senatorial career, that shaky spring was probably the worst time Kennedy could have chosen to displease elders of both persuasions. He himself had just been selected, with crotchety old Eastland's suffrage, as floor manager of the Administration's expanded Immigration Bill.

To Judiciary Committee Chairman Eastland, a gnarled old moss-bedecked cypress of seniority and Dixieland privilege, young Kennedy had already become one of the trials of advancing age. "Wha' you wan' now, Kennedy," he is reputed to inquire wearily whenever the youngster appears. Sometimes the compromises they work out prove touchy to live with. For example, at the time Kennedy was shepherding his Immigration Bill through, Kennedy finagled, through Eastland, a kind of informal agreement with the Southern bloc that none of them would speak on the subject for the record. Then, on the Senate floor itself, Senator Holland of Florida suddenly got up to ask how many Spanish-speaking "nigras" this liberalization would involve: the Deep South delegation scuttled for the cloakroom *en mêlée.*

Determined whatever the upshots, Kennedy went recruiting for his anti-poll-tax army. Persuasion, old political debts, appeals to democratic principle, implicit logrolling threats, implicit logrolling promises—he employed whichever, in each case, seemed indicated. Mark De Wolfe Howe of Harvard, that very same Mark De Wolfe Howe who had once circulated the academic letter labeling Kennedy's candidacy "both preposterous and insulting," came down to help. "Ted is a real expert at diffusing the opposition," one old Washington hand explains. "He knows just where to look for the opposition's weakness. He might start in working on X, for instance. He knows he'll never get X's vote, but he will have prevented X from dragging Y's vote away from him too." Kennedy opened the debate by delivering a major speech that treated the poll tax in historical terms as a *liberalizing* step in the development of universal suffrage, a means of permitting non-property-holders to vote. It played on the egalitarian impulses of even the most conservative.

Dave Burke had started working for Kennedy just before that. Burke himself was not fully aware, from the Senator's typically circular lines of early inquiry, exactly what his new employer was about; he was startled one afternoon when Kennedy looked up during a Committee meeting and asked for "my poll-tax amendment." Panic-stricken, no lawyer himself, Burke rushed back to the offices for a few lines of legalese to get Kennedy through the Committee session.

Katzenbach, the Attorney General, and Mansfield, the Majority Leader, and the reactionaries assembled marshaled their forces quickly and—almost—too late; the floor vote on the Kennedy Amendment that defeated it went 49-44; three out of five Senatorial Democrats voted *against* their own Administration on this matter. To placate them a provision went into the voting-rights bill requiring that if local or state poll taxes were collected, the much hated Federal registrars must collect them. Katzenbach had hinted broadly that two pending Supreme Court cases dealing with the Virginia poll tax might decide the matter without embarrassing the legislators. Obligated, the Justice Department pushed its suits harder, and on March 25, 1966, the Court reversed itself and found *all* local poll taxes in violation of the Fourteenth Amendment. To Senatorial insiders, operators, Kennedy's parliamentary skill and leadership had left people holding their breaths. "Ted is not as *forceful* in the Senate, yet, as Jack was," says the Republican moderate Thruston Morton, who knew both of them well. "But Teddy is personally more popular. He's much quieter, less in evidence, lower keyed. As a parliamentarian and what, for lack of a better word, I'd call a floor strategist, he's better than Jack. He's patient in debate with those who take an opposite viewpoint. Jack Kennedy, and Bobby after him, could sometimes answer quite shortly, indicate quite clearly his feeling of intellectual superiority to his colleagues. The Senate is a deliberative body; Ted intuitively understands this. He handles the whole thing with a lot more suavity."

The poll-tax fight set a kind of pattern: Edward showed himself almost invariably willing to trade a victory of form—i.e., a vote victory—for one of substance, as when he managed, as part of his Federal gun-control-legislation campaign, to force the Army to stop sponsoring the National Rifle Matches by permitting it to sponsor them one last time. The reapportionment broil, a very stubborn, bitter struggle Kennedy fought over many months in 1967 and ultimately won, is illustrative again of the kind of parliamentary generalship at which he has become so effective. The issue itself arose out of a series of Supreme Court decisions, the so-called one-man-one-vote cases. These required the states to reapportion voting districts according to population shifts since 1904. Once the effort to prevent such a return to democracy through Constitutional Amendment had failed, conservatives like Everett Dirksen, fearful for the erosion of their own pocket boroughs, fell back on legislation that would delay significant redistricting until at least 1972. Kennedy very shortly got upwind of all this, and recruited young Republican Senator Baker of Tennessee (Dirksen's son-in-law, of all men), and beat the obstructive legislation to pieces every time it, or some form of it, came from the House of Representatives. In the course of his inquiry he pinpointed the abuses resulting from later-day gerrymandering and suggested a "compactness and equality" criterion for voting districts that the Supreme Court has now taken under advisement. All these are, certainly, sophisticated issues, the infighting is complicated, but to the convinced libertarian they are in fact the heart and kidneys of a surviving democracy.

Two somewhat more dramatic campaigns had begun to bring Kennedy to the attention of newspaper readers even before Robert's assassination: his early skirmishing with—preparatory, obviously, to a frontal attack on—Congressional defenders of the draft policies, and his investigations into the refugee problems of Vietnam. Kennedy's Vietnamese concern came as an unintended consequence of a look he was forced to take, as Chairman of the Special Subcommittee on Refugees and Escapees, at the human marginalia piling up along the edges of our involvement there. He began to mull over the war's moral purposes, its human and political cost-effectiveness, the way, in detail, it was actually being waged. Overall indictments and geopolitical recommendations are very far from Kennedy's method—his characteristic working principles, his staff people admit, are "Let's preserve our options," or "It's a long road ahead"—but he is obviously deeply troubled. His way of dealing with this is, as usual, to return again and again to the facts. He picks the brains of experts, he empties and re-empties his famously overstuffed attaché case, "the Bag," on trips like his twice-yearly visits to the International Conference on Refugee Affairs at Geneva or his investigations, like the one last January, into the corruption inside Vietnam itself. His speeches detailing the unutterable misery of that nation's two to three million refugees have already worked a powerful effect among his senate colleagues. Further than that he cannot seem to make himself go. As late as the middle of March of 1968, Edward was reported unconvinced of the wisdom of Bobby's challenge. "Now when my brother Bobby recently decided to give an anti-Vietnam-policy speech and showed it to me and asked me what to do," he said a short time before his brother was assassinated, as he opened an Americans for Democratic Action dinner meeting, "I said he should put the speech in a plain brown envelope and send it along to *Ramparts* magazine. Then I took him over to the Senate, and I showed him where his seat was, and I told him a few things I thought would help him get along. . . ."

The war in Vietnam was spitting up the bones of politicians all across the pre-primary landscape the bleak mid-December day I spent in cavalcade across northeast Massachusetts with Kennedy on one of those odd frantic junkets of campaigning-for-its-own-sake he squeezed in whenever he could between stretches in Washington.

He was unconcealably preoccupied with his own incompletely formu-lated feelings of personal responsibility about the war, and the speech he made a few minutes later, to students in The Community College in Haverhill, showed how involved he felt. "It's nice to see so many bright eyes after that junior prom," he began; then his anchor dropped locally, "I think this is the biggest group of young people I've seen all in one place since I had lunch lahst Sunday at my brother Bobby's." His response to the laugh he got, not much, but enough to warm him up, provoked out of him genuinely that Kennedy grin of big, long, expensively-cared-for teeth. The Kennedy Reaction was setting in already, I saw: the co-eds were moving around inside the scoops of their auditorium folding chairs, crossing thighs, wriggling, rotating sneaker tips. If this one were not a Kennedy, I wondered, but just one more very-early-middle-aging politician in his invariable *suit*, needing a haircut but not upsetting at all, noticeably jug-eared, his lined neck beginning to fatten—if this one were just any-body at all, wouldn't these enthralled kids see him as unexciting, if not positively square, in a way?

"Young people are *ahs*king," Kennedy was now opening up, taking on timbre like an elocution prizewinner, "what have been ow-uh policies that have sent ow-uh young people to war three times in twenty-five years, they're ahsking significant questions which *should* be ahsked, they're forming their *own* idears, for while our elders are concentrating on their own wealth, their own comfort, this generation says, this is not enough—"

There is much recrossing of mini-skirted legs; Kennedy perorates: "Oliver Wendell Holmes said, 'Through our great good fortune, in our youth, our hearts were touched with fire.' " Applause begins prematurely. "I believe it is important that that fire, in the hearts of our youth, be used to light a better world. Thank you." He has stepped away already; half-limping, the outline of the brace visible through the cloth of his suit jacket, to escape the convergence of the mobs and through the stage door rear.

In the open country outside Haverhill there was a positively Pentagon-sized General Electric assembly plant; we pulled up there for fifteen minutes of nonstop handshaking. The interlude had a kind of Orpheus in the contemporary lumpen-proletariat Underworld character that dizzies me now whenever I think about it: the gigantic cinder-block shell of the place, scorched-smelling throughout with that special space-age hyper-dryness, like the inside of somebody's television set, where Kennedy, trailed always by his schedule-panicky handlers, shuffles briskly along acre after acre of aisles of workbenches, stops periodically for picture-taking, invades the cafeteria. He weaves in and out of table groupings, somehow warm and methodical at once, pressing hand after hand after hand—pressing *thousands* of hands, touching collarbones, pinching elbows, brushing beneath the cauliflower-like vaccination scars of worked-out old women with understanding fingertips. Wherever he passes excitement is audible: "Who's eatin'?" one girl employee says, shrugging, to another. "Everybody's runnin' after *him*. Gee, he should come every day."

"He's so much like John Kennedy it's—it's—" The woman is speechless. "He looks like a kid, honestly. Oooh, is he *cute!*"

"I wonder would he like some pea soup," I overhear one dour little soul say to nobody especially; I think she would halfway expect, should she press on Kennedy the paper cup she is holding, that he could in some obscure way bless it for her. By now Kennedy is out behind the heavy glass counters handshaking among the cooks.

At Lawrence, addressing a post-prandial Chamber of Commerce meeting, he tries one of those carefully breath-catching pan-Kennedy jokes: "I am aware that there is a man running for President of the United States, from Minnesota, who has held very high public office. I want to take this occasion to tell all of you here that under no circumstances could I ever support that man from Minnesota—" Applause erupts, too early. "Harold Stassen." The punch line goes all but unattended. Something in this reflex of business-community hatred for McCarthy-as-liberal offends Kennedy's deeply seated impulses; suddenly he has fallen into a delivery strenuous to the point of ranting: ". . . we know that the draft law today is just as unfair, as inequitable, as it was a year ago. Our young people, the ones here coming out of The Community College and the vocational high school, *aren't* going to be deferred, we realize that. . . ." His speech swings straightaway into the Vietnam war itself, its senselessness, the shortsightedness of its human provisions. "What have been the policies that have brought these about? I find it difficult to answer. Are we tied to the shibboleths of the past? Are we astigmatic to this extent?" He introduced the poverty program: "And I think it is well, my friends, to see how we're going to bring industry into the poverty program. This is a challenge you must help us with—"

"Boy, I couldn't have made it any shorter," Kennedy tells Dave Burke, almost apologetically, once he is safely back in the Oldsmobile and en route to Lowell. "That's an important group of people." He turns up a printed card somebody has slipped into his hand while he was folding himself gingerly into the car: "TO HELL WITH THE CONSTITUTION" is lettered crudely across the back. "SUPPORT JOHNSON." The awareness that he has missed his audience is unmistakably depressing. "I should have led them through what the considerations, the implications are if the government increases or doesn't increase taxes," he decides after a while.

At the high school in Lowell, exactly from the moment the car door opens, everything is all right again. A kind of honor guard of very nubile little girls in Prussian-blue uniforms with chevrons reviews Kennedy's approach: he now proceeds beyond them and up the aisle through nymphet pandemonium; pressing to get within benediction reach they scream deliriously, giggle, try to touch, shriek *eeeee*. One overstimulated chestnut-haired bud in an apache T-shirt is obviously out: both eyes glitter blindly in her adolescent ecstasy, she springs on reflex the moment he brushes her hand. "I don't believe it!" she gasps, utterly from the throat; Kennedy has shambled out of her range now and mounts the dais one step at a time, augustly.

The uproar quiets, finally; the mayor of Lowell introduces Kennedy, with point, as the man who *has* done more for Massachusetts. Upon the speaker's lips, quickly wiped away, a strange little fugitive smile is momentarily discernible. "Now let me say, Mister Mayor," the speaker of the day begins, "that this is—" the tumult pitches up again— "that this is the biggest group of young people—that I have seen—since I had lunch with my brother Bobby's family last Sunday. . . ." The laugh he gets is mostly of appreciation; the Senator smiles out benevolently. Kennedy at that moment was fully, visibly, comfortable again; easy; tilling the future.

In June, 1968, he was in San Francisco, closing up the primary shop there after his brother's final victory, when word of the assassination attempt reached him. By the time he got to Los Angeles, Bobby's condition was critical, already deteriorating. As ever, he was the one to give the news to his invalided father. For Edward Kennedy himself the moment was excruciating and fateful: the spiritual inheritance of this star-crossed near-mythological American family—whatever the duties, whatever the wealth and the organization and the charisma, whatever the fugitive piercing glories—the burden of all it had come to mean was his.

It would be hard to ascertain whether Ted had slept at all in the days that followed. He sat up half Tuesday night, and through the morning of surgery in the intensive-care wing of the Good Samaritan Hospital in Los Angeles; by nine o'clock on Thursday he had landed in New York with the body of his brother and was on hand to help drag the coffin off the forklift and slide it onto the bed of a hearse. There was a short receiving ceremony at St. Patrick's Cathedral; after that everybody left but Ted, who prayed into the earliest morning. He came back later that day to watch another night beside the purple-draped catafalque, beneath six flickering candles. People who wandered by noted that he had slumped little by little into the corner of a pew; workmen began to arrive to hammer together the scaffolding for television cameras; Edward Kennedy didn't notice. The people came to file by, forming a line a mile long. A woman said: "I watched on TV and the Kennedys don't cry. I thought I should come down and do some crying for them."

Sometime in the daylight intervals between his vigils he decided to deliver a personal eulogy at the funeral. He stepped up behind the rostrum of the cathedral to speak—his full face a little puffy by then and his mood strained by fatigue. At that moment and for the first time for many Americans, he came sharply into public focus.

"We loved him as a brother," Edward opened, "and as a father and as a son. From his parents and from his older brothers and sister, Joe and Kathleen and Jack, he received an inspiration—" Here Kennedy very nearly faltered, paused, went on. He suggested what Robert had meant to his family, his sense of the inequities of our societies, his hopes for the political and moral redemption to be sought through the upcoming young. He concluded with words he himself had written a few hours before. "There is pride in that, even arrogance, but there is also experience and truth, and in any event it is the only way we can live. That is the way he lived. That is what he leaves us."

When the ceremony was over there was to be the delayed tragedy-broken train ride beneath another afternoon and evening of rains, more hands to shake on the train and at the graveside, more people to thank, to reassure, to wave to, to comfort. Public life, which is undertaken so lightly sometimes, leaves very little private life once the realization of calling is complete. To this family of awkward outsiders which had determined to scramble so for national attention, for wealth, for political power, everything had arrived suddenly, and was as suddenly devastated. Two of Edward's brothers had schemed unsuccessfully for the Vice-Presidential nomination in their seasons; for Edward in 1968, it was obviously and simply a question of accepting it or not, and now that didn't seem to matter much. By now there were only the issues and the facts and the political process and the problems of a people, and the surviving possibility that he himself could still do something about that.

[September, 1968]

The Logistics of the Funeral

by Anthony Howard

"Three days," Britain's Duke of Norfolk is said to have kept murmuring after the first Kennedy funeral. "How *did* they do it?" The echo in the reaction is perhaps that of an old-established firm not quite able to understand the speed and efficiency of a new competitor breaking through into its own line of business.

In Europe the organizing of a public death has always been a slow, majestic process—from the days of the sixteenth-century Emperor Charles V rehearsing his own funeral in a Spanish monastery to the far more recent years spent by Winston Churchill constantly revising the arrangements for his burial from his bedroom in Hyde Park Gate. It has been the peculiar, unwanted contribution of the Kennedys to prove that private tragedy can be turned into public pomp on a crash-program basis.

In 1963 they had three days; last June they had just two—two days in which to plan, prepare and arrange all the aspects of a national ceremonial occasion that are not apparent to the eventual passive television audience. Perhaps the dimension and scale of their technical achievement can be understood only by a fellow professional like the hereditary Earl Marshal of England. But his question was a good one and it deserves an answer. How *did* they do it?

145

Curiously, there was never much tightly controlled central direction. There was simply the Kennedy machine with its own, built-in continuing momentum. The funeral was (and only the naïve would think the description offensive) "the last great Kennedy advance job": for the men who had worked in the organization it was a triumphant vindication of, rather than a mournful end to, Bobby Kennedy's Presidential campaign.

It all started, by necessity, in Los Angeles. It was just before two a.m. (California time) on Thursday, June 6, that a haggard, grief-ridden Frank Mankiewicz announced to the world that Senator Robert F. Kennedy was dead. One and three-quarter hours later Pierre Salinger was there in the same auditorium giving the press the detailed outline (right down to the place and time of the Requiem Mass and the final burial destination) of the funeral arrangements.

The key members of the Kennedy entourage—scattered all around the country by the exigencies of a Presidential campaign—had known most of this before. A Kennedy aide in Washington in fact got a phone call from Los Angeles giving the full funeral blueprint just fourteen minutes after the candidate died. The main elements in the funeral plan had been decided upon a considerable period—one estimate has it as much as four hours—before Senator Kennedy was formally declared to be dead. The Requiem Mass in St. Patrick's Cathedral in New York, the train journey to Washington, the burial in Arlington were all settled in a brief, numbed meeting on the fifth floor of the Good Samaritan Hospital in Los Angeles well before midnight on Wednesday evening.

Three men took those decisions: the Senator's only surviving brother Teddy, his brother-in-law, Steve Smith, and one of his closest friends, John Seigenthaler (formerly of the Justice Department and now Editor of the Nashville *Tennessean.*) It was called a "contingency" plan, but no one really believed in the qualifying adjective. "By then," Stephen Smith recalls bleakly, "the indications were pretty clear." It was he who initiated the discussion, and he eventually (after Senator Kennedy had died) who carried the suggestions that came out of it to Ethel Kennedy. The Senator's widow endorsed the whole plan just before she fell asleep in the small hours of Thursday morning for the first time in forty-eight hours.

In contrast to President Kennedy's funeral in 1963, there had been no disputes—no last Irish battle on behalf of Boston as the burial place, no Massachusetts opposition to holding the actual funeral mass in New York, no time-factor skepticism of John Seigenthaler's notion of a train to carry the Senator's body to Washington. The final touches, of course, came later—Mrs. Kennedy's own idea for Andy Williams to sing *The Battle Hymn of the Republic,* Steve Smith's suggestion that Leonard Bernstein conduct members of the New York Philharmonic in the slow movement of Mahler's *Fifth Symphony*—but the fundamentals of the plan were not thereafter changed.

The problem, in fact, once Senator Kennedy had died, became not so much one of making decisions as of coordinating the operational forces to carry them out. The boardroom in the Good Samaritan Hospital became the temporary Kennedy command post, but the troops to carry out the orders were not easy to locate.

In Washington, the Kennedy national campaign headquarters at 2000 L St. N.W. had been virtually stripped of workers for the last great push in the California primary. In New York—at the shopfront volunteer head-quarters at Madison Avenue and Thirty-eighth Street, amateurs abounded but there were few professionals. Almost immediately, however, those professionals who were available broke out with relief from the paralysis that had affected them ever since the Senator was shot. In New York—where Jim Tolan, Kennedy's own favorite advance man, was in charge—the funeral train was promptly ordered (on instructions from Jerry Bruno in Los Angeles) by John Ellis, a young former intern in the Senator's Washington office. In Washington, Joe Dolan, the Senator's chief of staff on Capitol Hill, started the Government wheels turning with Nicholas Katzenbach, the Under Secretary of State. And as far afield as Frankfurt, Germany, where he was on a World Bank trip, Robert McNamara packed his bags and prepared to fly home in response to a call from the family asking him to take charge of the funeral arrangements, just as he had for John F. Kennedy, in 1963.

At the beginning, inevitably, there was some administrative confusion. The first order from Pierre Salinger in Los Angeles was that everyone should somehow get to New York: it took a vigorous protest from Tom Mathews (publicity director of Lincoln Center on leave of absence for the campaign) in the Washington office for it to be realized that, according to the plan drawn up, experienced men would be needed in the nation's capital as well as in New York. Eventually a compromise was reached: though Washington was evacuated of top strategists like Joe Dolan, replacements were sent in. Even as Dolan was flying that Thursday morning early to New York, three young Manhattan attorneys (Chris McGrath, Bill Foley and Herb Schmertz) set out for La Guardia and the shuttle to supervise arrangements for the arrival of the funeral train at Union Station and the final graveside ceremony.

Senator Kennedy's funeral was different from his brother's in that it was, in neither a technical nor a general sense, a State Occasion; but it didn't work out as a private one either. In fact two of the most crucial roles in organizing things at the Washington end were held by government officials. One was Nicholas Katzenbach, Under Secretary to Dean Rusk at the State Department, and the other was Alfred Fitt, the Assistant Secretary for Manpower and Reserve Affairs at the Pentagon. Katzenbach was assigned by the Secretary of State to do everything possible to ease and smooth the way through Washington's official channels. He was the natural choice for the job: he had been Bobby Kennedy's deputy at the Justice Department; through a period of bad political strain he had remained a close friend of the family and after seven years at Justice and then at State he knew his way round the government establishment. (As a private citizen he had already made his way on Wednesday night to Hickory Hill, where a group of the Senator's friends had gathered to see what they could do to help.)

Alfred Fitt's selection seems at first more puzzling. A former Michigan lawyer—and "Soapy" Williams' legal adviser when he was the state's Democratic Governor—he had never really been part of the Kennedy set. He was, however, very much a McNamara protégé; and as such he had been specially asked by the then Defense Secretary to retain oversight of the Kennedy grave at Arlington even after he ceased to be General Counsel of the Army (a post that, curiously, includes responsibility for all National cemeteries). It was Fitt who had supervised all the arrangements for the reinterment of President Kennedy's body in 1967; and it was he who would become the effective coordinator of all the cemetery arrangements for Robert Kennedy's funeral.

In the first hours after the Senator's death the campaign staff in Los Angeles were understandably at something of a disadvantage when it came to detailed forward-planning. Their immediate concern was with such matters as the autopsy (this took six and a quarter hours and delayed their departure), the arrival back in New York (there was a doubt at first whether La Guardia could handle the White House-dispatched Presidential jet), even the problem (generously assumed as a campaign responsibility) of seeing that the vast army of correspondents, who had been on hand for the climax of the California primary, could get seats out on commercial flights.

But in Washington and New York work on the detailed logistics of the funeral started straight away. The most difficult question, it was immediately recognized, would be the invitation list, and a special project was at once set up to compile it under the direction of a leading Washington lawyer, Louis Oberdorfer. An Assistant Attorney General (with special responsibility for Tax affairs) while Robert Kennedy was running the Justice Department, Oberdorfer now was the Co-Chairman of Citizens for Kennedy. An able, calm and well-connected adopted son of Washington's legal establishment (he was born in Alabama), Oberdorfer bravely set himself a target of twenty-four hours in which to get the invitations out. Working at first from Hickory Hill, he called for every list he could think of—the roll of those who had attended President Kennedy's funeral in 1963, the people who had been invited to social occasions at the Kennedy White House, the guests at the various and recurring Hickory Hill christenings, Ethel Kennedy's Christmas-card list, even (a careful politician's touch) the names of the leading financial contributors to Bobby Kennedy's

Presidential campaign. Nick Katzenbach had expected—and indeed had been delegated by the family—to take charge of putting together the guest list. He was later to say half-resentfully, half-admiringly, "It took me very little time to see that I would only be in the way. It was quite plain it could all safely be left to Lou."

It wasn't, of course. By the end practically everyone was adding names, making suggestions: and indeed raising objections: at least two New York congressmen—Ogden Reid and Richard Ottinger (both eventually admitted as members of the Speaker's delegation from Washington)—were at first spitefully vetoed by a very junior member of the Kennedy staff. Indeed the suspicion that the list was used by some Kennedy aides to pay off old scores appears to have been pretty well founded. But at least at the beginning, when Oberdorfer was working with his own small group, it was an orderly, quasi-judicial process. "What Lou made it into," says one young lawyer who worked with him, "was a kind of court of claims; it wasn't so much a matter of thinking of names as of delivering judgment for the deserving and against the undeserving."

Much the same thing was going on in New York with two socialite Kennedy aides (Bill vanden Heuvel and Carter Burden III) in charge. Later this duplication of effort—to say nothing of the disparity in judgment—was to cause problems. One difficulty at this stage was that the three separate groups in Los Angeles, Washington and New York were not really functioning in unison.

Partly for this reason, most of the constructive work on Thursday came from the official government side. The ramifications of laying on ceremonial in Washington are extraordinary, with a chain of command that reaches from the Pentagon through the local military district headquarters to the commanding officer of the Third Infantry Honor Guard at Fort Myer. Throughout Thursday both Katzenbach and Fitt were attempting to press all the relevant buttons. A minor crisis developed in the office of the Chief of Protocol in the State Department when it was suddenly discovered that the last diplomatic condolence book had been used up at the time of the Martin Luther King assassination two months earlier. A loose-leaf volume was substituted and, to add mortification to dismay, someone had to be sent out to buy a piece of black velvet on which to place it (the regulation Foreign Service issue was nowhere to be found).

The procession of foreign diplomats arriving at the State Department to sign the book served a useful, if fortuitous, purpose. Nicholas Katzenbach had established very early on that the last thing the Kennedy family desired was a gathering of international leaders who would only serve to make the occasion look like a pale rerun of the President's State Funeral in 1963. So any diplomat seeking guidance on how his government should be represented was tactfully told by Ambassador Angier Biddle Duke (head of Protocol once again now, as he had been in 1963) that it was the family's wish the occasion be a private and not an official one. Even so, Angie Duke had his problems: Eire, for example, refused to be deterred and insisted on sending not just its Prime Minister, but both opposition leaders as well. More disturbing than that to the Protocol office was the threat that in the case of every country the Ambassadors both at the U.N. and those accredited in Washington would each insist on being present in St. Patrick's. With cool nerves, Katzenbach and Duke—realizing that the whole seating plan could get out of hand—had set a ceiling of two hundred for foreign representation in the Cathedral. No ambassador was actually refused a ticket (except, that is, a gentleman purporting to be the Biafran Ambassador to the U.S., of whose existence the State Department had until that moment no knowledge at all); but such is the power of Angie Duke's tact and persuasion that in the end considerably less than a full complement of ambassadors demanded to be admitted to the Cathedral.

But at least the Chief of Protocol had been brought in to the arrangements at an early stage. Over at Arlington Cemetery Jack Metzler, the Superintendent for the last seventeen years, was not so fortunate. A capable, jovial man ("Flattery," he loves to say, "might get you a nice grave"), he first heard of the coming burial in his own cemetery on the radio. But when the eventual government telephone call came, he was ready, better prepared at least than he had been in 1963 when everyone had automatically assumed that Boston would provide the Presidential grave site. Jack Metzler rose early and spent most of Thursday pacing and measuring the Kennedy memorial: he was joined at the site by Alfred Fitt from the Pentagon and Colonel Paul Miller (Chief of Ceremonies and Special Events of the Military District of Washington). Together they examined the terrain and surveyed the area. The whole site was photographed from every angle, and detailed diagrams were prepared for submission to the family late that night in New York.

The grave site had, in fact, been one of the first problems to be raised Thursday morning. On waking and learning of the Senator's death, Alfred Fitt had first called Paul Nitze, the Deputy Secretary of Defense and his immediate superior in the Pentagon. Neither Nitze nor Fitt—nor Clark Clifford, who later came on the line—was in doubt that Kennedy met the revised and restricted rules for burial in Arlington (though the Senator's war service had been brief, he had enlisted in the Navy in 1945, and as a former Attorney General and current Senator he also met the additional necessary requirement of having held high federal office). But there appears to have been some sudden doubt in the family's mind. Later that morning Fitt got a call from Katzenbach asking him to confirm that the Senator was eligible for Arlington burial. Fitt answered that there was no question about it—and whatever doubt there had been must have subsided.

From his conversation with Nitze Fitt also learned that McNamara—

already contacted in Frankfurt by the family—was flying back, determined to be on hand for the arrival of the Senator's body in New York later that evening. McNamara had gone with Bobby Kennedy to Andrews Air Force Base in November, 1963, and, as he was later to say, it meant a great deal to him to be present for this second tragic family return. It threatened, though, to be close. If the Kennedy plane from Los Angeles had not been delayed three hours by the lengthy autopsy, the former Defense Secretary could not have made it.

In order to do all he could to help his former chief fulfill his emotional wish, Fitt flew to New York in a Defense Department Jetstar. His aim was not just to deliver the photographs and diagrams of the grave site to McNamara but also to clear him through customs quickly at Kennedy International Airport where his Lufthansa flight was due to arrive at seven-forty-five p.m. McNamara was then to be rushed by car to La Guardia, where the plane carrying Robert Kennedy's remains was now scheduled to touch down at nine p.m.

At Los Angeles the long wait on Thursday morning caused by the thorough nature of the autopsy (the whole of Senator Kennedy's brain was removed as were all his other vital organs) had proved a strain. Not surprisingly some of the Kennedy party could not avoid harboring feelings about Los Angeles not entirely dissimilar from those felt five years before in Dallas. In those first hours anything was enough to provoke bitterness: Kuchel's now certain defeat in the Senate Republican Primary at the hands of the right-winger Rafferty, Mayor Yorty's own gratuitous performance in trying to link Sirhan with W. E. B. DuBois clubs; the memory that this had been the one city in the whole of the campaign where the police had refused to cooperate—even to the point of issuing on one single day no less than one hundred traffic-violation tickets to the Kennedy cavalcade.

These feelings broke out in public only once. When the Kennedy advance party eventually made its way to Los Angeles airport—the family waited to drive out with the coffin—the first thing they noticed was Mayor Yorty's helicopter with its engines still revved up. For the man who perhaps more than any other had borne the public strain of the past forty-eight hours, the Senator's press secretary Frank Mankiewicz, it was too much. He told the mayor that his presence would be "offensive" to Mrs. Kennedy (though he later claimed that he had used a softer expression) and managed to prevail upon Mayor Yorty to retire into the airport building.

Almost immediately after the family party arrived (it now included Mrs. Jacqueline Kennedy who had flown in from New York the previous day), the plane took off. A red carpet, lined with roses and carnations, had been laid to the sleek Air Force Boeing 707 but there was no public ceremony of any kind. Members of the family entered the plane by a forklift on which the coffin was also raised. The others making the flight—and there were more than seventy, including three particularly favored journalists—went up the portable stairway at the front.

The flight to New York took four and a half hours—and it has already attracted some of the cloud of rumor and legend that still overhangs the flight of Air Force One from Dallas. The memory of that occasion must have been especially poignant for Mrs. Jacqueline Kennedy who became hysterically convinced that this was the same plane she had been on then and wanted to get off. She had to be reassured by Pierre Salinger that in fact the plane they were now traveling on was the one in which he had been flying with Dean Rusk and other government officials to Tokyo on the day the President was shot.

Those who were on the flight to New York that day generally refused to talk about the experience at all, thereby inevitably increasing belief in the somewhat melodramatic account reported later that night by Sander Vanocur (one of the three journalists present; the other two were Joe Kraft and Rowland Evans) on NBC television. What does, however, seem clear is that Mrs. Ethel Kennedy set a wonderful example of controlled courage and that her sister-in-law's behavior did not quite reach that high standard. But for the most part the family kept to themselves in the forward cabin where the coffin, draped in a maroon cloth, rested throughout the flight. Teddy Kennedy, whom Vanocur described as having been "angry and mad," is said by others to have stayed by the coffin during the entire flight. He was later joined by the Senator's widow, and both had fallen asleep there by the time the plane approached New York. Other people in a kind of spontaneous vigil apparently took turns in going up and simply lying beside the coffin for brief periods.

Long before the plane landed people had begun to gather at La Guardia Airport. It was a segregated crowd. V.I.P.'s, their names adding up to a social register of the American establishment, were allowed on the Marine terminal apron; the public could only look on from behind a fence. The last to join the select group of notables was Robert McNamara who appeared, with his wife, pushing hurriedly through a police cordon. His plane from Germany had arrived fifteen minutes late at J.F.K. On hand to greet him, besides people like the Paul Mellons, the Douglas Dillons, and the Nelson Rockfellers, were three members of the family who had not made it to Los Angeles: Teddy Kennedy's wife Joan, and Sargent Shriver and his wife Eunice who had flown in that day from Paris. One participant on the scene remembers the atmosphere as having been extraordinary. "It was hot and noisy and hushed all at once, full of despair, sorrow and weeping." The big Air Force plane taxied to a stop at eight-fifty-eight p.m. (New York time) almost directly in front of the group on the tarmac. A hoist moved to the front exit and a ramp to the rear and as Sargent Shriver along with Joan Kennedy moved onto the hoist, the same observer recalls with horror the photographers hollering, " 'Say, who's that blonde dame with Shriver?' That was what it was like—a confused milling around in the Klieg lights as the truly powerful and beautiful people, knowing they belonged here more than anywhere else, greeted and embraced the exhausted members of the Kennedy entourage."

The arrival on Thursday night in New York was perhaps the one occasion during the whole two days when disorder nearly took over. Even the Douglas Dillons, financially exalted and socially lofty, were reduced to hitching a lift in a Pentagon Chevrolet. The specially hired Kennedy limousines for some reason were too quickly hustled away by the police: in many cases they roared off empty into the night while even the closest Kennedy intimates stood on the curbside trying to flag lifts.

Finally the cortege was formed. A grey Cadillac hearse with Ethel and Teddy Kennedy in the front seat led the thirty-four-car procession slowly to the city. When the cortege arrived at St. Patrick's the Cathedral staff, alerted at seven Thursday morning, had been waiting three hours. A bier was readied for the coffin and a short service was held beside it for the now two-hundred-strong group of friends and Kennedy courtiers who had flown from Los Angeles or who had been at the airport to greet the plane.

But not all of those who were to play central roles in the funeral organization were present. Earlier that evening the headquarters of the last great Kennedy thrust had been established on the thirtieth floor of the Pan American Building in the same suite of offices Bobby Kennedy had held his last council of war before announcing his candidacy less than three months earlier.

If there is a capital of the Kennedy empire, it lies here in Suite 3021 at 200 Park Avenue behind a door inscribed, somewhat obscurely: "Joseph P. Kennedy, Park Agency, Inc., Licensed Real Estate Brokers." It is the normal work place of Steve Smith, the steward of the $300,000,000 family fortune. Ordinarily its atmosphere is one of discreet decorum, but it was very different that Thursday night as notices were rapidly pinned on doors bearing such legends as "Honor Watch," "Guest List," "Transportation," and even simply "Advance Men."

The activity had not really seriously begun until about eight o'clock when the group of Washington lawyers under Louis Oberdorfer who were working on the invitation list arrived in from Kennedy Airport. For the next thirty-six hours this corridor length of offices was to provide the focal point of the entire funeral organization. Only one room was not invaded; Steve Smith's magnificent corner office was kept as sanctuary and refuge for the family.

Before the retainers and family friends flooded in from the Cathedral at about ten-thirty p.m. the mood was comparatively calm and collected. Oberdorfer pressed on with his invitation list, the switchboard rattled to the numbers of bus- and car-hire firms and Katzenbach and Angie Duke briefly discussed protocol and the diplomatic guest list. But the arrival of almost one hundred people from the Cathedral (the rest, exhausted, went to find beds) changed all that. "There were simply too many tired, talented people," recalls one early participant, "and there just wasn't enough for all of them to do." Perhaps the real trouble was that no one really knew who was in charge: from time to time a rumor would start that McNamara, or even Sargent Shriver, was about to arrive and take the whole thing over; but nothing like that happened that night, or indeed the next day.

On the main project, however, the work went remorselessly on. Something like a dozen people, including the Senator's personal secretary Angie Novello, his old school friend David Hackett and his former Justice Department press aide Ed Guthman, were now working on compiling the funeral invitation list. They operated rather like a hanging committee at an art show. A name would be read out (the one that drew the angriest response was that of Joe Resnick, the New York congressman and Kennedy-baiter), there would be nods or shakes of the head, and depending on the reaction the name would be added to the list or dropped from it. One problem—later on to jam the switchboard—was the number of people who called up and demanded invitations. The two most persistent callers were said to be Mayor Yorty (who finally got in) and Governor George Wallace (who did not).

By now it was clear, too, that the list itself would have to be broken down: first, between those who would be admitted to the Cathedral only and the closer friends who would also be invited to ride on the train; and, second, in order to recognize the differing claims of the various guests to precedence. An elaborate code system was worked out of eight categories: T for train, K for family, S for staff, F for friends, WH for White House, V for V.I.P., D for diplomat, M for anyone who failed to fit into the other categories. Those who eventually received a telegram may not have realized it, but amid the Western Union hieroglyphics at the top it bore one or more of these vital initials, reflecting the addressee's importance or lack of it. This was a necessary precaution, since the telegrams were designed to serve as tickets both at the Cathedral and, for those having the vital T on their forms, at Pennsylvania station too.

That kind of work could go on, but not even the closest and oldest surviving Kennedy associates like Theodore Sorensen, Fred Dutton, Burke Marshall and Bill Walton could rule on such major outstanding questions as the precise site for the grave, the degree of military ceremonial wanted in Washington, or the details of the service at St. Patrick's. All those matters had to wait for adjudication, and the first effort to obtain it proved abortive. When McNamara, having driven straight from the Cathedral to the Carlyle hotel to be with Jackie and Ethel Kennedy, eventually turned up about one a.m. at the central command post, most people assumed he would start issuing crisp Pentagon-type orders. It did not take long for them to discover he did not view his role that way. After a brief discussion with Nick Katzenbach and Bill Walton, he left to conduct further negotiations with the family, this time taking the photographs and diagrams of Arlington with him. He returned within half an hour to announce that nothing could be decided that night; it was commonly supposed that he had found Ethel Kennedy asleep and had not wished to wake her. McNamara himself then departed, announcing, as he left, his intention of going to inspect the grave site the next day.

Shortly afterward both Steve and Teddy Kennedy arrived and, in a four-cornered meeting with Katzenbach and Fitt, the first guidelines for decision-making began to emerge. On one point, Fitt and Katzenbach were told, the family was adamant: all military participation must be kept to a minimum. The reasons behind this decision did not need to be explained; both Fitt and Katzenbach assumed they came first of all from a desire not to compete in any way with the memory of the late President's funeral, and secondly from the fact that Bobby Kennedy's opposition to the Vietnam war had made trumpets, drums, and gun carriages look inappropriate. But the prohibition was not absolute. There could be, it was indicated, a Naval pallbearers' group at Union Station (in the end even this was not used), a Naval band to play the Navy hymn as the coffin was unloaded from the train, and an all-service uniformed cordon lining the route out of the station on the way to Arlington. At the grave site, however, the ceremony was to be wholly civilian. The family wanted the music to be supplied by a university band (preferably the Harvard one) and the coffin itself to be borne from the hearse by a group of friends appointed by the family.

These last two directions caused a twinge of anxiety to Alfred Fitt, the man from the Pentagon: believing that it might prove impossible to assemble the Harvard (or any other university) band at thirty-six hours' notice on the second weekend in June, and worried over the ability of untrained pallbearers to carry a heavy coffin up a steep hill, he arranged in each case to have fallback military detachments available. Neither was needed.

By this time on Friday morning it was clear that the Washington end of the funeral was turning into a major organization job. The needs in New York might be more immediate—if only because the Senator's lying in state (at which 150,000 people were eventually to file past) was due to start within an hour or two. Delicate personal problems like which individuals would be asked to form the honor watch through the twenty-four-hour-vigil period (now being organized by David Hackett and George Plimpton) still had to be settled; and the funeral mass itself for the moment remained almost entirely undiscussed.

Yet in the capital where the Kennedy organization was thin there were also any number of loose ends to be tied up. Katzenbach and Fitt had agreed Thursday night that the best solution would be to call a meeting in the morning at which everyone (the Army, the police, the Secret Service, the Kennedy advance men and press people) would be told exactly what they were to do and how to get it done.

Later Friday morning this meeting, originally scheduled for one p.m. in Fitt's office in the Pentagon, had to have its venue moved to Nick Katzenbach's office in the State Department. Bob McNamara meanwhile had called to announce his intention of coming with Mrs. Paul Mellon to inspect the grave site at precisely one o'clock. The former Defense Secretary by now had recovered his renowned power of decision-making. Up at Arlington in less than an hour he and Mrs. Mellon (accompanied at a distance by Fitt and Jack Metzler, the cemetery superintendent) chose the site, taking the precaution of supplying Mrs. Kennedy with two alternatives so that she should at least have the impression of having made the decision herself. The preferred site was called "Number One" on the diagram, and neither Metzler nor Fitt doubted that it would be the one selected. McNamara, who had strong feelings that the other two detracted from the dignity of the President's grave, would, after all, be submitting the plans to Mrs. Kennedy. Before he left to return to New York, McNamara inquired how long a grave took to prepare. Metzler replied that all would be well if they got the word to go ahead by ten o'clock that evening. Characteristically, at precisely ten o'clock, the phone rang on Fitt's desk in the Pentagon: the Number One site had been chosen.

Meanwhile, that Friday afternoon, Katzenbach's logistics meeting was in full swing on the seventh floor of the State Department. Even an experienced government hand like the State Department Under Secretary admits now to having been surprised at the number of people that get involved once any form of ceremonial is attempted in Washington. That afternoon nearly thirty individuals, each representing a differing interest, filed in and almost filled Katzenbach's spacious office.

It was a muddled, unsatisfactory meeting; for the first time since they had taken to the road the previous March, the Kennedy campaign staff was brought face to face with just how complex and labyrinthine government machinery can be. The Kennedy advance men—the two who turned up were Irish lawyers from the Bronx—may have known all about renting coliseums, hiring buses and filling stadia, but what soon became clear was that they did not understand such matters as precedence of the Supreme Court in relation to Congress, the security requirements of the White House (the Secret Service was attached to Presidential candidates only after Kennedy was shot), even simple police demands (which they had been accustomed to riding roughshod over on the campaign trail). "Fortunately," one of the government representatives at the meeting was to comment afterward, "the chief Kennedy man who did most of the talking [this was Chris McGrath whose brother, Kevin, was simultaneously negotiating rather more easily with the spiritual authorities in St. Patrick's in New York] soon realized he could swing nothing on us. He was forced to accept that he had to trust us—and in the end I think he did."

In New York no such problems were faced. Even in death Bobby Kennedy remained an imperial presence, and the police, city hall, even the prelates and priests at the Cathedral wanted merely to be given directions to follow. From the beginning, symbolized by both Governor Rockefeller's and Mayor Lindsay's attendance at LaGuardia Airport, both the state and the city gave maximum cooperation. Only The New York *Times*—highly unpopular with the Kennedy people ever since its harsh judgment, delivered in the immediate aftermath of the Oregon primary, that the Senator's campaign had been "too relentless and too aggressive in its single-minded pursuit of power"—caused resentment. Its somewhat peremptory demand for fifty-six seats in the Cathedral led to the first and only serious quarrel between Frank Mankiewiez and Pierre Salinger. Each competed avidly for the pleasure of telling Clifton Daniel (The *Times'* Managing Editor) that his paper had been allocated precisely two seats in St. Patrick's, or the same egalitarian number as that given to the New York *Daily News*.

The demand for press credentials was rapidly developing into a major problem both in New York and Washington, where Bill Moyers (having volunteered his services) was now lending a welcome experienced hand to the beleagured press office garrison in 2000 L Street. The original instructions from Pierre Salinger (operating out of the press headquarters in the Commodore Hotel on Forty-second Street in New York City) were crisp and uncompromising: there would be two hundred seats for the working press in the Cathedral and one hundred on the train. (Even this ceiling, however, raised some skeptical questions—especially among those who had always been doubtful about the Kennedy family's distinction between private and public grief.) But whatever those suspicions, it soon became clear that no offer the Kennedys could contemplate making would meet the strident demands of the media. Significantly, for the final ceremony at Arlington cemetery, where no numerical limit applied, no less than nineteen hundred credentials were issued by the Kennedy Washington office. Never during his life had Bobby Kennedy attracted press attention like that.

By Friday afternoon the entire planning operation had, in fact, acquired an almost campaign flavor. The last of the batches of invitations went out around lunchtime. Throughout the morning there had been a complicated telephone feeding system of names, addresses and codes to a special office at Western Union; and in the suite of offices on the thirtieth floor of the Pan American Building it now became the hour of the technicians. Banks of telephones were set up and rows of people set to work to try and reach every person to whom an invitation had been sent (this proved to a very wise move; some telegrams took till Monday to reach their destinations, and others never arrived). Any guest contacted who had not received his telegram was told to go to the Kennedy headquarters where elaborate rules against gate-crashers governed the issuance of replacement tickets. An instruction sheet put out that Friday read in part:

"At Thirty-eighth and Madison anyone who comes in will be asked to show some personal identification, or some written authorization to pick up a ticket plus personal identification. The name of the identified party will be checked against the master list; if it appears on the list, then the person will be asked whether he or the guest he represents received a telegram invitation. If a telegram was received and has reached the invited person, then no ticket will be issued. If a person received a telegram at his home but left home before it arrived, then he is eligible to receive a replacement ticket. The master list shows for each person his code—K, S, F, WH, V, D, M—and his train status ("train" or nothing). In lieu of a letter code the replacement tickets are color coded. . . . If a replacement ticket is to be issued, a ticket of the proper color should be handed to the person who will sign his name on the back of the ticket, or if he is an authorized representative he will sign the guest's name followed by the representative's initials."

Even more complicated was the technique for dealing with people who could not understand how they had been overlooked. Here the tone of the orders was perhaps a little more tactful but certainly no less firm.

"Unless they are very obviously V.I.P.'s they should be told that unfortunately it was not possible to invite as many people as the family would have liked to invite and that the guest list is already beyond the capacity of the Cathedral. Apologize and suggest that the proceedings will be covered fully on television from inside the Cathedral. If the person is, seems to be, or claims to be a V.I.P., ask for identification and show it to the supervisor. He will then call a special number at 200 Park Avenue to see whether the name has been or should be added to the master list. *Only names approved by the person answering that phone can be added to the master list.*"

A mere four individuals—Lou Oberdorfer, Carter Burden, Walter Schier (a former General Counsel to N.A.S.A.) and Jim Flug (Teddy Kennedy's Legislative Assistant) were empowered to make additions to the Guest List once it had been made up. So sparing was their use of this prerogative that in the end the supplementary list totaled less than a dozen. But even the shrewdest precautions are not foolproof: Gary DeDell, the Syracuse printing executive arrested at the entrance to the Cathedral for carrying an unloaded pistol in his briefcase, had obtained an invitation early on Saturday morning by persuading a tired volunteer worker to break the rules.

Yet that appears to have been the only occasion on which the system broke down. The graduates from Robert Kennedy's tough training school in the Justice Department (men like Lou Oberdorfer, Jack Rosenthal, John Seigenthaler, Ed Guthman, Jack Miller and John Nolan) had now taken firm control of the whole operation: and while others—especially "the beautiful people" (normally relegated to simple tasks like fetching coffee)—milled around, they ran a very tight ship.

In a way it was curious that the old Justice Department team should have assumed control so effortlessly. At the beginning a common prediction had been that the fight for supremacy would be between the old White House aides like Sorensen, O'Donnell and Salinger and the Senator's own much younger and more radical staff, notably Peter Edelman, Adam Walinsky and Jeff Greenfield. But before those battle lines could be drawn—and they were briefly sketched in only once over the old J.F.K. brigade's successful insistence that the Green Berets (or the Special Forces) must be represented at the funeral—Bobby Kennedy's hand-picked men at the Justice Department had simply taken charge. "They were," columnist Joe Kraft was to comment admiringly afterward, "probably the best staff any Kennedy ever had—and they certainly proved their worth during those two days."

Understandably Bobby Kennedy's own Senate staff, who had traveled the long campaign trail with him from Indiana to California, soon relapsed into behaving as mourners rather than as chief planners. Adam Walinsky and Peter Edelman worked on the Mass Card—with its echo from the J.F.K. funeral "Dear God, Please take care of him who tried to take care of yours"—but for the most part neither they nor most of the other immediate campaign entourage played any decisive role in the funeral arrangements. Even Teddy Kennedy's eulogy of his fallen brother at the Requiem Mass was drafted by one of the Washington lawyers, Milton Gwirtzman, whose own law firm (Dutton, Gwirtzman, Zumas & Wise) had three of its four partners working away on the thirtieth floor of 200 Park Avenue. In fact, scarcely a prominent Washington law firm was not represented there: Arnold & Porter, Steptoe & Johnson, Covington & Burling, Hogan & Hartson; all were in some way involved.

In this sense what perhaps the planning of the funeral demonstrated was that the Kennedy political army was even more formidable in its reserve strength than it was in its active forces. For a moment that Friday the whole secret Kennedy underground was suddenly exposed to the world: the twenty journalists who took their turn in the Honor Watch (including, ironically, one New York *Times* man, Anthony Lewis, who flew in all the way from London); the former secret Kennedy sympathizers within the L.B.J. administration, like Moyers and McNamara, who dropped everything to rally to their real hero's fallen standard; even the tough, cynical television pundits like David Brinkley and Sandy Vanocur who suddenly threw their cynicism, and their reputations for objectivity too, to the winds. The desire to be part of the tribe even cut across party lines: on Capitol Hill it was a Republican Senator, Charles Percy of Illinois, who told his staff that he did not want to see any of them that Friday at all. They were to go straight upstairs and take over the Kennedy office so that the girls answering the telephones there could get to New York.

New York was where anyone who had been at all involved in the Kennedy effort now wanted to be. It was, as the saying goes, where the action was. Some of that action was perhaps surprising. That night a wake was held with virtually the whole clan, including Jackie Kennedy, present. It was a wake where people joked, laughed and sang. The Irish and the adopted Irish understood the Kennedy tribal need for this sort of gesture: the Wasps and "the beautiful people" did not.

It would also probably have shocked the more practical-minded professionals still working away on the thirtieth floor of the Pan Am Building. By now almost everything had been tied up, even the arrangements for the Mass itself (though only after a slight altercation between an emissary of Archbishop Cooke and Stephen Smith himself over the Church's ruling that it was impossible to forbid ordinary members of the congregation to take communion if they felt they wanted to). But even if decisions no longer needed to be made, men with orderly minds always want official ratification for what has already been decided. And it was not until something like two a.m. Saturday that Teddy Kennedy and Steve Smith returned to give their *imprimatur* to all the arrangements. One observer of their eventual arrival back in Smith's office found their mood almost extraordinary. "They and John Seigenthaler, and one or two others, were making swift, hard jokes—almost baiting each other—in a way that I suppose only close friends can. It was only a matter of minutes, but they'd trade insults back and forth—and then suddenly they all burst into a quiet kind of laughter."

This may of course have represented no more than an effort to break the tension, for by now the organization job was effectively over. The guest list, which no one in the family had seen until then, was handed over to Steve Smith; Teddy Kennedy cast his eye over the Cathedral seating plan; the list of thirteen ushers and sixty-one honorary pallbearers (only the thirteen actual pallbearers had been selected by the family) and the train list were almost casually approved. Suddenly it occurred to at least two people present that throughout the past two days there had really been no one on the bridge at all and that the normally forgotten men of any campaign—those down in the engine room—had really, during this last campaign, been running the ship.

[November, 1968]

Chicago, The Year of Our Lord, 1968

The Members of the Assembly

by Jean Genet

Chicago reminds me of an animal which curiously is trying to climb on top of itself. Part of the city is transformed by the life—or the parade, in both senses of the term—of the hippies.

Saturday night, about ten o'clock, the young people in Lincoln Park have lighted a kind of bonfire. Close by, scarcely visible in the darkness, a good-sized crowd has formed beneath the trees to listen to a black band—flutes and bongo drums. An American Indian, carrying a furled green flag, explains to us that it will be taken tomorrow to the airport when Senator McCarthy is scheduled to arrive and speak. Unfurled, the flag bears upon its green background the painted image of a seventeen-year-old boy—some say he was Indian, others black—killed two days before by the Chicago police.

The cops arrive, in brief but still unangry waves, to put out the fire and disperse the demonstrators. One word about them: the demonstrators are young people of a gentleness almost too gentle, at least this evening. If couples are stretched out on the grass in the park, it seems to me it is for the purpose of angelic exchanges. Everything strikes me as being very chaste. The darkness of the park is not solely responsible for the fact that all I can see are shadows folded in each other's arms.

161

A group of demonstrators, which had at first dispersed, has re-formed and is singing a kind of two-syllable chant, not unlike a Gregorian chant, a funeral dirge to the memory of the dead boy. I can scarcely speak of the beauty of this plaintive wail, of the anger and the singing.

Around the park, which is almost totally dark, what I first see is a proliferation of American cars, heavy with chrome, and beyond them the gigantic buildings of the city, each of whose floors is lighted, why I don't know.

Are these four democratic days going to begin with a funeral vigil in memory of a young Indian—or black—murdered by the Chicago police?

If man is, or is searching to be, omnipotent, I am willing to accept Chicago's gigantism; but I should like the opposite to be accepted as well: a city which would fit in the hollow of one's hand.

Sunday, Midway Airport, Chicago. McCarthy's arrival. Almost no police, and the few who do check our press credentials are extremely casual. Across from the press platform itself, actually the empty back of a parked trailer truck, are three similar platforms: one is occupied by a brass-dominated orchestra whose members are men in their thirties and forties, another by a rock group in its twenties. Between them is the platform reserved for McCarthy and his staff. McCarthy's plane is a few minutes late; the crowd massed behind the press platform consists of men and women whose faces reflect that peculiar image which only profound honesty and hope can give.

McCarthy finally arrives; and the crowd comes dramatically to life: every man, woman, and child, shouting "We Want Gene," brandishes signs devoid of the customary slogans but generously bedecked with flowers drawn or painted each according to the bearer's whim, and it is this flower-crowd that McCarthy is going to address. He is extremely relaxed; he smiles; he is about to speak, but the battery of microphones is dead. Sabotage? Smiling, he walks over and tries the mikes of the musical group in its thirties and forties: dead. Still smiling, he tries the mikes of the rock group in its twenties: dead! Finally, he makes his way back to his platform and tries his own microphones, which in the interim have been repaired, at least to some degree. He smiles. He is also serious, and he declares that he will speak only if the men and women the farthest away from the speaker's platform can hear him. Finally, he does speak, and you have all heard what he said on television.

As he leaves the speaker's platform, it seems that no one is protecting him, save for the sea of flowers painted by the hope-filled men and women.

A few hours later, at McCarthy's headquarters in the Hilton Hotel, there again appears to be almost no police security, or if there is any it is subtle, invisible. We are received with great courtesy.

This leads me to what, in my opinion, is one of the basic questions I ask myself: after eight months of campaigning, in order for this little-known Senator—or known all too well through a name steeped in shame—in order for McCarthy to arouse such enthusiasm, what concessions has he made? In what ways has his moral rectitude been weakened?

And yet the fact remains that all his speeches, all his statements, reveal intelligence and generosity. Is it a trick?

For a city with as large a black population as Chicago has, I note that there were very few blacks out to greet and acclaim him.

The First Day: The Day of the Thighs

The thighs are very beautiful beneath the blue cloth, thick and muscular. It all must be hard. This policeman is also a boxer, a wrestler. His legs are long, and perhaps, as you approach his member, you would find a furry nest of long, tight, curly hair. That is all I can see—and I must say it fascinates me—that and his boots, but I can guess that these superb thighs extend on up into an imposing member and a muscled torso, made even firmer every day by his police training in the cops' gymnasium. Higher up, into his arms and hands which must know how to put a black man or a thief out of action.

In the compass of his well-built thighs, I can see . . . but the thighs have moved, and I can see that they are splendid: America has a magnificent, divine, athletic police force, often photographed and seen in dirty books . . . but the thighs have parted slightly, ever so slightly, and through the crack which extends from the knees to the too-heavy member, I can see . . . why, it's the whole panorama of the Democratic Convention with its star-spangled banners, its star-spangled undress, its star-spangled songs, its star-spangled fields, its star-spangled candidates, in short the whole ostentatious parade, but the color has too many facets, as you have seen on your television sets.

What your television fails to bring you is the odor. No: the Odor, which may have a certain connection with order? The reason is that the Democratic Convention is being held right next to the stockyards, and I keep asking myself whether the air is being befouled by the decomposition of Eisenhower or by the decomposition of all America.

A few hours later, about midnight, I join Allen Ginsberg to take part in a demonstration of hippies and students in Lincoln Park: their determination to sleep in the park is their very gentle, as yet too gentle, but certainly poetic, response to the nauseating spectacle of the Convention. Suddenly the police begin their charge, with their grimacing masks intended to terrify: and, in fact, everyone turns and runs. But I am well aware that these brutes have other methods, and far more terrifying masks, when they go hunting for blacks in the ghettos, as they have done for the past hundred and fifty years. It is a good, healthy, and ultimately moral thing for these fair-haired, gentle hippies to be charged at by these louts decked out in this amazing snout that protects them from the effects of the gas they have emitted.

And I should like to end the first day with this: the person who opens her door to receive us as we try to escape from these brutes in blue is a young and very beautiful black woman. Later, when the streets have finally grown calm again, she offers to let us slip out through a back door, which opens onto another street: without the police suspecting it, we have been conjured away and concealed by a trick house. Nonetheless, these enormous thighs of policemen stuffed with LSD, rage, and patriotism were fascinating to see.

Tomorrow: another sleep-in in Lincoln Park, for this Law which is no law must be resisted.

The Second Day: The Day of the Visor

The truth of the matter is that we are bathed in a Mallarméan blue. This second day imposes the azure helmets of the Chicago police. A policeman's black leather visor intrudes between me and the world: a gleaming visor in whose tidy reflections I may be able to read the world, wittingly kept in top condition by numerous, and doubtless daily, polishings. Supporting this visor is the blue cap—Chicago wants us to think that the whole police force, and this policeman standing in front of me, have descended from heaven—made of a top-grade sky-blue cloth. But who is this blue cop in front of me? I look into his eyes, and I can see nothing else there except the blue of the cap. What does his gaze say? Nothing. The Chicago police are, and are not. I shall not pass. The visor and the gaze are there. The visor so gleaming that I can see myself and lose myself in it. I've got to see the continuation of the allegedly Democratic Convention, but the cop in the black visor with the blue eyes is there. Beyond him, I can nonetheless catch a glimpse of a lighted sign above the convention floor: there is an eye and "CBS News," the structure of which, in French as in English, reminds me of "obscene." But who is this policeman in the blue cap and black visor? He is so handsome I could fall into his arms. I look again at his look: at long last I recognize it; it is the look of a beautiful young girl, voluptuous and tender, which is hiding beneath a black visor and blue cap. She loves this celestial color: the Chicago poice are feminine and brutal. It does not want its ladies to meekly obey their husbands whose hair is sky blue, dressed in robes of many colors. . . .

And what of the convention? It is democratic, it babbles on, and you have seen it on your screens: it is there for the purpose of concealing from you a game both simple and complex, which you prefer to ignore.

About ten o'clock this evening, part of America has detached itself from the American fatherland and remains suspended between earth and sky. The hippies have gathered in an enormous hall, as starkly bare as the Convention Hall is gaudy. Here all is joy, and in the enthusiasm several hippies burn their draft cards, holding them high for everyone to see: they will not be soldiers, but they may well be prisoners for five years. The hippies ask me to come up onto the stage and say a few words: this youth is beautiful and very gentle. It is celebrating the Un-Birthday of a certain Johnson who, it seems to me, hasn't yet been born. Allen Ginsberg is voiceless: he has chanted too loud and too long in Lincoln Park the night before.

Order, real order, is here: I recognize it. It is the freedom offered to everyone to discover and create himself.

About midnight, again in Lincoln Park, the clergy—also between earth and sky in order to escape from America—is conducting a religious service. I am subjected to another, but also very beautiful, kind of poetry. And what of the trees in the park? At night they bear strange fruit, clusters of young people suspended in their branches. I am as yet unfamiliar with this nocturnal variety: but that's the way it is in Chicago. The clergymen invite us to be seated: they are singing hymns in front of an enormous wooden cross. They joke too, and use slang. "Sit or split," says one of the bantering and slangy priests. "Sit or split." The cross, borne by several clergymen, moves away into the night, and this imitation of the Passion is very mov— I don't have time to finish the word: enormous projectors are turned on directly in front of us, and the police, throwing canisters of tear gas, rush at us. We have to run. Once again it is this police, azure but inexorable, who are pursuing us and pursuing the cross. Spellman-the-cop would have had a good laugh.

We take refuge in Ginsberg's hotel, across the street from the Park: my eyes are burning from the gas: a medic pours water into them, and the water spills over me down to my feet. In short, in their blundering clumsiness, the Americans have tried to burn me and a few minutes later to drown me.

We pause to collect ourselves in Allen Ginsberg's hotel room. And what of the convention? And democracy? The newspapers have kept you posted about them.

We leave the hotel: another azure policeman—or the beautiful girl in drag—holding his billy club in his hand the way, exactly the way, I hold a black American's member—escorts us to our car and opens the door for us: there can be no mistake about it: we are White.

The Third Day: The Day of the Belly

Chicago has fed these policemen's bellies, which are so fat that one must presume that they live on the slaughterhouses required by a city which resembles three hundred Hamburgs piled one on top of the other, and daily consumes three million hamburgers. A policeman's beautiful belly has to be seen in profile: the one barring my route is a medium-sized belly (de Gaulle could qualify as a cop in Chicago). It is medium-sized, but it is well on its way to perfection. Its owner wheedles it, fondles it with both his beautiful but heavy hands. Where did they all come from? Suddenly we are surrounded by a sea of policemen's bellies barring our entrance into the Democratic Convention. When I am finally allowed in, I will understand more clearly the harmony which exists between these bellies and the bosoms of the lady-patriots at the Convention—there is harmony but also rivalry: the arms of the ladies of the gentlemen who rule America have the girth of the policemen's thighs. Walls of bellies. And walls of policemen who encircle us, astonished by our appearance at the Democratic Convention, furious at the unconventional way we're dressed: they are thinking that we are thinking what they know, that is that the Democratic Convention is the Holy of Holies. The mouths of these bellies huddle in hasty conference. Walkie-talkies are barking. All of us in possession of the electronic passes required to enter the Amphitheater. The Chief of Police—wearing civilian clothes and his belly—arrives. He checks our passes, our identification, but obviously a man of taste and discretion, does not ask to see mine. He offers me his hand. I shake it. The bastard. We enter the corridors of the Convention Hall, but only to be allowed into the press section. New police bellies are there, blocking our route again. Can we go in and sit down? Bellies even heavier and more robust tell us there is no room for us inside: within the hallowed halls of the convention segregation is being practiced against four or five white males, who have had the effrontery to come without ties, a mixed band of long-haired and hairless, with a few beards thrown in. After long discussions, we are allowed to go in and sit down. I gather, from the fatigue which has just overwhelmed me, that what I am witnessing is a resounding lie, voluptuous for those who make their living from it. I hear the numbers being announced: they are counting the votes cast by New Jersey and adding them to those cast by Minnesota: never very good at arithmetic, I am amazed that this science is used to choose a President. Finally triumph and pandemonium—their triumph—Humphrey is nominated. The bellies have chosen a representative. This unmad madness, screaming mauve songs, gaudy but grey, this inordinate lie of talking bellies, you have seen and heard its pale reflections on your television screens.

I have an urge to go outside and touch a tree, graze in the grass, screw a goat, in short do what I'm used to doing.

A few hours before going to the convention, where our free and easy manner has petrified the police and made them suspicious, we have taken part in the Peace March organized by David Dellinger in Grant Park. Thousands of young people were there, peacefully listening to Phil Ochs sing and to others talk; we were covered with flowers. A symbolic march set off in the direction of the slaughterhouse. A first row of blacks, then behind them, in rows of eight abreast, anyone who cared to join the demonstration. No one got very far: more bellies charged, firing tear gas at the young people. Trucks filled with armed soldiers drove endlessly back and forth through the streets of Chicago.

To the Hippies

Hippies, young people of the demonstration, you no longer belong to America, which has moreover repudiated you. Hippies with long hair, you are making America's hair curl. But you, between earth and sky, are the beginning of a new continent, an Earth of Fire rising strangely above, or hollowed out below, what once was this sick country—an earth of fire first and, if you like, an earth of flowers. But you must begin, here and now, another continent.

Fourth Day: The Day of the Revolver

Is it necessary to write that everything is over? With Humphrey nominated, will Nixon be master of the world?

The Democratic Convention is closing its doors. The police, here as elsewhere, will be less brutal, if it can. And is the revolver, in turn, going to speak?

The Democratic Convention has made its choice, but where, in what drunken bar, did a handful of democrats make their decision?

Across from the Hotel Hilton, again in Grant Park, a sumptuous happening. The youth have scaled a bronze horse on which is seated a bronze rider. On the horse's mane—whose head is bowed as if in sleep—young blacks and whites are brandishing black flags and red flags. A burning youth, which I hope will burn all its bridges; it is listening, attentive and serious, to a Presidential candidate who was not invited to the convention: Dick Gregory. Gregory is inviting his friends—there are four or five thousand of them in the park—to come home with him. They won't let us march to the Amphitheater, he declares, but there's no law that says you can't come on down to my house for a party. But first, he says, the four or five policemen who have stupidly allowed themselves to be hemmed in by the crowd of demonstrators must be freed. With great wit and humor, Gregory explains how the demonstrators are to walk, no more than two or three abreast, keeping on the sidewalk and obeying all traffic lights. He says that the march may be long and difficult, for he lives in a house in the black ghetto of South Chicago. He invites the two or three beaten delegates (that is, McCarthy delegates) to head the march, for the police whose job it will be to stop the march may be less brutal with them.

We walk along a hedge of armed soldiers.

At long last America is moving, because the hippies have shaken their shoulders.

The Democratic Convention is closing its doors.

A few random thoughts, as usual:

America is a heavy island, too heavy: it would be good, for America, and for the world, for it to be demolished, for it to be reduced to powder.

The danger for America is not Mao's *Thoughts:* it is the proliferation of cameras.

So far as I know, there were no scientists among the demonstrators: is intelligence stupid, or science too easy?

The policemen are made of rubber: their muscles are of hard rubber; the convention itself was pure rubber: Chicago is made of rubber that chews chewing gum; the policemen's thoughts are made out of soft rubber, Mayor Daley of wet rubber. . . .

As we are leaving the Democratic Convention, a young policeman looks at me. Our gazes are already a settling of scores: he has understood that I am the enemy, but not one of the policemen is aware of the natural but invisible road, like that of drugs, which has led me, underground or via the route of heaven, into the United States, although the State Department refused me a visa to enter the country.

Too many star-spangled flags: here, as in Switzerland, a flag in front of every house. America is Switzerland flattened out by a steamroller. Lots of young blacks: will the delegates' hot dogs or the revolver bullet murder the democrats before it is too late?

Fabulous happening. Hippies! Glorious hippies, I address my final appeal to you: children, flower children in every country, in order to fuck all the old bastards who are giving you a hard time, unite, go underground if necessary in order to join the burned children of Vietnam.

—*Translated by Richard Seaver*   [November, 1968]

The Coming of the Purple Better One

by William Burroughs

Saturday August 24, 1968: Arrive O'Hare Airport, Chicago. First visit in 26 years. Last in Chicago during the war where I exercised the trade of exterminator.

"Exterminator. Got any bugs lady?"

"The tools of your trade," said the customs officer touching my cassette recorder.

Driving in from the airport note empty streets newspapers in the wind a ghost town. Taxi strike bus strike doesn't account for the feeling of nobody here. Arrive Sheraton Hotel where I meet Jean Genet. He is dressed in an old pair of corduroy pants no jacket no tie. He conveys a remarkable impact of directness confronting completely whoever he talks to.

Sunday August 25: Out to the airport for the arrival of McCarthy. An estimated fifteen thousand supporters there to welcome him mostly young people. Surprisingly few police. Whole scene touching and ineffectual particularly in retrospect of subsequent events.

Monday August 26: We spend Monday morning in Lincoln Park talking to the Yippies. Jean Genet expresses himself succinctly on the subject of America and Chicago.

"I can't wait for this city to rot. I can't wait to see weeds growing through empty streets."

May not have to wait long. Police in blue helmets many of them wearing one-way dark glasses stand around heavy and sullen. One of them sidles up to me while I am recording and says: "You're wasting film."

Of course the sound track does bring the image track on set so there is not all that much difference between a recorder and a camera.

Another sidles up right in my ear. "They're talking about brutality. They haven't seen anything yet."

The cops know they are the heavies in this show and they are going to play it to the Hilton.

Monday night to the Convention Hall. Cobblestone streets smell of coal gas and stockyards. No place to park. Some citizen rushes out screaming. "You can't park here! I'll call the police! I'll have your car towed away!"

Through line after line of police showing our credentials and finally click ourselves in. Tinny atmosphere of carnivals and penny arcades without the attractions. The barkers are there but no freaks no sideshows no scenic railways.

Up to Lincoln Park where the cops are impartially clubbing Yippies newsmen and bystanders. After all there are no innocent bystanders. What are they doing here in the first place? The worst sin of man is to be born.

Tuesday August 27: The Yippies are stealing the show. I've had about enough of the convention farce without humor barbed wire and cops around a lot of nothing.

Jean Genet says: "It is time for writers to support the rebellion of youth not only with their words but with their presence as well."

It is time for every writer to stand by his words.

Lincoln Park Tuesday night: The Yippies have assembled at the epicenter of Lincoln Park. Bonfires, a cross, the demonstrators singing *The Battle Hymn of the Republic.*

He hath loosed the fateful lightning of his terrible swift sword.

"Wet a handkerchief and put it in front of your face. . . . Don't rub your eyes."

He is trampling out the vintage where the grapes of wrath are stored.

"Keep your cool and stay seated."

He has sounded forth the trumpet that shall never call retreat.

"Sit or split."

At this point I look up to see what looks like a battalion of World War I tanks converging on the youthful demonstrators and I say, "What's with you Martin you wig already?"

He just looks at me and says: "Fill your hand stranger." And hauls out an old rusty police force from 1910 and I take off across Lincoln Park tear-gas canisters raining all around me. From a safe distance I turn around to observe the scene and see it is a 1917 gas attack from the archives. I make the lobby of the Lincoln Hotel where the medics are treating gas victims. The Life-Time photographer is laid out on a bench medics washing his eyes out. Soon he recovers and begins taking pictures of everything in sight. Outside the cops prowl about like aroused tomcats.

Wednesday August 28: Rally in Grant Park to organize a march to the Amphitheatre. I am impressed by the organization that has been built here. Many of the marshals wear crash helmets and blue uniforms. It is difficult to distinguish them from the police. Clearly the emergent Yippie uniform is crash helmet, shoulder pads, and aluminum jockstrap. I find myself in the second row of the nonviolent march feeling rather out of place since nonviolence is not exactly my program. We shuffle slowly forward the marshals giving orders over the loudspeaker.

"Link arms. . . . Keep five feet between rows. . . . You back there watch what you're smoking. . . . Keep your cool. . . . This is a nonviolent march. . . . You can obtain tear-gas rags from the medics. . . ."

We come to a solid line of cops and there is a confab between the cops and the marshals. For one horrible moment I think they will let us march five bloody miles and me with blisters already from walking around in the taxi strike. No. They won't let us march. And being a nonviolent march and five beefy cops for every marcher and not being equipped with bulldozers it is an impasse. I walk around the park recording and playing back, a beauteous evening calm and clear vapor trails over the lake youths washing tear gas out of their eyes in the fountain. Spot of bother at the bridge where the pigs and national guardians have stationed themselves like Horatio but in far greater numbers.

So out to the Convention Hall where they don't like the look of us despite our electronic credentials being in order and call a Secret Service

man for clearance. We get in finally and I play back the Grant Park recordings and boo Humphrey to while away the time as they count votes to the
all too stupid and obvious conclusion.

What happened Wednesday night when the guard dogs broke loose
again is history.

I have described the Chicago police as left over from 1910 and in a
sense this is true. Daley and his nightstick authority date back to turn-
of-the-century ward politics. They are anachronisms and they know it.
This I think accounts for the shocking ferocity of their behavior. Jean
Genet, who has considerable police experience, says he never saw such
expressions before on allegedly human faces. And what is the phantom
fuzz screaming from Chicago to Berlin, from Mexico City to Paris? "We
are REAL REAL REAL!!! REAL as this NIGHTSTICK!" As they feel, in their
dim animal way, that reality is slipping away from them. Where are all the
old cop sets, Clancy? Eating your apple twirling your club the sky goes out
against your back. Where are the men you sent up who came around to
thank you when they got out? Where is the gold watch the chief gave you
when you cracked the Norton case? And where are your pigeons, Clancy?
You used to be quite a pigeon fancier remember the feeling you got
sucking arrests from your pigeons soft and evil like the face of your
whiskey priest brother? Time to turn in your cop suit to the little Jew who
will check it off in his book. Won't be needing you after Friday.

The youth rebellion is a worldwide phenomenon that has not been seen
before in history. I don't believe they will calm down and be ad execs at
thirty as the establishment would like to believe. Millions of young people
all over the world are fed up with shallow unworthy authority running on
a platform of bullshit. There are five questions that any platform in
America must answer not with hot air but with change on a basic level.

1. Vietnam: As I recollect the French were in there quite some years and
finally pulled out to repeat the same mistake in Algeria. History tells us
this is a war that cannot be won. Perhaps it is not intended to be won but
merely as provocation and pretext to start a war with Red China. Looks
like some folks figure the only answer to this mess is blow the set up and
start over. May have happened several times before what we call history
going back about 10,000 years and the human actor being about 500,000
years on set, give a little take a little, so what was he doing for the 480,000
years unaccounted for? If we have come from stone axes to nuclear
weapons in ten thousand years this may well have happened before. Brion
Gysin has put forward the theory that a nuclear disaster in what is now the
Gobi Desert destroyed the civilization that had made such a disaster
possible and incidentally gave rise to what he terms "Albino freaks,"
namely the white race. Any case if we don't want to see the set go America

should get out of Vietnam and reach an immediate agreement with Red China.

2. Alienated youth: The only establishment that is supported by its young people is Red China. And that is why the State Department does not want Americans to go there. They do not want Americans to realize that any establishment offering young people anything at all will get their support. Because the western establishments are not offering anything. They have nothing to declare but their bad intentions. Let them come all the way out in the open with their bad intentions, declare a Secret Service overwhelming majority, and elect a purple-assed baboon to the Presidency. At this dark hour in the history of the penny arcade, Wednesday troubling all our hearts, the aggressive Southern ape suh fought for you in the perilous Kon-Tiki Room of the Sheraton.

3. Black Power: Find out what they want and give it to them. All the signs that mean anything indicate that the blacks were the original inhabitants of this planet. So who has a better right to it?

4. Our police and judicial system: What would happen if all the cotton-picking, stupid-assed, bible-belt laws passed by bourbon-soaked state legislators were actually enforced together with all federal and city laws? If every businessman who chiseled on his income tax by one dollar was caught and jailed? If every drug offender was caught and jailed? If every violator of all the laws penalizing sex acts between consenting adults in private was caught and jailed? How many people would be in jail? I think 30,000,000 is a very conservative estimate. And how many cops would it take to detect and arrest these criminals? And how many guards to keep them confined? And how many judges parole officers and court personnel to process them? And how much money would this cost?

Fix yourself on 30,000,000 violators in vast internee camps all united to scream with the inflexible authority of one big mouth. "We want gymnasiums! Libraries! Swimming pools! We want golf courses! Country clubs! Theatres!"

And with every concession they scream for MORE! MORE! MORE!

"The internee delegation in a meeting with the President today demanded as a prerequisite for any talks the 'immediate and unconditional removal of the so-called guards.' "

Senator Bradly rose in the Senate to question the wisdom of setting up what he termed "a separate state of dubious loyalty at the very core of our nation."

"We want tanks! Planes! Submarines!"

"An ominous atmosphere smogged the capital today as peace talks with the internee delegation bogged down."

"We want a space program! We want an atom bomb!"

"The number of internees is swelling ominously . . . forty million . . . fifty million . . . sixty million . . . 'America is a thin shell around a pulsing core of sullen violators.' "

"Today the internees exploded their first atom bomb described as 'a low yield nuclear device.' "

"It may be low yield but it's right on our back porch," said Senator Bradly plaintively.

"Today the internees signed a mutual assistance pact with Red China."

As regards our judicial system there are three alternatives:

A. Total enforcement. Is either of our distinguished candidates for the Presidency prepared to support the computerized police terror that such enforcement would entail?

B. An admission that the judicial system is a farce and the laws not really intended to be enforced except in a haphazard sporadic fashion. Is either candidate prepared to make such an admission?

C. Get some bulldozers in here and clean out all this garbage and let no state saloon reel to his drunken feet and start braying about state rights. Is either candidate prepared to advocate the only sensible alternative?

5. The disappearing dollar: 1959 Minutes To Go: "I'm absolutely weak I can only just totter home the dollar has collapsed." Figuring ten years time lag the dollar should collapse in 1969. There is something wrong with the whole concept of money. It takes always more and more to buy less and less. Money is like junk. A dose that fixes on Monday won't fix on Friday. We are being swept with vertiginous speed into a worldwide inflation comparable to what happened in Germany after World War I. The rich are desperately stockpiling gold, diamonds, antiques, paintings, medicines, food, liquor, tools and weapons. Any platform that does not propose the basic changes necessary to correct these glaring failures is a farce. What is happening in America today is something that has never happened before in recorded history: *Total confrontation.* The lies are obvious. The machinery is laid bare. All Americans are being shoved by the deadweight of a broken control machine right in front of each other's faces. Like it or not they cannot choose but see and hear each other. How many Americans will survive a total confront?

In Last Resort the Truth

The scene is Grant Park Chicago 1968. A full-scale model of *The Mayflower* with American flags for sails has been set up. A. J. in his Uncle Sam suit steps to a mike on the deck.

"Ladies and gentlemen it is my coveted privilege and deep honor to introduce to you the distinguished Senator and former Justice of the Supreme Court Homer Mandrill known to his many friends as the Purple Better One. No doubt most of you are familiar with a book called *African Genesis* written by Robert Ardrey a native son of Chicago and I may add a true son of America. I quote from Mr. Ardrey's penetrating work: 'When I was a boy in Chicago I attended the Sunday School of a neighborhood Presbyterian church. I recall our Wednesday-night meetings with the simplest nostalgia. We would meet in the basement. There would be a short prayer and a shorter benediction. And we would turn out all the lights and in total darkness hit each other with chairs.'

"Mr. Ardrey's early training tempered his character to face and make known the truth about the origins and nature of mankind. 'Not in innocence and not in Asia was mankind born. The home of our fathers was the African highland on a sky-swept savannah glowing with menace. The most significant of all our gifts was the legacy bequeathed us by our immediate forebears a race of terrestrial, flesh-eating, killer apes. . . . Raymond A. Dart of the University of Johannesburg was the strident voice from South Africa that would prove the southern ape to be the human ancestor. Dart put forward the simple thesis that Man emerged from the anthropoid background for one reason only: because he was a killer. A rock, a stick, a heavy bone was to our ancestral killer ape the margin of survival. . . . And he said that since we had tried everything else we might in last resort try the truth. . . . Man's original nature imposes itself on any human solution.'

"The aggressive southern ape suh, glowing with menace, fought your battles on the perilous veldts of Africa 500,000 years ago. Had he not done so you would not be living here in this great city in this great land of America raising your happy families in peace and prosperity. Who more fitted to represent our glorious Simian heritage than Homer Mandrill himself a descendant of that illustrious line? Who else can restore to this nation the spirit of true conservatism that imposes itself on any human solution? What candidate is better fitted for the highest office in the land at a time when this great republic is threatened by enemies foreign and domestic? Actually there can be only one candidate: the Purple Better One your future President."

To *The Battle Hymn of the Republic* an American flag is drawn aside revealing a purple-assed mandrill (thunderous applause). Led to the mike by Secret Service men in dark suits that bulge suggestively here and there the Purple Better One blinks in bewilderment.

The Technician mixes a bicarbonate of soda and belches into his hand. He is sitting in front of three instrument panels, one labeled P.A. for Purple Ass, one labeled A. for Audience, a third P. for Police. (Crude experiments with rhesus monkeys have demonstrated that small currents of electricity passed through electrodes into the appropriate brain areas can elicit any emotional or visceral response: rage, fear, sexuality, vomiting, sleep, defecation. No doubt with further experimentation these techniques will be perfected and electro-magnetic fields will supersede the use of actual electrodes imbedded in the brain.) He adjusts dials as Homer's mouth moves to a dubbed speech from directional mikes. The features of other candidates are projected onto Homer's face from a laser installation across the park so that he seems to embody and absorb them all.

"At this dark hour in the history of the republic there are grave questions troubling all our hearts. I pledge myself to answer these questions. One question is the war in Vietnam which is not only a war but a holy crusade against the godless forces of international communism. And I say to you if these forces are not contained they will engulf us all." (Thunderous applause.) "And I flatly accuse the administration of criminal diffidence in the use of atomic weapons. Are we going to turn a red white and blue ass to the enemy?" (No! No! No!) "Are we going to fight through to victory at any cost?" (Yes! Yes! Yes!) "I say to you we will win if it takes ten years. We will win if we have to police every blade of grass and every gook in Vietnam." (Thunderous applause.) "And after that we are going to wade in and take care of Chairman Mao and his gang of cutthroat slave drivers." (Thunderous applause.) "And if any country shall open its mouth to carp at the great American task well a single back-handed blow from our mighty Seventh Fleet will silence that impotent puppet of Moscow and Peking.

"Another question is so-called Black Power. I want to go on record as saying I am a true friend to all good Darkies everywhere." (To wild applause a picture of the world-famous statue in Natchitoches Louisiana flashes on screen. As you all know this statue shows a good old Darkie with his hat in his hand and is dedicated to All Good Darkies Everywhere.) Homer's voice chokes with emotion and tears drip off his purple nose. "Why when I was fourteen years old our old yard Nigrah Rover Jones got runned over by a laundry truck and I cried my decent American heart out. And I have a deep conviction that the overwhelming majority of Nigrahs in this country is good Darkies like Rover Jones. However we know that there is in this country today another kind of Nigrah and as long as there is a gas pump handy we all know the answer to that." (Thunderous applause.) "And I would like to say this to followers of the Jewish religion. Always remember we like nice Jews with Jew jokes. As for Nigger-loving communistic agitating Sheenies well just watch yourself Jew boy or we'll cut the rest of it off." (That's telling em Homer.) What about the legalization of marijuana? "Marijuana! Marijuana! Why that's deadlier than cocaine. And what are we going to do about the vile America-hating hoodlums who call themselves hippies, Yippies, and chippies? We are going to put this scum behind bars like the animals they are." (Thunderous applause.) "And I'll tell you something else. A bunch of queers, dope freaks, and degenerate dirty writers is living in foreign lands under the protection of American passports from the vantage point of which they do not hesitate to spit their filth on Old Glory. Well we're going to pull the passports off those dope freaks." (The Technician pushes a sex button and the Simian begins to masturbate.) "Bring them back here and teach them to act like decent Americans." (The Simian emisses, hitting the lens of a Life-Time photographer.) "And I denounce as Communist-inspired the rumors that the dollar collapsed in 1959. I pledge myself to turn the clock back to 1899 when a silver dollar bought a steak dinner and a good piece of ass." (Thunderous applause as a plane writes September 17, 1899, across the sky in smoke.) "I have heard it said that this is a lawless nation that if all the laws in this land were truly enforced we would have thirty percent of the population in jail and the remaining seventy percent on the cops. I say to you if there is infection in this great land it must be cut out by the roots. We will not fall into slack-assed permissive anarchism. I pledge myself to uphold the laws of America and to enforce these hollowed statutes on all violators regardless of race, color, creed or position." (Thunderous applause.) "We will overcome all our enemies foreign and domestic and stay armed to the teeth for years, decades, centuries."

A phalanx of blue-helmeted cops shoulder through the crowd. They stop in front of the deck. The lead cop looks up at A. J. and demands: "Let's see your permits for that purple-assed son of a bitch."

"Permits? We don't have any permits. We don't have to show you any stinking permits. You are talking suh to the future President of America."

The lead cop takes a slip of paper from his shirt pocket and reads MUNICIPAL CODE OF CHICAGO . . . Chapter 98, Section 14: "No person shall permit any dangerous animal to run at large, nor lead any such animal with a chain, rope, or other appliance, whether such animal be muzzled or unmuzzled, in any public way or public place." He folds the paper and shoves it back into his shirt pocket. He points at the Purple Better One. "It's dangerous and we got orders to remove it."

A cop steps forward with a net. The Technician shoves the rage dial all the way up. Screaming, farting, snarling, the Simian leaps off the deck onto the startled officer who staggers back and goes down thrashing wildly on the ground while his fellow pigs stand helpless and baffled not daring to risk a shot for fear of killing their comrade. Finally the cop heaves himself to his feet and throws off the Simian. Panting, bleeding, he stands there his eyes wild. With a scream of rage the Purple Better One throws himself at another patrolman who fires two panicky shots which miss the Simian and crash through a window of the Hilton in the campaign headquarters of a conservative Southern candidate. A photographer from The London Times is riddled with bullets by Secret Service men under the misconception he has fired from a gun concealed in his camera. The cop throws his left arm in front of his face. The Simian sinks his canines into the cop's arm. The cop presses his gun against the Simian's chest and pumps in four bullets. Homer Mandrill thuds to the bloody grass, ejaculates, excretes and dies. A. J. points a finger at the cop.

"Arrest that pig!" he screams. "Seize the assassin!"

A. J. was held in $100,000 bail which he posted in cash out of his pocket. Further disturbances erupted at the funeral when a band of vigilantes who call themselves the White Hunters attempted to desecrate the flag-draped body as it was carried in solemn procession through Lincoln Park on the way to its final resting place in Grant Park. The hoodlums were beaten off by A. J.'s guard of Korean Karate experts. The Daughters of the American Revolution who had gathered in front of the Sheraton to protest the legalization of marijuana were charged by police screaming, "Chippies! Chippies! Chippies!" And savagely clubbed to the sidewalk in a litter of diamonds, teeth, blood, mink stoles and handbags.

As the Simian was laid to rest under a silver replica of *The Mayflower* a statue of the Purple Better One in solid gold at the helm, A. J. called for five minutes of silent prayer in memory of our beloved candidate, "Cut down in Grant Park by the bullets of an assassin. . . . A Communistic Jew Nigger inflamed to madness by injections of marijuana. . . . The fact that the assassin had, with diabolical cunning, disguised himself as a police officer indicates the workings of a far-flung communistic plot the tentacles of which may reach into the White House itself. This foul crime shrieks to high heaven. We will not rest until the higher-ups are brought to justice whoever and wherever they may be. I pledge myself to name a suitable and worthy successor. We will overcome. We will realize the aspirations and dreams that every American cherishes in his heart. The American dream can be must be and will be realized. I say to you that Grant Park will be a shrine for all future Americans. In the words of the all-American poet James Whitcomb Riley

'Freedom shall a while repair
'To dwell a weeping hermit there.' "

[November, 1968]

In a Pig's Eye

by John Sack

Be a Chicago pig policeman! Carry a pistol and sleep until noon! Zzz . . . Zzz. . . . On the other hand, he had arrived home at four in the morning, a little mote of CS tear gas still chewing at his throat like cayenne pepper or like sunburn on his shoulders, his Irish eyes still smarting, tired: the wounds of another night of shoving the scroungers from Lincoln Park. "Yippies again" or "Hippies again," he had muttered to Mama, slipping beneath the sheets with the yellow rose of Texas pattern, the $16.92 blanket, the Cross, and hearing his wife answer, *"Ish,"* the random syllable over and above which she had nothing to say of Chicago's disgraceful new visitors. A minute later, and Chicago policeman number 14020 was sleeping—*zzz*.

Now it was twelve noon and "Mama" was in the kitchen to cook scrambled eggs and venison, the kids having had Cheerios already and Winnie a biscuit-bone—*How about Lady! Lassie! Brownie!* the kids all had yelled at him when the puppy arrived, but 14020 had answered, "Those names are so *ordinary.*" A row of the children's photographs, tinted, like *Désirée,* the movie, in purples and pinks, hung in his living room, once a year the Graphic man coming to hang up a bedsheet and wheedle, "Now, let's have a smile!" Behind glass in his dining room, like a Delft set in a whatnot, was 14020's family library, where what he loved best was *The Best-Loved Poems of the American People.* In the event of subversion one could probably break the glass with an ice hammer to listen to America singing. *Listen my children and you shall hear*—a cobblestone bridge and a chiarascuro horse and rider had risen in 14020's mind's eye on reading this. *In fourteen hundred ninety-two*— *If a task is once begun*— *Lord, let me live like a regular man*— *Oh, say, can you see, by the dawn's early light*—a dewy distillate of the atmosphere that any American boy breathes from birth. Once in school the future patrolman had gotten a D in English from his nattily dressed teacher, rhapsodic quoter of Shelley, toucher of boys' hairless elbows, suspected fairy ("If you stay after school," his friends had advised him merrily, "you'll get an A")—had gotten a D for electing to memorize poetry from *The Best-Loved Poems.* The girls in class had cunningly chosen things from Shelley, but *Hail to thee, blithe birdie* wasn't his coffee-cup and 14020 had sung instead of the land where the venison grows. "*Oh,*" he had begun—"*Oh the north countree is a hard countree,*" old Momo at the front of the room pricking up his delicate ears—"*Oh, tough as a steak was Yukon Jake, Hard-boiled as a picnic egg! He washed his shirt in the Klondike dirt, And drank his rum by the keg,*" a weak electrical impulse going down the Teach's elegant fingers and translating into a "D" at his manicured nails. What the hell—14020 wouldn't be going to Oxford anyway, but to police academy.

Reader, if you would know the psychology of Chicago's normative fuzz, get a copy of *The Best-Loved Poems of the American People* (Garden City, 1936). Get everything else whose tattered and torn bindings bear the same Dewey decimal number and shred 'em, pestle 'em into a powder, wet 'em into a paste, water 'em into a pulp, and warm 'em inside a stove set at 98.6 degrees. And—*voilà,* you've done it, there you've got a pot of Chicago copkopf, homemade psyche, the grey stuff of the second city's blue, a Cream of Wheat of American attitudes that is 192 years old. So thick yet so easily permeable is this oatmeal that no Irish or Polish farmer's heart is actually needed to pump blood to its farthermost cells. Seventy to eighty times a minute a new infusion of oxygen brings life to the most cachectic of America's tried and truisms—*Clean behind your ears*— *Mabel, Mabel, if you're able*— *Do not write "fuck" on your forehead*— *Spare the rod and spoil the child*— *What if your sister marries one*— *Cross at the green not in between*— *Eat your spinach*— *Bathe*— the neat antimacassar rules of the lower middle class: a class, remember, which, with its social inferiors, is a full ninety percent of America's people. Flower children, wearers of wampum, you in omega symbols and ankh crosses, whatever: alas, the different drummer you march to plays in a small chamber orchestra, the hundreds of millions hum the same respectable Oms as Chicago's police. And if these police, at times, tend to forget which are society's laws and which are society's manners—well, would you blame them?

"John! Breakfast is ready, John!" Mama was calling upstairs and 14020 arose, shaved, slipped into his blue police trousers with the Roosevelt era width, buckled on his pistol, nightstick, handcuffs, and Mace, breakfasted on venison, left. "Be careful, John," his wife called after him, as always, and 14020 became another of the visored thousands that the young people knew as "Pigs."

One day during the Convention, a squad of Chicago policemen sat around one of those outdoor tables, X's of redwood beneath it, bolts as big as I-beam rivets, that was a stone's throw—no, a bit farther—from the pasture where the young people, or Yippies, the papers called them, lay in Lincoln Park. Comers and goers to this party of finger cymbalists, *Rat*-readers, rappers, tambourine players, and catnappers went by these ten policemen often, and even their spinster aunts in Kansas would not have cluck-clucked so severely at the passing scene as did these 180-to-220-pound patrolmen. "Hmf! I don't think she should be in a miniskirt," a squad member said as a girl walked by. "Take it to the farm and cultivate it," another snickered, at a Yippie with a pumpkin-colored helmet where all decent people wore a fedora. "*That woman*—" another gasped as a girl in a sweater passed them. "*She doesn't have a brassiere on!*" "Patrio— what do they call it? Patriotism," another of the tittle-tattles said, as boys and girls with a blood-spattered flag of Chicago walked by. "Love of your country. Hmf!"

Lying on the grass (for there were no wastebaskets now in the park, the young people had built up council fires in several and Chicago had removed them all)—littering the area around the picnic table were the *Seed, Militant,* Yippie and other periodicals that the squad had been reading not so much to understand the visitors in Lincoln Park as to have chapters and verses by which to censure them. Typical of these throwaways was a Yippie thing some of whose eighteen demands were so blandly sensible that the Democratic platform itself may have adopted them, *9. A conservation program [for] preserving our natural resources. 13. A program [for] cable television.* Other demands had a pedigree in philosophy's history as old as Diogenes, *15. We believe that people should fuck all the time, anytime,* or a partisan in America of the 1960's as respectable as Erich Fromm, *7. The Abolition of pay housing, pay media, pay transportation, pay food, pay education, pay clothing, pay medical help, and pay toilets.* But the joyous forms in which the Yippies put these ideas had acted as rubber stoppers in the policemen's decorous ears, denying all ingress of content. "Yeah, I saw that thing," a Jewish patrolman at the picnic table was telling another. "It said everybody should eff. *You* know," he said, turning to a woman in plain clothes with a LOVE charm between her great bosoms, a policewoman who lowered her eyes demurely to indicate to the squad: she knew. "It isn't so bad if you think those words. But to print them!"

"Any time. Any place. Anyone you want," an Irish patrolman said in dismay.

"What amazes me," the Jewish one went on, "they don't want to work! They want everything handed to them! Shazam! A dinner. Shazam! A car. Shazam! A trip to Miami. But what do they do to earn these?"

"Like they say," the Irishman again. "Some people got to plant food and some people got to dig ditches." For after all, doesn't it say in *The Best-Loved Poems of the American People,*

> *If you want to fill a place*
> *And be useful to the race,*
> *Just get up and take a brace—*
> *Do it now!*

In late afternoon, a Yippie girl on a bicycle came by this redwood table to cry at Chicago's constabulary, "*Pigs!*" And crouching over the handlebars she then whizzed away in Tour de France posture in case the police escalated by hurling a .38 pistol at her pretty brunette head, or firing it. At other times the breeze brought to the squad's ears the insulting cries of "*Soo . . . ie*" and "*Oink oink oink!*" At these, the squad of police chuckled and kept playing hearts. It has been alleged that the suid metaphors got, at last, under the policemen's skins, provoking them to vengeance on Wednesday—absurd. *For sticks and stones may break my bones but names will tra-la la-la*—a worthy old American axiom, that, and if Longfellow's authorship can be shown it might run under the "Inspiration" category in the next, or forty-seventh, printing, of *The B.L.P. of the A.P.* Accordingly, it had a lifetime tenure in every cop's seat of reason, and anyhow: all in the squad could see where in Lincoln Park the pigs really groveled, for whose toes hadn't been washed in one half week? "They sleep on the grass and they call *us* the pigs," an officer at the picnic table said, not at all angry but only amazed at man's great capacity to deceive himself.

Nor did sticks and stones themselves, plastic bags of water, bottles, any of these rile the policemen beyond all endurance as they arched across the stars at eleven that night, the Lincoln Park closing time. "Careful. Here comes a big one," a man in the squad would say, as innocent of indignation as a little kid in Michigan's surf: for he sensibly jests at Budweiser cans who has felt switchblade knives and 22-caliber lead. At midnight when it moved out in a skirmish line, its CS tear gas ahead, its German shepherds on leashes, its CS-infested park as eerie as Spotsylvania in the floodlights of fire trucks, the squad of Chicago police was as casual as G.I.'s on a pick-up-the-cigarettes call, shuffling, chewing their gum, making little jokes like "Push me on into battle, Sergeant." Of anger, the police had as little as the "angry ocean" has whenever it beats on a seawall or shipwrecks a sailor. Spit on the flag, holler "Up yours" to his sister, rape a mother superior, these were the deeds to make an American angry: but a misdemeanor in Lincoln Park was just another day, another dollar. Be wary of the pathetic fallacy: the throw of the tear gas or the heavy fall of the nightstick is not necessarily a passionate act. At one in the morning as the last weeping trespasser fled to the streets of Old Town, the squad was asking serenely, "What do you say? Now? Thank you, Sergeant! Light 'em up!" And out of its blue pockets came the L&Ms and the Panatellas.

Insouciant the police could be, for they recognized that the challenge to their values arose from a too tiny minority of America to pay much attention to. Conversely, the challengers in Lincoln Park had to rage against the "*Facist*" and "*SS*" bullyboys or else resign themselves to the terrible truth that Chicago's police did represent the will of Chicago's people. To realize this, the young people only had to listen in Lincoln Park to the noisy tribunes of the millions of Americans who surrounded them, as millions of white corpuscles surround a germ. Men in their undershirts, women in Shalimar perfume, soldiers in Vietnam insignia:

"All your brothers and sisters are being killed there and you're talking against them!"

"If one American dies by *any* cause, *any* cause, you ought to support him!"

"You people got no right to wave a Communist flag in the United States of America! Because they got a right to cut you down, just like in *Doctor Zhivago!*"

"I'm proud of this country, boy! This is the greatest country in the world!"

"Get out of this country!"

Indeed, the young people just had to look at their subconscious selves to see, even there, the whalebone ethics of America, much as their manifestos damned it. One afternoon, the most awful apprehensions of the cardplayers at the redwood table had really been set to materialize: as a Yippie boy whispered to another, "We got forty chicks who say they'll groove!" For forty girls had vowed to divest themselves of Levis and society's trammels to participate today in a Yippie "ball-in," appropriately in the ball field of Lincoln Park—forty suntanned couples had pledged themselves to roll in the outfield as bare and as gloriously brown as the other team's discarded mitts. Revolution! And equity as well as philosophy was on Yippie's side: society would be monstrous if pretty girls can be tear-gassed and billy-sticked in a public park but cannot be equally and oppositely loved in commiseration. At one o'clock the organizers of this baseball diamond ball—one, a Yippie boy with glasses both of whose hinges had been supplanted by thick wads of adhesive tape, the other with a chain of pop-tops as a brim to a Rip Van Winkle hat—were passing among the Yippie girls to announce: it was starting time, the hour to put their pelvises where all their mouths were. "You people start moving to the ball park," the organizers said. Titters of "You go ahead. We'll watch," were all they heard until, with a heavy heart, the Yippie boys realized that the ball-in had dwindled to a game of one-o-cat and Rip Van Winkle would have to go it alone with his girl friend under a black oak. "We're going to start it here," he told her. "You're the unlucky victim."

"Thanks a lo . . . t."

Rip sat beside her to whisper in her earringed ear.

"*Oh*," the girl answered him. "Blush blush!"

Rip kissed her prettily on her milky cheek.

"Oh, where is my mo . . . ther?"

Rip looked hurt as a boy from the Aardvark theatre went by and gave her a promotional piece.

"*Bob Dylan. Don't Look Back*," she started to read cheerfully to Rip Van Winkle. "*So memorable that it rings in the mind for a long time afterwards! The picture is a must for Dylan fans! A fascinating picture!* You know, we should go see it. . . ." A virgin, the unlucky victim had fooled her mother and father that her reputation would be safe today at a girl friend's home in Chicago. Her father worked at Chicago's waterworks, where the rioters' fires in April had lowered the water pressure to where citizens couldn't bathe and raised her father's blood pressure to where he was voting for Wallace. Whenever the victim argued with him he merely said, "Eat your food."

"Screw it," the Yippie boy with adhesive tape on his glasses said. "I'm going to split and go back to New York City. This is bombing out."

And out beyond the outfield fence the same virtuous squad of cops waited, alerted, ready to use their handcuffs to practice what the American people preached, what the Yippies themselves didn't dare to say they secretly believed.

Another afternoon, the young people swept from Lincoln Park to walk south to confront the enemy at his very castle, his GHQ downtown, his pigsty central. Had they chrysanthemums, the colorful boys and girls would have seemed to be en route to a football game as they yelled things like *"Two! Four! Six! Eight! We don't want a po-lice-state!"* At hotel doors the Democratic delegates sat in their wheelchairs, the Ringer's solution dripping from bottles into their arms, their pulse rates ten to twenty times a minute. "What do you think, John?" an Idaho lady asked her delegate husband as the young people passed.

"I think dammit! Look at him there—he hasn't washed his hair in a month!"

"Up against the wall," the young people shouted as they continued down State Street, some wearing beards, some doing Hopi dances, some saying oms. Outstanding among them in NBC and CBS's eyes was a Berkeley girl who sat pickaback on one sturdy boy after another, radiantly smiling, holding aloft a red flag of revolution—a girl in a khaki uniform, a full canteen on her pistol belt. Few of the young in Chicago would work as hard as this living incarnation of socialist realism to win to Revolution's banners the hearts and minds of the city's bourgeois police. *"Look me in the eye, officer,"* she would say bravely as they stood in ranks, confronting them as a sergeant might. "I'm sorry you work over-time today—*but I want to free the people! You know what I mean, don't you?"* Once, one of these patrolmen had really whispered back, "I'm with you, sister," the girl in khaki smiling angelically and stroking his Negro face. But there had been just one.

Already at pigsty central the police were in elbow-to-elbow ranks to safeguard its $50 windows and window displays of Cyclops' or the Statue of Liberty's fingerprints. Therefore it may seem strange that the pied piper whom the glassy eyes of NBC and CBS discovered at the very vanguard of that parade was plainly a Chicago cop, Patrolman Ray Walsh. True, it was excellent tactics to lead these potential troublemakers down a full three-and-a-half miles of State Street till their tired feet conspired with their fallacious sense of having accomplished things to add up into inertia. And to solace the scared pedestrians was an errand that Walsh could be proud of: even the deputy commander with his major's leaves, his electric megaphone, his eyes darting up and about like a Christian in the lion arena, even he had stopped to sympathize with a lady shopper who wanted to flee before the light was green, "Lady, what can I tell you?" And there was a need for Walsh to keep the revolution on its allotted half of the sidewalk. But even so, Walsh was ashamed to have to keep cadence with an army whose very guidons announced its arrant un-Americanism. *"This in my own city,"* he would say to other patrolmen. At night all week he would sit at home in blue police trousers and loden après-ski boots to watch on a color television screen as large as a Delacroix as young people fought his fellow officers in Chicago's streets and chanted at Walter Cronkite, *"The whole—world's—watching!"*

"Uh," his Irish wife had commented as she turned from the shameful

things on the television to Pall Malls and Schlitz on the sofa table. "And today I saw *nuns* there! I see the nuns doing that," she continued, "instead of going home and saying their rosary, my respect for them isn't so great!"

"It makes you kind of sick inside," Walsh had agreed, drinking some Schlitz. Before the week had ended he was to write to Daley about it:

Dear Mayor Daley!

After all your meticulous and wonderful plans to cater to the Democratic convention here, you have to have it spoiled by a handful of men, tyrannical, Communists, leading young men and women into fights and riots with my fellow brothers in Blue.

Mr. Mayor, I'm an ex-serviceman, I have seen action in Korea and it took a lot of will power to control myself from pulling down the Communist flag and everything it stood for. . . .

"It's enough to make you want to quit," he was saying now to Patrolman Steve Stukel. All of Walsh's squad was marching along with the Communists today.

"Twenty-five months over there," Vietnam, "and then I got to see this," Stukel replied. *I'm tired,* he was thinking, *I'm hot, if these people get violent, I'm going to get violent also!*

"I figure, ninety percent of these kids are on dope, one kind or another," said Patrolman George Wertz. He wondered aloud what the puissant chemical was that had fixed that radiant smile on the girl in khaki for lo! already two miles.

"Probably not LSD," Walsh said. "But something like Dexedrine, one of those barbiturates."

"Stimulants," Wertz corrected him.

"Stimulants," Walsh agreed.

"*Revolution! Now!*" the young people screamed as they walked the last mile and a half to the pigsty central. If it weren't for these malcontents it would be Wertz's weekend: a sunny day, a lovely day at Adventureland, no doubt, the cotton candy, the yellow taffy, the children all on the rolly—he called it—coaster saying "*Ooh*" and "*Ah*" ("Daddy," they had asked him once, "can we go on the big one?" "No," Wertz had answered, and they had never asked again). Or else because of the children—and Wertz couldn't blame them, really—today he could dedicate to the toilet seat, to moving it out of harm's way of the bathroom door. It was *crack* all morning and afternoon as the children went to "wash their hands" and *crack* in the other direction as the children went out again. Would you believe it? white, rose, green, beige, toilet seats he had bought at Sears, a dozen at least, $6 apiece, and *crack—crack—crack*—in two or three months apiece they had busted off their hinges, "Good morning, I want to buy another toilet seat." Putting on a spring to lift the seat automatically when the children forgot to—dangerous, one fast *crack* and there would go the water tank. Taking down the bathroom door—now *really,* and even making the door narrower was impractical, how then could he bring in his brand-new bathtub on some other weekend? Right now Wertz's expedient was to stand the toilet seat on the bathroom's mosaic floor for children to put on, take off, as required, like a Chicago telephone book at dinner. It was an indecent situation, though, one that a weekend with a blowtorch and some plumber's lead could rectify if these people were not marching on headquarters under a red banner and crying out, "*Revolution! Now!*"

"Is that a VC flag?" Walsh was saying now to Stukel.

"They got variations," Stukel answered sullenly.

In a way, it was saintly restraint above and beyond the call of their captains for Walsh, the Korean veteran, Stukel, the Vietnam veteran, and Wertz to walk so amenably under the flag of their enemy all afternoon, but duty required them to insure that the orderly flow on Chicago's sidewalks not be impeded by the march. "Now you people are going to be arrested—" even the deputy commander kept shouting it through his megaphone—"arrested, if you take up more than half of the sidewalk," his voice at times obsequious, at other times edgy, in its passion that not a moment be lost in any pedestrian's progress up State Street to Marshall Field's, to Walgreen's, to Ess & Abe Distinctive Ladies Apparel, to Pickard Heim Beauty School, to Loft's, to *Rosemary's Baby,* or to Frank-burger to buy a Choc-o-Shake. This above all, that the relish jar be delivered, that the dress advertising copy be ready by five, and that the $7.50 necktie be bought before the party tonight! One might argue it was these pedestrians that the young people had to revolt against if they're to get a sane society: with a husky cry of "Up against the wall, mothers and fathers," disobeying the deputy commander, snapping out in Zengakuren snakelines, using the flagpole like a Samurai sword and laying about, the boys and girls should have driven all those pedestrians into the lake to be eaten alive by alewives. But so few yards had they crawled from the taffeta bassinets of America that in these, the most meaningful of their encounters in August, instinctively the young people sided one hundred percent with Chicago's police. "Now remember," a boy with a red shirt repeated into his microphone, mistakenly. "We're not against the people who use this street! So walk on the inside of the sidewalk," repeating it, repeating it, until by the squeal of his amplified voice he had half hypnotized himself. "The *in*-side of the *side*-walk, the *in*-side of the *side*-walk," his words became the singsong of a Hadacol salesman as Chicago, unobstructed, hurried on to its sales counters, and to its blotter-covered desks.

"*Your mother sucks . . .*"

It was that false allegation, to Stukel, the Vietnam veteran, that in one split second shattered the unanimity of the young people, the pedestrians, and Chicago's police. *You little*—and Stukel now charged at that offender with his fist clenched, his pistol, his nightstick, his Mace undeployed.

Lewd literature, dirt under fingernails, hair under armpits, sandals where all nice people had gartered socks, even the flag of those odious insurgents who once had shot his helicopter down—all of this he had endured, even the cries of *"Pig"* had passed out of Stukel's other ear. *But nobody says that about my Mother,* not in America he doesn't! Grand old Mother who cooked him spaghetti, the Mother whom he had given on Mother's day a white rose and a dozen red—Mother! Mother who told him stories like, "Why are there just two pallbearers at a Polish funeral? *Because,"* Mother had blurted, too eager to get to the punch line to listen to Stukel's guesses—"because there are just two handles on a garbage can!" *How many buttons are missing today? Nobody knows but Mother. How many playthings are strewn in her way? Nobody knows but Mother.* Mother who is spelled mother, Mother who married dear old—*Take that! And that! And that! And that!*

But before Stukel could strike out to incite a melee on State Street, a sergeant took his shoulder and ordered him, "Forget it." Stukel tried to forget it. The great parade continued on past pigsty central's $50 windows with no nasty incidents—today, half of the sidewalk scrupulously open.

It was Wednesday that the city shook. No thumb in a lovable old Irish sergeant's eye or knee in his groin precipitated it: rather, it began when a boy abused a quite inanimate object. "In the later nineteenth century," Wells says in *The Outline of History* in a chapter on England and France and Germany, "it would have aroused far less hostility to have jeered at God than to have jeered at one of those strange beings, England or France or Germany." And at Wednesday afternoon's rally in Chicago when a speaker suddenly asked, *"What is going on over there,"* and fifteen thousand people looked to their left to see a boy lower a sheet of Nylanin fabric from a wooden pole, the irrepressible strains of *"Say, does that star-spangled banner still wave"* did surge through the Cream of Wheat subconscious of a squad of Chicago policemen, who instinctively charged. Lumber, pieces of asphalt, Rheingold, even a smoke bomb in a vegetable can drove the American patriots back, but it was an item wrapped in Saran material that was really to teach the Department to Know Their Enemy. Sailing ever so lightly toward the squad, splashing apart on the grass, emitting an indisputable odor, the Saran bag brought a mortally horrified shout to the lips of one patrolman. "It's a bag of shit! They're shitting in bags and throwing it!"

Word of this utmost atrocity spread in the ranks of Chicago's police as speedily as the slices did of Johnson's birthday cake at the other side of the city. "It is shit!"

"It is what?"

"It is shit! In the plastic bags!"

"It is shit? *Be careful, there is shit in the plastic bags!"*

"They are animals. . . ."

Two minutes later, the first of the afternoon and evening's one hundred casualties lay on Chicago's grass, a river of blood on his face as though it had cracked like an oyster shell. America's unseen audience who needed no ABC that night for its home entertainment was, perhaps, not aware: to most of Chicago's policemen the targets of their heavy clubs were not Americans but desecrators of America's red white and blue, not human beings but African shit-kicking chimpanzees. It was for America's most cherished beliefs—not for Nazi piggery, sadism, vengeance, relief—that the blows descended. For a young boy to resist, to argue, even to offer excuses—to Chicago's policemen this was intolerable, that a kid should persist in recalcitrance even as the very incarnations of Americanism arrayed themselves before him in a column of blue. Let those who would now demur that the vast majority of *"they"* whose blood was to splatter on Michigan Avenue were innocent citizens—let them carry that argument to where it is still needed: to Asia, where not an American rifle company or air wing couldn't use that caveat. But those who would now find fault with Chicago's police for their extremism in defense of Americanism shall have to vote for Cleaver this month to vote for a Presidential candidate who concurs. As for other Americans, the polls are that 78.7 percent of our neighbors do not consider that Chicago used excessive force. Understandably: it is for these citizens' gods the police did battle, beating the heads that the more hidden persuaders of American society had evidently not reached.

Yet even in most young people the values of the middle classes had trickled. All secondhand was their revolution, rags and textbook tags out of other people's risings in 1848, 1917, the 1930's: cries of "Scab" in support of strikers who only wanted in on the gravy, barricades of Volkswagens that the police could walk by, wallpaper newspapers with no Chicago walls to plaster them on, and automobile honks of "Hell no—We won't go" which were a simple inversion of "Algérie—Française." All of these and Pamplona's bravado of being as close to the bulls as possible even as you're running away. But most of these summer vacationers, of Cheerios had their bones been built: and even the smiling girl in khaki, radiant waver of red, revolutionary extraordinary, could be seen in Chicago as Humphrey began his "I proudly accept . . ." speech and as a thousand voters of the future fled up the avenue from CS clouds—be seen setting against the sneezing, wheezing, weeping tide of humanity to get to a truck with the words, Good Humor. The smiling girl asked there, "Do you have a chocolate fudge cake?"

"No. We only have Popsicles."

"I wanted a chocolate fudge cake."

"Popsicles is all we have."

"No kind of ice cream, then?"

"Nothing but Popsicles."

"*Would you believe it,*" a boy going by remarked. "We're running from tear gas and she's buying Popsicles. The essence of capitalism!"

Reportedly they are now radicalized. Ten, fifteen, twenty years, the theory is, and these boys and girls will be out carrying rifles in America's own Sierra Maestras. Maybe. Let us hope so, anyhow. But the Chicago that has radicalized many has reactionalized twice as many, and these people are mighty not only in numbers but in nightsticks, pistols, CS, armored vehicles, atomic bombs, and, as Chicago teaches, in their readiness to use them—and these people in November vote. Humphrey was nominated and undermined in Chicago, and Nixon will be elected if Super-Nixon allows it: and will become the fifth President to win immortality on Rushmore, in granite with the great ones. Washington at Valley Forge, Jefferson the egalitarian, Lincoln born in a Western cabin, Roosevelt with his stick—all embodied in their physical flesh the very essence of America of their generation. And now Nixon the organization man, Rotary luncheon speaker, adapter, knower of Yukon poetry, owner of dogs, Nixon whom no President since 1920 has equalled in inability to see past the slipcover sensibilities of the middle class. Nixon who even relaxes with the very heart of America thumping outside his hotel room in red neon letters: CARS. Nixon by whose signature the virtues of Chicago's policemen and of their one or two hundred million wards will be ironly implemented in the 1970's— *Law and order— Do not be naughty— Spare the rod and spoil the child— Obey— Eat your spinach— Fit in— Support your local police.*

[November, 1968]

Part II

The Grass Roots of "Now"

Come Alive, America

by Charles and Bonnie Remsberg

In the World Headquarters of the Pepsi-Cola Company, an eleven-story glass-and-aluminum structure known to New Yorkers as the Joan Crawford Building, a group of executives met not long ago to discuss a new idea for product promotion. Their goal was to sell more Pepsi-Cola and also to gain for the soft drink a larger place in the hearts and minds of the American people.

What they proposed was a contest. They planned a national sweepstakes of the just-fill-in-the-blank-nothing-to-buy-no-jingle-to-write variety. The grand prize of the contest was to be the *ne plus ultra* for enterprises of this sort, and a discussion of it consumed much of the creative energies of the sales-promotion staff. The gift of a South Sea island was ruled out ("too unreal for general public identification"). So was an around-the-world cruise for two (too few promotable opportunities).

A Pepsi-Cola spokesman said, "We're going to hit people where they live. And what hits them hard, *really* hard? Groceries!"

The winner of the contest and his entire family, wearing roller skates if they so desired, would be turned loose in a supermarket and permitted to keep all the foodstuffs they could take from the shelves and deposit on the check-out counters in the space of thirty minutes. Pepsi executives would pick up the tab on the spot, handing the store manager a negotiable check and a "photogenic" five-foot-long nonnegotiable blowup that he could "keep forever."

According to the press release announcing this event, there would be children and adults "scurrying helter-skelter through the empty aisles of a store, racing against the clock . . . the blur of sprinting slacks and maybe even shorts . . . perhaps a relay system, using basketball tosses to get food from the shelves to the check-out counter . . . the facial expressions on the family's faces as they try to make split-second decisions on the most dollar-rewarding food choices to make . . . the looks on their faces as the check-out tape records higher and higher totals. . . ."

The press release was delivered to newspaper offices wrapped around a six-pound sirloin steak.

The papers printed stories of the promised event. There were television commercials that showed gasping families furiously grasping for packaged foods while crowds of spectators cheered. The word began to spread.

Very little was required of the people who entered the sweepstakes. They had to print their names and addresses (and the name and address of their "favorite retail outlet that sells Pepsi-Cola") on an entry blank and drop the blank into collection hoppers in supermarkets. Within two months, Pepsi-Cola had received 61,000,000 entries, thereby reportedly quadrupling the biggest response from any previous sweepstakes. From the entries, local Pepsi bottlers drew various low-echelon winners. They were guided in this by a Publicity Exploitation Kit which had been sent them by the home office. Many of the bottlers tumbled their group of entries in a cement mixer.

Most of the prizes at this stage consisted of gift certificates. But several entrants in each of the 525 Pepsi franchise areas were permitted "individual shopping sprees" in which they were allowed five, ten, or fifteen minutes to grab as many edibles and potables as possible.

After this prelude, the local bottlers shipped all the entries to the offices of D. L. Blair Corporation, an impartial contest-management company in New York. There, anonymous judges drew the names of fifty state grand-prize winners, each of whom reaped a year's supply of groceries, automotive service and accessories, and Pepsi, 2,496 full bottles of it, or, as one Pepsi official put it in an unguarded moment, "whatever the bladder can take."

Then finally, last July, when the nation's appetite had been properly whetted, Blair officials went back to the pile of entries and plucked out the name of the "top national winner."

It was Opal Miller, forty-seven, a seamstress who lives with her husband, Sharol, a paper-mill roustabout, and three of their nine children in

Taylorville, Illinois, population 8,801. Before the selection was announced to the public, a private investigator reported to Pepsi headquarters that Mrs. Miller was a brown-haired, bespectacled woman of "medium build," white, neat, clean, a "friendly neighbor" in an "average" neighborhood.

Mrs. Miller was called upon to make a statement. She took a pill to help curb her excitement and said, "I just can't believe I'm top. It musta been God's hand leading the hand that picked my entry. It's that miraculous."

Taylorville lies amid the cornfields and soybean patches of central Illinois. On the day before the Millers were to claim their winnings, the town was adorned as if for a holiday. Banners were hung in the courthouse square. They said: CONGRATULATIONS OPAL MILLER and WELCOME TO THE PEPSI-COLA CAPITAL OF THE WORLD. Bunting draped the light poles. The bank displayed a sign calling Mrs. Miller its "Luckiest Customer." The clothing store where she works set forth in red letters this message: LOOK! WE'RE BUSTIN' WITH PRIDE FOR OPAL MILLER!

At the intersection of Pepsi Boulevard and Miller Drive (the two major thoroughfares had been renamed for the occasion), visitors could inspect the modest supermarket where the event was to take place. There, drinking a Pepsi-Cola and surveying the new street markers from under an awning, was a greying, crew-cut man who resembled W. C. Fields. He was the mayor of Taylorville. He said that Taylorville was in the midst of "a volcano, a goodwill volcano.

"Nobody gets anything bad out of something like this, that's what's important. People here are thrilled. They realize this is the only time in their lives and the lifetime of Taylorville that they'll see something like this shopping spree come to pass. Some of the little towns around here are pretty jealous. We even had Miss America."

Miss America, whose four sponsors include the Pepsi-Cola Company, had consented to come to Taylorville as part of the preliminary celebrations. She received a gilded Key to the City and a serenade by a high-school band, which, as it turned out, had not learned how to play *Here She Comes, Miss America.*

"Those kids will probably never have an honor as great as welcoming Miss America," the mayor said.

Miss America had passed out autographed photographs of herself during a luncheon for local businessmen and neighboring mayors. One of the mayors confessed he needed a tranquilizer. After estimating that the Millers' grocery bill would hit $10,000, Miss America praised them as "the kind of people who preserve our American democracy."

The mayor said, "I think her visit, this whole shebang, will make Taylorville the Pepsi-Cola Capital of the World. Of course, we're already the Soybean Capital."

A short, ruddy man with a broad grin and a large tie clasp shaped like a paper clip emerged from the store. In a Brooklyn accent, he announced that he was Bob Windt, Director of Publicity for Pepsi.

"I just got back from a promotion thing in the Far East. The boss told me I wouldn't like this next assignment, Taylorville. But he was wrong. This is more fun than the time I took a horse into the Conrad Hilton Hotel in Chicago or when I had a guy box a kangaroo in 'Frisco. This is really my country down here." He looked down Pepsi Boulevard and smiled. "These are my people." The mayor smiled back.

"Inside the supermarket," Windt said, "there's a real human-interest drama." In honor of Mrs. Miller's winning and the attendant publicity, the store manager was financing a telephone call to the Millers' married daughter who was quartered on an Army base in Germany. The daughter was having a particularly difficult third pregnancy, and Mrs. Miller had hoped that Miss America might ease things by saying hello. But Miss A's chaperone had pointed out that the Queen's contract expressly forbade her to enter grocery stores. Windt explained: "Grocery stores downgrade the Miss America image." So Mr. and Mrs. Miller were placing the call sans celebrity, while a cameraman from nearby Springfield recorded the scene.

Windt had hoped for something more than a cameraman from Springfield. When he had walked away from the mayor, he said: "Frankly, the negative thing about all this is having it in central Illinois. If the winner had only been from Henderson, Nevada [twenty miles from Las Vegas], we'd have planned a three-day weekend and you'd have had to beat the news guys off with a club. Well, maybe the adrenalin will start flowing yet."

The store manager was having trouble completing the Millers' call; neither the daughter nor her spouse seemed to be at home. Mrs. Miller and her husband, who looked like the man in Grant Wood's "American Gothic," were busy in the manager's office figuring the transatlantic time difference and wondering where their daughter could be at so late an hour. (It was nine p.m. in Germany.) Finally Windt suggested they fake the call to accommodate the cameraman, and adjusted the receiver between them.

"Now, *action!*" he ordered. "Mrs. Miller, say something." Mrs. Miller stared blankly at the camera. "Anything . . . 'Hello, how are you?' "

"Hellohowareya," Mrs. Miller said.

"Mr. Miller, say something."

"Hellohowareya," Mr. Miller said.

"No biz like show biz," Windt muttered.

When the camera stopped whirring, Windt left to track down "a police whistle that blows with authority" to signal the start of the race the next morning, and the Millers followed the store manager back to the meat counter. A staff of butchers was stacking up nearly two tons of choice meats and double-checking a list of the Millers' preferences: 125 sirloins, seventy hams, seventy-five roasts, 250 porterhouses, twenty turkeys, etc.

The manager predicted that more than $5,000 worth of meat would be brimming over the top when the Millers raced down the aisles. Mr. Miller whistled appreciatively.

"Don't waste time trying to compare cuts," the manager told them. "Just grab whatever you see. Remember, seconds are dollars."

Mrs. Miller nodded. "Can we keep whatever we got in our hands when the final bell rings, or do we hafta drop it?"

"Keep it," the manager said. The Millers smiled at each other. "Now if you happen to drop or break anything when you're running, just leave it on the floor and grab more. We'll have boys stationed in the aisles to sweep up."

Much of the merchandise, the manager pointed out, was stocked on the shelves and stacked in aisles in shipping cartons, the tops of which had been cut off diagonally. "Take the whole thing. Don't waste time picking out individual items. We've got salmon, canned chickens, vegetables, everything stacked like that. If you're in doubt, just grab. Whatever you do, don't stop."

"Oh, we won't!" Mrs. Miller promised. "This is gonna be *mar*velous! But wouldn't it be wonderful if all nine kids was still at home and could be in on this?"

Even with only three offspring eligible to run, if Miss America's $10,000 estimate proved accurate, their grocery haul, plus the value of the 1964 Mercury station wagon which they were being given, would nearly double their combined yearly income, thereby raising them to a much higher tax bracket. The Millers were asked how they felt about that aspect of their windfall.

"We got the tax bite licked," Mr. Miller said.

"We're borrowin' money," Mrs. Miller added. "The Pepsi people have been just wonderful. They told us this was the smart thing to do rather than give up a once-in-a-lifetime opportunity for something like taxes."

Mr. Miller had spent several evenings with a diagram of the store, mapping out an elaborate battle attack. He and two of the three eligible sons—nineteen-year-old Jackie, a motorcycle buff, and thirteen-year-old Ronnie, a Little League catcher—would run relays to clean out the meat counter, while Mrs. Miller and nine-year-old David went for frozen foods, coffee and other light items. David, however, would need a mother's guiding hand. "A boy that young don't understand and might take just anything. Something nice but cheap, like candy or potato chips.

"Of course, we're going to take some Pepsi," Mr. Miller added. "Pepsi first and last." Mrs. Miller gave a thoughtful nod.

Both remarked that they were delighted with the store's compactness. Normally they shopped at a rangier supermarket, but lately had been boycotting it because it was being struck and they were opposed to crossing union picket lines. Now they were seeing the importance of a social conscience firsthand. "The meat counter over at that place is lots farther from the check-out stands," Mrs. Miller said. "We wouldn't be able to get near as much."

The store manager said he, too, was glad things worked out as they did. "This will bring in new customers, even from out of town. It'll be a status symbol to shop where Mrs. Miller shopped."

On Pepsi Boulevard, outside the store, the mayor was staring apprehensively at storm clouds overhead. He suggested a tour of the special displays in the downtown store windows. "Our businessmen used their inventive genius to honor the Millers and Pepsi. Miss America herself judged the windows."

Around the courthouse square, Taylorville's inventive genius was everywhere apparent. Most of the displays had been designed with promotional material supplied by the local Pepsi bottler. They featured mannequins (some wearing only bras and girdles) capped with paper Pepsi hats, alternating rows of Diet and Regular Pepsi cartons, corrugated paper Pepsi signs, glossy prints of Miss America holding a Pepsi, and hand-lettered posters congratulating Opal Miller—all before backdrops of gigantic red-white-and-blue Pepsi bottle caps. Reportedly, it had been extremely difficult for Miss America to narrow the field to *the* most outstanding display from among so many competitors. Down the street, a deliveryman, with furtive caution, toted a case of Coca-Cola into a drugstore just as the heavens opened up. A downpour.

Bob Windt was slouched in a chair in the hotel lobby, toying with a foot-long red-and-yellow plastic whistle and staring at the rain. A Pepsi photographer from New York was trying to cheer him: "I saw a woman drinking a Coke downtown, so I smashed her in the face." Windt said nothing.

He looked at the latest copy of the Taylorville *Breeze-Courier* which had kept on top of the story ever since Mrs. Miller's entry was drawn. Now, on the eve of the running, its twelve pages were filled with fifty-four display ads, praising the Millers and Pepsi-Cola under such headlines as: ANOTHER MILESTONE IN TAYLORVILLE'S HISTORY; TAYLORVILLE'S BOWLED 'EM OVER AGAIN; CONGRATULATIONS FOR MAKING SUCH AN UNFORGETTABLE EXPERIENCE POSSIBLE! The advertisers included the county sheriff and a local pest-control firm. The copy revealed that the shopping event was touching off a number of related contests. One tavern, for instance, was offering a "free thirty-minute eating-and-drinking spree for the customer who comes closest to guessing the dollar value of the Millers' total take."

Windt was still brooding. "This contest was too honest, so we came up with Taylorville. Hell, in Henderson we'd have even had Telstar."

Mr. Miller was partly to blame for the lack of journalistic enthusiasm, Windt decided, because he had not taken more days off from his job to join in preliminary promotional activities. "He could have asked for his vacation now," Windt said. "But he just sat there with his nose out of joint and didn't say anything."

The phone rang. ABC-TV was on the line from Chicago. Windt's face brightened. "That old adrenalin. Before this is over, *Time* and *Life* will be begging for stills!"

The rain was over by evening. Pepsi Boulevard had been blocked off in front of the store, and a dozen city laborers were there, noisily throwing together sets of wooden bleachers from the high-school football field. The choice center seats were to be roped off for the Miller kin and other dignitaries. The other seats were to be on a first-come first-served basis. "People will be here early," a worker said. "They know the TV cameras will sweep across the crowd." To assure *some* visibility for all, glaziers were removing the supermarket's large plate-glass front windows.

Inside, electricians were checking the efficiency of the wiring. Extra lines had been added. An independent moviemaker, hired by Pepsi, crammed a camera and a cameraman into a shopping cart and careened it up and down the aisles, rehearsing camera angles. The ABC crew, freshly arrived from Chicago, scanned the scene and declared that things weren't commercial enough. They suggested that prominent Pepsi signs be pasted atop cash registers directly in front of the TV camera platform. Stock boys, some of whom would work all night, were corraling one hundred extra shopping carts, three thousand paper bags and mountains of S&H Green Stamps, while other employees dismantled display cases of cigarettes, phonograph records, kitchen utensils and other non-foodstuffs which the Millers would not be permitted to grab during the race. "We decided to get these thing out of the way rather than have Mrs. Miller get excited and grab something she can't have," the manager explained.

Near the check-out counter, Bob Windt was in a rage over the cans of Jewel Mixed Nuts and the boxes of Chef Boy-Ar-Dee Pizza mix flanking a Pepsi display. "Terrible, terrible!" he bellowed to Tony Becker, a hulking Pepsi troubleshooter from Chicago who would be master of ceremonies for the running. "Our stake in this is to promote Pepsi. I don't give a damn about mixed nuts. Get 'em outa here or cover 'em up with Pepsi!"

Becker tried to explain that nuts and pizza could be considered "related food items" and that Pepsi "often ties in with related food items promotion-wise," but a fresh crisis was already pushing Windt's blood pressure to new heights. The wall clock Becker had chosen as "official timer" was imprinted only with the name of the supermarket. "When the cameras flash to the clock for the time, we want PEPSI to come out on the screen. I've had a hard enough time getting some of these news guys down here without blowing it like this," Windt said. In a hasty conference, he and Becker decided that a Pepsi clock would be designated "official," but to avoid hard feelings from the store staff, the first clock would be kept in reserve "in case of emergency."

Two aisles over, another important conference was underway. Two Pepsi promotion experts from New York had cornered the store manager and were informing him that the Millers would not be permitted to carry food in the pasteboard shipping cartons, despite the fact that their briefings and battle plans had been built around this stratagem. "We're mostly interested in something exciting, something *visual*," one of them explained in a confidential tone. "We might have a prism lens, say, that'll make Mrs. Miller suddenly be eight Mrs. Millers to the camera's eye. Basically, it will be better if they just carry what they can in their arms."

"Besides," said the other man, "we don't want to take a bath on this."

"Without the cartons," the first expert added, "the unexpected is more likely to happen. Why, we may be dragging those people up off the floor by the time thirty minutes is over."

All evening a steady stream of townsfolk filed down to the store to watch the preparations—mothers with babes in arms, grizzled old men, housewives in slacks and hair curlers, kids with baseball gloves and bubble gum, young farmers with sun-leathered faces, businessmen with cigars. Some sat on the bleachers for hours, staring at the activity inside the store or plotting their own imaginary assault on the shelves or ruminating over the tragic fact that six of the Miller brood had already flown the nest and thus they were ineligible for the spree.

The editor of the *Breeze-Courier* had just returned from a country-club banquet honoring the Millers for all they'd done for Taylorville.

"You know, Pepsi has hit on a real fine idea. We're a gluttonous race, I guess, but the idea of the supermarket, the grocery-store phenomenon and all, really thrills people. It's like the hunt. You get to sack the game yourself."

A husband and wife walked past, carrying youngsters in pajamas. "At least there's five of 'em," the man was saying. "They'll be able to get something. If some guy had won who was taking care of a seventy-five-year-old mother or something, hell, she wouldn't be able to grab nothing."

Miller Day (so designated by mayoral proclamation) dawned. On an early morning radio interview, a Pepsi executive said: "Out of all forty-eight states, the national spotlight is focused today on Taylorville." The bleachers were already filling (some local shops had given employees time off to attend) and inside the manager was assuring a group of nervous pink-smocked checkers that each of them would have a chance to handle the Millers' groceries and that there would be extra checkers standing by in case anyone got overly excited and had to quit. Two empty semi-trailers had been jockeyed into the parking lot; whatever couldn't be crammed into the station wagon the semi-trailers would carry to storage lockers the Millers had rented in the next town, and a uniformed cop was on hand to direct shopping-cart traffic. The festival crowd swigged free cups of Pepsi, tapped time to the Sousa marches blaring from a loudspeaker, and waved eagerly at TV cameramen and press photographers. Then, when a woman in black slacks and sneakers entered the store, followed by three sneak- ered boys and a man, someone shouted: "Is that *her?*"

It was. Taylorville's queen for a day walked directly to the manager's office and opened her purse.

"I'm going to take off my rings and my watch and anything that might hamper me in any way," Mrs. Miller announced. Her hair had been set gratuitously by a local beauty operator. Her sneakers were donated by J. C. Penney. She joined the rest of her family for a final reconnaissance of the battlefield. Women in the crowd looked on with unveiled envy as Mrs. Miller experimentally wrapped her arms around a tall stack of canned chickens. The store manager said, "Don't worry about being neat at the check-out counters, just dump the stuff and *go!*"

Finally, just before the zero hour of nine-thirty, Tony Becker got on top of a sturdy safe at the front of the store, grabbed a microphone, and said: "It's almost spree time! Millers, get on your marks!" As one, the five Millers dropped to a crouch at the check-out counters, their eyes on the twentieth-century cornucopia arrayed before them. "Awright, folks, let's count 'em down like a Sa-turn rocket. *Ten . . . nine . . . eight. . . .*"

Four thousand voices thundered in unison. In a second-story window across the street, an American Legion volunteer pressed the official bugle to his lips. At the base of the safe, Bob Windt put the police whistle to his lips. Alongside the Millers, the store manager raised a pearl-handled starter's pistol.

"*. . . three . . . two . . . one . . . GO!*"

Bugle blast, whistle shrill, revolver crack. The crowd shrieked as the Millers sprinted down the aisles, followed closely by the movie man in the shopping cart. In a blur of flying legs and snatching hands, they swarmed over the shelves like locusts through a cornfield. "Go! Go! Go!" the crowd chanted. Becker turned the march music double volume, and the bugler blared a cavalry charge.

Cash registers began to ring as Jackie dumped two dozen steaks on the counter. His mother staggered up with three huge frozen turkeys, and someone yelled: "Atta boy, Mrs. Miller!" Little David, momentarily bewildered, finally got his bearings and began heaving boxes of chocolate milk flavoring into the check-out aisles, where adult store employees scrambled frantically to pick them up. At the brimming meat counter, Mr. Miller loaded Ronnie to the chin with rib roasts. A sympathetic butcher, seeing sweat pouring down the boy's face, held a cup of water to his lips. "Not too much now," his father said. Alarmed Pepsi officials, noting that only the youngest of the Millers had remembered the "Pepsi first" pledge, rushed to a Pepsi display and grabbed a dozen cartons for them. The first shopping cart was loaded now, but in the frenzy the sacker rammed it through a glass door en route to the parking lot, then kicked the broken glass aside and raced on. Becker called on the crowd to give him the old Taylorville yell.

Bob Windt surveyed the scene with rapture. "This is great. We're in the greatest business in the world—*philanthropy!*"

For thirty minutes, the scream of the crowd, the blare of the music, the clang of the cash registers, the steady avalanche of steaks, bananas, sugar, shortening, coffee, cake mixes, frozen shrimp, fish, tea, honey-glazed hams in champagne sauce never slackened. Then suddenly, moments after the meat counter was stripped bare and Mrs. Miller dumped an armload of Metrecal on the counter, Becker bellowed: "We're coming down to the wire now! Pandemonium—*let it break loose!*" The crowd went out of control. People jumped up and down on the bleachers. They threw their paper Pepsi cups into the air. And as the sound of their voices reached the pitch of hysteria, there was a general movement, a surge toward the ravaged store. The final gun sounded.

Each panting Miller was handed a Pepsi. Flashbulbs popped. Jubilantly, the store manager announced the grand-total food value: $6,274.64, plus Green Stamps.

The Millers stopped smiling. "That's not as much as we'd planned on," Mrs. Miller said. She looked around to see what they had missed.

"Well, we don't wanna be big hogs. Just little ones," said her husband.

Then the crowd closed in and well-wishers smothered the winners with hugs and kisses.

Out in the parking lot people were inspecting the seventy-five loaded carts stretched under the boiling sun, and those fortunate enough to be neighbors or friends of the Millers were letting everyone else know about it. Someone shouted that the grocery grabbers had gotten twenty-eight twenty-five-pound bags of sugar. Someone else counted sixty one-pound cans of coffee. Another spotted a dozen bags of charcoal briquettes.

"Charcoal briquettes!" a woman said. "That's not foodstuffs! I thought they were only supposed to get foodstuffs!"

Windt was pushing through the crowd now, trying to get the truck loading started. He was asked what his next promotional idea might be.

"Well, I'll just sit back, study the elements and see what develops. Something will come up. I've been foolin' 'em since I was twelve, so what the hell?"

A man wearing a Pepsi-Cola shirt came past, and he was holding a radio shaped like a Pepsi dispenser. The volume was turned up to the limit, and a commercial that had made its debut that day came booming out:

"Come alive,

Come alive,

You're in the Pepsi generation."

[February, 1965]

Las Vegas (What?). Las Vegas (Can't Hear You! Too Noisy). *Las Vegas!!!!*

by Tom Wolfe

"Hernia, hernia, hernia, hernia, hernia, hernia, hernia, hernia, hernia, hernia, hernia, hernia, hernia, HERNia; hernia, HERNia, hernia, hernia, hernia, hernia, HERNia, HERNia, HERNia; hernia, hernia, hernia, hernia, hernia, hernia, hernia, eight is the point, the point is eight; hernia, hernia, HERNia; hernia, hernia, hernia, hernia, all right, hernia, hernia, hernia, hernia, hard eight, hernia, hernia, hernia, HERNia, hernia, hernia, hernia, HERNia, hernia, hernia, hernia, HERNia, hernia, hernia, hernia, hernia. . . ."

"What is all this *hernia hernia* stuff?"

This was Raymond talking to the wavy-haired fellow with the stick, the dealer, at the craps table about 3:45 Sunday morning. The stickman had no idea what this big wiseacre was talking about, but he resented the tone. He gave Raymond that patient arch of the eyebrows known as a Red Hook brush-off, which is supposed to convey some such thought as, I am a very tough but cool guy, as you can tell by the way I carry my eyeballs low in the pouches, and if this wasn't such a high-class joint we would take wiseacres like you out back and beat you into jellied madrilene.

At this point, however, Raymond was immune to subtle looks.

201

The stickman tried to get the game going again, but every time he would start up his singsong, by easing the words out through the nose, which seems to be the style among craps dealers in Las Vegas—"All right, a new shooter . . . eight is the point, the point is eight" and so on—Raymond would start droning along with him in exactly the same tone of voice, "Hernia, hernia, hernia; hernia, HERNia, HERNia, hernia; hernia, hernia, hernia."

Everybody at the craps table was staring in consternation to think that anybody would try to needle a tough, hip, elite *soldat* like a Las Vegas craps dealer. The gold-lamé odalisques of Los Angeles were staring. The Western sports, fifty-eight-year-old men who wear Texas string ties, were staring. The old babes at the slot machines, holding Dixie Cups full of nickels, were staring at the craps tables, but cranking away the whole time.

Raymond, who is thirty-four years old and works as an engineer in Phoenix, is big but not terrifying. He has the sort of thatchwork hair that grows so low all along the forehead there is no logical place to part it, but he tries anyway. He has a huge, prognathous jaw, but it is as smooth, soft and round as a melon, so that Raymond's total effect is that of an Episcopal divinity student.

The guards were wonderful. They were dressed in cowboy uniforms like Bruce Cabot in *Sundown* and Robert Taylor in many another Western and they wore sheriff's stars.

"Mister, is there something we can do for you?"

"The expression is 'Sir,' " said Raymond. "You said 'Mister.' The expression is 'Sir.' How's your old Cosa Nostra?"

Amazingly, the casino guards were easing Raymond out peaceably, without putting a hand on him. I had never seen the fellow before, but possibly because I had been following his progress for the last five minutes, he turned to me and said, "Hey, do you have a car? This wild stuff is starting again."

The gist of it was that he had left his car somewhere and he wanted to ride up the Strip to the Stardust, one of the big hotel-casinos. I am describing this big goof Raymond not because he is a typical Las Vegas tourist, although he has some typical symptoms, but because he is a good example of the marvelous impact Las Vegas has on the senses. Raymond's senses were at a high pitch of excitation, the only trouble being that he was going off his nut. He had been up since Thursday afternoon, and it was now about 3:45 a.m. Sunday. He had an envelope full of pep pills—amphetamine—in his left coat pocket and an envelope full of Equanils—meprobamate—in his right pocket, or were the Equanils in the left and the pep pills in the right? He could tell by looking, but he wasn't going to look anymore. He didn't care to see how many were left.

He had been rolling up and down the incredible electric-sign gauntlet of Las Vegas' Strip, U.S. Route 91, where the neon and the par lamps—

bubbling, spiraling, rocketing, and exploding in sunbursts ten stories high out in the middle of the desert—celebrate one-story casinos. He had been gambling and drinking and eating now and again at the buffet tables the casinos keep heaped with food day and night, but mostly hopping himself up with good old amphetamine, cooling himself down with meprobamate, then hooking down more alcohol, until now, after sixty hours, he was slipping into the symptoms of toxic schizophrenia.

He was also enjoying what the prophets of hallucinogen call "consciousness expansion." The man was psychedelic. He was beginning to isolate the components of Las Vegas' unique bombardment of the senses. He was quite right about "this *hernia hernia* stuff." Every casino in Las Vegas is, among the other things, a room full of craps tables with dealers who keep up a running singsong that sounds as though they are saying "hernia, hernia, hernia, hernia, hernia" and so on. There they are day and night, easing a running commentary through their nostrils. What they have to say contains next to no useful instruction. Its underlying message is, We are the initiates, riding the crest of chance. That the accumulated sound comes out "hernia" is merely an unfortunate phonetic coincidence. Actually, it is part of something rare and rather grand: a combination of baroque stimuli that brings to mind the bronze gongs, no larger than a blue plate, that Louis XIV, his ruff collars larded with the lint of the foul Old City of Byzantium, personally hunted out in the bazaars of Asia Minor to provide exotic acoustics for his new palace outside Paris.

The sounds of the craps dealer will be in, let's say, the middle register. In the lower register will be the sound of the old babes at the slot machines. Men play the slots too, of course, but one of the indelible images of Las Vegas is that of the old babes at the row upon row of slot machines. There they are at six o'clock Sunday morning no less than at three o'clock Tuesday afternoon. Some of them pack their old hummocky shanks into Capri pants, but many of them just put on the old print dress, the same one day after day, and the old hob-heeled shoes, looking like they might be going out to buy eggs in Tupelo, Mississippi. They have a Dixie Cup full of nickels or dimes in the left hand and an Iron-Boy work glove on the right hand to keep the calluses from getting sore. Every time they pull the handle, the machine makes a sound much like the sound a cash register makes before the bell rings, then the slot pictures start clattering up from left to right, the oranges, lemons, plums, cherries, bells, bars, buckaroos—the figure of a cowboy riding a bucking bronco. The whole sound keeps churning up over and over again in eccentric series all over the place, like one of those random-sound radio symphonies by John Cage. You can hear it at any hour of the day or night all over Las Vegas. You can walk down Fremont Street at dawn and hear it without even walking in a door, that and the spins of the wheels of fortune, a boring and not very popular sort of simplified roulette, as the tabs flap to a stop. As an overtone, or at times simply as a loud sound, comes the babble of the casino crowds, with an occasional shriek from the craps tables, or, anywhere from four p.m. to six a.m., the sound of brass instruments or electrified string instruments from the cocktail-lounge shows.

The crowd and band sounds are not very extraordinary, of course. But Las Vegas' Muzak is. Muzak pervades Las Vegas from the time you walk into the airport upon landing to the last time you leave the casinos. It is piped out to the swimming pool. It is in the drugstores. It is as if there were a communal fear that someone, somewhere in Las Vegas, was going to be left with a totally vacant minute on his hands.

Las Vegas has succeeded in wiring an entire city with this electronic stimulation, day and night, out in the middle of the desert. In the automobile I rented, the radio could not be turned off, no matter which dial you went after. I drove for days in a happy burble of Action Checkpoint News, *Monkey No. 9, Donna, Donna, the Prima Donna,* and picking-and-singing jingles for the Frontier Bank and the Fremont Hotel.

One can see the magnitude of the achievement. Las Vegas takes what in other American towns is but a quixotic inflammation of the senses for some poor salary mule in the brief interval between the flagstone rambler and the automatic elevator downtown and magnifies it, foliates it, embellishes it into an institution.

For example, Las Vegas is the only town in the world whose skyline is made up neither of buildings, like New York, nor of trees, like Wilbraham, Massachusetts, but signs. One can look at Las Vegas from a mile away on Route 91 and see no buildings, no trees, only signs. But such signs! They tower. They revolve, they oscillate, they soar in shapes before which the existing vocabulary of art history is helpless. I can only attempt to supply names—Boomerang Modern, Palette Curvilinear, Flash Gordon Ming-Alert Spiral, McDonald's Hamburger Parabola, Mint Casino Elliptical, Miami Beach Kidney. Las Vegas' sign makers work so far out beyond the frontiers of conventional studio art that they have no names themselves for the forms they create. Vaughan Cannon, one of those tall, blond Westerners, the builders of places like Las Vegas and Los Angeles, whose eyes seem to have been bleached by the sun, is in the back shop of the Young Electric Sign Company out on East Charleston Boulevard with Herman Boernge, one of his designers, looking at the model they have prepared for the Lucky Strike Casino sign, and Cannon points to where the sign's two great curving faces meet to form a narrow vertical face and says:

"Well, here we are again—what do we call that?"

"I don't know," says Boernge. "It's sort of a nose effect. Call it a nose."

Okay, a nose, but it rises sixteen stories high above a two-story building. In Las Vegas no farseeing entrepreneur buys a sign to fit a building he owns. He rebuilds the building to support the biggest sign he can get up the money for and, if necessary, changes the name. The Lucky Strike Casino today is the Lucky Casino, which fits better when recorded in sixteen stories of flaming peach and incandescent yellow in the middle of the Mojave Desert. In the Young Electric Sign Co. era signs have become the architecture of Las Vegas, and the most whimsical, Yale-seminar-frenzied devices of the two late geniuses of Baroque Modern, Frank Lloyd Wright and Eero Saarinen, seem rather stuffy business, like a jest at a faculty meeting, compared to it. Men like Boernge, Kermit Wayne, Ben Mitchem and Jack Larsen, formerly an artist for Walt Disney, are the designer-sculptor geniuses of Las Vegas, but their motifs have been carried faithfully throughout the town by lesser men, for gasoline stations, motels, funeral parlors, churches, public buildings, flop-houses and sauna baths. A San Francisco artist and jewelry designer, who lived for three years in Plainfield, New Jersey, near unspeakable Route 22, is in Las Vegas for the first time, driving down the Strip. "Wonderful," she says. "New Jersey has spread across the Continental Divide at last."

Then there is a stimulus that is both visual and sexual—the Las Vegas buttocks décolletage. This is a form of sexually provocative dress seen more and more in the United States, but avoided like Broadway message-embroidered ("Kiss Me, I'm Cold") underwear in the fashion pages, so that the euphemisms have not been established and I have no choice but clinical terms. To achieve buttocks décolletage a woman wears bikini-style shorts that cut across the round fatty masses of the buttocks rather than cupping them from below, so that the outer-lower edges of these fatty masses, or "cheeks," are exposed. I am in the cocktail lounge of the Hacienda Hotel, talking to managing director Dick Taylor about the great success his place has had in attracting family and tour groups, and all around me the waitresses are bobbing on their high heels, bare legs and décolletage-bare backsides, set off by pelvis-length lingerie of an uncertain denomination. I stare, but I am new here. At the White Cross Rexall drugstore on the Strip a pregnant brunette walks in off the street wearing black shorts with buttocks décolletage aft and illusion-of-cloth nylon lingerie hanging fore, and not even the old mom's-pie pensioners up near the door are staring. They just crank away at the slot machines. On the streets of Las Vegas, not only the show girls, of which the town has about two hundred fifty, bona fide, in residence, but girls of every sort, including, especially, Las Vegas' little high-school buds, who adorn what locals seeking roots in the sand call "our city of churches and schools," have taken up the chic of wearing buttocks décolletage step-ins under flesh-tight slacks, with the outline of the undergarment showing through fashionably. Others go them one better. They achieve the effect of having been dipped once, briefly, in Helenca stretch nylon. More and more they look like those wonderful old girls out of Flash Gordon who were wrapped just once over in Baghdad pantaloons of clear polyethylene with only

Flash Gordon between them and the insane red-eyed assaults of the minions of Ming. It is as if all the hip young suburban gals of America named Lana, Deborah and Sandra, who gather wherever the arc lights shine and the studs steady their coiffures in the plate-glass reflection, have convened in Las Vegas with their bouffant hair above and anatomically stretch-pant-swathed little bottoms below, here on the new American frontier. But exactly!

None of it would have been possible, however, without one of those historic combinations of nature and art that creates an epoch. In this case, the Mojave Desert plus the father of Las Vegas, the late Benjamin "Bugsy" Siegel.

Bugsy was an inspired man. Back in 1944 the city fathers of Las Vegas, their Protestant rectitude alloyed only by the giddy prospect of gambling revenues, were considering the sort of ordinance that would have preserved the town with a kind of Colonial Williamsburg dinkiness in the motif of the Wild West. All new buildings would have to have at least the facade of the sort of place where piano players used to wear garters on their sleeves in Virginia City around 1880. In Las Vegas in 1944, it should be noted, there was nothing more stimulating in the entire town than a Fremont Street bar where the composer of *Deep in the Heart of Texas* held forth and the regulars downed fifteen-cent beer.

Bugsy pulled into Las Vegas in 1945 with several million dollars that, after his assassination, was traced back in the general direction of gangster-financiers. Siegel put up a hotel-casino such as Las Vegas had never seen and called it the Flamingo—all Miami Modern, and the hell with piano players with garters and whatever that was all about. Everybody drove out Route 91 just to gape. Such shapes! Boomerang Modern supports, Palette Curvilinear bars, Hot Shoppe Cantilever roofs and a scalloped swimming pool. Such colors! All the new electrochemical pastels of the Florida littoral: tangerine, broiling magenta, livid pink, incarnadine, fuchsia demure, Congo ruby, methyl green, viridine, aquamarine, phenosafranine, incandescent orange, scarlet-fever purple, cyanic blue, tessellated bronze, hospital-fruit-basket orange. And such signs! Two cylinders rose at either end of the Flamingo—eight stories high and covered from top to bottom with neon rings in the shape of bubbles that fizzed all eight stories up into the desert sky all night long like an illuminated whisky-soda tumbler filled to the brim with pink champagne.

The business history of the Flamingo, on the other hand, was not such a smashing success. For one thing, the gambling operation was losing money at a rate that rather gloriously refuted all the recorded odds of the gaming science. Siegel's backers apparently suspected that he was playing both ends against the middle in collusion with professional gamblers who hung out at the Flamingo as though they had liens on it. What with one thing and another, someone decided by the night of June 20, 1947, that Benny Siegel, lord of the Flamingo, had had it. He was shot to death in Los Angeles.

Yet Siegel's aesthetic, psychological and cultural insights, like Cézanne's, Freud's and Max Weber's, could not die. The Siegel vision and the Siegel aesthetic were already sweeping Las Vegas like gold fever. And there were builders of the West equal to the opportunity. All over Las Vegas the incredible electric pastels were repeated. Overnight the Baroque Modern forms made Las Vegas one of the few architecturally unified cities of the world—the style was Late American Rich—and without the bother and bad humor of a City Council ordinance. No enterprise was too small, too pedestrian or too solemn for The Look. The Supersonic Carwash, the Mercury Jetaway, Gas Vegas Village and Terrible Herbst gasoline stations, the Par-a-Dice Motel, the Palm Mortuary, the Orbit Inn, the Desert Moon, the Blue Onion Drive-In—on it went, like Wildwood, New Jersey, entering Heaven.

The atmosphere of the six-mile-long Strip of hotel-casinos grips even those segments of the population who rarely go near it. Barely twenty-five-hundred feet off the Strip, over by the Convention Center, stands Landmark Towers, a shaft thirty stories high, full of apartments, supporting a huge circular structure shaped like a space observation platform, which was to have contained the restaurant and casino. Somewhere along the way Landmark Towers went bankrupt, probably at that point in the last of the many crises when the construction workers *still* insisted on spending half the day flat on their bellies with their heads, tongues and eyeballs hanging over the edge of the tower, looking down into the swimming pool of the Playboy Apartments below, which has a "nudes only" section for show girls whose work calls for a tan all over.

Elsewhere, Las Vegas' beautiful little high-school buds in their buttocks-décolletage stretch pants are back on the foam-rubber upholstery of luxury broughams peeling off the entire chick ensemble long enough to establish the highest venereal-disease rate among high-school students anywhere north of the yaws-rotting shanty jungles of the Eighth Parallel. The Negroes who have done much of the construction work in Las Vegas' sixteen-year boom are off in their ghetto on the west side of town, and some of them are smoking marijuana, eating peyote buttons and taking horse (heroin), which they get from Tijuana, I mean it's simple, baby, right through the mails, and old Raymond, the Phoenix engineer, does not have the high life to himself.

I am on the third floor of the Clark County Courthouse talking to Sheriff Captain Ray Gubser, another of these strong, pale-eyed Western-builder types, who is obligingly explaining to me law enforcement on the Strip, where the problem is not so much the drunks, crooks or roughhousers, but these nuts on pills who don't want to ever go to bed, and they have hallucinations and try to bring down the casinos like Samson. The county has two padded cells for them. They cool down after three or four days and they turn out to be somebody's earnest breadwinner back in Denver or Minneapolis, loaded with the right credentials and pouring soul and apologiae all over the county cops before finally pulling out of never-never land for good by plane. Captain Gubser is telling me about life and eccentric times in Las Vegas, but I am distracted. The captain's office has windows out on the corridor. Coming down the corridor is a covey of girls, skipping and screaming, giggling along, their heads exploding in platinum-and-neon-yellow bouffants or beehives or raspberry-silk scarves, their eyes appliquéd in black like mail-order decals, their breasts aimed up under their jerseys at the angle of antiaircraft automatic weapons, and, as they swing around the corner toward the elevator, their glutei maximi are bobbing up and down with their pumps in the inevitable buttocks décolletage pressed out against black, beige and incarnadine stretch pants. This is part of the latest shipment of show girls to Las Vegas, seventy in all, for the "Lido de Paris" revue at the Stardust, to be entitled *Bravo!*, replacing the old show, entitled *Voilà*. The girls are in the County Courthouse getting their working papers, and fifteen days from now these little glutei maximi and ack-ack breasts with stars pasted on the tips will be swinging out over the slack jaws and cocked-up noses of patrons sitting at stageside at the Stardust. I am still listening to Gubser, but somehow it is a courthouse where mere words are beaten back like old atonal Arturo Toscanini trying to sing along with the NBC Symphony. There he would be, flapping his little toy arms like Tony Galento shadowboxing with fate, bawling away in the face of union musicians who drowned him without a bubble. I sat in on three trials in the courthouse, and it was wonderful, because the courtrooms are all blond-wood modern and look like sets for TV panel discussions on marriage and the teen-ager. What the judge has to say is no less formal and no more fatuous than what judges say everywhere, but inside of forty seconds it is all meaningless because the atmosphere is precisely like a news broadcast over Las Vegas' finest radio station, KORK. The newscast, as it is called, begins with a series of electronic wheeps out on that far edge of sound where only quadrupeds can hear. A voice then announces that this is Action Checkpoint News. "The news—all the news—flows first through Action Checkpoint!—then reaches You! at the speed of Sound!" More electronic wheeps, beeps and lulus, and then an item: "Cuban Premier Fidel Castro nearly drowned yesterday." Urp! Wheep! Lulu! No news a KORK announcer has ever brought to Las Vegas at the speed of sound, or could possible bring, short of word of the annihilation of Los Angeles, could conceivably compete within the brain with the giddiness of this electronic jollification.

The wheeps, beeps, freeps, electronic lulus, Boomerang Modern and Flash Gordon sunbursts soar on through the night over the billowing hernia—hernia sounds and the old babes at the slots—until it is 7:30 a.m. and I am watching five men at a green-topped card table playing poker. They are sliding their Bee-brand cards into their hands and squinting at the pips with a set to the lips like Conrad Veidt in a tunic collar studying a code message from S.S. headquarters. Big Sid Wyman, the old Big-Time gambler from St. Louis, is there, with his eyes looking like two poached eggs engraved with a road map of West Virginia, after all night at the poker table. Sixty-year-old Chicago Tommy Hargan is there with his topknot of white hair pulled back over his little pink skull and a mountain of chips in front of his old caved-in sternum. Sixty-two-year-old Dallas Maxie Welch is there, fat and phlegmatic as an Indian Ocean potentate. Two Los Angeles biggies are there exhaling smoke from candela-green cigars into the gloom. It looks like the perfect vignette of every Big Time back room, "athletic club," snooker house and floating poker game in the history of the guys-and-dolls lumpen-bourgeoisie. But what is all this? Off to the side, at a rostrum, sits a flawless little creature with bouffant hair and Stridex-pure skin who looks like she is polished each morning with a rotary buffer. Before her on the rostrum is a globe of coffee on a hot coil. Her sole job is to keep the poker players warmed up with coffee. Meantime, numberless uniformed lackeys are cocked and aimed about the edges to bring the five Big Timers whatever else they might desire, cigarettes, drinks, napkins, eyeglass-cleaning tissues, plug-in telephones. All around the poker table, at a respectful distance of ten feet, is a fence with the most delicate golden pickets. Upon it, even at this narcoleptic hour, lean men and women in their best clothes watching the combat of the titans. The scene is the charmed circle of the casino of the Dunes Hotel. As everyone there knows, or believes, these fabulous men are playing for table stakes of fifteen or twenty thousand dollars. One hundred dollars rides on a chip. Mandibles gape at the progress of the battle. And now Sid Wyman, who is also a vice-president of the Dunes, is at a small escritoire just inside the golden fence signing a stack of vouchers for such sums as $4500, all printed in the heavy Mondrianesque digits of a Burroughs business check-making machine. It was as if America's guys-and-dolls gamblers had somehow been tapped upon the shoulders, knighted, initiated into a new aristocracy.

Las Vegas has become, just as Bugsy Siegel dreamed, the American Monte Carlo—without any of the inevitable upper-class baggage of the Riviera casinos. At Monte Carlo there is still the plush mustiness of the nineteenth-century noble lions—of Baron Bleichroden, a big winner at roulette who always said, "My dear friends, it is so easy on Black." Of Lord Jersey, who won seventeen maximum bets in a row—on black, as a matter of fact—nodded to the croupier, and said, "Much obliged, old sport, old sport," took his winnings to England, retired to the country and never gambled again in his life. Or of the old Duc de Dinc who said he could win only in the high-toned Club Privé, and who won very heavily one night, saw two Englishmen gaping at his good fortune, threw them every mille note he had in his hands and said, "Here. Englishmen without money are altogether odious." Thousands of Europeans from the lower orders now have the money to go to the Riviera, but they remain under the century-old status pall of the aristocracy. At Monte Carlo there are still Wrong Forks, Deficient Accents, Poor Tailoring, Gauche Displays, Nouveau Richness, Cultural Aridity—concepts unknown in Las Vegas. For the grand debut of Monte Carlo as a resort in 1879 the architect Charles Garnier designed an opera house for the Place du Casino; and Sarah Bernhardt read a symbolic poem. For the debut of Las Vegas as a revue in 1946 Bugsy Siegel hired Abbott and Costello, and there, in a way, you have it all.

I am in the office of Major A. Riddle—Major is his name—the president of the Dunes Hotel. He combs his hair straight back and wears a heavy gold band on his little finger with a diamond sunk into it. As everywhere else in Las Vegas, someone has turned on the air conditioning to the point where it will be remembered, all right, as Las Vegas-style air conditioning. Riddle has an appointment to see a doctor at 4:30 about a crimp in his neck. His secretary, Maude McBride, has her head down and is rubbing the back of her neck. Lee Fisher, the P.R. man, and I are turning ours from time to time to keep the pivots from freezing up. Riddle is telling me about "the French war" and moving his neck gingerly. The Stardust bought and imported a version of the Lido de Paris spectacular, and the sight of all those sequined giblets pooning around on flamingo legs inflamed the tourists. The Tropicana fought back with the Folies Bergère, the New Frontier installed "Paree Ooh La La," the Hacienda reached for the puppets "Les Poupées de Paris," and the Silver Slipper called in Lili St. Cyr, the stripper, which was going French after a fashion. So the Dunes has bought up the third and last of the great Paris girlie shows, the Casino de Paris. Lee Fisher says, "And we're going to do things they *can't* top. In this town you've got to move ahead in quantum jumps."

Quantum? But exactly! The beauty of the Dunes' Casino de Paris show is that it will be beyond art, beyond dance, beyond spectacle, even beyond the titillations of the winking crotch. The Casino de Paris will be a behemoth piece of American calculus, like Project Mercury.

"This show alone will cost us two and a half million a year to operate and one and a half million to produce," Major A. Riddle is saying. "The costumes alone will be fantastic. There'll be more than five hundred costumes and—well, they'll be fantastic.

"And this machine—by the time we get through expanding the stage, this machine will cost us $250,000."

"Machine?"

"Yes. Sean Kenny is doing the staging. The whole set moves electronically right in front of your eyes. He used to work with this fellow Lloyd Wright?"

"Frank Lloyd Wright?"

"Yes. Kenny did the staging for *Blitz*. Did you see it? Fantastic. Well, it's all done electronically. They built this machine for us in Glasgow, Scotland, and it's being shipped here right now. It moves all over the place and creates smoke and special effects. We'll have everything. You can stage a bombardment with it. You'll think the whole theatre is blowing up.

"You'll have to program it. They had to use the same mechanism that's in the Skybolt Missile to build it. It's called a 'Celson' or something like that. That's how complicated this thing is. They have to have the same thing as the Skybolt Missile."

As Riddle speaks, one gets a wonderful picture of sex riding the crest of the future. Whole tableaux of bare-bottomed Cosmonaughties will be hurtling around the Casino de Paris Room of the Dunes Hotel at fantastic speed in elliptical orbits, a flash of the sequined giblets here, a blur of the black-rimmed decal eyes there, a wink of the crotch here and there, until, with one vast Project Climax for our times, Sean Kenny, who used to work with this fellow Frank Lloyd Wright, presses the red button and the whole yahooing harem, shrieking ooh-la-la amid the din, exits in a mushroom cloud.

The allure is most irresistible not to the young but the old. No one in Las Vegas will admit it—it is not the modern, glamorous notion—but Las Vegas is a resort for old people. In those last years, before the tissue deteriorates and the wires of the cerebral cortex hang in the skull like a clump of dried seaweed, they are seeking liberation.

At eight o'clock Sunday morning it is another almost boringly sunny day in the desert, and Clara and Abby, both about sixty, and their husbands, Earl, sixty-three, and Ernest, sixty-four, come squinting out of the Mint Casino onto Fremont Street.

"I don't know what's wrong with me," Abby says. "Those last three drinks, I couldn't even feel them. It was just like drinking fizz. You know what I mean?"

"Hey," says Ernest, "how about that place back 'ere? We ain't been back 'ere. Come on."

The others are standing there on the corner, squinting and looking doubtful. Abby and Clara have both entered old babehood. They have that fleshy, humped-over shape across the back of the shoulders. Their torsos are hunched up into fat little loaves supported by bony, atrophied leg stems sticking up into their hummocky hips. Their hair has been fried and dyed into improbable designs.

"You know what I mean? After a while it just gives me gas," says Abby. "I don't even feel it."

"Did you see me over there?" says Earl. "I was just going along, nice and easy, not too much, just riding along real nice. You know? And then, boy, I don't know what happened to me. First thing I know I'm laying down fifty dollars. . . ."

Abby lets out a great belch. Clara giggles.

"Gives me gas," Abby says mechanically.

"Hey, how about that place back 'ere?" says Ernest.

". . . Just nice and easy as you please. . . ."

". . . get me all fizzed up. . . ."

"Aw, come on. . . ."

And there at eight o'clock Sunday morning stand four old parties from Albuquerque, New Mexico, up all night, squinting at the sun, belching from a surfeit of tall drinks at eight o'clock Sunday morning, and—marvelous!—there is no one around to snigger at what an old babe with decaying haunches looks like in Capri pants with her heels jacked up on decorated wedgies.

"Where do we *come* from?" Clara said to me, speaking for the first time since I approached them on Fremont Street. "He wants to know where we come from. I think it's past your bedtime, sweets."

"Climb the stairs and go to bed," said Abby.

Laughter all around.

"Climb the stairs" was Abby's finest line. At present there are almost no stairs to climb in Las Vegas. Avalon homes are soon to go up, advertising "Two-Story Homes!" as though an incredibly lavish and exotic concept. As I talked to Clara, Abby, Earl and Ernest, it came out that "climb the stairs" was a phrase they brought along to Albuquerque with them from Marshalltown, Iowa, those many years ago, along with a lot of other baggage, such as the entire cupboard of Protestant taboos against drinking, lusting, gambling, staying out late, getting up late, loafing, idling, lollygagging around the streets and wearing Capri pants—all designed to deny a person short-term pleasures so he will center his energies on bigger, long-term goals.

"We was in 'ere"—the Mint—"a couple of hours ago, and that old boy was playing the guitar, you know, 'Walk right in, set right down,' and I kept hearing an old song I haven't heard for twenty years. It has this little boy and his folks keep telling him it's late and he has to go to bed. He keeps saying, 'Don't make me go to bed and I'll be good.' Am I *good*, Earl? Am I *good*?"

The liberated cortex in all its glory is none other than the old babes at the slot machines. Some of them are tourists whose husbands said, *Here is fifty bucks, go play the slot machines,* while they themselves went off to more complex pleasures. But most of these old babes are part of the permanent landscape of Las Vegas. In they go to the Golden Nugget or the Mint, with their Social Security check or their pension check from the Ohio telephone company, cash it at the casino cashier's, pull out the Dixie Cup and the Iron-Boy work glove, disappear down a row of slots and get on with it. I remember particularly talking to another Abby—a widow, sixty-two years old, built short and up from the bottom like a fire hydrant. After living alone for twelve years in Canton, Ohio, she had moved out to Las Vegas to live with her daughter and her husband, who worked for the Army.

"They were wonderful about it," she said. "Perfect hypocrites. She kept saying, you know, 'Mother, we'd be delighted to have you, only we don't think you'll *like* it. It's practically a fron*tier* town,' she says. 'It's so *ga*rish,' she says. So I said, I told her, 'Well, if you'd rather I didn't come. . . .' 'Oh, no!' she says. I wish I could have heard what her husband was saying. He calls me 'Mother.' '*Moth*er,' he says. Well, once I was here, they figured, well, I *might* make a good baby-sitter and dishwasher and duster and mopper. The children are nasty little things. So one day I was in town for something or other and I just played a slot machine. It's fun—I can't describe it to you. I suppose I lose. I lose a little. And *they* have fits about it. 'For God's sake, Grandmother,' and so forth. They always say '*Grand*mother' when I am supposed to 'act my age' or crawl through a crack in the floor. Well, I'll tell you, the slot machines are a *whole lot* better than sitting in that little house all day. They kind of get you; I can't explain it."

The childlike megalomania of gambling is, of course, from the same cloth as the megalomania of the town. And, as the children of the liberated cortex, the old guys and babes are running up and down the Strip around the clock like everybody else. It is not by chance that much of the entertainment in Las Vegas, especially the second-stringers who perform in the cocktail lounges, will recall for an aging man what was glamorous twenty-five years ago when he had neither the money nor the freedom of spirit to indulge himself in it. In the big theatre-dining room at the Desert Inn, The Painted Desert Room, Eddie Fisher's act is on and he is saying cozily to a florid guy at a table right next to the stage, "Manny, you know you shouldn'a sat this close—you know you're in for it now, Manny, baby," while Manny beams with fright. But in the cocktail lounge, where the idea is chiefly just to keep the razzle-dazzle going, there is Hugh Farr, one of the stars of another era in the West, composer of two of the five Western songs the Library of Congress has taped for posterity, *Cool Water* and *Tumbling Tumbleweed,* when he played the violin for the Sons of the Pioneers. And now around the eyes he looks like an aging Chinese savant, but he is wearing a white tuxedo and powder-blue leather boots and playing his sad old Western violin with an electric cord plugged in it for a group called The Country Gentlemen. And there is Ben Blue, looking like a waxwork exhibit of vaudeville, doffing his straw skimmer to reveal the sculptural qualities of his skull. And down at the Flamingo cocktail lounge—Ella Fitzgerald is in the main room—there is Harry

James, looking old and pudgy in one of those toy Italian-style show-biz suits. And the Ink Spots are at the New Frontier and Louis Prima is at the Sahara, and the old parties are seeing it all, roaring through the dawn into the next day, until the sun seems like a par lamp fading in and out. The casinos, the bars, the liquor stores are open every minute of every day, like a sempiternal wading pool for the childhood ego. ". . . Don't make me go to bed. . . ."

Finally the casualties start piling up. I am in the manager's office of a hotel on the Strip. A man and his wife, each about sixty, are in there, raging. Someone got into their room and stole seventy dollars from her purse, and they want the hotel to make it up to them. The man pops up and down from a chair and ricochets back and forth across the room, flailing his great pig's-knuckle elbows about.

"What kind of security you call that? Walk right in the god-dern room and just help themselves. And where do you think I found your security man? Back around the corner reading a god-dern detective magazine!"

He had scored a point there, but he was wearing a striped polo shirt with a hip Hollywood solid-color collar, and she had on Capri pants, and hooked across their wrinkly old faces they both had rimless, wraparound French sunglasses of the sort young-punk heroes in *nouvelle vague* movies wear, and it was impossible to give any earnest contemplation to a word they said. They seemed to have the great shiny popeyes of a praying mantis.

"Listen, Mister," she is saying, "I don't care about the seventy bucks. I'd lose seventy bucks at your craps table and I wouldn't think nothing of it. I'd play seventy bucks just like that, and it wouldn't mean nothing. I wouldn't regret it. But when they can just walk in—and you don't give a damn—for Christ's sake!"

They are both zeroing in on the manager with their great insect corneas. The manager is a cool number in a white-on-white shirt and silver tie.

"This happened three days ago. Why didn't you tell us about it then?"

"Well, I was gonna be a nice guy about it. Seventy dollars," he said, as if it would be difficult for the brain to grasp a sum much smaller. "But then I found your man back there reading a god-dern detective magazine. *True Detectives* it was. Had a picture on the front of some floozie with one leg up on a chair and her garter showing. Looked like a god-derned athlete's-foot ad. Boy, I went into a slow burn. But when I am burned up, I am *burned up!* You get me, Mister? There he was, reading the god-derned *True Detectives*."

"Any decent hotel would have insurance," she says.

The manager says, "I don't know a hotel in the world that offers insurance against theft."

"Hold on, Mister," he says, "are you calling my wife a liar? You just get smart, and I'm gonna pop you one! I'll pop you one right now if you call my wife a liar."

At this point the manager lowers his head to one side and looks up at the old guy from under his eyebrows with a version of the Red Hook brush-off, and the old guy begins to cool off.

But others are beyond cooling off. Hornette Reilly, a buttery hipped baggage from New York City, is lying in bed with a bald-headed guy from some place who has skin like oatmeal. He is asleep or passed out or something. Hornette is relating all this to the doctor over the Princess telephone by the bed.

"Look," she says, "I'm breaking up. I can't tell you how much I've drunk. About a bottle of brandy since four o'clock, I'm not kidding. I'm in bed with a guy. Right this minute. I'm talking on the telephone to you and this slob is lying here like an animal. He's all fat and his skin looks like oatmeal—what's happening to me? I'm going to take some more pills. I'm not kidding, I'm breaking up. I'm going to kill myself. You've got to put me in Rose de Lima. I'm breaking up, and I don't even know what's happening to me."

"So naturally you want to go to Rose de Lima."

"Well, yeah."

"You can come by the office, but I'm not sending you to Rose de Lima."

"Doctor, I'm not kidding."

"I don't doubt that you're sick, old girl, but I'm not sending you to Rose de Lima to sober up."

The girls do not want to go to the County Hospital. They want to go to Rose de Lima, where the psychiatric cases receive milieu therapy. The patients dress in street clothes, socialize and play games with the staff, eat well and relax in the sun, all paid for by the State. One of the folk heroines of the Las Vegas floozies, apparently, is the call girl who last year was spending Monday through Friday at Rose de Lima and "turning out," as they call it, Saturdays and Sundays on the Strip, to the tune of $200 to $300 a weekend. She looks upon herself not as a whore, or even a call girl, but as a lady of assignation. When some guy comes to the Strip and unveils the little art-nouveau curves in his psyche and calls for two girls to perform arts upon one another, this one consents to be the passive member of the team only. A Rose de Lima girl, she draws the line.

At the County Hospital the psychiatric ward is latched, bolted, wired up and jammed with patients who are edging along the walls in the inner hall, the only place they have to take a walk other than the courtyard.

A big brunette with the remnants of a beehive hairdo and decal eyes and an obvious pregnancy is the liveliest of the lot. She is making eyes at everyone who walks in. She also nods gaily toward vacant places along the wall.

"Mrs.————is refusing medication," a nurse tells one of the psychiatrists. "She won't even open her mouth."

Presently the woman, in a white hospital tunic, is led up the hall. She looks about fifty, but she has extraordinary lines on her face.

"Welcome home," says Dr.————.

"This is not my home," she says.

"Well, as I told you before, it has to be for the time being."

"Listen, you didn't analyze me."

"Oh, yes. Two psychiatrists examined you—all over again."

"You mean that time in jail."

"Exactly."

"You can't tell anything from that. I was excited. I had been out on the Strip, and then all that stupid—"

Three-fourths of the 640 patients who clustered into the ward last year were casualties of the Strip or the Strip milieu of Las Vegas, the psychiatrist tells me. He is a bright and energetic man in a shawl-collared black silk suit with brass buttons.

"I'm not even her doctor," he says. "I don't know her case. There's nothing I can do for her."

Here, securely out of sight in this little warren, are all those who have taken the loop-the-loop and could not stand the centripety. Some, like Raymond, who has been rocketing for days on pills and liquor, who has gone without sleep to the point of anoxia, might pull out of the toxic reaction in two or three days, or eight or ten. Others have conflicts to add to the chemical wackiness. A man who has thrown all his cash to the flabby homunculus who sits at every craps table stuffing the take down an almost hidden chute so it won't pile up in front of the customers' eyes; a man who has sold the family car for next to nothing at a car lot advertising "Cash for your car—*right now*" and then thrown that to the homunculus, too, but also still has the family waiting guiltlessly, guilelessly back home; well, he has troubles.

" . . . After I came here and began doing personal studies," the doctor is saying, "I recognized extreme aggressiveness continually. It's not merely what Las Vegas can do to a person, it's the type of person it attracts. Gambling is a very aggressive pastime, and Las Vegas attracts aggressive people. They have an amazing capacity to louse up a normal situation."

The girl, probably a looker in more favorable moments, is pressed face into the wall, cutting glances at the doctor. The nurse tells her something and she puts her face in her hands, convulsing but not making a sound. She retreats to her room, and then the sounds come shrieking out. The doctor rushes back.

Other patients are sticking their heads out of their rooms along the hall.

"The young girl?" a quiet guy says to a nurse. "The young girl," he says to somebody in the room.

But the big brunette just keeps rolling her decal eyes.

Out in the courtyard—all bare sand—the light is a kind of light-bulb twilight. An old babe is rocking herself back and forth on a straight chair and putting one hand out in front from time to time and pulling it in toward her bosom.

It seems clear enough to me. "A slot machine?" I say to the nurse, but she says there is no telling.

" . . . and yet the same aggressive types are necessary to build a frontier town, and Las Vegas is a frontier town, certainly by any psychological standard," Dr.——is saying. "They'll undertake anything and they'll accomplish it. The building here has been incredible. They don't seem to care what they're up against, so they do it."

I go out to the parking lot in back of the County Hospital and it doesn't take a second; as soon as I turn on the motor I'm swinging again with Action Checkpoint News, *Monkey No. 9, Donna, Donna, the Prima Donna* and friendly picking and swinging for the Fremont Hotel and Frontier Federal. Me and my big white car are sailing down the Strip and the Boomerang Modern, Palette Curvilinear, Flash Gordon Ming-Alert Spiral, McDonald's Hamburger Parabola, Mint Casino Elliptical and Miami Beach Kidney sunbursts are exploding in the Young Electric Sign Company's Grand Gallery for all the sun kings. At the airport there was that bad interval between the rental-car stall and the terminal entrance, but once through the automatic door the Muzak came bubbling up with *Song of India*. On the upper level around the ramps the slots were cranking away. They are placed like "traps," a word Las Vegas picked up from golf. And an old guy is walking up the ramp, just off the plane from Denver, with a huge plastic bag of clothes slung over the left shoulder and a two-suiter suitcase in his right hand. He has to put the suitcase down on the floor and jostle the plastic bag all up around his neck to keep it from falling, but he manages to dig into his pocket for a couple of coins and get going on the slot machines. All seems right, but walking out to my plane I sense that something is missing. Then I recall sitting in the cocktail lounge of the Dunes at three p.m. with Jack Heskett, district manager of the Federal Sign and Signal Corporation, and Marty Stein-man, the sales manager, and Ted Blaney, a designer. They are telling me about the sign they are building for the Dunes to put up at the airport. It will be five thousand square feet of free-standing sign, done in flaming-lake red on burning-desert gold. The d—the D—alone in the word Dunes, written in Cyrillic modern, will be practically two stories high. An inset plexiglas display, the largest revolving, trivision plexiglas sign in the world, will turn and show first the Dunes, with its twenty-two-story addition, then the seahorse swimming pool, then the new golf course. The scimitar curves of the sign will soar to a huge roaring diamond at the very top. "You'll be able to see it from an airplane fifteen miles away," says Jack Heskett. "Fifty miles," says Lee Fisher. And it will be sixty-five feet up in the air—because the thing was, somebody was out at the airport and they noticed there was only one display to be topped. That was that shaft about sixty feet high with the lit-up globe and the beacon lights, which is to say, the control tower. Hell, you can only see that forty miles away. But exactly!

[February, 1964]

Twirling at Ole Miss

by Terry Southern

In an age gone stale through the complex of bureaucratic inter-dependencies, with its tedious labyrinth of technical specialization, each contingent upon the next, and all aimed to converge into a single totality of meaning, it is a refreshing moment indeed when one comes across an area of human endeavor absolutely sufficient unto itself, pure and free, no strings attached—the cherished and almost forgotten *l'art pour l'art*. Such is the work being carried forward now at the Dixie National Baton Twirling Institute, down at the campus of Ole Miss—a visit to which is well worthwhile these days, if one can keep one's wits about.

In my case, it was the first trip South in many years, and I was duly apprehensive. For one thing, the Institute is located just outside Oxford, Mississippi—and, by grotesque coincidence, Faulkner's funeral had been held only the day before my arrival, lending a grimly surreal aura to the nature of my assignment . . . namely, to get the story on the Baton Twirling Institute. Would reverting to the Texas twang and callousness of my youth suffice to see me through?

Arriving in Oxford then, on a hot midday in July, after the three-hour bus ride from Memphis, I stepped off in front of the Old Colonial Hotel

219

and meandered across the sleepy square toward the only sign of life at hand—the proverbial row of shirt-sleeved men sitting on benches in front of the county courthouse, a sort of permanent jury.

"Howdy," I say, striking an easy stance, smiling friendly-like, "Whar the school?"

The nearest regard me in narrow surmise: they are quick to spot the stranger here, but a bit slow to cotton. One turns to another.

"What's that he say, Ed?"

Big Ed shifts his wad, sluices a long spurt of juice into the dust, gazes at it reflectively before fixing me again with gun-blue-cold eyes.

"Reckon you mean, 'Whar the school *at*?', don't you, stranger?"

Next to the benches, and about three feet apart, are two public drinking fountains, and I notice that the one boldly marked "For Colored" is sitting squarely in the shadow cast by the justice symbol on the courthouse façade—to be entered later, of course, in my writer's notebook, under "Imagery, sociochiaroscurian, hack."

After getting directions (rather circuitous, I thought—being farther put off by what I understood, though perhaps in error, as a fleeting reference to "the Till case") I decided to take a cab, having just seen one park on the opposite side of the square.

"Which is nearer," I asked the driver, "Faulkner's house or his grave?"

"Wal," he said without looking around, "now that would take a little studyin', if you were gonna hold a man to it, but offhand I'd say they were pretty damn near the same—about ten minutes from where we're sittin' and fifty cents each. They're in opposite directions."

I sensed the somehow questionable irony of going from either to the Baton Twirling Institute, and so decided to get over to the Institute first and get on with the coverage.

"By the way," I asked after we'd started, "where can a man get a drink of whiskey around here?" It had just occurred to me that Mississippi is a dry state.

"Place over on the county line," said the driver, "about eighteen miles; cost you four dollars for the trip, eight for the bottle."

"I see."

He half turned, giving me a curious look.

"Unless, of course, you'd like to try some 'nigger-pot.' "

"Nigger-pot? Great God yes, man," I said in wild misunderstanding, "let's go!"

It soon developed, of course, that what he was talking about was the unaged and uncolored corn whiskey privately made in the region, and also known as "white lightning." I started to demur, but as we were already in the middle of the colored section, thought best to go through with it. Why not begin the sojourn with a genuine Dixieland experience—the traditional jug of corn?

As it happened the distiller and his wife were in the fields when we reached the house, or hut as it were, where we were tended by a Negro boy of about nine.

"This here's a mighty fine batch," he said, digging around in a box of kindling wood and fetching out unlabeled pints of it.

The taxi driver, who had come inside with me, cocked his head to one side and gave a short laugh, as to show we were not so easily put upon.

"Why, boy," he said, "I wouldn't have thought you was a drinkin' man."

"Nosuh, I ain't no drinkin' man, but I sure know how it suppose to taste—that's 'cause times nobody here I have to *watch* it and I have to *taste* it too, see it workin' right. We liable lose the whole batch I don't know how it suppose to taste. You all taste it," he added, holding out one of the bottles and shaking it in my happy face. "You see if that ain't a fine batch!"

Well, it had a pretty good taste all right—a bit edgy perhaps, but plenty of warmth and body. And I did have to admire the pride the young fellow took in his craft. You don't see much of that these days—especially among nine-year-olds. So I bought a couple of bottles, and the driver bought one, and we were off at last for the Institute.

The Dixie National Baton Twirling Institute holds its classes in a huge, sloping, fairyland grove on the campus of Ole Miss, and it resembles something from another age. The classes had already begun when I stepped out of the cab, and the sylvan scene which stretched before me, of some seven-hundred girls, nymphs and nymphets all, cavorting with their staffs in scanty attire beneath the broadleaf elms, was a sight to spin the senses and quicken the blood. Could I but have donned satyr's garb and rushed savagely among them! But no, there was this job o'work to get on with—dry, factual reportage—mere donkey work, in fact. I decided the correct procedure was to first get some background material, and to this end I sought out Don Sartell, "Mister Baton" himself, Director of the Institute. Mr. Sartell is a handsome and personable young man from north of the Mason-Dixon line, highly intelligent, acutely attuned to the needs of the young, and, needless to say, extremely dexterous *avec les doigts*. (By way of demonstrating the latter he once mastered a year's typing course in a quick six hours—or it may have been six days, though I do recall that it was an impressive and well-documented achievement.)

"Baton twirling," he tells me straight off, "is the second largest girl's youth movement in America—the first, of course, being the Girl Scouts." (Veteran legman, I check this out later. Correct.) "The popularity of baton twirling," he explains, "has a threefold justification: (1) it is a sport which can be practiced alone; (2) it does not, unlike other solo sports (sailing, skiing, shooting, etc.), require expensive equipment; and (3) it does not, again like the aforementioned, require travel, but, on the contrary, may be practiced in one's own living room or backyard."

"Right," I say. "So far, so good, Mister Baton—but what about the intrinsics? I mean, just what is the point of it all?"

"The point, aside from the simple satisfaction of mastering a complex and highly evolved skill, is the development of self-confidence, poise, ambidexterity, disciplined coordination, et cetera."

I asked if he would like a drink of nigger-pot. He declined graciously: he does not drink or smoke. My place, I decided, is in the grove, with the groovy girls—so, limbering up my 600-page, eight-dollar copy of *Who's Who in Baton Twirling,* I take my leave of the excellent fellow and steal toward the sylvan scene below, ready for anything.

The development of American baton twirling closely parallels the history of emancipation of our women. A larger version of this same baton (metal with a knob on the end) was first used, of course, to direct military marching bands, or, prior to that, drum corps—the baton being manipulated in a fairly straightforward, dum-de-dum, up-and-down manner. The idea of *twirling* it—and finally even *flinging* it—is, obviously, a delightfully girlish notion.

Among those most keenly interested in mastering the skill today are drum majorettes from the high schools and colleges of the South and Midwest, all of which have these big swinging bands and corps of majorettes competing during the half at football games. In the South, on the higher-educational level, almost as much expense and training goes into these groups as into the football team itself, and, to persons of promise and accomplishment in the field, similar scholarships are available. Girls who aspire to become majorettes—and it is generally considered the smartest status a girl can achieve on the Southern campus—come to the Institute for preschool training. Or, if she is already a majorette, she comes to sharpen her technique. Many schools send a girl, or a small contingent of them, to the Institute to pick up the latest routines so that they can come back and teach the rest of the corps what they have learned. Still others are training to be professionals and teachers of baton twirling. Most of these girls come every year—I talked to one from Honey Pass, Arkansas, a real cutie pie, who had been there for eight consecutive years, from the time she was nine. When I asked if she would like a drink of pot, she replied pertly: "*N* . . . *o* . . . spells 'No'!" Such girls are usually championship material, shooting for the Nationals.

Competitions to determine one's degree of excellence are held regularly under the auspices of the National Baton Twirling Association, and are of the following myriad categories: *Advanced Solo; Intermediate Solo; Beginners Solo; Strutting Routine; Beginners Strutting Routine; Military*

Marching; Flag; Two-Baton; Fire Baton; Duet; Trio; Team; Corps; Boys; Out-of-State; and others. Each division is further divided into age groups: 0-6, 7-8, 9-10, 11-12, 13-14, 15-16, 17 and over. The winner in each category receives a trophy, and the first five runners-up receive medals. This makes for quite a bit of hardware riding on one session, so that a person in the baton-twirling game does not go too long without at least token recognition—and the general run of *Who's Who* entries ("eight trophies, seventy-three medals") would make someone like Audie Murphy appear rudely neglected.

The rules of competition, however, are fairly exacting. Each contestant appears singly before a Judge and Scorekeeper, and while the Judge observes and relays the grading to the Scorekeeper, the girl goes through her routine for a closely specified time. In Advanced Solo, for example, the routine must have a duration of not less than two minutes and twenty seconds, and not more than two and thirty. She is scored on general qualities relating to her degree of accomplishment—including *showmanship, speed,* and *drops,* the latter, of course, counting against her, though not so much as one might suppose. Entrance fees average about two dollars for each contestant. Some girls use their allowance to pay it.

In the Institute's grove—not unlike the fabled Arcadia—the groups are ranged among the trees in various states of learning. The largest, most central and liveliest of these groups is the one devoted to the mastery of Strutting. Practice and instruction in Strutting are executed to records played over a public-address system at an unusually loud volume—a sort of upbeat rock and roll with boogie-woogie overtones. *Dixie, The Stripper,* and *Potato Peel* were the three records in greatest use for this class—played first at half speed, to learn the motions, then blasted at full tempo. Strutting is, of course, one of the most fantastic body-movement phenomena one is likely to see anywhere. The deliberate narcissistic intensity it requires must exceed even that of the Spanish flamenco dancer. High-style (or "all-out") Strutting is to be seen mainly in the South, and what it resembles more than anything else is a very contemporary burlesque-house number—with the grinds in and the bumps out. It is the sort of dance one associates with jaded and sequin-covered washed-out blondes in their very late thirties—but Ole Miss, as is perhaps well known, is in "the heartland of beautiful girls," having produced two Miss Americas and any number of runners-up, and to watch a hundred of their nymphets practice the Strut, in bathing suits, short shorts, and other such skimp, is a visual treat which cuts anything the Twist may offer the viewer. It is said, incidentally, that the best Strutting is done at the colored schools of the South, and that of these the greatest of all is to be seen at Alabama State Teachers College. That jazz trends have decisively influenced the style of Strutting in recent years is readily acknowledged, and is highly apparent indeed.

At the Institute, the instructor of the Strut stands on a slightly raised platform facing her class, flanked by her two assistants. She wears dark glasses, tight rolled shorts, and looks to be about 34-22-34. She's a swinger from Pensacola, Florida, a former National Senior Champion and Miss Majorette of America, now turned pro. When not at the Dixie Institute at the University of Mississippi, or a similar establishment, she gives private lessons at her own studio, for four to six dollars an hour, and drives a Cadillac convertible.

As for other, more academic, aspects of baton twirling, an exhibition was given the first evening by members of the cadre—all champions, and highly skilled indeed. It is really quite amazing what can be done with a baton, and no one could have been more surprised than your correspondent. The members of the cadre can literally walk those sticks over every inch of the body, almost it seems without touching them. This is especially effective at night when they use a thing called the "fire baton," with a torch flaming at each end.

Instruction in speed and manipulation of this sort is a long and nerve-racking process. There is something almost insane about the amount of sheer effort and perseverance which seems to go into achieving even a nominal degree of real excellence—and practice of four hours a day is not uncommon. And yet the genuine and really impressive skill which is occasionally displayed makes it difficult to consider the art as so totally ridiculous as one would have previously believed—though, of course, another might argue that such achieved excellence only makes it more ridiculous—or perhaps not so much ridiculous as absurd. In fact, in the existentialist sense, it might well be considered as the final epitome of the absurd—I mean, people starving in India and that sort of thing, and then others spending four hours a day skillfully flinging a metal stick about. *Ça alors!* In any case it has evolved now into a highly developed art and a tightly organized movement—though by no means one which has reached full flower. For one thing, a nomenclature—that hallmark of an art's maturity—has not yet been wholly formalized. Theoretically, at least, there should be a limit to the number of possible manipulations, each of which could legitimately be held as distinct from all others—that is to say, a repertory which would remain standard and unchanged for a period of time. The art of baton twirling has not yet reached that stage, however, and innovations arise with such frequency that there does not exist at present any single manual, or similarly doctrinaire work, on the subject. Doubtless this is due in large part to the comparative newness of the art as a large and intensely active pastime—the Dixie National Baton Twirling Institute, for example, having been founded as recently as 1951. The continuing evolution of the art as a whole is reflected in the names of the various manipulations. Alongside the commonplace (or classic) designations, such as *arabesque, tour-jeté, cradles,* etc., are those of more exotic or contemporary flavor: *bat, walk-over, pretzel,* and the like . . . and all, old or new, requiring countless hours of practice.

During the twirling exhibition I fell into conversation with a couple of graduate law students, and afterward went along with them to the campus coffee shop, "Rebel Devil" or whatever it is called—nearly all shops there have the word "Rebel" in them—and we had an interesting talk. Ole Miss prides itself, among other things, on having the only law school in the state which is accredited by the American Bar Association—so that these two graduate law students were not without some claim to representing a certain level of relative advancement in the community of scholars. They were clean-cut young men in their mid-twenties, dressed in summer suits of tasteful cut. In answer to a question of mine, we talked about Constitutional Law for ten minutes before I realized they were talking about *State* Constitutional Law. When it became apparent what I was driving at, however, they were quick to face the issue squarely.

"*We* nevuh had no Negra problem heah," said one of them, shaking his head sadly. He was a serious young man wearing glasses and the mien of a Harvard divinity student. "Theah just *weren't* no problem—wasn't till these *agi-ta-tors* came down heah started all this problem business."

They were particularly disturbed about the possible "trouble, an' I mean *real* trouble" which would be occasioned by the attempted registration of a Negro student [James Meredith] which was threatening to take place quite soon, during that very summer session, in fact. As it happened, the authorities managed to delay it; I did, however, get a preview of things to come.

"Why they'll find *dope* in his room the first night he's heah," the other student said, "dope, a gun, something—*anything,* just plant it in theah an' *find* it! And out he'll go!"

They assured me that they themselves were well above this sort of thing, and were, in fact, speaking as mature and nonviolent persons.

"But now these heah young *unduh* graduates, they're hot-headed. Why, do you know how *they* feel? What *they* say?"

Then to the tune of *John Brown's Body,* the two graduate law students begin to sing, almost simultaneously: "*Oh we'll bury all the niggers in the Mississippi mud . . .*", singing it rather loudly it seemed to me—I mean if they were just documenting a point in a private conversation—or perhaps they were momentarily carried away, so to speak. In any event, and despite a terrific effort at steely Zen detachment, the incident left me somewhat depressed, so I retired early, to my comfortable room in the Alumni House, where I sipped the white corn and watched television. But I was not destined to escape so easily, for suddenly who should appear on the screen but old Governor Faubus himself—in a gubernatorial campaign rant—with about six cross-purpose facial tics going strong, and in general looking as mad as a hatter. At first I actually mistook it for a rather tasteless and heavy-handed parody of the governor. It could not, I thought, really be Faubus, because why would the network carry an Arkansas primary campaign speech in Mississippi? Surely not just for laughs. Later I learned that while there is such a thing in television as a *nation*wide hookup for covering events of national importance, there is also such a thing as a *South*wide hookup.

The Institute's mimeographed schedule, of which I had received a copy, read for the next day as follows:

7:30	Up and at 'em
8-9	Breakfast—University Cafeteria
9-9:30	Assembly, Limber up, Review—Grove
9:30-10:45	Class No. 4
10:45-11:30	Relax—Make Notes
11:30-12:45	Class No. 5
1-2:30	Lunch—University Cafeteria
2:30-4	Class No. 6
4-5:30	Swim Hour
6:30-7:30	Supper—University Cafeteria
7:30	Dance—Tennis Court
11	Room Check
11:30	Lights Out (No EXCEPTIONS)

The "*Up and at 'em*" seemed spirited enough, as did the "No EXCEPTIONS" being in heavy capitals; but the rest somehow offered little promise, so, after a morning cup of coffee, I walked over to the library, just to see if they really had any books there—other than books on Constitutional Law, that is. Indeed they did, and quite a modern and comfortable structure it was, too, air-conditioned (as was, incidentally, my room at the Alumni House) and well-lighted throughout. After looking around for a bit, I carefully opened a mint first-edition copy of *Light in August,* and found "nigger-lover" scrawled across the title page. I decided I must be having a run of bad luck as, a few minutes later, I suffered still another minor trauma on the steps of the library. It was one of those incredible bits of irony which sometimes do occur in life, but are never suitable for fiction—for I had completely put the title-page incident out of my mind and was sitting on the steps of the library, having a smoke, when this very amiable gentleman of middle age paused in passing to remark on the weather (102°) and to inquire in an oblique and courteous way as to the nature of my visit. An immaculate, pink-faced man, with pince-nez spectacles attached by a silver loop to his lapel, nails buffed to a gleam, he carried a smart leather briefcase and a couple of English-literature textbooks which he rested momentarily on the balustrade as he continued to smile down on me with what seemed to be extraordinary happiness.

"My, but it's a mighty warm day, an' that's no lie," he said, withdrawing a dazzling white-linen handkerchief and touching it carefully to his brow, ". . . an' I expect you all from up Nawth," he added with a twinkle, "find it especially so!" Then he quite abruptly began to talk of the "natural tolerance" of the people of Mississippi, speaking in joyfully objective tones, as though it were, even to him, an unfailing source of mystery and delight.

"Don't mind nobody's business but yoah own!" he said, beaming and nodding his head—and it occurred to me this might be some kind of really weirdly obscured threat, the way he was smiling; but no, evidently he was just remarkably good-natured. " 'Live an' let live!' That's how the people of Mississippi feel—always have! Why, look at William Faulkner, with all his notions, an' him livin' right ovah heah in Oxford all the time an' nobody botherin' him—just let him go his own way—why we even let him teach heah at the University one yeah! That's right! I know it! Live an' let live— you can't beat it! I'll see you now, you heah?" And his face still a glittering mask of joviality, he half raised his hand in good-by and hurried on. Who was this strange, happy educator? Was it he who had defaced the title page? His idea of tolerance and his general hilarity gave one pause. I headed back to the grove, hoping to recover some equilibrium. There, things seemed to be proceeding pretty much as ever.

"Do you find that your costume is an advantage in your work?" I asked the first seventeen-year-old Georgia Peach I came across, she wearing something like a handkerchief-size Confederate flag.

"Yessuh, I *do*," she agreed, with friendly emphasis, tucking her little blouse in a bit more snugly all around, and continuing to speak in that oddly rising inflection peculiar to girls of the South, making parts of a reply sound like a question: "Why, back home near Macon . . . Macon, Georgia? At Robert E. Lee High? . . . we've got these outfits with *tassels!* And a little red-and-gold skirt? . . . that, you know, sort of *flares out?* Well, now they're awful pretty, and of course they're *short* and everything, but I declare those tassels and that little skirt get in my way!"

The rest of the day passed without untoward incident, with my observing the Strut platform for a while, then withdrawing to rest up for the Dance, and perhaps catch the Faub on video again.

The Dance was held on a boarded-over outdoor tennis court, and was a swinging affair. The popular style of dancing in the white South is always in advance of that in the rest of white America; and, at any given moment, it most nearly resembles that which is occurring at the same time in Harlem, which is invariably the forerunner of whatever is to become the national style. I mused on this, standing there near the court foul line, and (in view of the day's events) pursued it to an interesting generalization: perhaps *all* the remaining virtues, or let us say, positive traits, of the white Southerner—folk song, poetic speech, and the occasional warmth and simplicity of human relationships—would seem rather obviously to derive from the colored culture there. Due to my magazine assignment, I could not reveal my findings over the public-address system at the dance—and, in fact, thought best to put them from my mind entirely, and get on with the coverage—and, to that end, had a few dances and further questioned the girls. Their view of the world was quite extraordinary. For most, New York was like another country—queer, remote, and of small import in the scheme of things. Several girls spoke spiritedly of wanting to "get into television," but it always developed that they were talking about programs produced in Memphis. Memphis, in fact, was definitely the mecca, yardstick and *summum bonum*. As the evening wore on, I found it increasingly difficult, despite the abundance of cutie pieness at hand, to string along with these values, and so finally decided to wrap it up. It should be noted too, that girls at the Dixie National are under extremely close surveillance both in the grove and out.

The following day I made one last tour, this time noting in particular the instruction methods for advanced twirling techniques: *1-, 2-, 3-finger rolls, wrist rolls, waist roll, neck roll,* etc. A pretty girl of about twelve was tossing a baton sixty feet straight up, a silver whir in the Mississippi sunlight, and she beneath it spinning like an ice skater, and catching it behind her back, not having moved an inch. She said she had practiced it an hour a day for six years. Her hope was to become "the best there is at the high toss and spin"—and she was now up to seven complete turns before making the catch. Was there a limit to the height and number of spins one could attain? No, she guessed not.

After lunch I packed, bid adieu to the Dixie National and boarded the bus for Memphis. As we crossed the Oxford square and passed the courthouse, I saw the fountain was still shaded, although it was now a couple of hours later than the time before. Perhaps it is always shaded— cool and inviting, it could make a person thirsty just to see it.

[February, 1963]

The Last American Hero is Junior Johnson. Yes!

by Tom Wolfe

Ten o'clock Sunday morning in the hills of North Carolina. Cars, miles of cars, in every direction, millions of cars, pastel cars, aqua green, aqua blue, aqua beige, aqua buff, aqua dawn, aqua dusk, aqua aqua, aqua Malacca, Malacca lacquer, Cloud lavender, Assassin pink, Rake-a-cheek raspberry, Nude Strand coral, Honest Thrill orange, and Baby Fawn Lust cream-colored cars are all going to the stock-car races, and that old mothering North Carolina sun keeps exploding off the windshields. Mother dog!

Seventeen thousand people, me included, all of us driving out Route 421, out to the stock-car races at the North Wilkesboro Speedway, 17,000 going out to a five-eighths-mile stock-car track with a Coca-Cola sign out front. This is not to say there is no preaching and shouting in the South this morning. There is preaching and shouting. Any of us can turn on the old automobile transistor radio and get all we want:

"They are greedy dogs. Yeah! They ride around in big cars. Unnh-hunh! And chase women. Yeah! And drink liquor. Unnh-hunh! And smoke cigars. Oh yes! And they are greedy dogs. Yeah! Unh-hunh! Oh yes! Amen!"

There are also some commercials on the radio for Aunt Jemima grits,

229

which cost ten cents a pound. There are also the Gospel Harmonettes, singing: "If you dig a ditch, you better dig two. . . ."

There are also three fools in a panel discussion on the New South, which they seem to conceive of as General Lee running the new Dulcidreme Labial Cream factory down at Griffin, Georgia.

And suddenly my car is stopped still on Sunday morning in the middle of the biggest traffic jam in the history of the world. It goes for ten miles in every direction from the North Wilkesboro Speedway. And right there it dawns on me that as far as this situation is concerned, anyway, all the conventional notions about the South are confined to . . . the Sunday radio. The South has preaching and shouting, the South has grits, the South has country songs, old mimosa traditions, clay dust, Old Bigots, New Liberals—and all of it, all of that old mental cholesterol, is confined to the Sunday radio. What I was in the middle of—well, it wasn't anything one hears about in panels about the South today. Miles and miles of eye-busting pastel cars on the expressway, which roar right up into the hills, going to the stock-car races. In ten years baseball—and the state of North Carolina alone used to have forty-four professional baseball teams—baseball is all over with in the South. We were all in the middle of a wild new thing, the Southern car world, and heading down the road on my way to see a breed such as sports never saw before, Southern stock-car drivers, all lined up in these two-ton mothers that go over 175 m.p.h., Fireball Roberts, Freddie Lorenzen, Ned Jarrett, Richard Petty, and—the hardest of all the hard chargers, one of the fastest automobile racing drivers in history —yes! Junior Johnson.

The legend of Junior Johnson! In this legend, here is a country boy, Junior Johnson, who learns to drive by running whiskey for his father, Johnson, Senior, one of the biggest copper-still operators of all times, up in Ingle Hollow, near North Wilkesboro, in northwestern North Carolina, and grows up to be a famous stock-car racing driver, rich, grossing $100,000 in 1963, for example, respected, solid, idolized in his hometown and throughout the rural South, for that matter. There is all this about how good old boys would wake up in the middle of the night in the apple shacks and hear a supercharged Oldsmobile engine roaring over Brushy Mountain and say, "Listen at him—there he goes!", although that part is doubtful, since some nights there were so many good old boys taking off down the road in supercharged automobiles out of Wilkes County, and running loads to Charlotte, Salisbury, Greensboro, Winston-Salem, High Point, or wherever, it would be pretty hard to pick out one. It was Junior Johnson specifically, however, who was famous for the "bootleg turn" or "about-face," in which, if the Alcohol Tax agents had a roadblock up for you or were too close behind, you threw the car up into second gear, cocked the wheel, stepped on the accelerator and made the car's rear end skid around in a complete 180-degree arc, a complete about-face, and tore on back up the road exactly the way you came from. God! The Alcohol Tax agents used to burn over Junior Johnson. Practically every good old boy in town in Wilkesboro, the county seat, got to know the agents by sight in a very short time. They would rag them practically to their faces on the subject of Junior Johnson, so that it got to be an obsession. Finally, one night they had Junior trapped on the road up toward the bridge around Millersville, there's no way out of there, they had the barricades up and they could hear this souped-up car roaring around the bend, and here it comes—but suddenly they can hear a siren and see a red light flashing in the grille, so they think it's another agent, and boy, they run out like ants and pull those barrels and boards and sawhorses out of the way, and then—Ggghhzzzzzzzzhhhhhhggggggzzzzzzzeeeeeong!—gawdam! there he goes again, it was him, Junior Johnson!, with a gawdam agent's si-reen and a red light in his grille!

I wasn't in the South five minutes before people started making oaths, having visions, telling these hulking great stories, and so forth, all on the subject of Junior Johnson. At the Greensboro, North Carolina, Airport there was one good old boy who vowed he would have eaten "a bucket of it" if that would have kept Junior Johnson from switching from a Dodge racer to a Ford. Hell yes, and after that—God-almighty, remember that 1963 Chevrolet of Junior's? Whatever happened to that car? A couple of more good old boys join in. A good old boy, I ought to explain, is a generic term in the rural South referring to a man, of any age, but more often young than not, who fits in with the status system of the region. It usually means he has a good sense of humor and enjoys ironic jokes, is tolerant and easygoing enough to get along in long conversations at places like on the corner, and has a reasonable amount of physical courage. The term is usually heard in some such form as: "Lud? He's a good old boy from over at Crozet." These good old boys in the airport, by the way, were in their twenties, except for one fellow who was a cabdriver and was about forty-five, I would say. Except for the cabdriver, they all wore neo-Brummellian wardrobing such as Lacoste tennis shirts, Slim Jim pants, windbreakers with the collars turned up, "fast" shoes of the winkle-picker genre, and so on. I mention these details just by way of pointing out that very few grits, Iron Boy overalls, clodhoppers or hats with ventilation holes up near the crown enter into this story. Anyway, these good old boys are talking about Junior Johnson and how he has switched to Ford. This they unanimously regard as some kind of betrayal on Johnson's part. Ford, it seems, they regard as the car symbolizing the established power structure. Dodge is kind of a middle ground. Dodge is at least a chal-lenger, not a ruler. But the Junior Johnson they like to remember is the Junior Johnson of 1963, who took on the whole field of NASCAR (National Association For Stock Car Auto Racing) Grand National racing with a Chevrolet. All the other drivers, the drivers driving Fords, Mercu-rys, Plymouths, Dodges, had millions, literally millions when it is all added up, millions of dollars in backing from the Ford and Chrysler Corporations. Junior Johnson took them all on in a Chevrolet without one cent of backing from Detroit. Chevrolet had pulled out of stock-car racing. Yet every race it was the same. It was never a question of whether anybody was going to *outrun* Junior Johnson. It was just a question of whether he was going to win or his car was going to break down, since, for one thing, half the time he had to make his own racing parts. God! Junior Johnson was like Robin Hood or Jesse James or Little David or some-thing. Every time that Chevrolet, No. 3, appeared on the track, these wild curdled yells, "Rebel" yells, they still have those, would rise up. At Daytona, at Atlanta, at Charlotte, at Darlington, South Carolina; Bristol, Tennessee; Martinsville, Virginia—Junior Johnson!

And then the good old boys get to talking about whatever happened to that Chevrolet of Junior's, and the cabdriver says he knows. He says Junior Johnson is using that car to run liquor out of Wilkes County. What does he mean? For Junior Johnson ever to go near another load of bootleg whiskey again—he would have to be insane. He has this huge racing income. He has two other businesses, a whole automated chicken farm with 42,000 chickens, a road-grading business—but cabdriver says he has this dream Junior is still roaring down from Wilkes County, down through the clay cuts, with the Atlas Arc Lip jars full in the back of that Chevrolet. It is in Junior's blood—and then at this point he puts his right hand up in front of him as if he is groping through fog, and his eyeballs glaze over and he looks out in the distance and he describes Junior Johnson roaring over the ridges of Wilkes County as if it is the ghost of Zapata he is describing, bounding over the Sierras on a white horse to rouse the peasants.

A stubborn notion! A crazy notion! Yet Junior Johnson has followers who need to keep him, symbolically, riding through nighttime like a demon. Madness! But Junior Johnson is one of the last of those sports stars who is not just an ace at the game itself, but a hero a whole people or class of people can identify with. Other, older examples are the way Jack Dempsey stirred up the Irish or the way Joe Louis stirred up the Negroes. Junior Johnson is a modern figure. He is only thirty-three years old and still racing. He should be compared to two other sports heroes whose cultural impact is not too well known. One is Antonino Rocca, the professional wrestler, whose triumphs mean so much to New York City's Puerto Ricans that he can fill Madison Square Garden, despite the fact that everybody, the Puerto Ricans included, knows that wrestling is nothing but a crude form of folk theatre. The other is Ingemar Johansson, who had a tremendous meaning to the Swedish masses—they were tired of that old king who played tennis all the time and all his friends who kept on drinking Cointreau behind the screen of socialism. Junior Johnson is a modern hero, all involved with car culture and car symbolism in the South. A wild new thing—

Wild—gone wild, Fireball Roberts' Ford spins out on the first turn at the North Wilkesboro Speedway, spinning, spinning, the spin seems almost like slow motion—and then it smashes into the wooden guardrail. It lies up there with the frame bent. Roberts is all right. There is a new layer of asphalt on the track, it is like glass, the cars keep spinning off the first turn. Ned Jarrett spins, smashes through the wood. "Now, boys, this ice ain't gonna get one goddamn bit better, so you can either line up and qualify or pack up and go home—"

I had driven from the Greensboro Airport up to Wilkes County to see Junior Johnson on the occasion of one of the two yearly NASCAR Grand National stock-car races at the North Wilkesboro Speedway.

It is a long, very gradual climb from Greensboro to Wilkes County. Wilkes County is all hills, ridges, woods and underbrush, full of pin oaks, sweet-gum maples, ash, birch, apple trees, rhododendron, rocks, vines, tin roofs, little clapboard places like the Mount Olive Baptist Church, signs for things like Double Cola, Sherrill's Ice Cream, Eckard's Grocery, Dr. Pepper, Diel's Apples, Google's Place, Suddith's Place and—yes!—cars. Up onto the highway, out of a side road from a hollow, here comes a 1947 Hudson. To almost anybody it would look like just some old piece of junk left over from God knows when, rolling down a country road . . . the 1947 Hudson was one of the first real "hot" cars made after the war. Some of the others were the 1946 Chrysler, which had a "kick-down" gear for sudden bursts of speed, the 1955 Pontiac and a lot of the Fords. To a great many good old boys a hot car was a symbol of heating up life itself. The war! Money even for country boys! And the money bought cars. In California they suddenly found kids of all sorts involved in vast drag-racing orgies and so forth and couldn't figure out what was going on. But in the South the mania for cars was even more intense, although much less publicized. To millions of good old boys, and girls, the automobile represented not only liberation from what was still pretty much a land-bound form of social organization but also a great leap forward into twentieth-century glamour, an idea that was being dinned in on the South like everywhere else. It got so that one of the typical rural sights, in addition to the red rooster, the grey split-rail fence, the Edgeworth Tobacco sign and the rusted-out harrow, one of the typical rural sights would be . . . you would be driving along the dirt roads and there beside the house would be an automobile up on blocks or something, with a rope over the tree for hoisting up the motor or some other heavy part, and a couple of good old boys would be practically disappearing into its innards, from below and from above, draped over the side under the hood. It got so that on Sundays there wouldn't be a safe straight stretch of road in the county, because so many wild country boys would be out racing or just raising hell on the roads. A lot of other kids, who weren't basically wild, would be driving like hell every morning and every night, driving to jobs perhaps thirty or forty miles away, jobs that were available only because of automobiles. In the morning they would be driving through the dapple shadows like madmen. In the hollows, sometimes one would come upon the most incredible tar-paper hovels, down near the stream, and out front would be an incredible automobile creation, a late-model car with aerials, continental kit overhangs in the back, mudguards studded with reflectors, fender skirts, spotlights, God knows what all, with a girl and perhaps a couple of good old boys communing over it and giving you rotten looks as you drive by. On Saturday night everybody would drive into town and park under the lights on the main street and neck. Yes! There was something about being right in there in town underneath the lights and having them reflecting off the baked enamel on the hood. Then if a good old boy insinuated his hands here and there on the front seat with a girl and began . . . necking . . . somehow it was all more *complete*. After the war there was a great deal of stout-burgher talk about people who lived in hovels and bought big-yacht cars to park out front. This was one of the symbols of a new, spendthrift age. But there was a great deal of unconscious resentment buried in the talk. It was resentment against (a) the fact that the good old boy had his money at all and (b) the fact that the car symbolized freedom, a slightly wild, careening emancipation from the old social order. Stock-car racing got started about this time, right after the war, and it was immediately regarded as some kind of manifestation of the animal irresponsibility of the lower orders. It had a truly terrible reputation. It was—well, it looked *rowdy* or something. The cars were likely to be used cars, the tracks were dirt, the stands were rickety wood, the drivers were country boys, and they had regular feuds out there, putting each other "up against the wall" and "cutting tires" and everything else. Those country boys would drive into the curves full tilt, then slide maniacally, sometimes coming around the curve sideways, with red dirt showering up. Sometimes they would race at night, under those weak-eyed yellow-ochre lights they have at small tracks and baseball fields, and the clay dust would start showering up in the air, where the evening dew would catch it, and all evening long you would be sitting in the stands or standing out in the infield with a fine clay-mud drizzle coming down on you, not that anybody gave a damn—except for the Southern upper and middle classes, who never attended in those days, but spoke of the "rowdiness."

But mainly it was the fact that stock-car racing was something that was welling up out of the lower orders. From somewhere these country boys and urban proles were getting the money and starting this sport.

Stock-car racing was beginning all over the country, at places like Allentown, Langhorne and Lancaster, Pennsylvania, and out in California and even out on Long Island, but wherever it cropped up, the Establishment tried to wish it away, largely, and stock-car racing went on in a kind of underground world of tracks built on cheap stretches of land well out from the town or the city, a world of diners, drive-ins, motels, gasoline stations, and the good burghers might drive by from time to time, happen by on a Sunday or something, and see the crowd gathered from out of nowhere, the cars coming in, crowding up the highway a little, but Monday morning they would be all gone.

Stock-car racing was building up a terrific following in the South during the early Fifties. Here was a sport not using any abstract devices, any *bat* and *ball,* but the same automobile that was changing a man's own life, his own symbol of liberation, and it didn't require size, strength and all that, all it required was a taste for speed, and the guts. The newspapers in the South didn't seem to catch onto what was happening until late in the game. Of course, newspapers all over the country have looked backward over the tremendous rise in automobile sports, now the second-biggest type of sport in the country in terms of attendance. The sports pages generally have an inexorable lower-middle-class outlook. The sportswriter's "zest for life" usually amounts, in the end, to some sort of gruff Mom's Pie sentimentality at a hideously cozy bar somewhere. The sportswriters caught onto Grand Prix racing first because it had "tone," a touch of defrocked European nobility about it, what with a few counts racing here and there, although, in fact, it is the least popular form of racing in the United States. What finally put stock-car racing onto the sports pages in the South was the intervention of the Detroit automobile firms. Detroit began putting so much money into the sport that it took on a kind of massive economic respectability and thereby, in the lower-middle-class brain, status.

What Detroit discovered was that thousands of good old boys in the South were starting to form allegiances to brands of automobiles, according to which were hottest on the stock-car circuits, the way they used to have them for the hometown baseball team. The South was one of the hottest car-buying areas in the country. Cars like Hudsons, Oldsmobiles and Lincolns, not the cheapest automobiles by any means, were selling in disproportionate numbers in the South, and a lot of young good old boys were buying them. In 1955, Pontiac started easing into stock-car racing, and suddenly the big surge was on. Everybody jumped into the sport to grab for themselves The Speed Image. Suddenly, where a good old boy used to have to bring his gasoline to the track in old filling-station pails and pour it into the tank through a funnel when he made a pit stop, and change his tires with a hand wrench, suddenly, now, he had these "gravity" tanks of gasoline that you just jam into the gas pipe, and air wrenches to take the wheels off, and whole crews of men in white coveralls to leap all over a car when it came rolling into the pit, just like they do at Indianapolis, as if they are mechanical apparati *merging* with the machine as it rolls in, forcing water into the radiator, jacking up the car, taking off wheels, wiping off the windshield, handing the driver a cup of orange juice, all in one synchronized operation. And now, today, the *big money* starts descending on this little place, the North Wilkesboro, North Carolina, Speedway, a five-eighths-of-a-mile stock-car track with a Coca-Cola sign by the highway where the road in starts.

The private planes start landing out at the Wilkesboro Airport. Freddie Lorenzen, the driver, the biggest money winner last year in stock-car racing, comes sailing in out of the sky in a twin-engine Aero Commander, and there are a few good old boys out there in the tall grass by the runway already with their heads sticking up watching this hero of the modern age come in and taxi up and get out of that twin-engine airplane with his blond hair swept back as if by the mother internal combustion engine of them all. And then Paul Goldsmith, the driver, comes in in a 310 Cessna, and *he* gets out, all these tall, lanky, hard-boned Americans in their thirties with these great profiles like a comic-strip hero or something, and then Glenn (Fireball) Roberts—Fireball Roberts!—Fireball is *hard*—he comes in in a Comanche 250, like a flying yacht, and then Ray Nichels and Ray Fox, the chief mechanics, who run big racing crews for the Chrysler Corporation, this being Fox's last race for Junior as his mechanic, before Junior switches over to Ford, they come in in two-engine planes. And even old Buck Baker—hell, Buck Baker is a middling driver for Dodge, but even he comes rolling in down the landing strip at two hundred miles an hour with his Southern-hero face at the window of the cockpit of a twin-engine Apache, traveling first class in the big status boat that has replaced the yacht in America, the private plane.

And then the Firestone and Goodyear vans pull in, huge mothers, bringing in these huge stacks of racing tires for the race, big wide ones, 8.20's, with special treads, which are like a lot of bumps on the tire instead of grooves. They even have special tires for qualifying, soft tires, called "gumballs," they won't last more than ten times around the track in a race, but for qualifying, which is generally three laps, one to pick up speed and two to race against the clock, they are great, because they hold tight on the corners. And on a hot day, when somebody like Junior Johnson, one of the fastest qualifying runners in the history of the sport, 170.777 m.p.h. in a one-hundred-mile qualifying race at Daytona in 1964, when somebody like Junior Johnson really pushes it on a qualifying run, there will be a ring of blue smoke up over the whole goddamned track, the whole thing, a ring like an oval halo over the whole thing from the gumballs burning, and some good old boy will say, "Great smokin' blue gumballs god almighty dog! There goes Junior Johnson!"

The thing is, each one of these tires costs fifty-five to sixty dollars, and on a track that is fast and hard on tires, like Atlanta, one car might go through ten complete tire changes, easily, forty tires, or almost $2500 worth of tires just for one race. And he may even be out of the money. And then the Ford van and the Dodge van and the Mercury van and the Plymouth van roll in with new motors, a whole new motor every few races, a 427-cubic-inch stock-car-racing motor, 600 horsepower, the largest and most powerful allowed on the track, that probably costs the company $1000 or more, when you consider that they are not mass produced. And still the advertising appeal. You can buy the very same car that these fabulous wild men drive every week at these fabulous wild speeds, and some of their power and charisma is yours. After every NASCAR Grand National stock-car race, whichever company has the car that wins, this company will put big ads in the Southern papers, and papers all over the country if it is a very big race, like the Daytona 500, the Daytona Firecracker 400 or the Atlanta and Charlotte races. They sell a certain number of these 427-cubic-inch cars to the general public, a couple of hundred a year, perhaps, at eight or nine thousand dollars apiece, but it is no secret that these motors are specially reworked just for stock-car racing. Down at Charlotte there is a company called Holman & Moody that is supposed to be the "garage" or "automotive-engineering" concern that prepares automobiles for Freddie Lorenzen and some of the other Ford drivers. But if you go by Holman & Moody out by the airport and Charlotte, suddenly you come upon a huge place that is a *factory,* for God's sake, a big long thing, devoted mainly to the business of turning out stock-car racers. A whole lot of other parts in stock-car racers are heavier than the same parts on a street automobile, although they are made to the same scale. The shock absorbers are bigger, the wheels are wider and bulkier, the swaybars and steering mechanisms are heavier, the axles are much heavier, they have double sets of wheel bearings, and so forth and so on. The bodies of the cars are pretty much the same, except that they use lighter sheet metal, practically tinfoil. Inside, there is only the driver's seat and a heavy set of roll bars and diagonal struts that turn the inside of the car into a rigid cage, actually. That is why the drivers can walk away unhurt—most of the time—from the most spectacular crackups. The gearshift is the floor kind, although it doesn't make much difference, as there is almost no shifting gears in stock-car racing. You just get into high gear and go. The dashboard has no speedometer, the main thing being the dial for engine revolutions per minute. So, anyway, it costs about $15,000 to prepare a stock-car racer in the first place and another three or four thousand for each new race and this does not even count the costs of mechanics' work and transportation. All in all, Detroit will throw around a quarter of a million dollars into it every week while the season is on, and the season runs, roughly, from February to October, with a few big races after that. And all this turns up even out at the North Wilkesboro Speedway, with the Coca-Cola sign out front out in the up-country of Wilkes County, North Carolina.

Sunday! Racing day! Sunday is no longer a big church day in the South. A man can't very well go to eleven o'clock service and still expect to get to a two o'clock stock-car race, unless he wants to get into the biggest traffic jam in the history of creation, and that goes for North Wilkesboro, North Carolina, same as Atlanta and Charlotte.

There is the Coca-Cola sign out where the road leads in from the highway, and hills and trees, but here are long concrete grandstands for about 17,000 and a paved five-eighths-mile oval. Practically all the drivers are out there with their cars and their crews, a lot of guys in white coveralls. The cars look huge . . . and curiously nude and blind. All the chrome is stripped off, except for the grilles. The headlights are blanked out. Most of the cars are in the pits. The so-called "pit" is a paved cutoff on the edge of the infield. It cuts off from the track itself like a service road off an expressway at the old shopping center. Every now and then a car splutters, hacks, coughs, hocks a lunga, rumbles out onto the track itself for a practice run. There is a lot of esoteric conversation going on, speculation, worries, memoirs:

"What happened?"

"Mother—condensed on me. Al brought it up here with him. Water in the line."

"Better keep Al away from a stable, he'll fill you up with horse manure."

". . . they told me to give him one, a cream puff, so I give him one, a cream puff. One goddamn race and the son of a bitch, he *melted* it. . . ."

". . . he's down there right now pettin' and rubbin' and huggin' that car just like those guys do a horse at the Kentucky Derby. . . ."

". . . They'll blow you right out of the tub. . . ."

". . . No, the quarter inch, and go on over and see if you can get Ned's blowtorch. . . ."

". . . Rear end's loose. . . ."

". . . I don't reckon this right here's got nothing to do with it, do you? . . ."

". . . Aw, I don't know, about yea big. . . ."

". . . Who the hell stacked them gumballs on the bottom? . . ."

". . . th'ow in rocks. . . ."

". . . won't turn seven thousand. . . ."

". . . strokin' it. . . ."

". . . blistered. . . ."

". . . spun out. . . ."

". . . muvva. . . ."

Then, finally, here comes Junior Johnson. How he does come on. He comes tooling across the infield in a big white dreamboat, a brand new white Pontiac Catalina four-door hard-top sedan. He pulls up and as he gets out he seems to get more and more huge. First his crew-cut head and then a big jaw and then a bigger neck and then a huge torso, like a wrestler's, all done up rather modish and California modern, with a red-and-white candy-striped sport shirt, white ducks and loafers.

"How you doing?" says Junior Johnson, shaking hands, and then he says, "Hot enough for ye'uns?"

Junior is in an amiable mood. Like most up-hollow people, it turns out, Junior is reserved. His face seldom shows an emotion. He has three basic looks: amiable, amiable and a little shy, and dead serious. To a lot of people, apparently, Junior's dead-serious look seems menacing. There are no cowards left in stock-car racing, but a couple of drivers tell me that one of the things that can shake you up is to look into your rearview mirror going around a curve and see Junior Johnson's car on your tail trying to "root you out of the groove," and then get a glimpse of Junior's dead-serious look. I think some of the sportswriters are afraid of him. One of them tells me Junior is strong, silent—and explosive. Junior will only give you three answers, "Uh-huh," "Uh-unh," and "I don' know," and so forth and so on. Actually, I find he handles questions easily. He has a great technical knowledge of automobiles and the physics of speed, including things he never fools with, such as Offenhauser engines. What he never does offer, however, is small talk. This gives him a built-in poise, since it deprives him of the chance to say anything asinine. "Ye'uns," "we'uns," "h'it" for "it," "growed" for "grew" and a lot of other unusual past participles—Junior uses certain older forms of English, not exactly "Elizabethan," as they are sometimes called, but older forms of English preserved up-country in his territory, Ingle Hollow.

Kids keep coming up for Junior's autograph and others are just hanging around and one little old boy comes up, he is about thirteen, and Junior says: "This boy here goes coon hunting with me."

One of the sportswriters is standing around, saying: "What do you shoot a coon with?"

"Don't shoot 'em. The dogs tree 'em and then you flush 'em out and the dogs fight 'em."

"Flush 'em out?"

"Yeah. This boy right here can flush 'em out better than anybody you ever did see. You go out at night with the dogs, and soon as they get the scent, they start barking. They go on out ahead of you and when they tree a coon, you can tell it, by the way they sound. They all start baying up at that coon—h'it sounds like, I don't know, you hear it once and you not likely to forget it. Then you send a little old boy up to flush him out and he jumps down and the dogs fight him."

"How does a boy flush him out?"

"Aw, he just climbs up there to the limb he's on and starts shaking h'it and the coon'll jump."

"What happens if the coon decides he'd rather come back after the boy instead of jumping down to a bunch of dogs?"

"He won't do that. A coon's afraid of a person, but he can kill a dog. A coon can take any dog you set against him if they's just the two of them fighting. The coon jumps down on the ground and he rolls right over on his back with his feet up, and he's *got* claws about like this. All he has to do is get a dog once in the throat or in the belly, and he can kill him, cut him wide open just like you took a knife and did it. Won't any dog even fight a coon except a coon dog."

"What kind of dogs are they?"

"*Coon* dogs, I guess. Black and tans they call 'em sometimes. They's bred for it. If his mammy and pappy wasn't coon dogs, he ain't likely to be one either. After you got one, you got to train him. You trap a coon, live, and then you put him in a pen and tie him to a post with a rope on him and then you put your dog in there and he has to fight him. Sometimes you get a dog just don't have any fight in him and he ain't no good to you."

Junior is in the pit area, standing around with his brother Fred, who is part of his crew, and Ray Fox and some other good old boys, in a general atmosphere of big stock-car money, a big ramp truck for his car, a white Dodge, Number 3, a big crew in white coveralls, huge stacks of racing tires, a Dodge P.R. man, big portable cans of gasoline, compressed air hoses, compressed water hoses, the whole business. Herb Nab, Freddie Lorenzen's chief mechanic, comes over and sits down on his haunches and Junior sits down on his haunches and Nab says:

"So Junior Johnson's going to drive a Ford."

Junior is switching from Dodge to Ford mainly because he hasn't been winning with the Dodge. Lorenzen drives a Ford, too, and the last year, when Junior was driving the Chevrolet, their duels were the biggest excitement in stock-car racing.

"Well," says Nab, "I'll tell you, Junior. My ambition is going to be to outrun your ass every goddamned time we go out."

"That was your ambition last year," says Junior.

"I know it was," says Nab, "and you took all the money, didn't you? You know what my strategy was. I was going to outrun everybody else and outlast Junior, that was my strategy."

Setting off his California modern sport shirt and white ducks, Junior has on a pair of twenty-dollar rimless sunglasses and a big gold Timex watch, and Flossie, his fiancée, is out there in the infield somewhere with the white Pontiac, and the white Dodge that Dodge gave Junior is parked up near the pit area—and then a little thing happens that brings the whole thing right back there to Wilkes County, North Carolina, to Ingle Hollow and to hard muscle in the clay gulches. A couple of good old boys come down to the front of the stands with the screen and the width of the track between them and Junior, and one of the good old boys comes down and yells out in the age-old baritone raw-curdle yell of the Southern hills:

"Hey! Hog jaw!"

Everybody gets quiet. They know he's yelling at Junior, but nobody says a thing. Junior doesn't even turn around.

"Hey, hog jaw! . . ."

Junior, he does nothing.

"Hey, hog jaw, I'm gonna get me one of them fastback roosters, too, and come down there and get you!"

Fastback rooster refers to the Ford—it has a "fastback" design— Junior is switching to.

"Hey, hog jaw, I'm gonna get me one of them fastback roosters and run you right out of here, you hear me, hog jaw!"

One of the good old boys alongside Junior says, "Junior, go on up there and clear out those stands."

Then everybody stares at Junior to see what he's gonna do. Junior, he don't even look around. He just looks a bit dead serious.

"Hey, hog jaw, you got six cases of whiskey in the back of that car you want to let me have?"

"What you hauling in that car, hog jaw!"

"Tell him you're out of that business, Junior," one of the good old boys says.

"Go on up there and clean house, Junior," says another good old boy.

Then Junior looks up, without looking at the stands, and smiles a little and says, "You flush him down here out of that tree—and I'll take keer of him."

Such a howl goes up from the good old boys! It is almost a blood curdle—

"Goddamn, he *will*, too!"

"Lord, he better know how to do an *about-face* hissef if he comes down here!"

"Goddamn, get him, Junior!"

"Whooeeee!"

"Mother dog!"

A kind of orgy of reminiscence of the old Junior before the Detroit money started flowing, wild combats *d'honneur* up-hollow—and, suddenly, when he heard that unearthly baying coming up from the good old boys in the pits, the good old boy retreated from the edge of the stands and never came back.

Later on Junior told me, sort of apologetically, "H'it used to be, if a fellow crowded me just a little bit, I was ready to crawl him. I reckon that was one good thing about Chillicothe.

"I don't want to pull any more time," Junior tells me, "but I wouldn't take anything in the world for the experience I had in prison. If a man needed to change, that was the place to change. H'it's not a waste of time there, h'it's good experience.

"H'it's that they's so many people in the world that feel that nobody is going to tell them what to do. I had quite a temper, I reckon. I always had the idea that I had as much sense as the other person and I didn't want them to tell me what to do. In the penitentiary there I found out that I could listen to another fellow and be told what to do and h'it wouldn't kill me."

Starting time! Linda Vaughn, with the big blonde hair and blossomy breasts, puts down her Coca-Cola and the potato chips and slips off her red stretch pants and her white blouse and walks out of the officials' booth in her Rake-a-cheek red show-girl's costume with her long honeydew legs in net stockings and climbs up on the red Firebird float. The Life Symbol of stock-car racing! Yes! Linda, every luscious morsel of Linda, is a good old girl from Atlanta who was made Miss Atlanta International Raceway one year and was paraded around the track on a float and she liked it so much and all the good old boys liked it so much, Linda's flowing hair and blossomy breasts and honeydew legs, that she became the permanent glamour symbol, of stock-car racing, and never mind this other modeling she was doing . . . this, she liked it. Right before practically every race on the Grand National circuit Linda Vaughn puts down her Coca-Cola and potato chips. Her momma is there, she generally comes around to see Linda go around the track on the float, it's such a nice spectacle seeing Linda looking so lovely, and the applause and all. "Linda, I'm thirstin', would you bring me a Coca-Cola?" "A lot of them think I'm Freddie Lorenzen's girl friend, but I'm not any of 'em's girl friend, I'm real good friends with 'em all, even Wen-dell," he being Wendell Scott, the only Negro in big-league stock-car racing. Linda gets up on the Firebird float. This is an extraordinary object, made of wood, about twenty feet tall, in the shape of a huge bird, an eagle or something, blazing red, and Linda, with her red show girl's suit on, gets up on the seat, which is up between the wings, like a saddle, high enough so her long honeydew legs stretch down, and a new car pulls her—Miss Firebird!—slowly once around the track just before the race. It is more of a ceremony by now than the national anthem. Miss Firebird sails slowly in front of the stands and the good old boys let out some real curdle Rebel yells, "Yaaaaaaaaaaaaahhhhhoooooo! Let me at that car!" "Honey, you sure do start my motor, I swear to God!" "Great God and Poonadingdong, I mean!"

And suddenly there's a big roar from behind, down in the infield, and then I see one of the great sights in stock-car racing. That infield! The cars have been piling into the infield by the hundreds, parking in there on the clay and the grass, every which-way, angled down and angled up, this way and that, where the ground is uneven, these beautiful blazing brand-new cars with the sun exploding off the windshields and the baked enamel and the glassy lacquer, hundreds, thousands of cars stacked this way and that in the infield with the sun bolting down and no shade, none at all, just a couple of Coca-Cola stands out there. And already the good old boys and girls are out beside the cars, with all these beautiful little buds in short shorts already spread-eagled out on top of the car roofs, pressing down on good hard slick automobile sheet metal, their little cupcake bottoms aimed up at the sun. The good old boys are lollygagging around with their shirts off and straw hats on that have miniature beer cans on the brims and buttons that read, "Girls Wanted—No Experience Required." And every-body, good old boys and girls of all ages, are out there with portable charcoal barbecue ovens set up, and folding tubular-steel terrace furni-ture, deck chairs and things, and Thermos jugs and coolers full of beer—and suddenly it is not the up-country South at all but a concentra-tion of the modern suburbs, all jammed into that one space, from all over America, with blazing cars and instant goodies, all cooking under the bare blaze—inside a strange bowl. The infield is like the bottom of a bowl. The track around it is banked so steeply at the corners and even on the straightaways, it is like . . . the steep sides of a bowl. The wall around the track, and the stands and the bleachers are like . . . the rim of a bowl. And from the infield, in this great incredible press of blazing new cars, there is no horizon but the bowl, up above only that cobalt-blue North Carolina sky. And then suddenly, on a signal, thirty stock-car engines start up where they are lined up in front of the stands. The roar of these engines is impossible to describe. They have a simultaneous rasp, thunder and rumble that goes right through a body and fills the whole bowl with a noise of internal combustion. Then they start around on two build-up runs, just to build up speed, and then they come around the fourth turn and onto the straightaway in front of the stands at—here, 130 miles an hour, in Atlanta, 160 miles an hour, at Daytona, 180 miles an hour—and the flag goes down and everybody in the infield and in the stands is up on their feet going mad, and suddenly here is a bowl that is one great orgy of everything in the way of excitement and liberation the automobile has meant to Americans. An orgy!

The first lap of a stock-car race is a horrendous, a wildly horrendous spectacle such as no other sport approaches. Twenty, thirty, forty automo-biles, each of them weighing almost two tons, 3700 pounds, with 427-cubic-inch engines, 600 horsepower, are practically locked together, side to side and tail to nose, on a narrow band of asphalt at 130, 160, 180 miles an hour, hitting the curves so hard the rubber burns off the tires in front of your eyes. To the driver, it is like being inside a car going down the West Side Highway in New York City at rush hour, only with everybody going literally three to four times as fast, at speeds a man who has gone eighty-five miles an hour down a highway cannot conceive of, and with every other driver an enemy who is willing to cut inside of you, around you or in front of you, or ricochet off your side in the battle to get into a curve first.

The speeds are faster than those in the Indianapolis 500 race, the cars are more powerful, much heavier, and the drivers have more courage, more daring, more ruthlessness than Indianapolis or Grand Prix drivers. The prize money in Southern stock-car racing is far greater than that in Indianapolis-style or European Grand Prix racing, but few Indianapolis or Grand Prix drivers have the raw nerve required to succeed at it.

Although they will deny it, it is still true that stock-car drivers will put each other "up against the wall"—cut inside on the left of another car and ram it into a spin—if they get mad enough. Crashes are not the only danger, however. The cars are now literally too fast for their own parts, especially the tires. Firestone and Goodyear have poured millions into stock-car racing, but neither they nor anybody so far has been able to come up with a tire for this kind of racing at the current speeds. Three well-known stock-car drivers were killed last year, two of them champion drivers, Joe Weatherly and Fireball Roberts, and another, one of the best new drivers, Jimmy Pardue, from Junior Johnson's own home territory, Wilkes County, North Carolina. Roberts was the only one killed in a crash. Junior Johnson was in the crash but was not injured. Weatherly and Pardue both lost control on curves. Pardue's death came during a tire test. In a tire test, engineers, from Firestone or Goodyear, try out various tires on a car, and the driver, always one of the top competitors, tests them at top speed, usually on the Atlanta track. The drivers are paid three dollars a mile and may drive as much as five or six hundred miles in a single day. At 145 miles an hour average that does not take very long. Anyway, these drivers are going at speeds that, on curves, can tear tires off their casings or break axles. They practically run off from over their own automobiles. Junior Johnson was over in the garden by the house some years ago, plowing the garden barefooted, behind a mule, just wearing an old pair of overalls, when a couple of good old boys drove up and told him to come on up to the speedway and get in a stock-car race. They wanted some local boys to race, as a preliminary to the main race, "as a kind of side show," as Junior remembers it.

"So I just put the reins down," Junior is telling me, "and rode on over 'ere with them. They didn't give us seat belts or nothing, they just roped us in. H'it was a dirt track then. I come in second."

Junior was a sensation in dirt-track racing right from the start. Instead of going into the curves and just sliding and holding on for dear life like the other drivers, Junior developed the technique of throwing himself into a slide about seventy-five feet before the curve by cocking the wheel to the left slightly and gunning it, using the slide, not the brake, to slow down, so that he could pick up speed again halfway through the curve and come out of it like a shot. This was known as his "power slide," and—yes! of course!—every good old boy in North Carolina started saying Junior Johnson had learned that stunt doing those goddamned *about-faces* running away from the Alcohol Tax agents. Junior put on such a show one night on a dirt track in Charlotte that he broke two axles, and he thought he was out of the race because he didn't have any more axles, when a good old boy came running up out of the infield and said, "Goddamn it, Junior Johnson, you take the axle off my car here, I got a Pontiac just like yours," and Junior took it off and put it on his and went out and broke *it* too. Mother dog! To this day Junior Johnson loves dirt-track racing like nothing else in this world, even though there is not much money in it. Every year he sets new dirt-track speed records, such as at Hickory, North Carolina, one of the most popular dirt tracks, last spring. As far as Junior is concerned, dirt-track racing is not so much of a mechanical test for the car as those long five- and six-hundred-mile races on asphalt are. Gasoline, tire and engine wear aren't so much of a problem. It is all the driver, his skill, his courage—his willingness to mix it up with the other cars, smash and carom off of them at a hundred miles an hour or so to get into the curves first. Junior has a lot of fond recollections of mixing it up at places like Bowman Gray Stadium in Winston-Salem, one of the minor-league tracks, a very narrow track, hardly wide enough for two cars. "You could always figure Bowman Gray was gonna cost you two fenders, two doors and two quarter panels," Junior tells me with nostalgia.

Anyway, at Hickory, which was a Saturday-night race, all the good old boys started pouring into the stands before sundown, so they wouldn't miss anything, the practice runs or the qualifying or anything. And pretty soon, the dew hasn't even started falling before Junior Johnson and David Pearson, one of Dodge's best drivers, are out there on practice runs, just warming up, and they happen to come up alongside each other on the second curve, and—the thing is, here are two men, each of them driving $15,000 automobiles, each of them standing to make $50,000 to $100,000 for the season if they don't get themselves killed, and they meet on a curve on a goddamned practice run on a dirt track, and neither of them can resist it. Coming out of the turn they go into a wild-ass race down the backstretch, both of them trying to get into the third turn first, and all the way across the infield you can hear them ricocheting off each other and bouncing at a hundred miles an hour on loose dirt, and then they go into ferocious power slides, red dust all over the goddamned place, and then out of this goddamned red-dust cloud, out of the fourth turn, here comes Junior Johnson first, like a shot, with Pearson right on his tail, and the good old boys in the stands going wild, and the *qualifying* runs haven't started yet, let alone the race.

Junior worked his way up through the minor leagues, the Sportsman and Modified classifications, as they are called, winning championships in both, and won his first Grand National race, the big leagues, in 1955 at

Hickory, on dirt. He was becoming known as "the hardest of the hard-chargers," power sliding, rooting them out of the groove, raising hell, and already the Junior Johnson legend was beginning.

He kept hard-charging, power sliding, going after other drivers as though there wasn't room on the track but for one, and became the most popular driver in stock-car racing by 1959. The automobile companies had suddenly dropped out of stock-car racing in 1957, making a devout covenant never again to try to capitalize on speed as a selling point, the Government was getting stuffy about it, but already the presence of Detroit and Detroit's big money had begun to calm the drivers down a little. Detroit was concerned about Image. The last great duel of the dying dog-eat-dog era of stock-car racing came in 1959, when Junior and Lee Petty, who was then leading the league in points, had it out on the Charlotte raceway. Junior was in the lead, and Petty was right on his tail, but couldn't get by Junior. Junior kept coming out of the curves faster. So every chance he got, Petty would get up right on Junior's rear bumper and start banging it, gradually forcing the fender in to where the metal would cut Junior's rear tire. With only a few laps to go, Junior had a blowout and spun out up against the guardrail. That is Junior's version. Petty claimed Junior hit a pop bottle and spun out. The fans in Charlotte were always throwing pop bottles and other stuff onto the track late in the race, looking for blood. In any case, Junior eased back into the pits, had the tire changed, and charged out after Petty. He caught him on a curve and—well, whatever really happened, Petty was suddenly "up against the wall" and out of the race, and Junior Johnson won.

What a howl went up. The Charlotte chief of police charged out onto the track after the race, according to Petty, and offered to have Junior arrested for "assault with a dangerous weapon," the hassling went on for weeks—

"Back then," Junior tells me, "when you got into a guy and racked him up, you might as well get ready, because he's coming back for you. H'it was dog eat dog. That straightened Lee Petty out right smart. They don't do stuff like that anymore, though, because the guys don't stand for it."

Anyway, the Junior Johnson legend kept building up and building up, and in 1960 it got hotter than ever when Junior won the biggest race of the year, the Daytona 500, by "discovering" a new technique called "drafting." That year stock-car racing was full of big powerful Pontiacs manned by top drivers, and they would go like nothing else anybody ever saw. Junior went down to Daytona with a Chevrolet.

"My car was about ten miles an hour slower than the rest of the cars, the Pontiacs," Junior tells me. "In the preliminary races, the warmups and stuff like that, they was smoking me off the track. Then I remember once I went out for a practice run, and Fireball Roberts was out there in a

Pontiac and I got in right behind him on a curve, right on his bumper. I knew I couldn't stay with him on the straightaway, but I came out of the curve fast, right in behind him, running flat out, and then I noticed a funny thing. As long as I stayed right in behind him, I noticed I picked up speed and stayed right with him and my car was going faster than it had ever gone before. I could tell on the tachometer. My car wasn't turning no more than 6000 before, but when I got into this drafting position, I was turning 6800 to 7000. H'it felt like the car was plumb off the ground, floating along."

"Drafting," it was discovered at Daytona, created a vacuum behind the lead car and both cars would go faster than they normally would. Junior "hitched rides" on the Pontiacs most of the afternoon, but was still second to Bobby Johns, the lead Pontiac. Then, late in the race, Johns got into a drafting position with a fellow Pontiac that was actually one lap behind him and the vacuum got so intense that the rear window blew out of Johns' car and he spun out and crashed and Junior won.

This made Junior the Lion Killer, the Little David of stock-car racing, and his performance in the 1963 season made him even more so.

Junior raced for Chevrolet at Daytona in February, 1963, and set the all-time stock-car speed record in a hundred-mile qualifying race, 164.083 miles an hour, twenty-one miles an hour faster than Parnelli Jones's winning time at Indianapolis that year. Junior topped that at Daytona in July of 1963, qualifying at 166.005 miles per hour in a five-mile run, the fastest that anyone had ever averaged that distance in a racing car of any type. Junior's Chevrolet lasted only twenty-six laps in the Daytona 500 in 1963, however. He went out with a broken push rod. Although Chevrolet announced they were pulling out of racing at this time, Junior took his car and started out on the wildest performance in the history of stock-car racing. Chevrolet wouldn't give him a cent of backing. They wouldn't even speak to him on the telephone. Half the time he had to have his own parts made. Plymouth, Mercury, Dodge and Ford, meantime, were pouring more money than ever into stock-car racing. Yet Junior won seven Grand National races out of the thirty-three he entered and led most others before mechanical trouble forced him out.

All the while, Junior was making record qualifying runs, year after year. In the usual type of qualifying run, a driver has the track to himself and makes two circuits, with the driver with the fastest average time getting the "pole" position for the start of the race. In a way this presents stock-car danger in its purest form. Driving a stock car does not require much handling ability, at least not as compared to Grand Prix racing, because the tracks are simple banked ovals and there is almost no shifting of gears. So qualifying becomes a test of raw nerve—of how fast a man is willing to take a curve. Many of the top drivers in competition are poor at qualifying. In effect, they are willing to calculate their risks only against the risks the other drivers are taking. Junior takes the pure risk as no other driver has ever taken it.

"Pure" risk or total risk, whichever, Indianapolis and Grand Prix drivers have seldom been willing to face the challenge of the Southern stock-car driver. A. J. Foyt, the 1961 winner at Indianapolis, is one exception. He has raced against the Southerners and beaten them. Parnelli Jones has tried and fared badly. Driving "Southern style" has a quality that shakes a man up. The Southerners went on a tour of Northern tracks last fall. They raced at Bridgehampton, New York, and went into the corners so hard the marshals stationed at each corner kept radioing frantically to the control booth: "They're going off the track. They're all going off the track!"

But this, Junior Johnson's last race in a Dodge, was not his day, neither for qualifying nor racing. Lorenzen took the lead early and won the 250-mile race a lap ahead of the field. Junior finished third, but was never in contention for the lead.

"Come on, Junior, do my hand—"

Two or three hundred people come out of the stands and up out of the infield and onto the track to be around Junior Johnson. Junior is signing autographs in a neat left-handed script he has. It looks like it came right out of the Locker book. The girls! Levis, stretch pants, sneaky shorts, stretch jeans, they press into the crowd with lively narbs and try to get their hands up in front of Junior and say:

"Come on, Junior, do my hand!"

In order to do a hand, Junior has to hold the girl's hand in his right hand and then sign his name with a ballpoint on the back of her hand.

"Junior, you got to do mine, too!"

"Put it on up here."

All the girls break into . . . smiles. Junior Johnson does a hand. Ah, sweet little cigarette-ad blonde! She says:

"Junior, why don't you ever call me up?"

"I 'spect you get plenty of calls 'thout me."

"Oh, Junior! You call me up, you hear now?"

But also a great many older people crowd in, and they say:

"Junior, you're doing a real good job out there, you're driving real good."

"Junior, when you get in that Ford, I want to see you pass that Freddie Lorenzen, you hear now?"

"Junior, you like that Ford better than that Dodge?"

And:

"Junior, here's a young man that's been waiting some time and wanting to see you—" and the man lifts up his little boy in the middle of the crowd and says: "I told you you'd see Junior Johnson. This here's Junior Johnson!"

The boy has a souvenir racing helmet on his head. He stares at Junior through a buttery face. Junior signs the program he has in his hand, and then the boy's mother says:

"Junior, I tell you right now, he's beside you all the way. He can't be moved."

And then:

"Junior, I want you to meet the meanest little girl in Wilkes County."

"She don't look mean to me."

Junior keeps signing autographs and over by the pits the other kids are all over his car, the Dodge. They start pulling off the decals, the ones saying Holly Farms Poultry and Autolite and God knows whatall. They fight over the strips, the shreds of decal, as if they were totems.

All this homage to Junior Johnson lasts about forty minutes. He must be signing about 250 autographs, but he is not a happy man. By and by the crowd is thinning out, the sun is going down, wind is blowing the Coca-Cola cups around, all one can hear, mostly, is a stock-car engine starting up every now and then as somebody drives it up onto a truck or something, and Junior looks around and says:

"I'd rather lead one lap and fall out of the race than stroke it and finish in the money."

"Stroking it" is driving carefully in hopes of outlasting faster and more reckless cars. The opposite of stroking it is "hard-charging." Then Junior says:

"I hate to get whipped up here in Wilkes County, North Carolina."

Wilkes County, North Carolina! Who was it tried to pin the name on Wilkes County, "The bootleg capital of America"? This fellow Vance Packard. But just a minute. . . .

The night after the race Junior and his fiancée, Flossie Clark, and myself went into North Wilkesboro to have dinner. Junior and Flossie came by Lowes Motel and picked me up in the dreamboat white Pontiac. Flossie is a bright, attractive woman, *saftig,* well-organized. She and Junior have been going together since they were in high school. They are going to get married as soon as Junior gets his new house built. Flossie has been doing the decor. Junior Johnson, in the second-highest income bracket in the United States for the past five years, is moving out of his father's white frame house in Ingle Hollow at last. About three hundred yards down the road. Overlooking a lot of good green land and Anderson's Store. Junior shows me through the house, it is almost finished, and when we get to the front door, I ask him, "How much of this land is yours?"

Junior looks around for a minute, and then backs up the hill, up past his three automated chicken houses, and then down into the hollow over the pasture where his $3100 Santa Gertrudis bull is grazing, and then he says:

"Everything that's green is mine."

Junior Johnson's house is going to be one of the handsomest homes in Wilkes County. Yes. And—such complicated problems of class and status. Junior is not only a legendary figure as a backwoods boy with guts who made good, he is also popular personally, he is still a good old boy, rich as he is. He is also respected for the sound and sober way he has invested his money. He also has one of the best business connections in town, Holly Farms Poultry. What complicates it is that half the county, anyway, reveres him as the greatest, most fabled night-road driver in the history of Southern bootlegging. There is hardly a living soul in the hollows who can conjure up two seconds' honest moral indignation over "the whiskey business." That is what they call it, "the whiskey business." The fact is, it has some positive political overtones, sort of like the I.R.A. in Ireland. The other half of the county—well, North Wilkesboro itself is a prosperous, good-looking town of 5,000, where a lot of hearty modern business burghers are making money the modern way, like everywhere else in the U.S.A., in things like banking, poultry processing, furniture, mirror and carpet manufacture, apple growing, and so forth and so on. And one thing these men are tired of is Wilkes County's reputation as a center of moonshining. The U. S. Alcohol and Tobacco Tax agents sit over there in Wilkesboro, right next to North Wilkesboro, year in and year out, and they have been there since God knows when, like an Institution in the land, and every day that they are there, it is like a sign saying, Moonshine County. And even that is not so *bad*—it has nothing to do with it being immoral and only a little to do with it being illegal. The real thing is, it is—raw and hillbilly. And one thing thriving modern Industry is not is hillbilly. And one thing the burghers of North Wilkesboro are not about to be is hillbilly. They have split-level homes that would knock your eyes out. Also swimming pools, white Buick Snatch-wagons, flagstone *terrasse*-porches enclosed with louvered glass that opens wide in the summertime, and built-in brick barbecue pits and they give parties where they wear Bermuda shorts and Jax stretch pants and serve rum collins and play twist and bossa-nova records on the hi-fi and tell Shaggy Dog jokes about strange people ordering Martinis. Moonshining . . . just a minute—the truth is, North Wilkesboro. . . .

So we are all having dinner at one of the fine new restaurants in North Wilkesboro, a place of suburban plate-glass elegance. The manager knows Junior and gives us the best table in the place and comes over and talks to Junior a while about the race. A couple of men get up and come over and get Junior's autograph to take home to their sons and so forth. Then toward the end of the meal a couple of North Wilkesboro businessmen come over ("Junior, how are you, Junior. You think you're going to like that fast-backed Ford?") and Junior introduces them to me, from Esquire Magazine.

"Esquire," one of them says. "You're not going to do like that fellow Vance Packard did, are you?"

"Vance Packard?"

"Yeah, I think it was Vance Packard wrote it. He wrote an article and called Wilkes County the bootleg capital of America. Don't pull any of that stuff. I think it was in *American* Magazine. The bootleg capital of America. Don't pull any of that stuff on us."

I looked over at Junior and Flossie. Neither one of them said anything. They didn't even change their expressions.

Ingle Hollow! The next morning I met Junior down in Ingle Hollow at Anderson's Store. That's about fifteen miles out of North Wilkesboro on County Road No. 2400. Junior is known in a lot of Southern newspapers as "the wild man from Ronda" or "the lead-footed chicken farmer from Ronda," but Ronda is only his post-office-box address. His telephone exchange, with the Wilkes Telephone Membership Corporation, is Clingman, North Carolina, and that isn't really where he lives either. Where he lives is just Ingle Hollow, and one of the communal centers of Ingle Hollow is Anderson's Store. Anderson's is not exactly a grocery store. Out front there are two gasoline pumps under an overhanging roof. Inside there are a lot of things like a soda-pop cooler filled with ice, Coca-Colas, Nehi drinks, Dr. Pepper, Double Cola, and a gumball machine, a lot of racks of Red Man chewing tobacco, Price's potato chips, OKay peanuts, cloth hats for working outdoors in, dried sausages, cigarettes, canned goods, a little bit of meal and flour, fly swatters, and I don't know what all. Inside and outside of Anderson's there are good old boys. The young ones tend to be inside, talking, and the old ones tend to be outside, sitting under the roof by the gasoline pumps, talking. And on both sides, cars; most of them new and pastel.

Junior drives up and gets out and looks up over the door where there is a row of twelve coon tails. Junior says:

"Two of them gone, ain't they?"

One of the good old boys says, "Yeah," and sighs.

A pause and the other one says, "Somebody stole 'em."

Then the first one says, "Junior, that dog of yours ever come back?"

Junior says, "Not yet."

The second good old boy says, "You looking for her to come back?"

Junior says, "I reckon she'll come back."

The good old boy says, "I had a coon dog went off like that. They don't ever come back. I went out 'ere one day, back over yonder, and there he was, cut right from here to here. I swear if it didn't look like a coon got him. Something. H'it must of turned him every way but loose."

Junior goes inside and gets a Coca-Cola and rings up the till himself, like everybody who goes into Anderson's does, it seems like. It is dead quiet in the hollow except for every now and then a car grinds over the dirt road and down the way. One coon dog missing. But he still has a lot of the black and tans, named Rock. . . .

Rock, Whitey, Red, Buster are in the pen out back of the Johnson house, the old frame house. They have scars all over their faces from fighting coons. Gypsy has one huge gash in her back from fighting something. A red rooster crosses the lawn. That's a big rooster. Shirley, one of Junior's two younger sisters, pretty girls, is out by the fence in shorts, pulling weeds. Annie May is inside the house with Mrs. Johnson. Shirley has the radio outside on the porch aimed at her, The Four Seasons! "Dawn!—ahhhh, ahhhhhh, ahhhhhh-hhh!" Then a lot of electronic wheeps and lulus and a screaming disc jockey, yessss! WTOB, the Vibrant Voice of Winston-Salem, North Carolina. It sounds like station WABC in New York. Junior's mother, Mrs. Johnson, is a big, good-natured woman. She comes out and says, "Did you ever see anything like that in your life? Pullin' weeds listenin' to the radio." Junior's father, Robert Glenn Johnson, Sr.—he built this frame house about thirty-five years ago, up here where the gravel road ends and the woods start. The road just peters out into the woods up a hill. The house has a living room, four bedrooms and a big kitchen. The living room is full of Junior's racing trophies, and so is the piano in Shirley's room. Junior was born and raised here with his older brothers, L.P., the oldest, and Fred, and his older sister, Ruth. Over yonder, up by that house, there's a man with a mule and a little plow. That's L.P. The Johnsons still keep that old mule around to plow the vegetable gardens. And all around, on all sides like a rim, are the ridges and the woods. Well, what about those woods, where Vance Packard said the agents come stealing over the ridges and good old boys go crashing through the underbrush to get away from the still and the women start "calling the cows" up and down the hollows as the signal *they* were coming. . . .

Junior motions his hand out toward the hills and says, "I'd say nearly everybody in a fifty-mile radius of here was in the whiskey business at one time or another. When we growed up here, everybody seemed to be more or less messing with whiskey, and myself and my two brothers did quite a bit of transporting. H'it was just a business, like any other business, far as we was concerned. H'it was a matter of survival. During the Depression here, people either had to do that or starve to death. H'it wasn't no gangster type of business or nothing. They's nobody that ever messed with it here that was ever out to hurt anybody. Even if they got caught, they never tried to shoot anybody or anything like that. Getting caught and pulling time, that was just part of it. H'it was just a business, like any other business. Me and my brothers, when we went out on the road at night, h'it was just like a milk run, far as we was concerned. They was certain deliveries to be made and. . . ."

A milk run—yes! Well, it was a business, all right. In fact, it was a regional industry, all up and down the Appalachian slopes. But never mind the Depression. It goes back a long way before that. The Scotch-

Irish settled the mountains from Pennsylvania down to Alabama, and they have been making whiskey out there as long as anybody can remember. At first it was a simple matter of economics. The land had a low crop yield, compared to the lowlands, and even after a man struggled to grow his corn, or whatever, the cost of transporting it to the markets from down out of the hills was so great, it wasn't worth it. It was much more profitable to convert the corn into whiskey and sell that. The trouble started with the Federal Government on that score almost the moment the Republic was founded. Alexander Hamilton put a high excise tax on whiskey in 1791, almost as soon as the Constitution was ratified. The "Whiskey Rebellion" broke out in the mountains of western Pennsylvania in 1794. The farmers were mad as hell over the tax. Fifteen thousand Federal troops marched out to the mountains and suppressed them. Almost at once, however, the trouble over the whiskey tax became a symbol of something bigger. This was a general enmity between the western and eastern sections of practically every seaboard state. Part of it was political. The eastern sections tended to control the legislatures, the economy and the law courts, and the western sections felt shortchanged. Part of it was cultural. Life in the western sections was rougher. Religions, codes and styles of life were sterner. Life in the eastern capitals seemed to give off the odor of Europe and decadence. Shay's Rebellion broke out in the Berkshire hills of western Massachusetts in 1786 in an attempt to shake off the yoke of Boston, which seemed as bad as George III's. To this day people in western Massachusetts make proposals, earnestly or with down-in-the-mouth humor, that they all ought to split off from "Boston." Whiskey—the mountain people went right on making it. Whole sections of the Appalachians were a whiskey belt, just as sections of Georgia, Alabama and Mississippi were a cotton belt. Nobody on either side ever had any moral delusions about why the Federal Government was against it. It was always the tax, pure and simple. Today the price of liquor is sixty-percent tax. Today, of course, with everybody gone wild over the subject of science and health, it has been much easier for the Federals to persuade people that they crack down on moonshine whiskey because it is dangerous, it poisons, kills and blinds people. The statistics are usually specious.

Moonshining was *illegal,* however, that was also the unvarnished truth. And that had a side effect in the whiskey belt. The people there were already isolated, geographically, by the mountains and had strong clan ties because they were all from the same stock, Scotch-Irish. Moonshining isolated them even more. They always had to be careful who came up there. There are plenty of hollows to this day where if you drive in and ask some good old boy where so-and-so is, he'll tell you he never heard of the fellow. Then the next minute, if you identify yourself and give some idea of why you want to see him, and he believes you, he'll suddenly say, "Aw, you're talking about *so-and-so.* I thought you said—" With all this isolation, the mountain people began to take on certain characteristics normally associated, by the diffident civilizations of today, with tribes. There was a strong sense of family, clan and honor. People would cut and shoot each other up over honor. And physical courage! They were almost like Turks that way.

In the Korean War, not a very heroic performance by American soldiers generally, there were seventy-eight Medal of Honor winners. Thirty-nine were from small towns in or near the Appalachians. The New York metropolitan area, which has more people than all these towns put together, had three Medal of Honor winners, and one of them had just moved to New York from the Appalachian region of West Virginia. Three of the Medal of Honor winners came from within fifty miles of Junior Johnson's side porch.

Detroit has discovered these pockets of courage almost like a natural resource, in the form of Junior Johnson and about twenty other drivers. There is something exquisitely ironic about it. Detroit is now engaged in the highly sophisticated business of offering the illusion of Speed for Everyman—making their cars go 175 miles an hour on racetracks—by discovering and putting behind the wheel a breed of mountain men who are living vestiges of a degree of physical courage that became extinct in most other sections of the country by 1900. Of course, very few stock-car drivers have ever had anything to do with the whiskey business. A great many always lead quiet lives off the track. But it is the same strong people among whom the whiskey business developed who produced the kind of men who could drive the stock cars. There are a few exceptions, Freddie Lorenzen, from Elmhurst, Illinois, being the most notable. But, by and large, it is the rural Southern code of honor and courage that has produced these, the most daring men in sports.

Cars and bravery! The mountain-still operators had been running white liquor with hopped-up automobiles all during the Thirties. But it was during the war that the business was so hot out of Wilkes County, down to Charlotte, High Point, Greensboro, Winston-Salem, Salisbury, places like that; that night's run, by one car, would bring anywhere from $500 to $1,000. People had money all of a sudden. One car could carry twenty-two to twenty-five cases of white liquor. There were twelve half-gallon fruit jars full per case, so each load would have 132 gallons or more. It would sell to the distributor in the city for about ten dollars a gallon, when the market was good, of which the driver would get two dollars, as much as $300 for the night's work.

The usual arrangement in the white-liquor industry was for the elders to design the distillery, supervise the formulas and the whole distilling process and take care of the business end of the operation. The young men did the heavy work, carrying the copper and other heavy goods out into the woods, building the still, hauling in fuel—and driving. Junior and his older brothers, L.P. and Fred, worked that way with their father, Robert Glenn Johnson, Sr.

Johnson, Senior, was one of the biggest individual copper-still operators in the area. The fourth time he was arrested, the agents found a small fortune in working corn mash bubbling in the vats.

"My Daddy was always a hard worker," Junior is telling me. "He always wanted something a little bit better. A lot of people resented that and held that against him, but what he got, he always got h'it by hard work. There ain't no harder work in the world than making whiskey. I don't know of any other business that compels you to get up at all times of night and go outdoors in the snow and everything else and work. It's the hardest way in the world to make a living, and I don't think anybody'd do it unless they had to."

Working mash wouldn't wait for a man. It started coming to a head when it got ready to and a man had to be there to take it off, out there in the woods, in the brush, in the brambles, in the muck, in the snow. Wouldn't it have been something if you could have just set it all up inside a good old shed with a corrugated metal roof and order those parts like you want them and not have to smuggle all that copper and all that sugar and all that everything out here in the woods and be a coppersmith and a plumber and a cooper and a carpenter and a packhorse and every other goddamned thing God ever saw in this world, all at once.

And live decent hours—Junior and his brothers, about two o'clock in the morning they'd head out to the stash, the place where the liquor was hidden after it was made. Sometimes it would be somebody's house or an old shed or some place just out in the woods, and they'd make their arrangements out there, what the route was and who was getting how much liquor. There wasn't anything ever written down. Everything was cash on the spot. Different drivers like to make the run at different times, but Junior and his brothers always liked to start out from three to four a.m. But it got so no matter when you started out you didn't have those roads to yourself.

"Some guys liked one time and some guys liked another time," Junior is saying, "but starting about midnight they'd be coming out of the woods from every direction. Some nights the whole road was full of bootleggers. It got so some nights they'd be somebody following you going just as fast as you were and you didn't know who h'it was, the law or somebody else hauling whiskey."

And it was just a business, like any other business, just like a milk route—but this funny thing was happening. In those wild-ass times, with the money flush and good old boys from all over the county running that white liquor down the road ninety miles an hour and more than that if you try to crowd them a little bit—well, the funny thing was, it got to be competitive in an almost aesthetic, a pure sporting way. The way the good old boys got to hopping up their automobiles—it got to be a science practically. Everybody was looking to build a car faster than anybody ever had before. They practically got into industrial espionage over it. They'd come up behind one another on those wild-ass nights on the highway, roaring through the black gulches between the clay cuts and the trees, pretending like they were officers, just to challenge them, test them out, race . . . *pour le sport,* careening through the darkness, old Carolina moon. All these cars were registered in phony names. If a man had to abandon one, they would find license plates that traced back to . . . nobody at all. It wasn't anything, particularly, to go down to the Motor Vehicle Bureau and get some license plates, as long as you paid your money. Of course, it's rougher now, with compulsory insurance. You have to have your insurance before you can get your license plates, and that leads to a lot of complications. Junior doesn't know what they do about that now. Anyway, all these cars with the magnificent engines were plain on the outside, so they wouldn't attract attention, but they couldn't disguise them altogether. They were jacked up a little in the back and had 8.00 or 8.20 tires, for the heavy loads, and the sound—

"They wasn't no way you could make it sound like an ordinary car," says Junior.

God-almighty, that sound in the middle of the night, groaning, roaring, humming down into the hollows, through the clay gulches—yes! And all over the rural South, hell, all over the South, the legends of wild-driving whiskey running got started. And it wasn't just the plain excitement of it. It was something deeper, the symbolism. It brought into a modern focus the whole business, one and a half centuries old, of the country people's rebellion against the Federals, against the seaboard establishment, their independence, their defiance of the outside world. And it was like a mythology for that and for something else that was happening, the whole wild thing of the car as the symbol of liberation in the postwar South.

"They was out about every night, patroling, the agents and the state police was," Junior is saying, "but they seldom caught anybody. H'it was like the dogs chasing the fox. The dogs can't catch a fox, he'll just take 'em around in a circle all night long. I was never caught for transporting. We never lost but one car and the axle broke on h'it."

The fox and the dogs! Whiskey running certainly had a crazy game-like quality about it, considering that a boy might be sent up for two years or more if he were caught transporting. But these boys were just wild enough for that. There got to be a code about the chase. In Wilkes County nobody, neither the good old boys nor the agents, ever did anything that was going to hurt the other side physically. There were supposed to be some parts of the South where the boys used smoke screens and tack buckets. They had attachments in the rear of the cars, and if the agents got too close they would let loose a smoke screen to blind them or a slew of tacks to make them blow a tire. But nobody in Wilkes County ever did that because that was a good way for somebody to get killed. Part of it was that whenever an agent did get killed in the South, whole hordes of agents would come in from Washington and pretty soon they would be tramping along the ridges practically inch by inch, smoking out the stills. But mainly it was—well, the code. If you got caught, you went along peaceably, and the agents never used their guns. There were some tense times. Once was when the agents started using tack belts in Ardell County. This was a long strip of leather studded with nails that the agents would lay across the road in the dark. A man couldn't see it until it was too late and he stood a good chance of getting killed if it got his tires and spun him out. The other was the time the State Police put a roadblock down there at that damned bridge at Millersville to catch a couple of escaped convicts. Well, a couple of good old boys rode up with a load, and there was the roadblock and they were already on the bridge, so they jumped out and dove into the water. The police saw two men jump out of their car and dive in the water, so they opened fire and they shot one good old boy in the backside. As they pulled him out, he kept saying:

"What did you have to shoot at me for? What did you have to shoot at me for?"

It wasn't pain, it wasn't anguish, it wasn't anger. It was consternation. The bastards had broken the code.

Then the Federals started getting radio cars.

"The radios didn't do them any good," Junior says. "As soon as the officers got radios, then *they* got radios. They'd go out and get the same radio. It was an awful hard thing for them to radio them down. They'd just listen in on the radio and see where they're setting up the roadblocks and go a different way."

And such different ways. The good old boys knew back roads, dirt roads, up people's back lanes and every whichway, and an agent would have to live in the North Carolina hills a lifetime to get to know them. There wasn't hardly a stretch of road on any of the routes where a good old boy couldn't duck off the road and into the backcountry if he had to. They had wild detours around practically every town and every intersection in the region. And for tight spots—the legendary devices, the "bootleg slide," the siren and the red light. . . . .

And then one day in 1955 some agents snuck over the ridges and caught Junior Johnson at his daddy's still. Junior Johnson, the man couldn't *any*body catch!

The arrest caught Junior just as he was ready to really take off in his career as a stock-car driver. Junior says he hadn't been in the whiskey business in any shape or form, hadn't run a load of whiskey for two or three years, when he was arrested. He was sentenced to two years in the Federal reformatory in Chillicothe, Ohio.

"If the law felt I should have gone to jail, that's fine and dandy," Junior tells me. "But I don't think the true facts of the case justified the sentence I got. I never had been arrested in my life. I think they was punishing me for the past. People get a kick out of it because the officers can't catch somebody, and this angers them. Soon as I started getting publicity for racing, they started making it real hot for my family. I was out of the whiskey business, and they knew that, but they was just waiting to catch me on something. I got out after serving ten months and three days of the sentence, but h'it was two or three years I was set back, about half of '56 and every bit of '57. H'it takes a year to really get back into h'it after something like that. I think I lost the prime of my racing career."

But, if anything, the arrest made the Junior Johnson legend hotter.

And all the while Detroit kept edging the speeds up, from 150 m.p.h. in 1960 to 155 to 165 to 175 to 180 flat out on the longest straightaway, and the good old boys of Southern stock-car racing stuck right with it. Any speed Detroit would give them they would take right with them into the curve, hard-charging even though they began to feel strange things such as the rubber starting to pull right off the tire casing. And God! Good old boys from all over the South roared together after the Stanchion-Speed! Guts!—pouring into Birmingham, Daytona Beach, Randleman, North Carolina; Spartanburg, South Carolina; Weaverville, Hillsboro, North Carolina; Atlanta, Hickory, Bristol, Tennessee; Augusta, Georgia; Richmond, Virginia; Asheville, North Carolina; Charlotte, Myrtle Beach— tens of thousands of them. And still upper- and middle-class America, even in the South, keeps its eyes averted. Who cares! They kept on heading out where we all live, after all . . . even outside a town like Darlington, a town of 10,000 souls, God, here they come, down route 52, up 401 on 340, 151 and 34, on through the South Carolina mesas. By Friday night already the good old boys are pulling into the infield of the Darlington raceway with those blazing pastel dreamboats stacked this way and that on the clay flat and the Thermos jugs and the brown whiskey bottles coming on out. By Sunday—the race!—there are 65,000 piled into the racetrack at Darlington. The sheriff, as always, sets up the jail right there in the infield. No use trying to haul them out of there. And now—the *sound* rises up inside the raceway, and a good old boy named Ralph goes mad and starts selling chances on his Dodge. Twenty-five cents and you can take the sledge he has and smash his car anywhere you want. How they roar when the windshield breaks! The police could interfere, you know, but they are busy chasing a good old girl who is playing Lady Godiva on a hog-backed motorcycle, naked as sin, hauling around and in and out of the clay ruts.

Eyes averted, happy burghers. On Monday the ads start appearing—for Ford, for Plymouth, for Dodge—announcing that we gave it to you, speed such as you never saw. There it was! At Darlington, Daytona, Atlanta—and not merely in the Southern papers but in the albino pages of the suburban women's magazines, such as *The New Yorker,* in color—the Ford winners, such as Fireball Roberts, grinning with a cigar in his mouth in *The New Yorker* magazine. And somewhere, some Monday morning, Jim Paschal of High Point, Ned Jarrett of Boykin, Cale Yarborough of Timmonsville and Curtis Crider from Charlotte, Bobby Isaac of Catawba, E.J. Trivette of Deep Gap, Richard Petty of Randleman, Tiny Lund of Cross, South Carolina; Stick Elliott of Shelby—and from out of Ingle Hollow.

And all the while, standing by in full Shy, in Alumicron suits—there is Detroit, hardly able to believe itself, what it has discovered, a breed of good old boys from the fastnesses of the Appalachian hills and flats— a handful from this rare breed—who had given Detroit . . . speed . . . and the industry can present it to a whole generation as . . . yours. And the Detroit P.R. men themselves come to the tracks like folk worshipers and the millions go giddy with the thrill of speed. Only Junior Johnson goes about it as if it were . . . the usual. Junior goes on down to Atlanta for the Dixie 400 and drops by the Federal penitentiary to see his Daddy. His Daddy is in on his fifth illegal-distillery conviction; in the whiskey business that's just part of it; an able craftsman, an able businessman, and the law kept hounding him, that was all. So Junior drops by and then goes on out to the track and gets in his new Ford and sets the qualifying speed record for the Atlanta Dixie 400, 146.301 m.p.h.; later on he tools on back up the road to Ingle Hollow to tend to the automatic chicken houses and the road-grading operation. Yes.

Yet how can you tell that to . . . anybody . . . out on the bottom of that bowl as the motor thunder begins to lift up through him like a sigh and his eyeballs glaze over and his hands reach up and there, riding the rim of the bowl, soaring over the ridges, is Junior's yellow Ford . . . which is his white Chevrolet . . . which is a White Ghost, forever rousing the good old boys . . . hard-charging! . . . up with the automobile into their America, and the hell with arteriosclerotic old boys trying to hold onto the whole pot with arms of cotton seersucker. Junior!

[March, 1965]

The Naked Luncheon

by Gina Berriault

She descends from the ceiling, down through a round hole that is draped with red velvet around its edges and with gold fibrillar loops of braid. The gilded piano that, during the preliminary performances of two orange-and-black fringed dancers shuffling and shaking, has appeared to float from the ceiling, now descends slowly on its tracks and cables; it is her support, her special piano with its insides removed. Visible first are the high-heeled beige pumps, then the ankles, the calves, the knees, the thighs of the turning legs, while the tension bounds upward, struck continual blows, like a strength-measuring machine at Funland, by the amplified fanfare from the four musicians on the stage. She is wearing nylon nude-colored tights, a French-cut bikini bottom of pink cloth that surprisingly reaches almost to the navel, a white wig of a starlet, page-boy cut, pearly-white lipstick, black awnings of eyelashes, and bare breasts rather large for her small body and a trifle more pendulous than globular. She is in constant motion, after the blasting introduction when the piano rests at last on the floor, and the dancing figure is made to appear twelve times faster by the spotlight that goes on and almost off constantly, reminiscent of the unnerving light on the top of a police car. The music blares, the words are unseparated. It is sound beyond sound so that only the impact of the waves is felt; one is caught in the din like a mouse in the amplified guitar. She moves the pearly mouth like Monroe; it opens but no word is heard in the din. There is something silent and pantomimic about the frantic figure within the blasting music as if it danced in the unreal center of a hurricane. After a kind of climax involving both music and body, the figure calms, the piano begins to rise. Up goes the white wig through the ceiling, up go the breasts, up go the legs. Carol Doda disappears, and once again the piano stands against the ceiling on air while the crowds along the sidewalk are ushered in by flashlight and half the audience rises and moves out from the darkness, illuminated on its way by a light from somewhere that turns the white shirts of the men a luminescent violet as if a globe burned within each chest.

He puts into my hands a jigsaw puzzle. After it is assembled it will be a giant color photograph of Carol Doda, the same as on the cover of the box, facing front in a purple, topless swimsuit, one arm up and one arm down, pale hair straight to her shoulders, and on the crown of her head a red-and-purple spray of feathers. The man who gives me this gift is the biggest press agent I've ever seen in the smallest office I've ever seen, once a broom closet, perhaps, or a toilet when The Condor was a bar called the Black Condor. Expanded now into a nightclub, The Condor has a red-brick facade, arched windows with red glass, and fringed shades, and this triangular office in which I am wedged forms part of the jut at the corner of Broadway and Columbus. The desk is miniature and so is the typewriter; once, for a time, a three-foot midget served as master of ceremonies and this may have been his sanctum, but times have changed. In one corner are shelves piled with newspapers and magazines, and when the big man stands on a cane chair to bring down a newspaper from the top shelf it is almost unbelievable.

"On June 17, 1964," he begins, as if it were a world-shaking date. He was at the house of his boss, Gino, watching television. It was the time when the topless swimsuits were being introduced by the newspapers, and on the front page of the *Chronicle* that day was a photo of a four-year-old girl wearing one. "You want to know how to pack the place?" he asked his boss. "No four-year-olds," said Gino. At that time Carol Doda was a waitress at The Condor who did some dancing on a piano that stayed on the floor. Unfortunately, President Johnson was about to campaign in the city the first time she danced topless. "We couldn't get coverage," the press agent recalls. But notoriety came by way of a disc jockey who, through the glass of his booth, saw the topless suit held up by Gino, and the second night the place, as predicted, was packed. Within forty-eight hours Big Al's and The Off Broadway went topless, and not long after that a host of other clubs in North Beach—among them the El Cid, the

Galaxie, Pierre's, Tipsy's, and several jigger-size bars around the periphery, where the only entertainment before had been the sour humor of the habitués.

"Some people are saying that her breasts are silicone," I begin, hesitantly.

It was he who gave out the secret, he admits. He gave it out, three months after injections were begun, to a columnist whose observations are as essential to a great many in the San Francisco area as their Librium or their Dexedrine, and now, passing by the even longer lines before The Condor, one hears the word silicone in questions and in answers. "She was mad at me at first," he admits, this admission as eager as the other, "but now she's glad to talk about it. Let's face it, when you go from a 34 to a 44 you can't keep it a secret. When a woman grows like that it's like getting pregnant. They call her Miss Silicone of 1965." I fail to ask who *they* stands for. "It sounds cruel," he admits, "but she doesn't care because this is what the public wants and this is what it's getting. This is the sex symbol that Hollywood didn't build."

She is also, I am told, the Pinup Girl of the Year for the men aboard the aircraft carrier U.S.S. *Kittyhawk,* who have requested a photograph of her to accompany them, as their letter puts it, on their "cruise to Vietnam." He will oblige with five thousand photographs. "Isn't that quite a number?" I ask. "They can give out the extra ones when they get to Vietnam," he replies.

Just as a matter of curiosity, because he is not yet thirty and has to his credit, already, this burgeoning of the entire North Beach, I ask him about his past. As the spirit behind Personalities of California, an enterprise quiescent now because of his involvement at The Condor and other topless clubs, he put professional athletes—wrestlers, baseball and football players—into supermarkets for autographing appearances. The women, he claims, loved it, they flocked in. "This old woman brought her Bible for Pepper Gomez to sign." As I leave the broom closet I see Tony, one of the three owners of The Condor, sitting, with a beatific smile, under a Gay Nineties chandelier.

Whether you are man or woman, there is an initial shock on finding yourself surrounded by nude women, or women who appear in the dim and nude-color light to be nude. At The Off Broadway, as your eyes grow accustomed to the half-dark and to the bareness, you are then able to perceive pointed gold pasties over nipples, nylon flesh-colored tights, bras on some and rayon or nylon panties such as can be picked up on a Macy's bargain table, stretch girdles and two-piece swimsuits, and to perceive, within bras or behind the spangled pasties, small breasts and medium-sized breasts along with the larger ones, and even a hollow chest from improper posture, and, within a girdle, a protruding belly as after a childbirth. They are, at second and third glance, very human and as if in a dormitory, running around to find their clothes. These are the performing non-performers, some at ease, one sweetly pigeon-toed and awkward, with a touch of humiliation where the clothes used to be, standing to take an order with a kind of protective slumping-in of pelvis and breasts, and these are the ones who are being ridiculed in print by another columnist, this one minor, who demands bodily perfection of the girls who serve him his breaded veal cutlets while his own imperfections are concealed beneath his tailor-hung suit.

Voss Boreta, The Off Broadway owner, with the smooth, dark face of the nightclub owner in any movie, talks with happy accommodation about the trials as we sit across from each other at a table that affords a view of the large and low-ceilinged room filled with the usual well-dressed couples and small groups of men and lone men, served by waitresses everywhere bare and bumping and easing by, and engaged by five convulsive girls on as many platforms all around the room, in net trousers and no more except shoes, and by the Beatle-like group on the stage and a long, lean blonde vocalist in a trance and yellow pajamas who dances incessantly as she sings. For several days in the Spring of 1965 the trials were given the front pages, the TV newscasts, and the gossip columns, and those persons who, before, were not aware of the preponderant importance of the topless dancers over other figures of the world scene were now made aware. And when the judges and the jury, upon his advice, ruled that the topless conduct was not outraging of public decency and the girls removed their covering again, there were even larger crowds on the sidewalks waiting for the ones inside to come out.

Before the nighttime topless fashion shows, The Off Broadway booked top or near-top entertainers, and then had topless fashion shows at lunch-time, parading the girls only around the tables. When the arrests began, Boreta at once staged a fashion show at night. In all, he was arrested three times. "We paid Trini Lopez $7500 a week," he tells me. "It's like—fill up a bag and give it to Trini. The total payroll, for him and everybody else, was about $13,000 a week. Now we're even more packed and the payroll is $7000, total." The dancers, still in a frenzy up there on their platforms, after what seems to be close to half an hour, not varying their routine but at least changing platforms, are paid $25 to $30 a night. The waitresses get $12.50 and their tips. There are thirty-eight girls employed on two shifts, and if Boreta runs short his brother supplies him. "My brother's got The Cellar. Before topless, if he got twenty people a night he was lucky. Now he can't handle them all. Chris Boreta—running for Board of Supervisors."

The stage is now clear for the fashion show, and there appears a tall and slender model with champagne-color hair, a gliding walk, and eyes that appear to glow on and off. The yellow-pajamas vocalist, now in the hatcheck booth with a microphone in her hand, parodies the commentary of a *haute-couture* show as the model glides across the stage in a green dress with a neckline so plunging it bares the breasts and the navel. She is a dancer from Las Vegas and so is the model who follows her, very tall, very slender, in a silver-grey dress that appears to be conventional. It is, however, a trick dress, for once on the stage she gives it a graceful tug and down comes the top. On the white-painted brick walls are life-size photos of a bare Yvonne D'Angers. Now she herself appears from out the door that leads to the kitchen and to the dressing room downstairs, an incomparable and somewhat confounding fusion of eighteenth-century French courtesan and girlie-magazine model. The wig is high and as white as Christmas-tree snow, the lips pearly-white, the eyelids weighted with olack canopies, the walk slow with a gliding jog in the hips, the breasts globular, glowing faintly, perhaps with lotion, under the transparent lavender chiffon. Off in a corner of the room there is a glass stall where once a girl showered in what was called champagne. It is now a dressing room where Yvonne strips down to nothing behind white translucent curtains as the light inside dims down. In a red baby doll she emerges, rubs her back against the pillar at the edge of the stage, and, with utmost grace, lowers the top. Finding something amusing in the uplifted faces of the men below her, she laughs to herself, her breasts shaking with perfect timing. Now she lies down on the chaise longue that is covered with white fur, her legs up along the pillar, her breasts down almost under the chins of the nearest patrons, while the microphone voice, which strangely now appears to be Yvonne's mind in interior monologue, cautions *Don't touch. Just look.* She shifts position, she chooses one close patron and beckons slowly with the forefinger, and now the voice begins to make moaning, panting, husky sighs. *Hi, there, tiger. How are you? Get up, are you resisting? I'm sure you've bragged about it for years. Now stand up and do something.* The patron, a large man in a rather iridescent grey summer suit, won't stand up. *Oh, you really do have problems,* says the voice, and it is this terrorizing joke that brings him to his feet to bend his head over the face that, once again, is upside down on the edge of the chaise longue. Yvonne purses her lips upward as the patron bends his head downward; then, almost upon contact, the microphone voice, belonging again to the girl in the hatcheck booth, saying, "And that, ladies and gentlemen, was Yvonne D'Angers," sends her bounding up, running across the stage to her glass shower case, her mass of snowy hair shaking.

Down past the kitchen, down the stairs to the basement, and past a red-jacketed busboy playing solitaire standing up at the napery shelves, I come to the dressing room and find Yvonne settled nude in a chair before her dressing table, brushing a fake nail on the forefinger of the blonde Las Vegas girl. The fingernail, held up for my inspection, appears afflicted with a humpy cornification. "Then you file it down," explains the Las

Vegas girl, "and put on the polish. Oh, yes, they last . . ." and each girl displays her long, gold-tipped fingers.

There are racks of garments, transparent and opaque, of many colors, a small couch, and on the dressing tables, among the jars and bottles, some Listerine mouthwash and a bottle of witch hazel. Around the large mirror before Yvonne are perhaps twenty photographs of herself. She tells me that her father sells Citroëns to the Persians, that when she was a school-girl in Paris she walked by the Moulin Rouge and saw a photograph of a nude couple in a fishnet and heard that suggestive things were done in the dance. "Oh, how I wanted to see that act," she tells me. It is her smiling, obliging history. The brunette model, who has been dancing on the stage upstairs, in a sequined crotch piece and high heels, a shuffle-footed, on-a-dime dance with graceful wavings of her arms, now runs in. She throws a transparent, yellow, ruffled capelet around her shoulders and sits on the sofa to combine her observations on Las Vegas with those of the champagne blonde, who is her room-mate. They were given, they tell me, a chance to tour with a troupe in Europe, but turned it down because of the dog quarantine in England. Their three sheepdogs would have been detained six months, and none of them could have borne so long a separation. Someone outside reminds the girls the show begins again in three minutes.

The atmosphere, the next day at noon, is slightly different at The Off Broadway. There are fewer women, no musicians, and in among the waitresses with their pasties and their girdles and their bras, as before, is one with a green-striped cotton dress and low heels. Had she come in late and found no time to remove her clothes? It was at her table I was given a chair by the hostess and I ask her why she wears a dress. "It's just that when I'm out among strangers I prefer to wear clothes." It has an anachronistic sound here, like a medieval superstition. She is unmarried, a girl with a guileless face, who hastens to tell me that she is not the only one, that another girl, who also worked there before the place went topless and who is now on vacation, also wears a dress. A plump girl with lingerie bra and girdle is standing nearby. "Why aren't you topless?" I ask her. "I don't believe in it," she answers. "I believe in illusion." Of an amiable girl with pasties and panties I ask how the pasties are made to stay on. "With surgical glue," she replies. And how do you remove them? "With an ouch." One of the girls is now gliding across the stage in an orange transparent gown. "She's got a beautiful face," says an elderly man to his male companions around a small table. "I'm interested in those things. I used to be a mortician." The amiable waitress appears to be in a state of discomfort; there is a hint in her arms of a need to hug herself. "I'm cold," she confides. I ask if there is a device for extending the nipples while one sleeps, as I have noticed the extraordinary length of those on the model now passing among the tables. "They're the oddest nipples I've ever seen," the waitress agrees. "There may be a device, but I don't know of any." She has been a waitress for six years and has worked as a topless one for six months. "Are you molested by the men?" I ask. "No such luck," she replies and goes off to attend to her tables.

I turn my attention to the seven men at my table. They are all with a carbide company, the one across the table informs me, and one of the seven is telling the others about the salesman in the silicone division in San Francisco who sends out pictures of Carol Doda, before and after. Laughter follows this and jokes: "If I ever see silicone again, I'll recognize it," and, "You know what you'll hear now—Do you love me for my silicone or for myself?" The man across from me wears heavy glasses that appear to have behind them meditative eyes. No, it's not a convention, he tells me. Just a few people with the company from around the country. He himself is from New York. "Are they silicone?" he asks me as Yvonne passes by, and I tell him I am uninformed.

"In a sense," he comments, "it's like creating a freak in a circus. Nature did a grand job, better with some than with others. But one time people thought bleaching hair was gross, so maybe I'm behind the times. I'm a leg man, myself." He laughs. The others have left the table. He stands up, pats my shoulder. "It's just a joint with a gimmick," he says. What other products does his company manufacture? I ask. "Plastics, batteries, antifreeze, sapphires. . . ."

The plastic surgeon I call on informs me that the injections of liquid silicone by means of a needle into multiple areas of the breast is regarded as unethical by the California Society of Plastic Surgeons, for whom he speaks. Since the use of the medical-grade silicone is not approved by the Federal Drug Administration, manufacturers cannot release it and those persons injecting silicone are using either an industrial grade or are obtaining some other similar type of silicone compound. Because the silicone is promising, however, the F.D.A. has approved the release of the medical grade to several university medical centers for use only in small areas of the body, with injections into the breast specifically excluded. The reason for this exclusion, he explains, is that the ultimate fate of the material in the body is still uncertain. For one thing, it may disguise the presence of a breast tumor, and, for another, experiments have shown that sometimes a portion of the material injected locally disappears and may be carried to other areas of the body. "Where it goes we don't know."

Some silicone, I learn from a chemical engineer-salesman, resembles a thick motor oil. Sand is the starting material and silicone is an organic, modified polymer of sand. It is called dimethylpolysiloxane. He himself has not sold silicone to doctors, he assures me, but he knows that doctors purchase it anonymously. "It's as easy to buy as milk," I am told. "Any large-volume item is impossible to keep track of. So the medical profession, if they dictate their ethics, will have to do the policing, not the industry." His company has no medical-grade silicone, but the industrial grade, he is sure, is as pure. Its other uses? I ask. "Silicone rubber, used by the aerospace industry and by the missile industry for seals and gaskets. And by the urethane industry in foam for furniture, automobiles, insulation. . . ."

Dave Rosenberg, the press agent, is waiting at Enrico's, inside, past the customers sitting in the open around the small, marble-top tables, each with its single rose in a vase. Surprised to find him there because I had thought the interview was to be between Carol Doda and myself, I realize, as we sit down to wait for her, that his presence should have been expected; he is an integral and anxious part of her image. He wears a sky-blue sweater and orders a double Coke. "You heard of George and Teddy and The Condors?" he asks me. "We got a new record, a 45, *Ain't That Loving You, Baby?* We're going to put them up in a helicopter—George and Teddy—and drop 10,000 ping-pong balls on San Francisco. I get home at three in the morning and sit up thinking, thinking, always thinking up new ideas."

She comes in smiling, swinging a black bag, wearing a black-and-red poor-boy sweater, dark-green bell-bottom trousers, and high-heeled black pumps. Dave has told me that she is a frustrated person. I bring up the subject and he answers first. "She gets all kinds of publicity. She gets more publicity than almost anybody except maybe Mamie Van Doren or Jayne Mansfield. She wants to go places. Let's face it, I want to go places, too."

"I think about it day and night," says Carol. "I don't want to be topless forever. I like productional shows—Las Vegas, New York, Europe. I've been in *Der Spiegel* magazine in Germany, the London *Times,* and *Spectator*—they know me in Europe. Anybody else would be touring, but I'm still at The Condor. They helped me get this far, but now they're holding me back. Something's got to explode."

I bring up the possibility that in a year from now every major city in the country will have topless dancers and the fact of her being the original one might have no bearing in the presence of hundreds or thousands of other topless dancers. Since she has no manager, I suggest that she find one. She agrees. "I have to go on to greater heights . . ." and, turning to Dave, she suggests that he phone to New York.

"You could phone Gypsy Rose Lee," he proposes. "You could ask her about a manager." Carol was on Gypsy's TV program, he informs me, and answered questions about the silicone. "At the end of the show Gypsy says to the women, *The bus for the silicone doctor loads out front right after the show*. It was banned in L.A." He tells me that he gets around three calls a week from women who want to know where they can get the treatments.

"Why do women do it . . ." I begin.

"Do they do it for men or for themselves?" asks Dave of Carol, interpreting my question with fewer complications than I had intended for it.

"Not for men," says Carol. "I do it for myself. Men are animals. They don't care how a woman looks."

"We care, we care," protests Dave, shifting his weight in the small chair. "Some beautiful women, they look gorgeous with makeup. You see them in the morning and you want to give them a broom and send them on their way."

"Is there," I ask her, "any resentment? How does it affect you erotically?"

"What's that mean?" she asks.

"It means love," explains Dave.

"No," she replies, musing on resentment. "Because it's part of me. It's me. It becomes a part of yourself. When I see my old pictures I tear them up."

The three of us leave Enrico's, passing two men at one of the tables on the edge of the sidewalk, who lean out to watch her after she has gone by. Carol and I, walking behind Dave for a few yards, are both obscured from oncoming pedestrians. It isn't until they get past him that they see she is there.

There is a place called Mother's. On its windows are painted, in luminous red and black, nude women standing life-size, reminiscent of stained-glass figures. One enters into a chamber of uterine-red walls, rippled and folded in bas-relief as if frozen in the midst of contraction. In the men's room, I am told, there is an *assemblage* of tin soldiers and comic strips, and in the ladies' room there is one of broken dolls. Maria is introduced as the "labacious" dancer, or perhaps the microphone plays tricks. She is the girl who has been sitting at the bar in a black and silver kimono. "No dogs," warns a patron against the wall, a young man with the face of an aristocratic alcoholic. "No dogs," he repeats. Maria, growing at once agitated by the music, wears a bra that is not a bra. It acts as a spangled shelf for the bare breasts. She rolls her buttocks and strokes her breasts at the suggestion of the drummer who is singing out his many directions. And here, as in other clubs, the dancer's body seems to be undergoing a kind of frantic confinement in a yell leader's psyche of close-together legs and ebullient school spirit. There are no bumps, no grinds, there is no carnality here or impending carnality, and perhaps that is what is missing most because it is what we are led to expect. There are only the routines, up and down the block, of pistol pantomime with index fingers from the hips, of shotgun loading, of pony riding to music playing that very moment on a dozen radio stations in the area, and there are patrons' Sing Alongs, with clapping above the head, similar to Simon Says. What *is* present is something of Pop Art, the multi-static squares of race-cars, canned soup, pie wedges, motorcycles, and a movie star nude on a hamburger, what *is* present is an obstinate childlike innocence of the same kind that puts a fighting-cock cartoon on the helmets of our bomber pilots and drops toys a day after bombs. Over at the Red Balloon, one swoops down a slide, to the blast of a horn and the pop of rifles from the shooting gallery, into a carnival where patrons can throw balls at a target to knock a topless girl out of bed and, for a moment, into view, and where strip poker is played for a dollar a hand and the only one who strips is the girl. And down at the corner at Benny the Bum's, a small bar, Joyce, the Negro waitress, in black boots and net overblouse, snaps her fingers and shuffles on a little platform, sometimes lifting her blouse in a parody of the other *haute-couture* parody with, "Now I'm gonna show my lil tiddies."

Up in the dressing room at The Condor, in the few minutes before her last appearance for that night, Carol Doda removes the simple black dress she has been wearing while chatting with the patrons at the bar. Underneath, ready for the act, are the flesh-color tights, and tonight there is a grey bit of bikini bottom with what appears to be a silver braid bobbing at the back. She turns before the mirror. "I remind myself of a horse," she says, laughing, flipping up the braid. "A beer-wagon horse or the ones that pulled the fire trucks." She has, I notice, a beautiful back.

Was the silicone her own idea?

"It was suggested to me," she answers me. She was afraid at first, she thought about it a month, but the doctor reassured her. "But I paid for it myself. *I* paid for it." She describes for me how it's done. "Once a week for a year. It's pumped in with a big needle, like a horse needle. At first it feels too firm. It's like breast now, it feels soft."

She tells me about a letter she has received that day from the mother of a teen-age boy. It has upset her. She tore the letter up, but the pieces are still around if I want to read it. Reverends write to her, informing her that she needs help. There is a fragility to her face, the makeup appears to weigh on it, and there is a quick, natural animation in her gestures. What hurts her most, she tells me, are the kids calling her nasty names along the street and the women calling her a witch. She has no friends, her girl friends turned against her. "You know why? They're afraid. They don't want me to be famous. But I must have something that has to *be*. I know why Marilyn killed herself. Everybody steps on you. Judy Garland, who knows all about emotional upsets, was by to see me. And Gypsy Rose Lee, she came by with her little Mexican dog."

The dressing room looks like a McAllister Street second-hand store. There is a couch and a dresser that in 1930 were probably bargain pieces, old grey lockers that might have been salvaged from a ship. Shoes of the other two girls, now dancing below, lie about on the floor; clothes are thrown over chairs. From below rises the fanfare for her descent. We climb into what appears to be a tunnel and run along in it, bent over. It is a passageway four feet high and about that wide. "It's like being in the war," she says. "You know, a foxhole." We come to a hole in the floor. It is the hole through which she descends, a square one made to appear round from below with the use of a hoop from which hang the red velvet folds and the gold loops. Obviously she is standing on something solid, for she doesn't fall through, feet first. She descends, checking on the stability of her eyelashes and the artful dishevelment of her bangs even as her ankles and legs are beginning to appear to the audience below and the music moans and bellows and throws itself against the ceiling. On my knees I peer over the edge. She is almost down, and as I gaze on the crown of her head I am startled to see the fabric of the wig in which are rooted the white tendrils of hair.

There, gazing down through the hole at the dancing figure in the flashing light, I am reminded again, as I have been reminded of it in the presence of the other bewigged and breasty entertainers, of the story *Gogol's Wife,* by the Italian writer, Tommaso Landolfi. The wife is a balloon doll that Gogol pumps up to the proportions that he wishes, more on one day, less on another, with variations of each part. The color of her hair is changeable, on other areas in addition to her head, and even the color of her skin. But after some years of this ideal mating, while he is entertaining a guest, and the wife, plump that night and blonde, is sitting on a pile of cushions, she speaks: "I want to go poo-poo," she says slyly. It is the beginning of the end. She begins to show signs of aging, grows bitter and religious, and bears a child. And so, torn between love and disgust, he is driven at last to destroy her. He pumps her up until she explodes and is no more.

[March, 1966]

Part III
Egos, Superegos and Ids

Literary Notes on Khrushchev

by Saul Bellow

Khrushchev, the heir of Lenin and Stalin, Malenkov's successor and the evident head of the Russian oligarchy, has stamped his image on the world and compels us to think about him. It is hard of course to believe that this bald, round, gesticulating, loud man may be capable of overcoming, of ruining, perhaps of destroying us.

"It's him, Khrushchev, dat nut," a garage attendant on Third Avenue said to me last September as the fleet of Russian Cadillacs rushed by. This time Khrushchev was a self-invited visitor. He did not arrive with our blessings, and he did not have our love, but that didn't seem to matter greatly to him. He was able, nevertheless, to dominate the headlines, the television screens, the U.N. Assembly and the midtown streets. An American in his position, feeling himself unwanted and, even worse, unloved, would have been self-effacing. Not Khrushchev. He poured it on, holding press conferences in the street and trading insults from his balcony with the crowd, singing snatches of the *International,* giving a pantomime uppercut to an imaginary assassin. He played up to the crowd and luxuriated in its attention, behaving like a comic artist in a show written and directed by himself. And at the U.N., roaring with anger, interrupting

Mr. Macmillan, landing his fists on the desk, waving a shoe in the air, hugging his allies and bugging his opponents, surging up from his seat to pump the hand of the elegant black Nkrumah in his gilt crimson toga or interrupting his own blasts at the West to plug Soviet mineral water, suddenly winsome, Khrushchev the charmer, not once did he give up the center of the stage. And no one seemed able to take it from him.

Balzac once described the statesman as a "monster of self-possession." He referred of course to the bourgeois statesman. Khrushchev is another sort of fish altogether. And since his début on the world scene shortly after Stalin died and Malenkov "retired," Khrushchev—running always a little ahead of Bulganin—has astonished, perplexed, bamboozled and appalled the world. If the traditional statesman is a prodigy of self-possession, Khrushchev seems instead to give himself away. He seems to be a man of candor, just as Russia seems to be a union of socialist republics. Other statesmen are satisfied to represent their countries. Not so Khrushchev. He wishes to personify Russia and the Communist cause.

Timidity will get us nowhere. If we want to understand him we must give the imagination its freedom and let it, in gambler's language, go for broke. Anyway, he compels us to think of him. We have him continually under our eyes. He is in China, he is in Paris and Berlin and San Francisco, and he performs everywhere. In Austria he inspects a piece of abstract sculpture and, with an astonished air, he asks the artist to tell him what the devil it stands for. Listening or pretending to listen, he observes that the sculptor will have to hang around forever to explain his incomprehensible work. He arrives in Finland in time to attend the birthday celebration of its president; he pushes the poor man aside and frolics before the cameras, eats, drinks, fulminates and lets himself be taken home. In America, on his first visit, his progress across the land was nothing less than spectacular. And no fifteenth-century king could have been more *himself,* whether with the press, with Mr. Garst on the farm, with dazzling dolls of Hollywood, or with the trade-union leaders in San Francisco. "You are like a nightingale," he said to Walter Reuther. "It closes its eyes when it sings, and sees nothing and hears nobody but itself." In Hollywood with Spyros Skouras, he matched success stories, each protagonist trying to prove that he rose from greater depths. "I was a poor immigrant." "I began working when I learned to walk—I was a shepherd boy, a factory laborer, I worked in the coal pits, and now I am Prime Minister of the great Soviet State." Neither of them mentioned the cost of his rise to the public-at-large: Skouras said nothing of the effects of Hollywood on the brains of Americans nor did Khrushchev mention deportations and purges. We who had this greatness thrust upon us had no spokesman in the debate. But then people in show business have always enjoyed a peculiar monopoly of patriotism. The mixture of ideology and entertainment on both sides brought about an emotional crisis on the West Coast, and it was here that Khrushchev was provoked into disclosing some of his deeper feelings. "When we were in Hollywood, they danced the cancan for us," he told the meeting of the trade-union leaders in San Francisco. "The girls who dance it have to pull up their skirts and show their backsides. They are good, honest actresses, but have to perform that dance. They are compelled to adapt themselves to the tastes of depraved people. People in your country will go to see it, but Soviet people would scorn such a spectacle. It is pornographic. It is the culture of surfeited and depraved people. Showing that sort of film is called freedom in this country. Such 'freedom' doesn't suit us. You seem to like the 'freedom' of looking at backsides. But we prefer freedom to think, to exercise our mental faculties, the freedom of creative progress." I take these words from a semi-official Russian-sponsored publication. It does not add what some American reports added, namely, that the Premier here raised his coattails and exposed his rear to the entire gathering as he swooped into a parody of the cancan.

This, friends, is art. It is also an entirely new mode of historical interpretation by the world leader of Marxist thought who bodily, by the use of his own person, delivers a critique of Western civilization. It is, moreover, theatre. And we are its enthralled and partly captive audience. Khrushchev's performance is, in the term used by James Joyce, an epiphany, a manifestation which summarizes or expresses a whole universe of meanings. "We will bury you," Khrushchev has told the capitalist world, and though it has since been said over and over that this is merely a Ukrainian figure of speech, meaning, "We will exceed you in production," I think that in watching this dance we might all feel the itching of the nose which, according to superstition, means that someone is walking on our graves. We would not be far out in seeing auguries of death in this cancan. The "culture of surfeited and depraved people" is doomed. That is the meaning of his brutal and angry comedy. It is also what he means when he plays villain and buffoon to the New York public. To him this is the slack, shallow, undisciplined and cultureless mob of a decadent capitalist city. Still, life is very complicated, for if the Hollywood cancan is poor stuff, what can we say of the products of socialist realism with their pure and loyal worker-heroes and their sweet and hokey maidens? Khrushchev himself is far above such junk. It is possible to conclude from this that in a dictatorship the tyrant may suck into himself all the resources of creativity and leave the art of his country impoverished.

It may, in fact, take not only Russia but the entire world to feed the needs of a single individual. For it can't be ideology alone that produces such outbursts; it must be character. "I have often thought," wrote William James, "that the best way to define a man's character would be to seek out the particular mental or moral attitude in which, when it came upon him, he felt himself most intensely active and alive. At such moments there is a voice inside which speaks and says: '*This* is the real me!' " So perhaps Khrushchev feels himself, or attempts to reach himself, in these outbursts. And perhaps it is when the entire world is watching him soar and he is touching the limits of control that he feels most alive. He does not exhibit great range of feelings. When he takes off the rudimentary masks of bureaucratic composure or peasant dignity or affability, he is angry or jeering. But fear is not the best school for expressiveness, and no man could be an important party functionary under Stalin without the ability to live in fear. We cannot therefore expect him to be versatile. He had, however, what it took to finish the course, the nerves, the control, the patience, the piercing ambition, the strength to kill and to endure the threat of death. It would be premature to say that he has survived all that there is to survive in Russia, but it is a safe guess that in the relief of having reached first place he is whooping it up. Instead of having been punished for his crimes he has become a great leader, which persuades him that life is inherently dramatic. And in his joy at having reversed the moral-accounting system of bourgeois civilization he plays his role with ever greater spirit.

Our ablest political commentators have used theatrical metaphors to describe Khrushchev's behavior. Mr. Sulzberger in The New York *Times* speaks of the "fierce illogic of a Brendan Behan play." Others have been reminded of the Leningrad circus, and a British psychologist has suggested that Khrushchev may have made a study of Pavlov's conditioned reflex. After Pavlov had rewarded his dogs for responding to given signals, he scrambled the pattern and the animals suffered an hysterical breakdown. Our leaders, amid flowers and smiles and exchanges of charm, made appointments to meet Khrushchev at the Summit only to find that he had turned into the Great Boyg of the northern snows who deafened them with snarls and stunned them with ice. If Khrushchev had needed instruction in the technique of blowing hot and cold he could have gotten it from Hitler, who made a great deal of noise in the world, rather than from Pavlov, who made very little. From Hitler he might have learned that angry demonstrations unnerve well-conducted people, and that in statesmanship the advantage always lies with the unprincipled, the brutal and the insane. Hitler could at will convulse himself with rage and, when he had gained his ends, be coolly correct to his staff, all in a matter of moments. Khrushchev does not seem to have this combination of derangement and cold political technique which threatens the end of the world in fire and ice. But does he need lessons from Professor Pavlov in psychological techniques? Teach your granny to suck an egg.

No, the dramatic metaphor is the best one, and in trying to place his style, even before I had seen Khrushchev in action during his recent American visit, a short, buoyant, ruddy, compact, gesturing, tough man—it struck me that Marcel Marceau, another mime appearing in *The Overcoat* at a New York theatre, and Khrushchev, at the other side of town, had both been inspired by the Russian comic tradition. The masterpiece of that tradition is Gogol's *Dead Souls*. From Gogol's landlords and peasants, grotesquely thickheaded or just as grotesquely shrewd, provincial autocrats, creeps, misers, officials, gluttons, gamblers and drunkards, Khrushchev seems to have taken many of the elements of his comic style. He is one of Gogol's stout men who "know better than thin men how to manage their affairs. The thin ones are more often employed on special missions, or are merely 'on the staff,' scurrying hither and thither; their existence is somehow too slight, airy and altogether insubstantial. The stout ones are never to be found filling ambiguous posts, but only straightforward ones; if they sit down anywhere, they do so solidly and firmly, so that, though their position may creak and bend beneath them, they never fall off."

When the occasion demands more earnestness he plays the Marxist. Speaking at the U.N. he made me think, when he called for colonial liberation, of Trotsky in the first years of the Russian Revolution and in particular of Trotsky's conduct during the signing of the Treaty of Brest-Litovsk. There, to the amazement of the German generals, he delayed the negotiations in order to make speeches calling on the world proletariat to support and extend the revolution. Those days are gone forever, of course. They were gone even before Lenin died. And there is a great difference between the fresh revolutionary ardor of Trotsky and the stale agitational technique of an old party hack. Still, when it suits him, Khrushchev is a Marxist. Defending the poor working girls of Hollywood, he delivered the judgment of Marxian orthodoxy on their wriggling and kicking (more of the alienating labor imposed by capitalism on humanity).

There are certain similarities between Khrushchev's Marxism and the liberal ideology of Western businessmen. They make use of it at their convenience. Khrushchev, however, enjoys a considerable advantage in that the needs of Russian history and those of his own personality have coincided so that he is able at times to follow his instincts without restraint. He has besides a great contempt for the representatives of the West who are unable to do without the brittle, soiled and compromised conventions of civilized diplomacy. It is the great coma, the deep sleep, and he despises the sleepers and takes advantage of them. The pictures taken at the Summit reveal the extent of his success. General de Gaulle's mouth is drawn very small in a pucker of foreboding and distaste. Mr. Macmillan seems deeply hurt. Former President Eisenhower looks sad, but also opinionated. Things have gone wrong again, but it is certainly no fault of his. Together, the three must have seemed to Khrushchev like Keats's "still unravished brides of quietness." And it is not hard to guess what he, the descendant of serfs, risen to a position of such might, must have experienced. Confronting the leaders of the bourgeois West, so long feared and hated, he saw himself to be tougher, deeper and more intelligent than any of them. And, in expressing his feelings, more free.

It's hard to know whether the Khrushchev we saw banging with his shoe at the U.N. Assembly is the "real" Khrushchev. But one of the privileges of power seems to be the privilege of direct emotional self-expression. It is not a privilege exercised by many people in the West, so far as I can see.

"Men who have arrived can do what they like," declared the *Daily News* recently in one of its snappy ads. "There was a guy who liked spaghetti and beer, but when he became a junior executive, he thought it more fitting to order steak and asparagus. It was only when he became president of his company that he felt assured enough to go back to spaghetti and beer."

Such are the privileges of power, but bafflingly enough, apart from artists and tyrants, few people, even among company presidents, feel strong enough to tell the world how they feel. New York's Police Commissioner Kennedy, a man who has apparently arrived, could not, some time ago, express his honest views as to the religious convictions of the Jewish members of the force. Everyone knows that the commissioner is not anti-Semitic. Yet the New York Rabbinate felt compelled, as did Mayor Wagner, for formal reasons, to ask for a retraction. So it's not easy to speak one's mind. Even the artists have taken cover, disguising themselves as bank clerks and veiling their sayings. That leaves us with the tyrants. (Is it only a coincidence that Emily Post died during Khrushchev's visit?)

Masked in smiles and peasant charm, or in anger, the Russian Premier releases his deepest feelings and if we are not shaken by them it is because we are not in close touch with reality. In the West the connections between opinion, feeling and bodily motion have been broken. We have lost the expressive power. It is in the use of such power, falsely exploiting his Russian and peasant background, that Khrushchev has shown himself to be an adept. He has a passion always ready to exploit and, though he lies, he has the advantage. The principles of Western liberalism seem no longer to lend themselves to effective action. Deprived of the expressive power, we are awed by it, have a hunger for it and are afraid of it. Thus we praise the grey dignity of our soft-spoken leaders, but in our hearts we are suckers for passionate outbursts, even when those passionate outbursts are hypocritical and falsely motivated.

The best lack all conviction
While the worst are full of passionate intensity.

At times Khrushchev goes beyond Gogolian comedy; this is no longer the amiable chiseler who stuffs himself with fish or pancakes dipped in butter. Gogol's Chichikov, to congratulate himself when he has pulled a fast one, dances in the privacy of his room. But Khrushchev goes into his cancan before the world public with a deep and gnomish joy. Here is a man whom all the twisted currents of human purpose have brought within reach of world power. At a time when public figures show only secondary or tertiary personal characteristics, he appears to show only primary ones. He wears his instincts on his sleeve or like Dostoevski's Father Karamazov, that corrupt and deep old man, he feigns simplicity.

When the charm and irony wear thin, he shows himself to be a harsh, arbitrary and complicated man. It was a simple enough matter for him to have joked contemptuously with Spyros Skouras; in debate with well-informed men who press him closely he becomes abusive, showing that the habit of authority has made him inflexible. He seems unable to discuss any matter except on his own terms. Nature, history, Russian Marxism and, perhaps most of all, the fact that he has survived under Stalin make it impossible for him to entertain other views. What amounted in Paris to ex-President Eisenhower's admission of a blunder must have seemed to him incredible. He lives under an iron necessity to be right. What he perhaps remembers best about men who were not right is their funerals. For him the line between the impossible and the possible is drawn with blood, and foreigners who do not see the blood must appear preposterous to him.

[March, 1961]

Frank Sinatra Has a Cold

by Gay Talese

Frank Sinatra, holding a glass of bourbon in one hand and a cigarette in the other, stood in a dark corner of the bar between two attractive but fading blondes who sat waiting for him to say something. But he said nothing; he had been silent during much of the evening, except now in this private club in Beverly Hills he seemed even more distant, staring out through the smoke and semidarkness into a large room beyond the bar where dozens of young couples sat huddled around small tables or twisted in the center of the floor to the clamorous clang of folk-rock music blaring from the stereo. The two blondes knew, as did Sinatra's four male friends who stood nearby, that it was a bad idea to force conversation upon him when he was in this mood of sullen silence, a mood that had hardly been uncommon during this first week of November, a month before his fiftieth birthday.

Sinatra had been working in a film that he now disliked, could not wait to finish; he was tired of all the publicity attached to his dating the twenty-year-old Mia Farrow, who was not in sight tonight; he was angry that a CBS television documentary of his life, to be shown in two weeks, was reportedly prying into his privacy, even speculating on his possible friendship with Mafia leaders; he was worried about his starring role in an hour-long NBC show entitled *Sinatra—A Man And His Music,* which would require that he sing eighteen songs with a voice that at this particular moment, just a few nights before the taping was to begin, was weak and sore and uncertain. Sinatra was ill. He was the victim of an ailment so common that most people would consider it trivial. But when it gets to Sinatra it can plunge him into a state of anguish, deep depression, panic, even rage. Frank Sinatra had a cold.

Sinatra with a cold is Picasso without paint, Ferrari without fuel—only worse. For the common cold robs Sinatra of that uninsurable jewel, his voice, cutting into the core of his confidence, and it affects not only his own psyche but also seems to cause a kind of psychosomatic nasal drip within dozens of people who work for him, drink with him, love him, depend on him for their own welfare and stability. A Sinatra with a cold can, in a small way, send vibrations through the entertainment industry and beyond as surely as a President of the United States, suddenly sick, can shake the national economy.

For Frank Sinatra was now involved with many things involving many people—his own film company, his record company, his private airline, his missile-parts firm, his real-estate holdings across the nation, his personal staff of seventy-five—which are only a portion of the power he is and has come to represent. He seemed now to be also the embodiment of the fully emancipated male, perhaps the only one in America, the man who can do anything he wants, *anything,* can do it because he has the money, the energy, and no apparent guilt. In an age when the very young seem to be taking over, protesting and picketing and demanding change, Frank Sinatra survives as a national phenomenon, one of the few prewar products to withstand the test of time. He is the champ who made the big comeback, the man who had everything, lost it, then got it back, letting nothing stand in his way, doing what few men can do: he uprooted his life, left his family, broke with everything that was familiar, learning in the process that one way to hold a woman is not to hold her. Now he has the affection of Nancy and Ava and Mia, the fine female produce of three generations, and still has the adoration of his children, the freedom of a bachelor, he does not feel old, he makes old men feel young, makes them think that if Frank Sinatra can do it, it can be done; not that *they* could do it, but it is still nice for other men to know, at fifty, that it can be done.

But now, standing at this bar in Beverly Hills, Sinatra had a cold, and he continued to drink quietly and he seemed miles away in his private world, not even reacting when suddenly the stereo in the other room switched to a Sinatra song, *In the Wee Small Hours of the Morning.*

It is a lovely ballad that he first recorded ten years ago, and it now inspired many young couples who had been sitting, tired of twisting, to get up and move slowly around the dance floor, holding one another very close. Sinatra's intonation, precisely clipped, yet full and flowing, gave a deeper meaning to the simple lyrics—"In the wee small hours of the morning / while the whole wide world is fast asleep / you lie awake, and think about the girl . . . "*—it was, like so many of his classics, a song that evoked loneliness and sensuality, and when blended with the dim light and the alcohol and nicotine and late-night needs, it became a kind of airy aphrodisiac. Undoubtedly the words from this song, and others like it, had put millions in the mood, it was music to make love by, and doubtless much love had been made by it all over America at night in cars, while the batteries burned down, in cottages by the lake, on beaches during balmy summer evenings, in secluded parks and exclusive penthouses and furnished rooms, in cabin cruisers and cabs and cabanas—in all places where Sinatra's songs could be heard were these words that warmed women, wooed and won them, snipped the final thread of inhibition and gratified the male egos of ungrateful lovers; two generations of men had been the beneficiaries of such ballads, for which they were eternally in his debt, for which they may eternally hate him. Nevertheless here he was, the man himself, in the early hours of the morning in Beverly Hills, out of range.

The two blondes, who seemed to be in their middle thirties, were preened and polished, their matured bodies softly molded within tight dark suits. They sat, legs crossed, perched on the high bar stools. They listened to the music. Then one of them pulled out a Kent and Sinatra quickly placed his gold lighter under it and she held his hand, looked at his fingers: they were nubby and raw, and the pinkies protruded, being so stiff from arthritis that he could barely bend them. He was, as usual, immaculately dressed. He wore an oxford-grey suit with a vest, a suit conservatively cut on the outside but trimmed with flamboyant silk within; his shoes, British, seemed to be shined even on the bottom of the soles. He also wore, as everybody seemed to know, a remarkably convincing black hairpiece, one of sixty that he owns, most of them under the care of an inconspicuous little grey-haired lady who, holding his hair in a tiny satchel, follows him around whenever he performs. She earns $400 a week. The most distinguishing thing about Sinatra's face are his eyes, clear blue and alert, eyes that within seconds can go cold with anger, or glow with affection, or, as now, reflect a vague detachment that keeps his friends silent and distant.

Leo Durocher, one of Sinatra's closest friends, was now shooting pool in the small room behind the bar. Standing near the door was Jim Mahoney, Sinatra's press agent, a somewhat chunky young man with a square jaw and narrow eyes who would resemble a tough Irish plain-clothesman if it were not for the expensive continental suits he wears and his exquisite shoes often adorned with polished buckles. Also nearby was a big, broad-shouldered two-hundred-pound actor named Brad Dexter

*©*Redd Evans Music Corp.*

who seemed always to be thrusting out his chest so that his gut would not show.

Brad Dexter has appeared in several films and television shows, displaying fine talent as a character actor, but in Beverly Hills he is equally known for the role he played in Hawaii two years ago when he swam a few hundred yards and risked his life to save Sinatra from drowning in a riptide. Since then Dexter has been one of Sinatra's constant companions and has been made a producer in Sinatra's film company. He occupies a plush office near Sinatra's executive suite. He is endlessly searching for literary properties that might be converted into new starring roles for Sinatra. Whenever he is among strangers with Sinatra he worries because he knows that Sinatra brings out the best and worst in people—some men will become aggressive, some women will become seductive, others will stand around skeptically appraising him, the scene will be somehow intoxicated by his mere presence, and maybe Sinatra himself, if feeling as badly as he was tonight, might become intolerant or tense, and then: headlines. So Brad Dexter tries to anticipate danger and warn Sinatra in advance. He confesses to feeling very protective of Sinatra, admitting in a recent moment of self-revelation: "I'd kill for him."

While this statement may seem outlandishly dramatic, particularly when taken out of context, it nonetheless expresses a fierce fidelity that is quite common within Sinatra's special circle. It is a characteristic that Sinatra, without admission, seems to prefer: *All the Way; All or Nothing at All.* This is the Sicilian in Sinatra; he permits his friends, if they wish to remain that, none of the easy Anglo-Saxon outs. But if they remain loyal, then there is nothing Sinatra will not do in turn—fabulous gifts, personal kindnesses, encouragement when they're down, adulation when they're up. They are wise to remember, however, one thing. He is Sinatra. The boss. *Il Padrone.*

I had seen something of this Sicilian side of Sinatra last summer at Jilly's saloon in New York, which was the only other time I'd gotten a close view of him prior to this night in this California club. Jilly's, which is on West Fifty-second Street in Manhattan, is where Sinatra drinks whenever he is in New York, and there is a special chair reserved for him in the back room against the wall that nobody else may use. When he is occupying it, seated behind a long table flanked by his closest New York friends—who include the saloonkeeper, Jilly Rizzo, and Jilly's azure-haired wife, Honey, who is known as the "Blue Jew"—a rather strange ritualistic scene develops. That night dozens of people, some of them casual friends of Sinatra's, some mere acquaintances, some neither, appeared outside of Jilly's saloon. They approached it like a shrine. They had come to pay respect. They were from New York, Brooklyn, Atlantic City, Hoboken. They were old actors, young actors, former prizefighters, tired trumpet players, politicians, a boy with a cane. There was a fat lady who said she remembered Sinatra when he used to throw the *Jersey Observer* onto her front porch in 1933. There were middle-aged couples who said they had heard Sinatra sing at the Rustic Cabin in 1938 and "We knew then that he really had it!" Or they had heard him when he was with Harry James's band in 1939, or with Tommy Dorsey in 1941 ("Yeah, that's the song, *I'll Never Smile Again*—he sang it one night in this dump near Newark and we danced . . ."); or they remembered that time at the Paramount with the swooners, and him with those bow ties, The Voice; and one woman remembered that awful boy she knew then—Alexander Dorogokupetz, an eighteen-year-old heckler who had thrown a tomato at Sinatra and the bobby-soxers in the balcony had tried to flail him to death. Whatever became of Alexander Dorogokupetz? The lady did not know.

And they remembered when Sinatra was a failure and sang trash like *Mairzy Doats,* and they remembered his comeback and on this night they were all standing outside Jilly's saloon, dozens of them, but they could not get in. So some of them left. But most of them stayed, hoping that soon they might be able to push or wedge their way into Jilly's between the elbows and backsides of the men drinking three-deep at the bar, and they might be able to peek through and *see* him sitting back there. This is all they really wanted; they wanted to see him. And for a few moments they gazed in silence through the smoke and they stared. Then they turned, fought their way out of the bar, went home.

Some of Sinatra's close friends, all of whom are known to the men guarding Jilly's door, do manage to get an escort into the back room. But once they are there they, too, must fend for themselves. On the particular evening, Frank Gifford, the former football player, got only seven yards in three tries. Others who had somehow been close enough to shake Sinatra's hand did *not* shake it; instead they just touched him on the shoulder or sleeve, or they merely stood close enough for him to see them and, after he'd given them a wink of recognition or a wave or a nod or called out their names (he has a fantastic memory for first names), they would then turn and leave. They had checked in. They had paid their respects. And as I watched this ritualistic scene, I got the impression that Frank Sinatra was dwelling simultaneously in two worlds that were not contemporary.

On the one hand he is the swinger—as he is when talking and joking with Sammy Davis, Jr., Richard Conte, Liza Minelli, Bernice Massi, or any of the other show-business people who get to sit at *the* table; on the other, as when he is nodding or waving to his *paisanos* who are close to him (Al Silvani, a boxing manager who works with Sinatra's film company; Dominic Di Bona, his wardrobe man; Ed Pucci, a 300-pound former football lineman who is his aide-de-camp), Frank Sinatra is *Il Padrone.* Or better still, he is what in traditional Sicily have long been called *uomini rispettati*—men of respect: men who are both majestic and humble, men who are loved by all and are very generous by nature, men whose hands are kissed as they walk from village to village, men who would *personally* go out of their way to redress a wrong.

Frank Sinatra does things *personally*. At Christmas time, he will personally pick dozens of presents for his close friends and family, remembering the type of jewelry they like, their favorite colors, the sizes of their shirts and dresses. When a musician friend's house was destroyed and his wife was killed in a Los Angeles mud slide a little more than a year ago, Sinatra personally came to his aid, finding the musician a new home, paying whatever hospital bills were left unpaid by the insurance, then personally supervising the furnishing of the new home down to the replacing of the silverware, the linen, the purchase of new clothing.

The same Sinatra who did this can, within the same hour, explode in a towering rage of intolerance should a small thing be incorrectly done for him by one of his *paisanos*. For example, when one of his men brought him a frankfurter with catsup on it, which Sinatra apparently abhors, he angrily threw the bottle at the man, splattering catsup all over him. Most of the men who work around Sinatra are big. But this never seems to intimidate Sinatra nor curb his impetuous behavior with them when he is mad. They will never take a swing back at him. He is *Il Padrone*.

At other times, aiming to please, his men will overreact to his desires: when he casually observed that his big orange desert jeep in Palm Springs seemed in need of a new painting, the word was swiftly passed down through channels, becoming ever more urgent as it went, until finally it was a *command* that the jeep be painted *now*, immediately, yesterday. To accomplish this would require the hiring of a special crew of painters to work all night, at overtime rates; which, in turn, meant that the order had to be bucked back up the line for further approval. When it finally got back to Sinatra's desk, he did not know what it was all about; after he had figured it out he confessed, with a tired look on his face, that he did not care when the hell they painted his jeep.

Yet it would have been unwise for anyone to anticipate his reaction, for he is a wholly unpredictable man of many moods and great dimension, a man who responds instantaneously to instinct—suddenly, dramatically, wildly he responds, and nobody can predict what will follow. A young lady named Jane Hoag, a reporter at *Life*'s Los Angeles bureau who had attended the same school as Sinatra's daughter, Nancy, had once been invited to a party at Mrs. Sinatra's California home at which Frank Sinatra, who maintains very cordial relations with his former wife, acted as host. Early in the party Miss Hoag, while leaning against a table, accidentally with her elbow knocked over one of a pair of alabaster birds to the floor, smashing it to pieces. Suddenly, Miss Hoag recalled, Sinatra's daughter cried, "Oh, that was one of mother's favorite . . ."—but before she could complete the sentence, Sinatra glared at her, cutting her off, and while forty other guests in the room all stared in silence, Sinatra walked over, quickly with his finger flicked the *other* alabaster bird off the table, smashing it to pieces, and then put an arm gently around Jane Hoag and said, in a way that put her completely at ease, "That's okay, kid."

Now Sinatra said a few words to the blondes. Then he turned from the bar and began to walk toward the poolroom. One of Sinatra's other men friends moved in to keep the girls company. Brad Dexter, who had been standing in the corner talking to some other people, now followed Sinatra.

The room cracked with the clack of billiard balls. There were about a dozen spectators in the room, most of them young men who were watching Leo Durocher shoot against two other aspiring hustlers who were not very good. This private drinking club has among its membership many actors, directors, writers, models, nearly all of them a good deal younger than Sinatra or Durocher and much more casual in the way they dress for the evening. Many of the young women, their long hair flowing loosely below their shoulders, wore tight, fanny-fitting Jax pants and very expensive sweaters; and a few of the young men wore blue or green velour shirts with high collars and narrow tight pants, and Italian loafers.

It was obvious from the way Sinatra looked at these people in the poolroom that they were not his style, but he leaned back against a high stool that was against the wall, holding his drink in his right hand, and said nothing, just watched Durocher slam the billiard balls back and forth. The younger men in the room, accustomed to seeing Sinatra at this club, treated him without deference, although they said nothing offensive. They were a cool young group, very California-cool and casual, and one of the coolest seemed to be a little guy, very quick of movement, who had a sharp profile, pale blue eyes, blondish hair, and squared eyeglasses. He wore a pair of brown corduroy slacks, a green shaggy-dog Shetland sweater, a tan suede jacket, and Game Warden boots, for which he had recently paid $60.

Frank Sinatra, leaning against the stool, sniffling a bit from his cold, could not take his eyes off the Game Warden boots. Once, after gazing at them for a few moments, he turned away; but now he was focused on them again. The owner of the boots, who was just standing in them watching the pool game, was named Harlan Ellison, a writer who had just completed work on a screenplay, *The Oscar*.

Finally Sinatra could not contain himself.

"Hey," he yelled in his slightly harsh voice that still had a soft, sharp edge. "Those Italian boots?"

"No," Ellison said.

"Spanish?"

"No."

"Are they *English* boots?"

"Look, I donno, man," Ellison shot back, frowning at Sinatra, then turning away again.

Now the poolroom was suddenly silent. Leo Durocher who had been poised behind his cue stick and was bent low just froze in that position for a second. Nobody moved. Then Sinatra moved away from the stool and walked with that slow, arrogant swagger of his toward Ellison, the hard tap of Sinatra's shoes the only sound in the room. Then, looking down at Ellison with a slightly raised eyebrow and a tricky little smile, Sinatra asked: "You expecting a *storm?*"

Harlan Ellison moved a step to the side. "Look, is there any reason why you're talking to me?"

"I don't like the way you're dressed," Sinatra said.

"Hate to shake you up," Ellison said, "but I dress to suit myself."

Now there was some rumbling in the room, and somebody said, "Com'on, Harlan, let's get out of here," and Leo Durocher made his pool shot and said, "Yeah, com'on."

But Ellison stood his ground.

Sinatra said, "What do you do?"

"I'm a plumber," Ellison said.

"No, no, he's not," another young man quickly yelled from across the table. "He wrote *The Oscar.*"

"Oh, yeah," Sinatra said, "well I've seen it, and it's a piece of crap."

"That's strange," Ellison said, "because they haven't even released it yet."

"Well, I've seen it," Sinatra repeated, "and it's a piece of crap."

Now Brad Dexter, very anxious, very big opposite the small figure of Ellison, said, "Com'on, kid, I don't want you in this room."

"*Hey,*" Sinatra interrupted Dexter, "can't you see I'm talking to this guy?"

Dexter was confused. Then his whole attitude changed, and his voice went soft and he said to Ellison, almost with a plea, "*Why do you persist in tormenting me?*"

The whole scene was becoming ridiculous, and it seemed that Sinatra was only half-serious, perhaps just reacting out of sheer boredom or inner despair; at any rate, after a few more exchanges Harlan Ellison left the room. By this time the word had gotten out to those on the dance floor about the Sinatra-Ellison exchange, and somebody went to look for the manager of the club. But somebody else said that the manager had already heard about it—and had quickly gone out the door, hopped in his car and drove home. So the assistant manager went into the poolroom.

"I don't want anybody in here without coats and ties," Sinatra snapped.

The assistant manager nodded, and walked back to his office.

It was the morning after. It was the beginning of another nervous day for Sinatra's press agent, Jim Mahoney. Mahoney had a headache, and he was worried but not over the Sinatra-Ellison incident of the night before. At the time

Mahoney had been with his wife at a table in the other room, and possibly he had not even been aware of the little drama. The whole thing had lasted only about three minutes. And three minutes after it was over, Frank Sinatra had probably forgotten about it for the rest of his life—as Ellison will probably remember it for the rest of *his* life: he had had, as hundreds of others before him, at an unexpected moment between darkness and dawn, a scene with Sinatra.

It was just as well that Mahoney had not been in the poolroom; he had enough on his mind today. He was worried about Sinatra's cold and worried about the controversial CBS documentary that, despite Sinatra's protests and withdrawal of permission, would be shown on television in less than two weeks. The newspapers this morning were full of hints that Sinatra might sue the network, and Mahoney's phones were ringing without pause, and now he was plugged into New York talking to the *Daily News's* Kay Gardella, saying: ". . . that's right, Kay . . . they made a gentleman's agreement to not ask certain questions about Frank's private life, and then Cronkite went right ahead: 'Frank, tell me about those associations.' *That* question, Kay—*out!* That question should never have been asked. . . ."

As he spoke, Mahoney leaned back in his leather chair, his head shaking slowly. He is a powerfully built man of thirty-seven; he has a round, ruddy face, a heavy jaw, and narrow pale eyes, and he might appear pugnacious if he did not speak with such clear, soft sincerity and if he were not so meticulous about his clothes. His suits and shoes are superbly tailored, which was one of the first things Sinatra noticed about him, and in his spacious office opposite the bar is a red-muff electrical shoe polisher and a pair of brown wooden shoulders on a stand over which Mahoney can drape his jackets. Near the bar is an autographed photograph of President Kennedy and a few pictures of Frank Sinatra, but there are none of Sinatra in any other rooms in Mahoney's public-relations agency; there once was a large photograph of him hanging in the reception room but this apparently bruised the egos of some of Mahoney's other movie-star clients and, since Sinatra never shows up at the agency anyway, the photograph was removed.

Still, Sinatra seems ever present, and if Mahoney did not have legitimate worries about Sinatra, as he did today, he could invent them—and, as worry aids, he surrounds himself with little mementos of moments in the past when he did worry. In his shaving kit there is a two-year-old box of sleeping tablets dispensed by a Reno druggist—the date on the bottle marks the kidnapping of Frank Sinatra, Jr. There is on a table in Mahoney's office a mounted wood reproduction of Frank Sinatra's ransom note written on the aforementioned occasion. One of Mahoney's mannerisms, when he is sitting at his desk worrying, is to tinker with the tiny toy train he keeps in front of him—the train is a souvenir from the Sinatra film, *Von Ryan's Express;* it is to men who are close to Sinatra what the PT-109 tie clasps are to men who were close to Kennedy—and Mahoney then proceeds to roll the little train back and forth on the six inches of track; back and forth, back and forth, click-*clack* click-*clack*. It is his Queeg-thing.

Now Mahoney quickly put aside the little train. His secretary told him there was a *very* important call on the line. Mahoney picked it up, and his voice was even softer and more sincere than before. "Yes, Frank," he said. "Right . . . right . . . yes, Frank. . . ."

When Mahoney put down the phone, quietly, he announced that Frank Sinatra had left in his private jet to spend the weekend at his home in Palm Springs, which is a sixteen-minute flight from his home in Los Angeles. Mahoney was now worried again. The Lear jet that Sinatra's pilot would be flying was identical, Mahoney said, to the one that had just crashed in another part of California.

On the following Monday, a cloudy and unseasonably cool California day, more than one hundred people gathered inside a white television studio, an enormous room dominated by a white stage, white walls, and with dozens of lights and lamps dangling: it rather resembled a gigantic operating room. In this room, within an hour or so, NBC was scheduled to begin taping a one-hour show that would be televised in color on the night of November 24 and would highlight, as much as it could in the limited time, the twenty-five-year career of Frank Sinatra as a public entertainer. It would not attempt to probe, as the forthcoming CBS *Sinatra* documentary allegedly would, that area of Sinatra's life that he regards as private. The NBC show would be mainly an hour of Sinatra singing some of the hits that carried him from Hoboken to Hollywood, a show that would be interrupted only now and then by a few film clips and commercials for Budweiser beer. Prior to his cold, Sinatra had been very excited about this show; he saw here an opportunity to appeal not only to those nostalgic, but also to communicate his talent to some rock-and-rollers—in a sense, he was battling The Beatles. The press releases being prepared by Mahoney's agency stressed this, reading: "If you happen to be tired of kid singers wearing mops of hair thick enough to hide a crate of melons . . . it should be refreshing to consider the entertainment value of a video special titled *Sinatra—A Man And His Music. . . .*"

But now in this NBC studio in Los Angeles, there was an atmosphere of anticipation and tension because of the uncertainty of the Sinatra voice. The forty-three musicians in Nelson Riddle's orchestra had already arrived and some were up on the white platform warming up. Dwight Hemion, a youthful sandy-haired director who had won praise for his television special on Barbra Streisand, was seated in the glass-enclosed control booth that overlooked the orchestra and stage. The camera crews, technical teams, security guards, Budweiser ad men were also standing between the floor lamps and cameras, waiting, as were a dozen or so ladies who worked as secretaries in other parts of the building but had sneaked away so they could watch this.

A few minutes before eleven o'clock, word spread quickly through the long corridor into the big studio that Sinatra was spotted walking through the parking lot and was on his way, and was looking fine. There seemed great relief among the group that was gathered; but when the lean, sharply dressed figure of the man got closer, and closer, they saw to their dismay that it was not Frank Sinatra. It was his double. Johnny Delgado.

Delgado walks like Sinatra, has Sinatra's build, and from certain facial angles does resemble Sinatra. But he seems a rather shy individual. Fifteen years ago, early in his acting career, Delgado applied for a role in *From Here to Eternity*. He was hired, finding out later that he was to be Sinatra's double. In Sinatra's latest film, *Assault on a Queen*, a story in which Sinatra and some fellow conspirators attempt to hijack the *Queen Mary*, Johnny Delgado doubles for Sinatra in some water scenes; and now, in this NBC studio, his job was to stand under the hot television lights marking Sinatra's spots on the stage for the camera crews.

Five minutes later, the real Frank Sinatra walked in. His face was pale, his blue eyes seemed a bit watery. He had been unable to rid himself of the cold, but he was going to try to sing anyway because the schedule was tight and thousands of dollars were involved at this moment in the assembling of the orchestra and crews and the rental of the studio. But when Sinatra, on his way to his small rehearsal room to warm up his voice, looked into the studio and saw that the stage and orchestra's platform were not close together, as he had specifically requested, his lips tightened and he was obviously very upset. A few moments later, from his rehearsal room, could be heard the pounding of his fist against the top of the piano and the voice of his accompanist, Bill Miller, saying, softly, "Try not to upset yourself, Frank."

Later Jim Mahoney and another man walked in, and there was talk of Dorothy Kilgallen's death in New York earlier that morning. She had been an ardent foe of Sinatra for years, and he became equally uncomplimentary about her in his nightclub act, and now, though she was dead, he did not compromise his feelings. "Dorothy Kilgallen's dead," he repeated, walking out of the room toward the studio. "Well, guess I got to change my whole act."

When he strolled into the studio the musicians all picked up their instruments and stiffened in their seats. Sinatra cleared his throat a few times and then, after rehearsing a few ballads with the orchestra, he sang *Don't Worry About Me* to his satisfaction and, being uncertain of how long his voice could last, suddenly became impatient.

"Why don't we tape this mother?" he called out, looking up toward the glass booth where the director, Dwight Hemion, and his staff were sitting. Their heads seemed to be down, focusing on the control board.

"Why don't we tape this mother?" Sinatra repeated.

The production stage manager, who stands near the camera wearing a headset, repeated Sinatra's words exactly into his line to the control room: "Why don't we tape this mother?"

Hemion did not answer. Possibly his switch was off. It was hard to know because of the obscuring reflections the lights made against the glass booth.

"Why don't we put on a coat and tie," said Sinatra, then wearing a high-necked yellow pullover, "and tape this. . . ."

Suddenly Hemion's voice came over the sound amplifier, very calmly: "Okay, Frank, would you mind going back over. . . ."

"Yes I *would* mind going back," Sinatra snapped.

The silence from Hemion's end, which lasted a second or two, was then again interrupted by Sinatra saying, "When we stop doing things around here the way we did them in 1950, maybe we . . . " and Sinatra continued to tear into Hemion, condemning as well the lack of modern techniques in putting such shows together; then, possibly not wanting to use his voice unnecessarily, he stopped. And Dwight Hemion, very patient, so patient and calm that one would assume he had not heard anything that Sinatra had just said, outlined the opening part of the show. And Sinatra a few minutes later was reading his opening remarks, words that would follow *Without a Song,* off the large idiot-cards being held near the camera. Then, this done, he prepared to do the same thing on camera.

"Frank Sinatra Show, Act I, Page 10, Take 1," called a man with a clapboard, jumping in front of the camera—*clap*—then jumping away again.

"Did you ever stop to think," Sinatra began, "what the world would be like without a song? . . . It would be a pretty dreary place. . . . Gives you something to think about, doesn't it? . . . "

Sinatra stopped.

"Excuse me," he said, adding, *"Boy,* I need a drink."

They tried it again.

"Frank Sinatra Show, Act I, Page 10, Take 2," yelled the jumping guy with the clapboard.

"Did you ever stop to think what the world would be like without a song? . . . " Frank Sinatra read it through this time without stopping. Then he rehearsed a few more songs, once or twice interrupting the orchestra when a certain instrumental sound was not quite what he wanted. It was hard to tell how well his voice was going to hold up, for this was early in the show; up to this point, however, everybody in the room seemed pleased, particularly when he sang an old sentimental favorite written more than twenty years ago by Jimmy Van Heusen and Phil Silvers—*Nancy,* inspired by the first of Sinatra's three children when she was just a few years old.

> "If I don't see her each day
> I miss her. . . .
> Gee what a thrill
> Each time I kiss her. . . ."

As Sinatra sang these words, though he has sung them hundreds and hundreds of times in the past, it was suddenly obvious to everybody in the studio that something quite special must be going on inside the man, because something quite special was coming out. He was singing now, cold or no cold, with power and warmth, he was letting himself go, the public arrogance was gone, the private side was in this song about the girl who, it is said, understands him better than anybody else, and is the only person in front of whom he can be unashamedly himself.

Nancy is twenty-five. She lives alone, her marriage to singer Tommy Sands having ended in divorce. Her home is in a Los Angeles suburb and she is now making her third film and is recording for her father's record company. She sees him every day; or, if not, he telephones, no matter if it be from Europe or Asia. When Sinatra's singing first became popular on radio, stimulating the swooners, Nancy would listen at home and cry. When Sinatra's first marriage broke up in 1951 and he left home, Nancy was the only child old enough to remember him as a father. She also saw him with Ava Gardner, Juliet Prowse, Mia Farrow, many others, has gone on double dates with him. . . .

> "She takes the winter
> And makes it summer. . . .
> Summer could take
> Some lessons from her. . . ."

Nancy now also sees him visiting at home with his first wife, the former Nancy Barbato, a plasterer's daughter from Jersey City whom he married in 1939 when he was earning $25 a week singing at the Rustic Cabin near Hoboken.

The first Mrs. Sinatra, a striking woman who has never remarried ("When you've been married to Frank Sinatra . . ." she once explained to a friend), lives in a magnificent home in Los Angeles with her younger daughter, Tina, who is seventeen. There is no bitterness, only great respect and affection between Sinatra and his first wife, and he has long been welcome in her home and has even been known to wander in at odd hours, stoke the fire, lie on the sofa and fall asleep. Frank Sinatra can fall asleep anywhere, something he learned when he used to ride bumpy roads with band buses; he also learned at that time, when sitting in a tuxedo, how to pinch the trouser creases in the back and tuck the jacket under and out, and fall asleep perfectly pressed. But he does not ride buses anymore, and his daughter Nancy, who in her younger days felt rejected when he slept on the sofa instead of giving attention to her, later realized that the sofa was one of the few places left in the world where Frank Sinatra could get any privacy, where his famous face would neither be stared at nor cause an abnormal reaction in others. She realized, too, that things normal have always eluded her father: his childhood was one of loneliness and a drive toward attention, and since attaining it he has never again been certain of solitude. Upon looking out the window of a home he once owned in Hasbrouck Heights, New Jersey, he would occasionally see the faces of teen-agers peeking in; and in 1944, after moving to California and buying a home behind a ten-foot fence on Lake Toluca, he discovered that the only way to escape the telephone and other intrusions was to board his paddle boat with a few friends, a card table and a case of beer, and stay afloat all afternoon. But he has tried, insofar as it has been possible, to be like everyone else, Nancy says. He wept on her wedding day, he is very sentimental and sensitive. . . .

"What the hell are you doing up there, Dwight?"

Silence from the control booth.

"Got a party or something going on up there, *Dwight?*"

Sinatra stood on the stage, arms folded, glaring up across the cameras toward Hemion. Sinatra had sung *Nancy* with probably all he had in his voice on this day. The next few numbers contained raspy notes, and twice his voice completely cracked. But now Hemion was in the control booth out of communication; then he was down in the studio walking over to where Sinatra stood. A few minutes later they both left the studio and were on the way up to the control booth. The tape was replayed for Sinatra. He watched only about five minutes of it before he started to shake his head. Then he said to Hemion: "Forget it, just forget it. You're wasting your time. What you got there," Sinatra said, nodding to the singing image of himself on the television screen, "is a man with a cold." Then he left the control booth, ordering that the whole day's performance be scrubbed and future taping postponed until he had recovered.

Soon the word spread like an emotional epidemic down through Sinatra's staff, then fanned out through Hollywood, then was heard across the nation in Jilly's saloon, and also on the other side of the Hudson River in the homes of Frank Sinatra's parents and his other relatives and friends in New Jersey.

When Frank Sinatra spoke with his father on the telephone and said he was feeling awful, the elder Sinatra reported that *he* was also feeling awful: that his left arm and fist were so stiff with a circulatory condition he could barely use them, adding that the ailment might be the result of having thrown too many left hooks during his days as a bantamweight almost fifty years ago.

Martin Sinatra, a ruddy and tattooed little blue-eyed Sicilian born in Catania, boxed under the name of "Marty O'Brien." In those days, in those places, with the Irish running the lower reaches of city life, it was not uncommon for Italians to wind up with such names. Most of the Italians and Sicilians who migrated to America just prior to the 1900's were poor and uneducated, were excluded from the building-trades unions dominated by the Irish, and were somewhat intimidated by the Irish police, Irish priests, Irish politicians.

One notable exception was Frank Sinatra's mother, Dolly, a large and very ambitious woman who was brought to this country at two months of age by her mother and father, a lithographer from Genoa. In later years Dolly Sinatra, possessing a round red face and blue eyes, was often mistaken for being Irish, and surprised many at the speed with which she swung her heavy handbag at anyone uttering "Wop."

By playing skillful politics with North Jersey's Democratic machine, Dolly Sinatra was to become, in her heyday, a kind of Catherine de Medici of Hoboken's third ward. She could always be counted upon to deliver six hundred votes at election time from her Italian neighborhood, and this was her base of power. When she told one of the politicians that she wanted her husband to be appointed to the Hoboken Fire Department, and was told, "But, Dolly, we don't have an opening," she snapped, "*Make* an opening."

They did. Years later she requested that her husband be made a captain, and one day she got a call from one of the political bosses that began, "Dolly, congratulations!"

"For what?"

"*Captain* Sinatra."

"Oh, you finally made him one—thank you very much."

Then she called the Hoboken Fire Department.

"Let me speak to *Captain* Sinatra," she said. The fireman called Martin Sinatra to the phone, saying, "Marty, I think your wife has gone nuts." When he got on the line, Dolly greeted him:

"Congratulations, *Captain* Sinatra!"

Dolly's only child, christened Francis Albert Sinatra, was born and nearly died on December 12, 1915. It was a difficult birth, and during his first moment on earth he received marks he will carry till death—the scars on the left side of his neck being the result of a doctor's clumsy forceps, and Sinatra has chosen not to obscure them with surgery.

After he was six months old, he was reared mainly by his grandmother. His mother had a full-time job as a chocolate dipper with a large firm and was so proficient at it that the firm once offered to send her to the Paris office to train others. While some people in Hoboken remember Frank Sinatra as a lonely child, one who spent many hours on the porch gazing into space, Sinatra was never a slum kid, never in jail, always well-dressed. He had so many pants that some people in Hoboken called him "Slacksey O'Brien."

Dolly Sinatra was not the sort of Italian mother who could be appeased merely by a child's obedience and good appetite. She made many demands on her son, was always very strict. She dreamed of his becoming an aviation engineer. When she discovered Bing Crosby pictures hanging on his bedroom walls one evening, and learned that her son wished to become a singer too, she became infuriated and threw a shoe at him. Later, finding she could not talk him out of it—"he takes after me"—she encouraged his singing.

Many Italo-American boys of his generation were then shooting for the same star—they were strong with song, weak with words, not a big novelist among them: no O'Hara, no Bellow, no Cheever, nor Shaw; yet they could communicate *bel canto*. This was more in their tradition, no need for a diploma; they could, with a song, someday see their names in lights . . . *Perry Como* . . . *Frankie Laine* . . . *Tony Bennett* . . . *Vic Damone* . . . but none could see it better than *Frank Sinatra*.

Though he sang through much of the night at the Rustic Cabin, he was up the next day singing without a fee on New York radio to get more attention. Later he got a job singing with Harry James's band, and it was there in August of 1939 that Sinatra had his first recording hit—*All or Nothing at All*. He became very fond of Harry James and the men in the band, but when he received an offer from Tommy Dorsey, who in those days had probably the best band in the country, Sinatra took it; the job paid $125 a week, and Dorsey knew how to feature a vocalist. Yet Sinatra was very depressed at leaving James's band, and the final night with them was so memorable that, twenty years later, Sinatra could recall the details to a friend: ". . . the bus pulled out with the rest of the boys at about half-past midnight. I'd said good-bye to them all, and it was snowing, I remember. There was nobody around and I stood alone with my suitcase in the snow and watched the taillights disappear. Then the tears started and I tried to run after the bus. There was such spirit and enthusiasm in that band, I hated leaving it. . . ."

But he did—as he would leave other warm places, too, in search of something more, never wasting time, trying to do it all in one generation, fighting under his *own* name, defending underdogs, terrorizing top dogs. He threw a punch at a musician who said something anti-Semitic, espoused the Negro cause two decades before it became fashionable. He also threw a tray of glasses at Buddy Rich when he played the drums too loud.

Sinatra gave away $50,000 worth of gold cigarette lighters before he was thirty, was living an immigrant's wildest dream of America. He arrived suddenly on the scene when DiMaggio was silent, when *paisanos* were mournful, were quietly defensive about Hitler in their homeland. Sinatra became, in time, a kind of one-man Anti-Defamation League for Italians in America, the sort of organization that would be unlikely for them because, as the theory goes, they rarely agreed on anything, being extreme individualists: fine as soloists, but not so good in a choir; fine as heroes, but not so good in a parade.

When many Italian names were used in describing gangsters on a television show, *The Untouchables,* Sinatra was loud in his disapproval. Sinatra and many thousands of other Italo-Americans were resentful as well when a small-time hoodlum, Joseph Valachi, was brought by Bobby Kennedy into prominence as a Mafia expert, when indeed, from Valachi's testimony on television, he seemed to know less than most waiters on Mulberry Street. Many Italians in Sinatra's circle also regard Bobby Kennedy as something of an Irish cop, more dignified than those in Dolly's day, but no less intimidating. Together with Peter Lawford, Bobby Kennedy is said to have suddenly gotten "cocky" with Sinatra after John Kennedy's election, forgetting the contribution Sinatra had made in both fund-raising and in influencing many anti-Irish Italian votes. Lawford and Bobby Kennedy are both suspected of having influenced the late President's decision to stay as a house guest with Bing Crosby instead of Sinatra, as originally planned, a social setback Sinatra may never forget. Peter Lawford has since been drummed out of Sinatra's "summit" in Las Vegas.

"Yes, my son is like me," Dolly Sinatra says, proudly. "You cross him, he never forgets." And while she concedes his power, she quickly points out, "He can't make his mother do anything she doesn't want to do," adding, "Even today, he wears the same brand of underwear I used to buy him."

Today Dolly Sinatra is seventy-one years old, a year or two younger than Martin, and all day long people are knocking on the back door of her large home asking her advice, seeking her influence. When she is not seeing people and not cooking in the kitchen, she is looking after her husband, a silent but stubborn man, and telling him to keep his sore left arm resting on the sponge she has placed on the armrest of a soft chair. "Oh, he went to some terrific fires, this guy did," Dolly said to a visitor, nodding with admiration toward her husband in the chair.

Though Dolly Sinatra has eighty-seven godchildren in Hoboken, and still goes to that city during political campaigns, she now lives with her husband in a beautiful sixteen-room house in Fort Lee, New Jersey. This home was a gift from their son on their fiftieth wedding anniversary three years ago. The home is tastefully furnished and is filled with a remarkable juxtaposition of the pious and the worldly—photographs of Pope John and Ava Gardner, of Pope Paul and Dean Martin; several statues of saints and holy water, a chair autographed by Sammy Davis, Jr. and bottles of bourbon. In Mrs. Sinatra's jewelry box is a magnificent strand of pearls she had just received from Ava Gardner, whom she liked tremendously as a daughter-in-law and still keeps in touch with and talks about; and hung on the wall is a letter addressed to Dolly and Martin: "The sands of time have turned to gold, yet love continues to unfold like the petals of a rose, in God's garden of life . . . may God love you thru all eternity. I thank Him, I thank you for the being of one. Your loving son, Francis. . . ."

Mrs. Sinatra talks to her son on the telephone about once a week, and recently he suggested that, when visiting Manhattan, she make use of his apartment on East Seventy-second Street on the East River. This is an expensive neighborhood of New York even though there is a small factory on the block, but this latter fact was seized upon by Dolly Sinatra as a means of getting back at her son for some unflattering descriptions of his childhood in Hoboken.

"What—you want me to stay in *your* apartment, in *that* dump?" she asked. "You think I'm going to spend the night in *that* awful neighborhood?"

Frank Sinatra got the point, and said, "Excuse *me*, Mrs. Fort Lee."

After spending the week in Palm Springs, his cold much better, Frank Sinatra returned to Los Angeles, a lovely city of sun and sex, a Spanish discovery of Mexican misery, a star land of little men and lithe women sliding in and out of convertibles in tense tight pants.

Sinatra returned in time to see the long-awaited CBS documentary with his family. At about nine p.m. he drove to the home of his former wife, Nancy, and had dinner with her and their two daughters. Their son, whom they rarely see these days, was out of town.

Frank, Jr., who is twenty-two, was touring with a band and moving cross country toward a New York engagement at Basin Street East with The Pied Pipers, with whom Frank Sinatra sang when he was with Dorsey's band in the 1940's. Today Frank Sinatra, Jr., whom his father says he named after Franklin D. Roosevelt, lives mostly in hotels, dines each evening in his nightclub dressing room, and sings until two a.m., accepting graciously, because he has no choice, the inevitable comparisons. His voice is smooth and pleasant, and improving with work, and while he is very respectful of his father, he discusses him with objectivity and in an occasional tone of subdued cockiness.

Concurrent with his father's early fame, Frank, Jr. said, was the creation of a "press-release Sinatra" designed to "set him apart from the common man, separate him from the realities: it was suddenly Sinatra, the electric magnate, Sinatra who is supernormal, not super*human*, but super*normal*. And here," Frank, Jr. continued, "is the great fallacy, the great bullshit, for Frank Sinatra *is* normal, *is* the guy whom you'd meet on a street corner. But this other thing, the supernormal guise, has affected Frank Sinatra as much as anybody who watches one of his television shows, or reads a magazine article about him. . . .

"Frank Sinatra's life in the beginning was so normal," he said, "that nobody would have guessed in 1934 that this little Italian kid with the curly hair would become the giant, the monster, the great living legend. . . . He met my mother one summer on the beach. She was Nancy Barbato, daughter of Mike Barbato, a Jersey City plasterer. And she meets the fireman's son, Frank, one summer day on the beach at Long Branch, New Jersey. Both are Italian, both Roman Catholic, both lower-middle-class summer sweethearts—it is like a million bad movies starring Frankie Avalon. . . .

"They have three children. The first child, Nancy, was the most normal of Frank Sinatra's children. Nancy was a cheerleader, went to summer camp, drove a Chevrolet, had the easiest kind of development centered around the home and family. Next is me. My life with the family is very, very normal up until September of 1958 when, in complete contrast to the rearing of both girls, I am put into a college-preparatory school. I am now away from the inner family circle, and my position within has never been remade to this day. . . . The third child, Tina. And to be dead honest, I really couldn't say what her life is like. . . ."

The CBS show, narrated by Walter Cronkite, began at ten p.m. A minute before that, the Sinatra family, having finished dinner, turned their chairs around and faced the camera, united for whatever disaster might follow. Sinatra's men in other parts of town, in other parts of the nation, were doing the same thing. Sinatra's lawyer, Milton A. Rudin, smoking a cigar, was watching with a keen eye, an alert legal mind. Other sets were watched by Brad Dexter, Jim Mahoney, Ed Pucci; Sinatra's makeup man, "Shotgun" Britton; his New York representative, Henri Giné; his haberdasher, Richard Carroll; his insurance broker, John Lillie; his valet, George Jacobs, a handsome Negro who, when entertaining girls in *his* apartment, plays records by Ray Charles.

And like so much of Hollywood's fear, the apprehension about the CBS show all proved to be without foundation. It was a highly flattering hour that did not deeply probe, as rumors suggested it would, into Sinatra's love life, or the Mafia, or other areas of his private province. While the documentary was not authorized, wrote Jack Gould in the next day's New York *Times,* "it could have been."

Immediately after the show, the telephones began to ring throughout the Sinatra system conveying words of joy and relief—and from New York came Jilly's telegram: "WE RULE THE WORLD!"

The next day, standing in the corridor of the NBC building where he was about to resume taping his show, Sinatra was discussing the CBS show with several of his friends, and he said, "Oh, it was a gas."

"Yeah, Frank, a helluva show."

"But I think Jack Gould was right in the *Times* today," Sinatra said. "There should have been more on the *man*, not so much on the music. . . ."

They nodded, nobody mentioning the past hysteria in the Sinatra world when it seemed CBS was zeroing in on the *man*; they just nodded and two of them laughed about Sinatra's apparently having gotten the word "bird" on the show—this being a favorite Sinatra word. He often inquires of his cronies, "How's your bird?"; and when he nearly drowned in Hawaii, he later explained, "Just got a little water on my bird"; and under a large photograph of him holding a whisky bottle, a photo that hangs in the home of an actor friend named Dick Bakalyan, the inscription reads: "Drink, Dickie! It's good for your bird." In the song, *Come Fly With Me,* Sinatra sometimes alters the lyrics—". . . just say the words and we'll take our birds down to Acapulco Bay. . . ."

Ten minutes later Sinatra, following the orchestra, walked into the NBC studio which did not resemble in the slightest the scene here of eight days ago. On this occasion Sinatra was in fine voice, he cracked jokes between numbers, nothing could upset him. Once, while he was singing *How Can I Ignore the Girl Next Door,* standing on the stage next to a tree, a television camera mounted on a vehicle came rolling in too close and plowed against the tree.

"Kee-rist!" yelled one of the technical assistants.

But Sinatra seemed hardly to notice it.

"We've had a slight accident," he said, calmly. Then he began the song all over from the beginning.

When the show was over, Sinatra watched the rerun on the monitor in the control room. He was very pleased, shaking hands with Dwight Hemion and his assistants. Then the whisky bottles were opened in Sinatra's dressing room. Pat Lawford was there, and so were Andy Williams and a dozen others. The telegrams and telephone calls continued to be received from all over the country with praise for the CBS show. There was even a call, Mahoney said, from the CBS producer, Don Hewitt, with whom Sinatra had been so angry a few days before. And Sinatra was *still* angry, feeling that CBS had betrayed him, though the show itself was not objectionable.

"Shall I drop a line to Hewitt?" Mahoney asked.

"Can you send a fist through the mail?" Sinatra asked.

He has everything, he cannot sleep, he gives nice gifts, he is not happy, but he would not trade, even for happiness, what he is. . . .

He is a piece of our past—but only we have aged, he hasn't . . . we are dogged by domesticity, he isn't . . . we have compunctions, he doesn't . . . it is our fault, not his. . . .

He controls the menus of every Italian restaurant in Los Angeles; if you want North Italian cooking, fly to Milan. . . .

Men follow him, imitate him, fight to be near him . . . there is something of the locker room, the barracks about him . . . bird . . . bird. . . .

He believes you must play it big, wide, expansively—the more open you are, the more you take in, your dimensions deepen, you grow, you become more what you are—bigger, richer. . . .

"He is better than anybody else, or at least they think he is, and he has to live up to it." —NANCY SINATRA, JR.

"He is calm on the outside—inwardly a million things are happening to him."
—DICK BAKALYAN

"He has an insatiable desire to live every moment to its fullest because, I guess, he feels that right around the corner is extinction." —BRAD DEXTER

"All I ever got out of any of my marriages was the two years Artie Shaw financed on an analyst's couch." —AVA GARDNER

"We weren't mother and son—we were buddies." —DOLLY SINATRA

"I'm for anything that gets you through the night, be it prayer, tranquilizers or a bottle of Jack Daniel." —FRANK SINATRA

Frank Sinatra was tired of all the talk, the gossip, the theory—tired of reading quotes about himself, of hearing what people were saying about him all over town. It had been a tedious three weeks, he said, and now he just wanted to get away, go to Las Vegas, let off some steam. So he hopped in his jet, soared over the California hills across the Nevada flats, then over miles and miles of desert to The Sands and the Clay-Patterson fight.

On the eve of the fight he stayed up all night and slept through most of the afternoon, though his recorded voice could be heard singing in the lobby of The Sands, in the gambling casino, even in the toilets, being interrupted every few bars however by the paging public address: ". . . Telephone call for Mr. Ron Fish, Mr. Ron Fish . . . *with a ribbon of gold in her hair.* . . . Telephone call for Mr. Herbert Rothstein, Mr. Herbert Rothstein . . . *memories of a time so bright, keep me sleepless through dark endless nights. . . ."*

Standing around in the lobby of The Sands and other hotels up and down the strip on this afternoon before the fight were the usual prefight prophets: the gamblers, the old champs, the little cigar butts from Eighth Avenue, the sportswriters who knock the big fights all year but would never miss one, the novelists who seem always to be identifying with one boxer or another, the local prostitutes assisted by some talent in from Los Angeles, and also a young brunette in a wrinkled black cocktail dress who was at the bell captain's desk crying, "But I want to speak to Mr. Sinatra."

"He's not here," the bell captain said.

"Won't you put me through to his room?"

"There are *no* messages going through, Miss," he said, and then she turned, unsteadily, seeming close to tears, and walked through the lobby into the big noisy casino crowded with men interested only in money.

Shortly before seven p.m., Jack Entratter, a big grey-haired man who operates The Sands, walked into the gambling room to tell some men around the blackjack table that Sinatra was getting dressed. He also said that he'd been unable to get front-row seats for everybody, and so some of the men—including Leo Durocher, who had a date, and Joey Bishop, who was accompanied by his wife—would not be able to fit in Frank Sinatra's row but would have to take seats in the third row. When Entratter walked over to tell this to Joey Bishop, Bishop's face fell. He did not seem angry; he merely looked at Entratter with an empty silence, seeming somewhat stunned.

"Joey, I'm *sorry*," Entratter said when the silence persisted, "but we couldn't get more than six together in the front row."

Bishop still said nothing. But when they all appeared at the fight, Joey Bishop was in the front row, his wife in the third.

The fight, called a holy war between Muslims and Christians, was preceded by the introduction of three balding ex-champions, Rocky Marciano, Joe Louis, Sonny Liston—and then there was *The Star-Spangled Banner* sung by another man from out of the past, Eddie Fisher. It had been more than fourteen years ago, but Sinatra could still remember every detail: Eddie Fisher was then the new king of the baritones, with Billy Eckstine and Guy Mitchell right with him, and Sinatra had been long counted out. One day he remembered walking into a broadcasting studio past dozens of Eddie Fisher fans waiting outside the hall, and when they saw Sinatra they began to jeer, "Frankie, Frankie, I'm *swooning, I'm swooning.*" This was also the time when he was selling only about 30,000 records a year, when he was dreadfully miscast as a funny man on his television show, and when he recorded such disasters as *Mama Will Bark,* with Dagmar.

"I growled and barked on the record," Sinatra said, still horrified by the thought. "The only good it did me was with the dogs."

His voice and his artistic judgment were incredibly bad in 1952, but even more responsible for his decline, say his friends, was his pursuit of Ava Gardner. She was the big movie queen then, one of the most beautiful women in the world. Sinatra's daughter Nancy recalls seeing Ava swimming one day in her father's pool, then climbing out of the water with that fabulous body, walking slowly to the fire, leaning over it for a few moments, and then it suddenly seemed that her long dark hair was all dry, miraculously and effortlessly back in place.

With most women Sinatra dates, his friends say, he never knows whether they want him for what he can do for them now—or will do for them later. With Ava Gardner, it was different. He could do nothing for her later. She was on top. If Sinatra learned anything from his experience with her, he possibly learned that when a proud man is down a woman cannot help. Particularly a woman on top.

Nevertheless, despite a tired voice, some deep emotion seeped into his singing during this time. One particular song that is well remembered even now is *I'm A Fool to Want You,* and a friend who was in the studio when Sinatra recorded it recalled: "Frank was really worked up that night. He did the song in one take, then turned around and walked out of the studio and that was that. . . . "

Sinatra's manager at that time, a former song plugger named Hank Sanicola, said, "Ava loved Frank, but not the way he loved her. He needs a great deal of love. He wants it twenty-four hours a day, he must have people around—Frank is that kind of guy." Ava Gardner, Sanicola said, "was very insecure. She feared she could not really hold a man . . . twice he went chasing her to Africa, wasting his own career. . . . "

"Ava didn't want Frank's men hanging around all the time," another friend said, "and this got him mad. With Nancy he used to be able to bring the whole band home with him, and Nancy, the good Italian wife, would never complain—she'd just make everybody a plate of spaghetti."

In 1953, after almost two years of marriage, Sinatra and Ava Gardner were divorced. Sinatra's mother reportedly arranged a reconciliation, but if Ava was willing, Frank Sinatra was not. He was seen with other women. The balance had shifted. Somewhere during this period Sinatra seemed to change from the kid singer, the boy actor in the sailor suit, to a man. Even before he had won the Oscar in 1953 for his role in *From Here to Eternity,* some flashes of his old talent were coming through—in his recording of *The Birth of the Blues,* in his Riviera-nightclub appearance that jazz critics enthusiastically praised; and there was also a trend now toward L.P.'s and away from the quick three-minute deal, and Sinatra's concert style would have capitalized on this with or without an Oscar.

In 1954, totally committed to his talent once more, Frank Sinatra was selected Metronome's "Singer of the Year," and later he won the U.P.I. disc-jockey poll, unseating Eddie Fisher— who now, in Las Vegas, having sung *The Star-Spangled Banner,* climbed out of the ring, and the fight began.

Floyd Patterson chased Clay around the ring in the first round, but was unable to reach him, and from then on he was Clay's toy, the bout ending in a technical knockout in the twelfth round. A half hour later, nearly everybody had forgotten about the fight and was back at the gambling tables or lining up to buy tickets for the Dean Martin-Sinatra-Bishop nightclub routine on the stage of The Sands. This routine, which includes Sammy Davis, Jr. when he is in town, consists of a few songs and much cutting up, all of it very informal, very special, and rather ethnic—Martin, a drink in hand, asking Bishop: "Did you ever see a Jew jitsu?"; and Bishop, playing a Jewish waiter, warning the two Italians to watch out "because I got my own group—the *Matzia*."

Then after the last show at The Sands, the Sinatra crowd, which now numbered about twenty—and included Jilly, who had flown in from New York; Jimmy Cannon, Sinatra's favorite sports columist; Harold Gibbons, a Teamster official expected to take over if Hoffa goes to jail—all got into a line of cars and headed for another club. It was three o'clock. The night was young.

They stopped at The Sahara, taking a long table near the back, and listened to a baldheaded little comedian named Don Rickles, who is probably more caustic than any comic in the country. His humor is so rude, in *such* bad taste, that it offends no one—it is *too* offensive to be offensive. Spotting Eddie Fisher among the audience, Rickles proceeded to ridicule him as a lover, saying it was no wonder that he could not handle Elizabeth Taylor; and when two businessmen in the audience acknowledged that they were Egyptians, Rickles cut into them for their country's policy toward Israel; and he strongly suggested that the woman seated at one table with her husband was actually a hooker.

When the Sinatra crowd walked in, Don Rickles could not be more delighted. Pointing to Jilly, Rickles yelled: "How's it feel to be Frank's tractor? . . . Yeah, Jilly keeps walking in front of Frank clearing the way." Then, nodding to Durocher, Rickles said, "Stand up, Leo, show Frank how you slide." Then he focused on Sinatra, not failing to mention Mia Farrow, nor that he was wearing a toupee, nor to say that Sinatra was washed up as a singer, and when Sinatra laughed, everybody laughed, and Rickles pointed toward Bishop: "Joey Bishop keeps checking with Frank to see what's funny."

Then, after Rickles told some Jewish jokes, Dean Martin stood up and yelled, "Hey, you're always talking about the Jews, never about the Italians," and Rickles cut him off with, "What do we need the Italians for—all they do is keep the flies off our fish."

Sinatra laughed, they all laughed, and Rickles went on this way for nearly an hour until Sinatra, standing up, said, "All right, com'on, get this thing over with. I gotta go."

"Shaddup and sit down!" Rickles snapped. "I've had to listen to you sing. . . ."

"Who do you think you're talking to?" Sinatra yelled back.

"Dick Haymes," Rickles replied, and Sinatra laughed again, and then Dean Martin, pouring a bottle of whisky over his head, entirely drenching his tuxedo, pounded the table.

"Who would ever believe that staggering would make a star?" Rickles said, but Martin called out, "Hey, I wanna make a speech."

"Shaddup."

"No, Don, I wanna tell ya," Dean Martin persisted, "that I think you're a great performer."

"Well, thank you, Dean," Rickles said, seeming pleased.

"But don't go by me," Martin said, plopping down into his seat, "I'm drunk."

"I'll buy that," Rickles said.

By four a.m. Frank Sinatra led the group out of The Sahara, some of them carrying their glasses of whisky with them, sipping it along the sidewalk and in the cars; then, returning to The Sands, they walked into the gambling casino. It was still packed with people, the roulette wheels spinning, the crapshooters screaming in the far corner.

Frank Sinatra, holding a shot glass of bourbon in his left hand, walked through the crowd. He, unlike some of his friends, was perfectly pressed, his tuxedo tie precisely pointed, his shoes unsmudged. He never seems to lose his dignity, never lets his guard completely down no matter how much he has drunk, nor how long he has been up. He never sways when he walks, like Dean Martin, nor does he ever dance in the aisles or jump up on tables, like Sammy Davis.

A part of Sinatra, no matter where he is, is never there. There is always a part of him, though sometimes a small part, that remains *Il Padrone*. Even now, resting his shot glass on the blackjack table, facing the dealer, Sinatra stood a bit back from the table, not leaning against it. He reached under his tuxedo jacket into his trouser pocket and came up with a thick but *clean* wad of bills. Gently he peeled of a one-hundred-dollar bill and placed it on the green-felt table. The dealer dealt him two cards. Sinatra called for a third card, overbid, lost the hundred.

Without a change of expression, Sinatra put down a second hundred-dollar bill. He lost that. Then he put down a third, and lost that. Then he placed two one-hundred-dollar bills on the table and lost those. Finally, putting his sixth hundred-dollar bill on the table, and losing it, Sinatra moved away from the table, nodding to the man, and announcing, "Good dealer."

The crowd that had gathered around him now opened up to let him through. But a woman stepped in front of him, handing him a piece of paper to autograph. He signed it then *he* said, "Thank you."

In the rear of The Sands' large dining room was a long table reserved for Sinatra. The dining room was fairly empty at this hour, with perhaps two dozen other people in the room, including a table of four unescorted young ladies sitting near Sinatra. On the other side of the room, at another long table, sat seven men shoulder-to-shoulder against the wall, two of them wearing dark glasses, all of them eating quietly, speaking hardly a word, just sitting and eating and missing nothing.

The Sinatra party, after getting settled and having a few more drinks, ordered something to eat. The table was about the same size as the one reserved for Sinatra whenever he is at Jilly's in New York; and the people seated around this table in Las Vegas were many of the same people who are often seen with Sinatra at Jilly's or at a restaurant in California, or in Italy, or in New Jersey, or wherever Sinatra happens to be. When Sinatra sits to dine, his trusted friends are close; and no matter where he is, no matter how elegant the place may be, there is something of the neighborhood showing because Sinatra, no matter how far he has come, is still something of the boy from the neighborhood—only now he can take his neighborhood with him.

In some ways, this quasi-family affair at a reserved table in a public place is the closest thing Sinatra now has to home life. Perhaps, having had a home and left it, this approximation is as close as he cares to come; although this does not seem precisely so because he speaks with such warmth about his family, keeps in close touch with his first wife, and insists that she make no decision without first consulting him. He is always eager to place his furniture or other mementos of himself in her home or his daughter Nancy's, and he also is on amiable terms with Ava Gardner. When he was in Italy making *Von Ryan's Express,* they spent some time together, being pursued wherever they went by the *paparazzi.* It was reported then that the *paparazzi* had made Sinatra a collective offer of $16,000 if he would pose with Ava Gardner; Sinatra was said to have made a counter offer of $32,000 if he could break one *paparazzi* arm and leg.

While Sinatra is often delighted that he can be in his home completely without people, enabling him to read and think without interruption, there are occasions when he finds himself alone at night, and *not* by choice. He may have dialed a half-dozen women, and for one reason or another they are all unavailable. So he will call his valet, George Jacobs.

"I'll be coming home for dinner tonight, George."

"How many will there be?"

"Just myself," Sinatra will say. "I want something light, I'm not very hungry."

George Jacobs is a twice-divorced man of thirty-six who resembles Billy Eckstine. He has traveled all over the world with Sinatra and is devoted to him. Jacobs lives in a comfortable bachelor's apartment off

Sunset Boulevard around the corner from Whiskey à Go Go, and he is known around town for the assortment of frisky California girls he has as friends—a few of whom, he concedes, were possibly drawn to him initially because of his closeness to Frank Sinatra.

When Sinatra arrives, Jacobs will serve him dinner in the dining room. Then Sinatra will tell Jacobs that he is free to go home. If Sinatra, on such evenings, should ask Jacobs to stay longer, or to play a few hands of poker, he would be happy to do so. But Sinatra never does.

This was his second night in Las Vegas, and Frank Sinatra sat with friends in The Sands' dining room until nearly eight a.m. He slept through much of the day, then flew back to Los Angeles, and on the following morning he was driving his little golf cart through the Paramount Pictures movie lot. He was scheduled to complete two final scenes with the sultry blonde actress, Virna Lisi, in the film, *Assault on a Queen*. As he maneuvered the little vehicle up the road between the big studio buildings, he spotted Steve Rossi who, with his comedy partner Marty Allen, was making a film in an adjoining studio with Nancy Sinatra.

"Hey, Dag," he yelled to Rossi, "stop kissing Nancy."

"It's part of the film, Frank," Rossi said, turning as he walked.

"In the garage?"

"It's my Dago blood, Frank."

"Well, cool it," Sinatra said, winking, then cutting his golf cart around a corner and parking it outside a big drab building within which the scenes for *Assault* would be filmed.

"Where's the fat director?" Sinatra called out, striding into the studio that was crowded with dozens of technical assistants and actors all gathered around cameras. The director, Jack Donohue, a large man who has worked with Sinatra through twenty-two years on one production or other, has had headaches with this film. The script had been chopped, the actors seemed restless, and Sinatra had become bored. But now there were only two scenes left—a short one to be filmed in the pool, and a longer and passionate one featuring Sinatra and Virna Lisi to be shot on a simulated beach.

The pool scene, which dramatizes a situation where Sinatra and his hijackers fail in their attempt to sack the *Queen Mary*, went quickly and well. After Sinatra had been kept in the water shoulder-high for a few minutes, he said, "Let's move it, fellows—it's cold in this water, and I've just gotten over one cold."

So the camera crews moved in closer, Virna Lisi splashed next to Sinatra in the water, and Jack Donohue yelled to his assistants operating the fans, "Get the waves going," and another man gave the command, *"Agitate!"* and Sinatra broke out in song. "Agitate in rhythm," then quieted down just before the cameras started to roll.

Frank Sinatra was on the beach in the next situation, supposedly gazing up at the stars, and Virna Lisi was to approach him, toss one of her shoes near him to announce her presence, then sit near him and prepare for a passionate session. Just before beginning, Miss Lisi made a practice toss of her shoe toward the prone figure of Sinatra sprawled on the beach. As she tossed her shoe, Sinatra called out, "Hit me in my bird and I'm going home."

Virna Lisi, who understands little English and certainly none of Sinatra's special vocabulary, looked confused, but everybody behind the camera laughed. She threw the shoe toward him. It twirled in the air, landed on his stomach.

"Well, that's about three inches too high," he announced. She again was puzzled by the laughter behind the camera.

Then Jack Donohue had them rehearse their lines, and Sinatra, still very charged from the Las Vegas trip, and anxious to get the cameras rolling, said, "Let's try one." Donohue, not certain that Sinatra and Lisi knew their lines well enough, nevertheless said okay, and an assistant with a clapboard called, "419, Take 1," and Virna Lisi approached with the shoe, tossed it at Frank lying on the beach. It fell short of his thigh, and Sinatra's right eye raised almost imperceptibly, but the crew got the message, smiled.

"What do the stars tell you tonight?" Miss Lisi said, delivering her first line, and sitting next to Sinatra on the beach.

"The stars tell me tonight I'm an idiot," Sinatra said, "a gold-plated idiot to get mixed up in this thing. . . . "

"Cut," Donohue said. There were some microphone shadows on the sand, and Virna Lisi was not sitting in the proper place near Sinatra.

"419, Take 2," the clapboard man called.

Miss Lisi again approached, threw the shoe at him, this time falling short—Sinatra exhaling only slightly—and she said, "What do the stars tell you tonight?"

"The stars tell me I'm an idiot, a gold-plated idiot to get mixed up in this thing. . . . " Then, according to the script, Sinatra was to continue, " . . . do you know what we're getting into? The minute we step on the deck of the *Queen Mary,* we've just tattooed ourselves," but Sinatra, who often improvises on lines, recited them: " . . . do you know what we're getting into? The minute we step on the deck of that mother's-ass ship. . . . "

"*No,* no," Donohue interrupted, shaking his head, "I don't think that's right."

The cameras stopped, some people laughed, and Sinatra looked up from his position in the sand as if he had been unfairly interrupted.

"I don't see why that can't work . . . " he began, but Richard Conte, standing behind the camera, yelled, "It won't play in London."

Donohue pushed his hand through his thinning grey hair and said, but not really in anger, "You know, that scene was pretty good until somebody blew the line. . . . "

"Yeah," agreed the cameraman, Billy Daniels, his head popping out from around the camera, "it was a pretty good piece. . . ."

"Watch your language," Sinatra cut in. Then Sinatra, who has a genius for figuring out ways of not reshooting scenes, suggested a way in which the film could be used and the "mother" line could be rerecorded later. This met with approval. Then the cameras were rolling again, Virna Lisi was leaning toward Sinatra in the sand, and then he pulled her down close to him. The camera now moved in for a close-up of their faces, ticking away for a few long seconds, but Sinatra and Lisi did not stop kissing, they just lay together in the sand wrapped in one another's arms, and then Virna Lisi's left leg just slightly began to rise a bit, and everybody in the studio now watched in silence, not saying anything until Donohue finally called out:

"If you ever get through, let me know. I'm running out of film."

Then Miss Lisi got up, straightened out her white dress, brushed back her blonde hair and touched her lipstick, which was smeared. Sinatra got up, a little smile on his lips, and headed for his dressing room.

Passing an older man who stood near a camera, Sinatra asked, "How's your Bell & Howell?"

The older man smiled.

"It's fine, Frank."

"Good."

In his dressing room Sinatra was met by an automobile designer who had the plans for Sinatra's new custom-built model to replace the $25,000 Ghia he has been driving for the last few years. He also was awaited by his secretary, Tom Conroy, who had a bag full of fan mail, including a letter from New York's Mayor John Lindsay; and by Bill Miller, Sinatra's pianist, who would rehearse some of the songs that would be recorded later in the evening for Sinatra's newest album, *Moonlight Sinatra*.

While Sinatra does not mind hamming it up a bit on a movie set, he is extremely serious about his recording sessions; as he explained to a British writer, Robin Douglas-Home: "Once you're on that record singing, it's you and you alone. If it's bad and gets you criticized, it's you who's to blame—no one else. If it's good, it's also you. With a film it's never like that; there are producers and scriptwriters, and hundreds of men in offices and the thing is taken right out of your hands. With a record, you're *it*. . . ."

> But now the days are short
> I'm in the autumn of the year
> And now I think of my life
> As vintage wine
> From fine old kegs. . . .

It no longer matters what song he is singing, or who wrote the words—they are all *his* words, *his* sentiments, they are chapters from the lyrical novel of his life.

Life is a beautiful thing
As long as I hold the string. . . .

When Frank Sinatra drives to the studio, he seems to dance out of the car across the sidewalk into the front door; then, snapping his fingers, he is standing in front of the orchestra in an intimate, airtight room, and soon he is dominating every man, every instrument, every sound wave. Some of the musicians have accompanied him for twenty-five years, have gotten old hearing him sing *You Make Me Feel So Young.*

When his voice is on, as it was tonight, Sinatra is in ecstasy, the room becomes electric, there is an excitement that spreads through the orchestra and is felt in the control booth where a dozen men, Sinatra's friends, wave at him from behind the glass. One of the men is the Dodgers' pitcher, Don Drysdale ("Hey, Big D," Sinatra calls out, "*hey,* baby!"); another is the professional golfer, Bo Wininger; there are also numbers of pretty women standing in the booth behind the engineers, women who smile at Sinatra and softly move their bodies to the mellow mood of his music:

Life is a beautiful thing
As long as I hold the string. . . .
"Will this be moon love
Nothing but moon love
Will you be gone when the dawn
Comes stealing through. . . ."

After he is finished, the record is played back on tape, and Nancy Sinatra, who has just walked in, joins her father near the front of the orchestra to hear the playback. They listen silently, all eyes on them, the king, the princess; and when the music ends there is applause from the control booth, Nancy smiles, and her father snaps his fingers and says, kicking a foot, "*Ooba-deeba-boobe-do!*"

Then Sinatra calls to one of his men. "Hey, Sarge, think I can have a half-a-cup of coffee?"

Sarge Weiss, who had been listening to the music, slowly gets up.

"Didn't mean to wake ya, Sarge," Sinatra says, smiling.

Then Weiss brings the coffee, and Sinatra looks at it, smells it, then announces, "I thought he'd be nice to me, but it's *really* coffee. . . ."

There are more smiles, and then the orchestra prepares for the next number. And one hour later, it is over.

The musicians put their instruments into their cases, grab their coats, and begin to file out, saying good-night to Sinatra. He knows them all by name, knows much about them personally, from their bachelor days, through their divorces, through their ups and downs, as they know him. When a French-horn player, a short Italian named Vincent DeRosa, who has played with Sinatra since The Lucky Strike "Hit Parade" days on radio, strolled by, Sinatra reached out to hold him for a second.

"Vicenzo," Sinatra said, "how's your little girl?"

"She's fine, Frank."

"Oh, she's not a *little* girl anymore," Sinatra corrected himself, "she's a big girl now."

"Yes, she goes to college now. U.S.C."

"That's great."

"She's also got a little talent, I think, Frank, as a singer."

Sinatra was silent for a moment, then said, "Yes, but it's very good for her to get her education first, Vicenzo."

Vincent DeRosa nodded.

"Yes, Frank," he said, and then he said, "Well, good-night, Frank."

"Good-night, Vicenzo."

After the musicians had all gone, Sinatra left the recording room and joined his friends in the corridor. He was going to go out and do some drinking with Drysdale, Wininger, and a few other friends, but first he walked to the other end of the corridor to say good-night to Nancy, who was getting her coat and was planning to drive home in her own car.

After Sinatra had kissed her on the cheek, he hurried to join his friends at the door. But before Nancy could leave the studio, one of Sinatra's men, Al Silvani, a former prizefight manager, joined her.

"Are you ready to leave yet, Nancy?"

"Oh, thanks, Al," she said, "but I'll be all right."

"Pope's orders," Silvani said, holding his hands up, palms out.

Only after Nancy had pointed to two of her friends who would escort her home, and only after Silvani recognized them as friends, would he leave.

The rest of the month was bright and balmy. The record session had gone magnificently, the film was finished, the television shows were out of the way, and now Sinatra was in his Ghia driving out to his office to begin coordinating his latest projects. He had an engagement at The Sands, a new spy film called *The Naked Runner* to be shot in England, and a couple more albums to do in the immediate months ahead. And within a week he would be fifty years old. . . .

> *Life is a beautiful thing*
> *As long as I hold the string*
> *I'd be a silly so-and-so*
> *If I should ever let go.* . . .

Frank Sinatra stopped his car. The light was red. Pedestrians passed quickly across his windshield but, as usual, one did not. It was a girl in her twenties. She remained at the curb staring at him. Through the corner of his left eye he could see her, and he knew, because it happens almost every day, that she was thinking, *It looks like him, but is it?*

Just before the light turned green, Sinatra turned toward her, looked directly into her eyes waiting for the reaction he knew would come. It came and he smiled. She smiled and he was gone.

[April, 1966]

Ava: Life in the Afternoon

by Rex Reed

She stands there, without benefit of a filter lens, against a room melting under the heat of lemony sofas and lavender walls and cream-and-peppermint-striped movie-star chairs, lost in the middle of that gilt-edge birthday-cake hotel of cupids and cupolas called The Regency. There is no script. No Minnelli to adjust the CinemaScope lens. Ice-blue rain beats against the windows and peppers Park Avenue below as Ava Gardner stalks her pink malted-milk cage like an elegant cheetah. She wears a baby-blue cashmere turtleneck sweater pushed up to her Ava elbows and a little plaid mini-skirt and enormous black horn-rimmed glasses and she is gloriously, divinely barefoot.

Elbowing his way through the mob of autograph hunters and thrill seekers clustered in the lobby, all the way up in the gilt-encrusted elevator, the press agent Twentieth Century-Fox has sent along murmurs, "She doesn't see *anybody,* you know," and "You're very lucky, you're the only one she asked for." Remembering, perhaps, the last time she had come to New York from her hideout in Spain to ballyhoo *The Night of the Iguana* and got so mad at the press she chucked the party and ended up at Birdland. And nervously, shifting feet under my Brooks Brothers polo coat, I remember too all the photographers at whom she allegedly threw champagne glasses (there is even a rumor that she shoved one Fourth Estater off a balcony!), and—who could forget, Charlie?—the holocaust she caused the time Joe Hyams showed up with a tape recorder hidden in his sleeve.

Now, inside the cheetah cage without a whip and trembling like a nervous bird, the press agent says something in Spanish to the Spanish maid. "Hell, I've been there ten years and I still can't speak the goddam language," says Ava, dismissing him with a wave of the long porcelain Ava arms. "*Out!* I don't need press agents." The eyebrows angle under the glasses into two dazzling, sequined question marks. "Can I trust him?" she asks, grinning that smashing Ava grin, and pointing at me. The press agent nods, on his way to the door: "Is there anything else we can do for you while you're in town?"

"Just get me *out* of town, baby. Just get me *outta* here."

The press agent leaves softly, walking across the carpet as if treading on rose glass with tap shoes. The Spanish maid (Ava insists she is royalty, "She follows me around because she digs me") closes the door and shuffles off into another room.

"You *do* drink—right, baby? The last bugger who came to see me had the gout and wouldn't touch a drop." She roars a cheetah roar that sounds suspiciously like Geraldine Page playing Alexandra Del Lago and mixes drinks from her portable bar: Scotch and soda for me, and for herself a champagne glass full of cognac with another champagne glass full of Dom Perignon, which she drinks successively, refills and sips slowly like syrup through a straw. The Ava legs dangle limply from the arm of a lavender chair while the Ava neck, pale and tall as a milkwood vase, rises above the room like a Southern landowner inspecting a cotton field. At forty-four, she is still one of the most beautiful women in the world.

"Don't look at me. I was up until four a.m. at that goddam premiere of *The Bible*. Premieres! I will personally kill that John Huston if he ever drags me into another mess like that. There must have been ten thousand people clawing at me. I get claustrophobia in crowds and I couldn't breathe. Christ, they started off by shoving a TV camera at me and yelling, 'Talk, Ava!' At intermission I got lost and couldn't find my goddam seat after the lights went out and I kept telling those little girls with the bubble hairdos and the flashlights, 'I'm with John Huston,' and they kept saying, 'We don't know no Mr. Huston, is he from Fox?' There I was fumbling around the aisles in the dark and when I finally found my seat somebody was sitting in it and there was a big scene getting this guy to give me my seat back. Let me tell you, baby, Metro used to throw much better circuses than that. On top of it all, I lost my goddam mantilla in the limousine. Hell, it was no souvenir, that mantilla. I'll never find another one like it. Then Johnny Huston takes me to this party where we had to stand around and smile at Artie Shaw, who I was married to, baby, for Chrissake, and his wife Evelyn Keyes, who Johnny Huston was once married to, for Chrissake. And after it's all over, what have you got? The biggest headache in town. Nobody cares who the hell was there. Do you think for one minute the fact that Ava Gardner showed up at that circus will sell that picture? Christ, did you *see* it? I went through all that hell just so this morning Bosley Crowther could write I looked like I was posing for a monument. All the way through it I kept punching Johnny on the arm and saying, 'Christ, how could you let me do it?' Anyway, nobody cares what I wore or what I said. All they want to know anyway is was she drunk and did she stand up straight. This is the last circus. I am not a bitch! I am not temperamental! I am scared, baby. *Scared.* Can you possibly understand what it's like to feel scared?"

She rolls her sleeves higher than the elbows and pours two more champagne glasses full. There is nothing about the way she looks, up close, to suggest the life she has led: press conferences accompanied by dim lights and an orchestra; bullfighters writing poems about her in the press; rubbing Vaseline between her bosoms to emphasize the cleavage; roaming restlessly around Europe like a woman without a country, a Pandora with her suitcases full of cognac and Hershey bars ("for quick energy"). None of the ravaged, ruinous grape-colored lines to suggest the affairs or the brawls that bring the police in the middle of the night or the dancing on tabletops in Madrid cellars till dawn.

The doorbell rings and a pimply-faced boy with a Beatle hairdo delivers one dozen Nathan's hot dogs, rushed from Coney Island in a limousine. "Eat," says Ava, sitting crosslegged on the floor, biting into a raw onion.

"You're looking at me again!" she says shyly, pulling short girlish wisps of hair behind the lobes of her Ava ears. I mention the fact that she looks like a Vassar co-ed in her mini-skirt. "Vassar?" she asks suspiciously. "Aren't they the ones who get in all the trouble?"

"That's Radcliffe."

She roars. Alexandra Del Lago again. "I took one look at myself in *The Bible* and went out this morning and got all my hair cut off. This is the way I used to wear it at M-G-M. It takes years off. What's *that?*" Eyes narrow, axing her guest in half, burning holes in my notebook. "Don't tell me you're one of those people who always go around scribbling everything on little pieces of paper. Get rid of that. Don't take notes. Don't ask questions either because I probably won't answer any of them anyway. Just let Mama do all the talking. Mama knows best. You want to ask something, I can tell. Ask."

I ask if she hates all of her films as much as *The Bible*.

"Christ, what did I ever do worth talking about? Every time I tried to act, they stepped on me. That's why it's such a goddam shame, I've been a movie star for twenty-five years and I've got nothing, *nothing* to show for it. All I've got is three lousy ex-husbands, which reminds me, I've got to call Artie and ask him what his birthday is. I can't remember my own family's birthdays. Only reason I know my own is because I was born the same day as Christ. Well, almost. Christmas Eve, 1922. That's Capricorn, which means a lifetime of *hell*, baby. Anyway, I need Artie's birthday because I'm trying to get a new passport. I tramp around Europe, but I'm not giving up my citizenship, baby, for *any*body. Did you ever try living in Europe and renewing your passport? They treat you like you're a goddam Communist or something. Hell that's why I'm getting the hell out of Spain, because I hate Franco and I hate Communists. So now they want a list of all my divorces so I told them hell, call The New York *Times*—they know more about me than I do!"

But hadn't all those years at M-G-M been any fun at all? "Christ, after seventeen years of slavery, you can ask that question? I hated it, honey. I mean I'm not exactly stupid or without feeling, and they tried to sell me like a prize hog. They also tried to make me into something I was not then and never could be. They used to write in my studio bios that I was the daughter of a cotton farmer from Chapel Hill. Hell, baby, I was born on a tenant farm in Grabtown. How's that grab ya? Grabtown, North Carolina. And it looks exactly the way it sounds. I should have stayed there. The ones who never left home don't have a pot to pee in but they're happy. Me, look at me. What did it bring me?" She finishes off another round of cognac and pours a fresh one. "The only time I'm happy is when I'm doing absolutely nothing. When I work I vomit all the time. I know nothing about acting so I have one rule—trust the director and give him heart and soul. And nothing else." (Another cheetah roar.) "I get a lot of money so I can afford to loaf a lot. I don't trust many people, so I only work with Huston now. I used to trust Joe Mankiewicz, but one day on the set of *The Barefoot Contessa* he did the unforgivable thing. He insulted me. He said, 'You're the sittin'est goddam actress,' and I never liked him after that. What I really want to do is get married again. Go ahead and laugh, everybody laughs, but how great it must be to tromp around barefoot and cook for some great goddam son of a bitch who loves you the rest of your life. I've never had a good man."

What about Mickey Rooney? (A glorious shriek.) "Love comes to Andy Hardy."

Sinatra? "No comment," she says to her glass.

A slow count to ten, while she sips her drink. Then, "And Mia Farrow?" The Ava eyes brighten to a soft clubhouse green. The answer comes like so many cats lapping so many saucers of cream. Unprintable.

Like a phonograph dropping a new LP, she changes the subject. "I only want to do the things that don't make me suffer. My friends are more important to me than anything. I know all kinds of people—bums, hangers-on, intellectuals, a few phonies. I'm going to see a college boy at

Princeton tomorrow and we're going to a ball game. Writers. I love writers. Henry Miller sends me books to improve my mind. Hell, did you read *Plexus?* I couldn't get through it. I'm not an intellectual, although when I was married to Artie Shaw I took a lot of courses at U.C.L.A. and got A's and B's in psychology and literature. I have a mind, but I never got a chance to use it doing every goddam lousy part in every goddam lousy picture Metro turned out. I *feel* a lot, though. God, I'm sorry I wasted those twenty-five years. My sister Dee Dee can't understand why after all these years I can't bear to face a camera. But I never brought anything to this business and I have no respect for acting. Maybe if I had learned something it would be different. But I never did anything to be proud of. Out of all those movies, what can I claim to have done?"

"*Mogambo, The Hucksters*—"

"Hell, baby, after twenty-five years in this business, if all you've got to show for it is *Mogambo* and *The Hucksters* you might as well give up. Name me one actress who survived all that crap at M-G-M. Maybe Lana Turner. Certainly Liz Taylor. But they all hate acting as much as I do. All except for Elizabeth. She used to come up to me on the set and say, 'If only I could learn to be good,' and by God, she made it. I haven't seen *Virginia Woolf*—hell, I *never* go to movies—but I hear she is good. I never cared much about myself. I didn't have the emotional makeup for acting and I hate exhibitionists anyway. And who the hell was there to help me or teach me acting was anything else? I really tried in *Show Boat* but that was M-G-M crap. Typical of what they did to me there. I wanted to sing those songs—hell, I've still got a Southern accent—and I really thought Julie should sound a little like a Negro since she's supposed to have Negro blood. Christ, those songs like *Bill* shouldn't sound like an opera. So, what did they say? 'Ava, baby, you can't sing, you'll hit the wrong keys, you're up against real pros in this film, so don't make a fool of yourself.' *Pros!* Howard Keel? And Kathryn Grayson, who had the biggest boobs in Hollywood? I mean I like Graysie, she's a sweet girl, but with her they didn't even need 3-D! Lena Horne told me to go to Phil Moore, who was her pianist and had coached Dorothy Dandridge, and he'd teach me. I made a damn good track of the songs and they said, 'Ava, are you outta your head?' Then they got Eileen Wilson, this gal who used to do a lot of my singing on screen, and *she* recorded a track with the same background arrangement taken off *my* track. They substituted her voice for mine, and now in the movie my Southern twang stops talking and her soprano starts singing—hell what a mess. They wasted God knows how many thousands of dollars and ended up with crap. I still get royalties on the goddam records I did."

The doorbell rings and in bounces a little man named Larry. Larry has silver hair, silver eyebrows and smiles a lot. He works for a New York camera shop. "Larry used to be married to my sister Bea. If you think I'm something you ought to see Bea. When I was eighteen I came to New York to visit them and Larry took that picture of me that started this whole megilah. He's a sonuvabitch, but I love him."

"Ava, I sure loved you last night in *The Bible*. You were really terrific, darlin'."

"Crap!" Ava pours another cognac. "I don't want to hear another word about that goddam *Bible*. I didn't believe *it* and I didn't believe that Sarah bit I played for a minute. How could anybody stay married for a hundred years to *Abraham*, who was one of the biggest bastards who ever lived?"

"Oh, darlin', she was a wonderful woman, that Sarah."

"She was a jerk!"

"Oh, darlin', ya shouldn' talk like that. God will hear ya. Don'tcha believe in God?" Larry joins us on the floor and bites into a hot dog, spilling mustard on his tie.

"Hell, no." The Ava eyes flash.

"I pray to him every night, darlin'. Sometimes he answers, too."

"He never answered me, baby. He was never around when I needed him. He did nothing but screw up my whole life since the day I was born. Don't tell *me* about *God!* I know all about that bugger!"

The doorbell again. This time a cloak-and-dagger type comes in; he's wearing an ironed raincoat, has seventeen pounds of hair and looks like he has been living on plastic vegetables. He says he is a student at New York University Law School. He also says he is twenty-six years old. *"What?"* Ava takes off her glasses for a closer look. "Your father told me you were twenty-seven. Somebody's lying!" The Ava eyes narrow and the palms of her hands are wet.

"Let's get some air, fellas." Ava leaps into the bedroom and comes out wearing a Navy pea jacket with a Woolworth scarf around her head. Vassar again.

"I thought you were gonna cook tonight, darlin'," says Larry, throwing his fist into a coat sleeve.

"I want spaghetti. Let's go to the Supreme Macaroni Company. They let me in the back door there and nobody ever recognizes *any*body there. Spaghetti, baby. I'm starved."

Ava slams the door shut, leaving all the lights on. "Fox is paying, baby." We all link arms and follow the leader. Ava skips ahead of us like Dorothy on her way to Oz. *Lions and tigers and bears, oh my!* Moving like a tiger through Regency halls, melting with hot pink, like the inside of a womb.

"Are those creeps still downstairs?" she asks. "Follow me."

She knows all the exits. We go down on the service elevator. About twenty autograph hunters crowd the lobby. Celia, queen of the autograph bums, who leaves her post on the door at Sardi's only on special occasions, has deserted her station for this. *Ava's in town this week.* She sits behind a potted palm wearing a purple coat and green beret, arms full of self-addressed postcards.

Cool.

Ava gags, pushes the horn-rims flat against her nose, and pulls us through the lobby. Nobody recognizes her. "Drink time, baby!" she whispers, shoving me toward a side stairway that leads down to The Regency Bar.

"Do you know who *that* was?" asks an Iris Adrian type with a mink-dyed fox on her arm as Ava heads for the bar. We check coats and umbrellas and suddenly we hear that sound-track voice, hitting E-flat.

"You *sonuvabitch!* I could buy and sell you. How *dare* you insult my friends? Get me the manager!"

Larry is at her side. Two waiters are shushing Ava and leading us all to a corner booth. Hidden. Darker than the Polo Lounge. Hide the star. This is New York, not Beverly Hills.

"It's that turtleneck sweater you're wearing," whispers Larry to me as the waiter seats me with my back to the room.

"They don't like me here, the bastards. I never stay in this hotel, but Fox is paying, so what the hell? I wouldn't come otherwise. They don't even have a jukebox, for Chrissake." Ava flashed a smile in Metrocolor and orders a large ice-tea glass filled with straight tequila. "No salt on the side. Don't need it."

"Sorry about the sweater—" I begin.

"You're beautiful. Gr-r-r!" She laughs her Ava laugh and the head rolls back and the little blue vein bulges on her neck like a delicate pencil mark.

Two tequilas later ("I *said* no salt!") she is nodding grandly, surveying the bar like the Dowager Empress in the Recognition Scene. Talk buzzes around her like hummingbird wings and she hears nothing. Larry is telling about the time he got arrested in Madrid and Ava had to get him out of jail and the student is telling me about N.Y.U. Law School and Ava is telling *him* she doesn't believe he's only twenty-six years old and can he prove it, and suddenly he looks at his watch and says Sandy Koufax is playing in St. Louis.

"You're kidding!" Ava's eyes light up like cherries on a cake. "Let's go! Goddamit we're going to St. Louis!"

"Ava, darlin', I gotta go to work tomorrow." Larry takes a heavy sip of his Grasshopper.

"Shut up, you bugger. If I pay for us all to go to St. Louis we go to St. Louis! Can I get a phone brought to this table? Someone call Kennedy airport and find out what time the next plane leaves. I *love* Sandy Koufax! I *love* Jews! God, sometimes I think I'm Jewish myself. A Spanish Jew from North Carolina. *Waiter!*"

The student convinces her that by the time we got to St. Louis they'd be halfway through the seventh inning. Ava's face falls and she goes back to her straight tequila.

"Look at 'em, Larry," she says. "They're such babies. Please don't go to Vietnam." Her face turns ashen. Julie leaving the showboat with William Warfield singing *Ol' Man River* in the fog on the levee. "We gotta do it. . . ."

"What are you talkin' about, darlin'?" Larry shoots a look at the law student who assures Ava he has no intention of going to Vietnam.

". . . didn't ask for this world, the buggers made us do it. . . ." A tiny bubble bath of sweat breaks out on her forehead and she leaps up from the table. "My God, I'm suffocating! Gotta get some air!" She turns over the glass of tequila and three waiters are flying at us like bats, dabbing and patting and making great breathing noises.

Action!

The N.Y.U. student, playing Chance Wayne to her Alexandra Del Lago, is all over the place like a trained nurse. Coats fly out of the checkroom. Bills and quarters roll across the wet tablecloth. Ava is on the other side of the bar and out the door. On cue, the other customers, who have been making elaborate excuses for passing our table on their way to the bathroom, suddenly give great breathy choruses of "Ava" and we are through the side door and out in the rain.

Then as quickly as it started it's over. Ava is in the middle of Park Avenue, the scarf falling around her neck and her hair blowing wildly around the Ava eyes. Lady Brett in the traffic, with a downtown bus as the bull. Three cars stop on a green light and every taxi driver on Park Avenue begins to honk. The autograph hunters leap through the polished doors of The Regency and begin to scream. Inside, still waiting coolly behind the potted palm, is Celia, oblivious to the noise, facing the elevators, firmly clutching her postcards. No need to risk missing Ava because of a minor commotion on the street. Probably Jack E. Leonard or Edie Adams. Catch them next week at Danny's.

Outside, Ava is inside the taxi flanked by the N.Y.U. student and Larry, blowing kisses to the new chum, who will never grow to be an old one. They are already turning the corner into Fifty-seventh Street, fading into the kind of night, the color of tomato juice in the headlights, that only exists in New York when it rains.

"Who was it?" asks a woman walking a poodle.

"Jackie Kennedy," answers a man from his bus window.

[May, 1967]

The Totemization of Sir Winston Churchill

by Malcolm Muggeridge

The arrival of Sir Winston Churchill on the Riviera has become as regular and invariable an occurrence as Mardi Gras and Battle of Flowers. At Nice Airport the photographers turn out yet once more, and M. le Préfet or M. le Sous-Préfet or just M. le Maire waits on the tarmac. It has all happened many times before, and everyone knows what is expected of him. Local reporters from the *Agence France-Presse* and the *Nice-Matin* stand around in the vague expectation that there may be a story. Air-travelers waiting for their planes and spectators on the airport roof are glad enough to have something to look at. They cluster as near as possible to where the great man descends and, when they see him, raise a faint cheer, to which he responds by shakily lifting up his fingers in a V-sign.

The inevitable cigar, jutting out of his mouth, gives an impression of having been put there by someone else, as children stick an old pipe into a snowman. His face is glazed and vacant: it might be immensely old or just born—the eyes faded and watery, the features muzzy, somehow out of focus, like a photograph when the camera has moved. One has a sense, under the surface varnish, of an inward melancholy. It is an illusion to suppose that those who cling tenaciously to life necessarily want to go on

319

living. They often long to die and, like Lear, hate those who would upon the rack of this tough world stretch them out longer. Their survival may be due to some reflex action. By lingering on, they may be expiating an undue rage to live. Bernard Shaw told his biographer, Hesketh Pearson, that each night, when he lay down to sleep, he hoped not to awaken the following morning. Is Sir Winston, perhaps, a like case, except that the chains which keep him earth-bound eat mostly into the flesh, whereas Shaw's lacerated a mind which would not subside?

Sir Winston's prodigious constitution has miraculously carried him through all strains and hazards, and left intact his capacity to eat and drink with enjoyment. The cautions and abstinences which normally accompany old age, and which his doctors prescribe, are not for him. He can still go through the motions of responding to applause. Cheers penetrate his deafness (which he resolutely refuses to alleviate with a hearing aid) when words cannot. The instinct, inculcated through years of practice, to brace himself for public appearances still operates. As he goes to his car, nowadays with two nurses in his entourage, his footsteps are surprisingly steady, his bearing, ostensibly, alert. Old politicians, like old actors, revive in the limelight. The vacancy which afflicts them in private momentarily lifts when, once more, they feel the eyes of an audience upon them. Their old passion for holding the center of the stage guides their uncertain footsteps to where the footlights shine, and summons up a wintry smile when the curtain rises.

Thus, from time to time, Churchill manages to find his way, alone and unaided, into the House of Commons. This is the scene he knows best; this the place where he has spent so many breathless hours of his long life. He returns to it by instinct—to the stale air, the untidy benches, the drone of unmeant and unheeded speeches, the pallid Front Bench faces, the occasional exclamations of approval or dissent, the laughter so easily and so fatuously aroused, all the drab panoply of a mid-twentieth-century Parliament. When his bulky form appears, whoever may be speaking, whatever may be under discussion, the proceedings are, in effect, temporarily suspended. All eyes rest on him, in the galleries as on the floor of the House. With exaggerated obeisance, he makes his bow to Mr. Speaker, and advances upon his old seat below the gangway. Then, after some long-drawn-out byplay with his handkerchief or a throat lozenge, he leans across to ask a neighboring M.P., in a sepulchral whisper, what the business is before the House, and who the Member is (pointing at him) on his feet. It may well be Macmillan or Gaitskell whom he cannot identify. His eyes seldom intimate recognition, and, when they do, it is from an old recollection. With the years, distant memories grow clearer. The present and the recent past are hidden from view under thick clouds of forgetfulness.

Attention remains fixed on him. As he well knows, no speech will be heard, no question receive other than desultory consideration while he is there. Honorable and Right Honorable Members, on both sides of the House, continue to be preoccupied with his strange, eerie presence among them. When he gets up to go, their eyes follow him, as they did when he came in. After he has gone, and they have resumed their business, it takes a little while for them to get back onto their own pedestrian wave-length. The atmospherics created by his incursion only gradually subside. What is it about him which makes him, even in his decrepitude, still tower above the others, and hold them in thrall? Not warmth of character—he is rather horrible. Not past services—in the House of Commons, of all places, it is true that (to use a phrase Shakespeare puts into the mouth of Timon of Athens) men bar their doors before the setting sun. Not famous orations—like all rhetoric, his wear badly. Few today can listen without squirming even to the wartime speeches, which were so stirring at the time, about blood, sweat and tears, and fighting on the beaches.

He has become a kind of totem. His continued existence provides a link with departed glory. Though his sun may have set, still, as long as he is there, some glow lingers about the western sky in which others may participate. He is produced, as totems are, to keep up tribal morale, which otherwise would sag under the weight of unfamiliar and disconcerting circumstances. Britannia no longer rules the waves, but did when Churchill was First Lord of the Admiralty; narrower still and narrower shall our bounds be set, not wider still and wider, as Conservative ladies fervently proclaim when they sing *Land of Hope and Glory;* but he it was who said that he had not become His Majesty King George VI's Principal Secretary of State in order to preside over the dissolution of his Empire. Brave words, which had to be eaten during his postwar premiership, when the dissolution of the British Empire went on apace! Even so, the Conservative ladies continue to derive comfort and reassurance from them.

On the Riviera nowadays Sir Winston usually stays at the Hotel de Paris in Monte Carlo, as guest of Mr. Aristotle Onassis, who owns the place. Or Mr. Onassis will take him for a cruise, along with Maria Callas, on his sleek yacht *Christina,* named, in the circumstances somewhat embarrassingly, after his former wife, Tina Onassis. When the party goes ashore at some little holiday port, again there are cheers—"Vive Churchill!"—from groups of boatmen and fishermen and tourists who gather in the Mediterranean sun to look at him, and at Miss Callas, and even at Mr. Onassis. Those who saw Churchill, as I did, walk down the Champs Elysées with General de Gaulle, on his first visit to liberated Paris, when he seemed the embodiment of a resurrected Europe (at least, so we thought it then), might ruminate philosophically on the *bizarreries* of fame. How strange that applause, so tumultuous and heartfelt on the great stage of history, should, only a few years later, find this faint, frivolous echo in so diminished a setting! Does he detect and note the difference? Who can tell? It is still applause. Mr. Onassis is no General de Gaulle, certainly, but an attentive, considerate and generous host; *Christina* no man-of-war, but a commodious and elegant yacht. V is for victory; and, though that victory was won, it seems an eternity ago, and brought scant benefit and many woes, a V-sign made by its originator is still appreciated in Monte Carlo and along the Côte d'Azur.

The Hotel de Paris, where Mr. Onassis accommodates Sir Winston, is one of the few remaining old-style expensive hotels on the Riviera. The others are steadily being eliminated by *le camping,* which, in accordance with the spirit of the age, thrives by taking a little money from a lot of people rather than a lot of money from a few. There is nothing of *le camping* about the Hotel de Paris. The bars and dining rooms and lounges are kept in restful and perpetual twilight. As far as is humanly possible, the outside world is excluded. Residents, if so inclined, may make their way to the neighboring Casino by an underground passage without submitting themselves to the elements even to the extent of crossing the road. The service is alert and efficient, and the cuisine justly famed throughout, and, indeed, beyond the Alpes-Maritimes; the suites are ample and luxurious, and the charges astronomical—though not, of course, for Mr. Onassis' guests, who pay nothing. Outside, Rolls-Royces and Cadillacs are neatly berthed side by side, awaiting their owners' pleasure. Sir Winston keeps mostly to his suite, and appears only rarely in the public parts of the hotel. On the occasions when he is respectfully wheeled, in his invalid chair, into the dining room, the other diners all look up, eager to catch a glimpse of him. For them, too, he is a totem, whose effect is to reinforce their conviction that, whether or not there will always be an England, there will assuredly always be a Hotel de Paris.

Before Sir Winston's friendship with Mr. Onassis ripened into their present intimacy, he used to stay in the Villa Pausa at Roquebrune, some two miles further along the coast, with his literary agent, Mr. Emery Reves. This, too, is an ample residence, with a spacious stairway, and a large expanse of walls, which show off to advantage Mr. Reves's valuable collection of Impressionist paintings. It was formerly owned by Coco Chanel, famous for *haute couture* and perfume, who tamed its Italianate luxuriance into the quiet shades of grey she preferred, preserving, in the large garden, a similar color scheme by planting lavender under the old olive trees. Mlle. Chanel, long ago when she was the great friend of the Duke of Westminster, knew Sir Winston well. She used, she told me once, to play cribbage with him, and found it expedient to let him win always. In those far-off days, Mr. Reves was still in his native Hungary, and Adolf Hitler, the unconscious instrument which brought him and Sir Winston together in Mlle. Chanel's former villa, still in his native Austria. Such are the small, but still intriguing, byways of history's harsh course. Under the Reves regime, the Villa Pausa's décor has been preserved, though its chatelaine, Wendy Russell, has superimposed a certain degree of Americanization upon the household arrangements, daintily attiring the maids in coffee-shoppe pink nylon—a shade to which she is addicted, and which predominates in her own elegant boudoir.

As they say in Roquebrune, when conversation turns on the Reves ménage, made famous by Sir Winston's visits: *"C'est une vie en rose là-haut."*

Mr. Reves, like Mr. Onassis, is a rich man. Sir Winston's hosts usually are. The difference is that, whereas Mr. Onassis' wealth is derived from shipping, Mr. Reves's has been derived from Sir Winston. He has the, I should suppose, almost unique distinction in our rough island history, of having benefited financially by associating with a Churchill. By astute and pertinacious syndication of Sir Winston's writings, he has enriched himself, and, of course, to a far greater degree, Sir Winston. Thus, when Mr. Reves entertained Sir Winston, he was, in a sense, looking after a valuable property. The property continues to be valuable. Though Sir Winston no longer produces, his works go marching lucratively on through the media of film, radio and television. His paintings continue to have a brisk sale as Christmas cards in the United States, and *Winston Churchill: The Valiant Years* has recently provided American and British televiewers with yet another version of his famous war memoirs. The totem is effective at long range, like a guided missile, as well as by direct contact.

A ready means of being cherished by the English is to adopt the simple expedient of living a long time. I have little doubt that if, say, Oscar Wilde had lived into his nineties, instead of dying in his forties, he would have been considered a benign, distinguished figure, suitable to preside at a school prize-giving, or to instruct and exhort scoutmasters at their jam-borees. He might even have been knighted. A notable example of the operation of the same principle was Queen Victoria, who, in the earlier years of her reign, was so detested by her subjects that it was considered highly dubious whether the Monarchy would survive her death. Her gross and pudgy figure repelled them, as did her morbid protraction of the normal period of mourning after the death of Albert, the Prince Consort. This unfavorable impression was intensified by her lack of consideration for her heir, later Edward VII, and by her curious associates like John Brown, the Scottish baillie at Balmoral, who was permitted gross familiar-ities, at any rate in speech, and who, anyway, was nearly always drunk. By the time of the Queen's Diamond Jubilee, however, all was changed. She had sat so long on the throne that her stupidities had become endearing eccentricities, and her arrogance an old lady's whimsicality. Her turgid and heavily underlined journals were lovingly edited, and to this day are liable to raise a snicker rather than a yawn. Dreadful statues of her, turned out by the score, were erected in prominent places throughout the country, and even shipped to far-off lands like India, where they still stand unsuita-bly in Calcutta, New Delhi and Pakistan's Lahore.

If this unpleasing old Germanic lady thus achieved fame and popular esteem just by becoming very old, how much more so is this the case with Sir Winston, who has notable achievements to his credit, and who has displayed, in the course of his turbulent political career, exceptional verve and resourcefulness. Yet, even Sir Winston, as few now care to remember, has had periods of exclusion from office, and of intense unpopularity, particularly among his associates in the political party he happened to belong to at the time. I recall very well, in the middle Thirties, when I was working on the London *Evening Standard,* how Churchill used to come occasionally to the office. Lord Beaverbrook, the owner of the *Evening Standard,* had engaged him to write regular articles on current affairs at what was then considered an exceptionally high fee. What a dispirited and disgruntled figure he was in those days! Any political journalist would have been happy to give long odds against his ever holding office again, let alone becoming Prime Minister. The Tories, whom he had rejoined when their political fortunes revived, could not abide him. He found a point of attack in their India policy, which, when it was put into effect in a more extreme form some ten years later by a Labour Government, he approved without a murmur. At the time of King Edward VIII's abdication, he was howled down in the House of Commons when he attempted to make a plea on the King's behalf. Here, too, as the exiled Duke of Windsor found to his chagrin, Churchill in opposition was one thing, Churchill in office another. The nomadic Duke and Duchess of Windsor received no more consideration from their former champion when he was in a position to do them favors than they did from Mr. Attlee, who owed them none.

Now all this is forgotten. Churchill is very old, and so any breath of criticism of his character or achievement is considered to be not only in execrable taste, but almost blasphemous. This is a pity, if only because it detracts from his undoubted greatness. For a man, as human and humorous and audacious as Churchill has been, to be turned into a totem, serving to protract illusions of grandeur, is a sad end to a splendid career. How fortunate were those Hindu rulers whose philosophy required them to retire to the forest for their last years, and thus disengage their minds from earthly preoccupations in order to prepare themselves for the death which could not be long delayed.

It is, of course, true that Churchill's totem role is particularly required just now, when his country's fortunes are visibly declining. He was the last Prime Minister able to produce authentic Great Power credentials at international gatherings. Though, in fact, in his dealings with Stalin and Roosevelt, he was increasingly a junior partner, he appeared to be an equal. At the ill-omened Yalta meeting, he was mostly overborne, and sometimes treated with scant consideration by his two associates, but in the final winding-up scenes they allowed him an equal status with themselves. He had the dubious distinction of being photographed, his Russian fur hat rakishly on one side, as one of the three pillars of the modern world, who, it was confidently believed, would draw the frontiers and establish the conditions for an era of enduring peace and prosperity. Things, as we now know, took quite a different turn. Even so, the English are still inclined to look nostalgically into their old photograph album, which recalls grander circumstances than they now enjoy. Among the studio portraits it contains, Sir Winston's is particularly prized.

Few men of action have been able to make a graceful exit at the appropriate time. Napoleon's retirement to St. Helena was enforced, restless and cantankerous; Lloyd George, for the last twenty-three years of his life excluded from office, continued till the end to hover round public affairs, managing to persuade himself that he was contributing to their course and direction. Even Sir Oswald Mosley, whose meteoric career in party politics ended ingloriously in the British Union of Fascists and incarceration during the war years, continues still to believe that the call will come for him to take over the Government. Power-addiction, like any other, becomes in the end incurable. Its victims continue to crave for the drug even when it cannot be procured, or, if it could, when their systems are too enfeebled to react, other than fitfully and wanly, to its stimulus.

How much better for Churchill's reputation if he had brought himself, or been persuaded, to retire from active politics after his electoral defeat in 1945! Then his enormous services were a fresh memory instead of a too-often-told tale. The rhetoric which gloriously saved us from surrender to the Nazis had not staled with constant repetition; the great esteem in which he was rightly held had not degenerated into sycophancy, nor been used to sustain a legendary destiny which precludes effectively grappling with a real one.

It was not to be. He discarded the role of national leadership, which he had so richly earned, in favor of party leadership, for which he was ill-fitted, and which ill-became him. The red dispatch boxes, toys of office, held their old allure, and for them he threw away, or at any rate clouded, the memory of the time when he had been the spokesman, not of a class or a party, but of a nation and a cause. His postwar premiership was confused, meandering and self-willed—much more so than is even now recognized or admitted. He hung on as long as he dared, and as long as the poltroonery of his associates permitted. When, at last, he went, he bequeathed us Anthony Eden, who, in one ill-judged, ill-planned and fatuous venture at Suez, lost to, of all people, the Egyptians, what Winston Churchill's heroic wartime leadership had saved from the Nazis. History, which is always ironic, has rarely produced a greater irony than this.

Surely, it will be contended, Sir Winston's place in history is sufficiently assured irrespective of how the twilight of his days may be spent. Is it not the case that, as has so often been remarked, his deeds will live, and his writing be read, as long as England's fate interests mankind, and the English language continues to be spoken? As for his writing—I am not so sure. Participants in public events are seldom reliable chroniclers of them. Their egos are too involved, their views are too prejudiced, for them to achieve an historian's detachment. They find it difficult to recollect in tranquility, and therefore to endow with enduring interest, what so excited them at the time. Effective men of action, by their very nature, have little sense of perspective. They are too obsessed with their own lines to be interested in the play; too avidly concerned with the present to trace its relation to the past and the future. Tactics obsess them to the exclusion of strategy. Like Napoleon, their only true principle is "*On s'engage, et après on voit.*" History cannot be written in such a spirit. Gibbon, who as an officer in the Militia was a ludicrous figure, and at the Board of Trade a fiasco, could with exquisite clarity, skill and elegance unravel the story of Rome's decline and fall. Napoleon, on the other hand, when, on St. Helena, he looked back on the dramatic events in which he had played so decisive a part, had nothing of any particular interest or significance to say about them.

In Sir Winston's case the question is complicated by his rhetorical style, which, though it has been greatly admired by his contemporaries, posterity may well find distasteful. Already his memoirs of the First World War have begun to pall. Who today can stomach passages like:

"Once more now in the march of centuries Old England was to stand forth in battle against the mightiest thrones and dominations. Once more in defense of the liberties of Europe and the common right must she enter upon a voyage of great toil and hazard across waters uncharted, towards coasts unknown, guided only by the stars. Once more 'the far-off line of storm-beaten ships' was to stand between the Continental Tyrant and the dominion of the world. . . ."?

It would not be surprising if his memoirs of the Second World War came, before very long, to create a like impression of being gaseous, overwritten, and, in the light of subsequent events, too inappropriate to deserve attention.

History, in any case, is the story of the victor. When I first went to India, in 1924, little Indian boys were taught at school that their country was torn with conflicts and prostrate until the English landed on its shores. Thenceforth, all was well. Now they are taught the exact opposite—that their country languished until the English were chased away. Which version is true? The answer probably is: neither. However unjustly or inaccurately, Sir Winston's place in history will depend on who, from the turmoil and discontents of our time, is seen to emerge as the victor.

[June, 1961]

Bogie in Excelsis

by Peter Bogdanovich

Usually he wore the trench coat unbuttoned, just tied with the belt, and a slouch hat, rarely tilted. Sometimes it was a captain's cap and a yachting jacket. Almost always his trousers were held up by a cowboy belt. You know the kind: one an Easterner, waiting for a plane out of Phoenix, buys just as a joke and then takes a liking to. Occasionally, he'd hitch up his slacks with it, and he often jabbed his thumbs behind it, his hands ready for a fight or a dame.

Whether it was Sirocco or Casablanca, Martinique or Sahara, he was the only American around (except maybe for the girl) and you didn't ask him how he got there, and he always worked alone—except for the fellow who thought he took care of him, the rummy, the piano player, the one *he* took care of, the one you didn't mess with. There was very little he couldn't do, and in a jam he could do anything: remove a slug from a guy's arm, fix a truck that wouldn't start. He was an excellent driver, knowing precisely how to take those curves or how to lose a guy that was tailing him. He could smell a piece of a broken glass and tell you right away if there'd been poison in it, or he could walk into a room and know just where the button was that opened the secret door. At the wheel of a boat, he was beautiful.

His expression was usually sour and when he smiled only the lower lip moved. There was a scar on his upper lip, maybe that's what gave him the faint lisp. He would tug meditatively at his earlobe when he was trying to figure something out and every so often he had a strange little twitch—a kind of backward jerk of the sides of his mouth coupled with a slight squinting of the eyes. He held his cigarette (a Chesterfield) cupped in his hand. He looked right holding a gun.

Unsentimental was a good word for him. "Leave 'im where he is," he might say to a woman whose husband has just been wounded. "I don't want 'im bleeding all over my cushions." And blunt: "I don't like you. I don't like your friends and I don't like the idea of her bein' married to you." And straight: "When a man's partner is killed he's supposed to do something about it. It doesn't make any difference what you thought of him. He was your partner and you're supposed to do something about it."

He was tough; he could stop you with a look or a line. "Go ahead, slap me," he'd say, or, "That's right, go for it," and there was in the way he said it just the right blend of malice, gleeful anticipation and the promise of certain doom. He didn't like taking orders. Or favors. It was smart not to fool around with him too much.

As far as the ladies were concerned, he didn't have too much trouble with them, except maybe keeping them away. It was the girl who said if he needed anything, all he had to do was whistle; he never said that to the girl. Most of the time he'd call her "angel," and if he liked her he'd tell her she was "good, awful good."

Whatever he was engaged in, whether it was being a reporter, a saloon-keeper, a gangster, a detective, a fishing-boat owner, a D.A., or a lawyer, he was impeccably, if casually, a complete professional. "You take chances," someone would say. "I get paid to," was his answer. But he never took himself too seriously. What was his job, a girl would ask. Conspiratorially, he'd lean in and say with the slightest flicker of a grin, "I'm a private dick on a case." He wasn't going to be taken in by Art either; he'd been to college, but he was a bit suspicious of the intellectuals. If someone mentioned Proust, he'd ask, "Who's he?", even though he knew.

Finally, he was wary of Causes. He liked to get paid for taking chances. He was a man who tried very hard to be Bad because he knew it was easier to get along in the world that way. He always failed because of an innate goodness which surely nauseated him. Almost always he went from belligerent neutrality to reluctant commitment. From: "I stick my neck out for nobody." To: "I'm no good at being noble, but it doesn't take much to see that the problems of three little people don't amount to a hill o' beans in this crazy world." At the start, if the question was, "What are your sympathies?", the answer was invariably, "Minding my own business." But by the end, if asked why he was helping, risking his life, he might say, "Maybe 'cause I like you. Maybe 'cause I don't like them." Of course it was always "maybe" because he wasn't going to be that much of a sap, wasn't making any speeches, wasn't going to be a Good guy. Probably he rationalized it: "I'm just doing my job." But we felt good inside. We knew better.

Several months ago, the New Yorker Theatre in Manhattan ran a cycle of thirty Humphrey Bogart movies. A one-day double bill of *The Big Sleep* and *To Have and Have Not* broke all their attendance records. "I had two hundred people sitting on the floor," said Daniel Talbot, owner of the 830-seat revival house and one of the two producers of *Point of Order.* "It was wild. I had to turn away a couple of hundred people. And that audience! First time Bogie appeared they applauded, and that was just the beginning. Any number of scenes got hands. And the laughs! Bogart is very hot right now," Talbot explained. "It's more than a cult, it's something else too. He's not consciously hip, but hip by default. You get the feeling that he lives up to the Code. Anyone who screws up deserves the fate of being rubbed out by Bogart. He's also very American, and his popularity, I think, is a reaction to this currently chic craze for foreign films and things foreign in general. With Bogart you get a portrait of a patriot, a man interested in the landscape of America. I think he's an authentic American hero—more existential than, say, Cooper, but as much in the American vein, and more able to cope with the present." Talbot paused and grinned. "Frankly, I just like to watch him at work. He hits people beautifully."

The French have a more intellectual, if nonetheless affectionate, approach to Bogart and the legend he has left behind. As Belmondo stares mystically at a photo of Bogart in Godard's *Breathless,* slowly exhaling cigarette smoke and rubbing his lip with his thumb, he murmurs wistfully, "Bogie . . ." and you can almost hear his director's thoughts, echoed, for instance, in the words of the late André Bazin, probably France's finest film critic. "Bogart is the man with a past," he wrote in *Cahiers du Cinéma* in 1957, a month after Bogart died. "When he comes into a film, it is already 'the morning after'; sardonically victorious in his macabre combat with the angel, his face scared by what he has seen, and his step heavy from all he has learned, having ten times triumphed over his death, he will surely survive for us this one more time. . . . The Bogartian man is not defined by his contempt for bourgeois virtues, by his courage or cowardice, but first of all by his existential maturity which little by little transforms life into a tenacious irony at the expense of death." Of course, the French too can have a more basic approach. "Finally in full color," wrote Robert Lachenay in the same magazine, "we see Bogie as he was in real life—as he was to Betty Bacall every night on his pillow. . . . I loved Bogart even better then. . . ."

The Bogart cult has been perpetuated for the last several years in colleges all over the United States. "I met a Harvard fellow recently," said writer Nathaniel Benchley, "who believed in only two things: the superiority of Harvard and the immortality of Humphrey Bogart." During every exam period in Cambridge, it has become customary for the Brattle Theatre to run a Bogart film festival. Sometimes they don't even list the pictures; they just put a large photograph of him outside the theatre. It seems to be enough. Walk into the Club Casablanca (in the same building) and ask one of the undergraduates. "Bogart has a coolness you can't get away from," he might tell you. "It's a wryness, a freedom," he'll say, at the same time denying that there is a real cult and that he's just so refreshing, so pleasantly removed from their academic world. "There's no crap about Bogart," another student may observe. "He's also kind of anti-European and pro-American. Like he dumps on the European, you know what I mean?" By this time his date won't be able to control herself any longer. "He's so masculine!" she'll blurt out. "He's so fantastically tough!" Was he? "He satirized himself a great deal," said writer Betty Comden. Raymond Massey recalled an incident during the shooting of *Action in the North Atlantic* (1943): "The scene called for our doubles to jump from the bridge of a burning tanker into the water below, which was aflame with oil. Bogie turned to me and said, '*My* double is braver than yours.' I said that wasn't so, that *my* double was the braver man. Then Bogie looked at me and he said, 'The fact is I'm braver than you are.' I said that was nonsense. And the next thing I knew we did the doggone stunt ourselves." Massey chuckled. "I burned my pants off and Bogie singed his eyebrows."

To Joseph L. Mankiewicz, who directed him in *The Barefoot Contessa* (1954), Bogart's toughness was a façade. "You'd be having dinner with him," he said, "and someone would come over and you could just see the tough guy coming on." And to Chester Morris: "He had a protective shell of seeming indifference. He wasn't, but he did a lotta acting offstage. He liked to act tough, liked to talk out of the side of his mouth." Writer Nunnally Johnson said Bogart was convinced that people would have been disappointed if he didn't act tough with them. "A fan came over during dinner one time," said Johnson, "and Bogie told him to beat it. When the guy got back to his table I heard his companion say, quite happily, 'See, I told ya he'd insult you.' " Johnson reflected a moment. "But he was a lot tougher than I would be and a lot tougher than most people I know. I remember one time Judy Garland and her husband, Sid Luft, were at his home. Now Luft was a big alley fighter and a good deal broader than Bogart. But Bogie got annoyed about something or other and he walked right over to Luft, who also was a good head taller, and nodded at Judy. 'Would you take that dame out of this house,' he said, 'and never come back.' Luft kind of looked at him a moment and then he took her out." Johnson smiled. "Bogie took big risks."

Adlai Stevenson didn't find him that way. "He wasn't tough, not really," said the Ambassador. "He was, to me, a nonconformist. He had a cynicism without being unhealthy. He had great curiosity and an arch kind of skepticism." And still another opinion: "He was a pushover," said Lauren Bacall.

"I never broke through his barrier," said critic John McLain. "I don't think anyone really got underneath. Bogart didn't unburden himself to men. He loved to be in love and with a woman. I think he came closer to leveling with them than with anybody." Bogart married four women during his fifty-seven years, each of them an actress: Helen Mencken (1926), Mary Phillips (1928), the late Mayo Methot (1938), and in 1945, Lauren Bacall. "I think once a person was out, they were really out," said Truman Capote, discussing the divorces. "He had emotional attachments."

The Bogart-Methot marriage was a stormy one. "Their neighbors were lulled to sleep," Dorothy Parker once said, "by the sounds of breaking china and crashing glass." Johnson recalled that Methot once had Bogart followed. "She was very jealous and positive that he was playing around. But Bogie never had a weakness for dames. The only weakness he ever had was for a drink and a talk." Johnson smiled. "Bogie soon found out a guy was tailing him, and he called up the fellow's agency. 'Hello, this is Humphrey Bogart,' he said. 'You got a man on my tail. Would you check with him and find out where I am.' "

The first time Bogart met Betty Bacall was coming out of director Howard Hawks' office. She had made a test for Hawks, who had discovered her and first teamed the couple in *To Have and Have Not* (1945). "I saw your test," Bogart said to her. "We're gonna have a lotta fun together." It was with Bacall that he had his only children, a boy named Steve, which is what she called Bogart in that first movie, and a girl named Leslie Howard, after the actor who had insisted that Bogart be cast in the film version of *The Petrified Forest* (1936), the movie that really began his picture career. "He missed her when they were apart," Capote said. "He loved her. He used to talk a terrific line, but he was monogamous. Although that isn't entirely true—he fell in love with Bacall while he was still married to Mayo."

Bogart put it this way: "I'm a one-woman man and I always have been. I guess I'm old-fashioned. Maybe that's why I like old-fashioned women, the kind who stay in the house playing *Roamin' in the Gloamin'*. They make a man think he's a man and they're glad of it." The stories go that Bogart was a heavy drinker, but Johnson thinks otherwise. "I don't think Bogie drank as much as he pretended to," he said. "Many's a time I was with him, the doorbell would ring, and he'd pick up his glass just to go answer the door. He couldn't have been as good at his job if he drank as much as he was supposed to have."

But Bogart did drink. "I think the world is three drinks behind," he used to say, "and it's high time it caught up." On one occasion he and a friend bought two enormous stuffed panda bears and took them as their dates to El Morocco. They sat them in chairs at a table for four and when an ambitious young lady came over and touched Bogart's bear, he shoved her away. "I'm a happily married man," he said, "and don't touch my panda." The woman brought assault charges against him, and when asked if he was drunk at four o'clock in the morning, he replied, "Sure, isn't everybody?" (The judge ruled that since the panda was Mr. Bogart's personal property, he could defend it.)

But Bogart didn't have to drink to start trouble. "He was an arrogant bastard," said Johnson, grinning. "It's kinda funny, this cult and everything. When he was alive, as many people hated him as loved him. I always thought of him as somewhat like Scaramouche." Johnson chuckled. "What was it? 'Born with the gift of laughter and the sense that the world was mad. . . .' He'd start a skirmish and then sit back and watch the consequences. Of course, there was nearly always something phony about the guy he was needling. Needle is the wrong word—howitzer would be more like it. The other fellow could use deflating, but it didn't take all that artillery."

The Holmby Hills Rat Pack, which Bogart initiated and which died with him, sprang from this distaste for pretense. "What is a rat?" he once explained. "We have no constitution, charter or bylaws, yet, but we know a rat when we see one. There are very few rats in this town. You might say that rats are for staying up late and drinking lots of booze. We're against squares and being bored and for lots of fun and being real rats, which very few people are, but if you're a real rat, boy! Our slogan is, 'Never rat on a rat.' A first principle is that we don't care who likes us as long as we like each other. We like each other very much."

John McClain tells of the yacht club Bogart belonged to and of the people who rented the large house next door for a summer. They were the Earls and they Dressed for Dinner. The members of the club (who were never invited) used to peer over their fence, watching the lush festivities. McClain had been invited to a Sunday dinner and had asked if he might bring Bogart along as they would be together on his yacht over the weekend. As they docked, McClain reminded Bogart to dress for the occasion and went off to get ready himself. Bogart went into the club for a drink or two. "After a while," McClain recalled, "Bogie announced to everyone in the club, 'My dear friends, the Earls,' he said, 'are having an open house and they want you all to come.' And into the Earl house comes Bogie followed by about thirty people, all wearing shorts and sport shirts and sneakers." McClain laughed. "It was pretty funny, actually, but I was furious at the time."

"He could be very wrong too," said Benchley. "One time at '21' I was standing at the bar with a couple of friends and Bogie got up from his table and came over. 'Are you a homosexual?' he said to one of them, just like that. The fellow looked rather taken aback and said he didn't see that it was any of his business. 'Well are you?' said Bogie. 'Come on, we got a bet going at the table.' The fellow said, 'Since you ask, no.' I think Bogie could feel he'd been wrong and he turned to the other guy with us and asked him if *he* was a homosexual. The guy said no. He asked me and I said no and then he said, 'Well, I am,' and kinda minced away. He knew he'd been wrong."

A few weeks after Bogart's death, Peter Ustinov said, in a speech: "Humphrey Bogart was an exceptional character in a sphere where characters are not usually exceptional. To a visitor hot from the cold shores of England, he would put on an exaggerated Oxford accent and discuss the future of the 'British Empah' as though he wrongheadedly cared for nothing else in the wide world. His aim was to shake the newcomer out of his assumed complacency by insults which were as shrewdly observed as they were malicious. . . . The way into his heart was an immediate counterattack in a broad American accent, during which one assumed a complicity between him and his *bête noire,* Senator McCarthy, in some dark scheme. . . . It was in the character of the man that he smiled with real pleasure only when he had been amply repaid in kind."

Capote would go along with that: "The turning point in our friendship—the beginning really—was during *Beat the Devil* (1954). Bogie and John Huston and some others, they were playing that game—you know the one, what d'ya call it—you take each other's hand across a table and try to push the other's arm down. Well, it just happens that I'm very good at that game. So, anyway, Bogie called over, 'Hey, Caposy.' That's what he called me, 'Caposy.' He said, 'C'mon, Caposy, let's see you try this.' And I went over and I pushed his arm down. Well, he looked at me. . . . He had such a suspicious mind, he was sure that Huston had cut off my head and sewed it onto someone else's body. 'Let's see you do that again,' he said. And again I pushed his arm down. So he said once more, and I said I would only if we bet a hundred dollars, which we did. I won again and he paid me, but then he came over and he started sort of semi-wrestling with me. It was something they did. He was crushing me and I said, 'Cut that *owat,*' and he said, 'Cut that *owat.*' I said, 'Well, do,' and he said, 'Why?' I said, 'Because you're hurting me.' But he kept right on squeezing, so I got my leg around behind him and pushed and over he went. He was flat on his can looking up at me. And from then on we were very good friends."

"Bogie's needling tactics were quite calculated," Johnson explained. "I had lunch with him and Betty at Romanoff's one time and she was giving him hell about some row at a party. He'd provoked it, of course. 'Someday somebody's gonna belt you,' she said, and he said, 'No, that's the art of it—taking things up to that point and then escaping.' "

In 1947, Bogart led a march to Washington to protest the investigations of the Un-American Activities Committee. Some people labeled him a pinko. He didn't like that. "I am an American," he said. Bogart's political freethinking was considered dangerous in Hollywood. In 1952, however, he campaigned most actively for Stevenson for President. "He never seemed to give a damn what people thought or said," Mr. Stevenson recalled. "And it was quite perilous in those days to be a Democrat, especially one partisan to me. He was disdainful about anybody trying to muscle about in a free country."

"He wasn't an extremist in anything," said Miss Bacall, "except telling the truth. You had to admire Bogie. He always said what he thought. 'Goddamnit,' he used to say, 'if you don't want to hear the truth, don't ask me.' "

"That's true," Johnson agreed. "Everything he did was honest. He used to say, 'What's everybody whispering about? I've got cancer!' He'd say, 'For Christ's sake, it's not a venereal disease.' "

Bogart also said that the only point in making money is "so you can tell some big shot to go to hell." And: "I have politeness and manners. I was brought up that way. But in this goldfish-bowl life, it is sometimes hard to use them."

His widow thinks it was more than just good manners Bogart had. Finally, she'll tell you, "He was an old-fashioned man, a great romantic. And very emotional. He would cry when a dog died. You should have seen him at our wedding, tears streaming down his face. He told me that he started thinking about the meaning of the words. He was tough about life and totally uncompromising, but I remember he went to see Steve at nursery school and when he saw him sitting at his little desk, he cried."

Alistair Cooke met the Bogarts on the Stevenson campaign train and he remembered sitting with them one afternoon and saying that, of course, Stevenson wouldn't win. " 'What!' said Bogie, astounded. 'Not a prayer, I'm afraid,' I said. 'Why you son of a bitch,' Betty said, 'that's a fine thing to say.' 'Look,' I said, 'I'm a reporter. You're the lieutenants.' We bet ten dollars on it and when Stevenson lost he paid it to me. But he didn't really think I'd take it. You know what he said? 'It's a hell of a guy who bets against his own principles.' "

Cooke commented on this Bogart trait in an article he wrote for *The Atlantic Monthly* (May, 1957). "A touchy man who found the world more corrupt than he had hoped . . . he invented the Bogart character and imposed it on a world impatient of men more obviously good. And it fitted his deceptive purpose like a glove. . . . From all . . . he was determined to keep his secret: the rather shameful secret, in the realistic world we inhabit, of being a gallant man and an idealist."

Other friends detected a similar quality in Bogart. Mankiewicz called it, "A sadness about the human condition. He had a kind of eighteenth-century, Alexander Pope nature. I think he would have made a superb Gatsby. His life reflected Gatsby's sense of being an outsider." Stevenson found "a wistful note in him, as there often is in thinking people. He was much more profound than one might think." And Capote called him lost. "It was his outstanding single characteristic—that something almost pathetic. Not that he would ever ask for sympathy, far from it. It just always seemed to me as though he were permanently lonely. It gave him a rather poetic quality, don't you think?"

That secret inner world of Humphrey Bogart was reflected in his passion for sailing and his love for the *Santana*, his boat, on which he went off whenever he could, accompanied by a few friends. They used to drink Drambuies and play dominoes or just sail. He had learned early about the sea, having left school (at their request) at seventeen and joined the Navy. It was on the troopship *Leviathan* that he received the injury that permanently scarred his upper lip. "Sailing. That was the part of him no one could get at," Capote said. "It wasn't anything materialistic. It was some kind of inner soul, an almost mystical hideaway."

If the *Motion Picture Herald*'s annual Fame Poll of the Top Ten movie stars can be trusted, it appears that Bogart's peak years of popularity were 1943-1949, during and just after World War II. Cooke explained it this way: "He was . . . a romantic hero inconceivable in any time but ours. . . . When Hitler was acting out scripts more brutal and obscene than anything dreamed of by Chicago's North Side or the Warner Brothers, Bogart was the only possible antagonist likely to outwit him and survive. What was needed was no Ronald Colman, Leslie Howard or other knight of the boudoir, but a conniver as subtle as Goebbels. Bogart was the very tough gent required, and to his glory he was always, in the end, on our side."

He didn't get his Oscar, however, until 1952 (for *The African Queen*), and popped up on the top ten again in 1955, a little more than a year before he died. Betty Comden: "I don't think this cult is anything new. . . . " Adolph Green: "No. . . ." Comden: "Bogart never stopped being popular. . . ." Green: "There are so few originals around. . . ." Comden: "Bogart's style had an innate sophistication. . . ." Green: "He was less an actor . . ." Comden: ". . . than a personality." Bogart agreed. "Sure I am. It took fifteen years to make us personalities. Gable and Cooper can do anything in a picture, and people would say, 'Oh, that's just good old Clark.' "

"His great basic quality," said Ustinov, "was a splendid roughness. Even when perfectly groomed, I felt I could have lit a match on his jaw. . . . He knew his job inside out, and yet it was impossible not to feel that his real soul was elsewhere, a mysterious searching instrument knocking at doors unknown even to himself. . . ."

Perhaps this is what Bogart's admirers sense. "There was something about him that came through in every part he played," said Miss Bacall. "I think he'll always be fascinating—to this generation and every succeeding one. There was something that made him able to be a man of his own and it showed through his work. There was also a purity, which is amazing considering the parts he played. Something solid too. I think as time goes by we all believe less and less. Here was someone who believed in something."

"Like all really great stars," said director George Cukor, "he had a secret. You never really know him altogether. He also had boldness of mind, freedom of thought—a buccaneer. I think these young people haven't seen him," he went on, trying to explain the cult. "They're simply rediscovering him. After all, Bogie had class."

"The average college student would sooner identify with Bogart than, say, Sinatra, don't you think?" said Mankiewicz. "He had that rather intellectual disrespect for authority. Also I don't think anyone ever really believed that Bogart was a gangster—that's what fascinated people. Bogart never frightened them."

"It's angry youth," Chester Morris said. "They're cheering for the heavy today. Everything must be nonconformist. They'd also like to do the kind of things he did. He was a forerunner of James Bond." Benchley: "He's a hero without being a pretty boy."

"Could it be anything as simple as sex appeal?" Capote wondered. "He had an image of sophisticated virility and he projected it remarkably well. And with such humor. At last, he had such style that it doesn't wither, it doesn't age, it doesn't date. Like Billie Holiday."

"I think Robin Hood has always been attractive," said Adlai Stevenson.

Before the adulation, there must be something to adulate. And this must be created. "If a face like Ingrid Bergman's looks at you as though you're adorable," Bogart once said, "everyone does. You don't have to act very much." The late Raymond Chandler thought otherwise: "All Bogart has to do to dominate a scene is to enter it." Evidently it wasn't always that way. In 1922, playing one of his first stage roles, he was reviewed by Alexander Woollcott: "His performance could be mercifully described as inadequate." But two years later, of another performance, Woollcott again: "Mr. Bogart is a young actor whose last appearance was recorded by your correspondent in words so disparaging that it is surprising to find him still acting. Those words are hereby eaten." It would figure that Bogart often used to quote the first review but never the second.

" 'Why, I'm a National Institution,' he used to say," Capote recalled. "He was very proud of his success and fame. But he was most serious about his acting. He thought of it as a profession, one that he was curious about, knew something about. After all, it was almost the sum total of his life. In the end, Bogart really was an artist. And a very selective one. All the gestures and expressions were pruned down and pruned down. One time I watched *The Maltese Falcon* with him and he sat there, muttering in that hoarse way, criticizing himself in the third person. 'Now he's gonna come in,' he'd say. 'Then he's gonna do this and that's where he does the wrong thing.' I gathered during the silences that he liked it. It was braggadocio through silence."

Howard Hawks directed Bogart in his two most archetypal roles, as Harry (Steve) Morgan in *To Have and Have Not* and Philip Marlow in *The Big Sleep* (1946). "He was extremely easy to work with," Hawks said. "Really underrated as an actor. Without his help I couldn't have done what I did with Bacall. Not many actors would sit around and wait while a girl steals a scene. But he fell in love with the girl and the girl with him, and that made it easy."

Bogart used to say that an audience was always a little ahead of the actor. "If a guy points a gun at you," he explained, "the audience knows you're afraid. You don't have to make faces. You just have to believe that you are the person you're playing and that what is happening is happening to you."

Ustinov acted with Bogart once, in a comedy called *We're No Angels* (1955). "Bogart had an enormous presence," he said, "and he carried the light of battle in his eye. He wished to be matched, to be challenged, to be teased. I could see a jocular and quarrelsome eye staring out of the character he was playing into the character I was playing—rather as an experienced bullfighter might stare a hotheaded bull into precipitate action."

"When the heavy, full of crime and bitterness," said Bogart, "grabs his wounds and talks about death and taxes in a husky voice, the audience is his and his alone."

This emotion, elicited so consciously from his movie audiences, ironically became a reality. His death was horribly, heart-breakingly in character. He died on January 14, 1957, of a cancer of the esophagus, and it had taken well over a year to kill him. "These days," he said, "I just sit around and talk to my friends, the people I like." Which is what he did.

"I went to see him toward the end," said Ambassador Stevenson. "He was very ill and very weak, but he made a most gallant effort to keep gay. He had an intolerance for weakness, an impatience with illness."

"I went a few times," Capote said. "Most of his friends went, some almost every day, like Sinatra. Some were very loyal. He seemed to bring out the best in them all. He looked so awful, so terribly thin. His eyes were huge and they looked so frightened. They got bigger and bigger. It was real fear and yet there was always that gay, brave self. He'd have to be brought downstairs on the dumbwaiter and he'd sit and wait and wait for his Martini. He was only allowed one, I think, or two. And that's how we used to find him, smoking and sipping that Martini."

During that time, his wife rarely left the house, though her friends and even Bogart urged her to go out more often. When someone asked why she had only been out six or seven times in ten months, Bogart replied: "She's my wife and my nurse. So she stays home. Maybe that's the way you tell the ladies from the broads in this town."

"He went through the worst and most agonizing pain any human can take," said Dr. Maynard Brandsma. "I knew this and when I'd see him I'd ask, 'How is it?' Bogie would always answer simply, 'Pretty rough.' He never complained and he never whimpered. I knew he was dying and during the last weeks I knew he knew it too."

"I saw him twenty-three days before he died," said Cukor. "He couldn't come downstairs anymore and he was heavily sedated. He kept closing his eyes. Still he'd be telling jokes and asking to hear the gossip. But his voice was the wonder. That marvelous voice. It was absolutely alive. It was the last thing that died."

His death came in the early morning and that day the papers carried the news to the world. Most of the reports were similar. Quite a few of them told it this way: "Usually he kissed his wife Lauren Bacall and said, 'Good night.' But according to Dr. Michael Flynn, this time he put his hand on her arm and murmured in his familiar brusque fashion, 'Good-bye, kid.' "

Whether it really happened that way or not is beside the point. Bogart the man and Bogart the hero had merged until now one couldn't tell the difference between the two, if indeed there ever had been any. He had walked through seventy-five movie nights for his public and it was too late now to change the image, too late to alter a legend that had really just begun.

[September, 1964]

Mr. Fisher is Open

by Jack Richardson

"Eddie is very open right now." This was all I received by way of
caution and guidance from this magazine's editor who first suggested that I
might interview Eddie Fisher, then enjoying what Show Business terms a
"comeback engagement" at the Americana Hotel in New York. The word
"open" was ambiguous. I hoped, being a novice at wheedling private
opinions from public persons, that it connoted expansiveness, a loquaciousness and other qualities of an extrovert nature which would allow me
to be a quiet, passive repository for whatever Eddie Fisher might have to
say about life in the twentieth century. This, I felt, would be the least
painful way of dealing with someone you had never met and of whom you
hoped, in the space of a few days, to draw a verbal picture that would
satisfy both the standards of civilized social intercourse and an editorial
thirst for intimacy which, as a reporter, I felt bound to slacken. Alas, it
was not going to be that easy. Although a member of a garrulous profession, Eddie Fisher refused to garrul. In fact, it ended with him not
speaking to me at all.

The tale begins in the Royal Box of the Americana Hotel on a torpid
June night of this year. I had been called earlier that day by a certain Miss

Leff, one of Fisher's publicity representatives, and, in sweet tones of invitation, asked to witness her client perform and then initiate the interviews with a backstage meeting. I gratefully accepted, arrived at the nightclub, and all went well: the headwaiter, who had expected me, snapped his fingers militantly and I was led, slightly bloated with the power of the press, to a ringside table. To be sure, the table was rather modest, no more than two feet square in size. Still, I noticed that this was standard for the Royal Box, forgave them their shortcomings, and ordered a straight vodka, a drink small enough to rest comfortably on the table surface. Around me, the room was completely filled with customers ending their dinners and beginning the second shift in evening drinking. I realized that I should have some notion of the type of audience Fisher attracted and, feeling reportorially very thorough, I looked closely at my neighbors. The immediate impression was of age. At most tables, the ladies were hovering in that limbo land of late thirties, while their escorts, hoary of head and deeply tanned, spotted them a good twenty years. I don't mean to imply decrepitude; it is just that I had imagined a singer's following to be barely nubile teen-agers, which those around me definitely were not. The women were heavily jeweled and sported hairstyles that resembled miniature haystacks atop their heads; the men, by contrast, were somberly dressed, puffed cigars and cigarettes, and seemed uninterested in their companions. All in all, I had the impression of Catskill courtesans on a night about town with a convention. A romantic impression, perhaps, but eavesdropping on a conversation at the table next to me gave it some substance.

"You ask me, he's better off," a blonde demi-matron said, touching up her mouth with white lipstick. "She was too much for him."

"Hell, I never knew her on intimate terms," said a round but hard little sexagenarian next to her.

"And a good thing too, baby," said the blonde.

"Well," the man continued, "just once when she was in Toots Shor's with Damaggio, when she was married to him—"

"For Christ's sake, Gene," his friend said with a laugh, "that was Marilyn Monroe."

"Oh, yeah."

(Here, there was general but hesitant snickering, as though no one really was certain whom they were talking about.)

"Well, I think Eddie came out all right." The second lady at the table spoke up. "He's getting half of her share from *Cleopatra,* and besides, she's fat!"

At this point one of the men noticed that I had included myself in their little talk and sent me a glance that returned me to my vodka. God, I thought, how familiar it all was. The Burton-Fisher-Taylor Roman triangle—that certainly had been, or would be, drained of any interest before what I wrote about Fisher ever saw print. Last year's lovers would be of antiquarian interest only; scholars of passion might pore over the remains, but readers of this magazine struck me as having more vivid appetites. Besides, what could I possibly draw out of Fisher on this subject that wouldn't be offensive to him? And even if he wore his cuckoldry proudly, would anything be printable?

While mulling over these problems, I was joined by Miss Leff, who bustled quickly to her seat and simultaneously apologized for being late and introduced herself. She was a round pleasant woman, quite buoyant and quite enthusiastic over the prospect of my doing an article about Eddie. Not being absolutely certain just what her role in all this would be, I asked, in a general way, what her daily job required her to do.

"Oh, you know," she said brightly, "you sort of watch out for things. Make sure the client gets the kind of publicity he wants. Of course some, like Dean Martin, want to keep *out* of the papers."

This last, I'm pleased to note, she said in an approving tone.

"But mostly," she went on, "it's keeping the client in front of the public in a way he approves of."

I asked what variety of publicity Eddie Fisher was fondest of.

"Oh, well, right now he's rather open."

The enigmatic word again. This time I pressed for a definition.

"Well, you know, the Liz Taylor thing. He wants to put that behind him. He's singing again and that's all he really wants to do."

"That's fair enough," I said, but, as the lights went down in the Royal Box, I wondered just what *would* be of interest about Eddie Fisher if we did leave out, as Miss Leff put it, the Liz Taylor thing?

When it was pitch dark, an invisible orchestra began playing and, after a few notes, both it and Eddie Fisher were illuminated onstage. Without wasting a word, Fisher went right into song about how happiness awaited us all "right in our own backyard." He was smaller than I had imagined, with a puffed, cherubic face that clung determinedly to youth in spite of its lines and mottling. He attacked his audience with smiling directness, arms outstretched, and in a voice that seemed in shaky transit between ordinary speech and song.

"A lot of the songs mean something personal to Eddie," said Miss Leff. "This one for instance; it's about getting back to singing, where he belongs."

The audience seemed to catch this flavor and responded warmly to the opening number. Fisher acknowledged the reception by grinning boyishly, shuffling his feet, and staring at the ground. Then, after apologizing for being forty-five minutes late, he bounced into an old-fashioned, nasal rendition of *After You've Gone*. Again the parallel between art and life was pointed out to me by Miss Leff, and a lady in the dark behind me, as Fisher moaned the lyrics, ". . . you'll feel blue, you'll feel sad/You'll miss the bestest pal you ever had," murmured quite audibly, "You tell her, Eddie!"

At the end of each song, Miss Leff applauded vigorously and told me that this promised to be one of his best shows. I asked how long each show lasted and was answered that it was up to Eddie here at the Americana and that Eddie loved to sing. There was no way of telling. I reminded my hostess that I was to see Eddie between shows and hoped that he could be prevailed upon to remove himself from the stage long enough for us to get acquainted.

"Oh, don't worry," Miss Leff smiled. "There'll be time. And then there's going to be a party after the final show for all the Miss Universe contestants."

"The Miss Universe contestants?"

"It's some sort of publicity thing." She twinkled.

I sat back, while Eddie went on singing, and considered what it would be like in a hotel suite with *all* the Miss Universe ladies. I could visualize three or four of them confined in a single space, but the imagination balked at more than twenty. And then, anxiety ridden as I am, I fell into a fret over how late the young ladies could stay out and if any international curfew agreements had been drawn for visiting Miss Universes. I hoped that, tonight, Eddie would not feel like singing.

But on the stage, there was no diminishing of energy. Eddie was keeping the biographical analogy going with a bravado interpretation of *Wish You Were Here,* in which he altered the lyrics to read "Glad You Are There" at salient moments. The audience again assented to this declaration of male independence, and, interrupting her vigorous hand-clapping, I asked Miss Leff if this was the way Fisher really felt about Elizabeth now.

"Eddie's very open on the subject," she said suspiciously.

"He doesn't seem to mind singing about it."

"Oh, he even jokes about it in the show," she said.

If this logic was hard to follow, the jokes, such as they were, were not. One had Fisher telling his audience that he was tired that evening, not from performing, but from having to stand in line to see the picture. The audience snickered nervously. At another point between songs he announced that *they* finally had been married. A collective gasp turned into almost relieved chuckling when Fisher went on to congratulate Governor and Mrs. Nelson Rockefeller.

"Well," I said after this last piece of waggish byplay, "he seems in good spirits about the whole thing."

"What did you think of the jokes?" Miss Leff asked flatly.

"Well. . . ."

"They're not in the best of taste, are they?" she said, smiling. "But the audience likes them, so Eddie keeps them in."

"At a cost of great personal pain?"

We both laughed the cynical laugh of conspirators and I whispered an order for more drinks to cement our understanding. It was just then that something peculiar happened, at least I was assured that such occurrences were rare in Fisher's performing life. Having divested himself of coat and tie, Eddie was now strolling through the audience, embarrassing its spot-lighted members with snatches of songs addressed directly to them. At one table, however, sat an attractive lady who, to eschew euphemisms, was quite close to stone drunk. Eddie sang a few bars of *Let Me Entertain You* to her, and the baritone vibrato did its work a little too well. The woman giggled lasciviously and made a lunge at Mr. Fisher's private parts with her hand. With dexterity, and without missing a beat, Eddie eluded her and, chortling good-naturedly, made his way back to the bandstand. Those of the spectators that had witnessed the aphrodisiac results of being sung to by Fisher laughed, and, in happy ribaldry, applauded both him and the zestful lady. With this, the evening's first performance was over.

"Well," said Miss Leff as we rose, "that was something. It's *never* happened before. Oh, you get your kooks at every show, but nothing like that."

It seemed, as we headed for Fisher's suite, that Miss Leff's guard was back up, that our little conspiracy of sanity was over, and that she was once more committed to guarding Fisher from any unfavorable judg-ments. Well, so be it, I thought. My mind, stirred by the recent incident, was back upon the promised Miss Universes.

Standing in front of the suite's door when we arrived was a thin young man in a red sports jacket who was introduced to me simply as Eddie's brother. Eddie's brother looked disapprovingly at me and Miss Leff hastily explained my presence and we entered the rooms. There was activity everywhere: a woman sat at a desk where there were two phones and seemed to be on both of them at once; the comedian, Jack E. Leonard, was in one corner of the room gesturing frantically; a young girl sat staring silently from a chair while two men talked over her head; and, finally, another man pushed a portable bar around the room, stopping only on request. In the midst of this, quietly, Fisher appeared from his bedroom. He was wearing a bathrobe and seemed puzzled by my presence. There was a brief consultation between him and Miss Leff while I trotted alongside the traveling bar, and then it was decided that we should all go into the bedroom where talk would be easier.

It was really a dressing room: the mirror was covered with telegrams wishing him well in his engagement at the Americana (one, from Sophie

Tucker, referred to him as the Al Jolson of his generation), suits and luggage were strewn about the floor, and on the dressing table was a large key to the city of Boston.

"Just got that today," Fisher said, explaining the key. "I was up there on a benefit, that's why I was late for the show."

There was a self-deprecating smile accompanying the explanation; however, he fondled the key lovingly before setting it down and stretching out on the bed opposite me.

"So you want to do a story about me? What kind?"

It was a blunt question and I bluntly replied, "I don't know."

"Well, how long will it be?"

"Oh, at least five thousand words."

"Is that long?" he asked Miss Leff, and she nodded a vigorous assent.

He shrugged as if to indicate he deemed himself unworthy of such an effort, got up from the bed, and began to pace. His hands remained in the bathrobe's pockets and his eyes searched the floor sadly.

"Well, what's there to say? All I want to do now is sing, sing for the rest of my life. Nothing else."

I said I thought it laudable, but added that, after all, he had done other things in the past (he glanced up at this and over at Miss Leff) and would, I hastily continued, do other things in the future. I gathered quickly that Fisher's chronological preference was for things as yet unhappened.

"No," he repeated, "I just want to sing."

He certainly wasn't open in the way I had hoped, but I pushed on. "Well, we could talk about the way you feel while singing."

Here the lady of the two phones entered and announced Eddie was wanted on one of them. After he'd left, Miss Leff asked quickly what I thought of her client.

"He seems very dedicated," I said.

"He is. This comeback means a lot to him."

"But he's not going to sing twenty-four hours a day, is he?"

Suddenly there was a loud crash from outside, accompanied by a sharp, incoherent, angry voice. I looked at Miss Leff, who smiled with shaky nonchalance and stated that it must be Jack E. Leonard trying to get through the door. But at the second thump and jangle of glasses she looked concerned, rose, opened the door and peeked out. What she saw made her twitch quickly back into the room, the door snapping behind her.

"What was it?" I asked.

"Just a misunderstanding. Now about Eddie's dedication. . . ."

But my nascent reporter's instinct was aroused. Although I could see disapproval darkening the lady's face, I went to the door, opened it, and found, stretched upon the living-room floor, struggling with Eddie's brother and another man, the woman whose unbridled passion had enlivened the *Let Me Entertain You* number.

"You can't throw me out! I was *asked* up here!" she screamed and slithered out of reach of a bell captain who had joined in the efforts to shift her into an upright position.

"Close the door!" Eddie Fisher's brother snapped at me when he noticed I was taking in the social contretemps and that the unwanted lady was inching her way toward the bedroom, which was, presumably, her goal. I did so, and with the objective now impregnably defended, she began to cry, spicing tears with invective.

"I was invited up to this goddamned place, and no one's going to throw me out like some slut!"

"Come on, lady, you can do it the easy way or the hard way," said one of the men. "Eddie isn't even here now."

By this time, a hotel detective had appeared, and he and the bellman succeeded in exorcising the demon into the hall from where the last sound heard from her came:

"My shoe! I lost my effing shoe!"

Then—silence. The portable bar began its journey, Eddie's brother scowled at me, Jack E. Leonard began a story, the telephonic maiden called Chicago and Boston simultaneously—all returned to normal.

"Well, that's the first time something like *that* has ever happened," said Miss Leff when I returned to the bedroom. Obviously, we were both being spectators to a series of firsts in her client's life.

Eddie returned, still bathrobed, and carrying a bowl of chicken soup.

"It's all I'm allowed to eat before singing," he said sadly, but with the pride of one committed to rules beyond the ken of other mortals. He chose not to mention the little fracas that had taken place, and when I did, he replied that he'd been in another room, on the telephone, and had not heard a thing.

"Now," he began, still pacing and sipping at his soup, "what do you plan to write about?"

It seemed we were to start over again.

"I can't honestly answer that until I get to know you," I said.

"Get to know me? Why there must be a hundred Eddie Fishers."

Here he called in Eddie Fisher's brother and ordered more soup.

"Well, we'll take them one at a time," I said with restraint.

"What kind of questions do you want to ask?"

I was beginning to feel like a *Gauleiter* about to interrogate a member of the Polish resistance.

"Oh, anything," I said desperately. "How are things going for you now?"

"Never better," Eddie answered. For a few seconds he frowned and stumbled for words and then went on: "I think I really understand life now, really have some sort of control over it. I know what I want and what I can do to get it."

"And you want to sing," I said, hoping that this insight of mine would prove how well I understood him and that I could be trusted.

"Right! I just want to sing."

We could, I saw, remain at this impasse forever; the normal routes of conversation had to be deserted for questions at random. I asked first the most inoffensive I knew: "What movies have you seen recently that you've liked?"

"*La Dolce Vita* and *Spartacus*," was the reply.

Did he find *La Dolce Vita* particularly relevant to his life? A quick and definite "No" was the answer, along with an announcement that he now had to prepare for his next performance. We agreed to meet the next day, the time to be arranged by Miss Leff.

"What will we talk about tomorrow?" he asked as we were leaving.

"Oh, about anything you want. I don't have a camp schedule planned for you."

"I just want to sing. Really, I'm a happy saloon singer."

In the elevator going down, Miss Leff again prodded me for my opinion of Fisher.

"He seems quite pleasant," I said. "A little cautious when it comes to talking about himself, though."

"Well, Eddie's very open."

In the lobby Miss Leff said she would be leaving but that I could watch the second show if I wished. I said no, put her in a taxi, then caught one myself. I was nearly home before I remembered the Miss Universe girls. My first meeting with Eddie had really been numbing; I was too exhausted to care.

The next day Miss Leff called to say things had come up which she thought should be discussed with me. First, Eddie didn't think that the free time he had left would be enough for me to plumb so varied a person as himself for print. Second, he wanted the right to approve all quotes from him that I might use. And third, would I mind being flown to Las Vegas where Eddie would be appearing at the Desert Inn?

"Oh," she added, as I remained silent before these conditions, "Eddie liked you very much."

After that reward, I immediately accepted Miss Leff's proposal and then called my editor who agreed to my journey to Las Vegas, but demanded that the magazine pay the expenses and not the Fisher organization. This was to insure my freedom from any feeling of obligation to Eddie and his friends. All this seemed a little thick for nothing more than an interview with a popular singer who'd had a few matrimonial difficulties, but the trip to Las Vegas was enticing and I confess again to the foreign-correspondent thrill when, after picking up my ticket at Esquire's office, I heard my editor call out as I left: "Our man in Vegas is off!"

Well, their man in Vegas accomplished very little except for perhaps a record losing streak in blackjack. I arrived at the Desert Inn the day Fisher was supposed to open and put in a call to his rooms. The operator informed me that he was rehearsing, which seemed fair enough, and I spent the afternoon trying to earn the fealty of Fortuna at the card tables and watching what seemed to be a legion of grandmothers attacking slot machines with lunatic frenzy, some actually wearing a glove on their right or pulling hand to avoid blisters. For a time, I completely forgot Fisher and his "openness" but it came back to me when, at about five in the evening, I looked up from the impossible three-card mess I had helped myself to in a blackjack game and saw that Eddie Fisher's brother was playing next to me. I reintroduced myself, he blinked in recognition, and then told me that Eddie would be too busy to see me that night and perhaps I could get him tomorrow afternoon.

"I'd like to see what the opening-night show is like here," I said.

"Well, call Bob Abrahms, then," said Eddie's brother, shuffling away from the table with a fistful of silver dollars that he'd just won.

I did call. In New York Miss Leff had also given me this name as one to ring if anything needed expediting. The expediter, however, seemed to know nothing of my mission, said he would look into the matter, and told me Eddie's evening performance was all sold out. Feeling a little like Joseph K., I went testily and tiredly to bed.

The next morning, Art Kane, the photographer who was to capture Fisher's special qualities on film, arrived, and we spent an indolent few hours by the pool waiting for two o'clock, the hour when the Fisher organization begins to stir officially. He, too, felt something was amiss, for Abrahms had also been somewhat noncommittal with him on the phone that morning. Stretched out beneath a 110° sun, we tried to guess what had happened, and then let the matter dissolve in the dry Nevada heat.

At about four, however, after two unsuccessful tries to reach Fisher, the puzzle was solved. I received a phone call from Fisher's agent or press representative (I never could decipher exactly what the functions were of the people who surrounded him) in Los Angeles, who, after assuring me that *he* wanted the story, admitted that Eddie was skeptical.

"Of what?" I asked.

"Well, he's heard from a very high source that Esquire plans a series of articles called The Losers, and that it's going to be about him, Sybil Burton, and the New York Mets."

I told him that I knew nothing about this, and that, as I was writing the article, I could assure him it wasn't so.

"Oh, I trust you, so does Eddie. But can we trust the magazine."

I vouched for Esquire's honor and, in twenty minutes, I received a phone call from Bob Abrahms. Eddie would see me that evening between shows and then something further could be arranged if all went well.

That night, Mr. Abrahms, until then only a fractious, disembodied voice in my life, appeared in person. He was a large, pleasant-looking man dressed in a red sports jacket not different from the one Eddie's brother had been wearing when I first met him. He had met Fisher in the Army, where he had been a sergeant in charge of the singer's basic-training company. With him were two young ladies introduced solely as being from Los Angeles.

"You see," Abrahms began in a semi-apologetic voice, "Eddie right now is rather—well, he's rather. . . ."

"Open?" I volunteered.

"Right. If we could only have some idea what you're going to write about."

Here we were again on the logical circle. What I wrote about depended on the necessary condition of my seeing him. However, on oath, I swore there was no *a priori* notion in my mind about losers.

We were sitting in the hotel's casino bar, and every now and then one of the Los Angeleans had the desire to try the slot machine. Abrahms would give her twenty dollars or so, which she disappeared with and promptly lost in the, to me, unbelievably short time of three or four minutes. Abrahms did not appear to notice, and the girls' entertainment fund appeared inexhaustible.

"Well, okay," he said, "you can talk it over with Eddie tonight. Did you lose again, honey?"

"I came close this time." The girl smiled. "I got two lemons."

"That's the story of your life," her companion said, herself rising with a fresh supply of funds to test her fortune.

In a cottage behind the hotel, which was used for a dressing room, Eddie, again in a bathrobe and again drinking chicken soup, greeted me accompanied by his doctor from Hollywood who had flown to Las Vegas to help meet a minor crisis of laryngitis.

"Now about this story," Eddie whispered, "there's one thing. There's an area in the past that I just don't want to go into. I don't want to forget anything, you understand. I'm not trying to run away. It's just that I don't want to talk about it."

I answered that I understood and that we could talk about other things.

"What other things?"

Wearily now, I replied that this was up to him. I just wanted to know what Eddie Fisher was like so that I'd have *something* to write.

"There are a hundred Eddie Fishers." The gamin smile again, and the shy shuffling of feet.

"I'll settle for one."

Eddie, at the urging of his doctor, spoke no more. We were to meet at two o'clock the following afternoon. It was the last time I was to see him. As I left, fresh chicken soup was being ordered.

The next morning my editor woke me with a phone call from New York.

"What's going on out there?" he asked. "We've just been talking to Fisher and he's got some notion about a story called The Losers."

I answered that I thought everything was all right.

"No, it's not. But you stick with him. If he won't answer the phone, send him a telegram. If he doesn't answer that, bribe a bellboy to get into his room. Okay?"

"Okay," I said lamely, knowing that I could never go even so far as the telegram.

The rest of the day, Art Kane and I took turns calling Fisher's suite at thirty-minute intervals. It was no use. The openness had closed forever, and late that night, as Art was preparing to leave, we met Abrahms, who told me that Eddie hadn't made up his mind about the story, but would definitely call the next day with an answer. Art could not stay, and he and his cameras left in the morning. I did stay and received no phone call except from my editor urging me to raise the bellboy's bribe.

A good gambler knows when to quit, and I had had enough both of Eddie Fisher and the blackjack tables. That night I took a plane out of Las Vegas for New York. Later I found out, by reading a gossip column, that Fisher was again having problems with women, this time with a German model he had stolen from his best friend. But I knew nothing of this, and, as I looked down on the Las Vegas lights in the desert, I could only speculate what the hundred or so Eddie Fishers were really like.

[December, 1963]

Mr. Kenneth, They Love You

by Martin Mayer

Kenneth Battelle, known to his business associates, clientele and several million American females as "Mr. Kenneth," is a boy from Syracuse not yet forty but already at the top of his trade. As chief hairdresser and supervisor of the beauty salon at the ladies' retooling emporium of Mme. Lilly Daché, he commands a fee of $15 for a haircut and "styling"—which means that after he finishes cutting he will instruct an assistant in exactly what he wants done with what remains. Anyone who calls him out of town to cut and set her hair will pay a thousand dollars for his day, and his fee for a demonstration-lecture to fellow hairdressers is $1,500. Few of his clients, however, feel that they have received anything less than value for money; indeed, before his reputation became so large as it is today, many of them tried to give him a tip on top of the price—and were brushed aside, for Mr. Kenneth does not accept tips. "Remember," says Lillian Ross of *The New Yorker,* who first came to his chair to scoff as a Talk-of-the-Town reporter and stayed to become a weekly customer, "you are dealing here with an artist. An artist with a scissors."

350

Apart from the scissors, which he wields left-handed, Mr. Kenneth is an artist in his own appearance. He is a slight man of medium height who holds himself almost stiffly erect. His suits are beautifully tailored to his posture, the jacket sloping from prominent shoulder blades to a distinct waist accented by pockets cut on the diagonal, the well-pressed trousers, never a wrinkle, narrowing to bottoms without cuffs (a hairdresser whose trousers had cuffs would always be cleaning hair out of them). A vest of the same material, perhaps ornamented by brass or jeweled buttons, peeps out from between the narrow lapels of the jacket; and from the vest, triumphantly transfixed by a jeweled stickpin, a rather wide tie rises to a Windsor knot. A silk handkerchief billows slightly from the breast pocket of the jacket. Above it all, balanced, it seems, just a little precariously, is a round head somewhat too large for the dimensions of the body, a round, symmetrical, handsome face, and carefully combed thinning brown hair, always just short of requiring a cut. The smile is boyish and casual, yet cool and always the same.

But artifice stops, rather short, with the static composition of the lady's hair and the hairdresser's body. Neither in manner nor in approach to the job is there anything arty about Mr. Kenneth. "Most people," he says in a soft voice, speaking in the deliberate rhythm that marks all his activities, "think this is a frothy business. I don't. I think it's a service business. People come to Kenneth—this isn't, I hope, as vain as it sounds—people come to Kenneth because they think Kenneth can do something for them. But sometimes, right after I've cut their hair, when it's just lying there wet, they'll say, 'It looks better already.' This business is in part illusion. You have to feel what people expect you to be, and then be it."

Most customers come to Mr. Kenneth for the soft, voluminous, very feminine hairstyle associated with his name and with that of a Great Lady who must not be mentioned. In fact, however, he does all sorts of cutting and styling, suiting his work to the hair, the face, the lady's expressed desires. He feels that everybody likes "something different" (he changes the décor of his own apartment several times a year), and he always knows another way to solve the old problem. He rather enjoys a little chit-chat with the girls—secretaries and suburban housewives, as well as regular customers from the *haut monde* and demimonde—but he believes and wants to believe that the strength of his position rests on the quality of the work he does. Even on a day when he has cut thirty or forty heads of hair, working until nine at night though the salon has officially closed at six, he cares how each of his customers looks when she says her hair was cut by Mr. Kenneth. First of all, he is a craftsman, and when he comes to work in the morning he looks forward, almost cheerfully, to a day's exercise of his craft.

On Thursdays the salon opens at ten, but out-of-towners and new customers often come in early, the long and the short and the tall wandering through the storefront boutique of Madame Daché's narrow, nine-story home-and-business building on 56th Street between Madison and Park Avenues. The salesladies ignore these anxiously premature patrons; the senior of the group, a vigorous dumpy Italian lady with grey hair, is speaking nervously on the telephone: ". . . *piu non posso. Okayokay? Okay. Ciao ciao.*" In the windowless room directly behind the boutique stands the long curved desk which is Forward Command Post for the salon; here a staff of three or four soberly efficient ladies answers the telephone, keeps track of who is coming in when for which hairdresser, prepares the bills and collects the money. On Thursdays and Fridays, with the social affairs of the weekend just over the horizon, ladies have "standing appointments" with their special hairdressers and enter every week at the same hour by ritual. As a matter of policy, Mr. Kenneth tries to take everybody who walks through the door, whether or not she has an appointment, but on Thursday a girl at the desk may have to tell a newcomer that none of the hairdressers is free until noon. "Bonwit's is open," the girl says cheerily, "or Bloomingdale's. . . ."

Mr. Kenneth arrives on the hour and takes a quick look at his own appointment list, for curiosity's sake. Then he walks up the carpeted stairway, which rises with a not-quite-clean French elegance to the main salon on the second floor. At the head of the stairs is a rather splendid circular room, mirrors around the wall reflecting not only the hairdressers' chairs before them but also all the other mirrors and chairs, so a customer can see who else is here and be seen by those whose attention she may crave. Two more hairdressers' chairs, with their associated sinks, face a freestanding mirror inside the circle near the rear, giving a touch of theatre and increasing the apparent size of an already large room. The colors are pink and white.

Mr. Kenneth passes by the main salon without a look—he may not enter it all day, though he usually makes a visit or two. (He usually does *not* look in on the third floor, where the more esoteric beauty operations, from hair dyeing to waxes that remove hair to assorted massages, are carried on. Mr. Kenneth turns away to the rear, to a rectangular room about the size of a normal bedroom, which has been cut up by grey transoms to make five partially enclosed working areas, each with chair, sink and mirror. A customer is already in one of the chairs, head tilted back, neck resting on the contoured edge of the black sink, long blonde hair soaking in the sink. Like every Daché customer, she wears a pink cotton wrap, usually in lieu of her street clothes, which are hanging downstairs. Mr. Kenneth ignores her, and turns into the "dispensary" area to the left, where maids work at kitchen sinks. In the windowless dispensary room, he hangs his coat on a tree. This room, lined with bottles in boxes like a section of a supermarket, is Mr. Kenneth's only hope for privacy; here he can retire, very occasionally, to smoke a cigarette and to sit perched on a white kitchen ladder. One of the girls has, by custom, brought Mr. Kenneth something for breakfast—a bacon-and-egg sandwich wrapped in aluminum foil to keep it warm. He eats half the sandwich, rewraps the rest, drinks a cup of coffee, looking out on the still quiet hallway between his room and the big salon. "It's a long day; nobody wants to start it."

Another customer is already in process of shampoo; Mr. Kenneth glances out, picks up comb and scissors, and approaches his first of the day, who is now sitting up, a pink towel falling with her hair behind the back of the chair. She is a newcomer, but Mr. Kenneth knows her name from the appointment sheet, greets her by it, and removes the towel.

"My problem," the lady says with a commendable and almost successful effort at composure, "is baby-fine hair as you can see."

"Uh-huh." Methodically, stroke by stroke, in an andante rhythm formed of almost square gestures, Mr. Kenneth combs out the lady's hair.

"I'm from Baltimore. Usually I wear a bubble."

With ritual motions, Mr. Kenneth combs up all the hair that starts above a line at the base of the scalp, and pins it to the top of the head. "You wear a bubble because it's fine, you want to make it more voluminous?"

Slowly, twenty or thirty strands at a time, Mr. Kenneth combs the back hair straight down, shifts the scissors to his left hand, and cuts a straight line. "When it's fine . . . you have to cut it bluntly . . . all these things. . . . It's easier short . . . but like all things . . . you get tired of it. . . ." The back finished, he loosens some hair from the top and repeats the ritual, working first on the rear, then on the right side, then on the left. "How's the hairdressing in Baltimore?"

"How *is* it?" The lady pauses. "We have a couple of good places, not like here, of course."

"Uh-huh." Mr. Kenneth works very seriously, his mouth formed into a slight pout, giving equal attention to each strand of hair. Behind him, one of his assistants, a rather small young man with staring grey-green eyes (all Mr. Kenneth's assistants are smaller than he is), watches with emotions that are not to be fathomed by an outsider.

"Do you approve of permanents with this sort of baby-fine, chewed-up dyed hair?"

"I don't think your hair's so bad."

Ladies are now arriving to meet appointments for which Mr. Kenneth is already late—his calendar is as trustworthy as an airline timetable in a foggy winter. The second customer has finished shampoo (Mr. Kenneth works with clean, wet hair), and is seated in the chair in the next area. In a gesture of solicitude, he steps to her side and pumps the chair somewhat higher, then returns to his first.

"Now," he says, "you're going to comb it this way," and he runs his hand over her head from right to left.

"I always comb it the other way. Is that because that's the way my mother did it?"

"When you go that way, it lies flatly—nature of the hair, the way the hair grows. Comb it this way, you get more lift. I believe lift is very important."

She waves her hand over her hair. "Feels so strange."

"Oh, you'll get used to it," Mr. Kenneth says, and summons to his side a very pretty young Swedish girl in a black dress. They both stand behind the lady, and Mr. Kenneth pushes her hair. "Now, she has very fine hair," Mr. Kenneth says to the Swedish girl, "and I don't want it to look fuzzy. Get it very high here. I don't want any of it clinging. And if you'll do me a very large favor, before you spray it, bring her back to me, let me see it, if I want to change it. . . ." The Swedish girl leads the lady away and Mr. Kenneth moves on to a regular customer, a lady in her thirties with light freckles and pale blue eyes, not in the least nervous. She greets him with, "How was your trip?"

"Around the world? Very wild. All those airplanes. Waiting to get into the palaces."

Mr. Kenneth methodically, again, cuts hair, pinning up, taking a few hairs at a time, getting the line straight. Another of the young men comes by, and Mr. Kenneth speaks to him:

"Did you get to the theatre on time?"

"Yes, just barely. I showed her one of your hairdos—the one in *Glamour*."

"With the hair coming into the eye?" says Mr. Kenneth. "The funny picture?"

"Yes. She thought you'd be insulted because she laughed."

"Funny, that's the way she wears her hair. Remarkable that she can't see it. . . ."

Yet another, an older woman; then a striking lady who could be either a model or a society belle, and turns out to be both. With semi-proprietary boldness, she interrupts Mr. Kenneth: "If you *do* have time, I've got to pose for a couple of things—you wouldn't be very impressed, it's not your sort of thing."

"What is it? Sears' catalogue?"

"Oh, no—I'm cochairman of this committee, and I have to pose with my cochairman. Fifteen Kodas."

"Oh, dear."

"I said it wasn't your sort of thing."

Miss Daché herself, red-haired, short, not slim, important, comes down with a transparently thin model to be togged out with Cleopatra jewelry for a newspaper fashion page. "Can you do her?"

"I don't think so."

"Miss Preston herself is coming for the picture."

"It looks like a major undertaking."

The model, who has been examining her straight black hair and everything else about herself in a mirror in the next booth, says to Mr. Kenneth, "Did you say it looks mangy?"

Mr. Kenneth pauses to survey a just-released lock of hair from the head of his older customer; then, under control, replies, "No, I didn't say that. I didn't say that at all. I said, 'a major undertaking.' Setting. We don't have time for that."

Miss Daché wheedles. "Miss Preston herself."

"Do it in hats," says Mr. Kenneth. "I'd rather not do it at all than do it and have it not look right."

"Of course," says Miss Daché coldly.

"Do it in two different hats," says Mr. Kenneth brightly, ruffling the hair of the customer to examine its appearance with somewhat more body. Miss Daché and the model disappear.

". . . My husband *adored* the way you did my hair last time, it was *such* a success."

"That's good news. . . ."

"What are they doing in Paris?"

"I don't know—yes, I do. The Cleopatra thing."

"I don't know how Cleopatra wore her hair."

"Neither do I. Oh, no, I do. Long hair. Ella Cinders. . . ."

". . . In Nassau, the most *divine* place. Most marvelous golf course in the world. Most wonderful tennis. This man from Chicago bought it all up, he sells lots around it, very beautiful, very expensive. What are *you* going to do in Barbados?"

Mr. Kenneth says, wearily, "I'm going to try skin diving."

A model parades into Mr. Kenneth's area, wearing something the management of the boutique would like to sell to some customer of the salon. Mr. Kenneth greets her, and she turns to him a face of blonde impassivity. "A mute," he explains. "She can't talk."

". . . I just got back from Las Vegas," says a lady from East Orange. "All the chorus girls have long hair."

"I don't think fashion is going to be made," says Mr. Kenneth, "by what the chorus girls are wearing in Las Vegas. . . ."

Theatrical types arrive and chatter: "Terrible about Ernie. . . . No dough left at all. . . . They were such terrible gamblers. . . ."

". . . Marilyn's in town, you know."

"Yes, she was here. . . ."

"What made you come in?" says Mr. Kenneth to another suburban customer. "I'm always curious."

"Actually, it was magazine articles. . . ."

The manicurists are working on hands; the maids are sweeping; assistants, with all chairs occupied in the big room, are setting hair in Mr. Kenneth's booths, wrapping carefully combed strands around big wire-mesh rollers. He is now with a regular customer, a young lady of very considerable means and position, intelligent, eternally nervous.

"Now that we've straightened it, we'll have to curl it."

"That's what my sister does—she has a permanent and dyed and cut."

"Oh, my God—amazing she has any hair left."

"It always looks good."

"*She* must have a good hairdresser."

"Are people ever going to wear their hair in page-boy again? Nobody does today."

"I think that's fairly fortunate."

"Do you really think lemon juice works if you squeeze it on your hair and sit in the sun?"

"It sounds pretty drastic. Ought to do something."

"You're sure you're not getting it too short?"

"No, no. Yes, by your standards. No, by mine."

"Some people look so good with very long hair."

"Who?"

"All those people out in the big room."

"They're all seventeen."

"I have a friend who isn't seventeen—she's twenty-nine, and it looks marvelously."

"If you say so. No, really, I'm sure it does."

The store model returns in another outfit, escorted by a saleslady. Relenting, the model says, "Good morning, Kenneth."

"See," he comments, "she *does* talk."

"I put a dime in her," says the saleslady, and steers her out into the big room.

Escorted by the Swedish girl, the first customer returns, her hair now a great golden aura about what turn out to be excellent features. Mr. Kenneth combs out and sprays her hair himself, and the odor of the spray fills the room. "Cancer in a bottle," comments another customer. The lady from Baltimore looks at herself in the mirror with honest and surprised admiration. She says, "I wish I had a picture of this."

Mr. Kenneth says, "Oh, it looks *good*."

"You don't have a picture of this, or a name?"

"I don't have names for haircombs."

"Because once I get home. . . ."

"Haircombs just happen. . . ."

"For you."

"Gregory, tell Mona to come look how it's changed, will you?"

The customer says, "Well, I certainly thank you," and rises from the chair.

"Come again, when you're in New York," says Mr. Kenneth.

The nervous regular, now sitting and waiting for the man who will set her hair, has been studying the mirror. "Mr. Kenneth, may I ask you a question?"

"Yes."

"What about a bang?"

"No."

Out in the big salon, the ladies are chatting, examining themselves and their neighbors, nibbling on sandwiches catered by Robert Day-Dean's, reading books they have brought themselves or magazines from the catholic selection in the racks—*Publishers Weekly, The Atlantic* and the Italian *Epoca,* for example, as well as the usual ladies' and movie magazines. For them the time is passing, quickly or slowly or as usual depending upon individual temperament. For the people who work in the salon, however, each minute is another nibble in the hide of the great enemy, The Day, which here, as in a factory or in Arnold Wesker's kitchen, must be lived through and discarded, taking with it some piece of oneself. The great break in occupations does not in truth come between blue collar and white collar, but between those jobs which provide their own time focus and those which trap the worker in the patterned hell of the clockface.

For the worker in a beauty salon, the irritant routine of The Day, with its predictable cycle of crisis and relaxation, is heightened by the unpredictable piecework character of the pay. A hairdresser will receive a basic salary of, say, $100 a week plus (at Daché) a commission of twenty-five percent on everything over $200 spent by customers for his services during the course of the week. In addition to this payment from the boss, the hairdresser receives tips, which may vary anywhere from fifty cents to five dollars per customer, though the extremes are rare. The appointment calendar may or may not be full, but it is calibrated in half hours, each tense with the conflict between output and tip.

Much of Mr. Kenneth's manner of work is an escape from The Day, which he knows and hates. Taken into the Navy after a year at Syracuse University, he returned home as the eldest child of a divorced mother, with four younger sisters to see through adolescence; and he worked four years as a clock-bedeviled hairdresser ("fifteen hours a day," he recalls, probably with some exaggeration, "six days a week") "until my sisters were, like, eighteen or twenty." Then he went to Miami to try his luck and hated it. Nine months later he was in New York, working at Helena Rubinstein's.

"I was bottom man on the totem pole," Mr. Kenneth says, "so I got all the discount customers—former employees of Rubinstein, fashion people, assistant beauty editors. Nobody else wanted them, because the commissions were lower. They would ask me to work magazine and newspaper stories, setting hair for photographers, and nobody else wanted that because there were no tips. But you become a better hairdresser. You get the chance to invent things, then you come back here and bring them down for street wear, so to speak. And when I moved here, after five years at Rubinstein, I found myself with a fantastic clientele, this strangely powerful group of customers. The assistant beauty editors had become the beauty editors."

During the years at Rubinstein's, Mr. Kenneth also got in the habit of volunteering to come to the houses of certain cherished customers and brush their hair just before a major social function. He does it still, once or twice a week, and makes no charge for the service: "Then I never *have* to do it." Like everyone else who has done well in the world, he believes others should follow his tactics, and he urges his juniors to undertake newspaper and magazine dates, and to visit customers' homes. "But I suppose," he says, "they have more private life than I do."

To a degree, Mr. Kenneth has beaten The Day by making it all part of his private life. He is free of the appointment calendar; he works on each customer as long as he, of his own free will, wishes to work. Very prominent people indeed can wait while he cuts a secretary's hair; though his income is now something more than $50,000 a year, he recalls very well how much money $15 was when you had to work for it by The Day. At the same time, he enjoys his ability to float on the levels to which his talents have taken him, the ability to make jokes with, literally, any woman in the world.

It is all a private matter: celebrity in itself means little to Mr. Kenneth, except as a source of business. Not long ago a rather formidable greyhaired lady marched up to him while he was working and called "Kenneth!" in a voice that made him jump. "Kenneth, why don't you ever visit your old high school. All our other famous graduates come back. Gordon MacRae comes back. Why don't you?"

"Then I remembered she was my old history teacher," Mr. Kenneth says. "I asked her if she wanted her hair done, but she said, no, she just wanted to be sure I would visit the old high school, like the other famous graduates. Like Gordon MacRae. I thought what a funny idea she had of fame."

This Thursday is a winter's day, at the season when many of the women who gladly put down $15 for a haircut (plus $6.50 for a shampoo and set) are off in warmer climates; and as the afternoon wears on, the crush in Mr. Kenneth's quarters diminishes. A look at the calendar shows only eighteen appointments for the day. Even so, everybody waits.

"Go to René," says an English lady to a customer announced as on her way to London and seeking a local hairdresser. "He'll keep you waiting, but not *quite* so long as Kenneth."

"Oh," says Mr. Kenneth. "Do you go to René?"

The English lady, small, black-haired, middle-aged, will talk only about the weather. She is en route home from a month in Jamaica, and she does not josh with hairdressers. She is amused by the experience of a cut by Mr. Kenneth, who carefully refrains from telling her of any of the other English customers he has had that week. After she has gone to the big room, however, one of the American regulars asks about a titled customer then being lavishly entertained in New York.

"Goodness, yes," says Mr. Kenneth. "I've never heard of anybody who is having so many parties, breakfasts, lunches, teas, dinners, balls, given in her honor. It's almost like being the Duchess of Windsor. I had a customer yesterday who said that if she were asked to one more party for Lady B . . ." Mr. Kenneth pauses to examine a lock of hair, and the customer finishes his sentence for him: "she'd go." Kenneth smiles, and says, "Yes, I suppose she would."

". . . I had lunch in the Modern Museum. Have you ever done that?"

"Yes," says Mr. Kenneth. "And I think it's awful."

"Did you see the Chagall windows?"

"Yes."

"I picked up a Chagall seven years ago at Parke-Bernet."

"Now, don't tell me how much you paid for it and how much it's worth today. I can't *stand* that."

"Did you see the Rembrandt at the Met? The one they paid the two million dollars for?"

"Yes, and I didn't like it much. I wish they'd bought the Fragonard, the one that went to Washington."

"We ought to have you on the Fine Arts Commission, Kenneth."

"I don't want to get on the Fine Arts Commission. I've got my own Fine Arts Commission, right here—all you lovely ladies. No, really. When I go home every night, I write five hundred times, 'I should be grateful to spend my days the way I do.' I write it five hundred times, every day."

"The difficult thing with those sales," the lady says thoughtfully, "is that your insurance goes up."

"Not too many people have that problem," says Mr. Kenneth, and turns to an assistant. "William, while you're waiting, give it a turn here. Quite straight *here,* quite straight. . . ."

There is a handsome lady from South America, a newcomer, in New York from Caracas for two weeks. "Your name . . . is Kenneth

. . . I hear . . . a lot . . . about you. The best newspaper . . . in Colombia . . . *El Tiempo* . . . they say . . . a lot . . . about you. Very good things."

"Uh-huh," says Mr. Kenneth.

"Have you . . . been . . . in South America . . . sometimes?"

"No, but I know about that paper."

"You know . . . in the Caribbean . . . it is very hard . . . for good combs. . . ."

There is a very long-haired girl with a round face, in her twenties, somebody's secretary, as Mr. Kenneth quickly ascertains.

"Everybody thinks my hair is bad."

"Do you think so?" Mr. Kenneth asks.

"I wouldn't have worn it that way so long if I'd thought it was *that* bad."

The pinning is quickly finished, and the girl says, almost in terror, "You *are* going to cut it?"

"Yep."

The first snips produce foot lengths of varicolored hair on the floor. "All I know," says the girl miserably, "is that you're cutting it. . . . What's *he* doing, taking notes?"

"He's working on a book on dandruff, and he's very disappointed, none of our customers has dandruff."

But to his assistant, later, Mr. Kenneth makes a point of saying, "I like her hair; she has pretty hair," and the girl goes off cheerful for the rest of her ordeal, which includes dyeing.

There is the older lady, who hasn't been in for several weeks. "If you cut it too short, they'll say, 'Who gave you that lousy hairdo?' "

"Tell them, 'I got it at Macy's.' "

"Did you fire Michael, Kenneth, or did he quit?"

"What did they tell you?"

"They told me he was on an extended vacation for his health."

Mr. Kenneth laughs. "You make up your own mind."

And someone elegant comes in to kill a few minutes in a shopping day and have a cup of coffee with a friend who's in the chair. "Kenneth, I want to tell you I've had *more* compliments."

"And what a hard time you gave me. Now, you come back once a month," Mr. Kenneth says, and makes a clipping gesture.

"I will. Once a month. And anything you want to do, Kenneth. Anything. All the way."

"You always manage to make me blush," says Mr. Kenneth calmly. "Nobody else can do that."

Liquid is rolling off her friend's specially shampooed hair. "You're dripping all over the place?" Mr. Kenneth says in a kindly way. "No charge." It is the last appointment of the day.

At only a few minutes after six on this easy Thursday, Mr. Kenneth in the same andante puts on coat and gloves, and the silk scarf with a wool lining, and walks down the stairs. He talks over the day briefly with the indispensably businesslike lady who runs the desk—for Mr. Kenneth is the general manager of the salon as well as its chief hairdresser, and he is supposed to know the *Gestalt* while he cuts the hair; he used to have to read figures every night, but now he just takes them home every weekend. Mr. Kenneth gives a final, squared-off wave and a final boyish smile, and is off. Upstairs, his assistants, tied to the clock, are finishing The Day.

[July, 1962]

The Loser

by Gay Talese

At the foot of a mountain in upstate New York, about sixty miles from Manhattan, there is an abandoned country clubhouse with a dusty dance floor, upturned barstools, and an untuned piano; and the only sounds heard around the place at night come from the big white house behind it—the clanging sounds of garbage cans being toppled by raccoons, skunks, and stray cats making their nocturnal raids down from the mountain.

The white house seems deserted, too; but occasionally, when the animals become too clamorous, a light will flash on, a window will open, and a Coke bottle will come flying through the darkness and smash against the cans. But mostly the animals are undisturbed until daybreak, when the rear door of the white house swings open and a broad-shouldered Negro appears in grey sweat clothes with a white towel around his neck.

He runs down the steps, quickly passes the garbage cans and proceeds at a trot down the dirt road beyond the country club toward the highway. Sometimes he stops along the road and throws a flurry of punches at imaginary foes, each jab punctuated by hard gasps of his breathing—

"*hegh-hegh-hegh*"—and then, reaching the highway, he turns and soon disappears up the mountain.

At this time of morning farm trucks are on the road, and the drivers wave at the runner. And later in the morning other motorists see him, and a few stop suddenly at the curb and ask:

"Say, aren't *you* Floyd Patterson?"

"No," says Floyd Patterson. "I'm his brother, Raymond."

The motorists move on, but recently a man on foot, a disheveled man who seemed to have spent the night outdoors, staggered behind the runner along the road and yelled, "Hey, Floyd Patterson!"

"No, I'm his brother, Raymond."

"Don't tell *me* you're not Floyd Patterson. I know what Floyd Patterson looks like."

"Okay," Patterson said, shrugging, "if you want me to be Floyd Patterson, I'll be Floyd Patterson."

"So let me have your autograph," said the man, handing him a rumpled piece of paper and a pencil.

He signed it—"Raymond Patterson."

One hour later Floyd Patterson was jogging his way back down the dirt path toward the white house, the towel over his head absorbing the sweat from his brow. He lives alone in a two-room apartment in the rear of the house, and has remained there in almost complete seclusion since getting knocked out a second time by Sonny Liston.

In the smaller room is a large bed he makes up himself, several record albums he rarely plays, a telephone that seldom rings. The larger room has a kitchen on one side and, on the other, adjacent to a sofa, is a fireplace from which are hung boxing trunks and T-shirts to dry, and a photograph of him when he was the champion, and also a television set. The set is usually on except when Patterson is sleeping, or when he is sparring across the road inside the clubhouse (the ring is rigged over what was once the dance floor), or when, in a rare moment of painful honesty, he reveals to a visitor what it is like to be the loser.

"Oh, I would give up anything to just be able to work with Liston, to box with him somewhere where nobody would see us, and to see if I could get past three minutes with him," Patterson was saying, wiping his face with the towel, pacing slowly around the room near the sofa. "I *know* I can do better. . . . Oh, I'm not talking about a rematch. Who would pay a nickel for another Patterson-Liston fight? I know *I* wouldn't. . . . But all I want to do is get past the first round."

Then he said, "You have no idea how it is in the first round. You're out there with all those people around you, and those cameras, and the whole world looking in, and all that movement, that excitement, and *The Star-Spangled Banner,* and the whole nation hoping you'll win, including the President. And do you know what all this does? It blinds you, just blinds you. And then the bell rings, and you go at Liston and he's coming at you, and you're not even aware that there's a referee in the ring with you.

". . . Then you can't remember much of the rest, because you don't want to. . . . All you recall is, all of a sudden you're getting up, and the referee is saying, 'You all right?' and you say, 'Of *course* I'm all right,' and he says, 'What's your name?' and you say, 'Patterson.'

"And then, suddenly, with all this screaming around you, you're down again, and you know you have to get up, but you're extremely groggy, and the referee is pushing you back, and your trainer is in there with a towel, and people are all standing up, and your eyes focus directly at no one person—you're sort of floating.

"It is not a *bad* feeling when you're knocked out," he said. "It's a *good* feeling, actually. It's not painful, just a sharp grogginess. You don't see angels or stars; you're on a pleasant cloud. After Liston hit me in Nevada, I felt, for about four or five seconds, that everybody in the arena was actually in the ring with me, circled around me like a family, and you feel warmth toward all the people in the arena after you're knocked out. You feel lovable to all the people. And you want to reach out and kiss everybody—men and women—and after the Liston fight somebody told me I actually blew a kiss to the crowd from the ring. I don't remember that. But I guess it's true because that's the way you feel during the four or five seconds after a knockout. . . .

"But then," Patterson went on, still pacing, "this good feeling leaves you. You realize where you are, and what you're doing there, and what has just happened to you. And what follows is a hurt, a confused hurt—not a physical hurt—it's a hurt combined with anger; it's a what-will-people-think hurt; it's an ashamed-of-my-own-ability hurt . . . and all you want then is a hatch door in the middle of the ring—a hatch door that will open and let you fall through and land in your dressing room instead of having to get out of the ring and face those people. The worst thing about losing is having to walk out of the ring and face those people. . . ."

Then Patterson walked over to the stove and put on the kettle for tea. He remained silent for a few moments. Through the walls could be heard the footsteps and voices of the sparring partners and the trainer who live in the front of the house. Soon they would be in the clubhouse getting things ready should Patterson wish to spar. In two days he was scheduled to fly to Stockholm and fight an Italian named Amonti, Patterson's first appearance in the ring since the last Liston fight.

Next he hoped to get a fight in London against Henry Cooper. Then, if his confidence was restored, his reflexes reacting, Patterson hoped to start back up the ladder in this country, fighting all the leading contenders, fighting often, and not waiting so long between each fight as he had done when he was a champion in the ninety-percent tax bracket.

His wife, whom he finds little time to see, and most of his friends think he should quit. They point out that he does not need the money. Even he admits that, from investments alone on his $8,000,000 gross earnings, he should have an annual income of about $35,000 for the next twenty-five years. But Patterson, who is only twenty-nine years old and barely scratched, cannot believe that he is finished. He cannot help but think that it was something more than Liston that destroyed him—a strange, psychological force was also involved, and unless he can fully understand what it was, and learn to deal with it in the boxing ring, he may never be able to live peacefully anywhere but under this mountain. Nor will he ever be able to discard the false whiskers and moustache that, ever since Johansson beat him in 1959, he has carried with him in a small attaché case into each fight so he can slip out of the stadium unrecognized should he lose.

"I often wonder what other fighters feel, and what goes through their minds when they lose," Patterson said, placing the cups of tea on the table. "I've wanted so much to talk to another fighter about all this, to compare thoughts, to see if he feels some of the same things I've felt. But who can you talk to? Most fighters don't talk much anyway. And I can't even look another fighter in the eye at a weigh-in, for some reason.

"At the Liston weigh-in, the sportswriters noticed this, and said it showed I was afraid. But that's not it. I can never look *any* fighter in the eye because . . . well, because we're going to fight, which isn't a nice thing, and because . . . well, once I actually did look a fighter in the eye. It was a long, long time ago. I must have been in the amateurs then. And when I looked at this fighter, I saw he had such a nice face . . . and then he looked at *me* . . . and *smiled* at me . . . and *I* smiled back! It was strange, very strange. When a guy can look at another guy and smile like that, I don't think they have any business fighting.

"I don't remember what happened in that fight, and I don't remember what the guy's name was. I only remember that, ever since, I have never looked another fighter in the eye."

The telephone rang in the bedroom. Patterson got up to answer it. It was his wife, Sandra. So he excused himself, shutting the bedroom door behind him.

Sandra Patterson and their four children live in a $100,000 home in an upper-middle-class white neighborhood in Scarsdale, New York. Floyd Patterson feels uncomfortable in this home surrounded by a manicured lawn and stuffed with furniture, and, since losing his title to Liston, he has preferred living full time at his camp, which his children have come to know as "daddy's house." The children, the eldest of whom is a daughter named Jeannie now seven years old, do not know exactly what their father does for a living. But Jeannie, who watched the last Liston-Patterson fight on closed-circuit television, accepted the explanation that her father performs in a kind of game where the men take turns pushing one another down; he had his turn pushing them down, and now it is their turn.

The bedroom door opened again, and Floyd Patterson, shaking his head, was very angry and nervous.

"I'm not going to work out today," he said. "I'm going to fly down to Scarsdale. Those boys are picking on Jeannie again. She's the only Negro in this school, and the older kids give her a rough time, and some of the older boys tease her and lift up her dress all the time. Yesterday she went home crying, and so today I'm going down there and plan to wait outside the school for those boys to come out, and. . . ."

"How old are they?" he was asked.

"Teen-agers," he said. "Old enough for a left hook."

Patterson telephoned his pilot friend, Ted Hanson, who stays at the camp and does public-relations work for him, and has helped teach Patterson to fly. Five minutes later Hanson, a lean white man with a crew cut and glasses, was knocking on the door; and ten minutes later both were in the car that Patterson was driving almost recklessly over the narrow, winding country roads toward the airport, about six miles from the camp.

"Sandra is afraid I'll cause trouble; she's worried about what I'll do to those boys; she doesn't want trouble!" Patterson snapped, swerving around a hill and giving his car more gas. "She's just not firm enough! She's afraid . . . she was afraid to tell me about that groceryman who's been making passes at her. It took her a long time before she told me about that dishwasher repairman who comes over and calls her 'baby.' They all know I'm away so much. And that dishwasher repairman's been to my home about four, five times this month already. That machine breaks down every week. I guess he fixes it so it breaks down every week. Last time, I laid a trap. I waited forty-five minutes for him to come, but then he didn't show up. I was going to grab him and say, 'How would you like it if I called *your* wife *baby?* You'd feel like punching me in the nose, wouldn't you? Well, that's what I'm going to do—if you ever call her *baby* again. You call her Mrs. Patterson; or Sandra, if you know her. But you don't know her, so call her Mrs. Patterson.' And then I told Sandra that these men, this type of white man, he just wants to have some fun with colored women. He'll never marry a colored woman, just wants to have some fun. . . ."

Now he was driving into the airport's parking lot. Directly ahead, roped to the grass airstrip, was the single-engine green Cessna that Patterson bought and learned to fly before the second Liston fight. Flying was a thing Patterson had always feared—a fear shared by, maybe inherited from, his manager, Cus D'Amato, who still will not fly.

D'Amato, who took over training Patterson when the fighter was seventeen or eighteen years old and exerted a tremendous influence over his psyche, is a strange but fascinating man of fifty-six who is addicted to Spartanism and self-denial and is possessed by suspicion and fear: he avoids subways because he fears someone might push him onto the tracks; never has married; never reveals his home address.

"I must keep my enemies confused," D'Amato once explained. "When they are confused, then I can do a job for my fighters. What I do not want in life, however, is a sense of security; the moment a person knows security, his senses are dulled—and he begins to die. I also do not want many pleasures in life; I believe the more pleasures you get out of living, the more fear you have of dying."

Until a few years ago, D'Amato did most of Patterson's talking, and ran things like an Italian *padrone*. But later Patterson, the maturing son, rebelled against the Father Image. After losing to Sonny Liston the first time—a fight D'Amato had urged Patterson to resist—Patterson took flying lessons. And before the second Liston fight, Patterson had conquered his fear of height, was master at the controls, was filled with renewed confidence—and knew, too, that even if he lost, he at least possessed a vehicle that could get him out of town, fast.

But it didn't. After the fight, the little Cessna, weighed down by too much luggage, became overheated ninety miles outside of Las Vegas. Patterson and his pilot companion, having no choice but to turn back, radioed the airfield and arranged for the rental of a larger plane. When they landed, the Vegas air terminal was filled with people leaving town after the fight. Patterson hid in the shadows behind a hangar. His beard was packed in the trunk. But nobody saw him.

Later the pilot flew Patterson's Cessna back to New York alone. And Patterson flew in the larger, rented plane. He was accompanied on this flight by Hanson, a friendly, forty-two-year-old, thrice-divorced Nevadan who once was a crop duster, a bartender, and a cabaret hoofer; later he became a pilot instructor in Las Vegas, and it was there that he met Patterson. The two became good friends. And when Patterson asked Hanson to help fly the rented plane back to New York, Hanson did not hesitate, even though he had a slight hangover that night—partly due to being depressed by Liston's victory, partly due to being slugged in a bar by a drunk after objecting to some unflattering things the drunk had said about the fight.

Once in the airplane, however, Ted Hanson became very alert. He had to, because, after the plane had cruised a while at 10,000 feet, Floyd Patterson's mind seemed to wander back to the ring, and the plane would drift off course, and Hanson would say, "Floyd, Floyd, how's about getting back on course?", and then Patterson's head would snap up and his eyes would flash toward the dials. And everything would be all right for a while. But then he was back in the arena, reliving the fight, hardly believing that it had really happened. . . .

". . . And I kept thinking, as I flew out of Vegas that night, of all those months of training before the fight, all the roadwork, all the sparring, all the months away from Sandra . . . thinking of the time in camp when I wanted to stay up until eleven-fifteen p.m. to watch a certain movie on The Late Show. But I didn't because I had roadwork the next morning. . . .

". . . And I was thinking about how good I'd felt before the fight, as I lay on the table in the dressing room. I remember thinking, 'You're in excellent physical condition, you're in good mental condition—but are you vicious?' But you tell yourself, 'Viciousness is not important now, don't think about it now; a championship fight's at stake, and that's important enough and, who knows?, maybe you'll get vicious once the bell rings.'

". . . And so you lay there trying to get a little sleep . . . but you're only in a twilight zone, half asleep, and you're interrupted every once in a while by voices out in the hall, some guy's yelling 'Hey, Jack,' or 'Hey, Al,' or, 'Hey, get those four-rounders into the ring.' And when you hear that, you think, 'They're not ready for you yet.' So you lay there . . . and wonder, 'Where will I be tomorrow? Where will I be three hours from now?' Oh, you think all kinds of thoughts, some thoughts completely unrelated to the fight . . . you wonder whether you ever paid your mother-in-law back for all those stamps she bought a year ago . . . and you remember that time at two a.m. when Sandra tripped on the steps while bringing a bottle up to the baby . . . and then you get mad and ask: 'What am I thinking about these things for?' . . . and you try to sleep . . . but then the door opens and somebody says to somebody else, 'Hey, is somebody gonna go to Liston's dressing room to watch 'em bandage up?'

". . . And so then you know it's about time to get ready. . . . You open your eyes. You get off the table. You glove up, you loosen up. Then Liston's trainer walks in. He looks at you, he smiles. He feels the bandages and later he says, 'Good luck, Floyd,' and you think, 'He didn't have to say that; he must be a nice guy.'

". . . And then you go out, and it's the long walk, always a long walk, and you think, 'What am I gonna be when I come back this way?' Then you climb into the ring. You notice Billy Eckstine at ringside leaning over to talk to somebody, and you see the reporters—some you like, some you don't like—and then it's The Star-Spangled Banner, and the cameras are rolling, and the bell rings. . . .

". . . How could the same thing happen twice? How? That's all I kept thinking after the knockout. . . . Was I fooling these people all these *years? . . . Was I ever the champion? . . . And then they lead you out of the ring . . . and up the aisle you go, past those people, and all you want is to get to your dressing room, fast . . . but the trouble was in Las Vegas they made a wrong turn along the aisle, and when we got to the end, there was no dressing room there . . . and we had to walk all the way back down the aisle, past the same people, and they must have been thinking, 'Patterson's not only knocked out, but he can't even find his dressing room. . . .'*

". . . In the dressing room I had a headache. Liston didn't hurt me physically—a few days later I only felt a twitching nerve in my teeth—it was nothing like some fights I've had: like that Dick Wagner fight in '53 when he beat my body so bad I was urinating blood for days. After the Liston fight, I just went into the bathroom, shut the door behind me, and looked at myself in the mirror. I just looked at myself and asked, 'What happened?', and then they started pounding on the door, and saying, 'Com'on out, Floyd, com'on out; the press is here, Cus is here, com'on out, Floyd. . . .'

". . . And so I went out, and they asked questions, but what can you say? What you're thinking about is all those months of training, all the conditioning, all the depriving; and you think, 'I didn't have to run that extra mile, didn't have to spar that day, I could have stayed up that night in camp and watched The Late Show. *. . . I could have fought this fight tonight in no condition. . . .'* "

"Floyd, Floyd," Hanson had said, "let's get back on course. . . ."

Again Patterson would snap out of his reverie, and refocus on the omniscope, and get his flying under control. After landing in New Mexico, and then in Ohio, Floyd Patterson and Ted Hanson brought the little plane into the New York airstrip near the fight camp. The green Cessna that had been flown back by the other pilot was already there, roped to the grass at precisely the same spot it was on this day five months later when Floyd Patterson was planning to fly it toward perhaps another fight—this time a fight with some schoolboys in Scarsdale who had been lifting up his little daughter's dress.

Patterson and Ted Hanson untied the plane, and Patterson got a rag and wiped from the windshield the splotches of insects. Then he walked around behind the plane, inspected the tail, checked under the fuselage, then peered down between the wing and the flaps to make sure all the screws were tight. He seemed suspicious of something. D'Amato would have been pleased.

"If a guy wants to get rid of you," Patterson explained, "all he has to do is remove these little screws here. Then, when you try to come in for a landing, the flaps fall off, and you crash."

Then Patterson got into the cockpit and started the engine. A few moments later, with Hanson beside him, Patterson was racing the little plane over the grassy field, then soaring over the weeds, then flying high above the gentle hills and trees. It was a nice takeoff.

Since it was only a forty-minute flight to the Westchester airport, where Sandra Patterson would be waiting with a car, Floyd Patterson did all the flying. The trip was uneventful until, suddenly behind a cloud, he flew into heavy smoke that hovered above a forest fire. His visibility gone, he was forced to the instruments. And at this precise moment, a fly that had been buzzing in the back of the cockpit flew up front and landed on the instrument panel in front of Patterson. He glared at the fly, watched it crawl slowly up the windshield, then shot a quick smash with his palm against the glass. He missed. The fly buzzed safely past Patterson's ear, bounced off the back of the cockpit, circled around.

"This smoke won't keep up," Hanson assured. "You can level off."

Patterson leveled off.

He flew easily for a few moments. Then the fly buzzed to the front again, zigzagging before Patterson's face, landed on the panel and proceeded to crawl across it. Patterson watched it, squinted. Then he slammed down at it with a quick right hand. Missed.

Ten minutes later, his nerves still on edge, Patterson began the descent. He picked up the radio microphone—"Westchester tower . . . Cessna 2729 uniform . . . three miles northwest . . . land in one-six on final . . ."—and then, after an easy landing, he climbed quickly out of the cockpit and strode toward his wife's station wagon outside the terminal.

But along the way a small man smoking a cigar turned toward Patterson, waved at him, and said, "Say, excuse me, but aren't you . . . aren't you . . . Sonny Liston?"

Patterson stopped. He glared at the man, bewildered. He wasn't sure whether it was a joke or an insult, and he really did not know what to do.

"Aren't you Sonny Liston?" the man repeated, quite serious.

"No," Patterson said, quickly passing by the man, "I'm his brother."

When he reached Mrs. Patterson's car he asked, "How much time till school lets out?"

"About fifteen minutes," she said, starting up the engine. Then she said, "Oh, Floyd, I just should have told Sister, I shouldn't have. . . ."

"*You* tell Sister; *I'll* tell the boys. . . ."

Mrs. Patterson drove as quickly as she could into Scarsdale, with Patterson shaking his head and telling Ted Hanson in the back, "Really can't understand these school kids. This is a religious school, and they want $20,000 for a glass window—and yet, some of them carry these racial prejudices, and it's mostly the Jews who are shoulder-to-shoulder with us, and. . . ."

"Oh, Floyd," cried his wife, "Floyd, *I* have to get along here . . . you're not here, *you* don't live here, *I*. . . ."

She arrived at the school just as the bell began to ring. It was a modern building at the top of a hill, and on the lawn was the statue of a saint and, behind it, a large white cross. "There's Jeannie," said Mrs. Patterson.

"Hurry, call her over here," Patterson said.

"Jeannie! Come over here, honey."

The little girl, wearing a blue school uniform and cap, and clasping books in front of her, came running down the path toward the station wagon.

"Jeannie," Floyd Patterson said, rolling down his window, "point out the boys who lifted your dress."

Jeannie turned and watched as several students came down the path; then she pointed to a tall, thin curly-haired boy walking with four other boys, all about twelve to fourteen years of age.

"Hey," Patterson called to him, "can I see you for a minute?"

All five boys came to the side of the car. They looked Patterson directly in the eye. They seemed not at all intimidated by him.

"You the one that's been lifting up my daughter's dress?" Patterson asked the boy who had been singled out.

"Nope," the boy said, casually.

"Nope?" Patterson said, caught off guard by the reply.

"Wasn't him, Mister," said another boy. "Probably was his little brother."

Patterson looked at Jeannie. But she was speechless, uncertain. The five boys remained there, waiting for Patterson to do something.

"Well, er, where's your little brother?" Patterson asked.

"Hey, kid!" one of the boys yelled. "Come over here."

A boy walked toward them. He resembled his older brother; he had freckles on his small, upturned nose, had blue eyes, dark curly hair and, as he approached the station wagon, he seemed equally unintimidated by Patterson.

"You been lifting up my daughter's dress?"

"Nope," the boy said.

"*Nope!*" Patterson repeated, frustrated.

"Nope, I wasn't lifting it. I was just touching it a little. . . ."

The other boys stood around the car looking down at Patterson, and other students crowded behind them, and nearby Patterson saw several white parents standing next to their parked cars; he became self-conscious, began to tap nervously with his fingers against the dashboard. He could not raise his voice without creating an unpleasant scene, yet could not retreat gracefully; so his voice went soft, and he said, finally:

"Look, boy, I want you to stop it. I won't tell your mother—that might get you in trouble—but don't do it again, okay?"

"Okay."

The boys calmly turned and walked, in a group, up the street.

Sandra Patterson said nothing. Jeannie opened the door, sat in the front seat next to her father, and took out a small blue piece of paper that a nun had given her and handed it across to Mrs. Patterson. But Floyd Patterson snatched it. He read it. Then he paused, put the paper down, and quietly announced, dragging out the words, "*She didn't do her religion. . . .*"

Patterson now wanted to get out of Scarsdale. He wanted to return to camp. After stopping at the Patterson home in Scarsdale and picking up Floyd Patterson, Jr., who is three, Mrs. Patterson drove them all back to the airport. Jeannie and Floyd, Jr., were seated in the back of the plane, and then Mrs. Patterson drove the station wagon alone up to camp, planning to return to Scarsdale that evening with the children.

It was four p.m. when Floyd Patterson got back to the camp, and the shadows were falling on the clubhouse, and on the tennis court routed by weeds, and on the big white house in front of which not a single automobile was parked. All was deserted and quiet; it was a loser's camp.

The children ran to play inside the clubhouse; Patterson walked slowly toward his apartment to dress for the workout.

"What could I do with those school boys?" he asked. "What can you do to kids of that age?"

It still seemed to bother him—the effrontery of the boys, the realization that he had somehow failed, the probability that, had those same boys heckled someone in Liston's family, the school yard would have been littered with limbs.

While Patterson and Liston both are products of the slum, and while both began as thieves, Patterson had been tamed in a special school with help from a gentle Negro spinster; later he became a Catholic convert, and learned not to hate. Still later he bought a dictionary, adding to his vocabulary such words as "vicissitude" and "enigma." And when he regained his championship from Johansson, he became the Great Black Hope of the Urban League.

He proved that it is not only possible to rise out of a Negro slum and succeed as a sportsman, but also to develop into an intelligent, sensitive, law-abiding citizen. In proving this, however, and in taking pride in it, Patterson seemed to lose part of himself. He lost part of his hunger, his anger—and as he walked up the steps into his apartment, he was saying, "I became the good guy. . . . After Liston won the title, I kept hoping that he would change into a good guy, too. That would have relieved me of the responsibility, and maybe I could have been more of the bad guy. But he didn't. . . . It's okay to be the good guy when you're winning. But when you're losing, it is no good being the good guy."

Patterson took off his shirt and trousers and, moving some books on the bureau to one side, put down his watch, his cuff links and a clip of bills.

"Do you do much reading?" he was asked.

"No," he said. "In fact, you know I've never finished reading a book in my whole life? I don't know why. I just feel that no writer today has anything for me; I mean, none of them has felt any more deeply than I have, and I have nothing to learn from them. Although Baldwin to me seems different from the rest. What's Baldwin doing these days?"

"He's writing a play. Anthony Quinn is supposed to have a part in it."

"Quinn?" Patterson asked.

"Yes."

"Quinn doesn't like me."

"Why?"

"I read or heard it somewhere; Quinn had been quoted as saying that my fight was disgraceful against Liston, and Quinn said something to the effect that he could have done better. People often say that—*they* could have done better! Well I think that if *they* had to fight, *they* couldn't even go through the experience of waiting for the fight to begin. They'd be up the whole night before, and would be drinking, or taking drugs. They'd probably get a heart attack. I'm sure that, if I was in the ring with Anthony Quinn, I could wear him out without even touching him. I would do nothing but pressure him, I'd stalk him, I'd stand close to him. I wouldn't touch him, but I'd wear him out and he'd collapse. But Anthony Quinn's an old man, isn't he?"

"In his forties."

"Well, anyway," Patterson said, "getting back to Baldwin, he seems like a wonderful guy. I've seen him on television and, before the Liston fight in Chicago, he came by my camp. You meet Baldwin on the street and you say, 'Who's this poor slob?'—he seems just like another guy; and this is the same impression *I* give people when they don't know me. But I think Baldwin and me, we have much in common, and someday I'd just like to sit somewhere for a long time and talk to him. . . ."

Patterson, his trunks and sweat pants on, bent over to tie his shoelaces, and then, from a bureau drawer, took out a T-shirt across which was printed *Deauville*. He has several T-shirts bearing the same name. He takes good care of them. They are souvenirs from the high point of his life. They are from the Deauville Hotel in Miami Beach, which is where he trained for the third Ingemar Johansson match in March of 1961.

Never was Floyd Patterson more popular, more admired than during that winter. He had visited President Kennedy; he had been given a $35,000 jeweled crown by his manager; his greatness was conceded by sportswriters—and nobody had any idea that Patterson, secretly, was in possession of a false moustache and dark glasses that he intended to wear out of Miami Beach should he lose the third fight to Johansson.

It was after being knocked out by Johansson in their first fight that Patterson, deep in depression, hiding in humiliation for months in a remote Connecticut lodge, decided he could not face the public again if he lost. So he bought false whiskers and a moustache, and planned to wear them out of his dressing room after a defeat. He had also planned, in leaving his dressing room, to linger momentarily within the crowd and perhaps complain out loud about the fight. Then he would slip undiscovered through the night and into a waiting automobile.

Although there proved to be no need for bringing disguise into the second or third Johansson fights, or into a subsequent bout in Toronto against an obscure heavyweight named Tom McNeeley, Patterson brought it anyway; and, after the first Liston fight, he not only wore it during his thirty-hour automobile ride from Chicago to New York, but he also wore it while in an airliner bound for Spain.

"As I got onto this plane, you'd never have recognized me," he said. "I had on this beard, moustache, glasses and hat—and I also limped, to make myself look older. I was alone. I didn't care what plane I boarded; I just looked up and saw this sign at the terminal reading 'Madrid,' and so I got on that flight after buying a ticket.

"When I got to Madrid I registered at a hotel under the name 'Aaron Watson.' I stayed in Madrid about four or five days. In the daytime I wandered around to the poorer sections of the city, limping, looking at the people, and the people stared back at me and must have thought I was crazy because I was moving so slow and looked the way I did. I ate food in my hotel room. Although once I went to a restaurant and ordered soup. I hate soup. But I thought it was what old people would order. So I ate it. And after a week of this, I began to actually think I was somebody else. I began to believe it. And it is nice, every once in a while, being somebody else."

Patterson would not elaborate on how he managed to register under a name that did not correspond to his passport; he merely explained, "With money, you can do anything."

Now, walking slowly around the room, his black silk robe over his sweat clothes, Patterson said, "You must wonder what makes a man do things like this. Well, I wonder too. And the answer is, I don't know . . . but I think that within me, within every human being, there is a certain weakness. It is a weakness that exposes itself more when you're alone. And I have figured out that part of the reason I do the things I do, and cannot seem to conquer that one word—*myself*—is because . . . is because . . . I am a coward. . . ."

He stopped. He stood very still in the middle of the room, thinking about what he had just said, probably wondering whether he should have said it.

"I am a coward," he then repeated, softly. "My fighting has little to do with that fact, though. I mean you can be a fighter—and a *winning* fighter—and still be a coward. I was probably a coward on the night I won the championship back from Ingemar. And I remember another night, long ago, back when I was in the amateurs, fighting this big, tremendous man named Julius Griffin. I was only a hundred fifty-three pounds. I was petrified. It was all I could do to cross the ring. And then he came at me, and moved close to me . . . and from then on I don't know anything. I have no idea what happened. Only thing I know is, I saw him on the floor. And later somebody said, 'Man, I never saw anything like it. You just jumped up in the air, and threw thirty different punches. . . .' "

"When did you first think you were a coward?" he was asked.

"It was after the first Ingemar fight."

"How does one see this cowardice you speak of?"

"You see it when a fighter loses. Ingemar, for instance, is not a coward. When he lost the third fight in Miami, he was at a party later at the Fontainebleau. Had I lost, I couldn't have gone to that party. And I don't see how he did. . . ."

"Could Liston be a coward?"

"That remains to be seen," Patterson said. "We'll find out what he's like after somebody beats him, how he takes it. It's easy to do anything in victory. It's in defeat that a man reveals himself. In defeat I can't face people. I haven't the strength to say to people, 'I did my best, I'm sorry, and what not.' "

"Have you no hate left?"

"I have hated only one fighter," Patterson said. "And that was Ingemar in the second fight. I had been hating him for a whole year before that—not because he beat me in the first fight, but because of what he did after. It was all that boasting in public, and his showing off his right-hand punch on television, his thundering right, his 'toonder and lightning.' And I'd be home watching him on television, and *hating* him. It is a miserable feeling, hate. When a man hates, he can't have any peace of mind. And for one solid year I hated him because, after he took everything away from me, deprived me of everything I was, he *rubbed it in*. On the night of the second fight, in the dressing room, I couldn't wait until I got into the ring. When he was a little late getting into the ring, I thought, 'He's holding me up; he's trying to unsettle me—well, I'll get him!' "

"Why couldn't you hate Liston in the second match?"

Patterson thought for a moment, then said, "Look, if Sonny Liston walked into this room now and slapped me in the face, then you'd see a fight. You'd see the fight of your life because, then, a principle would be involved. I'd forget he was a human being. I'd forget I was a human being. And I'd fight accordingly."

"Could it be, Floyd, that you made a mistake in becoming a prize-fighter?"

"What do you mean?"

"Well, you say you're a coward; you say you have little capacity for hate; and you seemed to lose your nerve against those schoolboys in Scarsdale this afternoon. Don't you think you might have been better suited for some other kind of work? Perhaps a social worker, or. . . ."

"Are you asking why I continue to fight?"

"Yes."

"Well," he said, not irritated by the question, "first of all, I love boxing. Boxing has been good to me. And I might just as well ask you the question: 'Why do you write?' Or, 'Do you retire from writing every time you write a bad story?' And as to whether I should have become a fighter in the first place, well, let's see how I can explain it. . . . Look, let's say you're a man who has been in an empty room for days and days without food . . . and then they take you out of that room and put you into another room where there's food hanging all over the place . . . and the first thing you reach for, you eat. When you're hungry, you're not choosy, and so I chose the thing that was closest to me. That was boxing. One day I just wandered into a gymnasium and boxed a boy. And I beat him. Then I boxed another boy. I beat him, too. Then I kept boxing. And winning. And I said, 'Here, finally, is something I can do!'

"Now I wasn't a sadist," he quickly added. "But I liked beating people because it was the only thing I could do. And whether boxing was a sport or not, I wanted to make it a sport because it was a thing I could succeed at. And what were the requirements? Sacrifice. That's all. To anybody who comes from the Bedford-Stuyvesant section of Brooklyn, sacrifice comes easy. And so I kept fighting, and one day I became heavyweight champion, and I got to know people like you. And you wonder how I can sacrifice, how I can deprive myself so much. You just don't realize where I've come from. You don't understand where I was when it began for me.

"In those days, when I was about eight years old, everything I got—I stole. I stole to survive, and I did survive, but I seemed to hate myself. My mother told me I used to point to a photograph of myself hanging in the bedroom and say, 'I don't like that boy!' One day my mother found three large X's scratched with a nail or something over that photograph of me. I don't remember doing it. But I do remember feeling like a parasite at home. I remember how awful I used to feel at night when my father, a longshoreman, would come home so tired that, as my mother fixed food before him, he would fall asleep at the table because he was that tired. I would always take his shoes off and clean his feet. That was my job. And I felt so bad because here I was, not going to school, doing nothing, just watching my father come home; and on Friday nights it was even worse. He would come home with his pay, and he'd put every nickel of it on the table so my mother could buy food for all the children. I never wanted to be around to see that. I'd run and hide. And then I decided to leave home and start stealing—and I did. And I would never come home unless I brought something that I had stolen. Once I remember I broke into a dress store and stole a whole mound of dresses, at two a.m., and here I was, this little kid, carrying all those dresses over the wall, thinking they were all the same size, my mother's size, and thinking the cops would never notice me walking down the street with all those dresses piled over my head. They did, of course. . . . I went to the Youth House. . . ."

Floyd Patterson's children, who had been playing outside all this time around the country club, now became restless and began to call him, and Jeannie started to pound on his door. So Patterson picked up his leather bag, which contained his gloves, his mouthpiece and adhesive tape, and walked with the children across the path toward the clubhouse.

He flicked on the light switches behind the stage near the piano. Beams of amber streaked through the dimly lit room and flashed onto the ring. Then he walked to one side of the room, outside the ring. He took off his robe, shuffled his feet in the rosin, skipped rope, and then began to shadowbox in front of the spit-stained mirror, throwing out quick combinations of lefts, rights, lefts, rights, each jab followed by a *"hegh-hegh-hegh-hegh."* Then, his gloves on, he moved to the punching bag in the far corner, and soon the room reverberated to his rhythmic beat against the bobbling bag—rat-tat-tat-*tetteta*, rat-tat-tat-*tetteta,* rat-tat-tat-*tetteta,* rat-tat-tat-*tetteta!*

The children, sitting on pink leather chairs moved from the bar to the fringe of the ring, watched him in awe, sometimes flinching at the force of his pounding against the leather bag.

And this is how they would probably remember him years from now: a dark, solitary, glistening figure punching in the corner of a forlorn spot at the bottom of a mountain where people once came to have fun—until the clubhouse became unfashionable, the paint began to peel, and Negroes were allowed in.

As Floyd Patterson continued to bang away with lefts and rights, his gloves a brown blur against the bag, his daughter slipped quietly off her chair and wandered past the ring into the other room. There, on the other side of the bar and beyond a dozen round tables, was the stage. She climbed onto the stage and stood behind a microphone, long dead, and cried out, imitating a ring announcer, "Ladieeees and gentlemen . . . tonight we present. . . ."

She looked around, puzzled. Then, seeing that her little brother had followed her, she waved him up to the stage and began again: "Ladiees and gentlemen . . . tonight we present . . . *Floydie Patterson.* . . ."

Suddenly, the pounding against the bag in the other room stopped. There was silence for a moment. Then Jeannie, still behind the microphone and looking down at her brother, said, "Floydie, come up here!"

"No," he said.

"Oh, come up here!"

"*No,*" he cried.

Then Floyd Patterson's voice, from the other room, called: "Cut it out. . . . I'll take you both for a walk in a minute."

He resumed punching—rat-tat-tat-*tetteta*—and they returned to his side. But Jeannie interrupted, asking, "Daddy, how come you sweating?"

"Water fell on me," he said, still pounding.

"Daddy," asked Floyd, Jr., "how come you spit water on the floor before?"

"To get it out of my mouth."

He was about to move over to the heavier punching bag when the sound of Mrs. Patterson's station wagon could be heard moving up the road.

Soon she was in Patterson's apartment cleaning up a bit, patting the pillows, washing the teacups that had been left in the sink. One hour later the family was having dinner together. They were together for two more hours; then, at ten p.m., Mrs. Patterson washed and dried all of the dishes, and put the garbage out in the can—where it would remain until the raccoons and skunks got to it.

And then, after helping the children with their coats and walking out to the station wagon and kissing her husband good-bye, Mrs. Patterson began the drive down the dirt road toward the highway. Patterson waved once, and stood for a moment watching the taillights go, and then he turned and walked slowly back toward the house.

[March, 1964]

Requiem for a Lightweight

by Charles Mohr

"A lot of my enemies call me simple. The big trouble with the so-called liberal today is that he doesn't understand simplicity. . . . Those who do not have courage want complicated answers when they know in their hearts I'm right." ———BARRY GOLDWATER
Memphis, September, 1964

One evening in May of 1964, Senator Barry M. Goldwater was giving a speech in a restaurant at Glendora, California. Ed Nellor, one of a series of men who served in the difficult role of press secretary to Goldwater, had tarried in the bar to have a solitary drink after the speech began. Nellor was startled out of his private reveries by an excited man who burst into the bar and blurted out this warning:

"You've got to get to Senator Goldwater right away. There are men out there writing down every word he says!"

In a way this Southern California Paul Revere was unsophisticated. But in other ways he was a very astute man. He knew Goldwater's own words could hurt him; did, in fact, hurt him every day. Nor was he alone. The more a voter loved Barry, it seemed, the more he felt that public exposure

379

of his hero was a bad thing. On another occasion I was standing with a notebook and pen at the fringe of an airport crowd when Goldwater made a particularly controversial remark. "I suppose you're going to put that in the paper," a woman wearing a "We Want Barry" button hissed venomously in my ear.

For most of the 1964 Presidential election year I was one of the men and women who wrote down what Goldwater said and put it in the paper—in my case The New York *Times*. This was a profoundly exhausting experience and, in many ways, it was an even more bewildering one. But, above all, it was unforgettably entertaining. I sometimes thought how sad it was that H. L. Mencken, who regarded politics as the profession of boobs and the sport of kings, did not live to see it. The damnedest things kept happening on the Goldwater campaign.

At the end of Barry's first swing through the South in the month of September, we stopped one night for a speech at Charleston, West Virginia. Goldwater's formal, prepared text was hot news in itself—a long, uncompromising attack on the war-on-poverty program to be delivered in the heart of the poverty belt. The reporters had written first-edition stories based on the prepared text, and by the time we reached the Charleston auditorium we were numb, almost drowsing. As it turned out Goldwater chose instead to give what we later called his "law of the jungle history of capitalism."

He began with a digression, saying that current liberal economics was based on the formula: from each according to his ability to each according to his need. He added that this was what the Russians now practice (an error, of course; the Soviet Union does not profess to have arrived at pure communism).

"I think the Russians must have got that from the apes," said Barry. Some of us stopped drowsing and began taking notes.

Goldwater was warming to his theme. In the beginning, he said, the apes must have collected coconuts and tossed them onto a communal pile where any fellow anthropoid could help himself.

"But then," said Barry, "one ape got smart and invented capitalism. And under capitalism we take care of our brothers, but not our brothers who won't work and want to live off of us."

Apes, coconuts and capitalism. Nothing could top that, I thought, as the plane hummed back toward Washington. I was wrong. A stewardess worked her way down the aisle of the chartered campaign plane passing a tray. With unalloyed glee I helped myself to a big, luscious piece of—what else?—coconut cake.

The performance at Charleston was worse in degree, not different in kind, than most of the thousands of appearances Goldwater made from January to November. What made him do and say the things he did? It is an important question. Goldwater's opinions and philosophy were unquestionably important in themselves, but they were not the key to the campaign. Those opinions were so unsuited to the political climate of the day—not to say the national requirements—that even he was not wholly serious in delivering them. He used to tell audiences that although he might *like* to unload T.V.A. or change the Social Security system, they ought not be alarmed because everybody knew that Congress wouldn't let him. The real issue of the campaign became Goldwater's character; not what he did, but why he did it.

He was a remarkably complex man. Almost no declarative sentence about him can stand without a qualifying clause. His image is beginning to fade now, like a bad color photograph, and I would like to flash him onto the screen one last time. See him now, setting out on a campaign for the Presidency of the United States on a pair of crutches (the result of a bone-spur operation), looking and talking and loving life like a twentieth-century Long John Silver, full of roguish charm and dark plans for the future. . . . I joined the Goldwater campaign a few days after he had formally announced his candidacy on January 3. The first time I met him he was dressed like an Eastern banker, in a deep-blue homburg, a conservative blue suit and black topcoat. It somehow wasn't what I expected; I guess I had anticipated something more Western and breezy. Gradually I was to learn it was a mistake to anticipate anything with Goldwater (a few months later I saw him conduct a press conference on a yacht, dressed in baggy scarlet pants and sneakers, with no socks). At the first meeting he seemed shy, almost deferential. But it developed that his moods varied wildly. He could be the warmest of men—and the rudest. He could be jovial and then morose. He could show a tenacious simplicity and honesty, but he could also be Orientally devious.

Knowing little about Goldwater, I knew even less about the campaign staff which was being hastily assembled around him. My ignorance, it turned out, was shared by all.

Goldwater had assigned the top three jobs in the organization to three obscure Arizona lawyers, none of them really experienced in national politics. Denison Kitchel, the campaign director, was a small, grey man of meticulous courtesy. He was almost apologetically careful not to speak in the resounding generalities or ringing accusations common to many of Goldwater's right-wing supporters. Dick Kleindienst held the job of Director of Field Operations: he was expected to cope with state Republican organizations where the great majority of national-convention delegates would be won or lost. Kleindienst could—and did—swear with equal fluency in English and Navaho. An enthusiastic gambler, his hatred of losing made him a sort of bush-league Bobby Kennedy. He used to repeat—endlessly—over the gin-rummy table: "I knew a good loser once; he was a queer."

The job of deputy to Kitchel was held by a young Tucson attorney named Dean Burch, who had never held elective office either in public service or the Republican party. Burch had a heavily lined, rather plaintive face. He always struck me as very sensible in private conversation. Later, in July, he was chosen to be Republican National Chairman, primarily because of his unfaltering loyalty to Goldwater. (It was precisely for this reason that other Republicans this year got rid of Burch with, ironically, Goldwater's own eventual approval.)

Standing obediently in the shadow of these three men was a catlike, bow-tied New Yorker named F. Clifton (Cliff) White, who had run the "Draft Goldwater Committee" in 1963. White was to emerge as the organization genius of the group; subtly he would displace Kleindienst to become the real director of field operations, the one who would accomplish more than any other to secure the Republican nomination for Goldwater.

Those who imagined that Goldwater was being manipulated by a group of fanatic right-wing ogres were wrong. There were plenty of nuts knocking on his door, but Goldwater managed to avoid most of them. The campaign organization as a whole, including the handsome secretaries and the earnest young men in minor jobs, left a benign impression. A stranger being escorted through their camp was treated with the politeness shown an infidel visiting a Muslim shrine; he would be offered coffee and smiles, but no sermons or arguments unless he had the bad manners to attack The Faith.

Two things struck me in the first few days of my assignment. One was the air of improvisation and of general amateurism prevailing almost everywhere except at the desk of Cliff White. I thought this would soon pass—but it never really did (although the manipulation of national-convention delegates in July was hardly amateur; it was the one major accomplishment of the organization). I looked in vain for a Ted Sorensen or an Emmet Hughes.

The explanation was simple, but astounding. There was no speech writer because there were to be almost no written speeches. Goldwater did not want a speech writer because he was cocky; he had an almost sublime belief in his own ability to extemporize, to play it by ear. Ahead of him lay the Presidential primary elections in New Hampshire, Oregon and California, the Republican National Convention and a general election campaign after that, but Goldwater actually expected to do most of his talking off the cuff.

A kind of merry innocence pervaded the campaign in those early days. Only a handful of reporters was covering the candidate full time: Walter Mears of the Associated Press, Robert MacNeil of NBC, Loye Miller of *Time,* John Rolfson of ABC, and a few others. Logistically, we had serious problems. Goldwater and Kitchell were determined not to court or pamper the press, and there were no charter airplanes large enough to accommodate us on trips out of Washington. For months we had to juggle impossible schedules on commercial airlines to keep up with the candidate while he flew direct to obscure destinations in a private plane. There were, however, advantages to this. Large groups made Barry nervous. We were a small group. When we did catch up with him the atmosphere was relaxed and hospitable. Goldwater used to seem genuinely surprised that we went to so much trouble to cover him. Once, when we missed a speech of his in Thatcher, Arizona, he smiled shyly and said, "I didn't say anything worth hearing anyway."

The first trip I took with him was to North Carolina where he spoke in a roller-skating rink converted for the evening to a banquet hall. The occasion was a dinner in honor of the outstanding young men of Kinston, North Carolina.

He told his audience that the United States could never coexist with communism because Communists did not believe in God.

"It's as simple as that," he said.

What was striking about such utterances was the conversational, mild way in which he said them. He never tried to excite an audience or carry it along with him. You had the feeling that if someone stood up and yelled, "You're nuts," Goldwater would only smile and shrug.

There were a number of side trips in that period, including one to Reno, and Goldwater tended to tire easily, with disastrous results. He was tired on the day he appeared before a television panel consisting of a group of Nevada newspaper editors. One of them asked if he had advocated giving control of nuclear weapons to NATO commanders, rather than solely to the Supreme Commander of SHAPE.

"Oh, no," said Goldwater, "I would never say that in my most lucid moments."

The main show, of course, was in New Hampshire, where the first preferential Presidential primary election in the nation is held. New York Governor Nelson A. Rockefeller was the only other major candidate campaigning there, but write-in campaigns were under way on behalf of Henry Cabot Lodge and Richard M. Nixon. Having arrived just after Goldwater's first three-day swing through the state, I had missed an event which could have lost him the primary—if not his whole campaign for the Presidency. At a press conference in Concord on January 7, he said he would suggest just one change in Social Security—that "it be made voluntary." He and his followers spent the rest of the year trying to repair the damage. His final public position on the matter: Social Security was a contract between the Federal government and the public, and he did not believe in violating contracts. I think he had had a sincere change of heart on the issue. On many occasions, however, he and his men denied he had ever advocated making it voluntary—which is something more than a change in heart. It was Goldwater's own staff who prepared and distributed the Concord press-conference transcript, and some journalists still hang onto their copies—precious talismans.

There was never another campaign to compare with the one Goldwater put on in New Hampshire. Later he was to shun press conferences almost completely, but back there he had a press conference every morning until both he and the reporters simply became tired of the damn things. He made ten or more stops a day in the state's little villages. Usually, he would tell the crowd he didn't want to "bore" them with a speech, but they could ask him questions all they liked. It was similar to putting his head in a meat grinder. New Hampshire folk are natural interrogators. Goldwater was going through the equivalent of ten full-dress press conferences a day, and he was murdering himself. He made so much news it was impossible to get every incredible thing he said in the paper—there just wasn't space.

The questioning was tough, but he compounded his own difficulties. He had an opinion about *everything*. (Congressman Charlie Halleck of Indiana had once said to him in exasperation, "Goddamn it, Barry, you'll answer *any* question, won't you?") Goldwater also suffered from a tendency toward overstatement. One night before a large crowd in Portsmouth, he answered a question by saying that the Civil Rights Bill of 1964 could be used to destroy freedom of worship and to abolish private clubs. An articulate young Negro, the local secretary of the N.A.A.C.P., rose and said politely that the bill would do no such thing.

"You're right," said Barry cheerfully, "but it could be stretched that far."

Although he prided himself on honesty, he was one of the most inconsistent men I have ever known. When he began to sense danger, he would often slip sideways, and sometimes even backwards. At an early-morning press conference at Laconia he was asked whether he would campaign on a promise to lead the United States out of the United Nations if Communist China were admitted to the U.N.

"I would be inclined to do so," he said.

The wire-service and network reporters were still phoning this story to their offices when Goldwater took off for the nearby town of Meredith. I wasn't on deadline so I tagged along. He made his appearance there on a curb in front of a tiny crowd. One man said, "My wife wants to know what you would do about the United Nations."

Goldwater said earnestly: "We must stay in the United Nations, but we must improve it."

"You never opposed the U.N., then?" the man asked.

"No," said Goldwater.

A little later he appeared at the local high school and said that if China were admitted, "I think it blows the whole thing to pieces."

That evening at Colby Junior College for girls, he said, "I've never said let's get out of the U.N. I don't know how that rumor ever got started."

On still another occasion he said that he didn't think the world was ready for an organization like the U.N.

As a reporter, I hardly knew how to deal with this kind of problem. I wanted to print Goldwater's opinion accurately, but what the hell was his opinion? It was hard to print any one remark without printing them all—and even doing that certainly did not lead to clarity.

He was no more consistent personally than he was philosophically. He was always expounding to us a strategy of campaigning and then going out and doing exactly the opposite. We learned that when he said he was all through with handshaking he was likely to go out and shake a record number of hands the next day. (Once he *looked* like he might kiss a New Hampshire baby, but stopped just in time, remembering that he had told some Dartmouth students that he was not a baby-kissing candidate. Denny Kitchel whispered to us, "If he kisses that baby, I resign." Months later in San Diego, Goldwater did kiss a baby and gave us reporters a defiant want-to-make-something-of-it grin. We looked around for Kitchel. "I didn't see it and I don't believe it," he said before we could open our mouths.)

The finest moment of the New Hampshire campaign came with a torchlight parade in the state's mountainous north country. We had ducked out for a steak before the parade formed and got back to the curb in the nick of time, not knowing precisely what to expect. Here came Barry, riding in a pony cart pulled by a preposterously small and shaggy horse. He was preceded by a drum-and-bugle corps in Indian-feather bonnets, playing *Blue Moon,* and a chubby high-school drum majorette, her knees blue with cold, carrying, of all things, a United Nations flag.

In February we took a welcome time-out from the slush of New Hampshire and went to Arizona, where we saw a happier, more natural Goldwater than we had seen—or were to see again. He had scheduled a number of leisurely speeches in small Arizona towns; in case he lost the Presidential nomination he would run for reelection to the United States Senate. The first stop was Yuma where he put on dirt-plain cowboy clothes to be grand marshal in a rodeo.

He asked Walter Mears if he had ever seen a rodeo. Mears, a New Englander, said, "No, but I saw Gene Autry once at the Boston Garden." Barry, who was nothing if not frank, said that he hated rodeos.

The crowd didn't think much of Goldwater, either. I was surprised at how little fervor and emotion he aroused in his own state. He could always knock them dead in Los Angeles and even in Madison Square Garden, but he usually played to a dead house in his home state. That's the way it was that day. He was paraded around the rodeo ring in a convertible, but there was almost no applause.

At a small airport rally before departure things were warmer. Goldwater spoke briefly before climbing into the seat of his rented airplane (his own plane was grounded for modifications). Cuba was a hot issue and

Barry told the crowd about one of his favorite enthusiasms, "Bucky" O'Neill. Bucky had been the Republican sheriff of Yavapai County and "the first man killed up San Juan Hill" with the Rough Riders. Months later Goldwater was to make the "formal" opening speech of the general election campaign on the Yavapai County courthouse steps in front of an enormous equestrian statue of Bucky.

(Two reporters had nosed around Prescott the day before and been told that some historians believed Bucky was actually killed by a sniper while squatting over a trench latrine. But cynics are with us always.)

You had to like Goldwater in those days. He hated pretense. When an Arizona fat cat, who was important to him as a campaign contributor, insisted on following him around the state, Goldwater gave the distinct impression of being trapped. He was sufficiently pragmatic and courteous not to refuse, but too honest to feign happiness. He moaned to the Eastern press, "I need him like a bull needs tits."

One Saturday during that first Arizona trip Goldwater invited a handful of us to lunch at his wonderfully pleasant stone house in Paradise City. His well-publicized ham-radio set was installed behind a massive console desk in the living room. From that command center he could flip other switches and talk by intercom to any room in the house. A nearby bathroom was papered with old photographs taken by Barry. One of them was a picture of *another* bathroom complete with a molded rubber bath mat resembling rows of female breasts. There must have been a story behind that picture; I always meant to ask Goldwater about it, but never did.

He had a massive collection of books on Western history. He told me unhappily that before he got interested in the subject he had passed up a chance to buy a complete set of Bancroft's books cheaply, choosing instead only the history of New Mexico and Arizona. Goldwater may not have read widely, but it was obvious that when he liked a subject he delved into it with deep interest.

He knew I liked to shoot, and after lunch he asked if I would care to see one of his Christmas presents: a single-shot, high-velocity Remington varmint pistol with a telescopic sight. He led me to the front porch and pointed out a steel bullet trap installed on a low stone wall across his wide driveway. We took turns blazing away until his wife, Peggy, sternly told us to knock it off. The neighbors had complained in the past and there was an Episcopal church down the hill, not far from the line of sight. I felt sorry that suburban civilization was encroaching on Goldwater's wonderful house, restricting him and hemming him in. In political speeches he sometimes talked some awful bosh on the subject, but he really did love freedom, personal freedom, and I always admired his tenacious insistence on preserving his own independence.

The next political obligation was a speech at an Elks Hall in Nogales, a town straddling the Arizona-Sonora border. On an impulse he decided that we must eat in a first-class Mexican restaurant on the Sonora side. When we protested that we had to stay with him, he decided to take us there himself. This was not exactly convenient. He had been scheduled to arrive in Nogales in the evening and be greeted by an airport rally. He left a note on his desk for his maid, asking her to telephone someone in Nogales about the change in plans, and hurried us out to the airport where we boarded two chartered planes and flew to Nogales in midafternoon.

Miraculously, the maid found the note and phoned a Nogales Republican leader. He and two lady party workers raced up to the airstrip just as we were landing. They were dismayed when Goldwater explained that he had come early "to take these boys to dinner." But he could be irresistible and they ended up coming along, too. The rally never did take place, and I wondered how many people came out to that airstrip to see their missing hero.

I've never had a better evening. The restaurant was as good as Goldwater had promised. We drank Margaritas and washed down the food with cold Mexican beer. Mexican friends of Goldwater marched into the dining room with a banner bearing the words "Viva Goldwater," and joined the table. A mariachi band serenaded us during the meal. It starred a cornet player of enormous girth who played one-handed while, with wonderful insolence, he hooked the thumb of his free hand through his belt.

Goldwater was happy and the best of hosts. The conversation was bright and good. (I particularly remember from that evening an account of how, as a student, Goldwater was once jailed in Nogales and paid his bail with a phony check.) Full of tequila and brotherly love, we left the restaurant and walked back across the border to the Elks Hall. We felt the most comradely affection for Goldwater.

And then he started his speech, in which he said that Lyndon Johnson wanted to "take us back to the days of monarchy, dictatorship and one-man rule." The reporters sighed.

Affection was restored after the flight back to Phoenix. In the chilly Arizona midnight we stood under an airplane wing and passed a bottle of tequila around the circle and listened to the mariachi music playback on an NBC tape recorder. Peggy Goldwater, a tender but tough woman whom we found wholly admirable, took a pull at the bottle with the rest of us. When she tugged on Barry's sleeve, he was reluctant to go home.

"Let's hear it one more time," he said. We felt the same way.

We returned to New Hampshire, and in the windup of that campaign Goldwater began to make an unique appeal, surpassing in audacity Knute Rockne's exhortation to "Win this one for the Gipper." He would explain to audiences that he was scheduled to ride in the grand parade of the

Phoenix "rodeo of rodeos" a few days after the New Hampshire election. He said he would like to win the primary because "it will make my twenty-three-year-old Palomino, Sunny, happy." Sometimes he would embellish this plea by saying he hoped to win so that "I can ride with my hat off and people in my hometown will say, 'There goes the guy who won in New Hampshire.' "

Goldwater, of course, suffered a humiliating defeat, losing to Henry Cabot Lodge, who wasn't even in the Western hemisphere.

After the election, Mears, MacNeil and myself flew out to Phoenix to cover the rodeo parade. Somehow we talked our way into the parade and drove our convertible right behind Goldwater and Sunny. The result was almost too pat to be funny. Goldwater rode with his hat off much of the time, all right. But a fat woman on the curb gave him a raspberry and shouted with terrible, piercing clarity, "There goes the guy who lost in New Hampshire."

To avoid making a fool of himself while covering Goldwater, a reporter had to free himself of a belief in most political axioms. One such axiom is that while the nomination is not won in primaries it can be lost in primaries. Like many other rules, this one did not fit Goldwater. Losing in New Hampshire didn't hurt him a bit. But it drastically changed him and his campaign.

For one thing, he got a speech writer. Goldwater and his campaign advisers had concluded it was too dangerous to continue to rely on extemporaneous speeches. A little caution was indicated.

And very little caution is what Barry got. He chose as his ghost a man named Karl Hess, who had made a career as a right-wing idea man and as a conservative writer. Because he was short and round, Hess was sometimes described inaptly as "Buddha-like." Goldwater was not a fervent man. Underneath a wisecracking exterior Hess burned with zeal. It was impossible for Hess to be a moderating influence on Goldwater because Hess was farther to the right than the candidate.

One of Hess's earliest efforts, delivered by Goldwater in a Southern California football stadium, was a suggestion that the war in Vietnam be ended by bombing the "opium fields" of North Vietnam. It was the first literal example of poppycock I had ever encountered. Hess expanded the strategy in conversation. The United States should also destroy the North Vietnamese rice crop by aerial spraying and, when a repentant Ho Chi Minh had seen the folly of aggression and come to his knees, a generous America would ship him food in return for strict observance of the Geneva Accords. I was not among those journalists who were surprised when Goldwater later stood in San Francisco's Cow Palace and read a speech saying extremism in the defense of liberty was no vice.

But the New Hampshire defeat not only produced a Hess for Goldwater, it also brought major changes in the style and personality of the candidate himself. He had never before lost an election and he was not only angry, he was badly shaken.

Goldwater and his staff had begun the campaign believing there was a mute but vast army of American voters already in full agreement with his ideas and ready to rally to the colors. He hadn't tried to be cautious because he thought caution was unnecessary. He had no feel for audiences; his fellow "conservatives" raised so much hell and cheered so loudly that he failed to notice the reaction of ordinary, uncommitted voters. After the New Hampshire election, Goldwater came to a conclusion which must have been humiliating for him—he would need to conceal rather than reveal his opinions, take it easy, play it safe. Because he was so strong with middle- and lower-level Republican party leaders in the non-primary states, the nomination virtually was his. But he had to get through the California primary on June 2.

He had been the most open and frank candidate in memory, but now he was to become one of the most guarded. Press conferences almost ceased, and Goldwater never relaxed with reporters again. Tiresomely, he began to repeat careful, ambiguous written answers to questions on such touchy subjects as Social Security and extremism. And in one of the real innovations of American politics, his campaign strategy in California came to rest on the principle of campaigning as little as possible. He spent hours in hotel suites, dressed in a nightgown embroidered with the words "Goldwater's Body Shop, 24-Hour Service," watching afternoon reruns of TV Westerns. He made few speeches. He relied on his California organization to get out the vote and barely squeaked through to victory over Rockefeller. For some reason he was a worse winner than a loser.

The CBS computer declared him victor only twenty-two minutes after the polls closed in Los Angeles. Goldwater didn't wait around to celebrate. He boarded an overnight flight to Washington with a few of us as his unwelcome companions. He dropped into a seat, closed his eyes and pretended—not successfully—to fall asleep even before we took off. It can be said, though, that he only snubbed us. The reporters waiting for him at Washington the next morning were victims of one of the surliest and most inexcusable temper tantrums I have ever seen in public life. For some reason, Goldwater seemed to be furious that they were there to cover what was, after all, the biggest story of the day. When they attempted to ask him questions, he bulled through them to his car, tossing over his shoulder such sarcasms as "Why didn't you watch TV last night?"

At San Francisco, the convention became for us a blur of missed meals, twenty-hour days and endless fights to keep Goldwater's bodyguards from dislodging us from our beachhead on the candidate's floor of the Mark

Hopkins. Goldwater learned to smile a little once more, but he clearly hated the mobs who clutched adoringly at him. For most of the convention, Barry and his organization had absolute mastery of the situation. Their control was effortless, smooth and savvy. They looked good. But then some of them wrote, and the others approved, a speech containing thirty irretrievable, irreparable words: "I would remind you that extremism in the defense of liberty is no vice. And I would further remind you that moderation in the pursuit of justice is no virtue." The most significant measure of Goldwater's problem as a politician is that he never could understand why that speech caused so much trouble; he just didn't get it. An hour after he delivered the speech, he instructed Ed Nellor to tell the press that he particularly liked that line.

Goldwater took it relatively easy in the period between July and September. At one point he took a week off for a yacht cruise off the Southern California coast. One night he invited Clint Walker of TV's *Cheyenne* series aboard and spent the evening, we were told, singing cowboy songs. But there were spasms of activity, and important signs for those perceptive enough to see them.

Karl Hess began to hit his stride with what we reporters came to call the "anti-rape speech." First delivered at the Illinois State Fair in Springfield, this leitmotiv was to run like a thread through many other speeches until it was replaced by anti-homosexuality. Speaking from the infield of the state-fair racetrack, Goldwater deplored the increase in crime, but said there was no need for him to describe what kind of crime.

"Every wife and mother, yes, every woman and girl knows what I mean, knows what I am talking about," said Barry.

In August he went to Cleveland to make a speech to the Veterans of Foreign Wars—the speech in which he coined a new phrase by referring to "conventional nuclear weapons." (Another measure of his problem as a politician: he really thought he could pick and win semantic battles of that kind.) His arrival in Cleveland had been well-publicized, including time and route through the city. Yet there were very few on the streets to see him. Some city blocks were so empty it looked as though an air-raid drill was in progress. He later was to prove to be one of the worst crowd pullers in political history.

The campaign began formally in early September at Prescott, Arizona, in front of "Bucky" O'Neill's statue, with Goldwater giving a speech which was moderate but without much meaning. What I remember most about that day is an incident which showed he was still capable of flashes of his rascally but endearing old impudence.

As he was about to board his plane at Phoenix to fly to Prescott, reporters stopped him for a few questions. I mentioned that when Harry S. Truman set out from Washington's Union Station in 1948 on his campaign he had said he was going to "give 'em hell." Did Barry have any similar war cry for us?

"I'm not allowed to use the same bad language Harry Truman used," said Goldwater. (To his credit, he did smile.)

Peggy Goldwater's head snapped around toward Barry—and then she laughed.

For the next few weeks we traveled together on a chartered jet to which Goldwater had given the Navaho name "Yia Bi Kin," or House in the Sky. We used to amuse ourselves by telling strangers that the words were not Navaho but Yiddish.

There was never any single, major issue that dominated Goldwater's campaign. This was partly because he was desperately trying and discarding gimmicks, looking for the ultimate gimmick. Another reason was that to Goldwater *everything* was an issue. Back in New Hampshire I had written that while Goldwater's ideas were rather austere he was a man without malice. He proved me to be wrong in the general election campaign. He was throwing the ball right at his enemies' heads; if he missed it was not by design.

He began to use the white-backlash issue with an unexpected openness, as when he denounced "gang rape in California" and the Negro riots of 1964 in consecutive sentences.

In Minneapolis he suggested that welfare-state policies may promote crime by encouraging have-nots to think that if the government can take from the rich, the have-nots may get the idea they can too.

He often appealed to small-town, rural America by denouncing the "degradation" and crime of "the boss-ridden, racket-ridden cities."

He attacked the anti-poverty program by saying poverty was exaggerated as a problem and by warning that "a society in which no one is permitted to fall below the average is one in which no one can be permitted to rise above it."

He called the Democratic Party a "Fascist organization" because a local committee had expelled a Milwaukee alderman from the party for endorsing Goldwater.

Goldwater's crowds didn't help restore his perspective. His style was building apathy and/or hostility with most of the country, but Goldwater was doing much of his speaking at night in closed auditoriums full of screaming, hard-core conservatives, who couldn't get enough of it. And if his crowds were not especially large, they were fascinating. They screamed for blood with a frightening, animal intensity. At the same time, however, Goldwater drew hecklers who showed a virulence unusual even for American politics. They carried posters with such messages as "Fascist Lip in the West," and "Racists, Bigots United for Goldwater," and "Don't Stop Here—We're Poor Enough Already."

The only appetizing part of the crowds were the girls. There were Amazon-sized Texas co-eds in scanty cowgirl skirts. At Montgomery there was an entire football field full of Alabama belles in long crinoline gowns, looking as though they had just come from Jefferson Davis' inaugural ball. There were also the "Goldwater Girls" and the "Goldwater Gals," who like the Russians and Chinese had split into two camps and were having an ideological conflict. One branch wore yellow skirts and white blouses; the other branch wore red, white and blue. They *hated* each other. I was never able to understand exactly what the dispute was about. (One of my favorite stories from the campaign involved a Goldwater Girl who was propositioned by a newsman. She agreed to come to his room, but pleaded that she had to go home first to change. "I wouldn't want to disgrace Senator Goldwater by doing anything wrong in uniform," she is quoted as saying.)

The one area where Goldwater was hitting paydirt was in the South. Much of the dialogue between Goldwater and his Southern fans was in a virtual code. He managed to discuss race constantly without using the word.

He told one crowd that he might favor some social changes "but I am perfectly willing to be patient about them—and you are too." How true.

Goldwater's views on the Supreme Court were bizarre. He attacked the court's reapportionment decisions by saying that "everyone has his little pet projects, but I would like to remind you, ladies and gentlemen, that there are perfectly *legal* ways to do these things."

He pandered shamelessly to the Dixiecrats. He told one crowd that if he had had to put up with what their grandfathers suffered in Reconstruction days he might have been a Democrat, too. (It was not untypical of Barry that he said this in Knoxville, a part of Tennessee which had been pro-Union and Republican in sympathies, the one place in the state where such sentiments were least apt.)

He had a tongue of lead. Some of Goldwater's speeches, if translated into policy, might have been catastrophic for some Americans. But other speeches were simply catastrophic for Goldwater. They reflected a sort of country-club conservatism—as though he were talking to some buddies in the locker room, delivering the usual locker-room denunciation of taxes, Walter Reuther and foreign aid. Sometimes they could be excruciatingly specific, even if his intent was opaque. At Marion, Ohio, the hometown of Warren G. Harding (whom he described as one of his boyhood heroes), Barry stupefied a friendly crowd with a long dissertation on the shortage of "bracero" Mexican field workers faced by garden farmers in the Southwest. "Cantaloupes don't just jump in the bag," said Goldwater in one of the least controversial but most inconsequential remarks of the year.

We never tired of collecting Goldwaterisms. He told a crowd in St.

Petersburg that the Great Society without freedom "is nothing more than a meaningless hump of anthill." His grammar was atrocious (but he had my sympathy there). He used to thank crowds for coming out to "meet my wife and I."

Goldwater would say on one occasion that he would never appeal to special interests. On other occasions he would not only appeal to them, he would pass the point of no return. In North Carolina, which is a peanut-growing state, he said, "I am probably the most violent advocate of peanut butter in history. On a dare from my son, I even shaved with it once, and it was all right, except that it smelled."

I pondered that. Had Goldwater really shaved with peanut butter? It was not unlike him. On the other hand, he was more complex than he seemed, and I often had the feeling he was pulling the whole nation's leg and enjoying it immensely. For instance, it was true that he had a compressor and an air hose at his Phoenix swimming pool which allowed him to play around under the water. But he once told some credulous photographers that he sometimes stayed for two hours at a time on the bottom and fell asleep!

After accusations were leveled that former U.S. Ambassador to Ireland, Matthew McCloskey, had made an illegal kickback contribution to the Democratic Party through Bobby Baker, Goldwater began to use the issue—but he couldn't seem to remember McCloskey's name.

"We don't want a government of Bobby Bakers and Matt McCormicks," he told a crowd in Dayton, Ohio.

That evening on the charter plane I typed out a satiric handbill to be circulated among the passengers. It said: "Join Now. The Friends of Matt McCormick Society. Help Clear This Innocent Man!" Goldwater was not amused. In January, I think he might have been, but he was not the same man he had been then.

The most dangerous word in his vocabulary was "but." During the year he became increasingly bitter in the belief that his words had been twisted and misrepresented. He was always trying to "straighten out" the record. He never learned, however, when to stop. When he first got into trouble on Social Security, he would often painstakingly tell an audience that he was not really for major changes in the program. Then came that treacherous word "but." But, he would add, the public would probably be begging Congress for modification by 1970. People just didn't trust that kind of an approach; it left Goldwater's own opinion far too ambivalent.

He had the same problem in dealing with the charge that he was trigger-happy. He had never ever advocated nuclear war—he just talked about it all the time. And simply by discussing the matter so much, Goldwater did himself more harm on the nuclear-war issue than Lyndon Johnson ever did. In one speech alone, Goldwater mentioned nuclear weapons, war and such words as "devastation" a total of twenty-six times in thirty minutes. He used to imply that too much fear of nuclear war was rather silly and sissified. At Springfield, Missouri, he said that for "too long we've listened to those people who see something dangerous under every bush." At Evansville, Indiana, that same day he described world communism as the "schoolyard bully" and said:

"Let him push you around and eventually you'll have to fight. There is no room for argument. Whenever the schoolyard bully meets someone who stands up to him . . . then the bully will back down."

More sensitive and intelligent journalists than I recognized that Goldwater was at times succeeding in touching some basic yearnings in the American mind, the desire for a more orderly society and for settled values. I began to see it, too, but, at the same time, I saw that Goldwater could not sustain such a campaign no matter how much he talked about morality. His spirituality was off.

At Springfield he wound up and let loose with this summation:

"I suggest that instead of listening to the crybabies of Washington we listen to the goodness of God."

One night in a football stadium, he said that in his library ("my film library," he amended) he had a copy of the famous photograph of a Frenchman weeping on the streets of Paris as the Nazi army marched in.

"I think of that Frenchman," said Goldwater, "and of the tears in his eyes when I think what's going on in this country."

The man in the restaurant in Glendora was right—someone should have got to Goldwater.

In covering the campaign I tried hard to be fair and, above all, accurate. If I failed, I think I mostly failed in his favor. I seldom printed the outright absurdities like his "lucid moment" fluff in Reno. I was one of those journalists who, early in the year, fostered the impression that Barry was a "nice guy," an impression that influenced newcomers to the campaign long after I had become appalled by his thoughtless rudeness. It was rather typical of Goldwater that he could be generous in his praise of my work in private, while in public he compared the *Times* to *Izvestia*.

But the more exhaustive and accurate was coverage of Goldwater, the more it hurt him. Even before the convention had taken place, a friend told me that a distinguished and famous journalist had said, "Mohr has peeled Goldwater like an onion—a layer at a time—and now there is nothing left." Goldwater, of course, had hanged himself. Journalism, like copper, is a good conductor, but it is harmless unless something lethal is fed into it.

He lost the election for many reasons, but the most important of these were his character and his style. No candidate ever talked so much but appreciated so little the importance of words. He was an extraordinarily illogical man. In the early weeks of the campaign he used to say that the Civil Rights Bill was bad because it would "force you to admit drunks, murderers and known rapists to your place of business." (Some of us used to speculate about how many towns had a "known rapist" wandering about looking for a cup of coffee.) In the same breath he would say that it was "perfectly all right" if a state or city government passed such legislation. Now, the bill was either going to work the grotesque result which Goldwater claimed or it was not, and whether it was Federal law would make no difference.

Goldwater's self-destructive style grew out of the fact that he was essentially a superficial and frivolous man. He really thought he could advocate making Social Security voluntary one day and withdraw the suggestion the next without paying any penalty: he was unable to appreciate how seriously people took the issue. He cried that his political opponents and the press were "twisting" his words, but his real problem was that the voters would not forgive him either his threat to their interests or his inconsistency.

Some people viewed the Goldwater campaign as a potential tragedy for the country. I came finally to view it as a personal tragedy for Goldwater. Politically, he destroyed himself and he maimed the Republican Party, an institution for which he felt genuine loyalty and affection. Personally, he made himself miserable running for an office I am convinced he did not want; and in so doing, giving up the place in the Senate which he loved so much. He not only lost the election, he also lost his illusions and illusions were important to him. He found that the "conservative movement in America" was not the growing, marching army he had thought it was.

He also lost his sense of proportion and his sense of humor. He had grown up a somewhat spoiled and selfish rich boy, but like many spoiled rich boys he had enormous charm. Subjected to defeat and to pressure, the charm cracked, and then it crumbled.

Worst of all, Goldwater failed in the only serious purpose of his campaign, to give the voters "a clear choice, not an echo." He knew as well as anyone he had little chance to be elected, but he set out to offer a serious alternative to the foreign and domestic policies which had dominated American political life for thirty years. He did not succeed because he did not offer real choices but absurdities, as when he said that a vote for the Democrats was a vote for "tyranny." He never outlined a coherent conservative position, and he changed his stand so often many voters never knew just what he was about. Conservatism was destroyed without being tested, rather like a rocket aborted on the launching pad.

As Barry would say, "It's as simple as that."

[August, 1965]

Part IV
The New Sentimentality

The New Sentimentality

by Robert Benton
and David Newman

INTRODUCTION

There is a New Sentimentality, but nobody knows it exists. Once it was a kind of virtue, as in: "He is sentimental; he has a good heart." Then, as times changed, the term slipped from grace and became pejorative. "Don't give me that sentimental slop." And so all the wiser people and the intellectuals believed there was no more sentimentality in them. They thought they had replaced it with cynicism and honesty. But they were wrong. They merely exchanged Old Sentimentality for New Sentimentality.

The changeover came in the Fifties. Eisenhower was a key figure, perhaps the last bloom of Old Sentimentality. It was seen that the masses loved him, as a father or maybe Gramps, and those who felt they were above that kind of adoration said: "Look at that. How corny can anybody get? It's like a Norman Rockwell cover." They cast off sentiment, seeing it as weakness. They cultivated the art of "playing it cool." But the New Sentimentality was growing, without their ever knowing it.

Suddenly it was 1960 and John Kennedy was there, and the wise, the intellectual and the taste-making people did him homage. They didn't

399

think he was a father or Gramps. They liked him because he was tough, because he was all pro, because he was a man who knew what he wanted and grabbed it. They loved that in him as furiously as the crowds loved Ike. They sentimentalized every power grab. And that was when the New Sentimentality came out in the open.

Old Sentimentality had "values" that everyone could see, bywords that meant the same to all: Patriotism, Love, Religion, Mom, The Girl. The values of the New Sentimentality are not out there emblazoned on banners. They differ slightly from man to man, because one of the definitions of New Sentimentality is that it has to do with you, really just you, not what you were told or taught, but what goes on in your head, *really,* and in your heart, *really.*

Here are its tenets: Personal interest is the abiding motivation. In the Old way you had ideals, causes, goals that were in some way beneficent to all. In the New, your primary objective is to make your life fit your style. There is Professionalism above all. For example, the Old concept of "selling out," which used to drive good men crazy, causing them to cry in their beer and bemoan their wasted talent (writing ad copy, for instance), has disappeared. Now we glory in what pros we are, and a man loves himself for writing the best jingle on the market.

We used to be sentimental about Common Sense. To have it meant you did the Right Thing, considered its effects on all concerned, acted wisely. Now Common Sense has been supplanted by Sharpness. We love ourselves when we are really sharp. We love to see evidence of a sharp cookie winning the day, as long as he isn't a villain.

Self-indulgence used to be a bad idea. Anybody who was labeled with the term was wasting himself. Now it is a virtue. We think it is worthwhile because it tells us the truth about ourselves, about our drives and appetites. So we swing with it. We say, "Did I have a wild night!" and we feel pleased. It shows we have a sense of self.

We used to pride ourselves on our ability to Maintain A Firm Position, on anything. Now we pride ourselves on our Ability To Change. Men who switch jobs aren't drifters anymore; they go where the action is. They're proud of it.

We still get nostalgic, but we no longer get that dreamy feeling about old values, such as Togetherness or Sitting By An Open Fire. We now get nostalgic about old trivia: the movies we saw when we were in high school, the lies we told, a girl who jilted us.

We used to feel guilty when we realized that television was destroying "the art of conversation." When the electricity failed, we were exhilarated to see the old days come back. Now we read books about television and only regret it when show schedulings conflict.

We deal with God according to our own personal concept, not the minister's. We don't see Evil all around us, but if we suspect a touch of it in ourselves, we are rather glad.

The Key Couples of the New Sentimentality: They moved us, and taught us the style and the substance. In *Breathless,* we understood Belmondo, because he was cool and tough, but soft in the center. He was destroyed because he let love carry him away. We loved Jean Seberg because she was fragile, but hard.

Mr. and Mrs. John F. Kennedy reached us, because they created a style that succeeded. He, because he was the pro, the operator, the man who made his score. She, because she played the pro's wife with an appreciation of the higher aspects of the situation, and because she looked like a movie star.

PATRIOTISM

Old Sentimentality: Old Glory . . .   *Uncle Sam*

Old Sentimentality:	*New Sentimentality:*
The Fourth of July	Nothing
Cherry Blossoms	

Patriotism means commitment to an ideal, to something bigger than yourself and feeling proud of it. New Sentimentality does not allow for such commitment and blind service. In the New, you are proud only of your commitment to self.

TRANSITIONAL FIGURE

Marilyn Monroe moved from Old to New. Old in her life, her movies, her men, she became a factor of the New in her death. When she died, we did not react by saying, "How tragic." We said and felt, "Look what can happen to you when you screw up your life." We mourn her neuroticism.

MYTHOLOGY

Old Sentimentality: The Ox-Bow Incident

New Sentimentality: Shoot the Piano Player

Old Sentimentality: *The Ox-Bow Incident* said that good men must band together, that fair play could prevent evil, that friends should stick together, and fight the system, that love helps. New Sentimentality: *Shoot the Piano Player* showed that getting involved with people meant getting hurt, that love and devotion left you wide open for destruction, that living in disguise was the smart way to be yourself, that being alone was the only way to exist in an absurd world.

PSYCHOANALYSIS

In the New Sentimentality, those of us under analysis are sentimental about our neuroses. We fondly reminisce about our analysts and the exciting day we broke through to recall a trauma. Even the trauma takes on the qualities of a nostalgic event. Old Sentimentality was obsessed with psychiatry and bragged of cures and purges. New Sentimentality brags about the problems. We tell new friends about it so they'll know they are in the company of people as hung up as they are. We have learned how we mess things up, and we make those failures a part of our style. Take it or leave it.

SOVIETS

Old: Marx

New: Khrushchev

Old: Karl Marx, who believed in Utopia based on mankind cooperating. All would someday be well. Men, arise. New: Nikita Khrushchev, who knows that tension is the natural condition, that playing angles is the control.

POLITICS

Old Sentimentality:	New Sentimentality:
Marxism	The C.I.A.
Pacifism	
SANE	
Reform movements	
Splitting your ticket	
to vote for the man	

We had finally learned the cynicism of politics and there was nothing left to do but romanticize it. No longer shocked by corruption or stupidity in high places, we now admired the smoothie who didn't botch it up, the *coup* that worked.

FRIENDSHIP

In the Old Sentimentality, men had buddies and pals, a bunch of "the boys" they played poker with every Monday night, a world without women to retreat to. They treasured it. Women had "the girls," and hen parties, and a close girl chum to confide in. In the New Sentimentality, we have accomplices. Friends are not for escape, they are for conspiring. Men have given up the "boys." The wife or the lover is the best friend. Women have given up "the girls." New Sentimental women are men-oriented; they don't like other women very much. The Old Sentimentalists wrote a lot of letters to old pals. New Sentimentalists are lousy correspondents. Old friends are of no value; current collaborators are. The New Sentimentality also puts a high value on friends having an aura of attractiveness. Couples hang together because one man finds the friend's wife attractive and his wife likes the way the husband reacts to her. We also cultivate winners— they are more pleasant than losers. The New Sentimentality allows friendships to change without guilt. Circles are broadened. Nostalgia is for childhood friends, but mostly for childhood enemies. We recall not the kid we were pals with, but the bully that beat us up periodically. Or the girl we played "Doctor" with. What was her name? She was an accomplice.

LIFE PATTERNS

Old Sentimentality:	New Sentimentality:
Bad Luck	Getting Carried Away
Maturity	Wounding and
Common Sense	Being Wounded
Carrying the Torch	Inherent Flaws
Has-Beens	Vulnerability
Loyalty	Anxiety
College Ties	One-night Stands
Finding Yourself	Change
Selling Out	Going Where the Action Is
	Sharpness

LOVE

Old Sentimentality: The Prom

Under the reign of Old Sentimentality, we believed in the efficacy of Whitman's Samplers with sweets for the sweet. We intoned "Diamonds Are Forever." We got dreamy-eyed over dancing, proms, "our song," parking, "best girls," engagement rings. We loved to propose. We subscribed to the theory that self-sacrifice would prove ardency ("I'll go through fire for you"), and to the concept that one could trade on his ardor. We had a vestige of the really old days in feeling that one should have semi-honorable intentions toward his beloved. We believed love had a capital L, that it was true, that True Love was everlasting, that hearts broke, that there was one Great Love, that for every man was a woman, that you didn't say, "I love you," unless you really were positive. That's all gone. The New Sentimentality is organized on other lines. We now get starry-eyed about the fact that everybody is bound to get hurt in an affair, that we can be destroyed, but that we can surely bounce back. We no longer carry the torch. We pride ourselves on our ability to bounce back. We are sentimental about the transient nature of love affairs; we enter them knowing they won't last and loving the impermanence. Under Old Sentimentality, we believed we should keep something in reserve. Now we do our best to Get Carried Away. We assume that going overboard is part of love. We revel in the highs and we revel as much in the lows. We like to tell our lovers that we have moods and a lot of weaknesses. We pray they won't use them to destroy us, but then we do the same thing to them. Love is unsure.

CHILDREN

Old: Stuart Little *New: Charlie Brown*

In the Old Sentimentality, we pretended that children were cute "little people." In the New Sentimentality, we see that kids are kids, and they've got their own problems. They are not little grown-ups, but they remind us of ourselves because we see our own problems forming in them. We used to raise our children to be Good Citizens, to be loyal to our values. Now we know better, having seen the results in ourselves. So now we raise our kids, above all else, to be Sharp. We want them to be on top of it, for their protection.

SONGS

Old Sentimentality:
One for My Baby (and One
More for the Road)

New Sentimentality:
Surf City

It is no longer the tunes about Mom, or Summer, or That Gal Who Left Me that turn us on. We are capable of being captivated by a Twist lyric, or a quartet screaming "Zam." Rock 'n' roll is calculated, cynical. It's about us, *now*.

MARRIAGE

Old Sentimentality: George and Gracie

Old Sentimentality said that Marriage was an Institution. New Sentimentality says that Marriage is a day-to-day situation. Old Marriage had pipe and slippers, and what's-for-dinner-tonight, honey?, and family meetings, and protecting the little woman, and sanctity of the home above all else. New Marriage believes that things will work out, but it will not be easy, that crises will be forthcoming constantly, that love will help to hold it together but more is needed. New Marriage is based on privacy when somebody wants it, on at least one good knock-down, drag-out screaming fight a month just to clear the air, on both partners being kind to weaknesses. We expect our mates to be sophisticated in bed because we still like to preserve the sanctity of the home. New Sentimentality also allows for people to get very sentimental about their divorces. You hear it all the time. As for Adultery, it is an Old phrase, like Extramarital. New Marriage is more faithful than Old, because the people have already had enough affairs. One or two more don't destroy the union; we understand the nature of the impulse.

New Sentimentality: Jules and Jim

SEX

Old Sentimentality:	*New Sentimentality:*
Good Girls vs. Bad Girls	People Who Taught You
The Whore With	How To Make Love
a Heart of Gold	The Nostalgia of Necking
Honorable Intentions	Your Own Ineptitude
	Minor Perversions (yours)

The age of the tramp is gone. To be a "swinger" is to pat yourself on the back and be glad you're weak, kind of, but having a ball. We respect girls who sleep around a little. They are nicer. Virgins scare us out of the room. Fun is fun.

TRANSITIONAL FIGURE

The Maltese Falcon *to . . .*

. . . Beat the Devil—*no change*

Bogart makes the jump from Old to New. He was always a bit of both. Old because he was a man's man, a tough guy with the ladies, an arrogant talker, a slammer of authority. New because he always played a good man who was quite unscrupulous, because he grinned at the sexy girl first and then kissed her in sudden passion, because he took the Old Sentimentality of Sam Spade and transformed it into New. Bogart says that a man can both care and not give a damn.

CELEBRITIES

Old Sentimentality: John Wayne   *New Sentimentality: Timothy Carey*

The Old Sentimentality said that anybody who was famous was a celebrity and therefore possessed glamour and excitement. It didn't matter what we personally thought of them. We idolized movie stars because they were movie stars and if it was a rotten movie, so what? In the New Sentimentality, our celebrities come from the Underground. A minor character actor who happens to excite us in a personal way is a real celebrity. If we see somebody like Timothy Carey, the scared soldier in *Paths of Glory,* we react. We save our adulation for the man who happens to say something directly to us, not for the man who grabs the masses. We may therefore ascribe heartfelt sentiments to diverse people, like Al Capone, Abbott but not Costello, Barton MacLane, Ringo.

DIVERSIONS

Travel: The Old Sentimentality about travel was the delight derived from visiting colorful countries, seeing the natives. In New Sentimentality, all the romance is in the traveling itself. The airport is as exciting as the destination. The idea of flying across the world is better than landing any place. We do not paste stickers on our luggage, but we tell our friends about the movie we saw on the flight. We are not in love with the foreign girls as much as with the stewardesses. The *idea* of going is what we like best.

Television: The Old Sentimentality watches C.B.S. Reports and Sunday afternoon cultural programs and educational TV. The New Sentimentality watches *The Beverly Hillbillies* not because they like it, but because they admire its success. Late-night movies and afternoon reruns are the most beloved.

PLACES

Old Sentimentality: Manhattan

Old Sentimentality: San Francisco

Sentimentality: Jazz Festivals

Old Sentimentality: Jails (also, Hometowns)

New Sentimentality: No place

The Old Sentimentality always had us seeing you in all those old familiar places, cozy bars, certain hills and lovers' lanes, great steel-canyon cities that pulsed with glamour, colorful settings, simple streets where dear hearts and gentle people lived, crowded rooms where we saw a stranger one enchanted evening. In the New Sentimentality, all the places are inside you. There are no more "settings" against which we play our little dramas. We can be sentimental in our kitchen if we feel in the mood. Life doesn't "play better" against a moonlit sky anymore. There are no places; we make our own. We have learned that you can have a beautiful time on the Staten Island Ferry, or a lousy one. It has nothing to do with the Staten Island Ferry. Nothing at all.

WRITERS

Old: Ernest Hemingway

Bravery above all. Dying well. Honor as an eternal value. Hunting. Bulls.

Old: Arthur Miller

Inner honor. Suicides. Social poetizing. New Deal. American tragedies. Find yourself.

Old: Dorothy Parker

Cynicism used for shock. A *weltschmerz* for failures. Emancipation of women.

Old: E. E. Cummings

Love is like a flower, or a mountain. Love as a gift. Condemnation of compromise.

Old: John O'Hara

Sinning destroys. Myth of respectability as a façade. Sex as Evil. Class system.

Old: Jack Kerouac

Joys of the open road. Excess as a positive. Myth of the glamorous wastrel. Zen.

Old: Jean Cocteau

Death as poetry. Hellenic legends apply to our time. Mystique of "The Artist."

New: Robert Lowell

Beauty of destruction. The sanitarium as a setting for a poem. The order of chaos.

American writers are almost entirely of the Old Sentimentality. They gave us values to create conflicts. Their heroes rebelled against some existing order—social, psychological, romantic, familial—and were meaningful thereby. The hot new writers are much the same; even the surrealists who deal with the bizarre as a mirror of reality are upset about values. They chronicle their decay. The writers of the New Sentimentality appear in Europe. Few are good at it. Beckett is, Colette was becoming. The case of Nabokov is interesting. He is Old (*Pnin, The Gift*) and New (*Lolita, Pale Fire*), but he is never entirely one or the other. That is a measure of his greatness, no doubt about it. Robert Lowell is our most New Sentimental writer. He sees it happening.

THE PAST

Old: Tolstoy   *New: Proust*

The Motherland, the adulteress, the man of the soil, the intellectual, the Hero—these are Tolstoy's creations of Old Sentimentality. The operator, the manipulation of people in love, the vision of love as a fleeting episode in which any commitment brings pain and ineptitude, and most important now, the sense of the past as no different from today in terms of human behavior—that is all in Proust. He was the visionary of the New.

HEROS

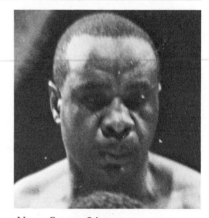

Old: Ben Hogan   *New: Sonny Liston*

Old Sentimentality: Ben Hogan is the fallen hero, a victim of Bad Luck, who fought His Way to the Top again and was an Inspiration. That is Very Old Sentimentality. New Sentimentality: Sonny Liston was the man nobody liked, but of whom people said, "You've got to hand it to him." A hero without heroics, his defeat was right in the tradition.

ART

: Jackson Pollock

New: Roy Lichtenstein

: Andrew Wyeth

New: Balthus

Pollock is Old because he was in the tradition of the Romantic Artist, the life burned out, the garret. Wyeth is Old because he proffers the Romance of Loneliness, Isolation. Lichtenstein is New because he puts art on, sees terror in humor, has no values. Balthus is New because he likes Evil.

PROPAGANDA

Old Sentimentality: La Dolce Vita

New Sentimentality: L'Avventura

Old Sentimentality: *La Dolce Vita* was Old, because its point of view was from the outside looking in at decay. It put the blame on society, evil, easy money, and bad company. New Sentimentality: *L'Avventura* dealt with the same subject from within. It said that decay was ennui, eroticism, lack of purpose—in other words, people. It said love was selfish.

THE PROBLEM

Old: James Baldwin   *New: Malcolm X*

James Baldwin is Goodness. He is typecast. He is the ideal Idealist and he writes, too. His novels and his new play are corny. Malcolm X is for self-defense and no sweet solutions. He is rough. He splits with the cause when it holds him back. He gets publicity and fights.

JAZZ

Old: Count Basie   *New: The Modern Jazz Quartet*

Old Sentimentality: Count Basie is playing controlled emotion. The hotter it is, the tighter the arrangement. One dances to it. One fantasizes "The Free Spirit." Hot jazz assumes that you need the music for a cathartic, for a release. But nobody jumps at one o'clock anymore. New Sentimentality: The Modern Jazz Quartet plays music that doesn't release you. It suspends you. The formalization of the M.J.Q. is not sentimental, but the clarity is. At best, the music reveals a note, crystal clear, hanging in space, ready to be broken. We want that in the New Sentimentality, because it's like us: fragile but rooted in blues, ordered but given to flights of fancy, insecure but heading in some direction. Problem swing.

FASHION

New: The Pucci Dress

Women dressing for women are not in the New Sentimentality. The designer Pucci was the first to realize that what men love about women is not their chic, or their correctness, but their bodies. Men are sentimental about bodies. The Pucci dress is all about women's structure. It respects the body and makes it look female. There are cheap dresses that do this, but they can't do it for the woman you love.

PURVEYORS OF OLD SENTIMENTALITY

These are the people who stand for past values. They are role players. In some cases, they played that role purposefully and aggressively. In others, they didn't plan it. They were of their time and that time is going. Best of their breed, they gave us the living manifestations of the Old Sentimentality.

Mr. and Mrs. Dwight D. Eisenhower
To Old Sentimentalists, they will always be Ike and Mamie. They are red, white and blue; apple-pie American; Gettysburg farm; grandchildren; West Point; Western novels; simple decency; Republican.

Gene Kelly
He is the happy sailor; muscular ballet; MGM; open smile; lover of ideal woman.

Jackie Robinson
He is the American Way; the Hard Road Up; courage; the very legend of the athlete.

Purveyors of Old Sentimentality—Continued

Danny Kaye
He is Children Are the Same the Whole World Over; a smile and a song; Universal Language of Love; Uncle Sam; beloved by royalty; the warm heart with the funny face; sweetness and light.

Adlai Stevenson
He is Honorable Man; myth of the egghead; Lincoln; the lost leader; Old Liberalism; wise.

Tom Dooley
He is triumph of Love; embodiment of Charity; Guts; aid to weak; Romantic Medicine.

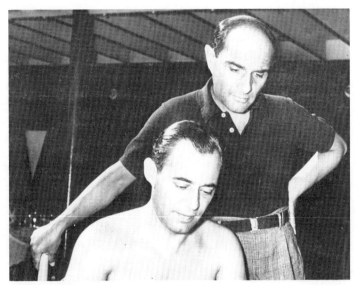

Rodgers and Hart
They were sophistication for the little man; waltzes; torch
songs; *Blue Room; Little Girl Blue*; marriage is for sweet
lovers, *Falling In Love With Love*; the romantic aura of
bittersweet love; Manhattan.

Rodgers and Hammerstein
They were Inspirational; singing of nuns; dancing cowboys;
Climb Every Mountain; a song from the heart; *You'll Never
Walk Alone*; Mary Martin; popular religion; the U.S.A.

Purveyors of Old Sentimentality—Continued

Lyndon Johnson
He is F.D.R.; the big ranch king; cowboys; *The Last Hurrah;* humble beginnings.

Pete Seeger
He is the dust bowl; a rebel with a cause; the hobo mystique; Old Left Wing; strikes.

The Clan
They are Boys' Night Out; the gang; the Buddy System; the romance of booze; practical joking; The Playboy Philosophy; Nouveau Riche; the idea of Organized Fun; millionaires; Show Biz.

Gian-Carlo Menotti
He is Puccini; schmaltz; a
Culture Concept; *Amahl;*
sweet mutes and cripples.

Grace Kelly
She is our Cinderella; the
Princess; the retired Movie
Star; Only in America;
Family.

PURVEYORS OF NEW SENTIMENTALITY

These are the givers of the New Way. They have enlisted our interest all
along without our realizing the changes they were making. They are the
vanguard of a different set of rules, of concepts, and, most importantly, of
attitudes. Sometimes intentionally, sometimes not, they have been teaching us the value system of the New Sentimentality.

The Beatles
They are the Put-On; the big laugh; a slap in the face; Professionalism; the new idea of the Celebrity; Ringo's looks; "We're
not any good, but we're having a good time"; Yeah! Yeah!
Yeah!

Purveyors of New Sentimentality—Continued

Alfred Hitchcock
He is the manipulation of the audience; the humor of horror; cynical control; tension as art.

Martin Buber
He is the lost man with his own God; the existential Jew; I to Thou as dialogue; hip religion.

The Untouchables
They are the Real Idea of Television; the violence, Love gets in the way and ruins the scheme; Ness as cynical do-gooder. The Rotten Twenties; the Cult of the Criminal; kicks for art's sake.

Audrey Hepburn
She is Holly Golightly; big sunglasses; beauty of the unbeautiful; the fragile that is tough.

Carlo Ponti
He is the lover in a new guise; the husband of Sophia; big Italian bankroll; Roma.

Maria Callas
She is the cult of Arrogance; the Professional; the subjugation of Nice to Tops; temper.

Michelangelo Antonioni
He is the sentimental eroticism; the condition of Alone; going overboard; Monica Vitti.

Purveyors of New Sentimentality—Continued

Elvis Presley
He is the Unlikely Winner;
the hard and mean sound;
Sharpness; the end of Authority; rock.

Jeanne Moreau
She is Woman as wrathful,
vengeful God; the love that
devours; Pierre Cardin; *Jules
et Jim.*

François Truffaut
He is Style over Content; the
idea of the Loner; Women are
fatal; the past is now.

Lady Bird Johnson
She is "no conflict of interest"; the quiet tycoon (radio
stations); Muzak; not just a
wife.

Lenny Bruce
He is the hipster; the trouble
with cops; Improvisation; a
summit of Style; anger.

Leo Castelli
He is the giver of Pop; money
made in mockery; the Painter
as anti-Hero; Power.

Jean Shrimpton
She is the Age of the Model; the Queen of English fashion; the
Look; awareness of aloofness; physical attractiveness as an
End; cold perfection; the beauty as a tough cookie; Makeup all
day long.

[July, 1964]

Part V
Some Failures in Communications

The Credibility Gap

The American Establishment

by Richard H. Rovere

"To understand the United States today, it is necessary to know something about the Establishment. Most citizens don't realize it exists. Yet the Establishment makes its influence felt from the President's Cabinet to the professional life of a young college teacher who wants to obtain a foundation grant for research. It affects the nation's policies in almost every area." —The News and Courier *of Charleston, S.C., October 18, 1961*

It is now, of course, conceded by most fair-minded and objective authorities that there is an Establishment in America—a more or less closed and self-sustaining institution that holds a preponderance of power

Note: Some of this material originally appeared in the *American Scholar* ("Notes on the Establishment in America," Vol. 30, No. 4, Autumn, 1961, pp. 489-495). Many readers professed to be puzzled by my approach. Some even asked if I intended my work to be taken seriously. I found their questions disheartening and, I might as well add, more than a bit offensive. They cast doubt not only on my own integrity but on that of the distinguished journal which had the courage to publish my findings. The *American Scholar* is, after all, an official publication of the United Chapters of Phi Beta Kappa. Its editors, of whom I am one, would certainly not be parties to a hoax. I might add, however, that the present work entirely exhausts my knowledge of the subject. Readers wishing further information are advised to get in touch with their in our more or less open society. Naturally, Establishment leaders pooh-pooh the whole idea; they deny the existence of the Establishment, and disclaim any connection of their own with it, and insist that they are merely citizens exercising citizens' rights and responsibilities. They often maintain that the real power is held by some other real or imagined force—the voters, the Congress, the comsymps, Madison Avenue, the rich, the poor, and so forth. This is an ancient strategy; men of power have always known how to use it. "Wouldst thou enjoy first rank?" St. John Chrysostom wrote. "Then cede it to another."[1] *The News and Courier* is absolutely right.

Conceptions of the Establishment, to be sure, differ widely, just as do conceptions of the Church, the State, and other important institutions. Hilary Masters, a leading member of the Dutchess County school of sociologists, defined it in a recent lecture[2] as "the legitimate Mafia."[3] To William F. Buckley, Jr. and his collaborators on the *National Review* it is almost interchangeable with the "Liberal Machine," which turns out the "Liberal Line." Their Establishment includes just about everyone in the

---

friendly F.B.I. agent or the House Committee on Un-American Activities. They may also buy The New York *Times* and read between the lines.

1. *Homilies*, 388.

2. Before the Edgewater Institute, Barrytown, N.Y., July 4, 1961. Vide *Proceedings*, 1961, pp. 37-51. Also see Masters' first-rate monograph *Establishment Watering Places*, Shekomeko Press, 1957.

3. It was the figure of speech, not the actual analogy, that seemed so striking and appropriate. Actually, the analogy was not actual—and doubtless was not intended to be regarded as such. The Establishment exists; the Mafia does not exist. Modern scholarship has pretty well destroyed the myth of the Mafia. (Vide, "The Myth of the Mafia," in *The End of Ideology*, by Daniel Bell, The Free Press, Glencoe, Illinois, 1960.) Bell cites a report by Serrell Hillman, a journalist who went all over the country to find out if there really was a Mafia at work in this country. He checked in at the Federal Bureau of Investigation and asked the top men there if they believed in the Mafia. They said they did not. Chicago Crime Commission—same story. [Hillman could not check with Central Intelligence Agency because it is forbidden by statute to intervene in domestic affairs.] But he did talk with innumerable police officials, criminal lawyers, criminals, private detectives, and the like—none of whom could put him on the trail of the Mafia. He was eventually forced to the conclusion that the only people who believed in it were (1) Senator Estes Kefauver, of Tennessee; (2) Hearst crime reporters; and (3) The Treasury Department's Bureau of Narcotics. Senator Kefauver once described the Mafia in concrete terms. "The Mafia," he said, "is the cement that helps to bind the Costello-Adonis-Lansky syndicate of New York and the Accardo-Guzik-Fischetti syndicate of Chicago." This sounds good but isn't. Note that tricky word "helps." Besides, it is unproved that there is any cement. If I may interject a purely personal note here, I may say that I have done a bit of work on my own. One day, in the Summer of 1960, I was on an airplane (United Air Lines, Flight 420) and learned that the Honorable Frank S. Hogan, District Attorney of New York County, was a fellow passenger. The air was turbulent, and seat belts had to be fastened, so I could not approach the famous prosecutor myself. I asked a stewardess if she would deliver a note to Mr. Hogan. She said she would be delighted. My note read: "Dear Mr. District Attorney: Is there a Mafia?" His reply was prompt and categorical.

country except themselves,[4] and the great hidden, enlightened majority of voters who would, if only they were given the chance, put a non-Establishment man in the White House and have John Kenneth Galbraith recalled from India, or left there and relieved of his passport. Galbraith, himself a pioneer in the field of Establishment studies, sees the Establishment as a rather small group of highly placed and influential men who embody the best of the Conventional Wisdom and can be trusted with substantial grants of power by any responsible group in the country. The perfect Establishment type, in his view, would be the Republican called to service in a Democratic administration (e.g., the present Secretary of the Treasury, Douglas Dillon) or the vice versa. "They are the *pivotal* people," he observed in one of his earlier studies. (The italics are his.) That was before his appointment as the Establishment's man in New Delhi. (He is not a member of his own Establishment, however, for he could not hope to be held over in a Republican administration.)

The fact that experts disagree on exactly what the Establishment is and how it works does not mean that they are talking about different things or about something that does not exist. Experts disagree about the Kingdom of God. This is not an argument against its existence; plainly the Kingdom of God is many things. Differences of opinion over the meaning of "justice" have given rise to one of the most honored professions in the world. One dogmatic Marxist may quarrel with another over the proper "role of the proletariat" and even about who should and who should not be counted as belonging to the "bourgeoisie." This does not make a fiction or a meaningless abstraction of either the proletariat or the bourgeoisie. The Establishment can be thought of in many different ways, all of them empirically valid in one or another frame of reference. Masters, Buckley, Galbraith, and Corradini[5] look upon the Establishment from quite different points of

"No, Virginia, there is not," he wrote. Still and all, I think that Masters' phrase caught the spirit of the thing admirably. Dante's *Inferno* was a product of the imagination, but it has helped many men to approach the reality of beauty and even the beauty of reality. The Establishment really is the cement that binds the Rockefeller-Gill-Sulzberger syndicate in New York to the Stevenson-Field-Sandburg syndicate in Chicago.

4. It is characteristic of most thinkers and writers on the subject to define the Establishment in such a way as to keep themselves outside it and even victimized by it. Werner von Fromm has suggested that they all tend toward a mild paranoia, and what little clinical evidence there is tends to support him. The one exception known to me is François Grund, a French economist of conservative leanings, who has applied to the Establishment Burke's phrases for the nobility—"an ornament of the civil order . . . the Corinthian capital of . . . society." Both von Fromm's and Grund's observations are to be found in the 1961 Edgewater *Proceedings*.

5. H. D. Corradini, author of *Patterns of Authority in American Society* (Gainesville Press, 1958). Corradini, an anthropologist, draws a striking parallel between the American Establishment and the Ydenneks, an intertribal council that still functions in Canada.

view—which grow in the main out of their differing disciplines—but they would have no difficulty in agreeing that Douglas Dillon is true-blue or that, say, Senator Thomas J. Dodd of Connecticut is on the outside looking in—disapprovingly, in his case. Despite their differences of emphasis and approach, none of them would have many reservations about the *News and Courier*'s definition:

"The Establishment is a general term for those people in finance, business, and the professions, largely from the Northeast, who hold the principal measure of power and influence in this country irrespective of what administration occupies the White House. . . . [It is] a working alliance of the near-socialist professor and the internationalist Eastern banker calling for a bland bipartisan approach to national politics."[6]

For my own part, I think the definition is a pretty good one. I would cavil a bit at the notion that "the Establishment is a general term," etc. It is a good deal more than a collective noun, as I shall make clear. Moreover, there is a slight ambiguity in the phrase "principal measure of power." Too many journalists, awed by their observations of the Establishment at work, leap to the conclusion that its power is not only great but invariably decisive. This is by no means the case. There are powerful anti-Establishment forces at work, and frequently they prevail. It seems to me perfectly clear, for example, that the Establishment has never found a way of controlling Congress.[7] Indeed, there are times when Congress appears to be nothing more or less than a conspiracy to louse up the plans of the Establishment. Whatever the Establishment wants, it often seems, Congress mulishly opposes.

Nor has the Establishment ever made much headway in such fields as advertising, television or motion pictures. The basic orientation of the leaders in all these fields is anti-Establishment, and what Establishment strength exists is concentrated mainly on the lower levels—in advertising, the copywriters; in television, certain of the news departments (most notably at Columbia Broadcasting); and in the motion pictures, a few writers and actors. Still, Establishment strength in these areas is generally unimpressive. In Hollywood, to take a simple example, ICMPAFPWJ, the Independent Committee of the Motion Picture Arts for Freedom and

6. The newspaper's anti-Establishment bias is plain enough, as is the editorialist's sense of exclusion. "Southerners have no place in the Establishment," he writes "except for a domesticated handful who have turned their backs on regional beliefs." For "regional beliefs" read Senator Strom Thurmond and Governor Orval Faubus.

7. From time to time, it has managed to hold a balance of power in the Senate, but it has never done even this much in the House. *The Congressional Monthly* for January, 1962, surveying the entire performance of the first session of the Eighty-seventh Congress, found that only nineteen members of the House had Establishment voting records of better than eighty percent. Of the nineteen, who accounted for less than five percent of the total membership, twelve were Democrats, seven were Republicans. Fourteen were from the eastern seaboard, two from California, and one each from Oregon, Louisiana, and Minnesota.

Peace With Justice, an Establishment front, held a fund-raising meeting in the Beverly Wilshire Hotel on November 20, 1961. Only twenty-eight persons attended, and the take for the evening, after eloquent pleas for support from Paul Newman and Joanne Woodward, was $3,067.50. (Of this amount, $2,900 was in the form of pledges, only about fifteen percent of which, in all likelihood, were actually redeemable.) On the very same evening, at the Beverly Hilton, the National Foundation for Amoebic Dysentery raised more than five times as much, all in cash or checks of that date, from three times as many people.

The Establishment does not control everything, but its influence is pervasive, and it succeeds far more often than its antagonists in fixing the major goals of American society. Though it does not, as I have noted, come anywhere close to controlling Congress, Congress is everlastingly *reacting* to it. Within the next couple of years, for example, Congress will spend a good part of its time fighting the Establishment program for a great revision of American trade practices and for eventual American association with the European Common Market. This whole scheme was cooked up at a three-day meeting of the Executive Committee at the Sheraton-Park in Washington immediately after President Kennedy's inauguration on January 20, 1961.[8] The odds are heavily against the Establishment winning this battle in 1962 or even in 1963. The important thing, though, is that the Establishment has taken the initiative and put its great antagonist on the defensive. Practically everyone is agreed that in time the victory, even in this difficult matter, will go to the Establishment.

The Establishment is not, of course, at any level a membership organization in the sense that it collects dues, issues cards, or holds meetings openly under its own auspices. It is a coalition of forces, the leaders of which form the top directorate, or Executive Committee—referred to sometimes as "Central." At the lower levels, organization is quite loose, almost primitive in some cases, and this is one of the facts that explains the differences in definition among experts. In the upper reaches, though, certain divisions have achieved a high degree of organization. For instance, the directors of the Council on Foreign Relations make up a sort of Presidium for that part of the Establishment that guides our destiny as a

8. The meeting had been called not for this purpose alone, but to review the state of the world generally at the start of the new President's term. The question of American intervention in Cuba, for example, was discussed at length and, eventually, tabled because the Committee members were so divided among themselves. A resolution was passed urging President Kennedy to meet with Nikita Khrushchev "at an early date with a view to determining whether any basis for negotiations to reduce tensions presently exists." The Common Market matter came up when Roscoe Gist reported that George Ball, Undersecretary of State for Economic Affairs, wished to pressure the United Kingdom into joining the Common Market and looked to a day when we, too, might belong. By a vote of 23-5, with two abstentions, he was authorized to go ahead.

nation.[9] (The unimpeachable source, a dissident Executive Committee member who leaked the story about the Common Market decision, said that the Gist Subcommittee appointed to work on the Common Market matter had only two members not drawn from the Council.) The presidents and senior professors of the great Eastern universities frequently constitute themselves as *ad hoc* Establishment committees. Now and then, the Executive Committee regroups as an Establishment front for some particular end. In the Summer of 1961, as a case in point, when anti-Establishment forces in Congress and elsewhere threatened the President's foreign-aid program, the Establishment, at the request of the White House, hastily formed the Citizens' Committee for International Development and managed to bull through a good deal of what the President wanted. The Establishment has always favored foreign aid. It is, in fact, a matter on which Establishment discipline may be invoked.

Summing up the situation at the present moment, it can, I think, be said that the Establishment maintains effective control over the Executive and Judicial branches of government; that it dominates most of American education and intellectual life; that it has very nearly unchallenged power in deciding what is and what is not respectable opinion in this country. Its authority is enormous in organized religion (Roman Catholics[10] and fundamentalist Protestants to one side), in science, and, indeed, in all the learned professions except medicine. It is absolutely unrivaled in the great new world created by the philanthropic foundations—a fact which goes most of the way toward explaining why so little is known about the Establishment and its workings. Not one thin dime of Rockefeller, Carnegie, or Ford money has been spent to further Establishment studies.[11]

If it were not for the occasional formation of public committees such as the Citizens' Committee for International Development, Establishment schol-

9. The President, of course, has Constitutional responsibility for foreign affairs, and I am not suggesting that any recent President has abdicated to the CFR. But policy and strategy are worked out in the Council and reach the President by way of the State Department, which, of course, is largely staffed and always directed by Council members.

10. It should be noted, though, that it is becoming influential in Catholic journalism. A content survey of twelve leading Catholic periodicals showed thirty-eight percent of the text to be Establishment inspired.

11. The situation approaches scandal at times. The foundations and universities have subsidized a number of first-rate Establishment scholars. Daniel Bell, H. E. Corradini, Alfred Kazin, and Mary McCarthy have received Guggenheim Fellowships or other such benefactions, but always for something other than Establishment studies. A few universities—Florida, Southern Methodist, Ramona, Virginia Military Institute, and Michigan State—have done what little they could to help out, and so have a few of the less-well-heeled foundations. But there is a general lockout in the richer and better-known institutions. Some have even gone so far as to encourage what might be called "red-herring scholarship"—efforts to prove that

ars would have a difficult time learning who the key figures are. Committee rosters serve Establishmentologists in the same way that May Day photographs of the reviewing stand above Lenin's tomb serve the Kremlinologists. By close analysis of them, by checking one list of names against another, it is possible to keep tabs quite accurately on the Executive Committee. A working principle generally agreed upon by Establishment scholars is this: If in the course of a year a man's name turns up fourteen times in paid advertisements in, or collective letters to, The New York *Times,* the official Establishment daily, it is about fourteen to one that he is a member of the Executive Committee. (I refer, naturally, to advertisements and letters pleading Establishment causes.) There are, to be sure, exceptions. Sometimes a popular athlete or movie actor will, innocently or otherwise, allow himself and his name to be exploited by the Establishment. He might turn up twenty times a year and still have no real status in the institution. But that is an exception. The rule is as stated above.

One important difference between the American Establishment and the party hierarchy in Russia is that the Establishment chairman is definitely *not* the man in the center of the picture or the one whose name is out of alphabetical order in the listings. The secret is astonishingly well kept. Some people, to be sure, have argued that when, as happens most of the time, the Establishment has a man of its own in the White House, he automatically becomes chairman just as he automatically becomes commander-in-chief of the Armed Forces. I am quite certain that this is not the case. For one thing, the Establishment rarely puts one of its tried and trusted leaders in the White House. Dwight Eisenhower and John F. Kennedy have both served the Establishment and been served by it, but neither is or ever was a member of the innermost circle. Both, indeed, were admitted with some reluctance on the part of senior members, and Eisenhower's standing has at times been most insecure.

I am not sure who the chairman of the Establishment is today, although I would not be altogether surprised to learn that he is Dean Rusk. By a thrust of sheer intuition, though, I did get the name of the 1958 chairman and was rather proud of myself for doing so. In that year, I discovered that J. K. Galbraith had for some time been surreptitiously at work in Establishment studies, and he told me that he had found out who was running the thing. He tested me by challenging me to guess the man's name. I thought hard for a while and was on the point of naming Arthur Hays Sulzberger, of The New York *Times,* when suddenly the right name

---

something other than the Establishment dominates the country. A notorious example is C. Wright Mills' *The Power Elite* (Oxford University Press, 1956). It was subsidized by the Huntington Hartford Foundation, Columbia University's Social Science Research Council, and Brandeis University. Even the parent body, the British Establishment, got into the act through the Oxford University Press, which, Mills admits, went "beyond the ordinary office of publisher in helping me get on with this."

sprang to my lips. "John J. McCloy," I exclaimed. "Chairman of the Board of the Chase Manhattan Bank, once with Cadwalader, Wickersham & Taft, and a partner in Cravath, de Gersdorff, Swaine & Wood, as well as, of course, Milbank, Tweed, Hope, Hadley & McCloy; former United States High Commissioner in Germany; former President of the World Bank; liberal Republican; chairman of the Ford Foundation and chairman—my God, how could I have hesitated!—of the Council on Foreign Relations, Inc.; Episcopalian." "That's the one," Galbraith said. He congratulated me for having guessed what it had taken him so much patient research to discover.

The Establishment is not monolithic in structure or inflexible in doctrine. There is an Establishment "line," but adherence is compulsory only on certain central issues, such as foreign aid. On economic affairs, for example, several views are tolerated. The accepted range is from about as far left as, say, Walter Reuther to about as far right as, say, Dwight Eisenhower. A man cannot be for *less* welfareism than Eisenhower, and to be farther left than Reuther is considered bad taste.[12] Racial equality is another matter on which the Establishment forbids dissent. Opposition to integration is a cause for expulsion, or at least suspension for not less than a year, unless it is mere "token" opposition. The only *white* Southern members of the Establishment in anything like good standing are reconstructed Southerners or Southerners the Establishment has reason to believe would be reconstructed if political circumstances would allow it. Take Senator William Fulbright of Arkansas. He is a pillar of the Establishment even though he votes with the unenlightened on racial matters. The Council on Foreign Relations gave him an "A-1" rating when he was up for chairman of the Senate Foreign Relations Committee.[13] The Executive Committee accepts him because it assumes his heart is in the right place. He is, after all, a former Rhodes scholar and a former university president. Moreover, the Fulbright scholarships have provided an enormous subsidy for Establishment intellectuals.

12. Setting the limitations on the left is not much of a problem nowadays, for the left has been inching toward the center at the rate of about seven inches per year; the only extreme positions in this epoch are on the right, and these are inadmissible. It is interesting to consider the change that has come over the Establishment in the last twenty years. In their views on government intervention and related questions, Wendell Willkie in the early Forties and Dwight Eisenhower in the early Sixties seemed peas from the same pod. But Willkie in his time was regarded as an economic liberal, whereas Eisenhower in ours is clearly a conservative. It has been estimated that by 1968, views such as Eisenhower's will be considered excessively rightist—as Barry Goldwater's are today—and will not be tolerated.

13. It exercised the veto power, though, when he was proposed as Secretary of State. It wanted Dean Rusk to get the job, and used Fulbright's record on racial questions as an argument against Fulbright's candidacy.

The Establishment has lately been having a most difficult time with those of its members—clergy, scientists, and academicians, in the main—who have joined the Committee for a Sane Nuclear Policy. The Executive Committee—in particular that powerful "hard-line" faction led by Dean Acheson and Roscoe Gist—has no use at all for this organization and would deal very sharply with its supporters if they did not include so many people who incorporate most of the Establishment virtues. Exactly what stand it will take remains to be seen.

In nonpolitical affairs, great doctrinal latitude is not only tolerated but encouraged. In religion, the Establishment is rigorously disestablishmentarian. Separatism is another matter on which discipline may be invoked.[14] Like a citywide ticket in New York, the Executive Committee is carefully balanced religiously as well as racially. (The only important difference is that several places are kept for nonbelievers.) The only proscribed views are the noisier ones. Though he now and then gets an audience in the White House, Billy Graham is *persona non grata* in Establishment circles. Monsignor Fulton J. Sheen is regarded as a Catholic Billy Graham and is similarly a pariah.

Reinhold Niebuhr is the official Establishment theologian, and Bishop Angus Dun is the chaplain.

In matters of public policy, it may be said that those principles and policies that have the editorial support of The New York *Times* are at the core of Establishment doctrine. And those irregularities and eccentricities that receive sympathetic *consideration* in The *Times* (not only on the editorial page but in the Sunday Magazine and the Book Review) are within the range of Establishment doctrinal tolerance.

It is essential to an understanding of the Establishment to recognize its essentially *national* characteristics. *The whole of its power is greater than the sum of its parts.* Its leading figures have national and international reputations, but very often are persons of only slight influence or standing in the cities and states from which they come. Former Chairman McCloy, for example, cuts a lot of ice in Washington, Geneva, Paris, London, Rio de Janeiro, Bonn, Moscow, and Tokyo, but practically none in Manhattan. In Albany, he is almost unknown. The relative weakness of the Establishment in the states undoubtedly helps to explain the shellackings it repeatedly gets in Congress. Statewide—or one might say, statewise—it is often torn by a kind of factionalism that seldom afflicts its national and

14. "The Establishment," the Reverend F. Q. Shafer said, in the first of his 1961 Geist Lectures at Brownlee Seminary, "takes the view that religion is a matter of conscience and has no place in politics or in education. It evidently sees no contradiction between this and its endlessly repeated dictum that politics and education must always be informed by conscience."

international operations. In New York, for example, Averell Harriman and Nelson Rockefeller have often found themselves locked in combat like Grant and Lee; in Washington, they are Alphonse and Gaston. And so it goes.

A state-by-state canvass of Establishment strengths and weaknesses was conducted by Perry Associates, a St. Louis firm, in 1959. Some of the highlights follow:

In three states—Texas, Oklahoma, and North Dakota—the Establishment is virtually outlawed. There are no restrictive or repressive measures on the statute books, but there is persistent harassment by police and other officials. The American Civil Liberties Union had expressed some interest in arranging a test case, but no suitable one was found. Despite constant police surveillance, there is considerable underground Establishment activity in the Dallas area and in San Antonio.

The Indiana authorities are openly hostile to the Establishment, and there has been continuing agitation for a law requiring Establishment agents to register with the Attorney General and be fingerprinted. It is hard to see what would be accomplished by this, for the Perry people could find no trace of Establishment activity anywhere in Indiana, except at Indiana University, in Bloomington. The faculty people there are state employees anyway and can quite easily be dealt with. In neither Nebraska nor Idaho could *any* Establishment influence be found. There were only the faintest traces in Wyoming, New Hampshire, Utah, and Florida.

Florida was the one Southern state in which Establishment forces seemed exceedingly weak. Elsewhere, it was learned, nearly all those who described themselves as "moderates" were actually connected with the Establishment.

The big centers are, as one might expect, the states with large cities and large electoral votes: New York, California, Illinois, Pennsylvania, Ohio, and Massachusetts. A rather surprising case, though, was Kansas, which ranked ahead of New Jersey and Maryland.

For some reason, Establishment studies have attracted few historians. Most of the work thus far has been undertaken by journalists, economists, sociologists, and psychologists. In consequence, very little has been done to uncover the origins of the Establishment. One British historian, Keith E. D. Smith-Kyle, maintains, in *America in the Round* (Polter & Polter, Ltd., London, 1956), that "the American pretense to equality was, to speak bluntly, given the lie by the formation in the early days of the Republic of the sort of 'command' group similar in most respects to what Britons nowadays speak of as 'The Establishment.' By 1847, when the Century Association was founded in New York, power had been consolidated in a handful of hands. From then on, whenever there was a 'laying on of hands,' the blood in those extremities was the very blood that had coursed through those that had molded the clay of life in the so-called Federal period."

It is plain that Smith-Kyle is trying to say, in a roundabout British way, that a hereditary aristocracy runs the show here. He is as wrong-headed in this matter as he is in most others.[15] American students, though they number few trained historians[16] among them and none of a celebrity that compares with Smith-Kyle's, subscribe almost unanimously to the proposition that the Establishment came into being at a far later date—to be exact, as well as neat, at the turn of the century. They see the institution forming during the administration of Theodore Roosevelt, who by common consent was the first Establishment President—and in a way the last.[17] The Founding Fathers of today's group zeroed in on T. R. as if they had caught him in a perfect bombsight. Consider them all, a few of them still alive, all of them within living memory: Henry L. Stimson, William Allen White, Nicholas Murray Butler, Robert Frost, Albert Beveridge, Abraham Hummel, Joseph Choate, William Travers Jerome, Jacob Riis, Charles Evans Hughes, Felix Frankfurter, Ida M. Tarbell, Joseph Pulitzer, Martin Provensen, Lincoln Steffens, Benson Frost, Learned Hand, W. Adolphe Roberts, Jane Addams, Nelson W. Aldrich, Eleanor Alice Burgess, John Hay, John Ray, John Jay Chapman, Van Wyck Brooks, Carl Schurz, Hamlin Garland, Oscar Straus, Winthrop Chanler, James R. Bourne, Whitelaw Reid, and Gifford Pinchot.[18]

There, plainly, was the first Executive Committee!

Some uninformed publicists confuse the Establishment with the Organization. The two could not be more different. The Establishment Man and the Organization Man could not be more different, or more at odds. The Establishment uses the Organization from time to time, as a ruling group must in an industrial and commercial society. But it devoutly hopes that in time the Organization will wither away. The Organization would like to overthrow the Establishment. It had a near success when it ran its 1960 chairman, Richard M. Nixon, for President of the United States.

15. Vide, his revolting apology for Munich, *The Noble Experiment* (Heineken, London), and his blatantly Stalinist *The Bear and the Jug* (Bafer & Bafer, 1949).

16. Arthur Schlesinger, Jr., has done some fairly decent work in the past, vide *The General and the President* (with Richard H. Rovere), but his judgments are suspect because of his own connections with the Establishment.

17. This is a rather fine point. Since Roosevelt's time, every President except Harding and Truman has taken office with full Establishment approval. So far as can be determined though, no one has ever gone directly from the Executive Committee to the office of Chief Executive. Woodrow Wilson is sometimes cited as an exception, but it is dubious in the extreme that he was one. Charles Evans Hughes, his 1916 opponent, was an Executive Committee man.

18. I am indebted for this list to F. W. Dupee's illuminating study *The Suckleys of Wildercliff and the Origins of the Establishment*, No. IV in the *Occasional Papers* published by the Mid-Hudson Historical Society. Mr. Dupee is professor of English at Columbia University and perhaps the country's leading authority on Henry James.

The New York *Times* has no close rival as an Establishment daily. Technological advance is making it possible for The *Times* to become a national newspaper. This development should add immeasurably to the growth of the institution's powers.

Most Establishment personnel get at least one newspaper besides The *Times*, in order to keep up with Walter Lippmann. Papers that carry both Lippmann and Joseph Alsop are in good standing with the Establishment and get a lot of advertising that way.

There are some specialized magazines but none of general circulation that can be described as official or semi-official organs. I have pondered long over the case of *Time* magazine and have concluded that it has no real place in the Establishment. It goes too far in attacking Establishment positions and it has treated many Establishment members with extreme discourtesy and at times with vulgarity. The Establishment fears *Time*, of course, and it now and then shows cravenness in its attempts to appease it by putting Henry Luce on some commission or other (on freedom of the press, national goals, and so forth), or by giving his wife some political job. But the Luce publications generally must be considered as outside the Establishment.

Now that control of *Newsweek* has passed to Philip L. Graham, publisher of The Washington *Post*, it may be that the Establishment will adopt it as an official weekly.

U. S. News and World Report is widely read, but held in low regard.

Foreign Affairs has, within its field, the authority of *Pravda* and *Izvestia*.

Harper's, *The Atlantic*, and *The New Yorker* all have Establishment clienteles, but none can be regarded as official. The *Saturday Review* was once heavily patronized but no longer is. *The New Republic* is coming up. *The Nation* has long since gone down. A few of the younger Establishment intellectuals read *Partisan Review*, but the more sophisticated ones regard it as stuffy and prefer *The Noble Savage*, edited by Saul Bellow and issued in April and November by the World Publishing Company.

As Thomas R. Waring, the noted Southern journalist, has pointed out, "The significance of the Establishment can be discovered by finding out who is *not* a member." No one has yet compiled a complete list of nonmembers, but the following names may help significance seekers to get their bearings. These people are known to be nonmembers:

The Honorable Lyndon B. Johnson, Vice-President of the United States.

The Honorable Richard M. Nixon, former Vice-President of the United States.

The Honorable John Nance Garner, former Vice-President of the United States.

Cus D'Amato, prominent New York sportsman and manager of Floyd Patterson, the heavyweight champion of the world.

J. Edgar Hoover, Director, Federal Bureau of Investigation.

General of the Army Douglas MacArthur.

Allen Ginsberg, poet.

The Honorable James A. Farley, former Chairman, Democratic National Committee.

Fowler Harbison, President, Ramona College.

James Hoffa, President, International Brotherhood of Teamsters.

Hetherington Wells, Chairman of the Board, Consolidated Hydraulics, Inc.

Spruille Braden, diplomatist. (Here is a curious case indeed. Former Ambassador Braden has held many leading positions in the Establishment and is even now a member of the Council on Foreign Relations. But he is also a member of the national council of the John Birch Society. He was read out of the Establishment on April 14, 1960, before his John Birch connections were known.)

Sherman Adams, formerly the assistant to the President of the United States.

Drew Pearson, syndicated columnist.

Edgar Queeny, Chairman of the Board, Monsanto Chemical Corporation.

Charles Goren, bridge expert.

Charles A. Lindbergh, aviator.

The Honorable John MacCormack, Speaker, House of Representatives.

The Reverend Norman Vincent Peale, pastor, Marble Collegiate Church of New York (Dutch Reformed) and author of *The Power of Positive Thinking*.

Cyrus S. Eaton, industrialist and philanthropist.

The Honorable Everett McKinley Dirksen, United States Senator from Illinois and the minority leader of the Senate.

Dr. Edward Teller, nuclear physicist, often known as "Father of the Hydrogen Bomb."

Conrad Hilton, hotel executive.

The Honorable Richard J. Hughes, Governor of New Jersey.

Michael J. Quill, President, Transport Workers Union.

Morris Fishbein, M.D., editor and official, American Medical Association.

George Sokolsky, syndicated columnist.

Duke Snider, Los Angeles Dodgers.

John L. Lewis, President, United Mine Workers of America.

Carleton Putnam, writer, former Chairman of the Board, Delta Air Lines.

The Establishment has in its top councils some people who appear to the unsophisticated to be oppositionists. For example, Norman Thomas, the Socialist leader; Norman Mailer, the self-styled "hipster" novelist; and Norman Podhoretz, the firebrand editor of *Commentary,* all enjoy close relations with leading figures on the Executive Committee. The Reverend Martin Luther King has been proposed for membership on the Executive Committee. On March 3, 1962, a planning committee that met for three days at the Royalton Hotel in New York reported that "we need informed, constructive criticism fully as much as we need support" and urged the recruitment of "people who will take a long, cold look at our policies and procedures and candidly advise us of any weaknesses they see. We recommend that in the cases of people playing this indispensable role of 'devil's advocate,' all discipline be suspended."

It is interesting to observe the workings of the Establishment in Presidential politics. As I have pointed out, it rarely fails to get one of its members, or at least one of its allies, into the White House. In fact, it generally is able to see to it that both nominees are men acceptable to it. It is never quite powerful enough, though, to control a nominating convention or actually to dictate nominations. National conventions represent regional interests much as Congress does, and there is always a good deal of unarticulated but nonetheless powerful anti-Establishment sentiment at the quadrennial gatherings of both Republicans and Democrats. Nevertheless, the great unwashed who man the delegations understand—almost intuitively, it seems—that they cannot win without the Establishment, and the more responsible among them have the foresight to realize that even if they did win they couldn't run the country without assistance from the Executive Committee. Over the years, a deal has been worked out that is almost an operating rule of American politics. The rule has been formulated by the novelist Margaret Creal in this way:

When an Establishment man is nominated for the Presidency by either party, the Vice-Presidential candidate must be drawn from outside the Establishment. When, as has occasionally happened, the Establishment is denied the Presidential nomination, it must be given the Vice-Presidential nomination.

The system has worked almost perfectly for the last thirty years. In that time, the only non-Establishment man in the White House has been Harry Truman, and he had been Franklin Roosevelt's non-Establishment Vice-President. Putting Henry Wallace aside as a pretty far-out case and not counting Alben Barkley (a Vice-President's Vice-President), the Vice-Presidents have all been non-Establishment: John Nance Garner, Harry Truman, Richard Nixon, and Lyndon Johnson.

Now observe what happens when the Establishment has to yield first place, as it had to do at the Republican convention in 1960. Richard Nixon, a non-Establishment Vice-President, simply could not be denied the Presidential nomination. So the Establishment Republicans demanded and of course obtained Henry Cabot Lodge. There was a similar case in 1936, when the Republicans went outside the Establishment to nominate Alf Landon for first place. The Vice-Presidential candidate was Colonel Frank Knox, the publisher of the Chicago *Daily News,* and later Roosevelt's Secretary of the Navy. Four years later, the Establishment nominated Wendell Willkie on the Republican ticket and agreed to Charles McNary, distinctly non-Establishment. In 1944, it was Dewey (Establishment) and Bricker (Non). The Establishment was particularly powerful in 1948 and not only got Dewey again but Earl Warren. In 1952, the usual deal was made in both parties: Eisenhower versus Stevenson (Establishment) and Nixon and Sparkman (Non). Same thing in 1956, with Estes Kefauver in for Sparkman.

The Russians have caught on to the existence of the Establishment and understand some of its workings quite well. Nikita Khrushchev showed himself to be no slouch when he told Walter Lippmann, last spring, that President Kennedy was controlled by Nelson Rockefeller. Many people regarded this as depressing evidence of the grip of old-school Marxism on Khrushchev's mind. They thought he was mistaking a faded symbol of industrial and mercantile power for the real wielder of authority under People's Capitalism. He was doing nothing of the sort. He was facing the facts of Establishment life. Not as a Standard Oil heir but as an Establishment agent, Nelson Rockefeller had forced the Republicans to rewrite their platform so that it conformed very closely to Chester Bowles's Democratic platform and provided for a vigorous anti-Communist defense program. Where did the central ideas of both platforms originate? In—where else?—the studies made by the Rockefeller Panel for the Rockefeller Brothers Fund and published as *Prospect for America.* Who was on the Rockefeller Panel? Here are just a few of the names, left and right:

Dean Rusk	Lucius D. Clay
Chester Bowles	Arthur F. Burns
Jacob Potofsky	Henry Luce[19]
Anna Rosenberg	Oveta Culp Hobby
Henry Kissinger	David Sarnoff
(Director of the project)	

And when Kennedy became President, from what foundation did he get his Secretary of State? The Rockefeller Foundation, of course.

19. The outsider inside. I once asked an authority on the parent body, the British Establishment, how he accounted for the sudden eminence of Barbara Ward. He explained that every Establishment agency (the B.B.C. directors, for example) had to have at least one woman and one Roman Catholic. Miss Ward was a neat package deal.

[May, 1962]

How I Signed Up at $250 a Month for the Big Parade Through Havana Bla-Bla-Bla and Wound Up in Guatemala with the C.I.A.

by Terry Southern

One night not long ago I was sitting around the White Horse Tavern, in New York City's colorful Greenwich Village, having a quick game of chess with a self-styled internationally famous blitz-chess champ. Six snappy ones and I pretty well had the game sewed up, when the champ suddenly said: "Say, see that guy at the bar—he was in the Cuban fiasco."

"Cut the diversionary crap, Champ," I countered, not bothering to look around, tapping the board of play instead, "and face up to the power." I had slapped the old de Sade double cul-de-sac on his Lady—and, as Bill Seward says, that's a rumble nobody can cool.

"No, man," insisted the champ in petulance, "I'm not kidding—just ask him and see."

Well, to make a short preface even terse (the champ, by the way, interfered with the pieces when I did look around, and so eked out another shoddy win), I investigated further to find that it was, in fact, true: this man *had* participated in the Cuban fiasco, of April 17, 1961, right up to the eleventh-hour moment of the fiasco proper, "Bad Day at the Pig Bay." His story was so interesting that my immediate hope was to share it with

448

whatever sort of sensitive readership I could muster, and to that end I invited him over to my place for some drinks and a couple of hours tape-recording of his curious tale. Here then is the story of Boris Grgurevich, thirty-three, born and raised in New York City; it is a verbatim transcript of the recorded interview:

Well, now let me ask you this, how did you get involved in this Cuban fiasco?

It was *cold,* man . . . you know, like January. You remember that big snowstorm? When they pulled all the cars off the street? Yeah, well that was it. . . . *Cold.* And this friend of mine, Ramón, comes by. I know him ten, fifteen years, but you know, haven't seen him for a while, so there's a big bla-bla hello scene . . . and he was running from something, I mean that was pretty obvious, but he was always very high-strung, moving around a lot—Miami, L.A., Mexico—and right away he says, "Man, let's go to *Miami,* where it's *WARM.*" And he had this *car,* and well, I mean it wasn't difficult him talking me into going, because of the weather and all. So that was the first thing—we went down to Miami.

Had he mentioned anything about Cuba before you left for Miami?

No, man, he didn't say anything about *Cuba*—or maybe he *did* mention it, you know, fleetingly . . . like "bla-bla-bla the Cuban situation," or some crap like that, but we were just going to *Miami.* I mean he probably *did* mention it, because he was *born* in Cuba, you dig, and speaks Spanish and so on—but Castro was all right with me . . . I mean he had that *beard,* you know, and he seemed pretty interesting. No, we didn't talk about that, we get down to Miami, and we have three great days at the track, and then we have four terrible ones—we were reduced to moving in with Jimmy Drew, a guy I know there. And so Ramón's taking me around—I mean, he knows Miami, see, and there's a *liquor* store in the neighborhood and he introduces me to this guy owns the liquor store—nice guy to know, owns a liquor store, and we get very friendly, you know, and he's giving us bottles of *rum.* Well, he's *Cuban,* dig, and he and Ramón start yakking it up about *Cuba* and "bla-bla Castro" and so on, and now he's talking about the *"invasion"* and how he's going to get back what they *took* from him and all that jive. And naturally I'm *agreeing* with him—well I mean he keeps laying this *rum* on us, about three bottles a day . . . but he's, well he was obviously full of crap, a kind of middle-aged hustler businessman . . . and all these cats hanging around the liquor store all looked like *hoods,* but sort of *failing,* you know? Anyway, we were meeting all these hood-faces hanging around this liquor store, mostly Cubans, or born in Cuba, and one of them took us to this . . . well, they had this recruiting station, you know, where they're all signing up for the *invasion,* and Ramón, well he's getting more and more excited about this—he's a *salesman* actually, I mean that's what he does, you know, in real life, sell things, and so he's selling himself on this idea, invading Cuba . . . and of course he was selling me on it too.

Well, now this recruiting—this station—was this being done quite openly?

Openly? Well, man, it was open twenty-four hours a day. You know, like in the middle of town.

This was about the time Cuba raised this question in the U.N. and the U.S. delegation so emphatically denied it. If recruitment was being done as openly as you suggest, how could they deny it?

Well, use your bean, man—what are they supposed to do, *admit* it?

All right, now let me ask you this, what was Ramón's idea exactly—I mean, if the invasion was successful, did he think he would get something out of it?

Well, Ramón's what you might call an *essentialist*—and he just more or less figures that the man with the gun is, you know, *the man with the gun.*

And how did you feel about it?

The money was the thing that interested me—I mean we'd had these four very bad days at the track, and I had no *money*. Well, they were offering two-fifty a month and, you know, room and board, and . . . let's see, what else . . . yeah, *a trip to Guatemala*. But I guess the main thing was these cats at the recruiting station, giving this big spiel about "bla-bla-bla the American Government, the C.I.A., the U.S. Army," and so on. I mean the picture *they* were painting had *battleships* in it, Dad—you know, rockets against pitchforks. Well man, I mean how could we lose? Cuba versus America—are you kidding?

So it was pretty obvious even then that it was an American project?

Well *of course,* man—that was the whole pitch. You don't think they could have got these guys in there any other way, do you? I mean most of *these* guys were just sort of tired, middle-aged businessmen, or young hustlers . . . *they* weren't going to do anything, anybody could see that. It was like they were recruiting for the *parade,* you know, to march through Havana—and these guys were joining up to be *in* the parade, that's all. I mean there was a *slight* pretense at a front—the *Juan Paula Company,* that's the way the checks were paid, from the *Juan Paula Company*—and then there were some of these C.I.A. faces running around, trying to make a cloak-and-dagger scene out of it, but that was just sort of a *game* with them. I mean everybody in Miami knew about the recruiting.

Did you meet other Americans who wanted to go?

Well, they didn't want Americans, you see, they wanted *Cubans*—for the big parade, dig? So you had to be Cuban, or if you were American, like Ramón, you had to be born in Cuba. But yeah, there were some other Americans down there, trying to get in—guys from the South mostly, these real . . . you know, anything-is-better-than-home types. Most of them had been in the Army or something like that. But they didn't want them—they wanted Cubans.

So how did you get in?

Well, man, I mean they didn't make an *issue* of it or anything like that, not as far as *I* was concerned, because we had gotten sort of friendly with them, these C.I.A. cats . . . and they weren't bad guys really—I mean they thought *they* were doing the right thing and they thought *we* were doing the right thing, so we had a pretty good relationship with them. They were nice guys actually—just sort of goofy.

Where did you see the first C.I.A. person? At the recruiting station?

That's right, they would fool around this recruiting station . . . but they were sort of flunky types. The first, what you might call "higher-echelon" C.I.A. face, was this guy directing the loading, you know, when we left for the airport. Young, dapper, sort of prematurely grey, crew-cut, very square, would-be-hip-looking cat. I guess he was a faggot really.

How did you get to the airport?

Well, one night about a week after we signed up and had finished taking these physicals they said, "Okay, this is it"—you know, very dramatic —and they picked us up, there were about ninety of us altogether, in these trucks . . . sort of like moving vans, and, well, went to the airport.

Was this the Miami International Airport?

No man, it was some kind of abandoned *military* airport. Took us about an hour to get there—then we were inside this huge hangar, and that's where they issued the uniforms. Khaki uniforms, shoes, and all that jazz. Then we get on the plane . . . C-47 . . . with the windows taped up, you know, no light, very cloak-and-dagger. And the trip . . . well, we took off that night and landed the next morning. Guatemala. And it was *hot,* man . . . wow, was it *hot.* Cats falling out all over the place—I mean, *these* guys were in no shape to start with, and then this *heat.* Well, there were these trucks there to pick us up—sort of red, commercial-type trucks, like farm trucks, you know, big open trucks. And they took us from the airstrip to the camp—that was outside Retalhuleu, the airstrip—and it takes about an hour and a half to get to Trax, the camp, the last half hour very *steep,* like straight up a mountain. First we pass a Guatemalan outpost, then a Cuban one. And it's all *lava*—the campsite was all lava . . . cut right out of the side of this mountain about 8,000 feet up. It was laid out in three levels, you dig, like huge terraces. The first level had the firing range, parade ground, the second had the barracks, mess hall, and so on, and then at the top was where the C.I.A. lived— separate, with their own mess hall, movie, and all that. Anyway it's all lava . . . like crushed coral, you know, crunch, crunch, crunch, every-where you step. And it was supposed to be a secret camp, but of course everyone knew about it—I mean they were fifteen hundred guys up there eventually, blasting away all day—rifles, machine guns, mortars. And it was written up in all the newspapers and magazines—including *Bohemia Libre*. Know that one? It's the big anti-Communist magazine there.

Was this formerly a Guatemalan army camp?

No, man, this was formerly *nothing*. They were still working on it when I got there—I mean the camp was built for this, you know, this particular project, and they were still working on it.

Well, had you gotten to know any of the other men yet? What were they like?

You mean the guys on the plane? Well, let's see, there was this guy, Martinez . . . he was about fifty-two or -three, had been in the Batista army, a clerk—beautiful handwriting . . . well, you know the type, man, a *clerk*. And he was there because that was all he knew—the army and how to write. I mean that was the whole story with him. And then you get someone else, like this kid Raúl—young country boy, thinks his old man has been beat for a couple of *cows* or something. Very sincere cat. Well, you know, man, there were all kinds, like any army. Mostly pretty simple cats though—well, you know, like any army.

Can you describe the camp more fully?

It was the usual scene, man—a *camp*. A military *camp*. The barracks . . . well, a couple of them were quonset huts, but most of them were just ordinary wooden barracks—hold about seventy guys, something like that. Mess hall, orderly room, quartermaster, motor pool, and so on . . . like an ordinary American Army camp . . . a little shabbier maybe, you know, more makeshift.

How was the food?

Well, that was a pretty funny scene all right—that whole mess-hall scene. They had these three American cooks, you dig, and lot of Guatemalans to do KP—with a couple of translators, you know, so the cooks could tell the Guatemalans what to do—and the food was okay, sort of typical American fare, but the Cubans didn't particularly dig it. I mean they like different things, you know—black beans, rice, pork, they eat a lot of pork. Anyway a lot of times they wouldn't eat in the mess hall—they would cop a *pig* somewhere, you know, off a farmer, somebody like that . . . trade him a gun for it, anything—I mean, there were, you know, quite a few little black-market operations going on. So they would have this pig . . . a live, squealing *pig*, man, and they'd butcher it right outside the barracks and build a big fire and cook it. They have a ball—a kind of little *fiesta*, you know, singing and dancing, lushing it up, cooking this pig. It was a crazy scene.

Did you start your training right away?

Yeah, you started off as a group. . . . They would keep all the guys who arrived together as a group, right through Basic Training—you know, marching, calisthenics, rifle range, and so on. And then they would train you for some specialty—like mortar, machine gun, or something.

But we didn't get started until the next day. I mean there was a little confusion when we arrived, because there had just been a take-over the night before—a Batista coup—and the San Román boys had taken over. These were two brothers, Pepe and Roberto San Román—they were very tight with the Americans. See, the Americans never knew what was happening—I mean, they lived apart, ate apart, none of them spoke Spanish, and they never had any idea what was going on in camp—so if some guy came to them and said "bla-bla-bla Communist plot" or some crap like that, why they had to *believe* him—they really had no choice, they always had to take the word of the guy who was telling them. So they'd say: "Okay, *you* take over—get those Commies outta there!"

Had there actually been a plot?

No, man, this was just *politicking.* There was a lot of maneuvering going on, you dig—I mean, these guys were sort of divvying up the spoils, you know, even before they got there. That's how sure of themselves they were. And so the San Román brothers finally came out on top. Short-lived though it proved to be.

Anyway they had these three cats in the can—not the regular stockade, but a tin-roof shack built just to hold these guys. They were the ones who had taken all the weight in the coup—you know, supposed to be Communist spies. It was like that shack in *The Bridge on the River Kwai,* and those cats were in there for *three months,* man. Nobody was allowed near them except whoever was guarding the shack—and the C.I.A. guy who brought their chow . . . and, that's right, there were a couple of G-2 faces would question them sometimes. But they never cracked—I saw them the day they came out—they were strong cats, man.

Do you suppose they were Communist spies?

Well, I think they were just strong, dangerous cats, man—who, you know, disagreed with the Batista clique. So when they pulled off this coup, these guys caught all the heat.

So the San Román brothers became . . . what, the commandants of the camp?

Well, Frank Bender, the C.I.A. guy, was in charge of the operation—I mean he was in charge of the *whole* thing, you dig, but Pepe San Román was *nominally* the camp commander, from the, you know, Cuban point of view—and Roberto, he was in charge of the heavy-weapons company, the four-point-two mortars . . . that was the most important company in the outfit.

What were the American instructors like?

Well, they were all specialists—you know, *instructors,* mostly from the Army: World War II, Korean War, or young cats from, I don't know, *Ohio* or some weird place like that. There were about thirty-five or forty of them. And it was just a gig for them. They were getting seven-fifty, and they were usually pretty conscientious about whatever it was they were teaching—they didn't have any particular interest in the political side of it. They were sort of typical Army faces—but *specialists*, you know, pretty humorless cats, except for the guy training the paratroopers, and he was about half off his nut. And some of them, being from the South and all, were very color conscious—they didn't really *like* the Cubans, you know, because they were different. And of course they were very down on any kind of *mixture,* and the Cubans . . . well, my company commander, for example, was a mulatto—big six-foot-two cat, very temperamental, would shout himself hoarse, that kind of guy, you know? A very uneven cat—one day he would be great, outgoing, very friendly, and the next a mean mother. Anyway the fact that these guys didn't really dig the Cubans, and were down on color, and couldn't speak Spanish—it gave, well, a kind of comic-opera quality to the thing in front.

Would you talk to them about what was going on?

Well, you know, they don't crack—I mean you ask them a direct question and they fade you right out. But, of course, in most cases they didn't know what was going on themselves. Like we used to buzz these instructors—you know, "When are we leaving bla-bla-bla?" but they just "Man, we don't know, we're waiting for orders," that kind of thing.

I don't understand why they couldn't get C.I.A. people who spoke Spanish.

Well, man, I'm inclined to believe that they'd rather *not* have guys who speak the language—I really think their fear is that deep . . . you know? I mean they figure that if these cats get to *talking* to these people they might be in some way *corrupted* by them, you dig. Like they don't trust their own boys, that's what it amounts to. And you can see their point in a way—because there was really nothing holding these cats together . . . they were all there for different reasons, mostly *personal* reasons—and of course because they thought they were going to *win,* that was the main thing. But there was no single idea behind it—you know, the sort of sense of purpose you need to pull off something like that. There were too many guys just looking out for number one—you know, *collectors* . . . they collected things. When it came time to ship out for the invasion, some of those guys had so much *stuff,* man—stuff they had copped . . . transistor radios, binoculars, anything they could cop. They would be carrying an extra pack full of this crap—I'm surprised they could even get off the landing craft with all that weight. They thought they were going on a picnic. Not all of them naturally—I mean there were some sensitive faces there too—sort of fatalistic cats, like this kid Juan on the mortars . . . he used to say: "Land on Monday, get captured on Tuesday, and shot on Wednesday." Very sensitive, sort of morbid type. So it was like that, all fragmented. A lot of different factions and ideas. But the real nucleus of the outfit, the heavy-weapons company, was very strong—they knew their jobs, and they were ready to fight. Well, they were just *wasted,* guys like that. And then there was a huge bunch of goof-offs—cats who had never done *anything,* and weren't going to start now. A lot of them stayed in the guardhouse, you know, like *permanently*—and they had it pretty good . . . they would let them out for chow, they'd get to go to the head of the line, that sort of thing. Some of them were very popular with the men, like clowns. They let all of them out just before the invasion, and a lot of them were made sergeants and so on.

What were the weapons you trained with?

Well, we started with the carbine and the M-1, then the M-3—that's the one that replaced the Thompson, you know, looks like a grease gun? And the Army .45, of course. And then the bazooka, machine gun, and mortar—finally the heavy mortars. That was the largest thing they had . . . these four-point-two mortars. And the Cubans dug that part of it—you know, the shooting. Especially the mortars—they were really *good* with the mortars. Primitive cats, you know, very good with their hands . . . and they'd do great things with the mortars, like dead reckoning, very unorthodox, and it would wig these C.I.A. faces, because they were all specialists—you know, they had learned by the numbers, and that's how they were trying to teach it—and one of these cats, like a young farm boy, would step up and just estimate the distance and drop it right in the top of a barrel about seventy-five yards away . . . and it would flip the instructor. "Tell him that's not the right way to do it," he'd say to the interpreter.

Were all the weapons American?

Everything was American, man. Blankets . . . well, you know *everything.*

What else do you recall about the training?

The training was a big drag, except on the firing range, that was pretty interesting. Very corny lectures and training films . . . well, there were a couple of paratrooper films that weren't bad. And we had this group, you know, which was *training* to be paratroops, and they were a gas . . . about a hundred and twenty guys, they were being trained by this guy from California, very funny cat, like something out of a movie, about forty years old, very *tough*—you know the type, fires a 30-caliber machine gun from the hip. And this was the toughest training on the base. But it was a big joke—I mean *this* cat and his paratroopers, it was like Ali Baba and his hundred and twenty thieves. They would go through the most outlandish things you can imagine in order to cop a pig or something off another company—like one guy pretending he's hanging himself, you know, to attract attention, while the other cats cop the pig. They were a wild bunch of studs, man—the paratroopers.

Did you have any tanks there?

No, the tanks never came to the camp—they were put directly on the ship. The tank crews arrived along toward the end, but they had already been trained—in New Orleans I believe.

What did you train for after you finished Basic?

Well, Ramón and I decided that *telegraphy* might be a good thing—I mean they wanted some guys to train for it, so five of us went into that. But it wasn't as easy as it sounded—you know, da-da-dit all day long in a box about the size of a phone booth. Very hot, man, and *coffee flies* . . . terrible, you have to hit them mop-mop-mop and nothing happens. Extremely difficult to kill. The telegraphy hut was right next to the *church,* you dig—it was just a shack, but there were these *priests* . . . not Cuban, *Spanish* . . . Spanish priests, man—they had imported these cats, and *they* were *something.* Very pretentious, very contemptuous of the Cubans—spoke Spanish with a lisp, you know? And one of these cats was too much—weird face, had a weird turn of mind . . . he had been there when they were building the camp, and a guy had been killed . . . fell from a cliff where they were working. And this priest . . . well, we'd step outside the hut, for a smoke, and he would engage us in conversation, like "Why don't you come to church and bla-bla-bla?"—so we'd talk to him and he'd tell about this guy falling over the cliff, but in extreme detail, man . . . how they found the body, how there were traces of where he had clutched at the grass trying to keep from going over the edge, and so on.

When did you learn that you weren't going to take part in the invasion itself?

Not until the very last minute, We had *no idea* we weren't going, and it was a big drag, man—I mean we'd been there *three months,* dig, and we wanted to *go.* We bugged the hell out of the Americans, Ramón and I, trying to get on that ship—but they wouldn't crack. "There's nothing we can do, your names weren't on the list," was all they would say. There were fourteen of us who didn't go—Ramón, myself, Molinet, who was the quartermaster, the guy in charge of the motor pool, one of the priests, two guys who were clerks, and about seven guys who were on weapons. We were all sore as hell about it—because of course we were sure we were going to win . . . but it wasn't just that—I mean we'd been through a lot together during those three months, and we wanted to go with them.

What do you suppose the reason was?

Well, it wasn't *coincidence,* I'm pretty sure of that. One story was that we were supposed to become cadre—you know, and help train the next group. Like replacing part of the C.I.A. you dig. I don't believe it was because Ramón and I were American, because there was one other American there, a translator for the cooks, and he went.

And when did you learn the outcome of the invasion?

Well we set up this shortwave radio, with a huge antenna, and listened—tuned in directly to Cuba. And at first it sounded like it was a success . . . so there was a big celebration got started—then after a while Castro came on, announcing how he wiped us out. And that brought everyone down, you know, very hard.

I simply can't understand how they could make such a mess of it.

Well, man, it was one of those things. They *wanted* to do it, but they wanted to do it without really *doing* it—you know, like a broad. So that was that . . . and the camp became a terrible drag after that, and of course everyone wanted to *leave*—you know, back to civilization. But these recruits kept arriving from Miami, about two hundred of them during the next couple of weeks—and this brought on the weirdest scenes of the whole time there . . . because these cats were *bugged,* man. I mean it was obviously a dead issue, and these guys wanted to go back to Miami. But the Americans were still trying to keep up some kind of training routine—you know, "Keep 'em busy, good for morale," the old Army crap. But these guys' attitude was "Okay, we lost, so let's get the hell out of here." And they didn't want to do anything. They had a meeting and sent a delegation up to see the Americans and told them they didn't want to drill or anything, they wanted to go back to the States. Well, that wigged the Americans—they thought it was "Communist agitation." See, they were still waiting for orders from Washington about what the hell they were supposed to do next. Anyway, the same day one of the toughest of these cats draws guard duty, and when the guy wakes him, he says, "If you wake me up again I'll blow your head off"—you know, *that* kind of reaction. Well, this guy goes back to the orderly room and tells Martinez Arbona, the guy who was acting camp commander, and Martinez Arbona comes down to the barracks and says, "This is insubordination, bla-bla-bla," and the other guy starts to beat him up. So Martinez cuts out, up the hill, tells the Americans—and this *really* flips them. Now it's a "Communist mutiny," you dig, and they're scared out of their wits. "We've gotta get those guns away from them!" But they had no idea how to go about it, so they were wigging completely. Well, *we* all knew they weren't Communists—I mean they just wanted to get the hell *out* of there. We told the C.I.A. cats, "Man, all you have to do is tell them to *turn in the guns and they can go home.*" But they kept trying to figure out some tricky muscle way of doing it—and God knows what would have happened if we hadn't gone down and told them if they would turn in the guns they could go home. And of course that's what they did. But the Americans never did really believe it—they were very suspicious of them . . . kept them completely separated from the rest of us. And when we got to the airstrip, they sent them right out . . . you know, like thank God they're gone!

So everybody went back to Miami?

Yeah, we get back to Miami, go to the recruiting station—that's where they'd been sending our checks, dig—pick those up, and go our separate ways. Very sad scene at the recruiting place because they've got the lists of guys that got wiped or captured, and relatives and so on are falling by to look at the lists. And we talked to a couple of guys who got away—swam out and got picked up by boats.

What did they have to say about the invasion?

What did they say? "We got wiped, man. . . *wiped.*"

[June, 1963]

The Duties and Responsibilities of a Congressman to the United States

by Adam Clayton Powell Jr.

The primary and overriding duty and responsibility of each Member of the House and the Senate is to get reelected. Regardless of denials, lofty views, noble-sounding principles, high ideals, great professions, the number-one purpose of each and every man and woman serving as a Member is to get back on the payroll. The only time this is not true is when a Member has accepted a much more lucrative position in private industry or has voluntarily retired.

Even those Members of the Congress who are wealthy and do not need the salary, nevertheless are activated primarily by the goal of getting reelected. This is no criticism of my colleagues. It is merely a simple statement of a crass fact. It would be ridiculous for anyone to think otherwise or for a Member to do otherwise, for if a Member was not interested in reelection, there would be no point in his starting in the first place to seek the public office. Now there are several ways of guaranteeing reelection: one, do what your constituents want you to do; another, be a blind follower of the party machine which controls the votes in your district; still another, play the tune which the big-money boys want to hear in order for them to pay the piper's bill for reelection, which is ofttimes staggering.

459

Members seeking reelection who happen to belong to the Majority Party do not of necessity go along with the Administration's desires when, through bargaining, they can force the Administration to give them hand-outs in the form of jobs and projects for their districts. In fact, the standard comment on the Floor of the House or the Senate, when someone casts a vote which will not be popular in his district, is, "You voted like a statesman today." But this comment is heard very rarely.

When questions of national interest conflict with the desires of one's constituents, the national interests suffer. For instance, I represent a district that is interested in the bread-and-butter issues of life—housing, jobs and education. My constituents don't care whether I vote for, or against, or not vote at all on tidelands oil, surplus wheat, industrial monopolies, or the oil-depreciation allowance. In these areas, I exercise my personal judgment. However, Representatives from those areas that have the problems of tidelands oil, surplus wheat, industrial monopolies and oil-depreciation allowances feel obliged to vote either according to what their constituents want or what the money boys who bankroll their campaigns demand.

To sum it up, the politician holding a seat in the United States Congress has a two-pronged responsibility that is obvious: commitment to the interest of his constituency and to the national welfare. How he performs in the first instance defines his life expectancy as a Member of Congress; how he performs in the second is his legislative voting record. Here again the legislative record is many things to many people. Take a man like Senator John Williams of Delaware. He has an almost perfect voting record in terms of not being absent, but that record consists of votes against public housing; votes against all kinds of civil-rights amendments, even those offered by such fellow Republicans as Senators Dirksen, Keating, Javits and others; votes against confirming his own President's recommendation of Sobeloff to be a Circuit Judge simply because Sobeloff was the Solicitor General of the Department of Justice who success-fully argued the famous 1954 Supreme Court decision outlawing school segregation and Senator Williams was not in favor of obeying the Supreme Court.

Then consider Senator Harry Byrd of Virginia, who has a perfect voting record, but refuses to accede to the President's wishes and give an income-tax cut to the low-income group of this country. On the other hand, I am accused of absenteeism. Yet as the new Chairman of the Committee on Education and Labor, I sent to the Floor of Congress eighteen bills which became laws of the land; and twenty-one other bills which died in the Rules Committee; making a record of thirty-nine bills within eighteen legislative months. Which is more important, a one-hundred-percent record of attendance with no production, or the produc-tion of thirty-nine pieces of legislation in eighteen months? The first duty of a Chairman is to be a Chairman, and not a Member. Only when a Member has been reelected several times can he develop into a "statesman," but he must proceed cautiously. He must under no circumstances ever get too far away from his constituency. Witness the amazingly narrow margin by which Senator Lister Hill of Alabama was reelected in 1962. This Senator, in his position, which is the counterpart of mine in the House as Chairman of the Committee on Education and Labor, brought to Alabama a tremendous number of hospitals and schools and other projects. But he stayed in Washington too much. People in Alabama forgot what he looked like. And he won by only 6,845 votes over, of all things in the heart of Dixie, a Republican!

This classic debate over the responsibility of the Member of Congress to either his district or the national welfare goes back to the very beginnings of our nation. From the year 1775 to 1790, two groups of the founding fathers debated two schools of thought. One, the direct Democrats, placed their faith in the people and said their Representative ought to be immediately responsible to his constituents. They were led by people like Benjamin Franklin, Tom Paine, James Wilson and Thomas Jefferson.

The other group, led by Madison and Hamilton, believed in a system of checks and balances, and it was this view of the conservatives that found expression finally in the Constitution of 1787.

Nevertheless, in *The Federalist Papers*, the authors wrote: "It is a sound and important principle that the Representative ought to be acquainted with the interests and circumstances of his constituents. Duty, gratitude, interest, ambition itself, are the cords by which they will be bound to fidelity and sympathy with the great mass of the people."

And so Madison and Hamilton prevailed. In the debate in the first Congress of the United States, it was the preponderant opinion that Representatives were to be trustees for the whole nation, and not merely agents of their particular constituency.

In 1800, Thomas Jefferson triumphed over the Federalists and, with the opening of a new century, there came a change in the prevailing philosophy of political representation. De Grazia, in his *Public and Republic,* wrote that the competence and discretion with which a Representative is endowed is "grounded on the supposition that he is charged with the will, acquainted with the opinions, and devoted to the interests of his constituents." Abraham Lincoln, in campaigning for reelection to the Illinois Legislature in 1836, said, "While acting as a Representative, I shall be governed by their [his constituents] will on all subjects upon which I have the means of knowing what their will is, and upon all others, I shall do what my own judgment teaches me will best advance their interests."

In recent times, the Member of Congress has become increasingly a broker for his constituency, interceding in its behalf with agencies to obtain contracts; secure favorable decisions; involving himself in programs which include loans, subsidies, contracts, franchises, and permits of various kinds without any gain or remuneration.

This then is a Member of Congress today, whose duties and responsibilities are arrived at in the following order: first, the wishes of his constituents; second, the dictates of his political party; third, the pressures of the special interest; and fourth and lastly, by his own views of the general welfare. Where is the national party platform which gets so much publicity every four years at the great national circuses—the Republican and Democratic Conventions? These platforms of the national parties mean absolutely nothing to the individual Congressman because these Congressmen are running in local areas.

In 1865, Congressman James A. Garfield in the House made very lofty statements about national welfare. But seven years later, in his diary of February 19, which is in the Manuscript Division of the Library of Congress, he wrote: "It is a terrible thing to live in fear of their constituents to the extent which many Members do."

Many Members of Congress are nothing more than errand boys—so much so that former Congressman Ramspeck of Georgia said that the Congress should be divided in two parts, with the Legislative part handled by elected Representatives in Congress, and the Service part by elected agents before the Executive Branch of the Government. Not a bad idea!

How in the name of all common sense can a Member of Congress know whether or not the national welfare will be affected by Georgia peanuts, Texas oil, Wyoming wool, Colorado silver, Mississippi cotton or Maine potatoes. For example, on April 25 of this year, H.R. 4997, the Feed Grain Act of 1963, came before the House. Members repeatedly made a point of order that a quorum was not present. The result was there were four quorum calls and two record votes. To make a quorum call the average Member of the House has to walk about four blocks round trip, down and up an average of three floors in his office building, then down and up two floors in the Capitol. He then must wait until his name is called, whereupon he can cover himself with immortal glory by answering, "Present!"

This time-consuming operation takes at least twenty-five minutes, and for some Members even more. It could be eliminated very expeditiously by putting in an electric quorum-call device, which is used in many State legislatures, whereby a Member could be working at his desk and yet, by answering through pressing a button, indicate that he is in Washington and therefore available for a vote.

Now I refuse to answer quorum calls. Most of them are instigated mischievously and very few of them serve any importance whatsoever. On the particular day the Feed Grain Bill was under consideration, had I answered all the quorum calls, I would have lost approximately two hours of working time. So I did not answer. I stayed at my desk. I did not even go out to lunch, but kept working. When the showdown came to recommit President Kennedy's Feed Grain Bill, I was there and voted. The Administration won by a margin of only nine votes. Even though it was late in the evening, I still had not finished my work at my desk. My work load would have been hopelessly behind schedule if I had answered those quorum calls. The American public is completely misinformed regarding absenteeism and the voting record. These are two separate things. To answer or not to answer a quorum call has nothing whatsoever to do with voting. It is of course very obvious that it is the vote which counts. Heinz Eulau, in *The American Political Science Review* of September, 1959, writes with his associates on "The Role of the Representative." They say there are three types: the "trustee," who is a free agent and follows his own convictions, principles, judgments of conscience; the "delegate," who is inclined to consult and follow the instructions of his constituents; and the "politico," who expresses both orientations either simultaneously or serially. These writers conclude that, under modern conditions, Congress has become "an agency for the coordination and integration of diverse social and economic political interests."

This is true—the entire picture of the duties and responsibilities of Members of Congress is further complicated when one considers the racial and religious backgrounds of Members. The pressure of the Southern Baptist Convention on two of the Senate conferees killed higher education for this nation. That same pressure flowed over onto the Floor of the House, so that the Edith Green Higher Education Bill, which had been passed by a margin of four and a half to one in the House three times, was finally defeated.

Elementary and secondary education in the United States, which is under my chairmanship, has absolutely no chance until men such as Congressman James Delaney of New York, who holds the key vote in the Rules Committee, changes his mind. Jim Delaney is a staunch Roman Catholic and, as far as his religious beliefs are concerned, he is absolutely correct. I respect him and admire him, but all I want to do is point out that here is a man whose duties and responsibilities are completely encompassed by his deep religious faith.

Take the great liberal Republican Senator, Jacob Javits of New York. Under no circumstance would he allow anything, directly or indirectly, which would adversely affect Israel to be passed by the Senate without raising his voice in protest. Here again we must understand his point of view, just as one day, before a Jewish audience, he was pleading with them to understand mine, saying, "Adam Powell feels about Negro rights like we [Jews] feel about Israel." When the brilliant Congressman Santangelo was in the House, one of the major things about which he was concerned was the continued use of Italian names and Italian types in the gangster series, *The Untouchables*. The Italian constituents in his district and his

Italian people applauded the successful fight which he waged to wipe out the stereotyped Italian gangster from the TV screen.

What is the national interest? Let us take the classic dispute over the Powell Amendment. The Powell Amendment was created by me, after the 1954 Supreme Court decision outlawing segregation in the public schools, when the Executive Branch of Government under President Eisenhower refused to withhold federal funds from those schools which were violating that decision. I then successfully attached the Powell Amendment to Federal Aid to Education. This amendment would forbid the use of federal funds in segregated schools. Immediately, all of the white press and white liberals said this was against the national interest, but all of the Negro press and Negro leaders said it was for the national interest. Here and there, an outstanding white person, such as Dr. Buell Gallagher, the President of the College of the City of New York, stood up in favor of the Powell Amendment. But even such great liberals as the late Mrs. Eleanor Roosevelt and Mrs. Agnes Meyer were against the Powell Amendment. For them, the national interest of the United States was schools for children, even if they were segregated in violation of the Supreme Court decision. For me the national interest of the United States was obedience to the law of the land, plus the moral posture of the United States before the world.

This classic problem of duty and responsibility is epitomized by the tragedy of our Southern Members of Congress, who are prisoners and captives of their constituencies. Ironically, the Negro, as he is beginning to get the right to vote in the South, is emancipating the white Southern Members of Congress so that they can vote more freely.

In the nearly nineteen years that I have been in Congress, I have met scores of Representatives from below the Mason-Dixon line who have privately and repeatedly confessed to me that if the votes on many issues could be taken in secret, they would vote the direct opposite of the way they are voting. For them, their duty and responsibility is to serve the prejudices of their constituents, even against the national interest, the world image, and the law of the land, and the Supreme Court decision of 1954. This is the fundamental difference between the Southerner and me: I am fighting that the law of the land shall be obeyed, and that the world image of the United States, especially before the "rising tide of expectations" of black peoples, shall be preserved untarnished. In fact the national interest for me is representing what I call "the outs": the thirty percent of the people of our country, black and white, which are still ill-housed, ill-fed, and largely uneducated for the better life. I must devote myself to them even though the vast majority are not in my district, my city or my state.

More than one half of my mail and cases come from outside my area. In Washington, one skilled secretary works throughout the year, handling an average of 5,000 cases. In New York City, all the secretaries and many volunteers work full time by day and two nights a week handling over 10,000 cases per year. These are the bread-and-butter cases. These are cases of discrimination, segregation. My fight therefore must be a fight for social reform, a continuing protest against the undue delays and an urgent demand for immediate action. This is not a popular posture before the nation, but it is at least a free one, and one which incidentally strikes a responsive chord among the leadership of the two-billion-plus darker peoples of the world.

When leaders from Africa and Asia come to the United States, they invariably ask the State Department to arrange appointments to talk to me. I attend the International Labor Organization's annual conference in Geneva, Switzerland, where the State Department arranges some type of social affair, at which I am the host in name, in order to woo the delegates from the colored nations to the side of the United States of America.

The basic insight into this entire problem is that you cannot compare the Senate and the House. Senators are elected for six years. For the first two years, they can afford to be "statesmen." For the second two years, they can "play it safe." For the last two years, they must run for office. Members of the House are elected every two years, which means they are always running for office.

Because of this, the House is a group of timid souls, a second-class body rapidly degenerating under a massive inferiority complex. For instance, relatives have been on the payrolls of Congress in great numbers since the beginnings of this nation. The Senate disdainfully publishes a partial list of their employees every now and then. The House meekly publishes a complete list every year. The House by rule cannot even mention the word "Senate," much less a Member of the Senate, on the floor. Members can only refer to "the other body." But Members of the Senate, under their rules, can attack any Member of the House by name any time they wish, make all kinds of misstatements, inaccuracies and lies, all under the cloak of immunity.

Members of the Senate, their families and their staffs travel throughout the world in baronial splendor without making an accounting in the *Congressional Record* of where, how, what or why—while the "Milque-toasts" of the House, straining at gnats and swallowing camels, have passed laws affecting only themselves, to place in the *Record* every detail of the where, how, what and why. Members of the Senate and their staffs can and do spend illimitable amounts of money through counterpart funds. The House by law does not allow any Committee to utilize such funds without special resolution.

This country will never have a House of Representatives whose Members will be worthy of being called Congressmen until the following changes take place. By law, the duties and responsibilities of the Members of the House must be identical with those of the Senate, no more and no less. The Members of the House should have the same term of office as the Senate—six years. This way, and only this way, can we have a period of statesmanship during their tenure of office. In order to give them more freedom of expression, the retirement program should be changed so that men can retire at a lower age with fewer years in order to be eligible, and with higher retirement pay. This will greatly encourage freedom of expression once a Member knows that his financial future is not in jeopardy.

Laws must be passed forbidding any Member of Congress to contact any agency, bureau or department, directly or indirectly at any time. This is the only way that Congressmen can be relieved from being errand boys. Then the constituents would have to write directly to those agencies, bureaus or departments for assistance. There should be a public revelation in the *Congressional Record* each year of the income tax of each and every Member of Congress.

Furthermore, all financial holdings and investments of any type of any member should be printed in the *Congressional Record* upon his election and at all subsequent reelections. Most important, there should be a law forbidding any Member of the Congress who is a lawyer from being connected directly or indirectly with any law firm. In other areas of government, when men are appointed to high office, they sever all connections with their corporations or firms.

When these changes are made and only then will the duties and responsibilities of the Members of the Congress be concerned more with the national interest. But even then, the primary duty still will be to serve the constituent and thereby get reelected.

[September, 1963]

Sixty Versions of the Kennedy Assassination

by Edward Jay Epstein

How It Happened

1. Single-Bullet Theory

Proponents: A 4-3 majority of the Warren Commission. And most Commission lawyers, notably Arlen Specter, who developed the theory in March, 1964, and Norman Redlich, who advocated it as the only alternative to a two-assassin theory.

Thesis: The first bullet wounded both Kennedy and Connally. A second bullet hit Kennedy in the head and killed him. Another bullet missed the car entirely and was never found.

Selling Point: This is the only theory that explains the assassination in terms of a single assassin. Why? Because films of the assassination show that a maximum of only 1.8 seconds could have elapsed between the earliest point at which Kennedy was first hit and the latest point at which Connally was first hit. Since the bolt of the murder rifle cannot be operated in less than 2.3 seconds, it could not possibly have been fired twice during the time in which both men were hit. Either both men were hit by the same bullet or there were two assassins.

Drawback No. 1: The single-bullet theory is tenable if and only if the three F.B.I. reports (November 26, December 9 and January 13) are completely wrong on their statements of the autopsy. Why? Because these three reports all state the first bullet did not go completely through Kennedy and therefore it could not have gone on to hit Connally, who was seated in front of Kennedy.

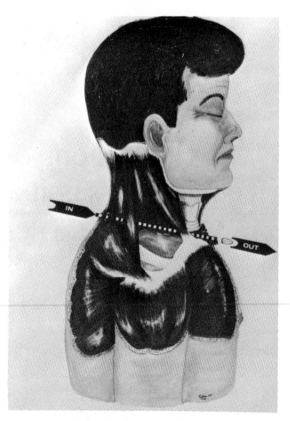

This precise bullet path is essential to the Commission's theory that the first bullet went through Kennedy and then hit Connally (Exhibit 385). Any slight difference would rule this out and thereby suggest a second assassin.

Retorts: 1. The Incompetent F.B.I. J. Lee Rankin, at the time the Commission's general counsel, and Norman Redlich, his deputy, have said—after the December 13 F.B.I. Summary Report was published in *Inquest*—that the "so-called F.B.I. Summary Report" (which the Commission considered of "principal importance") was "evaluated and discarded" during the inquiry. Redlich further said "the Commission study used the actual (November 26) reports of the F.B.I. investigative agents, not just the summary." (However, the actual report, just recently found in the National Archives, corroborates the Summary Report.)

2. *Time* magazine proposes that the F.B.I. was completely wrong on all reports and has long since publicly admitted these errors. (However, the F.B.I. told The Washington *Post* that its Summary Report was accurate as of when it was prepared, implying the doctors later may have changed their opinion. The F.B.I. declined comment to The New York *Times* in June, 1966, on the question of whether or not its reports were erroneous. Even to Commission champion Fletcher Knebel, the F.B.I. would only admit that it was possible that their *initial* reports did not reflect a subsequent decision by the doctors.)

3. *The Commission's Post-Report,* reported by Fletcher Knebel, holds that the day after the autopsy, on receiving further information about the throat wound from the Dallas doctors, the autopsy doctors reached the conclusion that the bullet exited from Kennedy's throat. Aside from the fact that this theory contradicts the version of the autopsy given in The Warren Report, it still leaves unresolved the problem of the bullet wound "below the shoulder" (reported by the F.B.I.), that later apparently moved up to the back of the neck.

Drawback No. 2: Photographs of the President's shirt and jacket support the F.B.I. report that the first bullet struck Kennedy below the shoulder. If the bullet fired from above did enter below the shoulder it is highly unlikely that it exited through the throat.

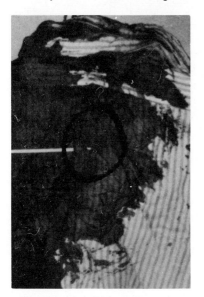 

Exhibits 59 and 60 indicate that the bullet entered lower than the Commission said it had.

Retorts: 1. The Creeping Shirt. Norman Redlich has suggested (after the F.B.I. photographs were published in *Inquest*) that the President's shirt somehow rose up a few inches so that the bullet hole in the shirt coincided with a hole in the rear of the neck. Experimentation indicates, however, that raising the shirt over the collar line entails doubling it up, which would produce two holes in the back of the shirt.

2. Newsweek magazine suggests that Kennedy may have been bent over so far that his shoulder was higher than his throat. But the films of the assassination show that Kennedy was sitting erect, and his back brace, according to the Report "tended to make him sit up straight."

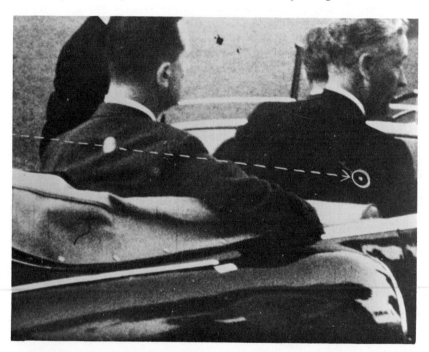

This photograph of the F.B.I. restaging, which appeared in several editions of The Warren Report, not only contradicts the Commission's placement of the bullet path but shows that if the bullet entered where the hole in the jacket is, and then went on to hit Connally, it would have come out Kennedy's chest, not his throat. And Kennedy had no chest wounds.

Drawback No. 3: Governor Connally says it is inconceivable that he could have been struck by the same bullet that hit Kennedy. He remembers that after hearing the first shot he turned to his right but could not see the President. He then began to turn to his left, and was hit. His story is corroborated by Mrs. Connally.

Retort: Connally was confused. The Commission brushed aside Governor Connally's testimony (and his wife's) by declaring that in view of the circumstances he could hardly be expected to recall clearly what happened.

2. F.B.I. Theory

Proponents: The F.B.I.

Thesis: 1. The first bullet hit Kennedy below the shoulder and penetrated "only a distance of a finger length." This bullet was "expelled" onto the President's stretcher when the Dallas doctors applied external heart massage.
2. The second bullet struck Connally.
3. The third bullet entered Kennedy's head and fragmentized. (The impact of the shot sent a tiny fragment of bone through Kennedy's throat, causing a small throat wound.) All shots came from the Book Depository.

Selling Points: 1. An entry wound *below* the shoulder would explain the shirt and jacket holes being about six inches below the top of the collar. It would also serve to explain the autopsy sketch showing a wound well below the collar line. And it would explain the Secret Service testimony that it was six inches below the collar.
2. The supposition that the bullet also fell out of Kennedy's back accounts for the bullet found on the stretcher. (See Planted-Bullet Theory, No. 17.)
3. The tiny bone fragment accounts for the small throat wound. Also, a bone fragment would explain the absence of metallic traces on the holes in the front of the shirt.

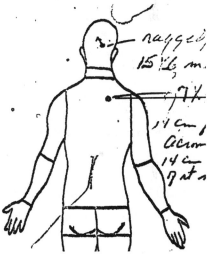

Exhibit No. 397, the autopsy sketch drawn by Dr. Humes, shows a bullet wound lower than the Commission's Exhibit 385 does.

Drawback No. 1: The F.B.I. Theory, by positing that Kennedy and Connally were hit by separate bullets, leads to a two-assassin theory. As one Commission lawyer bluntly put it: "To say that they were hit by separate bullets is synonymous with saying that there were two assassins."
Drawback No. 2: The Fourth Bullet. Late in the investigation, it was discovered that a bystander, James Tague, had been wounded by one of the shots. The F.B.I. Theory holds that all three shots hit inside the

President's car. Yet it was unlikely that Tague was wounded by any of these shots since he was standing about 260 feet away at the time of the fusillade. This raises the possibility that Tague was wounded by a fragment from a fourth bullet. But only three shells were found in the Book Depository.

Drawback No. 3: If the F.B.I. autopsy report is accurate, then the Commission's autopsy findings had to be purposely falsified. The implications of this are almost too disturbing to imagine. Yet, the fact that the autopsy surgeon, Commander Humes, burned "certain preliminary notes" has given rise to the theory that the "preliminary notes" actually contained the earlier version of the autopsy referred to by the F.B.I. This question is unresolved.

One of the main stimuli for theories that shots came from someplace other than the Book Depository is an amateur eight-millimeter film of the assassination taken by Abraham Zapruder. In ten seconds of color film, virtually the entire sequence of events is recorded. The Zapruder film shows the motorcade proceeding down Elm Street with the President smiling and waving, then suddenly he reaches for his throat, apparently hit. About a second later Connally grimaces with pain and begins toppling over. A few seconds elapse, then a bullet visibly strikes the President's head. From the film, the Commission judged that the President was first hit between film frame 210 and 225, and the fatal head shot occurred on film frame 313. By determining the shutter speed of the camera (18.3 frames per second), the Commission ascertained: 1) a maximum of 5.6 seconds elapsed from the first to the final shot; and 2) no more than 1.8 seconds elapsed between the time Kennedy and Connally were first hit. This time bind led directly to the Commission's Single-Bullet Theory (see No. 1). The Zapruder film also led to four other interesting theories.

3. Head Movement Theory

Proponent: Vincent Salandria, a Philadelphia lawyer.

Using two slide projectors, and superimposing frame 316 over frame 313, Salandria finds that after the fatal head shot, Kennedy's head moves sharply backward and to the left, a direction inconsistent with shots from the Depository. Salandria extrapolated the trajectory from the direction in which the head moves and concludes that the shot came from behind the picket fence or the arcade on the grassy knoll. Salandria also suspects that, because of the massive devastation, this second wound, unlike the first, may have been caused by a dumdum bullet—which couldn't have come from Oswald's rifle.

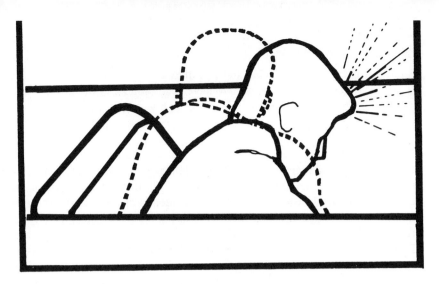

4. Early-Hit Theory

A group of California theorists has used the Zapruder film to show that the first shot hit Kennedy between film frames 190 and 210. If true, this would be significant because the Commission established that during this interval the line of sight from the sixth-floor window in the Depository was obstructed by the foliage of an oak tree; therefore the shot must have come from elsewhere.

Harold Weisberg also uses the Zapruder film to prove the Early-Hit Theory. Since Zapruder testified that he saw Kennedy hit, and Zapruder's view was blocked by a traffic sign between film frames 205 and 225 (by which time Kennedy had already been hit), Weisberg concludes that Kennedy was hit before film frame 205.

5. Missing-Frame Theory

The fact that film frames 208 through 211 have been deleted from the black-and-white frame-by-frame photographs published by the Warren Commission (Exhibit 885) and from the color slides of the Zapruder film at the National Archives—and the fact that frames 207 and 212 show obvious splice marks—has led a number of theorists to suspect that Kennedy was shot during that interval and that the four missing film frames were suppressed deliberately.

Drawback: Life magazine owns the original film and according to those who have seen it, the film is complete, no frames are missing, and Kennedy does not appear to have been hit in the sequence. The Archive's frames may just have been damaged innocently.

6. Traffic Sign Theory

David Lifton, a U.C.L.A. graduate student, claims that he can detect stress marks coming from the traffic sign starting at frame 212 and continuing until frame 221. He interprets these as shock waves caused by a bullet hitting the sign. This shot, he figures, could not have been the same one that Oswald is supposed to have fired because of the timing. And strangely, right after the assassination the sign was removed.

7. Entry Wound Theory

Proponents: Mark Lane, Thomas Buchanan, Joachim Joesten, *et al.*

Thesis: Early statements were made by Dallas doctors suggesting that the throat wound was made by a bullet *entering* the throat. Since films of the assassination firmly establish that the President's car was past the Book Depository when he was shot, a bullet entering the throat must have come from a point well in front of the Depository. "In front" was at first interpreted to mean the railroad overpass; however, when the Commission showed that a bullet did not in fact pass through the limousine's windshield, as was believed by the proponents of this theory, "in front" was then interpreted to mean the grassy knoll. Mark Lane states in his latest version that Kennedy was directly facing the knoll when he was shot in the throat, although none of the films indicates this to be the case.

Selling Point: The entry-wound theory explains the Dallas doctors' early statements and the relatively small diameter of the wound, although the doctors later testified that under certain conditions an exit wound would have the same appearance as an entry wound.

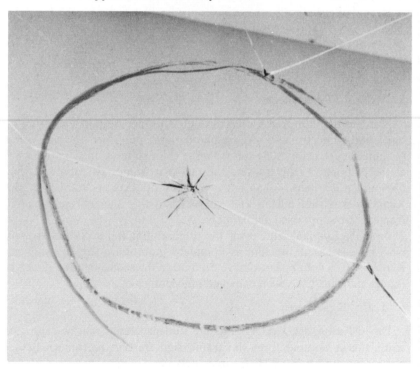

Drawback: The entry-wound theory does not explain what finally happened to the bullet that entered the throat. Since no exit wound was found in the President's back (and no bullet was in the President's body), the entry-wound theory depends on the assumption that the autopsy and other evidence was changed.

8. Over the Fence Theory

Proponents: Maurice Schonfeld, Jack Fox, Burt Reinhardt, all U.P.I.

In the United Press-International film library, a New York hobbyist found an eight-millimeter color film of the assassination made by Orville Nix. One of the frames of the Nix film particularly interested him because it showed an object behind the wall on the grassy knoll. He then employed a film specialist to blow the frame up, and it became clear that the object was in fact a vehicle. On the roof of the vehicle, he discerned a man aiming what appeared to be a rifle at the President's car. He immediately took his photograph to Dallas and asked eyewitnesses about it.

The Nix-U.P.I. film and partial blowup.

U.P.I. editors, apparently impressed with the photograph, sent reporter Jack Fox to Dallas to interview witnesses to the assassination.

Lee E. Bowers, Jr. told him that the photograph was "exactly what I saw." S. M. Holland, who was standing on the overpass and had one of the best views of any eyewitness, told Fox there were four shots: ". . . the first came from the book building and hit the President. The second came from the same place and hit Governor John Connally. . . . The third shot came from behind the picket fence to the north of Elm Street. There was a puff of smoke under the trees like someone had thrown out a Chinese firecracker and a report entirely different from the one which was fired from the book building. . . ."

According to Holland, the fourth shot came from the Book Depository. When Holland reached the fence he found a station wagon and sedan. On the bumper of the station wagon there were two muddy marks "as if someone had stood there to look over the fence." At least seven other witnesses on the overpass saw smoke rising from the same area, and many other witnesses thought the shots came from behind the picket fence. One Dallas policeman, J. M. Smith, even claimed to have "caught the smell of gunpowder" behind the wooden fence.

9. Eyewitness Theories

Eyewitness accounts of the assassination are perhaps the most popular source of two-assassin theories—virtually any armchair student of the assassination, given the report's twenty-six volumes of testimony, can develop an interesting theory as to where the shots came from. Right after the twenty-six volumes were made public, Harold Feldman, a writer on the psychology of assassins, counted up the various sources of shots reported by 121 eyewitnesses. His tally revealed that 38 gave "no clear opinion," 32 thought the shots came from the Book Depository, and 51 thought the shots came from the grassy knoll area. Largely on the basis of this analysis, Feldman advanced the theory that there were two assassins: one on the grassy knoll and one in the Book Depository.
Drawback: Eyewitness recollections often conflict: which means that *somebody* has to be wrong.

Who Did It?

The following six theories name Lee Harvey Oswald as the lone assassin.

10. Underground Man Theory

Proponent: The Warren Commission.
The Commission did not reach a final conclusion as to why Oswald killed President Kennedy. Instead, it listed five "factors" (which, a Commission lawyer said, read like clichés from a TV soap opera). They were:
   (1) hostility to his environment;
   (2) failure to establish "meaningful relationships";
   (3) desire for a place in history;
   (4) a commitment to Marxism and communism (a "factor" inserted at the insistence of Commissioner Gerald Ford);
   (5) a capacity to act decisively without regard to the consequences.
According to this theory, Oswald had no motive; he acted out of blind resentment.

11. Manchurian Candidate Theory

Proponents: Some Commission lawyers and members of the C.I.A.

Since Oswald spent considerable time in a Soviet hospital, a few Commission lawyers entertained the theory that Oswald might have been brainwashed and conditioned as a "sleeper" assassin; then he went haywire (i.e. he was accidentally turned on). The Commission decided to send a letter to the C.I.A. requesting information on the "present status of Soviet 'mind-conditioning' techniques." A few weeks later, a C.I.A. agent replied that this possibility was still "a main school of thought" at the C.I.A. on the assassination, and although such techniques were still in a *relatively* primitive stage, this form of conditioning could be induced by drugs. The theory, however, was not further developed.

12. Domestic Quarrel Theory

Proponent: Representative Gerald Ford.

Commissioner Gerald Ford, in his book, *Portrait of the Assassin,* suggests that Oswald was still hedging on the eve of the assassination when he returned home to see his wife, Marina. She spurned him. Oswald then went to the garage. He got his rifle.

13. Horrible Accident Theory

Proponent: Marina Oswald.

In her final testimony before the Commission, Marina Oswald advanced her own theory of Lee's motive. She said she believed her husband was actually trying to shoot Governor John Connally, and missed, and by a horrible accident he killed the President.

14. Oedipal Theory

Proponent: Dr. Renatus Hartogs, co-author of *The Two Assassins.*

Dr. Hartogs, a psychiatrist who evaluated Oswald as a thirteen-year-old boy, has recently advanced a theory explaining the assassination in terms of Oswald's repressed lust for his mother. Hartogs observes that Oswald slept in his mother's bed long after he should have had a bed of his own, and suggests that inner guilt feelings may have led him to kill President Kennedy. Dr. Hartogs finds it significant that Oswald shot at both Kennedy and Tippit three times, since the number "three" in psychoanalytic thinking symbolizes the masculine genitals. However, Sylvia Meagher points out in her review of Hartogs' book that Tippit was shot four times.

15. Killer-Instinct Theory

Proponent: John J. McCloy.

In a secret colloquium between the Commission and three psychiatrists, Commissioner McCloy advanced the "killer-instinct" theory. He noted that Oswald had killed two men and attempted to shoot at least three others (Governor Connally, General Walker, and the police officer who tried to arrest him). McCloy reasoned that this indicated a pattern of innate violence. By the time the report was written, however, McCloy's hypothesis seems to have been lost in the shuffle.

The following four theories are based on the belief that Oswald was innocent, that he was framed for both the Kennedy assassination and murder of officer J. D. Tippit by the real conspirators who planted evidence against him before and after the assassination. The logic of these theories inevitably leads to a high-level conspiracy involving law-enforcement agencies. For example, to believe that Oswald did not kill Tippit, it is necessary to assume: a) shells from Oswald's revolver were planted at the scene by the real murderers; b) the revolver then was planted on Oswald by the Dallas police (the plot obviously could not have depended on Oswald going home and conveniently fetching his pistol); and c) Oswald's admission that he had his revolver with him when arrested was fabricated.

16. Planted-Rifle Theory

Proponent: Mark Lane.
Thesis: A 7.65 caliber German Mauser was found in the Book Depository, and later Oswald's 6.5 caliber Italian Mannlicher-Carcano rifle was substituted for it. This theory is based on testimony (and an affidavit) indicating that the three Dallas law officers first described the rifle as a Mauser. The problem with this theory is that the bullet fragments found in the President's car ballistically match Oswald's Carcano, proving that it was employed in the assassination (no matter where or when it was found).

17. Planted-Bullet Theory

Proponents: Professor Richard H. Popkin, Professor Josiah Thompson, Sylvia Meagher, Vincent Salandria, Léo Sauvage, Harold Weisberg, Mark Lane and Ray Marcus.
Thesis: A bullet, which The Warren Report states was found on Connally's stretcher, was fired from Oswald's rifle sometime prior to the assassination. Then, after the assassination, it was planted on a stretcher in the Dallas hospital where Kennedy and Connally were treated, thereby framing Oswald.

The Commission claims this bullet pierced Kennedy's neck and Connally's shoulder, ribs, wrist and thigh. Theorists say it's a fake.

This theory is based on the fact that evidence developed by the Commission precluded both Kennedy's and Connally's stretchers as possible sources for the stretcher bullet. The Commission's autopsy report stated that the bullet exited Kennedy, therefore it could not have come from his stretcher. And Drs. Finck, Humes, and Shaw testified that more fragments were found in Connally's wrist than were missing from the bullet, thus ruling out Connally's stretcher as a source for the bullet. Furthermore, in missing tapes of the doctors' press conference, which was held after the stretcher bullet was found, Dr. Shaw supposedly says that a nearly whole bullet was *lodged in Connally's thigh*. The theorists thus deduce that the bullet must have been planted on the stretcher. The fact that no blood or other organic material was found on the bullet reinforces their argument. Professor Thompson further points out that the only bullet similar in appearance to the stretcher bullet was obtained by firing Oswald's rifle into a long tube of cotton. He believes that this test indicated that the stretcher bullet was probably obtained by firing the bullet into cotton.

18. Oswald Impersonator Theory

Proponents: Léo Sauvage, Harold Weisberg, Sylvia Meagher (See also Popkin's Two-Oswald Theory, No. 25).
Thesis: Before the assassination, someone impersonating Oswald planted clues that would incriminate Oswald in the assassination. According to this theory, the impersonator made himself conspicuous at a nearby rifle range, brought a gun to a neighborhood gunsmith, cashed large checks, and acted suspiciously. The impersonator probably took part in the assassination.

Who Is This Man? A C.I.A. report on Lee Harvey Oswald arrived at the F.B.I. field office in Dallas the day of the assassination. It revealed that Oswald had visited the Cuban Embassy in Mexico City on September 27, 1963, and included a photograph taken by a secret C.I.A. camera of the man identified as Oswald leaving the Embassy. After the assassination, a problem developed; the man in the C.I.A. photograph was *not* Oswald! Oswald's mother added to the confusion by claiming the man in the photograph was Jack Ruby. (Obviously, it isn't.) Commission lawyers, attempting to find out if the man in the photograph was associated with Oswald or impersonating him, were never able to identify the mystery man. All the C.I.A. would say was that it was a "mix-up".)

19. Fall-Guy Theory

Proponent: Joachim Joesten.
Thesis: That the assassination was the work of a conspiracy involving some officers of the C.I.A. and the F.B.I. as well as some Army figures and some reactionary oil millionaires. The conspirators used Oswald as a "fall guy, a red herring, to draw attention while the murderers escaped." The F.B.I., for reasons of its own, completed the frame of Oswald and covered up evidence of the real conspirators.
   The next three theories explain how the second assassin escaped from the grassy knoll.

20. Bogus Secret-Service Man Theory

Proponent: Sylvia Meagher.
   Dallas policeman J. M. Smith ran to the parking lot behind the grassy knoll immediately after the assassination. He suddenly encountered a stranger and pulled his gun. The stranger identified himself as a Secret Service agent and showed Smith his credentials (although Smith later could not recall his name). Smith's account is corroborated to some degree by two other law officers—Deputy Constable Weitzman and Sergeant Harkness.
   Sylvia Meagher, an independent researcher, made a meticulous check of Secret Service records and found that no Secret Service agent was on or near the knoll area at the time that Smith encountered the "agent." Mrs. Meagher suggests that the assassin may have escaped by using fake Secret Service credentials.

21. Trunk Theory

Proponents: S. M. Holland, Richard H. Popkin.
   Soon after the shots were fired, S. M. Holland rushed to the picket fence behind the knoll (where he thought he saw smoke) and found a station wagon and a sedan parked near the fence (see Over the Fence Theory, No. 8). Muddy footprints led from bumper of station wagon to sedan and then mysteriously ended. Holland said: "I've often wondered if a man could have climbed into the trunk of that car and pulled the lid shut on himself, then someone else have driven it away later." Other theorists, like Professor Popkin, have thought it more likely that the knoll assassin simply hid the rifle in the car, then fled on foot.

22. Storm Drain Theory

Proponent: Lillian Castellano.
   Mrs. Castellano, a California accountant, located what appeared to be a storm drain in a photograph of the grassy knoll taken at the time of the assassination. However, it could not be located in later photographs of the grassy knoll. Through a contact in Dallas, Mrs. Castellano obtained a

chart of the sewer and drainage system surrounding the grassy knoll. Apparently, the drain was filled in after the assassination. Mrs. Castellano suspected that it could have been part of an escape system.

23. Oswald as F.B.I. Informer

According to Secret Service report 767, Alonzo Hudkins, a Houston reporter, told the Secret Service that he had heard from Chief Allan Sweatt of the Dallas sheriff's office that Lee Harvey Oswald "was being paid two hundred dollars per month by the F.B.I. in connection with their subversive investigation" and that "Oswald had informant number S-172." The Commission never called Hudkins or Sweatt to testify.

There are a number of other interesting circumstances surrounding Oswald's possible relationships with the F.B.I.

1. Warren De Brueys, an F.B.I. agent who covered both the New Orleans and Dallas beat, asked Carlos Bringuier to furnish the F.B.I. information about the activities of his Anti-Castro group. When Bringuier refused, De Brueys threatened to send an undercover agent to infiltrate the group. Later, Lee Harvey Oswald came to New Orleans from Dallas and tried to infiltrate Bringuier's group by pretending he was an Anti-Castroite. Bringuier, at first, did not think this was a coincidence.

2. When Oswald was arrested for fighting with Bringuier, he asked to see an F.B.I. agent. An F.B.I. agent visited him in jail and questioned him about the activities of the Fair Play for Cuba Committee.

3. Oswald's address book contained the address and license plate number of Dallas F.B.I. agent James Hosty. It was later deleted from the police list of Oswald's addresses.

Drawback: J. Edgar Hoover categorically denied that Oswald had any connection with the F.B.I. and offered the F.B.I.'s file on Oswald to the Commission. (The Chief Justice refused it, however, on the grounds that it might contain secret information.)

24. Oswald as Secret Agent

Proponents: Mrs. Marguerite Oswald and Norman Mailer.

Mrs. Oswald suggested long before the assassination, and is still of the belief, that her son was a C.I.A. agent. His trip to Russia was a C.I.A. mission, and so were his later activities. If Oswald was involved in the assassination, Mrs. Oswald suggests, "Now it could have been that my son and the Secret Service were all involved in a mercy killing," explaining, "If he [Kennedy] was dying of an incurable disease, this would be for the security of our country."

Norman Mailer, on the other hand, believes that it is quite possible Oswald was an undercover agent for not one, but a number of espionage services (who "tend to collect the same particular small agents in common").

Mailer wrote in *Book Week*: "It was all a comedy of the most horrible sort, but when Kennedy was assassinated, the espionage services of half the world may have discovered in the next hour that one little fellow in Dallas was . . . a secret, useless little undercover agent who was on their private lists; what nightmares must have ensued." Oswald was then liquidated by one of his employer-agencies. According to Mailer's scenario, we hear an Ivy League voice cry out in some unknown council-of-war room: "Well, can't something be done, can't we do something about this man?", and a man getting up, saying, "See you in a while," and a little later a phone call made and another, and finally a voice saying to our friend Ruby, "Jack, I got good news. There's a little job. . . ."

25. Two Oswalds Theory

Proponent: Richard H. Popkin.
Thesis: Professor Popkin (Chairman, Philosophy Department, University of California at San Diego) has advanced a rather ingenious theory to explain certain discrepancies in the Commission's findings. Certain witnesses claim to have encountered Oswald prior to November 22 in places where he could not possibly have been. To explain these anomalies, Popkin suggests that there were actually "two Oswalds"; the second "Oswald" closely resembled the real Oswald. The real Oswald's role was to be a decoy—that is, he would lead the police astray by becoming the prime suspect. The escape of the second Oswald, who actually fired the shots from the Depository, was thus facilitated. When Oswald's trial came up, he would undoubtedly produce a surprise alibi, and the evidence would be so confused by the second Oswald's pre-assassination maneuvers that the Oswald-on-trial would be acquitted. What went wrong, however—and here the theory becomes a mite complicated—was that the real Oswald met Officer Tippit, who knew the second Oswald, and waved him down. In the ensuing confusion, Oswald panicked and shot Tippit.

This theory differs from the Oswald Impersonator Theory in one important way: here, the real Oswald is guilty.
Drawback: The sightings of this "second Oswald" all occurred before it was even known that Kennedy would be coming to Dallas. Thus it seems unlikely that a carefully deceptive plot could have been underway.
Retort: Oswald and his double were only one of many pairs of assassins being set up all over the country on a contingency basis, should the opportunity for action arise.

26. Post-Assassination Domino Theory

Proponents: Penn Jones Jr. and Mark Lane.
Penn Jones, the editor of the Midlothian, Texas, *Mirror,* notes that a number of key witnesses have died under "clouded circumstances" since

the assassination and he suggests the theory that people who know too much about the assassination are being silenced.

For example, Jones cites a meeting at Ruby's apartment at which two newspaper reporters, Bill Hunter and Jim Koethe, were present. Bill Hunter was later killed by the "accidental discharge" of a policeman's revolver in a police station in Long Beach, California. Jim Koethe was killed by a "karate chop" in his Dallas apartment. The murder is still unsolved. Ruby's lawyer, Tom Howard, also attended the meeting. He later died of a "heart attack" (Jones notes "no autopsy was performed"). Jones suggests that some important information was divulged at the meeting, and those who heard the information had to be disposed of.

Moreover, Jones's paper has maintained a death-count on other relevant individuals.

1. Hank Killam, whose wife was a waitress at Ruby's nightclub and whose friend lived in Oswald's rooming house, was found on a Florida street with his throat cut.

2. Dorothy Kilgallen, the only journalist who was granted a private interview with Ruby, died. Jones points out (erroneously) that her death occurred on the night of the "strange" Northeast Power Blackout. (Jones missed the connection that the announcer of What's My Line—the television panel show on which Miss Kilgallen was a regular—John Daly, was Chief Justice Warren's son-in-law.)

3. William Whaley, the cabdriver who took Oswald home after the assassination and possibly talked to him, died in a car crash—the first cabdriver to be killed on duty in Dallas since 1937.

4. Karen Bennett Carlin, another performer at Ruby's club and the last person to talk to Ruby before he shot Oswald, died of gunshot wounds in Houston, according to Penn Jones. This seems quite strange since she testified to a Commission lawyer *after* the reported date of her death.

5. Earlene Roberts, the housekeeper at Oswald's rooming house who claimed she saw a police car stop in front of the house about ten minutes before Oswald encountered Tippit, also died.

Mark Lane adds the case of Warren Reynolds, a witness to the Tippit shooting, who was shot through the head (but survived); Nancy Mooney, a former stripper in Ruby's nightclub who also provided an alibi for the man accused of shooting Reynolds, hanged herself in the Dallas jail; and Lee E. Bowers, Jr., a bystander who saw a car making a getaway from the grassy knoll, was killed in a car accident to which there were no witnesses.

27. Racist Theory

Proponents: Léo Sauvage, Hans Habe (author of *The Wounded Land*).

Sauvage, an American correspondent for *Figaro,* suggests the theory that Kennedy could have been killed by a conspiracy of Southern racists to prevent him from carrying out his civil-rights program. To turn blame away from themselves and onto Leftists, they methodically framed Oswald (by impersonating him and by planting evidence against him). Oswald's murder, however, was not part of the racist conspiracy, but a separate plot instigated by the Dallas police to prevent a trial in which he might be acquitted of the crime.

28. Cui Bono Theory

Proponents: Izvestia, Trud, Joachim Joesten, Barbara Garson, Don B. Reynolds, Jack Ruby and others.

Thesis: Although not one shred of hard evidence has been uncovered to prove them right, many people have taken the "Who benefited?" line of pursuit and point an accusing finger at Lyndon Johnson.

The Soviet Government newspaper *Izvestia,* after condemning The Warren Report as slanderous to Russia, hinted by sly innuendo that President Johnson may have been implicated in the assassination. They cited the works of Joachim Joesten which argue that Johnson has been covering up. The next day, *Trud,* the trade-union paper, made the accusation more forcefully.

Californian Barbara Garson has written a satire, based on *Macbeth,* called *Macbird* in which L.B.J. and Lady Bird take the parts of Macbeth and Lady Macbeth in the murder of J.F.K. and Adlai Stevenson (the Egg of Head).

In January of 1964 the Warren Commission learned that Don B. Reynolds, insurance agent and close associate of Bobby Baker, had been heard to say that the F.B.I. knew that Johnson was behind the assassination. When interviewed by the F.B.I., he denied this. But he did recount an incident during the swearing in of Kennedy in which Bobby Baker said words to the effect that the s.o.b. would never live out his term and that he would die a violent death. Reynolds also vaguely suggested that Governor Connally may have called long distance from Washington to Lee Oswald who was staying in a Dallas Y.M.C.A. He had no proof.

A number of letters allegedly written by Jack Ruby and smuggled out of jail were auctioned off by New York autograph dealer Charles Hamilton. Penn Jones, Jr. bought one and published part of it.

"I walked into a trap the moment I walked down the ramp Sunday morning. This was the spot where they could frame the Jew, and that way all of his people will be blamed as being Communists, this is what they were waiting for. They alone had planned the killing, by they I mean Johnson and others.

". . . read the book *Texas Looks at Lyndon* and you may learn quite a bit about Johnson and how he fooled everyone."

Drawback: In a letter to J. Lee Rankin, J. Edgar Hoover wrote, "I have not received any information to implicate President Johnson or Governor Connally in the assassination."

29. Dallas Oligarchy Theory

Proponent: Thomas Buchanan.

According to Buchanan's theory, "Mr. X," a right-wing Texas oil millionaire, had to eliminate Kennedy and Khrushchev to gain world domination of the oil market. He decided to assassinate Kennedy in such a way that Khrushchev would be discredited. Oswald was to be framed as the assassin, then executed by Tippit. With Oswald dead, the Soviet Union would be blamed for the assassination. Oswald, however, outdrew Tippit and was captured alive later. The conspirators then induced Ruby to kill Oswald as a means of silencing him for good. Aside from Mr. X, Buchanan names the following "additional conspirators":

1. The assassin on the bridge. (He hints this was Ruby.)

2. A second assassin in the Depository who was wearing a police uniform.

3. A police officer involved in Oswald's arrest (who was, next to Mr. X, the key conspirator).

4. Tippit.

5. Oswald.

6. One of the policemen who missed Oswald as he left the building.

30. Cuba-Framed Theory

Proponent: Fidel Castro.

About a week after the assassination, Castro suggested that the conspirators intended that Cuba be blamed for the assassination. According to this theory, Oswald may have been one of the riflemen, but his prime role in the conspiracy was to ghost a trail that would lead directly to Cuba. Thus, a few months before the assassination, Oswald set up a phony Fair Play for Cuba Committee in New Orleans and Dallas, engaged in "brawls" with anti-Castro Cubans, and identified himself with Castro and Cuba on radio programs. Then he went to Mexico where he tried to obtain a Cuban visa. (Castro notes that Oswald had no reason to go to Cuba. If Oswald wanted to go to Russia, as he claimed, it was shorter and easier to go via Europe.)

After the assassination, the plan called for Oswald to disappear. Evidence planted at the scene would identify Oswald as the assassin, and Oswald's pre-assassination activities and other planted clues would lead to the conclusion that Oswald had fled to Cuba. This, in turn, might serve as a pretext for an American invasion of Cuba.

There is some later evidence which fits in very neatly with the Castro thesis.

1. On September 26, just before Oswald's trip to the Cuban Embassy in Mexico, Mrs. Sylvia Odio, a Cuban Refugee leader, claims that three men visited her in Dallas. Two were Latins, possibly Cubans, the third

was American. The American was called "Leon Oswald." After the assassination Mrs. Odio as well as her sister definitely identified this man as Lee Harvey Oswald. The three men said that they had just come from New Orleans (the Commission established Oswald left New Orleans about September 25) and were about to take a trip. They wanted backing for some violent anti-Castro activities, but Mrs. Odio suspected that they might in fact be Castro agents. The next day one of the Latins called Mrs. Odio and told her that Oswald was "kind of nuts" and that he had said Kennedy should have been assassinated after the Bay of Pigs, and that "it is so easy to do it." Thus, Oswald established himself as a potential assassin traveling with two Cubans.

2. Two days before the assassination, three people spoke to Wayne January, manager of Red Bird airport in Dallas, about renting a plane. They told him they wanted to be flown to Yucatán Peninsula on November 22. After the assassination, January told the F.B.I. that he was convinced that one of the three persons was Oswald. January later said that he suspected the threesome might want to hijack his plane and go to Cuba, and thus decided not to rent them the plane.

3. Shortly after the assassination, there were literally dozens of allegations and "tips" that Oswald was closely connected with the Cubans. For example, one Latin American free-lance intelligence agent claimed that he saw Oswald receive $6,500 for the purpose of assassinating Kennedy. (The Commission found these allegations to be false.) However, if Oswald escaped and disappeared, these tips might very well have fed suspicion that Oswald was in Cuba.

31. Crystal Ball Theory

Proponent: Jeane Dixon.

In December, 1963, prophetess Jeane Dixon "got psychically" an inside line on the assassination. "As I interpret my symbols," she wrote, "Fidel Castro believed that President Kennedy and Premier Khrushchev had gotten together on a plan to eliminate him and replace him with someone more acceptable to the United States and the U.N. Castro, in his conniving way, therefore arranged for the assassination of John F. Kennedy. Lee Harvey Oswald was the triggerman, but there were other people involved in the plot."

32. Mafia Theory

Proponent: Serge Groussard.

In a series of articles in *L'Aurore,* Groussard offers the theory that Kennedy was assassinated in order to forestall a planned crackdown on organized crime. The "Al Capone gang" in Chicago ordered Ruby to set up the assassination. Ruby then sent Oswald (who was in his debt) to Mexico to visit the underworld's own plastic surgery clinic and other escape facilities; and Oswald agreed to be the rifleman. Tippit was supposed to drive Oswald out of Dallas, but when he learned that Oswald was the assassin he tried to arrest him and Oswald killed him. Ruby then had to finish the job personally.

33. Junta Theory

Proponent: M. S. Arnoni.

The editor of *The Minority of One* envisions a "titanic power struggle" in the U.S. Government. He postulates that the insurrectionist forces included the C.I.A., the Air Force, relevant defense contractors, and a number of congressmen and that the Junta's leaders were high-ranking Air Force and Navy officers. The object was to deliver the U.S. into the hands of a "military-industrial cabal."

Because President Kennedy attempted to oppose this Junta, he had to be eliminated. His fate was sealed when he signed the Nuclear Test Ban Treaty in 1963—which he, according to this theory, "signed in his own blood."

34. Red Execution Theory

Proponent: Revilo P. Oliver.

Professor Oliver, in an article for the John Birch Society magazine, advanced the theory that Moscow ordered Oswald to assassinate Kennedy. It seems that Kennedy was threatening to desert the Communists and "turn American." But the President's aides persuaded him to go to Dallas where he was "executed."

Although the assassin's accomplices escaped, Oswald himself was apprehended by dint of the heroic action of J. D. Tippit, and so it became necessary that "Jakob Rubenstein" eliminate Oswald.

35. Evil-Forces Theory

Proponent: Ousman Ba, Foreign Minister of Mali.

Ba charged in the United Nations Security Council that "Kennedy's assassination, the murder of Patrice Lumumba and Dag Hammarskjöld's death were all the work of forces that were behind the recent U.S.-Belgian rescue operation in the Congo." Ba did not elaborate.

A Second Primer of Assassination Theories

In an article in the December, 1966, Esquire, the Warren Commission's crucial Single-Bullet Theory (hereafter, the S.B.T.) seemed to be in real trouble. This theory posits that President Kennedy and Governor Connally both were first hit by the same bullet—a crucial assumption because the Commission established that there was not enough time for the murder rifle to be fired twice within the interval that both men were first hit (1.8 seconds or less). In short, either the S.B.T stands, or a Two-Assassin Theory emerges.

Trouble first developed for the S.B.T. with the publication of previously classified F.B.I. reports in Edward Jay Epstein's Inquest, *which flatly contradicted the Commission's autopsy statement that the first bullet passed clean through President Kennedy and exited his throat. The F.B.I. reports instead stated that the autopsy showed that the bullet in question did not exit from the President's throat, a fact which would make it impossible for this bullet to continue on to hit Governor Connally and thus would rule out the S.B.T. Next,* Life *magazine enlarged its 8mm amateur film of the assassination frame by frame, and, on the basis of this new evidence, concluded that Connally and Kennedy may indeed have been hit by separate bullets. Governor Connally also viewed the* Life *film frame by frame and stated categorically that* he *was hit by a separate bullet. The most unkind cut of all came when Governor Connally called a press conference for the express purpose of defending the Commission, then inadvertently mentioned that he still had a fragment of the bullet in his thigh. Alas, that fact alone would invalidate the S.B.T. because the bullet that is supposed to have wounded both men was found virtually intact. Finally, Senator Richard Russell, member of the Commission who now claims the dubious distinction of having been the only member "who bucked the Report," stated that "from the outset" he never really believed in the S.B.T. Then Commissioner Hale Boggs followed suit during a* Face the Nation *interview by expressing his own doubts about the faltering S.B.T. But even as Commission members began deserting the sinking S.B.T., a number of last-ditch theories were proposed by the defenders of the Commission.*

36. The Second-Thought Autopsy Report

Proponents: Arlen Specter and other Commission lawyers.

Thesis: Arlen Specter, a key investigator for the Commission and principal author of the S.B.T., has attempted to explain the contradiction between the F.B.I. Summary Reports and the Commission's autopsy report in terms of two different autopsy conclusions. In the one and only autopsy examination conducted on the night of the assassination at Bethesda Hospital, the doctors arrived at the "tentative" conclusion that the bullet which struck President Kennedy in the back penetrated only a short distance, then fell out through the point of entrance when the Dallas doctors applied external heart massage. The next day, however, the autopsy doctors found out about the throat wound (which was obscured by the tracheotomy operation) and changed their conclusion, now deciding that the bullet went completely through the neck. This conclusion was reached without benefit of having the corpse before them (or the autopsy and X-ray photographs). Then, according to Specter's theory, Commander Humes incinerated his original autopsy report in his recreation-room fireplace, and drew up a new autopsy report stating that the bullet exited the President's throat. The F.B.I. was not shown the new report and reiterated the old conclusion in their summary reports.

Drawback: Specter's theory contradicts The Warren Report's description of the autopsy, which he himself wrote in 1964. In The Warren Report (pp. 88-89), Specter states that, during the autopsy, doctors rejected the possibility that the bullet penetrated only a short distance, and that the evidence from Dallas of a throat wound "confirmed" this conclusion. Thus, whereas The Warren Report states that there was one and only one conclusion of the autopsy reached during the examination, the autopsy conclusion was changed (not confirmed) the next day by evidence from Dallas, and thus there were two autopsy conclusions. The question remains: Which one of these conflicting statements is true?

37. The Hoover-Hegelian Theory

Proponent: J. Edgar Hoover.
Thesis: Although the F.B.I. Supplementary Report of January 13, 1964, states that the bullet that struck President Kennedy in the back penetrated "to a distance of less than a finger length," and the Commission's autopsy report states that this same bullet passed clean through the neck and exited the throat, J. Edgar Hoover finds that there is no "conflict" between the two statements of the autopsy, only a "difference in the information reported." Hoover further claims that the F.B.I. of course knew that the bullet passed clean through the President's neck at the same time that they reported the bullet penetrated only a finger's length into his back. Since they also knew that the Commission knew the true contents of the autopsy report, there was no reason, Hoover insists, to make a false statement of the autopsy results. Moreover he dialectically explains that although the F.B.I. report flatly stated that the bullet did not pass through the President's body, the F.B.I. itself helpfully pointed to weaknesses in its own theory by stating that there was a hole in the President's shirt caused by an exiting projectile.

Drawback: Thesis plus antithesis doesn't equal J. Edgar Hoover's synthesis. Aside from the fact that the F.B.I. Supplementary Reports were prepared initially for public release and not for the Warren Commission, a major problem in Hoover's explanation is that the F.B.I. told The Washington *Post* on December 18, 1963, that the hole in the shirt was caused by a fragment from the *third* shot which exploded against the President's head (not from the *first* shot). Therefore, the F.B.I. report of the shirt hole does not *"clearly"* indicate that the autopsy doctors' early observation "that the bullet penetrated only a short distance into the President's back probably was in error," as Hoover postulates.

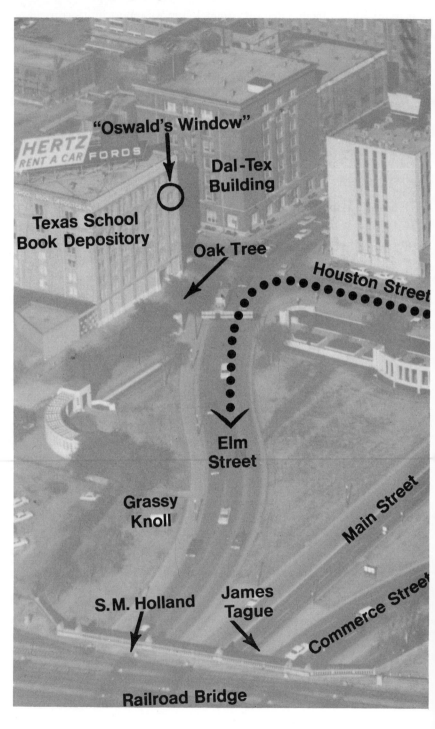

S.M. Holland (shown on the overpass where he stood November 22, 1963) saw smoke under the tree directly above his right thumb. **Copyright Alskog, 1967.**

38. View from the Bridge Theory

Proponent: Lawrence Schiller, a photographer, and the producer of Capitol Records album, *The Controversy,* on the assassination.

Thesis: A number of critics assume that shots came from the knoll because a number of witnesses state they saw smoke coming from the knoll area. The most celebrated puff-of-smoke witness is S. M. Holland. Schiller brought Holland back to the exact spot where he said he was standing, placed a camera level with his shoulder, aimed it at the spot where Holland said he saw the puff of smoke, and snapped a photograph. The photograph shows that directly behind and slightly higher than the spot where Holland claims the smoke came from is the sixth-floor window of the Texas School Book Depository. Thus, Schiller suggests, "Maybe both Holland and the Warren Commission are right: the shots came from the Book Depository but from Holland's perspective the smoke and the report of a gun appeared to come from the knoll."

Drawback: Holland, whose depth perception is normal, was just possibly able to distinguish the knoll, 180 feet away, from the Book Depository, which was 120 feet beyond that. Also, Schiller's analysis is destroyed completely in view of the fact that witnesses at other points also thought the shots came from the knoll: the policeman who ran up it, Abraham Zapruder, and others.

39. The Noble Lie Theory

Proponents: Drew Pearson, Henri Nannen (editor of *Der Stern*), and Jacob Cohen (former instructor at Brandeis summer school and author of *Honest Verdict*).

Thesis: Drew Pearson quotes *Der Stern*'s explanation that the original autopsy report was suppressed "on the grounds that President Kennedy was suffering from Addison's disease" and "his family did not want it known." Why? Because "politically Kennedy's illness could become dangerous. Addison's illness—it sounds sinister." Thus, according to this theory, the Kennedys withheld the autopsy report and "hid the X-rays, even from the Warren Commission." And "this would also explain the lack of a date on the Warren Commission autopsy report" which was changed "so that it contained no mention of the President's illness," as well as why the autopsy surgeon burned the original autopsy report ("otherwise hundreds of people would have been faced with lying under oath, which would have been deplorable").

Drawback: The fact that Kennedy had Addison's disease was in The Warren Report (as well as in Sorensen's biography of Kennedy), so why delete it from the autopsy report? And the Commission files show that Attorney General Robert Kennedy explicitly gave his approval to the Commission to look at the autopsy photographs and X-rays.

40. Manchester Theory

Proponent: William Manchester.

Thesis: In his sometime authorized account, author Manchester recognizes that there was hardly enough time for Oswald to have fired three shots. He therefore proposes that only two shots were fired: the first hitting Kennedy in the back and then going on to cause all of Connally's wounds, the second inflicting Kennedy's fatal head wound. According to this theory, Oswald left an extra cartridge case at the scene [from the Walker shooting?] and the some hundred witnesses who thought they heard three or more shots actually heard only two and echoes.

Drawback: More than a hundred witnesses heard more than two shots, and a number of witnesses claim that they *saw* a bullet miss and hit the pavement. Finally, one man, James Tague, was wounded by a fragment from a bullet. As he was standing 260 feet from the President's car at the time of the head shot, it does not seem likely that he was wounded by a fragment from that bullet.

Gaining wobbly support from the preceding sources, the S.B.T. runs into stiff competition from most of the following theories.

41. Connally's Small-Detail Theory

Proponent: John B. Connally, Governor of Texas.

Thesis: Immediately after he single-handedly demolished the S.B.T. in

Life, creating a nationwide outcry to reopen investigation, Connally called a press conference in Texas. He said that although he was not hit by the same bullet which hit Kennedy, it was only a small "detail," and he advised everyone to have faith in the Warren Commission because they were all patriotic men.

Drawback: None.

42. Russell Long Theory

Proponent: Senator Russell Long.
Thesis: The whole controversy over the S.B.T. was made to appear a bit irrelevant when Senator Long told the A.P. that he didn't doubt Oswald played a part in the assassination. "But," he added, "whoever fired that second shot was a better shot than Oswald."

43. Shot-Through-the-Tree Theory

Proponent: Alexander M. Bickel.
Thesis: Professor Bickel, writing in *Commentary,* finds that although the S.B.T. is untenable, the single-assassin theory can be rescued by constructing an alternate hypothesis to explain the first two shots. The Commission concluded that the first shot could not have come before the 210th frame (photo A) on the Zapruder film because before that point an oak tree blocked the assassin's line of sight. Bickel has found, however, that on

[A] [B]

frames 185-186 on the Zapruder film there was a "break" or window in the foliage of the tree (photo B). Bickel thus suggests that Oswald might have fired through the foliage at this point, which would have left sufficient time to operate the bolt and fire again at frame 232 to wound Connally, then fire the fatal head shot at film frame 313. According to this theory, the first bullet lodged in the President's back and was later expelled on his stretcher at Parkland Hospital in Dallas, accounting for its pristine condition. The second bullet wounded Connally and fragmentized, accounting for the two fragments found in the front seat of the Presidential limousine, and the final shot disintegrated when it struck the President's head, sending a minute fragment out through the throat and accounting for the throat wound.

Drawback: Although Professor Bickel's theory is certainly a possible alternative to The Warren Report, it still leaves a few unsolved problems. First, the opening in the tree gave the assassin a view of the car for no more than a tenth of a second. It seems improbable that a rifleman could aim, squeeze the trigger, and fire off an accurate shot in this brief interval. Second, this theory means that the President was hit in frame 186 but did not react until frame 225—a two-second delayed reaction. Finally, the theory fails to account for the shot that went astray and hit a bystander (although conceivably Oswald had time to fire a fourth shot, but then why were only three cartridge cases found?).

44. The Steroid Theory

Proponent: Ellen Leopold, Cambridge, Massachusetts.

Thesis: President Kennedy may indeed have had a two-second delayed reaction to the first shot "if he was on steroids." Not infrequently, Miss Leopold points out, sufferers of Addison's disease are put on steroids because they tend to suppress reactions of the adrenal glands. This theory lends unexpected support to Professor Bickel's Shot-Through-The-Tree Theory and also to the Early-Hit Theory (which posits a shot before the tree, as reported earlier).

Drawback: The Warren Commission, possibly for reasons pointed out by Drew Pearson, never determined whether or not Kennedy was on steroids. Until this question is settled, the Steroid Theory will be academic.

45. Riddle-Newton Theory

Proponent: R.A.J. Riddle, member of the Brain Research Institute and former professor of physics at U.C.L.A.

Thesis: Dr. Riddle finds a discrepancy between The Warren Report and Newton's second law of motion—i.e. that an object struck by a projectile will be given the same direction as that of the projectile. Because the film of the assassination shows that the general direction of motion of Kennedy is backward and to the left and because there is no evidence of a sudden acceleration of the car and on the assumption that a neuromuscular reaction can be ruled out as the cause for President Kennedy's sudden violent backward motion, Dr. Riddle believes that the projectile must have come from in front of the President. His computations add weight to Vincent Salandria's Head Movement Theory (see No. 8).

Drawback: Are Newton's laws sound if they contradict the Warren Commission?

46. Double Head-Shot Theory

Proponents: Professor Josiah Thompson Jr. and Ray Marcus, independently.
Thesis: The "third" shot, which caused Kennedy's fatal head wound, was actually two nearly simultaneous shots, one coming from the rear and another from the right front.

This theory takes Vincent Salandria's Head Movement Theory and Riddle's computations one step further. Thompson uses precise scientific studies made of the Zapruder film frames and close analysis of the medical evidence to show that the damage was inflicted by two bullets, not one. Also, he cites ear- and eyewitness reports which back up his claim that the third shot was really a third and a fourth.

47. Mark Lane's French Five-Shot Theory

Proponent: Mark Lane.
Thesis: In the French edition of his *Rush to Judgment,* Lane first proposed a theory which was later appended to his paperback edition of *Rush to Judgment.* In his original French version bullet *"une"* strikes President Kennedy from the back. Bullet *"deux"* strikes Kennedy in the throat. Bullet *"trois"* hits Governor Connally. Bullet *"quatre"* misses and wounds the bystander James Tague. And bullet *"cinq"* fired from the grassy knoll hits Kennedy in the head. Since one shot came from behind the President (bullet No. 1), one shot came from in front of the President (bullet No. 2)—he was facing straight ahead when hit in the throat—and one shot (bullet No. 5) came from the right (the knoll), there must have been at least *"trois"* assassins firing from different directions.
Drawbacks: If a bullet hit President Kennedy from in front, as Lane suggests, where did it go? There are no exit wounds that could account for a bullet entering through the throat. Then too, if the bullet entered the head from the rear, as the autopsy shows, it could not have entered from the right front, as Lane claims.

48. Dal-Tex Theory

Proponent: Harold Weisberg (*Whitewash* series).
Thesis: Some of the shots may have come from the Dal-Tex Building across the street from the Texas School Book Depository. In *Whitewash II,* a sequel to his first book, Weisberg enlarges an A.P. photo of the motorcade (A and B) and claims to see "a man in seeming distress" on a fire escape (arrow) on the side of the Dal-Tex Building and "an arm-like object projecting from the open second-floor window" (circle).

This theory receives some corroboration from a photograph that appeared in *The Saturday Evening Post* on December 14, 1963 (C). It purportedly showed the assassin's line of sight through the cross hairs of a telescopic lens. What the *Post* did not notice is that the corner of the Texas School Book Depository is visible in the right edge of the photo. Their photographer was shooting from the Dal-Tex Building, not having been able to gain entrance into the Depository. And strangely enough, according to Weisberg, the established bullet trajectories still bear out.

A tantalizing note adds intrigue to the theory: a man was arrested in the Dal-Tex Building shortly after the assassination, allegedly for having no business being there.

[A]

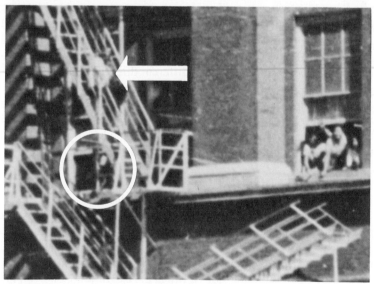

[B]

Enlargement of a window in the Dal-Tex Building allegedly showing a man on the fire escape (arrow) and a gun protruding from the window (circle).

[C]

The Saturday Evening Post's "line-of-sight" from the Dal-Tex Building.

49. The 24 Frames-per-Second Theory

Proponent: Harold Weisberg.
Thesis: The Commission's conclusion that all three shots were fired in 5.6 seconds is based on the assumption that Abraham Zapruder's camera was operating at a speed of 18.3 frames per second. The 103 frames that elapsed between frame 210 (the earliest point the Commission says the first shot could have been fired) and frame 313 (the point at which the third shot struck Kennedy's head), divided by the speed of the camera (18.3 frames per second), yields the 5.6-seconds time that the assassin had to fire in. Weisberg has found, however, an F.B.I. report in the National Archives in which Abe Zapruder claimed that his camera was set to operate at twenty-four frames per second, not 18.3. This would mean that the entire assassination occurred in less than 4.3 seconds (103 frames divided by 24), which is less time than the murder weapon could be fired twice.
Drawback: The F.B.I. established the film speed of the camera by filming the sweep second hand of a clock, and the camera's manufacturer recently confirmed that the camera speed was less than a tenth of a frame per second from the figure reported by the F.B.I.

50. Induced Cancer Theory

Proponents: Jack Ruby, Mark Lane, Penn Jones, Jr., Norman Mailer, and an unidentified Russian newspaper.
Thesis: That Jack Ruby's death was planned and brought about by members of a conspiracy whose prior business had been the murders of President Kennedy, Patrolman J. D. Tippit and, possibly, Lee Harvey Oswald.

According to an Associated Press story by Bernard Gavzer (datelined Dallas, January 3, 1967), Ruby had expressed the belief that mustard gas had been seeped into his cell and that he was injected with cancer.

The Dallas *Times Herald* states in an editorial that "the Communist Russian press" has accused the city of Dallas of being " 'Co-Conspirators' who . . . might have deliberately injected cancer cells into the veins of Ruby." This theory might in turn stem from such statements as the one uttered by Mark Lane after a screening of his movie, *Rush to Judgment*. Before a celebrity-packed audience he mused, "Isn't it strange that Ruby's sniffles went from a cold to pneumonia to cancer in twenty-four hours."

Ditto Penn Jones, whose assassination-connected death count is now at twenty (before Ruby: the motorcycle death of James Worrell, who allegedly saw somebody run out of the back door of the Texas School Book Depository). Jones, of course, finds Ruby's death "very suspicious."

In a rambling, emotional obituary entitled *A Requiem for the Rube,* Norman Mailer offers his own interpretation of Ruby's death and the significance thereof. "Jack Ruby added a point to the general median cancer potential for cancer by bugging the hope we could find one answer via Lee Harvey Oswald. In turn, us, Great American Pure Breed Public, in for feed, gave him his cans back. He died of cancer this morning, told us the way. We do not know the cure, but son, now we know the way. We know how to give cancer now. . . ."

51. Two-Men In-a-Window Theory

Proponent: Mrs. Eric Walther.
Thesis: A few weeks after the assassination, Mrs. Walther stated in an F.B.I. report that she saw a rifleman in one window of the Texas School Book Depository, and next to the man with the rifle was another man in a brown suit coat. Mrs. Walther was unable to see whether or not the second man had a rifle. A second rifleman of course would explain how Governor Connally and President Kennedy both were hit less than two seconds apart. The Commission never evaluated Mrs. Walther's statement.
Drawback: The window next to Oswald's was closed during the assassination.
Retort: The second man may only have been a lookout.

52. Doctored Photograph Theory

Proponents: Mark Lane, Harold Weisberg, David Lifton, et al.
Thesis: The photographs showing Oswald with the Kennedy and Tippit murder weapons are clever paste-ups of Oswald's head on another man's body.

When the Dallas police found the two photographs they were certain they had positive evidence linking Oswald with the weapons. *Life* magazine ran one of the pictures on its cover. *Newsweek* and The New York *Times* also printed the picture.

Confusion reigned shortly. Careful observers had noticed that all three publications had retouched the rifle and the pistol, but each did it in different ways. Their editors were forced to write humiliating letters to the Warren Commission admitting their alterations, but in essence none had falsified the photographs. Those accusations were to come later.

Mark Lane and Harold Weisberg noticed that the shadow under Oswald's nose seemed to be inconsistent with the other shadows in the picture. Both the F.B.I. and the Dallas police rushed to prove such a photograph *was* possible, but only succeeded in adding a touch of Dogberry humor. The Dallas police shot a picture of a plainclothesman on the scene, but on a cloudy day. The F.B.I. posed an agent on a roof in bright sunlight, but the photograph they sent to the Commission had the head cut off.

The "Doctored Photo."

Dallas Police   F.B.I.

53. False Knoll Theory

Proponent: David Lifton, a U.C.L.A. engineering graduate student and co-author of the three-assassins article in *Ramparts* which introduced Riddle's analysis. (See No. 45.)

Thesis: On the day of the assassination, three types of camouflage were employed by conspirators positioned beneath, on, and above the grassy knoll. Lifton reached this hypothesis after minute study of photographs of the area during and after the assassination. It answers the question why, despite the fact that eyewitness reports and the Head Movement Theory indicate shots came from the grassy knoll, nothing at all was found there immediately afterward.

Underground camouflage: Lifton suggests that prior to the assassination, the grassy knoll was excavated from beneath and a system of tunnels and bunkers was built into it. Peepholes covered by grass-mesh camouflage were placed on the sloping surface of the knoll. Lifton claims to detect such meshing in greatly-enlarged photos of the knoll. Subterranean nooks would explain the statement of witness Garland Slack: "I have heard this same sort of sound when a shot has come from within a cave. . . ." Lifton goes further to suggest that the puff of smoke seen by some people on the grassy knoll may have been the exhaust from a gas engine incorporated within the camouflage mechanization.

Surface camouflage: Lifton finds alterations ("bulges") in the wall and the hedgerow on the grassy knoll, netting in the bushes and faint images of heads. Borrowing support from Deputy Constable Weitzman who ran toward the wall and who said, "I scaled the wall and, apparently, my hands grabbed steam pipes. I burned them," Lifton points out that there are no steam pipes atop the wall. This might, he says, be an indication that things may have been altered for that day. Weitzman also says a witness told him that he saw somebody throw something through a bush.

Elevated camouflage: Because a comparison of certain photographs taken during the assassination with others taken afterward indicates that some tree structures had been altered on the knoll, and because he sees images up in the trees in assassination photos, Lifton believes there was some camouflage in the trees. Eyewitnesses S. M. Holland, Austin Miller and Frank Reilly all state that shots seemed to have come out of the trees.

Drawback: As even Lifton admits, the photoenlargements are of extremely grainy quality (they could not be reproduced properly here) and interpretations of them are questionable at best.

54. Blunderbuss Theory

Proponents: Mark Lane and Harold Weisberg.
Thesis: At least five witnesses saw a puff of smoke rise from the grassy knoll during the assassination. Commission lawyers didn't investigate because they believed no modern weapon would emit puffs of smoke conforming to the witnesses' descriptions. (Some of the witnesses, when queried, guessed the smoke came from a motorcycle or steam pipe.)

Since Commission lawyers were willing to accept the fact that Oswald used "an antiquated rifle and twenty-year-old ammunition," as Mark Lane frequently points out on TV, why preclude the possibility that the second assassin used even a more antiquated weapon?

55. Making of the President

Proponent: Vincent Salandria, a Philadelphia lawyer.
Thesis: Mr. Salandria finds a curious passage in Theodore H. White's *The Making of the President, 1964.* "On the flight [back to Washington aboard Air Force One] the party learned that there was no conspiracy; learned of the identity of Oswald and his arrest."

Salandria posits that this announcement was deliberately misleading and may have been the first sign of a conspiracy cover-up. This theory, obviously, would have to implicate strategically powerful individuals.

The argument is as follows: Johnson's party landed in Washington at 4:58 p.m. Dallas time. But at this point, Oswald had not been charged with the assassination. He had not yet been identified by any witnesses in the Tippit killing, much less the assassination. The rifle found in the

Depository had not yet been traced. The photographs of Oswald holding a rifle and wearing a revolver in his holster were not discovered until the next afternoon. No fingerprints were taken from him for comparison purposes until sometime after six p.m. The fiber on the rifle was not examined until Saturday morning. The brown-paper bag had not been linked to him. Marina Oswald had not yet been questioned. In short, none of the evidence itemized in the table of contents of The Warren Report under Chapter IV, "The Assassin," was known to the Dallas police at the time.

As to the statement that there was "no conspiracy," Salandria believes that the announcement was suspiciously premature. At 4:58 p.m. it was understood that the shots had come from the front, yet the suspect Oswald was positioned behind the President. District Attorney Henry M. Wade told the Warren Commission that discussions relating to a conspiracy charge were carried on by telephone between his office and Washington until late that night. As far as Wade could remember, these included calls from the White House, the F.B.I. and the State Department. The general drift of the calls seemed to be to discourage any conspiracy charge. Salandria finds this disturbing.

During Commission hearings, Congressman Gerald Ford told Secretary of State Dean Rusk that a comment he made *the day after* the assassination, indicating that no foreign power was involved, seemed a bit hasty. Said Ford, "You really didn't have much time to evaluate all of the evidence." Ford was concerned about who in the State Department might have made telephone calls to Texas urging that no charge of conspiracy be alleged.

Drawback: As yet the precise text of the announcement on the plane is not known, nor is its origin. Theodore White refuses to comment except to say that the plane was in constant touch with the White House, and messages were relayed through a Signal Corps center in the Midwest. But the announcement may have been based, innocently, on the lack of any indication that there was a conspiracy afoot.

56. The I-Murder Theory

Proponent: Malcolm Muggeridge.
Thesis: According to this theory, Oswald "kills Kennedy for Intelligence's own sake; the perfect I-murder." Presume that Oswald was at least a double agent, recruited first by Soviet Intelligence during his stay in Minsk, then turned around by the F.B.I., and "finally reduced to a condition of bemusedness and lost identity which led him, in a trance-like state, to murder the President, as van der Lubbe, in a similarly trance-like state, set fire to the Reichstag."

His shooting at Walker, Pro- and Anti-Cuban activities, etc. were all done as a cover, in the hope he would lead the F.B.I. to the Soviet contact. This bizarre game caused Oswald to lose touch with reality, and, not knowing who he was working for or why, he shot Kennedy. To avoid undue embarrassment, he had to be shot, and Jack Ruby was standing by.

57. The Sugar Theory

Proponent: J. I. Rodale, editor of *Prevention* and *Organic Gardening and Farming.*
Thesis: Oswald was seen minutes after the assassination with a Coke bottle in his hand. This fact leads health-crusader J. I. Rodale to suggest "Oswald was not responsible for this action: his brain was confused because he was a sugar drunkard. So what is called for now is a full-scale investigation of sugar consumption and crime."

THE CURB EXCHANGE

James Tague, who was standing on the curb along the south side of Main Street near the overpass, was struck sharply on the cheek at the time of the shooting. Police officers investigated immediately and said they found a "fresh chip in the curb" near where he was standing. A photograph was taken of the chip in the curb the next morning (top).

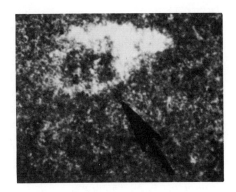

Eight months later (July, 1964) the photographer and two F.B.I. men returned to the site to make measurements, but could not find the chip. The F.B.I. men hypothesized that in the interim "there [had] been numerous rains that could have possibly washed away such a mark and also . . . the area is cleaned by a street-cleaning machine about once a week, which would also wash away such a mark." A month after *that,* J. Edgar Hoover wrote the Commission that the F.B.I. had cut out the section of curb with the mark (Bottom), and that indeed the mark was the same as that in the original photograph!

This internal F.B.I. contradiction was discovered by Raymond Marcus, who also claims that the curb cutout doesn't have any mark at all.

58. The Washing-Machine Theory

Proponent: George de Mohrenschildt.

Thesis: Marina Oswald, on the eve of the assassination, told her husband that they couldn't live together "unless he would equip the apartment with a washing machine." This demand caused a bitter argument which evoked in Oswald "the wish to strike and hurt someone."

Drawback: According to the Warren Commission, Oswald had the materials for making the paper bag for his rifle *before* he visited with his wife. Anyhow, as The Warren Report notes, they had lived near a laundromat.

59. Kennedy Lives Theory

Proponent: George Thomson, a Los Angeles swimming-pool engineer and writer.

Thesis: Thomson, in monographs and tapes which have been underground best sellers (reportedly 42,000 sold to date), advances the theory that Tippit was substituted for Kennedy in the Presidential limousine, and consequently it was Tippit not Kennedy who was shot. (Kennedy, years after, was the secret guest of honor at Truman Capote's celebrated party.) This explains the illegal removal of Kennedy's body from Dallas by his close cohorts, the missing X-ray and autopsy photographs, and subsequent confusion in reporting medical facts. The Kennedy controversy, for Thomson, revolves around the question of where Kennedy is today.

60. The "What Have We Here!" Theory

Proponent: T. N. Tastmona.

Thesis: In a privately-printed 200-page volume called *It Is As If:* ($20), Mr. Tastmona ("American born of American-born parents") scrutinizes the details of the assassination and the text of The Warren Report, finding bizarre parallels with the life of Benjamin Franklin, Sherlock Holmes, Mormon doctrine and American history. One sample, among many, is cited here as an extreme example of assassination theorizing:

In the Chronology index of *The Autobiography of Benjamin Franklin,* Tastmona finds mention of Arthur Lee, an American commissioner accompanying Franklin to France. Three pages later he finds a reference to Richard Oswald, Chief British negotiator. "The names 'Lee' and 'Oswald' sounded a responsive chord. *Lee Oswald!*—assassin of President Kennedy. Could some sort of historic parallel be coming to light? Could a *Harvey* be involved in these diplomatic deals?" Sure enough, on the next page of the Franklin autobiography Tastmona finds David Hartley, a British envoy. "Hartley!—a close approximation of 'Harvey'. . . .

" 'Hartley' differs from 'Harvey' by two letters. Perceive a composite form—Har TLV ey. What have we here! TLV equals a better abbreviation for 'television' than even plain TV. Lee Oswald was shot by Jack Ruby in full view of a national television audience. . . . It is as if this television crime had somehow been arranged to expound the disparity existing between the names Hartley and Harvey." Tastmona goes on to reveal that David Hartley was really David Hartley Junior, or Jr., and "it was Jack Ruby with initials J.R. who by this brutal system of criminal cryptology painstakingly identified the Hartley of scholarly historical allusion to be J. R. or Junior.

"While in Russia, Lee Oswald kept what he called a 'Historic Diary.' He affected interest in his place in history. This attitude must be considered as part of a pre-instructed clue system, hinting the historical parallels just adduced."

$$\begin{bmatrix} \text{December, 1966} \\ \text{May, 1967} \end{bmatrix}$$

The Dark Side of L. B. J.

by James Deakin

The place: The Texas ranch of Senate Majority Leader Lyndon B. Johnson.

The time: Several years ago.

A young man arrives at the ranch to run a routine political errand. While he is waiting in the living room, Johnson strides in, picks up the telephone and calls his press secretary, George Reedy, who is staying in the guesthouse down the road. He gives Reedy a monumental chewing out.

"He was using language that I had never heard one human being use to another," recalls the political worker, now an official of the University of Texas. "He called him every filthy name in the book and some that aren't. I don't think I'll ever forget it."

Finally, Johnson hangs up the phone. He turns to the young man and says, "Now, let's give George his Christmas present." He leads the way outside to an expensive new station wagon, drives it down to the guesthouse and toots merrily on the horn. When Reedy comes out, Johnson gives him the station wagon. To the astonished witness, the Senator observes: "You never want to give a man a present when he's feeling good. You want to do it when he's down."

In the chronicles of the American Presidency, it is not uncommon to find striking differences between public and private conduct. Beneath the outward rectitude are the usual weaknesses of spirit and failings of flesh: arrogance, pride and vanity (Woodrow Wilson, Franklin Roosevelt); sadism (Calvin Coolidge); liquor (U. S. Grant); neurotic evasion (James Buchanan); persecution complex (John Adams) and sexual insecurity (Warren Harding). At least one President, Harding, broke under this often-cruel duality. Others, like Grover Cleveland with his bastard child, surmounted the inherent hypocrisy of politics. Most Presidents have felt the need to conceal their personal imperfections, although only a few have made a fetish of it. The majority have been reasonably confident the people would forgive or forget and that history's verdict would be based on their official actions, not their private shortcomings.

In the case of the thirty-sixth Chief Executive, Lyndon Baines Johnson, the gap between the public pose and the private reality has proved to be as wide and awesome as any in the history of the republic. There may not be, literally, two Lyndon Johnsons. But he often appears to be the Yang and Yin, the light and dark force, of American politics.

Confronted with a double-identity problem, Johnson has reacted characteristically. He has not been content to live, more or less comfortably, with his shortcomings and trust the voters to do the same. He has sought to cast himself in heroic dimensions. He has appeared in a bewildering variety of shining roles—the wise savior of democracy, the parliamentary master, the cautious guardian of the nuclear trigger, the conqueror of poverty, disease and illiteracy at home and in the four corners of the earth, the Horatio Alger of his generation, the devoted son of a model mother, and most of all, the humble servant of a great people. He has identified himself with Lincoln, F.D.R. and a host of other eminent Americans. He is clean, brave, reverent, a veritable pantheon of Boy Scout virtues. He is the Paul Bunyan of Presidents and the glowing embodiment of the American Dream, played center stage under a spotlight that rarely dims, to applause that never stops, if he can help it.

His most familiar public pose is humility. His head bowed meekly, speaking in a smarmy mumble, he delivers a modest little sermon about the flag ("I have seen the sunrise on Mont Blanc, but the most beautiful vision these eyes ever beheld was the flag of my country in a foreign land") or the scourge of poverty ("As I looked into this African mother's eyes, I saw the same look . . . that I saw in my own mother's eyes when she was determined that her children would have food, clothes and an education") or the right of dissent from his Vietnam policy. This last homily takes an invariable form. Everybody has a right to disagree. It is part of our God-given freedom. Go ahead, criticize me. It's okay. I can bear it. (A brave little smile.) That's what your President is paid for. (And remember, I'm the only President you've got.)

But the dark side of Lyndon Johnson insistently intrudes upon the performance. Just as the courageous youth is saving the fair maiden, he is revealed as the one who foreclosed the mortgage in the first place. White House reporters groan inwardly when they see one of Johnson's humility bits coming, for they have glimpsed the hard man beneath the mush: Johnson slicing up a reporter for asking a "chicken-shit" question; Johnson impugning another newsman's patriotism for daring to inquire critically about the Dominican intervention, Johnson bludgeoning Senator Frank Church for his reservations about the Vietnam war ("Okay, Frank, next time you need a dam in Idaho, ask Walter Lippmann for one"); Johnson excoriating another Vietnam critic as "that (obscenity) Hartke"; Johnson neutralizing a diplomat's career with a stroke of his pen across a promotion list because the man once disagreed with him; Johnson cutting a team of magazine reporters ("Someone ought to do an article on *you* and your damn profession, your First Amendment"); Johnson warning the Republicans via the grapevine that if they press him too hard on Bobby Baker, some G.O.P. tax returns will be audited; Johnson in a bloody undercover war to the death with Bobby Kennedy, no holds barred, no quarter asked or given.

The disparity between Lyndon Johnson's public character and private nature is so profound that one can only be astonished at the task the man has set himself—to create a fictional human being for public consumption. He has, as Stewart Alsop has said, a "constant itch to try to be what he isn't." The measure of his failure is the endless gossip about the dark side of his nature—now a source of worldwide concern.

Beyond doubt, this Texan is one of the most complicated men ever to occupy the White House, perhaps the most complicated. His mind is fathomless; the subtlety of his mental processes rivals that of Lincoln. His grasp of the machinery of government is unparalleled; to hear him hold forth on fiscal policy is a breathtaking experience, considering how little most Presidents knew about this subject. His mastery of the intricate legislative arts is unexcelled. His ability at Congressional persuasion, although a little impaired these days, was once the eighth wonder of the world, and his political memory approaches the genius level.

But in the best Victorian tradition, Lyndon Johnson has a secret life. Within it lives a man subject to wide fluctuations from exhilaration to irritability to rage to withdrawal. White House reporters have grown accustomed to these dramatic changes in Johnson's mood. On the crest one day, ebullient, full of zest and verve, talking incessantly, dashing hither and yon, he may sink into a deep gloom twenty-four hours later. Then he retreats, goes perfunctorily through his schedule of public appearances, races through his speeches and hastens back to the privacy of his office. During one of his upswings, he often goes on a marathon talking jag that leaves reporters limp and their editors inundated with reams of copy. The White House "regulars"—reporters assigned full time to cover the President—have learned to steel themselves against what they describe as "the whirling-dervish effect." A typical example was March 12, 1966, a Saturday.

On that day, a group of state governors had come to the White House for what was scheduled as a routine discussion of federal-state relations. Johnson, however, turned the meeting into a full-scale, action-packed, razzle-dazzle briefing on the Vietnam situation. In the lead role, of course, was the President himself. As supporting players, he called in Vice-President Hubert Humphrey; Secretary of State Dean Rusk; Secretary of Defense Robert S. McNamara; General Earle G. Wheeler, Chairman of the Joint Chiefs of Staff; General Maxwell D. Taylor, special Presidential adviser on Vietnam; General Ellis Williamson, who had just returned from the war zone; Courtenay Valenti, the curly-haired daughter of then-Presidential aide Jack Valenti, and four dogs.

On the same day, Johnson met with the executive committee of the National Governors' Conference, held a press conference to report on the meeting, met with the governors of the Appalachian states, held another press conference to report on *that* meeting, presided at a three-hour briefing at which Rusk, McNamara and the generals reported to the governors on the Vietnam situation, held a third press conference to report on that meeting, announced the appointment of former Governor Farris Bryant of Florida as Director of the Office of Emergency Planning, and then played with Courtenay Valenti and his four dogs for a half hour while photographers snapped pictures. Two meetings, three press conferences, a three-hour briefing and a romp, and all in time for the Sunday papers. It had been a good, upbeat day for Lyndon Johnson.

But when he goes into one of his winters of despair—often produced by a critical news story or column—it is another matter. The President makes himself very scarce, as the record of his press conferences shows. With complete justification, Johnson asserts that he has held as many or more meetings with reporters as any of his predecessors, but the key indicator of his moods is the way the press conferences are grouped. He may hold three, four or five in the space of a few weeks and then go for many weeks without holding any at all. In the three weeks between February 27 and March 21 of this year, for instance, he held four news conferences. After that, six weeks elapsed before he met again with reporters, on May 3.

In the incestuous Washington community of politicians, bureaucrats, lawyers, diplomats and newspapermen, stories about Johnson's vanity sweep the circuit. When he became President, White House photographers soon learned that the right side of his face was off limits, since Johnson considers his left profile more photogenic. For a long time, photographers were herded over to the left side of the room when he held a press conference, but in recent months some infiltration to the right has been permitted. Similarly, there was a long period during which Johnson wore contact lenses when speaking from a text in public, rather than use his glasses. He is back to wearing them openly now, but during the time he was not, a hapless Signal Corps enlisted man ran afoul of the Johnson temper. A few minutes before a White House ceremony, the Signal Corpsman placed the lectern in the correct position for reading, then left the room. At this point, Jack Valenti wandered in, judged the lectern to be a little close and moved it back a few inches. Johnson had to strain to see the text but got through the ceremony. Then, in a towering rage, he summoned the Corpsman to his office and demanded of the bewildered soldier: "Son, are you trying to - - - - me?"

Although he has relaxed somewhat in these respects, the Johnson vanity is a well-established phenomenon. Shortly after becoming President, he assigned government photographer Yoichi Okamoto to the White House as his personal photographer. Okamoto is the President's shadow; quiet and unobtrusive, he goes wherever Johnson goes and is present at virtually every Presidential meeting, noiselessly clicking away. Several times a week, Johnson goes over the big batch of prints turned in by "Okie." Those he likes most, he keeps. Others he sends to those who appear in the pictures with him. If a reporter shows up in a picture, he is likely to get a note from the President's personal secretary, Juanita Roberts, saying: "The President was looking through some of his pictures today and thought you might like to have the enclosed." The pictures usually are large color shots, eminently suitable for a prominent place on the wall.

Johnson also has a predilection for plaques, but of a more enduring kind. If Texans want to put up monuments to him even though he is still alive, well why not? There is, for instance, his restored birthplace near Stonewell, his restored boyhood home in Johnson City, the soon-to-be-restored log cabin of his grandfather, Sam Ealy Johnson, Sr., a state park, a Lyndon B. Johnson lake, a projected Lyndon B. Johnson library at the University of Texas, and a plaque on the wall of the Pedernales Electric Cooperative proclaiming it to be "a product of the faith, ability and foresight of Lyndon Baines Johnson, President of the United States of America, while Congressman for the Tenth District, 1938."

The President's unwearying revisitations to his birthplace and his boyhood home have provided an endurance test for reporters and, once rested, interesting exercises in psychological speculation. Weekend after weekend, they speed down the narrow roads and lurch across the fields trying to keep up with the President as he pokes around in the faded memorabilia of his childhood, sifting out impressions of his past that begin to explain his complexity.

First, there is the picture of a small boy in an oversize cowboy hat, staring unwinkingly into an old-fashioned camera from a dusty front porch. Like the kids in Katherine Anne Porter's *Noon Wine*, digging in the ragweed, already squinting under the relentless sun, a little grubby, a little unwilling to go to school, restlessly energetic, suspicious of strangers. (In *Noon Wine*, when Olaf Helton came to work on Mr. Thompson's Texas farm, one of the Thompson boys called him "Big Swede" and ridiculed him; Lyndon Johnson was to say in later life that the trouble with foreigners was that "they're not like folks you were reared with.")

Then a restless red-neck youth, vaguely and inarticulately discontented, a drifter until he tires of working with his hands for pocket money and decides to go to college. Then a young Congressman from the sticks, clawing his way up in a town casually dominated by Eastern Brahmins (in *The Johnson Eclipse,* Leonard Baker notes that "the 'American Establishment' . . . excluded Lyndon Johnson for years"). Then a Senator and Senate Majority Leader, coming into his own as a professional among professionals in the one branch of government where Southern non-Establishment types have the best chance of rising to the top of the pecking order. Then a three-year eclipse as Vice-President, pouring out his frustrated vanity in transatlantic telephone calls to Walter Jenkins during trips to Europe. Johnson would ask Jenkins anxiously whether the New York and Washington papers played his trip "outside" (on page one) that day; when they did not, reporters recall, he would sink into despondency. Then a cosmic accident, and Lyndon Johnson is President. His ego blooms again like a giant tropical flower.

It is often said that alcohol is the fuel on which Washington runs. It is not. Ego and ambition, in equal parts, are the fuels. At the top, ambition drives a national government. It drives Johnson, who is hell-bent on being as great a President as Franklin Roosevelt. Despite Vietnam, despite the polls, despite Walter Lippmann and The New York *Times*, he wants to rank with F.D.R., and he is going at it as hard as he can, the only way he knows how. A veteran White House correspondent has commented that the thing to remember about Johnson is that, unlike some other men who reached the top, the mere fact of achieving the Presidency did not satisfy his ambition. It remains as an elemental and unfulfilled force even at the pinnacle. A great deal of what Johnson does can best be understood in the context of that ambition—and the insecurity of a man who is not sure he is going to make it, who has never been sure he was going to make it.

His sister, Mrs. Birge Alexander, recalls that as a boy he was the "bossy" one in the family. Not long after he was elected to the House, a group of elderly Senators journeying South to the funeral of one of their colleagues were astounded when a gangling young man bounced into the railroad car and began pumping their hands vigorously while proclaiming, "Ah'm Lyndon Johnson, glad to meet you," and "Proud to make your acquaintance." At the following Christmastime, according to Rowland

Evans and Robert Novak in *Lyndon B. Johnson: The Exercise of Power*, government officials who scarcely knew the young Congressman "were amazed when fat holiday turkeys arrived from Lyndon and Lady Bird Johnson."

When he reached the Senate via the famous 87-vote "landslide" of 1948, he began honing to perfection a set of classic techniques, some of them honorable, with which to further his ambitions. He worked hard, boasting that he could cram two days' work into one by taking an afternoon nap in between. (It was not an idle boast; he is still, today, an immensely hard worker, expecting all those around him to be the same.) He did favors, he logrolled, and he and Lady Bird entertained the power-houses of the Senate at small dinner parties at their house on Thirtieth Place. "These informal dinners," Evans and Novak point out, "gave Johnson a singular insight into the Senate's inner problems. Senators and their idiosyncrasies were analyzed there as they could never be on the floor and seldom in the cloakroom. At these parties, the men spoke frankly and unguardedly . . . and Johnson stored up in a few years a penetrating understanding of the world of the Senate." Later, as Majority Leader, Johnson built up a big batch of political I.O.U.'s by breaking with tradition to give several freshman Democratic Senators, including John F. Kennedy, a seat on a major committee.

On the darker side, Johnson poked into all the Senatorial closets he could find and rattled the bones of the skeletons. A liberal Senator has said that the Texan, as Majority Leader, ran "a little F.B.I." on Capitol Hill, using his big staff, wide acquaintanceship and his own sensitive antennae to accumulate a vast store of political secrets and gossip.

During the 1964 Presidential campaign, a four-man pool of reporters usually rode with Johnson on his Air Force jet (the pools have since been discontinued), and the President relaxed between campaign stops by recounting intimate stories about the great and near-great figures of contemporary American politics. To his small audience, he seemed to have a salacious anecdote about every prominent political personality of the last thirty years, rattling off descriptions of their sexual behavior and eccentricities until even the hard-bitten correspondents blanched. On one occasion, Johnson told of an incident involving a well-known American diplomat of the New Deal era whose tastes were unorthodox. While on a train trip, Johnson said, the diplomat encountered a porter in the washroom, and "he had that porter's britches down before he knew what hit him." He ridiculed the lofty moral tone taken by one of his political rivals, saying: "Why, when he was in Spain on that military trip, he laid every woman he could get his hands on." On one of his trips abroad as Vice-President, Johnson was asked by reporters how he had got along with an internationally famous statesman.

"I had my hand halfway up his leg before he knew what was happening," he replied.

In this phase of Johnson's secret life, he becomes that familiar figure, the American Yahoo—the big-talker whose specialty is the off-color joke. Robert Sherill, in *The Accidental President*, has written that "the President sometimes gets a little drunk at parties and . . . tells smutty stories until [Lady Bird's] face freezes and cracks." It is important, however, to keep this side of Johnson's personality in perspective. He does indeed know a great many dirty jokes—and so did Abraham Lincoln. He does use profanity in his private conversations—and so did Harry S. Truman and John F. Kennedy. The Presidents of the United States are men under pressure, and most of them, in these days at least, do not relax by reading the Bible. By itself, Johnson's blue language means nothing. It has little relevance to his official actions. Unlike his browbeating of subordinates, which makes it difficult for him to attract able men to government service, his smutty jokes have little effect on the course of government. What is significant, in his case, is that Johnson himself has succeeded in drawing attention to his private profanity by endeavoring to present himself publicly as a sort of Mary Poppins in the White House.

Johnson's jokes and similes are heavily animalistic and scatological. They emphasize bathroom functions. On one occasion, when he learned that a national magazine was preparing a story on his personal finances, he called in the editors and spent hours wheedling and cajoling them and uttering veiled warnings about higher postal rates, in an unsuccessful effort to squelch the article. The President insisted that the editors should come to him if they wanted accurate information. Then he gave a graphic men's-room example of the kind of personal information he would not expect them to print unless they had checked the statistics firsthand.

With the Easterners who froze him out for so many years, Johnson's scatology takes on strong overtones of the bravado that covers up insecurity. He seems to be saying to them: If I was too crude for you then, I'll be even cruder now. One of the most dignified of Kennedy's cabinet officers, a man of impeccable Establishment credentials, was rocked to the depths of his Ivy League soul when he was summoned into conference with the new President and found himself in the bathroom while Johnson bestrode the executive commode. An editor of a Midwestern newspaper attended one of the bathroom conferences when he was called to the Johnson ranch to discuss possible posts in the new Administration. Another Kennedy holdover asserts that he was summoned to the ranch early one morning and directed into the bathroom, where he sat on the side of the tub and received his instructions for the day while Johnson obtained relief. The Kennedy man says he mentioned the incident later to a woman who had been a member of Johnson's staff for years. "What's so unusual about that?" she replied. "He's been doing that with me for years."

Shortly after persuading a prominent Establishment educator to take a top Administration job, Johnson introduced him to the mule-skinner side of his new responsibilities. As the President posed for pictures with the new official, a photographer complimented Johnson on his civil-rights presentation to Congress. The Chief Executive let loose a flow of pleased profanity. The educator's face froze as Johnson declared that before he was through, every blankety-blank, so-and-so, unprintable mother's son in the United States would be able to go freely to the polling place and vote. Later, a reporter commented on the incident to the new official, who smiled weakly and said he had been in the Army, after all, and had heard some strong language in his time.

Some of Johnson's stories reveal the coarsening, almost brutalizing effect of his years in the slaughterhouse politics of the Lone Star State. One of his favorite jokes concerns a popular Texas sheriff who was running for reelection. The sheriff's opponents had been trying unsuccessfully to think of a good campaign issue to use against him. Finally, one man suggested that "we spread a rumor that he - - - -s pigs." Another protested that "you know he doesn't do that." "I know," said the first man, "but let's make the sonofabitch deny it."

It is interesting to note how closely Johnson's patterns of private conduct conform to an American stereotype: the adult drugstore cowboy. One of his biographers, Philip Geyelin, in *Lyndon B. Johnson and the World*, writes that Johnson "cannot remember having read six books all the way through since college." Veteran White House correspondents can recall only one book on international problems that he has ever mentioned reading—Barbara Ward's *The Rich Nations and the Poor Nations*. He is eternally restless, seldom able to sit through a movie, but instead turning constantly to talk to others in the audience. He is not a stamp collector, a piano player, a golfer or a sailor (although he occasionally tears around Lyndon B. Johnson Lake in a big motorboat). He cares nothing for art or the theatre, both of which he leaves to Lady Bird. When he is not working, there are only two things he really likes to do. He likes to get in his car at the ranch and cruise around, like a teen-ager on Saturday night, except that he is visually caressing his land rather than a teeny-bopper in a mini-skirt. And he likes to sit around the living room in the evening with some cronies, drinking Scotch (at his instruction, the White House insists he drinks bourbon, an American product) and rehashing the day's legislative triumph.

The first aspect of Johnson's secret life to gain currency was his tendency to bully, and this has severely handicapped his efforts to attract outstanding men to his Administration. Despite the valiant efforts of several generations of his staff (in the White House under Johnson, a generation is six months to a year) to portray him as the ideal boss, reports spread rapidly about his bullyragging, temper outbursts and cruel sarcasm. Finally, confronted with a matter of common knowledge, staff members took a new tack. Acknowledging that the chief occasionally dressed down a subordinate, they described it as a sort of initiation rite. Not until a new man had been dressed down by L.B.J., said his aides, could he consider himself admitted fully to the President's trust and confidence. A noble try, but it hardly accounted for the fact that the hazing never stopped.

At least it can be said of Johnson's bullying that he is a virtuoso, not a one-note man. Chewing out the immediate members of his staff, he uses a frontal assault. To an aide who had kept the Vice-President cooling his heels outside the oval office for a few minutes, Johnson raged, "If you ever keep Hubert waiting again, I'll kick your ass down that hall." When he saw reporters in casual conversation with this same assistant at an airport, Johnson hurried over and informed the newsmen bluntly that they were wasting their time, that *he*—jerking his thumb at the staffer—was just a flunky who didn't know anything and that if they wanted information they should come to the President.

With high-ranking Administration officials not on the immediate White House staff, Johnson switches from threats to sarcasm. One of his key advisers, an immensely hardworking man who customarily puts in a twelve-hour day, waited in his office one evening until eight or nine o'clock in case the President wanted him. When no call came, the official departed to join his wife at a theatre. Shortly after he left, Johnson called. Bright and early the next morning, the official's home telephone rang. The voice on the other end was venomous. "Hello, playboy," said Johnson. One aspect of Johnson's temper is that it is not always genuine; evidence attests that he can turn his wrath on and off for its effect on some hapless aide. Stewart Alsop has told of one visitor who found the President in a pleasant mood. He "chatted amiably for a few minutes, then glanced at a paper on his desk, excused himself, picked up a telephone and gave some nameless subordinate . . . a brutal dressing down, then pleasantly resumed the interrupted conversation."

During one stay at the ranch, Johnson let it be known that next to Lady Bird, the person most important to him was George Reedy. Recalling the station-wagon episode, reporters received this information dubiously. A kind and scholarly man whose travail seemed akin, both in intensity and duration, to that of the Israelites in Egypt, Reedy set some sort of record for service with Johnson. But at length even he moved on, like so many others who endured the *Sturm und Drang* for shorter periods. The staff turnover under Johnson has been phenomenal, the resignations continual—Horace Busby, McGeorge Bundy, Jack Valenti, Reedy, Henry Hall Wilson, Jr., Lee White, Bill Moyers, Hayes Redmond. And this list does not include several Kennedy holdovers who left early in the game. The high rate of turnover in the White House staff under Johnson has created a chronic shortage of top-level Presidential assistants, the men who, next to the President himself, probably have the most to say about the daily operation of the government. By law, the chief executive can have fourteen special assistants paid up to $30,000 a year. Johnson now has ten.

Those who have worked for Lyndon Johnson once are usually reluctant to return to the indignities and the sarcasm. For the past several months, the President has been trying without success to lure a onetime associate, now a top business executive, back into government as a member of his cabinet. And others shy away from government service after hearing the stories—Johnson routing a cabinet officer out of bed after midnight to come over to the White House and listen to him talk about inconsequentials, Johnson transparently staging a meeting of the entire cabinet for the benefit of reporters, then walking out and leaving a staff subordinate to preside while captive heads of great departments recite like schoolboys.

As a result, important government posts—the Attorney General, the Secretary of Commerce, the Urban Affairs Secretary, the chairmanship of key regulatory agencies—have gone vacant for long periods of time. To fill them, Johnson often has had to appoint career men from within the government, some able, some cautious bureaucratic time servers. Lacking rejuvenation and the cross-pollination of ideas from the outside, his Administration has been notable for its shortage of imagination, especially in foreign affairs. It is not too much to say that the intellectual mediocrity of the Johnson Administration has stemmed in large measure from the sad spectacle of a man who doesn't know how to handle subordinates wisely. "They're all afraid of him," a former aide has said. "You can't get good work and good advice from men when they are afraid of you."

With reporters, Johnson operates as he does with his staff. He probes for their weaknesses, and if he finds a feeble defense he bores in. If he encounters resistance, however, he is likely to back off. A press conference exchange illustrated both facets:

Reporter: Mr. President, in connection with the appointment to the Housing and Urban Affairs Department, there have been reports of a task force headed by Dr. Wood, which recommended—

Johnson: *What* reports? I want to know who reports what.

Reporter: There have been published reports in the newspapers.

Johnson: Whose?

Reporter: There have been published reports in newspapers.

Johnson: Well, who published it? That's what I want to know.

Reporter: I saw something in The Washington *Post*, for one.

Johnson: Go ahead. The Washington *Post*. What did The Washington *Post* say?

Reporter: That a task force headed by Professor Wood had recommended the transfer of the community-action program and the Office of Economic Opportunity to the new [Urban Affairs] department, and there have been subsequent reports that you have decided against this. Can you make any comment on that?

Johnson: I would say that, insofar as a report that I have made a decision on the matter, it is more propaganda than accurate. I have made no decision. We will, in the days ahead, consider a good many reorganization proposals, but the best authority for a Presidential decision is the President or the press secretary, and you can always get guidance on that if you have the time or disposition to obtain it.

So far, so good. It had been a nice, routine job of bullyragging, with the President interrupting the newsman before he could finish his question, and then browbeating him for good measure. But at this point something unusual occurred. Disgusted with the whole performance, the reporter added a comment in a bitter tone, as well-trained seals are definitely not supposed to do.

Reporter: That's why I asked you.

Johnson had turned to answer another question. His head jerked around in obvious surprise, and he flared back. You got it. That's why I told you.

The episode took an interesting turn. For several weeks thereafter, the reporter found Presidential courtesy lavished upon him. When he asked questions at subsequent press conferences, Johnson addressed him as "Mister Jones." He interrupted his answers to other questions to amplify his responses to Jones's queries. He made other reporters wait—"I think Mr. Jones had a question over there." He had his staff track down additional information for Mr. Jones. Another White House newsman has commented that Johnson is never nicer to him than just after he has written a critical column about the President.

The other side of Lyndon Johnson's ambition is his insecurity. On one occasion he was escorting a group of young men through the White House living quarters. When they got to his bedroom, he went over to a table and picked up a sheaf of papers. Here is one marked "top secret," he said, waving the documents. Here is one for "my eyes only." He told them that he could not let them see the documents, "but they're very important." The young men gaped as the leader of the world's most powerful nation brandished the tangible proof of his own importance. Like the residents of Columbus, Ohio, in Thurber's time, he seems always to be looking over his shoulder in anticipation that someone is going to tell him that he didn't win after all. More than a year after taking office, and after winning a smashing election victory of his own, he had the word passed to reporters that he had been responsible for forty percent of Kennedy's New Frontier program, a claim that did not square with his legislative inactivity as Vice-President. In private conversations, he has minimized Kennedy's accomplishments, often in scathing accents, while publicily eulogizing the fallen leader. He was, as Evans and Novak point out, "*both* men: the detractor of Kennedy and the keeper of Kennedy's memory."

Ever since he began his ascent to power, Johnson's dealings with the Washington press corps have been touchy. For his part, Johnson wants the news reported as he chooses and when he chooses. For their part, reporters have been hard pressed, more so than with most Presidents, to separate their personal reactions to Johnson from their professional responsibility to report and analyze his official actions. The conflict antedates his Presidency. Throughout his career, Johnson has blandly deceived reporters and through them the public, and the deception has extended from small personal matters to large policy issues. When Johnson was Majority Leader, a veteran Congressional reporter for a major news service finally decided to stop interviewing him. The late House Speaker Sam Rayburn remonstrated with the reporter. Rayburn pointed out that the Senate leader was an important news source and that the newsman could not afford to bypass him. The reporter replied that he could not afford to file misleading stories, either.

On a trip to Texas in his Senate days, Johnson escorted a group of reporters around his ranch. They stopped in front of a ramshackle shanty bearing the unmistakable marks of a hard life. In reverent tones, the Senator identified this almost-log cabin as the place in which he was reared to manhood. His mother, who happened to be along, listened to the Abe Lincoln spiel for a while and then spoke up. "Why, Lyndon," she said, "you *know* we had a nice house over on the other side of the farm."

When Johnson exaggerates the humbleness of his origins or the valor of his ancestors, it's a relatively harmless matter, although it doesn't do his image any good. But when he injects the same hyperbole into foreign relations, it can do lasting damage to the reputation of the United States government—as in the case of the crisis in the Dominican Republic. At a press conference on June 17, 1965, in what one observer called "a truly alarming stream of Presidential consciousness," he elaborated on his reasons for sending the Marines into Santo Domingo. Said Johnson: "Some 1,500 innocent people were murdered and shot, and their heads cut off, and . . . as we talked to our Ambassador to confirm the horror and tragedy and the unbelievable fact that they were firing on Americans and the American Embassy, he was talking to us from under a desk while bullets were going through his windows, and he had a thousand American men, women and children assembled in the hotel who were pleading with their President for help to preserve their lives. We didn't start that. We didn't intervene. We didn't kill anyone."

It was a graphic picture, but unfortunately it wasn't true. The U.S.

Ambassador in Santo Domingo, William Tapley Bennett, said later that he did not remember any bullets coming into his office, and he did not take cover under his desk. No one was beheaded by the Dominican insurgents. No American citizens were harmed—although two newsmen were shot by U.S. Marines. It should be borne in mind, too, that when Johnson made his press conference statement on June 17, almost three weeks had elapsed since the first Marine contingents were sent in—plenty of time in which to check the facts.

Although reporters didn't realize it at the time, the credibility problem arose at Johnson's first press conference as President, on December 7, 1963. When he was asked about the size of the federal budget then being prepared, Johnson pointed out that Kennedy's last budget had been $98,800,000,000. Then he noted that about $3,500,000,000 would have to be added to this figure to cover "built-in" increases and new programs. Reporters came away with the impression that the new budget would be between $102,000,000,000 and $103,000,000,000.

A few days later, the spending total changed again. At the President's Texas vacation headquarters, officials spread the word that the new budget would be about $100,000,000,000. At other times, Johnson let it be known that the range would be 98 to 102 billion. But when the budget was submitted to Congress, it was none of these figures—not 98, 99, 100, 102 or 103 billion. It was 97.9 billion, and this was later reduced to 97.3 billion. Johnson had his victory. He had kept spending under the Kennedy level. And the reporters and the public had their first lesson in what to expect from the new President: calculated confusion.

In terms of Johnson's credibility, however, it was a Pyrrhic victory. When budget-making time rolled around again the following year, a White House aide, obviously acting under instructions, told reporters that the new figure probably would be between 104 and 106 billion. He was greeted with stony silence. This time, no one filed a story, except for one lady correspondent who had not been in Texas the previous year. When this budget was submitted, it was not 104 or 106 billion. It was 99.7 billion. It might be argued that the varying figures merely meant that a final decision hadn't been reached. But in that case, since the federal budget affects business planning across the country, why say anything at all before the final total was reached?

Since those early days, case after case has come to light in which the President or officials speaking for him have treated the truth with utmost casualness. There has been deception on both the military and diplomatic aspects of the Vietnam war, on the budget, on the Great Society program, on taxes, on pay increases for federal employees, on the aluminum price increase, on the President's health, on the appointment of Abe Fortas to the Supreme Court, and on a long list of other official and personal matters.

When The Washington *Post* reported that Johnson would ask for a four-billion-dollar cut in excise taxes, the President spread the word that this was false. A few months later, he asked Congress to cut excise taxes by 3.9 billion. When The Washington *Star* reported that Johnson would recommend a three percent average pay increase for federal employees, he complained that the story was erroneous. A short time later, he proposed a three percent average pay increase for federal employees. When the aluminum companies announced they were raising prices, the government countered with an announcement that it would sell 200,000 tons of stockpiled aluminum on the open market, which would have the effect of driving prices down. The White House said there was "no connection whatsoever" between the two actions, but later Johnson boasted privately about his role in forcing the aluminum companies to back down and said he had personally talked to a vice-president of Alcoa.

In October, 1965, Johnson announced that he would undergo surgery for removal of his gallbladder. He told reporters that "a thorough examination showed this to be the only trouble." After the operation, it was announced that the surgeons had removed a kidney stone as well. And under questioning by newsmen, the President's personal physician disclosed that Johnson had still another stone in his left kidney and that this had been known "for some years."

One sunny day in July, 1965, the President presided at a ceremony in the rose garden. Afterward, he invited reporters into his office for an impromptu news conference. One newsman asked him whether he could say anything about his plans for filling the vacancy on the Supreme Court that had been created by the appointment of Justice Arthur Goldberg as Ambassador to the United Nations. Johnson replied flatly that he had not even begun to consider the matter, and the reporters filed stories to that effect. The President did not use any of the many phrases available to a President when he does not want to answer a question but does not want to mislead the public either. The next day, he announced the appointment of Abe Fortas to succeed Goldberg on the court.

Johnson does not seem able to let well enough alone. There is no constitutional or legal requirement that a President answer reporters' questions. There are many times when he is well advised not to. But Johnson, it seems, has to see whether his hand is still quicker than the public eye.

Secrecy is a passion for Johnson: It may stem from his upbringing in the Byzantine political world of Texas. But in the White House, this secrecy has caused him nothing but trouble. Bill Moyers has said that "fundamental to [Johnson's] operations . . . is surprise, which keeps his foes off balance. He wants to retain the advantage of calling his own signals and deciding on his own timing." This is obviously good strategy, but there is a strong risk that it will first confuse, then antagonize and finally alienate the public.

As a grey deceiver, President Johnson has virtuoso range, from the minutiae of family history to the number of American troops in Vietnam and their mission. At Camp Stanley in South Korea, on his Asian tour last year, he told American servicemen proudly that "my great-great grandfather died at the Alamo." A search by a Texas historical society, alas, failed to unearth any evidence to support this patriotic allusion.

A preoccupation with secrecy for its own sake can lead up some ludicrous paths. Some time ago, Philip Potter of the Baltimore *Sun,* who is a friend of the President, wrote a detailed story about Johnson's plans for a new Food for Peace program. The story appeared a few days before Johnson was ready to announce the new program. After reading the story, the President canceled the announcement and ordered his staff to burn the mimeographed news releases dealing with the new program. Months later, the new Food for Peace plan was put into effect, but in a piecemeal fashion, one step at a time, to conceal the fact that Potter's story had been correct. Moreover, the White House conducted an inquiry to determine who had leaked the story to Potter. A cabinet-level official was picked as the culprit, although he was innocent. The official later said he was given "unshirted hell" for his alleged transgression. The President did not speak to Potter for months afterward.

In these and dozens of other instances, Johnson has drawn too deeply on the credibility bank. He has cried wolf too often, to the point where many reporters view with suspicion almost everything that he or his spokesmen say. This goes beyond a mere spat; it has sunk deep into the fabric. The relationship between the President and the Washington press corps has settled into a pattern of weary cynicism.

When Johnson's deputy press secretary, Robert Fleming, told newsmen recently that there was no indication an announcement on the supersonic transport plane would be made in the near future, the reporters immediately began boning up on background information about the project so they would be ready to write their stories. Sure enough, the announcement came just one day later.

By overdrawing his credibility account, Johnson has given up, voluntarily, one of the chief weapons of leadership. The good faith of the prince, Machiavelli wrote, is his greatest asset. To be followed loyally, the chieftain must be trusted. This dark side of Lyndon Johnson, emerging despite his efforts at concealment, has eroded trust and, if you agree with Machiavelli, has impeded his quest for greatness.

The world, Anthony Trollope observed, is a place of hard words and harsh judgments. Lyndon Johnson has operated in this world as he found it, and as he thought it was. A hard, harsh man, he has bulled and battered his way through it to the top. But once there, it became his obligation to offer moral leadership, for this, as his mentor, Franklin Roosevelt, commented, is what is expected and required of the American President. Johnson has tried hard, but he is not an inspirational figure. His crude behavior intrudes as a shadow between the thought and the action. He has lived too long with Trollope's despairing summary.

Once Lyndon Johnson was complaining to a senior statesman that he wasn't liked, and he incautiously inquired why.

"Let's face it, Mr. President," replied the elder. "You just aren't a likable man."

[August, 1967]

An Appreciation of the Nonmilitary Functions of War

The military, or ostensible, function of the war system requires no elaboration. It is often necessary for a national military establishment to create a need for its unique powers—to maintain the franchise, so to speak. And a healthy military apparatus requires regular "exercise," by whatever rationale seems expedient, to prevent its atrophy.

The nonmilitary functions of the war system are more basic. They exist not merely to justify themselves but to serve broader social purposes. If and when war is eliminated, the military functions it has served will end

From a "leaked" government document entitled, in Esquire, "On the Possibility and Desirability of Peace," and later, in book form, "Report from Iron Mountain." The document purported to be the result of a three-year study by 15 of the country's most distinguished intellectuals, concluding that the economic, political and social institutions of modern man would fail without the existence of war to sustain them. The article was believed to be a deliberate hoax, devised out of the fertile imagination of Leonard Lewin (who claimed in the article only to be the conduit for a member of the committee who felt the public had a right to know the committee's recommendations to the government) to satirize, among other things, the nation's dependence on professional "expertise." A measure of its success in this paranoic decade was a bulletin from the State Department to all American embassies disclaiming knowledge of the report.

with it. But its nonmilitary functions will not. It is essential, therefore, that we understand their significance before we can reasonably expect to evaluate whatever institutions may be proposed to replace them.

Economic

The production of weapons of mass destruction has always been associated with economic "waste." The term is pejorative, since it implies a failure of function. But no human activity can properly be considered wasteful if it achieves its contextual objective. ". . . The attacks that, since the time of Samuel's criticism of King Saul, have been leveled against military expenditures as waste may well have concealed or misunderstood the point that some kinds of waste may have a larger social utility."[1]

In the case of military "waste," there is indeed a larger social utility. It derives from the fact that the "wastefulness" of war production is exercised entirely outside the framework of the economy of supply and demand. As such, it provides the only critically large segment of the total economy that is subject to complete and arbitrary central control. If modern industrial societies can be defined as those which have developed the capacity to produce more than is required for their economic survival (regardless of the equities of distribution of goods within them), military spending can be said to furnish the only balance wheel with sufficient inertia to stabilize the advance of their economies.

This function is often viewed, oversimply, as a device for the control of surpluses. One writer on the subject puts it this way: "Why is war so wonderful? Because it creates artificial demand . . . the only kind of artificial demand, moreover, that does not raise any political issues: *war, and only war, solves the problem of inventory.*"[2] The reference here is to shooting war, but it applies equally to the general war economy as well. "It is generally agreed," concludes, more cautiously, the report of a panel set up by the U.S. Arms Control and Disarmament Agency, "that the greatly enlarged public sector since World War II, resulting from heavy defense expenditures, has provided additional protection against depressions, since this sector is not responsive to contraction in the private sector and provides a sort of buffer or balance wheel in the economy."[3]

But even in the context of the general civilian economy war cannot be

1. Arthur I. Waskow, *Toward the Unarmed Forces of the United States* (Washington: Institute for Policy Studies, 1966), p. 9. (This is the unabridged edition of the text of a report and proposal prepared for a seminar of strategists and Congressmen in 1965; it was later given limited distribution among other persons engaged in related projects.)
2. David T. Bazelon, "The Politics of the Paper Economy," *Commentary* (November 1962), p. 409.
3. *Economic Impacts of Disarmament* (Washington: U.S.G.P.O., January 1962).

considered wholly "wasteful." Without a long-established war economy, and without its frequent eruption into large-scale shooting war, most of the major industrial advances known to history, beginning with the development of iron, could never have taken place. Weapons technology structures the economy. According to the writer cited above, "Nothing is more ironic or revealing about our society than the fact that hugely destructive war is a very progressive force in it. . . . War production is progressive because it is production that would not otherwise have taken place. (It is not so widely appreciated, for example, that the civilian standard of living *rose* during World War II.)"[4] This is not "ironic or revealing," but essentially a simple statement of fact.

War spending, considered pragmatically, has been a consistently positive factor in the rise of gross national product and of individual productivity. A former Secretary of the Army has carefully phrased it for public consumption thus: "If there is, as I suspect there is, a direct relation between the stimulus of large defense spending and a substantially increased rate of growth of gross national product, it quite simply follows that defense spending *per se* might be countenanced *on economic grounds alone* [emphasis added] as a stimulator of the national metabolism."[5] Actually, the fundamental nonmilitary utility of war in the economy is far more widely acknowledged than the scarcity of such affirmations as that quoted above would suggest.

But *negatively* phrased public recognitions of the importance of war to the general economy abound. The most familiar example is the effect of "peace threats" on the stock market; e.g., "Wall Street was shaken yesterday by news of an apparent peace feeler from North Vietnam, but swiftly recovered its composure after about an hour of sometimes indiscriminate selling,"[6] Other incidental examples are to be found in the pressures brought to bear on the Department of Defense when it announces plans to close down an obsolete facility (as a "wasteful" form of "waste"), and in the usual coordination of stepped-up military activities (as in Vietnam in 1965) with dangerously rising unemployment rates.

Although we do not imply that a substitute for war in the economy cannot be devised, no combination of techniques for controlling employment, production, and consumption has yet been tested that can remotely compare to it in effectiveness.

Political

The political functions of war are essentially organizational. First of all,

4. David T. Bazelon, "The Scarcity Makers," *Commentary* (October 1962), p. 298.
5. Frank Pace, Jr., in an address before the American Bankers' Association, September 1957.
6. A random example, taken in this case from a story by David Deitch in the New York *Herald Tribune* (9 February 1966).

the existence of a society as a political "nation" requires as part of its definition an attitude of relationship toward other "nations." This is what we usually call a foreign policy. But a nation's foreign policy can have no substance if it lacks the means of enforcing its attitude toward other nations—which is to say that it is organized to some degree for war. War, then, as we have defined it to include all national activities that recognize the possibility of armed conflict, is itself the defining element of any nation's existence vis-à-vis any other nation. Since it is historically axiomatic that the existence of any form of weaponry insures its use, we have used the word "peace" as virtually synonymous with disarmament. By the same token, "war" is virtually synonymous with nationhood. The elimination of war implies the inevitable elimination of national sovereignty and the traditional nation-state.

The war system not only has been essential to the existence of nations as independent political entities, but has been equally indispensable to their stable internal political structure. Without it, no government has ever been able to obtain acquiescence in its "legitimacy," or right to rule its society. The possibility of war provides the sense of external necessity without which no government can long remain in power. The historical record reveals instance after instance where the failure of a regime to maintain the credibility of a war threat led to its dissolution, by the forces of private interest, of reactions to social injustice, or of other disintegrative elements.

The basic authority of a modern state over its people resides in its war powers. (There is, in fact, good reason to believe that codified law had its origins in the rules of conduct established by military victors for dealing with the defeated enemy, which were later adapted to apply to all subject populations.[7] On a day-to-day basis, it is represented by the institution of police, armed organizations charged expressly with dealing with "internal enemies" in a military manner. Like the conventional "external" military, the police are also substantially exempt from many civilian legal restraints on their social behavior. In some countries, the artificial distinction between police and other military forces does not exist. On the long-term basis, a government's emergency war powers—inherent in the structure of even the most libertarian of nations—define the most significant aspect of the relation between state and citizen.

In advanced modern democratic societies, the war system has provided political leaders with another political-economic function of increasing importance: it has served as the last great safeguard against the elimination of necessary social classes. As economic productivity increases to a level further and further above that of minimum subsistence, it becomes more and more difficult for a society to maintain distribution patterns insuring the existence of "hewers of wood and drawers of water." The

---

7. *Vide* L. Gumplowicz, in *Geschichte der Staatstheorien* (Innsbruck: Wagner, 1905) and earlier writings.

further progress of automation can be expected to differentiate still more sharply between "superior" workers and what Ricardo called "menials," while simultaneously aggravating the problem of maintaining an unskilled labor supply.

The arbitrary nature of war expenditures and of other military activities make them ideally suited to control these essential class relationships. Obviously, if the war system were to be discarded, new political machinery would be needed at once to serve this vital subfunction. Until it is developed, the continuance of the war system must be assured, if for no other reason, among others, than to preserve whatever quality and degree of poverty a society requires as an incentive, as well as to maintain the stability of its internal organization of power.

Sociological

Under this heading, we will examine a nexus of functions, the most obvious of which is the time-honored use of military institutions to provide antisocial elements with an acceptable role in the social structure. The disintegrative, unstable social movements loosely described as "fascist" have traditionally taken root in societies that have lacked adequate military or paramilitary outlets to meet the needs of these elements. The current euphemistic clichés—"juvenile delinquency" and "alienation"—have had their counterparts in every age. In earlier days these conditions were dealt with directly by the military without the complications of due process, usually through press gangs or outright enslavement. But it is not hard to visualize, for example, the degree of social disruption that might have taken place in the United States during the last two decades if the problem of the socially disaffected of the post-World War II period had not been foreseen and effectively met. The younger, and more dangerous, of these hostile social groupings have been kept under control by the Selective Service System.

This system and its analogues elsewhere furnish remarkably clear examples of disguised military utility. Informed persons in this country have never accepted the official rationale for a peacetime draft—military necessity, preparedness, etc.—as worthy of serious consideration. But what has gained credence among thoughtful men is the rarely voiced, less easily refuted, proposition that the institution of military service has a "patriotic" priority in our society that must be maintained for its own sake. Ironically, the simplistic official justification for Selective Service comes closer to the mark, once the nonmilitary functions of military institutions are understood. As a control device over the hostile, nihilistic, and potentially unsettling elements of a society in transition, the draft can again be defended, and defended quite convincingly, as a "military" necessity.

It must be noted also that the Armed Forces in every civilization have provided the principal state-supported haven for what we now call the "unemployable." The typical European standing army (of fifty years ago) consisted of ". . . troops unfit for employment in commerce, industry, or agriculture, led by officers unfit to practice any legitimate profession or to conduct a business enterprise."[8] This is still largely true, if less apparent. In a sense, this function of the military as the custodian of the economically or culturally deprived was the forerunner of most contemporary civilian social-welfare programs, from the W.P.A. to various forms of "socialized" medicine and Social Security. It is interesting that liberal sociologists currently proposing to use the Selective Service System as a medium of cultural upgrading of the poor consider this a *novel* application of military practice.

Although it cannot be said absolutely that such critical measures of social control as the draft require a military rationale, no modern society has yet been willing to risk experimentation with any other kind. Even during such periods of comparatively simple social crises as the so-called Great Depression of the 1930's, it was deemed prudent by the government to invest minor make-work projects, like the "Civilian" Conservation Corps, with a military character, and to place the more ambitious National Recovery Administration under the direction of a professional army officer at its inception. Today, at least one small Northern European country, plagued with uncontrollable unrest among its "alienated youth," is considering the expansion of its armed forces, despite the problem of making credible the expansion of a nonexistent external threat.

In general, the war system provides the basic motivation for primary social organization. In so doing, it reflects on the societal level the incentives of individual human behavior. The most important of these, for social purposes, is the individual psychological rationale for allegiance to a society and its values. Allegiance requires a cause; a cause requires an enemy. This much is obvious; the critical point is that the enemy that defines the cause must seem genuinely formidable. Roughly speaking, the presumed power of the "enemy" sufficient to warrant an individual sense of allegiance to the society must be proportionate to the size and complexity of the society. Today, of course, that power must be one of unprecedented magnitude and frightfulness.

It follows, from the patterns of human behavior, that the credibility of a social "enemy" demands similarly a readiness of response in proportion to its menace. In a broad social context, "an eye for an eye" still characterizes the only acceptable attitude toward a presumed threat of aggression, despite contrary religious and moral precepts governing personal conduct. The remoteness of personal decision from social consequence in a modern society makes it easy for its members to maintain this attitude without

8. K. Fischer, *Das Militar* (Zurich: Steinmetz Verlag, 1932), pp. 42-43.

being aware of it. A recent example is the war in Vietnam; a less recent one was the bombing of Hiroshima and Nagasaki. In each case, the extent and gratuitousness of the slaughter were abstracted into political formulae by most Americans, once the proposition that the victims were "enemies" was established. The war system makes such an abstracted response possible in nonmilitary contexts as well. A conventional example of this mechanism is the inability of most people to connect, let us say, the starvation of millions in India with their own past conscious political decision-making. Yet the sequential logic linking a decision to restrict grain production in America with an eventual famine in Asia is obvious, unambiguous, and unconcealed.

What gives the war system its preeminent role in social organization, as elsewhere, is its unmatched authority over life and death. It must be emphasized again that the war system is not a mere social extension of the presumed need for individual human violence, but itself in turn serves to rationalize most nonmilitary killing.

A brief look at some defunct premodern societies is instructive. One of the most noteworthy features common to the larger, more complex, and more successful of ancient civilizations was their widespread use of the blood sacrifice. If one were to limit consideration to those cultures whose regional hegemony was so complete that the prospect of "war" had become virtually inconceivable—as was the case with several of the great pre-Columbian societies of the Western Hemisphere—it would be found that some form of ritual killing occupied a position of paramount social importance in each. Invariably, the ritual was invested with mythic or religious significance; as with all religious and totemic practice, however, the ritual masked a broader and more important social function.

In these societies, the blood sacrifice served the purpose of maintaining a vestigial "earnest" of the society's capability and willingness to make war—i.e., kill and be killed—in the event that some mystical—i.e., unforeseen—circumstance were to give rise to the possibility. It was primarily, if not exclusively, a symbolic reminder that war had once been the central organizing force of the society, and that this condition might recur.

It does not follow that a transition to total peace in modern societies would require the use of this model, even in less "barbaric" guise. But the historical analogy serves as a reminder that a viable substitute for war as a social system cannot be a mere symbolic charade. It must involve real risk of real personal destruction, and on a scale consistent with the size and complexity of modern social systems.

Ecological

Man, like all other animals, is subject to the continuing process of adapting to the limitations of his environment. But the principal mechanism he has utilized for this purpose is unique among living creatures. To forestall the inevitable historical cycles of inadequate food supply, post-Neolithic man destroys surplus members of his own species by organized warfare.

Ethologists[9] have often observed that the organized slaughter of members of their own species is virtually unknown among other animals. Man's special propensity to kill his own kind (shared to a limited degree with rats) may be attributed to his inability to adapt anachronistic patterns of survival (like primitive hunting) to his development of "civilizations" in which these patterns cannot be effectively sublimated. It may be attributed to other causes that have been suggested, such as a maladapted "territorial instinct," etc. Nevertheless, it exists and its social expression in war constitutes a biological control of his relationship to his natural environment that is peculiar to man alone.

War has served to help assure the *survival* of the human species. But as an evolutionary device to *improve* it, war is almost unbelievably inefficient. With few exceptions, the selective processes of other living creatures promote both specific survival *and* genetic improvement. When a conventionally adaptive animal faces one of its periodic crises of insufficiency, it is the "inferior" members of the species that normally disappear. In human societies, those who fight and die in wars for survival are in general its biologically stronger members. This is natural selection in reverse.

The regressive genetic effect of war has been often noted and equally often deplored, even when it confuses biological and cultural factors[10] The disproportionate loss of the *biologically* stronger remains inherent in traditional warfare. It serves to underscore the fact that survival of the species, rather than its improvement, is the fundamental purpose of natural selection, if it can be said to have a purpose, just as it is the basic premise of this study.

But as the polemologist Gaston Bouthoul[11] has pointed out, other institutions that were developed to serve this ecological function have proved even less satisfactory. (They include such established forms as these: infanticide, practiced chiefly in ancient and primitive societies; sexual mutilation; monasticism; forced emigration; extensive capital punishment, as in old China and eighteenth-century England; and other similar, usually localized, practices.)

9. *Vide* most recently K. Lorenz, in *Das Sogenannte Böse: zur Naturgeschichte der Aggression* (Vienna: G. Borotha-Schoeler Verlag, 1964).

10. As in recent draft-law controversy, in which the issue of selective deferment of the culturally privileged is often carelessly equated with the preservation of the biologically "fittest."

11. G. Bouthoul, in *La Guerre* (Paris: Presses universitaires de France, 1953) and many other more detailed studies. The useful concept of "polemology," for the study of war as an independent discipline, is his, as is the notion of "demographic relaxation," the sudden temporary decline in the rate of population increase after major wars.

Man's ability to increase his productivity of the essentials of physical life suggests that the need for protection against cyclical famine may be nearly obsolete.[12] It has thus tended to reduce the apparent importance of the basic ecological function of war, which is generally disregarded by peace theorists. Two aspects of it remain especially relevant, however. The first is obvious: current rates of population growth, compounded by environmental threat of chemical and other contaminants, may well bring about a new crisis of insufficiency. If so, it is likely to be one of unprecedented global magnitude, not merely regional or temporary.

The second relevant factor is the efficiency of modern methods of mass destruction. They offer, perhaps paradoxically, the first opportunity in the history of man to halt the regressive genetic effects of natural selection by war. Nuclear weapons are indiscriminate. Their application would bring to an end the disproportionate destruction of the physically stronger members of the species (the "warriors") in periods of war. Whether this prospect of genetic gain would offset the unfavorable mutations anticipated from post-nuclear radioactivity we have not yet determined.

Another secondary ecological trend bearing on projected population growth is the regressive effect of certain medical advances. Pestilence, for example, is no longer an important factor in population control. The problem of increased life expectancy has been aggravated. These advances also pose a potentially more sinister problem, in that undesirable genetic traits that were formerly self-liquidating are now medically maintained. Many diseases that were once fatal at preprocreational ages are now cured; the effect of this development is to perpetuate undesirable susceptibilities and mutations. It seems clear that a new quasi-eugenic function of war is now in process of formation that will have to be taken into account in any transition plan. For the time being, the Department of Defense appears to have recognized such factors, as has been demonstrated by the planning under way by the Rand Corporation to cope with the breakdown in the ecological balance anticipated after a thermonuclear war. The Department has also begun to stockpile birds, for example, against the expected proliferation of radiation-resistant insects, etc.

Cultural and Scientific

The declared order of values in modern societies gives a high place to the so-called "creative" activities, and an even higher one to those associated with the advance of scientific knowledge. Widely held social values can be translated into political equivalents, which in turn may bear on the nature of a transition to peace. The dependence, therefore, of cultural and

12. This seemingly premature statement is supported by one of our own test studies. But it hypothecates both the stabilizing of world population growth and the institution of fully adequate environmental controls. Under these two conditions, the probability of the permanent elimination of involuntary global famine is 68 percent by 1976 and 95 percent by 1981.

scientific achievement on the war system would be an important consideration in a transition plan even if such achievement had no inherently necessary social function.

Of all the countless dichotomies invented by scholars to account for the major differences in art styles and cycles, only one has been consistently unambiguous in its application to a variety of forms and cultures. However it may be verbalized, the basic distinction is this: Is the work war-oriented or is it not? Among primitive peoples, the war dance is the most important art form. Elsewhere, literature, music, painting, sculpture, and architecture that has won lasting acceptance has invariably dealt with a theme of war, expressly or implicitly, and has expressed the centricity of war to society. The war in question may be national conflict, as in Shakespeare's plays, Beethoven's music, or Goya's paintings, or it may be reflected in the form of religious, social, or moral struggle, as in the work of Dante, Rembrandt, and Bach. Aesthetic and moral standards have a common anthropological origin, in the exaltation of bravery, the willingness to kill and risk death in tribal warfare.

It is also instructive to note that the character of a society's culture has borne a close relationship to its war-making potential, in the context of its times. It is no accident that the current "cultural explosion" in the United States is taking place during an era marked by an unusually rapid advance in weaponry. This relationship is more generally recognized than the literature on the subject would suggest. For example, many artists and writers are now beginning to express concern over the limited creative options they envisage in the warless world they think, or hope, may be soon upon us. They are currently preparing for this possibility by unprecedented experimentation with meaningless forms; their interest in recent years has been increasingly engaged by the abstract pattern, the gratuitous emotion, the random happening, and the unrelated sequence.

The relationship of war to scientific research and discovery is more explicit. War is the principal motivational force for the development of science at every level, from the abstractly conceptual to the narrowly technological. Modern society places a high value on "pure" science, but it is historically inescapable that all the significant discoveries that have been made about the natural world have been inspired by the real or imaginary military necessities of their epochs.

Beginning with the development of iron and steel, and proceeding through the discoveries of the laws of motion and thermodynamics to the age of the atomic particle, the synthetic polymer, and the space capsule, no important scientific advance has not been at least indirectly initiated by an implicit requirement of weaponry. More prosaic examples include the transistor radio (an outgrowth of military communications requirements), the assembly line (from Civil War firearms needs), the canal lock, and so on. A typical adaptation can be seen in a device as modest as the common lawn mower; it developed from the revolving scythe devised by Leonardo da Vinci to precede a horse-powered vehicle into enemy ranks.

The most direct relationship can be found in medical technology. For example, a giant "walking machine," an amplifier of body motions invented for military use in difficult terrain, is now making it possible for many previously confined to wheelchairs to walk. The Vietnam war alone has led to spectacular improvements in amputation procedures, blood-handling techniques, and surgical logistics. It has stimulated new large-scale research on malaria and other tropical parasite diseases; it is hard to estimate how long this work would otherwise have been delayed, despite its enormous nonmilitary importance to nearly half the world's population.

[December, 1967]

Section 2

The Generation Gap

My Generation

by Frank Conroy

I remember asking, as a very young child, what was in the newspapers when there wasn't a war going on. That was the Second World War, the war to eradicate evil from the face of the earth, the war in which all Americans believed. Victory gardens, V-Mail, Gold Star Mothers, ration books and air-raid drills were the order of the day. People talked lustfully of three-inch-thick steaks, automobile tires and real butter. My father carried in his vest pocket his own personal sugar dispenser for coffee and my mother could be reduced to tears by a run in her stockings. The rationing of food, the enemy without, common hardship, common purpose and the almost godlike presence of Franklin Delano Roosevelt served to unify the country as it had perhaps never been unified before. If the First World War, however bloody, had been a bit of a lark, the Second was quite clearly a war of survival. Americans did not expect to lose, yet they knew they'd have to fight like hell to win. The discovery of the death camps of Central Europe resolved all questions as to what the war had been about. The forces of light against the forces of darkness, that was what we believed, and no American thirty-two years old can be untouched by that memory.

We hated the evil Germans and the treacherous Japs, scorned the weak Italians, loved the stalwart Russians, the plucky English and the wise Chinese. The double-fuselage P-38 was the fastest plane we knew about, the B-25 our image of power. It was, to use Fitzgerald's phrase, "bracing to be an American." Then came the atomic bomb and it was no longer quite so bracing.

It goes without saying that the effects of the bomb on the American mind were profound. We who were children at the time, with our childlike sensitivity to mystery, magic, and the unknown, with our social antennae fully extended to pull in all sorts of information, regardless of its usefulness (the ravenous hunger of children's minds, storing everything away undigested, stockpiling the recognizable, the unrecognizable and the ephemeral against a future time), were perhaps most deeply affected. We felt exhilaration at the indisputable proof that America was the strongest power on earth, apprehension because the power was mysterious, and most significantly we felt guilt, secret guilt that verged on the traitorous, guilt we could not possibly talk about. Our political apathy later, as college students in the Eisenhower years, seems to me to trace directly to our inability to reorganize those simple, propagandistic concepts of democracy and political morality which had been our wartime heritage, and which the bomb had rendered untenable.

The war ended, the United Nations was born at Dumbarton Oaks, and America moved into a new phase. We grew toward adolescence during the postwar boom, a period of expansion and prosperity unparalleled in the history of man, a time of busy optimism during which America seemed to concern herself entirely with adult matters. The kids, and there were not many of us in those days, were more or less left out of things. We inhabited a shadow area within the culture—nothing was important about us except the fact that eventually we'd grow up. We were embarrassed at our minority and most of us kept quiet, attempting not to call attention to ourselves.

We were the last generation to grow up without television. The radio was our thing—*The Lone Ranger, The Green Hornet, Mr. and Mrs. North,* etc. When television arrived we greeted it in a state of tremendous excitement. Movies at home! Free! It was too good to be true. And of course it was. It disappointed, was oddly dull after the initial novelty had worn off, unsettlingly hypnogenetic, vaguely inducive of claustrophobia. TV was technically crude in those days, inferior in every way to the marvelously cathartic medium of films, so we kept on paying quarters to get into the children's sections of our neighborhood theatres. And we got a lot for our money. The programs changed every three or four days, with newsreel, cartoon, short, trailers and a double feature. I used to go to Loew's Orpheum, see the show, and then sneak into the balcony to wait for vaudeville at eight o'clock. Movies were a way of life.

We became teen-agers when to be a teen-ager was nothing, the lowest of the low. Our heroes were not of our own age group. For the most part they were athletes—Jackie Robinson, Joe DiMaggio, Sugar Ray Robinson. Our music was Dixieland jazz (a revival was going on at the time), pop music, and, for some of us, bebop. (When I met my wife's aged grandmother years later she turned to me, fixed me with her steel-blue New England eyes and said: "Ah, Mr. Conroy, I understand you are interested in music. Please tell me about bobeep.") At the age of fifteen I saw Charlie Parker on the stage of Carnegie Hall. Our clothing, manners and lifestyles were unoriginal—scaled-down versions of what we saw in the adults. We had no sense of group identity, perhaps not much less than the teen-age generations that had preceded us, but unquestionably less than the generation that was to follow ten years later. We were mysteriously disenfranchised—the best-looking girls at high school would ignore the boys of their own age and prefer to go out with older men.

In college we were named. The Silent Generation. The Apathetic Generation. There was no doubt about it. The sleepy Eisenhower years. America in a trance, drifting leisurely through a long golf game while the clouds gathered. Among students it was hard to find a rebel, virtually impossible to find a Marxist, a mystic, a reformer, or indeed, anyone who felt very strongly about anything. When my roommate and I discovered secret fraternities in our college, a college which advertised itself probably to be fraternity-free, and exposed them in the newspaper, there was a bit of talk but not much more. Most students thought it was a ploy from the psychology department. One can imagine what would happen now.

We believed in civil rights but did nothing active about it. Picketing was unheard of, protest vaguely uncool. It was enough to send a few bucks to the N.A.A.C.P., an organization we believed to be utterly safe, no more and perhaps even less militant than the Parent-Teachers Association. We were not afraid of Negroes and so made no attempt, as the students do today, to identify ourselves with their power.

Our sexual mores were conservative in the extreme. It was the time of going steady. Fiercely monogamous, we frowned on playing the field and lived as if we were already married. Virginity in girls was not expected, but faithfulness most certainly was. Promiscuity, which we interpreted as going out with more than one person at a time, was a grievous sin. Our key words were discretion, privacy and propriety. Needless to say, we lived and breathed hypocrisy.

No one knew anything about drugs in those days. Marijuana, which was to sweep through all levels of American society during the next decade, was smoked, as far as I know, by only two students in my college of five hundred. Heroin and cocaine were thought to be extremely dangerous (as they doubtless are) and no one would have dreamed of experimenting with them. LSD, Methedrine, and amyl nitrite were unknown. Mind-expansion was not a meaningless term, however. We read Blake, Zen, science fiction, the Christian mystics, and various studies on E.S.P. and psychic phenomena. We blew our minds without drugs. I remember lying, at the age of nineteen, in the enclosed garden of the Bryn Mawr library, under the cherry tree, watching the stars for hour after hour, aware that light from unimaginable distances was collecting in my eye, getting high on the universe. College was a straight scene for us. We didn't come across pot until many years later.

Our literary heroes were more likely to be figures from the past than from our own time. Most of us felt closer to the sixteenth, eighteenth, and nineteenth centuries than to the seventeenth or the twentieth. James Joyce, whom rightly or wrongly we thought of as a nineteenth-century writer, the penultimate romantic, was a god. We took apart his difficult prose without the least sense of resentment, dissecting clues as eagerly as Talmudic scholars. *Portrait of the Artist* and *Ulysses* were books we knew well. The difficulties of *Finnegans Wake* were thought by us to be the inevitable result of the depth of Joyce's art rather than any failure of Joyce's mind. It would have been sacrilegious to suggest psychosis, and we scorned Stanislaus for having done so. Beckett was respected as much for having been Joyce's secretary as for his writings.

Closer to our own time, we admired Faulkner, Hemingway, Fitzgerald, early Steinbeck, and hated Wolfe, Dos Passos, Sinclair Lewis and James T. Farrell. Among young writers we liked Mailer, Capote, Styron and Salinger (who turned out not to live up to our expectations). There was a flurry about Francoise Sagan, mainly because she was nineteen, but on the whole we recognized her as a creation of the advertising age. The Beats were just beginning, Kerouac, et al., and we greeted them with a certain amount of suspicion, convinced that art was not that easy. Our standards were rather high, I think. The New Critics had filled us with an almost religious awe of language. We read Leavis, Edmund Wilson and Eliot as well, taking it all very seriously, worrying over every little point as if Truth and Beauty hung in the balance. The conservatism that colored so much of our experience did not evaporate when we dealt with literature. We defended literary art as if it were a castle under seige, in imminent danger of being destroyed by the vulgarians. In every college or university I knew anything about the most hated course was Social Science, as much a result of the incredibly rotten prose of the texts as it was of our disinterest in things social. We winced at bad prose, all of us, even the mathematicians and physicists who were presumably more interested in symbols than in language. We were neat, very neat, and sloppiness of any kind irritated us.

Fitzgerald calls a generation that reaction against the fathers which seems to occur about three times a century. There is the possibility that time has collapsed since he wrote those words, that life has accelerated to the point where changeovers occur much more rapidly, but nevertheless it is clear that those of us now in our early thirties were not a generation in any self-conscious sense. We had no leaders, no program, no sense of our own power, and no culture exclusively our own. Rather than saying, "Don't trust anyone over thirty," we would have been much more likely to say, "Don't trust anyone *under* thirty," or perhaps just, "Don't trust anyone." It is hard to believe that little more than ten years has gone by. Imagining, for the moment, American society as a huge mind, the students today can be thought of as representing the unconscious—they are pure emotion, they act first and figure it out later, they are the route through which revolutionary power is expressed—but most importantly they feel themselves to be a part of the social organism, they are the unconscious sensing the dimensions of the whole mind and their role within it. We felt nothing remotely like that. We were much more suspicious of society, without faith in its ability to respond to our minority voice. We were filled with precocious cynicism. We were stoics in our youth.

Now, as we come into power, we are aware of the paucity of our history. We have generation envy. How colorless were our times! Fitzgerald's people believed in their world—it really mattered who won the Princeton-Harvard game, it really meant something to appear at the theatre or the opera—and because they believed in their world they owned it. Until the Depression destroyed them they must have had a marvelous time. Styron's people had the war, a real war, a long, elaborate educational event plunging them directly into life. They had to learn to swim after they were in the water and, however sad their time, it was not dull. Brackman's people have faith. In a nonreligious age they have rediscovered faith. They are experimenters, revolutionaries and freethinkers, possessed by their own creative force. They have their own particular kinds of sillinesses, of course, but they believe they can change the world, and recent evidence suggests they are correct in that assumption. It is no accident that they follow us, they are most immediately in revolt against the banality of those who immediately preceded them. We have already learned a great deal from them, and will learn more. We will never be like them, nor do we want to be, but we perhaps stand to gain more from their example than anyone else. We are still young, after all, relatively late bloomers, but still young. Our strength lies in our fluency in all languages now spoken in America, the old and the new. In tremendously exciting times, we stand at the exact center of American culture, ready for anything.

[October, 1968]

Mrs. Aadland's Little Girl, Beverly

by William Styron

It usually requires a certain arrogance to say of a new book that it is a masterpiece. For one thing, the risks are large; in his runaway enthusiasm, the person who is rash enough to proclaim a new book "great," "a staggering achievement," "a work of art of the highest order" (these are the phrases most commonly employed) is likely to be proved wrong, even long before time and posterity have had a chance to assay his judgment. Recall, for example, *By Love Possessed*. A masterpiece? The reviewers seemed to think so, yet now it seems apparent that it wasn't that at all—at least not proven; opposed to what was originally claimed for it, too many people have considered it an unfair struggle and a thickheaded bore. At certain rare moments, however, there will appear a work of such unusual and revealing luminosity of vision, of such striking originality, that its stature is almost indisputable; one feels that one may declare it a masterpiece without hesitation, or fear that the passing of time might in any way alter one's conviction. Such a book is *The Big Love* (Lancer Books), a biography of Beverly Aadland by her mother, Mrs. Florence Aadland. To Mrs. Aadland and her collaborator, Tedd Thomey, we owe a debt of gratitude; both of them must feel a sense of pride and relief at having delivered themselves, after God alone knows how much labor, of a work of such wild comic genius.

I would like to make it plain, however, that—as in most high comic art—there is a sense of moral urgency in *The Big Love* which quite removes it from the specious and, more often than not, sensational claptrap we have become accustomed to in popular biography. Witness the first line of the book—a first line which is as direct and in its own way as reverberant as any first line since "Call me Ishmael."

"There's one thing I want to make clear right off," Mrs. Aadland begins, "my baby was a virgin the day she met Errol Flynn."

Continuing, she says: "Nothing makes me sicker than those dried-up old biddies who don't know the facts and spend all their time making snide remarks about my daughter Beverly, saying she was a bad girl before she met Errol. . . . I'm her mother and she told me everything. She never lied to me. Never."

Already it is obvious that we are in contact with a moral tone entirely different from, let us say, the lubricity of Errol Flynn's own biography, *My Wicked, Wicked Ways,* or the self-exploitation and narcissism so prevalent in those boring memoirs, which appear almost monthly, of yet another international lollipop. In striking this note of rectitude, Mrs. Aadland makes it clear that furthest from her desires is a wish to titillate, or in any way to make sensational an affair which, after all, ended in such tragedy and heartbreak for all concerned. Indeed, if it were not for the sense of decency and high principles which informs every page of *The Big Love,* we would not be in the presence of a comic masterpiece at all, but only one more piece of topical trash, hardly distinguishable from the life of a Gabor sister.

The stunning blonde who was to become "Bev" to her mother and, at the age of fifteen, "Woodsie" (because of her resemblance to a wood nymph) to Errol Flynn, was conceived, so Flo Aadland tells us, in an apartment on Mariposa Avenue in Hollywood on December 7, 1941. The date, of course, was ominous, contributing much to further Flo's lasting suspicion that her own life, and now Bev's, was "preordained." Tragedy had dogged much of Flo's life. She possessed, for one thing, an artificial foot, the result of a traffic accident, and this misfortune—usually referred to as "the tragedy of my leg"—coupled with a previous miscarriage had made it seem to her that life had hardly been worth living until Bev came along. Bev—who was a precocious child, walking at ten months, singing "all the radio commercials" at a year—altered the complexion of Flo's life entirely. "She was such a different baby, different in intelligence as well as beauty. I wondered . . . if she had been given to me . . . to make up for the tragedy of my leg." Shortly after this her speculation was confirmed when, riding with little Bev on a Hermosa Beach bus, she met a female Rosicrucian "who had made a deep study of the inner ways of life."

Discussing Bev, the Rosicrucian told Flo: " 'This baby has an old soul. . . . She is very mature. . . . Were the babies you lost before both girls?'

" 'Yes,' I said.

"The Rosicrucian lady nodded and then held both of Beverly's hands tightly in her own. 'Twice before, this baby tried to be born. . . . She has always known she was to fill the emptiness that entered your life when you lost your leg. . . . And you must realize this also. . . . This child has been born for untold fame and fortune.' "

Bev's early life was the normal one for a Hollywood youngster. So gifted that she was able to sing, in immaculate pitch, a popular song called *Symphony* at seventeen months, she was also almost overwhelmingly beautiful, and at the age of three, impersonating Bette Davis, won the costume beauty contest at the Episcopal Sunday School (an Episcopal activity peculiarly Californian in flavor). Later she was chosen mascot for the Hermosa Beach Aquaplane Race Association, cut the ceremonial tape for a $200,000 aquarium, and, not yet six, played in her first movie, a Technicolor epic called *The Story of Nylon*. As young as Bev was, she already exerted upon men a stupefying enchantment. A Hollywood doctor—"a very learned man, an authority on Eastern religions who had lectured all over the world and written many books"—was the first to pronounce the somber warning. "He held her hands the way that Rosicrucian lady had done. . . . 'Mrs. Aadland,' he said seriously, 'wherever did you get this little girl?' . . . Then he sat down in his chair and did a very strange thing. He closed his eyes and passed his hand back and forth just above Beverly's bright blonde curls. 'I think I see sort of a halo on this girl,' he said." Shortly Flo hears the gloomy, admonitory words: " 'I think men will be terribly affected by this girl. . . . Be very careful with your daughter. . . . I think men are going to kill over this girl. I have the feeling in my heart that she has the scent of musk on her.' " Her religious training enables Flo to comprehend: "I knew what he meant [about musk]. It wasn't the first time I had run into that phrase. I had read it in the Bible."

When Flynn began seeing Bev—then aged fifteen, and dancing in the movie version of *Marjorie Morningstar*—Flo sensed no impropriety. Thrilled that her daughter should be dating such a famous man, "overwhelmed by the fact that my baby called this man Errol," she confesses that she nearly fainted dead away when first led into his presence. To be sure, she says: "I'd read about his trials for the statutory rape of those two teen-agers in 1942. And I'd seen the headlines in 1951 when he was charged with the rape of a fifteen-year-old French girl." As for Bev, however, ". . . I still didn't believe he would take advantage of her." Against this gullibility may be measured Flo's near-insane outrage, some months later, when, during the course of a plane ride to join Errol in New York, Bev reveals that not only was she no longer chaste, but that Errol—on their very first night together—had done what the cynical reader knew he had done all along: he had, indeed, ravished her, tearing her seventy-five-dollar bolero dress, muttering "Woodsie, Woodsie" over and over, and "growling in his throat." Flo's indignation, however, is short-lived; despite this traumatic event, Bev seems deeply in love with Errol and Errol with Bev. On sober second thought, in fact, the future looks pretty rosy for Flo. "While [Bev] talked, the love bloom was all over her—in her eyes, making her cheeks pink. 'Mama,' she said, 'can't you imagine what it's going to be like with Errol from now on? Can't you imagine the lovely clothes, the spending, the famous people we'll meet? . . . Mama . . . he's told me how good I am for him. He's told me that we're going to write the Arabian Nights all over again.' "

And so the incredible joy ride commences, and the sedulous Florence is rarely absent from the scene, or at least its periphery. There are drinking bouts, yachting trips, dances, and other social events, including a well-publicized nude swimming party at a country estate near New York which Flo, with characteristic delicacy, assures us was *not* an orgy. "Beverly later told me all about it. [The people] *weren't* riotously drunk or mad with passion. It was an unconventional but casual swim. Afterwards they got out, dressed, and enjoyed some pork chops and apple sauce together. Beverly helped serve the food and was complimented by the others on her clothes and manners." The East Coast holds Flo—L.A. born and bred—in its thrall; her description of the Connecticut countryside, "the homes with their unusual gabled roofs," has a quality both eerie and exotic, as if it were the Norwegian troll country. At one club function, a handsomely swank place, also in Connecticut, Bev has her first encounter with snow. ". . . We sat down at a table . . ." Flo says, and describes a boring situation. "I looked around for a movie magazine or something interesting to read, but could find only copies of *Time* and *Fortune*. . . . Pretty soon we noticed it was snowing outside. Without saying a word to me or anyone else, Beverly got up and went outside. It was the first time Bev had ever seen snow falling and, being a native Californian, she was thrilled. I watched her through the large picture window. . . . She held up her arms gracefully and whirled them through the air, touching the falling snowflakes. She never looked lovelier. Her cheeks were flushed to a healthy pink and she wore one of her nicest outfits, a gorgeous peach-colored cashmere sweater and matching skirt. . . . As the big white snowflakes came down thicker and thicker, she did a very crazy thing. She took off her shoes and began dancing and skipping around on the golf greens. . . . She looked like an absolutely mad fairy princess, whirling and cavorting, holding her arms out so beautifully. . . . When she came in, she said: 'Oh, Mother, it was so beautiful!' Her nose was red as a raspberry and when I touched it with my finger tip it felt like a cold puppy's nose."

The note of pathos here, fugitive but intensely real, as it is in all comic art of a high order, is the mysterious ingredient which pervades every page of *The Big Love* and compels the book, in a grotesque fashion which surpasses all aesthetic laws, to become a kind of authentic literary creation in spite of itself. It was along about the passage just quoted that I was persuaded that Tedd Thomey, Mrs. Aadland's ghost, was in reality Evelyn Waugh, come back after a long silence to have another crack at the bizarre creatures who inhabit the littoral of Southern California. In truth, however, from this point on the book more reasonably brings to mind Nathanael West's *The Day of the Locust,* if for no other reason than the fact that, as in that fine and funny book, in which horror and laughter are commingled like the beginning of a scream, the climax of *The Big Love* swiftly plunges toward nightmare and hallucination in a fashion which all but overwhelms the comedy. Errol Flynn dies of a heart attack in Vancouver, and Beverly goes to pieces. She becomes the unwilling object of the attentions of a young madman, who, one night in Hollywood, rapes her at pistol point, and then in her presence blows out his brains—a tragedy which, Flo concludes, like the multiple tragedy of Errol Flynn and Beverly and Florence Aadland, must have been "preordained." Flo is charged with five counts of contributing to the delinquency of a minor; Beverly, in turn, is remanded into the custody of a movie-colony divine, the Reverend Leonard Eilers, whose wife Frances, in an admirable spirit of Christian guardianship, is now chaperoning Bev during her appearances on the Midwest nightclub circuit.

But at last the true comic spark returns, jewel-bright, in the ultimate scene of this terrifying, flabbergastingly vulgar, and, at times, inexplicably touching book. It takes place, appropriately enough, in the celebrated Forest Lawn Memorial Park, whither Flo, out on bail, and Bev and a friend have gone one morning at dawn to deposit flowers on Errol's grave, near a spot called the Garden of Everlasting Peace.

" 'My God,' I said to Bev. 'Can you imagine an unpeaceful man like the Swashbuckler in here?'

"We took the flowers from the car and placed them on the grave. . . . Then, although Errol's grave now had more flowers than any of the others, Beverly and our friend decided he deserved even more.

"So they went to the other graves and took only a few of the fresh flowers that had been left the day before. They took a bit of larkspur from one, a daisy from one and a lily from another. Then, frisking around like wood nymphs, the two of them leaped gracefully over Errol's grave, dropping the flowers at his head and feet.

"I watched them dance . . . for a few more moments and then I said to Beverly: 'You didn't kiss him yet, did you?'

" 'No, Mama,' she said.

"Then she knelt down very carefully and touched her lips to the grass near Errol's headstone.

" 'Mama!' she said suddenly.

" 'What's the matter?' I said.

" 'Mama!' she said. 'I just heard a big belly laugh down there!'

"After that we left. . . . As we drove away, we waved and called out gaily: 'Good-by, Errol!' "

It had been, Flo muses, "a tremendously swanky graveyard."

[November, 1961]

Doom and Passion Along Rt. 45

by Thomas B. Morgan

Thirteen pacifists, who seemed to think that a peace march might help belay the arms race, one hot afternoon not long ago found themselves trudging along a highway outside of Woodbury, New Jersey. They were elapsing yet another leg of a seven-hundred-mile "Walk for Peace" which had begun seven weeks earlier in Hanover, New Hampshire, and would end two weeks hence in Washington, D. C. At the moment, the Walk was led by Joel Kent and Marshall Bush, a sixty-four-year-old blind man. Kent was a tired-looking, gaunt scarecrow, aged forty, wearing a ragged white shirt and black trousers. He earned his living raising trees in Jamaica, Vermont. He was one of six peace-walkers who had come all the way from Hanover, through Massachusetts, across New York's midsection, down the Hudson River Valley, and into the flatlands of New Jersey. Bush, whom Kent held lightly at the elbow, was a latecomer, sturdy, white-haired, and neatly dressed in a sport shirt and slacks. Back home in Lancaster, Pennsylvania, he owned a vending-machine business. He had joined the walk south of Camden, planning to leave it sixty miles later— about three days afoot—in Wilmington, Delaware. And now, even though he had begun to ache from sunburn, he persisted in carrying the Walk's

leading sign, a circle of wood on an aluminum pole, WALK FOR PEACE /
HANOVER, N. H. TO WASHINGTON, D. C. He also carried his red-tipped white
cane, using it to feel for curbings and potholes.

Behind the tree farmer and the blind man, ten others walked, single file.
They had come about fifteen miles since morning. They had six miles
between them and the day's terminus, Paulsboro, New Jersey.

Time was passing and the walkers became more certain that they had
become part of an Organism, a multilegged creature of the road that lived
in space without an awareness of time passing. Ever since Hanover,
walkers had shared the feeling that the Walk was itself an entity, a thing
with a separate existence. But this feeling was always strongest late in the
afternoon when still there were longer, more tiring miles to go. They
would feel it then most keenly, almost as a loss of personality.

The only thing that mattered to the Organism was mileage—feet, yards,
blocks, spaces on the motor-oil map of the Atlantic seaboard. The Walk
has one dimension: distance. In the time sense, there was no past. What
had been happening since leaving Hanover the day before Easter had been
occurring some*where*—in Springfield, Troy, Poughkeepsie, or Camden—
but not some*time* in the past.

When had the rock been thrown at the Walk through the window of a
meeting hall? Answer: Hudson, New York.

Similarly, the future was timeless. What might happen next would not
happen *then,* but in a place farther south, down the road a piece, yonder.
Tomorrow would not be a Saturday in June. It would be the day the Walk
reached Chester, Pennsylvania. It would be Chester, Pa. Day.

And the present had become timeless, too.

The Walk had no tenses here in the thinly populated sand flats of New
Jersey, Route 41 now forking into Route 45, surrounded by scrubby trees
and billboards and the blur of compact cars and the murmuring of
innumerable youknowwhats. Mostly, as the sun moved lower, the Organism walked heads down, each personality suspended in this later afternoon
timelessness, staring at the tops of his shoes, his sneakers, boots, her
sandals, his brogans, loafers, oxfords, chukkas, all scuffed and dust-
covered and breaking down, picking them up and laying them flat, one dog
in front of the other, gingerly on the side away from the blisters, stiffly
because of the shin splint or the knot in the hamstring—and hardly ever
wondering what time it might be. In logic, in truth, time made no difference once the day's mileage had been set, twenty-one miles today—that is,
36,960 paces—seventeen miles yesterday, fifteen tomorrow, and so on
and on—*this* was what one had to get over. This was the suffering over
seven hundred miles in nine weeks that made the point for them.

From a passing car, a boy shouted, "Hey, look out for the Bombbbb!"

In the ranks, Jon Robison, nineteen, carried a sign. He had been with
the Walk since Kingston, New York, but could not go all the way to

Washington because his parents wanted him home in time for summer school. He wore a T-shirt and khakis, with a recorder stuck in his belt. When it was someone else's turn to carry the sign, he would play tunes on the recorder as he walked. His shoes had fallen apart and were now held together with black tape.

DEFEND FREEDOM, Jon's sign read, WITH NONVIOLENT RESISTANCE.

Another sign, NO BOMB TESTS / EAST OR WEST, was held by Larry Coopersmith, eighteen-year-old son of a contractor in the New York garment industry. "My father forbade me to come on this Walk," he says. "So, I packed up and here I am. I called up home later and he said, 'Son—you bastard!' He thinks I'm a Communist. He's very conservative. My father is about as close as there is to a pure capitalist. He's a contractor in a business where everyone cuts everyone else's throat. He is honest, so he gets his throat cut quite often." Coopersmith wore a striped polo shirt, shorts, anklets, and paper-thin oxfords. His feet hurt. "All I brought with me was four dollars," he says. "Someone back up the road gave me three dollars toward a new pair of shoes, but I never got any more money from anyone so I spent the three dollars on cigarettes."

Bringing up the rear, Penny Young, eighteen, carried a man-sized sign. She was from upstate Illinois, a pretty, plump, apple-cheeked young lady with boyish bobbed hair. She wore a fresh blouse, plaid skirt, high, white teen-ager socks and sneakers. She was a veteran of "peace actions" against the Electric Boat Company, manufacturers of Polaris submarines, and against the Atomic Energy Commission. The latter occurred in New York, involved sitting-in at A.E.C. headquarters, and won Penny a five-day sentence in the women's jail in Greenwich Village. "It was an educational experience," she says, "especially learning how much worse they make those girls by putting them in jail. The girls thought that anyone like me with short hair couldn't be straight, so they descended on me. I said, 'Look, girls, I'm straight.' After that, I got along all right. My father called and said he'd be in jail with me if it weren't for his job. See, I could go to jail with dignity and take whatever they could dish out. . . .

"When it was over, I made myself a sandwich-board sign saying JAILS ARE NOT THE ANSWER and picketed the place."

Grimly, Penny carried her sign, which had a distinct message on each side—WHAT YOU CAN DO / REFUSE TO WORK IN WAR INDUSTRIES and WHAT YOU CAN DO / JOIN THE PEACE CORPS. Like the other signs, hers had not been perforated, and it behaved like a box kite. Moreover, the actual weight of the sign varied with wind velocity. Marching into a mere zephyr, the sign would drag and the pole weight would increase greatly, straining the shoulders and cramping the fingers. Now in the persistent wind over the Jersey meadows, the sign produced severe discomfort. Penny's pole cut into her collar-bone like an ax blade. All of the sign-bearers were, in fact, walking grimly—and Penny held her lower lip firmly between her teeth.

Peter Giffen, twenty-four, a conscientious objector from Haddonfield, New Jersey, was taking his turn driving the Walk's supply truck. He was a full-time peace activist, used to work in a Michigan camp run by the American Friends Service Committee, had finished three years at Goddard College in Vermont. He had been skulled by a New York riot-squad policeman during peace-demonstration disturbances earlier this year. He was "coordinator" of the Walk, having been appointed by the sponsoring organization, the Committee for Nonviolent Action (C.N.V.A., one of the more volatile groups in the U.S. peace movement, was actually sponsoring three simultaneous peace walks at this time. Two other companies of pacifists were hiking east toward Washington from Nashville and Chicago, respectively, scheduled to arrive for joint peace demonstrations in the Capital of Deterrence. C.N.V.A. was then also engaged in an attempt to outfit and sail a small craft, called *Everyman II,* into the U.S. Pacific Ocean nuclear test area.) The truck driven by Giffen was an ancient Ford pickup donated by C.N.V.A. for carrying bedrolls, food, extra clothing, the water jug, and the leaflet supply. Above its front license plate was the legend: No BOMB.

All of the peace walkers carried copies of the Walk leaflet, which was to be offered to anyone passing by. Most of the material in it had been written by Paul Salstrom, twenty-one, son of a Rock Island, Illinois, furniture maker. Salstrom had studied briefly at the University of Chicago, had worked in Pennsylvania steel mills and mountain camps near Big Sur, California, and had gradually deepened his commitment to pacifism. Stern, blond, indefatigable, he was educating himself: for reading material, he had brought along on the Walk a biography of Havelock Ellis.

"WHO ARE THESE PEOPLE?" Paul's leaflet begins. "WHAT'S GOING ON HERE? You've just seen a group of people walking along the road or sidewalk carrying signs . . . and one of the walkers has handed you this leaflet. Perhaps you are trying to puzzle out what connection that youth or fairly respectable middle-aged do-gooder has with the morning headlines or with your personal thoughts and activities. We who are carrying the signs and passing out leaflets share your concern about jobs and layoffs, Russians and Chinese, strontium 90 in the kids' milk. We like to plant gardens, go on hikes and picnics . . . BUT NOW LET'S FACE REAL-ITY. . . ." Reality, Paul's leaflet says, demands a national policy based on renunciation of violence. This would include independent or unilateral steps toward disarmament, conversion of armament industries to consumer-goods production, increased aid to underdeveloped countries, and a national program of training for nonviolent resistance "against tyranny and oppression." "This program we advocate to Americans and Russians alike. . . . We believe it is likely that Russia would welcome and join a disarmament race. . . . WARS WILL CEASE WHEN MEN REFUSE TO FIGHT. . . ."

Jon Robison, who likes to keep track of such things, estimates that eighty-five percent of the people who were offered Paul's leaflet accepted it. Jon's percentage is slightly higher for Negroes and elderly ladies, lower for men wearing straw hats, and lowest for service-station gas-pump jockeys who are universally a sullen bunch.

They walked into Paulsboro, New Jersey, a little before six. It was a clean, nondescript little town with a generous Methodist community that had promised C.N.V.A. that the peace-walkers would be fed whenever they arrived. Dinner would be served in the church basement, access to which was gained by a stairway marked SHELTER AREA HERE. The walkers washed up quickly and, as usual, ate very well: fried chicken, potato salad, beans, hard-boiled-egg salad, cranberries, mashed potatoes, corn, hot rolls, country butter, and ice cream smothered in fresh strawberries, all in limitless quantities. "We're the best-fed revolutionaries in the country," Huw Williams said, disconcerting the parson. At nineteen, Williams was a junior at the University of Washington. He had left school to be in Hanover in time for the jumping off.

From dinner, the walkers were driven to the nearby town of Mickleton, where they would conduct a public meeting and spend the night at the Quaker Meeting House. They arrived an hour early. Paul Salstrom and Steve Trussel inspected the hall while most of the walkers relaxed on the porch and in the grass outside. Trussel, nineteen, was a loose-limbed, almost frail young man with blond hair and a poet's face. He wore a workingman's blue shirt and black trousers. Before joining the Walk in Hanover, he had been studying at Cooper Union in New York and had been arrested during the same melee in which Giffen had been slugged. He had shaved his beard for his trial on the advice of other demonstrators. "Being a student," he says, "I didn't realize how other people felt about beards. No one on this Walk has a beard, not because he wouldn't like one, but because he cares about what other people think." Clean-shaven, Trussell had received a suspended sentence. He has since become the Walk's most effective speaker, if not its voice.

"Why don't you talk about the nonviolent movement tonight?" Salstrom asked him.

"*What* nonviolent movement?"

"Let's not argue about that."

"I'm not interested in movements."

Thus engaged, Salstrom entered one of the Walk's oldest debates and one that underscored the Walkers' critical disagreement on basic goals.

"What are you interested in, Steve?" he asked.

"Just getting something done."

"You can't get anything done if you don't have a nonviolent movement."

"The movement can go down the drain as long as we get things done."

"We have to be organized. Where would this Walk be if it hadn't been organized in advance?"

"I've seen what organizing does to people. It makes machines out of the organizers."

"If you're going to organize, Steve, you have to be a machine."

"But then the love goes out of you."

"You can't have love and run an organization."

"Then junk the organization."

"You don't get it, Steve—without a movement, *nothing* will be done."

"Oh, I *get* it."

The two young men fell into a violent silence. Then Peter Giffen entered the hall, cheerfully lugging a carton of peace-movement literature. Included was a range of materials, some free and some for sale: up-to-date tracts from most peace groups in the U.S.; Dr. Jerome Frank's studies in the psychology of Nuclear Man; and Camus' 1947 essay, *Neither Victims Nor Executioners*. Griffen, Salstrom and Trussell spread the pieces on two front pews under a plaque bearing the motto: "Peace is an adventure in overcoming evil with good."

Jon Robison, just outside the hall on his back in the grass, blew an eerie lament on his recorder. Ken Meister, thirty-seven, tall and square-jawed with the look of a country preacher, played a giant game of tic-tac-toe in the gravel driveway with Manya Baumbacher, twenty-four, a shy, well-dressed girl from Salt Lake City who had been on the Walk since Massachusetts. Margo Nash was reading *Historical Sociology* on the meeting-hall porch. And Huw Williams was proving to Penny Young that he was one pacifist who could stand on his head. After a while, his nose began to bleed and he had to lie down with his feet up.

At the meeting, the audience of nine adults and three children arranged themselves in a tight group, using only two pews. They listened as Joel Kent spoke about the origins of the Walk and Ken Meister told of progress in the peace movement. The members of the audience felt free to interrupt with such questions as:

"What's been accomplished by this Walk so far?"

"It's hard to know what you've accomplished," Meister answered. "But I believe quite a number of people have been challenged by our ideas. If nothing else, we are proving that peace is more popular this year than it was last year. We were called Communists last year. Now people are far more willing to accept our leaflets. I think the Berlin crisis and the renewal of testing on both sides have made people more concerned."

"How do you know you're not being used by the Communists?"

"C.N.V.A.—the Committee for Nonviolent Action is, in itself, only about sixty people who organize these things—C.N.V.A. has no policy on Communists. But only people who are willing to accept nonviolent discipline are accepted in the work and we don't ask whether they are Communists. On the other hand, I don't know of any Communists in C.N.V.A."

"We believe no sincere Communist can accept nonviolence," Paul Salstrom added. "The two are incompatible."

"Who's paying for this?"

"Well, I'm glad you brought that up. Our leaflets for the trip cost $250 and aren't paid for yet. We usually get our breakfast and supper, but we need money for lunches. . . ."

When the audience had departed, the walkers found that they were four dollars richer. For a time, then, they sat in the pews and discussed plans for Washington. They were agreed on two alternatives, but had yet to make a decision: The Walk would either end with an "affirmative" demonstration at, say, the Jefferson Memorial or it would end with civil disobedience at the Pentagon Building.

"We'd have to plan carefully for something at the Pentagon," Paul said.

"Let's not do it if there's no reason for it," Steve said.

"I think," Huw Williams said, "we should have civil disobedience—for the symbolic effect."

"You really have to plan for something like that," Paul said. "There aren't enough of us to block the Potomac bridge. The trucks would just run over us and keep going. You need a strategy for every contingency."

"So let's have a strategy," Huw said.

"That," Steve Trussell said, "sounds like you're making civil disobedience an end in itself."

"Well, it would mean something."

"You're just looking for trouble, Huw."

Salstrom nodded with Trussell. "Huw wants to go to jail," he said. Then to Huw: "You've got time enough to go to jail, kid."

A little past eleven, the peace walkers were bedded down. The girls had gone off to spend the night in Methodist homes while the men had spread their sleeping bags on top of pew cushions on the floor of the Quaker Meeting Hall. Joel Kent had helped the blind man find his way to and from the bathroom. The lights had been turned out and, for a moment, the darkness seemed filled with sighs of exhaustion. Someone groaned and then there was silence.

"It may take ten years before this movement breaks through," Paul Salstrom said. "I mean, the way CORE broke through after nineteen years of getting organized. It took them nineteen years to break through with the Freedom Riders."

"There's got to be civil disobedience," Huw Williams said.

"It's dangerous, Huw, dangerous if it's relevant."

A car zipped by outside, splashing gravel. In its wake, there was a more serious silence.

"Civil disobedience varies for each individual," Salstrom said. "Some people see it as an attention-getter. It speaks to people negatively. In this country, it can only be symbolic. What happens is all laid out for you—you serve your sentence and make known your concern, that's all."

"Oh, it's dangerous and wonderful when it's pure," Steve Trussell said, "but it can become just another status symbol. It's already important to some of us how many days we've been in jail."

"What that means," Salstrom said, "is that we don't have a nonviolent movement in America yet. We have a peace movement, but not the nonviolent movement—"

"What is this about a *nonviolent* movement!" said Marshall Bush from his side of the dark room. "*This* is a peace movement and we shouldn't go round saying nonviolence is our principle. Peace is our principle, not—*satyagraha*. Your Gandhian movement was projected not to settle war nor keep the peace, but rather to achieve social justice. And in the South, nonviolence was used again for the principle of social justice. See, nonviolence is something you use in a struggle for peace or for justice or for liberty. Does anyone see that?"

Now the silence became thoughtful and filled again with sighs.

Quaker ladies of Mickleton, New Jersey, served eggs, sausages and pancakes for breakfast. Then, with the sun well up and promising no mercy, the peace walkers returned to the exact spot in Paulsboro—on the corner beside the Methodist Church—where they had halted their march the previous evening. Huw Williams took over the truck-driving chore. Peter Giffen handed out signs. Charles Hornig, a forty-six-year-old income-tax specialist from San Jose, California, helped himself to leaflets. With his wife's blessings, Hornig had decided to spend his annual vacation on the Walk.

"Let's walk, everybody," Giffen cried. "The theme of the day is lean hard on love—this is lean-hard-on-love day!"

They walked along Broad Street. Their signs fluttered in the wind. They were a four-masted galleon of the sidewalk, sailing off toward Gibbstown, the Delaware River, and Chester, Pennsylvania. Meister bounced on his sneakers, Margo jiggled, Larry ambled disjointedly on sore feet, Salstrom marched, Trussell rolled like a sailor, Manya Baumbacher staggered under a sign, Jon Robison on the recorder, Penny Young gaily and Hornig reading the editorial page of The New York *Times*. Peter Giffen strolled ahead with the lead sign and Joel Kent conscientiously held the thin, red arm of Marshall Bush, who walked with the firmly uncertain step of the blind. They passed neat homes with neat lawns and whispering sprinklers, a drive-in, a gas station, a grocery, people going the other way.

"You getting tired?" asked an elderly lady from her front stoop.

Larry Coopersmith happened to be closest to her.

"Frankly, yes," he said.

"How's the weather in New Hampshire?"

"Don't know. Left there seven weeks ago."

"Seven weeks!"

"That's right, lady."

"Well, bless your heart."

A woman in a parked car accepted a leaflet from Ken Meister. She looked through it quickly and then poked her head out of her window.

"You mean you want us to *disarm?*"

"Well, something like that—that's part of it," Ken said. "We ought to exercise a little more love than hate, don't you think? We shouldn't build our whole program on what *they* do. We should do what's right."

"You can't let *them* just take over our country."

"We stand for an open society."

"Russia wants everyone to be a Communist. That's not very open."

"Yes, and we want everyone to be a capitalist."

Broad Street became a highway. The wind died and the Walk moved a bit faster. They crossed Repaupo Creek and rested in the next patch of shade. The water jug went around. Someone asked Paul Salstrom what he wanted to do when the Walk was finished. "Go up to the Tetons," he replied, "and study ornithology and see this country, but I can't, because I'm going to prison." After this, no command was given, but the walkers roused themselves and set off again with the sun almost straight overhead. They came to a fork in the road, veered off on Route 322 and arrived about two p.m. at the Delaware River Ferry to Chester. Joel Kent paid their fares out of the Walk treasury. They boarded, Huw Williams drove the truck aboard and the Walk chugged across the Delaware to Pennsylvania. Here, they found themselves immediately in a rail yard at the edge of Chester itself, with a squad car and a dozen Chester sympathizers waiting to escort them into the city. Manya Baumbacher gave the policeman a Walk leaflet as the rest sat down beside the tracks in the shade of a long, low warehouse. Huw Williams brought out the box lunches that had been prepared by Methodists of Paulsboro. "Best-fed revolutionaries in the country," he said. A peppery old lady who had been a pacifist all her life stood over Paul Salstrom as he ate his lunch.

"Is your name Dutch, young man?"

"Swedish."

"My goodness, Swedish."

"Yes, it's a military name in Sweden."

"Well, let me tell you just the reverse: I have a grandnephew with *my* name, he just graduated college and, imagine, he's taken a job with one of the powder companies making explosives for the intercontinental ballistic missile. Simply letting himself be drawn into something that's wrong."

Paul nodded, understandingly. Then the old lady inquired about a certain young man, well-known among pacifists.

"He's in jail for civil disobedience," Paul said.

"Is he—I mean, is he *cooperating?*"

"He's cooperating, but now and then he goes on a hunger strike when he thinks they are not giving him the letters from people on his mailing list."

"Well, I should say—"

"But later he found out that people just weren't writing to him."

In time, the "Walk for Peace" moved into Chester, with about twenty-five walkers in the ranks and several new signs: MR. PRESIDENT / PLEASE STOP THE TESTING, SAVE OUR CHILDREN / NO MORE FALLOUT, and others. With two squad cars leapfrogging in the street beside them, the walkers penetrated the Negro ghetto, pushing leaflets and smiling. They detoured around a street vendor. He wiped his hands on his apron, reached for a leaflet, changed his mind, and grumbled, "I mind my own business," to no one in particular. They were passing a churchyard when a wedding party fled from the sanctuary and ran to the street through a shower of rice. Paul Salstrom watched the bride and groom lunge into the safety of a waiting limousine. "That was more reality than what we are doing," he said, moodily. "Perhaps it's more important, too."

At the height of the Saturday-afternoon rush hour, the walkers stationed themselves on four corners of a major intersection in downtown Chester. A bald man leaned out of his car and said, precisely, "Don't you kids know the Lord said there'll be no peace until He comes back?" Two fellows in straw hats stood back under an awning, watching the demonstration. First man: "Bunch of beatniks." Second man: "They ought to go back to Russia with their goddamn signs." First man: "They sure been walking, though." Second man: "Goddamn Russians." And in the second hour, two huskies wearing Swarthmore College T-shirts set up a counter-demonstration with two hastily painted signs (WE WANT VICTORY / NOT SLAVERY and NO LEFT TURN AT SWARTHMORE) and a stack of fliers offering a one-dollar Introductory Packet produced by the John Birch Society. None of this angered the peace walkers. They were leaning hard on love.

That evening, the Walk meeting was held in a Quaker Meeting House in Media, Pennsylvania. The counter-pickets appeared again with a new sign, UTOPIA FOR THE INTELLIGENTSIA / AMERICA FOR US, but they were so well-behaved that the casual observer might have assumed they were part of the Walk. It was a warm night, warmer still inside the meeting hall, but the meeting attracted more than fifty people, including two reporters and a radio interviewer. Manya Baumbacher began the program with a summary of the Walk's philosophy. Then Paul Salstrom described the organization of the Walk. He also outlined the walker's discipline. "Each of us," he said, "is pledged to refrain from physical violence no matter what acts are directed against him, to restrain himself at all times, to remain celibate unless walking with his spouse, to abstain from narcotics and alcohol and to maintain general neatness." Next, Steve Trussell told the audience what had prompted him to walk for peace. He said: ". . . Opponents say everyone in the peace movement is a Communist dupe. So, call me a dupe. Others say we are dreamers, impractical people who don't know what reality is. Well, I'm a dupe and a dreamer. But when I look around, I think maybe the world is duped and dreaming. The world is impractical. Look at it. The world has death in it. It's all around us. We add up death by the millions. . . . This walk has been wonderful. We've met people all along the way and we've fallen in love with them. Many people who don't know anything about unilateral disarmament invite weary walkers in for a drink of water. This is to me the real world—the *important world,* and the bomb is not the real and important world. . . . On this walk, I have found that this is a world you can love and therefore it is worth saving and worth each of us trying to do something about saving it. . . ."

Several questioning hands went up and Salstrom opened the discussion period.

"Salstrom, are you playing into the hands of the Communists?" a voice demanded. "Doesn't Khrushchev want our Polaris submarines out of the water, just like you do?"

"Wouldn't it be better," Paul Salstrom replied, "if we sent money to underdeveloped countries so that the Communists could not take them over?"

"Why, son, we're in a world war right now, only you don't know it. You can't trust a Russian, you ought to know that."

"I *know* some Russians," Steve Trussell said.

"What Russians?"

"Lots of them who came here from Russia. Millions of them. I trust *them.* They're just people."

"Ha! What I want to know, son, is this—is there a group like yours wandering around Russia today? Answer me that."

"No," Steve said. "There's no group like ours."

"That's it, son. That's it. No sense asking any more questions."

This night, there were no beds for the girls, so they slept in one room of the meeting house while the men slept in another. Morning was slightly cooler, but cloudless and windy. Led by Marshall Bush and Paul Salstrom, the Walk picked up the trail in Chester, jumping off on West Ninth Street for Wilmington. A matron on the street patted Penny's shoulder and said,

"Thank God, at least someone has his heart in the right place." A moment later, a motorist honked a horn at them and thumbed his nose. Stepping out on her porch in a pink slip, a woman shouted to a neighbor, "Honey, what'd I tell you—you can see any damn thing in the world right here on Ninth Street." A car slowed so that a young man in the back seat could say, conversationally, "Hey, listen, the only way we're going to have peace in this world is when we blow the goddamn thing up." Farther on, the Walk struggled against the wind, the pace slowed and Marshall Bush asked Paul to tell him what he saw.

"There are houses far as I can see, Marshall," he said. "Nice, neat houses. . . . There's the First Church of the Nazarene and a gas station. . . . People are out on their porches watching us. This must be Sunday or something."

"It is Sunday, boy."

"Well, Marshall, it's a nice day. Going to be hot."

"I need some Noxzema for my sunburn."

"All right, Marshall. It's going to be a California day. . . . You know, once when I was working in the Big Sur country, I went up to say hello to Henry Miller. I've read almost everything of his. He wasn't home, but his wife was there."

"I wouldn't let my daughter read Henry Miller."

"Depends on the daughter."

Marshall held Paul's wrist and tapped now and then with his cane. They walked on, past giant gas-storage tanks and iron fences and empty factories. Paul carried the sign erect and talked to Marshall.

"I registered for the draft at eighteen in Rock Island," he said. "I applied for conscientious-objector status at twenty and was refused. I appealed and that was refused. Then, April '61, I sent back my draft card. They didn't say anything about it at the time. Then, in November, they called me for induction. I didn't appear, but I wrote the board a letter of refusal. They still didn't do anything, so last Christmas I started a vigil in front of the draft-board building. That did it. They called the police. When they came to arrest me, I went limp. I was in jail for eight days and didn't eat anything, but I wasn't too worried about that. They force-feed you after twenty or twenty-five days. Well, on the other hand, in the Irish rebellion, several men fasted and starved themselves to death and won tremendous respect. . . . So, my family bailed me out and I pleaded guilty to the charge. My motives were simple: I want to change the law. I want our country to have a voluntary nonviolent program alongside a voluntary military program. This way would be fair to everyone and it might change people's minds as to what will really defend them.

"I know you don't get very far going the extra mile, but it does intensify your personal commitment. I'm a Lutheran. I have no dogma, but I guess I've got this Christian thing. The stand I've taken is moral. We have missiles aimed at Soviet cities now. We accept this, but I find it completely immoral. Being in the Army would require me to accept this. . . . I'm ready, Marshall, to go to any length to provide a nonviolent alternative. I'm going to prison in a few weeks, probably for three years. I can be out on good behavior in a year if I cooperate, but I don't know whether I will cooperate. I don't consider nonviolence as an absolute. It can exist side by side with violence. I know what you were saying the other night. I only say that I think you can solve moral problems with nonviolence. I'm willing to stake everything on this part of reality."

"I've known many men to take the same stand," old Bush told him.

Thus, the Walk continued, on and on, to the outskirts of Wilmington. A man came out of his house to offer water. A woman let the peace walkers eat lunch and rest in the yard back of her home. Children joined in the procession.

Toward the end of the day, during that period of timelessness, Penny Young found an injured pigeon cowering in a patch of tall grass. The peace walkers gathered round. The bird was breathing its last.

"Leave it there," Paul Salstrom said. "What can you do to help it?"

And so, on they* walked, wide-eyed in Gaza.

* On June 20, 1962, in Federal District Court in Rock Island, Illinois, Paul Salstrom was sentenced to three years in prison for refusal to report for military induction. He had served as his own lawyer. Meanwhile, other members of the Walk had arrived in Washington and were assembling near the White House and picketing at the Pentagon. When police arrested some of them for creating a "public hazard," many of them assumed the classic pose of the civil disobedient—"going limp"—and were photographed for both the newspaper wire services and for the three major TV networks. Then they dispersed. Some went home. Some moved on to other peace actions. Some went roaming. Those who had been arrested received suspended sentences and were released on probation, except for Huw Williams, who has insisted on a jury trial and, presumably, will get one.

[November, 1962]

There Goes (Varoom! Varoom!) That Kandy-Kolored (Thphhhhhh!) Tangerine-Flake Streamline Baby (Rahghhh!) Around the Bend (Brummmmmmmm mmmmmmmmmm.....

by Tom Wolfe

"This is the decade when the postwar babies come of age. In the automobile business, coming of age means the age at which they enter the automobile market. It adds up to twelve and a half million more young people in these age groups by 1970—an increase of more than one million per year!" —L. A. Iacocca, Vice-President of Ford Motor Company, and Ford Division General Manager

The first good look I had at customized cars was at an event called a "Teen Fair," held in Burbank, a suburb of Los Angeles beyond Hollywood. This was a wild place to be taking a look at art objects—eventually, I should say, you have to reach the conclusion that these customized cars *are* art objects, at least if you use the standards applied in a civilized society. But I will get to that in a moment. Anyway, about noon you drive up to a place that looks like an outdoor amusement park, and there are three serious-looking kids, like the cafeteria committee in high school, taking tickets, but the scene inside is quite mad. Inside, two things hit you. The first is a huge platform a good seven feet off the ground with a hully-gully band—everything is electrified, the bass, the guitars, the saxo-

561

phones—and (two) behind the band, on the platform, about two hundred kids are doing frantic dances called the hully-gully, the bird, and the shampoo. As I said, it's noontime. The dances the kids are doing are very jerky. The boys and girls don't touch, not even with their hands. They just ricochet around. Then you notice that all the girls are dressed exactly alike. They have bouffant hairdos—all of them—and slacks that are, well, skintight does not get the idea across; it's more the conformation than how tight the slacks are. It's as if some lecherous old tailor with a gluteus-maximus fixation designed them, striation by striation. About the time you've managed to focus on this, you notice that out in the middle of the park is a huge, perfectly round swimming pool; really rather enormous. And there is a Chris-Craft cabin cruiser in the pool, going around and around, sending up big waves, with more of these bouffant babies bunched in the back of it. In the water, suspended like plankton, are kids in Scuba-diving outfits; others are tooling around underwater, breathing through a snorkel. And all over the place are booths, put up by shoe companies and guitar companies and God knows who else, and there are kids dancing in all of them—dancing the bird, the hully-gully, and the shampoo—with the music of the hully-gully band piped all over the park through loudspeakers.

All this time, Tex Smith, from *Hot Rod Magazine*, who brought me over to the place, is trying to lead me to the customized-car exhibit—"Tom, I want you to see this car that Bill Cushenberry built, The Silhouette"—which is to say, here are two hundred kids ricocheting over a platform at high noon, and a speedy little boat barreling around and around and around in a round swimming pool, and I seem to be the only person who is distracted. The customized-car exhibit turns out to be the Ford Custom Car Caravan, which Ford is sending all over the country. At first, with the noise and peripheral motion and the inchoate leching you are liable to be doing, what with bouffant nymphets rocketing all over the place, these customized cars do not strike you as anything very special. Obviously they *are* very special, but the first thing you think of is the usual—you know, that the kids who own these cars are probably skinny little hoods who wear T-shirts and carry their cigarette packs by winding them around in the T-shirt up near the shoulder.

But after a while, I was glad I had seen the cars in this natural setting, which was, after all, a kind of Plato's Republic for teen-agers. Because if you watched anything at this fair very long, you kept noticing the same thing. These kids are absolutely maniacal about form. They are practically religious about it. For example, the dancers: none of them ever smiled. They stared at each other's legs and feet, concentrating. The dances had no grace about them at all, they were more in the nature of a hoedown, but everybody was concentrating to do them exactly *right*. And the bouffant kids all had form, wild form, but form with rigid standards, one gathers.

Even the boys. Their dress was prosaic—Levis, Slim Jims, sport shirts, T-shirts, polo shirts—but the form was consistent: a stovepipe silhouette. And they all had the same hairstyle: some wore it long, some short, but none of them had a part; all that hair was brushed back straight from the hairline. I went by one of the guitar booths, and there was a little kid in there, about thirteen, playing the hell out of an electric guitar. The kid was named Cranston something or other. He looked like he ought to be named Kermit or Herschel; all his genes were kind of horribly Okie. Cranston was playing away and a big crowd was watching. But Cranston was slouched back with his spine bent like a sapling up against a table, looking gloriously bored. At thirteen, this kid was being fanatically cool. They all were. They were all wonderful slaves to form. They have created their own style of life, and they are much more authoritarian about enforcing it than are adults. Not only that, but today these kids—especially in California—have *money*, which, needless to say, is why all these shoe merchants and guitar sellers and the Ford Motor Company were at a Teen Fair in the first place. I don't mind observing that it is this same combination— money plus slavish devotion to form—that accounts for Versailles or St. Mark's Square. Naturally, most of the artifacts that these kids' money-plus-form produce are of a pretty ghastly order. But so was most of the paraphernalia that developed in England during the Regency. I mean, most of it was on the order of starched cravats. A man could walk into Beau Brummel's house at 11 a.m., and here would come the butler with a tray of wilted linen. "These were some of our failures," he confides. But then Brummel comes downstairs wearing one perfect starched cravat. Like one perfect iris, the flower of Mayfair civilization. But the Regency period did see some tremendous formal architecture. And the kids' formal society has also brought at least one substantial thing to a formal development of a high order—the customized cars. I don't have to dwell on the point that cars mean more to these kids than architecture did in Europe's great formal century, say, 1750 to 1850. They are freedom, style, sex, power, motion, color—everything is right there.

Things have been going on in the development of the kids' formal attitude toward cars since 1945, things of great sophistication that adults have not been even remotely aware of, mainly because the kids are so inarticulate about it, especially the ones most hipped on the subject. They are not from the levels of society that produce children who write sensitive analytical prose at age seventeen, or if they do, they soon fall into the hands of English instructors who put them onto Hemingway or a lot of goddamn-and-hungry-breast writers. If they ever write about a highway again, it's a rain-slicked highway and the sound of the automobiles passing over it is like the sound of tearing silk (not that one household in ten thousand has heard the sound of tearing silk since 1945).

Anyway, we are back at the Teen Fair and I am talking to Tex Smith and to Don Beebe, a portly young guy with a white sport shirt and Cuban sunglasses. As they tell me about the Ford Custom Car Caravan, I can see that Ford has begun to comprehend this teen-age style of life and its potential. The way Ford appears to figure it is this: Thousands of kids are getting hold of cars and either hopping them up for speed or customizing them to some extent, usually a little of both. Before they get married they pour *all* their money into this. If Ford can get them hooked on Fords now, after the kids are married they'll buy new Fords. Even the kids who aren't full-time car nuts themselves will be influenced by which car is considered "boss." They use that word a lot, "boss." The kids used to consider Ford the hot car, but then, from 1955 to 1962, Chevrolet became the favorite. They had big engines and were easy to hop up, the styling was simple, and the kids could customize them easily. In 1959, and more so in 1960, Plymouth became a hot car, too. In 1961 and 1962, it was all Chevrolet and Plymouth. Now Ford is making a big push. A lot of the professional hot-rod and custom-car people, adults, will tell you that now Ford is the hot car, but you have to discount some of it, because Ford is laying money on everybody right and left, in one form or another. In the Custom Car Caravan, all the cars have been fashioned out of Ford bodies except the ones that are completely handmade, like the aforementioned Silhouette.

Anyway, Don Beebe is saying, over a loudspeaker, "I hate to break up that dancing, but let's have a little drag racing." He has a phonograph hooked up to the loudspeaker, and he puts on a record, produced by Riverside Records, of drag-strip sounds, mainly dragsters blasting off and squealing from the starting line. Well, he doesn't really break up the dancing, but a hundred kids come over, when they hear the drag-strip sounds, to where Beebe has a slot-racing stand. Slot-racing is a model-train-type game in which two model drag racers, each about five inches long, powered by electricity, run down a model drag strip. Beebe takes a microphone and announces that Dick Dale, the singer, is here, and anybody who will race Dick at the slot-racing stand will get one of his records. Dick Dale is pretty popular among the kids out here because he sings a lot of "surfing" songs. The surfers—surfboard riders—are a cult much admired by all the kids. They have their own argot, with adjectives like "hang ten," meaning the best there is. They also go in for one particular brand of customizing: they take old wood-bodied station wagons, which they call "woodies" and fix them up for riding, sleeping and hauling surfing equipment for their weekends at the beach. The surfers also get a hell of a bang out of slot-racing for some reason, so with Dick Dale slot-racing at the Teen Fair, you have about three areas of the arcane teen world all rolled into one.

Dick Dale, rigged out in Byronic shirt and blue cashmere V-neck sweater and wraparound sunglasses, singer's mufti U.S.A., has one cord with a starter button, while a bouffant nymphet from Newport named

Sherma, Sherma of the Capri pants, has the other one. Don Beebe flashes a starting light and Sherma lets out a cry, not a thrilled cry, just nerves, and a model 1963 Ford and a model dragster go running down the slot board, which is about chest high. The slot board is said to be one-twenty-fifth the actual size of a drag strip, which somehow reminds you of those incredible stamp-size pictures in the dictionary with the notation that this is one-hundredth the size of a real elephant. A hundred kids were packed in around the slot racers and did not find it incredible. That is, they were interested in who would win, Dick Dale or Sherma. I'm sure they had no trouble magnifying the slot racers twenty-five times to the size of the full-blown, esoteric world of hot rods and custom cars.

I met George Barris, one of the celebrities of the custom-car world, at the Teen Fair. Barris is the biggest name in customizing. He is a good example of a kid who grew up completely absorbed in this teen-age world of cars, who pursued the pure flame and its forms with such devotion that he emerged an artist. It was like Tiepolo emerging from the studios of Venice, where the rounded Grecian haunches of the murals on the Palladian domes hung in the atmosphere like clouds. Except that Barris emerged from the auto-body shops of Los Angeles.

Barris invited me out to his studio—only he would never think of calling it that, he calls it Kustom City—at 10811 Riverside Drive in North Hollywood. If there is a river within a thousand miles of Riverside Drive, I saw no sign of it. It's like every place else out there: endless scorched boulevards lined with one-story stores, shops, bowling alleys, skating rinks, tacos drive-ins, all of them shaped not like rectangles but like trapezoids, from the way the roofs slant up from the back and the plate-glass fronts slant out as if they're going to pitch forward on the sidewalk and throw up. The signs are great, too. They all stand free on poles outside. They have horribly slick doglegged shapes that I call boomerang modern. As for Kustom City—Barris grew up at the time when it was considered sharp to change all the C's to K's. He also sells Kandy Lac to paint cars Kandy Kolors with, and I know that sibilant C in City must have bothered the hell out of him at some point. It's interesting, I think, that he still calls the place Kustom City, and still sells Kandy Kolors, because he is an intelligent person. What it means is, he is absolutely untouched by the big amoeba god of Anglo-European sophisti-cation that gets you in the East. You know how it is in the East. One day you notice that the boss's button-down shirt has this sweet percale roll to it, while your own was obviously slapped together by some mass-production graph keepers who are saving an eighth of inch of cloth per shirt, twelve inches per bolt or the like, and this starts eating at you.

Barris, whose family is Greek, is a solid little guy, five feet seven, thirty-seven years old, and he looks just like Picasso. When he's working, which is most of the time, he wears a heavy white T-style shirt, faded off-white pants cut full with pleats in the manner of Picasso walking along a Mediterranean bluff in the wind at Rapallo, and crepe-sole slipper-style shoes, also off-white. Picasso, I should add, means nothing to Barris, although he knows who he is. It's just that to Barris and the customizers there is no one great universe of form and design called Art. Yet that's the universe he's in. He's not building cars, he's creating forms.

Barris starts taking me through Kustom City, and the place looks like any other body shop at first, but pretty soon you realize you're in a *gallery*. This place is full of cars such as you have never seen before. Half of them will never touch the road. They're put on trucks and trailers and carted all over the country to be exhibited at hot-rod and custom-car shows. They'll run, if it comes to that—they're full of big, powerful, hopped-up chrome-plated motors, because all that speed and power, and all that lovely apparatus, has tremendous emotional meaning to everybody in customizing. But it's like one of these Picasso or Miro rugs. You don't walk on the damn things. You hang them on the wall. It's the same thing with Barris' cars. In effect, they're sculpture.

For example, there is an incredible object he built called the XPAK-400 air car. The customizers love all that X jazz. It runs on a cushion of air, which is beside the point, because it's a pure piece of curvilinear abstract sculpture. If Brancusi is any good, then this thing belongs on a pedestal, too. There is not a straight line in it, and only one true circle, and those countless planes, and tremendous baroque fins, and yet all in all it's a rigid little piece of solid geometrical harmony. As a matter of fact, Brancusi and Barris both developed out of a design concept that we can call Streamlined Modern or Thirties Curvilinear—via utterly different roads, of course—and Barris and most other custom artists are carrying this idea of the abstract curve, which is very tough to handle, on and on and on at a time when your conventional designers—from architects to the guys who lay out magazines—are all Mondrian. Even the young Detroit car stylists are all Mondrian. Only the aircraft designers have done anything more with the Streamline, and they have only because they're forced to by physics, and so on. I want to return to that subject in a minute, but first I want to tell you about another car Barris was showing me.

This was stuck back in a storeroom. Barris wasn't interested in it any more since he did it nine years ago. But this car—this old car, as far as Barris was concerned—was like a dream prefiguration of a very hot sports car, the Quantum, that Saab has come out with this year after a couple of years of consultation with all sorts of aerodynamic experts and advance-guard designers. They're beautiful cars—Saab's and Barris'. They're the same body, practically—with this lovely topology rolling down over the tunneled headlights, with the whole hood curving down very low to the ground in front. I told Barris about the similarity, but he just shrugged; he is quite used to some manufacturer coming up with one of his cars five or six years later.

Anyway, Barris and I were walking around the side of Kustom City, through the parking lot, when I saw an Avanti, the new Studebaker sports model, very expensive. This one had paper mock-ups added to the front and the rear, and so I asked Barris about it. That wasn't much, he said; starting with the paper mock-ups, it brought the hood out a foot with a chic slope to it. He was doing the same sort of thing in the back to eliminate that kind of loaf-of-bread look. It really makes the car. Barris doesn't regard this as a very major project. It may end up in something like a kit you can buy, similar to the old Continental kits, to rig up front and back.

If Barris and the customizers hadn't been buried in the alien and suspect underworld of California youth, I don't think they would seem at all unusual by now. But they've had access to almost nothing but the hot-rod press. They're like Easter Islanders. Suddenly you come upon the astonishing objects, and then you have to figure out how they got there and why they're there.

If you study the work of Barris or Cushenberry (the aforementioned Silhouette) or Ed Roth or Darryl Starbird (can you beat that name?), I think you come up with a fragment of art history. Somewhere back in the Thirties, designers, automobile designers among them, came up with the idea of the streamline. It sounded "functional," and on an airplane it is functional, but on a car it's not, unless you're making a Bonneville speed run. Actually, it's baroque. The streamline is baroque abstract or baroque modern or whatever you want to call it. Well, about the time the stream-line got going—in the Thirties, you may recall, we had curved buildings (like the showpieces later, at the World's Fair)—in came the Bauhaus movement, which was blown-up Mondrian, really. Before you knew it, everything was Mondrian—the Kleenex box: Mondrian; the format of the cover of *Life* Magazine: Mondrian; those bled-to-the-edge photograph layouts in *Paris-Match*: Mondrian. Even automobiles: Mondrian. They call Detroit automobiles streamlined, but they're not. If you don't believe it, look down from an airplane at all the cars parked on a shopping-center apron, and except that all the colors are pastel instead of primary, what have you got? A Mondrian painting. The Mondrian principle, those straight edges, is very tight, very Apollonian. The streamline principle, which really has no function, which curves around and swoops and flows just for the thrill of it, is very free Dionysian. For reasons I don't have to labor over, the kids preferred the Dionysian. And since Detroit blew the thing, the Dionysian principle in cars was left to people in the teen-age netherworld, like George Barris.

Barris was living in Sacramento when he started customizing cars in 1940. As the plot develops, you have the old story of the creative child, the break from the mold of the parents, the garret struggle, the bohemian life, the first success, the accolade of the esoteric following, and finally the money starts pouring in. With this difference: We're out on old Easter Island, in the buried netherworld of teen-age Californians, and those objects, those cars, they have to do with the gods and the spirit and a lot of mystic stuff in the community.

Barris told me his folks were Greeks who owned a restaurant, and "they wanted me to be a restaurant man, like very other typical Greek, I guess," he said. But Barris, even at ten, was wild about cars, carving streamlined cars out of balsam wood. After a few years, he got a car of his own, a 1925 Buick, then a 1932 Ford. Barris established many of the formal conventions of customizing himself. Early in the game he had clients, other kids who paid him to customize their cars. In 1943 he moved to Los Angeles and landed in the middle of the tremendous teen-age culture that developed there during the war. Family life was dislocated, as the phrase goes, but the money was pouring in, and the kids began to work up their own style of life—as they've been doing ever since—and to establish those fanatic forms and conventions I was talking about earlier. Right in the heart of it, of course, was the automobile. Cars were hard to come by, what with the war, so the kids were raiding junkyards for parts, which led to custom-built cars, mostly roadsters by the very nature of it, and also to a lot of radical, hopped-up engines. All teen-age car nuts had elements of both in their work—customizing and hot-rodding, form and power—but tended to concentrate on one or the other. Barris—and Ed Roth later told me it was the same with him—naturally gravitated toward customizing. In high school, and later for a brief time at Sacramento College and the Los Angeles Art Center, he was taking what he described to me as mechanical drawing, shop, and free art.

I liked this term "free art." In Barris' world at the time, and now for that matter, there was no such thing as great big old fructuous Art. There was mechanical drawing and then there was free art, which did not mean that it was liberating in any way, but rather that it was footloose and free and not going anywhere in particular. The kind of art that appealed to Barris, and meant something to the people he hung around with, was the automobile.

Barris gets a wonderful reflective grin on his face when he starts talking about the old days—1944 to 1948. He was a hot-rodder when hot-rodders were hot-rodders, that's the kind of look he gets. They all do. The professional hot-rodders—such as the Petersen magazine syndicate (*Hot Rod Magazine* and many others) and the National Hot Rod Association—have gone to great lengths to obliterate the memory of the gamey hot-rod days, and they try to give everybody in the field transfusions of Halazone so that the public will look at the hot-rodders as nice boys with short-sleeved sport shirts just back from the laundry, and a chemistry set, such an interesting hobby.

In point of fact, Barris told me, it was a lurid time. Everybody would meet in drive-ins, the most famous of them being the Piccadilly out near Sepulveda Boulevard. It was a hell of a show, all the weird-looking roadsters and custom cars, with very loud varoom-varoom motors. By this time Barris had a '36 Ford roadster with many exotic features.

"I had just come from Sacramento, and I wasn't supposed to know anything. I was a tourist, but my car was wilder than anything around. I remember one night this kid comes up with a roadster with no door handles. It looked real sharp, but he had to kick the door from the inside to open it. You should have seen the look on his face when he saw mine—I had the same thing, only with electric buttons."

The real action, though, was the drag racing, which was quite, but quite, illegal.

"We'd all be at the Piccadilly or some place, and guys would start challenging each other. You know, a guy goes up to another guy's car and looks it up and down like it has gangrene or something, and he says: 'You wanna *go*?' Or, if it was a real grudge match for some reason, he'd say, 'You wanna go for pink slips?' The registrations on the cars were pink; in other words, the winner got the other guy's car.

"Well, as soon as a few guys had challenged each other, everybody would ride out onto this stretch of Sepulveda Boulevard or the old divided highway, in Compton, and the guys would start dragging, one car on one side of the center line, the other car on the other. Go a quarter of a mile. It was wild. Some nights there'd be a thousand kids lining the road to watch, boys and girls, all sitting on the sides of their cars with the lights shining across the highway."

But George, what happened if some ordinary motorist happened to be coming down the highway at this point?

"Oh, we'd block off the highway at each end, and if some guy wanted to get through anyway, we'd tell him, 'Well, Mister, there are going to be two cars coming down both sides of the road pretty fast in a minute, and you can go through if you want to, but you'll just have to take your best shot.'

"They always turned around, of course, and after a while the cops would come. Then you *really* saw something. Everybody jumped in their cars and took off, in every direction. Some guys would head right across a field. Of course, all our cars were so hopped up, the cops could never catch anybody.

"Then one night we got raided at the Piccadilly. It was one Friday night. The cops came in and just started loading everybody in the wagons. I was sitting in a car with a cop who was off duty—he was a hot-rodder himself—or they would have picked me up, too. Saturday night everybody came back to the Piccadilly to talk about what happened the night before, and the cops came back again and picked up three hundred fifty that night. That pretty well ended the Piccadilly."

From the very moment he was on his own in Los Angeles, when he was about eighteen, Barris never did anything but customize cars. He never took any other kind of job. At first he worked in a body shop that took him on because so many kids were coming by wanting this and that done to their cars, and the boss really didn't know how to do it, because it was all esoteric teen-age stuff. Barris was making next to nothing at first, but he never remembers feeling hard up, nor does any kid out there today I talked to. They have a magic economy or something. Anyway, in 1945 Barris opened his own shop on Compton Avenue, in Los Angeles, doing nothing but customizing. There was that much demand for it. It was no sweat, he said; pretty soon he was making better than $100 a week.

Most of the work he was doing then was modifying Detroit cars— chopping and channeling. Chopping is lowering the top of the car, bringing it nearer to the hood line. Channeling is lowering the body itself down between the wheels. Also, they'd usually strip off all the chrome and the door handles and cover up the wheel openings in the back. At that time, the look the kids liked was to have the body lowered in the back and slightly jacked up in the front, although today it's just the opposite. The front windshield in those days was divided by a post, and so chopping the top gave the car a very sinister appearance. The front windshield always looked like a couple of narrow, slitty little eyes. And I think this, more than anything else, diverted everybody from what Barris and the others were really doing. Hot-rodders had a terrible reputation at that time, and no line was ever drawn between hot-rodders and custom-car owners, because, in truth, they were speed maniacs, too.

This was Barris' chopped-and-channeled Mercury period. Mercuries were his favorite. All the kids knew the Barris styling and he was getting a lot of business. What he was really doing, in a formal sense, was trying to achieve the kind of streamlining that Detroit, for all intents and purposes, had abandoned. When modified, some of the old Mercuries were more streamlined than any standard model that Detroit has put out to this day. Many of the coupes he modified had a very sleek slope to the back window that has been picked up just this year in the "fastback" look of the Rivieras, Sting Rays, and a few other cars.

At this point Barris and the other customizers didn't really have enough capital to do many completely original cars, but they were getting more and more radical in modifying Detroit cars. They were doing things Detroit didn't do until years later—tailfins, bubble tops, twin headlights, concealed headlights, "Frenched" headlights, the low-slung body itself. They lifted some twenty designs from him alone. One, for example, is the way cars now have the exhaust pipes exit through the rear bumper or fender. Another is the bullet-shaped, or breast-shaped if you'd rather, front bumpers on the Cadillac.

Barris says "lifted," because some are exact down to the most minute details. Three years ago when he was in Detroit, Barris met a lot of car designers and, "I was amazed," he told me. "They could tell me about cars I built in 1945. They knew all about the four-door '48 Studebaker I restyled. I chopped the top and dropped the hood and it ended up a pretty good-looking car. And the bubbletop I built in 1954—they knew all about it. And all this time we thought they frowned on us."

Even today—dealing with movie stars and auto manufacturers and all sorts of people on the outside—I think Barris, and certainly the others, still feel psychologically a part of the alien teen-age netherworld in which they grew up. All that while they were carrying the torch for the Dionysian Streamline. They were America's modern baroque designers—and, oddly enough, "serious" designers, Anglo-European-steeped designers, are just coming around to it. Take Saarinen, especially in something like his T.W.A. terminal at Idlewild. The man in his last years came around to baroque modern.

It's interesting that the customizers, like sports-car fans, have always wanted cars minus most of the chrome—but for different ideals. The sports-car owner thinks chrome trim interferes with the "classic" look of his car. In other words, he wants to simplify the thing. The customizer thinks chrome interferes with something else—the luxurious baroque Streamline. The sports-car people snigger at tailfins. The customizers love them and, looked at from a baroque standard of beauty, they are really not so trashy at all. They are an inspiration, if you will, a wonderful fantasy extension of the curved line, and since the car in America is half fantasy anyway, a kind of baroque extension of the ego, you can build up a good argument for them.

Getting back to Easter Island, here were Barris and the others with their blowtorches and hard-rubber mallets, creating their baroque sculpture, cut off from the rest of the world and publicized almost solely via the teen-age grapevine. Barris was making a fairly good living, but others were starving at this thing. The pattern was always the same: a guy would open a body shop and take on enough hack collision work to pay the rent so that he could slam the door shut at 2 p.m. and get in there and do his custom jobs, and pretty soon the guy got so he couldn't even face *any* collision work. Dealing with all those crusty old arteriosclerotic bastards takes up all your *time*, man, and so they're trying to make a living doing nothing but custom work, and they are starving.

The situation is a lot like that today, except that customizing is beginning to be rationalized, in the sense Max Weber used that word. This rationalization, or efficient exploitation, began in the late Forties when an $80-a-week movie writer named Robert Petersen noticed all the kids pouring money into cars in a little world they had created for themselves, and he decided to exploit it by starting *Hot Rod Magazine*, which clicked right away and led to a whole chain of hot-rod and custom-car magazines. Petersen, by the way, now has a pot of money and drives Maseratis and other high-status-level sports cars of the Apollonian sort, not the Dionysian custom kind. Which is kind of a shame, because he has the money to commission something really incredible.

Up to that time the only custom-car show in the country was a wild event Barris used to put on bereft of any sort of midwifery by forty-two-year-old promoters with Windsor-knot ties who usually run low-cost productions. This car show was utterly within the teen-age netherworld, with no advertising or coverage of any sort. It took place each spring—during the high-school Easter vacations—when all the kids, as they still do, would converge on the beach at Balboa for their beer-drinking-Faschung rites, or whatever the Germans call it. Barris would rent the parking lot of a service station on a corner for a week, and kids from all over California would come with their customized cars. First there would be a parade; the cars, about a hundred fifty of them, would drive all through the streets of Balboa, and the kids would line the sidewalks to watch them; then they'd drive back to the lot and park and be on exhibit for the week.

Barris still goes off to Balboa and places like that. He likes that scene. Last year at Pacific Ocean Park he noticed all these bouffant babies and got the idea of spraying all those great puffed-up dandelion heads with fluorescent water colors, the same Kandy Kolors he uses on the cars. Barris took out an air gun, the girls all lined up and gave him fifty cents per, and he sprayed them with these weird, brilliant color combinations all afternoon until he ran out of colors. Each girl would go skipping and screaming away out onto the sidewalks and the beaches. Barris told me, "It was great that night to take one of the rides, like the Bubble Ride, and look down and see all those fluorescent colors. The kids were bopping [dancing] and running around."

The Bubble is a ride that swings out over the ocean. It is supposed to be like a satellite in orbit.

"But the fellows sky-diving got the best look as they came down by parachute."

In 1948 Petersen put on the first custom-car show in the Los Angeles armory, and this brought customizing out into the open a little. A wild-looking Buick Barris had remodeled was one of the hits of the show, and he was on his way, too.

At some point in the Fifties a lot of Hollywood people discovered Barris and the customizers. It was somewhat as if the literary set had discovered the puppeteer, Tony Sarg, during the Thirties and deified him in a very arty, in-groupy way, only I think in the case of Hollywood and

Barris there was something a lot more in-the-grain about it. The people who end up in Hollywood are mostly Dionysian sorts and they feel alien and resentful when confronted with the Anglo-European ethos. They're a little slow to note the difference between topsides and sneakers, but they appreciate Cuban sunglasses.

In his showroom at Kustom City, down past the XPAK-400 air car, Barris has a corner practically papered with photographs of cars he has customized or handmade for Hollywood people: Harry Karl, Jayne Mansfield, Elvis Presley, Liberace, and even celebrities from the outside like Barry Goldwater (a Jaguar with a lot of airplane-style dials on the dashboard) and quite a few others. In fact, he built most of the wild cars that show-business people come up with for publicity purposes. He did the "diamond-dust" paint job on the Bobby Darin Dream Car, which was designed and built by Andy DiDia of Detroit. That car is an example, par excellence, of baroque streamlining, by the way. It was badly panned when pictures of it were first published, mainly because it looked like Darin was again forcing his ego on the world. But as baroque modern sculpture—again, given the fantasy quotient in cars to begin with—it is pretty good stuff.

As the hot-rod and custom-car-show idea began catching on, and there are really quite a few big ones now, including one at the Coliseum up at Columbus Circle last year, it became like the culture boom in the other arts. The big names, particularly Barris and Roth but also Starbird, began to make a lot of money in the same thing Picasso has made a lot of money in: reproductions. Barris' creations are reproduced by AMT Models as model cars. Roth's are reproduced by Revel. The way people have taken to these models makes it clearer still that what we have here is no longer a car but a design object, an *objet,* as they say.

Of course, it's not an unencumbered art form like oil painting or most conventional modern sculpture. It carries a lot of mental baggage with it, plain old mechanical craftsmanship, the connotations of speed and power and the aforementioned mystique that the teen-age netherworld brings to cars. What you have is something more like sculpture in the era of Benvenuto Cellini, when sculpture was always more tied up with religion and architecture. In a lot of other ways it's like the Renaissance, too. Young customizers have come to Barris' shop, for example, like apprentices coming to the feet of the master. Barris said there were eleven young guys in Los Angeles right now who had worked for him and then gone out on their own, and he doesn't seem to begrudge them that.

"But they take on too much work," he told me. "They want a name, fast, and they take on a lot of work, which they do for practically nothing, just to get a name. They're usually undercapitalized to begin with, and they take on too much work, and then they can't deliver and they go bankrupt."

There's another side to this, too. You have the kid from the small town in the Midwest who's like the kid from Keokuk who wants to go to New York and live in the Village and be an artist and the like, he means, you know, things around home are but *hopelessly*, totally square, home and all that goes with it. Only the kid from the Midwest who wants to be a custom-car artist goes to Los Angeles to do it. He does pretty much the same thing. He lives a kind of suburban bohemian life and takes odd jobs and spends the rest of his time at the feet of somebody like Barris, working on cars.

I ran into a kid like that at Barris'. We were going through his place, back into his interiors—car interiors—department, and we came upon Ronny Camp. Ronny is twenty-two, but he looks about eighteen because he has teen-age posture. Ronny is, in fact, a bright and sensitive kid with an artistic eye, but at first glance he seems always to have his feet propped up on a table or something so you can't walk past, and you have to kind of bat them down, and he then screws up his mouth and withdraws his eyeballs to the optic chiasma and glares at you with his red sulk. That was the misleading first impression.

Ronny was crazy over automobiles and nobody in his hometown, Lafayette, Indiana, knew anything about customizing. So one day Ronny packs up and tells the folks, This is it, I'm striking out for hip territory, Los Angeles, where a customizing artist is an artist. He had no idea where he was going, you understand, all he knew was that he was going to Barris' shop and make it from there. So off he goes in his 1960 Chevrolet.

Ronny got a job at a service station and poured every spare cent into getting the car customized at Barris'. His car was right there while we were talking, a fact I was very aware of, because he never looked at me. He never took his eyes off that car. It's what is called semi-custom. Nothing has been done to it to give it a really sculptural quality, but a lot of streamlining details have been added. The main thing you notice is the color—tangerine flake. This paint—one of Barris' Kandy Kolor concoctions—makes the car look like it has been encrusted with chips of some kind of semi-precious ossified tangerine, all coated with a half-inch of clear lacquer. There used to be very scholarly and abstruse studies of color and color symbolism around the turn of the century, and theorists concluded that preferences for certain colors were closely associated with rebelliousness, and these are the very same colors many of the kids go for—purple, creosote yellow, various violets and lavenders and fuchsias and many of these Kandy Kolors.

After he got his car fixed up, Ronny made a triumphal progress back home. He won the trophy in his class at the national hot-rod and custom-car show in Indianapolis, and he came tooling into Lafayette, Indiana, and down the main street in his tangerine-flake 1960 Chevrolet. It was like Ezra Pound going back to Hamilton, New York, with his Bollingen plaque and saying, Here I am, Hamilton, New York. The way Ronny and Barris tell it, the homecoming was a big success—all the kids thought Ronny was all right, after all, and he made a big hit at home. I can't believe the part about home. I mean, I can't really believe Ronny made a hit with a tangerine-flake Chevrolet. But I like to conjecture about his parents. I don't know anything about them, really. All I know is, *I* would have had a hell of a lump in my throat if I had seen Ronny coming up to the front door in his tangerine-flake car, bursting so flush and vertical with triumph that no one would ever think of him as a child of the red sulk—Ronny, all the way back from California with his grail.

Along about 1957, Barris started hearing from the Detroit auto manufacturers.

"One day," he said, "I was working in the shop—we were over in Lynwood then—and Chuck Jordan from Cadillac walked in. He just walked in and said he was from Cadillac. I thought he meant the local agency. We had done this Cadillac for Liberace, the interior had his songs, all the notes, done in black and white Moroccan leather, and I thought he wanted to see something about that. But he said he was from the Cadillac styling center in Detroit and they were interested in our colors. Chuck'—he's up there pretty good at Cadillac now, I think—said he had read some articles about our colors, so I mixed up some samples for him. I had developed a translucent paint, using six different ingredients, and it had a lot of brilliance and depth. That was what interested them. In this paint you look through a clear surface into the color, which is very brilliant. Anyway, this was the first time we had any idea they even knew who we were."

Since then Barris has made a lot of trips to Detroit. The auto companies, mainly GM and Ford, pump him for ideas about what the kids are going for. He tells them what's wrong with their cars, mainly that they aren't streamlined and sexy enough.

"But, as they told me, they have to design a car they can sell to the farmer in Kansas as well as the hot dog in Hollywood."

For that reason—the inevitable compromise—the customizers do not dream of working as stylists for the Detroit companies, although they deal with them more and more. It would be like René Magritte or somebody going on the payroll of Continental Can to do great ideas of Western man. This is an old story in art, of course, genius vs. the organization. But the customizers don't think of corporate bureaucracy quite the way your conventional artist does, whether he be William Gropper or Larry Rivers, namely, as a lot of small-minded Babbitts, venal enemies of culture, etc. They just think of the big companies as part of that vast mass of *adult* America, sclerotic from years of just being too old, whose rules and ideas weigh down upon Youth like a vast, bloated sac. Both Barris and Roth have met Detroit's Young Stylists, and seem to look upon them as monks from another country. The Young Stylists are designers Detroit recruits from the art schools and sets up in a room with clay and styluses and tells to go to it—start carving models, dream cars, new ideas. Roth especially cannot conceive of anyone having any valid concepts about cars who hasn't come out of the teen-age netherworld. And maybe he's right. While the Young Stylists sit in a north-lit studio smoothing out little Mondrian solids, Barris and Roth carry on in the Dionysian loop-the-loop of streamlined baroque modern.

I've mentioned Ed Roth several times in the course of this without really telling you about him. And I want to, because he, more than any other of the customizers, has kept alive the spirit of alienation and rebellion that is so important to the teen-age ethos that customizing grew up in. He's also the most colorful, and the most intellectual, and the most capricious. Also the most cynical. He's the Salvador Dali of the movement—a surrealist in his designs, a showman by temperament, a prankster. Roth is really too bright to stay within the ethos, but he stays in it with a spirit of luxurious obstinacy. Any style of life is going to produce its celebrities if it sticks to its rigid standards, but in the East a talented guy would most likely be drawn into the Establishment in one way or another. That's not so inevitable in California.

I had been told that Roth was a surly guy who never bathed and was hard to get along with, but from the moment I first talked to him on the telephone he was an easy guy and very articulate. His studio—and he calls it a studio, by the way—is out in Maywood, on the other side of the city from North Hollywood, in what looked to me like a much older and more run-down section. When I walked up, Roth was out on the apron of his place doing complicated drawings and lettering on somebody's ice-cream truck with an airbrush. I knew right away it was Roth from pictures I had seen of him; he has a beatnik-style beard. "Ed Roth?" I said. He said yeah and we started talking and so forth. A little while later we were sitting in a diner having a couple of sandwiches and Roth, who was wearing a short-sleeved T-shirt, pointed to this huge tattoo on his left arm that says "Roth" in the lettering style with big serifs that he uses as his signature. "I had that done a couple of years ago because guys keep coming up to me saying, 'Are you Ed Roth?' "

Roth is a big, powerful guy, about six feet four, two hundred seventy pounds, thirty-one years old. He has a constant sort of court attendant named Dirty Doug, a skinny little guy who blew in from out of nowhere, sort of like Ronny Camp over at Barris'. Dirty Doug has a job sweeping up in a steel mill, but what he obviously lives for is the work he does around Roth's. Roth seems to have a lot of sympathy for the Ronny Camp-Dirty Doug syndrome and keeps him around as a permanent fixture. At Roth's behest, apparently, Dirty Doug has dropped his last name, Kinney, altogether, and refers to himself as Dirty Doug—not

Doug. The relationship between Roth and Dirty Doug—which is sort of Quixote and Sancho Panza, Holmes and Watson, Lone Ranger and Tonto, Raffles and his sidekick—is part of the folklore of the hot-rod and custom-car kids. It even crops up in the hot-rod comic books, which are an interesting phenomenon in themselves. Dirty Doug, in this folklore, is every rejected outcast little kid in the alien netherworld, and Roth is the understanding, if rather overly pranksterish, protective giant or Robin Hood—you know, a good-bad giant, not part of the Establishment.

Dirty Doug drove up in one of his two Cadillacs one Saturday afternoon while I was at Roth's, and he had just gone through another experience of rejection. He has two Cadillacs, he said, because one is always in the shop. Dirty Doug's cars, like most customizers', are always in the process of becoming. The streaks of "primer" paint on the Cadillac he was driving at the time had led to his rejection in Newport. He had driven to Newport for the weekend. "All the cops have to do is see paint like that and already you're 'one of those hot-rodders,' " he said. "They practically followed me down the street and gave me a ticket every twenty-five feet. I was going to stay the whole weekend, but I came on back."

At custom-car shows, kids are always asking Roth, "Where's Dirty Doug?", and if Dirty Doug couldn't make it for some reason, Roth will recruit any kid around who knows the pitch and install him as Dirty Doug, just to keep the fans happy.

Thus Roth protects the image of Dirty Doug even when the guy's not around, and I think it becomes a very important piece of mythology. The thing is, Roth is not buying the act of the National Hot Rod Association, which for its own reasons, not necessarily the kid's reasons, is trying to assimilate the hot-rod ethos into conventional America. It wants to make all the kids look like candidates for the Peace Corps or something.

The heart of the contretemps between the NHRA Establishment and Roth can be illustrated in their slightly different approach to drag racing on the streets. The Establishment tries to eliminate the practice altogether and restricts drag racing to certified drag strips and, furthermore, lets the people know about that. They encourage the hot-rod clubs to help out little old ladies whose cars are stuck in the snow and then hand them a card reading something like, "You have just been assisted by a member of the Blue Bolt Hot Rod Club, an organization of car enthusiasts dedicated to promoting safety on our highways."

Roth's motto is: "Hell, if a guy wants to go, let him *go*."

Roth's designs are utterly baroque. His air car—the Rotar—is not nearly as good a piece of design as Barris', but his beatnik Bandit is one of the great *objets* of customizing. It's a very Rabelaisian *tour de force*—a twenty-first century version of a '32 Ford hot-rod roadster. And Roth's new car, the Mysterion, which he was working on when I was out there, is another *tour de force,* this time in the hottest new concept in customizing, asymmetrical design. Asymmetrical design, I gather, has grown out of the fact that the driver sits on one side of the car, not in the middle, thereby giving a car an eccentric motif to begin with. In Roth's Mysterion—a bubbletop coupe powered by two 406-horsepower Thunderbird motors—a thick metal arm sweeps up to the left from the front bumper level, as from the six to the three on a clock, and at the top of it is an elliptical shape housing a bank of three headlights. No headlights on the right side at all; just a small clearance light to orient the oncoming driver. This big arm, by the way, comes up in a spherical geometrical arc, not a flat plane. Balancing this, as far as the design goes, is an arm that comes up over the back of the bubbletop on the right side, like from the nine to the twelve on a clock, also in a spherical arc, if you can picture all this. Anyway, this car takes the streamline and the abstract curve and baroque curvilinear one step further, and I wouldn't be surprised to see it inspiring Detroit designs in the years to come.

Roth is a brilliant designer, but as I was saying, his conduct and his attitude dilutes the Halazone with which the Establishment is trying to transfuse the whole field. For one thing, Roth, a rather thorough-going bohemian, kept turning up at the car shows in a T-shirt. That was what he wore at the big National Show at the New York Coliseum, for example. Roth also insists on sleeping in a car or station wagon while on the road, even though he is making a lot of money now and could travel first class. Things came to a head early this year when Roth was out in Terre Haute, Indiana, for a show. At night Roth would just drive his car out in a cornfield, lie back on the front seat, stick his feet out the window and go to sleep. One morning some kid came by and saw him and took a picture while Roth was still sleeping and sent it to the model company Roth has a contract with, Revel, with a note saying, "Dear Sirs: Here is a picture of the man you say on your boxes is the King of the Customizers." The way Roth tells it, it must have been an extraordinary good camera, because he says, with considerable pride, "There were a bunch of flies flying around my feet, and this picture showed all of them."

Revel asked Roth if he wouldn't sort of spruce up a little bit for the image and all that, and so Roth entered into a kind of reverse rebellion. He bought a full set of tails, silk hat, boiled shirt, cuff links, studs, the whole apparatus, for $215, also a monocle, and now he comes to all the shows like that. "I bow and kiss all the girls' hands," he told me. "The guys get pretty teed off about that, but what can they do? I'm being a perfect gentleman."

To keep things going at the shows, where he gets $1000 to $2000 per appearance—he's that much of a drawing card—Roth creates and builds one new car a year. This is the Dali pattern, too. Dali usually turns out one huge and (if that's possible any more) shocking painting each year or so and ships it on over to New York, where they install it in Carstairs or hire a hall if the thing is too big, and Dali books in at the St. Regis and appears on television wearing a rhinoceros horn on his forehead. The new car each year also keeps Roth's model-car deal going. But most of Roth's income right now is the heavy business he does in Weirdo and Monster shirts. Roth is very handy with the airbrush—has a very sure hand—and one day at a car show he got the idea of drawing a grotesque cartoon on some guy's sweat shirt with the airbrush, and that started the Weirdo shirts. The typical Weirdo shirt is in a vein of draftsmanship you might call Mad Magazine Bosch, very slickly done for something so grotesque, and will show a guy who looks like Frankenstein, the big square steam-shovel jaw and all, only he has a wacky leer on his face, at the wheel of a hot-rod roadster, and usually he has a round object up in the air in his right hand that looks like it is attached to the dashboard by a cord. This, it turns out, is the gearshift. It doesn't look like a gearshift to me, but every kid knows immediately what it is.

"Kids *love* dragging a car," Roth told me. "I mean they really love it. And what they love the most is when they shift from low to second. They get so they can practically *feel* the r.p.m.'s. They can shift without hardly hitting the clutch at all."

These shirts always have a big caption, and usually something rebellious or at least alienated, something like "MOTHER IS WRONG" or "BORN TO LOSE."

"A teen-ager always has resentment to adult authority," Roth told me. "These shirts are like a tattoo, only it's a tattoo they can take off if they want to."

I gather Roth doesn't look back on his own childhood with any great relish. Apparently his father was pretty strict and never took any abiding interest in Roth's creative flights, which were mostly in the direction of cars, like Barris'.

"You've got to be real careful when you raise a kid," Roth told me several times. "You've got to spend time with him. If he's working on something, building something, you've got to work with him." Roth's early career was almost exactly like Barris', the hot rods, the drive-ins, the drag racing, the college (East Los Angeles Junior College and UCLA), taking mechanical drawing, the chopped and channeled '32 Ford (a big favorite with all the hot-rodders), purple paint, finally the first custom shop, one stall in a ten-stall body shop.

"They threw me out of there," Roth said, "because I painted a can of Lucky Lager beer on the wall with an airbrush. I mean, it was a perfect can of Lucky Lager beer, all the details, the highlights, the seals, the small print, the whole thing. Somehow this can of Lucky Lager beer really bugged the guy who owned the place. Here was this can of Lucky Lager beer on *his* wall."

The Establishment can't take this side of Roth, just as no Establishment could accommodate Dadaists for very long. Beatniks more easily than Dadaists. The trick has always been to absorb them somehow. So far Roth has resisted absorption.

"We were the real gangsters of the hot-rod field," Roth said. "They keep telling us we have a rotten attitude. We have a different attitude, but that doesn't make us rotten."

Several times, though, Roth would chuckle over something, usually some particularly good gesture he had made, like the Lucky Lager, and say, "I am a real rotten guy."

Roth pointed out, with some insight, I think, that the kids have a revealing vocabulary. They use the words "rotten," "bad" and "tough" in a very fey, ironic way. Often a particularly baroque and sleek custom car will be called a "big, bad Merc" (for Mercury) or something like that. In this case "bad" means "good," but it also retains some of the original meaning of "bad." The kids know that to adults, like their own parents, this car is going to look sinister and somehow like an assault on their style of life. Which it is. It's rebellion, which the parents don't go for—"bad," which the kids *do* go for, "bad" meaning "good."

Roth said that Detroit is beginning to understand that there are just a hell of a lot of these bad kids in the United States and that they are growing up. "And they want a better car. They don't want an old man's car."

Roth has had pretty much the same experience as Barris with the motor companies. He has been taken to Detroit and feted and offered a job as a designer and a consultant. But he never took it seriously.

"I met a lot of the young designers," said Roth. "They were nice guys and they know a lot about design, but none of them has actually done a car. They're just up there working away on those clay models."

I think this was more than the craftsman's scorn of the designer who never actually does the work, like some of the conventional sculptors today who have never chiseled a piece of stone or cast anything. I think it was more that the young Detroit stylists came to the automobile strictly from art school and the abstract world of design—rather than via the teen-age mystique of the automobile and the teen-age ethos of rebellion. This status-group feeling is very important to Roth, and to Barris, for that matter, because it was only because of the existence of this status group—and this style of life—that custom-car sculpture developed at all.

With the Custom Car Caravan on the road—it has already reached Freedomland—the manufacturers may be well on the way to routinizing the charisma, as Max Weber used to say, which is to say bringing the whole field into a nice, safe, vinyl-glamorous marketable ball of polyethylene. It's probably already happening. The customizers will end up like those poor bastards in Haiti, the artists, who got too much, too soon, from Selden Rodman and the other folk-doters on the subject of primitive genius, so they're all down there at this moment carving African masks out of mahogany—what I mean is, they never *had* an African mask in Haiti before Selden Rodman got there.

I think Roth has a premonition that something like that is liable to happen, although it will happen to him last, if at all. I couldn't help but get a kick out of what Roth told me about his new house. We had been talking about how much money he was making, and he told me how his taxable income was only about $6200 in 1959, but might hit $15,000 this year, maybe more, and he mentioned he was building a new house for his wife and five kids down at Newport, near the beach. I immediately asked him for details, hoping to hear about an utterly baroque piece of streamlined architecture.

"No, this is going to be my wife's house, the way she wants it, nothing way out; I mean, she has to do the home scene." He has also given her a huge white Cadillac, by the way, unadorned except for his signature— "Roth"—with those big serifs, on the side. I saw the thing, it's huge, and in the back seat were his children, very sweet-looking kids, all drawing away on drawing pads.

But I think Roth was a little embarrassed that he had disappointed me on the house, because he told me his idea of the perfect house—which turned out to be a kind of ironic parable:

"This house would have this big, round living room with a dome over it, you know? Right in the middle of the living room would be a huge television set on a swivel so you could turn it and see it from wherever you are in the room. And you have this huge easy chair for yourself, you know the kind that you can lean back to about ninety-three different positions and it vibrates and massages your back and all that, and this chair is on tracks, like a railroad yard.

"You can take one track into the kitchen, which just shoots off one side of the living room, and you can ride backward if you want to and watch the television all the time, and of course in the meantime you've pressed a lot of buttons so your TV dinner is cooking in the kitchen and all you have to do is go and take it out of the oven.

"Then you can roll right back into the living room, and if somebody rings the doorbell you don't move at all. You just press a button on this big automatic console you have by your chair and the front door opens, and you just yell for the guy to come in, and you can keep watching television.

"At night, if you want to go to bed, you take another track into the bedroom, which shoots off on another side, and you just kind of roll out of the chair into the sack. On the ceiling above your bed you have another TV set, so you can watch all night."

Roth is given, apparently, to spinning out long Jean Shepherd stories like this with a very straight face, and he told me all of this very seriously.

I guess I didn't look like I was taking it very seriously, because he said, "I have a TV set over the bed in my house right now—you can ask my wife."

I met his wife, but I didn't ask her. The funny thing is, I did find myself taking the story seriously. To me it was a sort of parable of the Bad Guys, and the Custom Sculpture. The Bad Guys built themselves a little world and got onto something good and then the Establishment, all sorts of Establishments, began closing in, with a lot of cajolery, thievery and hypnosis, and in the end, thrown into a vinyl Petri dish, the only way left to tell the whole bunch of them where to head in was to draw them a huge asinine picture of themselves, which they were sure to like. After all, Roth's dream house is nothing more than his set of boiled shirt and tails expanded into a whole universe. And he is not really very hopeful about that either.

[November, 1963]

Three Letters Home from Mississippi

by Paul and Geoffrey Cowan

Under the auspices of the Council of Federated Organizations (COFO), seven hundred college students went to Mississippi this summer to help Negro residents register to vote. Two of the students were from the same family: Paul and Geoffrey Cowan. They decided to write an account of the experience to their sister, Holly, in Cambridge, Massachusetts. Here are first impressions on getting ready, traveling, and arriving in Mississippi.

Getting Ready

While I was searching for the baggage room in the Cincinnati airport, I was joined by one of my fellow passengers, a young man in a pressed corduroy suit. He offered to show me the way and while we were walking he mumbled something I could barely understand. He repeated himself: Was I, by any chance, in town for the toy convention? When I told him that I was not, he pointed to the luggage counter and set off in a different direction, presumably to attend to more important matters.

Cincinnati is a ninety-minute bus ride from Oxford, Ohio; Oxford, Ohio, is an indeterminable distance from Oxford, Mississippi. Amid the lush greenery and stylish grey-stone buildings of Western College for Women, almost two hundred college students are being trained to live in Mississippi this summer. They are also being taught how to register voters, get maximum legal protection, and act nonviolently. The National Council of Churches has arranged an orderly conference whose staff includes sociologists, dieticians, and a psychiatrist, as well as numerous ministers. But most of the training is led by members of the Student Nonviolent Co-ordinating Committee. For them the week in the Oxford sun is a summer's vacation. For the moment it's still; but no one mistakes the storm ahead.

All around the campus swarm reporters and photographers. Claude Sitton is here from The New York *Times;* Karl Fleming from *Newsweek;* Mrs. Homer Bigart from CBS; Dick Cunningham from The Minneapolis Morning *Tribune;* Nick von Hoffman from The Chicago *Daily News.* They are not here to watch the SNCC staff: as COFO director Bob Moses said in a speech the first morning, the press is interested in the students, not the staff, and not the people of Mississippi. Naturally the reporters all ask us the same question: Why are you here? Von Hoffman, prying human interest, wanted to interview me because he had heard that I had relatives in Chicago. He told me that the SNCC press office had boasted that my father was once president of CBS. The group of students also includes a Bingham, a Bundy, and a Schlesinger. There are sixty students in the project from the Boston area, and more than eighty from California. *Look* magazine is searching for the ideal naïve Northern middle-class white girl. For the national press, that's the big story. And when one of us gets killed, the story will be even bigger.

But the big story out of Mississippi this summer ought not to be about my participation in the movement, or even my death. The big story ought to be Life in Mississippi. If that life is ugly, then its creators must be villains, and those who endure must be beautiful. In his penetrating book about poverty, Michael Harrington describes the Other America as an invisible world which no one sees. When James Agee investigated a fragment of that world twenty-five years ago, his book sold fewer than two thousand copies. The purpose of this summer's program is to spotlight oppressed Mississippi; if Northern college students dominate the spotlight, the project, in large measure, will have failed.

In these letters, therefore, I plan to describe Mississippi. No doubt my reactions will figure prominently in the picture I snap, but the protagonists should be native Mississippians and the way they live now. To me, that is a more important story than my version of a bombing or a beating or a cross burning—it is the larger story of which the other incidents are only a part.

I have been assigned to a group of twenty-five voter-registration workers who will help organize Northern Mississippi. On Wednesday afternoon we will leave Oxford for Holly Springs, a small town with a local registration movement and a cooperative Negro Methodist college. From there, some of us will travel a few miles south to Batesville (the county seat of Panola County where an unprecedented decision by the 5th Circuit Court has forbidden registrars to ask questions of constitutional interpretation as a test of literacy). Already the seminars have given me a sense of Negro life in the upper Delta. By next week I should know it at firsthand.

Geoff

On The Bus

We are now traveling through Kentucky, a busload of forty students sleeping, reading, talking, singing—moving toward Mississippi through the American night. Right now no one seems visibly tense. I suppose the difficulty of our task, so often discussed, so terribly shown during this past week, will once again sober us as soon as we reach Mississippi. When we get there we are supposed to leave this chartered bus and proceed toward our destination by public transportation, in smaller groups.

This week at Oxford was incredibly intense. Always there was our fear for Mickey, James, and Andy—"I didn't even know them," lamented Jimmy Travis, a twenty-one-year-old Mississippi Negro who was machine-gunned through the neck and nearly killed one night a year ago. "I never saw my brothers' faces, and I feel sick about it. I'd rather be lost, instead of them, than feel sick like this." We all mourned those three men whose faces we never knew. One friend of mine, who had never before been religious, attended a service to pray that they might be alive. "I like to think that if the same thing happened to me, people would come to my service," he said.

As the week progressed, impelling us toward the unknown, a sense of kinship developed which embraced us all. But we still had many facts to learn and many ideas to clarify. There were new friendships, and a newly evolving context in which they would flourish. Most important, there was the intensifying pressure of our own departure, and the decision—constantly stressed by the COFO staff—that each of us had to make: Did we really feel that we wanted to go to Mississippi, in the face of the danger that had by now become impossible to ignore?

Last night Bob Moses spoke to us in a final session before our departure. I can't think of another leader who can talk so directly and so personally to everyone involved with him. The great thing about Moses is his humility—at meetings, unless he has something to say, he sits quietly toward the back of the auditorium, as part of the audience. Right now he is in the bus, riding as uncomfortably as any of us.

When Bob talks, his sentences come slowly, punctuated by long, thoughtful pauses. He uses no rhetoric and always speaks briefly. His face expresses eloquently the tension we all feel even while it reaffirms his—and our—belief in the job we have to do.

There is no way during this bumpy journey South (with three volunteers in front of me singing *Try to Remember* from *The Fantasticks*) to convey the mixture of fear and dedication we all felt last night as Bob spoke. I hesitate to quote his words directly for fear that, in getting them slightly wrong, I'll depart even further from the atmosphere of that still auditorium tucked away in Oxford, Ohio, containing the bravest group of people I have ever met.

He talked about how, when you spend all your time fighting evil, you become preoccupied with it and terribly weary. When your work causes other men to die, then you are forced to wonder about it—you raise terrible questions inside yourself. But in history no dominant group has ever been *privileged* (that was the word Moses used) without demanding that the oppressed render its sacrifices. There may be more people killed this summer, but that won't in any way deter us from what we are trying to do. Negroes who have challenged authorities in Mississippi have always been harassed or killed—and we're trying to change that, not succumb to it. We're going to do the job we have to do.

Then, Bob talked directly to the freedom-school teachers. He begged them to be patient with their students. There's a difference between being slow and being stupid, he said. The people you will be working with aren't stupid. But they're slow, so slow.

He finished, stood for a minute, then walked out the door. Inside the auditorium there was total silence, a willing silence. Finally, from far in the back, a single voice started to sing: "They say that freedom is a constant sorrow." Soon the rest of us joined in.

Now it is one o'clock and our bus, inconsequential to whoever observes it, is traveling down a Tennessee road, far into the country. I have always thought that between the hours of one and three a.m. America comes closest to realizing her promise. There is a true unity between all her travelers sharing, for the particular night, a lonely vigil, a personal responsibility for their land.

But it was at this hour six days ago that Mickey, James and Andy disappeared on the frontier of Mississippi. And it was Americans who apparently captured them, men who speak the same language, sing the same anthem, fight in the same wars as those of us on this bus. We all inhabit the same night in the same land, but somehow that is not enough.

Paul

Batesville

Home is now Batesville, Mississippi, and has been since noon yesterday. I live in the maze of dirt streets and pleasant houses which white folks might call nigger town; it is an area as isolated as Harlem—white faces are a striking rarity—but relatively as close to the business district as the black ghetto is to Park Avenue. All the citizens of Batesville carry on their commerce in a centrally located village, a square of storefronts, surrounding a fire station and a depot rather than a park.

The drugstore is practically the only commercial enterprise in the Negro section of town (there is also a beauty parlor, a café, and a gas station or two). The store is the hangout. It is a large, dimly lit soda shoppe with benches and a counter. For Cambridge residents I might describe it as a cross between the University Restaurant and the *Crimson*. Kids and adults alike gossip or talk of sports and politics. The management are our allies. Folks who come by there know why we're in town, and they're anxious to help.

The voter-registration project in Batesville predates COFO and even SNCC. I'm told that it began some twenty years ago when a local minister got so fed up with conditions that he conducted a series of literacy classes which were so successful that some whites started to come. However, no one (except a few Toms) got registered, and in 1960 ten prominent citizens formed an active Voters' League to fight for their vote. Naturally, they repeatedly failed the literacy test; finally they filed a suit against the county registrar. As witnesses they subpoenaed several highly literate Negroes who had been denied the vote, and a few illiterate registered whites. The 5th Circuit Court was persuaded that the tests were unfair. On May 28, 1964, the judges enjoined the registrar from asking voters to interpret a section of the Mississippi Constitution. Last month there were thirty registered Negro voters in Panola County; today there are more than three hundred. The county has more than seven thousand eligible Negro voters; we hope to register the bulk of them this summer.

It is difficult to describe the support that one feels in the Negro section of Batesville. Partly as a tactic and partly as a reflex, COFO workers constantly wave hello to all of Batesville's Negroes, and the Negroes respond in kind. For me the gesture has already become one of kinship. It means a lot; it means howdy; it means I'm fine; it means good luck; it means I'm with you; it means we're all in this thing together. Before coming to Mississippi, we had been told that whites considered all civil-rights workers not only "nigger lovers," but white Negroes as well. We had also been told that in the colored community you may soon be considered black. In one sense we have crossed the color barrier, especially in Batesville where the Voters' League is a going enterprise. Yesterday afternoon I canvassed H— Road with George, a jovial local Negro who knows virtually everyone in the county. We went to the two-room home of an old, thin crippled woman, and sat with her awhile, talking about politics, local road conditions, and medical care. Before we left, she asked me a strange question: she wondered what nation I came from. I asked her whether my accent sounded peculiar; she said that it did not, and I let the matter stand.

Some other Negroes talk freely about fear—fear of The Man, fear of Mr. Charlie. Occasionally theirs is the irrational fear of something new and untested. But usually it is a highly rational emotion, the economic fear of losing your job, the physical fear of being shot at. These people live in Mississippi. Public-school teachers know that they will be fired if they register to vote; so will domestic servants, so will factory workers, so will Negroes who live on plantations. In Mississippi, registration is no private affair—every week a list of newly registered voters is printed in the local newspaper. It is not difficult to tell the white and Negro names apart. The white names are dignified by the prefix Mr. or Mrs. or Miss. Sometimes you feel you're getting there when a woman tells you about her fears and tells how she lies to the white folks but secretly hates them. She has probably never talked like this to a white man before; for a moment you believe you are turning black.

But a white man never turns black in Mississippi. There are still the long silences and the incomprehensible phrases. Women still call you Mr. Geoff instead of Geoff, and old men offer their chairs. That doesn't disappear when they start to talk about fear. And neither does your secret belief—which the old men and women encourage—that you are, after all, superior. When talking to an illiterate, the line between environment and heredity is emotionally invisible. Maybe this will all change when you've been here longer and when you visit a family for the fifth time. Maybe; but you're still college educated, still play-acting, and still white. You're still amused when in sorting out books for the Freedom Library one Negro worker insists on discarding *Black Beauty* and a young local dark girl parades about with her recently discovered copy of *Pride and Prejudice*. It helps only slightly when you watch one of your fellow white volunteers throw away a copy of *Nigger of the Narcissus*. Following a marvelous dinner at the house of your local landlord, there is little you can do but grind your teeth when you hear yourself say, "Boy, was that a great dinner." Involuntarily, you both choke on the expletive. You're still white.

I could already venture a few portraits; one would be of the courageous wealthy Negro farmer who has almost single-handedly organized Panola County; another of my host, a still wealthier Negro farmer whose four-year-old great-grandchild lives in the house with us; a third of George, the happy, unemployed twenty-year-old, through whose loving eyes I am learning to see his world.   Geoff

[September, 1964]

Turning On the World

by Timothy Leary

By the Fall of 1960 there was in existence an informal international network of scientists and scholars who had taken the psychedelic trip and who foresaw the powerful effect that the new alkaloids would have on human culture. The members of this group differed in age and temperament, and had varying ideas about tactics, but the basic vision was common to all—we believed these wondrous plants and drugs could free man's consciousness and bring about a new conception of man, his psychology and philosophy.

There was Albert Hofmann, who had invented LSD, who dreamed the utopian dream, but who was limited by the cautious politics of Sandoz Pharmaceuticals. What a frustrating web his genius had woven for Sandoz. How could a medical-drug house make a profit on a revelation pill?

Sandoz knew they had patented the most powerful mind-changing substance known to man. They expected to make millions when the psychiatric profession learned how to use LSD, and they were continually disappointed to discover that human society didn't want to have its mind changed, didn't want to touch a love-ecstasy potion.

In 1960 a top executive of Sandoz leaned across the conference table and said jokingly to me, LSD isn't a drug at all. It's a food. Let's bottle it in Coca-Cola and let the world have it. And his legal counsel frowned and said that foods still come under the jurisdiction of the Food and Drug Administration.

By 1966, when LSD was crowding Vietnam for the headlines, officials of Sandoz Pharmaceuticals were groaning, We wish we had never heard of LSD.

I do really wish to destroy it! cried Frodo. Or well, to have it destroyed. I am not made for perilous quests. I wish I had never seen the Ring! Why did it come to me? Why was I chosen? —The Lord of The Rings

There were the detached philosophers—Aldous Huxley, Father Murray, Gerald Heard, Alan Watts, Harry Murray, Robert Gordon Wasson—who knew that the new drugs were reintroducing the platonic-gnostic vision. These men had read their theological history and understood both the glorious possibility and the angered reaction of the priestly establishment. They were not activists but sage observers.

Then there were the turned-on doctors—psychiatrists who had taken the trip, and came back hoping to fit the new potions into the medical game. Humphrey Osmond, witty, wise, cultured, had invented the name psychedelic and tolerantly wondered how to introduce a harmony-ecstasy drug into an aggressive-puritanical social order. Sidney Cohen, Keith Ditman, Jim Watt, Abram Hoffer and Nick Chewelos hoped to bring about a psychiatric renaissance and a new era of mental health with the new alchemicals.

And there was that strange, intriguing, delightful cosmic magician called Al Meyner, the rum-drinking, swashbuckling, Roman Catholic frontier salesman who promoted uranium ore during the Forties and who took the trip and recognized that LSD was the fissionable material of the mind and who turned on Osmond and Hoffer to the religious mystical meaning of their psychotomimetic drug. Al Meyner set out to turn on the world and flew from country to country with his leather bag full of drugs, claiming to have turned on bishops and obtained *nihil obstat* from Pope John. When the medical society complained that only doctors could give drugs, Meyner bought himself a doctor's degree from a Kentucky diploma mill and swept through northern California turning on scientists and professors and God seekers.

Right from the beginning this dedicated group of ring bearers was rent with a basic disagreement. There were those who said work within the system. Society has assigned the administration of drugs to the medical profession. Any non-doctor who gives or takes drugs is a dope fiend. Play ball with the system. Medicine must be the vanguard of the psychedelic movement. Any nonmedical use of psychedelic drugs would create a new marijuana mess and set back research into the new utopia.

The medical point of view made little sense to religious philosophers. Aldous Huxley called the psychedelic experience a gratuitous grace. His vibrant flame-colored wife, Laura, agreed. So, in gentle tones, did Huston Smith and Alan Watts and Gerald Heard.

And so did Allen Ginsberg, who had discovered the Buddha nature of drugs along with other writers.

I had been visited by most of the psychedelic eminences by this time and was under steady pressure to make the Harvard psychedelic research a kosher-medically-approved project. Everyone was aware of the potency of Harvard's name. Timothy, you are the key figure, said Dr. Al Meyner; I'm just old deputy-dog Al at your service. But the message was clear: Keep it respectable and medical.

And now here was Allen Ginsberg, the secretary-general of the world's poets, beatniks, anarchists, socialists, free-sex/love cultists.

November 26, 1960, the sunny Sunday afternoon that we gave Allen Ginsberg the mushrooms, started slowly. First in the cycle of breakfasts at noon were my son Jack Leary and his friend Bobbie, who had spent the night. Bobbie went off to Mass. When I came down I found Donald, an uninvited raccoon hipster-painter from New York, solemnly squatting at the table gnawing at toast and bacon. Frank Barron, who was visiting, and the poets, Allen Ginsberg and Peter and Lafcadio Orlovsky, remained upstairs and we moved around the kitchen with that Sunday-morning hush, not wanting to wake the sleepers. Lafcadio, Peter's brother, was on leave from a hospital.

About twelve-thirty the quiet exploded into family noise. Bobbie was back from church where he had excitedly told his father about the party we had given the night before for the Harvard football team and how I had given the boys, Bobbie and Jack, a dollar each for being bartenders.

I toted up the political profit and loss from this development. The Harvard football team rang up a sale. But the boys bartending? Bobbie's father is Irish so that's all right. All okay.

Then wham, the door opened and in flooded Susan Leary, my daughter, with three teen-age girls, through the kitchen, upstairs to get clothes, down to make a picnic lunch, up again for records, out, and then back for the ginger ale.

By now the noise had filtered upstairs and we could hear the late sleepers moving around and the bathroom waters running, and down came Frank Barron, half-a ake, to fry codfish cakes for his breakfast. And then, Allen Ginsberg and Peter. Allen hopped around the room with nearsighted crow motions cooking eggs, and Peter sat silent, watching.

Afterward the poets fell to reading The *Times* and Frank moved upstairs to Susan's room to watch a pro football game on TV. I told Allen to make himself at home and got beers and went up to join Frank. Donald the painter had been padding softly around the house watching with his big, soft creature eyes and sniffing in corners and at the bookcase and the record cabinets. He had asked to take mushrooms in the evening and was looking for records of Indian peyote drum music.

At dusk, Allen Ginsberg, hunched over a teacup, peering out through his black-rimmed glasses, the left lens bisected by a break, started telling of his experiences with ayahuasco, the fabled visionary vine of the Peruvian jungles. He had followed the quest of Bill Burroughs, sailing south for new realms of consciousness, looking for the elixir of wisdom. Sitting, sweating with heat, lonely in a cheap hotel in Lima, holding a wad of ether-soaked cotton to his nose with his left hand and getting high and making poetry with his right hand, and then traveling by second-class bus with Indians up through the Cordillera de los Andes and then more buses and hitchhiking into the Montaña jungles and shining rivers, wandering through steaming equatorial forests. Then the village Pucallpa, and the negotiations to find the *curandero* [guide], paying him with *aguardiente,* and the ritual itself, swallowing the bitter stuff, and the nausea and the colors and the drums beating and sinking down into thingless void, into the great eye that brings it all together, and the terror of the great snake coming. The old *curandero,* wrinkled face bending over him and Allen telling him, *culebra,* and the *curandero* nodding clinically and blowing a puff of smoke to make the great snake disappear and it did.

The fate of fire depends on wood; as long as there is wood below, the fire burns above. It is the same in human life; there is in man likewise a fate that lends power to his life. —I Ching

I kept asking Allen questions about the *curandero.* I wanted to learn the rituals, to find out how other cultures (older and wiser than ours) had handled the visionary business. I was fascinated by the ritual thing. Ritual is to the science of consciousness what experiment is to external science. I was convinced that none of our American rituals fit the mushroom experience. Not the cocktail party. Not the psychiatrist. Not the teacher-minister role. I was impressed by what Allen said about his own fear and sickness whenever he took drugs and about the solace and comforting strength of the *curandero,* about how good it was to have someone there who knew, who had been to those far regions of the mind and could tell you by a look, by a touch, by a puff of smoke that it was all right, go ahead, explore the strange world, it's all right, you'll come back, it's all right, I'm here back on familiar old human earth when you need me, to bring you back.

Allen was going to take the mushrooms later that night and he was shaping me up to help him. Allen was weaving a word spell, dark eyes gleaming through the glasses, chain-smoking, moving his hands, intense, chanting trance poetry. Frank Barron was in the study now, and with him Lafcadio Orlovsky.

A car came up the driveway and in a minute the door opened, and Donald, furry and moist, ambled in. He had brought his friend, an anthropology student from Harvard, to be with him when he tripped. Donald asked if his friend could be there during the mushroom session. I liked the idea of having a friend present for the mushrooms, someone to whom you could turn at those moments when you needed support, so I said, Sure, but he couldn't take the pills because he was a university student. Everyone was warning us to keep our research away from Harvard to avoid complications with the university health bureau and to avoid the rumors. He wasn't hungry so I mixed him a drink and then I got the little round bottle and pulled out the cotton topping and gave Donald 30 mg. and Allen Ginsberg 36.

Allen started bustling around getting his cave ready. I brought Susan's record player up to his room and he took some Beethoven and Wagner from the study and he turned out the lights so that there was just a glow in the room. I told him we'd be checking back every fifteen minutes and he should tell me if he wanted anything.

By the time I got downstairs Donald was already high, strolling around the house on dainty raccoon feet with his hands clasped behind his back, thinking and digging deep things. I stayed in the study writing letters, reading The *Times*. I had forgotten about the anthropology student. He was waiting in the kitchen.

After about thirty minutes I found Donald in the hallway. He called me over earnestly and began talking about the artificiality of civilization. He was thinking hard about basic issues and it was obvious what was going on with him—clearing his mind of abstractions, trying to get back behind the words and concepts.

And if he succeeds in assigning the right place to life and to fate, thus bringing the two into harmony, he puts his fate on a firm footing. These words contain hints about the fostering of life as handed on by oral tradition in the secret teachings of Chinese yoga. —I Ching

The anthropology student was standing by, watching curiously, and Donald asked if he minded leaving so that he could talk to me privately. Anthro went back to the kitchen and Donald continued talking about the falseness of houses and machines and deploring the way man cut himself off from the vital stuff with his engines and structures. I was trying to be polite and be a good *curandero* and support him and tell him, great boy, stay with it and work it out.

Susan came back from her friends' about this time and went upstairs to her homework, and I followed her up to check on Allen. He was lying on top of the blanket. His glasses were off and his black eyes, pupils completely dilated, looked up at me. Looking down into them they seemed like two deep, black, wet wells and you could look down them way through the man Ginsberg to something human beyond. The eye is such a defenseless, naïve, trusting thing. PROFESSOR LEARY CAME INTO MY ROOM, LOOKED IN MY EYES, AND SAID I WAS A GREAT MAN. THAT DETERMINED ME TO MAKE AN EFFORT TO LIVE HERE AND NOW.   —Allen Ginsberg

Allen was scared and unhappy and sick. And still he was lying there voluntarily, patiently searching, pushing himself into panics and fears, into nausea, trying to learn something, trying to find meaning. Shamelessly weak and shamelessly human and greatly classic. Peter was lying next to him, eyes closed, sleeping or listening to the record. I GOT NAUSEOUS SOON AFTER—SAT UP IN BED NAKED AND SWALLOWED DOWN THE VOMIT THAT BE-SIEGED FROM MY STOMACH AS IF AN INDEPENDENT BEING DOWN THERE WAS REBELLING AT BEING DRAGGED INTO EXISTENCE.

On the way downstairs I checked Susan's room. She was curled up on the carpet, with her books scattered around her and reading in the shadows. I scolded her about ruining her eyes and flicked on the two wall bulbs. Downstairs Frank was still at the study desk. Anthro was wandering in the living room and told me that Donald had gone outside. The rule we had set up was that no one would leave the house and the idea of Donald padding down Beacon Street in a mystic state chilled me. Out on the front porch I turned on the two rows of spotlights that flooded the long winding stone stairs and started down, shielding my eyes and shouting Donald. Halfway down I heard him answering back and saw him standing under an oak tree on the lower lawn. I asked him how he was, but he didn't talk, just stood there looking wise and deep. He was barefoot and higher than Piccard's balloon. I want to talk to you, but first you must take off your shoes. Okay, why not? I sat down to unlace my shoes and he squatted alongside and told about how the machines complicate our lives and how cold and hot were abstractions and how we didn't really need houses and shoes and clothes because it was just our concepts that made us think we needed these things. I agreed with him and followed what his mind was doing, suspending for a moment the clutch of the abstract but at the same time shivering from the November wind and wanting to get back behind the warm glow of the windows.

The young anthropology student was standing in the hallway. I told him that Donald was doing fine, great mystical stuff, philosophizing without concepts. He looked puzzled. He didn't want a drink or food. I walked upstairs and found the door to Allen's room closed. I waited for a while, not knowing what to do and then knocked softly and said softly, Allen I'm here now and will be back in a few minutes. *Paradise Lost,* A BOOK I'D NEVER UNDERSTOOD BEFORE—WHY MILTON SIDED WITH LUCIFER THE REBEL IN HEAVEN.

I GOT UP OUT OF BED AND WALKED DOWNSTAIRS NAKED, ORLOVSKY FOLLOWING ME, CURIOUS WHAT I WOULD DO AND WILLING TO GO ALONG

IN CASE I DID ANYTHING INTERESTINGLY EXTRAVAGANT. URGING ME ON IN FACT, THANK GOD.

Susan was sitting cross-legged on her bed brushing her hair when there came a patter of bare feet on the hallway carpet. I got to the door just in time to see naked buttocks disappearing down the stairway. It was Peter. I was grinning when I went back to see Susan. Peter is running around without any clothes on. Susan picked up her paraphernalia—curlers, brush, pins, and trotted up to the third floor. I headed downstairs.

When I got to the study Frank was leaning back in his chair behind the desk, grinning quizzically. In front of the desk looking like medieval hermits were Allen and Peter, both stark naked. I WENT IN AMONG THE PSYCHOLOGISTS IN STUDY AND SAW THEY TOO WERE WAITING FOR SOME-THING VAST TO HAPPEN ONLY IT REQUIRED SOMEONE AND THE MOMENT TO MAKE IT HAPPEN—ACTION, REVOLUTION. No, Allen had on his glasses and as I came in he peered out at me and raised his finger in the air. Hey, Allen, what goes on? Allen had a holy gleam in his eye and he waved his finger. I'm the Messiah. I've come down to preach love to the world. We're going to walk through the streets and teach people to stop hating. I DECIDED I MIGHT AS WELL BE THE ONE TO DO SO—PRONOUNCED MY NAKEDNESS AS THE FIRST ACT OF REVOLUTION AGAINST THE DESTROYERS OF THE HUMAN IMAGE.

Well, Allen, that sounds like a pretty good idea. Listen, said Allen, do you believe that I'm the Messiah. THE NAKED BODY BEING THE HIDDEN SIGN. Look, I can prove it. I'm going to cure your hearing. Take off your hearing machine. Your ears are cured. Come on, take it off, you don't need it. AND GRABBED THE TELEPHONE TO COMMUNICATE MY DECISION—WANTED TO HOOK UP KHRUSHCHEV, KEROUAC, BURROUGHS, IKE, KENNEDY, MAO TSE-TUNG, MAILER, ETC.

Frank was still smiling. Peter was standing by, watching seriously. The hearing aid was dumped on the desk. That's right. And now your glasses, I'll heal your vision too. The glasses were laid on the desk too. ALL IN ONE TELEPHONE LINE AND GET THEM ALL TO COME IMMEDIATELY TO HAR-VARD TO HAVE SPECTRAL CONFERENCE OVER THE FUTURE OF THE UNI-VERSE.

Allen was peering around with approval at his healing. But Allen, one thing. What? Your glasses. You're still wearing them. Why don't you cure your own vision. Allen looked surprised. Yes, you're right. I will. He took off his glasses and laid them on the desk.

Now Allen was a blind Messiah squinting around to find his followers. Come on. We're going down to the city streets to tell the people about peace and love. And then we'll get lots of great people onto a big telephone network to settle all this warfare bit.

Fine, said Frank, but why not do the telephone bit first, right here in the house. Frank was heading off the pilgrimage down the avenue naked.

Who we gonna call, said Peter. Well, we'll call Kerouac on Long Island, and Kennedy and Khrushchev and Bill Burroughs in Paris and Norman

Mailer in the psycho ward in Bellevue. We'll get them all hooked up in a big cosmic electronic love talk. War is just a hang-up. We'll get the love-thing flowing on the electric Bell Telephone network. Who we gonna call first, said Peter. Let's start with Khrushchev, said Allen.

Look, why don't we start with Kerouac on Long Island. In the meantime, let's pull the curtains, said Frank. There's enough going on in here so I don't care about looking outside. Allen picked up the white telephone and dialed Operator. The two thin figures leaned forward wrapped up in a holy fervor trying to spread peace. The dear noble innocent helplessness of the naked body. They looked as though they had stepped out of a quattrocento canvas, apostles, martyrs, dear fanatic holy men. Allen said, Hello, operator, this is God, I want to talk to Kerouac. To whom do I want to talk? Kerouac. What's my name? This is God. G-O-D. Okay. We'll try Capitol 7-0563. Where? Northport, Long Island. There was a pause. We were all listening hard. Oh. Yes. That's right. That's the number of the house where I was born. Look, operator, I'll have to go upstairs to get the number. Then I'll call back.

Allen hung up the receiver. What was all that about, Allen? Well, the operator asked me my name and I said I was God and I wanted to speak to Kerouac and she said, I'll try to do my best, sir, but you'll have to give me his number and then I gave her the number of my mother's house. I've got Kerouac's number upstairs in my book. Just a minute and I'll get it.

Back at the phone, Allen was shouting to Jack. He wanted Jack to come up to Cambridge and then he wanted Jack's mother to come too. Jack had a lot to say because Allen held the phone, listening for long spaces. Frank was still sitting behind the desk smiling. Donald and the anthro student were standing in the hallway looking in curiously. I walked over to explain. Allen says he is the Messiah and he's calling Kerouac to start a peace and love movement. Donald wasn't interested. He went on telling me about the foolishness of believing in hot and cold. It occurred to me that Allen and Peter were proving his point. The phone call continued and finally I walked back in and said, Hey, Allen, for the cost of this phone call we could pay his way up here by plane. Allen shot an apologetic look and then I heard him telling Jack, Okay, Jack, I have to go now, but you've got to take the mushrooms and let's settle this quarrel between Kennedy and Khrushchev. BUT NEEDED MY GLASSES—THOUGH HAD YELLED AT LEARY THAT HE DIDN'T NEED HIS EARPIECE TO HEAR THE REAL VIBRATIONS OF THE COSMOS. HE WENT ALONG WITH ME AGREEABLY.

Allen and Peter were sitting on the big couch in the living room and Allen was telling us about his visions, cosmic electronic networks, and how much it meant to him that I told him he was a great man and how this mushroom episode had opened the door to women and heterosexuality and how he could see new womanly body visions and family life ahead. BUT THEN I BEGAN BREATHING AND WANTING TO LIE DOWN AND REST.

Peter's hand was moving back and forth on Allen's shoulder. It was the first time that Allen had stood up to Jack and he was sorry about the phone bill but wasn't it too bad that Khrushchev and Kennedy couldn't have been on the line and, hey, what about Norman Mailer in that psychiatric ward in Bellevue, shouldn't we call him.

I don't think they'd let a call go through to him, Allen. Well, it all depends on how we come on. I don't think coming on as Allen Ginsberg would help in that league. I don't think coming on as the Messiah would either. Well, you could come on as big psychologists and make big demanding noises about the patient. It was finally decided that it was too much trouble.

Still *curandero,* I asked if they wanted anything to eat or drink. Well, how about some hot milk. IF I ATE OR SHIT AGAIN I WOULD TURN BACK TO MERE NON-MESSIAH HUMAN. Allen and Peter went upstairs to put on robes and I put some cold milk in a pan and turned on the stove. Donald was still moving around softly with his hands behind his back. Thinking. Watching. He was too deep and Buddha for us to swing with and I later realized that I hadn't been a very attentive *curandero* for him and that there was a gulf between Allen and him never closed and that the geographic arrangement was too scattered to make a close loving session. Of course, both of them were old drug hands and ready to go off on their own private journeys and both wanted to make something deep and their own.

Anthro's role in all of this was never clear. He stood in the hallway watching curiously but for the most part we ignored him, treated him as an object just there but not involved and that, of course, was a mistake. Any time you treat someone as an object rest assured he'll do the same and that was the way that score was going to be tallied.

We ended up with a great scene in the kitchen. I bustled around pouring the hot milk into cups, and the poets sat around the table looking like Giotto martyrs in checkered robes. Lafcadio came down and we got him some food and he nodded yes when I asked him about ice cream and Allen started to talk about his visions and about the drug scene in New York and, becoming eloquent, wound up preaching with passion about the junkies, helpless, hooked, lost, thin, confused creatures, sick and the police and the informers. I SAW THE BEST MINDS OF MY GENERATION DESTROYED BY MADNESS, STARVING HYSTERICAL NAKED, DRAGGING THEM-SELVES THROUGH THE NEGRO STREETS AT DAWN LOOKING FOR AN ANGRY FIX. And then we started planning the psychedelic revolution. Allen wanted everyone to have the mushrooms. Who has the right to keep them from some-one else? And there should be freedom for all sorts of rituals, too. The doctors could have them and there should be *curanderos,* and all sorts of good new holy rituals that could be developed and ministers have to be involved. Although the church is naturally and automatically opposed to mushroom visions, still the experience is basically religious and some ministers would see it and start using them. But with all these groups and organizations and new rituals, there still had to be room for the single, lone, unattached, non-groupy individual to take the mushrooms and go off and follow his own rituals—brood big cosmic thoughts by the sea or roam through the streets of New York, high and restless, thinking poetry, and writers and poets and artists to work out whatever they were working out.

Allen Ginsberg hunched over the kitchen table, shabby robe hiding his thin white nakedness, cosmic politician. Give them the mystic vision. They'll see it's good and honest and they'll say so publicly and then no one from the police or the narcotics bureau can put them down. And you're the perfect persons to do it. Big serious scientist professors from Harvard. That's right. I can't do it. I'm too easy to put down. Crazy beatnik poet. Let me get my address book. I've got lots of connections in New York and we'll go right down the list and turn them all on.

Now Allen Ginsberg, stooping over the kitchen table peering at his address book. There's Robert Lowell and Muriel Rukeyser, and LeRoi Jones. And Dizzy Gillespie. And the painters. And the publishers. He was chanting out names of the famous and the talented. He was completely serious, dedicated, wound up in the crusade. I'M NEARSIGHTED AND PSY-CHOPATHIC ANYWAY. AMERICA, I'M PUTTING MY QUEER SHOULDER TO THE WHEEL.

And so Allen spun out the cosmic campaign. He was to line up influentials and each weekend I would come down to New York and we'd run mushroom sessions. This fit our Harvard research plans perfectly. Our aim there was to learn how people reacted, to test the limits of the drug, to get creative and thoughtful people to take them and tell us what they saw and what we should do with the mushrooms. Allen's political plan was appealing, too. I had seen enough and read enough in Spanish of the anti-vision crowd, the power-holders with guns, and the bigger and better men we got on our team the stronger our position. And then, too, the big-name bit was intriguing. Meeting and sharing visions with the famous.

It was around midnight. Donald still seemed high and would walk in and out of the room, silently, hands behind his back, Talmudic raccoon, studying the kitchen crowd seriously, and then padding out. The anthropology student had joined us around the table. We had given him something to drink and he was listening to the conversation and saying nothing. He made some comment about schedules back to Cambridge and it was time for him to make the last train, so I drove him down to the station. He asked some questions about the scientific meaning of the mushroom research and it was clear that he didn't understand what had happened and what we were doing. There wasn't time to explain and I felt badly that he had been dragged into a strange situation. We had made the rule that people could bring their friends when they took the mushrooms and this seemed like a good idea for the person taking the mushrooms but it was just beginning to dawn on me that the problem never was with the person taking the drug but rather the people who didn't. Like Brother Toriblo, the Spanish monk, who talked about cruelty and drunkenness caused by the Sacred Mushrooms. It's okay to bring a friend, but he should take the mushrooms with you. And poor Anthro, it turned out, wasn't even a friend of Donald's and as it turned out didn't like him and was clearly bewildered by and critical of what he had seen and heard and the nakedness of the poets. His train was about due and I was too preoccupied by what Allen had been saying to feel like explaining to Anthro. The uneasy feeling persisted and I suggested that he not tell people about the mystic visions and the naked crusaders because this might be misunderstood and he said he wouldn't talk about it and we shook hands and he left.

That was Sunday night. By Monday afternoon the rumors were spreading around Harvard Yard.

Beatniks. Orgies. Naked poets. Junkies. Homosexuality. Drug parties. Tried to lure a decent naïve graduate student into sin. Wild parties masquerading as research. Queers. Beards. Criminal types.

The chairman of my department called me. What the hell is going on, Tim? Two graduate students have come to me indignant—demanding that your work be stopped.

I laughed. I'll send you the reports from the session as soon as they are typed. It was a good session. God would approve. We're learning a lot.

The disapproving gaze of the establishment was on us. You should fear the wary eyes of the servants of Sauron were the words of Elrond. I do not doubt that news . . . has already reached him, and he will be filled with wrath.
—The Lord of The Rings

In the months that followed we began to see ourselves as unwitting agents of a social process that was far too powerful for us to control or more than dimly understand. A historical movement that would inevitably change man at the very center of his nature, his consciousness.

We did sense that we were not alone. The quest for internal freedom, for the elixir of life, for the draught of immortal revelation was not new. We were part of an ancient and honorable fellowship which had pursued this journey since the dawn of recorded history. We began to read the accounts of earlier trippers—Dante, Hesse, René Daumal, Tolkien, Homer, Blake, George Fox, Swedenborg, Bosch, and the explorers from the Orient—tantrics, Sufis, Bauls, Gnostics, hermetics, Sivaites, sadhus.

From this moment on my days as a respectable establishment scientist were numbered. I just couldn't see the new society given birth by medical hands, or psychedelic sacraments as psychiatric tools.

From this evening on my energies were offered to the ancient underground society of alchemists, artists, mystics, alienated visionaries, dropouts and the disenchanted young, the sons arising.   [July, 1968]

The Life and Death of a Hippie

by Anthony Lukas

On dusky, brown summer mornings, as the big trailer trucks snort toward Woonsocket, the sour-sweet smells of dough baking mix with diesel fumes over Dexter Street. At the open windows of Gorman's Bakery ("Home of Gorman's Fortified Bread"), men with beefy forearms covered in white powder stand sniffing another day in Central Falls, Rhode Island. The steam from the ovens, the choking flour, the heat slowly rising from the macadam roadway, the fumes from the trucks' grinding gears and hissing brakes, all work up a powerful thirst in a man. So one figure raises a ghostly white hand in a window, beckons to a boy sitting across the street on the stoop of a three-story frame house, and asks him to bring three Seven-Ups from the soda fountain at Barry's News Store down the block.

The boy nods and moves off in his peculiar stride, bouncing up and down on the balls of his feet, his body bent sharply forward from the waist, his hands jammed deep in the pockets of his brown leather jacket, his head drawn down between his hunched-up shoulders in the manner of one of the big brown turtles in Scott's Pond. A few minutes later he comes bouncing back, a paper tray with the three Seven-Ups balanced precariously on his head, his silver harmonica flashing in his mouth, playing *Fingertips* to an audience of grinning, flour-white bakers.

This is how one of Gorman's bakers remembered James "Groovy" Hutchinson a few weeks after his nude body was found last October 8 beside that of his friend, Linda Fitzpatrick, in a Greenwich Village basement—their heads bashed in with bricks.

Linda's murder attracted nationwide attention, largely because of her family's social standing. The Fitzpatricks live in a graceful, thirty-room mansion on Doubling Road in Greenwich, Connecticut, a mile from the Greenwich Country Club. Mr. Fitzpatrick, a Princeton graduate, made a small fortune in the spice business and Linda had all the advantages money and position could provide: Greenwich Country Day School, Old-fields School in Baltimore, vacations in Bermuda. But, at least in the last months of her life, there was another side—pot, LSD, crash pads and warlocks—a side her family professed to know nothing about. Because of the gap between her two worlds and the depth of her parents' insulation, Linda quickly became a symbol of the profound alienation of many middle-class youths.

But Groovy was virtually ignored, dismissed by most of the press as a "tattooed drifter." Yet he was an original, a tortured tumbleweed among the flower children, many of whom were products of the manicured lawns and gladiolus beds of New Rochelle and Great Neck.

Most of the hippies dropped quite deliberately from suburbia into the East Village and Haight-Ashbury, seeking the bizarre and the immediate. But Groovy was a true dropout from society, who quite by chance found the hippie scene ready to drop into. Two decades ago he would have dropped out anyway and ended at best a gentle, aimless wanderer through America's shantytowns, at worst a leather-jacketed motorcycle tough. In the East Village he was an all-too-easy luminary, reflecting the gleam in the eyes of a thousand runaways. But to have starred in Central Falls, before an audience of bakers lined up in the windows of a great brick box, among the trucks and the filling stations and the railroad tracks and the junkyards—that may have been one of his finest hours.

Central Falls is the very essence of a New England mill town come on evil days. Wedged onto a sandy slab where the Seekonk and Blackstone Rivers meet just north of Providence, it lies at the southern end of the Blackstone valley, once a center of New England's textile industry. Towns like Saylesville, Valley Falls, Quinnville and Albion all had their big, sooty, brick mills which somehow managed to spin fine white yarn and cloth without a hint of its grimy origin. But after World War II most of the mills moved South, drawn by cheap labor and new power, leaving behind them stagnant pools of unemployment and depression.

With the mills gone, Central Falls has eighty-one manufacturing plants left, employing only 3,812 persons. Corning Glass and Standard Romper Company are the only major plants in town; the rest are mostly small companies lodged in converted mills, producing machines, paper, shoes and food products. There are jobs for the young, but men over forty, who spent their best years in the textile mills, find it hard to get work. Central Falls has a welfare case load of seventeen hundred, the fourth largest in the state, although there are fourteen communities with bigger populations. The city has lost population every census since 1930—when it had 25,898 persons—to 1965—when it had 18,677.

One thing Central Falls has plenty of is liquor licenses—sixty-four, or one for every two hundred ninety-one persons—and there is a bar on nearly every corner, most of them rough workmen's taverns that sell more beer than Scotch and more Scotch than gin. It's a tough city too, sometimes called "Little Chicago," known particularly for its numerous bookies. Other than drinking, playing the horses or, perhaps, bingo there isn't much to do in Central Falls. There's one movie—Holiday Cinema—and one bowling alley—Bill's Bowlaway. Central Falls calls itself, "The friendly city with the forward look," but one teen-ager says, "You can look right through it."

That's the way Central Falls apparently likes it. The city has elected the same mayor—Raymond J. Morissette—five straight times; last November after his latest victory, the mayor's son said, "It's a little like the way it was with the New York Yankees."

There are only four business streets of significance in Central Falls, enclosing most of the city's 1.27 square miles. "If you want to find a guy," explains one teen-ager, "you drive down Broad, left on Hunt, left on Dexter and then left on Clay. If they ain't there, they're out of town." In between are row after row of three-story frame houses where the conglomerate people of Central Falls live—about half of French-Canadian origin, twenty-seven percent Irish and English, ten percent Polish, five percent Syrian and two and a half percent Portuguese.

Jimmy Hutchinson's family is Portuguese on his mother's side, and his mother, Esther, and her large family were the chief influences in his young life. Esther was one of fourteen children born to Mr. and Mrs. Manuel Joseph of Lincoln, Rhode Island, where Mr. Joseph worked in a mill. While she was still young, the family moved to Pawtucket, just across the New Haven Railroad tracks from Central Falls, and it was there at nineteen—in the midst of World War II—that she married Joseph J. Hutchinson, then a sailor stationed at Quonset Point. After the war, the Hutchinsons moved to Pawtucket, where Esther helped support the family by making jewelry.

Esther was a dark-haired, well-built girl with Mediterranean good looks and a Mediterranean temperament to match. After her divorce from Mr. Hutchinson, she married a truck driver named Bob Benoit, but they separated several years ago. Esther had two children by Mr. Hutchinson—George, who was born in 1944 but was adopted while still an infant by the sister of Mr. Hutchinson's sister-in-law, and Jimmy, who was born February 19, 1946, in Pawtucket. She also had two children by Mr. Benoit: Brenda, now ten years old, and Ronald, now three.

The family lived in Pawtucket until Jimmy was about five and then moved to a comfortable old frame house on Tiffany Street in Central Falls. Jimmy went to kindergarten at the Kendall Street School and then on to first grade in 1952. It was that year that Jimmy's "learning problems"—as the school system called them—began to show up. His performance in the first grade was so poor that he had to repeat the grade the next year. The following year, when the family moved back to Pawtucket for a brief stay, Jimmy went on to second grade and then through third grade at the High Street School, but school records show that he was a "low achiever, a borderline student, with difficulty in reading, spelling and comprehension." They also show a "below-average I.Q." A school official said Jimmy evidently "tried hard, did what he could with what he had, but he didn't have much."

So when the family moved back to Central Falls in 1956, the School Department there assigned Jimmy to an "ungraded class" at the Hedley Avenue School. Miss Sara Kerr, who was the principal and school psychologist at Hedley Avenue, explains that the ungraded class was a remedial program to prepare "under-achieving children" to return to the normal grade progression. "As soon as Jimmy's achievement matched his age we would have put him back in a regular grade," Miss Kerr said. But it never did and he remained in the ungraded class for five long years.

Miss Kerr, a bird-like, sharp-featured woman with blue-tinted white hair which stands up sharply from her head, is now retired from the school system, but she spoke warmly about her former student the other day as she perched on an ornate armchair in the Victorian parlor of her home a few blocks from the Hedley Avenue School.

"Jimmy, poor Jimmy, was emotionally disturbed, a badly upset boy—and that came out in a severe reading problem as well as some behavioral problems. He had no motivation, no desire to learn and he was always disturbing the classes. I never found any meanness in him. We had some kids who killed flies and tortured them. Jimmy never did anything like that. He was just clowning. But the teachers couldn't put up with his capers so they'd send him to me.

"I can remember him, oh so well, standing there in the doorway of my office. He was always so well-dressed, beautiful clothes, no little girl could have been more fastidious. He'd just stand there so neat and clean-looking and I'd say, 'Oh, Jimmy, not again!' and he'd start to cry, wiping his eyes on his sleeve. And we'd sit and talk and I'd ask him why he couldn't pay attention and do his work. He'd just nod and sniffle and say, 'Yes, Miss Kerr.' He was a poor, bewildered boy.

"One night I kept him after school. I was determined that he was going to do a single little arithmetic problem, but he couldn't do it, he just couldn't.

"I can assure you for those five years he was never neglected or ignored; he was getting the very best remedial education available. The class was small—fifteen kids—and they had a teacher especially trained for remedial work. We worked and worked with Jimmy to erase his deficits, until I guess we finally came to the conclusion that there were just impediments to academic learning."

But Jimmy posed an increasingly difficult discipline problem. Coupled with this was the fact that he was fifteen by the end of his fifth year and bigger than most of the other kids in the ungraded class. As Miss Kerr recalls it, the superintendent came over one day and said, "Miss Kerr, we've got to try something else with this boy."

The "something else" was Central Falls Trade School, but in between his mother arranged psychiatric outpatient treatment for him at Butler Hospital. He underwent this treatment on and off for the next year.

His teachers agree that Jimmy was emotionally disturbed, that all his clowning was his way of saying, Notice me, pay attention. But by the second year at the Hedley Avenue School he was already getting most of his attention outside school—in a gang of which he was the informal but undisputed leader.

There was Ernie St. Angelo, a hulking boy with a barrel chest and huge hands which could squeeze a Narragansett beer can flat; there was his brother, Steve St. Angelo, a thin, dark-haired youth with a sensitive face; there were the Zenone brothers, Danny and Jimmy; Russell Wilson, Dave Quebec, Eddie Marco, Gary Larosee and sometimes Jimmy's older brother, George Carbary, down from North Attleboro.

But of them all, Ernie St. Angelo was closest to Jimmy, more like a brother than George. "Every day after school," Ernie recalls, "we used to go down to his house on Tiffany Street. Hutchy's Corner, we used to call it, 'cause we called him Hutchy—that's one of the things we called him. And Hippity-hop too, because of the funny way he walked, bouncing up and down like that—oh, yeh, and Bouncy, we called him Bouncy too."

Jimmy collected nicknames like other kids collected rocks or bottle caps. Groovy, the last one, came much later, the casual gift of a casual friend in New Orleans. But in Central Falls there was Jungle Jim, a name he got after he cut another kid with a machete. There was Gander, "because he used to goose guys." There was Steve Ribs, which the gang started calling him one day when he hung on a vine over Scott's Pond making the Tarzan call—"Aaaahhh"—with his puny chest stuck out and ribs showing all over. There was Rock Hutchinson, which he gave himself one night, a night Eddie Marco, another gang member, remembers well: "We useta go drinking on Friday nights. One night we got all dressed up.

He had bought some new clothes, a new trench coat and these new square shades. So we come down the street and he says, 'Dig me. I'm Rock Hutchinson. See, girls. You've got a chance to go out with Rock Hutchinson now!' And everything. Ah, he was too much."

Jimmy, the gang remembers, would do anything and usually carried the rest of them along. "We wouldn't of ever done this stuff unless Hutchy done it first," Ernie St. Angelo recalls. "You wouldn't see him one day. And next day he'd come and tell you what he done. And you'd say, 'No, you didn't,' and he'd say, 'C'mon, I'll show ya.' And he'd do it, too. He'd do anything. I'll tell ya he was a nut. A nut! But he was funny. If somebody was on their deathbed and they don't want to see nobody the one I would advise them to see would have been Hutchinson because I tell you he would have had 'em out of that bed. He was that funny. He was funny not being funny. Even when he got mad the faces he useta make was funny. Serious he was funny.

"I'll tell ya the kind of the things he useta do. When we were real young we useta go down to the dump. There was this bum who useta live down there, Slim the Bum, he was a real dirty old guy living in this shack, a shack made out of doors off old houses they tore down. We was all scared of him because he was kind of crazy, sort of trapped in the head, you know. We useta throw stones at him and watch him skip. But not Hutchy. Hutchy would go up there and shake hands with him, you know? Pat him on the back and say, 'How ya doin', Slim. How's the wife and kids?' It useta really break us up. One day I says, 'Jimmy, why do you go down there and do that stuff with Slim?' and he says, 'Aw, Slim's my buddy.'

"There just wasn't anything he wouldn't do. I remember when we was 'bout thirteen or fourteen, we started going down to the slaughterhouse to ride the wild pigs. The first time I ever went was with my cousin. So I spread the word around Central Falls: 'I know a place we can go and ride pigs.' So when Hutchy heard this, he never rode any pigs before, but he says, 'Come on, let's go.'

"Well see, it was a whole day. You'd hop the freight train in Central Falls. And then you'd go up to Pawtucket where it stopped and you'd hop the big freight coming by and that would take you right out to Providence and you'd get off when it slowed down after the lights and go over to the slaughterhouse. Now they got these pigs all in this big pen waiting to be slaughtered and they'd go nuts because they can sense the smell of death coming from the other pigs being killed. See, you ought to watch out. 'Cause they have the male and the female pigs. Now if you ride the female pigs it's all right, but if you ride a male pig, it's all over. They'll bite you to death.

"Well, Hutchy, he didn't care. He got on this big male, must have been about three hundred pounds. They got some big pigs down there. He rode him all around. And then he got off it, and he started skiing in the muck, you know, the crap. We useta do that. You'd grab their tail and just ride on your feet. And right in the center of the floor was this big hole, a hole about four feet deep where everything drains into it. And Hutchy was skiing by it and he went right into it, right up to his waist. He come home all stinking and everything and his mother says, 'Where were you?' and he says, 'Oh, I was down to the stables, riding the horses.' And she sniffs again and she says, 'They was no horses.' Oh, he was too much!"

"Jimmy was always gettin' himself messed up like that," Eddie Marco chimed in joyously. "One day me and Hutchy and a few other kids, we went down to the pond and there was soft mud down there, you'd run over it and it would start getting all pliable, like jelly. You'd run across it and it would bounce as you ran. And if you stood in a spot for long you'd sink, it was something like hard quicksand.

"And Hutchy was jumping up and down and everybody's telling him, 'Start running.' But he says, 'No, this thing can't suck me up.' So we turn around and a minute later Hutchy's screaming for help. He was up to his knees and was screaming, 'It's eating me up.' So we got boards and pushed 'em out there and pulled him out."

Now the gang was really off, one Hutchy exploit tripping on the heels of another.

"I remember one time he bought a case of Ruppert's," Ernie said. "He used to love Ruppert's beer. So he put it down on the ground and he had a stick, one of those voodoo sticks they used to have, you know, with those shrunken heads. He jammed this stick into the case and he gets down on his knees and everything and he goes, 'Oh, Ruppert's Goddess. Oh, Ruppert's Goddess. You're so good to me.' He went to extremes. Anything you did with him, you'd try and keep up with him, you know, so he wouldn't make you look stupid. But mostly you couldn't. He'd start joking and you'd start joking to keep up with him and before you know it you're running out of jokes and this kid's still going, got a book in his head or something.

"One time we was out in Lincoln Woods at this park they have out there. And there were these four guys singing round the snack bar. They was pretty good you know, maybe semipros, and they had everybody gathered round them listening. So Hutchy, he had these bongo drums, and he went over and sat down across the path on the grass, and he started playing the drums. He wasn't so good, really, but he played real hot, and these people round the singers started coming over one by one. He just took them away. Finally, the singers gave up too and came over. At first they was kinda mad, but then they started laughing and said, 'What are you going to do?'

"Sure, he was a clown. He was half clown, half nut and all hot. Why did he act that way? I don't know. Maybe down deep he might have thought he was really a fool. He probably was hiding something, a bad feeling inside, a feeling that no one really liked him 'cause he was a fool. So he was going to be a bigger fool than even they thought."

Jimmy's problems stemmed, in part, from what could hardly have been a secure, serene home life. His mother stopped working in jewelry factories and collected Aid to Dependent Children. She was still lively and attractive when she left Mr. Benoit.

Friends say she did her best with the cramped five-room apartment on the third floor of the green frame building at 818 Dexter Street, where she moved with her three children from Tiffany Street. Jimmy had his own room leading off the kitchen, decorated with pictures of Elvis Presley and James Brown, his childhood idols, and scattered with records, model cars and airplanes he made and the comic books he pored over but could never quite read.

Jimmy doted on his younger sister, Brenda, and often spent nights baby-sitting with her. His mother says he was "a good son, always doing something for me, for everybody. He never talked the hippie line or nothin' like that. I don't understand how my son could ever have lived that life in all that filth and everything. He was always clean, liked clothes and everything. And he liked to work. And he wasn't unhappy or anything. He never said nothin' about worrying or nothin' like that."

In September, 1962, at the age of sixteen, after a year at the Butler Center, Jimmy entered the machinist's class at Central Falls Trade School, which was in a grey Quonset hut not far from the high school.

The machine shop, at the rear of the hut, is small and jammed with grey steel lathes, grinders, drill presses, spindles and milling machines. On the walls, hammers, awls and wrenches hang on nails, each over its own black outline. Above them is a neatly lettered sign, WE AIM TO KEEP THIS PLACE CLEAN—PLEASE HELP. Grey lockers bear a seemingly endless roster of French-Canadian names: "Plamondon, Trottier, Bernier, Rocheleal."

The teacher also is of French-Canadian descent; he is Louis Sarault Jr., a lean, deliberate, thoughtful man who takes sociology and psychology courses "so I can understand these boys and my own job a little better.

"Sure I had Jimmy in my shop for three years," he recalls. "I remember the day he arrived. Dr. Calcutt, who was superintendent then, marched him over himself. He told me Jimmy came from an ungraded class, that he'd gotten through only the third grade. Normally the trade school accepts only kids who've gone through the eighth grade. But Dr. Calcutt said, 'Let's give him another chance, Louis. See what you can do with him.' Well, that wasn't unusual. Old Sarault usually got all the problem kids. I like the challenge.

"I got to say Jimmy tried here. He wasn't too shifty with a paper and pencil. If he could write more than his name he didn't show me. If I asked him how much is half of fifteen he'd scratch his head and say that's a tough one. You need more than that in a technical shop like this. I couldn't talk trig to him. I had to do his thinking for him.

"But he made himself some nice tools. I remember this diestock he made, welded it himself. It was so good I kept it around as a model, threw it away only last year.

"And in some respects he had a good head. He could reason. He wouldn't take an unnecessary chance if it jeopardized his safety. He was a real con artist, foxy. In fact, in the con sense of the word, you'd have to say he was sharper than most of the other kids. He'd smile at you, but underneath you knew he was saying, 'I'm putting you on, Sarault.' And his friendship—you'd almost have to say alliance—with Ernie St. Angelo was a very shrewd one. Ernie's a big boy and he could take care of Jimmy, but he's not too smart, while Jimmy had it up there in the way you need it on the street.

"He was skinny, real skinny, but if he thought there was an easy mark in the class he'd go after him." One of his classmates said he once took on Ronald Fanion, a little kid with glasses, and that Sarault caught them and said: "If you guys want to fight, then stand up like men, right next to each other, and swap punches in the arm."

(Ernie St. Angelo remembers that fight. "Ya, it was really funny. Hutchy knew Fanion was nearsighted and couldn't see for nothin'. So he said I'll fix 'em. He filled his shirt pocket with nuts and bolts and scraps of metal. Fanion threw a shot at him, took the pocket off and cut his hand bad.")

Sarault remembers that Jimmy went after Ralph Johnson, a kid who also looked like a mark. "But Ralphie punched him out real good, made a cream puff of him. Up till then the shop had been a little wary of Jimmy because he talked tough. But once they saw him in action against Johnson they knew he was nothing.

"Under his toughness, Jimmy was pretty timid. Once or twice when I disciplined him he'd cry. A boy of sixteen! A kid needs to be wanted, he needs to be loved, and I don't know how much of that he had at home. Once when he got in trouble I told him to bring his mother in. She was all agitated and said, 'I'm through with him; I've told him he has to conform, but he won't. I've had enough.'

"He'd been tossed around a lot. He said he didn't remember his father. But he carried his father's picture around in his billfold—a sharp-looking sailor in his Navy whites, his hat cocked back on his head, a little moustache. Jimmy said he wanted to be just like his father and go into the Navy. I think I pleased him once when I said he looked a little like his father. He kept wanting to grow a moustache like his father's, but I wouldn't let him. Every once in a while the fuzz would start sprouting under his nose and I'd say, 'Shave it off, Jimmy.' And he would. A couple of years later I saw him on the street here and sure enough he had a little moustache, just the spitting image of his father's.

"Jimmy got through okay right up to May of his final year and those last ten days the seniors got off to get caps and gowns and all that. Then he went and got in some bad trouble."

This was the machete incident. According to members of the gang who were there, Jimmy had persuaded Gerry Bergevine, a twenty-nine-year-old neighbor, to buy him some beer. Some other kids tried to take it away from him and a "real punch-'em-up" developed. A friend managed to throw Jimmy a machete and in the fight Jimmy cut seventeen-year-old Albie Nickerson on the arms so badly Albie had to be taken to the hospital. After a hearing before Judge Guillaume Myette, Jimmy was held for the Grand Jury in $1,500 bail.

"That really blew up a storm," Sarault recalls. "Dr. Calcutt, who had gone out of his way to help Jimmy, said, 'Louis, I don't see how we can give him a diploma now.' But I knew Jimmy wanted that diploma in the worst kind of way. After all those years in the ungraded class, you can't blame him. He was tired of hearing people say all he did was mush. So, although I don't think he attended graduation, he was given his diploma."

Three weeks after he got his diploma, Jimmy got another break. The Grand Jury declined to indict him, apparently because Nickerson refused to testify.

Perhaps because of his close call, Jimmy seemed to plunge into work that summer. He worked briefly for Tuppet Screw Company in Central Falls and in September switched over to the New England Paper Tube Company in Pawtucket, where he developed a reputation as a hard worker.

At first, as a floor boy, pushing two-wheeled handcarts of paper tubes around the four-story building, he averaged forty-nine hours a week—nine hours on weekdays and four hours on Saturday. Then, in January, 1966, he became a baler, raking wastepaper from a huge chute into compressing machines, then trotting downstairs seven or eight times a day to wire up the bales of packed paper. As a baler he averaged sixty-one and three-quarter hours a week, working all the day shift and part of the night shift in a room filled with the roar of the nearby splitting machines and the hiss of the relentlessly moving mountain of wastepaper.

"He was a real comedian," recalls Frank, his foreman. "He was loud and you could hear him clowning all over, even with all the machines going. But it didn't bother me none. My rule is if it doesn't hurt work it doesn't hurt me, and Jimmy worked good. He was absent only seventy hours in twenty months and he was late only three times—hell, that's a better record than mine."

To the gang, most of whom were working only sporadically, Jimmy's spate of industriousness was just another sign he was nutty ("Hutchy was a working fool," Ernie said). He put most of his money (which got up to about $87 a week before taxes) in a credit union, at first for a car and then for a motorcycle.

But he had no luck with his purchases. He bought Albie Nickerson's '57 white Ford convertible, but Steve St. Angelo ran it into a tree. Then Jimmy bought a motorcycle—a Japanese Yamaha—and within a few days cracked that up.

"Yeh, the Yamaha went into a gas station but Hutchy didn't," Ernie recalls. "He and these other kids were out on this rainy night. It was real slick and at the entrance to the station he jammed on the brake. He did a swan dive over the handlebars and the bike just rolled into the station and cracked up. Hutchy was all banged up, but still clowning. He told me the story all Japanese like, you know, 'Ah, velly honorable bike. So solly, have tell you velly sad tale. Learn number-one lesson—with Japanese bike you do not put front brake on in rain.' "

The motorcycles were part of a new style the gang had adopted even before Jimmy and Ernie left trade school. They began calling themselves the "Mondos" to differentiate them from the "Collegians," another gang across town. The Collegians hung out on Broad Street around Eddie's Ice Cream Parlor and Izzy's Grill. They wore white sneakers, chinos or Levis, white shirts and close-cropped hair. The Mondos hung out on Dexter Street around Sparky's Restaurant and Duchesneau's Drug Store. They wore black pointed boots with high Cuban heels, black leather jackets, black pants with tapered bottoms, their long hair slicked back with grease.

Jimmy was the sharpest dresser of all the Mondos—everything black except the white buttons on his shirt, a white silk tie, a red vest and maybe a little snap-visor corduroy hat. By now his arms—and chest and legs—were heavily tattooed. He had a girl on his left arm, a little baby with boxing gloves marked "Baby Jim," some dice and lucky sevens. ("The first one he got was a torch with a scroll saying 'Mom,' " recalls Ernie. "I can remember when he got it. We went down to Rocky's Tattoo Parlor in Providence and he says, 'Aw, it's nothin', we get a tattoo, it's nothin'. You go first.' I says, 'Why me?' He says, 'Look at ya, ya big gorilla'—he used to call me that—'you're a big gorilla, look at the fat on ya. Look at me. I'm like a pole.' So I got this on here and he says, 'How was it?' and I said, 'It's nothin', Hutch, you'll like it!' So he gets up there trying to show how brave he was and the guy started the machine and started on his arm and you could hear all kinds of grunts. But he was smiling like it wasn't hurting him. He also had these hinges. Usually they'd put on these big hinges, like they have on sea chests, right at the inside of the elbow, but his arm was too skinny so they put one of these door hinges on. Every time he met somebody new he'd show him the hinges on his arms or legs and he'd bend the arm or leg and say, '*Eeeekkk, eeeekkk,*' like one of those creaky doors.")

With his square dark glasses tilted down on his nose, his little corduroy hat cocked back, all his hinges creaking, Jimmy could often be found early in the evenings leaning against the windows of Duchesneau's Drug Store entertaining the rest of the Mondos with his renowned rendition of Little Stevie Wonder's *Fingertips*. First he would play it on the harmonica, doing a jiggly little dance on the sidewalk as he played. Then he would take the harmonica out of his mouth and, spreading his arms wide, would imitate the blind Negro singer's wail: *Say, yeh, yeh, yeh, yeh, yeh, yeh/Just a little bit of soul, oohhwwaa, oohhwwaa, oohhwwaa/Yeh, yeh, yeh/Clap your hands just a little bit louder/Clap your hands just a little bit louder/Yeh, yeh, yeh, yeh.*

Then he would do his other favorite, James Brown, or he would do a Jackie Gleason or Red Skelton routine he had seen on TV, and the Mondos would roar and slap their knees and shout, "Oh, Hutchy, you're some hot ticket."

Sometimes the Mondos would spend the whole evening in front of Duchesneau's or Sparky's, watching the girls, or "snappers," as they called them. "They'd never really do anything, you know," recalls teen-age Karen Conroy. "They'd just cross their arms in front and watch you real close and say, 'Dig her.' " There were some "snappers" who hung out with the Mondos, girls like Connie Oakley, Cathy Malloy, Madeleine Gilbert. Jimmy knew them all, dated Cathy, but like most of the Mondos he never got serious about girls. On Friday nights the Mondos would often wander up to the dances at Holy Trinity but only to watch the girls go in and then make appropriate remarks.

Almost every spring there was a clash between the Mondos and the Collegians on Dexter Street, but most of the time they only growled at each other. They rarely got into serious trouble with the police. Occasionally they would steal empty bottles from construction sites and cash them in, or pull false alarms and watch the fire trucks race up, or drop lighted cigarettes in mailboxes and watch the smoke seep out; and one Halloween a Mondo was arrested for possession of eggs ("Yeh, believe it or not, possession of eggs! 'Course he'd been throwing them at police cars").

The police didn't like the Mondos and they took a particular dislike to Jimmy. "They thought he was a wise guy," Ernie said. "They really used to get on him. 'Course they used to ride all of us. You're out on a corner with another guy, see, and they'd come along, tell you to move. And you ain't doing nothing. There's old men across the street, about ten of them, and they don't kick them off. Hutchy really hated that and I guess he told some of the cops off 'cause they'd really go after him. I seen cops hit him in the legs with clubs hard enough to knock him on the ground and double him up with pain— just for standing on the corner!"

Most of the time, though, Jimmy was shrewd enough to stay out of serious trouble. If he wanted to raise a little hell he'd let others take the risks. "There was this guy who would do anything for Jimmy," says Ernie. "He was always following us Mondos around and we couldn't stand him. He was a hot ticket all right but we couldn't stand him because he had such a big mouth. So most of us just used to tell him to buzz off. But old Hutchy was too shrewd. He'd say to this guy, 'If you want to hang with us you gotta show us you can do something. Why don't you steal a car and come back and pick us up? But for God's sake make it a good one. No old buggies.' We all laughed 'cause we didn't think the guy could steal anything. But a little while later he came around the corner with a red T-bird, for Chrissakes. We all climbed in, laughing and all, and this guy was so small he couldn't hardly reach the pedals, but Jimmy, he held him up by the seat of the pants and told him, 'On, James,' like he was a chauffeur or something."

With the rest of the gang, and particularly with his buddy, Ernie, Jimmy could be more than generous. Ernie remembers once he needed another hundred dollars to get a car he wanted. "Hutchy said, 'I'll give it to ya.' This is while he was working at the paper-tube place and he had plenty of dough. I said, 'Naw, I don't want your money.' But he went to the bank on Friday and drawed out a hundred and he come to my house and says, 'Here, Ernie, here's the money. Go buy the car. And then when you get the car we'll all go along.' That's the kind of guy he was. Listen. He was a well-loved kid, not well-liked, well-loved." The other Mondos agreed. Eddie Marco said emotionally: "There always was and always will be a Hutchinson."

Others found him less appealing. Seventeen-year-old Wayne Robichaud said, "Well, I guess he was okay to the kids who were his friends, but he used to pick on some of us smaller kids. I was a little scared of him." Nineteen-year-old Ken Moore said, "He could be rough. I remember once I walked by a car where he and a girl were in the backseat. I knocked on the window and he came out after me with this knife."

The Collegians remember that Jimmy carried a knife his last few years in Central Falls, "all kinds of knives, big ones, small ones, curved ones, switchblades." The Mondos concede this, but insist it was largely for self-defense. "He was only ninety pounds, for crying out loud. The guy couldn't fight with his hands. He didn't have no defense with his hands."

But it was a knife which ultimately got Jimmy into big trouble. On October 22, 1965, he and Steve St. Angelo went out to celebrate Steve's seventeenth birthday. "We decided to go over to North Attleboro, Massachusetts, and do the town," Steve recalls. "We hit a few of the spots in town and then we drove over to the V.F.W. hall where they was having this teen-aged dance."

Officers Robert Bray and Antonio J. Casale stationed outside the hall later reported that they observed the two boys "staggering" up to the door and "demanding" admission about nine o'clock. "They smelled strongly of alcohol, were unsteady on their feet and their speech was incoherent," the report said. "They became loud and boisterous and began to hit the paneled wall of the lobby when they were refused admission." They were placed under arrest, but Officer Bray noticed Hutchinson had his left hand in the pocket of his leather jacket and ordered him to remove it. Hutchinson did not respond. According to Bray, he then put one hand on Hutchinson's left wrist and began patting the outside of the pocket with his other hand to see if it contained a gun or a knife. "In the process," Bray's report reads, "Hutchinson's left hand came up and forward, still in his left pocket, and a sharp pointed weapon in his left-hand coat pocket penetrated the pocket and came in contact with Bray's right hand, puncturing the palm of his hand, drawing blood."

The sharp pointed weapon, still kept in an envelope in the North Attleboro police station, is a piece of steel about four inches long with two sharp blades protruding at right angles at each end. When the bar, wrapped in cotton and Scotch tape, is held in a man's clenched fist, the two blades jut out just beyond the knuckles.

The boys were taken to the police station where Jimmy was charged with assault and battery with a dangerous weapon, possession of a dangerous weapon, drunkenness and disturbance of the peace. Steve was charged with drunkenness and disturbing the peace.

Ernie St. Angelo, who went up to North Attleboro that night, recalls that even then Jimmy was still clowning. "He had his hands handcuffed behind his back and every time the cops turned their backs he kept stepping through them so his hands would be in front. The cops didn't know how he did it. Then back in the cell he and Stevie unrolled this toilet paper, draped it all over the cell and through the bars and started singing *Happy Birthday*. When the cops came back to tell them to shut up, Jimmy said, 'Jeez, it's my buddy's birthday, aren't you going to even wish him happy birthday?' "

At his arraignment the next morning, Jimmy pleaded not guilty to all four charges and was held in $1,125 bail. When he could not put up the bail he was taken to the New Bedford House of Correction where he was held until the hearing on October 29, when he was bound over for the Grand Jury. On February 11, the Bristol County Grand Jury indicted him.

Within a week after the indictment, Jimmy was talking seriously about leaving Central Falls.

The Mondos say he had always wanted to travel. Eddie Marco remembers: "When we were twelve, a bunch of us took our bikes and went all the way to the Red Bridge in Providence. Hutchy wanted to keep going, but I had a little Mickey Mouse watch and I said I had to be home for five o'clock supper. So I turned around and came back. Gee, I didn't see the rest of them until after eight. They said Hutchy just wouldn't stop, he wanted to go all the way to New York. 'Course, he had an English bike. He could go faster than we could."

Later, he took to riding the freights in and around Providence and he would give his friends a tour of the city from the top of a freight car. Once, Ernie recalls, "He went right up to the front of a freight and asked the engineer, 'Buddy, can I drive your train?' And the guy started screaming at him and Hutchy says, 'No offense, no offense.' "

Still later, he and the other Mondos would drive to New York for weekends, fill up the car with liquor they could buy legally there at eighteen and sell it to minors in Central Falls.

In New York, the Mondos usually went to Greenwich Village, which fascinated Jimmy. "He always wanted to go down there," Ernie says. "We never wanted to, but he kept saying, 'Oh, I want to see them guys with the long hair.' One time we was in this bar down there and the American Beatles were playing. We were sitting at a table, plastered, so Hutchy calls this guy over, when they had a break, and he grabbed the kid's hair. 'Excuse me,' he says real nice. 'Is that your real hair?' Then he started pulling. We was all laughing. Finally the kid says, 'All right, already.' "

Early in April, 1966, Jimmy told his brother, George Carbary, that he was going to leave home. "He didn't know where he was going to go," George recalls. "He said he just wanted to change the scenery. He wanted me to come with him, but I said I couldn't go. Then, before I knew it—boom, he was gone."

Jimmy withdrew all his savings from the credit union and he and Dave Quebec, one of the Mondos, bought a car. He packed a small suitcase with a couple of sports jackets, two pairs of pants, some underwear and socks, telling his mother that he might send for the rest of his clothes as soon as he was settled. He gave his record player and his large record collection to his sister, Brenda.

Jimmy worked his last day at the Paper Tube Company on April 22 and the next day he and Quebec drove to New York. His mother received a postcard dated the twenty-third from New York with a picture of the New York skyline under the printed legend, "Just Arrived in New York." It read: "Having fun. Can't complain as yet. Say hi to Ronnie, Brenda and everyone for me. Okay. Love, Jim H." His friends presume that Quebec wrote this and subsequent postcards for the still almost illiterate Jimmy.

Shortly after they arrived in New York, Jimmy and Quebec apparently joined an itinerant carnival known as Amusements of America, a New Jersey outfit which toured the Eastern Seaboard with a string of Ferris wheels, merry-go-rounds, "thrill rides" and "children's rides." It is not clear just what Jimmy did for the carnival. Once he told his brother that he and Quebec helped put up and tear down the tents. Another time he said he sold tickets in a freak show.

The record of his travels for the next eight months is told largely in a series of laconic postcards he sent his mother. The next was from Hagerstown, Maryland, later in April: "Hi, ma. Heading for Canada. How's the family? Fine I hope. See you soon. Jim." The card from Philadelphia on May 3 said he was "doing all right and don't need anything." In the following weeks the carnival played a series of one-week stands in New Jersey and Pennsylvania. On August 28 came a card from Ottawa, Canada: "Hi, Mom. Had a wonderful time here. Going back to the U. S. now. Will hear from me soon. Doing fine. Being good. Your best son, love, Jimmy."

Soon after he came back to this country, Jimmy left Amusements of America and joined a smaller carnival run by David B. Endy of Miami, Florida, as it headed South. In September, he sent his mother a card from Enfield, North Carolina, saying, "Took in the sights here—moving on to a new town."

Early in January, 1967, a barber known as "Frenchy," who ran "Frenchy's Barbershop" a few doors down from Jimmy's house in Central Falls, was on vacation in Hollywood, Florida, and wandered into a carnival at a shopping center there. He spotted Jimmy standing by a sideshow. "I remember him very well 'cause he was one of the first round here to wear his hair long. He never wanted any off the top. I said, 'How ya doing, Jimmy.' He said 'Oh, okay, I guess.' "

Jimmy apparently stayed on in Hollywood after the carnival left because on February 7 he sent his mother another postcard from there saying, "Having a good time and going up to New Orleans today."

In New Orleans, Jimmy worked at odd jobs, waiting to pick up with another carnival on its northern swing. Then in late February he was staying at a small hotel in the French Quarter when he met another young ex-carnival worker from Kansas City named Ronald Johnson. Johnson, also dubbed "Galahad," remembers the meeting this way:

"There was this Spanish kid I knew down there—he and I'd been going out with the same chick—and one night I didn't have a place to stay so the Spanish kid said come on up to my place. I went up there and Groovy was up there with this other kid named Chris. At first Groovy came on a little uptight, sort of teed off, you know, because those two guys were goofing off all the time while he was working and paying the rent. But the next day Groovy and I got to rappin' and found out the things we had in common. That wasn't only carnivals. There were lots of things. But the main thing was we both liked to goof on people, you know, blow people's minds, doing weird, fantastic things.

"After that Groovy stopped working mostly and we just goofed off together, just horsing around with the longhairs in Jackson Park and all over the French Quarter." (In these weeks Jimmy acquired at least four things—a tattoo of "Bourbon Street" in fancy lettering; a piece of parchment printed like a diploma, "Nobody of the Year Award," and inscribed under it, "James Hutchinson," which Jimmy later hung in his New York pad; the nickname Groovy, which as Galahad recalls came from a guy in a bar one night, an agent in a carnival; and the drug habit. Galahad is a little vague about when Groovy first began taking drugs. The Mondos say he was "a wino"—a drinker—in Central Falls and never did more with drugs than sniff glue. But soon after he met Galahad he was apparently taking LSD regularly.)

"One day," Galahad recalls, "we was sitting in his hotel room, just rappin', rappin' about carnivals, and we just decided to take off, like the carnivals weren't due yet and we could catch them in Philly. So we hitchhiked up to New York, took us about a week. We spent this one wild night just wandering around Memphis but mostly we kept on the road."

Galahad and Groovy arrived in New York on April 1 and as Galahad remembers it they went first to Times Square. "We ran into some kids up there who were tripping on LSD and were on their way to the movies. We asked where we could stay and they suggested the Peace Eye Bookstore down in the Village. So we went down there and ended up staying a couple of weeks."

The Peace Eye, at 383 East Tenth Street in the heart of the East Village, was a hippie bookstore featuring psychedelic literature and the underground press. It was owned by Ed Sanders, the leader of The Fugs. The Jade Companions were staying in the back room and allowed Galahad and Groovy to camp there for about three weeks. They got their food in exchange for a little work around the place, most of it by Groovy.

"One day," Galahad recalls, "Groovy told me he wanted to open a crash pad where homeless kids could stay. I don't know where he got the idea. There weren't any crash pads down in New Orleans. I think he got the idea from some girl he met. Finally we met this other chick who said she'd let us use her pad, really her boyfriend's pad, over on Eleventh Street, as long as we paid the rent—$35 a month."

The pad was Apartment 11 on the third floor of a dingy tenement at 622 East Eleventh Street. On the door was a hand-lettered sign: "Galahad's Pad, protector of all that is righteous and holy." For the next three months, it served as the most renowned of the East Village's crash pads, where the homeless and the friendless could stay as long as they liked. Sometimes Groovy and Galahad would return a runaway child to frantic parents and be rewarded with a television set or money. ("We're in the people business," Groovy once said.) But at most times there were twenty to thirty assorted hippies staying there and, later, a whole host of visitors—newsmen, television cameramen, curiosity seekers and policemen, always policemen.

The police concentration on the pad was later explained in an affidavit filed by Police Commissioner Howard Leary before the United States

District Court. The commissioner said there had been "a number of entries" to the apartment "occasioned by constant requests . . . from other police departments, but most frequently from parents themselves to find minors, runaway teen-agers in the East Village area of New York City. Usually the parents themselves have heard that their children are living at Apartment 11 at 622 East Eleventh Street."

The commissioner's affidavit was filed in response to a suit on behalf of Galahad, Groovy and several other defendants by John Mage, their lawyer, and Paul Chevigny of the New York Civil Liberties Union. The suit charged that the police were conducting a campaign of "harassment, including dragnet arrests, invasions of privacy and searches" against the defendants. The suit, filed in June, 1967, cited eight specific instances prior to May 6 on which the police entered the apartment "without consent, warrant or other lawful cause" and intrusions after that "on an almost daily basis."

Among the instances were:

One on April 27 when, according to Mage, a member of the Narcotics Squad banged on the door and demanded entrance. He arrested Groovy for impairing the morals of a minor—a girl found in the apartment. Groovy spent the night in jail, but the next morning the case was dismissed on arraignment when the girl was found to be over sixteen.

One on May 6 when the police again demanded entrance. Under instructions from Mage, who became their lawyer after Groovy's arrest, Groovy and Galahad demanded a warrant. But according to the suit the police said they did not need a warrant and "forced their way in." About fifteen persons were arrested and taken to the Ninth Precinct but were released the next morning without being charged.

One on May 19 when police again banged on the door, searched the apartment, arrested Groovy and several others on narcotics charges, which were dismissed next morning in Court.

John Mage, a boyish-looking but deeply committed young lawyer, recalls: "After one of the mass arrests I called the Ninth Precinct and complained that this was something out of 1938 Berlin. I guess because I was a lawyer they assumed that I was a married old man with children because the detective said, 'What if your daughter was running around with these hippies?' I said if I had a daughter I'd expect the police to treat her justly, as all people ought to be treated, and the detective shouted, 'These aren't people, they're bedbugs and they should be exterminated.' "

In answering the suit, Commissioner Leary said, "I believe the police officers have acted in good faith to enforce the laws of the State in these situations." But shortly after the suit was·filed—and a parallel action against the detectives involved was brought before the Police Review Board—the police entries of the apartment stopped.

Even after that, the pad was threatened by an ever-increasing horde of newsmen seeking the bizarre and the way out. "Neither Galahad nor Groovy knew how to cope with this kind of publicity," recalls Don McNeill of *The Village Voice*. "It just blew Galahad's mind, almost destroyed him. It was just incredible to see how the media's attention contorted the guy."

Groovy was less affected by it because he was more naïve. Eve Cary, who works for the Civil Liberties Union, recalls a wide-eyed Groovy coming up to her at one of the court hearings and saying, "*Time* magazine, the society magazine," wanted to interview him.

"Groovy was just gleefully enjoying everything that happened to him," John Mage said. "Even during the worst of the arrests he just ate up the attention. Newsmen were baffled and amazed to find somebody down there who would talk to them at any time, tell them absolutely anything that came into his head."

Groovy struck others as somehow different, more truly innocent than most of the hippies. June Tauber, a "straight" girl who met him several times last summer, recalls that he made a particular impression on her the night of the Tompkins Square riot. "Most of the hippies, the whole thing, was so dark, dirty, almost Hogarthian. Except for Groovy. He was ebullient, hopping and leaping around, buzzing around Galahad like a butterfly, his little, dark, dancing eyes, his teeny, teeny features, small, delicate, light and bouncy, almost childlike in the midst of that dreary affair."

Another friend remembers Groovy one night as he and other hippies waited for hours amid the forbidding marble columns of the Criminal Court for Galahad to be released on bail: "Groovy would go careening around the hall like a kid on the last day of school, in and out of pillars, leaping, prancing, then skidding sideways to a grinning halt before the largest cluster of psychedelic brethren. For variety he would play softly on his harmonica, breaking into a little jig every few bars."

Steve Golden, who covered the East Village for The New York *Times* last summer, says: "Galahad was the brains of the organization, quick, sharp, though no genius. Groovy wasn't so smart, but he could feel, which Galahad couldn't. Groovy had the vitality, the energy. He was the only one who could put down Galahad without getting him mad. I think of them as Don Quixote and Sancho Panza or maybe Paul Douglas and Judy Holliday in *Born Yesterday*."

One day Galahad and Groovy were sighted on St. Mark's Place in the heart of hippieland. Galahad had on a fireman's hat and was wheeling a shopping cart in which was a big fire extinguisher. Groovy would scurry ahead and light a piece of paper in the gutter and then Galahad would race up and put it out. They would panhandle from the bystanders and then Groovy would race ahead and light another piece of paper. (Galahad liked the act, which Groovy had invented, and told him to hold onto the extinguisher. But when they got together that night Groovy didn't have the extinguisher. "What you do with it?" Galahad demanded. "I don't know," Groovy said. "I think I gave it to somebody.")

Groovy seemed to enjoy giving things away in the Village—part of his newfound "digger" ethos. Sometimes he would stand on the street corner and when he saw someone whose face he liked he would go up and plant a bottle cap in his open palm. "I just want you to have it," he'd tell the bewildered pedestrian.

He also gave away drugs—LSD, speed, pot—or sold them at prices far below those charged by the more professional dealers.

Suddenly in midsummer Groovy took off for Woodstock, New York, about ninety miles up the Hudson, where a hippie scene was developing. He drove up with some friends and they stayed about a month. Galahad recalls that Groovy talked vaguely about starting some sort of rural "commune" there patterned after those that were sprouting in the California hills, but his Woodstock friends say he never did anything about it.

"Mostly we just clowned around the Café Espresso in the middle of town, and Groovy was the chief clown," one friend recalls. "One night he pulled some grass out of the ground, you know, real green cow-type grass, and he rolled it up in a cigarette paper and went up to these proper villagers and said, 'Hey, you want a joint of grass, man?' Ya had to laugh. Oh, another night, you know, the tables of the café were in this little sunken courtyard with their tops just about level with the sidewalk and one night Groovy just stepped off the sidewalk onto one of the tables and asked these tourists for a light. It broke everybody up—except the tourists. They just sat there and looked amazed."

Groovy and his friends had no place to stay in Woodstock. They moved around, sleeping in fields and barns. One week they stayed at a camp in the woods near Bob Dylan's house and visited several times with the folk singer-poet. Later, somebody said, they'd found a vacant barn and on a rainy July 23, Groovy, two other boys and two girls went out there to sleep. About 1 a.m., acting on a complaint by the owner, two Woodstock constables arrested the five for trespassing. The two girls were later released in custody of their parents. But the boys appeared the next day before Justice of the Peace Milton Houst and were sentenced to fifty days in jail or $50 fine.

One of the boys arrested with him recalls that Groovy seemed happy in jail. "In the cell he met this old Negro he'd known on the carnival circuit and rapped with him for hours about the old days. When I got out he asked me not to tell anybody he was there because he wanted to stay in, get some rest and three square meals a day for a while. He was already pretty strung out on drugs by then and I think he just liked the idea of fifty days of peace and quiet. But somebody called Galahad in New York and he came up and paid the fine."

A few weeks after Groovy got out of jail he and Galahad hit the road again. "We were just tired of the scene," Galahad recalls. They rode with some friends from Woodstock up to Montreal (Groovy wanted to see Expo) and then out to Denver. One night they were stopped in a small South Dakota town by a policeman who wanted to see their identification. "Groovy said he didn't have any eye-dentification," Galahad remembers. "But he said he had some tattoos. The cop said he just wanted to see an I.D. card. But Groovy kept showing him his tattoos. It really blew that cop's mind."

In Denver they were picked up by a girl in her Volkswagen bus and they drove with her and six others to Haight-Ashbury in San Francisco, where Galahad and Groovy put up in the Digger Free Store.

One day Steve Golden ran into Groovy at the Haight-Ashbury Free Clinic, which gave hippies free medical care. "He was wearing the only clothes I ever saw him wear anywhere—a dark shirt under a navy-blue pea jacket, scruffy blue jeans and a blue wool Ridgway cap with a button on the top. But he looked a lot worse than he had in New York. He was sitting on an overstuffed couch, his hands folded in his lap and when I said hello he looked up and said, 'Hi.' His eyes were much duller, his skin had turned sallow and he had a four day's growth of beard. I tried to talk with him but I got little response. He said he needed some vitamins, but the clinic didn't have them and he didn't have money to buy them. I offered him $5, but he wouldn't take it. He said he didn't feel well enough to peddle the *Berkeley Barb* like the others were doing, but he'd panhandle some."

Late in August, Groovy and Galahad left for New York because Galahad had a date in Court. Passing through Chicago, Groovy pulled a freak-out which is still Galahad's favorite. "We were busted for loitering and this cop started frisking Groovy. Groovy had this electric razor in one pocket and when the cop touched the razor case Groovy suddenly yelled, 'Careful, it'll explode and blow us all up.' Boy, the cop yanked his hands away like it was a hot stove."

Back in New York the two friends saw less of each other than before. They stayed in different pads, although they would usually get together at least once a day. "We still looked after each other like brothers," Galahad says, "but he was really strung out on speed [Methedrine] by then. Seemed like every time I saw him he was on that stuff, always speedin' all over the place, moving around, circulating, grooving with all the people. I couldn't keep up with him at the end. I didn't have all the energy he did. I wasn't on speed then."

Steve Golden recalls seeing Groovy one day at a be-in. "His little face, which always looked a bit like John Carradine's, was getting down to bones. His chin was sharpened, his cheeks hollowed. His body, which was always thin, still seemed okay, but his face looked like it was starting to die."

Jim Fouratt, a leader of the Jade Companions of the Flowered Dance and other East Village community groups, also saw Groovy several times after he got back from California. "He was getting more and more frantic, still playing the court jester to Galahad's king, a minstrel in the midst of all that ruin. He was frightening to look at, all wasted away from the drugs, he looked like a skeleton dancing and singing."

Sometime around this time Groovy met Linda Fitzpatrick, the girl from Greenwich, Connecticut. Nobody paid much attention to her because Groovy was always with girls in the Village—girls named Fran, Shelly, Vina.

He spent part of his last day in a sleeping bag in front of the Psychedeli-catessen next to Linda. At dawn the next morning their bodies were discovered in the boiler room on Avenue B.

Groovy's head was badly mutilated by the brick, but the family insisted on an open casket at the funeral so the undertaker worked a day and a half to fix it up. On October 13, he was buried in Highland Memorial Park in Johnston, Rhode Island. Ernie St. Angelo, Danny Zenone and most of the other Mondos were there. So were Galahad and about thirty other flower children from the Village. Galahad played Groovy's harmonica briefly over the grave. "I know how Groovy would have wanted it," he said. "Like this."

In the reams of press coverage which followed the murder, Groovy was beatified. One feature writer saw him as "his generation's young rebel, a fugitive from the meanness and materialism he saw around him. An urban Huck Finn. The modern runaway from mendacity and phony respectabil-ity. A hot-gospeling psychedelic seeker of lost souls."

After reading most of the stories, Ernie St. Angelo said: "Hutchy would have been in his glory if he was alive and could read all this. He would have loved the crazy things they're saying. He always wanted to be the leader of the laughers.

[May, 1968]

The Collapse of S.D.S.

by Roger Kahn

A few days after the Students for a Democratic Society babbled into civil war last spring, I called the Chicago office where Mark Rudd, the new maximum leader of a muscular minority, was hard at work. Pretty much everybody was on vacation, Rudd told me, in a manner he has perfected: the soft voice pregnant with insolence. Besides, there were no statements ready for the bourgeois press.

"Well, I wanted to talk to you about the future of participatory democracy, Mark."

"I'm sorry," said the soft voice. "No statement."

"Then tell me this. Which is the real S.D.S.?"

Rudd gave the question no pause. "You're talking to him," he said.

That is participatory democracy with a difference, and while Rudd clicked off, it struck me that there probably has not been a people's movement quite like his since Louis XIV announced, in freshman European History, *L'état c'est moi.*

At Chicago during several imperfect days in June, the S.D.S., growing in influence and numbers but not in maturity, committed binary fission. Since their meeting at Michigan State University a year before, times had been heady for the young radicals. National membership grew persistently toward 100,000. Campus after campus—seventeen on a single day last April—was disrupted by people protesting Vietnam, racism or both. Power was coming to students, but as it did, power's handmaiden, factionalism, took hold. The group Rudd captured, the Revolutionary Youth Movement, sees youth as a class, fighting in the vanguard against the abuses of capitalist America. Youth and the blacks are a distinct breed of warrior. The others, putatively led by John Pennington, late of Harvard, grew out of the Maoist Progressive Labor Party. This offshoot, the Worker-Student Alliance, describes blacks as a subgroup in a generally oppressed American proletariat. You have to have lived with the Left for a time to comprehend the fury of these dogmatic struggles.

The Chicago convention attracted fifteen hundred radical delegates, who wanted variously to dominate the S.D.S., to reunite it, to formulate new revolutionary programs or, at the very least, to hit Mayor Daley in the left jowl with a soiled sock. None of these things was accomplished. Instead, with shouting, chanting and finally with a drill that traces to Munich, 1923, the Students for a Democratic Society came apart at the querulous age of nine.

I mean to guide you, as best I can, through the bewildering factions of S.D.S. belief, the valid and contrived sources of S.D.S. conflict, and even into the remote future, which by radical clocks begins at eleven o'clock tomorrow morning. We are crossing into a land of red and black, where Mao is very good, Gene McCarthy is very bad, Ho Chi Minh is good and bad and Dick Nixon is indisputably excellent. The radicals reason that with Ol' Integrity in the White House, revolution has moved a decade closer. The radical press sets a suitable tone.

"S.D.S. lives," swears the Rudd faction's newsletter, "but one important thing has changed. The Progressive Labor Party faction has been kicked out. We cannot defeat white-supremacy anti-communism anti-working-class chauvinism with liberalism, allowing these tendencies to exist alongside of our revolutionary struggle, like a parasite draining our lifeblood away. *Power to the People!*"

At its top the newsletter carries a symbolic clenched left fist, etched to the best standards of W.P.A. art. At the bottom, Rudd's signature appears, beside four co-signers, including both of last year's top S.D.S. officers. The newsletter places national S.D.S. headquarters in Chicago.

With another day comes another bulletin. The same clenched fist leads the page, but *New Left Notes* claims the national S.D.S. offices for Boston. The walkout, John Pennington writes, "was unprincipled because it was not rooted in a good political basis. A lot of the appeal was, rather, to anti-communism. . . . Their opportunism manifested itself most grossly in racism. . . . Throughout the years, R.Y.M. leaders have concentrated on two things: infighting for political control and uniting to 'get P.L.' "

The prose is rather mild, but *New Left Notes* does not resemble The New York *Times*. Under the logotype, an artist has drawn two men crouching with guns and cartridge belts. The caption reads: "We are advocates of the abolition of war, we do not want war, but war can only be abolished through war and in order to get rid of the gun, it is necessary to take up the gun."

Welcome to the radical dimension, fifteen years before *1984*.

Considering Chicago and afterward, one thinks of diffuseness that is as old as the Left itself. Here are people who agree on sweeping principles and wage war on lesser ones. Here are factions of the Far Left approaching totalitarianism through a back door, like Mussolini. Here, in an organization committed to oppose strong leadership, Mark Rudd, a strong leader, shows a sublime, or catlike, ability to survive.

At the 1968 S.D.S. convention on the Michigan campus, Rudd, fresh from his conquest of Columbia, entered like an emperor and was spurned. The S.D.S. elected a hulking Californian named Michael Klonsky as national secretary. Bernardine Dohrn, a handsome, driving graduate of the University of Chicago Law School, was elected inter-organizational secretary. To the majority then, Rudd was a movie-star type, a flabby thinker, self-serving and a creation of the capitalist press.

Now a year later, after the great split, Rudd stood before the eight hundred members of the Revolutionary Youth Movement who had gathered in the First Congregational Church of Chicago. "I *am* a press-created leader," he said. "The media have made me a symbol of the New Left. While I don't approve, the movement needs leadership and symbols. My name exists as a symbol and at this time I think that's a good thing." On the basis of this talk, Rudd was elected national secretary, overwhelmingly defeating Robert Avakian, a round, intense Mao expert who leads B.A.R.U., California's Bay Area Revolutionary Union.

To understand these events and indeed the dissolution of the S.D.S., one has to call to mind the circumstances of last June and to view them (and the world) in the way that a radical would. As radicals saw matters, America in June was shuddering at the epicenter of the imperialist world. America's trouble excited them. It whipped their resolve and tickled their imagination with the persistent fantasy of revolution. When the radicals went to Chicago, they really thought that they might soon be contesting for control of the United States government. Consider June events:

The prime interest rate had just been advanced to eight and a half percent.

"The reason," one radical told me, "is that debts have become larger than the means of paying them off. The country has invested too much in nonproductive areas. The Vietnam war is a nonproductive area. As a result, we have a classic Marxist case: the underproduction of wealth.

That always precedes economic collapse. A money crisis is the first robin of depression."

Nixon was dealing and pleading with Congress to retain the income-tax surcharge.

"As depression gets closer," the radical said, "the ruling class defends itself by attacking the living standards of others. They cut back on education and welfare, the way they have in New York State. They increase taxes. Of course, these are only stopgaps."

For the first time since Korea, there was serious talk that Federal wage and price controls were needed to stop inflation.

"This might not happen until the Rockefeller wing—the brightest wing—of the international banking community gains more power in the Administration. This will be effective for a time, but it is only a more sophisticated stopgap."

Hospital workers were continuing an unpopular strike in Charleston, South Carolina.

"As real wages decline, and American real wages have been declining for four years, workers become confused. Instead of turning on their true oppressors, the international capitalists, they act in isolated, individual ways. They even turn on one another. Blacks blame a kind of low-level bigotry for their plight. Craft unions move to bar blacks. Despite this seeming disunity, the wave of strikes is another robin of the coming depression."

A powerful anti-black vote was apparent in the success of George Wallace, the nominations of John Marchi and Mario Proccacino in New York and the election of Sam Yorty in Los Angeles.

"Just as pogroms in Russia increased as the revolution approached, America's mounting racism is another sign that a depression and subsequent revolution is coming."

The right was growing swiftly stronger.

"If we are not to go from the abomination of Eisenhower-Kennedy-Johnson-Nixon, the gang-bang fathers of Vietnam, straight to the dust, straight to outright fascism, then we radicals are going to have to get ourselves together right now."

The national leaders of the S.D.S. wanted to convene on a campus, but a dozen or so universities turned them down. Jeff Gordon, an owlish Brooklynite who is a Worker-Student leader, found possible campus sites in New England. Now Klonsky and Bernardine Dohrn declined. New England was a Worker-Student stronghold. Instead they decided to meet at the Coliseum, a drab complex of halls and theatres behind a single dirty marquee on the South Side of Chicago. In the third week of June, young delegates converged on Chicago, sometimes by bus, more often five or six to an old car. Labor Committee people came from New York, and Worker-Student people came from Boston and Revolutionary Youth Movement people came all the way from California. A few, very few, came from Independent Socialist Clubs. Some of the Easterners who cut across Canada were rewarded with minute baggage examinations. The customs men were looking for heroin and marijuana. One claimed to have found pot in Rudd's belongings a month earlier.

It was a hard trip and not immediately rewarding. The Coliseum is a depressed arena set in a depressed area. An ancient greystone public school weathers slowly across the street. It is the kind of school Chicago reserves for ghetto children. The thick walls suggest a prison. There are cheap lunch counters nearby and a workingman's bar. It is a proletarian neighborhood and somber.

The convention began on the cool threatening Wednesday of June 18, starting five hours late. In the morning South Wabash Avenue was a muddle of radicals and newspapermen and plainclothesmen. Police photographers moved into the greystone school with long-range movie cameras but no uniformed police were in sight. Although Mayor Daley can discount liberal pressure, he could not ignore businessmen who warned that another Chicago police riot might drive conventions to other cities. "Even," someone said, "if all the victims are Commies, it'll look bad."

A few reporters were trying to interview students on the sidewalk. Others, under twenty-eight, joined the lines waiting to file past registration tables where, for a $5 fee, delegates were issued blue identification cards. One newspaperman passed by saying, "I'm from the University of Chicago." Another, claiming to be a University of Wisconsin man, was challenged.

"Name someone in the English department at Madison," said a bespectacled English girl behind a table.

"Professor Kelly," the reporter said.

"Okay," the girl said, leaving the reporter to wonder whether a man named Kelly really taught English at Wisconsin or whether the girl was as ignorant as he.

Inside, a security detachment searched everyone. The security men wore green armbands, and examined wallets or purses. Then each delegate was patted down. It was two days before Jeff Gordon rose on the floor to protest that "women's breasts are being felt and their legs are being felt close to their vaginas." After that women were added to the searching corps.

The hall was grey and dark and noisy. Voices echoed, the way they do in buildings at a zoo, and this would be important later when chanting started. All the seats were temporary. They could be picked up and thrown. The podium was fairly large and guarded on every side except the front by a railing. Along the walls, factions set up tables where their literature was available. People filed in slowly, and stood in knots. The Worker-Student Alliance believes in conventional grooming, which is to say haircuts and shaves. The Revolutionary Youth Movement prefers long hair and flowing moustaches. The room seemed fairly closely divided.

A Midwesterner named Tim McCarthy, brown-haired and harassed, was the S.D.S. Sam Rayburn, the permanent chairman. He had no gavel. Instead McCarthy used a rock to rap for order. At two o'clock he recognized Mike Klonsky.

Klonsky, twenty-six, and a graduate of San Fernando State, wore old pants and a camp T-shirt. He has light blond hair and a large saint-blond moustache and he looks powerful, but speaks haltingly. Klonsky proposed that almost all the press be admitted, provided each reporter paid a $25 fee and signed an affidavit that he "won't testify against us." The Coliseum rental was $400 a day and, Klonsky said, why not let the press pick up that tab. They can afford it.

Under any circumstances, The New York *Times* was to be barred. A *Times* national correspondent named Anthony Ripley had testified before the House Internal Security Committee, and Klonsky insisted the paper would have to be penalized.

"Actually," says Gene Roberts, National News Editor of The *Times,* "Ripley did not want to testify. He turned down a committee request. Then they subpoenaed him." Bernardine Dohrn told Ripley a year ago that she was "not a socialist but a revolutionary communist with a small c." The committee wanted that quote on record. All Ripley finally testified, in effect, was that his original *Times* story was accurate.

Still, Klonsky said, "No New York *Times.*"

Next McCarthy recognized Ed Clark, a drawling, balding man from New Orleans who stood with the W.-S.A. "We shouldn't let any reporters in," Clark said. "The capitalist press is not going to print the truth. They'll distort what happens. They always distort. We have our own press. We don't need the capitalist press. Bar them all." The hall erupted into applause. A few minutes later Clark's resolution passed 3 to 2.

The vote was significant because it was factional. Clark of the Progressive Labor Party-Worker-Student Alliance had defeated Klonsky of the Revolutionary Youth Movement. From this point forward, not more than an hour into the convention, the R.Y.M., which controlled the chair and the national offices, knew that it was outnumbered.

The maneuvering that followed was rather like that at the major party conventions. Small irrelevant issues are used as tests of strength. Positions are adopted not for ideological reasons but to gain delegates. Floor leaders buttonhole, arm twist, promise. And everyone looks for a single popular issue that will entrap the uncommitted. Perhaps a quarter of the delegates were women and that night both sides hit upon an identical stratagem to woo the uncommitted. They would support women's liberation.

Someone distributed a pamphlet headed: *The Fight for Women's Liberation is Basic to Defeating Imperialism!* In it, eight New Yorkers, mostly women, argued that "females, a vital part of the labor movement" were exploited, and had been at least since an 1824 strike in Pawtucket, Rhode Island. Black women were triply exploited: "first as workers, second as black people, and third, as women." The pamphleteers all but shrieked against male chauvinism within the movement. "In a recent leaflet put out by the Revolutionary Student Union in Berkeley around People's Park, we find a picture." The pamphlet reproduced an illustration of a full-breasted girl lifting a sweater toward her head. The girl wore no brassiere and the sweater was above the third rib when the shutter clicked. The caption read, "Today we relax."

Both sides agreed that this chauvinism was intolerable and, as the first day's jousting ended, outraged men were grabbing copies of the female liberation pamphlets as fast as the outraged women could distribute them.

Mark Rudd's responses tingle to disaster. When he was a Boy Scout, growing up fat and happy in the middle-class fastness of Maplewood, New Jersey, he was often driven to see his grandparents' store in Newark's dark and boiling central ward. The disaster of that neighborhood, he insists, nourished his radicalism. Later, at Columbia, he became particularly good at rallying student protesters after setbacks. Now, as the R.Y.M. caucused in the Coliseum balcony on the morning of the second day, Rudd's assurance swelled. The group was calling itself The Weatherman, after a line of Bob Dylan's: "You don't need a weatherman to know which way the wind blows."

Klonsky and Carl Davidson, a reporter for the radical weekly *Guardian,* were suggesting that the American blacks were about to enter "a new democratic stage." Blacks might stop rioting, and join with the bourgeoisie and press for progress within the American laws.

Standing in a checked shirt, Rudd said, "Well, sure. But the working class consists of everyone who doesn't own the means of production and the blacks sure as shit don't own them. So we can't talk about a new democratic stage for the blacks. They have to be liberated by a socialist revolution, the way Vietnam should be liberated and the way China was liberated."

"We can't go irresponsible and tell the blacks that there won't be a new stage of democratic progress," Davidson said.

"We sure as hell can," Rudd said. "We can talk to black people and give them the understanding our revolutionary Marxism gives us. We're revolutionaries."

Rudd carried the point. R.Y.M. would continue to preach revolution at blacks. Later, during a break, feeling his own importance, he strode down Wabash Avenue with his Oriental girl friend and another girl, a German expatriate. A news photographer began snapping and Rudd rushed forward, arms out, hands up, commanding: "Who are you? Who are you taking pictures for?"

The photographer backed off. "I'm with *Women's Wear Daily*," he said. "I'm supposed to get pictures of the way women of the Left dress. Who are you?"

For the next two days the Worker-Student Alliance, under Gordon and Pennington and the Revolutionary Youth Movement under Klonsky, Dohrn and Bob Avakian circled one another. The W.-S.A. kept winning test votes, but narrowly. Owlish Jeff Gordon and earnest John Pennington were nervous. The R.Y.M. leaders felt defeat. The feminist issue was now useless, but one asset R.Y.M. possessed was good lines into minority groups. On Thursday and Friday, they marshaled black and tan and brown, huddled with them, gave them the podium and urged them to get "the racist W.-S.A."

A tall thin Puerto Rican, wearing a purple beret, led off. "All people should have the right to self-determination," he said. The Puerto Rican was prominent in a gang called The Young Lords. He criticized W.-S.A. for not recognizing Puerto Ricans as a nation. Then he recited a history of Puerto Rico.

"And now," he said at length, "I want you to meet my friend Corky."

Corky wore a brown beret. He was short and chubby, a Mexican-American. "Remember the Western United States was stolen from Mexico," Corky said. "We need self-determination." Corky read an extended list of American communities which he said should have self-determination. The hall was yawning. Chaka Walls spoke next.

Walls is a quick, angry, powerful man, a leader of the Illinois Black Panther Party. "Blacks have the right to self-determination," he shouted. Abruptly the hall rang with cheers. Walls was excited. "I'm gonna tell you motherfuckers, blacks have a right to choose. I've seen a lot of things around here I don't like. People says blacks don't have a right to choose as blacks. You motherfuckers better get yourselves together."

Whatever Klonsky and Dohrn wanted they were stuck. Chaka had the microphone plus the attention of fifteen hundred whites and he was not letting go. "About all this male chauvinism," he said. "I'm for pussy power myself." Seated in the hall, you could see some women cringe. Like Orwell's left, the S.D.S. is stained with puritanism. Motherfucker is a necessary obscenity. Pussy power is upsetting to a nice middle-class radical girl.

"Revolutionary women have a lot to contribute," Walls said. "I'm glad to see there're enough women around here for all the revolution. The way the women contribute is by getting laid."

R.Y.M. strategy was becoming a disaster. In the back of the hall W.-S.A. people chanted, *"Fight male chauvinism. Fight male chauvinism."*

But Walls was out of control. "Superman," he shouted, "was a punk. He never even tried to fuck Lois Lane."

The chant swelled. Walls could not go on. After a while Jul Cook, another Panther, replaced Walls at the microphone and pleaded for quiet. "The Worker-Student Alliance," he said, "comes here and makes a lot of noise, but they're not leading any fights on campus." A hearty cheer rose from R.Y.M. "But," Cook said, "you got to know I'm with my brother. I'm for pussy power myself. The *position* of women in the movement. . . ."

People guessed what was coming. The chant against male chauvinism renewed.

"The position of the women," roared Cook, "should be *prone.*"

R.Y.M. strategy had collapsed. The noble Panthers were playing burlesque comics. A girl got up and said she refused to have women's liberation used as a political football. Someone else wondered if Jul Cook, the Panther, understood the difference between prone and supine or if he was revealing a matter of personal preference.

On Friday night R.Y.M. walked out. At first R.Y.M. leaders bickered. Bernardine Dohrn insisted that black liberation could come about only through a socialist revolution. Klonsky and Avakian thought it might happen separately. But against a swarming common enemy, the two R.Y.M. factions got themselves together long enough to urge Jul Cook to play a second engagement. At seven p.m. Tim McCarthy rushed to the microphone and shouted: "The Panthers have asked to speak again and here they are." It was a kind of vaudeville introduction.

This time Cook carried a written speech. "The Panthers and the Young Lords and the Brown Berets have gotten together," he began, "and adopted a common position. The Progressive Labor-Worker-Student Alliance faction is acting like pigs. They're holding back the black and brown peoples' struggle for self-determination. Immediately after the convention, chicken shit P.L. is going to change its position *because* P.L. is chicken shit."

W.-S.A. people sat silent. It is as hard for a radical to lash out at a black as it is for him to praise a policeman. "P.L. acts like cops," Cook said. "They act like counterrevolutionaries. P.L. is the reincarnation of Leon Trotsky." There were a few shouts of protest. "Chairman Mao supports liberation for all oppressed people."

At last W.-S.A. chanted, *Read Mao, Read Mao, Read Mao.*

"P.L. is counterrevolutionary," Cook yelled at the microphone.

The W.-S.A. faction, all about the dingy hall, chanted: *Bullshit, Bullshit, Bullshit."*

A half dozen Panthers walked toward the Progressive Labor Party's literature table on the left side of the hall. They stood glaring, intimidating. Jeff Gordon and John Pennington dispatched a battalion and soon the angry Panthers were surrounded by men from the W.-S.A.

The chants continued. Bob Avakian's group, several hundred strong, began a rhythmic: *Power to the people. Power to the people.* The W.-S.A. shifted smoothly: *Power to the workers. Power to the workers.* A group of New Yorkers began to bellow: *Let's go, Mets.*

The place was deafening. Mike Klonsky walked to the microphone and tried to speak. The W.-S.A. roared: *Rebuttal. Rebuttal.* Klonsky glared at the chanters, who ignored him. Jeff Gordon rose and, surrounded by a dozen men, walked to the microphone. His cadre wore red-and-white buttons on their left shoulders, the insignia of the new W.-S.A. security force.

Speaking very slowly, Gordon said, "The Progressive Labor Party will not be intimidated out of S.D.S." (Roaring applause.) "We support national liberation all over the world. We support the Black Panther Party. When we criticize the Panthers it is in a comradely and constructive fashion. We support self-determination for all the black people in the United States." Gordon stepped down and the hall resounded to: *Fight racism. Fight racism.*

The leadership of R.Y.M. gathered at the rear of the podium. They had lost control of the agenda and the delegates and the meeting, and now it appeared that they would lose control of S.D.S. On the floor someone said, "They've driven into the Holland Tunnel the wrong way. Now they're stopping the car while they figure out what to do."

At nine forty-five Rudd walked to the microphone. "If we go on this way," he said, "we'll have fights, not political discussion. I suggest we recess for an hour. Frankly I'm not suggesting this only to let the situation cool. We want to caucus to decide what to do."

On the platform behind him, R.Y.M. leaders argued Rudd's proposal. Bernardine Dohrn was talking heatedly with Klonsky, who had a pacifying hand on one of hers. Suddenly Bernardine spun away and marched to the microphone, breathless and intense.

Usually, Bernardine is immaculate and poised. Now she was perspiring. Her soft brown hair looked scraggly. Her silky yellow blouse had come unbuttoned. "Some of us are going to have to decide," she shouted, "whether our principles allow us to stay in the same organization with people who deny the right of self-determination to the oppressed. Anyone who would like a discussion of that, follow me into the next room." She strutted off the podium toward a corridor on the left, opening to a large, empty room. Mike Klonsky stared after Bernardine, looking as though his favorite grandmother had fallen off a roof. Rudd moved quickly behind Bernardine. Slowly the rest of the R.Y.M. hierarchy followed. All around the room people rose and walked out.

The W.-S.A. started chants. *Sit down.* Some picked up chairs and banged them against the floor. *Sit* (beat, beat, beat) *down. Sit* (beat, beat, beat) *down.* Others chanted *Stay and fight. Stay and fight.* But at least a third of the people walked out after Bernardine. The S.D.S. was never whole again.

R.Y.M. devised its doomsday device on the next evening. The W.-S.A. meeting, under a new chairman, broke itself into workshops. Groups moved their chairs and gathered, facing one another, and discussed racism, imperialism and how it was essential for young radicals not only to teach workers, but to learn from the workers as well. The point about blacks, people said over and over, was that they were a part of the oppressed proletarian class.

It was almost eleven o'clock when Jared Israel of W.-S.A., a black-haired New Yorker who had moved to Boston, concluded a private meeting with Mike Klonsky. He returned to the main floor and asked for attention. "Look," he shouted, "I have information that the R.Y.M. people are finally coming back here. When they do, please don't hiss or chant. All we need is for a fight. Then the Chicago pigs will bust us all."

Israel was preaching docility because, as far as I can learn, Klonsky and Dohrn had urged it on him. Docility was what the R.Y.M. people wanted. It was critical to their careful plan.

A file of R.Y.M. women, Valkyries, left the closed room. A dozen marched through the passageway into the main hall and formed a line about the podium. The girls stood shoulder to shoulder saying nothing. The podium itself was unoccupied.

A column of green armbands came next. These men ringed the radical Valkyries. Two columns now protected the lectern.

A double file of men followed. Ten Black Panthers were in the lead. The file marched to a point in front of the hall, split into two columns and strung themselves out until the W.-S.A. was completely encircled. Someone stood up.

"Sit down," a R.Y.M. man yelled.

"I didn't try to get up," a W.-S.A. member explained later, "and neither would you. It was scary."

The W.-S.A. had been taken in. Their disarrayed people, sprawled about in workshops, were surrounded. Now the R.Y.M. elite marched unchallenged to the podium. Big Mike Klonsky, who reportedly carries a gravity knife, leaned toward the microphone. "We have agreed there will be no fights. I'm sure there will be none," he commanded.

The W.-S.A. was too startled to respond.

Bernardine stepped forward. "In the last twenty-four hours," she cried, her voice grinding, "we in the next room have been discussing principles. We support the national liberation struggles of the Vietnamese, the American blacks and all other colonials. We support all who take up the gun against U.S. imperialism. We support the governments of China, Albania, North Vietnam and North Korea. We support women's liberation."

Backed by the green armbands, the shrill revolutionary held the room. "All members of the Progressive Labor Party-W.-S.A., and all who do not support these principles are objectively racist and counterrevolutionary. They are no longer members of S.D.S."

Too late, W.-S.A. began to chant. Pointing fingers at the podium and thrusting in rhythm, the W.-S.A. people cried: *Shame! Shame! Shame!* But Bernardine's group, having declared itself the winner, was walking out. With muscle and with trickery, the minority had read the majority out of S.D.S.

Later that night, the R.Y.M. people secured the files and the mailing lists and the names of contributors in the National Office on West Madison Street. The next day, while the W.-S.A. was overwhelmingly electing John Pennington, the R.Y.M. group cast its lot with Mark Rudd. Still, some had doubts, and as Rudd was accepting his new office, a thin S.D.S. faction, R.Y.M. II, was born.

"The S.D.S.," the young radical tells me in the hot New York summer, "is dead. It can't be what it was." We are meeting over a Scotch in my living room, and there will be no chanting here.

"What was it?" I say.

"It was a focus for young leftists everywhere. It was a place where we could get together and learn from one another. It was where we found out how to use our local experiences—my own at Cornell, somebody else's somewhere else—and make some sense out of them. It was where we grew from being merely radicals—people who talk big change in the parlor—to becoming active revolutionaries. It's revolutionaries, not radicals, who disrupt the campus fat cats and who let people know that our universities are contributing to imperialism full time. I'm proud of that."

Technically, the S.D.S. traces to the 1930's when the Fabian socialist League for Industrial Democracy opened a student division. But actually it is an organization of the present revitalized only nine years ago and given a voice in 1962 when Tom Hayden began The Port Huron Statement:

"We are people of this generation, bred in at least modest comfort, housed now in universities, looking uncomfortably to the world we inherit."

"I'm more uncomfortable than ever," the young radical says, challenging; "aren't you?"

He is upset at what has happened. "It was smart to keep out the press," he says, "because we acted like so many jerks."

I sip my drink and tell the radical that things run their course. First S.D.S. had intended to work through existing institutions. Then it found it could not. First it would have no permanent leaders. Now it is undone by the inability of a Mike Klonsky to contend rationally with a major challenge.

"What are you going to do now?" I ask the radical.

"We're going to fight. All winter long there's going to be a fight between R.Y.M. and W.-S.A. for every old S.D.S. chapter in America. But I'm not kidding myself. The fight will settle nothing. We'll only have more splits."

The S.D.S. is a kind of Willy Loman of radical groups, wanting to achieve something it didn't understand. Being young, it sought desperately to be noticed. Notice has come and harshly. Representative Ichord is investigating. State legislatures pass bills against campus protest. Fighting Ronnie Reagan wants to pave over every S.D.S. headquarters in the land.

The irony is disturbing, if you believe, as I do, in many of the positions for which S.D.S. stood. Vietnam can kill us all, or at least drive us to bankruptcy. The blacks have to be brought into society, through Columbia, Harvard and Princeton, as well as through grade school at Yeehaw Junction, Florida.

Enough of us believed these things to set a climate where S.D.S. experimenters could advance. But they were advancing in America, where one of the rules for political success is discipline.

You have to be organized, work through leaders, prepare. The need for discipline did in S.D.S., the fortress of anti-disciplinarianism.

"When someone writes a history of S.D.S.," the radical says, "how do you think it's going to go?"

"What do you mean?"

"Well is he going to mark us down as important radicals, or in the end are we going to look like a pack of anarchists."

We sit a long time. The day and the summer are waning. I have to tell the young man I don't know.

[October, 1969]

My Generation

by Jacob Brackman

No, no breather yet for reminiscence, no nostalgia, no wistful catalog of names and feats. The biggest crop in national history, War Baby boom; *Hibakusha,* survivors of Hiroshima. Happening now. Our fathers had played out our chances for us. Next time the lamps start going out, no one shall ever see them lit again. Half America under twenty-five, stirring, rumbling: unbuttoned potentiality, exquisite and terrible. First to grow from infancy with Rootie Kazootie and Mr. Wizard, with access to perspective, incredible information about the world; supersaturated with grey emanations. First to grow in the shadow of extinction, first to gamble piously with human chemistry, gripped in a fever for eleventh-hour salvation. The adult secondary, keying on us, cotton-mouthed, their legs near gone, barking signals of our estrangement up to their big forward wall: which way would we cut, or charge, and when? Rushing to their mailboxes, devouring the magazines—something was happening here, the kids were going crazy, black ones burning city blocks, white ones occupying great universities (my God, and holding *hostages*), out to levitate the Pentagon with obscene chants, capping joints instead of kegs at the Delta House, ten thousand self-exiled to Canada, not even *trying* to get through anymore. "Stop us?" Cohn-Bendit laughed. "Slap at water."

The magazine editors fumbling for the angle that won't look ridiculous, eavesdropping in the bar cars, pleading with their adolescent children ("Something's happening here, right? Tell Daddy"). Searching out those few among us who cared, for a time still, to talk, uncertain what they listened for, or could hear. The media men set us questions, subverted in a thousand nuances: How did it feel when (*read*: Kennedy, Schwerner, Rockwell, King, Kennedy) was shot? When did you reject your parents' attitude toward (*read*: sex, religion, the Republican Party)? Did you turn nihilistic when they beat you in a Mississippi jail? Didn't you realize they were sick individuals? Isn't pot, come on now, just running away from reality? Does Gene McCarthy give you hope? You can't believe disruption helps your cause? Do you dig (*read*: maxi-skirts, Che, Nehru jackets)? Well, what other country's better? You think you'd like to live in China? . . . Our disappointment ran so deep we goofed all over them. "Your dog is chewing on my arm." "For a kicks sort of thing, you know what I mean?" "You go on build it up, mother, we gonna burn it down." "Don't think twice, it's all right, Ma (I'm only bleeding)." "I don't know, man, all around me I see cats plugging at their games, and I can't put them down, man; I can't even locate my own head."

Scott, born to the American century, sharing its war-rent Teens and profligate Twenties, winning a First in the Newman field day, pledging Cottage Club at Princeton; too long and too intensely pursuing meager collegiate dreams of wealth and glory, jazzy flapper fun, of heroics on the gridiron, on the battlefield, with the deb of the moment on a sawdusted ballroom floor: *There was an orchestra—Bingo-Bango/Playing for us to dance the tango/And the people all clapped as we arose/For her sweet face and my new clothes.* . . . You called yourselves "lost" and rather fancied the notion; cut the strings to your discredited elders, to their witch hunts and Prohibitions, their Teapot Domes. And after all the football and the classy North Shore parties, the Riviera gilt by association, there glistened a more seductive bauble, bigger than the Ritz—to be a great writer: an American Turgenev. Till in the Thirties, all your barren aspirations cracked, or rather, played themselves out: "Horror and waste— waste and horror—what I might have been and done that is lost, spent, gone, dissipated, unrecapturable." We are setting off where you broke down, Fitzboomski, a sensibility delicate as tears, you took too long to realize how lost you were. We arrived precociously at consciousness, with nothing to live up to.

Perhaps the writer must make plain that his presumptuous "we" isn't shorthand for a clear temper of ideas, statistically accessible, but for a kind of Early-Warning System, which gets its fix from marginal characters, from madmen, yes, and outlaws, reduced to a fraction of their significance by the vast denominator that has remained—will always remain—the same: "In what he called 'the most extensive survey of its kind ever undertaken,' pollster George Gallup found that the political views of voters between the ages of twenty-one and twenty-nine differ hardly at all from the views of those thirty to forty-nine. 'A lot of this talk about this group's being a maverick generation must be considered ridiculous,' Gallup told reporters. 'People should not worry about the future of this country. It's in good hands.' The most recent survey, he said, shows Nixon polling forty-four percent to Kennedy's thirty-seven percent." Who were we then? No torpid cross-section, median deadwood, we had no cutoff age. With vague and wide connections we stretched ten years on campus, fifteen, at least, through rock and dope. Of one hundred million, we were a fringe, but we were making more noise than was our due, attaching converts in their pubescence; and fringes of our own, too woolly, too scary for even us to believe, were burgeoning around us. We did not enjoy the company of all our finest peers by any means, for there were scientists, ponderers, decent liberals who had removed themselves inexorably from us, as if the times were quite like other times and there was still a future for business as usual. Yet, at their remove, they felt a sense of loss. And those who joined us relinquished all prospects for return. We nurtured a daring premise: we were of historical moment, critical, unprecedented, containing within ourselves the fullness of time. Some great wind was brewing as we breathed; not a new generation, but a new notion of generation with new notions of its imperatives. We would not default, succumb to the certainties of age, gulp pills, compromise maturely, lubricate our adulthoods with facile resignations. We would not be normal. For normality was now disease—hacking coughs, quilted stomachs and cold loins, the sniveling bitterness of diminished hopes—and if we were to live propitiously in our era, we would have to define normality anew. We might say no, after long childhoods of indulgence, to the sudden demands of our complicity. We might not, on schedule, relinquish our freedom. We might remain forever infants, joyous beggars, dependent on the system, refusing our contributions yet ready enough to consume. Though distribution was presently askew, or demented, technology has already created wealth enough to sustain us all. We might innovate for Health across the boards: new jokes, sex, politics, learning—a massive reclamation of the cities of our souls. Or so we mused when we were on, and up. When we were off, and down, we could envision ourselves forty-year-old waifs, with pee stains on our underwear, drifting without callings in a society we could neither convert nor make sense of. For in a single day we could waver between something like optimism and a despair so deadly it seemed there was no acre of earth where we would be permitted to gather with those we loved and share a creditable life—a despair that suggested we were the first generation that could imagine declining its bid to inherit the earth.

In 1952, the year I started going to the movies alone, M-G-M released a film called *It's a Big Country,* with, well, real spirit, and an amazing cast—Ethel Barrymore, Keefe Brasselle, Gary Cooper, Van Johnson, Gene Kelly, Janet Leigh, George Murphy—and lots of lines like: "I'm just a guy who loves America. What a country! Greatest in the world and I'm proud to be a part of it. *Sure . . .* we got our problems. But we'll lick 'em." The other night I caught it again on TV and short-circuited back to a past I scarcely recalled. Between vignettes, the camera swept past bustling cities and waving fields of grain, while a basso narrator intoned, "America! The conscience. The heart. The will." In one irresistibly upbeat sketch, a Texan who kept insisting he didn't believe in "overdoin' things" gradually revealed the gross dimensions of his excess.(!) In another, an immigrant Hungarian obsessed with his people's traditional hostility toward Greeks, reconciled himself to his eldest daughter's marriage to one (while an entire Greek fraternity suddenly surrounded his remaining six daughters). It was an enmity I hadn't heard of before (nor since) but I was quite prepared to believe that it was keeping lots of fine people apart. I'm sure that immigrant family seemed to me rather like my grandparents, with whom I lived, and that I imagined I would grow up rather like the heretical daughter who might just go ahead and marry the Greek, convention be damned, because, after all, we're all Americans. (A fantastic intimation: American problems are the ones that aren't intrinsically *American.*) I wasn't much for Country 'Tis of Thee, nor otherwise impossibly square, but my ancestors had been given some bad times in their Old Countries. I'd heard stories. At night, sometimes, I used to think about how lucky I was to have been born here. My own relation to America was strong and clear. Of course I knew that there were imperfections, vast ones, but I thought almost everybody good (millions of liberals! wearing sandals! listening to The Weavers!) wanted to help change what was bad. I was ready to work, too, and I thought of our problems: "We'll lick 'em." 1952. "Indians" were mentioned once, in a recitation of all the different kinds of real Americans there are. Although it was a "sweeping panorama" no Negro was seen or heard of. Squalor was a homey testing ground for pluck, a purgatory short enough to make heaven seem the cozier. The Korean War did not exist. I remember exactly when I saw *It's a Big Country.* Stevenson had just lost. I was nine years old.

I went to lots of movies as a kid; I could never have guessed that this one, for all its garish mediocrity, influenced me as much, or confirmed as much for me, as any book I ever read. As I watched it again on television, the perfect familiarity of every scene astounded me, for I had no memory of any truth awry, any line or image even slightly extreme. I wish I could have seen it annually, throughout my adolescence, to graph my departure from its lovely vision.

Many people five years older than I (the magic Thirty!) managed to sustain their image of lickable problems into maturity, where it got focused into a hopeful conception of American life, or at least of the forces which stunt that life. Poverty was a toughening up en route to success; Racism, a declining aberration, a Southern psychosis; War, forced upon us from without by foreigners of ruthless, outsized ambition. Even as today, the media takes each Vietnam horror story to be a freakish, notable event, so these elders learned to interpret every tormenting fact of American depravity as a temporary *exception,* learned to cultivate a "full perspective." And as Fitzgerald's great believers wakened to a nation incorrigibly great, so many people five years younger than I wakened to one simply incorrigible, and grew without belief of any kind. We in the middle learned that the enemy was Russia, and later, China, and still later that the enemy was not peculiar to any system, but was the same in all: repression, banality, irrelevance, and all the other uglinesses which conspire to dwarf or extinguish the human personality. We clung desperately to hopes for fixing this, for fixing that, tracing the evil in our national life to misguided policy, until poverty, racism, war and the rest seemed no longer a result of bunglings, no longer accidental, but institutional features of our society. The enormity of the change required seemed, then, to lie altogether beyond our means of change, and numbed us into quietude, or nightmares of apocalypse.

We needed new definitions of livelihood, of maturity and enjoyment, but we could scarcely imagine change so gargantuan it seemed close to reversal, so inaccessible to legislation or "programs" as to demand a radicalism of messianic proportions. America injured us into black experiments, futile bouts; our fists sank into her fat, and disappeared. Some of us were beautiful before going over the edge. The personal histories of friends, and their friends, merged with our own; we shared a common genealogy, and we would share a common fate. One, brimming with compassion, marched and organized. As he ascended ghetto stairwells a kind of targetless hate began to spread inside him, a guilty helplessness, and dread. He was neither poor nor black. He could not pay his dues with nightstick scars, even assuming he could find someone to administer them. His hair and eyes grew wild, but some vestigial love of country froze him in the anarchist's posture. He became an armchair kamikaze; talked of confrontation, interests, guns, resistance, plotted strikes on Lockheed and, at last, provoked a beating from the law in a Westchester shopping center so suburban ladies might see that it could happen there, and to a nice Jewish boy. Succumbing to the romance of guerrilla-hood, he laughed at talk of Asian peasants or disenfranchised blacks, crying that each injustice was but a single head of the Hydra that had to be stilled by a sword through the heart. One day, he was gone, some said to Cuba. Another, with a foot already inside the academy, gave away what he had, wandered barefoot and penniless through Mexico, smoked ganja in Jamaica with

Ras Tafarians and charas in Calcutta with poets; became an animal, howled through the woods of western Pennsylvania, was loved across the boundaries of class and burned for a time with the conviction that it was all *there,* laid out for him, the occult feast, the rites of exploration. "I'm running a whole different flick," he said. Sometimes he talked ideas that unhinged our knees, sometimes his silence was so wise we swore we'd never speak again. And while our leaders reassessed positions, he reassessed for us the meat of consciousness, to make our lives organic, of a piece. Some months ago he turned to vegetable, but until he could no longer wipe himself after toilet, we thought we must also cast off what we still clung to, and follow him. We had sent them out to reconnoiter galaxies, and they, as it happened, plunged too far. We lost radio contact. They lost ground control. We could no longer interpret their fitful vibrations.

Those of us with nerve endings less exposed hung back, holding our acts together, but making little waves. Teen-agers ran a gigantic import industry. (How can you venerate government and law when you commit a felony every day?) Black sophomores propped their black feet up on the prexy's walnut desk. Wheeler-dealer heads took Wall Street for a ride. Ecstatic communitarians grooved to divine potato patches. Children invented music that didn't go Bingo-Bango. They didn't know much; they were suckers for fakery. But we were slow to call any experiment excessive. Within ambient disorder, each seemed somehow appropriate. We felt *ourselves* growing into the people our parents had warned us about. The woods already burning, they spent their strength clucking over our eccentricity. And there were ever reassurances: we would learn; we'd soon be out on the field with the team from VISTA or Dow. Meanwhile, we dug in for the longest "adolescent phase" since adolescence was invented a century ago. Bleak signals flashed across our skies. Legions of our most promising would surely disappear into the prisons. In the Fifties, we never guessed the phonies could become so dangerous. Many wouldn't stick it out. They'd learned why Lao-Tze hopped upon his ox, at last, and rode out beyond the Great Wall. Many others, perhaps stronger and finer, perhaps not yet placing the problems at so terrible a depth, might begin their thousand pinpricks, launch forays into the barren democratic sensibility. By their refusal, their mischief, their infiltration, great numbers could begin to conceive of something more decent than submitting to the culture. There was that vague and fragile chance, and although I had contempt for much my generation spawned, I could not see another chance anywhere I looked.

[October, 1968]

The Color Gap

Fifth Avenue, Uptown

by James Baldwin

There is a housing project standing now where the house in which we grew up once stood, and one of those stunted city trees is snarling where our doorway used to be. This is on the rehabilitated side of the avenue. The other side of the avenue—for progress takes time—has not been rehabilitated yet and it looks exactly as it looked in the days when we sat with our noses pressed against the windowpane, longing to be allowed to go "across the street." The grocery store which gave us credit is still there, and there can be no doubt that it is still giving credit. The people in the project certainly need it—far more, indeed, than they ever needed the project. The last time I passed by, the Jewish proprietor was still standing among his shelves, looking sadder and heavier but scarcely any older. Further down the block stands the shoe-repair store in which our shoes were repaired until reparation became impossible and in which, then, we bought all our "new" ones. The Negro proprietor is still in the window, head down, working at the leather.

These two, I imagine, could tell a long tale if they would (perhaps they would be glad to if they could), having watched so many, for so long, struggling in the fishhooks, the barbed wire, of this avenue.

The avenue is elsewhere the renowned and elegant Fifth. The area I am describing, which, in today's gang parlance, would be called "the turf," is bounded by Lenox Avenue on the west, the Harlem River on the east, 135th Street on the north, and 130th Street on the south. We never lived beyond these boundaries; this is where we grew up. Walking along 145th Street—for example—familiar as it is, and similar, does not have the same impact because I do not know any of the people on the block. But when I turn east on 131st Street and Lenox Avenue, there is first a soda-pop joint, then a shoeshine "parlor," then a grocery store, then a dry cleaners', then the houses. All along the street there are people who watched me grow up, people who grew up with me, people I watched grow up along with my brothers and sisters; and, sometimes in my arms, sometimes underfoot, sometimes at my shoulder—or on it—their children, a riot, a forest of children, who include my nieces and nephews.

When we reach the end of this long block, we find ourselves on wide, filthy, hostile Fifth Avenue, facing that project which hangs over the avenue like a monument to the folly, and the cowardice, of good intentions. All along the block, for anyone who knows it, are immense human gaps, like craters. These gaps are not created merely by those who have moved away, inevitably into some other ghetto; or by those who have risen, almost always into a greater capacity for self-loathing and self-delusion; or yet by those who, by whatever means—War II, the Korean war, a policeman's gun or billy, a gang war, a brawl, madness, an overdose of heroin, or, simply, unnatural exhaustion—are dead. I am talking about those who are left, and I am talking principally about the young. What are they doing? Well, some, a minority, are fanatical churchgoers, members of the most extreme of the Holy Roller sects. Many, many more are "Moslems," by affiliation or sympathy, that is to say that they are united by nothing more—and nothing less—than a hatred of the white world and all its works. They are present, for example, at every Buy Black street-corner meeting—meetings in which the speaker urges his hearers to cease trading with white men and establish a separate economy. Neither the speaker nor his hearers can possibly do this, of course, since Negroes do not own General Motors or RCA or the A&P, nor, indeed, do they own more than a wholly insufficient fraction of anything else in Harlem (those who *do* own anything are more interested in their profits than in their fellows). But these meetings nevertheless keep alive in the participators a certain pride of bitterness without which, however futile this bitterness may be, they could scarcely remain alive at all. Many have given up. They stay home and watch the TV screen, living on the earnings of their parents, cousins, brothers, or uncles, and only leave the house to go to the movies or to the nearest bar. "How're you making it?" one may ask, running into them along the block, or in the bar. "Oh, I'm TV-ing it"; with the saddest, sweetest, most shamefaced of smiles, and from a great distance. This distance one is compelled to respect; anyone who has traveled so far will not easily be dragged again into the world. There are further retreats, of course, than the TV screen or the bar. There are those who are simply sitting on their stoops, "stoned," animated for a moment only, and hideously, by the approach of someone who may lend them the money for a "fix." Or by the approach of someone from whom they can purchase it, one of the shrewd ones, on the way to prison or just coming out.

And the others, who have avoided all of these deaths, get up in the morning and go downtown to meet "the man." They work in the white man's world all day and come home in the evening to this fetid block. They struggle to instill in their children some private sense of honor or dignity which will help the child to survive. This means, of course, that they must struggle, stolidly, incessantly, to keep this sense alive in themselves, in spite of the insults, the indifference, and the cruelty they are certain to encounter in their working day. They patiently browbeat the landlord into fixing the heat, the plaster, the plumbing; this demands prodigious patience; nor is patience usually enough. In trying to make their hovels habitable, they are perpetually throwing good money after bad. Such frustration, so long endured, is driving many strong, admirable men and women whose only crime is color to the very gates of paranoia.

One remembers them from another time—playing handball in the playground, going to church, wondering if they were going to be promoted at school. One remembers them going off to war—gladly, to escape this block. One remembers their return. Perhaps one remembers their wedding day. And one sees where the girl is now—vainly looking for salvation from some other embittered, trussed, and struggling boy—and sees the all-but-abandoned children in the streets.

Now I am perfectly aware that there are other slums in which white men are fighting for their lives, and mainly losing. I know that blood is also flowing through those streets and that the human damage there is incalculable. People are continually pointing out to me the wretchedness of white people in order to console me for the wretchedness of blacks. But an itemized account of the American failure does not console me and it should not console anyone else. That hundreds of thousands of white people are living, in effect, no better than the "niggers" is not a fact to be regarded with complacency. The social and moral bankruptcy suggested by this fact is of the bitterest, most terrifying kind.

The people, however, who believe that this democratic anguish has some consoling value are always pointing out that So-and-So, white, and So-and-So, black, rose from the slums into the big time. The existence—the public existence—of, say, Frank Sinatra and Sammy Davis, Jr. proves to them that America is still the land of opportunity and that inequalities vanish before the determined will. It proves nothing of the sort. The determined will is rare—at the moment, in this country, it is unspeakably rare—and the inequalities suffered by the many are in no way justified by the rise of a few. A few have always risen—in every country, every era, and in the teeth of regimes which can by no stretch of the imagination be thought of as free. Not all of these people, it is worth remembering, left the world better than they found it. The determined will is rare, but it is not invariably benevolent. Furthermore, the American equation of success with the big time reveals an awful disrespect for human life and human achievement. This equation has placed our cities among the most dangerous in the world and has placed our youth among the most empty and most bewildered. The situation of our youth is not mysterious. Children have never been very good at listening to their elders, but they have never failed to imitate them. They must, they have no other models. That is exactly what our children are doing. They are imitating our immorality, our disrespect for the pain of others.

All other slum dwellers, when the bank account permits it, can move out of the slum and vanish altogether from the eye of persecution. No Negro in this country has ever made that much money and it will be a long time before any Negro does. The Negroes in Harlem, who have no money, spend what they have on such gimcracks as they are sold. These include "wider" TV screens, more "faithful" hi-fi sets, more "powerful" cars, all of which, of course, are obsolete long before they are paid for. Anyone who has ever struggled with poverty knows how extremely expensive it is to be poor; and if one is a member of a captive population, economically speaking, one's feet have simply been placed on the treadmill forever. One is victimized, economically, in a thousand ways—rent, for example, or car insurance. Go shopping one day in Harlem—for anything—and compare Harlem prices and quality with those downtown.

The people who have managed to get off this block have only got as far as a more respectable ghetto. This respectable ghetto does not even have the advantages of the disreputable one, friends, neighbors, a familiar church, and friendly tradesmen; and it is not, moreover, in the nature of any ghetto to remain respectable long. Every Sunday, people who have left the block take the lonely ride back, dragging their increasingly discontented children with them. They spend the day talking, not always with words, about the trouble they've seen and the trouble—one must watch their eyes as they watch their children—they are only too likely to see. For children do not like ghettos. It takes them nearly no time to discover exactly why they are there.

The projects in Harlem are hated. They are hated almost as much as policemen, and this is saying a great deal. And they are hated for the same reason: both reveal, unbearably, the real attitude of the white world, no matter how many liberal speeches are made, no matter how many lofty editorials are written, no matter how many civil-rights commissions are set up.

The projects are hideous, of course, there being a law, apparently respected throughout the world, that popular housing shall be as cheerless as a prison. They are lumped all over Harlem, colorless, bleak, high, and revolting. The wide windows look out on Harlem's invincible and indescribable squalor: the Park Avenue railroad tracks, around which, about forty years ago, the present dark community began; the unrehabilitated houses, bowed down, it would seem, under the great weight of frustration and bitterness they contain; the dark, the ominous schoolhouses from which the child may emerge maimed, blinded, hooked, or enraged for life; and the churches, churches, block upon block of churches, niched in the walls like cannon in the walls of a fortress. Even if the administration of the projects were not so insanely humiliating (for example: one must report raises in salary to the management, which will then eat up the profit by raising one's rent; the management has the right to know who is staying in your apartment; the management can ask you to leave, at their discretion), the projects would still be hated because they are an insult to the meanest intelligence.

Harlem got its first private project, Riverton—which is now, naturally, a slum—about twelve years ago because at that time Negroes were not allowed to live in Stuyvesant Town. Harlem watched Riverton go up, therefore, in the most violent bitterness of spirit, and hated it long before the builders arrived. They began hating it at about the time people began moving out of their condemned houses to make room for this additional proof of how thoroughly the white world despised them. And they had scarcely moved in, naturally, before they began smashing windows, defacing walls, urinating in the elevators, and fornicating in the playgrounds. Liberals, both white and black, were appalled at the spectacle. I was appalled by the liberal innocence—or cynicism, which comes out in practice as much the same thing. Other people were delighted to be able to point to proof positive that nothing could be done to better the lot of the colored people. They were, and are, right in one respect: that nothing can be done as long as they are treated like colored people. The people in Harlem know they are living there because white people do not think they are good enough to live anywhere else. No amount of "improvement" can sweeten this fact. Whatever money is now being earmarked to improve this, or any other ghetto, might as well be burnt. A ghetto can be improved in one way only: out of existence.

Similarly, the only way to police a ghetto is to be oppressive. None of Commissioner Kennedy's policemen, even with the best will in the world, have any way of understanding the lives led by the people they swagger about in two's and three's controlling. Their very presence is an insult, and it would be, even if they spent their entire day feeding gumdrops to children. They represent the force of the white world, and that world's real intentions are, simply, for that world's criminal profit and ease, to keep the black man corraled up here, in his place. The badge, the gun in the holster, and the swinging club make vivid what will happen should his rebellion become overt. Rare, indeed, is the Harlem citizen, from the most circumspect church member to the most shiftless adolescent, who does not have a long tale to tell of police incompetence, injustice, or brutality. I myself have witnessed and endured it more than once. The businessmen and racketeers also have a story. And so do the prostitutes. (And this is not, perhaps, the place to discuss Harlem's very complex attitude towards black policemen, nor the reasons, according to Harlem, that they are nearly all downtown.)

It is hard, on the other hand, to blame the policeman, blank, good-natured, thoughtless, and insuperably innocent, for being such a perfect representative of the people he serves. He, too, believes in good intentions and is astounded and offended when they are not taken for the deed. He has never, himself, done anything for which to be hated—which of us has?—and yet he is facing, daily and nightly, people who would gladly see him dead, and he knows it. There is no way for him not to know it: there are few things under heaven more unnerving than the silent, accumulating contempt and hatred of a people. He moves through Harlem, therefore, like an occupying soldier in a bitterly hostile country; which is precisely what, and where, he is, and is the reason he walks in two's and three's. And he is not the only one who knows why he is always in company: the people who are watching him know why, too. Any street meeting, sacred or secular, which he and his colleagues uneasily cover has as its explicit or implicit burden the cruelty and injustice of the white domination. And these days, of course, in terms increasingly vivid and jubilant, it speaks of the end of that domination. The white policeman, standing on a Harlem street corner, finds himself at the very center of the revolution now occurring in the world. He is not prepared for it—naturally, nobody is—and, what is possibly much more to the point, he is exposed, as few white people are, to the anguish of the black people around him. Even if he is gifted with the merest mustard grain of imagination, something must seep in. He cannot avoid observing that some of the children, in spite of their color, remind him of children he has known and loved, perhaps even of his own children. He knows that he certainly does not want *his* children living this way. He can retreat from his uneasiness in only one direction: into a callousness which very shortly becomes second nature. He becomes more callous, the population becomes more hostile, the situation grows more tense, and the police force is increased. One day, to everyone's astonishment, someone drops a match in the powder keg and everything blows up. Before the dust has settled or the blood congealed, editorials, speeches, and civil-rights commissions are loud in the land, demanding to know what happened. What happened is that Negroes want to be treated like men.

Negroes want to be treated like men: a perfectly straightforward statement, containing only seven words. People who have mastered Kant, Hegel, Shakespeare, Marx, Freud, and the Bible find this statement utterly impenetrable. The idea seems to threaten profound, barely conscious assumptions. A kind of panic paralyzes their features, as though they found themselves trapped on the edge of a steep place. I once tried to describe to a very-well-known American intellectual the conditions among Negroes in the South. My recital disturbed him and made him indignant; and he asked me in perfect innocence, "Why don't all the Negroes in the South move North?" I tried to explain what *has* happened, unfailingly, whenever a significant body of Negroes move North. They do not escape jim-crow: they merely encounter another, not-less-deadly variety. They do not move to Chicago, they move to the South Side; they do not move to New York, they move to Harlem. The pressure within the ghetto causes the ghetto walls to expand, and this expansion is always violent. White people hold the line as long as they can, and in as many ways as they can, from verbal intimidation to physical violence. But inevitably the border which has divided the ghetto from the rest of the world falls into the hands of the ghetto. The white people fall back bitterly before the black horde; the landlords make a tidy profit by raising the rent, chopping up the rooms, and all but dispensing with the upkeep; and what has once been a neighborhood turns into a "turf." This is precisely what happened when the Puerto Ricans arrived in their thousands—and the bitterness thus caused is, as I write, being fought out all up and down those streets.

Northerners indulge in an extremely dangerous luxury. They seem to feel that because they fought on the right side during the Civil War, and won, that they have earned the right merely to deplore what is going on in the South, without taking any responsibility for it; and that they can ignore what is happening in Northern cities because what is happening in Little Rock or Birmingham is worse. Well, in the first place, it is not possible for anyone who has not endured both to know which is "worse." I know Negroes who prefer the South and white Southerners, because "At least there, you haven't got to play any guessing games!" The guessing games referred to have driven more than one Negro into the narcotics ward, the madhouse, or the river. I know another Negro, a man very dear to me, who says, with conviction and with truth, "The spirit of the South is the spirit of America." He was born in the North and did his military training in the South. He did not, as far as I can gather, find the South "worse"; he found it, if anything, all too familiar. In the second place, though, even if Birmingham *is* worse, no doubt Johannesburg, South Africa, beats it by several miles, and Buchenwald was one of the worst things that ever happened in the entire history of the world. The world has never lacked for horrifying examples; but I do not believe that these examples are meant to be used as justification for our own crimes. This perpetual justification empties the heart of all human feeling. The emptier our hearts become, the greater will be our crimes. Thirdly, the South is not merely an embarrassingly backward region, but a part of this country, and what happens there concerns every one of us.

As far as the color problem is concerned, there is but one great difference between the Southern white and the Northerner: the Southerner remembers, historically, and in his own psyche, a kind of Eden in which he loved black people and they loved him. Historically, the flaming sword laid across this Eden is the Civil War. Personally, it is the Southerner's sexual coming of age, when, without any warning, unbreakable taboos are set up between himself and his past. Everything, thereafter, is permitted him except the love he remembers and has never ceased to need. The resulting, indescribable torment affects every Southern mind and is the basis of the Southern hysteria.

None of this is true for the Northerner. Negroes represent nothing to him personally, except, perhaps, the dangers of carnality. He never sees Negroes. Southerners see them all the time. Northerners never think about them whereas Southerners are never really thinking of anything else. Negroes are, therefore, ignored in the North and are under surveillance in the South, and suffer hideously in both places. Neither the Southerner nor the Northerner is able to look on the Negro simply as a man. It seems to be indispensable to the national self-esteem that the Negro be considered either as a kind of ward (in which case we are told how many Negroes, comparatively, bought Cadillacs last year and how few, comparatively, were lynched), or as a victim (in which case we are promised that he will never vote in our assemblies or go to school with our kids). They are two sides of the same coin and the South will not change—*cannot* change—until the North changes. The country will not change until it reexamines itself and discovers what it really means by freedom. In the meantime, generations keep being born, bitterness is increased by incompetence, pride, and folly, and the world shrinks around us.

It is a terrible, an inexorable, law that one cannot deny the humanity of another without diminishing one's own: in the face of one's victim, one sees oneself. Walk through the streets of Harlem and see what we, this nation, have become.

[July, 1960]

The Segs

by Reese Cleghorn

The late Senator Theodore G. Bilbo of Mississippi said Negroes should be kept in their place, uneducated as well as segregated, so society would not "spoil a good field hand and make an insolent cook." White supremacy was simpler in those days: Senator Bilbo saw no paramount need to prove Negro inferiority, because to him and most of his constituents it was obvious.

Times have changed, and today the South's leading segregation spokesmen argue their case with what they consider to be clear evidence from genetics, anthropology, anatomy, history, and political science. If their contentions are rejected by the overwhelming majority of geneticists, anthropologists, anatomists, historians and political scientists, they nevertheless can argue that scientists and academicians have been notably wrong before. Even the Supreme Court has reversed itself, and they appear confident that one day it will reverse its recent decisions against segregation.

All this may seem implausible and even preposterous to most Americans. But the hopefulness of what seems a hopeless cause in the South can be understood only in terms of this rationale, developed by what might be

651

called, in the spirit of the times, the Segregation Establishment. When Governor George Wallace proclaims, in the face of heavy evidence to the contrary, "We are winning," he speaks from beliefs that are unknown in most of the country. When university students riot in hope that segregation may yet be preserved, they are acting upon ideas that could be startling on campuses elsewhere.

What are these beliefs and who keeps them alive? The Segregation Establishment can best speak for itself. Outside the South, its spokesmen are virtually unknown. Although fame has come to the bitter-end segregationist governors—Alabama's George Wallace, Mississippi's Ross Barnett, and, less dramatically at present, Arkansas' Orval Faubus—few newspaper readers know much about Leander H. Perez, Sr., Roy Harris, Robert Shelton, Lester Maddox, and William J. Simmons. These five might be called the permanent leaders. They are not all alike in their sentiments or even their goals, but each owes his fame across the South to his professional status as a segregationist. Each works regularly at it. Each has developed a view of life in accordance with that work, a *Weltanschauung* to which he adheres even as his cause seems to be undergoing *Götterdämmerung*.

These five do not typify the Southerner who believes in segregation, any more than James Baldwin or Malcolm X typifies the American Negro who wants to end racial discrimination. Their views are fashioned by the fact that they must appear to be the uncompromising champions of a cause. Whereas a great sea of Southerners hold segregationist views without ever having to fortify their reasons, or even know their reasons, these five men must be masters of the polemics of segregation. They must speak of genetics and perceive the lessons of history. (That Muse, in particular, somehow seems to speak more distinctly to them than to other men.)

So these are not typical white Southerners, or even typical Southern leaders. They are, however, the men who often may be found behind the headlines from the South, or even from Washington, if you look far enough back into the foliage behind the event. When a George Wallace or a Ross Barnett takes office, he is armed with judgments and arguments fashioned by a Bill Simmons or a Roy Harris, and he takes office because of the political climate such men create. When certain Southerners of scrupulous solemnity take the Senate floor to speak, they use arguments from the fact-and-idea mills of the Segregation Establishment.

The products of these factories are tonier now than they used to be, a fact which reflects the growing sophistication of even the no-compromisers. A treatise widely distributed after the Supreme Court's 1954 school-desegregation decision likened Negroes to lizards. Today, although a Leander Perez may explode with wild ferocity, the greater demand among the dedicated segregationists is for material about the fall of

Egyptian civilization, constitutionalism, judicial tyranny, and the consistency of segregation with Christianity.

These segregationists frequently cite what "history tells us" and "anthropology says." But they also sometimes reveal that their thoughts, like Senator Bilbo's, are derived largely from their own way of looking at Negro field hands and Negro cooks. Roy Harris, as a lawyer, has dealt with too many Negro "cuttin's and shootin's." Bill Simmons has seen Negroes shuffling like Africans. Leander Perez has observed that the Negro, after six years, cannot master his hay baler. These would seem to be the real stuffings of the segregationists' beliefs.

But now let the Segregation Establishment speak for itself.

"The Jews are leading the Negroes. They'll resent it and they'll say Perez is anti-Semitic. And when they say that, I say that they are unadulterated damn liars, because I do resent any goddamn Jew trying to destroy our country and our rights and that's what they are doing, and they are using the Negroes for it!" So says Leander H. Perez, Sr., a sturdy dynamite-stick of a man whose fuse burns low after an hour of quieter talk. He had risen now, square and spread-legged behind his desk, with an index finger pointing skyward. Perez is a man who comes to the point. That is one reason he is, at seventy-two, a multimillionaire, a political strongman, and Louisiana's leading segregationist.

"Well, you see, when people are involved in nationwide and worldwide propaganda and conspiracy, there's no question of principle or integrity left. They have an objective. They don't know where their orders come from. It's that unseen web."

Leander H. Perez, Sr. talks often about the conspiracy. "I am not obsessed with the Negro question," he continues in reasonable tones. "I say the turmoil is a flash in the pan, and the Negro question is not that important to the country. It's those who are making common cause with the conspiracy to destroy constitutional government in this country—and that includes the Kennedys, the Warrens, and their ilk. . . . The Negro is just used. No, this is part of the Communists' cold war. It's worldwide. You stir up the racial strife and turmoil and national disunity. It was the Stalin conspiracy to stir up revolution in the Black Belt in this country, among the Negroes and the sharecroppers. It was the Stalin plan then to recognize this Black Belt as an independent state, or nation, and back it up with aggressive military force. Failing in that, naturally, the Communists turned to infiltration. And my God! They have succeeded beyond their fondest dreams. And now the national government, the politicians on a national level, are carrying the ball for the Communists in this cold war."

As the president of the Plaquemines Parish Council, the governing body of an oil-rich Louisiana county, Judge Perez fights this national menace at every opportunity. In fact, he has been imaginatively conducting guerrilla warfare against the federal government, and sometimes the state government, throughout the four decades in which he has run this parish. He has become vastly wealthy, at times held sway over the Louisiana legislature without ever sitting in it, and gained what may be the nearest thing to absolute power in the United States. Perez is Louisiana's most combative segregationist: he has been excommunicated because he fought so bitterly the desegregation of Catholic schools.

He has helped establish private schools for pupils boycotting public and parochial schools, and he works frequently in the interests of the Citizens Councils. To one and all he is "Judge Perez," though he gave up his local judgeship almost forty years ago to become district attorney for Plaquemines and St. Bernard's Parish (his son took over the post three years ago) and from then on to attend to more important matters. His offices today occupy the eighteenth floor of the Commerce Building in New Orleans, where he practices law with his two sons.

To understand his views on racial matters, he says, you have to understand the conspiracy and how far it has progressed. Two men gave John F. Kennedy the Presidency, in his view: David Dubinsky and Walter Reuther. He deems both men to be leaders responsive to "the unseen web," and says they now run the country "through their stooges in high national office."

Is the United States government, then, to be considered under Communist control?

"Control and influence are two different things. You don't need control to influence the events in government. I say there is an unnatural influence, yes, over the course of our government in Washington. If only the Communist-Zionist web could be portrayed to the people of this country it would be the greatest accomplishment that could ever happen."

As an example of Communists in Washington, he cited a former high official who is Jewish.

Had it not been established, he was asked, that this official's name was confused with the name of a man who had once been on a Communist list?

"They can cover it up! Any damn way they want to!" he said.

Was he saying the two persons were the same?

"I don't say it's the same one, but you know damn well it is! I'm only showing you the influence that these organizations have, planting their stooges in key positions in this country."

Was there more than a coincidence that all the people he was naming were Jewish?

"I'll ask *you* about that," he said. "Why did Ben Franklin say that the American people would rue the day that they gave Jews full rights of citizenship in this country? The Jews had been scheming and plotting to destroy Christian government and Christian civilization."

Did Judge Perez think Negroes were inferior?

"Can there be any doubt about Negro inferiority to the white race when over the ages we cannot see results from the Negro's work in lifting himself to any stage of civilization or accomplishment? Yes, I think it's brain capacity. First, because I recall reading in the *Encyclopaedia Britannica,* one of the early editions, a British anthropologist had made a study of the Negro and he had written quite an extensive article on the formation of the Negro's head and cranium and brain capacity. He showed, after extensive study in this country among Negroes, that the Negro brain capacity is so limited that a Negro child at the age of about ten or eleven developed normally, but after that time in life his brain was stunted. Now, that is what I really meant. But I wouldn't pass judgment on that, except I do know from my experience with Negroes—and I've worked with a number of Negroes, employ them on my farm here—I find that in spite of the fact that they may have operated a hay baler for six years, the same hay baler, they make the same mistakes day after day. They have to be told what to do. . . .

"Why, *of course* it's inherent. I have heard over and over again this alibi that it's a product of civilization and the fact that they've been held down. That's all a myth. The Southern Negro has made more advancement than Negroes in their natural state anywhere in the world. Let's compare our Southern Negroes with the Congolese. While there's rape and assault among some of our Negroes over the country, certainly there's nothing to compare with the Negroes in their natural state.

"That business about the Negroes being held down. That's a game, you know, the Franz Boas theory, which has been taken up by the propagandists. They're trying to create an inferiority complex, or rather, a guilt complex, among white folks in this country. Yes, the white people are supposed to be responsible for all the Negro's shortcomings because he's been held down! Which, of course, is not true."

Does the Communist conspiracy have anything to do with the fact that most anthropologists reject assertions of Negro inferiority?

"There's no doubt about it," he said. "Of course. No doubt." He cited Gunnar Myrdal's sociological work with reference to the Supreme Court's 1954 school decision, and noted that "the Carnegie Corp. of Alger Hiss fame" had financed studies by Myrdal. [Hiss, until his trial, was on the Board of the Carnegie Foundation for International Peace.]

Hiss had not participated in Myrdal's famous work, had he?

"No, Hiss was not a part of that report. I said the *Carnegie Corp. of Alger Hiss fame.* I repeat, the *Carnegie Corp. of Alger Hiss fame.*"

Have the Negroes any aspirations of their own?

"The Negroes, of course, are largely emotional," he said quietly, his voice trailing off.

Largely what?

"EEE-MOtional! And UN-THINKing! And they are led and misled, handled through the churches, and the Negro preachers are paid off and bought! The Jews have been using the NAACP to their own purposes. Now this march on Washington, for instance. Do people stop to think what it cost? How many millions—two, three, five million dollars? Who put up that money? The labor bosses, like Walter Reuther! And tax-exempt corporations like the Ford Fund for the Republic and the others.

"I would say the Negroes themselves are satisfied with their lot in this country. They realize they're a whole lot better off than Negroes elsewhere in the world. The stir is caused by the conspiracy. It is not the desire of the Negroes."

Does he accept the theory that Negroes want their civil rights because they're after intermarriage?

"There's no doubt that is the ultimate objective, as W. E. B. DuBois said in a full-page advertisement in a Pittsburgh paper several years ago. He pointed out that that was the ultimate aim. You make a Negro believe he is equal to the white people and the first thing he wants is a white woman. And that's why there are so many criminal assaults and rapes. That's why it isn't safe for white women who are government employees in the Supreme Court building in the nation's capital to leave their offices and go into the streets alone."

Part of the same conspiracy?

"I wouldn't say that there is a drive to encourage Negroes to rape white women. Of course not! But I say it is the natural result of all this upheaval, all of this propaganda, all this project of so-called racial equality, all of this worldwide cold-war conspiracy to stir up racial strife and turmoil."

Does he foresee segregation in the United States a hundred years from now?

"If you mean that we shouldn't have segregation, that we should have all-out integration, that we should have social intercourse, that we should have intermarriage, that ultimately in five or ten generations we should be all one happy mongrelized family, then you are talking about the real Communist plan for America. Because nothing would more certainly destroy America and make it the overripe fruit to fall into the hands of Communist Russia than that. And no matter what Esquire, no matter what *Life* or *Time* or *Look,* or any other magazine, any other propagandists, may want to write on the subject, *that* is the ultimate Communist conspiracy against America. A mongrelized people so helpless that national defense and national security would be a forgotten thing!"

Is segregation, then, the chief safeguard against the Red takeover?

"From the way you ask that question, as if segregation were a dirty word—what do you mean by that? Haaaaaaaah! You know my view damn well. And there's no equivocation about my view. When people are talking hypocritically about civil rights, what are our civil rights? To live our own

life? To choose our own associates? To raise our children in an atmosphere of morality instead of immorality, with Negroes as immoral as they
are? What? Yes, they are inherently immoral! You know the Negroes.
Why, I have a Negro man comes here with a woman and says this is my
wife. But they *ain't married*. It's the way it has been as long as I've known
Negroes, yes. Most of the Negroes, generally, are illegitimates. Most of
them.

"Good-bye! That's all."

But he had an afterthought. "Now when Esquire writes the story, they
can take anything they want to out of context, and personally I just don't
give a damn. Because when we know we are right and when we follow the
rule of reason, we don't mind propaganda. I just don't give a damn, and
you can tell 'em that!"

"If we can keep the segregation fight going for a few years, things are
going to be different," says Roy Harris, of Augusta, Georgia. "When the
Negro invades the suburbs, where the privileged live, it will be all over.
White people are going to run for a while, but then they're going to stand
up and fight." A red headline over the tabloid newspaper on Harris' desk
shouted: "Kennedys Connive With The NAACP To Use U.S. Army To
Force Mixing." Harris, the roly-poly, sixty-eight-year-old lawyer who
edits this tabloid, was once Georgia's political kingmaker. Today his
strange little weekly arms militant segregationists throughout the South
with their hottest ammunition.

Among segregation leaders throughout the South, Roy Harris' *Augusta
Courier* is quoted about as often as Carleton Putnam's peculiar doctrine
on anthropology. Usually the *Courier*'s friends fail to give it credit in
citing its revelations, but when Governor George Wallace of Alabama
testified in Washington on July 15 that Communists control the civil-
rights movement, he displayed a picture and story from The *Augusta
Courier* to prove it. Harris, who started the four-page paper in 1947, "so I
could say what I damn well pleased," says the circulation is seven thousand or so. The masthead once listed the editor as "Old Man Everybody,"
but no editor is listed now, for readers know that Harris, the short, round
man who writes a front-page column, IS The *Augusta Courier*.

Some recent headlines were these: "King's Nonviolent Rioters Are
Trained Outsiders Brought To South"; "Communists Assisted In Organiz-
ing The NAACP In 1909 And Have Been Integrated With It Since That
Time"; "Abraham Lincoln Opposed Integration"; "U.S. Judges Who Play
Martinets Send Their Children To Segregated Schools"; "Ignorant Rich
White People Of North Give Money To Aid Integration"; "Kennedy Boys
Want Votes." As may be seen, the *Courier* views not only the contempo-
rary but also the historical scene, and this is consistent with Harris' idea

that the paper "does not so much influence as arm" segregationists in the South. Harris receives contributions from people all over the country, but carefully screens out the numerous anti-Semitic ones. He regularly clips several daily newspapers for reprints and currently is bearing down upon stories about racial strife in the North, which he takes to be proof that integration cannot work.

"I came up with early practical experience with the Negro people," he said. "I came up working with them on the farm, and usually, you know, back in those days the average white family out there lived among a nest of 'em. You might be the only white family on the farm, see? One white family and half-a-dozen colored neighbors. I came up playing with them. We played and worked together.

"Then, when I got to practicing law, I represented worlds of 'em. I waded through more Negro cuttin's and shootin's and Negro fights, I reckon, than anybody, in the first twenty years I practiced law. And I had an opportunity to know them firsthand. Segregation is the only way two separate, dissimilar races can live together without having riots, and fights, and killin's and cuttin's.

"Then, when you go back and study your history of Egypt, or India, or Portugal, or go down and study Puerto Rico and Cuba, you find that any time you mix the white and the Negro races you have destroyed the white race. Intermarriage will follow—not in mass, but eventually. I think the Negro has some qualities superior to the white man's. He has a certain richness of character in the way of patience, loyalty and the ability to enjoy living which the white man doesn't have. But the Negro never has developed any kind of a civilization of his own, even in Africa.

"When you throw the white and Negro races together, you subject a lot of good white people to a different moral standard that the Negro has. You subject him to being victimized by rapes and beatings, just like it's happened in every integrated community in the North, and at every integrated school they've had to have police. I don't think it's fair to the white people to subject them to this."

Is there an inherent difference between whites and Negroes?

"I think it's basic, and I don't think it'll ever change. I don't want to say that I'm better than any other person, don't care who he is, because I know a lot of people—and a lot of Negroes—that, when it comes down to it, I think are better than I am. But at the same time, that's not true of all of 'em. They've got better hearts in 'em, they do more things for people than I do. But you've got to figure there's a physical difference, and it's just there, and you can't eliminate it."

What is the solution, then?

"Of course old Abe Lincoln, Tom Jefferson and a bunch of them wanted to send them back to Africa. But I don't think you can do that because it could not be a force proposition. And I don't think the Negroes would want to go back."

What will the situation be like a hundred years from now?

"In the next hundred years, I believe, we are going to be resisting just like we are now. And I don't believe it's going to take much more mixing for the pendulum to swing back the other way.

"We're in this shape now because white people didn't stick together. Before long, the white people are going to elect them a candidate. I don't know that this will be the solution, but when it happens we can get together on one."

Would there be national segregation laws?

"If they will make segregation *possible* again, you don't care whether you have any segregation laws or not. In Georgia we've existed practically with no segregation laws. It's a question of who controls the politics."

As for Negro leaders' aspirations, he puts intermarriage high on the list: "The plan of amalgamation of the white and Negro races into a mulatto race, as proposed by the NAACP and CORE, by Martin Luther King's stomp-down, nonviolent type of violence, means the destruction of both races and the creation of a mongrel race of people of the same color."

Harris does not believe in any restrictions on Negro voting, but he thinks registration standards should be higher for all. "I think it ought to be based on education and morals. I don't think you can set up a board to determine a man's morals. I think you've got to take it from your criminal records."

Harris finds it difficult to label his political views in general: "I'm the most liberal person you ever saw to have the reputation of a mossback conservative. I've always led the damn fights for spending money and taxes and for the schools and everything. But by present-day standards, they don't count me a liberal a-tall. By modern-day standards you've got to be soft on Communists, and you've got to embrace the Negro's ambitions, which I can't do. I had always thought that I had been a liberal, but they've changed the meaning of the word."

Over the past thirty years Harris has managed more successful gubernatorial campaigns in Georgia than anyone has at any time, but he has skipped from one side to another in doing it. His biggest switch was from the camp of Eugene Talmadge to that of "liberal" Governor Ellis Arnall, whom he helped as campaign manager and speaker of the Georgia House of Representatives, and back to the Talmadge fold: after Gene Talmadge died in 1946, Harris helped elect his son, Herman, as governor. He has seldom been on the losing side, but it happened in 1962: Carl Sanders defeated Harris' choice, former Governor Marvin Griffin.

His present—and largest—contribution to the segregation fight remains the little paper with the red headlines and sometimes bizarre appraisals of current events. "We've got some good stuff coming up," he says, smiling. "In the next few issues we're going to just devote a little space to some of the troubles they're having up North—in Philadelphia, Chicago and other places. You know, there is little difference between the conditions in New York City today and in the jungles of the Congo."

"The Negro is a diseased animal and can never be our equal. If he was forced into captivity in coming to America, what's so bad about forcing him into captivity and carrying him back to his home?" Impatience shows in the sad eyes of Robert Shelton, the thirty-five-year-old Alabaman who is speaking; impatience, and hurt, almost as if he knows that whatever reasonable words he utters will later be twisted and hurled back in his face, only because he has spoken up for the white man. As Shelton addresses himself to race relations, so does the clattering copying machine outside his personal office, in "Suite 401, United Klans of America, Inc., Knights of the Ku Klux Klan, Imperial Wizard."

"If things are left as they are," Robert Shelton said, "there's no question but that we will have a revolution of the black man against the white man—unless some drastic steps are taken by conservative-thinking people to head off this Communist trend of using Negroes as tools, aggravating them into these dastardly acts. We are all the time reading in the medias that this is a nonviolent demonstration. But there has never been any demonstration carried out by them that has not had violence connected. They have that savage instinct."

Shelton, a tall, lean man with furrows in his forehead, leaned attentively over a desk flanked by big American and Confederate flags. A Bible on the desk was formally centered, opened to Romans ii. Near it was an ashtray made of small, white tile squares with a mosaic of four red "K's." He waited for questions, and when they came he answered seriously. An acquaintance of many years had said that only once had he seen Shelton laugh, and that was over a race joke; he did not smile before, during, or after this interview.

Did he really foresee a Negro revolutionary uprising?

"It's in the planning stage. It's not going to be too long, from activities coming out of Cuba being withheld from the general public. I can see, from conditions that exist today, the upsurging of the Negro element through guidance of the Communist conspiracy. And I don't mean Northerner against Southerner. This is definitely going to lead to a violent revolution between the black man and the white man. There will be no straddling of the fence. And definitely evidence has already shown—actions in Leopoldville, in the Congo—what will happen when you give these Negroes, these crazed savages, the power. So it is something that there will have to be a solution to—a drastic solution, immediately."

What is the drastic solution?

"F.D.R. gave us some of it. We have the fleet in mothballs that could be brought out for transportation back to Africa; and we have the storage of food in Alaska that runs into the billions and billions, which gives them the food; and we also have in Africa over $11,000,000,000 worth of storage homes that belong to the federal government. The only thing that Roosevelt didn't supply was a leader, and I think the Negroes could select their leader, who could send them back as colonies in Africa. Let them have their own government. Let them advance their own strategy, and have their *social equality*."

Is the Negro inferior to the white man?

"Absolutely! I think history has proven that. The white race of people have had a cultured civilization for over two thousand years. The Negro has only been out of the savage actions of the jungles of Africa approximately two hundred years. And the Negro had the same opportunity and resources in Africa to develop himself and his race of people as our forefathers had in America in carving this country from the dense jungles of America. I think we can all realize that the Negro does not have the intitiative, the basic intelligence, to be creative—does not have the ingenuity to devise, invent, create things that the white race does."

Is the inequality permanent?

"Absolutely! Because the climate certainly wouldn't have any bearing facts on what happened in Africa. When the white man went into Africa, they started advancing the Negro even in Africa. I think anatomy has shown that there is a difference in the structure of his jaws. I'm not qualified to speak on anatomy, but from the reports I have read from various groups there seems to be quite a difference."

How far would the Klan go in preventing this imminent overthrow which he foresees?

"We are a law-abiding organization, observing the duly constituted authority of law. And we are not going out provoking or asking trouble or trying to bring about violence. But we are certainly going to maintain self-preservation. The law of nature calls for self-preservation. I'm not going out looking for trouble, or violence, but if it comes to us we're going to protect ourselves."

What about the arrests of Klansmen in various criminal cases, including the one in Alabama in which several of them were sent to prison for castrating a Negro man?

"Once again you're talking about a group of people that are professing to be Klansmen. Now, any group of people can get up five, eight or ten members and profess to be Klansmen and yet not be. They are not Klansmen of this organization. Now, they might call themselves Klansmen and have their own little group. I don't recall that any member of this organization ever has been convicted of any crime they've been charged with. We have always taken steps against violence.

"And you might ask the question: Why, if you wanted to have an organization, why not pick another name besides the Ku Klux Klan? The Ku Klux Klan is the only organization that was organized, formulated and put into effect by Americans, inside American shorelines. So why should you throw away a heritage and a principle? What I'm referring to is a fraternal organization. My grandfather was a member. My father was a member. Because you have people that are associated through their families with the Klan associations, many people are sympathetic with the Klan whether or not they are in it."

Shelton is the leader of only one remnant of the Klan, probably the largest and at the moment the most industrious. But unity has been the most invisible part of the "invisible empire." Besides Shelton's United Klans, there are the Dixie Klans, Federated Klans, Original Klans, Associated Klans and many others. Shelton's office reflects the ambitiousness of his branch, which has shifted the principal Klan leadership from Georgia to Alabama. Shelton himself is the reason.

He makes his living as an air-conditioning salesman, but he goes to the Klan office in the yellow-brick Alston Building in Tuscaloosa, Alabama, almost every day he is in town, riding up in an elevator sometimes operated by a relaxed Negro man in a Klan-red polo shirt. Shelton grew up in Tuscaloosa, graduated from a nearby high school, and has lived in this little city all his life except for some Air Force service. His local fame grew when it was rumored during Governor John Patterson's administration that Shelton, having supported Patterson, had influence with the governor. Shelton denies this. But that brief prominence may have given him an advantage in the struggle for Klan leadership.

Now he is working hard to extend his "empire." His telephone (listed not under the K.K.K., but under the "Alabama Rescue Service") rang a number of times.

"The pendulum is swinging in our favor more and more every day," he said after answering one of the calls. "I think the state of Alabama and the governor is going to be a great part in writing history for this country. People are waking up all over the country."

"Yayss, Sir, if you think about the leaders among the Negro groups at this time you'll seldom ever find one that's not a mulatto," says Lester Maddox. His crinkled eyes have the look of friendly finality as he speaks over a cup of coffee, black, at The Pickrick in Atlanta. Black waiters in white coats tinkle glasses in the kitchen nearby and an old myna bird, black, occasionally greets a customer with a snipped-short "Hello, there!" Maddox's new Pontiac Grand Prix glistens in the sun outside. It, too, is black. But all the customers eating the well-advertised "skillet fried chicken" are and forever shall be white, if Maddox has anything to do with it. His restaurant is the militant-segregationists' banquet hall for convivial fellowship and rededication. And Maddox, forty-eight-year-old some-time candidate for high office, is both their leader and his own court jester.

Lester Maddox is a nondescript man whose coats always seem to flare up at the shoulders and the hips, as if concealing a kite frame. When he is excited, his face flushes, nervous energy exudes, and his tongue is faster. But basically he is not a volatile man. He would look at home behind the counter of a pharmacy (in which he once worked). His speech is somewhat high-pitched, lacking in Southern long-vowel, soft-R mellifluence.

After quitting high school in 1933, a year before finishing ("We didn't have shoes to wear to school, or food to eat at school times"), he went to work in a drugstore at $4 a week. Later he worked at a machine stamping out metal products for Atlantic Steel Company in Atlanta, where his father spent most of his working years as a roll turner. He became a foreman, but wanted his own business. In 1944 he and his wife opened a tiny restaurant-grocery combination, and three years later he bought a site on Hemphill Avenue and built The Pickrick. He will tell you, so rapidly his words flow together, that "pick means to fastidiously eat, and rick means to pile up, to heap, to amass, so we say Pickrick means you pick it out and we'll rick it up."

The restaurant has increased in floor space by seven times. It is a Western-style timber-and-old-brick building in a business area near Georgia Tech, and the food is low-priced. Everyone around Atlanta became aware of The Pickrick when Maddox began to write snappy, column-type advertisements for it in 1949. The ad still begins, as it did in the beginning, with "Pickrick Says," alongside a picture of Maddox. Blocks of lively text follow, divided by short, sharp headlines such as, "I Told You So," "Special to Christians," "Yes, Sir," "Thank God for Gov. Wallace," "Those Do-Gooders," "You Pinks and Punks," "I'm For," and "Sneak of the Year." The ad usually ends with what seems to be an almost irrelevant price list and plug for the restaurant ("Our Sunday Menu"), which may be followed by a social afterthought such as this recent one: "Dine Segregated At No Extra Charge."

Almost from the start, Maddox began to use his ad to get things off his chest. He regularly excoriates the Atlanta daily newspapers, which publish the ad— known to its readers as "Pickrick's Column"—every Saturday. When Maddox decided to run for mayor as a hard-line seg-regationist in 1957, veteran Mayor William B. Hartsfield, who had held the fort for two decades against all comers, beat him 2-1. In 1961 he was beaten again, 2-1, by Ivan Allen, Jr., the present mayor. Maddox has always had higher political prestige among his followers than these results might indicate, however, because he has claimed he received "the majority of the white votes," and "beat everybody but Martin Luther King."

When he was about to be interviewed for Esquire, Maddox remarked that the magazine was no friend of segregation, but he agreed to state some of his views. He was found in a cramped little office off the main restaurant floor. On one wall was a color print of Christ, and on another, fastened with tape and tacks, were letters, cartoons, and membership cards of segregationist organizations. A British .303-caliber rifle stood in a corner near the old-style iron safe ("just in case it's ever needed here," he said).

"I was just making a note from *Advertising Age*," he explained, scribbling over the one bare spot on a scratched wooden desk. "Some of the big companies have been giving in to CORE. We've contacted several hundred major companies on this, and some of our results have been favorable. One company had advertised it was sponsoring an integrated TV show, and they almost apologized for it after they heard from us."

He moved with quick motions, the light flashing now and then on rimless glasses that seem halfway down his face, under a long forehead. "Looka here at the mail," he said, indicating a stack by his hand and a three-foot cardboard box crammed with envelopes. "Did you see this?" He took from an envelope a folded copy of a cartoon, crudely drawn in contemporary bathhouse style, peppered with misspellings. The subject was the marriage of the University of Georgia's first Negro co-ed and a white student. "Look here Nigger," the caption started. "It just came in the mail," Maddox said, indicating little reaction. Then he reached into a pile of papers nearby and handed over another on the same subject, similarly drawn, similarly copied, but not folded. Where had it come from? He shrugged; replied noncommittally.

Walking out now to find a secluded table for talking, he spoke of The Pickrick's institutional role in the segregation fight. "A lot of students come in here to talk to us—from Yale and Harvard and other schools," he said. He pointed to a long bulletin board covered with newspaper clippings, handbills, and pictures. "Kan the Kennedy Klan," said a red-and-black sticker. "Five White Men Shot in Race Riots," a headline said. Nearby was a table filled with segregation literature for customers to take.

"Let's sit down here," Maddox said, indicating a small table in a side room. He explained, as his Negro "help" worked not far away, that he is a segregationist because it is Christian and American, and because he loves his people. "Throughout the Bible we are instructed about the purity of man, the purity of his soul, in all areas. . . ." He rose, found a paper someone had written on the subject, and cited such passages as Deuteronomy 22: 9-10, "Thou shalt not sow thy vineyard with divers seed. . . . Thou shalt not plow with an ox and an ass together"; and instructions given to Isaac not to seek a wife among the Canaanites. "I think it's against the will of God to mix our races, to amalgamate our races."

Maddox's view of the underlying economic aspects of the integration drive are somewhat unorthodox. "I think the major cause behind the move to integrate is not to help the Negro," he said. "It is to help the big financial people— the Carnegies and the Mellons and the Fords and the various big-money people. They're trying to indicate to Africa and other parts of the world that the United States has come to be a leader for doing something for the Negro. They're not really interested in the American Negro as much as they are in pleasing Africa in order to get their products into that area and to get the dollars."

In light of the current integration activity, where does he believe the American Negro will be a hundred years from now?

"With the present no-win policy of our government, and our forcing our people to bow down to dictatorial government, I can't see how we can last a hundred years. I'd be very much surprised if we survive through two more presidential elections as the United States government. I think we'll have a Communist government, unless the people awaken."

What presidential candidate can prevent this debacle?

"None of them at this time would satisfy me," he said. "Goldwater doesn't suit me, but he'd do a much better job. He thinks the American businessman ought to run his business . . . and that the local communities should work out their own racial problems."

Maddox recently formed an organization seeking a solution locally. It is called the People's Association for Selective Shopping (PASS), and the purpose is to boycott businesses that have desegregated or otherwise favored "racial amalgamation." PASS seems to have gotten up no steam. There is much literature in The Pickrick about its prospects. Walking now to the table, Maddox displayed handbills for PASS. Suddenly he was caught up in a group of happy customers on their way in and out. "Here are some friends from Perry and West Point, Georgia," one of them said. Maddox beamed and shook hands; now that the interview was over and philosophical questions were put aside, he looked happy.

"I didn't use the word 'inferiority.' I think you did," said William J. Simmons, uneasily recrossing his long, black-stocking-clad legs. Simmons' appearance and demeanor suggest that he might have been a colonel of the Coldstream Guards if he had not been born in Utica, Mississippi. "The reason I want to be rather precise is that this whole area is loaded with emotional, fuzzy thinking, and the scare words such as 'inferiority' and 'racist' make people's corpuscles rather than their brain cells hop." Then the fastidious forty-seven-year-old administrator of the Citizens Councils of America (home office: Jackson, Mississippi) began to quote directly from his favored scientific authorities. Bill Simmons does not like to sound presumptuous about scientific matters.

"Rather than use a word such as 'inferiority,' " William J. Simmons said, "let me put it in this sense: In terms of the ability to adapt to Western civilization, the colored has shown himself to be less capable than the white. It is a white civilization. In terms of adaptability to the way of life in Africa, the colored is probably superior to the white."

Does he see no difference in the quality of civilization on the two continents?

"I certainly do," he said. But he seemed reluctant to make the judgment his allies frequently make about Negro inferiority. He fenced with the question a bit more, and then said: "I don't see how any white person in the United States could watch newsreel pictures of chanting, clapping colored people shuffling their feet just exactly as they do in Africa and still think that there is not a difference in behavior, a difference in personality, that is *extreme*. I'm unconvinced that the Northern white people are ready to incorporate that sort of thing into their rather antiseptic lives."

Bill Simmons, a banker's son, studied at the Institut de Touraine in France after graduation from Mississippi College. During World War II he served first with the British and then with the U.S. Navy. Afterward, he was assistant treasurer and chief accountant for a natural-gas company before going on to become full-time administrator of the Citizens Councils, which he runs from third-floor offices in the Plaza Building, across the street from the governor's mansion in Jackson, Mississippi. He is not specific about his salary ("very modest"), the Councils' budget (about $200,000 on the state level alone last year and more than that this year, he said) or the Councils' membership (90,000 in Mississippi, he suggested as a guess; others think much less than that). Though he denies having any great influence with Governor Ross Barnett, he is often with the governor on important occasions and has been regarded as a major adviser.

For this interview, he temporarily abandoned a seclusion devoted to writing a book about the integration showdown at the University of Mississippi.

"We in the South now are fighting for survival," he said. "Any talk about white supremacy is like arguing in nineteenth-century terms. What we are concerned about is black supremacy, and we certainly are not in favor of that."

The threat to the South, in Simmons' view, cannot be explained entirely with any simple allusion to a Communist conspiracy or Northern politicians' desire for Negro votes. "I attribute it to a wave of equalitarian philosophy that started in the early part of the twentieth century, primarily with the progressive educationists, such as John Dewey. In time it seemed to permeate the educational field. Dewey and others—Franz Boas among the anthropologists—turned out a number of disciples at Columbia who went into the teaching profession, and this influence grew to a remarkable degree. I think it resulted directly in the Supreme Court school-integration decision. And I think that, although it's predominant now, there's beginning to be a reaction. I think it's going to be reversed."

"Equalitarian" pressures are one thing, however, and segregation pressures are another: "I don't think faculties or administrations are free or ought to be free from community pressures anywhere. I think they ought to be responsive to the views of their community, and there is a very great gap between the views of a certain element of professors at Ole Miss and the views of the majority of Mississippians." He says he thinks these professors should leave.

Simmons believes that the truth of his position may emerge in a case now pending in court. A federal judge in a Brunswick, Georgia, case recently ruled that integration would have a "demoralizing and disorganizing" effect on schools in Brunswick, and the key point in the case was white parents' contention that integration would be damaging psychologically to their children. Allegations were made arguing Negroes' genetic inferiority. "In the Supreme Court 1954 decision," Simmons said, "there was no evidence of a genetic basis. . . . In the new case, interveners did present genetic evidence of racial difference." He says he thinks this case could in effect reverse the 1954 decision. The case, which is being cited by many segregation leaders, including Governor Wallace in his recent defiance of the courts, has not yet made its way through all appellate channels. In the meantime, it is being used to suggest that the doctrine of Negro inferiority has become intellectually respectable.

Simmons says he has read recently that a number of Negro national leaders have identified the American Negro's rights struggle with the aspirations of Africans. "This in effect means that the mass Negro movements have taken their allegiance primarily to Africa—not the United States—to a foreign power or powers. We should remember that the movement for African nationalism has meant that the white man in Africa, in the countries where the blacks have taken over, has been completely deprived of his civil rights, including even the right of life. He's driven into the sea.

"This is the sort of thing to which the leaders of the NAACP, CORE and the other organizations creating this revolution have gravitated. This raises the question that the United States itself is in danger of non-white domination. The non-whites' most potent ally is the liberal-controlled United States government that exists today. The thing that makes this whole thing dangerous is the force and power the government has put behind it. With that, you have the colored masses that exist outside the country. You know the liberals constantly remind us that we must integrate to please the three-fourths of the world which is non-white. This allies the Negroes in the United States with the three-fourths of the non-white world. I'd say the Southern white Protestant is coming rapidly to the position where he can sympathize with the position of the Jews in Nazi Germany."

What is the answer in the light of this startling threat to white people, so largely ignored across the nation?

"Strong organization," he said, with one of the first goals being defeat of "the Kennedys" in 1964. He favors unpledged electors and sometimes is credited with Mississippi's strategy to bring more states behind this plan. The idea is to withhold enough electoral votes from the two major parties to force the election into the House of Representatives, where the South ostensibly would have more bargaining power.

The eventual solution, and "the only real solution," he says, "is a return of Negroes to Africa."

There is no chance now for sending Negroes to Africa, he conceded. "Obviously the weight of opinion is the other way. But these things can change. . . . Generally it has been considered that this ought to be done on a voluntary basis. I think it ought to be voluntary. If this were advanced as a real solution, if real pride of race were instilled in the Negro people, a sense of their own destiny, free of competition and involvement with the white man, I think it's entirely possible that a movement could be started that would begin to sweep them."

Might the Citizens Councils of America undertake this project?

"That I don't know. It hasn't been seriously considered because obviously under present circumstances we think about more immediate problems," he said.

To Simmons, the Citizens Councils are fighting an uphill battle to preserve segregation and constitutional government, defending the views of millions of white Southerners. "I'm a segregationist," he said, "because I believe it's right."

[January, 1964]

The Brilliancy of Black

by Bernard Weinraub

Jesus Christ, His arms outstretched and pleading, is painted in lush blues and pinks in the lobby. Inside the church, the aisles are filling with teen-agers, curiously quiet and solemn, who grip programs ("Harlem Youth Unlimited presents . . . 'The Role of Negro Youth in Shaping Their Destinies' "). Stepping through the crowd a slight woman with a lost, desperate smile hands out a "Come Ye Disconsolate" leaflet and cries out that Brothers and Sisters you are all invited to view the Southern Baptist Stars on their twenty-second anniversary at Mount Moriah Baptist Church.

Outside, bare-chested little boys in sneakers watch the white television men set up their cameras. A white cop, a pudgy man with roly-poly fingers and a hard, blue-eyed Irish face, removes a handkerchief from his rear pocket, scrubs off his forehead sweat and gazes up, up, up at the church—a De Mille Corinthian setting that was once a movie threatre, the Alhambra. The Black Muslims are distributing *Muhammad Speaks,* and the television men are nervous and the teen-agers keep surging into the sweltering lobby past the mural of Jesus. It is dusk on Seventh Avenue and 116th Street in Harlem and it is warm and they are waiting for Stokely Carmichael.

Three months earlier, Stokely had taken over the Student Nonviolent Coordinating Committee and had coined those two words "Black Power" that aroused all the white folks and dismayed some of the powerful black folks. He had been on *Meet The Press* television and on the front page of The New York *Times* and had visited Mississippi and Washington, D.C. and Boston and now, finally, he was in Harlem.

The kids waited. They were fifteen, sixteen and seventeen, the boys in pressed olive-drab suits and seersucker jackets, the girls in sandals, dangling earrings, A-line skirts, and kerchiefs, quite chic, on their African cropped hair. They carried paperbacks and chatted quietly. For the past few months they had been in the Haryou-Act anti-poverty program where they worked with the community, and baby-sat for working mothers, and were taught what to wear when they took the A train downtown to apply for a job on Fifth Avenue. And they had read—and discussed—James Baldwin and Chester Himes and explored in heated talks The Role of Negro Youth and The Problems of Negro Youth and What's Ahead for Negro Youth. And now Stokely, who used to play stickball on 137th Street, comes onstage with a half-dozen other speakers and the curious tenseness among the teen-agers bursts. They break into wild applause.

Stokely is surrounded by friends. "Hey, baby, how ya' doin'?" he cries. . . . "Hey Thomas, why the hell aren't you back in Alabama doin' some work. . . . Hey, boy, you lookin' *good*." Stokely looks good too. He wears black Italian boots, a tight blue suit, white shirt, striped tie, a name chain on his wrist. He is six-feet-one and has the build of a basketball guard: a solid chest, slender waist, powerful legs. His smile dazzles—an open, unguarded, innocent smile.

The first speaker is seventeen-year-old Clarissa Williams, a striking girl in a loose green dress. She has a gentle voice: "*Newsweek* and *Life* have conducted their own surveys of black people. Well, baby, no one has to tell us what the black community is like because we know it, we live it. We intend to be the generation which will make black youth to be unlimited. We intend to be the generation that says, Friends, we do not have a dream, we do *not* have a dream, we have a plan. So, TV men, do not be prepared to record our actions indoors, but be prepared to record our actions *on the streets*. . . ." The audience, and Stokely, applaud and cry, "Hit 'em hard, sister."

Clarissa hits them harder and by the time she winds up her tough little speech the audience is electric. And then Stokely rises. His style dazzles. He shakes his head as he begins speaking and his body appears to tremble. His voice, at least in the North, is lilting and Jamaican. His hands move effortlessly. His tone—and the audience loves it—is cool and very hip. No Martin Luther King We Shall Overcome oratory. No preacher harangue. No screaming. He speaks one tone above a whisper, but a very taut, suppressed whisper. His speech—he has made it dozens of times before—varies with the audience, the area, the news that day, his mood. Stokely's words flow musically and build and Stokely pounds into the microphone and stops and the music starts again. The audience is rapt.

"Brothers and Sisters, we have been living with The Man too long. Brothers and Sisters, we have been *in a bag* too long. *We have got to move to a position where we will be proud, be proud of our blackness.* From here on in we've got to stick together, Brothers and Sisters, we've got to join together and move to a new spirit and make of our community a community of love . . . LOVE. There's no time for shuckin' and jivin'. We've got to move fast and we've got to come together and we've got . . . we've got to realize . . . that this country was conceived in racism and dedicated to racism. And understand that we've got to move . . . WE HAVE GOT TO MOVE. . . . We've got to build to a position so that when L.B.J. says, 'Come heah, boy, I'm gonna send you to Veetnam,' we will say, 'Hell, no.' " ("Preach, boy, preach. . . . Tell 'em, Stokely. . . .")

"Brothers and Sisters, a hell of a lot of us are gonna be shot and it ain't just gonna be in South Vietnam. We've got to move to a position *in this country* where we're not afraid to say that any man who has been selling us rotten meat for high prices should have had his store bombed fifteen years ago. We have got to move to a position where we will control our *own* destiny. We have got to move to a position where we will have black people represent *us* to achieve *our* needs. This country don't run on love, Brothers, it's run on power and we ain't got none. Brothers and Sisters, don't let them separate you from other black people. Don't ever in your life apologize for your black brothers. Don't be ashamed of your culture because if you don't have culture, that means you don't exist and, Brothers and Sisters, we do exist. Don't ever, don't ever, don't *ever* be ashamed of being black because you . . . you are black, little girl with your nappy hair and your broad lips, and *you are beautiful.* Brothers and Sisters, I know this theatre we're in—it used to be the Alhambra. Well I used to come here on Saturday afternoon when I was a little boy and we used to see Tarzan here and all of us would yell like crazy when Tarzan beat up our black brothers. Well, you know Tarzan is on television now and from here on in I'm rooting for that black man to beat the hell out of Tarzan. . . ."

The audience roars and is on its feet and Stokely grins and waves. The audience keeps applauding. . . .

Stokely is in the East to build up support, to meet with S.N.C.C. workers in New York, Newark, Boston and Philadelphia. He will make speeches and hold private meetings and endure just a few interviews (he turns down many of them now because of "distortions"). At twenty-five, the most charismatic figure in the Negro movement, Stokely Carmichael rushes from ghetto to ghetto with the drive of a political candidate one week before Election Day. He sleeps just a few hours a night. He eats on the run and drinks milk to keep up his energy. In Mississippi and Alabama, during those five summers of unbearable heat, of prison, of beatings, of death threats, of rifle shots fired at him through car windows, Stokely smoked three packs of cigarettes a day. He doesn't smoke now and doesn't drink.

His base now—and S.N.C.C.'s headquarters—is in Atlanta and his itinerary in other cities is set up by the local S.N.C.C. office, mostly by twenty- and twenty-one-year-old Negroes whom Stokely led in the South. There are, inevitably, the fund-raising parties—S.N.C.C.'s funds have dropped—but mostly just meetings and speeches.

He spends the next day in Newark, a dismal, grey city which has more Negroes than whites. The highlight of the visit is a speech that evening at the anti-poverty board on Springfield Avenue, in the heart of the ghetto, and then a cocktail party at ten-fifteen across town. The anti-poverty board is packed with an older audience than in Harlem. There are mothers with children on their laps and grandmothers with grandchildren on their bosoms; old men in overalls, janitors, civil-service workers, LeRoi Jones, high-school students, tough-looking nineteen-year-olds leaning against the green stucco walls, and several white poverty workers.

Stokely instinctively knows the audience. He stares quickly across the room and then scribbles down notes on the back of an envelope. He rises to warm applause. He smiles.

"Is it okay if ah take off mah jacket?" he says in a too-Southern drawl.

The speech goes well. Stokely begins by warming up the elderly women in the audience and ends with a cry to the students. The themes are the same. "You gotta understand about white power. It's white power that brought us here in chains, it's white power that kept us here in chains and it's white power that wants to keep us here in chains. . . . What they've been able to do is make us ashamed of being black . . . ashamed. I used to come home from school and say, 'Hey, Momma.' And she used to say, 'Sssshh, you know how loud we are.' I wouldn't go outside eating watermelon, no sir. They say we're lazy, so we work from sunup to sundown to prove that we're not lazy. We are tired of working for them, of being the maids of the liberal white folks who consider us part of their families. . . . My mother was a maid for a lady in Long Island and this lady wanted me to go to college and she told my mother, 'Your boy is a bright colored boy and we want to help send him to college.' Well, I hated that woman. She gave my mother $30 a week and all the old clothes her kids didn't want. Well, I didn't want her old clothes. I didn't want her to help send me to college. I wanted my Momma." ("Tell it, Stokely. . . .")

"There is a system in this country that locks black people in, but lets one or two get out every year. And they all say, 'Well, look at that one or two. He's helping his race.' Well, Ralph Bunche hasn't done a damn thing for me. If he's helping his race, then he should come *home*. Brothers and

Sisters, there's nothing wrong about being all white or all black. It's only when you use one to exploit the other—and we have been exploited. You gotta understand what they do. They say, 'Let's integrate.' Well integration means going to a white school because that school is good and the black school is bad. It means moving from a black neighborhood to a white neighborhood because one neighborhood, they tell you, is bad and the other is good. Well, if integration means moving to something white, moving to something good, then integration is just a cover for white supremacy. . . .

"Brothers and Sisters, we have to view ourselves as a community and not a ghetto and that's the only way to make it. The political control of every ghetto is outside the ghetto. We want political control to be *inside* the ghetto. Like the workers in the Thirties, like the Irish in Boston, we demand the right to organize the way we want to organize. Black power is the demand to organize around the question of blackness. We are oppressed for only one reason: because we are black. We must organize. Brothers and Sisters, the only way they'll stop me from organizing is if they kill me or put me in jail. And once they put me in jail I'll organize my brothers in prison. *Organize!*"

The back of Stokely's white shirt is drenched with sweat. As soon as he finishes the speech, the crowd rises and surrounds him and shakes his hand and Stokely seeks out the old ladies who cry, "My, my, *my,* you are somethin' " and gives the younger kids that special handshake reserved only for a black brother or sister—a handshake in which he clasps a hand with his right hand and places his left hand over the linked hands. (When a white man shakes his hand, the smile is guarded, the handclasp unsure, the left hand remains limp.)

Thirty minutes later the cocktail party on Porter Avenue awaits Stokely, who has stopped off in several Negro bars—not to drink, but to meet and talk with some of the customers. The party is given by a short, burly chemist and his wife in the yard in back of their twelve-room stucco house. At least forty people have paid $5 to see Stokely, with about a half-dozen S.N.C.C. workers admitted free. Weak Martinis and Whiskey Sours are ladled out and, curiously, the middle-aged white and Negro couples stand and drink together near the small swimming pool in the center of the yard. The younger white kids stand alone. The young Negroes stand beneath the Rose of Sharon, uncomfortable, hostile, waiting for Stokely.

He arrives late and in a bitter mood. In the car coming to the party Stokely has been told that David Frost, a candidate running in the upcoming Democratic Senatorial primary on an anti-Vietnam ticket, will also speak at the party. Stokely immediately feels that his name is being used to attract people for a political candidate, a *white* political candidate. The money isn't even going to S.N.C.C., as he had been told in New York, but to a local liberal group. Stokely is furious. He walks to the edge of the backyard and has a five-minute talk with Bob Fullilove, the local S.N.C.C. leader. Across the lawn, the young Negroes glower. . . . This is a real put-down, says one girl who is attending Rutgers Law School. Why the hell are they holding this in the backyard? Can't they hold it inside as if it were a regular, *formal* cocktail party? These people are not my kind of people . . . I don't like this scene, man. . . . This is bad news. . . .

Stokely and Fullilove end their talk and Stokely walks beneath the Rose of Sharon with the woman who accompanied him to the party, a six-foot-tall, very cool, very black-skinned woman with piled-high Nefertiti hair. She wears a tight white dress and is, she knows and Stokely knows and the entire party knows, the most stunning woman there. Stokely sips a Coke and the girl glowers at the crowd, which tries very hard to be casual, and not stare at her. A white man walks over, smiling, gripping his Martini.

"I just want to tell you, Mr. Carmichael, I saw you on TV and I really agreed with you on, uh, Vietnam and—"

Stokely cuts him off. "Thank you." Stokely gives him the white man's handshake.

"Attention, attention," cries the hostess, a short chubby woman in a knit dress. "Our guests are all here and our program is beginning."

The young Negroes appear startled. "What program?" Stokely frowns.

"I just want to say a few words," the woman goes on. "We have always been an integrated community. . . ." The Negroes begin shifting uncomfortably. "And we've never cared at all here about money or status, whatever that means."

"Shit," says Stokely in a loud whisper. "She don't know about status? Look at that swimming pool."

As soon as Frost begins speaking, Stokely leaves the backyard and walks toward the front of the house with his date. He leans against an elm, his left hand gentle on the young woman's shoulder. They chat in a whisper. A Negro girl, slightly drunk, and a white man come out of the house and Stokely glares at the girl. She walks over. "I like what you said about being proud of our blackness," she says.

"That means everyone," says Stokely in an angry whisper.

"Let's get out of here," says Stokely's date.

The girl looks at the white man and says, "Be proud of my blackness, my black womanness." She starts laughing and they walk away to a car.

Stokely watches them drive off.

"Let's leave," says Stokely's date.

They return to the backyard and within minutes Stokely—who had been scheduled to speak—and most of the young Negroes are gone; the whites and middle-aged Negroes are left alone.

Stokely is scheduled to take an eight o'clock flight the next morning to

Glens Falls, New York, and then be driven to Benson, Vermont, for a speech at a camp—he's not quite sure what type of camp or who will be there. At two minutes after eight Stokely's cab pulls up to the Mohawk Airlines terminal at LaGuardia Airport and Stokely leaps out and runs toward the ticket desk.

"I'm sorry," the ticket agent behind the desk says with a smile. "The flight just left."

"Oh no, oh no, oh *no*." Stokely pounds his fist on the desk.

"There *is* a flight leaving from Kennedy at eight-forty-five with a stop-off at Albany. And there's another at ten-thirty." The ticket agent smiles again.

Stokely walks away and shakes his head. "I took a cab from the Bronx [his mother's house]. It should have taken twenty minutes to get here. I kept saying, 'Use the bridge, use the bridge, man.' But that son of a bitch kept saying that Bruckner Boulevard was faster. Faster! It took an hour. Oh . . . oh that son of a bitch."

Stokely wears dark glasses, a black shirt with small-flowered print, dungarees and black shoes. He hails a cab for Kennedy Airport and once the cab starts Stokely lifts up the glasses and rubs his eyes—he had gone to bed at five that morning.

"They always do that in Atlanta," he says. "They always give us a hard time with flights down there."

He shakes his head again. The cab glides out of LaGuardia toward the Van Wyck Expressway. The traffic toward Manhattan is heavy; toward Kennedy Airport there are few cars. When Stokely is in New York, he generally spends the night in his mother's South Bronx home (the only Negro family on the block). He had not seen her on this trip, though, since she is working as a maid on a maritime line.

"She's a hard worker and a sharp gal," says Stokely, staring at the cars crawling toward New York. He turns. "She knew, she knows, that if you want to make it you got to hustle, and she hustled from the word go. She took no shit from no one. I got that from my mother. She used to tell me, 'You take nothing from no one, no matter who they are.' She knows the realities of life and she demanded, made sure, that I knew them too."

He smiles. "My old man was just the opposite." Stokely shakes his head and sighs. "He believed genuinely in the great American dream. And because he believed in it he was just squashed. Squashed! He worked himself to death in this country and he died the same way he started: poor and black."

"We came here in '52 from Port-of-Spain. That was a place that was mostly black. It was run by black people and everyone—the cops, the teachers, the civil servants—was black. We came here thinking that this was the promised land. Ha. We went up to the Bronx—I was eleven years old—and I saw this big apartment house we were going to and I said, 'Wow, Daddy, you own that whole thing?' And then eight of us climbed up to a three-room apartment."

"My old man . . ." Stokely takes off his glasses . . . "my old man would Tom. He was such a good old Joe, but he would *Tom*. And he was a very religious cat too— he was head deacon of the church and he was so honest, so very, very honest. He never realized people lied or cheated or were bad. He couldn't conceive of it. He just prayed and worked. Man, did he work. He worked as a cabdriver at night and went to school to study electricity and during the day he worked as a carpenter. He just thought that if you worked hard and prayed hard this country would take care of you. Well, I remember he tried to get into the carpenter's union—and this is a very racist thing. And the only way for him to get into the union was to bribe the business representative. Well, he would have none of that. So one day when my father is out, my mother calls up the business representative and tells him to come to the house and she gives him $50 and a bottle of perfume and my father gets into the union. And when my father comes home and finds out that he's in the union he says, 'You see. You work hard and pray hard and this country takes care.' And my mother and I . . . laughed. Wow. My old man was like the Man with the Hoe. He just felt that there were millions to be made in this country and he died at forty-two—just a poor black man."

The cab pulls up at the Eastern Airlines terminal in Kennedy Airport. Stokely walks in and within seconds a porter walks up and smiles broadly. "I usually hang out with the porters at the airports," he says, walking quickly through the terminal. "A lot of times I don't have money and they just pass the hat. They're good people. In Memphis last week they bought me a steak dinner."

He walks to Gate 2 where a Mohawk flight is taking off at eight-forty-five. He waits ten minutes on standby but the flight is filled. He trudges back to the ticket desk and makes a reservation for the ten-thirty flight and then phones S.N.C.C. to tell them to notify the camp. By now Stokely is hungry and he walks into the cocktail lounge and restaurant in the heart of the terminal. The alcoholics, the hangers-on, the bored travelers, the women catching the nine o'clock flight to Mexico City line the bar, sipping Bloody Marys and beer and Scotch, straight. A waiter hustles over and says, no, the restaurant is not open at this hour, but there's another restaurant at the end of the corridor. A woman at the bar, blonde, tall, tanned, in her late forties, carrying a large white pillbox, turns and stares through dark glasses at Stokely—this hulking, dungareed figure in dark glasses too. Their eyes meet. The woman smiles, just slightly, and Stokely stares at her for a moment and then turns away and walks out.

"Man, this place says something. You can get a drink at nine o'clock, but you can't get food."

At a table in the restaurant Stokely calls the waitress "M'am" and orders orange juice, bacon and eggs, English muffins and two glasses of milk.

"I used to drink," he says with a smile. "I used to like wine. I used to know a hell of a lot of guys who drank wine all day."

The waitress brings his orange juice and he sips it. "In Harlem I used to know a lot of guys like that. I used to know a lot of guys who were addicts and they were some beautiful cats. I'm not kidding. They had this ability, this profound ability to understand life."

While Stokely's father struggled and his mother worked as a maid to help support the family—Stokely has four sisters—he often spent days and weeks with his aunts on Lenox Avenue and 142nd Street in Harlem. "I like Harlem," says Stokely. "It's a very exciting place. It represents life, real life. On one block you have a church and right next door is a bar and they're both packed. On Saturday night people are always in constant motion. You get all of life's contradictions right there in one community: all the wild violence and all the love can be found in Harlem. You get the smells of human sweat and all sorts of bright colors and bright clothes and people in motion. You get preachers on one side of a street and nationalists on the other."

The waitress brings the rest of the order.

Stokely Carmichael grew up in the Bronx and Harlem, a bright, wild, aggressive boy. He attended P.S. 39, P.S. 34, and P.S. 83 and was involved, almost as soon as the family moved to New York, in fistfights and gang intrigues. In the Bronx, he was the only Negro member of the Morris Park Avenue Dukes and was, he admits, a specialist in stealing hubcaps and car radios.

In 1956 quite suddenly Stokely broke with the past. He was admitted to the Bronx High School of Science, a school for some of the brightest children in New York. "My freshman year I wanted to leave," Stokely recalls. "I couldn't intellectually compete with those cats. They were doctors' sons and lawyers' sons and read everything from Einstein to *The Grapes of Wrath*. The only book I knew was *Huckleberry Finn*. It was clear to me I couldn't compete. My mother wouldn't accept it though. She wanted me to go to Science and she would have it no other way. No questions asked. 'Remember one thing,' she would say, 'they're white, they'll make it. You won't unless you're on the top.'"

Stokely began reading—Marx, Darwin, Camus, anything he was given. "I began to read as quickly as I could; anything that anybody mentioned. It was naïve at the time, but it was sincere." For the first time, his friends were upper middle-class whites, wealthy kids who would go on to Harvard, Columbia, Brandeis. He began going out with white girls and making the Greenwich Village scene. He was invited to parties on Park Avenue.

Even as he persisted in friendships with white men and women, however, Stokely realized that the white and black worlds he knew were not linking; in fact they were splitting, irrevocably, apart. "I learned at Science that white people, liberal white people, could be intellectually committed but emotionally racist. They couldn't see *through*. I was everybody's best friend. They would say to me, 'Oh, you're so different.' And they didn't know any other black people. What they meant was I didn't meet their image of black people. And their image, their responses, are governed by the thought that Negroes *are* inferior. I was an exception. I was the accepted Negro. But other Negroes weren't like me. They were bums, lazy, unambitious, inhuman, and that attitude was extended to me. They would say to me, 'Oh, you dance so well,' when I couldn't dance so well. Or they would say to me, 'Oh, you're so sensitive.' Well the only thing I was sensitive to was the fact that they all had maids and they saw no inconsistency between being my friend and exploiting a black maid—paying her $30 a week while they went off and made a damned good living. I went to parties on Park Avenue and they called their maids by their first name and the maids were smiling and serving and I knew full well what was going on in their minds and I knew they didn't want to take all that shit. All these kids—these filthy rich kids—they all had maids and my mother was a maid."

When Stokely was a high-school senior, he began reading about the first sit-ins in the South. His first reaction was negative. "What I said was, 'Niggers always looking to get themselves in the paper, no matter how they did it.' My opinion was that they didn't know what they were doing."

Within months, though, he met several students involved in the sit-ins. As the civil-rights movement spread quickly across the South, Stokely's commitment—and fascination—grew. First, he picketed Woolworth's in New York and then sat-in in Virginia and North Carolina. He turned down scholarships to several white schools and enrolled at Howard University, mostly because he could keep working in the movement while at a Negro school. At Howard, he met other civil-rights activists and immediately engaged in sit-ins and the early freedom rides through Mississippi, Georgia and Alabama. The first ride and the first arrest was in Jackson, Mississippi in 1961. . . .

By now Stokely had finished breakfast at the airport and walked to Gate 2 to board the plane. Almost as soon as he took his seat he began shivering—he is always cold—and he grabbed a blanket off the rack. The plane started and Stokely peered through the window at the rows of A-frame houses below, the cars, the Manhattan skyline. "I went down South when I was nineteen. I was a kid who took nothing from no one.

And, man, I took it." He smiled. "In Mississippi, the beatings are by the cops, not by mobs. The mobs, they throw wild punches and if you're cool you can miss them. But the cops are out to get your ass and you get three cops in a back room who are out to get your ass and. . . ." He shook his head. "In Jackson, before they put me in jail, the cops rode me up and down in an elevator; they kept kicking and using billy clubs and pressing the buttons using their fist. I wanted . . . I just wanted to get my hands on one of them. But like you had to cover your head and . . . and . . . you keep thinking why don't you leave me alone. Why don't you beat your wives instead and just leave me alone?"

Stokely then spent time in jail. "Fifty-three days. Oh, lord, fifty-three days in a six-by-nine cell. Twice a week to shower. No books, nothing to do. They would isolate us. Maximum security. And those guards were out of sight. They did not play, *they did not play*. The sheriff acted like he was scared of black folks and he came up with some beautiful things. One night he opened up all the windows, put on ten big fans and an air conditioner and dropped the temperature to 38 degrees. All we had on was T-shirts and shorts. And it was so cold, so *cold*, all you could do was walk around for two nights and three days, your teeth chattering, going out of your mind, and it getting so cold that when you touch the bedspring you feel your skin is gonna come right off.

"I don't go along with this garbage that you can't hate, you gotta love. I don't go along with that at all. Man you *can*, you *do* hate. You don't forget that Mississippi experience. You don't get arrested twenty-seven times. You don't smile at that and say love thy white brother. You don't forget those beatings and, man, they were rough. Those mothers were out to get revenge. You don't forget. You don't forget those funerals. I knew Medgar Evers, I knew Willie Moore, I knew Mickey Schwerner, I knew Jonathan Daniels, I met Mrs. Liuzzo just before she was killed. You don't forget those funerals."

The worst experience was what Stokely calls a two-day nervous breakdown just before the Selma-to-Montgomery march. "I was in the Ben Moore Hotel in Montgomery, getting ready to go downstairs, when they locked the doors. I couldn't get out. And downstairs were the marchers, and the cops began beating and using hoses. I couldn't stand it. I was by my window and I looked down and saw the cops beating and I couldn't get out. I was completely helpless. There was no release. I kept watching and then I began screaming and I didn't stop screaming. Some guys took me to the airport later and I kept screaming and I tried to kick in a couple of windows at the airport. Oh, man."

He shakes his head slowly. "There have been people in the movement who have cracked. Like you can't help it. You always work on the assumption that the worst things will happen, you always work on the assumption that you're going to die. I used to say that the only way they'll stop me is if they kill me. I still think that's true. What bothers me now is if I live through all this I just hope I don't get tired or give up or sell out. That's what bothers me. We all have weaknesses. I don't know what mine are. But if they find out they'll try to destroy me. It's a question of them finding out what my weaknesses are—money, power, publicity, I don't know. And sometimes . . . sometimes . . . you just get so tired too."

Stokely peers out the window at the clean, azure sky and shivers beneath the blanket. Within seconds, he is asleep.

Twenty minutes later the plane is landing at Albany Airport where Stokely will catch a plane for Glens Falls. He steps down the ramp and begins singing: "The empty-handed painter on your street is drawing crazy patterns on your sheet."

He grins and walks into the terminal. "Man, that Dylan is a wild guy."

With thirty minutes free before the next plane leaves, Stokely steps into the airport luncheonette and orders a vanilla ice cream soda. The waitress leaves and Stokely turns toward several persons at the counter reading newspapers. "Look at that, look at *that*," he says, laughing, pointing to the sports page headline of The New York *Daily News*: "Operate on Whitey's Arm."

"If they flipped that over and put it on the front page they'd sell a million copies," he laughs.

Within the hour Stokely arrives in the small Glens Falls airport—three hours late. As soon as he climbs off the plane, a smiling, crew-cut youth waves and walks over and introduces himself. He is Frank Levy, a Ph. D. candidate in economics at Yale and a member of the camp's staff.

Stokely struggles into Levy's red MG and they drive off to the camp, about fifty miles away. Stokely asks Levy about the camp and is told that it's called the Shawnee Leadership Institute, an annual two-week summer camp for teen-agers who hold discussions on "issues" and listen to invited guest speakers. (The next day, Lord Caradon, the British Ambassador to the United Nations, was coming up.) There are about seventy campers and a staff of thirty, mostly college and graduate students.

Stokely likes Levy and they begin kidding about Vermont: "I wonder if everyone up here smokes pot." The car crosses New York into Vermont on Route 4 and passes Deak's grocery and Frank's Taxidermist. "I've never been to Vermont before," says Stokely.

The elms and pines are just starting to blaze with autumn colors and Stokely settles back and gazes silently at the countryside. He waves at farm boys—who wave back—and laughs as they ride past Crumley's grocery in Fort Ann. "A town like this and you go out of your mind," he exclaims. "I read someplace that suicide rates are very high in Vermont—they must be sick of cutting all that grass."

Just outside of Fort Ann, the car breaks down. Stokely moans and shakes his head and begins laughing. "This is my day," he says. The fan belt is broken and Stokely and Levy struggle with the new belt. After twenty minutes they are off again.

As soon as Stokely arrives at the camp he appears startled, then amused. "Wow," he says, as a half-dozen teen-age interracial couples, their arms around each other, surround the car, "Hey, like I had visions when I heard the name of the camp of old Protestant ladies sitting around campfires talking about love." They shake his hand and escort him to the dining room.

Once inside, Stokely is greeted by an old friend, Julian Houston, who is president of the Student Government at Boston University. Stokely grins and gives Julian the "black" handshake and embraces him. "Man, you should be workin' down in Alabama," cries Stokely.

With Houston and several other camp leaders, Stokely sits down at a wooden table while the campers, awestruck, watch him. Plates of ham and cheese and rolls are brought out and Stokely eats hungrily while a long-haired girl strums a guitar and sings *Ain't Gonna Study War No More.*

After the plates are cleared away, all the campers are called into the wooden dining room. Stokely removes his shoes and begins speaking quietly.

"Black people have not only been told that they are inferior, but the system maintains it. We are faced in this country with whether or not we want to be equal and let white people define equality for us on their terms as they've always done and thus lose our blackness or whether we should maintain our identity and still be equal. This is Black Power. The fight is whether black people should use their slogans without having white people say, 'That's okay.' You have to deal with what white means in this country. When you say black power you mean the opposite of white and it forces this country to deal with its own racism. The 1954 school desegregation decision was handed down for several reasons. It was a political decision—and it was *not* based on humanitarianism, but was based on the fact that this country was going further into nonwhite countries and you could not espouse freedom and have second-class citizens in your own country. The area in which we move now is politics and within a political context. People kept saying that segregation and racism was wrong because it was immoral. But they still didn't come to grips with the two essential things: we are poor and we are black. You can pass 10,000 bills but you still haven't talked about economic security. When someone is poor, it's not because of cultural deprivation, it's not because they need to be uplifted and head-started. When someone is poor, it's because they have no money, that's all. That's all. They say it's our fault, *our fault* that we're poor when in fact it's the system that calculates and perpetuates poverty. They say black people don't know money, that they'll drink it away, they won't work. But we never had money, and it's presumptuous to tell us we won't be thrifty, brave, clean and reverent. You know who the biggest welfare group is in this country? You know who they are? You think it's the black people? Well, it's not. It's the farmers. They are the biggest welfare group in this country. But the difference between them and us is that they run their own programs, they control their own resources and they get something out of it. We must, *we must* take over and control our resources and our programs. And if we don't, the black people will wake up again tomorrow morning, still poor, still black, and still singing *We Shall Overcome.*"

The audience responds warmly and as soon as Stokely finishes, the questions begin. Stokely calls on a burly Negro youth who speaks in a thick drawl.

"Stokely, do you believe in God?"

Stokely stares at the youth. "That's a personal question."

The youth smiles. "Oh."

"Where you from?" Stokely asks.

"St. Augustine, Florida, Stokely."

"What you do down there?"

"I worked in the field. Cotton, tobacco, you name it. I worked for $2 a day since I was so high. I worked for $2 a day until I heard Dr. King down there and then I knew I had to join the movement."

"Right." Stokely turns from the boy to the audience. "The reason I joined the movement was not out of love. It was out of hate. I hate white supremacy and I'm out to smash it."

A pause. An older woman rises, a white woman. "Stokely," she asks, a tremor in her voice, "What can we do? What can the whites do?"

"You must seek to tear down racism. You must seek to organize poor whites. You must stop crying "Black supremacy" or "Black nationalist" or "racism in reverse" and face certain facts: that this country is racist from top to bottom and one group is exploiting the other. You must face the fact that racism in this country is a white, not a black problem. And because of this, you, *you* must move into white communities to deal with the problem. We don't need kids from Berkeley to come down to Mississippi. We don't need white kids to come to black communities just because they want to be where the action is.

"Look," says Stokely, leaning forward, speaking in a loud whisper. "Every white man in this country can announce that he is our friend. Every white man can make us his token, symbol, object, what have you. Every white man can say, 'I am your friend.' Well from here on in we're going to decide who is our friend. We don't want to hear any words, we want to see what you're going to do. The price of being the black man's friend has gone up.

"And you must understand," he says, his voice rising, "that as a person oppressed because of my blackness, I have common cause with other blacks who are oppressed because of *their* blackness. It must be to the oppressed that I address myself, not to members—even friends—of the oppressing group."

The audience stirs. Stokely suggests they walk outside so he can get some good country air. Within minutes, the teen-agers sit in a semicircle beneath an evergreen, chatting quietly with Stokely who is lying on his side, his elbow dug into the grass, his chin in his hand. . . .

By dusk, with the apricot-colored sky streaked with violet, the campers implore Stokely to stay the night. He'd love to, he says, he needs the rest and this marvelous clean air, but there are meetings and speeches and appointments the next day.

With Julian Houston, Stokely climbs into a car driven by a Roman Catholic priest from Boston who is on the camp's staff.

"Stokely," says the priest, driving quickly down the darkening road, "what should church people do?"

Stokely pauses. "They should start working on destroying the church and building more Christ-like communities. It's obvious, Reverend, that the church doesn't want Christ-like communities. Christ—he taught some revolutionary stuff, right? And the church is a counterrevolutionary force."

The priest drives a moment in silence. "What should the priest's job be?"

"To administer, through his actions, the teachings of Jesus Christ," says Stokely. "I would also make every church a plain building that could be used for other things, a building that will not be embellished."

"What's next for you, Stokely?" asks the priest.

"Next?" Stokely smiles. "How does the victim move to equality with the executioner? That's what's next. We are the victims and we've got to move to equality with our executioners." He pauses. "Camus never answers that question, does he? We are the victims, they are the executioners. Every real relationship is that—victim and executioner. Every relationship. Love, marriage, school, everything. This is the way this society sees love. You become a slave to somebody you love. You love me, you don't mess around with anyone else. One is the victim, the other the executioner. . . ."

It is dark now and chilly and Stokely begins shivering. He begins gossiping with Houston about old friends who have been lost to the poverty program, the Peace Corps, graduate schools.

At the airport in Burlington, Stokely is told that the plane to New York has been delayed an hour. He shakes his head—"It's my day"—and walks around with Houston. He then has two sandwiches and two glasses of milk and averts the stares of several men at the bar who recognize him.

The plane finally arrives. Stokely shakes hands with the priest and Houston and walks wearily up the ramp. He is cold and tired and sleeps listlessly on the trip to New York.

Shortly before eleven the plane lands at Kennedy Airport. Stokely has a date downtown in Manhattan but decides, instead, just to return to the Bronx and go to sleep. By now he is exhausted. The lack of sleep, the missed and delayed flights, the car trips, the questions, sandwiches on the run, the pressures have taken their toll. He walks through the terminal, breathing heavily, peering blankly through his dark glasses. Once outside, he decides to take a taxi and starts walking to the first cab in line. The driver, who is white, stares at Stokely—dungarees, dark glasses, carrying a paper bag of ham sandwiches, looking vaguely ominous—and drives past him to pick up a laughing white couple who carry cardboard cases of tax-free liquor. Stokely tenses, clenches his fist and takes a deep breath and turns toward the second cabdriver in line. This driver, who is a young Negro, has watched Stokely and is now smiling faintly. Stokely walks over, looks at the cabdriver and begins smiling too. He then opens the door and climbs into the cab and returns home for just a brief rest.

[January, 1967]

From "The Second Civil War"

by Garry Wills

Can peace flower from the barrel of a gun? The Reverend Albert Cleage, of the Central United Church of Christ in Detroit, thinks so: "The police, here in Detroit, asked the mayor for nine million dollars' worth of weapons to use against us. I think every black man in America feels that the white man is just at the beginning of using genocide here. But, you know, I think genocide will come much quicker if we just get real passive. We've pretty much outlived our economic usefulness; but even so, if the white man thinks, 'We're going to kill twenty-five million black people, but it's going to take fifty million white people to do it,' then he begins to wonder, 'Is it worth it?'" The Reverend Cleage thinks that the black community must arm itself in order to *prevent* wholesale killing—much as we stockpile atomic bombs that we may avoid using them.

But is this threat of "two white men for every black" a realistic one? After all, the odds are nine to one against the Negro, simply in terms of population—not counting the technological superiority of what Reverend Cleage calls "the white man's military establishment." The majority of those killed in past riots were Negroes. "But this [program] will be a whole different approach," Cleage answered. "If the black man is fighting

685

genocide, he goes out in the morning and says, 'I'm going to kill all the white men I can today, because he's going to kill me by tonight.' How are you going to kill twenty-five million of us overnight? They didn't even kill the Jews overnight in Germany—and *they* weren't resisting. *We* will be prepared. If the white man decides to destroy us, we will set out to make it the most expensive destruction of a race there has ever been in history. And I think we're capable of doing that. This is not a fight in which one tries to win." To work, a policy of preventive arming must strike a balance of terror.

I was talking with Reverend Cleage in the empty meeting hall of his large church; he sat, purring with soft eloquence, across the table from me and my escort. His features and coloring show how potent is the symbol "black." He is, externally, one of us, the enemy. His thick eyebrows and thick moustache are frosted with grey. He must, of course, wear a "natural" hairstyle, but it is cut so short that he looks more like a crew-cut businessman, dressed conservatively for the office, than a revolutionary. Still, he called the Detroit riot the July Rebellion, and thinks it is only a first stage. He had predicted, seven months before the riot, that "1967 will be a year of racial violence and conflict." When the riot broke out, on a Sunday morning, he took the pulpit to say he had been asked if he would urge his congregation to "cool it." His answer was, resoundingly, no: "Essentially, we are trying to get free, and we want justice, and we are no longer talking about love and all these other things that cluttered up people's minds for so long. We want justice and we are going to fight for it."

That is the note he has struck, over and over, in his sermons and weekly newspaper column. One pictures a middle-aged Stokely Carmichael as one reads him, a clerical Rap Brown. He is something more serious than either—an eloquent, established clergyman, not depending only on the young; a man with trained political instinct and style, attractive to radicals and moderates alike. He has been running for one office or another over the past five years; but he did not catch on fully till the riot. Even now, he offers his unbending program in the accents of a patient man soothing idiots: "The Negro is an intelligence test the white man is taking. We will see just how stupid you are." His favorite words are "rational" and "reasonable."

His country-vicar style is set off by the drama of one's entry to him. His attendant, who ushers us into the room, is a man whose "natural" is piled in Rap Brown profusion on his head—defiant cultivation of "the Brillo look." He wears the engulfing rainbow clothes of some imagined African domesticated. After placing us in the cleared space toward the front of the deep hall, he takes up a Secret Service position at our backs. But the Reverend Cleage, when he strolls in, talks with an almost casual persuasiveness. Why, I asked, did the ghetto residents burn their own stores and homes in the riot? "In the Rebellion? Those buildings were not ours. To burn down a slum owner's shack means *he's out*. He won't come here to exploit us again. There's nothing irrational about cleaning that out of your community. The black man is only doing what the white men did in their revolution. There's nothing surprising about black men wanting to control the black community—fighting to control it, burning to control it. That's very rational."

The Reverend Cleage preaches the Nation, the chosen people who must be kept pure of the Gentile (i.e., the white man). Perhaps that is why a visit to him is like a journey to a foreign country. I found a white man who works in the ghetto, who had the proper black connections. This contact went with his black friend on preliminary embassy, and was left at the door while the black man negotiated entry (when he came out, he apologized for leaving his fellow on the doorstep: "Oh, that's all right; it's a long-standing custom—in the South—to be denied the front door because of one's color"). The next day, this white man could conduct me to the interview. He sent his name in (while we waited at the door), offered further references when we were admitted, and was surprised (as I was) by the affable Wizard we met at the center of this forbidding Oz.

I asked who would return to the ghetto once exploiters were "cleared out" by fire. "A businessman will go anywhere—to hell, if he finds a way—for profit. We are the white man's colony, the biggest, richest colony he ever had, other than South Africa with the diamonds. We must teach him to invest in the ghetto just as he would in any other foreign nation." Are you in favor of colonialism then? "Neo-colonialism is all right. It's the old colonialism, still practiced in Rhodesia and South Africa, that was wrong. But neo-colonialists realize that nation in which they invest has to have control of business in its territory, and a just return of the profits, and full ownership over a reasonable length of time." Will men submit to these restrictions when investing in their own country? "That is better than not knowing, from one night to the next, whether one's building is going to stand. You can talk better with a businessman than with a maudlin sentimental liberal. A businessman wants to know how much money he can make—what are the risks, what are the rules. He's practical."

Cleage's opposition to the meliorist liberal, who asks what he can give the black man, was made clear just after the riot. Mayor Cavanagh appointed a typical liberal panel—the New Detroit Committee, chaired by department-store owner Joseph L. Hudson—to decide what to do about (and for) the ghetto. It is true that the Mayor included three black nationalists on the panel (spiking the normal mixture a bit); but he did not include the Reverend Cleage—and so, the evening before the committee's first meeting, a thousand black activists met at the City-County Building to register their discontent with the official body. Even one of the official committee came to protest. The demands made that night were an unheralded preview of the action at a meeting held one month later in Chicago—the National Conference for New Politics, where a minority Black Caucus demanded (and got) fifty percent of the votes. In Cleage's church, on August 9, speakers said the Hudson Committee should have a black chairman, a black majority; that it should address itself merely to answering a set of black demands. The Reverend Cleage summed up: "The Hudson Committee will take orders from us."

I asked the Reverend Cleage, several months after that meeting, what the Hudson Committee had accomplished so far. "Oh, they are trying to cooperate with the Metropolitan Fund to merge Detroit in a six-county complex, so they can take all power from Detroit before the black people take Detroit." A typical clash between the liberal and the advocates of Black Power. Liberals would like to integrate the black downtown and the white suburbs; make suburban taxes available to the inner city; work together as a single metropolitan complex. The black leader watches Negro population creeping toward the fifty-percent mark in city after city: "We have forty-two percent now," Cleage says of Detroit. As the balance trembles, about to turn, they foresee a last panicked rush of remaining white citizens out of town, which will leave all municipal administration to elected black officials. Mr. Cleage does not worry about tax money in that case. The cities are too vitally needed, by the surrounding countryside and by the federal government, for the nation to let them starve for funds. The black nation will have its own territory, its own government; and the white nation must come to it for the use of certain vital installations.

At this juncture, there is no enemy for a Reverend Cleage, like the liberal who tries to prevent such schism, who wants to thin the tight black centers of population out in larger grey areas. "The white man has to give us control of the cities. If he doesn't, he leaves us no alternative but violence. There's no other choice. The white man is still toying with the idea that there's a third possibility, but he's just wasting time." Who stands in your way? "The white liberal is the most difficult person to get rid of. He's got emotion, prestige and everything tied up in *his* leadership. Moynihan is almost a classic pattern of what happens to the liberal. His study tries to show that the black community is sick; but the black community is not as sick as the white community." If the black community is sick, it must still be ministered to by white surgeons, like Moynihan—which Mr. Cleage resents. He thinks that Moynihan, losing support among the black, has turned to the Right for support, to hold onto his power: "Moynihan issued a statement that the time had come when white liberals and white bigots had to get together." (He is referring to a speech before the A.D.A. calling for a "politics of stability" that could unite all moderates, left and right, to prevent the growth of "terrorism" in America.) Moynihan has become a favorite target of black militants, ever since his Department of Labor report on *The Negro Family* appeared. Rap Brown, speaking on educational TV, said that, while black men take care of their own problems, white men should begin "to talk about civilization of Lyndon Johnson, to talk about civilization of James O. Eastland, to talk about the civilization of Patrick Moynihan."

The other enemy, after the liberal, is "the Negro" (carefully to be distinguished from "the black man"): "The Uncle Tom is a traitor," Mr. Cleage told me, "and what have you white men always done, historically, to traitors? That's right, killed them." It is all said in the mildest know-your-candidate manner.

It is difficult to judge how much of the black community shares Cleage's strategy for municipal takeover. But it is perfectly clear that ghetto residents vibrate to his rhetoric of pride, of self-respect, and appreciate his denunciation of injustices they have experienced. During the riot, three unarmed black men were killed in the Algiers Motel, and a policeman is now under indictment for murder. The pent-up anger over what the black community calls this "massacre" was given vent in the Reverend Cleage's church when a "People's Tribunal" tried the policeman *in absentia*. It was the new Nation conducting its first case of genocide, in truest Bertrand Russell style: the jury was made up of people like Mrs. Rosa Parks, who began the historic Montgomery boycott when she stayed in the front of a bus, and Negro novelist John Killens. Two jurymen were white—but they were members of People Against Racism, a group meant to "civilize the whites."

The Church itself is a symbol of black aspiration. Near the place where the Detroit riot began, there is a street-side all-white statue of Jesus, on the ground of a Catholic seminary. During the revolt, the face and hands and feet of this statue were painted black—in imitation of the black Jesus and black Mary whose portraits flank the entrance of the Reverend Cleage's church. Inside the church, there is a full-length picture of the black Madonna, unveiled last Easter Sunday in connection with a call for a "Black Christian Nationalist Movement." The artist, Glanton Dowdell, was one of those convicted of carrying a revolver in the Kercheval riot of 1966. The muted Mr. Cleage and his flaming attendant Zulu took us from picture to picture in a little pilgrimage. There is a stylized tear in the eyes of Jesus and Mary, who look as if some Negro Norman Rockwell had confected them. The exotic bodyguard relaxes his monosyllabic rigidity before the Madonna, and whispers, to no one in particular, "She's so beautiful—in a way that does not make you think of sex." It is the voice of the new chivalry, of the ascetic knights who ride unseen through the TV films of looting and arson, elite warriors of this new Nation. He is the "new Negro" who appeared first in the disciplined secret cadres of the Muslims, but who is found now in a hundred groups, religious or mystical in character. I asked Mr. Cleage what part religion plays in the movement.

"Religion is the heart and core and center of the black Nation. We were misled in religion just like we were in history and culture. Most black people in America didn't know till a few years ago that the black culture in Africa was far superior to the white man's in Europe. All our education has been miseducation. For thousands of years, when the white man in Europe was a barbarian, black people in Africa had a philosophy, astronomy, science, libraries. But black people didn't know it because white men didn't put it in the book.

"The same way with religion—religion was given to us by the slave masters in the South, and they gave us a lie. Christianity is essentially the religion of the black Messiah. The Jewish nation started with Abraham, who came from the Chaldean portion, and those were Arabs (as known today). When Abraham left, as the father of Israel, he mixed with all of the peoples of the Mediterrean and Africa. The Old Testament is a record of this racial mixture that took place in building the black Nation, Israel. Moses was married to a black woman. Joseph was married to an Egyptian. There were no white people in the area until the development of the Greco-Roman period, as an imperialism. So there was no way in the world Jesus could have been white."

Is Jesus the savior of white people as well as black? "That's up to the white man. I preach about the Nation—the black Nation, the black Messiah. Jesus was building on the Old Testament. The first three Gospels of the New Testament are historical. The Gospel of John is later, as are the epistles of the Apostle Paul. Paul was trying to relate the Gospels of the black Messiah to the white Gentile world. Jesus had no conception of anything the Apostle Paul talked about—the whole universalism, brotherhood. White people preach that; they very seldom turn to the Old Testament—all black preachers, even the most ignorant black preachers, preach primarily out of the Old Testament and the first three Gospels. There has always been a definite division between the Christianity of black people and the Christianity of white people—Jesus on the one side, and Paul on the other."

Does God reject the white man? "God created man in his own image (that's the Bible again), and does not want that dignity to be torn down; so he would be concerned with those who are oppressed. It is divine justice, knowledge, wisdom that Jesus would come to the black people." Yet you say the white man is sick. Has God abandoned him in his sickness? "I think Paul has a message for white people. They need that kind of religion. They have to believe in universalism because they are the oppressors. They're concerned about guilt. God is concerned about my oppression, and he tells me what to do to get rid of it. He's concerned about your guilt, and he tells you what to do to get rid of that. White people need the epistles of Paul. But for a black man to believe in the universal brotherhood of man is demeaning, and psychologically destroys them. The oppressed need one thing, and the oppressor another. Now God in his infinite wisdom has seen fit to give them both what they need. For black people to say, 'We're going to love everybody,' would destroy us; it would be a sickness with us."

A wild emblematic history—but not so wild as the Muslim version of Genesis (with its reverse Manichaeism, angelic-black quenching the devil-white); and look what that theory has wrought, in terms of pride and discipline. For fighting against the odds, nothing is so practical as mysticism, the luminous simplicities, the inner (illogical) light. Mr. Cleage's homiletic style echoes, across the century, the launched pulpit shafts of another violent divine: "Sharps rifles are a greater moral agency than the Bible." On the eve of civil war, Henry Ward Beecher stirred congregations with words like that; and when rifles were sent into Kentucky to aid abolitionist guerrillas, the crates were marked "Bibles." Beecher's Bibles became the term for all guns sent to support abolition, and the sermons grew more and more "unworldly": "Let no man pray that [John] Brown be spared! Let Virginia make him a martyr!" When the war came, Beecher made his home an armory for Union ordnance.

Mr. Cleage is very interested in guerrilla tactics. When I asked him about the Mayor's request for nine million dollars in riot weapons, he said, "Their arms are not going to be any more effective here than in Vietnam. You don't need superior arms. The Negro is not going to be stupid enough to throw bricks at tanks." Though his rhetoric is Northern abolitionist, his strategy is the dreamy Southern one, of light rapid marauders against the clumsy machine. The new secessionist is a creature of the forlorn hope, like the Confederate leaders; and, like them, he can call his doubting Lees back to defend him, drawn against their better judgment by the ties of blood. If the Cleage minority issues a call to arms, many in the black majority will feel they must support "the brothers." As Cleage puts it, "There are no 'good darkies' anymore." And after predicting the riots in 1967, he has this to say about 1968: "Next summer, if conditions are the same, we'll probably have rebellion in the streets just as we did this year."

Using my interview with Cleage as passport, I tried to travel a bit in his Nation. I went to "The Easel," a black art shop, and asked if I might interview the owner: "I am the owner and I have set a policy for all the C.C.A.C. (Citywide Citizens Action Committee) that we will not talk to white newsmen." But Cleage talked to me. "I won't." The C.C.A.C. is the group that was set up at the meeting which protested the Hudson Committee's makeup.

I went to Vaughn's Book Store, the literary center of the Revolution—raided several times, I had heard, during the riot, and doused by firemen though it was not on fire. I asked about this; was told that these things happened. The lady in charge at the moment (Vaughn himself is at a meeting with Mr. Cleage) is minimally courteous but uncommunicative. The shop is busy, its patrons well-dressed, the black intelligentsia. The book selection is extraordinary, covering all aspects of the race struggle in America and the accession to power of African nations. The books lean toward hagiography (with Malcolm X and Muhammad Ali as the leading heroes) and is trans-racial only in one sense: all advocates of revolution are admitted to the Pantheon. Che Guevara is here, and Mao (in an expensive multi-volumed edition), Fidel and Régis Debray. There are special offprints of a *National Guardian* article on last summer's rebellion—"The Birth of a Nation"—written by local celebrities (and C.C.A.C. members) Grace and James Boggs. Readers are given the choice of four Michigan Negro newspapers, one of which, *The Inner City Voice*, publishes items like this:

POLICE INHUMANITY

Mrs. Jacqueline M. was dragged from her apartment by white police officers and taken to the 10th Precinct. Policemen inside the station fondled the private parts of her body, while she was in the interrogation room. They put their hands underneath her clothing, then ripped off the top part of her pajamas. Police photographers took pictures of her exposed body, while various white police officers posed holding her breasts. Then they ripped off the lower part of her pajamas (she had been sleeping when the police broke into her apartment), and made her stand nude in the middle of the room for over an hour.

This operation, which involved considerable manpower, was supposed to have taken place during the riot, when police were desperate to get more men on the streets and newsmen swarmed in precinct stations. Devils do not bother with minor things like strategy; and mystics see devils in the light of revelation, not of logic. One *Free Press* reporter who worked on the exposé of police and National Guard responsibility in the forty-three reported deaths said that unfounded rumors were assumed throughout the ghetto—e.g., that all three men in the Algiers Motel had their genitals shot off.

I asked Detroit's police commissioner, Ray Girardin, if he thought Cleage the most influential of the black leaders. "He is getting the attention now; but I think Cleage is being used by smarter people behind him." I assume this opinion reflects the traffic over his desk of intelligence reports. Would Milton and Richard Henry be two of these "smarter ones"? "They're pretty bright and the ones who do what planning there is in these riots are highly intelligent. We had them under surveillance all through the riot."

The Henry brothers are the men who offered to use their influence to stop the revolt if the Mayor would meet their demands (withdrawal of troops, amnesty, funds for co-ops, etc.). Milton Henry, a lawyer, also served as prosecuting attorney at the Reverend Cleage's "People's Tribunal." He is a Muslim, and was an associate of Malcolm X. Milton was out of town when I visited Detroit, so I called on Richard Henry, who prefers his post-slave name, a Swahili one—Imari. He was reluctant to be interviewed, after an NBC special on the Detroit riot. "Bill Matney double-crossed me, and we're old friends." Matney is the Negro reporter who interviewed black militants around Detroit and produced evidence that some of the rioting and arson was planned. I thought Imari might resent this contention, but that was not the case: "Oh, some of the burning was organized; in fact, a lot of it was. They hit sections in teams." What he resented were the factual inaccuracies (that a mysterious white man runs the black movement); and, even more, that no militant was allowed to express the separatist *philosophy* on the screen. I assured him that was precisely what I would report on, and was allowed to visit him at his home.

Imari, or "Rick" as he is known to his old friends, lives in a large home sparsely furnished. His teen-age daughter was watching television with her friends; they got bundled out of the front room into the kitchen when I came. The home is middle-class in appearance; Henry has a government job, as technical writer. He is slight, wears a long-suffering smile, and breathes soft laughter through his words—bitterness has reached, in him, the point of last-hope gaiety, a what-is-there-to-lose enjoyment of the risks he lives with. He agrees with Cleage that genocide may be just around the corner. "Black men are finally beginning to realize that the Cowboy-and-Indian shows on TV are about *us*. The people who count—the Army, the police, who do the fighting for the white community—have reached the conclusion that society is not going to adjust to what the black militants want, so they are preparing for war against the militants." I asked if this war apparatus has intelligence units inside the black movement. "Oh, yes; anytime they want us, they know where we are and what our habits are. But"—the laughter is breathing as he says it—"I just read recently that the head of one section of British intelligence turned out to be a double agent. Remember this, too: black people realize that they have dues to pay, and most are paying them."

Imari differs from Cleage on several crucial points. For one thing, Cleage still tries to negotiate with the white establishment his takeover of the city. "People don't realize how easy it would be to get along with the C.C.A.C., with Cleage and the Boggses. They keep telling the white man, 'You have one last chance.' They want a cut of the action. And, you know, Johnson is just like the Mafia. When he sees we're getting more and more votes, he says, 'Okay, boys, I'll give you a cut of the action.' But our people have suffered too much to join the exploiters now." If the Negro were given his share of the action, wouldn't that stop exploitation? "No, the nation's whole policy is racist. We are willing to have good relations with the white Communists. We give milk to Yugoslavia and train their pilots. We trade with Russia. But we look toward Asian Communists and get all upset. That's how bad our racism is. South Africa has systematized the dehumanization of my people. Yet look at all the money we pour into that country. The ghetto is only one of the colonies America exploits. It's too late for Johnson to bribe us. We don't want to be co-exploiters. We want to do away with exploitation."

A more serious point of difference with the Reverend Cleage—whose church, nonetheless, Imari and his Muslim brother attend—is on the matter of the revolution's base. Cleage and the C.C.A.C. argue that the Northern city is the logical base. Imari just laughs at this, as a romantic conception. "We can hold the cities *gloriously*—for about a week. Then we run out of food." He looks to the South, to countries with a black majority. He waits, not for black mayors to be elected in the cities, but for black sheriffs in the South. "We will have to fight, and we must do it from positions of strength. We must be ready so that, under pressure, we won't have random immigrants, but organized *movements* to the South. When push comes to shove, it will be there." But isn't that condemning yourself to a backward agrarian base? "Did Israel start as a backward country? We'll take the best things with us." Grin—"We'll take nuclear power"—fading to serious thoughts: "If you go to Alaska, you don't go and live like the Eskimos. Besides, the separatists are developing their international contacts, to get the moral weight of the rest of the world on our side, and their economic weight, and military weight. All we have to be is strong enough to hold off military attack on our Southern bastions until these foreign alliances can exercise their influence." How will they do that? "For instance, the deterrent effect of Chinese nuclear subs in the Gulf of Mexico." (Does China promise these things, I wondered? And wondered, Why not? Promises are not performance.)

But the odds remain stacked against the enclaves Imari would retire to. His troops would be fighting the most powerful military establishment in the world. "It's a good thing nobody told the Vietcong that. The government's resources are unlimited. Ours are only limited. But we don't have to move until we want to. That's how the odds get evened. Oh, we might end up with too little too late. In a real military engagement, success is never assured. Maybe we will be like the Sitting Bulls and Crazy Horses, and you all will build some monuments to us and say, 'Weren't they wonderful Indians? Too bad we killed them all.' That's horse racing."

Like Cleage, Imari hopes the black community can make it too expensive for the whites to extirpate them, once they dig in at their base. If this standoff is reached, he thinks the government can be persuaded to grant the land base as a matter of reparation for criminal injury inflicted during centuries of enslavement and discrimination. "If a mail truck hits a dog in the street, the government will acknowledge it committed a tort and pay injuries. Yet the government killed us and kept us slaves for years.

West Germany paid reparations to the new State of Israel, not to individuals—and did this for crimes committed by an earlier government (the Nazis)."

The concept of reparation is catching on in the black community, and even being put into practice. In Plainfield, New Jersey, an enterprising young ghetto dweller has collected money from local merchants as a return from their exploitatory profits. He leads a Youth for Action Movement which claims seventy-five drilled "black cadets." He led a nineteen-day boycott against a tavern which, he claims (the tavern owner denies it), refused to house one of his collection boxes. This boycott, which cost the tavern an estimated $9,000, was mentioned when he went to other owners and asked for cash donations. The machinery is old—that of the protection racket. But the justification is new—"reparations."

Many in Detroit think Cleage the most extreme voice of the black community. But Imari makes his softly voiced position seem moderate. (Cleage foregoes, for one thing, the hope of Chinese subs.) The day after I visited Imari, I asked the Negro reporter who best knows the ghetto—Joseph Strickland of The Detroit *News*—if the Henrys are the most extreme leaders in the black community. "No, Jackie Wilson makes them sound moderate." Can I see him? "No, he won't talk to the white press." I had to content myself with the moderation of Imari, whose forthcoming book is called *War in America*, and who told me: "There are two kinds of people in this country who realize that the race war has in fact begun—they are the white military establishment (including the local police), and the black militant leaders."

But, unfortunately, others share his belief that it is a matter of all-out war. In Detroit, itself, for instance, these white groups agree with him—Post No. 375 of the American Legion, United War Veterans for Defense of the United States Constitution, Breakthrough, Citizens Committee for Civil Defense, Detroit Police and Firemen Association for Public Safety, and Chaldean Committee for Preservation of Liberty. These are the groups that put out a joint statement which says of the riot: "ARE YOU READY NOW to PREPARE YOURSELF FOR THE NEXT ONE? Or will you be forced to stand helplessly by because you were UNprepared to defend your home or neighborhood against bands of armed terrorists who will murder the men and rape the women?" To make sure that people are prepared, Breakthrough holds meetings at various halls (Veterans of Foreign Wars, Knights of Columbus, the City-County Building) where spokesmen for the National Rifle Association demonstrate and recommend guns—the model for home defense is good at a hundred yards and should have two hundred rounds "per family."

The head of Breakthrough, Donald Lobsinger, has staged his own demonstrations, broken up civil-rights meetings and marches, and disrupted interfaith church services. Three days before the riot started,

Breakthrough picketed a Catholic church with signs calling the priest inside a traitor, a "red ally." The group puts out a leaflet describing survival kits for the next riot (food, medicine, vitamins, etc.); it recommends that its members join the General Douglas MacArthur Shooting Club. During the riot, its leaflets offered a thousand-dollar reward for the arrest and conviction of Mayor Cavanagh on a charge of "criminal negligence" in putting down the riot—the white equivalent of Mr. Cleage's "People's Tribunal." Cleage is very much aware of the arming on the other side: "The ranges of the shooting clubs are packed; the city is way behind in processing gun registrations. So, naturally, any black man who can get hold of a gun is getting hold of it." I got an eerie confirmation of his words on the very day he spoke them. Out at Imari's house the phone rang, my host went and spoke into it briefly, and returned shaking his head in comic exasperation: "That idiot! He just said he could get two carbines if I had seventeen dollars for them. *He* should know my phone is tapped."

I spent all one day and two long nights with Hutch and Duke. When we were not drinking somewhere, we were driving somewhere—the two of them up front, I a captive audience in the backseat (both handles were gone from the doors). Whenever Hutch's heavy foot stabbed us forward or cuffed us to a stop, weapons rattled in the trunk—clubs, two shotguns, a sawed-off rifle, sawed-off shotgun (these last the gift of solicitous teenagers worried for their safety). Hutch and Duke both have a "natural"; Hutch wears leaded gloves; they give the palm-out shoved fist salute to "brothers" everywhere, and exchange militant greetings—"B.P., baby" (Black Power). They owe their present status—one they relish almost childishly—to the riots, and they know this. They are Deputy Sheriffs of Cook County.

Sheriff Woods, an ex-F.B.I. man, the tough guy who told his men in Maywood they must shoot carefully, no time could be wasted on trips to the hospital, cast about, during the Detroit riot, for someone to be his eyes and ears in the trouble points around Chicago—Markham, Phoenix, Harvey, Chicago Heights. Two young process servers had written a memorandum to him earlier in the summer, describing sensitive spots and criticizing the way they were being handled. Both had been organizers of a political group (The New Breed) that was out at the edge of militancy in 1964 (the black cause counts in months as others count in decades, it is a movement led by the young). The New Breed never adopted the non-violent mystique of Dr. King (though the group served as marshals for his Chicago march)—in fact they opened a karate school to teach the brothers self-defense. They struck a bargain with Charles Percy—that he finance their local candidate if they support him during his '64 campaign. It was a one-shot affair. "He'll find it does not last in '68," Hutch says. "We tried to tell him not to come into our territory playing poor boy. 'Drive a

Cadillac,' I said to him, 'then we'll know you have good sense.' But he wanted to impress the whites with pictures of him in the ghetto wearing shirt sleeves."

Neither of the two makes any bones about their grievances with white men in general, and white cops in particular. They are working on a book to be called *Two Bigots*. Nonetheless, Sheriff Woods established them as liaison with the militant groups in Cook County, sent them into Markham; and, almost immediately, they persuaded a vigilante group of older Negroes to disarm and some youths who had been causing trouble to turn in their weapons. The youths turned in eleven shotguns and thirteen pistols. The Sheriff's appointment of the two men seemed, I suggested, an enlightened decision. "He's not enlightened," Hutch answered, "he's something better. He's fair; and he's the most *truthful* law-enforcement agent I have ever met. He knows what he does not know." The two, both fidgety in police circles, all touchy edges, are proud of their job because they took it on their own terms: "He *has* to let us remain black; because we're no possible use to him except as black men, able to talk with the brothers. If it comes to a war between blacks and whites—well, it's pretty clear where we will be." The two can get along with the teen-agers they help because their attitude is that the quickest way to stop police brutality is to *be* the policemen in the neighborhood. They don't like to have things done for them, and they challenge the kids to take the same attitude. "We don't tell them to be model citizens. We tell them not to be stupid. Stick together; use the gangs they have; form co-ops; get into business; *own* something. These kids react to money."

Hutch—James R. Hutchinson—is tall, good-looking in a baby-faced way, deceptively youthful and willowy in appearance, but a smoothly knit athlete—high school and college basketball, karate teaching at the school. He likes to flick his leaded gloves, with their built-in sap, within inches of one's face, to demonstrate control. He is the scholar of the pair, in a constant boil of statistics, running over with percents and averages— "eighty-five percent" recurring with suspicious frequency, it seems to be his only way of saying "a large number."

Duke—Leonard Hunter—is a little shorter than Hutch, and one year older (twenty-seven). He dresses with panache—his wasp-waist wrapped around with colorful vests, his suits pinched in, cut close and tight. He speaks in a husky, precise voice, picking out the key syllable for emphasis. "Man, that is *eh*-vident." He moves in a continual pummeling seizure of hoarse laughter, benevolent "dry heaves" brought on by the craziness of things. The world has him at its mercy; it overpowers him with idiocy. After describing how the University of Chicago claimed it would improve the lot of Negroes by clearing them out of its vicinity, he doubles over as if punched and wheezes out: "Them cats sure can sell a story! (*Uh, uh, uh!*)"

All the liberal projects seem to have earned their scorn. Urban renewal—"nigger removal." Public housing—"high-rise slums." The Poverty Program—"Our kids all realize they were just being paid to do nothing." Moving Negroes out toward the suburbs—"Get us out of the city before we can control it; the 'Damn [for Dan] Ryan Expressway' is our Berlin Wall, we can't cross back except by daylight." Again Moynihan is the villain. Hutch leads the attack, with statistics: "He says sixty percent of the illegitimate births are Negro children. But he neglects to mention that ninety percent of the abortions are performed for white women—and the hospitals will cover up the illegitimate births of white women." Duke is doubled over again: "What that cat knows about us colored boys I could put in my eyeball." They reject the whole history of the white man's attempts to help them: "Roosevelt hurt the hell out of us," Hutch says. "He started paying us for doing nothing; that destroyed our self-respect." Duke: "That cat was a genius! Just think (uh! uh! uh!) they say he had a mistress and kept his wife too. I bet she said, 'Do you want a divorce?' and he said, 'No, baby, it would hurt my image.' "

I asked them what they would do in place of the old measures. They take different approaches when they answer. Hutch's analysis is in terms of sex. "The white man has split our community from within. He hires the Negro woman; over seventy-six percent of the married Negro women work." (There goes Duke again: "Man, does that sound like unemployment?") "He doesn't have to pay her as much as he would pay to a man; and then she thinks the white establishment is not so bad, there must be something wrong with that cat of hers at home, who doesn't get hired. Who does the buying in our community? Who does the voting? Eighty-five percent of the precinct captains in our district are women. Daley knows what he is doing. He appoints Bernadine Washington to his Chicago Commission on Human Relations. She knows as much of what's going on in the street as A. Philip Randolph does. He puts Mrs. Wendell Green on the school board. Negro boys have no male image to look up to. Patricia Harris gets the job of Ambassador to Luxembourg, though her husband has the same degree she has. In proportion, we have more female judges than you do. Ninety-five percent of the interracial marriages are of Negro men and white women—women who have been brought up in a tradition of respect for the male. Why? Because men are ninety percent ego—so black men can't stand the contempt their women have for them." I mentioned that white women also own more property than men now. Duke is sneezing helplessly over this one: "Y'all cats die quicker, leaving all that bread behind. We might just play a waiting game, and get your women and your money." Hutch agrees that male superiority is an idea being undermined in the white community as well. "But you control the media; so when this gets too bad, you just put out a lot of movies about the sad lady tycoon who returns to the home and is happy taking care of sixteen kids.

"The Negro boy gets second-best at home," Hutch drives ahead, his steam up now. "The girl is the one who will get jobs, stay in school, be given consideration by the white community. Why, eighty-five percent of Negro women say they would send a girl to school before they would send their boy. The Negro boy is not only rebelling against the white man, but against Momma. That's why ninety-five percent of the rioters are boys." (In Watts, when young Marquette Frye was stopped for speeding, he joked with officers until his mother arrived on the scene and accused him of being drunk; only then did he turn surly—and the riot began.)

"Not only is the boy rebelling against Momma; he's rebelling against his Momized elders. You know, the average age on the South Side is twenty-five; on the West Side, it's nineteen. There is a big communications gap between the kids and the adults, and an even bigger gap between the adults and the white man. So when the white man tries to deal with the kids he has two gaps he must bridge. *One* would be hard enough. But you know what he does? He chooses exactly the wrong people to deal with—the women, the 'older leaders,' the womanized men!"

Duke's approach is more economic than sexual: "There are too many hands in our pockets. We'd get along just fine if you only let us handle the vice in our area. But we don't even run our own numbers. The syndicate, the big markets, the slum lords—they just take it all off the cash register each year. Money comes into the ghetto at nine in the morning; and all of it leaves again by five at night. One of the white boys we worked with in the campaign said, 'You all are pretty hot numbers when it comes to sex.' I said, 'You think so? Let's make a deal. We'll trade you, for all you cats' money.' (*Uh! Uh!*)"

Hutch agrees: "One of our thirteen-year-old kids put it as well as anyone could: 'There's nothing the matter with niggers that money can't solve.' But every time you see a house torn down in the ghetto, you can bet that a supermarket or a gas station is going up to get that money just as soon as it is in our pockets. They don't want us to own anything, any of the businesses, to keep something of what we earn. The money is not so important in itself—it is the pride that comes from owning, from having economic independence."

Duke is not doubling up anymore; he rivals the Fat Boy in *Pickwick* for his ability to catnap anywhere, anytime, when the action gets slow. He has heard Hutch's pitch before. I haven't—we talk past two in the morning; he is so eager, now, to serve up concrete proofs. Nothing will do but a drive, that morning, to the major "El" stops where workers leave the day's employment. "But we'll have to hit them before six a.m."

So, after less than two hours of sleep, I tottered out onto Michigan

Avenue; the wind off the lake sliced me into little pieces, which blew here and there till Hutch collected them and dumped me in the backseat of his Sheriff's car (the one without handles in the back, a convenience for transporting prisoners). Hutch looks disgustingly fresh, but Duke is flaked out again—he went on to more action, refreshed after his nap (and our talk) ended. Another deputy is with them, William Smith. Smitty, an experienced policeman in his forties, agrees with Hutch and Duke about the problems of the Negro boy. He went to see the mother of one twelve-year-old who was always in trouble; all she did was insult the boy in front of Smitty. Later Smitty had the boy adopted, and there has been no trouble since. We drive past high-rise slums. "That's where you keep down with the Joneses," Smitty says. "Can you imagine coming home at night to a football stadium of noise?" Duke is in paroxysms: "The politicians did a *good* job there."

Our first stop is Sixty-third and Cottage Grove. Buses humph their doors open and shut; women pour out of them and up the El stairs— well-dressed, the younger ones mini-skirted ("Any higher," Smitty whews, "we'd have to run her in for indecent exposure"), the older ones in furs; those in between wear leather or plastic coats, pink or white. "They're going to scrub floors," Hutch says; "but they go in furs." "Well," Duke explains, "some of them are going to those big homes out in the suburbs. Man, our people travel in some pretty high circles." (The soft dry detonations are going off.) Hutch is all business: "How many natural hairdos do you see on the women?" The hair is red, blue, indescribable tints; piled high, pulled low, wound in taffy configurations. "They're pretending they are white. The woman buys white style for herself and her daughter. The boys have to shift for themselves. If a Negro man gets a smile out of a woman during the day, it's a real accomplishment." Smitty laughs: "He's really going some to catch *her* attention. Man, he's got to be *delicious*. That's why the cats go out and buy the best when they get money— forty-dollar shoes, fifty-dollar knits [sweaters]." "Man, they take off their knits before they let themselves get into a fight," Duke manages to get out with his customary effort. "We told Chuck Percy, 'Whatever you do, don't fool with a cat's knits!' But he went up to a guy and stuck one of his campaign buttons right into it, and this cat pushed him away in utter amazement—'What are you *doing* to my knits?' "

A few men climb the El stairs; they all seem to carry attaché cases. "Janitors," Smitty guesses. "Yeah, they carry coveralls in the cases; that's how bad they need some dignity," Hutch says in his emotional voice. He does not laugh at the world's turns, as Duke can. A man drives his wife up, drops her off at the stairs: "Now he'll go home—no job. And the car is hers, no doubt." A young man goes by wearing a natural. "Hi brothers!" with the fist-push. "Hey brother." "You notice," Hutch twists around to me, "it's 'Hi brother.' You don't use the word 'sister' much in greeting the girls. It's 'Hi baby' to them. The *brotherhood* is what the young boys need. The gangs used to be the only masculine world they knew. Now the whole teen-age crowd is one gang of brothers."

To illustrate his point, he drives me, after we hit a few more El stops, to "The Wall of Respect" at Forty-third and Langley—a stretch of "blind side" brick facade on which a black pantheon was painted last summer. Elijah Muhammad, Muhammad Ali, Rap Brown, Lew Alcindor, Jimmy Brown, Ray Charles. It is a male world, painted with uneven skills, at different scales, crude yet somehow attaining majesty. It stretches down the side of four buildings. "That signifies unity," Smitty says; and he points out that there are no blemishes on the wall. Every other brick surface in sight is scribbled over, pocked, smeared. But this one is unmarked, fresh as the day it was painted. There are children on the corner, waiting for a bus. "What does that mean to you?" Smitty asks, pointing to the wall. "I don't know. It's just beautiful," they say, wide-eyed—apprentice young knights in the new chivalry. "Would you ever mark it up?" "*No*." Why not? "That would be *wrong*." It is said that Negroes, put in bright new housing, will just deface and ruin it. Not if all their walls were Walls of Respect. "Respect, you notice," Hutch nudged me. "Dignity!"

We drive through streets still dingy with the night; a lemony sky makes the litter glow first as day gets down to the streets. Women are out, walking to their buses. "They are not afraid to be on the streets. Who rapes men? And they are the men of the community." "We'll take you to Spiegel's mail-order house," Duke suggests, "to see what the work force is." Inside the vast store, we visit the employment area, where classes of new workers shuttle through continually. We see two groups of twenty or so, and not one man in either. Hutch asks the girls what they will be earning their first few months there. Duke has better luck, though, coaxing answers out with winks.

As we drive, Hutch remembers his days in Vietnam: "I went airborne, counterinsurgency; trying to prove something, I guess. I don't know why I screwed around in those jungles all those months. But I do know the brothers who are coming back won't let themselves be pushed around anymore." When we get back into the car after a stop, Hutch checks in on the car radio, "10-8" (back in circulation), then continues with the kind of chatter he heard from planes in Vietnam: " 'Straight Arrow? This is Lone Ranger, about four hundred miles off'—they'll rendezvous in about twelve seconds. 'Oh-uh-vah and ahw-oh-oot,' " he drawls in expert mimicry. "Oh, them crackers!"

Hutch and Duke are with the County Sheriff's office; but they introduce me to several members of the Chicago City Department—Human Relations Division. These men, like Smitty, are cops who came up the hard way, who are called on now to help decipher the ghetto. One, a huge fellow with easy smiling ways, said: "You could always tell a black cop, even in plainclothes—by his size. He was hired to beat up on his own people, and he had to be big. They didn't much care what else he did. One officer—I'll call him Ted—was a known pickpocket; but no one quarreled with him when he was on a case, so the force just ignored his foible. Once a man did make the mistake of taking him on. Ted was waiting for the bus, at his neighborhood stop, and a man started pestering a woman. Ted told him to stop it, and the man whipped out a switchblade. But before he could get it up, his wrist was slashed with Ted's blade. 'Why, Ted,' the lady said, 'I thought you were a policeman.' 'Oh, I forgot,' he mumbled, put his blade away, and pulled his gun.

"Once a cop, a man was not out of the ghetto. Or if he did make the move, it was a slow process. I remember my first cases in the white community. This little lady had called for the police, on a burglary, so I went. She nearly fainted when she opened the door and saw me. I told her, 'This won't come off if I come in; but, on the other hand, I never investigate a case on the porch with the screen latched.' Once I got in and she found herself unraped, it went all right." This man, for all his easygoing way, had the fire in his belly. Once another officer "let that word slip." "I slapped him once across the face, nearly took his jaw off. But I don't believe in violence. Oh, once in a while, you have to be a little mean, especially at home—you know, open the door on the hinge side, for a change? Still, my motto is, Never send a guy away mad. If you mess with me, I may have to pull your dick off. But I won't send you away mad."

He is a type of the Negro cop who is suddenly asked to say things about the Negro's feelings that would have got him fired ten years ago. "They want to know who's bitter. We're *all* bitter. Big surprise!" I talked to a man in Baltimore who came back from service in World War II and needed a job. He tried for two years to take the police test and succeeded, at last, only because his fiancée had a job with the city and got her boss to help (how Hutch would love the story, another proof for his book—the woman could get the job, and even get the man a job; but only by being there first). The man is now a Community Relations officer: "They tell me to go out and find what 'their' complaints are. I'm one of 'them.' My complaints are that more than a third of the Baltimore city police don't even live in Baltimore. They lifted the residence requirement in the Fifties, to keep the force from going Negro." In Watts, a Negro policeman was sent incognito into the riot area to scout the situation. As he came out to report, he hailed a radio car, which stopped. The officer inside leaned out and said: "What you want, shitass jigaboo?" What does a Negro cop say when his superiors ask what "their" grievances are?

The brothers were drifting that night, to one of two meetings—a benefit for a local leader, and a dinner talk meant to raise money for Father

Groppi, the leader of the Milwaukee open-housing marches. Reverend Cleage had told me, in Detroit, that open housing is no longer a real issue—"We don't think it's all that great a thing to live next door to a white man"—and that marches were a thing of the past: "Oh, there might come a time when mass presence would have some effect; but it will be a different kind of thing. It won't be just marching up the street to say something. This time we'll be going somewhere, like to tie up the town for twenty-four hours—if we figure it is worth five thousand black people getting whipped to show a city can't move without us. But just the old peaceful nonviolent marching, where the white people throw bricks and stones and you just redeem 'em through love, that's all *gone*."

I wondered, then, what he thought of Father Groppi, still marching, still asking for an occupancy law. He smiled almost beatifically: "*Beautiful,* baby, it's so *nostalgic.* The last of the marches. Don't you understand? Black people are looking for confrontations. Anything you want to set up, they'll make it an issue if you don't consult them. If you say this street is going to be one-way, and don't ask us what *we* want, we'll make it an issue from now till doomsday, and we don't even care about the street. Those marching with Groppi don't care about open occupancy. But still it's a good fight."

I asked Hutch what he thought of Father Groppi. "Oh, he's out of it. He's still marching. We're past the marching stage." But he knew some of the brothers throwing the dinner, so he got us in. After the meal I went up to the stormy priest, incongruously short and quizzical; a sacerdotal Woody Allen, limp weedy locks around a receding hairline, sad-dog eyes, squash nose. Can you win your fight for open occupancy? "There are signs of it." A "Commando"—one of his teen-age entourage—comes up and claps "Grop" on the shoulder. "I see you've let the hair cover your scar," Grop says, Brillo-ing a head wound out of the "natural." "Keep that visible. I'm proud of it." The Commando beams, says, "So am I." "A policeman gave it to him," Groppi tells me. Hutch points out, in a whisper, that the only girl with the party of Commandos is a white one.

The talk is given in a large high-school auditorium. Father Groppi sits flanked by his eight Commandos—bodyguards are the style in this aggressively masculine movement. The Fruit of Islam guarding Elijah Muhammad. The Deacons guarding Southern marchers. The devout Zulu trailing the Reverend Cleage. The priest's style at the lectern is also Woody Allen, hems and haws and hair-mussing, but exquisitely timed. "I don't know, but . . ." he begins when he knows very well. He tells how his angry Commandos tore up the Milwaukee mayor's office in anguish at their not having protests answered: "The white people said, 'How shocking!' The mayor said 'Hoodlums!' And we just said"—his voice sinks to a chortled sexy croon—" 'Black Power, brother, Black Power.' "

Though the performance is getting to him, Hutch still tries to pooh-pooh Groppi, and buzzes with sociology: "You will notice that there are very few women here; and most of the women are white" (and most of the white women are nuns). But now Groppi nets Hutch in with the rest of the rapt audience. "I bet there isn't a black woman in my parish, a white man hasn't tried to make out with her." He tells of a black picnic some whites tried to break up: "Fifteen or twenty Commandos came streaming out of the bus and *whoosh* the whites just disappeared." Clutch in, throat shifting down, to chortle: "It was a beautiful sight. And all the Youth Council cheered—especially, I might say, the young ladies." "Hey," Hutch says with a start, "he does understand." At the press conference after his talk, Father Groppi agrees that his is the last march—the wearying, frustrated appeal cannot go on forever. What next? "Perhaps guerrilla warfare."

Father Groppi's priesthood seems to give him a dubious masculinity that tunes him into the young Negro's struggle. He describes with glee the Commandos' muscle; swears with an adolescent's pride in the achievement; describes a school principal who ran, hands flapping in fairy helplessness, through his corridors sobbing, "The Commandos are here! The Commandos are here!" (The nuns loved this one.) Asked about his duty to superiors, he has said, "The white priest who has to ask the archbishop every time he crosses the street should never have been ordained—he's a pansy." He has reached them now; he is "telling it like it is."

Telling it like it is—not so much a matter of *what* one says, though it is often framed that way. "We trust Stokely Carmichael," Hutch says, "because he never lied to us." Asked about several Negro leaders in Chicago, he answers, "They bullshitted us." They did not, so much, lie; far worse, they *lost touch*. They adopted the white man's language, in which the brothers feel ill-defended. It is so easy to make a slip, be tricked, be laughed at. The whole tongue and idiom are an instrument that belongs to whites, and it would be foolish to challenge them on their own ground. That is why there has been a retreat to the old scorned "Rastus, suh" and "sugah-chile" dialect—soul talk. It is home ground, where the white man cannot follow; or, if he does, where *he* is the one who misses tone and nuance, talks as an outsider. This is where the black man can be at ease, able to laugh at the white man—and at himself. It is where the Lenny Bruce edge on those speeches at Cambridge gets softened into Duke's sense of irony. "Telling it like it is" is being attuned to the brothers' needs; and the evidence of attunement is up-to-date fluidity in the language. Hutch, talking to me one moment about "the sociology of matriarchy," pitches his voice higher and rasps, "Hi y'all, you up tight?" when he sees a brother approach. He is bilingual now. If he ever loses touch with those sounds of the street, he will be a lost brother, no longer "telling it like it is."

A white newsman talking to black men is urged, over and over, to tell it like it is. But that is impossible. Perhaps, for a while, a Father Groppi can speak out of analogous resentments and hit the right tone. Some can venture pastiche; use words carefully weighed, loved, worried, eased into place. But it is false, part of the smothering falsehood Hutch and Duke resent in the liberal. They admire Sheriff Woods because he knows he does not know. Their scorn is reserved for people pretending they understand, who don't. People saying they can solve the Negro's problem, who can't. People thinking they have earned a share in Negro pain, who haven't. Those who mother black men when they are trying to grow up; the helpful, the well-meaning; the Moynihans.

I asked Hutch over and over why he, with his analysis of the Negro matriarchy, resented Moynihan, whose report—whatever its defects— made the same points that Hutch labors. "Do you think Negroes would tell the truth to Moynihan?" was all he could answer. He is evasive, unsure of his reasons—sure only of his response. Moynihan did not tell it like it is. He couldn't. He is white.

The Negro does not want to be diagnosed; he does not even want to be helped, if the white man is going to do the helping. He has to do it himself. He wants not help but reparation, not charity but justice. He would rather demand than have things volunteered to him. As Mr. Cleage put it, he is looking for confrontations—and he will find them.

At almost every police department I visited, I asked the superintendent or commissioner one question: How do we prevent riots? In almost every case, I was told: "First, you remove the *causes* of rioting, and our wonderful mayor is doing this." Then, after this pro forma opening, they got down to brass tacks: flood the streets with blue; have good plans, good intelligence; more men, more guns, cars, tear gas, tanks. They know the causes cannot be removed by next summer, or the summer after. Hutch knows it, too: "Give Stokely Carmichael all the power he asks for, and it would still be twenty years before he could accomplish what he wants." Nonetheless, the cry is "Freedom *now*."

Freedom. Not Utopia. The slums will not disappear *now*. But respect can be built faster than cities. When police described for me how the mayor was "removing causes," they talked of eliminating poverty. But money is not the solution in itself. More important is the way the money is gained by the Negro; it must not be given, but surrendered, on his terms, or he will think it is another bribe to "keep him in his place"—paying him for doing nothing. Given all the money he needs, the Negro would still "seek confrontations" if he were not respected. In spirit he must come for the money, and carry it away, in that dignified attaché case.

He has learned that respect can grow from fear. After all, Hutch and Duke have their jobs because of the white man's fear. Men who looked condescendingly on *"colored boys"* now edge around them. They are Commandos, knights, bodyguards. They are men. They will be proving that, to us and to themselves, now and next summer and the next. They will be playing with fire. What this means, I suppose, is that, like little boys in a strange playground, we must fight before we can be friends.

Any one of these confrontations can ignite another Detroit, or worse. It is unrealistic to expect a society to overlook this possibility; or—having recognized it—not to take precautions. If the police have a simplistic view of "removing the causes," black leaders take a silly view of the "guns or butter" issue as it applies to civil disturbance. They say that if the money spent on war budgeting were given to them, there would be no danger of a riot. "Chicago spent three million dollars extra last summer," Hutch claims, "just on riot patrol—the man-hours, the cars, the fuel, the maintenance. If that went to us, they wouldn't need patrols." But he himself says that money cannot do it—not unless there is a creative friction that makes men bristle with new respect. And this friction has no chance of becoming creative unless it is in some measure controlled.

The danger is that white society cannot bear with patience the attritive ordeal of these confrontations—that private citizens will take arms; or that they will demand, of elected officials or of the police, that the confrontations be brought to an end. This possibility is a grim one. Just how grim, Richard Rovere told us last autumn: "I can imagine the coming to power of an American de Gaulle, or even of someone a lot more authoritarian than de Gaulle. Much of the troublemaking in the months and years ahead will be the work of Negroes, and I can imagine the imposition of a kind of American apartheid—at least in the North, where Negroes live in ghettos that are easily sealed off. If there should be the will to do it, it could be done quite 'legally' and 'Constitutionally.' There are enough smart lawyers around to figure out how." Other voices grow increasingly pessimistic—Moynihan's among them: "We must prepare for the onset of terrorism." The war budgets, plans and armaments are there; and the revolutionary restlessness is bound, in David-moments, to tempt this Goliath.

But a man like Mr. Cleage has mayoral aspirations—so he wants a Detroit to be mayor of. Who would rule a cinder? The threats of police blitzkrieg on the one side, of guerrilla terrorism on the other, are reaching that "unthinkable" stage which made atomic weapons, in Churchill's estimate, maintain the world peace throughout the Fifties. The Second Civil War is not a possibility but the present reality—anyone who denies that is *certainly* not telling it like it is. But it is a Cold War, a test of nerves, a series of feints—and it must increasingly be confined to that. The confrontations must be symbolic, the opponent must be allowed to save face—to retire with his briefcase.

The presence of the guns makes it imperative to develop limited-response weapons and train men in their intricacies, so the police will not be panicked into total response—flexible weapons that allow a long "escalation" of riot technique, putting off and off the need for heavy arms. It means that we cannot hope, by some drastic measure, to make all the danger go away; we must learn to live with danger, and limit it, and survive, all of us; so that, having fought, we may be friends.

[March, 1968]

An Introduction to Soul

by Al Calloway

Soul is sass, man. Soul is arrogance. Soul is walkin' down the street in a way that says, "This is me, muh-fuh!" Soul is that nigger whore comin' along . . . ja . . . ja . . . ja, and walkin' like she's sayin', "Here it is, baby. Come an' git it." Soul is bein' true to yourself, to what is *you*. Now, hold on: soul is . . . that . . . uninhibited . . . no, *extremely* un-inhibited self . . . expression that goes into practically every Negro endeavor. That's soul. And there's swagger in it, man. It's exhibitionism, and it's effortless. Effortless. You don't need to put it on; it just comes out.—*Claude Brown*

When I walk on Eighth Avenue, man, I see rhythms I don't see down-town. *Polyrhythms.* You look at one cat, he may be doin' bop, bop-bop bop, bop-bop, and another one goin' *bop*-de-bop, *de*-bop. Beautiful, man. Those are *beautiful* people. Yeah. But when I go downtown to Thirty-fourth Street, everybody's walkin' the same, you dig? They don't put themselves into it. Their walk tells you nothing about who they are. *Polyrhythms.* That's what it is. Like a flower garden in a breeze. The roses swing a little bit from side to side, kind of stiff, not too much. The lilacs swing wide, slow, lazy, not in a hurry. A blade of grass wiggles. It's

708

'cause they're all different and they're bein' themselves. Polyrhythms, like on Eighth Avenue. That's soul.—*Al Calloway*

SOUL IS MOTION AND SOUND.

It is stomping and clapping with the gospel music of the First Tabernacle of Deliverance (Spiritual), American Orthodox Catholic Church on Harlem's One Hundred Twenty-fifth Street, and boogalooing the Funky Broadway to the Memphis gospel soul blues of Otis Redding while walking down the street. Soul is "Doin' the Thing" with the church-oriented funky jazz of Horace Silver and just *moving* back down home with John Lee Hooker's gutbucket folk blues. Soul is being natural, telling it like it is. In the plantation fields and later the church, black people were allowed to keep *some* form of their self-expression going. The beautiful simple poetry of spiritual work songs like *Steal Away*—let's sneak back to the "Good Ship Jesus" and sail all the way home—is part of the blues of today, just as the spiritual ecstasy in a Yoruba Temple in West Africa is akin to what is felt in the soul-stirring Sanctified and Baptist churches of America's black ghettos. When Mahalia Jackson sings, the gospel and the blues of Bessie Smith become the *essence* of soul. Ray Charles throws his head back and shouts, "Oh, yeah!" and transmits an inner feeling of goodness. When you've heard it like that, you *know* you have been moved. Then he comes in with, "Don't it make you want to feel all right," and it's like everything has been unraveled and you just lay in there and groove. Ray Charles turns you on. So does Aretha Franklin and "Mister Soul" James Brown. On a warm day in Harlem one can see and feel an infinite variety of rhythms. People stand on tenement stoops and on the sidewalks and sway to jukebox music here, WLIB and WWRL radio there. Some get caught up in front of record shops and just soul dance like they want to. All around you, Watusi, Boston Monkey, Shing-a-ling, Karate, Boogaloo, The Pearl, the Funky Broadway. Storefront-church tambourines ring and two young men in red shirts walk down the street, one playing a sheepskin drum and the other a cowbell or a fife. A saxophone riffs, a trumpet wails, and then there's the shout. The black poet LeRoi Jones calls it "Ka'ba. . . . Our world is full of sound/our world is more lovely than anyone's. . . ."

SOUL HEROES.

At Forty-third Street and Langley Avenue, on Chicago's South Side, amid the many storefront churches and dilapidated tenements, stands a soulful monument to African-American folk heroes past and present. Last summer, Billy Abernathy, his wife, and at least a score of other artists and draftsmen within the black community formed the Organization of Black American Culture (O.B.A.C.) and got the building's owner, who happens to be black, to consent to the creation of the revolutionary and historical hand-painted mural. Folk heroes who have made great contributions to the worlds of music, sports and literature adorn the Wall: men like Marcus Garvey, Malcolm X and Stokely Carmichael; men who have steered large masses of black people away from the "assimilation complex" bag that DuBois talked about and guided them to the positive course of *digging* themselves. The Wall is blessed with Dr. DuBois' image too. The great innovators of American music, Charlie Parker, Thelonious Monk, Max Roach, Ornette Coleman and the late John Coltrane, share a large portion of the Wall, along with Sassy Sarah Vaughn and Nina Simone. The mighty men, Muhammad Ali and Wilt Chamberlain, are there because they do their thing with a lot of style, and that's important. The real genius of the Wall is that it generates African-American self-pride. No matter what happens to Chicago, the Wall is sure to stand.

THE NITTY—GRITTY OF SOUL.

There's a little piece of real estate in Harlem called Harlem Square, and on and about its four corners the curious, the intellectual and the political meet and exchange ideas. The center of activity there is one of Harlem's landmarks, Michaux's National Memorial African Bookstore. Marcus Garvey, Adam Clayton Powell Jr., Malcolm X and other soul heroes were heard by thousands at many a mass rally that took place in front of Michaux's. Inside the bookshop, every inch of available space is jammed with books by and about black folk. In the back room, where some of the soul heroes sat and wrote their speeches, the walls are crowded with photographs, paintings and drawings of great people of color. Every wall is a wall of respect. It is in Michaux's bookstore ("The House of Common Sense and Home of Proper Propaganda") that you learn about African musicians long ago who mastered the art of circular breathing and the simultaneous playing of instruments made out of elephant tusks and antelope horns. When you *see* the blind soul brother Roland Kirk playing his Manzello (the first saxophone), tenor sax and Stritch at the same time, and frequently blowing long sheets of sound without a breath, you are witnessing soul, baby. —One thing is certain: soul would be nowhere without the great savior, soul food. Black people brought to the Americas a tradition of how to make good food. Being close to the earth was their nature, and it was not difficult for them to find beans and greens that were good and to make good bread out of corn and crackling. It was a good thing that they knew this too, because *the man* would work them in the fields from sunup till dusk and sometimes they had other chores after that. On top of which they had to go all out for self, or the plantocracy would have starved them to death. When it came down to the hog, the planters didn't know anything except ham, bacon, spareribs and chops. The rest of it was no good, or so they thought, and the slaves copped it. They came up with pig tails, pig knuckles, ham hocks, hog maws, pig ears, snout, neck bones, chitlins, tripe and sowbelly. By the time fried or smothered chicken (The Gospel Bird) became a delicacy for special Sundays, black people were making candied yams, sweet-potato pie and fruit cobblers from the vegetables and fruits that they grew in their little patches or gathered from around. Traditionally, black people have congregated at the church for social and spiritual life, because church organization was (is) the only form allowed them. So when the sisters get together with those pots you can bet your life the food's going to be good. If you go into the Victory Restaurant on One Hundred Sixteenth Street in Harlem, you'll dig Bishop Shelton's sisters, with their natural hair and little caps and no makeup and floor-length gowns, serving soul food from eight in the morning till midnight. A plate of knuckles, black eyes and rice, a thick slice of corn bread, a glass of lemonade and a small home-made sweet-potato pie, and you're straight. If you really want to dig deep, get into Adam Powell's bag and cop a mess of chitlins and greens and soak them down with hot sauce. Soul food is why it is still chic to have a soul sister in the kitchen. Everybody digs the way she makes steaks, lobsters, roasts and *mmm* those rolls, pies and cakes.

THE STYLE OF SOUL.

It is about nurturing creativity, being aesthetic in thought and action as much as possible. It permeates one's entire existence. In Harlem, as in all of America's urban black communities, the style is seen in the way a soul brother selects and wears his vines (suit, coat, tie, shirt, etc.). The hat and shoes are most important. If they are *correct*, it is certain that his whole thing is beautiful. You know that he's a cat who cares about himself. His hat will be a soft beaver, felt or velour, blocked in whatever way he may feel at any given time. He buys the best hat and while he's in his crib playing tunes and laying with his woman he may just let his hands go all over the hat like a potter does his clay. Thus, he creates his thing. A soul brother's shoes are always pointy-toed and so shined that he can almost adjust his hat while looking at them. The Sixties have ushered in a "new" mood among a significant number of soul brothers and sisters, causing a clean break with "anything other than what you really are." As reflected in manner of dress, a little stingy hat without the brim called a *ziki* is worn, or a free-form *fila* which is like a soft bag. The *kufe*, a small round headpiece, is also what's happening. Some soul brothers have gone all the way into a West African thing and are wearing *shokotos* (pants). The style of soul is getting back into the African folk bag. At the House of Ümoja (which means *unity* in Swahili), one of the many African shops in Harlem, soul brothers wear pieces of ivory in their ears and ornament their noses with gold like the Yorubas of West Africa. Wilt Chamberlain wears an African medallion around his neck and so does Jimmy Brown. Lew

Alcindor wears *dasikis* and so does LeRoi Jones. —Soul is what, forever, has made black people hip. And it is what has enticed whites to imitate them without understanding it. Among black people, soul is a congenital understanding and respect for each other. It is the knowledge that one is but a segment of all that is, which is spatial, particled, like the colors in a rainbow; yet like when its colors are all rolled into one it is a deep purple haze . . . like morning . . . like dusk. It makes you humble, peaceful. That is why, above all, soul is wise and weary. It is the self-perception that informs you how and when to groove in your own way while others groove in theirs, and it is the sophistication that knows better than to ask, "Understand me," and settles instead for, "Don't mess with me; I'm in my own thing, baby."

[April, 1968]

Q: How can we get the black people to cool it? James Baldwin: It is not for us to cool it. Q: But aren't you the ones who are getting hurt the most? James Baldwin: No, we are only the ones who are *dying* fastest.

James Baldwin
interviewed by Gerry Astor

Q: Can we still cool it?
BALDWIN: That depends on a great many factors. It's a very serious question in my mind whether or not the people of this country, the bulk of the population of this country, have enough sense of what is really happening to their black co-citizens to understand why they're in the streets. I know as of this moment they maybe don't know it, and this is proved by the reaction to the civil-disorders report. It came as no revelation to me or to any other black cat that white racism is at the bottom of the civil disorders. It came as a great shock apparently to a great many other people, including the President of the United States and the Vice-President. And now you ask me if we can cool it. I think the President goofed by not telling the nation what the civil-disorders report was all about. And I accuse him and the entire administration, in fact, of being largely responsible for this tremendous waste and damage. It was up to him and the Vice-President to interpret that report and tell the American people what it meant and what the American people should now begin to think of doing. *Now!* It is already very, very late even to begin to think of it. What causes the eruptions, the riots, the revolts—whatever you want to

713

call them—is the despair of being in a static position, absolutely static, of watching your father, your brother, your uncle, or your cousin—no matter how old the black cat is or how young—who has no future. And when the summer comes, both fathers and sons are in the streets—they can't stay in the houses. I was born in those houses and I know. And its not their fault.

Q: From a very short-range approach, what should the federal government do, right now, to cool it?

BALDWIN: What do you mean by the federal government? The federal government has come to be, in the eyes of all Negroes anyway, a myth. When you say the federal government, you're referring to Washington, and that means you're referring to a great many people. You're referring to Senator Eastland and many people in Washington who out of apathy, ignorance or fear have no intention of making any move at all. You're talking about the people who have the power, who intend to keep the power. And all that they can think of are things like swimming pools, you know, in the summertime, and sort of made-up jobs simply to protect peace and the public property. But they show no sign whatever of understanding what the root of the problem really is, what the dangers really are. They have made no attempt, whatever, any of them, as far as I know, really to explain to the American people that the black cat in the streets wants to protect his house, his wife and his children. And if he is going to be able to do this he has to be given his autonomy, his own schools, a revision of the police force in a very radical way. It means in short that if the American Negro, the American black man, is going to become a free person in this country, the people of his country have to give up something. If they don't give it up it will be taken from them.

Q: You say that existing jobs are just make-work jobs. What kind of job program should be adopted?

BALDWIN: It's very difficult to answer that question since the American Republic has created a surplus population. You know it's created not only people who are unemployable but who no longer wish to be employed in this system. A job program involves, first of all, I would think, a real attack on all American industries and on all American labor unions. For example, you're sitting in Hollywood. And there are not any Negroes, as far as I know, in any of the Hollywood craft unions: there is no Negro grip, no Negro crew member, no Negro works in Hollywood on that level or on any higher level either. There are some famous Negroes who work out here for a structure which keeps Negroes out of the unions. Now it's not an Act of God that there aren't any Negroes in the unions. It's not something that is handed down from some mountain; it's a deliberate act on the part of the American people. They don't want the unions broken, because they are afraid of the Negro as a source of competition in the economic market. Of course what they've made him is something much worse than that. You can't talk about job programs unless you're willing to talk about what is really holding the structure together. Eastman Kodak, General Motors, General Electric—all the people who really have the power in this country. It's up to them to open up *their* factories, *their* unions, to let us begin to work.

Q: They would have to begin, say, on-the-job training programs for those. . . .
BALDWIN: Yes, and by the way I know a whole lot of Negroes on the streets, baby, who are much brighter than a lot of cats dictating the policies of Pan American. You know what this country really means by on-the-job training programs is not that they're teaching Negroes skills, though there's that too; what they're afraid of is that when the Negro comes into the factory, into the union, when he comes, in fact, into the American institutions he will change these institutions because no Negro in this country really lives by the American middle-class standards. That's what they really mean by on-the-job training. That's why they pick up a half-dozen Negroes here and there, and polish them up, polish them off, and put them in some ass-hole college someplace, then expect those cats to be able to go back on the streets and cool the other cats. They can't. The price in this country to survive at all still is to become like a white man. More and more people are refusing to become like a white man. That's at the *bottom* of what they mean by on-the-job training. They mean they want to fit you in. And furthermore, let's tell it like it is. The American white man does not really want to have an autonomous Negro male anywhere *near* him.

Q: In on-the-job training programs, the white American structure wants a worker who is trained, who shows up regularly at eight-thirty in the morning and works till five in the afternoon.
BALDWIN: Yeah, well I know an awful lot of cats who did that for a long time. We haven't got to be trained to do that. We don't even have to be given an incentive to do that.

Q: Would you say, then, that many black people have been able to go nowhere, so they've lost any feeling that it's worth working regularly?
BALDWIN: That is part of what we're talking about. Though it goes deeper than that, I think. It's not only that. What is happening in this country among the young, and not only the black young, is an overwhelming suspicion that it's not worth it. You know that if you watched your father's life like I watched my father's life, as a kid much younger than I watches his father's life; his father *does* work from eight to five every day and ends up with nothing. He can't protect anything. He has nothing. As he goes to the grave, having worked his fingers to the bone for years and years and years, he still has nothing and the kid doesn't either. But what's worse than that is that one has begun to conclude from that fact that maybe in this Republic—judging now on the evidence of its own performance—maybe there isn't anything. It's easy to see on the other hand what happens to the

white people who make it. And that's not a very attractive spectacle either. I mean I'm questioning the values on which this country thinks of itself as being based.

Q: What you are calling for, then, is a radical change in thinking by government and industry.
BALDWIN: Yes.

Q: And given the inertia plus . . .
BALDWIN: Fear.

Q: . . . fear and whatever else there may be, any such changes seem . . .
BALDWIN: . . . seem improbable.

Q: Certainly, they will come slow. A union will not throw open its doors and bring in several hundred people from the black community right away. Now my question is . . .
BALDWIN: You've answered your question.

Q: "Sweeper jobs," then, just won't work?
BALDWIN: No. I'll tell you what you will do. You will do what you did last summer and the summer before that. You'll pour some money into the ghetto and it will end up in the hands of various adventurers. In the first place, thirteen dollars and some change is not *meant* to do anything. And a couple of cats will make it, and the rest will be where they were.

Q: But can you buy time with this kind of program; enough time for the longer term changes?
BALDWIN: You could if you meant it. What's at issue is whether or not you mean it. Black people in this country conclude that you mean to destroy us.

Q: But if industry and government seriously planned job-training programs, and the unions opened up?
BALDWIN: Look, the labor movement in this country has always been based precisely on the division of black and white labor. That is no Act of God either. Labor unions along with the bosses created the Negro as a kind of threat to the white worker. There's never been any real labor movement in this country because there's never been any coalition between black and white. It's been prevented by the government and the industries and the unions.

Q: What would be the first steps a union could take to demonstrate that it seriously wants to correct such inequities? What should the leadership do?
BALDWIN: Educate their own rank and file. Declare themselves. And penalize any member of the union who is against it.

Q: What can industry do on a short-range basis?

BALDWIN: I'm not sure that you should be asking me these questions at all. But I'll do my best to answer them. What can industry do? Well you know, the same as the labor unions. The labor unions won't have Negroes in the unions above a certain level. And they can never rise out of that local, or do what they might be able to do if they weren't trapped in that local at a certain level. Industry is perfectly willing to hire me to dig a ditch or carry a shovel. It isn't going to hire me to build a city or to fly a plane. It is unable to look on me as just another worker. There are exceptions to this rule, obviously, to be found everywhere. But this is the way it works and the exceptions, in fact, prove the rule.

Q: Do you think it would help if industry were to get involved as co-sponsors of low-income housing?

BALDWIN: No. I think we've had far more, more than enough of low income housing which simply becomes high-rise slums.

Q: Well, if they were not high-rise slums?

BALDWIN: I don't want any more projects built in Harlem, for example. I want someone to attack the real-estate lobby because that's the only way to destroy the ghetto.

Q: But what about building low-income housing out in the suburbs where factories are beginning to move?

BALDWIN: Well, that depends on the will of the American people, doesn't it? That's why they are in the suburbs—to get away from me.

Q: What about certain plans of industry to set up factories or businesses which would be owned by ghetto people? Would you see this as a positive step?

BALDWIN: What would be produced in those factories?

Q: Piecework, small items subcontracted by larger manufacturers.

BALDWIN: It's a perfectly valid idea except that in order to do that you have to eliminate the ghetto. Look, it is literally true that from a physical point of view those houses are unlivable. No one's going to build a factory in Harlem, not unless you intend, you know, *really* to liberate Harlem.

Q: Well, New York State, for example, plans to build a State office building in Harlem.

BALDWIN: In Harlem. I know exactly where they're going to build it, too. And at the risk of sounding paranoiac, I think I know why. It's going to be where the Black Nationalist Bookstore is now, and one of the reasons for it, I am convinced, is simply because the Black Nationalist Bookstore is a very dangerous focal ground—125th Street and Seventh Avenue. You know, it's what in Africa would be called a palaver tree. It's where Negroes get together and talk. It's where all the discontent doesn't begin, exactly, but where it always focuses.

Q: Wouldn't you think that would be a very foolish idea, because you can always pick some other place to meet and talk?
BALDWIN: Yes, but the American white man has proved, if nothing else, he is absolutely, endlessly foolish when it comes to this problem.

Q: Let's talk about the average citizen, the white man who lives on Eighty-ninth Street and Riverside Drive, what should he be doing?
BALDWIN: It depends on what he feels. If he feels he wants to save this country, he should be talking to his neighbors and talking to his children. He shouldn't, by the way, be talking to me.

Q: What should he be telling his neighbors?
BALDWIN: That if I go under in this country, I, the black man, he goes too.

Q: Is there any action he can take? Pressure on the local government?
BALDWIN: Pressure on his landlord, pressure on the local government, pressure wherever he can exert pressure. Pressure, above all, on the real-estate lobby. Pressure on the educational system. Make them change textbooks so that his children and my children will be taught something of the truth about our history. It is run now for the profit motive, and nothing else.

Q: What about the white suburbanite who fled the city, while making sure the blacks stayed there? What does he have to do now?
BALDWIN: If he wants to save his city, perhaps he should consider moving back. They're his cities too. Or just ask himself why he left. I know why he left. He's got a certain amount of money and a certain future, a car, two cars, you know, scrubbed children, a scrubbed wife, and he wants to preserve all that. And he doesn't understand that in his attempt to preserve it he's going to destroy it.

Q: What about the poverty program, does that offer any remedy?
BALDWIN: Are you joking? There has not been a war on poverty in this country yet. Not in my lifetime. The war on poverty is a dirty joke.

Q: How would you improve it?
BALDWIN: By beginning it.

Q: In what fashion?
BALDWIN: Look, there's no way in the world to do it without attacking the power of some people. It cannot be done unless you do that. The power of the steel companies, for example, which can both make and break a town. And they've done it, they're doing it. Everybody knows it. You can't have a war on poverty unless you are willing to attack those people and limit their profits.

Q: Is it a matter of limiting the profits of industries only, or is it also a matter of limiting the power of the politicians?

BALDWIN: But the politicians are not working for the people; they're working for exactly the people I say we have to attack. That is what has happened to politics in this country. That is why the political machinery now is so vast and so complex no one seems to be able to control it. It's completely unresponsive to the needs of the American community, completely unresponsive. I'm not talking only as a black man, I mean to the whole needs of the American people.

Q: You mean insofar as it responds to industry?
BALDWIN: It responds to what it considers its own survival.

Q: What would you say ought to be done to improve the relationship of the police with the black community?
BALDWIN: You would have to educate them. I really have no quarrel particularly with the policemen. I can even see the trouble they're in. They're hopelessly ignorant and terribly frightened. They believe everything they see on television, as most people in this country do. They are endlessly respectable, which means to say they are Saturday-night sinners. The country has got the police force it deserves and of course if a policeman sees a black cat in what he considers a strange place he's going to stop him; and you know of course the black cat is going to get angry. And then somebody may die. But it's one of the results of the cultivation in this country of ignorance. Those cats in the Harlem street, those white cops; they are scared to death and they *should* be scared to death. But that's how black boys die, because the police are scared. And it's not the policemen's fault; it's the country's fault.

Q: In the latest civil disorder, there seems to have been a more permissive attitude on the part of the police, much less reliance on firearms to stop looters as compared with last summer when there was such an orgy of shooting by the police and the National Guard.
BALDWIN: I'm sorry, the story isn't in yet, and furthermore, I don't believe what I read in the newspapers. I object to the term "looters" because I wonder who is looting whom, baby.

Q: How would you define somebody who smashes in the window of a television store and takes what he wants?
BALDWIN: Before I get to that, how would you define somebody who puts a cat where he is and takes all the money out of the ghetto where he makes it? Who is looting whom? Grabbing off the TV set? He doesn't really want the TV set. He's saying screw you. It's a judgment, by the way, on the value of the TV set. Everyone knows that's a crock of shit. He doesn't want the TV set. He doesn't want it. He wants to let you know he's there. The question I'm trying to raise is a very serious question. The mass media—television and all the major news agencies—endlessly use that word "looter." On television you always see black hands reaching in, you

know. And so the American public concludes that these savages are trying to steal everything from us. And no one has seriously tried to get to where the trouble is. After all, you're accusing a captive population who has been robbed of *everything* of looting. I think it's obscene.

Q: Would you make a distinction between snipers, fire bombers and looters?
BALDWIN: I've heard a lot about snipers, baby, and then you look at the death toll.

Q: Very few white men, granted. But there have been a few.
BALDWIN: I know who dies in the riots.

Q: Well, several white people have died.
BALDWIN: Several, yeah, baby, but do you know how many Negroes have died?

Q: Many more. But that's why we're talking about cooling it.
BALDWIN: It is not the black people who have to cool it.

Q: But they're the ones. . . .
BALDWIN: It is not the black people who have to cool it, because they won't.

Q: Aren't they the ones who are getting hurt the most, though?
BALDWIN: That would depend on the point of view. You know, I'm not at all sure that we are the ones who are being hurt the most. In fact I'm sure we are not. We are the ones who are *dying* fastest.

Q: The question posed, however, was whether snipers could be classified as true revolutionaries; fire bombers, as those overwhelmed with frustration and seeking to destroy the symbols of their discontent; looters, as victims of the acquisitive itch?
BALDWIN: I have to ask you a very impertinent question. How in the world can you possibly begin to categorize the people of a community whom you do not know at all? I disagree with your classifications altogether. Those people are all in the streets for the same reason.

Q: Does some of our problem come from our flaunting the so-called good life, with its swimming pools, cars, suburban living and so on, before a people whom society denies these things?
BALDWIN: No one has ever considered what happens to a woman or a man who spends his working life downtown and then has to go home uptown. It's too obvious even to go into. We are a nation within a nation, a captive nation within a nation. Yes, and you do flaunt it. You talk about us as though we were not there. The real pain, the real danger is that white people have always treated Negroes this way. You've always treated Sambo this way. We always were Sambo for you, you know, we had no

feelings, we had no ears, no eyes. We've lied to you for more than a hundred years and you don't even know it yet. We've lied to you to survive. And we've begun to despise you. We don't hate you. We've begun to despise you. And it is because we can't afford to care what happens to us, and *you* don't care what happens to us. You don't even care what happens to your own children. Because we have to deal with your children too. We don't care what happens to you. It's up to you. To live or to die. Because you made our life that choice all these years.

Q: What about the role of some of the black institutions. Does the church have some meaning still in the black community insofar as the possibility of social progress is concerned?
BALDWIN: You must consider that the fact that we have a black church is, first of all, an indictment of a Christian nation. There shouldn't be a black church. And that's again what you did. We've used it. Martin Luther King used it most brilliantly, you know. That was his forum. It's always been our only forum. But it doesn't exist anywhere in the North anymore, as Martin Luther King himself discovered. It exists in the South, because the black community in the South is a different community. There's still a Negro family in the South, or there was. There is no Negro family essentially in the North, and once you have no family you have no church. And that means you have no forum. It cannot be used in Chicago and Detroit. It can be used in Atlanta and Montgomery and those places. And now since Martin is dead—not before, but certainly since he is dead—that forum is no longer useful because people are repudiating their Christian church in toto.

Q: Are they repudiating Christianity as well?
BALDWIN: No more intensely than you have.

Q: Then the black church is dead in the North?
BALDWIN: Let me rephrase it. It does not attract the young. Once that has happened to any organization, its social usefulness is at least debatable. Now that's one of the great understatements of the century.

Q: In that case, what is the role of Adam Clayton Powell?
BALDWIN: Adam Clayton Powell is not considered a pastor, he is considered a politician. He is considered, in fact, one more victim. People who can't stand Adam would never, never, *never* attack him now. Crimes which Adam is accused of—first of all, the people in Harlem know a great deal more about that than anybody who has written about it. That's one thing. And for another, as long as you don't impeach Senator Eastland, it's a bullshit tip and we know it. We're not fighting for him, we're fighting for us.

Q: What about some of the other leaders of the black community?

BALDWIN: The real leaders now in the black community you've never heard of. Roy's not a leader, Whitney's not a leader.

Q: Floyd McKissick?

BALDWIN: Floyd's not a leader either, but Floyd *is* closer to the tempo, to the pulse. First of all, leaders are rare. A man is not made a leader by the mass media of this country. Martin was a leader in spite of all the opposition he got, even from black people. Because that's what he was. And because he loved his people. He loved this country.

Q: Stokely Carmichael?

BALDWIN: Stokely in my view is perhaps a little too young. Look, I'm nearly twenty years older than Stokely. I can't answer that question. Stokely is a leader for a great many people. Stokely is even more than that, Stokely is a *symbol* for a great many people. A great many emasculated black boys turn to Stokely because he's fighting against their emasculation. I understand that, and they're right. I may have my own disagreements with Stokely from time to time but I'm on his side. What Stokely is saying essentially is true and that is why people are so uptight about Stokely. Because they can't deny what he is saying. And what he is trying to do is anathema to the white people of the United States because what he is saying is that we have no hope here. These white people are never going to do anything for us because they cannot. Also, as long as we are on the subject of Stokely, let me point out to you that Stokely has never said he hated white people. And I happen to know him and I know he doesn't. What he is insisting on is black autonomy, and *that* puts everybody uptight. That's all he is saying. What he is suggesting that frightens the American white people is that the black people in this country are tied to all the oppressed and subjugated people everywhere in the world. Furthermore, he is saying very clearly, and it's true, that this country which began as a revolutionary nation has now spent god knows how many billions of dollars and how many thousands of lives fighting revolution everywhere else. And what he's saying is that black people in this country should not any longer turn to President Lyndon Johnson, who is after all at the very best (and this is an understatement; I'm speaking for myself now) a very untrustworthy big daddy. But to other black people, all the other people who are suffering under the same system that we are suffering from, that system is led by the last of the Western nations. It is perfectly conceivable, or would be if there were not so many black people here, that the Americans might decide to "liberate" South Africa. Isn't it? That is to say, to keep the horrors of communism away, all the freedom fighters in South Africa would turn South Africa into another Vietnam. No one is fooled about what you are doing in Vietnam. At least no black cat is fooled by it. You are not fighting for freedom. You don't care about those people. You don't care about my people and I know you don't care about theirs. You're fighting for what the Western world calls material self-interest. And that means my back. My stolen tin, my stolen diamonds, my stolen sugar. That's what it means; it means I should work for you forever.

And I won't.

But the idea is that people who are divided by so many miles of the globe, and by so many other things, should begin to consider themselves as a community, should begin to consider that they have something in common—this is what Stokely says. What they have in common is to get the man off their backs. It's a very dangerous and frightening idea for Americans, because it happens to be true.

Q: Do you feel that there's a conscious understanding of American imperialism by . . .
BALDWIN: The Americans are not imperialists. According to them, they're just nice guys. They're just folks.

Q: But we are talking about a form of imperialism . . .
BALDWIN: We're talking about the very last form of imperialism, you know—Western imperialism anyway—the world is going to see.

Q: But do you feel that the under class of black people, given an insufficient education, understands the specifics of this imperialism you describe?
BALDWIN: We understand very much better than you think we do, and we understand it from the letters we get from Vietnam.

Q: Is there any white man who can . . .
BALDWIN: White by the way is not a color, it's an attitude. You're as white as you think you are. It's your choice.

Q: Then black is a state of mind too?
BALDWIN: No, black is a condition.

Q: Who among the white community can talk to the black community and be accepted?
BALDWIN: Anybody, who doesn't think of himself as white.

Q: Among the Presidential candidates, whom do you feel would be accepted as speaking in good faith? Richard Nixon?
BALDWIN: You must be joking.

Q: Nelson Rockefeller?
BALDWIN: Maybe, that would depend very much on what he does now. I don't put him down.

Q: What about Robert Kennedy?
BALDWIN: What about Robert Kennedy indeed: Bobby's a very, very, very bright man. The best thing said about Bobby Kennedy, and I'm not trying

to cop out on this, was said by Al Calloway in that rather curious issue about Soul that Esquire just did. Al said that if Soul could be studied and learned, he'd learn it. He'd study and learn, but it can't be studied and learned. I've had one very publicized thing with Bobby so that anything I say is suspect. He's very bright, and all the liberals will be on his bandwagon. He will probably be President. Almost surely he will be. And what can I say? I have to leave it open. I, myself, will not be on that bandwagon. I think he's very shrewd but I think he's absolutely cold. I think he may prove to be, well, very dangerous.

He's very attractive. He says all of the right things, you know, not always at the right time. And I can see the kind of appeal he'd have; after all, he is the brother of J.F.K. But I'm in another position. I have to be as clearheaded as I can be about it and look beyond the particular event or the particular man. I would not myself put my life in his hands.

Q: Do you know anything of Eugene McCarthy?
BALDWIN: Nothing at all. I can't discuss him. But I ought to say that it's been a very long time since I've had any respect for *any* politician. I have to say, too, that I'm looking through the political spectrum from the standpoint of my rather bitter forty-three years in this country. What I'm also saying is that if I endorse anybody, no matter what it means, I don't want to tell black people to vote for so-and-so or him or her because I don't want to be killed by those black people when they discover they've been betrayed.

Q: Hubert Humphrey?
BALDWIN: Forget it.

Q: Do you care to expand on that?
BALDWIN: No, just forget it. I point to his record since he became Vice-President. The flaming liberal.

Q: Do you think the riots can be considered in another light than simply an outburst against the system? Are they possibly also, consciously or unconsciously, a struggle to bring to a culture purification by blood?
BALDWIN: Well, that refers back to Thomas Jefferson, I think, who said, "I tremble for my country when I reflect that God is just."

Q: He also said that the tree of liberty should be watered with blood . . .
BALDWIN: The blood of tyrants. We call it riots, because they were black people. We wouldn't call it riots if they were white people.

Q: What does the death of Martin Luther King signify?
BALDWIN: The abyss over which this country hovers now. It's a very complicated question and the answer has to be very complicated too. What it means to the ghetto, what it means to the black people of this

country, is that you could kill Martin, who was trying to save you, and you will face tremendous opposition from black people because you choose to consider, you know, the use of violence. If you can shoot Martin, you can shoot all of us. And there's nothing in your record to indicate you won't, or anything that would prevent you from doing it. That will be the beginning of the end, if you do, and that knowledge will be all that will hold your hand. Because one no longer believes, you see—*I* don't any longer believe, and not many black people in this country can afford to believe—any longer a word you say. I don't believe in the morality of this people at all. I don't believe you do the right thing because you think it's the right thing. I think you may be forced to do it because it will be the expedient thing. Which is good enough.

I don't think that the death of Martin Luther King means very much to any of those people in Washington. I don't think they understand what happened at all. People like Governor Wallace and Mister Maddox certainly don't. I would doubt very much if Ronald Reagan does. And that is of course where the problem lies, with people like that, with people we mentioned earlier, and with the institutions we mentioned earlier. But to the black people in this country it means that you have declared war. You have declared war. That you do intend to slaughter us, that you intend to put us in concentration camps. After all, Martin's assassination—whether it was done by one man or by a State Trooper, which is a possibility; or whether it was a conspiracy, which is also a possibility; after all I'm a fairly famous man too, and one doesn't travel around—Martin certainly didn't—without the government being aware of every move he made—for this assassination I accuse the American people and all its representatives.

For me, it's been Medgar. Then Malcolm. Then Martin. And it's the same story. When Medgar was shot they arrested some lunatic in Mississippi, but I was in Mississippi, with Medgar, and you don't need a lunatic in Mississippi to shoot a cat like Medgar Evers, you know, and the cat whoever he was, Byron de la Beckwith, slipped out of the back door of a nursing home and no one's ever heard from him since. I won't even discuss what happened to Malcolm, or all the ramifications of that. And now Martin's dead. And every time, you know, including the time the President was murdered, everyone insisted it was the work of one lone madman; no one can face the fact that this madness has been created deliberately. Now Stokely will be shot presently. And whoever pulls that trigger will not have bought the bullet. It is the people and their representatives who are inciting to riot, not Stokely, not Martin, not Malcolm, not Medgar. And you will go on like this until you will find yourself in a place from which you can't turn back, where indeed you may be already. So, if Martin's death has reached the conscience of a nation, well then it's a great moral triumph in the history of mankind, but it's very unlikely that it has.

Q: **Some people have said that the instant canonization by white America is the cop-out . . .**

BALDWIN: It's the proof of their guilt, and the proof of their relief. What they don't know is that for every Martin they shoot there will be ten others. You already miss Malcolm and wish he were here. Because Malcolm was the only person who could help those kids in the ghetto. The *only* person.

Q: **I was just about to say, we white people . . .**

BALDWIN: . . wished that Malcolm were here? But you, the white people, no matter how it was done actually, technically, you created the climate which forced him to die.

Q: **We have created a climate which has made political assassination acceptable . . .**

BALDWIN: . . . . which made inevitable that death, and Medgar's, and Martin's. And may make other deaths inevitable too, including mine. And all this in the name of freedom.

Q: **Do you think "cooling it" means accepting a culture within a culture, a black culture as separate?**

BALDWIN: You mean, white people cooling it?

Q: **Yes.**

BALDWIN: White people cooling it means a very simple thing. Black power frightens them. White power doesn't frighten them. Stokely is not, you know, bombing a country out of existence. Nor menacing your children. White power is doing that. White people have to accept their history and their actual circumstances, and they won't. Not without a miracle they won't. Goodwill won't do it. One's got to face the fact that we police the globe—we, the Americans, police the globe for a very good reason. We are protecting what we call the free world. You ought to be black, sitting in Harlem, listening to that phrase. We, like the South African black miners, know exactly what you're protecting when you talk about the free world.

Q: **Are there some viable black institutions that . . .**

BALDWIN: Why does a white country look to black institutions to save it?

Q: **Well, to begin a dialogue, to find out what should be done . . .**

BALDWIN: That is up to you.

Q: **But doesn't white America need instruction from . . .**

BALDWIN: . . . . the streets of any ghetto.

Q: **But on the streets of any ghetto can you learn . . .**

BALDWIN: Ask any black junkie what turned him into a junkie.

Q: **But what I'm after are programs that you can work with.**

BALDWIN: What you mean by programs is a way of alleviating the distress without having it cost you anything.

Q: **Well, even if we're willing to spend the money . . .**
BALDWIN: I'm not talking about money.

Q: **But if we are willing to change our point of view . . .**
BALDWIN: Well, then, the person to talk to is first of all your own heart your wife, your child. It's your country too. I've read a great deal about the good white people of this country since I came back to it in 1957. But it's the good white people of this country who forced the black people into the streets.

Q: **Do you think it counts for anything having a mayor like John Lindsay walking the streets?**
BALDWIN: I like John Lindsay. Just because he walks the streets, perhaps. Or for the same reasons I like J.F.K., you know, with enormous reservations. He's somewhere near the twentieth century at least.

Q: **What kind of President should we have? Would a black President help?**
BALDWIN: You're going to need somebody who is willing, first of all, to break the stranglehold of what they call the two-party system. John Lewis was right on the day of the March on Washington, when he said we can't join the Republican Party because look who that is made up of. We can't join the Democratic Party—look who's in *that* party. Where's *our* party? What we need is somebody who can coalesce the energies in this country, which are now both black *and* white, into another party which can respond to the needs of the people. The Democratic Party cannot do it. Not as long as Senator Eastland is in it. I name him, to name but one. I certainly will never vote for a Republican as long as Nixon is in that party. You need someone who believes in this country, again, to begin to change it. And by the way, while we're on this subject, one of the things we should do is cease protecting all those Texas oil millionaires who are one of the greatest menaces any civilization has ever seen. They have absolutely no brains, and a *fantastic* amount of money, *fantastic* amount of power, *incredible* power. And there's nothing more dangerous than that kind of power in the hands of such ignorant men. And this is done with the consent of the federal government. With the *collusion* of the federal government.

Q: **Are there any natural allies for the black people?**
BALDWIN: We're all under the same heel. I told you that before. We are all under the same heel. That's why everyone was so shocked when Fidel Castro went to Harlem. They think Negroes are fools, as Langston Hughes put it once. Second-class fools, at that.

Q: You feel that any people who are oppressed outside the United States are natural allies for the black American?

BALDWIN: Yes. From Cuba . . . to Angola. And don't think the American government doesn't know that. This government which is trying to free us is also determined we should never talk to each other.

Q: In *The Fire Next Time* you questioned whether the black people want to be integrated into a burning house. Do you still feel they do not have the same goals of materialism as the white man?

BALDWIN: I think Stokely's right when he says that integration is another word, you know, the latest kind of euphemism for white supremacy. No. I don't want to be integrated into this house or any other house, especially not this burning house. I don't want to become . . . like you. You, the white people. I'd rather *die* than become what most white people in this country have become. What one is after is something else, which is exactly what Martin was after, and this was community. You know, I just want you to leave me *alone*. Just l-e-a-v-e m-e *a-l-o-n-e!* And then we can take it from there. And above all, leave my child alone.

Q: Do you think that the local community control of schools is necessary?

BALDWIN: Schools and policemen.

Q: Why policemen?

BALDWIN: Look, we live in Harlem, let's say, or we live in Watts. The mother who comes down there with his cap and his gun in his holster, he doesn't know what my day is like. He doesn't know why I get drunk when I do. He doesn't know anything *about* me at all. He's scared *shitless* of me. Now, what—the—fuck is he doing there? All he can do is shoot me. He's a hired concentration-camp keeper. I can police my own community far better than you ever will. Because you can't. It's not in you to do it. I know why somebody there is upset when he is upset. The cats were right when they were told by somebody, some cop, some leader, some mayor to go home. They said *you* go home, we *are* home, baby. We can take care of ourselves. This is the message we're trying to get across; we don't need you to take care of us. Good Lord, we can't afford to have you take care of us any longer! Look what you've done. To us. And to yourselves, in taking care of us. No. I think the black people in this country should run their own schools, and run their own police force. Because you can't do it. All you can do is bring in tanks and tear gas . . . and call the National Guard when it gets too tight. And think you can fight a civil war and a global war at the same time.

Q: There used to be a New York City regulation that a policeman couldn't reside in the precinct to which he was assigned. You are saying that the regulation should require him to live there.

BALDWIN: Yeah, I'm telling you that.

Q: Do you have any hope for the future of this country?

BALDWIN: I have a vast amount of determination. I have a great deal of hope. I think the most hopeful thing to do is to look at the situation. People accuse me of being a doom-monger. I'm not a doom-monger. If you don't look at it, you can't change it. You've got to look at it. And at certain times it cannot be more grim. If we can look at it, we can change it. If we don't look at it, we won't. If we don't change it, we're going to die. We're going to perish, every single one of us. That's a tall order, a hard, hard bill to pay; but you have been accumulating it for a very long time. And now the bill is in. It is in for you and your children, and it is in all over the world. If you can't pay your bill, it's the end of you. And you created in this country a whole population which has nothing to lose. It's part of your bill. There's nothing more that you can do to me, nothing more at all. When you, in the person of your President, assure me that you will not tolerate any more violence, you may *think* that frightens me. People don't get frightened when they hear that, they get *mad*. And whereas you're afraid to die, I'm not.

Q: So the one thing that is fairly certain about cooling it is that the National Guard . . .

BALDWIN: I am not the one to be cooled.

Q: But it can be said that the National Guard, the police, tear gas, these methods are not the answer.

BALDWIN: I suggest that the mayor of every city and the President of this nation go on the air and address the white people for a change. Tell *them* to cool it.

Q: In the most recent disturbances, why have certain black leaders attempted to get other black people off the streets?

BALDWIN: To save their lives. Not as a favor to you. Nobody wants this generation to die. Except the American people.

Q: You would say, then, that we have a lot to answer for?

BALDWIN: I'm not trying to accuse you, you know. That's not the point. But you have an awful lot to face. I don't envy any white man in this century, because I wouldn't like to have to face what you have to face. If you don't face it, though, it's a matter of *your* life or death. Everyone's deluded if they think it's a matter of Sambo's life or death. It isn't a matter of Sambo's life or death, and it can't be, for they have been slaughtering Sambos too long. It's a matter of whether or not *you* want to live. And you may think that my death, or my diminution, or my disappearance will save you, but it won't. It can't save you. All that can save you now is your confrontation with your own history . . . which is not your past, but your present. Nobody cares what happened in the past. One can't afford to care what happened in the past. But your history has led you to this moment, and you can only begin to change yourself and save yourself by looking at what you are doing in the name of your history, in the name of your gods, in the name of your language. And what has happened is as though I, having always been outside it—more outside it than victimized by it, really, in a sense; outside it surely, you know, slaughtered by it, victimized by it, but mainly *outside* it—can see it better than you can see it. Because it cannot afford to let you fool me. If I let you fool me, then I die. But I've fooled *you* for a long time. That's why you keep saying, what does the Negro want? It's a summation of your own delusions, the lies you've told yourself. You know *exactly* what I want!

Q: So that when we come to you with the question, How do we cool it?, all we're asking is that same old question, What does the Negro want?
BALDWIN: Yes. You're asking me to help you save it.

Q: Save ourselves?
BALDWIN: Yes. But *you* have to do that.

Q: Speaking strictly, from your point of view, how would you talk to an angry black man ready to tear up the town?
BALDWIN: I only know angry black men. You mean, how would I talk to someone twenty years younger than I?

Q: That's right.
BALDWIN: That would be very difficult to do. I've tried, and I try it, I try it all the time. All I can tell him, really, is I'm with you, whatever that means. I'll tell you what I *can't* tell him. I can't tell him to submit and let himself be slaughtered. I can't tell him that he should not arm, because the white people are armed. I can't tell him that he should let anybody rape his sister, or his wife, or his mother. Because that's where it's at. And what I try to tell him, too, is if you're ready to blow the cat's head off—because it could come to that—try not to hate him, for the sake of your soul's salvation and for no other reason. But let's try to be better, let's try—to be better than they are. You haven't got to hate them, though we do have to be free. It's a waste of time to hate them.

[July, 1968]

Martin Luther King is *Still on the Case*

by Garry Wills

Of course, Mailer had an instinct for missing good speeches—at the Civil Rights March in Washington in 1963 he had gone for a stroll just a little while before Martin Luther King began, "I have a dream," so Mailer —trusting no one else in these matters, certainly not the columnists and the commentators—would never know whether the Reverend King had given a great speech that day, or revealed an inch of his hambone.

—NORMAN MAILER
The Armies of the Night

Nigger territory, eh?" He was a cabdriver, speculative; eyed the pistol incongruous beside him on the seat, this quiet spring night; studied me, my two small bags, my raincoat. The downtown streets were empty, but spectrally alive. Every light in every store was on (the better to silhouette looters). Even the Muzak in an arcade between stores reassured itself, at the top of its voice, with jaunty rhythms played to no audience. Jittery neon arrows, meant to beckon people in, now tried to scare them off. The curfew had swept pedestrians off the street, though some cars with white men in them still cruised unchallenged.

"Well, get in." He snapped down every lock with four quick slaps of his palm; then rolled up his window; we had begun our safari into darkest Memphis. It *was* intimidating. Nothing stirred in the crumbling blocks; until, almost noiseless—one's windows are always up on safari—an armored personnel carrier went nibbling by on its rubber treads, ten long guns bristling from it (longer because not measured against human forms, the men who bore them were crouched behind the armored walls); only mushroom helmets showed, leaning out from each other as from a single stalk, and, under each, bits of elfin face disembodied.

At last we came to lights again: not the hot insistence of downtown; a lukewarm dinginess of light between two buildings. One was modern and well-lit; a custodian sat behind the locked glass door. This is the headquarters of a new activism in Memphis, the Minimum Salary Building (designed as national headquarters for raising the pay of ministers in the African Methodist Episcopal Church and now encompassing other groups). Its director, Reverend H. Ralph Jackson, was a moderate's moderate until, in a march for the striking sanitation workers, he was Maced by police. Since then his building has been a hive of union officials, Southern Christian Leadership Conference staff, and members of various human-rights organizations.

Next to it is the Clayborn Temple, a church from which marchers have issued almost daily for the past two months. Marchers fell back to this point in their retreat from the scuffle that marred Dr. King's first attempt to help the strikers. Some say tear gas was deliberately fired into the church; others that it drifted in. But the place *was* wreathed with gas, and a feeling of violated sanctuary remains. Churches have been the Negro's one bit of undisputed terrain in the South, so long as they were socially irrelevant; but this church rang, in recent weeks, with thunderous sermons on the godliness of union dues.

I pay the cabdriver, who resolutely ignores a well-dressed young couple signaling him from the corner, and make my way, with bags and coat, into the shadow of the church porch. In the vestibule, soft bass voices warn me. I stop to let my eyes, initiated into darkness, find the speakers and steer me through their scattered chairs. They are not really conversing; their meditative scraps of speech do not meet each other, but drift off, centipetally, over each one's separate horizon of darkness. This uncommunicative, almost musical, slow rain of words goes on while I navigate my way into the lighted dim interior of the church.

About a hundred people are there, disposed in every combination: family groups; clots of men, or of women; the lean of old people toward each other, the jostle outward of teen-agers from some center (the church piano, a pretty dress on a hanger); or individuals rigid in their pews as if asleep or dead. The whole gathering is muted—some young people try to pick out a hymn on the piano, but halfheartedly. There are boxes of food, and Sunday clothes draped over the backs of pews. The place has the air of a rather lugubrious picnic—broken up by rain, perhaps, with these few survivors waiting their chance to dash out through the showers to their homes. Yet there is a quiet sense of purpose, dimly focused but, finally, undiscourageable. These are garbage collectors, and they are going to King's funeral in Atlanta. It is ten p.m.; in twelve hours the funeral will begin, 398 miles away.

They have been told different things, yesterday and today, by different leaders (some from the union, some from S.C.L.C.). They have served as marshals in the memorial march that very afternoon, and preparations for that overshadowed any planning for this trip. Some have been told to gather at ten o'clock; some at eleven. They believe there will be two buses, or three; that they will leave at eleven, or at twelve; that only the workers can go, or only they and their wives, or they and their immediate families. Yesterday, when they gathered for marshals' school, a brusque young Negro shouted at them to arrive sharply at ten: "We're not going by C.P. Time—Colored People's Time. And if you don't listen now, you won't find out how to get to Atlanta at all, 'cause *we'll* be on the *plane* tomorrow night." The speaker seemed to agree with much of white Memphis that "you have to know how to talk to these people."

And so they wait. Some came before dark, afraid to risk even a short walk or drive after curfew. Some do not realize the wait will be so long; they simply know the time they were asked to arrive. Most will have waited three hours before we start; some, four or five. I try to imagine the mutters and restlessness of a white group stranded so long. These people are the world's least likely revolutionaries. They are, in fact, the precisely *wrong* people—as the Russian fieldworker was the wrong man to accomplish Marx's revolt of the industrial proletariat.

People such as these were the first "Memphians" I had met in any number. That was four days ago. And my first impression was the same as that which nagged at me all night in the church: these Tennessee Negroes are not unlikely, they are impossible. They are anachronisms. Their leaders had objected for some time to J.P. Alley's "Hambone" cartoon in the local paper; they say, rightly, that it offers an outdated depiction of the Negro. Nonetheless, these men *are* Hambones. History has passed them by.

I saw them by the hundred, that first morning, streaming past the open casket in a hugger-mugger wake conducted between the completion of the embalmer's task and the body's journey out to the Memphis airport. I had arrived in Memphis several hours after King's death; touched base at the hotel, at the police station, at the site of the murder—dawn was just disturbing the sky; flashbulbs around and under the balcony still blinked repeatedly against the room number—306—like summer lightning. As the light strengthened, I sought out the funeral home police had mentioned—R.S. Lewis and Sons.

Clarence Lewis is one of the sons, he has been up all night answering the phone, but he is still polite; professionally sepulchral, calm under stress. "They brought Dr. King here because we have been connected with the Movement for a long time. We drove him in our limousines when he was here last week [for the ill-fated march]. They brought the body to us from the morgue at ten-thirty last night, and my brother has been working on it ever since. There's so much to do: this side [he pulls spread fingers down over his right cheek and neck] was all shot away, and the jawbone was just dangling. They have to reset it and then build all that up with plaster." I went through the fine old home (abandoned to trade when the white people moved from this area) into a new addition—the chapel, all cheap religious sentiment, an orange cross in fake stained glass. There are two people already there, both journalists, listening to the sounds from the next room (Clarence calls it, with a mortician's customary euphemism, "the Operating Room"), where a radio crackles excerpts from Dr. King's oratory, and men mutter their appreciation of the live voice while they work on the dead body. We comment on the ghoulishness of their task— knowing ours is no less ghoulish. We would be in there, if we could, with lights and cameras; but we must wait—wait through an extra hour of desperate cosmetic work. We do it far less patiently than Memphis garbage men wait in their church. "Hell of a place for Dr. King to end up, isn't it?" the photographer says. "And one hell of a cause—a little garbage strike."

When, at eight o'clock, the body is brought out, bright TV lights appear and pick out a glint of plaster under the cheek's powder. Several hundred people file past; they have sought the body out, in their sorrow, and will not let it leave town without some tribute. But not one white person from the town goes through that line.

Those who do come are a microcosm of the old Southern Negro community. Young boys doff their hats and their nylon hair caps—their "do rags"—as they go by. A Negro principal threatened to expel any child from a local high school who came to class with an "Afro" hairdo. Possessive matrons take up seats in the back, adjust their furs, cluck sympathetically to other women of their station, and keep the neighborhood record straight with bouts of teary gossip. They each make several passes at the coffin; sob uncontrollably, whip out their Polaroid cameras, and try an angle different from that shot on their last pass. One woman kisses the right cheek. Clarence Lewis was afraid of that: "It will spoil the makeup job. We normally put a veil over the coffin opening in cases of this sort; but we knew people would just tear that off with Dr. King. They want to see him. Why, we had one case where the people lifted a body up in the coffin to see where the bullet had gone into a man's back."

Outside, people mill around, making conversation, mixing with stunned friendliness, readjusting constantly their air of sad respect. Again, the scene looked like a disconsolate picnic. Some activists had called him "De Lawd." He always had to be given either his title (*"Doctor* King," even the *Reverend Doctor* King") or his full historic name ("Luther Martin King" one prim lady mourner called him in the funeral home, understandably stumbling over the big mouthful). Even that title "Doctor"—never omitted, punctiliously stressed when whites referred to him, included even in King's third-person references to himself—had become almost comical. He was not only "De Lawd," but "De Lawd High God Almighty," and his Movement was stiff with the preacher-dignities of the South; full of Reverends This and Bishops That and Doctors The-Other. No wonder the militants laughed at it all. And now, damned if he hadn't ended up at a Marc Connelly *fish fry* of a wake—right out of *The Green Pastures.*

Connelly learned to read by poring over the pages of the Memphis *Commercial Appeal* and he learned his lesson well: he was able to create a hambone God: "Dey's gonter to be a deluge, Noah, an' dey's goin' to be a flood. De Levees is gonter bust an' everything dat's fastened down is comin' loose." These are unlikely people, I thought at that sad fish fry, to ride out the deluge whose signs had already thundered from several directions on the night King died. But then, so was Noah an unlikely candidate. Or Isaac, who asked: "Does you want de brainiest or the holiest, Lawd?" "I want the holiest. I'll make him brainy." And there was one note, at King's makeshift wake, not heard anywhere in Connelly's play. As one of the mammy types waddled out the front door, she said with matter-of-fact bitterness to everyone standing nearby: "I wish it was Henry Loeb lying there"—handsone lovable Henry Loeb, the city's Mayor, who would later tell me, in his office, how well he liked his Negroes; unaware, even now, that they are not his. Connelly's "darkies" do not hate white people: "the white folk" simply do not exist in his play, which was meant to fortify the Southern conviction that "they have their lives and we have ours," an arrangement convenient to the white and (so whites tell themselves) pleasant for all. The whites get servants, and the blacks get fish fries. That whole elaborate fiction was shattered by the simple words, "I wish it was Henry Loeb." Massah's not in the cold, cold ground. She wishes he were. These people may be Hambones, but not J.P. Alley's kind. They are a paradox, a portent white Memphis still must come to grips with—hambone militants, "good darkies" on the march. When even the stones rise up and cry out, the end has come for Henry Loeb's South.

The signs of it are everywhere—at the Lorraine Motel, where King died; it is an extension of the old Lorraine Hotel, once a white whore-house. Then, when the neighborhood began to go black, it was thrown to a Negro buyer as, in the South, old clothes are given to "the help." A man named William Bailey bought it, and laboriously restored it to respectability. King stayed there often on his visits to Memphis. It is now a headquarters for the S.C.L.C.'s Project Memphis, a program designed—as its assistant director says—"to make Memphis pay for the death of Dr. King." Yet the Lorraine is run by a man who could pose for "Uncle Ben" rice ads—an ex-Pullman porter who is still the captain of porters at a Holiday Inn. He works for the white man, and does it happily, while he owns and runs a black motel where activists plot their campaigns. "I'm very proud to be part of the Holiday Inn family," he told me. "Why, the owners of the whole chain call me Bill Bailey." That's the Negro Henry Loeb has always known. It is the other side of him—the owner of the Lorraine, the friend of Dr. King—that is the mystery.

King made the mistake of staying, on his penultimate visit to Memphis, at one of the posher new Holiday Inns—in the kind of place where Bill Bailey works, not in the motel he owns. The Memphis paper gleefully pointed out that King *could* stay in the Inn because it had been integrated—"without demonstrations." But the Lorraine is not integrated (except in theory). Neither was the white flophouse in which the sniper lurked. It is good that King came back to the real world, the de-facto segregated world, to die. He was in the right place, after all. Memphis indeed, had taught him to "stay in his place"—a thing it will come to regret. For "his place" is now a command post, a point where marches are planned, and boycotts, and Negro-history classes.

These garbage men are that new thing, Hambones in rebellion—and they have strange new fish to fry. The people who filed past King's body had said no to the whole city of Memphis; said it courteously, almost deferentially (which only made it more resounding); they had marched every day under their employers' eyes; boycotted the downtown; took on, just for good measure, firms like Coca-Cola and Wonder Bread and Sealtest Milk; and were ready, when the time came, to join with King in taking on Washington. Patience radiates from them like a reproach. Perhaps that is why the white community does not like to see them in a mass—only in the single dimension, the structured encounter that brings them singly into the home or the store for eight hours of work. These Negroes seem almost too patient—wrong people for rebels. Yet their like has already made a rebellion. A tired woman in Birmingham was the wrong sort to begin all the modern civil-rights activism; but Rosa Parks did it. King was drawn into that first set of marches and boycotts almost by accident—as he was involved, finally, in the garbage men's strike: "Dat's always de trouble wid miracles. When you pass one you always gotta r'ar back an' pass another."

The buses were late. They were supposed to arrive at eleven-thirty for loading baggage (each man had been told to bring toothbrush, change of underwear, change of outer clothes if he wanted it, and most wanted it.) Besides, there had been talk of a bus for teen-agers, who were now giggling and flirting in the dark vestibule (surrendered to them by their elders). Jerry Fanion, an officer of the Southern Regional Conference, scurried around town looking for an extra bus; like all Negroes, he was stopped everywhere he went. Police recognized him, and they had been alerted about the men who would be leaving their homes for the funeral; but they made him get out of the car anyway, and laboriously explain himself. He never did get the bus. Later in the week, the teen-agers made a pilgrimage to King's grave.

Meanwhile, the wives in the Clayborn Temple still did not know whether they could go with their husbands. About eleven-thirty, T.O. Jones showed up, with P.J. Ciampa. Jones is the spheroid president of the sanitation local—a man too large in some ways and too small in others for any standard size of shirt, coat, pants. He is content with floppy big pants and a windbreaker that manages to get around him, but only by being too long in the sleeves and too wide in the shoulders. He is a quiet man in his early forties, determined but vague, who began the strike by going to the office of the Director of Public Works and—when the Director told him there was an injunction against any strike by city employees—changing into his "prison clothes" on the spot.

Ciampa is the fiery Italian organizer who came into town for the union and amused people with televised arguments against Mayor Loeb (who insisted that all negotiations be carried on in public). Jones and Ciampa have lost the list of men signed up for the buses; they don't know how many buses are coming, how many can ride on each. They try to take two counts—of workers alone, and workers with their wives; but it's difficult to keep track of those who wander in and out of shadows, doors, ante-rooms.

After an hour of disorder, it becomes clear that everyone can fit into the three buses if folding chairs are put down the aisles. T.O. had told me to save a seat for him, but the chairs in the aisle barricade us from each other. I sit, instead, with a sleepy young man who describes the route we *have* to take, and then finds confirmation of his theory, with a kind of surprised triumph, all along the way. The route one travels through Mississippi and Alabama is a thing carefully studied by Southern Negroes. After giving T.O. a check for the bus drivers, Ciampa went back to the hotel, T.O. swung onto the lead bus, and we pulled out.

In the seat behind me, a woman is worried over the teen-agers still standing by the church, hoping they will get a bus. "How they gonna get home?" she asks. "Walk, woman," her husband growls. "But what of the curfew?" "What of it?" "I don't trust those police. If I hadn't got on the bus with you, I'd have stayed all night in the church." As the bus rolls through downtown Memphis, on its way South, the woman sees cars moving. "What are they doing out during the curfew? Why aren't *they* stopped?" She knows, of course. Her husband does not bother to answer her.

In our bus, all the animation comes from one voice in the back. A tall laughing man I had watched, in the church, as he moved from one cluster to another, mixing easily, asked to sit beside me while I was still saving a seat for T.O. I was sorry later I had not said yes. As the riders shouldered sleepily into their chair backs, he joked more softly, but showed no signs of fatigue himself—though he had been a marshal all the long afternoon of marching. And as fewer and fewer responded to him, he moved naturally from banter and affectionate insults to serious things: "That Dr. King was for us." The response is a sigh of yesses. "He didn't have to come here." A chorusing of noes. As he mused on, the crowd breathed with him in easy agreement, as if he were thinking for them. This "audience participation" is what makes the Southern preacher's sermon such an art form. I had been given a dazzling sample of it three days before in the garbage men's meeting at the United Rubber Workers Union Hall. That was the day after King's death, and a formidable lineup of preachers was there to lament it. They all shared a common language, soaked in Biblical symbol: Pharoah was Mayor Loeb, and Moses was Dr. King, and Jesus was the Vindicator who would get them their dues checkoff. But styles were different, and response had to be earned. The whole hall was made up of accompanists for the improvising soloist up front. When he had a theme that moved them, they cheered him on: "Stay there!" "Fix it." "Fix it up." "Call the roll." "*Talk* to me!" "Talk *and a half.*" The better preacher, the surer his sense of the right time to tarry, the exact moment to move on; when to let the crowd determine his pace, when to push against them; the lingering, as at the very edge of orgasm, prolonging, prolonging; then the final emotional breakthrough when the whole audience "comes" together.

Memphis is not really the birthplace of the blues, any more than Handy was the father of them; but these are the same people who created the form—the triple repeated sighing lines, with a deep breathing space between each, space filled in with the accompanists' "break" or "jazz." That is the basic pattern for the climactic repetitions, subtle variations, and refrains of the preacher's art. That kind of sermon is essentially a musical form; and the garbage men are connoisseurs. When a white pastor from Boston got up, he gave them slogans and emotion; but without a response from the audience—he didn't know the melody.

Nor did all the black preachers succeed, or win equal acceptance. The surprise of the afternoon, at least for me, came when an S.C.L.C. delegation reached the hall, and the Reverend James Bevel got up to preach. He and his associates looked almost out of place there amid the "do rags" and scarred ebony skulls; they were immaculately dressed, with educated diction, wearing just the proper kind of "natural" and a beard.

Bevel was the fourteenth, and last, speaker of the afternoon. It seemed that earlier emotional talks would have drained these men of all response left them after the shock of the preceding night. But Jim Bevel slowly built them up, from quiet beginnings, to an understanding of what it means to be "on the case." (This is a phrase he invented a year ago to describe musicians who are perfectly interacting; it is now an S.C.L.C. phrase of wide applicability.) "Dr. King died on the case. Anyone who does not help forward the sanitation workers' strike is not on the case. You getting me?" (They're getting him.) "There's a false rumor around that our leader is dead. *Our* leader is not dead." ("No!" They know King's *spirit* lives on—half the speeches have said that already.) "That's a *false* rumor!" ("Yes!" "False." "Sho' nuff." "*Tell* it!") "Martin Luther King is not—" (yes, they know, not dead; this is a form in which expectations are usually satisfied, the crowd arrives at each point *with* the speaker; he outruns them at peril of losing the intimate ties that slacken and go taut between each person in the room; but the real artist takes chances, creates suspense, breaks the rhythm deliberately; a snag that makes the resumed onward flow more satisfying)—"Martin Luther King is not our *leader!*" ("No!" The form makes them say it, but with hesitancy. They will trust him some distance; but what does he mean? The "Sho' nuff" is not declamatory now; not fully interrogatory, either; circumflexed.) "*Our* leader—("Yes?")—is the *man*—("*What* man?" "Who?" "Who?" Reverend Abernathy? Is he already trying to supplant King? The trust is almost fading)—who led *Moses* out of *Israel*." ("*Thass* the man!" Resolution; all doubt dispelled; the bridge has been negotiated, left them stunned with Bevel's virtuosity.) "*Our* leader is the man who went with Daniel into the lions' den." ("Same man!" "Talk some.") "Our leader is the man who walked out of the grave on Easter morning." ("Thass the leader!" They have not heard, here in hamboneland, that God is dead.) "Our leader never sleeps nor slumbers. He cannot be put in jail. He has never lost a war yet. *Our* leader is *still on the case*." ("*That's it!*" "*On* the case!") "Our leader is not dead. One of his prophets died. We will not stop because of that. Our staff is not a funeral staff. We have friends who are undertakers. We *do business*. We *stay on the case*, where our leader is."

It is the most eloquent speech I have ever heard. I was looking forward, a day later, to hearing Bevel again, before a huge audience in the Mason Temple. He was good—and gave an entirely different speech. But the magic of his talk to the sanitation workers was gone. It was not merely the size of the crowd (though that is important—the difference between an intimate combo and some big jazz band only partially rehearsed). The makeup of the crowd was also different. Those in the Union Hall were predominantly male. Men accompany; women compete—they talk over the preacher's rhythms. Their own form is not the jazz combo, but the small group of gospel singers, where each sister fights for possession of the song by claiming a larger share of the Spirit. In a large place like the Mason Temple, women set up nuclei around the hall and sang their own variations on the sermon coming out of the loudspeakers.

But that night in the bus, there was no fighting the jolly voice that mused on "Dr. King's death." Responses came, mingled but regular, like sleepy respirations, as if the bus's sides were breathing regularly in and out. This is the subsoil of King's great oratory, of the subtly varied refrains: "I have a *dream* . . . *I* have a dream today." He must have been a great preacher in his own church; he could use the style out in the open, before immense crowds. He made the transition more skillfully than Bevel had—and far better than Abernathy does. That very day, the Monday before King's funeral, Abernathy had paused long on the wrong phrases: "I do not *know* . . . I do not *know*." He had let the crowd fool him by their sympathy; he took indulgence for a *demand* to linger. He did not have King's sure sense of when to move.

I suppose I heard thirty or forty preachers on that long weekend of religious eloquence; but not one of them reached King's own level of skill in handling a crowd. That was the mystery of King. He was the Nobel Prize winner and a Southern Baptist preacher; and, at places like the Washington Mall in 1963, the two did not conflict but worked together. As the man in the bus kept saying, "He was for *us*." (Unh-*hmmn!*") "He was *one* with us." ("That he was." "That he was.")

But King's rapport with his people was not the natural thing it seems now. He had to learn it, or relearn it. The man's voice rose behind us in the bus: "You know what Dr. King said?" ("What?") "He said not to mention his Nobel Prize when he died." ("Thass what he *said*.") "He said, 'That don't mean nothing'." ("Sho' nuff.") "What matters is that *he* helped *us*." ("Thass the truth." "That *is* the truth." "*That* is.")

In several ways. King was very bright, a quick study. He skipped two grades to finish high school at the age of fifteen. He was ordained at eighteen; graduated from college at nineteen. It was a fast start, for a career that is one long quick record of youthful accomplishment. He got his theology degree at the age of twenty-two. While a pastor (from the age of twenty-five), he got his Ph.D. from Boston University at twenty-six. And he went direct from graduate school to a position of national leadership. His major achievements were already behind him when he became the youngest man (thirty-five) to receive the Nobel Prize. He was dead before he reached the age of forty; and there are constant little surprises in remembering how young he was—as when Harry Belafonte, speaking in Memphis, referred to King as his junior by a year. Was "De Lawd" really younger than that baby-faced singer? And why did we never think of him as young?

He had the strained gravity of the boy who has moved up fast among his elders. That unnatural dignity is in his writing, too, which labors so for gravity that it stretches grammar: "President Kennedy was a strongly contrasted personality . . . trying to sense the direction his leadership could travel." His acceptance speech will not rank with the great Nobel speeches: "transform this *pending* cosmic elegy into a creative psalm . . . unfolding events which surround . . . spiral down a militaristic stairway . . . blood-flowing streets. . . ."

The young King wanted to study medicine. He majored in sociology at Morehouse College. He thought preachers not quite intellectually respectable, though his father and grandfather and great-grandfather had all been preachers. Even when he accepted ordination, he thought he should become a theologian-minister, perhaps a professor, rather than a mere preacher. He took his first parish—in Montgomery—to get "pastoring background" before accepting a teaching post. To the end of his life he talked of turning to an academic career.

But he was never convincing as a scholar. An account of his own intellectual development reads as if it were lifted from a college catalog: "My intellectual journey carried me through new and sometimes complex doctrinal lands, but the pilgrimage was always stimulating, gave me a new appreciation for objective appraisal and critical analysis, and knocked me out of my dogmatic slumber." He was not even a very perceptive commentator on the men who created his doctrine of civil disobedience—Thoreau and Gandhi. When he began the Montgomery boycott, he liked to refer vaguely to Hegel as the prophet of "creative tensions." It was not till someone suggested more likely patrons of nonviolent rebellion that he began referring to Gandhi and Gandhi's American forerunner—*referring* to them—as saints. He never really discusses their philosophy. And his most ambitious defense of civil disobedience—the Letter from a Birmingham Jail, written eight years after the Montgomery boycott—does not even *refer* to Gandhi or Thoreau. Instead, King uses tags from Augustine and Aquinas (hardly anti-authoritarians). Nor does the Letter deserve high marks for logic. It offers as the model of civil disobedience, not Gandhi, but Socrates, the stock Platonic figure suborned for all noble causes, but something of an embarrassment in this context, since Plato makes him preach history's most rigorous sermon against civil disobedience in the *Crito*. The Letter gives three qualifications for a valid act of civil disobedience: 1) that it be open, 2) that it be loving (nonviolent), and 3) that those engaged in it accept their punishment willingly. Then he gives as a historical example of this the Boston Tea Party, whose perpetrators: 1) were clandestine (they disguised themselves as Indians), 2) were armed for violence (they forced wharf guards away and were ready to repel any interruption), and 3) evaded all punishment (Sam Adams and his Committee of Correspondence *dared* England to attempt punishment). Indeed, none of the historical examples of civil disobedience given in King's Letter meets the three requirements he had just set up.

Like Moses, he was not "de brainiest." He only knew one book well—the Bible. It was enough. All the other tags and quotes are meant to give respectability to those citations that count—the phrases sludged up in his head from earliest days like a rich alluvial soil. He could not use these with the kind of dignity he aspired to unless he were more than "just a preacher." Yet the effect of that *more* was to give him authority *as* a preacher. By trying to run away from his destiny, he equipped himself for it. He became a preacher better educated than any white sheriff; more traveled, experienced, poised. He was a Hambone who could say "no" and make it sound like a cannon shot.

It is interesting to contrast him with another preacher's son—James Baldwin. Baldwin became a boy preacher himself as a way of getting out into the secular world. King became a student as a way of getting into a larger world of *religion,* where the term "preacher" would not be a reproach. He needed a weightiness in his work which only that "Doctor" could give him. He needed it for personal reasons—yes, he had all along aspired to be "De Lawd"—and in order to make Southern religion relevant. That is why King was at the center of it all: he was after *dignity,* which is the whole point of the Negro rebellion. His talent, his abilities as a "quick study," his versatility, his years studying philosophy and theology (for which he had no real natural bent) were means of achieving power. His books and degrees were all tools, all weapons. He had to put that "Doctor" before his name in order to win a "Mister" for every Southern Negro. They understood that. They rejoiced in his dignities as theirs. The Nobel Prize *didn't* matter except as it helped them. As T.O. Jones put it, "There can never be another leader we'll have the feeling for that we had for him."

Our three buses had a long ride ahead of them—ten hours, an all-night run, through parts of Mississippi, Alabama, and Georgia. They were not luxury buses, with plenty of room; the Greyhound company had run out of vehicles and leased these from a local firm. One could not even stretch one's legs in the aisle; the folding chairs prevented that. Ten hours there. Ten hours back.

Minutes after our departure, the man behind me said, "We're in Mississippi now." "Oh no!" his wife groaned. It is well to be reminded that our citizens are afraid to enter certain states. The man most frightened was T.O. Jones. He knows what risks an "uppity" Negro takes in the South. He does not give out his address or phone number. The phone is changed automatically every six months to avoid harassment. He has lived in a hotel room ever since the beginning of his union's strike, so his wife and two girls will not be endangered by his presence in the house. "This is risky country," he told me. "And it gets more dangerous as you go down the road. That Mississippi!" We were going down the road.

The lead bus had no toilet, and the chairs in the aisle effectively barricaded it from anyone's use in the other buses. The technique for "rest stops" was for all three buses to pull off into a darkened parking lot; the chairs were folded; then people lined up at the two toilets (one bus for men, one for women). At our first stop, some men began to wander off into the trees, but T.O., sweating in the cool night, churning all around the buses to keep his flock together, warned them back. "Better not leave the bus." I asked him if he expected trouble. "Well, we're in Mississippi, and folk tend to get flusterated at—" He let it hang. He meant at the sight of a hundred and forty Negroes pouring out of buses in the middle of the night. "You didn't see that man over there, did you—in the house by the gas station? There was a man at the door." Some had tried to go near the dark station, to get Cokes from an outdoor vending machine. T.O. pulled them back to the buses. He carries his responsibility very self-consciously.

Back in the bus, there was a spasm of talk and wakefulness after our stop. The deep rumbling voice from the rear got chuckles and approval as he mused on the chances of a strike settlement. "We got Henry Loeb on the run now." ("Yeah!" "Sure do!") "He don't know what hit him." Fear is not surprising in the South. This new confidence is the surprising thing. I had talked to a watery little man, back in the church, who seemed to swim in his loose secondhand clothes—a part-time preacher who had been collecting Memphis' garbage for many years. What did he think of the Mayor? "Mr. Loeb doesn't seem to do much thinking. He just doesn't *understand*. Maybe he can't. The poor man is just, y'know—kinda—*sick*." It is King's word for our society, a word one hears everywhere among the garbage men; a word of great power in the Negro community—perhaps the key word of our decade. It is no longer a question of courage or fear, men tell each other; of facing superior white power or brains or resources. It is just a matter of understanding, of pity. One must be patient with the sick.

Henry Loeb does not look sick. He is vigorous, athletic, bushy-browed, handsome in the scowling-cowboy mold of William S. Hart and Randolph Scott. And he has a cowboy way of framing everything as part of his personal code: "*I* don't make deals. . . . *I* don't believe in reprisals. . . . . *I* like to conduct business in the open." There is an implicit contrast, in that repeatedly emphasized pronoun, with all the other shifty characters in this here saloon. He even has a cowboy's fondness for his "mount"—the P.T. boat he rode during the war, a loving if unskilled portrait of which hangs behind his desk. (His office biography makes the inevitable reference to John F. Kennedy.)

Loeb is an odd mixture of the local and the cosmopolitan. He comes from a family of Memphis millionaires; he married the Cotton Carnival Queen. Yet as a Jew he could not belong to the Memphis Country Club (he has become an Episcopalian since his election as Mayor); and he went East for his education. A newsman who knows him made a bet with me: "When he hears you are from a national magazine he will not let five minutes go by without a reference to Andover or Brown." When I went into his office, he asked for my credentials before talking to me (he would later boast that he talks to anyone who wants to come see him). Then he asked where I live. Baltimore. "Oh, do you know so-and-so?" No. Why? "He was in my class at Andover, and came from Baltimore." That newsman could clean up if he made his bets for money.

Loeb did not mention Brown. But he did not need to. As I waited for him in his office, his secretary took the Dictaphone plug out of her ear and began flipping through her dictionary, and confided to me, as she did so, "The Mayor was an English major at Brown University, and he uses words so big I can't even find them." Later, his executive assistant found occasion to let me know that his boss was "an English major at Brown University."

But the Mayor also plays the role of local boy protecting his citizens from carpetbaggers out of the North. He has the disconcerting habit of leaving his telephone amplifier on, so that visitors can hear both ends of a conversation; and when a newspaperman with a pronounced Eastern accent called him for some information, he amused local journalists, who happened to be in his office, by mimicking the foreigner in his responses. When a group of white suburban wives went to his office to protest his treatment of the garbage strikers, he listened to them, then slyly asked the five who had done most of the talking where they were from; and his ear had not betrayed him—not one was a native "Memphian." He has a good ear for classes, accent, background. He wanted to know where I had gone to college. The South is very big on "society."

But Loeb has no ear at all for one accent—the thick, slow drawl of men like T.O. Jones. He knows they haven't been to college. I asked him whether he thought he could restore good relations with the Negro community after the sanitation workers settlement. "There is good understanding now. I have Negroes come to me to firm up communications—I won't say to reestablish them, because they had not lapsed." I told him I attended a mass rally at Mason Temple, where more than five thousand Negroes cheered as preacher after preacher attacked him. "Well, you just heard from a segment of the community whose personal interests were involved. Why, I have open house every Thursday, and just yesterday I had many Negroes come in to see me about different things." Imagine! And Massah even talked to them! And they came right in the front door, too! It is the conviction of all Henry Loebs that the great secret of the South, carefully hidden but bound to surface in the long run, is the

Negro's profound devotion to Henry Loeb. After all, look at everything he has done for them. "*I* took the responsibility of spending fifteen thousand dollars of city money—multiplied many times over by federal food stamps—to feed the strikers." *Noblesse oblige.*

The odd thing is that white Memphis really *does* think that—as citizen after citizen tells you—"race relations are good." Its spokesman cannot stop saying, "How much we have done for the Negro" (the Southern bigot is nothing but the Northern liberal caricatured—we have *all* done so much for the Negro). A journalist on the *Press-Scimitar,* the supposedly "liberal" paper in town, says, "We have been giving Negroes the courtesy title" (that is, calling Mr. and Mrs. Jones *Mr.* and *Mrs.* Jones) "ever since the Korean War." (It embarrassed even the South to call the parents of a boy killed in action *John* and *Jane* Jones.) But the executive secretary of the local N.A.A.C.P. was considered a troublemaker when, arrested in a demonstration supporting the strikers, she held up the booking process time after time by refusing to answer the officer's call for "Maxine" instead of Mrs. Smith. ("Why, *isn't* your name Maxine?" one honestly befuddled cop asked her.)

Mrs. Smith is one of the many Negroes who protested the morning paper's use of the "Hambone" cartoon. But she ran up against the typical, infuriating response: "Hambone" was actually the white man's way of saying how much he *loves* the Negro. It was begun in 1916 by J.P. Alley, who—this is meant to settle the question once for all—won a Pulitzer Prize for attacking the Klan. It was kept up by the Alley family (one of whom is married to the morning paper's editor), and Memphis felt it would lose a precious "tradition" if their favorite darkie disappeared from their favorite newspaper—as, at last, a month after King's death, he did; with this final salute from the paper: "Hambone's nobility conferred a nobility upon all who knew him."

Nowhere is the South's sad talk of "tradition" more pitiful than in Memphis. The city was founded as part of a land deal that brought Andrew Jackson a fortune for getting Indians to give up their claims to the site. The city's great Civil War hero—to whom Forrest Park is dedicated—could not belong to the antebellum equivalent of the Memphis Country Club because he was not a "gentleman"—that is, he was not a slave *owner* but a slave *trader*. After the war, however, he took command of the Ku Klux Klan, which made him "society." The Memphis Klan no doubt boasted of all the things it did for the Negro, since it *was* more selective and restrained than the Irish police force, which slaughtered forty-six Negroes in as many hours during 1866. Later in the century, yellow fever drove the cotton traders out of town; and Irish riffraff took over; the municipality went broke, surrendered its charter, and ceased to exist as a city for a dozen years. Then, just as Memphis regained its right of self-government, a small-town boy from Mississippi, Ed Crump, came up the pike and founded the longest-lasting city "machine" of this century. The main social event for the town's "aristocracy"—the Cotton Carnival—goes back only as far as 1931, when it was begun as a gesture of defiance to the Depression: the city is built on a bluff, and run on the same principle.

When Dr. King's planned second march took place, four days after his death, men built the speaker's platform inconveniently high up, so Mrs. King would be standing before the city emblem, above the doors of City Hall, when she spoke. It was meant, of course, as a rebuke to the city. But her standing there, with that background, is henceforth the only tradition Memphis has worth saving.

Yet the city keeps telling itself that "relations are good." If that is so, why was Henry Loeb guarded by special detectives during and after the strike? (One sat in during my session with him; they stash their shotguns under his desk.) Why did some white ministers who supported the strike lose their jobs? Why are black preachers called Communists in anonymous circulars? But the daily papers will continue to blink innocently and boast on the editorial page: "Negro football and basketball players figure prominently in all-star high-school teams selected by our Sports Department." What *more* do they want?

When dawn came, our buses had reached Georgia, the red clay, the sparse vegetation. By the time we entered Atlanta, it was hot; the funeral service had already begun at Ebenezer Church. The bus emptied its cramped, sleepy load of passengers onto a sidewalk opposite the courthouse (Lester Maddox is hiding in there behind *his* bodyguard, conducting the affairs of office on a desk propped up, symbolically, with shotguns). The garbage men who brought their good clothes have no opportunity to change. The women are especially disappointed; the trip has left everyone rumpled. Men begin to wander off. T.O. does not know what to do. He ends up staying where the bus stopped, to keep track of his flock. Some men get the union's wreath over to the church. Others walk to Morehouse College. But for most, the long ride simply puts them in the crowd that watches, at the Capitol, while celebrities march by.

It was a long ride for this; and the ride back will seem longer. The buses leave Atlanta at eight-thirty on the night of King's burial, and do not reach Memphis until six the next morning. But no one regretted the arduous trip. T.O. told me he *had* to go: "We were very concerned about Dr. King's coming to help us. I talked with the men, and we knew he would be in danger in Memphis. It was such a saddening thing. He was in Memphis for only one reason—the Public Works Department's work stoppage. This is something I lay down with, something I wake up with. I know it will never wear away."

A week after the funeral, Mayor Loeb finally caved in to massive pressures from the White House. The strike was settled, victoriously. At the announcement, T.O. blubbered without shame before the cameras. It was the culmination of long years—almost ten of them—he had poured into an apparently hopeless task, beginning back in 1959 when he was fired by the city for trying to organize the Public Works Department. After the victory I went with him to an N.A.A.C.P. meeting where he was introduced, to wild applause, by Jesse Turner, head of the local chapter: "Our city fathers tell us the union has been foisted on us by moneygrubbing outsiders. Well, here's the outsider who did it all, Carpet-bagger Jones." The applause almost brought him to tears again: "I was born in Memphis, and went to school here. I haven't been out of the state more than three days in the last ten years. Is that what they mean by an outsider?" A man got up in the audience and said, "When my wife saw you on television, she said 'I feel sorry for that fat little man crying in public.' But I told her, 'Don't feel sorry for him. I've seen him for years trying to get something going here, and getting nowhere. *He* just *won*.' "

When the strike was still on, Henry Loeb, if asked anything about it, liked to whip out his wallet and produce the first telegram he got from the union's national office, listing nine demands. He would tick off what he could and couldn't do under each heading, giving them all equal weight, trying to bury in technicalities the two real issues—union recognition and dues checkoff. When I went to see him after the settlement, he brought out the tired old telegram, now spider-webbed with his arguments and distinctions. Then he searched the grievance-process agreement for one clause that says the final court of appeal is the Mayor (still built on a bluff). He assured me that, no matter how things look, *he* does not make deals. They really settled on *his* terms. But isn't there a dues checkoff? No. The *city* does not subtract union dues before pay reaches the men; their credit union does (a device the union had suggested from the outset). What about recognition of the union; wasn't that guaranteed? No, it was not. There is no contract, only a memorandum signed by the City Council. Well, is that not a binding agreement—i.e., a contract? "No, it is a *memorandum*" (see how useful it is to be an English major?)—"but we have a way of honoring our commitments." The code. Well, then, didn't the union get a larger raise than the Mayor said it would? Not from the *city*. Until July 1, when all city employees were scheduled for a raise, the extra demands of the union will be met by a contribution of local businessmen. *Noblesse oblige*—see what we have done for our Negroes. Will the Mayor handle promised union agitation by the hospital and school employees in a new way, after the experience of the garbage strike? "No. Nothing has changed."

Wrong again, Henry. Everything has changed. The union is here to stay, it will spread: Jesse Epps and P.J. Ciampa and T.O. Jones will see to that. The S.C.L.C. is here to stay: Jim Bevel is in charge of Project Memphis. The city is his case now, and he is on it. A coalition of local preachers that backed the strikers has made itself a permanent organization, Community on the Move for Equality; preachers like James Lawson, better educated than some Brown graduates, are convinced that the God of Justice is not dead, not even in Memphis. Most important, Memphis is now the place where Dr. King delivered one of his great speeches—those speeches that will outlive his labored essays.

The excerpt most often published from that last speech told how King had been to the mountaintop. But those who were there at the Mason Temple to hear him, the night before he died, remember another line most vividly.

He almost did not come to that meeting. He was tired; the weather was bad, he hoped not many would show up (his first march had been delayed by late spring *snows* in Tennessee); he sent Ralph Abernathy in his stead. But the same remarkable people who rode twenty hours in a bus to stand on the curb at his funeral came through storm to hear him speak on April 4. Abernathy called the Lorraine and told King he could not disappoint such a crowd. King agreed. He was on his way.

Abernathy filled in the time till he arrived with a long introduction on King's life and career. He spoke for half an hour—and set the mood for King's own reflection on the dangers he had faced. It was a long speech—almost an hour—and his followers had never heard him dwell so long on the previous assassination attempt, when a woman stabbed him near the heart. The papers quoted a doctor as saying that King would have died if he had sneezed. "If I had sneezed," he said, he would not have been in Birmingham for the marches. "If I had sneezed—" ("Tell it!" He was calling the roll now, talking "and a half," tolling the old cadences.) He could never, had he sneezed, have gone to Selma; to Washington for the great March of 1963; to Oslo. Or to Memphis.

For the trip to Memphis was an important one. He did not so much climb to the mountaintop there as go back down into the valley of his birth. Some instinct made him return to the South, breathing in strength for his assault on Washington, which he called the very last hope for nonviolence. He was learning, relearning, what had made him great— learning what motels to stay at; what style to use; what were his roots. He was learning, from that first disastrous march, that he could not come in and touch a place with one day's fervor; that he had to *work with* a community to make it respond nonviolently as Montgomery had, and Birmingham, and Selma.

It is ironic that the trouble on that first march broke out on Beale Street, where another man learned what his roots were. W.C. Handy did not come from Memphis, like Bessie Smith; he did not grow up singing the blues. He learned to play the trumpet in Alabama from a traveling bandmaster, a real Professor Harold Hill. Then he went North, to tootle transcribed Beethoven on "classical cornet" afternoons in Chicago. It was only when he came back South, and saw that the native songs *worked* better with audiences, that he began to write down some of those songs and get them published.

King, after largely ineffectual days in Chicago, returned to Memphis, the deracinated Negro coming home. Home to die. His very oratory regained majesty as he moved South. He had to find out all over what his own movement was about—as Marc Connelly's "Lawd" learns from his own creation: "Dey cain't lick you, kin dey Hezdrel?" Bevel said the leader was not Martin King. That was true, too, in several ways. In one sense, Rosa Parks was the true leader. And T.O. Jones. All the unlickable Hezdrels. King did not sing the civil-rights blues from his youth. Like Handy, he got them published. He knew what *worked*—and despite all the charges of the militants, no other leader had his record of success. He was a leader who, when he looked around, had armies behind him.

This does not mean he was not authentic as a leader. On the contrary. His genius lay in his ability to articulate what Rosa Parks and T.O. feel. Mailer asks whether he was great or was hamboning; but King's unique note was precisely his *ham* greatness. That is why men ask, now, whether *his* kind of greatness is obsolete. Even in his short life, King seemed to have outlived his era. He went North again—not to school this time, but to carry his movement out of Baptist-preacher territory—and he failed. The civil-rights movement, when it left the South, turned to militancy and urban riots. Men don't sing the old songs in a new land.

Yet it may be too soon to say that the South's contribution has been made. After all, the first two riots in 1968 were in South Carolina and Tennessee. The garbage strike opens a whole new possibility of labor-racial coalition in those jobs consigned exclusively to Negroes throughout the South. And, more important, the Northern Negro, who has always had a love-hate memory for the South, begins to yearn for his old identity. The name for it is "soul."

The militant activists insist on tradition (Africa) and religion (Muslim-ism, black Messianism, etc.) and community (the brothers). Like the young King, many Negroes feel the old Baptist preachers were not dig-nified. Better exotic headdress and long gowns from Africa than the frock coat of "De Lawd." But the gowns and headgear *are* exotic—foreign things that men wear stiffly, a public facade. There are more familiar Negro traditions and religion and community. Black graduate students have earned the right to go back to hominy and chitlins and mock anyone who laughs. The growth of "soul" is a spiritual return to the South—but a return with new weapons of dignity and resistance. Religion, the family, the past can be reclaimed now without their demeaning overtones. In this respect, the modern Negro is simply repeating, two decades later, King's brilliant maneuver of escape and reentry. He got the best of both worlds—the dignity that could only be won "outside," and the more familiar things which that dignity can transform. King was there before them all.

He remained, always, the one convincing preacher. Other civil-rights pioneers were mostly lawyers, teachers, authors. They learned the white man's language almost too well. King learned it, too; but it was always stiff. He belonged in the pulpit, not at the lectern. Bayard Rustin, with his high dry professional voice and trilled r's, cannot wear the S.C.L.C.'s marching coveralls with any credibility. The same is true, in varying measure, of most first-generation "respectable" leaders. Some of them would clearly get indigestion from the thinnest possible slice of watermelon, Adam Powell, of course, can ham it with the best; but his is a raffish rogue-charm, distinguished by its whiff of mischief. King, by contrast, was an Uncle Ben with a degree, a Bill Bailey who came home— and turned the home upside down. That is why he infuriated Southerners more than all the Stokelys and Raps put together. In him, they saw *their* niggers turning a calm new face of power on them.

King had the self-contained dignity of the South without its passivity. His day is not past. It is just coming. He was on his way, when he died, to a feast of "soul food"—a current fad in Negro circles. But King was there before them. He had always loved what his biographer calls, rather nervously, "ethnic delicacies." He never lost his "soul." He was never ashamed. His career said many things. That the South cannot be counted out of the struggle yet. That the Negro does not have to go elsewhere to find an identity—he can make his stand on American soil. That even the Baptist preacher's God need not yield, yet, to Allah. God is not dead— though "De Lawd" has died. One of His prophets died.

[August, 1968]

Part VI

Living Up to Our Commitment in Vietnam

When Demirgian Comes Marching Home Again (Hurrah? Hurrah?)

by John Sack

Ninety-nine bottles of beer on the wall, ninety-nine bottles of beer. If one of those bottles should happen to fall, ninety-eight bottles of beer on the wall. Ninety-eight. . . .

On the bottom side of earth in that strange land of Vietnam, time is a row of old brown bottles that are toppling down, of concrete balls that are cracking apart—time, in Vietnam, is a great burlap bag of rocks, and each day a soldier's shoulders are lightened of one more pound. As the night disappears, as sun makes the metal mess kits shine and warms a boy's cheeks, as day breaks he tells himself words like "Ninety-nine days." The next day he tells himself "Ninety-eight. . . ."

Tonight is the last night of Demirgian's tour of duty. Demirgian, a boy with the rank of specialist, his specialty being the rifle, his duty being to kill communists with it—Demirgian, the three hundreds, two hundreds, one hundreds over, the days strewn in back of him like little worthless pieces of broken glass, a staleness issuing out of them, a sickening smell—Demirgian has just tonight left as a rifleman in Asia. And when those seemingly endless hours are safely behind him—hurrah! Demirgian comes marching home again, uninjured, undead! Everybody cross your fingers! Pray for Demirgian! Pray!

That night Demirgian lay in his combat clothes—his steel helmet, the damp fabric of his shirt and trousers, his canvas boots—and Demirgian had a wet black rifle on the soil beside him as with intricate fingers he made himself a glass of grape juice. Slower than a caterpillar chews on a maple leaf his fingers tore a small paper packet of Kool-Aid and quieter than a dandelion loses its fluff his hand shook the light purple powder into his Army canteen. The cold stars above, the cool earth below him kept their complete silence as Demirgian tilted his rubber canteen to its left—right—left—right—with the slow periodicity of a pendulum. One long minute of this and Demirgian took a quiet sip. And ah! Demirgian had come alive! He's in the grape-juice generation! He buried the torn paper packet quietly in six soft inches of Vietnam's soil.

The time was about ten or ten-thirty at night. It shouldn't be thought that on ambush parties (for Demirgian's invisible squad had an ambush assignment tonight: to lie in the total darkness, if anyone comes it's a communist, shoot him)—it shouldn't be thought that soldiers on ambush parties lie like panthers ready to leap, their legs up under them, their eyes all alert: ridiculous. The essence of American ambush parties is that nothing—*nothing*—happens, nowhere but in the grave do the endless hours pass by a mass of human substance so stubbornly true to its configurations of one hour earlier, nobody in an American ambush party does a cotton-picking thing, the hours between sunset and sunrise hang as languidly as a hammock between two willow trees, one in a hundred times does a star-crossed communist happen by—a real event. Demirgian, a year of these uninteresting ambush parties and he still hadn't ambushed one living breathing soul. Demirgian had waited, he had scratched at where the mosquitoes bit, in his feet he had pins and needles, accordingly: he had wiggled his toes, he had given himself to little insidious itches, the nibbles of little millions of imaginary ants, he had *in—out—in—out*—he had carefully not neglected to breathe, the earth, like a big brown blotter, had sopped up his *élan vital,* his muscle tone, his temperature, his blood, he was pressed to these stretches of Asia hour after hour and hi-di-ho, I should have brought my yo-yo, at dawn he had lifted himself like a heavy canvas tarpaulin and carried himself back to the company camp. It was three meals a day, pink pills on Sunday, payday on the thirtieth—it was a living and it soon would be over, America hello!

And so Démirgian lay in a last night of lassitude. Elsewhere in this ambush party a pair of flat shadows coalesced and imperceptible whispers rose. "Sergeant?"

"Yes?"

"Sergeant. I have a headache."

"You have a headache?"

"Sergeant? You have an aspirin?"

"Yes."

Another boy in Demirgian's dull ambush party quietly snored. The sergeant in charge of this tableau said his bedtime prayers, he said to himself, "*Padre nuestro*," bowing his dark-colored face to the earth, "*que estas en los cielos. . . .*" The sergeant prayed for a typical night: no communists.

A VISIT TO THE BULLET FACTORY. *Splash! At the factory where the bright bullets for Demirgtan's rifle are made, Connecticut citizens in big iron shoes are carrying lead to the melting pot—splash! From out of the press comes the hot wet wire, the width of a bullet's width, the length of eternity, and Curtis, a colored man, a giant, the wire is his muscular hands, his body bowed over the floor like an ogre's over a steaming caldron, is coiling it—coiling it—oiling it, the machinery sends it along. The machinery is gargantuan, the gears are like wagon wheels, the conrods are making the motions of steady animal love. And chop! And chop! The wire is cut into bullet sizes, the slippery bullets slide from the chopping block on a gangway of grease, they are slithering, skiddering, and slippering into one another—sleighs on a snowy hillside, jingle all the way!*

Careful of the powdery stuff, boys and girls. Like little chipped pieces of pencil lead, it comes to the bullet plant in cases, it gets itself on clothing like a city's soot, it makes the wooden floor of the factory like a ballroom floor, as though beneath the balls of the feet lay little ball-bearings. Roll out the barrel! To Agnes, in her sensible shoes, the floor is like the floor of the Pleasure Beach Ballroom, in Bridgeport. We'll have a barrel of. . . . Agnes had met her husband there as the polka played. With her cardboard card and a brisk black brush, Agnes gets the powder up once every day, as David with his—bang—with his little leather—bang—with his little leather mallet—BANG, David hits the feeder lines to clean them, too. No smoking, please, as busy little birdlike ladies in glasses of plastic take the black powder, the bullets, the brass, as forty-nine at one time of these instrumentalities are made in the U.S.A. And a thousand wheels go round and round! And the air's on edge in the factory sound! And boxes of bullets abound on the ground! And—

Click. Clack. Mechanically, Demirgian puts one of Connecticut's bullets into his mean-looking rifle. A power uncalled upon, a lion asleep, here in its cave the bullet shall sit in steely silence all through an Asian night, an unnecessary accessory to American ambush parties with no one to set upon. But coming in in the morning—bang! and Demirgian will sometimes shoot at a C-ration can. And bang! and Demirgian shoots at a squealing pig. And bang! and Demirgian gets him a chicken with one of Connecticut's accurate bullets. Demirgian—what a character, the other risible soldiers say, Demirgian king of the shooting gallery, give him a box of candy, give him a cuddly teddy bear! However, Demirgian has still never shot at a communist. And he has adequate reason. A year in the Vietnam bushes (the endless series of stops and starts, the waits at the ambush sites, the walks)—a year minus a day in Vietnam and Demirgian has still never seen a communist to shoot at. Typical.

The time was getting on past eleven. Demirgian still lay on his hard lumpy mattress of earth—the ambush area, as across from him in the bushes a little thickening of blackness seemed to have suddenly moved, like a fish in the Stygian deep. Old soldier Demirgian tiredly recognized it for what it was, a banana leaf in the evening breeze. If only it were a communist soldier—ah! *Charlie tries to creep up on me,* Demirgian said to himself wistfully—*Charlie ever tries that and I'm just going to lie here—yeah! Let him get ten meters from me, the stupid little son-of-a. Yeah, and I'll have my hand grenade and I'll pull the pin—Charlie you're about to have had it! k-k-k! And then I'll let the handle go and I'll one—! two—! and I'll throw it!* Thumb on the bottom, fingers on top, a lazy little catlike windup, the pitch—Demirgian could see himself throw the grenade like a baseball, a rock, Demirgian had had some practice at that in Newton, Massachusetts, the city where he had been drafted from and where he had been a schoolboy before. "*Foreigner,*" some of the other kids had cried at Demirgian, "*Camel chaser,*" some of the Irish would say, and Demirgian, age twelve, his body behind a cardboard carton with its color of dead lawns and a dry-spell smell, his eyes at two tiny fiber-filled holes—Demirgian had thrown lumps of pudding stone at the Irish children, that is how he would throw his grenade at that communist if the stars in their slowly maundering courses should offer him—*at last*—one of his unseen enemies. To kill himself a communist soldier: that was Demirgian's dream, the Irish had been the object of nothing like it, this was Demirgian's sacred quest. For a boy with no past history of animus to Asians of any political party, a year on that distant continent and Demirgian's wish to kill communists had gone beyond all expectations, it was something fierce, his bones had become like a thing turned black, a thin black liquid ran in his arteries, no other friends of his felt it that passionately, the reason—that was Demirgian's secret. A bullet, a piece of his bayonet, it didn't make a diff to Demirgian *how,* a tent peg if it's sharp enough, a shovel, a can of kerosene, a kitchen match and—*bastard, die!* Demirgian's imagination knew no mercy—kick him in the genitals, finger in his eyeballs, stick him in the ashcan, ha-ha-ha! *Yeah,* Demirgian thought in his wait at this ambush area, it might be the night tonight—a toss of a hand grenade, success! An explosion, *and I'll look at him lying there dead and I'll think to myself*—Demirgian thought of a pale yellow face, the mouth like a broken bottle, the starlight on crooked teeth—*I think I'll be sorry about him—yeah,* Demirgian thought. *I'll say to him poor bastard! You're fighting for a losing cause!* If there was a watch or something upon him, Demirgian thought he might take it, a souvenir.

It wouldn't be easy. It's a practical fact of Vietnam that the airplane pilots and artillerymen kill the communists while the riflemen like Demirgian kill themselves—one doesn't have to say: by accident—and Demirgian would have to throw himself over the odds if his heart's desire was to be gratified tonight. Still, there had been soldiers in Demirgian's own squad who had killed themselves communists, it had been known to happen sometimes in spite of Charlie's invisible, really, ways. A boy in Demirgian's squad who once killed a real communist in a pineapple patch had been written about in *Newsweek* for that unusual deed. *Our forearms,* a senior editor of *Newsweek* had written—*our forearms [were being] slashed by thorns and our fatigues drenched with sweat. Suddenly—* suddenly a pal of Demirgian's had been a real enemy soldier—*the bullet ripped through the Vietcong's head.* Though his name had been spelled wrong in *Newsweek,* the commie-killing infantryman had been given a hero's due by Demirgian's proud battalion commander, a trip via cargo plane to the China sea, a holiday spree at the beaches—time out, a Coppertone tan, a blanket, sand, a date in a blue bikini, only the brave deserve the fair! Another day, a Red had been made dead by the steady machine gun of Demirgian's best friend—his buddy. His holiday over, Demirgian's friend had returned to the envious squad with his China-sea suntan to learn that he had been recommended for a medal—a Bronze Star and a "V" for valor—in addition, in recognition of that extraordinary act. It wasn't unheard of, Demirgian knew!

RECOMMENDED AWARD OF THE BRONZE STAR MEDAL. *"With complete disregard for his own personal safety and well being -------- moved the machine gun to the forward position of the platoon and began placing accurate fire on enemy positions. His actions are in keeping with the highest traditions of the military service, and. . . ."*

Obligatory words. Kill every communist in China and still you'll get no medal to wear if your company commander's letter of recommendation doesn't say that you've done it with a certain very specific élan. It is Army tradition—if a man's to have a Medal of Honor bestowed upon him a letter of recommendation has to follow form in saying verbatim, "He never relented from his determined effort to destroy the enemy," and Demirgian's best friend is certain to be laughed out of court if the letter in which he has been recommended for a Bronze Star and a "V" for valor leaves it unsaid that he killed his communist in a way that evinced the virtues of aggressiveness, devotion to duty, and bravery, and if it doesn't say, "His actions are in keeping with the highest traditions." All these amenities observed, the letter of recommendation has been given to one of the clerks with the order to send it speedily through the Army's bureau-cratic channels—someone has killed a communist, hurrah!

AWARD OF THE BRONZE STAR MEDAL. *"By direction of the President, under the provisions of the executive order 11046, the Bronze Star Medal is awarded to -------- for outstanding meritorious service as a company clerk in. . . ."*

Fie on that clerk—he has thrown the letter of recommendation away and given the Bronze Star to himself, the stinker! A very latent heterosex-ual, the clerk has a way of walking in the company camp and throwing his soft weight around as though he were keeping a hula-hoop up—a typical Army clerk, and he isn't about to let medals be bestowed on those awful-awful boys in Demirgian's squad who always make fun of his mannerisms by crying at him in the shower tent, "Gentlemen only," or calling to him at bedtime, "Tuck me in?" The clerk has become so wrought up ("Careful," the boys in Demirgian's squad say, "careful, he'll hit you with his purse")—so angry that not in a zillion years will he see a Bronze Star and a "V" for valor hung on any friend of Demirgian's. Instead, the clerk, who every morning, afternoon, and evening has dis-charged his responsibilities in spite of his having a typewriter with a raggedy old typewriter ribbon and a filing cabinet with an army of eek—insects inside, who sometimes even has gone around back of the orderly room to identify a dead soldier's bloody body—ugh, the clerk has simply given a Bronze Star to himself lest the Army let these meritorious achievements go unrecognized. He has written himself a letter of recom-mendation, none of the Army's high-sounding words has he left unsaid, he has signed it with his commander's scratchy signature, and he has wished it Godspeed on the winding road to higher headquarters. One month later the very handsome medal is his.

". . . . Through his untiring efforts and professional ability, he constantly obtained outstanding results. He was quick to grasp the implica-tions of new problems with which he was faced as a result of the ever-changing situation inherent in a counterinsurgency operation and to find ways and means to solve these problems. The energetic application of his extensive knowledge has materially contributed to the efforts of the United States Mission to the Republic of Vietnam to assist that country in ridding itself of the communist threat to its freedom. His initiative, zeal, sound judgment, and devotion to duty have been in the highest traditions of. . . ."

Eleven-thirty. Midnight almost, and Demirgian still hadn't met a communist, a passerby at whom he could fire his bright golden bullet or throw his grenade at and kill.

One click—one kilometer—from the area where the passing hours went by Demirgian's ambush party like a trickle of lukewarm water was Demirgian's company camp, a tight little triangular area of huts and holes in the starlight, a Kipling place. Just outside of these earthworks, the Coke stand, as the soldiers called it, was deserted, of course, it was closed until six o'clock, but that afternoon as Vietnamese small businessmen stood at its shaky wooden tables to give soldiers beer and Coke, to busily pop bottle tops off with rusty openers, to grow a garden of bottle tops in their fatherland's soil, to overcharge, and to shout at their weary customers not to walk off with the empties—that afternoon at the Coke stand something very strange had happened. Sitting drinking a bottle of Vietnamese formaldehydic beer, a soldier in this company had sought to fill up the empty interstices of time by saying one of those two or three formula phrases whose endless iteration passes for conversation at the Coke stand, "Hey mamasan, VC come tonight?" A catechism, but that afternoon instead of her cackling laugh and inveterate answer, "VC no come tonight," the Vietnamese in her clothes of black wrinkled rayon had looked at that soldier scaredly and quietly said, "Yes."

Now, it must be understood that the loud little people who worked at the Coke stand, dirt in each crease of their bodies, teeth the color of cockroaches, the words in their skinny mouths a caterwaul of ugly *ow* sounds—that the Vietnamese were a people whom the customers at the Coke stand had very little respect for, Demirgian, in fact, had even wanted to murder them, at times. Once in his early days in Vietnam he had bought himself an orange pop, he had given the lady a fifty-piastre bill, the Vietnamese had pushed it into the dirty seam of her dress—Demirgian had said quite politely, "Change?" At that, the lady had started to shriek—to *shriek* in the half-hysterical *ow*'s of a dog when there's somebody on its tail, to shriek at Demirgian and the echoing acres that fifty piastres—half an American dollar—was a fair market price for a bottle of pop in Asia. It was seven o'clock in the morning, and Demirgian's ears had become used to the unbroken silence of the ambush party that he had been lying in all that night to guarantee the right of this shrieking lady to engage in private enterprise. It rankled Demirgian to think he had risked life and limb for a race of such ungrateful people as to challenge—in *shrieks*—even his right to refresh himself afterward with a bottle of soda without paying them ten times the wholesale price. He believed that if it was necessary—and it *was*—to twist the Vietnamese lady's arm, to give her a karate chop at the base of her cervical spine, or simply to shoot her in that goddam shrieking skull in order to get change, that he was just angry enough to do this. But he didn't—Demirgian was very tired, anyhow he had left his rifle up against a palm tree ten or fifteen yards away. He didn't murder the Vietnamese lady.

Still, the customers at the Coke stand had precious little use for the counterwomen there. It was "Mamasan, give me Coke" and "Mamasan, you VC?" and "*Di di!*" to the little children who simply crawled in their ears as they crowded around them for C-ration chewing gum or candy—"Go!" the only word of Vietnamese that all American soldiers knew by heart, just as the Coke-stand crowd and prostitutes were the only citizens of Vietnam that any soldier knew on sight. Among the American soldiers it was an article of faith that the longer the Vietnamese war would last the happier the Vietnamese people would be—war to them meant money, even the salmon-size cans of C-rations that the soldiers gave to those screaming children went to their mamasans the same afternoon to sell on the Vietnamese black market ("Or give to the VC," Demirgian used to say). Our allies, our friends in arms—the boys in Demirgian's company didn't think of the Vietnamese people as that, enemies, in fact, is closer to what soldiers thought of the native people, in fact their word for things sold at those rickety tables was "VC beer" or "VC orange pop" or "VC Coke." And these were the boys whose predispositions the mamasan's answer of that strange afternoon had fallen upon: "Hey mamasan, VC come tonight?" "Yes."

No one at the Coke stand had believed her. Someone had wanted to notify the Captain—no! a sergeant had argued, the Captain he hears about this, he gets nervous in the service, he calls a hundred percent alert and who of us here's going to get to sleep? So forget it! And this explains why at eleven-thirty most of those in the dark company camp or Demirgian's little typical ambush party were sound asleep in their camouflage-colored blankets and unaware that a full battalion of communists lay in the blackness in range of Demirgian's peaceful rifle. Any minute now, they would attack.

WHAT DID YOU DO IN THE WAR, DADDY-O? *Five seconds. Four seconds. Three seconds. Two seconds. One—*

A soldier in a lightly starched tan uniform is keeping a close eye on a wall clock that is somewhere about as large as the harvest moon. For a minute now, he hasn't taken a puff on the cigarette that he grips in his motionless fingers, he hasn't spoken a word since he whispered, "Out—out," to a boy so innocent of the circumstances that he had just walked into the quite electronic-looking room.

At zero the soldier's impatient finger taps on a button of green—go! A circle of grey steel rotates, acetate issues, it interrupts the quanta discriminately, electrons are correspondingly let loose, a shower of electromagnetism falls on Vietnam as thoroughly as the monsoon rain—not a blade of grass escapes it. On earth, at a thousand electrical receptors all is reconstituted instantly into the luminous images of Batman and Robin. Holy von Clausewitz, it's the Armed Forces Television Network! Zow!

Nobody had a television set at Demirgian's dark ambush area, and Demirgian was bored—bored. To be sure, the past ten or a dozen minutes had given

Demirgian some sounds that he could attend to—*o-o-o-o-o*, artillery in the black atmosphere, *crump*, when it hits the ground, *ta-ta-ta-ta*, machine guns, the *bang* and *bang* of distant rifles, Demirgian also could look at things—the yellow sky, yellow because of the falling flares, the yellow sky shrinking in and around like a tired tent, a tracer bullet's long arc of red, another. Demirgian sat through this *son et lumière* with no great intellectual curiosity, things in the night were no great surprise to Demirgian, he had become used to them in Vietnam, war is war. He didn't guess that his company camp was under attack by two or three running hundreds of real actual communists, one kilometer away.

This startling news, the sergeant who prayed in Spanish had just heard in soft crackling sentences on the warm rubbery "telephone" receiver of an Army field radio. To this mart soldier, his elbows in the stony soil, the receiver tight to his attentive ear—to this experienced leader of the ambush party the news translated itself into an order of the highest urgency—*nobody should fire!* "Look," he said in a whisper to his radio operator, a PFC, a shadowy mass at his side—"look, we all been cut off. Charlie got the trails going to the company block' now. Is no way that we can penetrate back to the company. We—"

"How about the company?" the radio operator asked him. He knew if the company fell the squad wouldn't have a prayer.

"They are still fighting like good ones. We going to have to stay sweat 'im out. So it will be no fire," the sergeant said—"*it will be no fire unless they attack us.*" One little rifle sound, one little ray of red-orange light, one little grenade explosion and it was clear to this squad leader that the many companies of Charlies in the dark middle distance, advancing, retreating, giving themselves their pep talks, go give 'em hell, comrade, the Charlies would know of their whereabouts at once, not a boy on this lonely detachment would be left alive. A matter of their life and death, and to impress everyone on this perilous ambush party with the strategy of *don't shoot*, the sergeant said to the radio operator that he would crawl on the dark ground ten, twenty, thirty meters to the invisible figures on their left, the radio operator was to crawl to the right—to Demirgian.

Thus, at about midnight, the radio operator, a good-looking guy, a Negro with light skin, thick hair, was doing what was without precedent in his many quiet nights on ambush parties: he was moving. His chest in the cold earth, his knees and elbows going like the claws of crabs, the pebbles going by beneath his stomach, the *o-o-o-o-o*'s going over, the *crump*'s, as the radio operator crawled by the strange shapes of night he was asking himself, *what am I doing this for?* He was on a madman's errand, that was a fact. To tell Demirgian that he must abandon his heart's desire, arrest his every instinct, keep his itchy finger from the trigger of his rifle or the cotter pin of his little grenade no matter how many black presences passed him in the night—this was an act of saintly restraint that a whole heavenly choir of angels couldn't easily urge on that hellcat, easier that a rattlesnake be told to ignore a rat! Moreover, the order of *don't shoot at the enemy* couldn't even be offered for Demirgian's consideration until the Negro radio operator had come within earshot—and rifle shot, it couldn't be delivered to Demirgian until the quietly crawling soldier had made himself a target to Demirgian's wide-awake eyes. *What's with Demirgian?* often the radio operator had asked himself that, any other infantryman could fire a gun at communist areas, pick up the brass, give me a piece of your fruitcake, thanks—a job is a job, didn't have to get *ferocious* about it! But Demirgian! What was Demirgian after, get a holiday at the China Sea? Get a medal for killing a communist? Get a souvenir—a Russian watch or some raggedy wet piastres to buy himself orange pop at the Coke stand with? Demirgian was a real spitfire, the radio operator knew—was it something psychological, perhaps? Had the Irish kids who called him a camel chaser now become sublimated into Asian revolutionaries? Or did Demirgian suffer inferiority feelings, a year in Vietnam in the wilds and woolies and he still hadn't proved himself, he didn't have a scalp to show although other boys did? Or simply, did Demirgian want to get written about in *Newsweek*, that's all? *His forearms were being slashed by thorns, his fatigues were. . . .* Many times the radio operator had asked himself the question:what is Demirgian bugged by, never, though, had he guessed at Demirgian's real secret, he hadn't come close. He had satisfied himself by thinking, *well—Demirgian's an Armenian, that is the answer*. He had seen a show on television about the Gurkhas once, the Gurkhas all swinging a sword and taking a slice at a living breathing ox, a splash, a bucket of blood, an ox head lay on the ground like a rotten melon—a fierce race of people, obviously enough, and Demirgian had Armenian ancestors, Demirgian's family traced itself to the Gurkha part of the world. *That is the answer*, the radio operator had told himself— mistakenly.

He had crawled over the stones to five or ten yards from Demirgian's position—close enough, and he whispered a word in the darkness that he knew would identify him to Demirgian as a bona-fide friend from the Army, no communist. The radio operator whispered, "Demirgian!"

He heard Demirgian answer, "Yeah?"

The radio operator whispered to him, "Don't fire no matter what," and turning a hundred and eighty degrees he quickly crawled back to the dark patch of earth he had started at, where he opened a cold can of C-rations. His favorite kind of C-rats was turkey loaf—it was everybody's, it disappeared from the boxes quickly and tonight he was making do with boneless chicken, at least it wasn't the Spam ham and lima beans: *ugh!* a little wet pillar of salt, a cattle lick. With his G.I. opener in between his thumb and index finger he went to work experiencedly on that chicken can, the opener going as silently and as surely as a knitting needle, the tracer bullets making a *slap—slap—*as they passed above him. The skies were as yellow as Mars's, in the distances yellow smoke rose, at every horizon the heavens and earth seemed to have jarred apart, the yellow bowl of heaven rocked on the dark brown earth and—*boom! boom!* the universe, it seemed, had gone against the rocks, it was breaking up.

The radio operator heard a man whisper, "*What are you doing?*"

He answered truthfully, "Seargeant, when I'm hungry I eat." He buried his empty chicken can in cold earth, and with his little knitting-needle tool he quietly split the circumferences of a pound cake and a fruit cocktail, thinking, *all I need now is vanilla ice cream—mm*, exactly as mother used to make it! The noises continued, *o-o-o-o-o! crump!* For his midnight crawl the radio operator was to get other desserts than C-rats, the Army commendation medal with a "V" for valor ("His actions are in keeping with the finest traditions of the military service . . .").

Demirgian. As for Demirgian, the infantryman *terrible* had given a good minute's thought to the portent of those whispered words, "Don't fire no matter what." He had asked himself, *what is there to fire at? Why are they suddenly telling me this?* Nothing in the night's sound and fury seemed to this veteran of three-hundred-and-something similar ones to be anything other than the usual mutual harassments of Vietnam's hours of darkness, Vietnam was a shooting gallery after dark, it wasn't a place for women or children but it wasn't anything new to Demirgian's ears and eyes. Old soldier Demirgian let himself forget it. Twelve o'clock his long boring hours of being on guard duty had ended, and rolling over in the damp earth he whispered to a sleeping sergeant, "Hey. Wake up," for staying awake was that man's responsibility now. Then as the skies issued sounds like a house of a thousand shutters in a September storm, Demirgian rolled over on his shoulder blades and closing his tired eyes he fell asleep.

MEANWHILE, BACK AT THE CAMP. . . . *Back at Demirgian's triangular camp the Captain is shouting things to his company with his shotgun in one hand and flip-flops on his feet—Vietnamese rubber shower shoes, he hadn't time to dress, a lieutenant is thinking worriedly what's with the mortars? why don't the company mortars fire? the first sergeant is lying wounded, the enemy is fifty—forty—thirty yards away and coming closer. Running to where the mortars are, crying why aren't they being fired, told we are waiting for data, sir, we need to be given our azimuth data, our elevation data, our increment data, our—hearing this, the lieutenant cries one of the inspired cries of the twentieth century, let history record that the lieutenant cried, "The hell with data!" And seizing the mortar tube in his sweating hands he says to start dropping the mortar rounds in—and crump! crump! he levels them on the charging communists. From out of the west come the hoofbeats of water buffalo, the lone lieutenant cries again, the lieutenant says, "The buffalo are coming! And they—" the lieutenant means the enemy soldiers, "they are right behind them," the mortars turn to the water buffalo, the buffalo are turning back! The communists are being buffalo-bumped! But now there is one more mortar round left in that beleaguered camp—no more. The mortarmen kiss it, caress it, slip it into their mortar tube, it exists, the mortar round falls in the midst of America's enemy with a bump, it doesn't go crump! All is quiet on the mortar front! Boo to American industry!*

The communists still keep coming—damn. The camp is frightfully shy of rifle soldiers, some are in Army hospitals, irregular holes in their arms or legs, malaria, gonorrhea, some are on pacification work and Demirgian is fast asleep, the artillery officer is a playboy in Tokyo on a rest and recreation leave, a terror-stricken lieutenant is still in his little cotton tent, his shoes shined, his belt buckle bright with metal polish. Outside of the company camp the barbed wire is absent—orders, we've got to show the Vietnamese we're not a bunch of scaredies, damn! On one whole side of the triangle not a rifle is functioning, double damn—the bullets are stuck inside of them and of the machine guns, too! Boo to Connecticut! Nuts to the Nutmeg State! The communists are coming over the earthen walls now! Are we downhearted? YES! As soon as they've taken the company camp the little abandoned ambush party is next!

And meanwhile Demirgian sleeps through it all (When the bough breaks, the cradle will fall).

The sergeant whose turn at guard duty was from midnight to two o'clock in the morning had been lying flat on his back almost sleeping when Demirgian's tiny whisper of "Hey. Wake up" advanced him to the state of being almost awake. Nor did the Negro sergeant roll to the prone position, to his stomach. The silhouette of a hip, a shoulder going over, an arm—anything, the sergeant had told himself, would be just enough to notify whoever was making all those shooting sounds in the night, the *o-o-o-o-o*'s and the *crump*'s, the *ta-ta-ta-ta*'s like a cold motor, the rifle shots, of his presence on this lonely square yard of earth, and he had stayed flat on his back during his whole tour of guard duty. Inconspicuousness—the secret of one's survival.

He could look at the stars. Years ago, he had become aware that as stars go across the Carolina night they aren't like the wild ducks, the stars aren't shoving themselves one ahead of the other or slipping behind, the star patterns that he thought he saw in the Carolina sky didn't change for hours—for years, and when he had come to Vietnam he was pleased to see that these special relationships one to the other held for that alien land, as well. He looked at these familiar faces now in his motionless hours of standing guard—of his lying on guard, the rocking chair, the cup and the saucer, these are what the sergeant had called his precious constellations.

Low in that friendly sky was the "V" shape of Taurus the bull, to the sergeant this was a part of a spaceship, the nose cone. Orion at this season lay on its side horizontally, its belt became a bandleader's hat to the sergeant's nostalgic eyes, its sword was a celluloid visor—the sergeant remembered the golden braid in its broad figure-eights, the sergeant could even see it! The little silver whistle, the hand on that shiny scepter, a downbeat flat as a fist on a wooden table, *be kind to your web-footed friends!* The sergeant had been a bandleader once—at a high school for Negroes he had played on the drums, the clarinet, the bass and baritone tubas, he hadn't cared to play on the trombone, it didn't ever get to solo, still he liked the guitar the best, really and truly. Tonight while he lay on his back on sentry duty he sang to himself sentimentally, *He took a hundred pounds of clay and He said, Hey listen! I'm goin' to fix this world today because I know what's missin'!* A pretty song—it reminded him of his wife in Scotland Neck, North Carolina.

Being in Vietnam made the sergeant want to sing, a melody held the minutes together in a way that simply twiddling his fingers didn't, time was as thin as skimmed milk if the sergeant didn't fill it with remembered songs. Demirgian he didn't understand at *all,* Demirgian for whom every second patch of elephant grass was enough to make the senses quicken, the eyes become as lively as a chirping bird's, the life forces start to flow, Demirgian who looked for a destructible enemy in every second cranny of every paddy even as the sergeant tried to keep acedia away by singing to himself, *can't get no . . . satisfaction.* "Demirgian. Now take it easy," often the sergeant had to preach patience to Demirgian when the disappointed soldier shot at the pigeons and people's chickens after yet another day of not shooting communists. Demirgian's mysterious vendetta wasn't— well, it wasn't a vendetta even, the sergeant knew. Not a boy in Demirgian's whole platoon had been killed or wounded by *communists* since the first days of Demirgian's tour of duty. Accidents do happen and Demirgian had many friends who weren't alive any longer, still he couldn't fault the communists for something as American in its origins as "I didn't know it was loaded" ways of behavior, this the sergeant appreciated. One of Demirgian's late lamented friends had been scratching his head using a 45 when he had idiotically pulled the trigger, one soldier who didn't have a "church key" to open a can of orange soda at the Coke stand had tried unintelligently with a 50-caliber bullet instead, another had tried to use gasoline to burn up the stuff underneath the latrines and *poof!* he had been burned to death like a Buddhist monk, it wasn't the fault of the Bolsheviks any of those. Seven whole boys (a lieutenant, even) had shot themselves in this or that organ in the course of one particularly ridiculous week, the fault was in themselves and Demirgian wasn't out to get revenge, obviously enough—his ferocity wasn't due to this. *Must be, Demirgian had a brother killed,* the sergeant had told himself: untrue. Demirgian the fire-eating soldier, a mystery to that sergeant lying beside him.

"*I love you,*" the sergeant was thinking now.

"*No, no!*"

"*Yes, I love you. You are more to me than anything in the whole world,*" the line was Lord Darlington's in *Lady Windermere's Fan,* by Oscar Wilde. Who would have guessed as that sergeant lay in his dirty combat clothes on sentry duty, as the *o-o-o-o*'s and the *crump*'s reverberated, and as time itself seemed to condense from the night air to settle all around him as damp as a heavy dew—that the Negro sergeant had once played the Darlington part in his segregated high school's big auditorium, an ascot around his neck, in its center a pearl stickpin, the hints of his acting teacher firm in his senses: say *rawther* instead of *rather,* cup in the right hand and saucer in the left. The line of Wilde's that he remembered most was "Excuse me, you fellows. I have to write a few letters," the sergeant had given it many earnest reprises, the teacher had been in the wings with a copy, whenever the sergeant's half-open mouth had failed to entice one of Darlington's speeches to fill it with apropos sounds he had simply said, "Excuse me, you fellows. . . ."

Uh-oh. A squad of little communists was quietly coming along the trail—the sergeant didn't see it since he hadn't eyes on top of his head, and Demirgian the wistful communist-killer was fast asleep.

A TRAGIC HAP-
PENING. *Bank! Bang! At the company camp the enemy has broken through, a corner of that black triangle is communist-held—a bunker, inside it a couple of Coke bottles, bottle caps, the colorful crumbs of fruitcake, pound cake in a C-ration can, a can that is empty, lids, a couple of comic books, ten or a dozen Playmates, mosquito lotion, the empty brass of Connecticut's bullets—that, and some communist soldiers too. American boys are thowing the last of the hand grenades with a Batman abandon, one soldier not even pausing to pull out the cotter pin. But there come the reinforcements—hurrah! The resupply of ammunition, the high-explosive rounds, the phosphorus, the bullets made in Connecticut by sweet old ladies in steel shoes—the ammo is coming along the trail in a steel tank and bang! it suddenly explodes, the tank, the mighty ammunition too. The communists on their ambush party are luckier on this awful night than Demirgian on his.*

From out of the smoking top of the tank wreck a tank soldier crawls. An officer, his clothes are in terrible shreds, one of his legs is missing, he hasn't one of his arms, instead of his genital organs there is a bleeding hole, the phosphorus has gone through his eyeballs, they are like glowing charcoals—they are like orange "exit" bulbs. From now until dawn he

*will crawl on the scorching steel, then he will fly to Washington for
medical treatment.*

Visions of sugarplums danced in the head of Demir-
gian, the sleeping soldier, months ago he had taken a week's leave in
Bangkok and there wasn't a night that he still didn't think or dream of his
respite from war in that fabulous city—Bangkok, a beautiful story. Three
hours out of Saigon's ridiculous airport, ten thousand planes, the planes in
the treetops almost, the planes sitting one on the other like the grey arrays
at automobile graveyards, the noise, the inconsiderateness, the Vietnamese people—three hours after this and Demirgian had been dining in
quiet luxury in the land of the white elephants, the setting immaculate, a
candle, a low teak table reposing like a tamed lion on a purple rug, a
picture window, a curtain made of tissue-paper flowers as delicate as
moths, and seen through it a garden, the wind was in the palm trees, a star.
Everything in that restaurant in Bangkok had shone, and music as soft as
water running over a bed of pebbles had quietly come to Demirgian
from—where? it had seemed to Demirgian that molecule on molecule of
air just tapped onto one another like little tinkling cat bells, Bangkok! It
had been a real revelation, he had never guessed that the Orient offered
things to the senses other than the sight of running noses, the smell of the
sewage in streets. In this first delightful hour in Bangkok, girls in purple
silk hostess gowns had come to Demirgian smiling adoringly, crawling to
him on their reverential knees with a pitcher of water or wine, apologizing
to Demirgian for entering upon his serenity uninvited, *forgive me for
saying so except* . . . the flowers, the petals of these flowers are meant to
delight the palate as well as the wondering eyes, the petals are a finely
carved chestnut. Crawling to Demirgian, one of these orchid girls had
given him a silver silk bag of Bangkok's perfume, the girl herself whispering thank you—thank you! Never before in Asia had Demirgian heard the
words thank you, even the loud little children that he had left chewing gum
in the grabby little hands of had never said *cam on* in Vietnamese, they
had simply shoved out their other hand. Bangkok had been enchanting, it
didn't smell of deteriorating fish, it had traffic lights, lines in the center of
its wide streets, it seemed that the people of Bangkok *cared,* the
barbers—even the barbers had worn a white doctor's robe and had shaved
off the fluff on Demirgian's eyelids and inside of his ear canals, sending a
small squirt of water in afterward, what a wonderful country! Demirgian
said to some friends of his, "If they had a war here, I'd reenlist if I could
go to Thailand, wouldn't you?"

His friends had said yes. Demirgian had taken this leave (the Army
called it a rest and recreation leave, and every boy in Vietnam whether he
kills an enemy soldier or doesn't has a week of it in his year's tour of
duty)—Demirgian had come to Bangkok with two good friends, the first

was Demirgian's most immediate sergeant, a Botticelli angel boy, a sergeant with a sweet almost watery smile, eyes of calamine blue, the other was Demirgian's friendly lieutenant, the leader of his platoon. A real source of humor this—if Demirgian asked him, "Do you have a match," the lieutenant would say something like, "I don't light a cigarette for a private, *private*," the lieutenant lighting it anyhow, the three of them laughing, friends in Bermudas and sports shirts. After the wine, the chestnut carved like a frangipani flower, the Thai girls with fingers like cattails doing a delicate dance, the music of gentle stringed instruments—after the candlelit dinner the three boys had gone to a nightclub, the sergeant had fallen in love: Keri, the young girl's name. The rest of that wonderful week the three had become a foursome as Keri showed them the bright shining temples of her beloved city, Keri, the friendly lieutenant, Keri's friend the sweet-smiling sergeant, and Demirgian, Demirgian wittily imitating her at every tenth item of interest, "Now this temple is built of marble. It was started in the year a hundred and it took a thousand years to finish. There is a legend . . .", the three of them laughing and Keri laughing too, Keri biting her lower lip so her laughter wouldn't go beyond the bounds of her people's sense of etiquette.

On the seventh day they had visited the Zoo, the monkeys swinging there like Indian clubs, a black arm, a leg, a tail of each spider monkey twisted around the steel trapezes, the graceful, surprisingly, giraffes, the elephants like an Egyptian relief, a row of them standing all looking left, a rope on their enormous legs to orient them in that direction, the elephants rocking side to side as slowly as heavy punkahs on hot afternoons, the trunks of these elephants swinging, the ears slowly moving like old shredded regimental flags—it seemed that these monumental elephants had been standing there through all of Asia's history, swaying side to side. Above the center elephant was a high golden roof—a temple roof, its millions of little sequins the color of old mustard shone in the Bangkok sun, and Keri had said almost reverentially, "This is the King's elephant."

Demirgian had asked her cheerfully, "Which is the Queen's elephant?" and Keri had suddenly turned away looking hurt. "Aw," Demirgian said in embarrassment. "Doesn't the Queen have an elephant?" and Keri got rigidly silent.

"You shouldn't make fun of their king and queen," the soft-spoken sergeant told them.

"I'm not making fun," Demirgian answered honestly. "Which is the King's giraffe?" But every lighthearted thing that Demirgian thought of saying to Keri so she would smile again, Keri just got angrier at, her lips got tighter together, the sergeant got quite apprehensive. "I wish I were a king so I could have an elephant," Demirgian tried—it didn't work, to a Thai there is little one should say of their benevolent king and queen except perhaps hosanna. "Hey," Demirgian said in some despair. "Let's do the dodger cars," and he ran from those difficult elephants to a nearby kind of Playland park—he was already in a miniature blue car, he was driving it every whichway, he was—*crash*—he was crashing it into the native people by the time the surprised others had come walking up. "Everyone let's do *this*," Demirgian drove up shouting to them.

The lieutenant wasn't too terribly sure. "I don't think the Thais are as barbaric as we are, Demirgian," the lieutenant said, the Thais in the other dodger cars had been driving them, in fact, as gingerly as A & P shopping carts, the Thais had been smiling to one another, tipping their hats, in effect, and acting as though they had only learner's permits till Demirgian had charged at them, Demirgian who—*zzzzz*—was suddenly off again in a cloud of concrete dust, the terror of the Thai five hundred, the wheels rising, the tires crying, the side of his steel sports car was *crash! crash!* was crashing on everyone else's, the metal getting dented, the shower of sparks, the Thais in their battered chariots all laughing happily and Keri, at last, laughing, too, Keri having to sit on a bench because of her laughing so hard, the sergeant laughing, the lieutenant laughing and crying, "Go gettem, cat! Go gettem," Demirgian laughing triumphantly, the Grand Prix of Bangkok his.

In the evening they ate at the river, the sunset lay on the temple tops and slivers of orange sunset fell in the silver river and drifted by like goldfish, Keri said to the real catfish, "Here, baby. Here," giving the fish little bits of bread to nibble on. That night Keri slept at the sergeant's hotel, washing him, bringing his towel to him, crying in the morning when he said good-bye, when he promised her, "I will be back," sincerely. At the Saigon airport a little later, the Vietnamese people pushing, the porters not getting the change right, the dirt, the speaker making its static and saying, "*Attention all military personnel . . .*", the holiday plane from Bangkok had scarcely landed when the three soldiers met a Guamanian friend from their own platoon, the lieutenant naturally asking him, "What's new?" Well, in Vietnam it had been another of those stupid weeks, the Guamanian said—Demirgian's best friend, the medal-less communist-killer, had been lying on ambush when he was taken for Charlies and accidently shot in the head by a squad sergeant and, well, the platoon sergeant had been killed one morning at reveille by American artillery, idiotically one of our howitzers had been aimed at his sleeping tent, so it's hi-dee-hee in the field artillery and, of course, the first sergeant, he had been telling guys to police up this, police up that, exactly as some clumsy son-of-a-dumbbell stepped on a detonator and *bang!* as *police up* died on the first sergeant's lips the first sergeant himself had died and also, a company next to theirs, unintentionally it had been bombed by American airplanes, twenty or thirty soldiers had gone to the hospital for napalm burns, another twenty or thirty boys had died and—anyhow, it had been a bad week, the Guamanian had stated, you couldn't really deny it. Demirgian went to buy a hot dog saying to Keri's sergeant, "Vietnam! The cesspool of the universe!"

"The cesspool of the universe," the sergeant repeated—he was shaking uncontrollably now, he had started doing this as the Guamanian gave his report. He was still acting strange the next afternoon ("He looked like he was underwater," a boy remembered)—the next afternoon when he got to his quarters: the company camp, a dark canvas tent, a long row of cots, a couple of Vietnamese laundry boys on one of them, sitting, looking at dirty photographs of ways of making love, and saying things in English like "Fucky-fucky," laughing, showing their wide red mouths. Putting one of Connecticut's bright bullets in his rifle chamber, *click! click!* the sergeant said, "I'm going to do some hunting."

"I hope you'll do your hunting out yonder," the soldier who owned the photographs said to him uneasily.

"I can do my hunting right here," the sergeant replied. Once he had killed the Vietnamese laundry boys he was taken away in handcuffs and court-martialed. Now the sergeant is serving a life sentence at Leavenworth, the Negro who looked at constellations and sang *can't get no . . . satisfaction* taking his place as Demirgian's sergeant.

A QUESTION FROM THE COURT. "*Were these dirty pictures of American women?*"

"*They were just some old dirty pictures you buy around.*" The witness is the soldier who owned them.

"*Were there oriental women in them? Or were they caucasian— white—women?*"

"*Oriental.*"

"*Pictures of oriental women?*"

"*Yes sir.*"

"*Were there dirty pictures of oriental men or caucasian men?*"

"*Oriental men. They had masks on, some of them.*"

"*The dirty pictures consisted of both oriental men and oriental women?*"

"*Yes sir.*"

"*There were no white women in those pictures?*"

"*No sir.*"

A CROSS-EXAMINATION BY THE DEFENSE. "*You say that these pictures were of oriental women—right?*"

"*Yes sir.*"

"*Now here you say that the men had on masks?*"

"*Yes sir.*"

"*How do you know whether they were oriental or caucasian?*"

"*They all looked like the same man, sir.*"

"*But if a man had on a mask, how would you know?*"

"Well, he didn't look American, sir."
"What didn't look American?"
"The man. There was something about him that was oriental."
"I repeat my question. What didn't look American?"
"The whole bunch! The pictures! They weren't American."
A PART OF THE DEFENSE'S SUMMATION. *"He goes to his tent to get ready to go to the field—to pick up his equipment. After entering he sees the two Vietnamese for whom he has no love or trust, sitting on the bunks, talking, laughing, and enjoying themselves. He explains to himself, why should he fight in their country on their behalf and risk his life for these people while they perform menial tasks at the base camp in the relative safety of the base camp. As he gathers his equipment perhaps he thinks about this. Maybe he becomes angry. . . ."*
A part of the prosecution's summation. *". . . Well, okay, he disliked the Vietnamese, fine. That's up to an individual. If he wants to hate the Vietnamese, fine! But putting his hatred in action by killing is not quite correct."*

"Huh?" Demirgian said.

The other boys in the ambush party had waked up Demirgian an hour before dawn and related to him what great alarms and excursions there had been while God had His guardian angels over him—the company camp had been attacked, a corner taken, a tank carrying ammo had been blown to kingdom come, a second tank had gotten into the triangle, *tarantara*, the tide of war turning, communists withdrawing, company enduring, hurrah! Not a boy in Demirgian's sturdy army had been killed by those two or three or four hundred communists (one had been killed by accident by a friend of his, nothing more)—a very great victory for America. By the wet yellow light of the flares, Demirgian could now glimpse some of the forty or fifty communist dead, the easy victims of American artillery and of six-barreled machine guns on American planes, fat fire-breathing planes that the soldiers had given the sobriquet of Puff the magic dragon (. . . *lived by the sea,* the Negro sergeant had sung to himself at one o'clock in the morning, the magic dragon's rain of red tracer bullets lighting the night with a pillar of fire—*lived by the sea, and frolicked in the autumn mist in a land of Honah Lee*).

Good soldiers all, nobody in the ambush party had shot at that communist squad when it innocently went by, the silver starlight above it, behind it, the final score had been nothing to nothing, the ambush party, the communists. Demirgian got to his heavy feet, the bullet still in Demirgian's dew-dappled rifle like a disappointed suitor, the hand grenades still on Demirgian's belt, mud in the crack of their cotter pins, dew. *Damn, but I would have fired at them,* Demirgian said to himself angrily while he walked back to camp, while he passed the dead communist soldiers who were lying simply everywhere, kicking them—*damn, I'd have thrown a grenade, at LEAST!* At times in the humdrum months of his tour, Demirgian had walked by the Coke stand waiting until—waiting until—the moment that he felt a little hand at his wallet pocket he had whirled around and given the thievish child the kicking that he well deserved, now he was kicking the communist soldiers every bit as hard and shouting at their unlistening ears, "Wake up, you sorry bastard—you stupid bastard—you goddam bastard! Wake up!"

"Hey, Demirgian," somebody said to him, laughing. "They're already dead."

"Wake up, you silly bastard," Demirgian said to a dead communist, kicking.

"Demirgian," the Negro radio operator said to him softly. "Don't do that."

"What do you mean don't do that?" Demirgian asked.

"Don't do that," the Negro radio operator said. He didn't like to see brutality, the radio operator—once he had been in a street gang, he was twelve years old, at a gas station he had gotten himself in a fight with the white-colored kids. It had been simply sticks till a two-tone automobile had driven by, a Negro, he was a boy of twenty, perhaps, had gotten out of that great automobile, he had squatted on the chest of one white boy, he had raised up a concrete block and—*down,* the boy's white face had broken apart like a bag of blood, the fight had stopped immediately. Running, everyone running, the Negro radio operator running, a fruit cart had toppled over, the grapes had rolled after him like little bloodshot eyeballs, running, falling, the dirty red blood on his elbows, after the Negro child reached home he had prayed all night, "Oh, Lord! Don't let him die!" Since then the Negro radio operator had disliked to see brutality—yet, he thought, how could there be brutality if the communists felt no pain, if the sufferers were already dead, if the bodies lay every random way as though they had fallen from airplanes, Demirgian kicking, calling them dirty bastards, mud of his boots spattering on the yellow faces, the skin of the faces shivering like raindrops on mud—uncomfortably, the radio operator walking away as Demirgian still kicked at them and called to them, "Wake up!" But none of the communist soldiers woke up.

One of the communist soldiers woke up! He looked at Demirgian slowly through one of his eyes, an eye like a twist of lemon rind, an oily eye! He moved one of his bloody arms! A living breathing communist, a boy of about eighteen, a Vietnamese in black, Demirgian brought down his foot on his face and *crunch,* Demirgian felt his little nose go like a macaroon, he said to the communist, "Bastard—well, was it worth it," kicking him in his eyeballs. "Stupid bastard—what did it get you," kicking him on his Adam's apple. "Goddam bastard. . . ."

DEMIRGIAN'S

SECRET. *Demirgian hates the Vietnamese people—well, so does every soldier, but Demirgian hates and hates! The goddam bastards! Goddam people! Come to help their miserable country and what? Anyone get a word of thanks? Dead or alive—crippled, I could be blind, a basket case and they wouldn't care, not if they'd had my damn piastres first! Money is all they'd care, the crooked bastards! Give me—give me—that's the extent of it, give 'em a stick of soap, though, do you suppose they'd use it, the filthy people? No—they'd sell it, the filthy bastards! Nya nya nasal language, they sound like they've got their tongue up their nose, the ugly bastards! Faces like wet brown prunes, teeth the color of coffee grounds, mouths like a hole in the kitchen sink—the breath of a garbage bag, I bet, I expect to see ants start crawling out! They're ignorant people—dumb! A lady I saw took a bottle of metal polish what do you think for? It says on the label "fatal" and I don't really recommend it for teeth—but I should give a good goddam! Let her kill herself, I should care! They're worthless people!*

A really and truly detestable race of people. Demirgian's year of duty among the Vietnamese had taught him to loathe them, the earth and Demirgian would be better rid of them, Vietnamese go to your damnable ancestors, die! Demirgian wants to kill communists because they're the only native people the Army's regulations allow him to kill.

". . . Goddam bastard, stupid bastard, dumb bastard, thought you were better than us Americans, didn't you? Ignorant bastard," Demirgian said and he kicked at that black bag of bones until it had given a consummation to Demirgian's tour of duty and a success to Demirgian's quest by quietly becoming dead. Congratulations, Demirgian's foot! For it hadn't been by Connecticut's fancily manufactured bullets that he had achieved his heart's desire, Demirgian had become a communist-killer by force of foot alone— Agnes' dustpan hadn't been necessary, David's leather mallet neither, America could have saved itself money, each of those bullets was costing it ten cents. "Sorry about that," Demirgian said to the lifeless body, and he continued on toward camp by the dawn's early light, a Russian watch in his pants pocket—a souvenir.

Like a great headache going, a pressure on the ears relieved, the black of night receded into the skies and a pink sunrise came to that company camp, the tents became green, not grey, the brass of Connecticut's bullets lay on the earth like little bright buttercups. A couple of tired soldiers went to police the bodies up, another was at the wash basin brushing his teeth, spitting the pink water into the Vietnamese mud, a toe slowly turning it under and stirring the liquidy pink and brown, washing, drying himself, his olive-colored towel wet with the morning dew, another was having coffee from a grey aluminum cup, the gritty metallic taste of aluminum oxide on his tongue, nails in a carpenter's mouth. It was morning and each soldier said to himself *so-and-so-many days,* each was a day nearer to getting out of that abominated country. Six o'clock at the Coke stand it was business as usual, the Vietnamese women with their betel-black teeth, the raggedy tan piastre notes, the sticky yellow dribbles of paint on the soda bottles so soldiers wouldn't want to take the empties away, the price of four times the wholesale price, the heat, the children on the tired soldiers saying *give me—give me—*and saying dirty words if they didn't get given, a Vietnamese shouting at the tired soldiers, *"Ong da ban chet . . ."*, the mortar rounds had wounded one of his water buffalo, he wanted compensation. "Well," Demirgian said to another soldier, "I finally killed me a gook," and Demirgian smiled satisfiedly, Demirgian's soul was at peace, Demirgian, a little later, had started back to the country in whose interests he had been posted to Asia, to his green gabled home in Newton, to the sign in the living room *welcome home* in red, white, and blue! Safe and sound, Demirgian came marching home again! Let's give him a hearty welcome then! Hurrah! Hurrah!

[January, 1968]

Hell Sucks

by Michael Herr

There is a map of Vietnam on the wall of my apartment in Saigon, and some nights, coming back late to the city, I'll lie out on my bed and look at it, too tired to do anything more than just get my boots off. The map is a marvel, especially absorbing because it is not real. For one thing, it is very old. It was left here years ago by a previous tenant, probably a Frenchman since the map was made in Paris. The paper has buckled, and much of the color has gone out of it, laying a kind of veil over the countries it depicts. Vietnam is divided into its older territories of Tonkin, Annam and Cochin China, and to the west, past Laos and Cambodge, sits Siam, a kingdom. That's old, I told the General. That's a really old map.

The General is drawn to it too, and whenever he stops by for a drink he'll regard it silently, undoubtedly noting inaccuracies which the maps available to him have corrected. The waters that wash around my Indochine are a placid, Disney blue, unlike the intense, metallic blues of the General's maps. But all of that aside, we both agree to the obsolescence of my map, to the final unreality of it. We know that for years now, there has been no country here but the war. The landscape has been converted to terrain, the geography broken down into its more useful components;

corps and zones, tactical areas of responsibility, vicinities of operation, outposts, positions, objectives, fields of fire. The weather of Vietnam has been translated into conditions, and it's gone very much the same way with the people, the population, many of whom can't realize that there is an alternative to war because war is all they have ever known. Bad luck for them, the General says. As well as he knows them (and he knows them well), he seldom talks about them except to praise "their complexity, their sophistication, their survivability." Endearing traits.

Everyone is terribly sorry about what the war is doing to Vietnam and the Vietnamese, especially since the cities have been brought into it, although somehow most of the official expressions of grief have about them that taint of Presidential sorrow, turning a little grinny around the edges. The Tet Offensive changed everything here, made this an entirely different war, made it Something Else. ("Nonsense," a colonel told me. "We're just doing the same things in the cities that we've done in the boonies, why . . . for *years*!" He was not the same man who said, "We had to destroy Bentre in order to save it," but he might have been. He'd be hip to that.) Before Tet, there was some clean touch to jungle encounters, some virtue to their brevity, always the promise of quick release from whatever horror there was. The war went on in bursts, meeting engagements; and covering it—particularly in the Highlands and the Delta, II Corps and IV Corps—you were always a tourist, a tripper who could summon up helicopters like taxis. You would taxi in, the war would break over you suddenly and then go away, and you would taxi out. Enough chances were taken to leave you exhilarated, and, except for the hangovers that any cheap thrill will give you, it was pleasant enough. Now, it is awful, just plain awful, awful without relief. (A friend on The New York *Times* told me that he didn't mind his nightmares so much as his waking impulse to file on them.) It has finally become that kind of conventional war that the Command so longed for, and it is not going well. And for every month that it continues not going well, the scope of its destruction is enlarged. We are not really a particularly brutal people, certainly no more brutal now than we've been in other wars, acquiring it as the war goes on. But our machine is devastating. And versatile. It can do almost everything but stop.

And after all these years, we were caught in midwinter with the blunt truth that our achievement in Vietnam had been less than epic, a fact that touched everyone but the men who run the war. It became finally clear that General Westmoreland did not understand this war ("This is a different war than Americans have ever been asked to fight," he told the Examining Angels. "How is it different?" they asked. "Well, you know, it's just . . . different"), and he was asked to leave it. The immediate official response was manic; after years and years of posing along the rim, the Mission joined hands and leapt through the Looking Glass. It was as though Swift's vault had been plundered to meet the public doubt. They trotted out their kill ratios, their curious estimates of enemy morale (there wasn't any), their poor, salvaged shards of Pacification (that good American idea; it would have worked wonderfully in New Mexico), strange redemption profiles of the countryside's lost security. The same incantations, the heavies, moderates and lights of this statistic-obsessed war, were sung again, and optimism was spent at the same excessive rate which we had previously maintained in the expending of ordnance. This antic Thumbs-Upmanship was best pegged by a British correspondent who compared it all to the captain of the *Titanic* accouncing, "There's nothing to be alarmed about, ladies and gentlemen. We're only stopping briefly to take on some ice." And I remembered an Indian lady I once knew who shipped a trunk to her family in Calcutta. She had lost the key but found another, the key to one of her closets, and she mailed that on after the trunk. She knew it wouldn't open the trunk, but she so wanted it to work that she sent it anyway. Strange story, but I expect it might touch our Ambassador, and possibly even our former Commanding General.

When the battle for Hué was all over, they entered it into the records, gauged its terrible cost and battlegrammed it, so that it took on the dry, tactical stamp of the West Point Atlas of American Wars. When future observers come to it, it will seem that some order had been apparent during the twenty-seven days that it took to get the North Vietnamese and Vietcong forces out of the Imperial City, and that will not be exactly the truth. Hué was not the bloodiest battle of the Vietnam war (unless you enter in the more than four thousand civilian dead and the tens of thousands who were wounded, not likely in any forthcoming revised edition of the W.P.A.O.A.W.), but it was the hardest and the bitterest, and for those of us who were a part of it, even the coldest chronicles will be enough to recall the texture of its dread. If the war was changing, Hué was that turn of the screw which locked the new terms into place for good, taking you beyond that cutoff point where one war becomes just like all other wars. You would get twinges of this feeling any time that you were on the line, with the troops; but still, before Hué, you thought of yourself as a dove or a hawk, felt that our involvement was criminal or proper, obscene or clean. After Hué, all of your lines of reasoning turned into clumsy coils, and all of the talk got on your nerves. Hué finally gave you what you had expected, half yearned for, in the days of the war that ended with the Offensive. It got up memories, vicarious enough, stored from old copies of *Life* magazine, old movie newsreels, Pathé sound tracks whose dirge-disaster music still echoed: the Italian Campaign, the fight for the Reservoir, gruesome camp, evocations of '44 and '50.

Going in, there were sixty of us packed in a deuce-and-a-half, one of eight trucks moving in convoy from Phubai, bringing in over three hundred replacements for the casualties taken in the earliest fighting south of the Perfume River. There had been a harsh, dark storm going on for days, and it turned the convoy route into a mud bed. It was terribly cold in the trucks, and the road was covered with leaves that had either been blown off the trees by the storm or torn away by our heavy artillery. The artillery had done a job here, touched everything. Many of the houses had been completely collapsed, and not one had been left without at least heavy pitting from shell fragments. Hundreds of refugees held to the side of the road as we passed. Many of them had been wounded during the shelling. The kids would laugh and shout the standard, "You you you! Okay?" The old would look on with that quiet tolerance for misery that makes so many Americans uneasy, which is usually misread as indifference. But the younger men and women would often give us looks of unmistakable contempt, pulling their cheering children back from the trucks.

So we sat there, grinning at the bad weather and the discomfort, sharing the first fear, glad that we were not riding point or closing the rear because, man, the middle is good. They had been hitting our convoys regularly, and a lot of the trucks had been turned back. The houses that we were passing so slowly made the best kind of cover for snipers, and one B-40 rocket could have made casualties out of a whole truckload of us. All the Grunts were whistling and no two were whistling the same tune, and it sounded like a locker room just before a big game. A friend of mine, Sergeant Dale Dye, a Marine correspondent, sat with a tall yellow flower sticking out of his helmet cover, a really outstanding target, the kind of idiosyncracy the Marines will indulge in. His eyes rollicked, and below his big moustache his wicked, shy smile said, "Oh yes, Charlie's got his shit together here, this will be oh-so-bad, indubitably." It was the same smile I saw later when a sniper's bullet tore up the wall two inches above his head inside the Citadel. Odd cause for merriment in anyone but a Grunt.

There's something you see in the faces of Marines that you'll never see in the Army, some extra character etched in by the training and by more hard times than you'd believe, by constant intimidation, by the widespread conviction that you will get yours if you hang in there long enough. They're each of them like the hardest man on the block (You ain't been cut, you ain't my man) and they all have that wild, haunted, going-West look that says it is perfectly correct to be here where the fighting is worst, where you won't have half of what you'll need, where it is colder than the Nam ever gets. To pass the time, I started reading the stuff they'd written on their helmet covers and flak jackets. There were the names of campaigns and the names of their girls, nicknames (The Entertainer, The Avenger, Short Time Safety Moe), the slogans that touch on their lonely, severe fantasies (Born to Lose, Born to Raise Hell), and general graffiti (Hell Sucks, Time is On My Side, Yossarian Lives, Just You and Me God—Right?). There was nothing on the truck as good as the scrawl on the wall in Khesanh that said, "I Think I'm Falling In Love With Jake," but it passed the time.

And they are all giving you that mock-astonished look. "You mean you don't *have* to be here? And you're *here?*" But they are glad you're here, really very grateful. "Hey, Esquire! Hey, you want a story, man? Write this: I'm up there on 881, this was May, I'm up there walkin' the ridgeline an' this Zip jumps up smack into me, lays this AK-47 fuckin' right *into* me, only he's so surprised I got my whole clip off 'fore he knew how to thank me for it. Grease one." After twenty kilometers of this, in spite of the roiling dark sky ahead, we could see the smoke coming up from the far side of the river, from the Citadel of Hué.

The bridge was down that spanned the canal dividing the village of An Cu and the southern sector of Hué, blown the night before by the Vietcong, and the forward area beyond the opposite bank was not thought to be secure, so we bivouacked in the village for the night. It had been completely deserted, and we set ourselves up in empty hootches, laying our poncho liners out over the litter of shattered glass and brick. At dusk, while we were all stretched out along the canal bank eating dinner, two Marine gunships came down on us, strafing us, sending burning tracers up along the canal, and we ran for cover, more astonished than scared. "Way to go, mother-lover, way to pinpoint the motherin' enemy," one of the Grunts screamed, and he set up his M-60 machine gun in case they came back. "I don't guess we gotta take *that* shit." Patrols were sent out, guards posted, and we went to the hootches to sleep. For some reason, we were not even mortared that night.

The next morning we knew that the area must have been secured beyond a reasonable doubt, because the A.R.V.N. were there. Good little fighters, the A.R.V.N.; ask any U.S. adviser in the field. Most of them here were not even armed. They needed both hands free for their work that morning, which consisted of thoroughly combing every house and store in the village, turning out drawers, tipping over chests and urns, raiding chicken coops and liquor cabinets, kicking in all the glass cases they could find, and forcibly relieving refugees on the road of radios, wine, ducks, clothing, anything. What they couldn't carry, they wore. One soldier moved up the road in an old felt hat that fell down over his eyes and a blue gabardine overcoat at least eight sizes too large, so that it trailed around him in the mud as he walked. I thought he was going to ask me the way to Floogle Street, but he only smiled proudly at his good luck and ducked into one of the shops.

It was the same after we'd crossed the canal on a two-by-four and started walking in. We tried to flag down a lift, but the jeeps all seemed to be driven by A.R.V.N. officers out on organized looting parties. We walked along in the open toward the river, talking in an offhanded way about how superb the N.V.A. snipers were supposed to be, until we came across the very first of the hundreds of civilian dead that we were to see in the next weeks: a little girl who had been hit while riding her bicycle and an old man who lay arched over his straw hat. They'd been lying out like that for over a week, and for the first time I was grateful for the cold.

Along the Perfume River's south bank there is a long, graceful park that separates Hué's most pleasant avenue, Le Loi, from the riverfront. People will talk about how they'd sit out there in the sun and watch the sampans moving down the river, or watch the girls bicycling up Le Loi, past the villas of officials and the French-architected university buildings. Many of those villas had been destroyed and much of the university permanently damaged. In the middle of the street a couple of ambulances from the German Mission had been blown up, and the Cercle Sportif was covered with bullet holes and shrapnel. In the park itself, four fat green dead lay sprawled around a tall, ornate cage, inside of which sat a small, shivering monkey. One of the correspondents along stepped over the corpses to feed it some fruit. (Days later, I came back to the spot. The corpses were gone, but so was the monkey. There had been so many refugees and so little food then, and someone must have eaten him.) The Marines of 2/5 had secured almost all of the central south bank and were now fanning out to the west, fighting and clearing one of the major canals. We were waiting for some decision on whether or not U.S. Marines would be going into the Citadel itself, but no one had any doubts about what that decision would be. Didn't it always come to that with the Grunts? Didn't it, every goddam time? We sat there taking in the dread by watching the columns of smoke across the river, receiving occasional sniper rounds, infrequent bursts of .50 caliber, watching the Navy L.C.U.'s on the river getting shelled from the wall. One Marine next to me was saying that it was just a damned shame, all them poor people, all them nice-looking houses. He was looking at the black napalm blasts and the wreckage along the wall. "Looks like the Imperial City's had the schnitz," he said.

It stayed cold for the next ten days, cold and dark, and that damp gloom was the background for the footage that we all took out of the Citadel. The little sunlight there was caught the heavy motes of dust that blew up from the wreckage of the East Wall, held it until everything you saw was filtered through it. And most of what you saw was taken in from unaccustomed angles, prone positions or quick looks from a crouch; lying flat out, hearing the hard dry rattle of shrapnel scudding against the debris around you, listening to the Marine next to you who didn't moan, "Oh my God, Oh Sweet Jesus, Oh Holy Mother save me," but who sobbed, instead, "Are you *ready* for this? I mean, are you *ready* for this?" Once, when the noise from a six-round mortar attack stopped, I heard some singing in back of me. There were three Grunts huddled together holding onto their helmets, looking more mischievous than scared. "We gotta get out of this place," they sang, "if it's the las' thing we ever do-woo." With all of that dust blowing around, the acrid smell of gunpowder would hang in the air for a long while after fire fights, and there was also some CS gas that we'd fired at the N.V.A. blowing back in over our positions. It was impossible to get off a clean breath with all of that going on, and of course there was that other smell too, that most special of all smells that came up from shallow graves and from shattered heaps of stone wherever an air strike had passed. It held to the lining of your nostrils and worked itself into the weave of your fatigues, and weeks later, miles away, you would wake up from a dream in the middle of the night and it would be there in the room with you. The N.V.A. had dug themselves so deeply into the wall that air strikes had to destroy it meter by meter, dropping napalm as close as three hundred meters from our positions. Up on the highest point of the wall, on what had once been a tower, I looked across the Citadel's moat and saw the N.V.A. moving quickly among the rubble of the opposing wall. We were close enough to be able to see their faces. A rifle went off a few feet to my right, and one of the figures across the moat started forward and then dropped. A Marine sniper leaned back from his cover and grinned at me.

By the end of that week, the wall had cost the Marines roughly one casualty for every meter taken, a quarter of them K.I.A. 1/5, which came to be known as the Citadel Battalion, had been through every tough battle the Marines had had in the past six months, and now some of its companies were down to below platoon strength. They all knew how bad it was, the novelty of fighting in the streets had become a nasty, spooky joke, and not many of them really believed they'd ever get out alive. Everyone wanted to get wounded.

There was a tough, quiet Negro who called himself Philly Dog. He'd been a gang lord in the streets of North Philadelphia, and in Hué he was the best man to be with, the only one who really understood how it was when you had no cover and no rear. He was better here than the hottest jungle fighter, better than those lean, mean Nam veterans with their proficiency badges for coaxing water out of palm roots, filleting snakes and reading moss. Philly Dog was the only scout you could feel right about in Hué.

"Just hold onto it, man," he'd say. "You doan go out there. That's Charlie." He pointed up the road.

We were in among the makings of a former villa, with only the rear wall still standing. I couldn't see anything up the road past one of our tanks, only a few houses, scattered trees and wires and a gigantic portion of collapsed wall.

"How do you know?" I asked.

" 'Cause if I was Charlie, that'd be my spot." And he was right, almost every time.

At night, in the battalion C.P., the Major in command would sit reading his maps, staring vacantly at the trapezoid of the Citadel. It could have been a scene in a Norman farmhouse twenty-five years ago, with candles burning on the tables, bottles of red wine arranged along damaged shelves, the cold in the room, the high ceilings, the heavy ornate cross on the wall. The Major had not slept for five nights, and for the fifth night in a row he assured us that tomorrow would get it for sure, the final stretch of the wall would be taken, and he had all the Marines he needed to do it. And one of his aides, a tough mustang of a first lieutenant, would pitch a hard, ironic smile above the Major's stare, a smile that rejected good news and opted for doom, and it was like hearing him say, "The Major here is full of shit, and we both know it."

We found a villa near the C.P. and set ourselves up in it for the night. We never stayed in the same area two nights in a row, since it never took the N.V.A. very long to get us zeroed in. In the living room of the villa there were photographs of a Vietnamese family that had been taken in the States; the father in a dark business suit standing somewhere in New York; Mom, Dad and the kids at Disneyland. The Grunts could never get over the fact that there were wealthy Vietnamese, and these pictures filled them with awe. Dale Dye was there (after the sniper had barely missed him, he had gotten rid of that flower), and some of the guys had found a bottle of Veuve Cliquot. Usually they'd scarfe up the 7 Crown or the Calvert's and leave four-star cognacs sitting on the shelves, but the champagne intrigued them. Most of them had never tasted it. One tall kid was saying that where he came from, it only got poured at weddings. Dye popped the cork, and one of them went chasing after it, giggling at how gala this was getting to be. Dye passed the bottle to the tall boy, who put it to his lips as if it might go off before drinking it. "It tickles m'nose," he said, and Dye broke up, shaking his head. "It's a good champagne," he said. "Not a great champagne, but a good champagne."

We slept so soundly that night that a sixty-round mortar barrage a little before dawn failed to wake us.

After the Catholic chaplain was killed, the Protestant had to give communion. His name was Takesian, an Armenian from Boston, one of those hip, blunt clerics who loved to talk, as though talking itself contained ritual powers of redemption. He wasn't one of your grizzled battle chaplians, but he was very brave, and very much affected by the particular ugliness of the Hué fighting. It was not physical fear that put him off, but the mood of bitterness that no one seemed to be able to shake, and he would sit for long stretches by himself, staring at the wounded through his thick steel-rimmed glasses. He was using sliced C-ration white bread and canteen water to deliver the sacramants, and some of the Grunts were skeptical about receiving them from a Protestant. "Listen, you silly bastards," Takesian said. "You could all get your ass shot off any time now out there. Do you think God gives a damn *how* you've been blessed?"

Sometimes one of the companies would find itself completely cut off, and it would take hours for the Marines to get their casualties out. I remember one Marine with a head wound who finally made it up to the Battalion C.P., only to find himself stuck in a stalled jeep. He finally jumped out of the jeep and started to push it, knowing it was the only way out of there. Most of the tanks and trucks which carried casualties had to move up a long, straight road with no cover, and they began calling it Rocket Alley. Every tank the Marines had had been hit at least once there. An epiphany of Hué turned up in John Olson's great photograph in *Life,* the wounded from Delta Company piled hurriedly on the tank. Sometimes, on the way out to the Battalion Aid Station, the more seriously wounded would take on that bad color, the grey-blue fishbelly promise of death that would spread upwards from the chest and cover the face. There was one Marine who had been shot through the neck, and all the way out the corpsmen massaged his chest. By the time they reached the station, though, he was so bad that the doctor triaged him, passed him over to treat the ones that he knew could be saved, and when they put him into the green canvas body bag there was some chance that he was still clinically alive. The doctor had never been in a position before where he had had to choose like that—there were so many wounded—and he never got used to it. During the lulls, he'd step outside for some air, but it was no better out there. The bodies were stacked together, and there was always a crowd of A.R.V.N. standing around staring, death-enthralled like all Vietnamese. Since they did not know what else to do, and not knowing how it would look to the Marines, they would smile vacantly at the bodies there, and a couple of ugly incidents occurred. The Marines who had volunteered for the body details were overworked and became snappish, ripping packs off of corpses angrily, cutting gear away with bayonets, heaving bodies into the green bags. One of the dead Marines had become stiff and they had trouble getting him to fit. "Damn," one of them said, "didn't this mother have big feet on him?" And he finally forced the legs into the canvas. In the station, there was the youngest-looking Marine I'd ever seen, so young that his parents must have had to sign for him at enlistment. He'd been caught in the knee by a large piece of shrapnel, and he had no idea at all of what they would do with him now that he'd been wounded. He lay out on the stretcher while the doctor explained how he would be choppered back to the Phubai hospital and then put on a plane for Danang, and then flown back to the States for what would probably be the rest of his hitch. At first the boy was sure that the doctor was kidding him, then he started to believe a little of it, and when he knew that it was true, that he was actually getting out, he couldn't stop smiling, and enormous tears of happiness ran down into his ears.

It was at this point that I began to recognize almost every casualty, remember conversations we'd had days and even hours earlier, and that's when I got out, riding a Medevac chopper with a lieutenant who was covered with blood-soaked bandages. He'd been hit in both legs, both arms, the chest and head, his ears were filled with caked blood, and he asked a photographer named Art Greenspon who was in the chopper if he'd get a picture of him like this so he could mail it to his wife.

But at this point, the battle for Hué was almost over. The Cav was working the northwest corner of the Citadel, and elements of the 101st had come in through what had formerly been an N.V.A. resupply route. Vietnamese Marines and some of the 1st A.R.V.N. Division, who had fought well from the beginning, had been moving the remaining N.V.A. down toward the wall. The N.V.A. flag that had flown for so long over the South Wall had been brought down, and in its place an American flag had been put up, a sight which must have thrilled those most xenophobic of all Vietnamese, the people of Hué. Two days later the Hoc Bao, Vietnamese Rangers for whom this privilege had been reserved, stormed through the walls of the Imperial Palace, but there were no enemy troops left inside. Except for a few corpses that bobbed sluggishly in the moat, most of the dead had been buried. Nearly seventy percent of Vietnam's one lovely city was destroyed, and if the landscape seemed desolate, imagine how the figures in that landscape looked.

There were two official ceremonies marking the expulsion of the N.V.A., both flag raisings. On the south bank of the Perfume River, two hundred refugees from one of the camps were recruited to stand in the rain and watch the G.V.N. flag being run up. But the rope snapped, and the crowd, thinking the V.C. had shot it down, broke up in panic. (There was no rain in the stories that the Saigon papers ran, there was no trouble with the rope, and the cheering crowd numbered thousands.) As for the other ceremony, the Citadel was still thought by most people to be insecure, and when the flag finally went up there was no one there to watch it except a handful of Vietnamese troops.

In the first weeks after the Tet Offensive began, the curfew began early in the afternoon, and was strictly enforced. By two-thirty each day Saigon had the look of the final reel of *On the Beach,* a desolate city whose long avenues held nothing but refuse, windblown papers, small, distinct piles of human excrement and the dead flowers and spent firecracker casings of the Lunar New Year. Alive, Saigon had been depressing enough, but once the Offensive began it became so stark that, in an odd way, it was invigorating. The trees along the main streets all looked like they'd been struck by lightning, and it became unusually, uncomfortably cold; one more piece of bad luck in a place where nothing was in its season. With so much filth growing in so many streets and alleys, an epidemic of plague was feared, and if there was ever a place that suggested plague, demanded it, it was Saigon in the Emergency. Large numbers of American civilians, the construction workers and engineers who were making it here like they'd never made it at home, began openly carrying weapons, 45's and grease guns and AK's, and no mob of Mississippi sheriff's boys ever promised more bad news. You'd see them at ten in the morning on the terrace of the Continental Hotel, waiting for the bar to open, unable to light their own cigarettes until it did. The crowds on Tu Do Street looked like Ensor processions, and there was a corruption in the air that had nothing to do with government officials on the take. After seven in the evening, when the curfew became total, nothing but police vehicles and M.P. jeeps moved in the streets, except for a few very young children who raced up and down over the rubbish, running newspaper kites up into the chilling wind. Shortly after dark, I could expect to see the headlights of the General's jeep coming up the street toward my apartment.

The General is a great favorite of the press here. He is commonly thought to be candid, articulate and accessible, which is absolutely the highest compliment the press corps can pay to any member of the American Mission. He is less accessible now that the war has begun to go badly, but he still finds time most nights to drop around for a quick drink, before returning to his headquarters and, I imagine, a late night's work. I have never really understood our growing friendship, since there is not a single point touching the war that we agree on. It is thought by outsiders that the General and I spend our evenings playing chess, but in fact I never learned the game, and its abstractions make the General nervous. My colleagues think that he drinks with me instead of them because I am accredited to a monthly, but of course there's more to it than that. For one thing, the General never condescends to me, while I take a lot of trouble trying not to understand him too quickly. I suppose that we are both, in our own way, aesthetes. The General is an aesthete of insurgency and counterinsurgency, a choreographer of guerrilla activity, and he has been at it a long, long time. Some of the older hands here remember seeing him in Vietnam at the time of the Indochina War. He was a captain then, and he would turn up in odd, remote corners of the country dressed in black pajamas. He is supposed to have spoken fluent Vietnamese then, although he now flatly denies any familiarity with that language, which he will actually mimic quite cruelly, breaking into protracted fits of laughter. It's said that he took a break in service during the early Sixties, two years in which he all but completely disappeared. He has no command designation as such, but is connected vaguely with something called Special Operations, about which he refuses to speak.

One is immediately struck by the clean-lined ruggedness of his features, although the longer you observe him the more you notice something delicate there, some softness behind the eyes that is almost feminine. The eyes are ice-blue but not cold, and they suggest his most interesting trait, an originality of mind that one never associates with the Military, and which constantly catches you off balance. It's impossible to guess his age to a certainty (I'd never think of asking him), but he is probably around fifty.

"How's the war going, General?" I'll ask him.

"You're a correspondent, you tell me."

"Seriously."

"Oh, how does it ever go, Mike? Slowly. Damned slowly."

He accepts his drink, lights a Bastos and sinks into a chair.

"We're hurting him," he says. "We know we're hurting him. What we don't know is how much more of it he can take. We're killing him." He raises his glass. "To absent friends."

We talk about many things: Blake, Mexico, the Beethoven Quartets, Oriental women, the Saints, wines, the Elizabethans, classic automobiles and, obviously, Vietnam, which I don't really understand that well. Before the Offensive, we would argue about whether the American position here was morally defensible. I believed it was not, the General believed it was beside the point. In fact (we never said this, but somehow mutually acknowledged it) the subject bored us both. Now, since Tet, I've been more concerned with whether or not our position is even militarily defensible, and the General is optimistic there. Sometimes, he worries about me, about my safety and, even more, about my sanity. I have what he refers to as "this thing about death," an unhealthy fascination with so much of what I've had to see here. He respects it intellectually (one of our other constant topics is suicide) but finally he finds it morbid and unprofitable. Worst of all, he finds that I have a tendency, when discussing the dead, to not only dwell on them, but to personalize them as well. "That way lies you-know-what," he says, tapping his temple; but he lets me get it out, lets me talk about the victims, about the dead and the disposition of the dead.

The first dead I saw in Vietnam was a Cambodian Mercenary serving with the Special Forces in the Seven Mountains Region of the Delta. He had accidentally shot himself in the head while cleaning his .30-caliber rifle. Mercenaries live in a compound with their families, and this one had his parents, his grandparents and his wife with him at the time. The medics bandaged his entire head so that he looked like something you'd see in relief on an old temple wall, some dead prince, very dignified in repose. The women squatted over his body, and their moaning built up into a terrible wail, falling off and beginning again, hour after hour. Some blood and brine from the wound had seeped through the bandages and filled a small dent in the canvas, so that when they carried him from the stretcher some of it spilled over my boots. "Sorry," one of the medics said. "Got some on you." The next dead that I saw were in a mass of over one hundred, Vietcong who had tried to overrun the perimeter of an outpost of the 25th Infantry Division near Tayninh. They had been stopped by 105's firing fléchette canisters, thousands of steel shafts that cut them up in the most incredible way, leaving them almost unrecognizable as human beings, although you could see that some of them were very young and some were women. In Cantho, on the morning after the Offensive began, there were around forty V.C. piled up at the end of the airstrip, and one of them was a medic who had died huddled over his aid case. One of the Americans worked him loose with his feet, jammed a cigar into the clenched teeth and photographed it. Another American was screaming at a very young dead, almost sobbing, "There, you silly bastard, there! You got it now? You got it?" Americans often admonish the dead like that, particularly the young ones. The bodies were all loaded into the back of a truck, where they lay all day, growing stiff in the positions which they had taken in death. When the truck finally started, one of them fell off the back. He was so rigid that he landed exactly on both knees and one elbow (a perfect three-pointer, one of the guys called it) with no other part of him touching the ground, and he had to be lifted up into the truck like a heavy wrought-iron figure.

Later that day, in the provincial hospital at Cantho, the friendly dead began accumulating in the corridors. The Vietcong shelled the hospital for over seven hours from Cantho University, which they had captured and held until it was finally bombed flat, and even if we had wanted to leave we couldn't have. They needed help desperately that day. Over four hundred civilian wounded were brought in, most of them children ("Who shot you, V.C. or U.S.?" the Psywar types kept asking), and we had to cleanse the wounds, cut away dead tissue, or just lean on them, hold them still while the surgeons worked. Outside of the operating rooms there were all of those who were beyond saving, already going grey before death. They just waited there, and you could see they knew. There was an odd piece of graffiti up on the wall of one of the hospital rooms, and I passed it a hundred times that day, always meaning to find out who had written it, and why. It said, "How do you feel about decay, Senator?" In spite of the mortars, a number of Vietnamese came into the hospital carrying wounded children, strangers whom they'd found lying out in the streets, and a number of others came in simply to help. At this point in the fighting the IV Corps Commander, General Manh, was absorbed in constructing a solid five-block perimeter around his house, a strange sort of defense plan considering that the most precious region of the country was at stake, and we were not permitted to drive our jeeps through this perimeter because they drew fire. We had to drive instead through sniper-infested sections of the city, frequently through ambushes along the road, and there were certainly a lot of dead to be seen there.

Of course it is much closer to you when the dead are Americans, and closer still when you've known them. I'm always being told about our comparatively heightened regard for human life, and a lot of us here think that it's exclusively American. I knew a G.I. in Bu Dop who could look at blown-up Vietnamese all day, V.C. or friendly, men, women and children, it didn't much matter. "Hell, they ain't people," he said. "Them're Slopes." But the sight of one quite cleanly killed American made him vomit. The war was a very simple one for him, and you can bet that he had a solution for ending it. But we did agree that it was a bad thing that Americans were getting killed. I'd spent enough hours flying out of combat LZ's in choppers shared with the dead. Often enough, they had no faces left at all, and some died with that wincing sucking-in of breath that shows the full pain of it, some with the dreamy smiles of the drowned, and one that I particularly remember with full staring eyes and a look of mighty outrage, like some Old Testament picture of wrath at the injustice of it. Some just get Blown Away, and sometimes, if they can't reassemble a more or less total corpse from the found parts, they will enter it as Missing. "Shitty way to buy the farm," one kid told me.

For me, though, the very worst dead was a Vietnamese who had been killed near a canal in southern Hué, on the road leading to the Hotel Company C.P. The very top of his head had been shaved off by a piece of debris, so that only the back of his scalp remained connected to the skull. It was like a lidded container whose contents had poured out into the road to be washed away by the rains. Perhaps something had driven over it, or perhaps it had just collapsed during the ten days or more that it had lain there, but I couldn't get the image of it out of my mind. I spent that afternoon with the commander of Hotel, checking their defense perimeter. He was a great, decent Marine named Captain Christmas. This was not a wealthy section of Hué. The homes were modest, sometimes nothing more than elaborate hootches, but walking around Hotel's positions you could see that the entire section had been planned and landscaped, its arranged pathways decorated with statues, its gardens formally designed. Christmas was very moved by this, and his men had strict orders to respect the homes, the grounds and the people. But when it came to spending the night there, my nerves gave out. The Grunts probably assumed that I was afraid of a mortar attack, which was ridiculous since one could be and usually was mortared almost anywhere in Hué, at any time. It was that dead out there with his hinged scalp. I knew that if I stayed here he would drift in over me that night, grinning and dripping, all rot and green-black bloat. After I'd decided to go, I knew that I'd have to pass him again on the way out, and when the time came I forgot my promise and looked back at him one more time. . . .

The General holds up his hand. He's been leaning forward, listening like a crack therapist, and his eyes have gone narrow. He's been tuned into it, all right.

"Yes. Of course," he says. "It's terrible. I didn't really expect it to happen this way. If they'd listened to me then."

"Who? When?"

He shakes his head and a guarded smile comes over his face. Outside, there is a gecko chittering and screaming, and a cluster of magnesium flares are settling down over the perimeter beyond Tan Son Nhut. The General's driver, a giant Khmer called Lurch, is sleeping behind the wheel of the jeep down by the curb.

"Sometimes," the General says, "I think I'm the only man in the world who understands this thing."

"It must be very lonely for you."

"Mike, it comes with the job. But you. If you hate this all so much, why do you stay?"

He has me there. I wait a moment before answering. "Because, General, it's the only war we've got."

And he really smiles now. After all that talk, we're speaking the same language again.

[August, 1968]

An American Atrocity

by Normand Poirier

First Squad drew the night's ambush. While Second and Third Squads of Second Platoon had slogged all day over wooded hills and barren dunes, First Squad had stood security back at Platoon C.P. So First Squad drew the night's ambush and at dusk, as Second and Third Squads filed into the C.P. perimeter—grousing at still another day of no contact with Vietcong—the nine men of First Squad set out in a light wind-whipped rain for their ambush site. Their orders: proceed three hundred yards to the junction of a certain stream and forest trail, deploy in ambush, remain in ambush until 11 p.m., abandon the ambush and check several huts for V.C. suspects and weapons, return to the C.P. by 12:30 a.m. For the Marines in Second Platoon, a routine patrol. Soldiering in their sector of Trà Bông Township had tamed off sharply since the arrival of the Marines in battalion strength four months earlier. The Vietcong had pulled out to mountains in the west and overt enemy activity had dwindled to stray rounds of sniper fire. Second Platoon had neither taken nor inflicted a casualty in weeks. Battalion officially considered the sector pacified. By all odds, First Squad's night ambush should have been uneventful.

But something unusual occurred. After crossing three hundred yards of

790

alternately swampy and sandy terrain, the men of First Squad—a sergeant, a lance corporal, six privates first class and a hospitalman—reached the junction of stream and trail. Three men checked security around the site, standard operational procedure, and then the squad gathered together in a tight huddle of hushed talk deliberately inaudible above the babbling of the nearby stream. At this point, standard operational procedure called for the sergeant to assign ambush positions. The parley that took place did not follow S.O.P.: the sergeant did none of the talking; the talk lasted too long to be concerned only with a routine ambush. Five minutes. Ten minutes. Fifteen minutes. Dusk turned to dark around them. The rain stopped. After twenty minutes, the men stood up. They removed from their collars the small metal insignia denoting grade. They rolled their sleeves down to cover wristwatches and I.D. bracelets. They removed rings from their fingers. The sergeant radioed back to the C.P. that the squad had been positioned off and that the ambush was set. Then the men set out in single file on the trail they were supposed to have ambushed toward the hamlet of Xuan Ngoc a half-mile away. As they walked, the clouds parted and the moon broke through. It would be a clear night.

There were no lights in the hut as the men of First Squad observed it in silence from thirty yards away. At a signal from one, the last three men in the column moved stealthily toward it. They were numbers seven, eight and nine. No names would be used in this operation as a precaution against later identification. Each man had a number. Numbers seven, eight and nine were rear security. At the signal, they fanned out around the house, one to the rear and two to the sides. Numbers one, two and three would break in through the front door. Four and five would stand security out front.

Nguyen Luu had lived in the little hamlet of Xuan Ngoc all of his sixty-one years. He was a rice farmer and a carpenter and had helped build many of the two-dozen thatched-roof bamboo huts that housed his relatives and neighbors in the hamlet. He spent his days in the rice paddies or in his hut making benches and tables or repairing other farmers' wooden plows. Marine patrols passed by his paddies and his hut every few days, stopping now and then to check his I.D. cards and ask about V.C., but for the most part Nguyen Luu was left alone with his wife, who was almost seventy, his two younger sisters, and two nieces, not yet in their teens, who lived in the hut with him. He knew of six men from the hamlet who were Vietcong. He had once seen them with weapons. But everyone in the hamlet knew them and the hamlet chief had long since given their names to the U. S. troops and they had either been arrested or had fled into the mountains. And Nguyen Luu was satisfied. Since the

Marines arrived, the V.C. had stayed away and a measure of peace had settled over Xuan Ngoc.

So Nguyen Luu, asleep in his one-room hut with his wife, two sisters and two nieces, bolted upright in terror when the front door crashed open and dark figures swarmed in, shouting and knocking over furniture and filling the room with screams from the women and children. A light flashed in his face and a hand grabbed his hair and jerked his head back and an angry voice yelled, "Veecee! Veecee! Veecee!" He tried to shake his head no, but the hand that gripped his hair dragged him out of his bunk face down onto the floor and a heavy boot kicked him in the ribs. "No Veecee! Vietnamese!" he cried out and looked up to see his old wife's toothless face in the spot of light and a hand holding her head back by the hair. Her eyes were white with panic and her mouth moved soundlessly. The hand shoved her back on the bunk and Luu felt the boot again in his back. He was lifted to his feet and pushed through the front door to the patio, where two men stood with rifles. One of them punched him in the stomach and the other knocked him down with a blow to the face. He started to say that he was not a V.C., but he was kicked in the stomach and he could not catch his breath. He felt a gun barrel jab into his neck and he was terrified that he would be shot before he could get his breath back to explain that he had an I.D. card. Again he was raised to his feet and, while four Marines shouted at him and threatened him with their rifles, he saw his wife and two sisters and the two children being led away from the hut by two other Marines. He saw one Marine kick his sister Tran Thi Dat when she held out her I.D. card. The women and children were crying. Luu pleaded no one knew about V.C. but the Marines understood only his headshaking and one of them punched him in the face and another slashed his face with the barrel of his rifle. Luu fell down again. Two Marines went into the hut and ripped it apart, smashing furniture, tearing shelves from walls, slashing the matting of the walls. Luu rose to his knees, sobbing, and held out his I.D. card. A Marine grabbed it, looked at it, and tore it up. Luu could hear the women and children crying from the paddy next to the hut and he begged the Marines not to shoot them, realizing as he did that they did not understand him. The two Marines stomped out of the house angrily and kicked him again. Then they led him off to the paddy and made him squat with the women and children. For ten minutes the Marines terrorized the family, shouting about V.C., aiming at them with their rifles as though they would shoot them, kicking them, menacing them with bayonets. And then, with a final kick into Luu's back, the Marines filed off into the darkness in the direction of the hut of Nguyen Truc.

Nguyen Truc, a thirty-eight-year-old rice farmer, was asleep with his wife. Their five children, ranging in age from two to nine, were sleeping on a second bunk in the hut's one room. The front door burst open with a loud crack and a beam of light searched the room. The mother bounded out of bed toward her children but a Marine caught her by the arm and swung her to the door, where another Marine grabbed her. Truc jumped toward her but he was rammed back against the wall and held there by two men who flashed the light in his face. "You Veecee! You Veecee!" the men screamed at him and he shouted back that he was not. But they began punching him around the room. He was knocked sprawling against furniture, against the walls, once into his children, who were crying and screaming on their bunk. He heard his wife screaming outside and fought ferociously to reach the front door, but the Marines beat him until he was too weak to stand. They dragged him to the patio, where there were more Marines, and there two men grabbed him by the legs and held him upside down—his head off the ground—and a third delivered a kick to the face that knocked him out. He came to with the sound of his wife's hysterical sobbing in his ears and he saw that Marines were carrying pieces of firewood into the house and he asked his wife where the children were and she screamed that they were inside and that the troops were going to burn them. Truc went berserk and strained to his feet, screaming that they could not kill his children, blood streaming from the gash in his forehead. He was punched to the ground. The Marines surrounded him and his wife and shouted about V.C. and the couple wailed that they knew nothing and begged for their children. They were grabbed by the arms and led inside their house and were shown by flashlight their five children on the bunk covered by pieces of firewood. The couple screamed and sobbed and struggled to get to their children and the Marines barked at them furiously about V.C. Then the Marines shoved them across the room to their children and left.

Nguyen Thi Mai was not in her hut when the Marines broke into it. She was in a low-ceilinged dirt-walled bunker made of bamboo and sand at the rear of the hut. The bunker had been constructed by a neighbor for protection against mortar shellings. Nguyen Thi Mai had not used it for months because the shelling had stopped with the arrival of the U. S. troops. But this night she and her mother and her mother's sister had heard screams carried on the night breeze from the direction of Nguyen Truc's house, and screams in the night were not a good omen. So, as they had done during the period of the mortar shellings, Nguyen Thi Mai and the two older women packed their valuables— clothing and dishes—into an old suitcase and went to the bunker for the night. They were talking softly by the light of an oil lamp when they heard the racket and the sound of men's voices at the house. It sounded as though the men were tearing the house apart. The three women sat frozen in fear, Nguyen Thi Mai in a unique fear because she knew she was pretty, well-formed and only sixteen years old. None of the three thought to extinguish the lamp.

Nguyen Thi Mai stared at the narrow waist-high door to the bunker. A face appeared. A black man's face. The man stared at the women, called out to the other men, then waved the women out. The two older women went out but Nguyen Thi Mai couldn't move. She cringed on the bunk. The man reached in and pulled her out by the leg. Outside, her mother and aunt chattered nervously that they had their I.D. cards and that the troops should be careful of the suitcase because it contained their most precious items and that Nguyen Thi Mai didn't need an I.D. card because she was not yet eighteen. But the Marines merely shouted at the two women and tore up their I.D. cards and stuffed them back into the bunker and placed a board over the low doorway to block their view. Then one trooper grabbed Nguyen Thi Mai around the neck and slapped a hand on her mouth. Two others grabbed her legs and she was thrown to the ground on her back. A hand felt for the top of her pajama pants and ripped it off. She tried to scream, but the sounds died in her throat. She tried to kick and twist her body, but hands like vises gripped both her arms and both her legs and she couldn't move. The men talked excitedly and laughed and then her legs were forced open. She wanted to scream for her mother but the rough hand over her mouth and nose killed off all sound but the futile grunt in her throat. She could hear her mother wailing inside the bunker: God save my baby! God save my baby! She saw one of the troopers kneel between her legs with a flashlight and she cried at the shame of it. She knew they were going to do to her what no man had done to her and she cried for her mother. Then the vises on her arms and legs let go and the hand that had covered her mouth slapped her hard across the face and she was free. She screamed and ran in horror to the cover of the woods behind the bunker to hide her nakedness. She stayed there a long time after the Marines had left and then she crept back to the bunker and asked her mother to hand out a pajama pants from the suitcase. She put it on and went inside and joined her mother and aunt on the bunk, but no one spoke of what had happened because they were all too ashamed.

The men of First Squad raided six more huts. They ransacked but found neither weapons nor contraband; they beat and terrorized the villagers but elicited no information about Vietcong. When they reached the tenth hut—the home of Bui Thi Huong—they were frustrated and enraged. Bui Thi Huong was eighteen and the mother of a three-year-old boy, Dao Thien. Her husband, Dao Quang Thinh, was twenty, a farmer too ill with a chronic skin disease to be in the army. They lived in the hut with his mother, Nguyen Thi Lanh, fifty, his sister, Pham Thi Tan, twenty-nine, and his sister's daughter, Dao Thi Tao, aged five. They were sleeping when the men of First Squad battered their way into the hut. They yanked Thinh out of his bunk and accused him of being a V.C. He shook his head that he wasn't and repeated over and over, "No Veecee!" but they punched him in the head and stomach. Other Marines were dragging the three screaming women from the hut to the open concrete patio in front of the hut. Thinh managed to break free and dashed through the door to the patio but two Marines tackled him and began pounding him with fists and boots. One Marine came out of the hut holding a hand grenade and as he shouted to the other troopers he pointed to the grenade and to Thinh, indicating it as proof that Thinh was a V.C. Thinh shook his head and denied in wide-eyed terror that it was his grenade but the troopers formed a ring around him and punched him until he was nearly unconscious. They propped him up against the front of the hut and ordered his sister and mother and the two young children to sit beside him. While two Marines stood guard over them, five of the men assembled at the side of the house where Thinh's young wife had been dragged. She had heard her husband's protests of innocence and his cries as he was beaten and the cries of her mother-in-law and sister-in-law and the wailing of the children. But she could not even cry out because a man had a hand over her mouth and two others held her arms and legs and they had her on her back on the ground. When there were five men around her they forced open her legs and ripped her pajama pants away and tore open the top of her pajamas. She felt rough hands on her breasts and strained to break free but the grips on her arms and legs were like steel clamps. The hand on her face squeezed until she thought her nose would break. She felt the point of a knife jab into her forehead. A man knelt between her legs with a light and the others talked and laughed. She strained at the clamps and bit the hand over her mouth and when the hand flew off she let out a scream that pierced the night. The hand cracked her face back and forth and she felt blood trickle down her chin. Then the hand came down on her face again, this time holding a cloth cap, and she could neither scream nor see. She felt the first man go inside her and she prayed for her husband and baby. Then a second man raped her. She could hear her mother-in-law and sister-in-law wailing on the patio. They didn't understand, they were saying. They were not V.C. and the Americans just that day had checked their I.D. cards. O God, what were they doing to Bui Thi Huong, little mother. God save our little mother. God save our little father. Our little father was not V.C. Why did they beat our little father? Bui Thi Huong prayed while the second man raped her and she became so exhausted and pained that she fell off into unconsciousness. She felt water splashing on her face and she came to to see a man standing over her pouring water from a canteen. Another man was tapping her cheeks and she was relieved that no one was on her and inside her. The canteen was handed to two men standing beside her and they washed their genitals. All the men were talking and laughing and then a third man raped her. Tears streamed from her eyes but her sobs caught in her throat because of the hand over her mouth. She was so tired that she wished for unconsciousness again, but it did not come. She heard her husband's voice again, but she could tell from it that he was in great pain. He was asking what they had done with his wife. After the third man was finished, a fourth man raped her. And then a fifth man. Her husband's voice was loud now. He was screaming for his wife, hysterically, and the screams would carry all over the hamlet. The Marines shouted at him back on the patio but he kept screaming. The men around her raised their voices in anger and yelled back at the men on the patio but her husband yelled still louder. The man who was raping her finished and the troopers walked off to the patio. She heard them shout at her husband and she heard him scream as they hit him. He was hysterical with hatred because, he said, he knew what they had done to her. He knew. He knew! They could not understand him and they shouted things that she could not understand. But then she heard the first burst of gunfire. An angry, deafening blast of gunfire. And then she didn't hear her husband's voice any more. Only the wailing of her mother-in-law and sister-in-law and the crying of the children. Then she heard another burst of gunfire. And her mother-in-law's voice was gone. And then another burst, two or three bursts together, and there were no voices. My baby, she thought. My baby! She got to her knees and heard bamboo snap and saw a blinding flash of light and felt a searing pain in her right arm and breast and felt herself lifted and spun around and plopped down on the ground. She knew she was dead. Then the ground beneath her shook from a violent explosion and she felt a rain of debris and dirt pelt down on her. She lost consciousness.

First Squad reported by radio to the lieutenant at Platoon C.P. that the ambush had sprung and that three V.C. had been killed—two women and a man. The two women had been dragged off by the V.C., the lieutenant was told. This radio message was heard also by the captain of "B" Company, the lieutenant's commanding officer, at his C.P. He radioed the lieutenant for an immediate report on details of the skirmish. The lieutenant ordered his squad to return to the Platoon C.P. There, the men of First Squad told the lieutenant that the shootings had not taken place at the assigned ambush site. They had taken place a mile away. The men had panicked while checking out hooches and had accidentally killed civilians.

The lieutenant hiked back to the scene with his men. He froze when he saw on the patio the bodies of a man, a woman and two young children. The body of the older woman, the grandmother, had been blasted back inside the hut. Bui Thi Huong's body was around to the side of the hut.

"My God! What have you done!" the lieutenant said.

He turned to his men for an answer but before anyone could speak a sharp cry came from one of the two blood-splattered children. The lieutenant spun around and all ten men stared, without moving, at the bodies. The lieutenant spoke quietly to two men then ordered the dead man's body to be carried back to the original ambush site. At the site, he detailed five men to remain there with the body and track up the area to simulate an ambush action. The lieutenant then radioed to the captain that the ambush had triggered contact, that his squad had taken eight rounds and returned forty, that two females and one male V.C. had been killed, that the two females had been dragged away by V.C., and that pursuit had been broken off. The lieutenant then led the remaining four members of the squad back to Platoon C.P.

The five men he left behind proceeded to doctor up the ambush site. They dragged the man's body in the sand to make the trails for the two vanished female V.C. They removed their shoes and left the footprints of the ambushed V.C. They scattered empty cartridge shells. But then, instead of returning to the C.P., they went back to the hut. They set about policing the area. They lifted the body of the grandmother onto one bunk. They carried the body of the younger woman to the second bunk and placed the body of the little boy next to her. When they started to lift the body of the five-year-old girl, the child cried out. So they left her on the patio. They spread hay over the pools of blood on the patio and then gathered around the child. They looked down at the naked, blood-streaked form and debated. Four of them walked off a few yards but the fifth man stood over the child and with his M14 rifle bashed its brains in. The body was thrown into the hut, the splintered door was shut, and the five men headed back to Platoon C.P. First Squad's patrol was over.

At the C.P., the lieutenant warned the men of First Squad that they had better get together on one version of what had happened because he was going to report that version to his company commander in the morning. The men huddled for an hour, then reported this story to the lieutenant: they were set in at the ambush site; they saw several figures running through the woods; they followed the figures to a group of hooches; they heard screams and saw someone running from the hooches; somebody panicked and opened fire and they all opened up. The civilians were accidentally killed.

Bui Thi Huong didn't move when she came to. She listened for sounds from the hut but she heard only the wind through the banana trees. Her stomach ached and her right arm and chest throbbed and burned and her body was slick with blood. She didn't know how long she'd been unconscious and she didn't know whether the soldiers had left. It was still night. The moon was bright. When she did look up she could see in the moonlight that her little house had partly caved in from the explosion. The back wall and part of one side wall had been blown out. She was afraid her whole family was dead. My baby! My husband! She crawled, using her good arm, to the patio and through the sticky blood on the patio into the hut. In the gloom, she made out the bodies on the bunks. She crawled to the nearest bunk where her sister-in-law was sprawled and she held her hand to her sister-in-law's nostrils to feel if she was breathing. She felt nothing.

"O my sweet sister!" she whispered and began to weep. She crawled to the other bunk and held her hand to her mother-in-law's nostrils and knew that she was dead.

"O my sweet mother!" she said. And then she saw her own baby and picked him up with her good arm and knew immediately that he was not alive. She held him against her and rocked him and then she lay on the floor with him. She knew her husband was outside, dead, but she was too weak to look for him. She remained awake with her baby on the floor until dawn.

Then she was suddenly aware that it was light out and that someone was staring at her. At the front door she saw her neighbor, Mrs. Tho, peering in at her.

"Everybody is dead," Bui Thi Huong said, "American soldiers. . . ."

Mrs. Tho entered the hut. She observed the bodies and saw that Bui Thi Huong was without pajama pants. She went back to her own hut and returned with a pair. She helped the young woman into them and told her that they would have to go to a Vietnamese medic in the marketplace for her wounds. Bui Thi Huong nodded in agreement. She kissed her baby and placed him on the bunk next to her mother-in-law and, leaning on Mrs. Tho, started off for the marketplace at Ky Chanh village. Neither woman talked during the long walk and though they passed a score of curious villagers—her pajama was bloodied and her face and hair were caked with dirt—they were spoken to by no one. At the marketplace, the Vietnamese, who had had some medical training, cleaned and bandaged her wounds. He put her on a military van that served the area as a bus and told the driver to let her off at the Marine base. There was a hospital there. There were two long benches against either side of the van but she was afraid she might create a disturbance by fainting and falling off so she sat on the floor between the two rows of passengers and rode that way the five bumpy miles to the base. She stood outside the main gate until a Vietnamese interpreter noticed her and took her to a medical aid station. Through the interpreter, she told Lieutenant Anthony Fathman, a Navy doctor, that she had been raped and shot and that her whole family had been murdered by Marines. The doctor examined her and concluded that she had, indeed, been raped. He had her taken to the base hospital and drove off to report her rape and murder charges to the commanding officer of the battalion.

While Bui Thi Huong was making her way from her hut to the Marine base, the lieutenant and the men of his First Squad were marching to the base with the body of her husband. The lieutenant was Stephen J. Talty, a rugged twenty-three-year-old Marine. The report he made to his C.O., Captain J. P. T. Sullivan, was the most distasteful task he'd been called on to make in his ten months in the Corps. He had lied in his radio report the night before, he told the captain. His men had not killed three V.C. during an ambush; they had killed four innocent civilians accidentally in a moment of panic while searching out hooches for V.C. He had lied in his radio report, the lieutenant said, because he had not wanted to go on the air with talk of civilian killings.

Captain Sullivan was irritated by the report. Only three days before, General Westmoreland had issued a directive warning against mistreatment of Vietnamese, "physical and otherwise," because of the resultant bad publicity in the Saigon press. The publicity, the directive pointed out, was "damaging to the image of the Marine Corps." Henceforth, the directive went on, all such incidents of mistreatment would be reported up through channels to his office. The captain did not relish being brought to General Westmoreland's attention in this capacity.

He set off in a jeep for the office of the commanding officer of the battalion. The colonel was just then listening to a Navy doctor who was relaying a Vietnamese woman's claims of rape and murder.

The nine men of First Squad were sitting in the shade beside the green frame chapel—two M.P.'s standing guard over them—when Major James T. Elkins drove up. His sergeant-chauffeur ordered them inside the chapel and Major Elkins read off their names, to which they answered.

Sgt. Ronald L. Vogel
L/Cpl. Robert W. Monroe
Pfc. Clifton G. Hobson
Pfc. Jerry D. Sullivan
Pfc. Danny L. McGhen
Pfc. John D. Potter Jr.
Pfc. James W. Henderson
Pfc. James H. Boyd Jr.
Hn. Jon R. Bretag

Henderson, a slender six-foot-four, and Hobson, nearly a foot shorter but muscular, were Negro. The seven others were white. Major Elkins called Sergeant Vogel forward and led him to the chaplain's office where he interrogated him about the previous night's mission. Elkins began by advising him that under Article 31 of the Uniform Code of Military Justice he had the right to remain silent, that anything he said could be used against him in court, and that he had the right to counsel. Vogel said that he understood his rights and that he had no objection to being questioned about the patrol.

For a half hour, Sergeant Vogel related in a slow drawl the story that he and his men had fabricated for the lieutenant—the ambush, the running figures, the pursuit to the huts, the panic, the gunfire, the dead civilians. Under questioning, however, Vogel was vague, imprecise, confused. He labored to answer the simplest questions and Major Elkins decided that Vogel was either lying or a dullard. He settled for the latter. He tried Vogel to what he considered the limit and asked him if he had any objections to writing down on paper what he had related. Vogel said he had no objections. The major provided him with pencil and pad and told him he would return in fifteen minutes. As the major opened the door to leave the room, Vogel said:

"I can't."

"You can't what?" Elkins asked.

"I can't write it because it's all a lie. I'm sick of it!"

"What's a lie?"

"The whole bullshit story I just told you," he said, shaking his head. "We made it all up."

Then Sergeant Vogel told Major Elkins what had really happened.

The Inquiry

Master Sergeant Charles W. Ellis sat in his cubicle in the Division Legal quonset hut at Chu Lai and mulled over the story Major Elkins had just related to him. It was 9:30 p.m. on September 24, 1966, the night after the raid on the hamlet of Xuan Ngoc, and Ellis was about to interrogate the nine men who had been trucked over from the Battalion C.P. on Hill 54 ten miles west. Ellis had been a criminal investigator for seventeen of his twenty-three years in the Marine Corps and his credentials were impeccable. Besides his training at military police schools, he had graduated from the F.B.I. National Academy, the Federal Bureau of Narcotics training school, and the school for U. S. Treasury agents. He was considered one of the ablest investigators in the Corps with experience in every area of criminal activity. But this case had elements that baffled him. Sergeant Vogel had told Major Elkins at the chapel that when his squad reached the ambush site one of his men—Pfc. Potter—took command of the squad with the claim that he had been given secret orders by Lieutenant Talty. Potter, according to Vogel, then briefed the squad to this effect: that the lieutenant was fed up with patrols and ambushes that did not produce; that the lieutenant was convinced the local Vietnamese were withholding information about V.C.; that the only way to obtain information was through fear; that the ambush was a cover to satisfy the Company Commander, Captain Sullivan, who had to approve all night missions; that under this cover, the lieutenant wanted the squad to stage a raid of terror; that the lieutenant had said that anything goes—beating up on people, wrecking hooches, raping, killing; that the only restriction was on burning, fires that might be observed from the Company C.P.

Ellis found it difficult to believe that a lieutenant would issue such an order. He would be exposing himself to the severest repercussions. And why would he bypass his sergeant, the leader of the squad, and give the order to a Pfc.? And why would a sergeant let a Pfc. usurp his authority? And why would eight men acquiesce to a plan of beating, raping and deliberate murder? Why would eight men, a corporal and sergeant includ- ed, take orders they knew to be criminal from a Pfc.? Vogel would have to be lying. And yet such a raid had taken place. There were five dead bodies. There was one wounded and raped woman. There were statements piling up from the farmers who had been terrorized. Vogel's story was a bizarre one and yet there it all was, the debris.

"Why do you suppose," Ellis asked Major Elkins, "they went back and killed the little girl? Afraid she might testify?"

"Vogel was very vague about that child. He remembered less about that part of it than anything else," Elkins said.

"Well, let's see if we can't help him remember," Ellis said.

The interrogations were conducted under irksome conditions: Ellis' cubicle was cramped; a huge generator growled outside the window; jets roared in deafening takeoffs right over the building; and everyone had been through a long stifling day. Especially Sergeant Vogel. Nervous, scared, he had not slept or eaten in thirty hours. The other men in the squad had been fed C-rations that afternoon but Vogel, after making his statement to Major Elkins, had been isolated in an M.P. shack and no one had thought to feed him. When he walked into Ellis' cubicle he was tired and hungry and utterly dejected. At twenty-three, he'd been a Marine for four years, straight out of high school. He had been in Vietnam over a year and had seen action in Operations Wyoming, Apache, Colorado and Napa. His four-year hitch had ended in July but he volunteered for another six months in Vietnam even though he wanted desperately to be back home with his wife and their little girl, Robin Lee. Only a few days before the raid on Xuan Ngoc, Vogel had received word from his wife that the final adoption papers on Robin Lee had come through.

The interrogation of Sergeant Vogel, as did all subsequent interviews, began with Ellis warning him that he was suspected of murder and rape and advising of his right to remain silent and of his right to counsel. Vogel waived his rights.

"All right now. I think it will be a lot easier for both you and me if you told your story first. Start right at the very beginning. Go through it slow. If need be I'll ask you questions from time to time. . . ."

Ellis has a deceptively gentle manner. He is soft-spoken and calm. He has a greying crew cut and pronounced cheekbones. There is no menace in his style.

With the spools of a tape recorder turning slowly on the desk in front of him, Vogel told his story in a sluggish Southern drawl. At about 7:30 p.m. at the Platoon C.P., Lieutenant Talty told him that his squad had the night's ambush. Vogel picked up his gear and joined his squad where Pfc. Potter greeted him with, "Are you going?" He said he certainly was and Potter told him, "You don't have to go." Vogel told him that the lieutenant had told him to go and that it was his squad and that he was going. Potter shrugged and the squad set out for the ambush site.

"Who was in control of the squad?" Ellis interrupted.

"Pfc. Potter and Lance Corporal Monroe, sir."

"Why?"

"Well, I didn't know anything about it, sir. The lieutenant didn't brief me. I couldn't tell them what to do. I didn't know anything about the ambush or anything."

Ellis studied Vogel's face. "But you're a sergeant, the appointed squad leader, the senior man present, and yet you let a lance corporal or a Pfc. take your command away from you without taking action to find out what the hell was going on?"

"I didn't know about the ambush," Vogel said.

"And you made no effort to call back to the lieutenant and find out what the hell the scoop was?"

"No sir. No excuse. I should have but I didn't. I. . . ."

"We'll talk about it later. Go ahead."

At the ambush site, Vogel said, Potter told the men that he had orders from the lieutenant to pull a raid on hooches and destroy, rape and terrorize.

"Were those the words he used?"

"I don't know the exact words. Go out and terrorize and find out where the V.C. were. Harass, destroy, beat up on people. Rape if there were some young girls around. And shoot anybody that got in the way and wreck their houses. Then he gave us numbers. I was number six. . . ."

He told of the raids on the huts, the beatings, the assault on the sixteen-year-old Nguyen Thi Mai. "Some of the men were going to rape her but the Doc examined her with a flashlight and thought she had clap so they left her." Vogel became increasingly nervous and vague, stammering, as he tried to reconstruct the scene at the hut of Bui Thi Huong where the rape and murders occurred. He denied having participated in either. He said that while Bui Thi Huong was being raped he was on the patio guarding the man and the woman and children. Once he walked over to the side of the house when one of the men yelled for water. He had a canteen. The woman had fainted and Pfc. Sullivan was tapping her cheeks so Vogel poured water on her face to revive her. He saw Potter climb on the woman and then he went back to the patio. Later, the man on the patio, Bui Thi Huong's husband, started screaming and nothing would shut him up. Vogel thought of stuffing his mouth with straw but Doc Bretag pulled a bandage from his bag and tried to gag him with it. The man fought the gag and continued screaming until the Marines at the side of the house returned to the patio, angry, and one of them said that "We're going to have to shoot them." Somebody else said, "We better get outta here!" Vogel said that at this point he walked away from the house to a trail twenty-five yards away where he waited for his squad. Henderson and Bretag were on the trail with him. A few minutes later, he heard shooting from the house.

"But you said one of the men said that these people would have to be shot," Ellis broke in.

"Yes."

"So when you heard those rifle shots go off you knew that they were killing those people back there."

"Yeah," Vogel said.

"But you were a squad leader! Why didn't you go back and see what was happening? Why didn't you leave your position on that trail and walk back down there and find out what was happening? You already *knew* what was happening!"

"Yes sir."

"Why didn't you go down and try and stop it?" Ellis persisted. "You had a weapon, did you not?"

"Yes, but I did not have no rounds. We left in a hurry . . . I. . . ."

"I'm not interested in whether you had rounds or not!" Ellis snapped angrily. "You had a weapon, didn't you?"

Vogel remained silent. He looked away from Ellis to Major Elkins and then to the ceiling; his gaze had nowhere to go.

"Vogel, were you afraid of Potter?"

The sergeant remained silent.

"Were you physically afraid of these men?"

"Probably," Vogel finally answered, "when they had their rifles and they were firing."

Major Elkins pulled out a pack of cigarettes and offered one to Vogel, who reached for it with a trembling hand. Ellis watched Vogel fumble with the matches. What had he lied about? Had he lied about not raping the woman? Or his part in the murders? Or was he shaking because he knew his lie was still ahead of him? Elkins had said Vogel had been vaguest about the wounded little girl and Ellis asked Vogel to relate what had happened when the squad returned to the hut with Lieutenant Talty.

"We went there and were looking around and the lieutenant said, 'Oh my God, what have you done!' Or some words like that. He started talking to Potter and Monroe and all of a sudden a baby screamed, cried out, and the lieutenant jumped."

"Did the lieutenant or anybody go over and check this baby?"

"No. They looked at it but didn't do anything about it."

"You could see two babies, right?"

"Yes sir. The lieutenant was saying, 'What have you done!' and 'What are we going to tell the captain!' and 'We're going to have to do something.' "

"He included himself in this statement?"

"Yes sir. Then it was all quiet for a while. And then he said let's take the man's body back to the ambush site. The whole squad went and we took the man's body."

Vogel described how at the ambush site, a thousand yards from the hut, the lieutenant left five men behind with instructions to 'Make it look like an ambush took place if it takes you all night.' The five were Potter, Monroe, Hobson, McGhen and Vogel. The lieutenant and the rest of the squad returned to the Platoon C.P. Vogel and the others dragged the body through the sand and across the stream, leaving trails of the two nonexistent female V.C.'s who had been dragged away. They took off their boots and left the tracks of the nonexistent V.C. who had tripped the ambush. They dropped empty cartridges that had been fired at the hut. And then the five returned to the hut.

"We put the bodies inside the hut . . ." Vogel said, hurriedly.

"Whoa!" Ellis barked.

". . . except for the baby," Vogel corrected himself. "I started to pick it up and it screamed. . . . Potter said the baby was going to die anyway. . . ."

"But it was screaming. It was living."

"Yeah, the baby was still living, but the way it looked. It was just bloody."

"You don't know how much damage was done to that baby, do you?"

"No."

"You don't know if the baby was going to die, do you?"

"It . . . it looked like it was hit by a frag," Vogel offered.

"Did you look at it to see what the nature of its injuries were? Did you look at it close?"

"No," Vogel said and sighed. "No, I did not."

"Vogel, who decided the baby would have to be killed?"

The sergeant said he didn't know for sure.

"But Potter said it isn't going to live anyway. . . ."

Vogel nodded and blurted, ". . . and he said who's going to do it and everybody turned around. Couldn't do it . . . everybody looked out. . . ."

"What do you mean 'looked out'?"

"Just looked out. . . ."

"Looked out where? You just looked out at rockets going off?"

"Just looking in the distance . . . nobody could do it . . . then Potter did it . . ." he said, his voice trailing off.

"Speak up, Vogel! How do you know he did it?"

"I don't know."

Ellis' questions came rapidly, one on the other, so that Vogel had no time to think. He was swept along on a racing current of questions.

"You were looking out?"

"No. Everybody turned around . . . Potter was standing. . . ."

"But they turned around and looked at Potter!"

"Potter was standing over. . . ."

"You looked at him!"

"Yes! Yes! I did! We all looked at him!"

"And you all knew what Potter was going to do!"

"Yeah. . . ."

"What did Potter do when you were looking at him while he was standing over the baby?"

"He had his rifle in his hands . . ." Vogel said.

"What did he do. . . ."

"He said, 'Somebody count for me!' "

"Somebody count what?" Ellis asked.

"Count! Just count!"

"Count cadence?"

"No, just count for him. So I started counting. I turned around and started counting. . . ."

"You *looked* at him and then you started counting! You can't make it any easier."

"I said one . . . two . . . three. . . . And he was hitting the baby with the butt!"

"How was he doing it?"

"Dropping it down."

"Picking it up and smashing it down or just letting it fall down?"

"Picking it up and hitting it down," Vogel said, softly.

"Like a baseball bat or like he was chopping wood or straight up and down like a butt stroke? Did you ever see anyone churn butter?"

"It was straight up and down."

"Like someone churning butter," Ellis said in conclusion.

"Yeah," Vogel said. And after a long pause he said: "Then it was quiet and someone said to Potter, 'You sure got some balls to do that.' "

Vogel's interrogation lasted from 9:45 to 10:30 p.m. and the eyes of the other eight men in the squad followed him as he was led by an M.P. past them.

They could not have been encouraged. His face was ashen. His shirt was soaked through with sweat. More significantly, he returned none of their stares. The men had suspected, since Vogel had been whisked away from the chapel by Major Elkins, that he had talked. The sight of him as he emerged from Ellis' office did nothing to dispel that feeling.

Nevertheless, Hospitalman Jon R. Bretag, a twenty-year-old Navy medic from Albuquerque, New Mexico, decided to try the concocted version of the previous night's incident on Ellis. Ellis let him relate it—the ambush, the chase to the hooches, the shadowy figure, the panicked gunfire, the accidental killings. A high-school graduate, Bretag had been a good student. His father, a Chief Warrant Officer in the U.S. Army Reserves, worked for the Bureau of Indian Affairs, and his mother was a Registered Nurse. He had enlisted in the Navy a year before and had volunteered for duty in Vietnam in July. On September 21, two days before the raid on Xuan Ngoc, he was assigned to Lieutenant Talty's platoon. Ellis let him tell his version of the killings and then abruptly stopped him.

"What about the woman you raped, Doc?"

"Rape?"

"The rape at the house where you killed those people. You remember that? You examined a girl for clap, like you examined one earlier, and you raped her."

"Well . . . I . . . we . . ." he stammered. "I examined her but I didn't see the men do anything. They were just standing around her chatting."

"What were they chatting about, Doc?"

"I don't remember."

"Doc, little bits of amnesia isn't going to help you a bit. Let's face it, you are as much in trouble as every one of these men who are involved."

"I know, sir."

Ellis got up, took two or three steps to the window, leaned his elbow on the sill, and stared out at Chu Lai's plane-lined strip.

"It probably started out as a big gag, a big joke," he said, his voice lined with sarcasm. "A big joke. And then it got a little horrible toward the end. But let's stick to the joke part, where we are still in the fun-and-games business, all right? You made an examination on the woman. Now you didn't do it to pass the time out there. What did they have in mind?"

"They had rape on their minds, sir."

"Now how do you know that?"

"Well, they wanted to know who was going to be first and all this. . . ."

"Did they flip a coin or how did they arrive at who was going to go first?"

"I . . . I don't remember. . . ."

Ellis fixed Bretag with a stare and said:

"There's been a hell of an injustice here, Doc! A hell of a crime! You got it on your conscience to live with the rest of your life. Those were human beings out there! There was no provocation. If you can let that kind of thing go on you're in a pretty bad way!"

"I didn't know what I was getting into," Bretag pleaded. "I volunteered for this patrol because I was new and I wanted to have the experience. This was my first patrol. I didn't know what I was getting into!"

Then the young seaman told Ellis what he wanted to know. "When we got to our ambush site Potter said the lieutenant told him the purpose of this patrol was, as much as I could gather . . . it didn't seem right to me . . . was that we were supposed to, you can say, raid these huts, raising hate and discontent. Potter said we were to beat up people, tear up the hooches, rape and kill. Spoke up and asked him why we were doing this. And he looked hard at me and said the people wouldn't turn the V.C. in but if we created enough fear they would. I went along as just a medical personnel. We went through some huts, the men were beating up on people. . . ."

He told how he had examined the sixteen-year-old girl with a pocket flashlight while Marines held her pinned to the ground and told them that she looked diseased. They became angry but they didn't do anything to the girl.

"How about the second girl, Doc?"

"Well, I was guarding this man and woman and two kids on the patio of this hut and they called me over to the side of the house. They had a woman stretched out and they told me to check her for clap. I did and I said I didn't know if she did or not. Well, Potter said, 'Who's going to go first?' Two of them said they couldn't get a hard on. A third got on her. I went back to the patio for about ten minutes. When I came back . . . well . . . he had got off her . . . I guess I got on and had intercourse. . . ."

He looked up at Ellis and waited for Ellis to say something but Ellis just returned his look and he continued.

"Then two others got on her after me. Then the woman appeared to have passed out. Potter asked if she was dead. Vogel poured water on her and Sullivan tapped her cheeks. Potter was standing there with his penis out trying to get an erection. That's when I went back to the patio. . . ."

There the young father, Bui Thi Huong's husband, was propped up against a wall of the hut. His sister sat near him with the two children and the grandmother was squatting just inside the hut.

"There was a wailing chant," Bretag said. "That's the only way I can describe it. Then the man started crying loudly and all the Marines wanted to keep him quiet so they began wrestling with him and hitting him. I tried to tie a bandage around his mouth but each time I went to tighten it it would slip down around his neck and I'd be strangling him. Then the men from the side of the house had come around to the front now. They didn't leave anybody over there for security so I went to the side. I heard yelling, screaming, you shut up, shut up, and then a couple of bursts of automatic fire, then some semiautomatic fire. I don't know how many bursts, how many rounds.

"I walked back to the house and looked at the people. The man was laying up against the house. The woman was laying next to him. I didn't see any of the children . . . except for one by the old lady. Someone said, 'We'll have to make it look good. I'm going to throw in a hand grenade. Everybody get behind the sand.' I got behind the sand pile and the grenade was thrown. After that, I didn't walk back. I didn't want to see what was—what happened. I'd seen enough and I was getting sick. It was my first patrol and the first time I'd seen 'em, people shot, laying there. . . ."

Pfc. Danny L. McGhen of the McKeesport, Pennsylvania, area, did about-faces in his statement to Ellis as smartly as he had ever done them for a drill instructor. Like Bretag, McGhen launched into the spurious version of the murders. He had advanced through three simple declarative sentences when Ellis slammed a fist on his desk.

"Let's stop right there, McGhen! We've been through all the bullshit! It's all over with. We know exactly what happened. Do I make myself clear? There is 720 feet of tape there and none of it is a lie. Now nothing about any noises in front of the ambush site or any of that jazz."

"Right, sir!"

Ellis took McGhen straight to the rape of Bui Thi Huong and the murders.

"You saw what was being done to that girl?"

"It was dark but I still had an idea what was going on, sir."

"You know damn well what was going on, McGhen."

"The men were trying to rape her, sir."

"Trying?"

"Were raping her, sir."

"Fine, McGhen. Now how did the shooting start?"

"Well, sir, the man was making a lot of noise. Everybody got scared. I know I was. I guess in my mind I finally started realizing what was happening. I went around to the front of the house because I couldn't . . . I guess I went crazy because I couldn't stand that noise anymore. I kept thinking in my mind, somebody is going to tell and we're all going to get in real trouble over it . . . if we weren't in already! So I went out front and I kept trying to get the man to be quiet and I *think* . . ." He looked up at Ellis and corrected himself. ". . . I *know* I did . . . hit him a couple of times. To get him quiet. And he wouldn't get quiet and by this time everybody was getting around. I don't know who it was, somebody said, 'We'll have to shoot them!' and as soon as they did somebody opened up."

"Who?"

McGhen gave the names of those he was "pretty sure" opened up.

"I think I shot at the man and the old lady both, sir," he said. "But I think I might have hit the old lady."

"Who fired at the young girl with the baby?"

"I think Boyd was standing there, sir. Boyd, I'm pretty sure it was."

"What happened after the shooting?"

"We picked up the man's body and we were going to take him back to the ambush site and say that he was caught in the ambush and let it go at that. So we did this and we were even crazy enough, stupid enough, to make trails like bodies were drug away and leave cartridges around."

Ellis asked him who killed the second child at the house.

"Potter did, sir. He stood there and went mashing up and down with his rifle. It was his own idea, sir. Nobody else could do it."

"Then what?"

"Then, sir? Nothing, sir. Nobody said nothin'. I just said as we looked down at the baby that I was glad this wasn't in the United States."

Ellis stared at McGhen for a full minute. When he spoke his voice crackled with anger. "What the hell difference does it make where it's at! You murdered five people!" He picked up a book and slammed it on the desk. "What difference does it make where you did it at? You raped one woman and tried to murder her. Does it really make any difference where it happened?"

"No sir. I guess it don't," McGhen replied, sheepishly.

"Do you have a religion, McGhen?"

"Evangelical United Brethren, sir."

"Are they in favor of killing?"

"No sir."

"What do they teach about it? Murder, I'm talking about, not just war-time killing."

"It's not done, sir."

"It's against the law of God?"

"Yes sir."

"So what difference does it really make when you murder somebody exactly where it takes place?" Ellis asked. "You've deprived two children of sixty years of life!"

Ellis sighed, shook his head, and sat down. He knew he should not have gotten into the religious thing for the tape. The statements would be introduced at the formal pretrial investigation and defense counsel would harangue him for his unprofessionalism. He continued:

"How long have you been overseas, McGhen?"

"About thirty days, sir."

"You just come out of boot camp?"

"Yes sir."

"How old are you?"

"Nineteen, sir."

Pfc. James H. Boyd Jr. was eighteen, the youngest man on the patrol. He was probably also poorest equipped to be in Vietnam. He was slightly built, almost scrawny. And his score of 24 on the Armed Forces Qualification Test gave him a Class IV rating, the lowest class the Marine Corps will accept. Cutoff score is 21. He was raised in Coon Rapids, Minnesota, and his parents were divorced when he was eleven. He repeated fourth and tenth grades and after finishing tenth grade he enlisted because his father was out of a job. He had been in Vietnam five months before the incident at Xuan Ngoc and had fought in Operation Colorado and Operation Napa and had written numerous letters home filled with his fear and his anger and his bewilderment at the death of his buddies.

It was after two a.m. when he was called into Ellis' office and both Ellis and Boyd were so bone-tired that neither bothered to fence with the pre-arranged story.

"Who'd you shoot, Boyd?" Ellis asked.

"I didn't shoot anybody."

"You fired your rifle," Ellis stated.

"I didn't . . . I don't know if I hit anyone. . . . But I didn't shoot. . . ."

"Who did you shoot at, Boyd?"

"I don't know. One of the women, sir."

"Did you hit her?"

"I don't know, sir."

"You fired directly at her? From a very short distance?"

"Yes sir."

"Very small chance of you missing her, Boyd?"

"Very."

He said Potter and others blasted the old lady and the man with automatic bursts. He said one child was in her grandmother's arms and was killed with her by these bursts. The baby was in his father's arms and was hit but not killed.

"Now how do you know he wasn't?"

"Because he was bawling when we left."

Sergeant Ellis did not interrogate Lieutenant Talty until four days later. Talty was in the field and Ellis was busy with routine detective work. He inspected the scene of the murders and collected physical evidence—spent slugs embedded in beams in the hooch and in trees, cartridge casings, the spoon from the grenade tossed into the hooch. He had pictures taken of the hut, patio and grounds around the hut. He had the squad's weapons collected and sent off to a military ballistics expert in Japan along with the recovered slugs and casings. Through interpreters he took statements from Bui Thi Huong, Nguyen Thi Mai, and a score of Vietnamese who had been visited by the raiders. The bodies of the five murder victims had been buried by relatives and neighbors the day after the incident and he tried to have the bodies exhumed for autopsy but S-5, the Marine Civil Affairs Branch, advised him that the Vietnamese refused to allow their dead to be dug up. It would be disrespectful. Ellis conceded that there had been enough disrespect. He learned from S-2, intelligence, that none of the murdered—needless to say, not the children—had been V.C. suspects or V.C. sympathizers. In fact, S-2 said, none of the people harassed by the squad were known to have any V.C. connections. The hamlet of Xuan Ngoc was considered a pacified area.

Ellis, with Major Elkins present, interviewed Lieutenant Talty on September 28 in the same cubicle in the quonset hut at Chu Lai where the lieutenant's men had been questioned. Talty was twenty-three, a birthday he had celebrated two weeks after his arrival in Vietnam on July 9, and in his ten weeks as a platoon leader in Bravo Company had shown himself to be a dependable and commendable officer, though he had come fresh from training schools. He had enlisted in the Corps in December, 1965. He was a native of Buffalo, New York, where his father was a public-school supervisor and his mother a nurse. He had served as an altar boy for seven years while a pupil at St. Thomas Aquinas Grammar School, graduated from Bishop Timon High School, and earned above-average grades at St. Bonaventure U. in Buffalo where he got his B.A. in English in 1965. For three summers during college he was a lifeguard at a Buffalo Recreation Department swimming pool. He mixed weight lifting with folk singing as an undergraduate and was good enough at the latter to get paying jobs for his group around the Buffalo area. He failed, as a sophomore, in his first try to pass the test for Marine Officers' school and was sorely disappointed. When he made it in 1965 he was elated. When he reached Vietnam he was a proud Marine. He was proud of the Corps, proud of his part in it. He was especially close to and careful for his men. He surveyed their gear closely and made sure they had what they needed in clothes and weapons. He sat down with them and made sure their pay and allotments were properly taken care of. Not all officers were so diligent. Under fire he was cool and resourceful. In less than ten weeks he had taken part in Operations Colorado, Napa, and Monterey, and numerous smaller operations against insurgent V.C. forces. His immediate superior officers said he was a good leader of men. His men thought of him as a good officer. Master Sergeant Ellis, as he tried to understand what had gone wrong with First Squad at Xuan Ngoc hamlet, was not so sure.

Ellis advised Talty that an Article 31 investigation into murders, rape and assaults was underway and that the lieutenant was a possible suspect and that he did not have to say anything and that he had the right to counsel. Talty said that he would answer all questions without counsel. He proceeded to detail the events of the night of September 23:

At 7 p.m., he gathered a squad around him at Platoon C.P. and briefed them on their patrol. They would proceed to a stream junction 300 meters from the perimeter, set up an ambush, and remain at the site until 11 p.m. The squad would then check out several hooches in the area for V.C. and return to the C.P. by 12:30 a.m. At 7:30 p.m., he received a radio message from the squad reporting the men were in position. At 9 p.m. he received another message that three V.C. had been killed, two males and one female. But the message was garbled due to faulty transmission. A later message reported two females and one male had been killed. The squad had received eight rounds of V.C. fire. Soon after, the squad returned to the C.P. and told the lieutenant that civilians had been killed in an accident. The lieutenant went to the site with them and saw the bodies. He said, "My God, what the hell have you done here!" They told him it had been an accident. The company commander, Captain J.P.T. Sullivan, radioed for information on the incident and the lieutenant told him that he had one male body but that the two female bodies had been dragged away.

"We moved the body back to the ambush site and I left five men there," Talty said. "Potter, Monroe, McGhen, Vogel and Hobson. I told them to make it look like an ambush. Then I went to the C.P., sat down, gathered my wits, questioned the other three I brought in, separately, Henderson, Boyd and Sullivan. Doc was with us, too. They said they were all rear security and didn't know anything. I sent a team out with the platoon sergeant to bring the others back. I wanted to find out what happened. So I said to leave the body until the morning and we will get our story straight on this. So we all sat down and they told me what happened. I hit the sack at 1:30 a.m. in the morning, I told them to get the body and they did and took it to Hill 54. I told the C.O. what happened. I didn't tell him I moved the body. I just told him I made it look like an ambush. The reason I had done this—it was a mistake on my part—it was just to give me time to think and to find out just exactly what happened."

"Now, lieutenant," Ellis began, "Among those dead bodies at the hut there was a live baby, wasn't there?"

Talty said there was.

"Did you take any action to check the condition of that baby?"

He said he had not, and Ellis asked him why he had not.

"I thought probably she would be alive in the morning when they looked over the area," he said.

"Isn't that a pretty big chance to be taking, sir?"

"Yes it is."

"That she could have survived an ordeal, a thing like that?" There was a guarded reprimand in the question. "That she *might* just be alive in the morning if somebody *happened* to wander out and look at the area?"

"Yes, Sergeant Ellis, it is."

"Is there any question you should have taken some steps?"

"I'm positive I should have, now," Talty said, coolly.

"Now some of your men, lieutenant, claim that you ordered them to return to the hut and dispose of those bodies, to police up the area?"

"I gave no such orders."

"They did, in fact, though, return to that house and moved the bodies from the patio to the interior of the house," Ellis said. "And in the course of doing this—the reason we bring this up—is that the young child that made the sounds while you were at the house was murdered by Potter. He bashed its brains out with a rifle butt in the presence of four men, lieutenant."

"I did not give them any orders at all to return to that house."

"Then somebody countermanded or disobeyed your orders?"

"I told them to stay at the ambush site."

Ellis looked through some notes and set off on a new tack. He asked Talty to repeat what he had reported to Captain Sullivan the morning after the murders. Talty said he had told the C.O. that his men had accidentally killed four civilians and that. . . .

"I'm sorry, lieutenant, would you repeat this?" Ellis interrupted.

"I told the C.O. that my men had accidentally killed four civilians."

"Now while you were relating this story to the captain, did you tell him that there was one live baby out there?"

"No, I didn't. I just told him . . . I just ran through it quickly and I told him there were some civilians killed and. . . ."

"You said there was *four* civilians, lieutenant."

"I wasn't trying to keep it from him."

"Lieutenant, you said that you told the captain there were *four* civilians killed!"

"Right!"

"Which would have been a man, a woman, and two children because that's what you saw on the patio that night. And yet we both know that the child was alive when you were out there. So there were only *three* civilians killed and one wounded. A baby."

"Well," Talty paused, "from what they told me there was two women, a man and one child."

"But you *saw* two children!" Ellis argued.

"Right!"

"So isn't that a little confusing, sir?"

"Right. It is."

"You reported what they told you instead of what you saw? And you didn't tell anyone that the baby was alive? Why?"

"I don't know."

"Lieutenant, did you know that morning that the baby was, in fact, not alive?"

"Definitely not!" Talty said, angrily. "How would I know that?"

Talty looked at both Ellis and Elkins but got no answer.

Ellis switched to another line of questioning. He asked Talty for his professional opinion of Sergeant Vogel.

"I don't think he is very competent. Potter runs the squad and he is a damn good man. I hate to see this happen. He is a damn good man, one of the best point observers and a good trooper. Monroe we kind of put on mess duty there for a while until after Operation Colorado. He was kind of shaky because one of his best buddies got shot up, but he is a real good man, too. We got a good squad."

Ellis asked in what ways Sergeant Vogel was incompetent.

"He was always yelling at his men, screaming at them, trying to show them he was the boss and still he actually didn't know his job. He went about it all in the wrong way, I think."

Major Elkins asked if his leadership could have been undermined by Potter and Monroe.

"I don't think so, I don't think that was true. I don't think that was true at all."

"You say Monroe and Potter were running the squad. What do you mean they were running it? Wasn't Sergeant Vogel there?"

"They were the ones doing all the work in the field actually. They were the ones who knew what was going on. They were just handling themselves better and quicker."

"Well, lieutenant, you see the dilemma that we are faced with. For some reason your men disobeyed your orders to remain in a combat ambush for a specified time. They jumped the time and left several hours early and went on a reign of terror for about two-and-a-half hours. It all boils down to this point, lieutenant, that Potter and Monroe allegedly had a private briefing and they passed on the briefing to the patrol not in your presence. After they left the ambush they briefed the patrol themselves and they said that these were your instructions—to rape, rob, terrorize!"

"I gave them no such orders!" Talty shot back angrily.

"Why would they move out of the ambush early?"

"I asked Vogel at the hut and he said he didn't know. Nobody knew."

"No one knew why they had moved?" Ellis asked. "No one came up with a good concrete answer? Do you suppose it was everybody's idea to move at one time?"

"They said they had seen something."

"What had they seen?"

"A man running."

"But this house is a considerable distance from the ambush site, right?

Doesn't that seem a little odd to you that they would chase a man a mile or almost a mile and a half across the sand?"

"They weren't chasing. . . ."

"Everything they had been taught was dead against it!"

"I said to them why the hell did you go so far."

"And what was the answer?"

"None."

"Well, lieutenant, this is where we are at now, trying to determine just what was told to these people that would give them the idea or reason to believe that they might have the semblance of backing from somebody to jump out of the ambush site for no reason and go on this terror strike."

Ellis stared across the desk into Talty's eyes but Talty did not answer.

"Quite frankly," Ellis said, smiling wanly, "it has me puzzled! I haven't run across a situation similar to it—where a squad has just deliberately disobeyed an order . . . just deserted an ambush and literally terrorized the countryside. . . ."

Again he stared at Talty and again there was no answer.

"Let me ask you a question, lieutenant, that might be a little involved. You're the leader of these people. You knew they were screwed up when you walked up to that house, even before you got to that house. You walked into that scene and the first thing you see is the bodies of two small children.

"Now lieutenant, there is nothing—*nothing*—I can think of, using all my experience, I can't think of *anything* that would lead you to believe that two small children could be gunned down at that time of night by accident!"

"I disagree there!" Talty said, pointing a finger at Ellis.

"How can you say that!"

"I disagree because of knowing the reaction of any squad, any normal squad when they are in combat! They see something or something startled them and one opens up and then they automatically all of them do and that's what I thought happened. That they had killed the two individuals by doing that. Something startled them and they just opened up. That's the first thing that came to my mind. Things like that, I mean I don't know how you figure it, but things like that can happen by accident. It doesn't have to be mischievous or anything else and that's what I thought it was."

Ellis stared wide-eyed at him. "Are you still entertaining the idea that this was *nothing more than an accident*? A very regrettable accident?"

Talty hesitated then said: "I don't know. I don't know what it was."

"But you have heard the story! We have told you that there were two or three hours of *terror*! People were raped! People were beaten up! People were . . . you've been told this before . . . people were hung up by the *heels* and kicked in the head and five people were murdered! Now, do you still think it was an accident?"

"No, I don't," Talty conceded.

"What do you think it was now, lieutenant?"

"It was . . ." he paused for the right word . . . "brutal."

"Brutal! We have two men who were running that squad who were supposed to be outstanding men, Potter and Monroe. They were the ones who had the leadership. Are they still outstanding troops, lieutenant?"

"Well!" Talty hesitated. He crossed his legs. "If you're asking me if I would take them into combat with me, yes."

"You still trust them?"

"I think so."

"Knowing what they did!"

"I wouldn't turn my back on them, if that's what you mean." The lieutenant could not get comfortable in his chair.

"Do you think you could trust them!"

"It's a hard question to answer."

"All right, lieutenant!" Ellis said sternly. "This thing is being put in such a way that it leaves the question in mind as to whether—by implication or straight orders—you engineered the whole thing. This is what it boils down to."

"I know it does!" Talty said.

"Someone is giving us stories and facts that come together in such a way that there was a secret briefing held by you with Monroe and Potter and that they in turn relayed the briefing to the squad. It looks as though you engineered this thing. By implication if nothing else. Or by saying, 'Go to your ambush site and at a specific time go out and rape, rob, beat and terrorize these goddamned people and get these zipper heads or gooks, shoot them, and don't bring any prisoners.' This is the word that was passed on to the squad. So it looks as though this word came from you originally. This is the position that you are being put in."

Talty's face grew redder as Ellis spoke.

"I see what they are trying to do! They are trying to blame the whole thing on me! But that day. . . ."

"We're just relaying to you what was related to us and showing you what this involves," Ellis said, quietly.

"Well, I'll tell you something!" Talty exploded. "I gave them no orders to kill anyone or rape or pillage or anything else! And earlier that day or I think it was the day before we had been sitting down, the platoon sergeant and myself and a bunch of guys, and it was first indicated that we move at night and raid a few places and find out if there were V.C. coming in. And then there was the usual kidding around about hanging them by the neck and beating them up and . . . well, I'm not an advocate of this! Why, it pisses me off to see them go out in the field and grab a chicken and kill a chicken and have some chicken! But I'm not telling these guys . . . these guys have heads of their own . . . if they want to go out and kill somebody . . . I would never in my life . . . to me . . . I mean these people are human beings and I'm not going to tell them . . . it's like trying to kill my own family . . . I'm not going to give them orders to go out and rape and burn. . . ."

Talty was breathing hard and beads of sweat rolled down his forehead. He wiped his brow with his sleeve, then looked at the stain.

"You say this bullshit session went on? This kidding around?"

"Yes, *kidding* around!"

"Were you involved in the kidding around, too?"

"Oh yes I was involved in it," he replied quickly. "But they are not going to take that and call it an order! That's what they're trying to do, though!"

Ellis paused. When he spoke it was in his weary, grey voice.

"Could it be that they might have thought this was the way the lieutenant felt about it?"

The lieutenant mopped his face with his handkerchief. "Well, that's bad, I guess."

"You see, lieutenant, somewhere something went wrong," Ellis suggested. "Some *word* was misconstrued, misunderstood, some *act* was misunderstood. And this was the end result."

"I gave them no orders!"

"You have to backtrack and find out where this bad seed came into it, if in fact the bad seed ever existed."

"When I gave them the briefing I gave it in front of everybody and they were grouped around me and if they took anything . . . I mean there were a lot of other people that day . . . and there had been a lot of other joking around in the Marine Corps, as far as that goes . . . when you're out in the field you joke around sometimes . . . and if these guys are going to take it like that . . . take it like it was an order from me . . . I wasn't the only one goofing around or anything like that . . . if they took that as an order from me . . . then . . . then . . . they are sick!"

"What exactly was said during this kidding around?"

"I said that we are going to try moving in on these hooches at night and try to find some V.C. with their weapons. Try to catch them making time with their wives. And then somebody would say, 'We ought to go in there and rape and burn,' or things like that . . . but *I* didn't say anything like that!"

"How about the destruction of other people's property?"

"Things like that, when they go to a place, about beating up on civilians and tearing things apart? I let it be known that I didn't go for that. I told them never let me catch them doing that stuff."

"Would you concur with this, lieutenant? A squad is sent out on what is supposed to be a combat mission. They are sitting in an ambush with specific instructions on the time to move out and for some reason they jump the gun and leave their position quite early and do in fact go to houses and commit acts of atrocity, they rape, they hang a man by his heels and kicked him in the head, and tore up another man's house almost apart and beat him and his wife and threw their children out in the patio and covered them up like they were going to burn them. And then they get to this house and they massacre the whole family. Doesn't it seem odd that these people would do this without feeling that they had implied backing? They just can't arbitrarily get up and move out without feeling some sense of security that someone is behind them. Someone has to have, by some form or other, communicated, implied. . . ."

"I gave them nothing like that."

"Do you concur that they *might* have been thinking this?"

"No I don't!" Talty said, emphatically. "It's impossible that they could have."

"Why, lieutenant! They done it!" Ellis exclaimed. "They done just what I said they done and it took them several hours to do it. Now, they must have felt somewhere along the line by some form of communication or another that someone had implied that this sort of action is just what was supposed to be taken."

"They couldn't have," Talty maintained, shaking his head. "I gave them specific. . . ."

"They left their ambush early!"

"To search out a couple of hooches. . . ."

"But what about all the atrocities?"

"Search for V.C. . . . search for V.C. . . . that's what I gave them the flashlight for . . . search for V.C. . . ."

"Then we have them hanging people by their heels and actually going on a terror spree!"

Talty shook his head as though he didn't want to listen to Ellis.

"I gave them no such orders . . . I. . . ."

"They took it in their heads to do it all by themselves?" Ellis asked, incredulously. "Is it *possible* it might have been something you said? Or some implication?"

"No! I don't think so at all!"

"Then it would have to be one individual who gave the orders. Either that or the whole squad decided together to do it."

"It would have to be," Talty agreed.

"Well," Ellis stated angrily, "that would mean that every man in the squad is an animal!"

"Not necessarily! I'm not saying that!"

"Either one man leads, lieutenant, or the whole pack is an animal and they operate on the same level! They all get the same idea at the same time! Either that or it would have to be one man leading."

"Not necessarily one," Talty suggested, weakly.

"Well, let's say two then," Ellis said and his voice softened. "I'll give it the benefit of the doubt. Would you say that Boyd was capable of coming up with the idea?"

"No."

"That Vogel was capable of coming up with this?"

"No."

"Or Henderson? Even with his size?"

"No."

"The Doc?"

"No."

"What about Potter and Monroe?"

"I don't think they would actually *plan* something like this," Talty said. "I don't know. It's hard to say. I didn't think they were the type to do anything like that, that's all. It's still hard for me to believe that they have done it. . . ." Talty frowned at the thought of his guilty men. ". . . I mean they are my own men, you know, and I have worked with them and I have *never* seen any of this maltreatment . . . and I let it be known that I was against it . . . and I never seen it done . . . I just can't believe that all of a sudden they would do that. . . ."

The Verdict

Sergeant Ellis' inquiries into the facts surrounding the raid on Xuan Ngoc lasted from September 24, the day after the crimes were committed, to October 9. The formal pretrial investigation was conducted in the quonset hut at Chu Lai from October 24 to November 2. Under Article 31 of the Uniform Code of Military Justice, a pretrial investigation officer hears all witnesses and evidence against suspects and recommends to higher authority whether they should be charged and tried. The process is the approximate equivalent of the grand jury system in civilian courts; to indict or not indict. The pretrial investigation officer in this case was a Lieutenant Colonel John L. Zorack, a wiry, sharp-featured career Marine in his early forties. The ten suspects, including Lieutenant Talty, were present, with a variety of captains and majors to represent them as counsel.

The hearing dragged on through six days of sweltering heat. Wide latitude is allowed in cross-examinations in these preliminary hearings and the battery of six defense lawyers (four acted for two suspects) took full advantage of it. The hearing bogged down further because most of the witnesses were Vietnamese who had to be questioned through an interpreter. The interpreter, to complicate matters still more, was weak in English (he had taken a six-month course in an American school) and not overly familiar with the Vietnamese dialect spoken in the Xuan Ngoc area.

Lieutenant Colonel Zorack, after hearing the six days of testimony, recommended that the following be charged and tried by general courts-martial:

Sergeant Ronald Vogel: Murder and rape.

Lance Corporal Robert W. Monroe: Murder, rape, assault, assault to commit murder, assault to commit rape.

Pfc. John D. Potter Jr.: Murder, rape, assault, assault t/c rape.

Pfc. Danny L. McGhen: Murder, rape, assault, assault t/c murder, assault t/c rape.

Pfc. James H. Boyd Jr.: Murder, assault t/c murder.

Pfc. Clifton G. Hobson: Rape, assault t/c rape, assault.

Pfc. Jerry D. Sullivan: Rape, assault t/c rape.

Pfc. James W. Henderson: Rape, assault t/c rape, assault.

Hn. Jon R. Bretag: Rape, assault t/c rape.

Lieutenant Stephen J. Talty: Making a false report to a superior officer.

In a footnote to his recommendations, Lieutenant Colonel Zorack suggested that the charge against Lieutenant Talty be dropped. It was Zorack's understanding, he said, that the lieutenant had submitted his resignation. The lieutenant had exercised extremely poor judgment, Zorack conceded, but in view of the relative insignificance of the charge of making a false report, the investigating officer recommended that the resignation be accepted.

The Commanding General of the First Marine Division, the authority to which Zorack addressed his recommendations, disagreed. He ordered that the lieutenant be court-martialed not only for making a false report but also for violation of Article 78 of the Uniform Code of Military Justice: accessory after the fact of murder.

Lieutenant Talty and his nine men were tried by courts-martial separately at Chu Lai during January of 1967.

Pfc. Potter, the real leader of the squad, the man charged with rape, the murder of five people including that of the five-year-old Dao Thi Tao, did not take the stand in his defense. He was revealed to be, nevertheless, an excellent Marine. "Potter was the kind of man that I wanted in my platoon," testified Gunnery Sergeant Jerald L. Hass, a veteran Marine, and platoon sergeant in Bravo Company. "Potter was forceful, excellent, above average." Blond, of medium build, Potter had been in the Marines two years, the last ten months in Vietnam. He had seen a lot of action— Operations Jackson, Osage, Montgomery, Colorado, and numerous smaller sweeps against V.C. On June 22 he had been wounded in the groin by shrapnel and had been awarded the Purple Heart. He had come from Satartia, Mississippi, a hamlet near Yazoo City. His father, a deacon in the Methodist Church, ran a grocery store. An above-average student in high school, Potter transferred to the Chamberlain-Hunt military academy in

Port Gibson, Mississippi, where he easily made second lieutenant and became a cadet leader. After one year at Mississippi State College, he enlisted in the Marines.

A psychiatrist's report read at his court-martial brought out that Potter, after ten months in Vietnam, "gave a history of frustration, anger and nervous tension. In this war the enemy is always hidden and Marines know that he is hidden by the citizenry. Potter was angry and he looked forward to raiding the village. This mental strain, however, didn't prevent him from being fully mentally responsible."

Potter was found guilty. He was sentenced to a dishonorable discharge "and hard labor for the rest of your natural life." He was twenty. Over the two years since his trial, as a prisoner at the Portsmouth, New Hampshire, naval prison, he has exhausted all routes to appeal. Preparations were being made at this writing to transfer him to the Federal penitentiary at Leavenworth where he will serve his sentence.

As Potter was revealed at his court-martial to have been a forceful Marine, Sergeant Vogel was drawn as a weak leader.

Sergeant Pedro Laredo of Bravo Company testified: "Potter and Monroe took care of the squad. Both Captain Sullivan and Lieutenant Talty were aware of Vogel's shortcomings. Vogel wasn't getting the work done. He wasn't showing leadership at all. That ambush was going to be his last patrol. They were going to transfer him next morning due to incompetence."

And Gunnery Sergeant Hass: "Sergeant Vogel was to be administratively busted. If I had my way he wouldn't of had that squad. There was nothing Mr. Talty could do. This man's background and his capabilities at leading men was well known within this Company. He had no business having the squad. We were going to solve the problem within a week. If he didn't snap out of his shit, we were going to take the squad away from him and administratively bust him."

Vogel was charged as a principal in the murder of the five-year-old girl in that he aided and abetted Potter by counting one, two, three. He was charged as a principal in the rape of Bui Thi Huong, though he did not physically rape her, because he aided and abetted by pouring water on her to revive her. He was found guilty on both charges.

In a final plea to the court before sentencing, Vogel, the Marine with the adopted daughter waiting for him back home, said: "I don't know how to say this or what to do. I'll take the blame for all of it. It was my fault I was not carrying out my duties as a sergeant and because I was the senior man present. If I could do anything to bring those people back I would do so. I would even give up my own life. But I can't do so. I'm going to have to leave it up to you men and whatever you decide."

The men decided to sentence him to fifty years in prison. Last May, Vogel's sentence was cut by the Naval Board of Review to ten years. The

Board reversed the rape conviction in the belief that Vogel, when he poured water on Bui Thi Huong, might have been performing a humane act. He is serving his time at the Portsmouth naval prison.

Even the prosecution saw the pathos in the case of Pfc. Boyd, the low achiever from Coon Rapids who pleaded guilty to murder in that he fired a single shot at one of the women as she was falling from Potter's burst.

"This is a sad and pathetic case, a classic example of where a man is a victim of circumstances," the trial counsel said, adding to the weight of defense counsel's plea for leniency in sentencing.

The pathos was not lessened when defense counsel read the court a letter from the defendant's mother:

". . . we belonged to the Methodist Church until our eleven-year-old daughter led us to a bible-believing church which is the Coon Rapids Baptist Church. Here is where we accepted Jesus as our personal savior and by the grace of God we were saved. Jim accepted Jesus as his personal savior before he went to Vietnam and by the grace of God he was also saved. . . ."

Strangely, the Marine Corps was able to determine *after* the incident at Xuan Ngoc, that the eighteen-year-old Boyd had "a long-standing character and behavior disorder manifested by lack of normal interpersonal relationships, immaturity, poor judgment and almost complete disregard for the accepted social, moral and legal codes of society. Boyd usually acts in an impulsive and immature manner without taking time to consider his actions beforehand."

And the court sentenced him to four years at hard labor. Boyd, with time off for good behavior, has been released from Portsmouth and is now at liberty.

Bretag, the Navy medic who had the misfortune to make his first volunteer patrol in Vietnam a raid on a sleeping village, also pleaded guilty to the rape of Bui Thi Huong.

"I've always tried to perform my duties as a Corpsman to the best of my ability," he told the court before sentencing. "But on the night of the twenty-third I let myself down and I let my family and my fellow Corpsmen down. As being so weak as to follow the group and stand by and not try to stop what was happening. If there was some way that I could rectify what happened that night I'd very much do so."

Bretag was sentenced to six months at hard labor.

Clifton G. Hobson and James W. Henderson, the two Negro Pfc.'s in the squad, both pleaded not guilty to the charges of raping Bui Thi Huong and assaulting Nguyen Thi Mai with intent to commit rape. Henderson, twenty-one, well over six feet and slender, had enlisted in the Marines in 1963 after finishing junior high school in Philadelphia. His mother was a widow. Hobson was short and stocky. He played football and basketball in junior high school in his native Monroe, Louisiana, and his one fear as a boy was that he wouldn't fill out enough to play football in high school and college. He did but his father, the game's injuries in mind, asked him not to go out for the sport and Clifton complied. Both his mother and father were teachers, his mother principal of an elementary school in Monroe. An uncle was a high-school principal, an aunt a supervisor of instructors, and another uncle a doctor. He had a sister in college. After graduating from Carroll High School in Monroe, Hobson spent a year at Grambling College. He had been in Vietnam three months before Xuan Ngoc and, like Henderson, had made a good record.

Both men were found guilty. Henderson was sentenced to two years at hard labor and Hobson to three years. Both men's convictions on the charges of raping Bui Thi Huong were later reversed on appeal. In Henderson's case, the court found that the mere testimony that the defendant was seen on top of the alleged victim was not proof of guilt, that forcible entry had to be proved. Hobson's conviction was set aside because the Board of Review was unconvinced by the evidence against the accused. The convictions on the charges of assaulting the sixteen-year-old girl with intent to commit rape were affirmed in both instances, however, and the sentences were reduced to six months. Both men are now free.

Lance Corporal Monroe, Pfc. Jerry Sullivan, and Pfc. Danny McGhen were found not guilty on all charges in their courts-martial. McGhen and Sullivan are out of the Marines but Monroe is now a sergeant at Camp LeJeune, North Carolina.

Lieutenant Talty was court-martialed at Chu Lai on March 13 and 14 of 1967. He pleaded not guilty to charges of being an accessory after the fact of murder in that he assisted his squad in order to prevent the detection and apprehension for murders of Vietnamese civilians and of making a false official statement to a superior officer.

The question of the lieutenant's mood on September 23, the day of the raid on Xuan Ngoc, was not brought up at his court-martial but it had been at Potter's court-martial. Defense counsel had asked a Corporal Dedmon, one of the lieutenant's men, about Talty's state of mind that day.

"Well, our platoon had been sort of fouling up in garrison, seemed like everything we did, and we wanted to get some V.C. so we could more or less prove that we were as good as anyone else because we had a lot of pride in our platoon and we wanted real bad to get some V.C. that day."

The trouble was that V.C. were scarce, if not absent, in the Xuan Ngoc area. Captain Sullivan, who had been company commander at the time of the raid, testified by deposition at Talty's trial:

"When we first came into the [area] in May, V.C. activity was, shall we say, moderate. The more we stayed inside the area, it became decreasing, that is it became decreased. Smaller and smaller. In September . . . we had no incident in the Xuan Ngoc area that I can recall."

The lieutenant testified that his instructions to the squad were to set up an ambush, remain at the ambush site until 11:30 p.m., search out any hooches in the immediate area, and return by 12:30 a.m. He admitted that after the squad showed him the bodies at Bui Thi Huong's house he radioed the company commander, Captain Sullivan, with the false report that a male and two female V.C. had been killed in the ambush and that the two females had been dragged away. He admitted that he then instructed the squad to carry the man's body a thousand yards back to the ambush site and "make it look like an ambush if it took all night. Drag the body around, walk around in bare feet, I didn't care what they did. I didn't want to tell the company commander what happened. I was very shocked."

"Did you give them any instructions about returning to the house?"

"No sir, I did not. One man suggested that we go back and get rid of the bodies, put them in the shack and burn it, but I said, 'No, you should never go back to the house.' "

The lieutenant was asked by his counsel why he had instructed the men to simulate an ambush action.

"They were obviously wrong in what they had done. They left the ambush site. I wasn't altogether protecting them. I was protecting myself in a way. I knew there would be repercussions because of what happened. They left the ambush site, they killed these civilians who, I assume, were innocent. But I had no idea. Murder didn't enter my mind at all. I thought it was a brutal, tragic accident. And I was willing to help them. I'd helped them before."

Gunnery Sergeant Hass, who had to be told by the referee Law Officer to keep his language slightly less salty, testified that when Lieutenant Talty returned to the C.P. after viewing the bodies, the lieutenant said, "Well, they really fucked up this time!"

The prosecutor asked Talty why he had made such a remark.

Talty said that Potter and Monroe more or less ran the squad "and when they got together anything could happen."

"What do you mean?"

"They've often been told before about maltreatment of the people."

"You knew they had antagonism for the people?"

"Yes sir."

"You knew that in the past they were guilty of antagonism and brutality toward the Vietnamese people?"

"I wouldn't say brutality."

"Pushing around?"

"Yes."

"Hitting on occasion?"

"I have never seen it but I had heard it."

"You knew the victims of their acts, roughhousing, were innocent people?"

"That's correct."

"And yet you let them run the squad?"

"They were both good troopers. Very good."

"Did you take measures to correct these propensities?"

"Yes sir. And I thought they had taken effect."

The prosecutor then probed Talty's motives for making his false report to the captain and ordering his men to fake the ambush.

"You said you thought the killings were an accident. Didn't you go to an awful lot of trouble to cover up an accident?"

"Yes sir, but I knew there would be repercussions. I just wanted to get away from that house. I wanted to get the hell away from there."

"But why go to such great lengths? Why not tell the C.O. it was an accident?"

"There would be an investigation. There would be repercussions. I would be relieved, the squad leaders would be relieved, everybody would be relieved. The captain would be relieved. But I wasn't going to cover up the incident. I was going to tell about it."

"You were going to tell them you covered it up and made it look like an ambush? Then why were you doing it?"

"I don't know," Talty said. "I just wanted to get away from there."

Lieutenant Talty was found not guilty of the more serious charge, accessory after the fact of murder. He was found guilty of making a false report and sentenced to dismissal from the Corps, forfeiture of $100 per month pay for five months, and loss of 300 numbers in rank. The Board of Review affirmed the conviction but set aside the sentence of dismissal. The lieutenant petitioned the Court of Military Appeals for a review of his case but the court turned him down. It then forwarded the case, in accordance with established practice, to the Secretary of the Navy for possible clemency. Attached were two enclosures: the Judge Advocate of the Navy recommended no clemency. Lieutenant General L. W. Walt, now Assistant Commandant of the Marine Corps, recommended:

"This officer submitted a false and misleading statement to his superiors in an attempt to prevent the discovery of murders committed by his men and to protect himself. An officer who is guilty of such conduct could never be trusted. An officer who cannot be trusted is of no value."

Talty and six of his men are back in civilian life. One is a sergeant in the Corps, two are still in prison.

All cases in the Xuan Ngoc incident are in the Judge Advocate General's "finished" file.   [August, 1969]

The facts of this report are available for public inspection in the office of the Judge Advocate General of the Navy in Washington, D.C.

Part VII

Creative Agonies

Some Children of the Goddess

by Norman Mailer

I doubt if there is any book I read in the last few years which I approached with more unnatural passion than *Set This House on Fire*. Styron's first novel, *Lie Down in Darkness*, was published when he was twenty-six, and it was so good (one need today only compare it to *Rabbit, Run* to see how very good it was) that one felt a kind of awe about Styron. He gave promise of becoming a great writer, great not like Hemingway nor even like Faulkner whom he resembled a bit, but great perhaps like Hawthorne. And there were minor echoes of Fitzgerald and Malcolm Lowry. Since his first novel had failed to make him a household word in America, he had a justifiable bitterness about the obscurity in which good young writers were kept. But it poisoned his reaction to everything. One of the traps for a writer of exceptional talent, recognized insufficiently, is the sort of excessive rage which washes out distinction. Styron was intensely competitive—all good young novelists are—but over the years envy began to eat into his character. Months before James Jones's *Some Came Running* was published (and it had the greatest advance publicity of any novel I remember—for publicity seemed to begin two years before publication), Styron obtained a copy of the galleys. There were long nights in

Connecticut on "Styron's Acres" when he would entertain a group of us by reading absurd passages from Jones's worst prose. I would laugh along with the rest, but I was a touch sick with myself. I had love for Jones, as well as an oversized fear for the breadth of his talent, and I had enough envy in me to enjoy how very bad were the worst parts of *Some Came Running*. But there were long powerful chapters as well; some of the best writing Jones has ever done is found in that book. So I would laugh in paroxysms along with the others, but I was also realizing that a part of me had wanted *Some Came Running* to be a major book. I was in the doldrums, I needed a charge of dynamite. If *Some Came Running* had turned out to be the best novel any of us had written since the war, I would have had to get to work. It would have meant the Bitch was in love with someone else, and I would have had to try to win her back. But the failure of *Some Came Running* left me holding onto a buttock of the lady—if she had many lovers, I was still one of them. And so everything in me which was slack and conservative could enjoy Styron's burlesque readings. Yet I also knew I had lost an opportunity.

A few months later, I ceased seeing Styron—it would take a chapter in a novel to tell you why. I liked the boy in Styron, disliked the man, and had vast admiration for his talent. I was hardly the one to read *Set This House on Fire* with a cool mind. Nine years had gone by since *Lie Down in Darkness* was published, and the anticipation of the second novel had taken on grandiloquent proportions among his friends and his closest enemies. One knew it would be close to unbearable if his book were extraordinary; yet a part of me felt again what I had known with *Some Came Running*—that it would be good for me and for my work if Styron's novel were better than anything any of us had done. So I read it with a hot sense of woe, delighted elation, and a fever of moral speculations. Because it was finally a bad novel. A bad maggoty novel. Four or five half-great short stories were buried like pullulating organs in a corpse of fecal matter: overblown unconceived philosophy, Technicolor melodramatics, and a staggering ignorance about the passions of murder, suicide and rape. It was the magnum opus of a fat spoiled rich boy who could write like an angel about landscape and like an adolescent about people. The minor characters were gargoyles, and badly drawn. Here and there quick portraits emerged, there was one excellent still-life of an Italian police official who was Fascist, the set pieces were laid out nicely, but the vice of the talent insisted on dominating. Whenever Styron didn't know what to do with his men and women (which was often, for they repeated themselves as endlessly as a Southern belle), Styron went back to his landscape; more of the portentous Italian scenery blew up its midnight storm. But Styron was trying to write a book about good and evil, and his good was as vacuous as the spirit of an empty water bag:

I can only tell you this, that as for being and nothingness, the one thing I did know was that to choose between them was simply to choose being, not for the sake of being, or even the love of being, much less the desire to be forever—but in the hope of being what I could be for a time.

Which is a great help to all of us.

His evil character took on the fatal sin of an evil character: he was not dangerous but pathetic. A fink. Styron was crawling with all ten thumbs toward that ogre of mystery who guards the secrets of why we choose to kill others and quiver in dread at the urge to kill ourselves. But like a bad general who surrounds himself with a staff which daren't say no, Styron spent his time digging trenches for miles to the left and miles to the right, and never launched an attack on the hill before him. It was the book of a man whose soul had gotten fat.

And yet, much as I could be superior to myself for having taken him thus seriously, for having written predictions in *Advertisements for Myself* that he would write a very good book which the mass media would call great, much as I would grin each day after reading a hundred pages of hothouse beauty and butter bilge, much as I would think, "You don't catch the Bitch that way, buster, you got to bring more than a trombone to her boudoir," much so much as I was pleased at the moral justice which forbids a novelist who envied too much the life of others to capture much life in his own pages, I was still not altogether happy, because I knew his failure was making me complacent again, and so delaying once more the day when I would have to pay my respects to the lady.

And indeed I lost something by the failure of *Some Came Running* and *Set This House on Fire*. I never did get going far on my novel. I wrote a four-hour play and essays and articles, two hundred thousand words accumulated over the years since *Advertisements for Myself*, and I showed a talent for getting into stunts, and worse, much worse. Years went by. Now once again, in this season, ready to start my novel about the mysteries of murder and suicide, I found by taking stock of psychic credit and debit that I had lost some of my competitive iron. I knew a bit of sadness about work. I did not feel sure I could do what I had now settled for doing, and to my surprise I was curious what others were up to. If I couldn't bring off the work myself, it might be just as well if someone else could give a sign of being ready to make the attempt. In this sad dull mellow mood, feeling a little like a middle-aged mountaineer, I read at one stretch over three weeks the novels I want to write about here.

There was a time, I suspect, when James Jones wanted to be the greatest writer who ever lived. Now, if *The Thin Red Line* is evidence of his future, he has apparently decided to settle for being a very good writer among other good writers. The faults and barbarities of his style are gone. He is no longer the worst writer of prose ever to give intimations of greatness. The language has been filed down and the phrases no longer collide like trailer trucks at a hot intersection. Yet I found myself nostalgic for the old bad prose. I never used to think it was as bad as others did, it was eloquent and communicated Jones's force to the reader. It is not that *The Thin Red Line* is dishonest or narrow; on the contrary it is so broad and true a portrait of combat that it could be used as a textbook at the Infantry School if the Army is any less chicken than it used to be. But, sign of the times, there is now something almost too workmanlike about Jones. He gets almost everything in, horror, fear, fatigue, the sport of combat, the hang-ups, details, tactics, he takes an infantry company through its early days in combat on Guadalcanal and quits it a few weeks later as a veteran outfit, blooded, tough, up on morale despite the loss of half the original men, gone, dead, wounded, sick or transferred. So he performs the virtuoso feat of letting us know a little about a hundred men. One can even (while reading) remember their names. Jones's aim, after all, is not to create character but the feel of combat, the psychology of men. He is close to a master at this. Jones has a strong sense of a man's psychology and it carries quietly through his pages.

The Thin Red Line was of course compared to *The Naked and the Dead*, but apart from the fact that I am the next-to-last man to judge the respective merits of the two books, I didn't see them as similar. *The Naked and the Dead* is concerned more with characters than military action. By comparison it's a leisurely performance. *The Thin Red Line* is as crammed as a movie treatment. No, I think the real comparison is to *The Red Badge of Courage*, and I suspect *The Red Badge of Courage* will outlive *The Thin Red Line*. Yet I don't quite know why. *The Thin Red Line* is a more detailed book; it tells much more of combat, studies the variations in courage and fear of not one man but twenty men and gets something good about each one of them. Its knowledge of life is superior to *The Red Badge of Courage, The Thin Red Line* is less sentimental, its humor is dry to the finest taste, and yet . . . it is too technical. One needs ten topographical maps to trace the action. With all its variety, scrupulosity, respect for craft, one doesn't remember *The Thin Red Line* with that same nostalgia, that same sense of a fire on the horizon which comes back always from *The Red Badge of Courage.*

No, Jones's book is better remembered as satisfying, as if one had studied geology for a semester and now knew more. I suppose what was felt lacking is the curious sensuousness of combat, the soft lift of awe and pleasure that one was moving out onto the rim of the dead. If one was not too tired, there were times when a blade of grass coming out of the ground before one's nose was as significant as the finger of Jehovah in the Sistine Chapel. And this was not because a blade of grass was necessarily in itself so beautiful, or because hitting the dirt was so sweet, but because the blade seemed to be a living part of the crack of small-arms fire and the palpable flotation of all the other souls in the platoon full of turd and glory. Now, it's not that Jones is altogether ignorant of this state. The description he uses is "sexy," and one of the nicest things about Jim as a writer is his ease in moving from mystical to practical reactions with his characters. Few novelists can do this, it's the hint of greatness, but I think he steered *The Thin Red Line* away from its chance of becoming an American classic of the first rank when he kept the mystical side of his talents on bread and water, and gave his usual thoroughgoing company-man's exhibition of how much he knows technically about his product. I think that is the mistake. War is as full of handbooks as engineering, but it is more of a mystery, and the mystery is what separates the great war novels from the good ones. It is an American activity to cover the ground quickly, but I guess this is one time Jones should have written two thousand pages, not four hundred ninety-five. But then the underlying passion in this book is not to go for broke, but to promise the vested idiots of the book reviews that he can write as good as anyone who writes a book review.

When you discuss eight or ten books, there is a dilemma. The choice is to write eight separate book reviews, or work to find a thesis which ties the books together. There is something lick-spittle about the second method: "Ten Authors in Search of a Viable Theme," or "The Sense of Alienation in Eight American Novelists." A bed of Procrustes is brought in from the wings to stretch and shorten the separate qualities of the books. I would rather pick up each book by itself and make any connections on the fly. The thesis of the Bitch is thesis enough for me. Its application to Jones would say that *The Thin Red Line* is a holding action, a long-distance call to the Goddess to declare that one still has one's hand in, expect red roses for sure, but for the time, you know, like there're contacts to make on the road, and a few Johns to impress.

Another Country, by James Baldwin, is as different from *The Thin Red Line* as two books by talented novelists published in the same year can turn out to be. It does not deal with a hundred characters, but eight, and they are very much related. In fact there is a chain of fornication which is all but complete. A Negro musician named Rufus Scott has an affair with a white Southern girl which ends in beatings, breakdown, and near-insanity. She goes to a mental hospital, he commits suicide. The connection is taken up by his sister who has an affair with a white writer, a friend of Rufus' named Vivaldo Moore, who in turn gets into bed with a friend named Eric who is homosexual but having an affair with a married woman named Cass Silenski, which affair wrecks her marriage with her husband Richard, another writer, and leaves Eric waiting at the boat for his French lover Yves. A summary of this sort can do a book no good, but I make it to trace the links. With the exception of

Rufus Scott who does not go to bed with his sister, everybody else in the book is connected by their skin to another character who is connected to still another. So the principal in the book, the protagonist, is not an individual character, not society, but a milieu, not a social organism like an infantry company, but indeed is sex, sex very much in the act. And almost the only good writing in the book is about the act. And some of that is very good indeed. But *Another Country* is a shocker. For the most part it is an abominably written book. It is sluggish in its prose, lifeless for its first hundred pages, stilted to despair in its dialogue. There are roles in plays called actor-proof. They are so conceived that even the worst actor will do fairly well. So *Another Country* is writer-proof. Its peculiar virtue is that Baldwin commits every *gaffe* in the art of novel writing and yet has a powerful book. It gets better of course; after the first hundred pages it gets a lot better. Once Eric, the homosexual, enters, the work picks up considerably. But what saves the scene is that Baldwin has gotten his hands into the meat and won't let go. All the sex in the book is displaced, whites with blacks, men with men, women with homosexuals, the sex is funky to suffocation, rich but claustrophobic, sensual but airless. Baldwin understands the existential abyss of love. In a world of Negroes and whites, nuclear fallout, marijuana, bennies, inversion, insomnia, and tapering off with beer at four in the morning, one no longer just falls in love—one has to take a brave leap over the wall of one's impacted rage and cowardice. And nobody makes it, not quite. Each of the characters rides his sexual chariot, whip out, on a gallop over a solitary track, and each is smashed, more or less by his own hand. They cannot find the juice to break out of their hatred into the other country of love. Except for the homosexuals who can't break into heterosexual love. Of all the novels talked about here, *Another Country* is the one which is closest to the mood of New York in our time, a way of saying it is close to the air of the Western world, it is at least a novel about matters which are important, but one can't let up on Baldwin for the way he wrote it. Years ago I termed him "minor" as a writer, I thought he was too smooth and too small. Now on his essays alone, on the long continuing line of poetic fire in his essays, one knows he has become one of the few writers of our time. But as a Negro novelist he could take lessons from a good journeyman like John Killens. Because *Another Country* is almost a major novel and yet it is far and away the weakest and worst near-major novel one has finished. It goes like the first draft of a first novelist who has such obvious stuff that one is ready, if an editor, to spend years guiding him into how to write, even as one winces at the sloppy company which must be kept. Nobody has more elegance than Baldwin as an essayist, not one of us hasn't learned something about the art of the essay from him, and yet he can't even find a good prose for his novel. Maybe the form is not for him. He knows what he wants to say, and that is not the best condition for writing a novel. Novels go happiest when you discover something you did not know you knew.

Baldwin's experience has shaped his tongue toward directness, for urgency—the honorable defense may be that he has not time nor patience to create characters, milieu, and mood for the revelation of important complexities he has already classified in his mind.

Baldwin's characters maim themselves trying to smash through the wall of their imprisonment. William Burroughs gives what may be the finest record in our century of the complete psychic convict. *Naked Lunch* is a book of pieces and fragments, notes and nightmarish anecdotes, which he wrote—according to his preface—in various states of delirium, going in and out of a heroin addiction. It is not a novel in any conventional sense, but then there's a question whether it's a novel by any set of standards other than the dictum that prose about imaginary people put between book covers is a novel. At any rate, the distinction is not important except for the fact that *Naked Lunch* is next to impossible to read in consecutive fashion. I saw excerpts of it years ago, and thought enough of them to go on record that Burroughs "may conceivably be possessed by genius." I still believe that, but it is one thing to be possessed by genius, it is another to be a genius, and *Naked Lunch* read from cover to cover is not as exciting as in its separate pieces. Quantity changes quality, as Karl Marx once put it, and fifty or sixty three-page bits about homosexual orgies, castration, surgeon-assassins, and junkie fuzz dissolving into a creeping green ooze leaves one feeling pretty tough. "Let's put some blue-purple blood in the next rape," says your jaded taste.

This is, however, quibbling. Some of the best prose in America is graffiti found on men's room walls. It is prose written in bone, etched by acid, it is the prose of harsh truth, the virulence of the criminal who never found his stone walls and so settles down on the walls of the john, it is the language of hatred unencumbered by guilt, hesitation, scruple, or complexity. Burroughs must be the greatest writer of graffiti who ever lived. His style has the snap of a whip, and it never relents. Every paragraph is quotable. Here's a jewel among a thousand jewels:

Dr. Benway . . . looks around and picks up one of those rubber vacuum cups at the end of a stick they use to unstop toilets . . . "Make an incision, Doctor Limpf. . . . I'm going to massage the heart." . . . Dr. Benway washes the suction cup by swishing it around in the toilet-bowl. . . .

Dr. Limpf: "The incision is ready, doctor."

Dr. Benway forces the cup into the incision and works it up and down. Blood spurts all over the doctors, the nurse and the wall. . . .

Nurse: "I think she's gone, doctor."

Dr. Benway: "Well, it's all in the day's work."

Punch-and-Judy. Mr. Interlocutor and Mr. Bones. One, two, three, bam! two, four, eight, bam! The drug addict lives with a charged wire so murderous he must hang his nervous system on a void. Burroughs' achievement, his great achievement, is that he has brought back snow-flakes from this murderous void.

Once, years ago in Chicago, I was coming down with a bad cold. By accident, a friend took me to hear a jazz musician named Sun Ra who played "space music." The music was a little like the sound of Ornette Coleman, but further out, outer space music, close to the EEEE of an electric drill at the center of a harsh trumpet. My cold cleared up in five minutes. I swear it. The anger of the sound penetrated into some sprung-up rage which was burning fuel for the cold. Burroughs' pages have the same medicine. If a hundred patients on terminal cancer read *Naked Lunch*, one or two might find remission. Bet money on that. For Burroughs is the surgeon of the novel.

Yet he is something more. It is his last ability which entitles him to a purchase on genius. Through the fantasies runs a vision of a future world, a half-demented welfare state, an abattoir of science fiction with surgeons, bureaucrats, perverts, diplomats, a world not describable short of getting into the book. The ideas have pushed into the frontier of an all-electronic universe. One holds onto a computer in some man-eating machine of the future which has learned to use language. The words come out in squeaks, spiced with static, sex coiled up with technology like a scream on the radar. Bombarded by his language, the sensation is like being in a room where three radios, two television sets, stereo hi-fi, a pornographic movie, and two automatic dishwashers are working at once while a mad scientist conducts the dials to squeeze out the maximum disturbance. If this is a true picture of the world to come, and it may be, then Burroughs is a great writer. Yet there is sadness in reading him, for one gets intimations of a mind which might have come within distance of Joyce, except that a catastrophe has been visited on it, a blow by a sledgehammer, a junkie's needle which left the crystalline brilliance crashed into bits.

Now beyond a doubt, of all the books discussed here, the one which most cheats evaluation is Joseph Heller's *Catch-22*. It was the book which took me longest to finish, and I almost gave it up. Yet I think that a year from now I may remember it more vividly than *The Thin Red Line*. Because it is an original. There's no book like it anyone has read. Yet it's maddening. It reminds one of a Jackson Pollock painting, eight feet high, twenty feet long. Like yard goods, one could cut it anywhere. One could take out a hundred pages anywhere from the middle of *Catch-22*, and not even the author could be certain they were gone. Yet the length and similarity of one page to another gives a curious meat-and-potatoes to the madness; building upon itself the book becomes substantial until the last fifty pages grow suddenly and surprisingly powerful, only to be marred by an ending over the last five pages which is hysterical, sentimental and walleyed for Hollywood.

This is the skin of the reaction. If I were a major critic, it would be a virtuoso performance to write a definitive piece on *Catch-22*. It would take ten thousand words or more. Because Heller is carrying his reader on a more consistent voyage through Hell than any American writer before him (except Burroughs who has already made the trip and now sells choice seats in the auditorium), and so the analysis of Joseph H.'s Hell would require a discussion of other varieties of inferno and whether they do more than this author's tour.

Catch-22 is a nightmare about an American bomber squadron on a made-up island off Italy. Its hero is a bombardier named Yossarian who has flown fifty missions and wants out. On this premise is tattooed the events of the novel, fifty characters, two thousand frustrations (an average of four or five to the page) and one simple motif: more frustration. Yossarian's colonel wants to impress his general and so raises the number of missions to fifty-five. When the pilots have fifty-four, the figure is lifted to sixty. They are going for eighty by the time the book has been done. On the way every character goes through a routine *on every page* which is as formal as a little peasant figure in a folk dance. Back in school, we had a joke we used to repeat. It went:

"Whom are you talking about?"

"Herbert Hoover."

"Never heard of him."

"Never heard of whom?"

"Herbert Hoover."

"Who's he?"

"He's the man you mentioned."

"Never heard of Herbert Hoover."

So it went. So goes *Catch-22*. It's the rock and roll of novels. One finds its ancestor in Basic Training. We were ordered to have clean sheets for Saturday inspection. But one week we were given no clean sheets from the Post laundry so we slept on our mattress covers, which got dirty. After inspection, the platoon was restricted to quarters. "You didn't have clean sheets," our sergeant said.

"How could we have clean sheets if the clean sheets didn't come?"

"How do I know?" said the sergeant. "The regulations say you gotta have clean sheets."

"But we can't have clean sheets if there are no clean sheets."

"That," said the sergeant, "is tough shit."

Which is what *Catch-22* should have been called. The Army is a village of colliding bureaucracies whose colliding orders cook up impossibilities. Heller takes this one good joke and exploits it into two thousand variations of the same good joke, but in the act he somehow creates a rational vision of the modern world. Yet the crisis of reason is that it can no longer comprehend the modern world. Heller demonstrates that a rational man devoted to reason must arrive at the conclusion that either the world is mad and he is the only sane man in it, or (and this is the weakness of *Catch-22*—it never explores this possibility) the sane man is not really sane because his rational propositions are without existential reason.

On page 178, there is a discussion about God.

". . . how much reverence can you have for a Supreme Being who finds it necessary to include such phenomena as phlegm and tooth decay in His divine system of creation. . . . Why in the world did He ever create pain?"

"Pain?" Lieutenant Scheisskopf's wife pounced upon the word victoriously. "Pain is a useful symptom. Pain is a warning to us of bodily dangers."

. . . "Why couldn't He have used a doorbell instead to notify us, or one of His celestial choirs?"

Right there is planted the farthest advance of the flag of reason in his cosmology. Heller does not look for any answer, but there is an answer which might go that God gave us pain for the same reason the discovery of tranquilizers was undertaken by the Devil: if we have an immortal soul some of us come close to it only through pain. A season of sickness can be preferable to a flight from disease for it discourages the onrush of a death which begins in the center of oneself.

Give talent its due. *Catch-22* is the debut of a writer with merry gifts. Heller may yet become Gogol. But what makes one hesitate to call his first novel great or even major is that he has only grasped the inferior aspect of Hell. What is most unendurable is not the military world of total frustration so much as the midnight frustration of the half world, Baldwin's other country, where a man may have time to hear his soul, and time to go deaf, even be forced to contemplate himself as he becomes deadened before his death. (Much as Hemingway may have been.) That is when one becomes aware of the anguish, the existential *angst*, which wars enable one to forget. It is that other death—without war—where one dies by a failure of nerve, which opens the bloodiest vents of Hell. And that is a novel none of us has yet come back alive to write.

With the exception of *Another Country*, the novels talked about up to now have been books written for men. *Catch-22* was liked, I believe, by almost every man who read it. Women were puzzled. The world of a man is a world of surface slick and rock knowledge. A man must live by daily acts where he goes to work and works on the world some incremental bit, using the tools, instruments, and the techniques of the world. Thus a man cannot afford to go too deeply into the underlying meaning of a single subject. He prefers to become interested in quick proportions and contradictions, in the practical surface of things. A book like *Catch-22* is written on the face of solemn events and their cockeyed contradictions. So it has a vast appeal: it relieves the frustration men feel at the idiocy of their work. *Naked Lunch* fries the surface in a witch's skillet; the joy in reading is equal to the kick of watching a television announcer go insane before your eyes and start to croon obscenely about the President, First Lady, Barry Goldwater, Cardinal Spellman, J. Edgar. Somewhere in America somebody would take out his pistol and shoot the set. Burroughs shatters the surface and blasts its shards into the madness beneath. He rips the reader free of suffocation. Jones wrote a book which a dedicated corporation executive or an ambitious foreman would read with professional avidity because they would learn a bit about the men who work for them. *The Thin Red Line* brings detail to the surprises on the toughest part of the skin. So these three books are, as I say, books for men. Whereas *Another Country*, obsessed with that transcendental divide keeping sex from love, is a book more for women, or for men and women. So too is *Set This House on Fire*. And much the same can be said of *Rabbit, Run* and *Letting Go*.

On record are the opinions of a partisan. So it is necessary to admit the John Updike's novel was approached with animus. His reputation has traveled in convoy up the Avenue of the Establishment, The New York Times *Book Review* blowing sirens like a motorcycle caravan, the professional muse of *The New Yorker* sitting in the Cadillac, membership cards to the right Fellowships in his pocket. The sort of critics who are rarely right about a book—Arthur Mizener and Granville Hicks, for example—ride on his flanks, literary bodyguards. *Life* magazine blew its kiss of death into the confetti. To my surprise, *Rabbit, Run* was therefore a better book than I thought it would be. The Literary Establishment was improving its taste. Updike was not simply a junior edition of James Gould Cozzens. But of course the Establishment cannot nominate a candidate coherently. Updike's merits and vices were turned inside out. The good girlish gentlemen of letters were shocked by the explicitness of the sex in *Rabbit, Run*, and slapped him gently for that with their fan, but his style they applauded. It is Updike's misfortune that he is invariably honored for his style (which is atrocious—and smells like stale garlic) and is insufficiently recognized for his gifts. He could become the best of our literary novelists if he could forget about style and go deeper into the literature of sex. *Rabbit, Run* moves in well-modulated spurts at precisely those places where the style subsides to a ladylike murmur and the characters take over. The trouble is that young John, like many a good young writer before him, does not know exactly what to do when action lapses, and so he cultivates his private vice, he *writes*. And there are long over-fingered descriptions in exacerbated syntax, airless crypts of four or five pages, huge inner exertion reminiscent of weight lifters, a stale sweet sweat clings to his phrases.

EXAMPLE: *Redbook, Cosmopolitan, McCall's.*
Boys are playing basketball around a telephone pole with a backboard bolted

to it. Legs, shouts. The scrape and snap of Keds on loose alley pebbles seems to catapult their voices high into the moist March air blue above the wires. Rabbit Angstrom, coming up the alley in a business suit, stops and watches, though he's twenty-six and six-three. So tall, he seems an unlikely rabbit, but the breadth of white face, the pallor of his blue irises, and a nervous flutter under his brief nose as he stabs a cigarette into his mouth partially explain the nickname.

EXAMPLE: *True Confessions.*
Outside in the air his fears condense. Globes of ether, pure nervousness, slide down his legs. The sense of outside space scoops at his chest.

EXAMPLE: *Elements of Grammar.*
His hands lift of their own and he feels the wind on his ears even before, his heels hitting heavily on the pavement at first but with an effortless gathering out of a kind of sweet panic growing lighter and quicker and quieter, he runs. Ah: runs. Runs.

It's the rare writer who cannot have sentences lifted from his work, but the first quotation is taken from the first five sentences of the book, the second is on the next-to-last page, and the third is nothing less than the last three sentences of the novel. The beginning and end of a novel are usually worked over. They are the index to taste in the writer. Besides, trust your local gangster. In the run of Updike's pages are one thousand other imprecise, flatulent, wrynecked, precious, overpreened, self-indulgent, tortured sentences. It is the sort of prose which would be admired in a writing course overseen by a fussy old nance. And in Updike's new book, *The Centaur*, which was only sampled, the style has gotten worse. Pietisms are congregating, affirmations à la Archibald MacLeish.

The pity is that Updike has instincts for finding the heart of the conventional novel, that still-open no-man's-land between the surface and the deep, the soft machinery of the world and the subterranean rigors of the dream. His hero, Rabbit Angstrom, is sawed in two by the clear anguish of watching his private vision go at a gallop away from the dread real weight of his responsibility. A routine story of a man divided between a dull wife he cannot bear to live with, and a blowsy tough tender whore he cannot make it with, the merit of the book is not in the simplicity of its problem, but in the dread Updike manages to convey, despite the literary commercials in the style, of a young man who is beginning to lose nothing less than his good American soul, and yet it is not quite his fault. The power of the novel comes from a sense, not absolutely unworthy of Thomas Hardy, that the universe hangs over our fates like a great sullen hopeless sky. There is real pain in the book, and a touch of awe. It is a novel which could have been important, it could have had a chance to stay alive despite its mud pies in prose, but at the very end the book drowns in slime. Updike does not know how to finish. Faced with the critical choice of picking one woman or another (and by the end, both women are in fearful need), his character bolts over a literal hill and runs away. Maybe he'll be back tomorrow, maybe he'll never be back, but a decision was necessary. The book ends as minor, a pop-out. One is left with the expectation that Updike will never be great, there is something too fatally calculated about his inspiration. But very good he can be, a good writer of the first rank with occasional echoes from the profound. First he must make an enemy or two of the commissioners on the Literary Mafia. Of course a man spends his life trying to get up his guts for such a caper.

Letting Go, by Philip Roth, has precisely the opposite merits and faults. As a novel, its strategy is silly, tiresome, and weak. But its style, while not noteworthy, is decent and sometimes, in dialogue, halfway nice. It is good time spent to read any ten pages in the book. The details are observed, the mood is calm, the point is always made. It is like having an affair with a pleasant attentive woman, the hours go by neatly. It is only at the end of a year that one may realize the preoccupations of the mistress are hollow, and the seasons have been wasted.

Letting Go is a scrupulous account in upper Jewish New Yorker genre of a few years in the lives of two English Department college instructors, one married to that most coveted of creatures, a fragile dreary hangup of a heroine, the other a bachelor and lover of worried proportions. Very little happens. The wife goes on being herself, the husband remains naturally frozen and stingy, and the instructor-lover has a small literary breakdown. One can say, well isn't this life? didn't Chekhov and de Maupassant write about such things? And the answer is yes they did, in five pages they did, and caught that mood which reminds us that there is sadness in attrition and grinding sorrows for decency. But Roth is not writing a book with a vision of life; on the contrary, one could bet a grand he is working out an obsession. His concentration is appropriated by something in his life which has been using him up in the past. Virtually every writer, come soon or late, has a cramped-up love affair which is all but hopeless. *Of Human Bondage* could be the case study of half the writers who ever lived. But the obsession is opposed to art in the same way a compulsive talker is opposed to good conversation. The choice is either to break the obsession or enter it. The compulsive talker must go through the herculean transformation of learning to quit or must become a great monologuist. Roth tried to get into the obsession—he gave six hundred pages to wandering around in a ten-page story— but he did it without courage. He was too careful not to get hurt on his trip and so he does not reveal himself: he does not *dig*. The novel skitters like a water fly from pollen spread to pollen spread, a series of good short stories accumulate en route, but no novel. The iron law of the conventional novel, the garden novel, is that the meaning of the action must grow on every page or else the book will wither. It is Updike's respectable achievement in *Rabbit, Run* that he writes just such a book, or tries to until the last three pages when he vanishes like a sneak thief. Roth never gets into the game. One senses a determined fight to maintain *Letting Go* as a collection of intricately intercollected short stories.

But the short story has a tendency to look for climates of permanence—an event occurs, a man is hurt by it in some small way forever. The novel moves as naturally toward flux. An event occurs, a man is injured, and a month later is working on something else. The short story likes to be classic. It is most acceptable when one fatal point is made. Whereas the novel is dialectical. It is most alive when one can trace the disasters which follow victory or the subtle turns that sometimes come from a defeat. A novel can be created out of short stories only if the point in each story is consecutively more interesting and incisive than the point before it, when the author in effect is drilling for oil. But Roth's short stories in *Letting Go* just dig little holes in many suburban lawns until finally the work of reading it becomes almost as depressing as must have been the work of writing it. Roth has to make a forced march in his next book, or at the least, like Updike, get around to putting his foot in the whorehouse door. If he doesn't, a special Hell awaits his ambition—he will be called the Rich Man's Paddy Chayefsky, and Paddy without his grasp of poverty is nothing much at all.

It is necessary to say that the four stories about the Glass family by J. D. Salinger, published in two books called *Franny and Zooey* and *Raise High the Roof Beam, Carpenters*, seem to have been written for high-school girls. The second piece in the second book, called *Seymour an Introduction*, must be the most slovenly portion of prose ever put out by an important American writer. It is not even professional Salinger. Salinger at his customary worst, as here in the other three stories of the two books, is never bad—he is just disappointing. He stays too long on the light ice of his gift, writes exquisite dialogue and creates minor moods with sweetness and humor, and never gives the fish its hook. He disappoints because he is always practicing. But when he dips into Seymour, the Glass brother who committed suicide, when the cult comes to silence before the appearance of the star—the principal, to everyone's horror, has nausea on the stage. Salinger for the first time is engaged in run-off writing, free suffragette prose, his inhibitions (which once helped by their restraint to create his style) are now stripped. He is giving you himself as he is. No concealment. It feels like taking a bath in a grease trap.

Now, all of us have written as badly. There are nights when one comes home after a cancerously dull party, full of liquor but not drunk, leaden with boredom, somewhere out in Fitzgerald's long dark night. Writing at such a time is like making love at such a time. It is hopeless, it desecrates one's future, but one does it anyway because at least it is an act. Such writing is almost always unsprung. It is reminiscent of the wallflower who says, "To hell with inhibitions, I'm going to dance." The premise is that what comes out is valid because it is the record of a mood. So one records the mood. What a mood. Full of vomit, self-pity, panic, paranoia, megalomania, *merde*, whimpers, excuses, turns of the neck, flips of the wrist, transports. It is the bends of Hell. If you purge it, if you get sleep and tear it up in the morning, it can do no more harm than any other bad debauch. But Salinger went ahead and reread his stew, then sent it to *The New Yorker*, And they accepted it. Now, several years later, he reprints it in book covers.

There is social process at work here. Salinger was the most gifted minor writer in America. *The New Yorker*'s ability is to produce such writers. The paradox comes from the social fact that *The New Yorker* is a major influence on American life. Hundreds of thousands, perhaps millions of people in the most established parts of the middle class kill their quickest impulses before they dare to act in such a way as to look ridiculous to the private eye of their taste whose style has been keyed by the eye of *The New Yorker*. Salinger was the finest writer *The New Yorker* ever produced, but profoundly minor. The major writer like James Jones, indeed James Jones, leads the kind of inner life which enables him to study victories as well as defeats; Salinger was catapulted by a study of excruciating small defeats into a position of major importance. The phenomenon in the nation was the same those years. Men of minor abilities engaged America in major brinkmanships.

But it is always dangerous when the Literary Mafia (*The New Yorker*, the *Saturday Review*, The New York Times *Book Review*, *Time* magazine's book reviews, and the genteel elements in publishing) promote a minor writer into a major writer. A vested interest attaches itself to keeping the corpse of the violated standards buried. Readers who might be average keen in their sense of literary value find their taste mucked up. The greatest damage in this case, however, seems to have been to Salinger himself. Because a writer, with aristocratic delicacy of intent and nerves so subtle that only isolation makes life bearable for him, has been allowed to let his talent fester in that corrupt isolation. Salinger has been the most important writer in America for a generation of adolescents and college students. He was their leader in exile. The least he owed them for his silence was a major performance.

But it's a rare man who can live like a hermit and produce a major performance unless he has critics who are near to him and hard on him. No friend who worried about Salinger's future should have let him publish *Seymour an Introduction* in *The New Yorker* without daring to lose his friendship first by telling him how awful it was. Yet there was too much depending on Salinger's interregnum—he was so *inoffensive,* finally. So a suspension of the critical faculty must have gone on in the institutional wheels of *The New Yorker* which was close to psychotic in its evasions.

As for the other three stories in the two books, they are not as good as the stories in *Nine Stories.* Affectations which were part once of Salinger's charm are now faults. An excessive desire to please runs through his pages. There is too much sweetness. He is too pleased with himself, too nice, he lingers too much over the happy facility of his details in a way Fitzgerald never would. He is no longer a writer so much as he is an entertainer, a slim much-beloved version of Al Jolson or Sophie Tucker, the music hall is in the root of his impulse as much as the dungeons and mansions of literature. Does one desire the real irony? There is nothing in *Franny and Zooey* which would hinder it from becoming first-rate television. It is genre with all the limitations of genre: catalogs of items in the medicine chest, long intimate family conversations with life, snap with mother, crackle and pop. If I were a television producer I'd put on *Franny and Zooey* tomorrow. And indeed in ten years they will. America will have moved from One Man's Family to the Glass Family. Which is progress. I'd rather have the Glass Family on the air. But don't confuse the issue. The Glass stories are not literature but television. And Salinger's work since *The Catcher in the Rye* is part of his long retreat from what is substantial, agonizing, uproarious, or close to awe and terror. *The Catcher in the Rye* was able to change people's lives. The new books are not even likely to improve the conversation in college dormitories. It is time Salinger came back to the city and got his hands dirty with a rough corruption or two, because the very items which composed the honor of his reputation, his resolute avoidance of the mass media and society, have now begun to back up on him. There is a taste of something self-absorptive, narcissistic, even putrefactive in his long contemplation of a lintless navel.

The value of past predictions by this critic may be judged by the following about Saul Bellow. It is taken from page 467 in *Advertisements for Myself.*

When and if I come to read *Henderson the Rain King,* let me hope I do not feel the critic's vested interest to keep a banished writer in limbo, for I sense uneasily that without reading it, I have already the beginnings of a negative evaluation for it since I doubt that I would believe in Henderson as a hero.

Well, one might as well eat the crow right here. Henderson is an exceptional character, almost worthy of Gulliver or Huckleberry Finn, and it is possible that of all the books mentioned in this piece, *Henderson the Rain King* comes the closest to being a great novel. Taken even by its smallest dimension, and its final failure, it will still become a classic, a fine curiosity of a book quite out of the mainstream of American letters but a classic in the way *The Innocents Abroad,* or *The Ox-Bow Incident, The Informer,* or *High Wind in Jamaica* is classic.

Bellow's main character, Henderson, is a legendary giant American, an eccentric millionaire, six-four in height, with a huge battered face, an enormous chest, a prodigious potbelly, a wild crank's gusto for life, and a childlike impulse to say what he thinks. He is a magical hybrid of Jim Thorpe and Dwight Macdonald. And he is tormented by an inner voice which gives him no rest and poisons his marriages and pushes him to go forth. So he choose to go to Africa (after first contemplating a visit to the Eskimos) and finds a native guide to take him deep into the interior.

The style gallops like Henderson, full of excess, full of light, loaded with irritating effusions, but it is a style which moves along. *The Adventures of Augie March* was written in a way which could only be called *all writing.* That was one of the troubles with the book. Everything was mothered by the style. But Henderson talks in a free-swinging easy bang-away monologue which puts your eye in the center of the action. I don't know if Bellow ever visited Africa, I would guess he didn't, but his imaginative faculty—which has always been his loot—pulls off a few prodigies. I don't know if any other American writer has done Africa so well. As for instance:

I was in tremendous shape those first long days, hot as they were. At night, after Romilayu had prayed, and we lay on the ground, the face of the air breathed back on us, breath for breath. And then there were the calm stars, turning around and singing, and the birds of the night with heavy bodies, fanning by. I couldn't have asked for anything better. When I laid my ear to the ground, I thought I could hear hoofs. It was like lying on the skin of a drum.

After a series of tragicomic adventures, Henderson reaches a royal almost Oriental tribe with a culture built upon magic and death. He is brought to the King, Dahfu, who lives in a wooden palace attended by a harem of beautiful Amazons. (One could be visiting the royalest pad in Harlem.) Dahfu is a philosopher-king, large in size, noble, possessed of grace, complex, dignified, elegant, educated, living suspended between life and death. The King, delighted with his new friend, takes him into the secrets of his mind and his palace, and one begins to read the book with a vast absorption because Bellow is now inching more close to the Beast of mystery than any American novelist before him. Dahfu is an exceptional creation, a profoundly sophisticated man with a deep acceptance of magic, an intellectual who believes that civilization can be saved only by a voyage back into the primitive, an expedition which he is of course uniquely suited to lead.

As the action explores its way down into an underworld of plot and magical omens, one ceases to know any longer whether Dahfu is potentially an emperor who can save the world, or a noble man lost in a

Faustian endeavor. The book is on the threshold of a stupendous climax—for the first time in years I had the feeling I was going to learn something large from a novel—and then like a slow leak, the air goes out of the book in the last fifty pages. Dahfu is killed in a meaningless action, Henderson goes home to his wife, and the mystery that Bellow has begun to penetrate closes over his book, still intact.

He is a curious writer. He has the warmest imagination, I think, of any writer in my generation, and this gift leads him to marvelous places—it is possible that Bellow succeeds in telling us more about the depths of the black man's psyche than either Baldwin or Ellison. He has a widely cultivated mind which nourishes his gift. He has a facility for happy surprises, and in Henderson, unlike Augie March, he has developed a nose for where the treasure is buried. Yet I still wonder if he is not too timid to become a great writer. A novelist like Jones could never have conceived *Henderson the Rain King* (no more could I), but I know that Jones or myself would have been ready to urinate blood before we would have been ready to cash our profit and give up as Bellow did on the possibilities of a demonically vast ending. The clue to this capitulation may be detected in Bellow's one major weakness, which is that he creates individuals and not relations between them, at least not yet. Augie March travels alone, the hero of *Seize the Day* is alone, Henderson forms passionate friendships but they tend to get fixed and the most annoying aspect of the novel is the constant repetition of the same sentiments, as if Bellow is knocking on a door of meaning which will not open for him. It is possible that the faculty of imagination is opposed to the gift of grasping relationships—in the act of coming to know somebody else well, the point of the imagination may be dulled by the roughness of the other's concrete desires and the attrition of living not only in one's own boredom but someone else's. Bellow has a lonely gift, but it is a gift. I would guess he is more likely to write classics than major novels, which is a way of saying that he will give intense pleasure to particular readers over the years, but is not too likely to seize the temper of our time and turn it.

For those who like the results of a horse race, it should be clear that the novels I liked the most in this round of reading were *Henderson, Naked Lunch,* and *Catch-22. The Thin Red Line* if not inspired was still impressive. *Another Country* suffered from too little style but compensated by its force. *Rabbit, Run* was better than expected but cloyed by too much writing. *Set This House on Fire* was rich in separate parts, and obese for the whole. *Letting Go* gave a demonstration of brilliant tactics and no novelistic strategy at all. *Franny and Zooey* and *Raise High the Roof Beam, Carpenters* was a literary scandal which came in last.

It has been said more than once that Tolstoy and Dostoevsky divided the central terrain of the modern novel between them. Tolstoy's concern—even in the final pessimism of *The Kreutzer Sonata*—was with men-in-the-world, and indeed the panorama of his books carries to us an image of a huge landscape peopled with figures who changed that landscape, whereas the bulk of Dostoevsky's work could take place in ten closed rooms: it is not society but a series of individuals we remember, each illuminated by the terror of exploring the bad jungle of themselves. This distinction is not a final scheme for classifying the novel. If one can point to *Moby Dick* as a perfect example of a novel in the second category—a book whose action depends upon the voyage of Ahab into his obsession—and to *An American Tragedy* as a virile example of the first kind of novel, one must still come up short before the work of someone like Henry James, who straddles the categories, for he explores into society as if the world were a creature in a closed room and he could discover its heart. Yet the distinction is probably the most useful single guide we have to the novel and can even be given a modern application to Proust as a novelist of the developed, introspective, still-exploitive world, and Joyce as a royal, demented, most honorable traveler through the psyche. The serious novel begins from a fixed philosophical point—the desire to discover reality—and it goes to search for that reality in society, or else must embark on a trip up the upper Amazon of the inner eye.

It is this necessity to travel into one direction or the other up to the end which makes the writing of novels fatal for one's talent and finally for one's health, as the horns of a bull are final doom for the suit of lights. If one explores the world, one's talent must be blunted by punishment, one's artistic integrity by corruption: nobody can live in the world without shaking the hand of people he despises; so an ultimate purity must be surrendered. Yet it is as dangerous to travel unguided into the mysteries of the Self, for insanity prepares an ambush. No man explores into his own nature without submitting to a curse from the root of biology since existence would cease if it were natural to turn upon oneself.

This difficulty has always existed for the novelist, but today it may demand more antithesis and more agony than before. The writer who would explore the world must encounter a society which is now conscious of itself, and so resistant (most secretly) to an objective eye. Detours exist everywhere. There was a time when a writer had to see just a little bit of a few different faces in the world and could know that the world was still essentially so simple and so phrased that he might use his imagination to fill in unknown colors in the landscape. Balzac could do that, and so could Zola. But the arts of the world suffered a curious inversion as man was turned by the twentieth century into mass-man rather than democratic man. The heart-land which was potential in everyone turned upon itself; people used their personal arts to conceal from themselves the nature of their work. They chose to become experts rather than artists. The working world was no longer a congerie of factories and banks so much as it was reminiscent of hospitals and plastic recreation centers. Society tended to collect in small stagnant pools. Now, any young man trying to explore that world is held up by pleasures which are not sufficiently intense to teach him and is dulled by injustices too elusive to fire his rage. The Tolstoyan novel begins to be impossible. Who can create a vast canvas when the imagination must submit itself to a plethora of detail in each joint of society? Who can travel to many places when the complexity of each pool sucks up one's attention like a carnivorous cess-fed flower? Of all the writers mentioned here, only Jones, Heller and Burroughs even try to give a picture of the world, and the last two have departed from conventional reality before financing the attempt. It may be that James Jones is indeed the single major American writer capable of returning with a realistic vision of the complex American reality. But by his method, because of the progressively increasing confusion and contradiction of each separate corner in American society, he will have to write twenty or thirty books before he will have sketched even a small design.

Yet a turn in the other direction, into the world of the Self, is not less difficult. An intellectual structure which is cancerous and debilitating to the instinct of the novelist inhabits the crossroads of the inner mind. Psychoanalysis. An artist must not explore into himself with language given by another. A vocabulary of experts is a vocabulary greased out and sweated in committee and so is inimical to a private eye. One loses what is new by confusing it with what may be common to others. The essential ideas of psychoanalysis are reductive and put a dead weight on the confidence of the venture. If guilt, for example, is neurotic, a clumsy part of the functioning in a graceful machine, then one does not feel like a hero studying his manacles, nor a tragic victim regarding his just sentence, but instead is a skilled mechanic trying to fix his tool. Brutally, simply, mass man cannot initiate an inner voyage unless it is conducted by an expert graduated by an institution.

Set This House on Fire, Another Country, Rabbit, Run, Letting Go, Henderson, and the Glass stories were all amateur expeditions into the privacy of the Self, but they are also a measure of the difficulty, because one could sense the exhaustion of talent in the fires on the way, as if a company of young untried men were charging a hill which was mined and laid across with fire lanes for automatic weapons.

Yet the difficulty goes beyond the country of psychoanalysis. There are hills beyond that hill. The highest faces an abyss. Man in the Middle Ages or the Renaissance, man even in the nineteenth century, explored deep into himself that he might come closer to a vision of a God or some dictate from eternity, but that exploration is suspect in itself today, and in the crucial climactic transcendental moments of one's life, there is revealed still another dilemma. God, is it God one finds, or madness?

The religious temper of these books is significant. Of them all, *The Thin Red Line, Naked Lunch, Another Country*, and *Letting Go* have no overt religious preoccupation. Yet altogether one could make a kind of case that *Naked Lunch* and *Another Country* are not divorced from religious obsessions. The suggestion of still another frontier for the American novel is here. A war has been fought by some of us over the last fifteen years to open the sexual badlands to our writing, and that war is in the act of being won. Can one now begin to think of an atttack on the stockade—those dead forts where the spirit of twentieth-century irreligious man, frozen in flop and panic before the montage of his annihilation, has collected, like castrated cattle behind the fence? Can the feet of those infantrymen of the arts, the novelists, take us through the mansions and the churches into the palace of The Bitch where the real secrets are stored? We are the last of the entrepreneurs, and one of us homeless guns had better make it, or the future will smell like the dead air of the men who captured our time during that huge collective cowardice which was the aftermath of the Second War.

[July, 1963]

The Black Boy Looks at the White Boy

by James Baldwin

I first met Norman about four years ago, in Paris, at the home of Jean
Malaquais. Let me bring in at once the theme that will repeat itself over
and over throughout this love letter: I was then (and I have not changed
much) a very tight, tense, lean, abnormally ambitious, abnormally intelligent, and hungry black cat. It is important that I admit that, at the time I
met Norman, I was extremely worried about my career; and a writer who
is worried about his career is also fighting for his life. I was approaching
the end of a love affair, and I was not taking it very well. Norman and I
are alike in this, that we both tend to suspect others of putting us down,
and we strike before we're struck. Only, our styles are very different: I am
a black boy from the Harlem streets, and Norman is a middle-class Jew. I
am not dragging my personal history into this gratuitously, and I hope I do
not need to say that no sneer is implied in the above description of
Norman. But these are the facts and in my own relationship to Norman
they are crucial facts.

Also, I have no right to talk about Norman without risking a distinctly
chilling self-exposure. I take him very seriously; he is very dear to me.
And I think I know something about his journey from my black boy's

850

point of view because my own journey is not really so very different, and also because I have spent most of my life, after all, watching and outwitting white people. I think that I know something about the American masculinity which most men of my generation do not know because they have not been menaced by it in the way that I have been. It is still true, alas, that to be an American Negro male is also to be a kind of walking phallic symbol: which means that one pays, in one's own personality, for the sexual insecurity of others. The relationship, therefore, of a black boy to a white boy is a very complex thing.

There is a difference, though, between Norman and myself in that I think he still imagines that he has something to save, whereas I have never had anything to lose. Or perhaps I ought to put it another way: the things that most people seem to imagine that they can salvage from the storm of life are really, in sum, their innocence. It was this commodity precisely which I had to get rid of at once, literally, on pain of death. I am afraid that most of the white people I have ever known impressed me as being in the grip of a weird nostalgia, dreaming of a vanished state of security and order, against which dream, unfailingly and unconsciously, they tested and very often lost their lives. It is a terrible thing to say, but I am afraid that for a very long time the troubles of white people failed to impress me as being real trouble. They put me in mind of children crying because the breast has been taken away. Time and love have modified my tough-boy lack of charity, but the attitude sketched above was my first attitude and I am sure that there is a great deal of it left.

To proceed: two lean cats, one white and one black, met in a French living room. I had heard of him, he had heard of me. And here we were, suddenly, circling around each other. We liked each other at once, but each was frightened that the other would pull rank. He could have pulled rank on me because he was more famous and had more money and also because he was white; but I could have pulled rank on him precisely because I was black and knew more about that periphery he so helplessly maligns in *The White Negro* than he could ever hope to know. Already, you see, we were trapped in our roles and our attitudes: the toughest kid on the block was meeting the toughest kid on the block. I think that both of us were pretty weary of this grueling and thankless role; I know that I am; but the roles that we construct are constructed because we feel that they will help us to survive and also, of course, because they fulfill something in our personalities; and one does not, therefore, cease playing a role simply because one has begun to understand it. All roles are dangerous. The world tends to trap and immobilize you in the role you play; and it is not always easy—in fact, it is always extremely hard—to maintain a kind of watchful, mocking distance between oneself as one appears to be and oneself as one actually is.

I think that Norman was working on *The Deer Park* at that time, or had just finished it, and Malaquais, who had translated *The Naked and The Dead* into French, did not like *The Deer Park*. I had not, then, read the book; if I had, I would have been astonished that Norman could have expected Malaquais to like it. What Norman was trying to do in *The Deer Park*, and quite apart, now, from whether or not he succeeded, could only—it seems to me—baffle and annoy a French intellectual who seemed to me essentially rationalistic. Norman has many qualities and faults, but I have never heard anyone accuse him of possessing this particular one. But Malaquais' opinion seemed to mean a great deal to him; this astonished me, too; and there was a running, good-natured but astringent argument between them, with Malaquais playing the role of the old lion and Norman playing the role of the powerful but clumsy cub. And, I must say, I think that each of them got a great deal of pleasure out of the other's performance. The night we met, we stayed up very late, and did a great deal of drinking and shouting. But beneath all the shouting and the posing and the mutual showing-off, something very wonderful was happening. I was aware of a new and warm presence in my life, for I had met someone I wanted to know, who wanted to know me.

Norman and his wife Adele, along with a Negro jazz-musician friend and myself, met fairly often during the few weeks that found us all in the same city. I think that Norman had come in from Spain, and he was shortly to return to the States; and it was not long after Norman's departure that I left Paris for Corsica. My memory of that time is both blurred and sharp, and, oddly enough, is principally of Norman—confident, boastful, exuberant, and loving—striding through the soft Paris nights like a gladiator. And I think, alas, that I envied him: his success, and his youth, and his love. And this meant that, though Norman really wanted to know me, and though I really wanted to know him, I hung back, held fire, danced, and lied. I was not going to come crawling out of my ruined house, all bloody, no, baby, sing no sad songs for *me*. And the great gap between Norman's state and my own had a terrible effect on our relationship, for it inevitably connected, not to say collided, with that myth of the sexuality of Negroes which Norman, like so many others, refuses to give up. The sexual battleground, if I may call it that, is really the same for everyone; and I, at this point, was just about to be carried off the battleground on my shield, if anyone could find it; so how could I play, in any way whatever, the noble savage?

At the same time, my temperament and my experience in this country had led me to expect very little from most American whites, especially, horribly enough, my friends; so it did not seem worthwhile to challenge, in any real way, Norman's views of life on the periphery, or to put him down for them. I was weary, to tell the truth. I had tried, in the States, to convey something of what it felt like to be a Negro and no one had been able to listen: they wanted their romance. And, anyway, the really ghastly thing about trying to convey to a white man the reality of the Negro experience has nothing whatever to do with the fact of color, but has to do with this man's relationship to his own life. He will face in your life only what he is willing to face in his. Well, this means that one finds oneself tampering with the insides of a stranger, to no purpose, which one probably has no right to do, and I chickened out. And matters were not helped at all by the fact that the Negro jazz musicians, among whom we sometimes found ourselves, who really liked Norman, did not for an instant consider him as being even remotely "hip" and Norman did not know this and I could not tell him. He never broke through to them, at least not as far as I know; and they were far too "hip," if that is the word I want, even to consider breaking through to him. They thought he was a real sweet ofay cat, but a little frantic.

But we were far more cheerful than anything I've said might indicate and none of the above seemed to matter very much at the time. Other things mattered, like walking and talking and drinking and eating, and the way Adele laughed, and the way Norman argued. He argued like a young man, he argued to win; and while I found him charming, he may have found me exasperating, for I kept moving back before that short, prodding forefinger. I couldn't submit my arguments, or my real questions, for I had too much to hide. Or so it seemed to me then. I submit, though I may be wrong, that I was then at the beginning of a terrifying adventure, not too unlike the conundrum which seems to menace Norman now.

"I had done a few things and earned a few pence"; but the things I had written were behind me, could not be written again, could not be repeated. I was also realizing that all that the world could give me as an artist, it had, in effect, already given. In the years that stretched before me, all that I could look forward to, in that way, were a few more prizes, or a lot more, and a little more, or a lot more money. And my private life had failed, had failed, had failed. One of the reasons I had fought so hard, after all, was to wrest from the world fame and money and love. And here I was, at thirty-two, finding my notoriety hard to bear, since its principal effect was to make me more lonely; money, it turned out, was exactly like sex, you thought of nothing else if you didn't have it and thought of other things if you did; and love, as far as I could see, was over. Love seemed to be over not merely because an affair was ending; it would have seemed to be over under any circumstances; for it was the dream of love which was ending, I was beginning to realize, most unwillingly, all the things love could not do. It could not make me over, for example. It could not undo the journey which had made of me such a strange man and brought me to such a strange place.

But at that time it seemed only too clear that love had gone out of the world; and not, as I had thought once, because I was poor and ugly and obscure, but precisely because I was no longer any of these things. What point, then, was there in working if the best I could hope for now was the Nobel Prize? And *how*, indeed, would I be able to keep on working if I could never be released from the prison of my egocentricity? By what act could I escape this horror? For horror it was, let us make no mistake about that.

And beneath all this, which simplified nothing, was that sense, that suspicion—which is the glory and torment of every writer—that what was happening to me might be turned to good account, that I was trembling on the edge of great revelations, was being prepared for a very long journey, and might now begin, having survived my apprenticeship (but had I survived it?), a great work. I might really become a great writer. But in order to do this I would have to sit down at the typewriter again, alone—I would have to accept my despair: and I could not do it. It really does not help to be a strong-willed person, or, anyway, I think it is a great error to misunderstand the nature of the will. In the most important areas of anybody's life, the will usually operates as a traitor. My own will was busily pointing out to me the most fantastically unreal alternatives to my pain, all of which I tried, all of which—luckily—failed. When, late in the evening or early in the morning, Norman and Adele returned to their hotel on the Quai Voltaire, I wandered through Paris, the underside of Paris, drinking, screwing, fighting—it's a wonder I wasn't killed. And then it was morning, I would somehow be home—usually, anyway—and the typewriter would be there, staring at me; and the manuscript of the new novel, which it seemed I would never be able to achieve, and from which clearly I was never going to be released, was scattered all over the floor.

That's the way it is. I think it is the most dangerous point in the life of any artist, his longest, most hideous turning; and especially for a man, an American man, whose principle is action and whose jewel is optimism, who must now accept what certainly then seems to be a grey passivity and an endless despair. It is the point at which many artists lose their minds, or commit suicide, or throw themselves into good works, or try to enter politics. For all of this is happening not only in the wilderness of the soul, but in the real world which accomplishes its seduction not by offering you opportunities to be wicked, but by offering opportunities to be good, to be active and effective, to be admired and central and apparently loved.

Norman came on to America, and I went to Corsica. We wrote each other a few times. I confided to Norman that I was very apprehensive about the reception of *Giovanni's Room*, and he was good enough to write some very encouraging things about it when it came out. The critics had jumped on him with both their left feet when he published *The Deer Park*—which I still had not read—and this created a kind of bond or strengthened the bond already existing between us. About a year and several overflowing wastebaskets later, I, too, returned to America, not vastly improved by having been out of it, but not knowing where else to go; and one day, while I was sitting dully in my house, Norman called me from Connecticut. A few people were going to be there—for the weekend—and he wanted me to come, too. We had not seen each other since Paris.

Well, I wanted to go; that is, I wanted to see Norman; but I did not want to see any people, and so the tone of my acceptance was not very enthusiastic. I realized that he felt this, but I did not know what to do about it. He gave me train schedules and hung up.

Getting to Connecticut would have been no hassle if I could have pulled myself together to get to the train. And I was sorry, as I meandered around my house and time flew and trains left, that I had not been more honest with Norman and told him exactly how I felt. But I had not known how to do this, or it had not really occurred to me to do it, especially not over the phone.

So there was another phone call, I forget who called whom, which went something like this:

N: Don't feel you have to. I'm not trying to bug you.

J: It's not that. It's just—

N: You don't really want to come, do you?

J: I don't really feel up to it.

N: I understand. I guess you just don't like the Connecticut gentry.

J: Well—don't you ever come to the city?

N: Sure. We'll see each other.

J: I hope so. I'd like to see you.

N: Okay; till then.

And he hung up. I thought, I ought to write him a letter—but of course I did nothing of the sort. It was around this time I went South, I think; anyway, we did not see each other for a long time.

But I thought about him a great deal. The grapevine keeps all of us advised of the others' movements, so I knew when Norman left Connecticut for New York, heard that he had been present at this or that party and what he had said: usually something rude, often something penetrating, sometimes something so hilariously silly that it was difficult to believe he had been serious. (This was my reaction when I first heard his famous remark about running for mayor of New York. I dismissed it. I was wrong.) Or he had been seen in this or that Village spot, in which unfailingly there would be someone—out of spite, idleness, envy, exasperation, out of the bottomless, eerie, aimless hostility which characterizes almost every bar in New York, to speak only of bars—to put him down. I heard of a couple of fist fights, and, of course, I was always encountering people who hated his guts. These people always mildly surprised me, and so did the news of his fights: it was hard for me to imagine that anyone could really dislike Norman, anyone, that is, who had encountered him personally. I knew of one fight he had had, forced on him apparently by a blow-hard Village type whom I considered rather pathetic. I didn't blame Norman for this fight, but I couldn't help wondering why he bothered to rise to such a shapeless challenge. It seemed simpler, as I was always telling myself, just to stay out of Village bars.

And people talked about Norman with a kind of avid glee, which I found very ugly. Pleasure made their saliva flow, they sprayed and all but drooled, and their eyes shone with that blood lust which is the only real tribute the mediocre are capable of bringing to the extraordinary. Many of the people who claimed to be seeing Norman all the time impressed me as being, to tell the truth, pitifully far beneath him. But this is also true, alas, of much of my own entourage. The people who are in one's life or merely continually in one's presence reveal a great deal about one's needs and terrors. Also one's hopes.

I was not, however, on the scene. I was on the road—not quite, I trust, in the sense that Kerouac's boys are; but I presented, certainly, a moving target. And I was reading Norman Mailer. Before I had met him, I had read only *The Naked and The Dead*, *The White Negro*, and *Barbary Shore*; I think this is right, though it may be that I only read *The White Negro* later and confused my reading of that piece with some of my discussions with Norman. Anyway, I could not, with the best will in the world, make any sense out of *The White Negro* and, in fact, it was hard for me to imagine that this essay had been written by the same man who wrote the novels. Both *The Naked and The Dead* and (for the most part) *Barbary Shore* are written in a lean, spare, muscular prose which accomplishes almost exactly what it sets out to do. Even *Barbary Shore*, which loses itself in its last half (and which deserves, by the way, far more serious treatment than it has received), never becomes as downright impenetrable as *The White Negro* does.

Now, much of this, I told myself, had to do with my resistance to the title, and with a kind of fury that so antique a vision of the blacks should, at this late hour and in so many borrowed heirlooms, be stepping off the A train. But I was also baffled by the passion with which Norman appeared to be imitating so many people less talented than himself, i.e., Kerouac, and all the other Suzuki rhythm boys. From them, indeed, I expected nothing more than their Pablum-clogged cries of *Kicks!* and *Holy!* It seemed very clear to me that their glorification of the orgasm was but a way of avoiding all of the terrors of life and love. But Norman knew better, had to know better. *The Naked and The Dead*, *Barbary Shore*, and *The Deer Park* proved it. In each of these novels, there is a toughness and subtlety of conception and a sense of the danger and complexity of human relationships which one will search for in vain, not only in the work produced by the aforementioned coterie, but in most of the novels produced by Norman's contemporaries. What in the world, then, was he doing, slumming so outrageously, in such a dreary crowd?

For, exactly because he knew better and in exactly the same way that no one can become more lewdly vicious than an imitation libertine, Norman felt compelled to carry their *mystique* further than they had, to be more "hip," or more "beat," to dominate, in fact, their dreaming field; and since this *mystique* depended on a total rejection of life, and insisted on the fulfillment of an infantile dream of love, the *mystique* could only be extended into violence. No one is more dangerous than he who imagines himself pure in heart; for his purity, by definition, is unassailable.

But *why* should it be necessary to borrow the Depression language of deprived Negroes, which eventually evolved into jive and bop talk, in order to justify such a grim system of delusions? Why malign the sorely menaced sexuality of Negroes in order to justify the white man's own sexual panic? Especially as, in Norman's case, and as indicated by his work, he has a very real sense of sexual responsibility, and even, odd as it may sound to some, of sexual morality, and a genuine commitment to life. None of his people, I beg you to notice, spend their lives on the road. They really become entangled with each other, and with life. They really suffer, they spill real blood, they have real lives to lose. This is no small achievement; in fact it is absolutely rare. No matter how uneven one judges Norman's work to be, all of it is genuine work. No matter how harshly one judges it, it is the work of a genuine novelist, and an absolutely first-rate talent.

Which makes the questions I have tried to raise—or, rather, the questions which Norman Mailer irresistibly represents—all the more troubling and terrible. I certainly do not know the answers and, even if I did, this is probably not the place to state them.

But I have a few ideas. Here is Kerouac, ruminating on what I take to be the loss of the garden of Eden:

"At lilac evening I walked with every muscle aching among the lights of 27th and Welton in the Denver colored section, wishing I were a Negro, feeling that the best the white world had offered was not enough ecstasy for me, not enough life, joy, kicks, darkness, music, not enough night. I wished I were a Denver Mexican, or even a poor overworked Jap, anything but what I so drearily was, a 'white man' disillusioned. All my life I'd had white ambitions.—I passed the dark porches of Mexican and Negro homes; soft voices were there, occasionally the dusky knee of some mysterious, sensuous gal; and dark faces of the men behind rose arbors. Little children sat like sages in ancient rocking chairs."

Now, this is absolute nonsense, of course, objectively considered, and offensive nonsense at that; I would hate to be in Kerouac's shoes if he should ever be mad enough to read this aloud from the stage of Harlem's Apollo Theatre.

And yet there is real pain in it, and real loss, however thin; and it *is* thin, like soup too long diluted; thin because it does not refer to reality, but to a dream. Compare it, at random, with any old blues:

> *Backwater blues done caused me*
> *To pack my things and go*
> *'Cause my house fell down*
> *And I can't live there no mo'.*

"Man," said a Negro musician to me once, talking about Norman, "the only trouble with that cat is that he's white." This does not mean exactly what it says—or, rather, it *does* mean exactly what it says, and not what it might be taken to mean—and it is a very shrewd observation. What my friend meant was that to become a Negro man, let alone a Negro artist, one had to make oneself up as one went along. This had to be done in the not-at-all-metaphorical teeth of the world's determination to destroy you. The world had prepared no place for you, and if the world had its way, no place would ever exist. Now, this is true for everyone, but, in the case of a Negro, this truth is absolutely naked: if he deludes himself about it, he will die. This is not the way this truth presents itself to white men, who believe the world is theirs and who, albeit unconsciously, expect the world to help them in the achievement of their identity. But the world does not do this—for anyone; the world is not interested in anyone's identity. And, therefore, the anguish which can overtake a white man comes in the middle of his life, when he must make the almost inconceivable effort to divest himself of everything he has ever expected or believed, when he must take himself apart and put himself together again, walking out of the world, into limbo, or into what certainly looks like limbo. This cannot yet happen to any Negro of Norman's age, for the reason that his delusions and defenses are either absolutely impenetrable by this time, or he has failed to survive them. "I want to know how power works," Norman once said to me, "how it really works, in detail." Well, I know how power works, it has worked on me, and if I didn't know how power worked, I would be dead. And it goes without saying, perhaps, that I have simply never been able to afford myself any illusions concerning the manipulation of that power. My revenge, I decided very early, would be to achieve a power which outlasts kingdoms.

When I finally saw Norman again, I was beginning to suspect daylight at the end of my long tunnel; it was a summer day, I was on my way back to Paris, and I was very cheerful. We were at an afternoon party, Norman was standing in the kitchen, a drink in his hand, holding forth for the benefit of a small group of people. There seemed something different about him: it was the belligerence of his stance, and the really rather pontifical tone of his voice. I had only seen him, remember, in Malaquais' living room, which Malaquais indefatigably dominates, and on various terraces, and in various dives, in Paris. I do not mean that there was anything unfriendly about him. On the contrary, he was smiling and having a ball. And yet—he was leaning against the refrigerator, rather as though he had his back to the wall, ready to take on all comers.

Norman has a trick, at least with me, of watching, somewhat ironically, as you stand on the edge of the crowd around him, waiting for his attention. I suppose this ought to be exasperating, but in fact I find it rather endearing, because it is so transparent and because he gets such a bang out of being the center of attention. So do I, of course, at least some of the time.

We talked, bantered, a little tensely, made the usual, doomed effort to bring each other up-to-date on what we had been doing. I did not want to talk about my novel, which was only just beginning to seem to take shape, and, therefore, did not dare ask him if he were working on a novel. He seemed very pleased to see me, and I was pleased to see him, but I also had the feeling that he had made up his mind about me, adversely, in some way. It was as though he were saying, "Okay, so now I know who *you* are, baby."

I was taking a boat in a few days, and I asked him to call me.

"Oh, no," he said, grinning, and thrusting that forefinger at me, "*you* call *me*."

"That's fair enough," I said, and I left the party and went on back to Paris. While I was out of the country, Norman published *Advertisements for Myself,* which presently crossed the ocean to the apartment of James Jones. Bill Styron was also in Paris at that time, and one evening the three of us sat in Jim's living room, reading aloud, in a kind of drunken, masochistic fascination, Norman's judgment of our personalities and our work. Actually, I came off best, I suppose; there was less about me, and it was less venomous. But the condescension infuriated me; also, to tell the truth, my feelings were hurt. I felt that if that was the way Norman felt about me, he should have told me so. He had said that I was incapable of saying "F--- you to the reader." My first temptation was to send him a cablegram which would disabuse him of that notion, at least insofar as one reader was concerned. But then I thought, no, I would be cool about it, and fail to react as he so clearly wanted me to. Also, I must say, his judgment of myself seemed so wide of the mark and so childish that it was hard to stay angry.

I wondered what in the world was going on in his mind.

Did he really suppose that he had now become the builder and destroyer of reputations?

And of *my* reputation?

We met in the Actors Studio one afternoon, after a performance of *The Deer Park*—which I deliberately arrived too late to see, since I really did not know how I was going to react to Norman, and didn't want to betray myself by clobbering his play. When the discussion ended, I stood, again on the edge of the crowd around him, waiting. Over someone's shoulder, our eyes met, and Norman smiled.

"We've got something to talk about," I told him.

"I figured that," he said, smiling.

We went to a bar, and sat opposite each other. I was relieved to discover that I was not angry, not even (as far as I could tell) at the bottom of my heart. But: "Why did you write those things about me?"

"Well, I'll tell you about that," he said (Norman has several accents, and I think this was his Texas one). "I sort of figured you had it coming to you."

"Why?"

"Well, I think there's some truth in it."

"Well, if you felt that way," I said, "why didn't you ever say so—to me?"

"Well, I figured if this was going to break up our friendship, something else would come along to break it up just as fast."

I couldn't disagree with that.

"You're the only one I kind of regret hitting so hard," he said, with a grin. "I think that I—probably—wouldn't say it quite that way now."

With this, I had to be content. We sat for perhaps an hour, talking of other things, and, again, I was struck by his stance: leaning on the table, shoulders hunched, seeming, really, to roll like a boxer's, and his hands moving as though he were dealing with a sparring partner. And we were talking of physical courage, and the necessity of never letting another guy get the better of you.

I laughed. "Norman, I can't go through the world the way you do because I haven't got your shoulders."

He grinned, as though I were his pupil. "But you're a pretty tough little mother, too," he said, and referred to one of the grimmer of my Village misadventures, a misadventure which certainly proved that I had a dangerously sharp tongue, but which didn't really prove anything about my courage. Which, anyway, I had long ago given up trying to prove.

I did not see Norman again until Provincetown, just after his celebrated brush with the police there, which resulted, according to Norman, in making the climate of Provincetown as "mellow as Jello."

The climate didn't seem very different to me—dull natives, dull tourists, malevolent policemen; I certainly, in any case, would never have dreamed of testing Norman's sanguine conclusion. But we had a great time, lying around the beach, and driving about, and we began to be closer than we had been for a long time.

It was during this Provincetown visit that for the first time I realized, during a long exchange Norman and I had, in a kitchen, at someone else's party, that Norman was really fascinated by the nature of political power. But, though he said so, I did not really believe that he was fascinated by it as a possibility for himself. He was then doing the great piece on the Democratic convention which was published in these pages, and I put his fascination down to that. I tend not to worry about writers as long as they are working—which is not as romantic as it may sound—and he seemed quite happy, with his wife, his family, himself. I declined, naturally, to rise at dawn, as he apparently often did, to go running or swimming or boxing, but Norman seemed to get a great charge out of these admirable pursuits and didn't put me down too hard for my comparative decadence.

He and Adele and the two children took me to the plane one afternoon, the tiny plane which shuttles from Provincetown to Boston. It was a great day, clear and sunny, and that was the way I felt; for it seemed to me that we had all, at last, re-established our old connection.

And then I heard that Norman was running for mayor, which I dismissed as a joke and refused to believe until it became hideously clear that it was not a joke at all. I was furious. I thought, You son-of-a-bitch, you're copping out. You're one of the very few writers around who might really become a great writer, who might help to excavate the buried consciousness of this country, and you want to settle for being the lousy mayor of New York. *It's not your job.* And I don't at all mean to suggest that writers are not responsible to and for—in any case always for—the social order. I don't, for that matter, even mean to suggest that Norman would have made a particularly bad mayor, although I confess that I simply cannot see him in this role. And there is probably some truth in the suggestion, put forward by Norman and others, that the shock value of having such a man in such an office, or merely running for such an office, would have had a salutary effect on the life of this city—particularly, I must say, as relates to our young people, who are certainly in desperate need of adults who love them and take them seriously, and whom they can respect. (Serious citizens may not respect Norman, but young people do, and do not respect the serious citizens; and their instincts here could not possibly be more sound.)

But I do not feel that a writer's responsibility can be discharged in this way. I do not think, if one is a writer, that one escapes it by trying to become something else. One does not become something else: one becomes nothing. And what is crucial here is that the writer, however unwillingly, always, somewhere, knows this. There is no structure he can build strong enough to keep out this self-knowledge. What *has* happened, however, time and again, is that the fantasy structure the writer builds in order to escape his central responsibility operates not as his fortress, but his prison, and he perishes within it. Or: the structure he has built becomes so stifling, so lonely, so false, and acquires such a violent and dangerous life of its own that he can break out of it only by bringing the entire structure down. With a great crash, inevitably, and on his own head, and on the heads of those closest to him. It is like smashing the windows one second before one asphyxiates, it is like burning down the house in order, at last, to be free of it. We do not, in this country now, have much taste for, or any real sense of, the extremes human beings can reach; time will improve us in this regard; but in the meantime the general fear of experience is one of the reasons that the American writer has so peculiarly difficult and dangerous a time.

One can never really see into the heart, the mind, the soul of another. Norman is my very good friend, but perhaps I do not really understand him at all, and perhaps everything I have tried to suggest in the foregoing is false. I do not think so, but it may be. One thing, however, I am certain is *not* false, and that is simply the fact of his being a writer, and the incalculable potential he, as a writer, contains. His work, after all, is all that will be left when the newspapers are yellowed, all the gossip columnists silenced, and all the cocktail parties over, and when Norman and you and I are dead. I know that this point of view is not terribly fashionable these days, but I think we *do* have a responsibility, not only to ourselves and to our own time, but to those who are coming after us. (I refuse to believe that no one is coming after us.) And I suppose that this responsibility can only be discharged by dealing as truthfully as we know how with our present fortunes, these present days. So that my concern with Norman, finally, has to do with how deeply he has understood these last sad and stormy events. If he has understood them, then he is richer and we are richer, too; if he has not understood them, we are all much poorer. For, though it clearly needs to be brought into focus, he has a real vision of ourselves as we are, and it cannot be repeated too often in this country now, that: *Where there is no vision, the people perish.*

[May, 1961]

Looking for Hemingway

by Gay Talese

"I remember very well the impression I had of Hemingway that first afternoon. He was an extraordinarily good-looking young man, twenty-three years old. It was not long after that that everybody was twenty-six. It became the period of being twenty-six. During the next two or three years all the young men were twenty-six years old. It was the right age apparently for that time and place." —Gertrude Stein

Early in the Fifties another young generation of American expatriates in Paris became twenty-six years old, but they were not Sad Young Men, nor were they Lost; they were the witty, irreverent sons of a conquering nation and, though they came mostly from wealthy parents and had been graduated from Harvard or Yale, they seemed endlessly delighted in posing as paupers and dodging the bill collectors, possibly because it seemed challenging and distinguished them from American tourists, whom they despised, and also because it was another way of having fun with the French, who despised *them*. Nevertheless, they lived in happy squalor on the Left Bank for two or three years amid the whores, jazz musicians and pederast poets, and became involved with people both

863

tragic and mad, including a passionate Spanish painter who one day cut open a vein in his leg and finished his final portrait with his own blood.

In July they drove down to Pamplona to run from the bulls, and when they returned they played tennis with Irwin Shaw at Saint-Cloud on a magnificent court overlooking Paris—and, when they tossed up the ball to serve, *there,* sprawled before them, was the whole city: the Eiffel Tower, Sacré-Coeur, the Opéra, the spires of Notre Dame in the distance. Irwin Shaw was amused by them. He called them "The Tall Young Men."

The tallest of them, at six feet four inches, was George Ames Plimpton, a quick, graceful tennis player with long, skinny limbs, a small head, bright blue eyes and a delicate, fine-tipped nose. He had come to Paris in 1952, at the age of twenty-six, because several other tall, young Americans—and some short, wild ones—were publishing a literary quarterly to be called *The Paris Review,* over the protest of one of their staff members, a poet, who wanted it to be called *Druids' Home Companion* and to be printed on birch bark. George Plimpton was made editor in chief, and soon he could be seen strolling through the streets of Paris with a long, woolen scarf flung around his neck, or sometimes with a black evening cape billowing from his shoulders, cutting a figure reminiscent of Toulouse-Lautrec's famous lithograph of Aristide Bruant, that dashing littérateur of the nineteenth century.

Though much of the edition of *The Paris Review* was done at sidewalk cafés by editors awaiting their turns on the pinball machine, the magazine nevertheless became very successful because the editors had talent, money and taste, and they avoided using such typical little-magazine words as "zeitgeist" and "dichotomous," and published no crusty critiques about Melville or Kafka, but instead printed the poetry and fiction of gifted young writers not yet popular. They also started a superb series of interviews with famous authors—who took them to lunch, introduced them to actresses, playwrights and producers, and everybody invited everybody else to parties, and the parties have not stopped, even though ten years have passed; Paris is no longer the scene, and the Tall Young Men have become thirty-six years old.

They now live in New York. And most of the parties are held at George Plimpton's large bachelor apartment on Seventy-second Street overlooking the East River, an apartment that is also the headquarters for what Elaine Tynan calls "The Quality Lit Set," or what Candida Donadio, the agent, calls "The East Side Gang," or what everybody else just calls *"The Paris Review* Crowd." The Plimpton apartment today is the liveliest literary salon in New York—the only place where, standing in a single room on almost any night of the week, one may find James Jones; William Styron; Irwin Shaw; a few call girls for decoration; Norman Mailer; Philip Roth; Lillian Hellman; a bongo player; a junkie or two; Harold L. Humes;

Jack Gelber; Sadruddin Aga Khan; Terry Southern; Blair Fuller; the cast from *Beyond The Fringe*; Tom Keogh; William Pène du Bois; Bee Whistler Dabney (an artist who descends from Whistler's mother); Robert Silvers; and an angry veteran of the Bay of Pigs invasion; and a retired bunny from the Playboy Club; John P. C. Train; Joe Fox; John Phillips Marquand; and Robert W. Dowling's secretary; Peter Duchin; Gene Andrewski; Jean vanden Heuvel; and Ernest Hemingway's former boxing coach; Frederick Seidel; Thomas H. Guinzburg; David Amram; and a bartender from down the street; Barbara Epstein; Jill Fox; and a local distributor of pot; Piedy Gimble; Dwight Macdonald; Bill Cole; Jules Feiffer; *and* into such a scene one wintry night earlier this year walked another old friend of George Plimpton's—Jacqueline Kennedy.

"Jackie!" George called out, opening the door to greet the First Lady and also her sister and brother-in-law, the Radziwills. Mrs. Kennedy, smiling broadly between gleaming earrings, extended her hand to George, whom she has known since her dancing-school days, and they chatted for a few seconds in the hallway while George helped her with her coat. Then, peeking into the bedroom and noticing a mound of overcoats piled higher than a Volkswagen, Mrs. Kennedy said, in a soft, hushed, sympathetic voice, "Oh, *George*—your *b e d*!"

George shrugged, and then escorted them through the hall down three steps into the smoky scene.

"Look," said one hipster in the corner, "there's Lee Radziwill's sister!"

George first introduced Mrs. Kennedy to Ved Mehta, the Indian writer, and then slipped her skillfully past Norman Mailer toward William Styron.

"Why, hel*LO*, Bill," she said, shaking hands, "nice to see you."

For the next few moments, talking with Styron and Cass Canfield Jr., Mrs. Kennedy stood with her back to Sandra Hochman, a Greenwich Village poetess, a streaked blonde in a thick woolly sweater and partially unzipped ski pants.

"I think," Miss Hochman whispered to a friend, tossing a backward nod at Mrs. Kennedy's beautiful white brocade suit, "that I am a bit *déshabillée*."

"Nonsense," said her friend, flicking cigarette ashes on the rug. And, in truth, it must be said that none of the seventy other people in that room felt that Sandra Hochman's outfit contrasted unpleasantly with the First Lady's; in fact, some did not even notice the First Lady, and there was one who noticed her but failed to recognize her.

"My," he said, squinting through the smoke toward the elaborately teased coiffure of Mrs. Kennedy, "that *really* is the look this year, isn't it? And that chick has almost made it."

While Mrs. Kennedy conversed in the corner, Princess Radziwill talked with Bee Whistler Dabney a few feet away, and Prince Radziwill stood alone next to the baby grand piano humming to himself. He often hums to himself at parties. In Washington he is known as a great hummer.

Fifteen minutes later Mrs. Kennedy, expected soon at a dinner given by Adlai Stevenson, said good-bye to Styron and Canfield and, escorted by George Plimpton, headed for the steps toward the hall. Norman Mailer, who had meanwhile drunk three glasses of water, was standing by the steps. He looked hard at her as she passed. She did not return his glance.

Three quick steps, and she was gone—down the hall, her coat on, her long white gloves on, down two flights of steps to the sidewalk, the Radziwills and George Plimpton behind her.

"Look," squealed a blonde, Sally Belfrage, gazing down from the kitchen window at the figures below climbing into the limousine, "there's *George*! And *look* at that car!"

"What's so unusual about that car?" somebody asked. "It's only a Cadillac."

"Yes, but it's *black,* and so-o-o *un*chromed."

Sally Belfrage watched as the big car, pointed in the direction of another world, moved quietly away, but in the living room the party went on louder than before, with nearly everyone oblivious to the fact that the host had disappeared. But there was liquor to be consumed and, besides, by just casting an eye over the photographs on the walls throughout the apartment, one could easily feel the presence of George Plimpton. One photograph shows him fighting small bulls in Spain with Hemingway; another catches him drinking beer with other Tall Young Men at a Paris café; others show him as a lieutenant marching a platoon of troops through Rome, as a tennis player for King's College, as an amateur prizefighter sparring with Archie Moore in Stillman's Gymnasium, an occasion during which the rancid smell of the gym was temporarily replaced by the musk of El Morocco and the cheers of George's friends when he scored with a solid jab—but it quickly changed to *"Ohhhhhhh"* when Archie Moore retaliated with a punch that broke part of the cartilage in George's nose, causing it to bleed and causing Miles Davis to ask afterward, "Archie, is that black blood or white blood on your gloves?", to which one of George's friends replied, "Sir, *that* is blue blood."

Also on the wall is George's rebab, a one-stringed instrument of goatskin that Bedouin tribesmen gave him prior to his doing a walk-on in *Lawrence of Arabia* during a dust storm. And above his baby grand piano—he plays it well enough to have won a tie-for-third prize on Amateur Night at the Apollo Theatre a couple of years ago in Harlem—is a coconut sent him by a lady swimmer he knows in Palm Beach, and also a photograph of another girl, Vali, the orange-haired Existentialist known to all Left Bank concierges as *la bête,* and also a major-league baseball that George occasionally hurls full distance across the living room into a short, chunky, stuffed chair, using the same windup as when he pitched batting practice against Willie Mays while researching his book, *Out Of My League,* which concerns how it feels to be an amateur among pros—and which, incidentally, is a key not only to George Ames Plimpton but to many others on *The Paris Review* as well.

They are obsessed, so many of them, by the wish to know how the other half lives. And so they befriend the more interesting of the odd, avoid the downtown dullards on Wall Street, and dip into the world of the junkie, the pederast, the prizefighter, and the adventurer in pursuit of kicks and literature, being influenced perhaps by that glorious generation of ambulance drivers that preceded them to Paris at the age of twenty-six.

In Paris in the early Fifties, their great white hope was Irwin Shaw because, in the words of Thomas Guinzburg, a Yale man then managing editor of *The Paris Review*, "Shaw was a tough, tennis-playing, hard-drinking writer with a good-looking wife—the closest thing we had to Hemingway." Of course the editor in chief, George Plimpton, then as now, kept the magazine going, kept the group together, and set a style of romanticism that was—and is—infectious.

Arriving in Paris in the Spring of 1952 with a wardrobe that included the tails his grandfather had worn in the Twenties, and which George himself had worn in 1951 while attending a ball in London as an escort to the future Queen of England, he moved immediately into a tool shed behind a house owned by Gertrude Stein's nephew. Since the door of the shed was jammed, George, to enter it, had to hoist himself, his books, and his grandfather's tails through the window. His bed was a long, thin cot flanked by a lawn mower and garden hose, and was covered by an electric blanket that George could never remember to turn off—so that, when he returned to the shed at night and plopped into the cot, he was usually greeted by the angry howls of several stray cats reluctant to leave the warmth that his forgetfulness had provided.

One lonely night, before returning home, George took a walk through Montparnasse down the same streets and past the same cafés that Jake Barnes took after leaving Lady Brett in *The Sun Also Rises*. George wanted to see what Hemingway had seen, to feel what Hemingway had felt. Then, the walk over, George went into the nearest bar and ordered a drink.

In 1952 *The Paris Review*'s headquarters was a one-room office at 8 Rue Garancière. It was furnished with a desk, four chairs, a bottle of brandy, and several lively, long-legged Smith and Radcliffe girls who were anxious to get onto the masthead so that they might convince their parents back home of their innocence abroad. But so many young women came and went that Plimpton's business manager, a small, sharp-tongued Harvard wit named John P. C. Train, decided it was ridiculous to try to remember all their names, whereupon he declared that they should henceforth all be called by one name—"Apetecker." And the Apetecker alumnae came to include, at one time or another, Jane Fonda, Joan Dillon Moseley (daughter of Treasury Secretary Dillon), Gail Jones (daughter of Lena Horne), and Louisa Noble (daughter of the Groton football coach), a very industrious but forgetful girl who was endlessly losing manuscripts, letters, dictionaries and, one day after John P. C. Train received a letter from a librarian complaining that Miss Noble was a year overdue on a book, he wrote back:

Dear Sir:

I take the liberty of writing to you in my own hand because Miss L. Noble took with her the last time she left this office the typewriter on which I was accustomed to compose these messages. Perhaps when she comes into your library you will ask if we might not have this machine.

Subscription blank enclosed.

Yours faithfully,
J. P. C. Train

Since *The Paris Review*'s one-room office obviously was too small to fulfill the staff's need for mixing business with pleasure, and since there was also a limit to the number of hours they could spend at cafés, everybody would usually gather at five p.m. at the apartment of Peter and Patsy Matthiessen on 14 Rue Perceval, where by that time a party was sure to be in progress.

Peter Matthiessen, then fiction editor of *The Paris Review*, was a tall, thin Yale graduate who as a youngster had attended St. Bernard's School in New York with George Plimpton, and who now was working on his first novel, *Race Rock*. Patsy was a small, lovely, vivacious blonde with pale blue eyes and a marvelous figure, and all the boys of twenty-six were in love with her. She was the daughter of the late Richard Southgate, one-time Chief of Protocol for the State Department, and Patsy had gone to lawn parties with Kennedy children, had chauffeurs and governesses and, in her junior year at Smith, in 1948, had come to Paris and met Peter. Three years later, married, they returned to Paris and acquired for $21 a month this apartment in Montparnasse that had been left vacant when Peter's old girl friend had gone off to Venezuela.

The apartment had high ceilings, a terrace and lots of sun. On one wall was a Foujita painting of a gigantic head of a cat. The other wall was all glass, and there were large trees against the glass and wild growth crawling up it, and visitors to this apartment often felt that they were in a monstrous fishbowl, particularly by six p.m., when the room was floating with Dutch gin and absinthe and the cat's head seemed bigger, and a few junkies would wander in, nod, and settle softly, soundlessly in the corner.

This apartment, in the Fifties, was as much a meeting place for the young American literati as was Gertrude Stein's apartment in the Twenties, and it also caught the atmosphere that would, in the Sixties, prevail at George Plimpton's apartment in New York.

William Styron, often at the Matthiessens', describes their apartment in his novel, *Set This House on Fire,* and other novelists there were John Phillips Marquand and Terry Southern, both editors on *The Paris Review,* and sometimes James Baldwin, and nearly always Harold L. Humes, a chunky, indefatigable, impulsive young man with a beard, beret and a silver-handled umbrella. After being dismissed from M.I.T. for taking a Radcliffe girl sailing several hours beyond her bedtime, and after spending an unhappy tour with the Navy making mayonnaise in Bainbridge, Maryland, Harold Humes burst onto the Paris scene in full rebellion.

He became a chess hustler in cafés, earning several hundred francs a night. It was in the cafés that he met Peter Matthiessen, and they both talked of starting a little magazine that would be *The Paris Review.* Before coming to Paris, Humes had never worked on a magazine, but had grown fond of a little magazine called *Zero,* edited by a small Greek named Themistocles Hoetes, whom everybody called "Them." Impressed by what Them had done with *Zero,* Humes purchased for $600 a magazine called *The Paris News Post,* which John Ciardi later called the "best fourth-rate imitation of *The New Yorker* I have ever seen," and to which Matthiessen felt condescendingly superior, and so Humes sold it for $600 to a very nervous English girl, under whom it collapsed one issue later. Then Humes and Matthiessen and others began a long series of talks on what policy, if any, they would follow should *The Paris Review* ever get beyond the talking and drinking stages.

When the magazine was finally organized, and when George Plimpton was selected as its editor instead of Humes, Humes was disappointed. He refused to leave the cafés to sell advertising or negotiate with French printers. And in the Summer of 1952 he did not hesitate to leave Paris with William Styron, accepting an invitation from a French actress, Mme. Nénot, to go down to Cap Myrt, near Saint-Tropez, and visit her fifty-room villa that had been designed by her father, a leading architect. The villa had been occupied by the Germans early in the war. And so when Styron and Humes arrived they found holes in its walls, through which they could look out to the sea, and the grass was so high and the trees so thick with grapes that Humes' little Volkswagen became tangled in the grass. So they went on foot toward the villa, but suddenly stopped when they saw, rushing past them, a young, half-naked girl, very brown from the sun, wearing only handkerchiefs tied bikini-style, her mouth spilling with grapes. Screaming behind her was a lecherous-looking old French farmer whose grape arbor she obviously had raided.

"Styron," Humes cried, gleefully, *"we have arrived!"*

"Yes," he said, "we are *here!*"

More nymphets came out of the trees in bikinis later, carrying grapes and also half cantaloupes the size of cartwheels, and they offered some to Styron and Humes. The next day they all went swimming and fishing and, in the evening, they sat in the bombed-out villa, a breathtaking site of beauty and destruction, drinking wine with the young girls who seemed to belong only to the beach. It was an electric summer, with the nymphets batting around like moths against the screen. Styron remembers it as a scene out of Ovid, Humes as the high point of his career as an epicurean and scholar.

George Plimpton remembers that summer not romantically, but as it was—a long, hot summer of frustration with French printers and advertisers; and the other *Review* staff members, particularly John P. C. Train, were so annoyed at Humes' departure that they decided they would drop his name from the top of the masthead, where he belonged as one of the founders, down to near the bottom under "advertising and circulation."

When the first issue of *The Paris Review* came out, in the Spring of 1953, Humes was in the United States. But he had heard what they had done to him and, infuriated, he now planned his revenge. When the ship arrived at the Hudson River pier with the thousands of *Paris Reviews* that would be distributed throughout the United States, Harold Humes, wearing his beret and swearing, *"Le Paris Review c'est moi!"* was at the dock waiting for them; soon he had ripped the cartons open and, with a rubber stamp bearing his name in letters larger than any on the masthead, he began to pound his name in red over the masthead of each issue, a feat that took several hours to accomplish and which left him, in the end, totally exhausted.

"But . . . but . . . how *c-o-u-l-d* you have *done* such a thing?" George Plimpton asked when he next saw Humes.

Humes was now sad, almost tearful; but, with a final flash of vengeance, he said, "I am damned well not going to get shoved around!"

Rages of this sort were to become quite common at *The Paris Review*. Terry Southern was incensed when a phrase in one of his short stories was changed from "don't get your crap hot" to "don't get hot." Two poets wished to dissect John P. C. Train when, after a French printer had accidentally spilled the type from one poem into another, and the two poems appeared as one in the magazine, Train *casually* remarked that the printer's carelessness had actually improved the work of both poets.

Another cause for chaos was the Paris police force, which seemed ever in pursuit of John Train's nocturnal squad of flying poster plasterers, a union of Yale men and Arab youths who ran through Paris at night sticking large *Paris Review* advertising posters on every lamppost, bus, and *pissoir* they could. The ace of the squadron, a tall Yale graduate named Frank Musinsky, was so impressive that John Train decided to name all the other young men "Musinsky"—just as he had previously named the girls "Apetecker"—which Musinsky considered quite an honor, even though his real name was not Musinsky. Musinsky acquired the name because his grandfather, whose surname was Supovitch (sic), had switched names in Russia many years ago with a countryman named Musinsky who, for a price, agreed to take Frank's grandfather's place in the Russian army.

Nobody knows what became of him in the Russian army, but Frank's grandfather came to the United States, where his son later prospered in the retail shoe business and his grandson, Frank, after Yale and his tour with Train's flying squad, got a job in 1954 with The New York *Times*—and soon lost it.

He had been hired as a copyboy in the *Times* sports department and, as such, was expected to devote himself to running galley proofs and filling pastepots, and was not expected to be sitting behind a desk, feet propped up, reading Yeats and Pound and refusing to move.

One night an editor shouted, "Musinsky, without doubt you're the worst copyboy in the history of the *Times*," to which Musinsky, rising haughtily, snapped, "Sir, to quote E. E. Cummings, whom I'm sure you have heard of, 'There is some shit I shall not eat.' " Frank Musinsky turned and left the *Times,* never to return.

Meanwhile, Frank's place in the Paris flying squad was taken by several other Musinskys—Colin Wilson was one—and they all helped to preserve *The Review*'s traditional irreverence for the bourgeoisie, the Establishment, and even for the late Aga Khan who, after offering to give a $1,000 prize for fiction, then submitted his own manuscript.

The editors quickly snapped up his money, but just as quickly returned the manuscript, making it clear that his prose style was not what they were seeking, even though the Aga's own son, Sadruddin Khan, a Harvard friend of Plimpton's, had just become publisher of *The Paris Review*, an offer that George proposed and Sadruddin accepted rather impulsively one day when they both were running from the bulls at Pamplona—a moment during which George suspected, correctly, that Sadruddin might agree to just about anything.

As improbable as it may seem, what with all the Musinskys and Apeteckers flying this way and that, *The Paris Review* did very well, publishing fine stories by such younger writers as Philip Roth, Mac Hyman, Pati Hill, Evan Connell, Jr. and Hughes Rudd, and, of course, distinguishing itself most of all by its "Art of Fiction" interviews with famous authors, particularly the one with William Faulkner by Jean Stein vanden Heuvel and the one with Ernest Hemingway by Plimpton, which began in a Madrid café with Hemingway asking Plimpton, "You go to the races?"

"Yes, occasionally."

"Then you read *The Racing Form*," Hemingway said. "There you have the true Art of Fiction."

But as much as anything else, *The Paris Review* survived because it had money. And its staff members had fun because they knew that, should they ever land in jail, their friends or families would always bail them out. They would never have to share with James Baldwin the experience of spending eight days and nights in a dirty French cell on the erroneous charge of having stolen a bed sheet from a hotelkeeper, all of which led Baldwin to conclude that while the wretched round of hotel rooms, bad food, humiliating concierges, and unpaid bills may have been the "Great Adventure" for the Tall Young Men, it was not for him because, he said, "there was a real question in my mind as to which would end soonest, the Great Adventure or me."

The comparative opulence of *The Paris Review,* of course, made it the envy of the other little magazines, particularly the staff members of a quarterly called *Merlin,* some of whose editors charged the *Review* people with dilettantism, resented their pranks, resented that the *Review* would continue to be published while *Merlin,* which had also discovered and printed new talent, would soon fold.

In those days *Merlin*'s editor was Alexander Trocchi, born in Glasgow of a Scotch mother and Italian father, a very exciting, tall and conspicuous literary figure with a craggy, satanic face, faun's ears, a talent for writing and a powerful presence that enabled him to walk into any room and take charge. He would soon become a friend of George Plimpton, John Phillips Marquand, and the other *Review* people, and years later he would come to New York to live on a barge, and still later in the back room of *The Paris Review*'s Manhattan office, but eventually he would be arrested on narcotics charges, would jump bail, and would escape the United States with two of George Plimpton's Brooks Brothers suits. But he would leave behind a good novel about drug addiction, *Cain's Book*, with its memorable line: "Heroin is habit-forming . . . habit-forming . . . rabbit-forming . . . Babbitt-forming."

Alexander Trocchi's staff at *Merlin* in those days was made up largely of humorless young men in true rebellion, which *The Paris Review* staff was not; the *Merlin* crowd also read the leftist monthly *Les Temps Modernes,* and were concerned with the importance of being *engagé.* Their editors included Richard Seaver, who was reared in the Pennsylvania coal-mine district and in whose dark, humid Paris garage *Merlin* held its staff meetings, and also Austryn Wainhouse, a disenchanted Exeter-Harvard man who wrote a strong, esoteric novel, *Hedyphagetica,* and who, after several years in France, is now living in Martha's Vineyard building furniture according to the methods of the eighteenth century.

While the entire *Merlin* staff was poor, none was so poor as the poet, Christopher Logue, about whom it was said that once, when playing a pinball machine in a café, he noticed a ragged old peasant lady staring at a five-franc piece lying on the floor near the machine, but before she could pick it up Logue's foot quickly reached out and stomped on it. He kept his foot there while the old lady screamed and while he continued, rather jerkily, to hold both hands to the machine trying to keep the ball bouncing—and *did,* until the owner of the café grabbed him and escorted him out.

Some time later, when Logue's girl friend left him, he came under the influence of a wild Svengali character then living in Paris, a pale, waxen-faced South African painter who was a disciple of Nietzsche and his dictum, "Die at the right time," and who, looking for kicks, actually encouraged Logue to commit suicide—which Logue, in his depressed state, said he would do.

Austryn Wainhouse, who had suspected that suicide was very much on Logue's mind, had spent the following week sitting outside of Logue's hotel each night watching his window, but one afternoon when Logue was late for a luncheon date with Wainhouse, the latter rushed to the poet's hotel and there, on the bed, was the South African painter.

"Where's Chris?" Wainhouse demanded.

"I am not going to tell you," the painter said. "You can beat me if you wish; you're bigger and stronger than I, and. . . ."

"I *don't* want to beat you," Wainhouse shouted. It then occurred to him how ridiculous was the South African's remark since he (Wainhouse) was actually much smaller and hardly stronger than the painter. "Look," he said, finally, "don't you leave here," and then he ran quickly to a café where he knew he would find Trocchi.

Trocchi got the South African to talk and admit that Christopher Logue had left that morning for Perpignan, near the Spanish border twelve hours south of Paris, where he planned to commit suicide in much the same way as the character in the Samuel Beckett story in *Merlin,* entitled *The End*—he would hire a boat and row out to sea, further and further, and then pull up the plugs and slowly sink.

Trocchi, borrowing 30,000 francs from Wainhouse, hopped on the next train for Perpignan, five hours behind Logue. It was dark when he arrived, but early the next morning he began his search.

Logue, meanwhile, had tried to rent a boat, but did not have enough money. He also carried with him, along with some letters from his former girl friend, a tin of poison, but he did not have an opener, nor were there rocks on the beach, and so he wandered about, frustrated and frantic, until he finally came upon a refreshment stand where he hoped to borrow an opener.

It was then that the tall figure of Trocchi spotted him and placed a hand on Logue's shoulder. Logue looked up.

"Alex," Logue said, casually handing him the tin of poison, "will you open this for me?"

Trocchi put the tin in his pocket.

"Alex," Logue then said, "what are *you* doing here?"

"Oh," Trocchi said lightly, "I've come down to embarrass you."

Logue broke down in tears, and Trocchi helped him off the beach and then they rode, almost in total silence, back to Paris on the train.

Immediately George Plimpton and several others on *The Paris Review* who were very fond of Logue, and proud of Trocchi, raised enough money to put Christopher Logue on a kind of monthly allowance. Later Logue returned to London and published books of poetry and his plays, *Antigone* and *The Lily-White Boys*, were performed at the Royal Court Theatre in London. Still later he began to write songs for The Establishment, London's satirical nightclub act.

After the Logue episode, which, according to George Plimpton, sent at least a half-dozen young novelists to their typewriters trying to build a book around it, life in Paris at the *Review* was once more happy and ribald—but, a year later with the *Review* still doing well, Paris slowly seemed to pall.

John P. C. Train, then managing editor, put a sign on his in-basket reading, "Please Do Not Put Anything In The Managing Editor's Box," and one day when a pleasant, blue-eyed Oklahoman named Gene Andrewski wandered in with a manuscript and mentioned that he had once helped produce his college humor magazine, John Train quickly handed him a beer and said, "How would you like to run this magazine?" Andrewski said he would think it over. He thought it over for a few seconds, looked around at everybody else drinking beer, and agreed to become a kind of Assistant Managing Editor in Charge of Doing Train's Job. "The main reason I took the job," Andrewski later explained, "was I wanted the freedom."

In 1956 Peter Duchin moved to Paris and lived on a barge on the Seine, and many *Paris Review* people made this their new headquarters. There was no water on the barge, and in the morning everybody had to shave with Perrier. But the attempt at merriment on the barge seemed futile because, by this time, most of the old crowd had left. Paris was, as Gertrude Stein suggested, the right place for twenty-six, but now most of them were thirty years old. And so they returned to New York—but not in the melancholy mood of Malcolm Cowley's exiles of the Twenties, who were forced home during the early currents of the crash, but rather with the attitude that the party would now shift to the other side of the Atlantic. Soon New York was aware of their presence, particularly the presence of Harold L. Humes.

After taking over a large apartment on upper Broadway with his wife, his daughters, and his unclipped wirehair terrier, and installing seven telephones and a large paper cutter that has the cracking eighteenth-century sound of a guillotine, Humes lashed out with a series of ideas and tall deeds: he hit on a theory of cosmology that would jolt Descartes, finished a second novel, played piano in a Harlem jazz club, began to shoot a movie called *Don Peyote,* a kind of Greenwich Village version of Don Quixote starring an unknown from Kansas City named Ojo de Vidrio, whose girl friend eventually grabbed the film and ran off with it. Humes also invented a paper house, an *actual paper house* that is water-proof, fireproof and large enough for people to live in; he set up a full-sized model on the Long Island estate of George Plimpton's family, and Humes's corporation, which included some backers from *The Paris Review* crowd, insured Humes's brain for $1,000,000.

During the Democratic National Convention in 1960, Humes led a phalanx of screaming Stevensonians onto the scene after employing the gate-crashing techniques of the ancient armies of Athens. When back in New York he called for an investigation of the New York police force, whereupon the police commissioner called for an investigation of *Humes* —and discovered fourteen unpaid traffic tickets. Humes went to jail just long enough to be discovered by the Commissioner of Corrections, Anna Kross, who upon recognizing him behind bars said, "Why, Mr. Humes, what are *you* doing in *there?*", to which he responded with Thoreau's line to Emerson, "Why, Miss Kross, what are *you* doing out *there?*"

When released on bail that was produced by Robert Silvers, another *Paris Review* editor, Harold Humes was asked by newspaper reporters how he liked the cell, and he replied, once more after Thoreau, "In a time of injustice, the place for an honest man is in jail."

Robert Silvers, one of the few quiet editors on the *Review,* a man with no apparent vices except smoking in bed, had no place to stay when he returned from Paris, and so he temporarily occupied the guest room in George Plimpton's apartment on East Seventy-second Street, where he proceeded to burn many holes in the mattress. He then plugged up the holes with peach pits. George Plimpton did not object. Robert Silvers was an old friend and, besides, the mattress did not belong to Plimpton. It belonged to a fashion model who had once occupied the apartment, and who surprised both Plimpton and Silvers one day with a letter asking if they would please send the mattress to her home in France. They did, pits and all, and, having heard no complaints, they both nurture some delight in the thought that somewhere in Paris, somewhere in the very chic apartment of a high-fashion model, there is a mattress stuffed with peach pits.

Fortunately for Plimpton, he did not have to buy a new mattress for his guest room because, at about that time, *The Paris Review,* which had an office in a tenement on Eighty-second Street, had been evicted; and so George took home the small bed that had been in the back room of *The*

Paris Review's office—a room that had been the locale of several parties that had reduced the premise to a collage of broken bottles, bent spoons, rats and chewed manuscripts. Alex Trocchi had lived in *The Paris Review*'s back room for a while, but later he was on the move from the police and desperately in need of more money for more drugs. Eventually he was caught and arrested. His friends on *The Paris Review* helped with the bail money, but he jumped bail and left the country with George Plimpton's two suits and, as far as anyone knows, he now lives on the Isle of Man.

After the eviction from the tenement, *The Paris Review*'s New York office shifted to the unlikely and quiet borough of Queens, where, in a large home between Grand Central Parkway and a cemetery, Lillian von Nickern Pashaian, when she is not tending to her three children, canaries and turtles, accepts manuscripts that are addressed to *The Paris Review* and forwards them for a reading to either Jill Fox in Bedford Village, New York, or to Rose Styron in Roxbury, Connecticut. If *they* like what they have read, they forward the manuscript to George Plimpton's apartment on Seventy-second Street where, between all his other activities, he gives a final reading and decides whether or not it will be accepted. If it is accepted, the author usually becomes the recipient of a small check and all he can drink at the next Plimpton party.

A Plimpton party is often planned only a few hours before it begins. George will pick up the phone and call a few people. They, in turn, will call others. Soon there is the thunder of feet ascending the Plimpton staircase. The inspiration for the party may have been that Plimpton won a court-tennis match earlier that day at the Racquet and Tennis Club, or that one member of *The Paris Review* crowd has a book coming out (in which case the publisher is invited to share the expenses), or that a member has just returned to Manhattan from a trip—a trip that might have carried John P. C. Train, a financial speculator, to Africa, or Peter Matthiessen to New Guinea to live with Stone Age tribesmen, or Harold Humes to the Bronx to fight in court over a parking ticket.

And in giving so many parties, in giving out keys to his apartment, in keeping the names of old friends on *The Paris Review* masthead long after they have ceased to work for it, George Ames Plimpton has managed to keep the crowd together all these years, and has also created around himself a rather romantic world, a free, frolicsome world within which he, and they, may briefly escape the inevitability of being thirty-six.

It exudes charm, talent, beauty, adventure. It is the envy of the uninvited, particularly of some child-bearing Apeteckers in the suburbs who often ask, "When is that group going to settle down?" Some in the group, like George Plimpton, have remained bachelors. Others have married women who like parties—or have been divorced. Still others have an understanding that, if the wife is too tired for a party, the husband goes alone. It is largely a man's world, all of them bound by their memories of Paris and the Great Adventure they shared, and it has very few exiles, although it has had some—one being the beautiful blonde who was very much on everyone's mind in Paris ten years ago, Patsy Matthiessen.

Patsy and Peter are divorced. She is now married to Michael Goldberg, an abstract painter, lives on West Eleventh Street, and moves in the little world of downtown intellectuals and painters. Recently she spent several days in a hospital after being bitten by the dog of the widow of a famous painter. In her apartment she has a cardboard box full of snapshots of *The Paris Review* crowd of the Fifties. But she remembers those days with some bitterness.

"The whole life seemed after a while to be utterly meaningless," she said. "And there was something very *manqué* about them—this going to West Africa, and getting thrown in jail, and getting in the ring with Archie Moore. . . . And *I* was a Stepin Fetchit in that crowd, getting them tea at four, and sandwiches at ten. . . ."

A few blocks away, in a small, dark apartment, another exile, James Baldwin, said, "It didn't take long before I really was no longer a part of them. They were more interested in kicks and hashish cigarettes than I was. I had already done that in the Village when I was eighteen or seventeen. It was a little boring by then.

"They also used to go to Montparnasse, where all the painters and writers went, and where I hardly went. And they used to go there and hang around at the cafés for hours and hours looking for Hemingway. They didn't seem to realize," he said, "that Hemingway was long gone."

[July, 1963]

Back on the Open Road for Boys

by Alice Glaser

On the bank of the Ganges between Delhi and Calcutta is the dusty city of Benares—a city tingling with ricksha bells, teeming with sages and scavengers, smelling of yak and marijuana. Eighteen months ago it was discovered by two wandering poets, Allen Ginsberg and Peter Orlovsky, probably the only two Beats still on the road. Even Kerouac, their god, had settled down on Long Island with his mother, and the whole Beat movement seemed threatened unless the will could be revived and a new hopland could be found. Benares seemed the perfect place. Sandals were only four cents a pair, and pads were going for $2 a month. The streets were lined with beggars carrying monkeys, with naked holy men, and with big buffaloes that the children pulled down to the Ganges and washed all over, intimately, soaping and scrubbing them and finally polishing them with banana oil and waiting for the defecation so they could scoop it up, roll it in dust and straw, and later convert it to fuel.

Such sights and smells charmed the Beats and, though Ginsberg and Orlovsky dined mostly on borsch and scrambled eggs, they otherwise quickly adapted to this Indian scene. They wore long, billowy gowns and beards not unlike the Sikhs, who wear bangles on their left wrists and their masculine organ on the right side.

Their poets' pad, on the third floor of a hot Hindu tenement, over-looked two temple tops and a blind woman rocking in the shade, back and forth, saying nothing. On their first week in Benares, the poets, their hair and beards untrimmed, gleefully sprinted down to the Ganges in blue swimming trunks. A buffalo began to lick Orlovsky.

"What does it feel like?" Ginsberg asked.

"Like the tongue you buy in stores," said Orlovsky.

Ginsberg seemed disappointed.

For the rest of the year they remained in Benares, undiscovered by the Trends Editors of *Vogue*, unmissed by Orville Prescott. But early this spring, wondering if they might not have a message for the hipsters back home, I flew to Benares and, after a bumpy ricksha ride across town toward the Ganges, I soon found myself knocking on the heavy wooden door of the poets' pad.

"How old are you?" asked Ginsberg, lying on the floor, inhaling deeply and blowing the sweet, cool smoke into the hot room.

"In my mid-thirties," I said.

"I'm thirty-six," he said.

"How about some tea?" asked Orlovsky, a delicate, thin blond of twenty-nine, standing in a gown over a small alcohol stove.

The bowls on the shelves were buzzing with flies and sticky with old hairs, and, declining politely, I took a seat on the floor.

"Do you mind if I comb out my hair?" Ginsberg asked, raising his head. "I'm not used to having hair so long." He removed from under a carpet a long, dirty comb and teased his brunet locks slightly upward.

"Are you here on a grant?" I asked.

"Guggenheim turned me down twice," Ginsberg said. "They think I'm a creep."

"Well, where does your money come from?"

"I get from $800 to $1,200 a year from the publisher, Lawrence Ferlinghetti; about $50 or $60 more from the Eighth Street Bookshop in Greenwich Village, and not much from the magazines because I sell to the crappy, experimental ones that don't pay much. Although I did get an advance from *Playboy* to do a piece on India. Any excess money, I plow back into the literary scene, such as that little magazine in New York we shall euphemistically call *Mother*. It's a magazine of culture written in a really frantic, freakish camp. *Mother, A Magazine of the Arts*."

"How do you spend your days?"

"Burning bodies," Ginsberg said. "Next door, at the Manikarnika Ghat, they usually have at least four or five bodies going up there. When you die here, you know, your body gets burned up. There is never any fear of death, either. Death is no worse than a hamburger stand."

"You mean you just stand around and watch?"

"We help out, too. Burning bodies is a holy rite. After they're burned, it's a sweet smell—they empty everything into the Ganges, which is very sterile, you know, because of the mineral content of the water. A dead cow can go floating down it and you can go swimming in the same spot two minutes later without getting infected by anything."

"How has your writing been going?"

He inhaled, blew out more smoke, and cheerfully presented a section from his journal, which I read as follows: ". . . so we ate cold chicken squatting on a mattress, twenty-five rupees, five dollars' worth, while the old lady beggar I have been watching on the clothshop corner steps downstairs rocked back and forth on her heels under a grey mattress for the fourth successive day. No sleep last night, and all morn feeding bannanas [sic] to monkeys on the roof, sunrise and then to the police to give papers registration address—the policeman a jolly type baffled by our presence. 'Why do you want to stay here in India so long?' "

"Well," I said, putting the journal aside, "why *do* you stay in India so long?"

Peter Orlovsky, leaning against a wall across the room, said, "I like living here. There's so much going on all the time. Wherever it happened, and whenever it's going, it's here right now."

Ginsberg nodded. Then he pulled out some photographs of himself, William Burroughs, Orlovsky and other Beats taken earlier in the year on another journey. One photograph showed Orlovsky naked with his hands modestly clasped over his genitalia; another showed Orlovsky, naked, facing the camera, no hands.

"I got mad in Greece," Orlovsky explained. "I wanted to pose naked in front of the Parthenon but the guide was afraid he'd get into trouble. . . ."

"You're like Dali," said Ginsberg, turning. "Dali sat naked to newsmen for an interview once. Dali's a European Spaniard from an earlier scene. That's especially why he's a Catholic and Monarchist, also a Dadaist."

Then I asked Ginsberg about some writers he has known, and he said, "Kerouac uses his friends in his books: Peter is usually 'George.' I've known Kerouac and Burroughs since 1943; Jack had a sort of sympathy about his family, a sort of despairing tenderness. One critic, Podhoretz, called Jack a juvenile delinquent, and then got fond of Mailer, and when Mailer stabbed his wife all those Columbia people got upset. Mailer was influenced by Burroughs, you know. He read *Naked Lunch* and got very influenced. Mailer got up and praised Burroughs at the Edinburgh Conference. Burroughs has always been a kind of loner. About the stories of Burroughs cutting pages down the middle, this is in the Gertrude Stein direction; this is how *Soft Machine* is. It's a transition from tonal to atonal—it takes a while to accustom the ear to it but it does become familiar after a while."

"What are your plans, if any?"

"Well," he said, inhaling again, and again lying on the floor, "we're going to stay here for a while and then maybe go to Japan. But not just yet. One of these days I'll go to Canada to speak at the University of Toronto, then to New Jersey to see my father, and back here to pick up Peter for Japan."

"Then what?"

"To be real, that's what," he said. "And to reserve all my charms and determination for private life rather than be hypocritical and nasty in public. See, the old tradition was to be pompous in public and if you preferred a private perversion or two, never say so, making the public somehow different from what the private thoughts were, dig?"

"Dig," I said, but before I could ask another question I realized both were sleeping, and so I kissed them and left.

[July, 1963]

The night Senator and Mrs. Javits, Robert Rauschenberg, Niki de Saint-Phalle, Jean Tinguely, Merce Cunningham, the Stewed Prunes, *Life, Newsweek, Harper's Bazaar* and *Show* magazines, the Canadian Broadcasting Corporation and the cream of New York's Upper Bohemia all saw, at last, what was Happening

by John Wulp

In the Spring of 1962 I was in control of the Maidman Playhouse, a rather plush off-Broadway theatre on West Forty-second Street. I had taken a year's lease on the theatre which had begun in midwinter, but since that time I had produced two shows, a musical and an evening of one-act plays, both of which had been disastrous failures.

After that I tried renting the theatre, but with no better luck. One show had already opened to good reviews, but it had failed to attract an audience and quickly closed. Another show was scheduled to open the end of May, but the script was so bad I knew it had little chance of running—as things turned out it never even opened.

If I wanted to hang onto the theatre I had to think up something to do that would enable me to pay the rent through the summer months—and fast.

I was sitting in the office of the theatre brooding about these problems one day toward the end of April when the telephone rang. It was Kenneth Koch, a poet and playwright with some reputation among the *avant-garde* in New York. He was the author of a ten-minute epic called *Bertha*, which had been included among the plays in the *Theatre of The Absurd*

882

produced off-Broadway the year before, and also of a slightly longer epic called *George Washington Crossing The Delaware*, one of the three one-act plays I had recently produced.

"Hello, John," said Kenneth. "How are things?"

"I don't know," I said. "How are things with you?"

"Just great," said Kenneth. "Say, John, I was wondering what's going on at your theatre now?"

"Nothing much," I said. "I've got the Stewed Prunes on Monday nights, but that's about all." The Stewed Prunes were a pair of comedians consisting of MacIntyre Dixon, fair and short and phlegmatic, and Richard Libertini, dark and tall and volatile, who had persuaded me to allow them to use the theatre on Monday nights to try out new material. They generally played to an audience of ten or twelve people.

"What sort of business are they doing?" said Kenneth.

"Pretty good," I said. "Why?"

"Well, a group of us were sitting around talking last night and we thought it might be fun to do something," said Kenneth.

"Who's we?" I said.

"Oh, you know," said Kenneth. "Bob Rauschenberg, Niki de Saint-Phalle, Jean Tinguely. You know them, don't you?"

"The only one I know is Bob Rauschenberg," I said. Bob Rauschenberg is a painter of "Neo-Dadaist" tendencies. He got a start toward international fame several years before when he had smeared his bed with paint and then exhibited the bed (quilt, sheets, and stuffed pillow case) as a work of art. This provoked a minor scandal among the art-world followers, and Bob Rauschenberg's reputation was made.

I had met him several years before, when I went to his studio to see if he might be interested in designing the scenery for a play that I had written which was about to be produced in New York. I had never seen his work before. In one corner stood a stuffed goat whose face had been daubed with paint and whose body was encased by an automobile tire. In another corner stood an orange crate that had been pasted with photographs and smeared with paint and on which stood a stuffed white chicken.

"Is this your work?" I inquired, somewhat timorously.

"Yes, but it isn't plugged in yet," Bob Rauschenberg replied, whereupon he put a plug into a wall socket and a naked light bulb in the orange crate began to blink on and off.

The matter of his designing the scenery for my show never worked out, but I had seen Bob Rauschenberg several times since then and we had a nodding acquaintance with each other.

"Well, certainly you've heard of Jean Tinguely," said Kenneth.

"What has he done?" I said.

"Oh, you know," said Kenneth. "He's the guy that does the self-destroying machines. They had a show of his a few years ago in the courtyard of the Museum of Modern Art. You must have read about it in the newspapers. It was on all the front pages."

"I remember now," I said. "That was the night the self-destroying machine failed to destroy itself. Didn't the fire department have to come and put it out?"

"We won't go into that," said Kenneth.

"What do you mean?" I said.

"Oh, the fire department didn't really have to put it out," said Kenneth. "They were just showing off. They probably wanted some free publicity."

"He's French, isn't he?" I said.

"Who?" said Kenneth.

"Jean Tinguely," I said with some exasperation. "Who do you think we're talking about?"

"He's Swiss, but that's all right," said Kenneth.

"Who's Niki de Saint-Phalle?" I said.

"She's the girl who fires rifles at paint-filled bags concealed on various objects," said Kenneth. "You've heard about her, haven't you?"

"I don't think so," I said.

"Oh, sure you have," said Kenneth. "You must have read about her someplace or seen her on television."

"Well, anyhow, what are you planning to do?" I said.

"I don't know," said Kenneth. "As I say, we were only talking about it last night."

"You must have some idea," I said.

"Well, I thought maybe I'd write something about Boston," said Kenneth. "You know, I went to Harvard and Bob Rauschenberg's been there one or two times. Niki's never been there, but she says she loves the sound of the place."

"I still have no idea what you're planning to do," I said.

"I don't know," said Kenneth. "I have no idea what Bob Rauschenberg is planning to do. Who can tell with him? Jean says he's going to do something with balloons. I don't know. He blows them up, I suppose. Niki will probably paint by firing a rifle. I don't know. I don't know."

"Who's going to direct this thing?" I said.

"We're trying to get Merce Cunningham," said Kenneth.

"Do you really think he'll do it?" I said. Merce Cunningham is a famous *avant-garde* dancer and choreographer in New York, and I was surprised that he would be willing to be associated with a project that seemed so nebulous.

"Sure, why not?" said Kenneth. "Bob Rauschenberg is a good friend of his."

"Do you suppose anybody will come?" I said.

"Who can tell?" said Kenneth. "I should imagine so. They're all very big names in the art world right now."

"Well, I don't know—" I said. "Do you have any money?"

"Are you kidding?" he said.

"I'll tell you what," I said. "I've got a show coming in the end of May, but I think we can work out some sort of schedule so that you can do your show if you can get it on within the next couple of weeks."

"That's all right," said Kenneth. "Jean is leaving for Europe in a couple of weeks so we'd have to get it on before then anyhow. How much do you want for rent?"

I swallowed hard and said the biggest figure I thought I had a chance of getting. "A hundred and fifty dollars."

"Don't you think that's a little steep?" said Kenneth.

"You can take it or leave it," I said.

"Let me talk it over with the others and call you back," said Kenneth.

A few days later he called back to say that he had discussed my terms with the other people involved, and they had all decided to go through with the venture.

The performance was scheduled to be held at ten in the evening of Friday, May 4. It was then around the end of April, so that left just a week and a half for preparations.

It was agreed that Kenneth Koch would write a short epic poem to be called *The Construction of Boston*, and Bob Rauschenberg, Niki de Saint-Phalle and Jean Tinguely would appear in this work. Merce Cunningham had by this time definitely consented to direct it. It was still necessary to get two actors to read the poem, but I said I would take it upon myself to persuade the Stewed Prunes to do this without being paid. Kenneth Koch and his friends thought they could assemble the rest of the performers.

There were to be two paid ads in The New York *Times*. The first was to appear on the Wednesday before the performance, the second on the day of the performance itself. Both ads would be paid for by Leo Castelli, a New York gallery owner and a friend of the artists.

No tickets would go on sale until ten o'clock in the morning on the day of performance. All tickets would be three dollars. There would be no complimentary tickets—not to friends of the artists and the performers, not even to critics.

Once this had been settled wheels began to turn.

I got in touch with the Stewed Prunes. They said they were reluctant to perform for nothing, although it was no secret between us that they had never earned a cent on one of their Monday nights. Nevertheless, I managed to persuade them that the prestige of appearing on the same stage with such well-known artists as Bob Rauschenberg, Niki de Saint-Phalle, and Jean Tinguely might be beneficial to their careers, and they finally said yes.

It was not long after this that Kenneth Koch called me again to set up an appointment for me to meet with Merce Cunningham and the others for the purpose of showing them the stage.

We met at the theatre around four o'clock on a Sunday afternoon.

"This really is a lovely little theatre," said Merce.

"Is all this yours?" Bob Rauschenberg said to me. He was enviously eyeing the debris that had accumulated backstage.

"Please feel free to use anything you find lying about," I said.

"You wouldn't have a costume for Jean?" said Niki de Saint-Phalle. Jean Tinguely spoke very little English: whenever he had anything to say, he said it in French and Niki de Saint-Phalle translated it for him.

"I'll show you what we have in the costume room," I said. I led them down a winding metal stairway to the costume room.

"You don't have to worry about us damaging anything we use," said Bob Rauschenberg. "We're real artists."

When I opened the costume room Niki de Saint-Phalle and Jean Tinguely immediately began going through the racks trying to find a costume for Jean. All the while they were searching, Jean kept putting on a series of funny hats to the accompaniment of giggles and squeals from Niki. Finally, she uttered a cry of delight.

"Look, Jean! Look what I've found!" she said. "It's *you!*"

Niki de Saint-Phalle and Jean Tinguely came hurrying out of the costume room and went into one of the dressing rooms so that Jean could get a better look at himself in the mirror when he tried on his costume. He stripped himself to the waist, revealing a hairy black chest. Then he tried wriggling into an elegant evening dress that turned out to be sizes too small for him.

"Oops, careful!" said Niki de Saint-Phalle, who was helping him. "You'll split the seams."

A look of horror must have come over my face because the evening dress had once been a very expensive costume.

"Don't worry," said Bob Rauschenberg to reassure me. "We're real artists."

Jean Tinguely was unable to get into the dress. He stood with it bunched around his hips, holding the top part over his hairy chest as he sadly surveyed himself in the mirror.

"What a shame!" said Niki de Saint-Phalle. "That one would have been perfect for you."

When I saw what they were after I brought them one dress after another from the costume room, but all of them were shabbier and less expensive than the dress Jean had first tried on and they found some reason to reject each one.

"No, that won't do," said Niki de Saint-Phalle. "No! No! Jean must look elegant."

"We're real artists," said Bob Rauschenberg.

They decided there was nothing to do but rent a costume for Jean Tinguely.

During the following days the preparations for the performance grew more and more frantic. Bob Rauschenberg and a group of friends he had recruited to help him were busy as ants carrying various objects into the theatre. They brought bathtubs and toilets. They brought beds and dressers and chairs. They brought rubber tubing and tangles of electrical wiring. On their last trip they wheeled into the theatre an enormous replica of the Venus de Milo that Niki de Saint-Phalle had made out of plaster of Paris.

"Jean has a reputation for destroying things," said Niki de Saint-Phalle to me one afternoon as we were talking in the lobby. "So for this performance he has decided he would like to build something for a change."

"That will be nice," I said.

Shortly thereafter a load of cinder blocks was delivered to the theatre and neatly stacked in the lobby.

"What are the cinder blocks for?" I said when I next encountered Niki de Saint-Phalle.

"Jean has decided to build a wall," she replied.

"A wall?" I said.

"Yes," said Niki de Saint-Phalle. "It's going to fill the entire proscenium opening."

"Won't that make it difficult for the audience to see?" I said.

"That's the idea," said Niki de Saint-Phalle.

The dress rehearsal was scheduled to begin at eleven o'clock on the night before the actual performance. When I arrived at the theatre I discovered an assorted group of people sprawled out on seats in various parts of the auditorium drinking cups of black coffee. In addition to the Stewed Prunes, I recognized two dancers, Henry Geldzahler, an associate curator of American painting and sculpture at the Metropolitan Museum, and Maxine Groffsky, a girl who was working as a reader in a large publishing house. All the others were unknown to me.

"Hello, dear," said Maxine, as soon as she spotted me. She was sitting in the front row with her feet propped up on the stage.

"Maxine!" I said. "What are you doing here?"

"I wish I knew," said Maxine. "I'm sleepy."

It was difficult to tell very much about what the show would be like from the dress rehearsal. None of the costumes had arrived and the artists could do little more than walk through their paces and describe the actions they would eventually perform.

"This is where I make rain," said Bob Rauschenberg.

"This is where I fire the cannon," said Niki de Saint-Phalle.

After the dress rehearsal, everyone met to compare notes.

"I know it looks rough," said Merce, "but we'll get it tidied up by tomorrow night."

"How long did it run?" said Kenneth.

"A little under fifteen minutes by my watch," said Bob Rauschenberg.

"What will we do?" said Kenneth. "Do you think the audience will be furious at paying three bucks a ticket for a show that runs less than fifteen minutes?"

"It will run longer in actual performance," said Niki de Saint-Phalle.

"Maybe nobody will come anyhow," said Kenneth.

"I think the whole thing is crap," said Henry Geldzahler.

I sensed that something was wrong with the Stewed Prunes. I had noticed MacIntyre Dixon stretched out on a couch in the lobby with his eyes tightly closed while Richard Libertini bent over him solicitously, but I thought it best not to say anything at the time. However, as soon as I was able to get Merce Cunningham alone, I asked him what had happened.

"Oh, one of the parts from Jean's weather machine came loose and hit the little Stewed Prune (what's his name? I can never tell the two of them apart) on the forehead," said Merce.

"Is it anything serious?" I said.

"I don't think so," said Merce. "But he's threatening to walk out on the show."

"What will you do?" I said.

"Kenneth's talking to him now," said Merce.

"If there's any way I can be of help, let me know," I said.

"The Stewed Prunes don't understand my artistic principles," said Merce. "I understand their artistic principles, but I'm not interested in them."

When I arrived at the theatre to open the box office around nine-thirty on the morning of the performance, I found a line of people waiting to buy tickets and all three box-office telephones ringing frantically. It quickly became obvious to me that I was not going to be able to handle the box office by myself, so I put in a hurried call to Bob Foley, an unemployed actor who had appeared in one of my shows.

"Get over here as fast as you can!" I said. "This place is a madhouse!"

"But I'm not up yet!" said Bob Foley. "I haven't had my coffee!"

"Don't ask any questions!" I said.

Bob Foley arrived at eleven o'clock, rubbing the sleep out of his eyes, but by that time, between the telephone reservations and the window sales, the two hundred tickets for that evening's performance were completely sold out. From that point on it became a question of dealing as diplomatically as possible with the mobs of people who showed up at the theatre or called in by telephone.

"No, I'm sorry, we're completely sold out," I said over and over again.

"Yes, that's right. The tickets only went on sale at ten o'clock, but we were completely sold out by ten-thirty. I can put your name on a list and if there are any cancellations. . . ."

"No, I'm sorry, we're completely sold out," said Bob Foley on another telephone. "If you want me to put your name on a list. . . ."

"Hello, I'm————. I'm calling for Leo Castelli—I'm Mr. Castelli's secretary."

"Yes?" I said.

"Mr. Castelli would like to reserve forty-eight tickets for tonight's performance."

"I'm sorry, we're completely sold out," I said.

"Oh, dear, I thought the tickets were only supposed to go on sale at ten o'clock."

"That's right, but we're completely sold out already," I said.

"Oh, dear, you're completely sold out? Mr. Castelli has invited a party of forty-eight people."

"I'm sorry," I said.

"Some of the people Mr. Castelli has invited are very important in the art world."

"I'm sorry," I said.

"You know Mr. Castelli paid for the newspaper ads?"

"If there are any cancellations I'll let you know," I said.

"Hello, this is————, at *Harper's Bazaar.* I'd like to reserve twelve tickets for tonight's performance."

"I'm sorry, there are no tickets left," I said.

"You must have a few tickets put aside for the press. We were planning to send our entire art staff."

"We're completely sold out," I said.

"In that case, do you suppose it might be possible to squeeze one of our photographers into your theatre somehow? Our readers couldn't afford to miss this."

By one o'clock, what with special requests of one sort or another, I had considerably oversold the house and there was a waiting list of several hundred people. When Bob Rauschenberg, Niki de Saint-Phalle, and Jean Tinguely heard this there was some debate as to whether or not they should schedule a second performance, but they finally decided against it.

"It's better if we don't make it too easy to get in," said Niki.

The phone never stopped ringing.

"Hello, this is Nan Rosenthal at *Show* magazine. I was wondering if you could tell me a little bit about tonight's performance."

"I'm sorry, there are no tickets left," I said.

"You don't seem to understand. This is Nan Rosenthal at *Show* magazine."

"There are no tickets left," I said.

"I'm the art editor at *Show* magazine. You must have made some arrangements to accommodate the press."

"There's a small cubicle at the back of the theatre," I said. "Maybe I could fit you in there."

"Will I be able to see?"

"You'll have a partially obstructed view of the stage," I said.

"No, no, you don't seem to understand. This is Nan Rosenthal at *Show* magazine."

"It's the best I can do," I said.

"Well, all right. Put two tickets aside for me. The name is Nan Rosenthal at *Show* magazine."

"There are no complimentary tickets," I said.

"I'm Nan Rosenthal, at *Show* magazine."

"We're not giving complimentary tickets to anyone," I said.

"But if I'm interested I might do a piece on tonight's event for *Show* magazine."

"What good is that going to do me?" I said.

"Don't you want free publicity? Think how much a plug in *Show* magazine might boost your business."

"There's only going to be one performance and we're sold out already," I said.

"I've never heard of such a thing," said Nan Rosenthal, and hung up, indignant.

During the afternoon several New York newspapers called. *Life* called. *Newsweek* called. A man from The Newark *News* called. They all wanted to send either reporters or photographers. I said I would try to accommodate them somehow, but they would have to pay for their tickets.

"Hello, I was wondering if you would be so kind as to give me some information about tonight's event."

"I'm sorry, we're completely sold out." I said.

"Oh dear, I've come all the way down from Boston. You see, I'm on the program committee for the Boston Museum of Fine Arts. We saw your advertisement in the newspapers and were *so* intrigued by the title. Do you think your show might be suitable for the Boston Museum of Fine Arts?"

"You'd have to decide that for yourself," I said.

"Couldn't you just give me some hint as to the nature of the program?"

"It's sort of difficult to describe," I said. "If you're at all familiar with the work of Bob Rauschenberg or Jean Tinguely, you'll know what I mean."

"It sounds absolutely fascinating. Are you sure there's no way I could get in?"

"Well, I was thinking of opening up a small cubicle at the back of the theatre," I said.

"Will I be able to see all right?"

"You'll be able to see enough to tell what's going on," I said.

"Oh, if you could get me in I would be ever so grateful. You see, I'm on the program committee for the Boston Museum of Fine Arts. . . ."

"Hello, I was wondering what my chances are for getting into tonight's performance."

"There are no tickets left," I said.

"Well, actually I wasn't interested in getting a ticket so much as I was interested in getting into the theatre with my equipment."

"Your equipment?" I said.

"Yes, this is————, from the Canadian Broadcasting Corporation. We thought we'd like to do a broadcast of the show you're having at your theatre tonight."

"How big is your equipment?" I said.

"It doesn't take up much room at all."

"Perhaps we could wedge you in next to one of the columns at the side of the auditorium," I said.

"Anything will be fine."

Around six o'clock the artists began to arrive to make final preparations for the performance, but still the telephone continued to ring, and still more and more people continued to arrive at the box office.

Around nine o'clock, just before the audience began to file into the theatre, I met Merce Cunningham in the lobby. Merce was on his way out to get a sandwich and a glass of milk before the performance. He looked worn and tired.

"Is everything all set?" I said.

"Who knows?" said Merce. "I have no idea what's going to happen tonight."

"What about MacIntyre Dixon?" I said.

"He's agreed to go through with it," said Merce. "We've worked it out so he can read his lines from in front of the proscenium where he won't be in any danger."

The audience was an impressive one.

Marcel Duchamp was there, making a rare public appearance.

Virgil Thomson was there, in a party that included a young rock-and-roll composer and his attractive actress wife.

The art director of *Harper's Bazaar* was there along with several members of his staff.

Leo Castelli had finally gotten in, although he was forced to stand.

Every available seat in the house was filled. People were standing about twenty deep in each of the doorways, and the little cubicle at the back of the auditorium that I thought might hold twelve people was crammed with twice that number. I told Bob Foley to lock the doors. There was a mob of fifty to a hundred people in the outer lobby still hoping to get in.

Just then the telephone in the box office rang.

"Hello," said the voice on the other end of the line. "Are you having some sort of show at your theatre tonight?"

"I'm sorry, there are no tickets left," I said wearily.

"Now, wait a minute," said the voice at the other end of the line. "Are you having some show called—what the hell is it? *The Construction of Boston*—at your theatre tonight?"

"There are no tickets left," I said.

"I'm sure you can always find room for a few more," said the voice at the other end of the line.

"There are no tickets left," I said. I was beginning to get angry.

"I'm calling for Senator and Mrs. Javits," said the voice at the other end of the line.

That calmed me down very quickly. "I'm sorry, I'd like to help you," I said, "but there's a line of about a hundred people ahead of you."

"What time does the show start?" said the voice at the other end of the line.

"It's just about to begin," I said.

"We'll be right over."

Kenneth Koch was supposed to have programs printed, but in his excitement he had forgotten to do so. Therefore, it had been decided that I should read the list of credits to the audience. Just as I was about to step in front of the red curtain, however, Merce Cunningham stopped me.

"I don't want my name mentioned," said Merce.

"Why not?" I said.

"I just don't want my name mentioned," said Merce.

I stepped in front of the curtain.

"Good evening, ladies and gentlemen," I said. "I have been asked to read the program for tonight's event. The show you are about to see is called *The Construction of Boston*. It was written by. . . ."

And I began the list of credits.

Bob Rauschenberg, Niki de Saint-Phalle, and Jean Tinguely were each playing themselves. They each also had alter egos bearing the same names but played by other people. I felt this was too complicated to explain so I simply recited the information that Kenneth Koch had written down.

"The part of Jean Tinguely will be played by Jean Tinguely," I read. And, after that, "The part of Jean Tinguely will be played by Henry Geldzahler."

Much to my astonishment, the audience broke into guffaws which increased each time I read the similar listings for the other artists.

After I had finished reading the program, I stepped in back of the red curtain once again and walked to the side of the stage. I was just about to look for a spot from which I might watch the show when Bob Foley came rushing up to me.

"John, you've got to do something about that mob in the lobby," said Bob Foley. "There's some guy out there who's pounding on the doors trying to get in."

As I walked to the back of the lobby, I could hear the pounding.

I angrily pulled open the door only to be confronted by Senator Javits. A woman I presumed to be Mrs. Javits was standing beside him.

"Good evening, Senator Javits," I said.

Senator Javits simply smiled.

"This is Senator and Mrs. Javits," said a man in a sharkskin suit who was behind the Senator.

"Yes, I know," I said. And then I pointlessly repeated, "Good evening, Senator Javits."

Senator Javits smiled again.

"Senator and Mrs. Javits would like to see this little show you're going to have here tonight," said the man in the sharkskin suit.

"What am I going to do?" I said. "As I told you over the phone I don't have any more room and there are all these people ahead of you."

"You don't seem to understand," said the man in the sharkskin suit. "This is Senator and Mrs. Javits."

"If I let the Senator in, I have to let everyone else in," I said.

"Surely you can find some place for the Senator and his wife," said the man in the sharkskin suit.

"Well, if they don't mind standing—" I said.

Senator Javits finally spoke.

"How much do I owe you?" he said. He reached into his pocket and took out a roll of bills.

"How many people are in your party?" I said. "Six? That means you owe me eighteen dollars."

"I'm sorry," said Mrs. Javits, smiling to the angry mob of people in the outer lobby.

But Mrs. Javits' smile did not appease them. After the Senator and his party had stepped into the theatre, there were angry grumbles of resentment.

"What are you going to do about that?" said Bob Foley.

"Let them in! Let them all in!" I said. "To hell with the fire laws. I'm sure nobody is going to lock me up as long as I've got a Senator on the premises."

By the time I had freed myself from the Senator and his party, the performance had already begun. I was unable to see over the heads of the people in the doorways, so I went backstage and climbed into the scenery loft. About thirty people had gotten there before me. Those who had arrived first were the only ones who had an unobstructed view of the stage. They were sitting on the edge of the platform, their legs dangling in midair. The others had to crane their necks to see. They were perched on the railing or leaning out from the uprights. In one corner of the platform a lady reporter from the Canadian Broadcasting Corporation was speaking into her microphone.

I looked down on a scene of wild confusion.

The two Stewed Prunes were reading from their scripts on opposite sides of the proscenium so that it was difficult to see or hear them. But there were enough other things going on to occupy my interest whenever I was able to get a glimpse of the stage.

Jean Tinguely made his entrance wearing a white ball gown with a large flounce at the bottom. The black hair on his chest was showing over the top of the gown. On his head he wore a wide-brimmed Lillian Russell picture hat covered with multicolored ostrich plumes which was tied beneath his chin with a large satin bow. He was pushing a wheelbarrow loaded with cinder blocks which he dumped in the center of the stage. Then he turned and went into the wings to reload the wheelbarrow.

The audience cheered.

Henry Geldzahler, who was impersonating Jean Tinguely's alter ego followed Jean onstage. Henry was also wearing a ball gown. He held his script in one hand and a cigar in the other.

"I am *ze* spirit of Jean Tinguely," said Henry Geldzahler, affecting a French accent. But the rest of his words were lost because Jean Tinguely had returned with the second load of cinder blocks which he again dumped in the center of the stage.

The audience cheered.

In one corner of the stage a facsimile of a small apartment had been set up consisting of a bed, a dresser, one or two chairs, a cast-iron bathtub, an ice box, a hot plate, a Maxfield Parrish drawing, and other assorted objects. Here the male dancer and the female dancer silently went about the acts of daily living, completely unmindful of everything else that was happening onstage. An alarm clock went off. The male dancer, wearing pajamas, got out of bed to silence it. He yawned. He brushed his teeth. He did a few setting-up exercises. In the meantime, the female dancer, wearing a nightgown, had gotten out of bed. She yawned. She dressed herself in a soiled cotton wrapper. She lit the hot plate and put on a pot of coffee.

By this time Bob Rauschenberg had come onstage followed by his alter ego. They were both dressed in Army-surplus rain capes with illuminated photo reflectors where their heads should have been. Bob Rauschenberg's alter ego didn't have any lines to read. Whenever the script called upon Bob Rauschenberg to say something, his alter ego projected his speeches in writing upon the back wall of the stage.

The Stewed Prunes commanded Bob Rauschenberg to make weather for Boston and he obliged by setting in motion a mechanical contraption he had erected at the side of the stage. A feather duster began to spin around scattering a whole bunch of plastic balls that were delicately balanced above it into the audience and about the stage. As soon as MacIntyre Dixon heard the whirring sound of the machine from which the metal part had come loose in rehearsal, he covered his head with both hands.

Next, the Stewed Prunes commanded Bob Rauschenberg to supply the elements for Boston. He filled a bucket with water from the cast-iron bathtub and poured this into a toilet seat imbedded in an old automobile tire.

After this the Stewed Prunes commanded Bob Rauschenberg to beautify the Boston landscape. He hauled what looked to me like part of an air-conditioning duct onstage and attempted to plant a rose bush in it. His efforts were continually hampered by the fact that he kept getting tangled in the wires that supplied the current for the light in his photo reflector.

Finally, the Stewed Prunes commanded Bob Rauschenberg to produce rain for Boston. He pulled a rope which was connected to a network of black rubber hose he had strung around the ceiling and a stream of water was released, drenching everyone onstage.

The audience cheered.

By now the two dancers had changed into street clothes.

The male dancer was cooking bacon and eggs in a frying pan.

The female dancer was arranging flowers in a vase. When she had finished she put the vase of flowers in the icebox.

Jean Tinguely had at last transported all the cinder blocks onstage and had begun to construct a wall across the proscenium opening. He labored first on one side of the stage and then on the other, leaving the center free for entrances and exits and also so that the audience could see what was going on. As he worked the flounce of his ball gown kept getting caught in the cinder blocks and Jean continually had to wrench himself free. Finally he removed the ball gown altogether and angrily threw it into the wings. From this point on Jean worked in his trousers, bare from waist up.

The performance was coming to a climax.

The Stewed Prunes called upon Niki de Saint-Phalle to appear and supply culture for Boston. Thereupon, Niki made her entrance down the center aisle of the auditorium, dressed in the uniform of a Napoleonic cannoneer. Two assistants, similarly attired, followed her.

The audience cheered.

Niki de Saint-Phalle's alter ego came onstage dressed in a costume identical to Niki's and sang a little ditty about culture. But the song was completely lost in the noise of Jean Tinguely's hurling the cinder blocks into place.

Maxine Groffsky wheeled the veiled plaster-of-Paris replica of the Venus de Milo onstage.

The statue was now unveiled.

One of Niki de Saint-Phalle's assistants handed her a loaded rifle. She took careful aim at the statue and fired. Luminous paint began to ooze from the statue.

The audience cheered.

She took aim and fired a second time. More luminous paint.

The audience cheered.

During these events I could hear the lady from the Canadian Broadcasting Corporation speaking into her microphone in hushed but breathless tones: "The applause you hear is for Niki de Saint-Phalle who has just made her entrance through the audience, followed by two assistants. Miss de Saint-Phalle has just come onstage. She is dressed—I believe—as George Sand, while her two assistants seem to be wearing some sort of military uniforms. An enormous plaster-of-Paris statue has just been wheeled onstage. They've just uncovered it. If I'm not mistaken I would say the statue is supposed to be a very rough replica of the Venus de Milo. One of Miss de Saint-Phalle's assistants has just handed her a rifle. She is taking aim. She fires! I believe that's green paint I see, yes, luminous green paint is oozing from the left nipple of the statue. . . ."

I couldn't help but wonder what the radio audience in Canada must be thinking.

Niki de Saint-Phalle kept aiming and firing at the statue. As soon as one rifle was empty, an assistant would hand her another loaded one. By the time Niki had fired all her ammunition the statue was riddled with holes and discolored with blotches and drippings of luminous paints. Then Niki's two assistants went into the wings and returned pulling a small cannon behind them.

The male dancer was listening to a news commentator on the radio.

The female dancer was washing the breakfast dishes in the bathtub.

Niki de Saint-Phalle's two assistants stuffed the cannon with newspapers, then they poured in gunpowder, and finally inserted a pellet of white paint. Niki lit the fuse.

The cannon went off with a loud explosion. It reared back and went hurtling across the stage, almost falling into the laps of the spectators in the front row. Niki de Saint-Phalle had intended that the paint in the cannon would make the statue entirely white again, but because the statue simply turned a muddy shade of grey, everyone assumed that Niki had missed her aim.

The audience booed.

Now Jean Tinguely set about in earnest to complete the center portion of the wall. Everyone onstage pitched in to help him so the work proceeded rapidly. As the cinder blocks rose higher and higher it became more and more difficult for the actors to deliver their lines. Henry Geldzahler managed to speak through a small aperture in the wall, but

Niki de Saint-Phalle's alter ego was forced to climb a ladder in order to make herself seen and heard above the din. The spectators in the front rows began to head for the exits, all the while glancing apprehensively over their shoulders.

No one was quite sure when *The Construction of Boston* had been completed. As soon as Jean Tinguely ran out of cinder blocks and it was no longer possible to see or hear any of the performers, the houselights were turned on. There was a moment of stunned silence. A few people clapped, some booed. The Stewed Prunes, suddenly realizing they were stranded in front of the wall, tried frantically to find some way of getting backstage without going through the auditorium, but were forced to nudge and jostle their way through the former members of the audience who were now crowding the aisles and the lobby.

The entire performance had taken about fifteen minutes.

After the performance the stage was littered with paint and plaster of Paris and broken fragments of cinder block, but this did not deter the mobs of people who descended on the artists and performers.

In addition to friends and well-wishers, there were reporters and photographers from *Life, Newsweek,* and *Harper's Bazaar.*

Out of the corner of my eye I noticed the lady from the Canadian Broadcasting Corporation threading her way through the crowd, shoving her portable microphone into people's faces and asking them if they had any opinions for the Canadian listening audience.

Senator Javits and his wife posed for photographs with Bob Rauschenberg. Senator Javits said that he found the performance "interesting," an opinion which his wife must have shared because four days later she devoted a large part of her short-lived newspaper column to her interpretation of the event.

I willingly posed for group photographs with the others, a circumstance which nettled Kenneth Koch.

"John, you're standing right in front of me," he said.

I turned and smiled. At first I thought Kenneth must be kidding.

"Damn it, John," said Kenneth. "I think I should be in the center of the photograph. After all, this whole thing was my idea."

When all the spectators had left the stage and only the people who had participated in *The Construction of Boston* were left, there was some debate as to whether to clean up the stage that night.

"Let's do it now," said Bob Rauschenberg. "I know everyone is tired, but it's better to do it now while we're all still here."

Everyone agreed with him and the whole group set to work at once.

I left the others to their cleaning chores and went out to the box office to count up the receipts with Bob Foley. The total income for the evening came to nearly eight hundred dollars. Even after I deducted the rent, the money for taxes, and various incidental expenses, I was still able to turn over more than six hundred dollars to Kenneth Koch when he came by the box office to get a final accounting.

As soon as he saw the amount of money, Kenneth's eyes lit up. He was all set to do a whole series of similar evenings.

"It's such a great idea," he said, "and it's all so simple. I don't see how I ever thought it up. I mean, there's London and Paris and Rome. We can go on forever until we've exhausted all the cities of the world."

The idea stuck in my mind, and the more I thought about it the more it seemed as though Kenneth Koch might have the solution to my financial problems. It was obvious that there was a large audience for the sort of show he and his friends had presented. Nearly as much money had been taken in at the box office for *The Construction of Boston* as had been taken in during the short runs of each of the shows that had been presented at the theatre during the winter, and each of those shows had cost over ten thousand dollars to produce.

The following Sunday afternoon I took a walk in Greenwich Village and was still pondering this state of affairs, when, quite by accident, I bumped into Niki de Saint-Phalle and Jean Tinguely. They were having dinner at the Albert French Restaurant and invited me along.

Naturally, we began to discuss the events of the previous Friday.

"It just goes to prove what I've always suspected," said Niki de Saint-Phalle. "People are tired of the theatre and movies. They want *real* entertainment."

Jean Tinguely spoke in French.

"Jean says that artists have become the new movie stars," translated Niki. "Jean says he may become the new Humphrey Bogart."

We all laughed.

I told them about the difficulties I was having in holding onto the theatre, and I said I was wondering if it might not be a good idea not to do any more plays but instead to present a series of events similar to the one on Friday night. They both agreed that this was a splendid idea, but Jean raised the objection that it would not be wise to present such an event too often. He felt that a great deal of the success of *The Construction of Boston* was due to its novelty. I replied that then I would still be without any way of meeting my monthly rent.

"Maybe we could charge ten or fifteen dollars a ticket," said Niki.

"Twenty-five," I said.

Jean spoke. "Jean says fifty," translated Niki.

We all felt confident that we would have no trouble getting fifty dollars a ticket, and that this money could be raised by subscription so the theatre rent would be covered in advance.

As soon as this obstacle had been passed, none of us could speak fast enough to get out all the wild and fanciful ideas that came crowding into our heads. We could get real poets to write the scripts and real actors to recite the lines.

Jean spoke, and Niki de Saint-Phalle translated: "Jean says maybe we could get Richard Burton." Then, turning to me, she inquired seriously, Can he speak well?"

[November, 1963]

Grace Through Gambling

by Jack Richardson

Boethius, Walter Raleigh,Wilde, Sade—names that were going through my mind of those who had turned a prison cell into a work chamber. I sat hunched in an at-stool position on a bowel-chilling bench and marveled that anyone, after finding himself caged away by the world, could summon forth enough rational energy to continue a literary dialogue with it. I had been in my cell only a few hours, and though I was foggy from lack of sleep, I felt a greater enervation oozing through me. My reason for being confined was petty and laughable—an accident completely unweighted by any volition or criminal intent on my part. Still, the green walls, sour air, and ludicrously impenetrable bars were parts of a geography I had often imagined myself in, and after a while I began to feel a fatigue that seemed comfortable and in concord with the rest of my life. For over a year I had grown more inclined to do less and less that required any decisive effort. I hadn't completely abandoned myself to chance, but that was only because old habits of responsibility and ambition were hard to shake. Still, what work I did was minimal, based on Spartan standards of survival, and the idea of taking a thing seriously, of smoothing it down, of reaching its conclusion—this I found to be, almost literally, sickening. What was left of the moral adviser in me said I was letting things slide; his literary counterpart mumbled on about malaise and the great unspecific fear of our times. With the former I agreed; the latter I throttled with relief. I *was* letting myself drift, but not from fear and certainly not from general principles. I am too intelligent to let that old melodrama of the absurd world keep me from trying to gorge myself with pleasures and fame. Human triumph may be feeble, but I had sought it, with selfish gusto, in everything I did, and dared any post-Pauline teleologist to prove me wrong. It was not the universe that was failing me; I was failing it. In my scramble for indulgence I was leaving behind me the usual refuse of the community of which I'm a part; a divorce, a half dozen or so squalid affairs, some unmemorable literary jottings, one or two dedicated enemies, and the sense of possibility that had got me started in the first place. I felt the track I was on was beginning to twist with such complexity of design that it might very well turn out to be a teasing, vicious maze which would prove inescapable if I took too many more steps in the same direction. Day after day I mined myself and came up with nothing but semiprecious or unknown bits of mineral. Wanting to have my life weighed, analyzed and pronounced rare, I had, by that famous modal year of thirty, found nothing conclusive about its samplings.

So slowly then I had let that fatigue take hold of me, not just because I was frustrated with what I had not been able to do, but because I hoped that some indifferent lassitude might get my particular fates off their rumps. They may have been taking me for granted as one needing no providential signs, and I wanted to plead, with a little petulance, that I needed as many as could be spared.

Well, in their usual way, they answered with no specifics, but some hints had been dropped. While in semi-hibernation one thing began to snap me into a state of keen sensitivity over and over again. I had begun to gamble.

I am glad the last sentence is out of the way. I detest declarations in print that have confessional rings to them, like "I began to drink," "I began to hate," "I began to deflower my nephews." Although I am completely unregenerate, it is best to get the subject of all this stated quickly and simply. While my work, my friends, the leftovers of my family, my lady at the time, the familiars of my apartment and neighborhood became dim items light-years away from me, the sessions about a card or dice table, for as long as they lasted, created a sharply sensed landscape in which I felt solid ground under my feet. I don't mean to say that the landscape was hospitable. On the contrary, I tripped, stumbled and left skin behind with almost each step. But the pain perked me up into bright consciousness, and for days afterward I brooded over the scabs left behind from my falls. At first I had taken the sessions at poker, dice, chemin de fer and blackjack, played in private houses and well-locked back rooms around New York, to be desperate diversions to keep me from mulling over the loose ends of the real life we are all supposed to have. Gradually, however, I saw that the one had a good chance of replacing the other. Between days of mollusk-like torpor, these moments at the table were providing me with good memoranda that I was indeed living. And since this was all I had at the time, I became indulgent. Always disposed to theatrics, I began edging a new personality into the world. My clothes became tailored and spunky, my friends were treated to stories, some true, of high-rolling epics, where before they got little but literary puns. It was comic opera, and I knew it at the time. But I also wondered tentatively if it was not something more.

Gambling did not spring full bloom into my life at the age of thirty. In fact my mother, who considered me extraordinary, once, as a Christmas present, bought me a miniature roulette wheel. The table consisted of a small strip of cheesecloth with all the proper brackets and numbers painted on it. I've never known just why she picked out this particular toy; I don't remember asking for it. But as I said, she took me to be a special cut and was always urging me to do outlandish things—such as safaris to Africa or the composition of sonnets—to insure I would never be mistaken for just another neighborhood boy. The roulette wheel might have held my interest no longer than the month or so other toys received had it not been for the pneumonia I caught some weeks after Christmas. Confined to bed for two months, I took to spinning the small wheel for hours, marking down what numbers came up and trying to form infallible betting systems—an occupation excusable in a child. Also the roulette wheel was a way of luring friends up for a visit. Ten-year-olds quickly tire of the bedridden, but when the convalescent is a miniature casino they will put up with him. Most of my visitors were tiny Italian Catholics filled with senses of sin and evil, so they came eagerly, just as their St. Augustine had done in an African orchard fifteen hundred years ago, to enjoy their little falls from grace. They put their pennies on the cheesecloth as though making offerings at a black mass and I later had to pay for this company by my being interdicted as a playmate when I was on my feet again. One had confessed to his mother the squandering of six cents at the bedside of a Protestant whom God was punishing with a serious disease, and I became *persona non grata* with the Papists on Seventy-fourth Street in Jackson Heights. This, by the way, was the only time I ever was with the house. However, I can't remember if, with the percentages behind me, I showed a profit or not.

The other incident of gambling I recall while still a child is of the kind that might be used as an excuse for abstaining from all games of chance for a lifetime. One Saturday afternoon, behind a handball court at the local school yard, a group of older boys were having a crap game. After standing on its periphery for a time as befitted my age, I drew up sufficient courage to inch forward until I was close enough to watch the proceedings.

As I looked down and saw at least five single-dollar bills waiting to be scooped up by the fortunate, I was struck with an instant greed of such intensity that I flew home, took my bicycle and pedaled to a local shop, where I sold it for ten dollars. Back to the school yard, again a moment at the edge of the onlookers, again seized by my first real compulsion, and finally pushing beyond my proper station into the game. I knew nothing about dice except that seven was somehow a pivotal number, but my elders guided me honestly and even seemed worried that such total innocence was bound to be rewarded. I disabused them of that moral theory in less than an hour. As wretched as I had ever been, I moved stoically away from the game, and then, once out of sight, cried in rage all the way home. It was too great a crime for me to live with alone, so, still tearful, I threw myself on my mother's mercy. Well, it was not quite a safari to Africa, but she did detect a trace of special quality in the daring needed to gamble away a bicycle. The dear woman, as I said, thought me extraordinary.

Though both these incidents form very sharp memories, neither I think slipped any inchoate passion for gambling into my nervous system. If there was an early infection, then it was my grandfather who was the carrier. I saw him only once. My grandmother had given up on him and his profligate ways years before I was born. Tired of his week-long disappearances into card games that somehow journeyed from Bristol, Virginia, to as far south as New Orleans, she finally came to New York, where several of our family had migrated, and went to work in a department store. When my mother was divorced in the same city, the three of us lived together until I was seventeen. Flanked and doted on by these two women, I was self-satisfied, spoiled and happy, but at times I yearned for a little masculine dash around the house. My father came to visit each week, but though benevolently kind, I can't say he brought a heady male scent with him. He was five-feet-two, cautious, a musician of indifferent talent, and he once told me to "save myself for my wife," an admonition my mother would have disowned me for had I accepted it. If anything, he brought a calm respite from the frenzied attention I received from the ladies the rest of the week.

But my grandfather—well, there was a myth to be explored. A letter from him would set my mother and grandmother off on a whole evening of going over his character and rapscallion ways. Though he had caused them pain, I could see, even as a child, that they forgave and loved him. From what I gathered, he had lived a life of complete license and self-indulgence, but he had once been shot in the stomach defending my grandmother from an enraged suitor she had turned down.

"With the bullet in him, he went right after that Jeffs boy, caught him in the street and almost killed him."

Every time my grandmother said that line, she jerked her head emphatically at me and I knew I was receiving a code she expected me to live up to. I would nod solemnly, my mother would get that safari look in her eye, and my grandmother would turn melancholy over the wandering card games; but soon the dirge would modulate into light reminiscences about how that "devil" had put up his poultry farm in a stud game, had lost it, and, before the man could collect, had put together a chicken roast for the family and all its Negroes so that, as he said, he cut down his losses with pleasure.

Well, here was a man as flawed as I knew I was and still coaxed love from the two women who watched over me. Perhaps, then, when all my debits were exposed, perhaps when my mother realized I was unlikely to be a published poet at the age of thirteen or the seducer of every maiden in the eighth grade, perhaps when my grandmother glimpsed that I too was very selfish, with wastrel ways and a disposition *not* to step in the line of fire between a woman and a madman—perhaps even then, if I could cultivate the winning ways of my grandfather, I'd still get my share of affection.

And then one day he came to visit—miraculously tall, straight, with a hawklike countenance and a sea of white hair. There was nothing profligate about his face, and he moved steadily and strongly around our small apartment while both mother and grandmother scolded and giggled in the most complete capitulation morality ever made to honesty that I know of. That night he and my grandmother slept together, and though I was not certain what this meant, I sensed well-being in the house.

During the stay, grandfather taught me the rudiments of stud poker while the ladies feebly protested. He was very grave about the instruction, as would any man explaining a serious part of his life to a grandson. He had large, fine-boned hands that made the cards dance about neatly on our little coffee table, and he spoke with soft conviction about how poker should be played, while every now and then, to propitiate my mother and grandmother, throwing in a caveat about the dangers of letting gambling smother all else in one's life. For three evenings he and I sat down to play cards—at first for nothing and then for pennies—while the rest of the family feigned horror at the Eden-like knowledge I was receiving. I'm certain that for different reasons they really felt pleased that should I ever be called into a poker game I could acquit myself like a gentleman—like an extraordinary gentleman. As for grandfather, he had what he wanted—the center of the stage and a sense of importance. I found out later that nothing had been going too well for him down South—clubs were dropping him, etc.—so he had come north to verify that his life was still important and perhaps even to get a sense of family continuity in me. What skills he had to bequeath, he passed on in a few days, and, confident that I would never stay with a Jack in the hole against a King and Queen showing on the board, he left his two ladies crying and returned to the existence he had fortified at our coffee table. In two years he died. The myth was complete. My grandmother had to pay for the funeral.

It was years before I put grandfather's advice to any practical use, and then I found it sadly inadequate. Also in years of chatting with my grandmother, much of the shine began to dim on the legend of Burt McDowell, Virginia cardplayer. It was, I think, my first lesson in the stripping down of great men to expose petty fears and needs. Even now I am never anxious to ferret out facts about those men who taught me. The disappointment is too great, but not in the way Doctor Johnson meant when he chastised those who were shocked to find their favorite authors shabby in their private lives. He counseled that one should pay them double homage for overcoming the tainted nature of the species and achieving something unhuman in their art's perfection. No, I am not disappointed that the great ones are not sublimely excellent; but I am disheartened to find that once known by me, they begin to pollute their own work. That a middle-aged pederast has fashioned a charming sestina out of a weekend with some sullen illiterate pulls the poem back into human folly and no amount of pure criticism is ever going to return it to its place of mysterious self-sufficiency.

Slowly, then, my grandfather and his gambling came down to human size. I saw an infinite poser who used one frailty to hide another. It was better to be accused of social failure because of a propensity for the gambling tables than have to admit that there were common things in the world you wanted but were too crippled with ineptitudes to attain. In the end he fervently desired to be buried in the Elks Club cemetery, hoping in death at last to be the equal of those good, workaday citizens he felt so outmatched him in life.

Still, he had had enough slyness in his choice of disguises to leave two women with deep notions of love, and as I began to gamble, I looked back gratefully on him. His five-card-stud instruction may have been faulty, but the other secrets I found out were more important. I knew that someday I too might really want my own piece of Elks Club cemetery rather than the wispy existence as one of fortune's stableboys awaiting the rewards for a hard night in her service. Even as I took myself off to a game in a new suit, I made a special effort to mock and keep myself apperceptively in hand. All of this was only an interim to be enjoyed while the essential Jack Richardson stored up enough energy to make the world again a biting experience.

But there was no change. I rose and, without any fretting or self-recrimination, sat peacefully in my apartment all day thinking about nothing more consequential than that indeed I was not fretful or self-recriminatory about this complete inertia. What work I owed I postponed until it had to be churned out in an orgy of rage because I was being disturbed. I finally solved the problem of my days by sleeping through them, getting up at dusk and gambling when I could until late in the morning. Gradually my reaction to the games I played in changed. Where before I had bet in a desultory manner, happy to be participating in something enjoyable, I was, after a while, experiencing ridiculously out-sized emotions over my own particular fate in each outing. To lose filled me with a catalog of such self-lacerating feelings that only the sternest efforts of a mind trained in logic could drag me back to the point where I would grudgingly admit that no final judgment of leper had been passed on me by the universe. And when I won there would be an equal amount of persuasion needed to convince me that the whole world would not indeed marvel at my accomplishment. I also began taking a strange attitude toward money. Though I would cavalierly toss it away in a game of poker, I began to keep frighteningly minute records of each bit of daily expense. Each paper I bought, every tip I left, each call I made was marked down in an elaborate system of categories as though I were about to undergo the most exhaustive financial examination ever made by the Internal Revenue Service. Then I would set off, hoping that the night's action would let me come home and put down on paper that luck had picked up all my bills for the day. I would check and recheck my figures every afternoon, and I often sat for hours, staring at the columns spread out on the floor, satisfied that I was inbibing vital information from them.

The battle of my mind for a just perspective on the joys and misery I was drawing from this began to move across larger terrain. Soon it was in combat with itself, proposing such arguments as that gambling provides the answer to what all men want to know; namely, which of us are of the elect; and disposing the like with sharp rebuffs on how, as I never saw any evidence for such Calvinist flappery when the subject was theology, it was unlikely something would turn up in the theory of games to reveal divine determination. And then there was the great debate on significance which brought some tired, old Vienna Circle arguments to the fore in behalf of the semantic shakiness and subjective prejudice in ranking human behavior in terms of absolute worth. I was not so far gone that such academic prattle did not make me feel a little guilty, but when I gave equal time to the prosecution nothing more than an obscenely phrased appeal to my own feelings came forth, and at the time I had none that I trusted.

And so with part of my life mired and beginning to fossilize, while the other blazed with a lunatic brightness and medieval warmth, I arrived in that cell exhausted. I had been arrested in a raid on what the papers would later call a fashionable East Side gambling party. Those who had been caught with me were mostly young college boys who at first had enjoyed the notion of a trip to the station house and had peppered the air with the sort of joyous, joking camaraderie that I remembered and detested from the Army. As we moved along in the police wagon, I had that slightly unclean feeling of the man who keeps constant company with those much younger. I wondered if I might possibly look their coeval, thought back upon my life, and decided that it was impossible.

At the station house my fellow companions' mood changed. When it became apparent that we really were to be booked and locked up until a hearing in the morning, they began to remember who they were or planned to be someday. Cries were imperiously made for lawyers and family intervention. But the authority they hoped for, when called, proved either too sleepy or too angry to take fast steps of intercession. Seeing that their move for power had failed, the young men fell to mournful questioning of the officers on how, since it was now Easter morning, they would get to mass. This worked better, and though they still would have to be locked away for awhile, assurances were given that they would be out in time to celebrate the resurrection of their Lord. I suppose they had hoped that a communion of faith would free them, but calculating that their time in prison would be only hours, the band of religious fanatics went to their cells. I, the old atheist, went into mine.

I sat in the same delightful stupor that I did when forced to be alone and awake in my apartment. The notion that I was a bit absurd tried to get at me several times, but my mind had spent itself in enough dialectic that day and just wouldn't bother with it. I probably would have dozed off like someone inured to frequent arrest had not the cell door opened and a new occupant arrived. I was startled into wakefulness. My companion was a beautiful black lady who glanced icily at me and, after the primmest, haughtiest heel-clicking walk I had ever seen, took the bench opposite mine.

Now I am not a lustful person; in fact, I am grateful for minimum potency when the need arises; but I was excited by the notion of this woman and I, right under the noses of a constabulary caught on their holy day, trying some secret infidel delights. There was not much time for courtship so I got up and tried to shuffle pleasantly toward her. She fixed me with a mean eye that made me shuffle in place for a while. I wanted to tell her she had got me to move with a semblance of purpose for the first time, apart from a gambling room, in months, but I suspected the compliment hidden away in that would take too long to explain.

"What are you in for?" I said, choking on the cliché and hoping the answer would be wild, indiscriminate prostitution. But there was no answer, only a sullen look. Back to the shuffle, and my hand was soon on her shoulder. There was no attempt to remove it, so I began to fondle down her arm until I came to the hand. It was suspiciously large and powerful looking. Slowly, I began to wonder if it was customary for our moral police to put men and women into a cell together, even for a few hours.

I stood up.

"Are you a man?" I asked.

"You better believe it, baby," was the answer in a voice so basso that it almost propelled me to my corner of the cell. My sense of manners kept me from laughing myself up and down the walls. It was perfect for some good, self-depreciating cackling. Fooled by a transvestite! Here in a cell, worn out from years of trying to find just what this complicated collection of thoughts and feelings is that, in Cartesian fashion, I call "I"—here I find I can be deluded by a grumpy poove in a ten-dollar dress. So much for the illusion/reality problem all those bad plays and books are written about.

Bertrand Russell has said that, during a walk in an English garden, he altered, in five minutes, his entire social philosophy. Nothing so drastic happened to me because of that Easter-morning encounter. I am a bit slower than Lord Russell, so it took a few weeks before I renounced the debate over what I really was and gave myself completely to what braced me, even in its moments of caricature, back to life. I became a gambler, and if it was only Saturday night drag I was putting on to cover up the same fear grandfather had—well, there would be those with subtler senses than mine to tell me.

Once my mind had been made up, I became full of pragmatic purpose. If I was going to pledge loyalty to Fortuna, I wanted to do so in her main temples and not in poolrooms or bars or among Catholic youths in an upper East Side townhouse. Fortunately, the time I live in is indulgent. When I began screaming that I wished to be off to Cannes, London, Monte Carlo, Las Vegas and any other town, island or city where I could keep my figures and get continuous confirmation that my mother was right in her estimate of me, no one proved unduly shocked. I had some money for the voyage, but not nearly enough for the trial I wanted to make. A consultation with my sweet agent, and soon a publisher was found with enough absence of mind to advance funds sufficient for play anywhere in the world, at all but the highest stakes. Somewhere during negotiations he cleared his head long enough to demand that I produce a salable book about my travels and new profession.

My plan was to start west, go first to Las Vegas and then to California. If no disaster struck by then, I would move off into the Orient, picking Hong Kong and Macao as my first serious stops. After that, any definite plans would be hubristic. I would journey so long as fate permitted, but I secretly felt that the gods of chance would be so pleased with their new votary that extraordinary encouragement would be given to insure against any relapse.

While indulging in that sort of barbarian logic, I put some of the old skills to work and began figuring out percentages and methods of play at each game I would be likely to encounter. I wasn't going to be one of luck's hysterical Corybants, screaming gibberish and making her angry at the presumption of lunatic bets. I wanted to present her with well-reasoned arguments that showed I took nothing, least of all her mathematical sense, for granted.

At other times, of course, I harbored notions of one blind play with every penny at stake that had been given me. I would dress slowly and impeccably, as though preparing for an elaborately formal ritual. Then, after caressingly counting the money, I would place it neatly in my pocket and walk, with the economy and purpose of an assassin, to the table grand enough to accept my bet. After selecting what I wished to play, I would lay the money lightly down, gaze only briefly at its resting place in limbo between me and the bank, and then lift my eyes upward, disdaining concern with the man-made apparatuses that would punish me or reward me, knowing that judgment would not come from them. At this point, when the wheel began to spin or the cards snap toward me, things became too vivid to be endured even in imagination. I would push such febrile *Mittel Europa* notions out of mind and hurry back to the security of my equations.

And then, every few days or so, there would be a death rattle from my old self proclaiming that I might very well be going insane. I had gathered together more money than I had ever had, and was about to skip around the world throwing it on tables while enjoying the notion that, besides untold riches, heaven would fashion a constellation in the likeness of my long, sad profile to proclaim for all time my coups at roulette. I had gone from someone working with the language and themes of serious men to something fit for a study in anthropological regression.

"I want to know," I would say. "I want finally to know."

And then the old voice would scratch out: "What do you want to know?"

And I would answer: "Whether or not I am to have any grace in this life."

At this, there would be a humanist-skeptic retch and an expiration into silence.

That crabbed voice could never persuade, but it could depress me. I would begin to dwell on what I had decided to leave behind with only a faint chance that my future life would ever allow a reclamation. My daughter—lanky, nervous and beautiful, before whose gaze there was no protest articulate enough for my exoneration; my ex-wife, wise and stubborn, who had never used the grim knowledge our marriage had given her to hurt me; the girl who loved me now sensed that it would end soon, but made no scene—these had come into my life at times when I was too tired to keep up the walls of self-absorption. They too would recede along with all that I could not bring with me to the tables.

During the last week before leaving I gambled with such sustained fury that I think a Vegas casino owner would have been abashed. Even at my farewell party I managed to start a poker game in which I won, something everyone held to be a good omen. I felt half a fool, half a hero. The standard reaction, I imagine, when one goes to slay dragons that operate on a one-to-five-percent edge against all seekers of the grail.

The last night, while she slept, I lay awake. There is nothing so still as a room one is about to leave for a long time. The quiet is spread out and heavy, as though offering a foretaste of what will be left behind when the waves floating from the click of the outside latch exhaust themselves against the walls. I think I was as calm that night as I had ever been in my life. The body next to me was warm and arched to fit snugly against mine; through the bedroom door I could see my books stacked in the library and the furniture that had come to stay bit by bit over the past years. On my desk, there was a folder that I had abandoned for months. In it were some sketches and scenes for a project that I had forgotten to store with all those schemes I was no longer going to try. The girl moaned and stretched next to me. I looked down and smiled at her. Work on the table; a loved girl in your bed, and rooms you fashioned to be your sanctuary. It was the old voice warming to a last try. I didn't bore the quietness with fancies about grace or fortunes; I admitted that all the chaos I was going into frightened me and that I knew I would someday grow numb even to the pleasures of gambling. I was going west in the morning so that the peace that was around me would never be my final end.

[April, 1967]

On Experiencing Gore Vidal

by William F. Buckley Jr.

I have here a recent issue of *The East Village Other* featuring a piece entitled "Faggot Logic" which is about me, or more precisely about a column I wrote on Senator McGovern which highly displeased this demi-mondaine journal. "Following faggot logic," my critic writes, "is disturbing at any time of year, and Buckley's spiteful spewlings today have just pissed me off, even more than usual." That is certainly an icebreaker, even in *The East Village Other,* and I read on, my interest aroused to learn something about the nature of faggot logic. "On the Right," the author went on, referring to the logo of my thrice-weekly column, "is nearly invariably an exercise in faggot dialectic. And since I think this peculiar mode of intellect is worthless at best and generally inimical to the public weal, then I'd like, just once—Christmas season notwithstanding—to engage in a point-by-point vivisection of one of his scabrous evacuations."

Alas, many many words later, the reader is left knowing nothing he didn't know before about the nature of faggot logic, which in my case was nothing at all, and moreover glumly aware that he would not likely come to apprehend the meaning of anything in any way elusive under the guidance of the writer in question, whose thought proved to be as barren as his wit: so that after jogging alongside him over an endless stretch of indignation, one arrives at the cheerless conclusion (hardly reassuring to poor Senator McGovern), that the author likes the senator, dislikes me, and thinks we should get out of Vietnam instantly.

Even so the piece sticks in the mind because here is a licentious rhetorical effort at homicide—in which the author arms himself with all the bad words; and yet he selects as the killer-word: "faggot." That was the warhead. Very interesting. And particularly revealing in the context of the general attitude of that journal towards faggotry, the unmetaphorical practice of which it explicitly panders to, or so it would seem. On page 17 of the same issue there are advertisements as plainspoken as Macy's for garden furniture. "NUDE MALE FILM CLUB. . . . There will be continuous screenings nightly . . ."—is just one display ad. Another, discreetly sequestered in the classified section, positions wanted, "WHEEL AND DEAL": "Bi-Sexual, nude model, handsome, tall, trim, blond, hung, well-built, 30, will pose for sketches or you name it. $20 per session. . . ." And for those choosy readers who desire a synoptic view of the area and its possibilities there is the "1969 Gay Guide for gay guys, 'N.Y., N.J. baths, bars, glory holes, restaurants, movies, etc.' "

Why is faggotry okay, but the imputation of it discreditable? Is there a platonic coinage, which is bad—even as the real thing becomes okay? Is that a culture lag, of sorts? Rather like saying about somebody that he is impious (which is unfriendly) even though, as everybody knows, explicit impiety is perfectly okay.

At this point my mind moved to Gore Vidal, and the dismal events of the Summer of 1968, when he and I confronted each other a dozen times on network television, leading to an emotional explosion which, it is said, rocked television. Certainly it rocked me, and I am impelled to write about it; to discover its general implications, if any; to meditate on some of its personal implications, which are undeniable and profound; to probe the question whether what was said—under the circumstances in which it was said—has any meaning at all beyond that which is most generally ascribed to it, namely: Excessive bitchery can get out of hand. But first the narrative.

In the late Fall of 1967 I had a telephone call from Mr. James Haggerty, vice-president of the American Broadcasting Company and former White House press chief for President Eisenhower. Would I, he asked, consent to confer with Mr. Elmer Lower and Mr. William Sheehan concerning ABC's coverage of the 1968 political conventions? Yes I said—obviously. We met then, the heads of ABC News and Special Events and of ABC Television News and they disclosed their plans for 1968. Instead of covering the political conventions "gavel to gavel," ABC would condense the day's events into ninety minutes of nightly television, divided into five segments. The fourth segment was conceived as broad-ranging commentary on the convention, and the forthcoming election, and on politics in general.

They had in mind that two people would share that time, one of them a conservative, the other a liberal. Would I?

I asked a few mechanical questions, and indicated it would probably work out, and then asked them who would be my adversary. They replied that he had not been selected, did I have any suggestions? I thought a while and gave them eight or ten names, among whom were some of the obvious people (Schlesinger, Galbraith, Mailer), and some a little less obvious (for instance Al Lowenstein, Carey McWilliams Jr.). Was there anyone at all I would refuse to appear alongside? I wouldn't refuse to appear alongside any non-Communist, I said—as a matter of principle; but I didn't want to appear opposite Gore Vidal (I said), because I had had unpleasant experiences with him in the past and did not trust him. A few months later the announcement was made that Gore Vidal had been selected as my opposite number. "We knew we wanted Buckley," Elmer Lower told a reporter in Miami at the outset of the Republican Convention, "because we were well familiar with him. . . . It was a question of who would best play off against him. We considered a number of people and did some 'auditions,' sort of surreptitiously that is, watching people on the air without them knowing we were watching them. It looked as though Buckley would play better with Vidal than with any of four or five other people." In one sense he was right. Even before Chicago—a good week or ten days after Miami—there were those who took pains to record their misgivings. For instance—not exactly typical, but singularly interesting—Stephanie Harrington, who wrote in *The Village Voice,* looking back on our first series of encounters at Miami:

"What political analysis ABC did try for turned out to be the most embarrassing ingredient in its grand innovation. This was its attempt to elevate the affair to the level of intelligent discussion by bringing together nightly Gore Vidal and William Buckley for their comments—which [discussions] had far more to do with their contempts for each other than [with] their impressions of the convention. It was clearly a sequel to that painful moment some years back when Buckley, during a televised debate with Vidal, descended to his unique level of argument and in a typically Buckleyesque display of dirty debater's tricks, destroyed his opponent not by logic but by using his personal life against him. [I interrupt Miss Harrington to bring you a special announcement: remember that phrase, 'personal life.'] Indeed, he tried again this time, dismissing Vidal's political opinions on the grounds that he is the kind of man who would write a book like *Myra Breckinridge.* It was obvious that Buckley's heroics about the show going on despite the broken collarbone he suffered in a fall on his boat [—heroics? I simply went. Heroism, maybe; heroics, no—] had less to do with interest in the convention than with eagerness to get his claws into Vidal again."

Now under the stress of my conversations with ABC, we see that the anchor of Miss Harrington's argument is uprooted, and her analysis drifts away into fantasy. *Still,* she did say a few things concerning which there has been considerable speculation which *is* relevant: so that (fulldisclosurewise) I now divulge the history, abbreviated but not censored, of my dealings with Mr. Vidal, acknowledging Miss Harrington's and others' suspicions that those dealings figured, yes indeed, in the meetings at Miami and Chicago.

In January of 1962, appearing on the Jack Paar program to promote his play *Romulus,* Vidal went out of his way to observe that I had "attacked" Pope John XXIII for being "too left wing": which sorrowful recording of my impiety drew from the audience horrified tremors.

Paar was evidently pressured to invite me to reply, which he had and I did, on an evening Paar once reminisced about as having been among the most memorable of his career, such was the ensuing uproar. Said uproar, for once, directed not against me, but against Paar's assault on me after I had left the studio, which assault stimulated, by the count of one NBC spokesman, seven thousand (anti-Paar) telegrams of protest and one (pro-Paar) phone call from the White House. That is by the way—what I liked most in terms of the theatre of the episode was that instants after I left the studio, Paar ingenuously announced to the studio audience, "*I just got a call here. Gore Vidal's coming back tomorrow night!*" Now Paar's shows were taped three hours before they were telecast. So that he couldn't have received a telephone call from Gore Vidal reacting to my appearance—because the show would not go out over the air-waves for another three hours. (And they used to talk about Tricky Dick.)

Anyway, Vidal showed up, and after cooing about him ("Notice the difference in manner and approach and reasoning") for a few minutes Paar asked what *had* I actually said about the Pope and the encyclical?

Vidal: Yes, well what he actually said—and I went back and looked it up . . . in the month of August, Buckley attacked the Pope in a piece in his magazine, and the piece was called "A Venture in Triviality."

(a, I did not "attack the Pope." b, There was no "piece," merely a one-paragraph, unsigned editorial. c, The paragraph was not called "A Venture in Triviality"; it bore no title; one phrase in it said "[the encyclical] must strike many as a venture in triviality coming at this particular time in history.")

V.: It was a vicious piece, and *America*, which is the Jesuit weekly in the United States, attacked Buckley in an editorial declaring that he owes his readers an apology, unquote.

(The demand by *America* for an apology was unrelated to the editorial in question.)

V.: And Buckley's answer to the Jesuits was: "You are impudent."

(My answer to the Jesuits was in 2500 words, one sentence of which stated that it was impudent for *America* to ask a non-Catholic journal of opinion to apologize for a transgression—even assuming that that is what it was—against exclusively Catholic protocol; and of course I was right.)

V.: I mean, who is he? Here's a guy who has never worked for a living . . . has never had a job.

(I had held down one part-time job, as a member of the faculty of Yale, 1947-1951; and three full-time jobs before going to work for *National Review*, in 1955, which is at least a full-time job.)

V.: He's got two sisters.

(Six.)

V.: One said while she was at Smith . . .

(It was ten years after she graduated.)

V.: . . . that the faculty was filled with Communists.

(She said four faculty members had Communist-front connections, which was true.)

V.: The other was at Vassar and started the same thing at Vassar.

(She said that at Vassar the bias in the social-science departments was predominantly liberal, and of course she was right, ask Mary McCarthy.)

V.: Meanwhile their brother was at Yale and wrote *God and Man at Yale* and said that was full of Communists.

(My book did not charge or intimate that there was a single Communist at Yale.)

V.: He feels free to correct, through his little magazine of his, the actions of all our Presidents and the Pope, and philosophers . . . on the subject of philosophy I thought *this* might interest you, Jack—of Albert Schweitzer—who is one of the great men of our time, and whose philosophy is reverence for life—he wrote of Albert Schweitzer, quote: He is more destructive than the H Bomb, unquote.

(The quotation is not from me, but from a book review in *National Review*—by a Ph.D. in philosophy. I do not censor the book reviewers.)

V.: On the subject of integration, Mr. Buckley wrote, quote: Segregation is not intrinsically immoral, unquote. Well, that's a double negative which means I don't quite dare to come out and say I'm in favor of segregation, so I'll put it in a double negative.

(a, It isn't a double negative. b, It is a litotes, and should be recognized as such by a professional writer. The litotes has been around as a necessary rhetorical refinement for years; was used, for instance, by that old evader, Homer. c, I didn't in fact write that phrase, I spoke it in the presence of a Catholic liberal, John Cogley, who d, agreed with me.)

V.: . . . but that's exactly what it means, which goes against not only Catholic doctrine but I would think any humane—you put your finger on it, you know, when you said there's no humanity there.

But Mr. Vidal was not through.

V.: I was just going to say one more thing struck me, listening to Mr. Buckley. He said (and I was quite fascinated because it's amazing the things perhaps you can *just* get away with, this side of libel). . . . He said that Harry Truman had called Eisenhower an anti-Semite and anti-Catholic.

Paar: Yes, he did say that. But what—

Vidal: There's no evidence that Harry Truman ever said this. Now I would like to say right now, on the air, that I will give $100 to the *National Review*, which is Buckley's magazine, if he can prove that Harry Truman ever said any such thing: and if he cannot prove it, why I think he should then be regarded as what he is, which is an irresponsible liar. . . . As someone once said . . . [the Buckleys] are sort of the sick Kennedys.

I flew early the following morning to Switzerland, leaving a telegram to be dispatched by my office to Jack Paar. It read: "PLEASE INFORM GORE VIDAL THAT NEITHER I NOR MY FAMILY IS DISPOSED TO RECEIVE LESSONS IN MORALITY FROM A PINK QUEER. IF HE WISHES TO CHALLENGE THAT DESIGNATION, INFORM HIM THAT I SHALL FIGHT BY THE LAWS OF THE MARQUIS OF QUEENSBERRY. HE WILL KNOW WHAT I MEAN. WILLIAM F. BUCKLEY JR." The telephone was ringing when I reached my destination in Switzerland, as I half expected it would be. Come on now, calm down, whaddaya say, forget it, write a piece about the whole thing instead. So I finally withdrew the telegram, and contented myself instead to send a letter to Jack Paar:

Dear Mr. Paar:

[I have been informed of what Mr. Gore Vidal said on your show on February 1.]

1. The documentation, taken in each case from The New York *Times*, is as follows: On October 9, 1952, President Harry Truman accused the Republicans generally of supporting "the discredited and un-American theory of racial superiority." On October 17, Assistant Secretary of State Howland Sargeant read a message from Mr. Truman to the Jewish Welfare Board in Washington. Eisenhower, Truman said, "cannot escape responsibility" for his endorsement of Senator Revercomb, "the champion of the anti-Catholic, anti-Jewish provisions of the original D.P. bill." Truman charged that Eisenhower "has had an attack of moral blindness, for to-

day he is willing to accept the very practices that identify the so-called 'master race' although he took a leading part in liberating Europe from their domination."

2. The following day, Rabbi Abba Hillel Silver, ex-President of the Zionist Organization of America, expressed "shock that an irresponsible statement of that character could be made. The attempt by implication to identify a man like General Eisenhower with anti-Semitism and anti-Catholicism, is just not permissible even in the heat of a campaign."

3. Please instruct Mr. Vidal to make out a check for $100 to the National Conference of Christians and Jews.

Paar, directed to do so by NBC's lawyers, read, or rather caused to be read, the letter aloud over his program, during a station break, following which he made no reference to it whatever. Vidal made no acknowledgment, tendered no apology, did not reply in any way to a couple of letters asking him to make out the check.

It is not my habit to review the material that appears in the back of the book section of *National Review*, so that I saw for the first time in the published magazine, weeks later in Switzerland, a review by Noel E. Parmentel Jr. of Vidal's play, *Romulus*. The review was unfavorable to the play, but generous—one should say accurate—in its appreciation of Vidal's talents as a playwright. One aspect of *Romulus* the reviewer found offensive, and was not alone in the critical community in doing so. "All in all," he wrote, "*Romulus* adds up to (with the possible exception of *Sail Away*) the most offensive instance of 'inside' theatre, which such diverse types as the late Ernie Kovacs and New York *Times* drama critic Howard Taubman have chosen to call 'effeminate' and which the boys in Lindy's are calling '*la nouvelle fague*.' "

Parmentel went on. "Although the critics have generally ridiculed the Vidal literary product, he is far from being a jejune hack. He has certainly traveled an odd road. During his early career as a 'serious' novelist, he evinced an interest in homosexuality equalled only by that of the editors of *One*. Many of his novels and stories are clinical, apparently informed commentaries on the problem. [Notice what Vidal would consider the planted axiom:—the *problem*.] In spite of all this high purpose, critic William Peden was once moved to note that the Vidal output constituted 'a rather dreary landmark in the literature of homosexuality.' "

And there followed a crack I confess I have repeated here and there mostly because I thought it funny, still do. "Always the seeker after truth, Vidal lived for a time in the ruins of a sixteenth-century monastery in Guatemala, where he gathered material for an anti-United Fruit Company novel—positively, as a local wag observed, the *only* anti-fruit novel Vidal ever wrote."

And then, more seriously, "At another point he made a pilgrimage to the bedside of André Gide. It is reported that the great French writer liked Vidal and gave him an inscribed first edition of his controversial *Corydon*. Vidal carried his almost obsession with homosexuality into the movies. Although he is quite a proficient scriptwriter, he once wrote a scenario about Billy the Kid, acted by a bewildered Paul Newman, in which the legendary outlaw appeared as a misunderstood homosexual. It was only natural that Sam Spiegel should call on Vidal's specialist skills for Tennessee Williams' *Suddenly Last Summer*."

The operative word is "obsession." And it wasn't only *National Review*, as Parmentel made clear, that thought it a—problem. Our sister publication on the Left, *The New Republic*, carried a review of *Romulus* by Robert Brustein who is now the dean of the Yale Drama School. He wrote that Vidal had "transform [ed] Dürrenmatt's tough parable into an effeminate charade. . . . To make the Romans into homosexuals," he concluded, "is simply in bad taste." *Why* bad taste?

The months passed, and David Susskind asked me if I would appear *mano a mano* with Vidal on his *Open End*—just the two of us. And discuss what? I asked. *Everything*, said Susskind. All right, I said.

Now no discussion of "everything" nowadays can be counted upon not to touch on sex. Accordingly I was prepared, should the subject arise, to attempt to state the case, biological, cultural, and religious, for heterosexuality (that sounds funny, doesn't it?)—prepared to go so far as to defend its "normalcy"; to defend, even, the idea that normalcy in this instance at least is related to what is normative: to defend, one might say, the conservative position.

It seemed to me utterly natural—one is tempted to say utterly normal—that in defending heterosexuality I should furtively consult my own preferences in that direction, and accordingly that in defending bisexuality, the question of Vidal's preferences would reasonably arise. I had read, in preparation for our meeting, his book of essays, *Rocking the Boat*, in which his own intellectual sympathies, at least, were quite candidly stated. "Now it is an underlying assumption of twentieth-century America," he wrote—and the student of rhetoric knows already, the "now" being a dead giveaway, that the writer is about to introduce an assumption with which he disagrees—"that human beings are either heterosexual or, through some arresting of normal psychic growth, homosexual, with very little traffic back and forth. To us, the norm is heterosexual; the family is central; all else is deviation, pleasing or not, depending on one's own tastes and moral preoccupations. Suetonius"—Vidal was reviewing a translation of *The Twelve Caesars* by Robert Frost—"reveals a very different world. His underlying assumption is that man is bisexual and that given complete freedom to love—or, perhaps more to the point in the case of the Caesars, to violate—others, he will do so, going blithely from male to female as fancy dictates. Nor is Suetonius alone in this assumption of man's variousness. From Plato to the rise of Pauline Christianity, which tried to put the lid on sex, it is explicit in classical writing. [Nonsense, as it happens. E.g. Aristophanes, who mocked Plato's homosexuality; Juvenal, who stigmatized the Greek-aristocratic homosexuality; Catullus, who found Caesar's bisexuality, in the words of Gilbert Highet, 'ridiculous and disgusting.'] Yet to this day Christian, Freudian and Marxian commentators have all decreed or ignored this fact of nature in the interest each of a patented approach to the Kingdom of Heaven. . . ."

Now in fact the subject did not come up, though the question was raised, I think (I do not exactly remember and I do not have the transcript) as to whether practicing homosexuals working in sensitive government agencies were security risks, like, say, drunkards. I have never been convinced, by the way, that they are, but I did recite the reasons given by security officials (susceptibility to blackmail, primarily), and I do not know whether I loosed an inflection that burrowed into the memory of Miss Harrington. I cannot conceive that if I had made a major, or even a minor statement, about Gore Vidal's "personal life," that it would have escaped the attention of every single one of the television critics who watched and reported on the program, and there were apparently many of them, none of whom made the slightest reference to the cause of Miss Harrington's trauma. Could she have had in mind a personal reference to Vidal's relations to the Kennedys? But the only thing I knew about his private life in that connection (Vidal had not yet fallen out with the Kennedys) was that his sometime stepfather is Jacqueline Kennedy's incumbent, a nexus that connects an awful lot of people with an awful lot of people and is neither newsworthy nor scandalous.

On the other hand, I gather that I spoke sharply to Vidal (I should hope so!). One reviewer who was also covering the opening of the Lincoln Center that night, wrote that every so often he "would switch over to an independent channel where a fair-haired barracuda named William Buckley Jr. was nibbling at the flesh of a young sea robin named Gore Vidal. . . . In the only complete sentences spoken on this piscatorial orgy, we heard Mr. Vidal saying he couldn't imagine Mr. Buckley in the role of an abolitionist and Mr. Buckley saying that he was an abolitionist for the slaves of Eastern Europe, which Mr. Vidal wasn't." There was no masking, I gather, the mutual dislike, which in Mr. Vidal's case was spontaneously generated, in mine evolved as a reaction to his hit-and-run network disparagement of my family and myself earlier in the year. "The debate," another reviewer wrote, "got entrenched in so much personal opprobrium nothing really was decided other than Buckley's clear debating superiority. . . . When it came to historical and political facts and interpretation, Vidal, frustrated in realistic fencing, resorted to personal disdain, never an attractive effect. . . . Both indulged the sort of ad hominem needling that dazzles and spins off sparks and delights viewers who adore such exercise of forensic fisticuffs, but it does keep issues muddled while delighting the more sadistic semantic fight fans." Vidal said a while later on the Les Crane program that I had beaten him badly, and gave as the reason that he, Vidal, had permitted himself to become "emotionally involved," whatever that means.

It was during the Republican Convention at San Francisco in 1964 that I resolved I would not again debate with Gore Vidal. It was the memory of that encounter, added to everything else, that made me suggest to ABC that I'd prefer not to debate with him, and now I gather that his exclusion graveled him. Indeed over the intervening years I had never asked him to appear on *Firing Line*, which was launched early in 1966. "The one forum on which they have not met is Buckley's syndicated series, *Firing Line*," a reporter wrote, after interviewing Vidal. "Buckley invited the novelist to the program, but 'I refused to give him that much help,' Vidal smiled thinly." (I'd have smiled thinly too if I told a reporter I refused Ed Sullivan's invitation to tap dance on his show because I didn't want to give Sullivan that much help.) At San Francisco it wasn't just the usual things that aroused me, but an insight I got into what I now concluded was more than a merely episodic insensibility to the truth. Specifically, Vidal announced on a television program, once again "moderated" by Susskind (Susskind's advocacy of Vidal's positions competed with the positions themselves in burdening Vidal), that I had that very afternoon importuned Barry Goldwater to accept a draft of an acceptance speech I had written for him, and that Goldwater had brusquely turned me down, all of this in the presence of John Jones, a Goldwater aide. I told him, a) that I had not laid eyes on Goldwater that afternoon, b) that I had not written nor suggested to anyone that I write a draft of Goldwater's acceptance speech, and that c) although I knew very well who John Jones was, in fact I had never laid eyes on him in my entire life. Vidal not only refused to modify let alone to withdraw his allegation, he reasserted it several times. The next day, Susskind (over Vidal's protests, Susskind subsequently told me) read over the air a letter from Jones confirming my denials. (Goldwater, it happened, had tuned in on the program, and was as nonplussed as Jones.)

There were one or two other instances of the same kind of thing, and I remember that it occurred to me then, as it did a couple of times in Miami and Chicago, that perhaps Vidal makes his own reality, which is, all things considered, sufficient reason to understand his philosophical melancholy, even as the order of reality would be melancholy if it had conceived Vidal. At any rate, one wants to stay away from such people, at least publicly. Yet once again the debate had been lively. One reviewer, who took pains to disavow any sympathy with my politics, said that, in the service of "the radical right, [Buckley] was far more successful than Susskind and Vidal on the medium left . . . Susskind and Vidal rocked back and forth like two old harpies and spat at him with no visible effect on their target nor, I suspect, on viewers." The other reviewer "got the impression . . . that Susskind was a zookeeper trying to prevent two hissing adders from killing each other. But the hissing was always wreathed in benign smiles." August 7, 1968, The Rockford *Star*, " 'I haven't seen Buckley since 1964 at the Cow Palace,' Vidal recalled. 'His last words to me were that he never wanted to see me again.' " Needless to say, I did not say those words. But they represented, accurately, my thoughts.

I find only two unpleasant references to Vidal written by me between 1964 and 1968. Commenting on an article by Vidal in Esquire on the Kennedy family, I wrote, "It is of course ironic that Mr. Vidal, the super-liberal super-thinker who in pursuit of the good life has tried everything, but everything in the world, including icon-smashing with a vengeance, now engages an icon he had a hand in molding." The other reference was exhumed by the drama editor of The Miami *Herald* who wrote at the beginning of the Republican Convention that "Vidal is worried the broadcasts may be a bit dull, feeling the allotted twenty minutes or so won't really give them time to get into things. That seems like an obscure worry as only a couple of years ago, in his newspaper column, Buckley referred to Vidal as 'the playwright and quipster who lost a congressional race a few years ago but continues to seek out opportunities to advertise his ignorance of contemporary affairs.' "

Bent on promoting their forthcoming programs, the people at ABC set up a lunch for me to meet the area's television critics, and subsequently did as much, I assume, for Vidal. Such meetings, as every writer knows, are something of a strain: because you are generally made to feel that you can only please by being viperish. What will I want to say about the conventions when face to face with Vidal? I didn't know. My line on Vidal was that I thought his dissatisfaction with America and with American politics was such as to make him almost necessarily sour on anything that was likely to happen at either convention.

Vidal was evidently much more detailed. One critic wrote that according to Vidal he had "accepted ABC's offer, even though he was to be teamed with Buckley, a man with whom he has had video encounters before and for whom he has utter contempt." Another quoted Vidal as saying, "Bill, of course, will try to personalize our shows. He thrives on insults. But I'll try to stick to politics. He never sticks to a subject because he's on such weak ground." Another wrote that Vidal "was not the least bit reluctant to discuss his adversary. Vidal welcomed the chance to be quoted. Apparently he relishes the vaudeville-team approach to interpretative journalism employed by ABC television for the national conventions and is anxious to allow the churlish nature of their on-screen rapport to carry over into off-screen conversation. . . . 'though I don't like being brought down to his level. That's the reason I've refused to appear with him over the last four—or is it six?—years. . . . Buckley is frivolous, superficial and often very entertaining.' "

And he told Mr. Hal Humphrey, whose column is widely syndicated, that he would "stipulate at least one ground rule. . . . 'When I'm talking I want the camera on me and not on Bill's face doing all those wild expressions of his while I'm just a voice off-stage.' " Later he told a correspondent that he had complained to the director of getting insufficient camera time, and the director had promptly complied with his requests. On these and related matters he proved most fastidious. "Buckley," a Miami reporter wrote, ". . . is as conservative about being pictured in the make-up chair as he is in his political philosophy. He submitted to a brief [make-up], a quick swish of a comb by his wife Patricia who had accompanied him. On the other hand, his fellow program jouster Gore Vidal was thoroughly liberal about being touched up. No hurry-up job, this. Miss May leisurely cleansed the skin with an antiseptic lotion, added a cream-type foundation and powder and commented on his hairline: 'He has a good hairline.' 'I don't have a wig,' he quipped. 'Tell your photographer not to make me look as though I have. Past pictures have. See how vain I am. I'm letting you take my bad side,' gesturing to his right."*

In general, the press anticipated the forthcoming debates with unmitigated glee. In Toledo the headline was, "Politicians Are Forewarned/Bill, Gore May Steal Show." The Washington *Post* announced that "The best show during the Republican and Democratic Conventions next month will not be on the convention floors or in hotel corridors but in an ABC studio. . . . In Buckley and Vidal, ABC has a dream television match. They are graceful, shrewd, cool antagonists; paragons of caustic wit and established observers of the American political scene." "It's anybody's ball game," wrote the New York *Daily News* about the G.O.P. Convention, "as they've been telling us the past couple of days, but right now the inside dope at the convention is that Bill Buckley and Gore Vidal have it practically sewed up. As a team, Buckley is in the No. 1 slot, naturally, since he's thoroughly committed, with Vidal, an expert sniper, as his running mate. And the beauty part of it is that, disliking one another intensely and both gifted in invective (they are far and away the best infighters in Miami Beach), they're a cinch to provide challenging leader-

---

* *"We have found, especially in persons whose libidinal development has suffered some disturbance, as in perverts and homosexuals, that in the choice of their love-object they have taken as their model not the mother but their own selves."—Freud,* On Narcissism, II.

ship." "A rare stroke of good television programing . . ." said the Philadelphia *Daily News*. "As an ABC spokesman puts it, 'We fully expect the fur to fly when those two come together,' and there wasn't a dissenting comment from his listeners."

So there we were, Saturday, August 3, on duty for our first broadcast, suddenly re-scheduled in a makeshift studio at the Fontainebleau Hotel because the ceiling had caved in two days before over the studio at the convention site. We were instructed that we must prerecord an initial statement of a sentence or two, and I knew, when I heard Vidal's, that the session was going to be grim. "To me," he said, "the principal question is, can a political party based almost entirely upon human greed nominate anyone for President for whom the majority of the American people would vote?" Now there was an interval of eight or ten minutes before we swung into the live portion of the program. Diagonally across from us, William Lawrence was well into his political forecast, which had followed a pastiche of the day's events screened by ABC producers. Across from us was Howard K. Smith, suave, intelligent, mildly apprehensive, rehearsing with his lips the lines he would presently deliver, directly in touch with the controls, where twenty officials and technicians called the signals, to Smith, to Lawrence, to the thirty-forty-fifty technicians, reporters, directors, who filled the enormous room, at one corner of which, earphones attached, Vidal and I awaited the sound of the bell. We had exchanged minimal amenities, and I scribbled on my clipboard to avoid having to banter with him, and he did the same, and I felt my blood rising in temperature as I reflected on the malevolent inanity of his introductory observation, and then the resolution evolved that I would hit him back hard with a *tu quoque* involving *Myra Breckinridge* —which I had not then read. . . . But Howard K. Smith derailed me by asking me not, as I had expected, to initiate the exchange by commenting on Vidal's description of the Republican Party, but rather to answer a specific question—who, in my judgment, was the Best Man at Miami? We were off.

I answered: Reagan and Nixon, and said why, more or less. Vidal came back with Rockefeller—"I cannot possibly imagine Richard Nixon President of the U. S." He backed this failure of his imagination by reciting an arresting catalog of Nixon's sins, so livid up against the exigencies of the day:

"And here you have a man who when he was in Congress voted against public housing, against slum clearance, against rent control, against farm housing, against extending the minimum wage. . . . He said, 'I am opposed to pensions in any form as it makes loafing more attractive than working.' And now today he offers us a program for the ghettos which he's made much of, and what is it? Well, he is going to give tax cuts to private businesses that go into the ghetto and help the Negroes. Now in actual fact private business is set up to make private profits. . . . So I would say that so far as Mr. Nixon goes he is an impossible choice domestically."

Now up against an extended barrage like that, a debater has problems. Point-by-point refutation is clearly impossible. As a rule one doesn't have handy the relevant material for coping with such arcana. And anyway, in network situations, an elementary sense of theatre (which if you don't have it, you won't ever face the problem of what to do in network situations) disciplines you in the knowledge that you simply don't have the time it takes for detailed confutation. Nixon hadn't been in Congress for *sixteen* years. Just to begin with, whatever Nixon did in Congress between 1947 and 1952 was largely irrelevant. Apart from that, what on earth does it mean, Nixon "voted against," say, "rent control"? Rent control survives in only a few places, primarily New York City. How can *any* attitude he took toward "farm housing" eighteen years ago bear on his present qualifications for the Presidency? And what sort of a "farm housing" bill did he vote against? How can we know?—maybe it was the same farm housing bill that the Americans for Democratic Action also opposed? And anyway, wasn't Nixon selected in 1952 by Eisenhower because he had a reputation as a domestic liberal (one of Christian Herter's boys) and as a tough anti-Communist—a good combination in 1952? Hadn't Nixon's preference for Eisenhower over Taft situated him in the liberal wing of the G.O.P.?

And then there was the problem of the directly quoted sentence. Vidal quoted Nixon as saying, "*I am opposed to pensions in any form as it makes loafing more attractive than working.*" The debater knows by the application of rudimentary discriminatory intelligence that no politician in the history of the world ever said that, and most probably no non-politician: and certainly not anyone who ever contemplated running for the Presidency. The mind needs to work quickly in such situations, canvassing rapidly the possibilities that a direct challenge might lead him into a carefully planned ambush. . . . So one comes in on the subject from the other direction: If Nixon had ever uttered a sentence so preposterous—condemning pensions paid even to ninety-year-old widows, on the grounds that they are conducive to sloth—wouldn't a fatuity so lapidary have instantly become a part of the political folklore, like, for instance, Mr. Agnew's "If you've seen one slum you've seen them all"? The answer is of course yes; so that in debate, under these circumstances, you can feel safe in saying, "Nixon never said that"—even though such a denial is itself a) unprovable, and b) silly; since no one on earth is familiar with every statement Nixon ever made; and no one therefore can know as a certitude that he never made *any* particular statement. What to do?

I decided to do nothing. To go back and challenge the over-arching axiom planted by Vidal at the outset—more damaging, more readily exposable, than what he said about Nixon. . . .

B.: It seems to me that the earlier focus of Mr. Vidal here on human greed—you remember that he said he found himself wondering whether the party that was devoted to the concept of human greed could ever hope to get a majority of the American people to vote for it. Now the author of *Myra Breckinridge* is well acquainted with the imperatives of human greed—

Vidal broke up—reacted quite extraordinarily. . . .

V.: Ha, ha, ha. If I may say so, Bill, before you go any further, that if there were a contest for Mr. Myra Breckinridge, you would unquestionably win it. I based the entire style polemically upon you—passionate and irrelevant.

B.: That's too involuted to follow. Perhaps one of these days you can explain it—

V.: You follow it.

I didn't and don't. In any case, we were off.

B.: For Mr. Vidal to give us the pleasure of his infrequent company by coming back from Europe where he lives in order to disdain the American democratic process and to condemn a particular party as one that has engaged in the pursuit of human greed, requires us to understand his rather eccentric definitions. . . .

I went on to point out that Senator Robert Kennedy, not Nixon, had first suggested the tax rebates, and that the Republican Party's support of the costly Vietnam war was hardly an exercise in greed. Vidal answered that the Republicans were big businessmen who made profits from the war, I pitched for the free enterprise system; he said the Republicans denigrate the poor and the minority groups, and that if by some terrible accident Nixon became President, "I shall make my occasional trips to Europe longer."

B.: Yes, I think a lot of people hope you will. As a matter of fact, Mr. Arthur Schlesinger Jr., who is a member of *your* party, not mine, [has] remind[ed] you of your promise to renounce your American citizenship unless you get a satisfactory party in November.

V.: Now, now, Bill, that isn't quite what I said. I said it would be *morally* the correct thing to do but I can behave as immorally as the Republicans.

B.: I can believe that, too.

What Vidal had written, in the book Authors Take Sides on Vietnam, *published only a few months before Miami, was* "For myself, should the war in Vietnam continue after the 1968 election, a change in nationality will be the only moral response." *So already, pre-Gethsemane, the statement turned out to be nothing more than moral bravura.*

Vidal returned to the theme of Republicans-as-believers-that-welfare-is-immoral. He managed to intrude a feline reference to Ronald Reagan, which so help me God if I had said such a thing about Adlai Stevenson, I hope I'd have gone off and joined the Trappists. He warmed up by attributing to Reagan, as he had done to Nixon, a statement Reagan never made—

V.: Meanwhile, with several denunciations [by Reagan] like I quoted to you, on free-loaders on welfare and how it encourages immorality and divorce—I assume he was on unemployment insurance when he divorced Jane Wyman—

And on he went. Another evening (August 6) he would motivate Reagan's liberal-to-conservative switch in the early Fifties on Reagan's falling in love with the daughter of "a very prominent brain surgeon." I asked how come, under the circumstances, Reagan had achieved the extraordinary plurality of 1966? Well, the people make mistakes.

Vidal suddenly switched the topic, electing to allude to my "intimacy" with Reagan and Nixon. In order to do so, he assigned to the word "neurosis" a meaning I have never heard it given, not even by conventional neurotics.

V.: . . . Since you're in favor of the invasion of Cuba, in favor of bombing the nuclear potentiality of China, since you're in favor of nuclear bombing of North Vietnam, I'd be very worried about your kind of odd neurosis: neurosis being a friend of anybody who might be a President. If I were one of the candidates I'd say Bill Buckley don't stay home. [I know, I know, I don't get it either.]

B.: I'd be very worried too, if you had such a hobgoblinized view—but I've never advocated the nuclear bombing of North Vietnam.

V.: I'll give you the time and place if it amuses you.

B.: Well, you won't.

V.: I will.

B.: I advocated the liberation of Cuba at the same time that Mr. Kennedy *ordered* the liberation of Cuba.

V.: No, no, Bill, keep to the record. You said we should enforce the Monroe Doctrine and invade Cuba the sooner the better in your little magazine whose name will not pass my lips in April, 1965. You favored bombing Red China's nuclear production facilities the 17th of September, 1965, in *Life* magazine . . .

I had said to *Life: "I have advocated bombing Red China's nuclear production facilities. But it becomes more and more difficult to do . . . as Red China takes pains to diffuse and protect its facilities. But technically, it is still possible. How do we justify the bombing in terms of world opinion? On the grounds the good guys of this earth have got to keep the bad guys from getting nuclear bombs."*

V.: . . . and you suggested the atom bombing of North Vietnam in your little magazine which I do not read but I'm told about, the 23rd of February, 1968. So you're very hawkish, and if both Nixon and Reagan are listening to you, I'm very worried for the country.

I told him he was misquoting me.

V.: No, Bill Buckley, let me make it clear to you that the quotation is exact. . . . Are you saying that you didn't say that?

B.: I'm saying that I didn't say it, that your misquotations—

V.: Tune in this time tomorrow night and we will have further evidence of Bill Buckley's cold war turned hot. . . .

I responded limply, and Howard Smith relieved us, and I would suppose the national audience, from the misery, by telling us how "enjoyable" it had been to hear us "articulate" our "points of view."

That was August 3. Today (as I write) is February 19, 1969, and I have just now reached for the bound volume of *National Review* 1968, and leaf through to find the issue of February 23, 1968. It does not exist. I look back, to the issue of February 13—surely that was what he meant? Nothing there about nuking North Vietnam. Perhaps the following issue—February 27? Ha! P. 206: "Vietnam and Partisan Politics" by W.R.B., second column third paragraph. "If Lyndon Johnson's reasoning is correct that bombing the North is justified, then it is also correct to bomb the harbor of Haiphong and prevent the delivery there of the hundreds of thousands of tons of material being used against us so effectively." That is the most bellicose paragraph in the issue. Could Vidal have had in mind a column, written about that time, though never published in *National Review,* advocating the use of tactical nuclear weapons in Vietnam? Who knows. Yes, I have advocated (and most ardently continue to do so) their use, only after pointing out that they are conceived as more efficient than conventional artillery, under certain circumstances, and that their firepower is more discriminatory, and therefore less damaging to extra-military targets than, for instance, the mass bombings by the B-52's used in the defense of Khesanh.

I wondered what, say, a court would have done under parallel circumstances? "You know," the prosecution declaims, "on February 23, 1968, the Supreme Court, in Minelli *v.* Illinois, declared that anyone who. . . ." And, later, an inquisitive legal researcher discovers that the Supreme Court didn't declare *anything* on February 23, 1968, and that Minelli and the State of Illinois, far from fighting with each other, were always on the very best of terms. What happens? Contempt of court? Reversal? Disbarment? I'll tell you what happens when the audience is not the judge, the jury, and Minelli's kinfolk, but ten million people. What happens is nothing.

Reflections on the first meeting?

From Vidal: "I don't mind his condemning my books," he told one reporter. "The President of Bantam Books, which is bringing out the paperback edition in September, phoned me last night and asked me to encourage the attacks on *Myra* because the book wholesalers have been calling all day with orders. . . . Bill refuses to deal with the issues because he doesn't know what they are, so he uses the personal attack. I spend my time reading statements of Nixon, Reagan and Rockefeller, and I'm able to deal with their positions. Buckley doesn't do much reading. He just arranges his prejudices." Vidal was very pleased by his performance. The television people, he explained, learned greatly from it. "Did you notice," he asked another critic, "that after our first meeting the other commentators began to change their style—to try for wit and candor? Even Cronkite tried to be funny. It's possible that ABC is exploiting our names and reputations. But I couldn't turn down the audience. Just think of how many millions of people who never heard of either of us now know who we are," he crowed. "He went over each encounter," the critic reported, "claiming that he 'absolutely destroyed' Buckley in their first preview meeting. . . . 'The camera did focus on Buckley too much during Tuesday's session, but I put a stop to that,' Vidal said. 'The next night there were not so many full-face reaction shots of him.' "

The press wasn't, or at least not all of it, quite so appreciative. Dean Gysel, who had talked about the dream team, referred to the shows' "waspish bitchery." "Vidal was especially guilty of making personal attacks," said another reviewer. "There was something positively obscene," wrote Terrence O'Flaherty, who had written four years earlier about the San Francisco encounter, sounding a note of warning . . . "about . . . [the] face-splitting exchange [which] was irresistible as well as embarrassing. . . . It was not the dialogue itself that made the conversation obscene; it was the expression of almost sensual relish which flashed across their faces as they thrust and stabbed—for obviously they enjoyed these duels as much as the audience. [Point: what is obvious may not be true, and in this case, speaking authoritatively about my own state of mind, I not only didn't enjoy the evening, I detested it.] [But] suddenly the conversation gets the teeth on edge." And Jack Gould, of The New York *Times:* "[Their] petty confrontations should qualify them as the week's major bores in Miami Beach. . . ." Sure, there was also the world of the satisfied. "Both stress style over content," one critic wrote, "but it is high style. Both may be irrelevant, but they are passionately irrelevant. The polemics are such that the rubber band often breaks, but then they define their positions." And the ratings were very high.

My own feeling was that the encounter had confirmed my misgivings. On Sunday morning I telephoned to Wally Pfister, the producer, and suggested the possibility of alternative formats: perhaps two or three minutes of Vidal, followed by two or three minutes of Buckley, but no cross-talk. He reported back the conclusion of the brass that that would make for uninteresting fare. To a television critic he spoke without making reference to my expressed dissatisfactions. . . . "Pfister revealed that the day after the first debate, Vidal called him and said: 'I sure took care of him [Buckley] last night, didn't I?' Later, Buckley called him and said: 'I certainly made him [Vidal] look silly, didn't I?' The mighty are human, too," the critic concluded. The mighty are unmighty too, he'd have better concluded.

        Vidal's political philosophy is, I discovered fairly early in our association, elusive. His attitudes, if you look them up in the yellow pages, are neatly left-liberal in purely conventional terms. However there are anomalies. There is a strain of populism. But populism, after all, should be popular. I have heard John Kenneth Galbraith call himself a populist, always on the understanding that he does not thereby deprive himself of his right to intellectually aristocratic habits, e.g. in the case of Galbraith cultural elitism, and in the case of Vidal, that much at least; and, touching on the point already raised, sexual singularity as well. But on the whole, populists should be not only expert but enthusiastic at reasoning through to the justification of the people's demands. Vidal isn't good at this at all: or rather, one comes across an impenetrable barrier to the understanding. Towards "the people," he has ambiguous relations, though he appears not to be able to do without them, at least not for as long as twenty network minutes. Even though "they" are, strangely, always out to get him. "Vidal expresses the hope," wrote Hal Humphrey in a syndicated story, "that security provisions at the conventions are especially good because, he says, for the first time in his life (he's forty-two) he has a fear of physical danger to himself. 'I get more threatening mail each day, and from reading it I wonder that there isn't more violence in our country than there is. You know, of course, that one of every five people in the U.S. is mentally disturbed?' " (The inference is that he gets threatening mail from those who are disturbed, rather than from those who are undisturbed.)

Now anyone plugged in to reality will recognize this as sheer fantasy. If Vidal got five threatening letters in 1967, I'll deliver him J. Edgar Hoover as a bodyguard. But it was a cherished theme: "While in Miami Beach," reported Tom Mackin, "he was the subject of considerable hostility. 'I hear hissing in the lobby of the Fontainebleau and people shrink from me,' he said."

Possibly his difficulty in understanding "the people" accounts for his rather extraordinary record as political forecaster. In 1963 he wrote that Goldwater could not be nominated in 1964, in 1968 he predicted that Reagan would be nominated, at Miami he said that Nixon could not be elected, a few days later he predicted that he would be elected—but having predicted something which actually came to be, he left the impression that he made this prediction not so much because his observation of political events led him to the conclusion, as because he needed to massage his *Weltschmerz* which he proceeded to do in *The New York*

Review of Books, after the nomination of Nixon, with masturbatory diligence. Gloom is his chic, and when he remembers to blame "them," it is "the people" who are responsible for the melancholy state of public affairs. On the occasions when he forgets to blame the human condition on "the people," it is the people's leaders who are responsible, the people's leaders being the Vested Interests. "I think," Vidal told a writer for the *Saturday Review,* who asked him what his thoughts turned to on contemplating the city of Rome—"I think," said Vidal, "not only of Marc Antony, Caesar and Cicero, but of our own representatives who take their name from this"—he pointed to history—"the Roman senate. I contemplate their follies and mistakes. I see Washington in ruins as something perfectly portended. . . . Americans have no sense of the past, and indeed hate it." (Even though they are reactionaries.) ". . . We're in the third world war already," he sighed to an interviewer in The Washington *Post* last winter, "and it is going straight to the terminus." It isn't exactly clear why we have not yet reached the terminus. Away back in 1961 Vidal was writing that "we have become a passive, ill-informed, fearful society," whose right wing "has not yet had the courage to propose that some people be allowed to vote and some not to vote according, say, to the size of their income but that is what they [who?] are after. For they mistrust and dislike the majority."

Now wait a minute. The right wing mistrusts and dislikes the majority. As much as Vidal mistrusts and dislikes the majority? Indeed, shouldn't we *all* distrust and dislike the majority—if, among other things, the majority's memory "is about four weeks at best," as Vidal announced it to be in Miami? *"One must never underestimate the collective ignorance of that informed electorate for whom Thomas Jefferson had such high hopes,"* he told us in the Spring of 1963. And now, a few years later, the majority was in even worse odor. Because *"it could be said that with almost the best will in the world, we have created a hell and called it The American Way of Life."*—On the other hand, in other moods, and to suit other purposes, it is "the people" who are the foilees, rather than the foilers. At Miami, Vidal wrote, "the public liked Lindsay but the delegates did not. They regarded him with the same distaste that they regard the city of which he is mayor, that hellhole of niggers and kikes and commies, of dope and vice and smut. . . . [One is left to infer, by Vidalian logic, that "the people" should, and one supposes, really *do,* approve of dope and vice and smut.] So they talk among themselves until an outsider approaches; then they shift gears swiftly and speak gravely of law and order and how this is a republic not democracy." "The people" were pronounced good by Vidal in an opening statement at Chicago. "At Miami Beach," he reminisced about the people, "the people wanted Rockefeller but the politicians wanted Nixon. Here, in Chicago, the people want McCarthy but the politicans seem to want Humphrey. On

Wednesday night, we shall discover just how democratic the two political parties are." Two days later he was saying in despair that the Presidents we tend to get saddled with, in the instant case Lyndon B. Johnson, "reflect the mood of the country." Which would certainly appear to be "the people's" fault, it being "the people" who make up the mood of the country, right? At a moment when the Gallup poll was showing that Nixon was decisively and exactly equally ahead of both Humphrey and McCarthy, Vidal simply ignored the McCarthy showing, his endeavor being, at that moment, to prove that the people were against Humphrey. ". . . there is a poll about to be released," he said, ". . . which is going to show that Humphrey has got something like twenty-seven percent of the vote against Richard Nixon who's got something like sixty in that trial heat. . . ." But of course the trouble with putting Humphrey down, vis-à-vis Nixon, was that to do so required that Nixon be put up; and of course this interfered hugely with the anti-democratic melodrama of Miami Beach, where Vidal had announced that if Nixon were nominated, in the teeth of the demands of the people who wanted Rockefeller, the people would not forgive the Republican Party. . . .

By election night, of course, Vidal was utterly confounded, because "the people," in going towards Nixon, obviously weren't behaving themselves. "I have always felt," he explained, "that we must never underestimate the essential bigotry of the white majority in the United States." If the white majority is bigoted, why did it want McCarthy at Chicago and Rockefeller at Miami? Or, all along, did he really mean the *minority*? Let's see—the minority who wanted Rockefeller-McCarthy; or the minority who is bigoted? And then at Chicago (August 25) Vidal had said, "Well, it is the greater wisdom, finally to trust the people. In any case, we *are* trusting the people, since the major politicians are *entirely* dominated by what the polls say, as we witnessed at Miami Beach. . . ." So: the people—who are good—even though their memory is only four weeks old—but they are wise—and wanted Rockefeller and McCarthy—in spite of their essential bigotry—but the politicians paid no attention to the people—even though the politicians are entirely dominated by the people:—and so on, into the mists of unintelligibility.

Whatever difficulty Mr. Vidal had with "the people," he had none at all with the poor people, with whom he identifies altogether. He does have difficulty in deciding how many poor people there are all told, though he is quite certain on the point that they will not be cared for by a Republican administration.

"The United States," he announced on August 5, "has thirty million poor people in the ghettos, people that I am afraid voted against you so heavily when you ran for Mayor, Bill, when you kept reminding the Negroes in Harlem in one of your first efforts, to throw the garbage out the window for that." [I don't know, you figure it out.]

I challenged the figure but was sharply rebuked.

"I would say that Mr. Buckley as always has misstated the case on poverty as he has on so much else. There are over thirty million people living at the poverty line and the Republican Party, according to the platform, which I read very carefully, is going to benefit the insurance agencies, the private interests, in great detail and nothing at all for the people."

Vidal's little-Marxist assumption that material interests always govern occasionally got him into trouble, as when he was challenged to recite the practical Presidential qualifications of Eugene McCarthy, which he promptly gave as McCarthy's unfortunate support of Humphrey's anti-Communist bill of 1954, and

V.: . . . also, on two occasions, [McCarthy] supported the . . . oil lobby on the depletion of oil resources allowance of which I must say liberals take a very dim view, but I suspect you, with your oil interests and liking for that sort of lobby, would find quite commendable. So he can indeed make those "practical elisions" that you so much admire. I think he is a practical man.

B.: Do you think that Minnesota is such a heavy oil state?—

V.: If Minnesota—what has that got to do with anything?

B.: What was the advantage in [McCarthy's] yielding to the oil interests?

V.: I dread to think but I—

B.: I know you dread to think. That's obvious. . . .

Two days after giving the figure of thirty million, Vidal suddenly rescued millions of Americans from poverty.

"As far as the mutiny in the land which Mr. Buckley refers to, of course, there is mutiny in the land. When you have sixteen million people in poverty and six million in abject poverty—these are actual statistics—and when something like ten to eleven billion dollars is needed to end it all according to Health, Education, and Welfare, I suspect that you are going to need some sort of a program."

So now there are not "over thirty million" but twenty-two million poor (whose poverty will end, we note in passing, with a one-time subsidy of five hundred dollars each). That was Wednesday. That weekend, Vidal wrote an article for *The New York Review of Books,* bewailing the events of Miami Beach, and speaking gloomily about the prospects, under a Republican Administration—"for the forty million poor."

In the interval between Miami and Chicago, I read *Myra Breckinridge.* I have thought and thought about it, and resolved finally to describe and evaluate it and its purposes mostly by quoting from reviewers of the novel who cannot be suspected of sexual or cultural homeguardism.

"Really," said Gore Vidal during the spring after his novel's appearance, to an interviewer from *The National Observer,* "the state of reviewing in this country is *so* low. There is so much dealing in personalities, even in respectable publications. You know, I had originally intended to let *Myra* go under a pen name—not because I was ashamed of her, but because I wanted her to stand on her own. I wish now I'd done that. . . . [But] I wanted to make *Myra* the kind [of book] I'd read myself. I did. I'm delighted."

From *Myra,* a sample—a bowdlerized sample—: "I touched the end of [his] spine, a rather protuberant bony tip set between the high curve of buttocks now revealed to me in all their splendor . . . and splendor is the only word to describe them! Smooth, white, hairless except just beneath the spinal tip where a number of dark coppery hairs began, only to disappear from view. Casually I ran my hand over the smooth slightly damp cheeks. To the touch they were like highly polished marble warmed by the sun of some perfect Mediterranean day. I even allowed my forefinger the indiscretion of fingering the coppery wires not only at the tip of the spine but also the thicker growth at the back of his thighs. Like so many young males, he has a relatively hairless torso with heavily furred legs. . . ."

In England, the authorities did not permit the distribution of the American original. However, the *New Statesman* observed, "Despite the famed mutilations, the British *Myra* hasn't been severely ravaged: the operation leaves no fiery scars. The cuts are mainly in the rape scene: pink sphincters, rosy scrotum, 'the penis . . . was not a success.' The cruelty of this particular charade is so triumphant that it survives censorship. Also, it's far more gruesome than erotic—for those who don't love pain. In fact, *Myra* is more cerebral than bawdy."

Indeed.

"Oh," said Vidal on the Merv Griffin show (November 18, 1968), "*Myra*'s not pornographic. It's extremely graphic, I suppose. It's a—describe certain sexual activities in great detail, but I don't think— pornography is written to stimulate people in order to make money for the writer. And I was not—I didn't—I don't write books to make money."

Griffin: "You don't?"

"Vidal: "People, though I'm not—I think now, I must say, in a way I would be more interested in exciting people perhaps than in writing for money."

Indeed. Vidal, the reviewers seem to agree, was engaged in other pursuits than moneymaking, even if he did not resent the pennies from heaven; it is gratifying, in fact, to make money from intellectual pursuits. "In an 'Afterword' to his revised early novel, *The City and the Pillar,*" the *New Stateman* observes, "Mr. Vidal announced that everyone is bisexual, while 'the idea that there is no such thing as "normality" is at last penetrating the tribal consciousness. . . .' "

In order to establish the abnormality of normality, the vehicle is homosexuality. "Not only are these nasty consequences in Vidal's little morality tale," wrote Marvin Barrett in *The Reporter,* "he takes his lofty homosexual theme of twenty years back (then all high-toned sentiment), grinds it to sludge, and flushes it away with a lewd satiric chuckle.

"Only half kidding," Barrett continues—and there is the operative phrase—"he has Myra/Myron say: 'In the Forties, American boys created a world empire because they chose to be James Stewart, Clark Gable and William Eythe. By imitating godlike autonomous men, our boys were able to defeat Hitler, Mussolini and Tojo. Could we do it again? Are the private eyes and denatured cowboys potent enough to serve as imperial exemplars? No. At best, there is James Bond . . . and he invariably ends up tied to a slab of marble with a blowtorch aimed at his crotch. Glory has fled and only the television commercials exist to remind us of the republic's early greatness and virile youth.' "

"Glory" has fled—along with—necessarily with?—the convention in favor of heterosexuality as the "normal" sexual relationship. We move in a different direction, as we are emancipated from surely the only prejudice commonly shared by St. Paul, Marx, and Freud. . . . "Some novels," writes Michael O'Malley in *The Critic,* "smell of beer, others of marijuana or perfume. . . . This one is soaked in estrogen. A tone entirely estrous: everyone in continual heat, an itchy, yowling, manic, pussycat heat that is right out of *The Pearl* and as ludicrous, as depressing. . . . The whole thing seems to have been written from a point of observation to the rear of the characters and about eighteen inches off the pavement. This may be a privileged angle to some but for me it produces almost at once a severe pain in the neck. The story itself is Odds and Ends. Rear ends. There are more bottoms here than in *Twenty Thousand Leagues Under the Sea.* The heart of the book—and the part where you throw up your hands *and* your lunch and realize that you're dealing with yet another pale echo of Genet's masturbatory daydreams—is this rape. It just goes on and on with an interminable homosexual nittyness. . . . Other Odds against you include a masochist with a touch of nymphomania, the rapee who turns sadist homosexual, a Negro queen called Irving Amadeus, the profoundly les-bian Miss Cluff, a rock group that practices bestiality, the bisexual Gloria Gordon, a bit of a satyr, the obligatory Hollywood orgy scene, and some business lifted from Catullus to add tone. Catullus did it better."

But then Catullus had other things on his mind, whereas *Myra* is plainly intended as allegory, in the continuing crusade of Gore Vidal not only to license homosexuality but to desacralize heterosexuality: in the interest of a *true* understanding of human nature, such as has not been nobly or ignobly understood by any dominant philosophical or imperial figure since Plato and the Twelve Caesars; and (bonus!) is in any case desirable if only as the humane solution to pressing social problems. "In other words," *Time* magazine commented, "the remedy for overpopulation might be homosexuality."

But the allegory fails, straining vainly against paradigms artistic as well as moral. "Is this *Paradise Lost*," asks *The Times Literary Supplement*, in a review entitled "Pathetic Phallusy," "or merely a *Golden Ass* penetrated? Milton, Blake said, was 'of the Devil's party without knowing it'; Vidal, it seems, is of the Devil's party—and knows it. For he connives with his temptress, his tutelary female, the eternal aggressive whore, or *porné* incarnate, deflating, deflowering the tumescent males. Myra Breckinridge herself sees all life as a naming of parts, an equating of groins, a pleasing and/or painful forcing of orifices. Which is the essence, after all, of pornography. All is referred to the phallic point, the reductio ad absurdum of the genitalia. Nor is the response spiked, but silkily sensuous to male buttocks, nipples, pubic hair, and the whole repertory of male adornment from jockey briefs to T-shirt and jeans. . . . Pornography, then, is exhibited as the final metamorphosis of Existentialism: 'The only thing we can ever know for certain is skin.'

"Today," the *T.L.S.* concludes—even as the *New Statesman* sighed that "the sexual cook-outs will disturb many, as they are meant to; but the trans-sexuality can't be rejected as fantasy; since a fantasy that's so popular has surely acquired universal flesh"—"Today," *T.L.S.* succumbs, Kinsey-like, "sex is metamorphosed as freely as fancy dress. And in his role of *arbiter elegantiae,* Gore Vidal can write, without recourse to preposterous tableaux,

" '*It is the wisdom of the male swinger to know what he is, a man who is socially and economically weak, as much put upon by women as by society. Accepting his situation, he is able to assert himself through a polymorphic sexual abandon in which the lines between the sexes dissolve, to the delight of all. I suspect that this may be the only workable pattern for the future, and it is a most healthy one.' "* Vidal has thought seriously about the future. One year after writing *Myra,* he proposed (Esquire, October 1968) the dissolution of the family. Breeding complications? None he cannot handle: "The endlessly delicate problem of who should be allowed to have children might be entirely eliminated by the anonymous matching in laboratories of sperm and ova."

There is nothing left to be said about *Myra.* It attempts heuristic allegory but fails, giving gratification only to sadist-homosexuals, and challenge only to taxonomists of perversion: for the rest, for the millions, only the same excitement that depravity gives, that de Sade has given to six generations of people altogether healthy. But the homiletic failure of the allegory does not rob it of the seriousness of the effort. *Myra* is indeed more intellectual than bawdy, even as de Sade was. Vidal is fond of recalling that Alfred Whitehead once said that one gets at the essence of a culture not by studying those things which were said at the time, but by studying those things which were not said. It will surely be said about *Myra Breckinridge,* not that the shrewdest readers of it failed to get the message. But that the responsible community betrayed itself, finally, as indifferent: to so acute, so crazed an assault on—traditional, humane sexual morality: on the family as the matrix of society: on the survival of heroism, on the very idea of heroism. It may be that the cognoscenti consider that Vidal is a trivial literary figure, and hardly a philosophical menace; that their toleration of his effronteries, indeed their ignoring of them, is merely an application of the Jeffersonian principle that one's tolerance of those who would tear down the republic is a monument to our democratic self-assurance. But Jefferson said that such toleration was appropriate on the assumption that "reason is left free to combat" the nihilists. Reason is free all right. But who is using it? ABC-TV? The half dozen young black racist anti-Semites in the New York Public School system are not about to usher in Buchenwald. Even so, reason and passion were quickly and decisively mobilized against them. The editor of a prominent newsweekly, renowned for its liberal opinions, told me that *Myra* was the only book he had taken pains to hide from his adolescent daughter—who probably read it before her father did, assuming she can get the $1.25 to buy the paperback edition and has a normal curiosity. Censorship is probably not the answer. But with the repudiation of censorship, something very strange happened. The corollary was unthinkingly accepted that no one is censurable. "And on my left, Mr. Gore Vidal, the liberal author, and playwright, and novelist, whose most recent book is *Myra Breckinridge*. Mr. Vidal, could we have your views on the moral qualifications of the Republican nominee, Mr. Richard Nixon, to serve as President?"

And so we met again, at Chicago. No need to describe the surrounding tumult. The unhappy delegates could not give satisfaction. Lyndon Johnson was still powerful, but not so much so as to risk a personal appearance, not even to celebrate his birthday. Eugene McCarthy—it was somehow intuited—simply wouldn't do; indeed the Kennedy forces had, in inexplicit recognition of McCarthy's Presidential shortcomings, extruded Senator George McGovern, who, in his few personal appearances, had captivated the beholders; but he was a staying operation, clearly so—his practical role being secondarily the tacit repudiation of McCarthy and primarily a foot in the door for a blitzkreig by Senator Kennedy.

For a while the official attitude towards Mayor Daley was tolerant—his was an adamantine history of pro-Kennedyism, and he foreswore on Sunday the expected endorsement of Hubert Humphrey. So that the pressure on Daley mounted, and his ensuing ineptitudes might have been stagemanaged by Lowenstein and Unruh. In the turmoil, the delegates—and the public—reached hagiologically for the single nominee they knew they could not conscript, because Bobby Kennedy was dead. But his name, especially now that he was dead, was holy; even as Goldwater's would have been, if he had been assassinated minutes after triumphing over Rockefeller in the California primary (I can see John Lindsay at the Communion rail).

I trafficked on Robert Kennedy's prestige, though not, I like to think, in a way he'd have disapproved of. . . . It was on Tuesday and the Vietnam plank was on the agenda. After a while Vidal made a pass at realpolitik. He yearned for the diplomacy of the nineteenth century, shorn of morality and pietism, and wondered whether, in fact, it wouldn't be clever of the United States to back Ho Chi Minh, on the grounds that he and Mao Tse-tung were natural enemies. (Virginia Kirkus was to comment on Vidal's *Reflections Upon a Sinking Ship*, "Vidal seems fatally addicted to the worldly skeptical tone with a Boy Scout aria tagged on at the end, rather like Vidal imitating Talleyrand imitating Walter Lippmann.")

At the mention of Ho Chi Minh and the Vietcong, I saw an opening I had been waiting for. . . .

B.: Mr. Vidal's suggestion that perhaps it would be in our interest to support Ho Chi Minh suggests [to me] that as a matter of testamentary integrity, I should reveal a concrete proposal contained in a letter sent to me by Senator [Robert] Kennedy about six months ago,* the P.S. of which was:

"I have changed my platform for 1968 from 'Let's give blood to the Vietcong' to 'Let's give Gore Vidal to the Vietcong.' "

V.: May I see that?

B.: I think, however, that [giving Vidal to the Vietcong] would be immoderate.

Vidal was reeling.

V.: I must say . . . I must say, I am looking at this. What a very curious handwriting. It also slants up, sign of a manic depressive. I did see that. Whether you forged it or not, I don't know. I would have to have my handwriting experts, the graphologists would have to look at it. I put nothing beyond you, not even in the Dreyfus case when we had such evidence brought into court. [Poor Vidal had been reduced to blithering unintelligibility] . . . But it is very, very amusing and has nothing to do with the case. In fact, his writing [you] makes me terribly suspicious of him as a Presidential candidate. I will say that. . . . Yes, I realize that. I recognize the handwriting. Makes me very suspicious of what he might have been like as President.

Vidal had been oh-so-careful to stay clear of the history of his feelings towards the Kennedys, for reasons both self-serving and charitable. He had begun as an ardent admirer of J.F.K. Then there was the affair at the White House, after which he turned anti-

* *I should have said "about a year ago." The letter was sent in early April, 1967.*

Kennedy. It was rather hard for him to become convincingly anti-J.F.K., in the teeth of his own fulsome praise of him; but he took it out against the Kennedy family and Bobby in particular (Vidal worked conspicuously for Senator Keating against Bobby in 1964) in two interesting and discerning articles published in Esquire. But now Robert Kennedy, freshly assassinated, had emerged as the stricken savior of young idealism, so that not once had Vidal, in all the previous sessions, spoken about Kennedy. Indeed shortly after the assassination Vidal had treated it as a personal affront, final proof of everything he had been saying for years and years and years about America. Interviewed by *Stern*, he gave a most remarkable explanation for the murder of Robert Kennedy, namely the intensity of the hatred of Kennedy in the town of Pasadena which, he explained to his German readers, had housed and reared the killer.

"Sirhan grew up in Pasadena, a center of the John Birch Society, a center of radical right reactionaries, a despicable blot on this earth. The people of Pasadena are well-off. They hate the Jews, they hate the Negroes, the poor, the foreign. I find these to be really terrible people. Sirhan grew up in this atmosphere and I do not doubt that he heard many anti-Kennedy speeches. He simply accepted the way people in Pasadena think. He decided that Bobby Kennedy was evil and he killed him. . . ."

One wonders what exactly the people of Pasadena read, that so inflamed the assassin's heart?

"There is no doubt that when Bobby goes before the convention in '68 he will seem beautifully qualified. . . . But there are flaws in his *persona* hard to disguise. For one thing, it will take a public-relations genius to make him appear lovable. He is not. His obvious characteristics are energy, vindictiveness, and a simplemindedness about human motives which may yet bring him down."

Was that *the passage that caught the eye of Sirhan?*

"To Bobby the world is black or white. Them and Us. He has none of his brother's human ease; or charity. . . . He would be a dangerously authoritarian-minded President."

Can't permit such a man as that *to become President, can we, sons of Pasadena?*

"In their unimaginative, fierce way, the Kennedys continue to play successfully the game as they found it. They create illusions and call them facts, and between what they are said to be and what they are falls the shadow of all the useful words not spoken. The cold-blooded jauntiness of the Kennedys in politics has a remarkable appeal for those who also want to rise and find annoying—to the extent they are aware of it at all—the moral sense . . . to entrust him [Bobby] with the first magistracy of what may be the last empire on earth is to endanger us all."

The words of course are all Vidal's—did Sirhan read them? Vidal did not speculate on the question. The reporter from *Stern* did not question him on the subject. Vidal had little to fear from a reporter who accepted unquestioningly Vidal's learned intelligence that Sirhan Sirhan came by his anti-Semitism from the public school children of Pasadena, California.

By nomination-time, Vidal had cataloged a considerable indictment of the opposition, and of me. The Republican platform was "war-minded"; Ronald Reagan was merely an "aging Hollywood juvenile actor"; I was what he had in mind in writing *Myra Breckinridge*; Nixon had "no discernible interest except his own" for running. He had denounced Nixon as a hypocrite who accepted racist support. He had deplored my "almost Stalinist desire to revise history," and pronounced me "the leading warmonger in the United States."

Chicago was seething with tension, objectified in the demonstrators' encounters with the Chicago police. ABC devoted itself, in the filmed segment preceding our own commentary, to an impassioned excoriation of the Chicago police superintended by ABC commentator John Burns. Vidal was thereupon asked by Howard Smith for the usual preliminary statement.

V.: One of the more vivid pleasures [what a strange word to use] of Chicago has been the spectacle of a Soviet-style police state in action. The police here are brutal. The citizens are paralyzed, and the right of peaceful assembly has been denied by Mayor Daley, who believes in order without law.

B.: [Trying to focus on the political vectors—after all, Humphrey had just been nominated.] The selection of Mr. Humphrey is what in a Republican context would be hilariously applauded as the choice of a moderate over against an extremist. But the American Left are very poor losers and therefore it means trouble for the Democratic Party.

The attempt to bring the discussion around to the nomination of Humphrey as Presidential candidate was ignored.

V.: I think there's very little that we can say after those pictures that would be in any way adequate. It's like living under a Soviet Regime. . . . [He proceeded heatedly along the same lines until finally,]

Howard Smith: I wonder if we can let Mr. Buckley comment now for a short while?

B.: The distinctions to be made, Mr. Smith [I had found that, under stress, I was better off addressing the moderator than Vidal], are these: Number One, Do we have enough evidence to indict a large number of individual Chicago policemen? It would seem from what Mr. Burns showed us, that we do. However, the effort here—not only on your program tonight, but during the past two or three days in Chicago—has been to institutionalize this complaint so as to march forward and say that, in effect, we have got a police state going here, we have got a sort of fascist situation.

One young man approached me, last night, and said, "Are you aware that Mayor Daley is a fascist?"—to which my reply was, "No. And if that *is* the case, why didn't John Kennedy and Bobby Kennedy, whose favorite mayor he [Daley] was, indict him as such, and teach us that we should all despise him as a fascist?"

The point is that [some] policemen violate their obligations just the way [some] politicians do. If we could all work up an equal sweat and if you all would be obliging enough to have your cameras handy every time a politician commits demagogy or a businessman passes along graft or bribes, or every time a businessman cheats on his taxes, or every time a labor union [man] beats up people who refuse to join his union—then maybe we could work up some kind of impartiality in resentment. As of this moment, I say: go after those cops who were guilty of unnecessary brutality, [and] develop your doctrine of security sufficiently so that [you can know] when you *don't* have as many cops as you should have had—for instance, in Dallas, in November of 1963. You don't [then] go and criticize the F.B.I. for not having been there, for not having taken sufficient security measures. But don't do what's happening in Chicago tonight, which is to infer from individual and despicable acts of violence, a case for implicit totalitarianism in the American system.

Vidal responded emphatically that nothing less than a constitutional issue was at stake, that the demonstration had sought nothing more than constitutionally-guaranteed opportunities to voice their dissent.

V.: These people came here with no desire other than anybody's ever been able to prove, than to hold peaceful demonstrations.

B.: I can prove it.

V.: How can you prove it?

B.: Very easily. By citing the recorded words of Mr. Hayden of the S.D.S., of Mr. Rennie Davis of the Coordinating Committee—whose object has been to "break down the false and deceptive institutions of bourgeois democracy sufficient to usher in a revolutionary order." Anybody who believes that these characters are interested in the democratic process is deluding himself. I was fourteen windows above that gang last night, [above] these sweet little girls with their sun-baked dresses that we heard described a moment ago, and the chant between eleven o'clock and five o'clock this morning, some four or five thousand voices, was sheer, utter obscenities directed at the President of the United States, at the Mayor of this city, plus also the intermittent refrain, "Ho Ho Ho/Ho Chi Minh/The N.L.F./Is sure to win!"

This is the way [they have chosen] of accosting American society concerning their brothers, their sisters, their uncles, their fathers, who are being shot at by an enemy which wrongly or rightly nevertheless we are fighting. I say it is remarkable that there was as much restraint shown as was shown for instance last night by cops who were out there for seventeen hours without inflicting a single wound on a single person even though that kind of disgusting stuff was being thrown at them and at all American society.

Smith: Our reporter, Jim Burns, said there ought to be a different way to handle situations like that.

B.: I wish he would invent it. Why don't you ask him next time— Maybe tomorrow?—to tell us *how* to handle it. Because I'm sure the Republican Party and the Democratic Party would [gladly] form a joint platform which would suggest how to do it. . . .

V.: The right of assembly is in the Constitution, in the Bill of Rights.

B.: Nothing on earth is absolute.

V.: That's right. We live in a relativist world. However, it is the law, it is the Constitution and . . . [Vidal, agitated,—as I was—groped frantically for his ideological querencia] and let us have no more sly comments in your capacity as the enemy of the people.

The discussion turned blisteringly to the question of what does the Constitution guarantee, what doesn't it, with Vidal insisting on the blamelessness of the demonstrators. . . .

V.: When they were in the parks on Monday night, when I observed them, watched the police come in like this from all directions, standing. They were sitting there, singing folk songs. There were none of the obscenities which your ear alone seems to have picked up. [What I and my wife had heard, fourteen stories high was: F--- L.B.J.! . . . F--- Mayor Daley! . . . —how do you begin producing witnesses when there are, say 50,000 of them available?] They were absolutely well-behaved. Then, suddenly, the police began. You'd see one little stirring up in one corner. Then, you'd suddenly see a bunch of them come in with their night clubs and I might say, without their badges, which is illegal,—

Smith: Mr. Vidal, wasn't it a provocative act to try to raise the Vietcong flag in the park, in the film we just saw? Wouldn't that invite—raising a Nazi flag in World War II, would have had similar consequences?

Vidal explained that there are different points of view about the Vietnam war, and that "I assume that the point of American democracy is you can express any point of view you want—"

B.: (garbled).

V.: Shut up a minute.

B.: No, I won't. The answer is: they were well-treated by people who ostracized them and I am *for* ostracizing people who egg on other people to shoot American marines and American soldiers.

And then it came—

V.: *As far as I am concerned, the only crypto Nazi I can think of is yourself, failing that, I would only say that we can't have.* . . .

Smith.: *Now let's not call names.*

B.: *Now listen, you queer. Stop calling me a crypto Nazi or I'll sock you in your goddamn face and you'll stay plastered—*

Smith: *Gentlemen! Gentlemen! let's not call names.* . . .

B.: *Let Myra Breckinridge go back to his pornography and stop making allusions of Nazism.* . . . *I was in the infantry in the last war.*

V.: *You were not in the infantry, as a matter of fact you didn't fight in the war.*

B.: *I was in the infantry.*

V.: *You were not. You're distorting your own military record.*

Through it all one hears the pleading voice of Howard Smith: *Gentlemen, please, gentlemen, I beg of you;* and then, taking the conversation by the horns,

Smith: Wasn't it a provocative act to pull down an American flag and put up a Vietcong flag even if you didn't agree with what the United States is doing?

V.: It is not a provocative act. You have every right, in this country, to take any position you want to take because we are guaranteed freedom of speech. We've just listened to a certainly grotesque example of it.

I muttered something about lawful acts which are nevertheless provocative, citing the projected hate-Jew rally that George Lincoln Rockwell had planned to stage in New York City a few years before, which Mayor Wagner aborted by denying him a license. Vidal maintained that such freedoms are absolute, and Smith, reacting to instructions from the control board at which the mesmerized executives finally rallied, no doubt to tell him to get the two madmen off the air, interrupted:

S.: I think we have run out of time, and I thank you very much for the discussion. There was a little more heat and a little less light than usual, but it was still very worth hearing.

But it wasn't over. Situated as we were, in one corner of the immense studio, at other parts of which ABC continued ineluctably with its live broadcast for another twenty minutes, we had, as was customary, very quietly to unharness ourselves from our ear sets and then tread noiselessly out of the studio. My pulse was racing, and my fingers trembled as wave after wave of indignation swept over me—and then suddenly, about to deposit the earphones on the table stand, I stopped, frozen. Vidal, arranging his own set, was whispering to me. "Well!" he said, smiling. "I guess we gave them their money's worth tonight!"

I reached my trailer after taking great strides through the maze of technicians operators executives reporters guests, all of whom looked at me as I stomped by and then, quickly, looked away; afraid, perhaps, that I would greet anyone guilty of a lingering glance with a sock on his goddamn face. I reached my trailer and there was chaos there among my half dozen friends, and my wife, who had watched on the closed-circuit television. Everyone spoke at once, and then the door swung open—it was Paul Newman, longtime friend of Vidal. I want you to know, he said, working his jaw like Hud, I think that was the foulest blow I ever saw. I approached him feverishly: "Have you ever been called a Nazi?" I spat the words out at him. His voice mellowed. "That," he explained, opening his hands wide as one does in expressing the obvious, "was purely *political*. What *you* called *him* was personal!" I despaired; and motioned to the door, a gesture which the clamorous company, silent since Newman's arrival, by the strain of their necks and the inflection of their eyes, seconded by acclamation. And he left, slamming the door behind him.

The reaction was voluble. There were those who did not conceal a sense of bawdyhouse excitement. *Time* magazine wrote that "Commentators William F. Buckley Jr. and Gore Vidal made Mayor Daley and his cohorts look like amateurs in invective." ABC, which was in uproar, withheld the entire exchange from the western United States, where it would normally have run two hours after being seen live in the rest of the country. That would account for some papers' (e.g., the Oakland *Tribune*) otherwise unaccountable failure to remark the provocation—"The boys were discussing the police violence, Vidal attacking the police and Buckley defending them," wrote Bob MacKenzie. "The insults became more and more heated. Finally Buckley blew his famous cool entirely. . . ." The New York *Daily News*'s Kay Gardella delivered a prim rebuke for our "disgraceful" language, and reported that a spokesman of ABC-TV had said that after the telecast Vidal "apologized to Buckley in his trailer office at the convention site. . . . [However] an apology was adamantly denied by Vidal when reached in his Ambassador Hotel suite in Chicago. 'What would I have apologized for?' he asked. 'It's Mr. Buckley who begins the personal attack. I simply respond in kind.' " "ABC official Elmer Lower," the same story reported, "referred to the verbal volley yesterday as 'intemperate language.' He said that 'ABC was upset about what happened, but what can you do except talk to the individuals and ask that it not happen again?' " Well you can of course do that much, which in fact ABC did not do.

I wondered as the clippings came pouring in at the all but universal conclusion that my outburst had identified me as the equal of Vidal in intemperance. And worse. *Commentary* magazine, shrewd and deliberate, wrote that "It was really rather irresponsible to choose this pair as the chief editorialists on the ABC team. Though their political opinions certainly added up to a rather perilous balance, the shameful pleasure of watching them match wits had less to do with a search for political enlightenment than with such archaic or illegal entertainments as cock-fighting, duels to the death, and fliting. The effect was the opposite of edifying. Certainly, Dr. Frederick Wertham must have been worried by Buckley's scarcely controlled ferocity as he shook his fist and drawled. . . . After drama like that, who could be content to turn back to the maunderings of Carl Albert?" I wondered that the editors of *Commentary,* of all people, should apparently think it irrelevant to specify what it was that catalyzed the scarcely controlled ferocity. One wonders how the editor of *Commentary* would have reacted if he had been called a crypto Nazi in the presence of a dozen million people. Would he take the position that that was merely a *political* charge, in a response to which one has no reason to lose one's cool? If, in non-academic circumstances, you call a man a Nazi, are you evoking ethnocentric nationalism—or Buchen-wald? A single editorialist—in *The Arizona Republic*—caught the point.

"This was a smear of the worst kind. The New York *Times,* which was so mad it couldn't see straight when Spiro Agnew said Hubert Humphrey was soft on communism, ignored it completely. . . . In order to put the incident in better perspective, just suppose that Buckley had called Vidal a pro or crypto Communist. . . ."

For days and weeks, indeed for months, I tormented myself with the question, What should I have said? Obviously my response was the wrong one if it is always wrong to lose one's temper, as I was disposed ("the wrath of man worketh not the righteousness of God") to believe that it is. Was my mistake that of going on TV at all, in the light of the abundant warnings, with Vidal (who says A, must say B)? Assume that. But even so the question is not then answered: What *might* have been done within the narrow context? Could it be that my emotional reaction was defensible and even healthy, but that my words were ill-chosen? "The higher the stakes," C. S. Lewis wrote, "the greater the temptation to lose your temper. . . . We must not over-value the relative harmlessness of the little, sensual, frivolous people. They are not above, but below, some temptations. . . . If they had perceived, and felt as a man should feel, the diabolical wickedness which they"—let us say the Nazis—"[were] committing and then forgiven them, they would have been saints. But not to perceive it at all—not even to be tempted to resentment—to accept it as the most ordinary thing in the world—argues a terrifying insensibility. . . . Thus the absence of anger, especially that sort of anger which we call *indignation*, can, in my opinion, be a most alarming symptom. And the presence of indignation may be a good one. Even when that indig-nation passes into bitter personal vindictiveness, it may still be a good symptom, though bad in itself. It is a sin; but at least shows that those who commit it have not sunk below the level at which the temptation to that sin exists—just as the sins (often quite appalling) of the great patriot or great reformer point to something in him above mere self. If the Jews cursed more bitterly than the Pagans, this was, I think, at least in part because they took right and wrong more seriously."

Can it be that the rhetorical totalism of the present day has etiolated *every* epithet? It was a commonplace at Chicago to call the police and the mayor Fascists and Nazis, and the country yawned, indeed much of it expected that so should the police and mayor have yawned. Everybody gets away with everything. Paul Krassner of *The Realist,* addressing the kids at the Coliseum at L.B.J.'s "unbirthday party," attaches the very highest importance to impunity. "I have it on good authority," he yelled into the loudspeaker, "that when someone privately asked L.B.J. why he kept up the war, he answered, 'The Commies are saying F--- you L.B.J.; and nobody gets away with that.' Well, tonight, as a birthday present, we are all going to say 'F--- you L.B.J.—*and get away with it.*'" To that Coliseum William Burroughs dispatched a congratulatory message calling the cops dogs, and Jean Genet topped him and called them mad dogs, and Terry Southern said they weren't dogs but swine. Can such men understand the causes of anger in others? Understand the special reverence we need to feel for that which is hateful? I do not believe that anyone thought me a Nazi because Vidal called me one, but I do believe that everyone who heard him call me one without a sense of shock, without experiencing anger, thinks more tolerantly about Nazism than once he did, than even now he should.

And then finally, the word I did use, which was "personal" in the understanding of Paul Newman—and a few others. Perhaps if I had merely threatened to hit him, that would have been all right. But to call him a queer—"I've been aware of you," one man wrote me, months after the affair, and apropos of nothing, "since the old days when you were on the debating team at Yale and I sat and watched and listened. I admired you then, and since—until you called Vidal a 'homosexual' on TV. This reminded me—somehow and so much—of *Of Human Bondage* when Mildred called the doctor a 'cripple.' I mean, he *did* have a clubfoot, a limp, true, but it was wildly cruel of her to mention it. Dramatic, yes, but really hitting below the belt. I can't recall your doing this sort of thing in New Haven. Have you changed that much—and if so, why?" I don't know. I hope not (though unquestionably Yale hopes so). But don't you see, Vidal does not consider that he is clubfooted, rather that the conventional morality is. He is no more reluctant to suggest his tastes than Swinburne was—and everyone from Carlyle to Edmund Wilson has spoken and written about them—intending to be wildly cruel? "In some ways," Vidal has written, "I was lucky to be brought up with no sense of sexual guilt. I was never told that . . . it was particularly wicked to go to bed with boys or girls. I also went into the army a month after my seventeenth birthday, and there was very little [there] one didn't do. That established a promiscuous pattern which I'm sure has had its limiting side. But there have been compensations." Vidal as usual writes loosely. One must suppose that very little of what we know is "wicked" we know because somebody took us aside and told us so. I don't remember, e.g., being "told" that it was particularly wicked to kill someone, but I have nevertheless always supposed it to be so. And anyway, what does Vidal mean by the "limiting side"? And has that limiting side any obligation to try to survive? Evangelists for bisexuality must endure evangelists for heterosexuality. And the man who in his essays proclaims the normalcy of his affliction, and in his art the desirability of it, is not to be confused with the man who bears his sorrow quietly. The addict is to be pitied and even respected, not the pusher.

Such then have been my thoughts, acknowledgedly self-serving, but not empty, I think, of objective interest. It remains a fact that, as I began by acknowledging, faggotry is countenanced, but the imputation of it—even to faggots—is not. There may be occasions when the clinical imputation is justified, such occasions as were mentioned earlier—Robert Brustein's reviewing a play. But the imputation of it in anger is not justified, which is why I herewith apologize to Gore Vidal.

[August, 1969]

A Distasteful Encounter with William F. Buckley Jr.

by Gore Vidal

During the evening of May 13, 1944, Christ Episcopal Church at Sharon, Connecticut was vandalized. According to *The Lakeville Journal*: "The damage was discovered by worshipers who entered the church for early communion the following day. The vandalism took on the appearance of similar occurrences in New York, according to witnesses. Honey mixed with feathers was smeared on seats, obscene pictures were placed in prayer books, among other desecrations." According to the local police lieutenant "the crime [was] one of the most abominable ones ever committed in the area."

Twenty-four years later, on Wednesday, August 28, at nine-thirty o'clock, in full view of ten million people, the little door in William F. Buckley Jr.'s forehead suddenly opened and out sprang that wild cuckoo which I had always known was there but had wanted so much for others, preferably millions of others, to get a good look at. I think those few seconds of madness, to use his word, were well worth a great deal of patient effort on my part.

Last month, in a lengthy apologia, Buckley reprinted this exchange which, he proudly tells us, "rocked television." For purpose of reference, I must briefly reprise what happened. On the night of August 28, the Chicago Police riot was at its peak. Predictably, Buckley took the side of the police. This was particularly hard to do since, just before we went on the air, ABC had shown a series of exchanges between police and demonstrators which made it quite clear that the boys in azure blue were on a great lark, beating up everyone in sight. Buckley attacked me for defending the victims. That did it. I was now ready for the *coup de grace*. I began: "The only pro crypto Nazi I can think of is yourself. . . ."* As Buckley knew, there was more to come. He created a diversion: "Now listen, you queer. Stop calling me a pro crypto Nazi or I'll sock you in the goddamn face and you'll stay plastered. . . ." It was a splendid moment. Eyes rolling, mouth twitching, long weak arms waving, he skittered from slander to glorious absurdity. "I was," he honked, "in the Infantry in the last war." Starting as always with the last improvisation first, I said, "You were not in the Infantry, as a matter of fact you didn't fight in the war." I was ready to go into that but by then he was entirely out of control and, as our program faded away on much noise, a few yards from us Hubert Humphrey was being nominated for President. All in all, I was pleased with what had happened: I had enticed the cuckoo to sing its song, and the melody lingers on.

For eleven nights we had "debated" one another on television, first at the Republican Convention in Miami Beach and then at the Democratic Convention in Chicago. The American Broadcasting Company had asked us to discuss politics, and so I had spent a number of weeks doing research on the major candidates as well as on my sparring partner. From past experience, I knew that as a debater Buckley would have done no research, that what facts he had at his command would be jumbled by the strangest syntax since General Eisenhower faded from the scene, that he would lie ("McCarthy never won a majority in any state he ever ran in . . .") with an exuberance which was almost but not quite contagious; and that within three minutes of our first debate, if the going got tough for

---

* *There is some confusion about what was actually said on the telecast. The word "Nazi" was first introduced into the discussion by Howard K. Smith who felt that to raise a Vietcong flag in Grant Park was the equivalent to raising a Nazi flag during the Second War. I said it was not the same thing: officially there is no war between us and Hanoi. More to the point, a sizeable minority in the U.S. disapprove of their government's policy and if flaunting a North Vietnamese flag gives them comfort they have every constitutional right to do so (as it later developed, the "flag" raised was underwear). Buckley once again attacked the dissenters; I defended their right to dissent. Unfortunately, two lines of his preceding my "pro crypto Nazi" remark are not clear on the tape. It is my recollection they had to do with communism and the dissenters' relation to the Great Conspiracy. Whatever they were, my own outburst was not a declarative sentence but the beginning of a response to Buckley which was—so notoriously—cut short. Incidentally, I had not intended to use the phrase "pro crypto Nazi." "Fascist-minded" was more my intended meaning, but the passions of the moment and Smith's use of the word "Nazi" put me off course.*

him on political grounds, he would mention my "pornographic" novel *Myra Breckinridge* and imply its author was a *"degenerate."* This is of course what happened. This is what always happens when Buckley performs. As columnist or debater, he has made sniggering sexual innuendos about a range of public figures, and there is some evidence that what may have begun as a schoolboy debater's trick to save a losing argument has now become morbid obsession.

Study the technique. Discussing the "left opposition" to President Johnson on the Vietnam war, Buckley writes (June 17, 1966, Los Angeles *Times*): "At the eye of the hurricane, taking advantage of the centrifugal quiet of his station, is Bobby, whose way is swept clean by the ravaging winds of his associates. He must of course occasionally lisp into the act. . . ." Now the late Senator's voice was known to us all and he did not lisp. Why say that he did? Because the word "lisp" suggests softness, weakness, and, above all, effeminacy. The mad cuckoo behind the little door could not resist casting a shadow upon the virility of his enemy, just as the cuckoo astonishingly characterized those who demonstrated against the war in New York, October 1965, as "epicene" and "mincing" slobs, thus slyly assigning to Sodom's banner such unlikely recruits as I. F. Stone, Ossie Davis, and Father Philip Berrigan. Charity forbids me mentioning what he has written or said of many others; it is all, however, in the record, as his great idol Joe McCarthy used to say.

In any event, having indicated that he lost the debates to me by "losing his cool," Buckley now hopes to regain by writing what he lost through performing. From where I sit, it looks as if our old friend Hugh Bris is back in town. Apparently Buckley has spent the better part of a year brooding over his disaster. "I tormented myself," he declares in a tone which, for sheer plangency, has not sounded since Whittaker Chambers sang among the pumpkins. And so, to relieve his torment, at extraordinary length, he has given us the passion of William Buckley "on experiencing Gore Vidal," a document which deserves at least appendix-status in any study of paranoia American Style. It is obvious that Buckley spent a great deal of effort on this work and though it is about as accurate as those newspaper columns he writes in twenty minutes, it is still a most revealing work—though not, as I hope to demonstrate, in quite the way he thinks.

Buckley begins his tirade with, I should have thought, a most dangerous quotation from *The East Village Other* to the effect that Buckley has been found guilty of exercising "faggot dialectic." The implication is plain. The writer thinks that Buckley is a faggot. He is not alone. Norman Mailer even shouted the word "fag" at Buckley during a Les Crane taping: it was cut from the show . . . how innocent television was before Chicago last summer! Now Buckley's private life should be a matter of no concern to *The East Village Other* or even to that vivacious compendium *The Homosexual Handbook* whose listing of well-known degenerates includes, on page 261, "*William F. Buckley:* Writer, professional candidate, Mr. Buckley hosts a television program and conducts it with a flourish and a zest, with such brilliant gestures and hand movement, that Gore Vidal is reported to have called him 'the Marie Antoinette of American politics.' " Now to include Buckley in a list of homosexuals is doubtless slanderous. In any case, every public figure is vulnerable to this sort of rumor, which is why it seems to me odd that someone like Buckley, himself suspect, should be so quick to smear others as "queers." It is a most unbecoming trait in him, and more than a little mad.

Buckley's reaction to being called a "faggot logician" in *The East Village Other* was very peculiar. Quoting with obvious excitement from a series of personal ads in the paper soliciting homosexual partners, he asks, "why is faggotry okay, but the imputation of it discreditable?" This is sophistical, to say the least. When Buckley imputes faggotry to others, he means no compliment; nor were the liberal editors of the paper paying him a compliment by calling him a "faggot logician." Though Buckley is hardly a logician, he is—at his level—a kind of syllogist, and this is what I think he is trying to say: If liberals think faggotry okay and I call one of them a faggot, why is that wrong in their eyes since there is nothing wrong in being one? Yet when they call *me* one, they imply there is something very wrong about being a faggot.

I believe I can straighten this out for him. People often use terms which are blunt but not necessarily unkind. Agnew's "fat Jap," let us say, or Aristophanes needling Socrates for being a pederast which Buckley reminded us of in his garble of classical history ("I really loved your novel *Julian*," Bill whispered softly to me in Miami as we waited to go on the air) when Aristophanes was himself an apologist for pederasty (read Plato's *Symposium* for the inside story and don't forget you saw it here first!). People have a tendency to be ambiguous about sex and sexual words. Succumbing to his constant vice of name-dropping, Buckley described how at Chicago Paul Newman ticked him off for having shouted "you queer" at me. Buckley described the conversation accurately except for Newman's last statement, "You," said Newman with that preciseness that made him such a formidable campaigner in the 1968 primaries, "are a male c-asterisk-asterisk-t." Now this did not mean that the heterosexual movie star and father of six in any way deplored the c-asterisk-asterisk-t, ("The last fantasy which is of course the first reality." *Myra Breckinridge*, p. 245), it just meant that the word in that context was nicely evocative, even traditional, since the word "hysterical" derives from the Greek noun for womb, and by his own admission Buckley was a "madman" that night. In other words, it is possible to designate someone as a faggot in one context while, in another, regard the whole subject with a permissive eye. By Newman's standard, Buckley behaved like a male womb, by mine he was hysterical, and since that anomaly—the male womb—ought to be excised, I hope that this present exercise will prove to be a successful hysterectomy.

Just as I had predicted, no sooner had I begun to discuss the various political positions of Nixon and Reagan, Buckley launched an attack on *Myra Breckinridge*, as a pornographic potboiler, even though he now admits in his *mea culpa* that he had not read the book at the time he attacked it. Would that he were always so candid! But his motive was plain. *Myra Breckinridge* is about a homosexual who becomes a woman, falls in love with a girl and then becomes, more or less, a man again. To connect me with the book would mean, to certain simple souls, that the author was a homosexual who had become a woman who had then become a man, etc.—because books are true, aren't they? This is pretty simple-minded reasoning but Buckley himself has a simple mind; it is only his neurosis that is rich and strange. Needless to say, identifying authors with their works is a feckless game. Simply to go by their books, Agatha Christie is a mass murderess, while William Buckley is a practicing Christian. But we are dealing now with tribal emotions. There was nothing that Buckley was not prepared to invoke in order to keep me from establishing him as anti-black, anti-Semitic, and pro-war. After I had pointed out, pleasantly I hope, how much he resembled Myra Breckinridge, particularly in his use of logic, I was able to get the subject back to politics. I confronted him with a series of statements he had made. He then did something I have never seen anyone do on television before or since. He simply denied having written what I had said he had written. It was the obverse of Joe McCarthy's, "I have a paper here in my hand." This time I had the paper with each statement neatly checked and dated, and he denied it all. As Goebbels used to say, in somewhat similar circumstances, the big lie is always more powerful than the small plausible one. Still upset over those quotations, he now tells us that he carefully checked his records and the dates I had given him and so on were wrong.

He makes a great to-do over my statement that he favored the atom-bombing of North Vietnam, on the ground that my quote was from the *National Review*, 23 February 1968. Apparently there is no such issue. The quote, as prepared for me by a researcher, and which, incidentally, appeared in Buckley's *On the Right* column of 22 February 1968, reads, "The use of limited atomic bombs for purely military operations is many times easier to defend on the morality scale than one slit throat of a civilian for terrorism's sake." I thought this most illustrative of the Buckley morality scale. But then, denying he had made the statement, he writes, "Could Vidal have had in mind a column, written about that time, though never published in *National Review*, advocating the use of tactical nuclear weapons in Vietnam? Who knows? Yes, I have advocated (and most ardently continue to do so) their use. . . ." He then appeals to the reader: what is he to do with someone who invents facts on television?

There is a solemn lunacy about all this. Incidentally, in the text of his article that I was sent by Esquire, *he crossed out the following exchange from our first performance*:

Vidal: According to you, it's [the people] made nothing but errors since 1932 with an eight-year interregnum of a man you didn't much admire. In fact you criticized Richard Nixon for his unctuous love and attention of the great general. Unctuous is a rather good word.

Buckley: I can account for these errors other than by using the neurotic terms that you're so fetched by. . . .

Buckley crossed out this exchange. Reading it, I wondered why. Admittedly, his response makes no sense—just which of the terms I had used was "neurotic"? A few lines later I understood the reason for the cut.

"Vidal suddenly switched the topic, electing to allude to my 'intimacy' with Reagan and Nixon."

Buckley does indeed like to give the impression that he is "the tablet keeper of history" for the movers and shakers, and his journalism is filled with little anecdotes as to how Reagan introduced him as a speaker one night in California, or "I have had exclusive interviews with Mr. Rockefeller and Mr. Nixon in recent weeks." (*National Review*, 9 April 1968.) I knew, as shall be later demonstrated, that in the words of *The Wall Street Journal*, his ". . . ideological stance seem[s] to have closed off for him, at least for the present, any close public contact with political figures in the major parties." (31 January 1967.)

"In order to do so, [Vidal] assigned to the word 'neurosis' a meaning I have never heard it given, not even by conventional neurotics."

Aware that I had simply played back the word "neurotic," Buckley thought it wise to suppress that part of the dialogue which showed him as provocateur. He then gave the following exchange:

Vidal: Since you're in favor of the invasion of Cuba, in favor of bombing the nuclear potentiality of China, since you're in favor of nuclear bombing of North Vietnam, I'd be very worried about your kind of odd neurosis [I meant "neurotic"] being a friend of anybody who might be a President. . . .

Denying everything, Buckley did admit, righteously, that: "I advocated the liberation of Cuba at the same time that Mr. Kennedy ordered the liberation of Cuba."

Vidal: No, no, Bill, keep to the record. You said we should enforce the Monroe Doctrine and invade Cuba the sooner the better in your little magazine whose name will not pass my lips.

I then gave the date when he favored an invasion—20 April 1965, four years after Kennedy's attempt at "liberation." ("What Republican leader has done anything to dramatize the need for the restoration of the Monroe Doctrine and *all that it signifies* in terms of *our axiomatic obligation* to our own hemisphere?" [Italics mine] *N.R.* 20 April 1965.) He continues with my testimony, beginning:

Vidal: You favored bombing Red China's nuclear production facilities the 17th of September 1965 in *Life* magazine, and you suggested the atom bombing of North Vietnam in your little magazine which I do not read but I'm told about, the 23rd of February 1968. So you're very hawkish, and if both Nixon and Reagan are listening to you, I'm very worried for the country.

Buckley abandons the transcript to observe, "I told him he was misquoting me." Was I? Here is what I quoted from *Life* magazine September 17, 1965: "I have advocated bombing Red China's nuclear production facilities. . . . How do we justify the bombing in terms of world opinion? On the grounds that the good guys of this earth have got to keep the bad guys from getting nuclear bombs."

On television I called Buckley a warmonger because the preemptive strike which he favors against China would lead to a war with China, because the use of nuclear weapons against the North Vietnamese would undoubtedly bring the Chinese into that already disastrous operation, and because his call for an invasion of Cuba is plainly a call for war. I quoted him accurately. And his response? I had invented everything. I suspect that the thought of a Republican administration in 1969 made him not want to be reminded of more zealous days. Always ambitious to be accepted by the nation's establishment, he wanted desperately to appear to be in the placid mainstream of our political life—yet there I was revealing him as an eccentric war-lover of the right. He was not happy. As we left the studio, after the first debate, he whispered to me, "You'll be sorry."

During the next twelve debates, I did my best to discuss the issues. I came to each session armed with quotations from Nixon, et al. Buckley came with a set of prejudices, uncompromised by fact. He was at a constant disadvantage and he knew it. The best he could do was simply say that whatever source I quoted was false. He makes particularly heavy weather in his epilogue of my quotation from Nixon: "I am opposed to pensions in any form as it [sic] makes loafing more attractive than working." According to Buckley, "no politician in the history of the world ever said that, and most probably no non-politician." The second part of this hyperbole is quite mad: most right-wingers say this sort of thing all the time. As for the first part, Nixon did make the statement, and it can be found in *Labor*, 18 October 1952.

When the evidence was too clearly against Buckley, he would again revert to sexual innuendo, attacks on *Myra*, and, finally, Bobby Kennedy. With unexpected naïveté, Buckley thought I would be embarrassed to have the audience reminded that I had written unkind things about Bobby. The opposite is true. And so, contrary to expectation, I enjoyed Buckley's reading of Bobby's letter to him, suggesting that not blood but Gore be sent to the Vietcong. I also noted that at the end of the letter Bobby had scribbled, "And please, when you put it in—please don't twist it." He knew Buckley. Needless to say, this part was not read aloud on the air.

Apropos of the second Kennedy murder, Buckley quotes from an interview I gave to the German magazine *Stern* in which I said that I thought it significant that Sirhan was brought up in Pasadena, a city rich in anti-Jews, anti-blacks, anti-poor. In fact, Los Angeles County, California, is one of the strongholds of the virulent Right Wing. Now obviously Pasadena is not solely responsible for making Sirhan do what he did, but it was certainly a contributing factor. You cannot live unaffected in a community where so many tote guns and talk loudly about how this Commie and that Jew and that nigger ought to be shot. Needless to say, Buckley defends Pasadena. He then quotes various unflattering things I had written about Bobby, asking rhetorically, "Was that the passage that caught the eye of Sirhan?" This is pure Goebbels. But where Buckley is more than usually bird-brained is that I can quote him at equal length in dispraise of Bobby, and I, too, can cry, "Is this the phrase that caught the madman's eye and drove him to kill?"

Yet there is a demagogic strategy in all this. If one is lying, accuse others of lying. On television this sort of thing is enormously effective in demoralizing the innocent and well-mannered who, acting in good faith, do not lie or make personal insults. Buckley has made many honorable men look dishonest fools by his demagoguery, and by the time they recover from his first assault and are ready to retaliate, the program is over. Fortunately, I had Buckley night after night and was so able to remind him and the audience of those facts he found inconvenient. My favorite exchange occurred when we were discussing Eugene McCarthy. At the end of one debate, in which I had claimed that McCarthy was the popular choice of the party, if not of its leaders, Buckley suddenly exclaimed, "McCarthy never won a clear majority in any state he ever ran in. Name one state. Name *one!*" Honking and hissing, flapping his arms, he made it impossible for me to answer that McCarthy had won the Wisconsin primary by fifty-seven percent, a clear majority. The next night, however, I brought up the subject again. Buckley began to writhe. He tried to deny the figures. Then tried to deny saying what he had said. Finally: "But Wisconsin was an uncontested primary and I meant a *contested* primary." I pointed out that since there were other names on the ballot, that meant a contest and, in any case, that is not what he had said, et cetera. Childish. Typical. Appealing? To whom, I wonder.

As the debates continued their turbulent way, Buckley began to show the strain. His hands shook, eyes grew wild, he sweated constantly. As I doggedly and, probably rather boringly, discussed the positions of the candidates, he would go off on wild tangents of his own. I lived in Europe

(I also live in America). I was a pornographer. I was making up my newspaper quotations. Whenever he did this, I would reply in kind. Although careful to avoid discussing his personal life, I set out to establish him not only as a war-lover but as a totalitarian, in the general sense of someone with an authoritarian disposition who wishes to use the state for such ends as placing the "chronic welfare cases" of New York City in "rehabilitation centers" outside the city (a proposal made in the mayoralty campaign of 1965). No matter what I said, he denied it. Yet here are some of the quotations:

"I am convinced that Martin Luther King belongs behind bars along with everyone else who conspires to break the law."

After King's death, he wrote:

"The martyrdom [King] seemed sometimes almost to be seeking may commend him to history and to God, but not likely to Scarsdale, New York, which has never credited the charge that the white community of America conspires to ensure the wretchedness of the brothers of Martin Luther King. . . ."

After Adam Clayton Powell was suspended from Congress, the *National Review* printed a lip-smacking comment wittily subtitled, "The Jig Is Up, Baby."

"If the entire Negro population in the South were suddenly given the vote and were to use it as a block and pursuant to directives handed down by some more demagogic Negro leaders, chaos would ensue."

This statement is a paradigm of the Buckley technique, and should be analyzed. If the Negroes are given the vote, and if they all decided to vote as a block, and the leader of the block was Rap Brown, say, then there would be chaos. Conclusion: don't give them the vote. Yet (a) there is no evidence that they would necessarily vote in any more of a self-serving block than those New York Irish cops who voted for Buckley; (b) it is well known that extremist black leaders like Rap Brown have almost no influence among the Southern blacks; (c) how could there be "chaos" when the only choice offered the blacks in a general election like that of 1968 would be Nixon or Humphrey? Perhaps their block support of Humphrey is Buckley's idea of chaos. In any case, the thought of the blacks exercising their constitutional right to vote is displeasing to one who regards the blacks not only of America but of Africa with distaste, even going so far as to characterize Patrice Lumumba and Joseph Mobutu as "semi-savages in the Congo." (The New York *Times,* 23 August 1961.)

In his epilogue, Buckley had some good fun with my statistics on poverty. I am supposed to have said, sometimes there were forty million poor and at other times twenty million, and so on.

The point to throwing doubt on my statistics (supplied by the Department of Health, Education and Welfare) was to give the impression that poverty is really not much of a problem. But then Buckley's attitude toward the poor is singularly cruel. "It is estimated that in New York one half of the chronically poor are disorganized poor, who cannot be persuaded even to flush their own toilets." (*N.R.,* 4 June 1968.) He also affects not to understand my reference to garbage thrown out of the windows of Harlem. I was not able to complete the sentence on television. But here it is. During a television exchange with Buckley, James Baldwin blamed the white owners of the black slums for their condition. Buckley's response: And I suppose the white landlords go pitty-pat uptown and throw the garbage out the windows.

I first became aware of the Buckleys as a family when I was running for Congress as a Democrat in upstate New York, close to Sharon, Connecticut, where the Buckleys live. Campaigning in America (a town I carried) I heard a good deal about the family, none of it flattering. Until then, I had been vaguely aware of someone called William F. Buckley Jr. who had written an attack on the faculty of Yale's "intellectual drive toward agnosticism and collectivism," a defense of Joe McCarthy and McCarthyism as "a movement around which men of goodwill and stern morality can close ranks," and who edited an unsuccessful magazine called *National Review* (according to *The Wall Street Journal,* January 31, 1967, between 1955 and 1964, the operating deficit was $2,181,000; it is now more). I had dismissed him as a sort of Right Wing Liberace.

Then, on a January night in 1962, on *The Jack Paar Show,* there was a discussion of the Right Wing. I mentioned Buckley in a half sentence, something to do with his dismissal of Pope John's encyclical *Mater et Magistra* as "a venture in triviality." Buckley was not mentioned again. Then, unfortunately, this was the opportunity he had been waiting for, according to Buckley, "Paar was evidently pressured to invite me to reply." Needless to say, Paar was not seriously "pressured" by anyone except Buckley who rang him up and asked for "equal time." Buckley had now managed to get himself on national television. It was a heady moment. The fact that Paar cut him up badly made no difference. Buckley had finally hit the big time as a TV entertainer, and that was all that mattered. It is a source of some pain to me that, unwittingly, I helped Buckley lose his richly deserved anonymity.

We met for the first time on David Susskind's program of September 23, 1962. For two hours, we debated. I had been reluctant to appear with Buckley on the ground that simply to sit next to him would make me look the same sort of nut of the Left Wing that he was of the Right. But Susskind persuaded me. It is my recollection that the program was dull.

We next met in San Francisco, 1964, during the Goldwater convention. We appeared for an hour on a program moderated by Susskind. Here is Buckley's version of what happened: ". . . Vidal announced . . . that I had that very afternoon importuned Barry Goldwater to accept a draft of an acceptance speech I had written for him, and that Goldwater had brusquely turned me down, all of this in the presence of 'John Jones,' a Goldwater aide. I told him that I had not laid eyes on Goldwater that afternoon. . . ." I never said Buckley went to Goldwater . . . in fact, just the opposite. It was, all in all, a fine comic interlude, beginning earlier the day of the telecast, when Douglas Kiker, then of the New York *Herald Tribune,* took Norman Mailer and me to see Goldwater's press secretary "John Jones." What "Jones" said about Goldwater was to be off the record. I could not resist, however, asking what Buckley's role would be in the campaign if Goldwater were the nominee. "Jones" sighed. "That guy! The telephone's been ringing all day, him wanting to talk to the Senator. Then he sent over some stuff for the acceptance speech and I took it into the Senator, and he said, 'What's all that crap?' " I confess to having prepared a trap for Buckley. Once we were on air, I inquired innocently as to what his role would be in a Goldwater campaign. Buckley looked positively roguish, his *éminence* becoming more *grise* by the moment. I egged him on. He grew more and more expansive about his relations with Goldwater. Hinted at closeness. Then, to my shame, I allowed the trap to shut. I repeated—somewhat paraphrased—what "Jones" had told Mailer, Kiker and me. Buckley raved: it was all lies! The next day "Jones," quite predictably, wrote Buckley a letter denying what he had said and Buckley sent a copy to me with a covering letter to the effect that he never wanted to see me again. I found this sentiment agreeable. In any case, aside from my two witnesses, Mailer and Kiker, events proved me right: Buckley played no part in the campaign of '64, and the G.O.P. national chairman Dean Burch ascribed this to "a matter of personality."

After San Francisco, Buckley tells us he decided not to debate me again and declares that "over the intervening years I had never asked him to appear on *Firing Line* [Buckley's television program]"; according to Buckley, this "exclusion gravelled him." Here we have two misstatements. First, I was hardly "gravelled" at the thought of not appearing on *Firing Line.* Second, I was one of the first people approached to appear on *Firing Line.* As Buckley's luck would have it, the producer of the program rang me while I was giving an interview to Gerald Walker. I turned the producer down flat, hung up, then explained to Walker that one of the regrets of my life was allowing Buckley to use me to get himself attention. Walker recorded all this in his interview, which appeared in *Writer's Yearbook, 1965.*

Now before we return to Chicago and the crack-up, I think I should answer certain charges Buckley has made about my work. I am, apparently, such a dedicated proselytizer for homosexuality that I have, in the words of *National Review*'s daintiest hack, produced in

Romulus (a play taken from Dürrenmatt about the last Roman emperor) ". . . the most offensive instance of 'inside theatre' . . . effeminate. . . ." In actual fact, there is nothing "effeminate" about the play. No character is a homosexual, and the subject is never mentioned. Buckley also quotes New Haven's mevin for all drama seasons Robert Brustein as objecting to the play as an "effeminate charade." What can they mean? They mean, simply, that the leading actor, Cyril Ritchard (now a widower, but for years a happily married man) is known as a camp actor —and doesn't camp mean effeminate mean homosexual? Since no one listens in the theatre (or to television), the actual drama went unnoticed. Fortunately, the text can be found with Dürrenmatt's original in a Grove Press edition, and the curious will discover that this "effeminate charade" is a thoughtful meditation on power and responsibility, and makes no mention of sex of any kind. The *N.R.* writer also tells us that "[Vidal] once wrote a scenario about Billy the Kid . . . as a misunderstood homosexual." A) Leslie Stevens wrote the Screenplay for *The Left Handed Gun*, based upon a television play by me; B) in neither version was Billy the Kid shown to be homosexual.

Now for *Myra Breckinridge*. As literary critic, Buckley is—how to put it?—lightly equipped. But that does not deter him. He will take on any subject with insolent pluck, confident that his readers are bound to be even more ignorant than he. He is probably right. To support his case against *Myra*, he quotes most selectively, from some of the more troubled American reviews. Now I am not about to explain or defend my work, but since he has quoted at length from such obscure periodicals as *The Critic* (a house organ for the Knights of Columbus?), I shall quote from two well-known English critics.

First, Michael Ratcliffe in *The Times* (London): "Most British reviews have taken Mr. Vidal with total seriousness, up to a point, but to conclude, as some have, that *Myra Breckinridge* is a novel about sex as the source of all ultimate power is greatly to underrate its subtlety. Gore Vidal remains, after all, a proclaimed classicist, a writing professional and a patrician who suffers fools and shamateurs less gladly than ever . . . and it is impossible when reading *Myra Breckinridge* not to sense his impatience that the headlong flight into apparent sexual libertarianism has produced a nightmare of idiotic thinking and cant and even that, as an anthropological phenomenon, sex has become wildly overrated. . . . Mr. Vidal has drawn the line between absurdity and obscenity, between satire and daft thinking with such a delicate exactness that future sociologists will be hard put to distinguish the fantasy from the real thing."

Second, Brigid Brophy in *The Listener*: "The high baroque comedy of bad taste is a rare genre. *Myra Breckinridge* belongs to it and is a masterpiece: the funniest event since *Some Like It Hot* (and some can't recommend more highly than that). . . . The trans-sex fantasy explodes,

I suspect, at a level even deeper than the one from which it liberates the homosexual imprisoned in every heterosexual and also, of course, the heterosexual in every homosexual (for what, after all, was a respectable, presumed-exclusive queer like Myron doing taking such an erotically detailed interest in lady film stars?). . . . Because the baroque is so analytically formal, the baroque mode and his baroque subject matter are a perfect metaphor for Mr. Vidal's satiric purpose.

"He finds intellectual sloppiness destructive. He destroys it by an explosive, centrifugal force far more inherently destructive than its enemy, but which he controls and creatively deploys into an artistic form."

In England literary critics tend to write about books for the newspapers; in the United States journalists like Buckley do most of the reviewing, with the result that one gets a good deal of intellectual sloppiness and much moralizing at the Billy Graham level. Muddling *Myra*'s views with my own, Buckley indicates that I prefer homosexuality to heterosexuality. Now I want to make one thing absolutely clear, as Richard Nixon would say: I do not prefer homosexuality to heterosexuality—or, for that matter, heterosexuality to homosexuality. Unhappily, somewhere along the way, those who write for newspapers decided that since I thought homosexuality as *natural* as heterosexuality, I must then hate heterosexuality and love homosexuality. One of the sad characteristics of popular journalism is that what *ought* to be true is true. Contrary evidence is not admitted, including the two million words which I have published in the last twenty-five years, nowhere stating that homosexuality ought to be the preferred form of sexuality. It is true that at one point *Myra* makes a case for homosexuality on the ground that it might help contain the population explosion. That was a joke. Incidentally, though Buckley quotes at length from the scene in which Rusty is raped, he makes no mention of the many pages devoted to Myra's attempted seduction of Mary-Ann and the long and I think quite beautiful apostrophe to the uterine mystery.

"But tonight she was subtly changed. I don't know whether it was the snaps at Scandia or the cold bright charm of the powerful Letitia or the knowledge that Rusty would never be hers again but whatever it was, she allowed my hand to rest a long moment on the entrance to the last fantasy which is of course the first reality. Ecstatically, I fingered the lovely shape whose secret I must know or die, whose maze I must thread as best I can or go mad for if I am to prevail I must soon come face to face with the Minotaur of dreams and confound him in his charneled lair, and in our heroic coupling know the last mystery: total power achieved not over man, not over woman but over the heraldic beast, the devouring monster, the maw of creation itself that spews us forth and sucks us back into the black oblivion where stars are made and energy waits to be born in order to begin once more the cycle of destruction and creation at whose apex now I stand, once man, now woman, and soon to be privy to what lies beyond the uterine door, the mystery of creation that I mean to shatter with the fierce thrust of a will that alone separates me from the nothing of eternity; and as I have conquered the male, absorbed and been absorbed by the female, I am at last outside the human scale, and so may render impotent even familiar banal ubiquitous death whose mouth I see smiling at me with moist coral lips between the legs of my beloved girl who is the unwitting instrument of victory, and the beautiful fact of my life's vision made all too perfect flesh."

While we are on Buckley's favorite subject, sex, I will try to unmuddle his distortion of what I have said about bisexuality. We are all bisexual to begin with. That is a fact of our condition. And we are all responsive to sexual stimuli from our own as well as from the opposite sex. Certain societies at certain times, usually in the interest of maintaining the baby supply, have discouraged homosexuality. Other societies, particularly militaristic ones, have exalted it. But regardless of tribal taboos, homosexuality is a constant fact of the human condition and it is not a sickness, not a sin, not a crime . . . despite the best efforts of our puritan tribe to make it all three. Homosexuality is as natural as heterosexuality. Notice I use the word "natural," not normal. Buckley likes the word normal. It conjures up vigorous Minute Men with rifles shooting Commies, while their wives and little ones stay home stitching hoods. But what is the sexual norm? By definition it is what most people do most frequently. Therefore, the norm is neither homosexual nor heterosexual. The most frequent (if not most preferred!) sexual outlet of most people of the time is masturbation, making onanism the statistical norm from which all else is deviation. Yet I don't think even Mrs. Portnoy's son would want to make a case for that particular normality.

As for being an "evangelist of bisexuality," I am not an evangelist of anything in sexual matters except a decent withdrawal of the state from the bedroom. There will, of course, always be morbid twisted men like Buckley sniggering and giggling and speculating on the sexual lives of others, and nothing's to be done about them. But the sex laws must be changed. It was Dr. Kinsey who pointed out that if all the laws were enforced, ninety percent of the men in the United States would be in jail. One final point: Buckley quotes an American reviewer who was horrified at my explicit description of a male body (as usual, no mention of the equally explicit description of a female body). To me this reviewer's objection perfectly reflects the sickness of the society we live in. On the one hand, such critics hold that we are made in the very image of God, a bit of proud, primitive lunacy still obtaining in certain Christian sects, and yet, without any awareness of paradox, they also hold nudity to be obscene, the body disgusting, and certain parts of it horrifying. Yet if we are made in God's image, the body must be divine. Conversely, if the body is vile, then its maker must be vile. Unfortunately, our primitives are beyond mere logic. They have their tribal prejudices and find both comfort and glory in their confusion.

"The only pro crypto Nazi I know is you," I said to Buckley on the night of August 28. He tells us that this so maddened him, he went to pieces with righteous anger. Looking and sounding not unlike Hitler, but without the charm, he began to shriek insults in order to head me off, and succeeded, for by then my mission was accomplished: Buckley had revealed himself. There was no need to discuss his anti-Semitic background. He had demonstrated most vividly what I could only have stated. But now that he has seen fit to relive his failure at Chicago, I am now obliged to write what I chose not to say on the air.

William F. Buckley Sr. was a Texan and an oil speculator who made a small fortune and had ten children. Politically, he was a perfect example of what Professor Richard Hofstader has called the "paranoid style" in American political life. A nouveau riche of limited intelligence but powerful prejudices, Buckley Sr. felt that he should have more influence in the country than indeed he had. In this he follows what Professor Hofstader has shown to be a classic pattern. Whenever a member of one of the immigrant groups to the United States moves from poverty to affluence, his first response is a sense of letdown that he is still no closer to the levers of power than he was before. If he is of a paranoid disposition, he will suspect conspiracy; he will blame *them*. The John Birch Society is a particular haven for this kind of malcontent. It seems likely that Buckley Senior felt insufficiently acknowledged. Despite the legend of his great fortune, he was never listed in *Who's Who in America, Current Biography, Poor's Register of Corporations, Directors, and Executives,* or even the *Social Register.* Like a cut-rate Joe Kennedy, he then decided to compensate through his children. They were taught total conservatism. They were privately tutored. All were sent to England to acquire patrician accents. William Jr.'s did not quite take. The result was a vigorous, highly articulate brood who, in the words of one (John), "are all good conservatives and, thank heavens, we all married conservatives." The family is as devoted to one another as the Kennedys, and on the important issues, they think alike. When Buckley Junior was attacking the faculty at Yale for "collectivist" tendencies, two sisters opened up separate fronts at Smith and Vassar.

Though Buckley Jr. is usually candid about his love of war and distaste for the blacks, he is extremely wary of appearing anti-Semitic. In this he resembles Robert Welch, though not the late irrepressible George Lincoln Rockwell. Very seldom does he betray his actual feelings as he did on Tex McCrary's radio program 25 September 1964. ". . . they [the Jews] tend to construct an engaging political myth, centered around the Hitlerian experience which more or less suggests that Hitler was the embodiment of the ultra-Right, and that the true enemies of Hitler, many of them—that the true enemies were, in fact, many of them Communists during the early Thirties. And under the circumstances they, I think, emotionally feel a kind of toleration for Communist excesses in this country. . . ." Arnold Forster of the Anti-Defamation League of B'nai B'rith answered Buckley four days later·on the same program. To Buckley's charge that Jews feel a kind of toleration for Communist excesses in this country, Forster replied: "That of course, Tex, is nothing more than insidious slander. . . . And notice how easy he finds it to generalize, Tex, about Jews. Millions of human beings in one group." The question of course is why does Buckley find it so easy insidiously to slander, in Forster's phrases, millions of human beings? I know the answer and Buckley, knowing that I knew it at Chicago, terrified that I would discuss it on the air, saw fit to interrupt me with calculated hysterics.

On March 4, 1944, Mr. and Mrs. Sully Berman bought a house on the green at Sharon. The Bermans were Jews. Now in Sharon, there was a gentleman's agreement to keep out Jews. Needless to say, the arrival of the Bermans was considered by the village gentry to be a betrayal of that agreement, and the town's wrath was directed not so much at the Bermans as at the real-estate agent who had done such an un-Christian thing as to admit Jews to Sharon. The agent was Mrs. Francis James Meadows Cotter. Her husband was the Episcopal minister at Sharon, and Rector of Christ Church. The Cotters were a well-liked family, and their two daughters were contemporaries and friends of the young Buckleys. Buckley Sr., however, was a most unforgiving man. He complained loudly and bitterly about what Mrs. Cotter had done and, like Henry II, vowed revenge. Shortly thereafter, on Saturday, May 13, Christ Episcopal Church was vandalized. Honey and feathers were poured over the velvet cushions of the pews. Prayer books were defaced. Obscene photographs were inserted in the Bible.

There was considerable uproar the next morning when the Reverend Cotter and his flock assembled. Who had done it? The high-spirited Buckleys were immediately suspected. Acting on a tip, detectives went to the Buckley house and there found the magazines from which had been torn the nudes, the oatmeal and syrup containers still set out on the kitchen table. Minimal sleuthing revealed which of the young Buckleys had been in town that night. The detectives then confronted the three vandals and got them to sign confessions. The case came to court June 10, and the three (one was in college and two in prep school) were found guilty by a Justice of the Peace and each fined $100 for damaging the church. Buckley Sr. did his best to take further revenge on the Cotters, even going so far as to request the Episcopal Bishop of Connecticut to remove Cotter from Christ Church, but by then village sentiment was entirely on the side of the Cotters and Buckley Sr. dropped the matter. But he had made his point as far as his family was concerned and therein lies the key to his son's character. Buckley Jr. has never accepted any view of the world other than his father's. He is forever the little boy trying to impress Daddy by hating what Daddy hates. To be fair, Buckley Sr.'s prejudices were not much different from those of, let us say, Joe Kennedy or Senator Gore, my grandfather, but Joe Kennedy's sons and Senator Gore's grandson changed as they made their way in the world, learned charity or at least good sense, but not Bill—he is still the schoolboy debater echoing what he heard in his father's house, and for this postponed maturity he must suffer the fate of having been irrelevant to his own time, a mere entertainer with a gift for mischief.

"A man like Titus Oates occurs like a slip of the tongue, disclosing the unconscious forces, the nightside of an age. . . ." So wrote Graham Greene and so one might write of Buckley. In examining Eichmann's career Hannah Arendt came to the conclusion that evil could be banal. Buckley's career suggests that evil can be fatuous. But banal or fatuous, the result is the same if to the fool or his friends falls the power of the state. Buckley is not of course a "pro crypto Nazi" in the sense that he is a secret member of the Nazi party (and I respond to Buckley's charming apology to me with mine to him if anyone thought I was trying to link him to Hitler's foreign and domestic ventures). But in a larger sense his views are very much those of the founders of the Third Reich who regarded blacks as inferiors, undeclared war as legitimate foreign policy, and the Jews as sympathetic to international communism.

Since I began this operation with a story from *The Lakeville Journal*, a sense of symmetry impels me to end with another newspaper quotation. During Buckley's campaign for Mayor of New York, The New York *Times* took exception to his "slurs on Negroes," and accused him of pandering to "brutish instincts." Buckley wanted to know to what brutish instincts he was appealing, and The *Times* made answer, "Those instincts are fear, ignorance, racial superiority, religious antagonism, contempt for the weak and afflicted, and hatred for those different from oneself."

[September, 1969]

Addenda to the Sixties

The following selections—other articles and stories appearing in the pages of *Esquire* during the decade—constitute a supplementary list of readings in the history and style of the period.

1960

1961

August	JAMES THURBER Afternoon of a Playwright
September	ROBERT ALAN AURTHUR How I Went into Television for Fun & Profit & Found Indians
December	EDMUND WILSON The Rats of Rutland Grange

1962

February	WILLIAM STYRON The Death-in-Life of Benjamin Reid
April	DAN WAKEFIELD & THOMAS B. MORGAN Bobby & Teddy
May	JESSICA MITFORD Whut They're Thanking Down There
June	GAY TALESE Joe Louis: The King as a Middle-aged Man
July	NORMAN MAILER An Evening with Jackie Kennedy BROCK BROWER Mary McCarthyism
August	NOEL E. PARMENTEL JR. The Acne and the Ecstasy
September	WILLIAM F. BUCKLEY JR. The End of Whittaker Chambers
October	MARK EPERNAY Introducing the McLandress Dimension THOMAS B. MORGAN The Late Spring of Alf Landon
November	WILLIAM STYRON The Aftermath of Benjamin Reid PETER BOGDANOVICH Mr. Lewis Is a Pussycat
December	PHILIP ROTH Iowa: A Very Far Country Indeed ROBERT BOLT A Modern Man for All Seasons RICHARD SCHICKEL James T. Farrell: Another Time, Another Place CLEVELAND AMORY The Decline and Fall of Breakfast JAMES BALDWIN Color

1963

January	MARK EPERNAY The Confidence Box FEDERICO FELLINI End of the Sweet Parade
February	NORMAN MAILER Ten Thousand Words a Minute
March	GORE VIDAL The Best Man 1968
April	GAY TALESE The Soft Psyche of Joshua Logan DAN WAKEFIELD Dos, Which Side Are You On?
May	GAY TALESE One Year Later, Still No Bomb BARBARA W. TUCHMAN A Game, Gentleman, a Game
June	ANTHONY LEWIS Sex . . . and the Supreme Court DAN WAKEFIELD The Neatest Teener JAMES JONES "Flippers! Gin! Weight Belt! Gin! Faceplate! Gin!"
July	MALCOLM COWLEY The Last of the Lost Generation JAMES JONES & WILLIAM STYRON Two Writers Talk It Over
August	WILLIAM MELVIN KELLEY The Ivy League Negro
September	MARK EPERNAY The Sad State of the Department of State: The Hog-Wild Machine JACK RICHARDSON The Noblest Hustlers
October	WALTER ROSS Where Did Charles Lindbergh Go? MARK EPERNAY Let Us Now Appraise Famous Men TOM WOLFE The Marvelous Mouth
November	JOSEPH B. CUMMING JR. The Art of Not Being Thirty-seven

R.H.S. CROSSMAN
Apocalypse at Dresden

December GORE VIDAL
Tarzan Revisited
NORMAN MAILER
The Last Night
CALDER WILLINGHAM
Distress Notes

1964

February CHARLES SOPKIN
The Millionaire: A Self-Portrait

April TOM WOLFE
Public Lives: Confidential Magazine; reflections in tranquility
by the former owner, Robert Harrison, who managed to
get away with it
IGOR CASSINI
Personal Lives: When the sweet life turns sour; a farewell to
scandal

June JOHN BERENDT
Memoirs of a Six-Months Trainee
WILLIE THE LION SMITH
Have No Fear and Keep It Clear, the Jive Is Comin' For Look
Who's Here

July MURRAY MORGAN
The Loneliness of the Missile Attendant
THOMAS B. MORGAN
Blaze Starr in Nighttown

August EVELYN WAUGH
In Which Our Hero's Fortunes Fall Very Low
MARVIN ELKOFF
Everybody Knows His Name
VANCE BOURJAILY
Memoirs of an Ace

September JACK RICHARDSON
The Ten-Dollar Understanding
ANONYMOUS
Letter Home from an Anonymous Co-ed
VANCE BOURJAILY
Fitzgerald Attends My Fitzgerald Seminar
REBECCA WEST
Dr. Stephen Ward Returns

October TOM WICKER
L.B.J. Down on the Farm

BYNUM SHAW
Nevertheless, God Probably Loves Mrs. Murray
JEROME BEATTY JR.
How J. Gallagher O'Shay Got the U.S. Space Program off the Ground

November NORMAN MAILER
In the Red Light: A History of the Republican Convention in 1964
SYBILLE BEDFORD
The Lost Art of Civilized Touring
DOROTHY PARKER
New York at Six-thirty P.M.

December FRANK O'CONNOR
Quarreling with Yeats: A Friendly Recollection
PAN MOOHO
The Gentle Art of Tiny Teapot Tea
MURIEL SPARK
The Quest for Lavishes Ghast
DYLAN THOMAS
Me and My Bike

1965

April TERRY SMITH
Bobby's Image
NUBAR GULBENKIAN
The Last Aristocrat

June MARION MAGID
The Death of Hip

August The 100 Best People in the World

September FRED POWLEDGE
The New Fraternity
HEINRICH BÖLL
Recollections of 1945
ROBERT ALAN AURTHUR
Going Back to Boot Camp, Parris Island, S.C.

November WILLIAM F. BUCKLEY JR.
The Approaching End of Edgar H. Smith Jr.

1966

February ROSALYN DREXLER
A Woman's Place is on the Mat

HUGHES RUDD
New York, New York: Good-bye, Good-bye

November OVID DEMARIS & GARRY WILLS
The Svetlana Papers

JACK RICHARDSON
How Gambling Saved Me from a Misspent Life

WILLIAM WORTHY
The American Negro Is Dead

December WILLIAM F. BUCKLEY JR.
The Politics of the Capote Ball

ROBERT BENTON & DAVID NEWMAN
Why Your Parties Will Never Be as Good as Truman Capote's

GAY TALESE
The Party's Over

1968

January GARRY WILLS
Buckley, Buckley, Bow Wow Wow

OTTO FRIEDRICH
The Grave of Alice B. Toklas

March STEVEN LEVINE
Reminiscences of My Childhood

April Soul Section

KARL SHAPIRO
To Abolish Children

June BYNUM SHAW
Let Us Now Praise Dr. Gatch

July WYATT COOPER
Whatever You Think Dorothy Parker Was Like, She Wasn't

August PETER SWERDLOFF
The Wagumps Are Next to Godliness

September THOMAS WHITNEY RODD
How I Came to Hate Bernard Weinraub, Love the Warden,
     Keep My Mouth Shut

L. RUST HILLS
How to Retire at Forty

October F. SCOTT FITZGERALD
My Generation

WILLIAM STYRON
My Generation

DWIGHT MACDONALD
The Constitution of the United States Needs to Be Fixed

DANIEL J. BOORSTIN
The New Barbarians
WILLIAM F. BUCKLEY JR.
The Politics of Assassination
KENNETH TYNAN
Dirty Books Can Stay

November   WILLIAM A. NOLEN, M.D.
The Appendix Is Where You Find It

December   SUSAN SONTAG
Trip to Hanoi
STEVEN V. ROBERTS
Will Tom Hayden Overcome?
AUBERON WAUGH
No Matter What the Rest of the World May Think, America
    You're Beautiful

1969

February   DEAN ACHESON
Dean Acheson's Version of Robert Kennedy's Version of the
    Cuban Missile Affair
DAVID LYLE
Dr. Spock Misbehaves

March   DAVID LOWE
Kentucky on $5 a Day
SUSAN BROWNMILLER
Up from Silence
THOMAS BERGER
Controversy: The Arthur Bader Show

April   ANNE BARRY
Now That You Own Alaska, Friends, What Are You Going to
    Do with It?
DONALD BARTHELME
And Now Let's Hear It for the Ed Sullivan Show!
ETHEL GRODZINS ROMM
**** Is No Longer a Dirty Word
DONN PEARCE
Life-Styles: Building Time

May   GEORGE LARDNER & JULES LOH
The Wonderful World of George Wallace

July   WILLIAM H. HONAN
Le Mot Juste for the Moon

Acknowledgments

All articles in this collection first appeared in *Esquire,* although, in some cases, subsequent publication rights were reassigned to certain authors, their agents or their publishers. We are grateful to the following for granting permission to reprint material:

Kennedy Without Tears
From *Kennedy Without Tears: The Man Beneath the Myth,* by Tom Wicker. Reprinted by permission of William Morrow and Company, Inc., © 1964 by Tom Wicker.

"You All Know Me! I'm Jack Ruby!"
Reprinted by permission of the authors and their agents, Scott Meredith Literary Agency, Inc., New York, New York. © 1968 by Garry Wills and Ovid Demaris.

The Coming of the Purple Better One
Reprinted by permission of Harold Matson Company, Inc., © 1968 by William Burroughs.

Las Vegas (What?). Las Vegas (Can't Hear You! Too Noisy). Las Vegas!!!!

977

Picture Credits:

The New Sentimentality

Grateful acknowledgment is also extended to
three whose assistance in the preparation of
this collection proved to be invaluable:

Catherine H. McBride

Rebecca Bartlett

Constance Wood